BUSINESS LAW
Text and Cases

BUSINESS LAW
Text and Cases

Jonathan M. Purver, LL.B.

William D. Farber, J.D., LL.M.

Jimmie E. Tinsley, J.D.

Christian C. Bjorklund, J.D.

Harcourt Brace Jovanovich, Publishers
San Diego   New York   Chicago   Atlanta   Washington, D.C.
London   Sydney   Toronto

Bancroft-Whitney Company
San Francisco

ISBN: 0-15-505621-2
Library of Congress Catalog Card Number: 82-81961
Printed in the United States of America

PREFACE

A basic understanding of the law, while important for every member of society, is *essential* for the businessperson. It is unwise to enter the field of business—and impossible to remain in it—without adequate knowledge of one's legal rights, duties, and responsibilities. There are simply too many potential pitfalls for the unwary. *Business Law* was planned and written as an effective and practical source of legal knowledge—for the business student, for the student who studies business law to further his or her general education, and for the businessperson who has recognized the need for additional education.

The text focuses on the practical aspects of doing business and the effects of the law on the conduct of business. The book is based on the premise that if persons engaged in business activities are aware of their legal rights and obligations, they can avoid most adverse consequences. *Business Law* emphasizes this kind of *preventive law*. It is concerned with both the legal rules governing business and the environment in which these rules operate.

Business Law contains 55 chapters, divided into 11 parts. Each part opens with brief Introductory Comments about the topics that follow and their place in the business milieu. No two instructors are likely to cover the topics in precisely the same order and *Business Law* may be studied in a different order than is presented in the book. With few exceptions (Part One is best covered first), there is no single "right" path through the book.

Business Law covers all the traditional subjects taught in an introductory business law course. In addition, new or increasingly important areas of the law with which the business student must become familiar are included or given more emphasis than in other texts. For example, *Business Law* contains chapters on administrative law, the creditor–debtor relationship, bankruptcy, personal property and equipment leasing, real property, franchising, white-collar crime, and products liability.

Preventive law—how to anticipate and avoid legal problems—is emphasized by the use of *precautionary notes*. Such notes, set off throughout the text by the symbol ⊘ in the margin, highlight these important points for the students' attention.

In addition to its preventive orientation, *Business Law* offers several other distinctive features. Many legal rules and situations are illustrated by *examples* that are set off from the rest of the text. These examples aid the students' understanding of difficult legal concepts; they make the text more interesting to read and show legal rules at work in real-life settings. Also, many *cross-references* make the text more useful, both for current study and for later reference.

A feature that *Business Law* shares with other legal textbooks is the inclusion of *case material*—excerpts from published judicial opinions. While cases have their proper place in the study of business law, their value is somewhat limited and easily overestimated. Thus, the authors have selected and edited cases with great care before integrating them into the body of the text. Some are business law classics, but many are fresh cases used for the first time in a business law text. A bracketed summary of the facts and, when appropriate, the procedural background precede each case, to help the students grasp the point of the case quickly. The disposition of the case is also prominently noted.

The text of each chapter concludes with Key Concepts and Terms. This unique listing summarizes the chapter and enables students to review and gauge their comprehension of the material. Each chapter ends with Questions and Case Problems that test students' understanding of basic legal rules and their application to situational problems.

Following the chapter material are six appendixes—one of which includes the complete Uniform Commercial Code —a comprehensive glossary, a table of statutes cited, and a volume index.

A full set of supporting materials is available with *Business Law*. A Study Guide for students contains a list of objectives for each chapter, an outline review, and a self-test comprehension check, with answers provided. An Instructor's Manual includes for each chapter an outline, teaching strategies, case briefs, answers to questions and case problems, and five additional case problems, with answers for class discussion or tests. The Test Book contains two sets of fifteen multiple-choice questions for all text chapters, plus five additional case problems per chapter, with answers.

Business Law is the result of a joint venture between two major publishing houses: Harcourt Brace Jovanovich, Inc., and Bancroft-Whitney Company (a subsidiary of Lawyers Cooperative Publishing Company). The authors are experienced attorneys who are members of Bancroft-Whitney's editorial staff, the same staff that serves the legal profession with such publications as *American Law Reports* (ALR), *American Jurisprudence 2d* (Am Jur 2d), and the dozens of other titles that are published under the Lawyers Cooperative/Bancroft-Whitney logo. Two of the authors are former adjunct professors of law. They have all brought to *Business Law* their unique talents as professional legal researchers and writers. Special appreciation is given to Alison C. Treanor, whose contribution included copy editing the manuscript. Her efforts added significantly to the quality of the book. The authors also acknowledge the contribution of David A. Winn, formerly managing editor at Bancroft-Whitney, under whose guidance *Business Law* became a reality.

The following reviewers offered helpful suggestions as to the subjects to cover, organization, and other matters, and their assistance is appreciated: H. M. Bohlman, Arizona State University; Charles M. Foster, North Texas State University; Madelyn M. Huffmire, University of Connecticut; Duane R. Lambert, California State University, Hayward; George Spiro, University of Massachusetts; Susan Stiner, Nebraska State Bar; and Jon E. Stuebbe, San Francisco State University.

Business Law is the result of thousands of hours of planning, research, writing, and editing. We hope that it serves the educator and the student well. Through it, the student should come to agree that, as stated by the late United States Supreme

Court Justice William O. Douglas, "The law is not a series of calculating machines where definitions and answers come tumbling out when the right levers are pushed." Rather, law is a continually changing and growing process, one that the businessperson must consider and anticipate in many aspects of his or her work.

Christian C. Bjorklund
Bancroft-Whitney Company

Contents

PART FOUR
Sales 267

PART FIVE
Commercial Paper   345

PART SIX
Creditor–Debtor Relationship 429

PART SEVEN
Property   571

PART EIGHT
Insurance 723

PART NINE
Business Organizations 763

PART TEN
Employment Relationships   921

BUSINESS LAW
Text and Cases

PART ONE

Law and the Legal Process

Introductory Comments

Law is a dynamic process. Through law, society establishes values and goals. Supreme Court Justice Felix Frankfurter said American society is a "legal state" in the sense that almost everything that takes place will sooner or later raise legal questions. The purpose of American business law is to bring reason, fairness, and stability to the marketplace. In understanding business law, the businessperson becomes aware of the means to prevent disputes and, thus, to avoid lawsuits. It is essential for the businessperson to be able to anticipate the legal consequences of his or her actions. The preventive aspect of business law is the polestar that should guide the businessperson through every transaction and management decision.

Part One discusses the historical foundations of law (Chapter 1) and how the legal process is carried out in the American judicial system

and in a lawsuit (Chapter 2). Part One also examines the law that governs administrative agencies—the so-called "invisible fourth branch of government"—which are increasingly active in regulating the marketplace (Chapter 3). The last chapter in this part concerns criminal law and sets forth the elements of a crime and the defenses and constitutional safeguards against a criminal charge. The specific aspects of business-related crimes, the so-called "white-collar crimes," are treated in another part of this book (Chapter 55).

An important section in this part of the book is the one that describes relationships of the businessperson and the attorney (1:6). This section tells how a businessperson should select and use counsel, and discusses the attorney's role and responsibilities in the context of business.

1 Nature and Sources of Law

The law embodies the story of a nation's development through many centuries, and it cannot be dealt with as if it contained only the axioms and corollaries of a book of mathematics. In order to know what it is, we must know what it has been, and what it tends to become.

Oliver Wendell Holmes, Jr., *The Common Law*

1:1 What Is Law?

Every government is the exact symbol of its people, said the historian Thomas Carlyle. So it is with law: The laws and legal system of a society reflect the values of its people. The fairness of a nation's laws and the extent to which the legal system justly administers the laws is a measure of the enlightenment, humanity, and degree of civilization of its people. .What was said by the legal scholar John Dillon nearly a hundred years ago has particular meaning today: Ethical considerations can no more be excluded from the administration of justice, which is the end and purpose of all laws, than one can exclude the vital air from his room and live.[1]

Law consists of the whole body of rules applied and enforced under the authority of established government in determining what conduct is proper and should be permitted and that which should be denied or penalized. In a country such as the United States, most social questions ultimately become *legal* questions, as explained by constitutional scholar Paul Freund:

> More than a century ago Alexis de Tocqueville remarked, with characteristic perception and clairvoyance, that the major issues of American life sooner or later appear as questions for decision by the courts. In the succeeding years this observation has lost none of its validity. Across the forum of the Supreme Court there have passed, like figures in a morality play, most of the great forces whose conflict and resolution have been the themes of American history: the opening of a continent and local rivalries in transportation and trade, the expansion of commerce and business and the pressures for its control, slavery and civil war, organized industry and organized labor, social welfare legislation, taxation, public compulsory military service and internal security, church and state, a free press and public order, efficient law enforcement and the right to a fair trial.[2]

---

[1]J. Dillon, *Laws and Jurisprudence of England and America*, Lecture I (1894).
[2]P. Freund, "The Supreme Court," in *Talks on American Law*, 71 (1961).

Functions of Law   Without law, there would be anarchy. Law is the means through which society is able to exist by providing protection for the individual; by establishing and maintaining order, health, and safety; by providing a peaceful means of dispute resolution; by providing stability and flexibility in economic relations between people; and by prohibiting conduct destructive to society. Rules of law reflect the society and time in which they operate. Growth of law has been pragmatic, developing from society's need for reasonableness and flexibility in its day-to-day working.

Law as a Dynamic Process   Law is a dynamic process. It is a flow, constantly changing, continually expanding. In a sense, law is similar to language: It consists of rules and has a pattern, but the rules and pattern change as they are used over a period of time. Law is best understood by viewing the legal system as a *process*—a means of pulling together society's needs and goals and translating them into guides for fairness and reasonableness in conduct. Courts, through judicial decisions, reflect the controlling and important social, economic, and political goals and needs of the society in which they function.

Law as an Instrument of Business   Law plays a vital and stabilizing role in business transactions and relationships. Businesspersons can, for example, enter into a valid contract, knowing that the agreement is enforceable in court. Law as an instrument of business may be traced to the law merchant, a body of commercial law embracing the usage of merchants in many countries (see Chapter 19).

Each business transaction, each commercial contact, involves people. The extent to which persons can trust one another and bargain in confidence that the other will act in good faith is the measure of the success of a nation's commerce. The subject of law must never be viewed as a series of isolated technical rules, but should be seen as a system for bringing reason and fairness into the marketplace.

1:2   Common Law and Equity

The English system of law, on which the American legal system is based, developed after the Norman Conquest in the eleventh century. Upon conquering England, the Normans found themselves attempting to govern a land with no uniform nationwide system of law or means for the consistent administration of justice. Such laws as existed were based on the local customs of each township, and in many cases force was the "law." In his goal to unify the legal system of England, William the Conqueror replaced the local, and highly varied, systems of law, with a uniform—or "common"—system of law. This system was administered by royal judges sent out into the land to listen to controversies, disputes, and accusations which arose. This centralized and uniform system for the administration of justice was continued by the Norman kings. By the early thirteenth century, the Norman judicial system had replaced the various local methods of dispute resolution.

When they began the centralization of justice, the Norman kings' royal judges had no body of rules on which to rely. They drew from customs, traditions, business practices, and community standards to create the principles on which to decide cases. Over the years, as the court system grew and became more finely attuned to the needs of society, a system of judge-made rules began to develop. These rules became known as "the common law," because they were common to all the people in the land.

Common law developed at the township level, changing as it developed:

> Common law . . . makes itself up as it goes along; it sets precedents but they are never unalterable, because they are derived ultimately, not from a book of rules, but from a judge's intuitive feeling for equity and fair play—from a man rather than a machine. Code law assumes a pattern laid down once and for all; common law assumes a freely developing pattern which is nevertheless consistent with itself, like the development of a living language.[3]

The Courts of Equity   Because of the extremely rigid, frequently overly technical procedural requirements (such as having to use particular phraseology in a request for relief) of the common-law systems, people were sometimes unable to obtain fair relief in the courts. Furthermore, the common-law judges viewed all relief in terms of money; that is, a royal judge might award money damages, but would not prevent or compel a person's action. In time, some persons who felt that the form of relief was inadequate petitioned the King directly. These petitions were turned over to the King's Lord Chancellor. By the late fifteenth and early sixteenth centuries, this practice gave rise to a second court system, called the Court of Chancery. Remedies granted by the Court of Chancery were known as *equity*, from the Latin word *aequitas*, which means fairness or justice.

While a judge under the common-law system would only award money damages for violation of a legal right, an equity chancellor (as the judges of the equity court were called), could fashion a variety of remedies. An equity chancellor, when it was fair to do so, might enjoin (prevent) a person from performing certain activities, or might require a person to perform certain activities. If, for example, a person were obligated under a contract to convey property to the plaintiff, a chancellor in the equity court would order him to make the conveyance. A common-law judge, however, would not be apt to render such an order but would attempt to ascertain an amount of damages for the defendant's failure to convey the property.[4]

Adoption of English Common-law and Equity Systems in the United States   The English colonists who settled North America based their legal system on what they had previously experienced, the common-law and equity systems of Europe. Although the *United States Constitution* reflected strong anti-British sentiment and embodied a new, highly untraditional system of laws, the new nation preserved large portions of the British legal heritage.

The colonies, and later the states (with the exception of Louisiana, a former French colony, whose laws are still based on French civil law), established separate court systems to administer law and equity, as had England. Subsequent reform of

---

[3]A. Watts, *Psychotherapy East and West*, 202 (1969).
[4]Legal remedies are discussed in Chapter 18.

American court systems in the nineteenth century resulted in simplification of judicial procedures and elimination of equity courts as separate courts in most states. While the two court systems have been joined in most states, the terminology in law and equity cases may remain different. For example, in a "lawsuit," the "plaintiff" initiates an action by bringing a "complaint." In an equity case, the person bringing the suit is a "petitioner," who brings a "bill in equity." The law judge renders a "judgment," while the equity judge renders a "decree."

1:3 Statutory Law

While the common-law and equity systems of jurisprudence in England resulted from judge-made decisions from the period following the Norman Conquest, the primary growth of law in the United States has resulted from *statutes* enacted by state legislatures and by Congress. Under the federal Constitution and the constitutions of all 50 states, it is the function and duty of the legislative branch of government to enact the laws (statutes) under which we live.

There exists, side by side, then, in the American legal system, the common law and statutory law. Through historical development, some areas of law have resulted in less control by statutes than by judicial decisions. The law of contracts, for example, was developed extensively by the common-law judges during the growth of England's legal system. This is not to say that there is no legislation in this area. Legislatures have indeed enacted statutes covering contracts, but the legislation has been phrased broadly and it is the common-law rules which fill out the details of the statutes. Other areas of law, particularly business law, are entirely the result of statutes. For example, corporation and antitrust laws are created by legislation, not court decisions.

Uniform and Model Laws and the Restatement During the latter half of the nineteenth century, considerable variety arose among the various state laws. As commerce between states increased, it became clear that some degree of uniformity of legislation was essential, particularly in the business community. The combined effort of several states resulted in the creation of the National Conference of Commissioners on Uniform State Laws in 1891, which still exists today. The commissioners, a distinguished group of attorneys, propose statutes in various areas of law which might be adopted, in whole or in part, by the state legislatures to secure *uniformity of laws* among the states.

Another way statutes have become more uniform throughout the United States has been through model acts drafted by various committees of the American Bar Association. These model acts, like the various uniform acts, are not statutes until they have been enacted by the states. One example of a model act that has had a significant impact on business law is the Model Business Corporation Act (MBCA), first drafted in 1960. It has gone through several revisions and has been adopted in substance in more than 35 states. Major portions of the act are being followed in many other states.[5]

---

[5]The MBCA is set forth in Appendix C and is discussed in Chapters 42–45.

To promote uniformity in basic principles of law in many fields, the American Law Institute (ALI) was organized in the 1920s by several law professors, judges, and practicing attorneys. In contrast to the National Conference of Commissioners, the ALI is primarily concerned with nonstatutory rules of law. The ALI writes and publishes books containing statements of what it believes to be the proper rules of law in many areas. These books are entitled Restatements of Law, and although the *Restatements* do not constitute actual law, the courts give weight to the principles set forth in them.

How and why a uniform law governing business was created can be seen in the development of the Uniform Commercial Code (UCC).[6] Rapid change and expansion in many areas of commercial life created a demand for broad, flexible, and uniform statutory law. The National Conference of Commissioners on Uniform State Laws and the American Law Institute jointly commenced an intensive research and study program in 1945 with a view toward formulating a uniform law dealing with most aspects of commercial transactions. The outcome of the program was promulgation of the Uniform Commercial Code in 1952. As a result of further studies, refinements, and revisions, the Uniform Commercial Code was ultimately adopted in all states, except Louisiana, which adopted only certain portions.

Ordinances   One type of statutory law consists of *ordinances*, which are enactments by the legislative body of a municipal corporation (city). An ordinance is a municipal law of a general and permanent nature. Examples include fire codes, parking regulations, provisions for health and food inspections, provisions for city tax revenues, and city elections. City governments arise only by the power given to them under a state constitution or statute. Therefore, the scope of a city ordinance may not exceed its constitutional or legislative limits.

Treaties   A treaty, another form of statutory law, is a written contract between nations executed with the formality customary in dealings between nations, although not necessarily in a particular and prescribed form. In the United States, the power to make treaties with foreign nations is, under the Constitution, given to the President, acting with the advice and consent of the Senate. Treaties require the concurrence of two-thirds of the Senate. Trade treaties have a substantial impact on private business in the United States. The states are prohibited from entering into any treaty without the consent of Congress.

1:4   The Constitution and the Federal–State System

From the time of the American Revolution until the adoption of the United States Constitution, the main concern of the colonists was "limited government." They argued that certain inherent rights belonged to the people and could not be divested by government. Thus, the members of the Constitutional Convention resolved to form a central government with broad powers designed to preserve the rights of the individual. Rather than establish a unitary government, the framers

---

[6]The UCC is set forth in Appendix B.

of the Constitution formed a system under which governmental powers were divided between the central (or federal) government and other self-governing parts (the states). This system of government is known as *federalism*. The Tenth Amendment of the Constitution states that the powers not delegated to the United States (federal government) by the Constitution, nor prohibited by the Constitution to the states, are reserved to the states or to the people. The power of the federal government is thus expressly limited by the Constitution.[7]

Supremacy Clause   The division of power between the states and the federal government under the Constitution creates the possibility of a conflict for supremacy between them. The framers of the Constitution, realizing such conflict might arise, provided for its resolution with the Supremacy Clause (Article VI, § 2), which states that the Constitution, laws, and treaties of the United States "shall be the supreme law of the land," anything in the Constitution or laws of any state to the contrary notwithstanding. Hence, whenever the federal government exercises a power granted by the Constitution, any conflicting exercise of power by the states must yield to the federal power.

Delegated Powers Doctrine   Article I, § 1, of the Constitution lodges all legislative power in Congress. The powers of Congress are specifically enumerated. Since the federal government is one of delegated powers only, every federal statute must have as its basis one of these enumerated powers. Article I, § 8, sets forth many congressional powers, such as the power to lay and collect taxes, to regulate interstate and foreign commerce, and to declare war. The amendments also grant powers to Congress. For example, the Fourteenth Amendment, guaranteeing due process and equal protection of the law, has been held to grant Congress the power to legislate the preservation of these guaranties.

Necessary and Proper Clause   The specific powers of Congress may be enlarged by the Necessary and Proper Clause of the Constitution (Article I, § 8), which provides that Congress has the power "to make all laws which shall be necessary and proper for carrying into execution the foregoing powers."

Commerce Clause   Federal power with respect to the regulation of commerce is derived from the Commerce Clause (Article I, § 8, Clause 3), which grants to Congress the power to "regulate commerce with foreign nations and among the several states." The Commerce Clause is read in conjunction with the Necessary and Proper Clause. Federal economic regulation began in 1887 with Congressional enactment of the Interstate Commerce Act. The Commerce Clause was relied on as the basis for the affirmative exercise of federal power over national commerce. Since 1937, the Supreme Court's position has been that Congress has the power to regulate any activity—whether it is interstate or intrastate in nature—as long as it has any appreciable effect on interstate commerce. This is known as the affectation doctrine.

---

[7]The Constitution is reprinted in Appendix A.

Protection of Rights of the Individual   There are express and implied limitations on the exercise of governmental power which emanate from the Constitution. Principal among the express limitations which protect individual rights are those contained in the *Bill of Rights*, the first ten amendments to the Constitution.[8]

The Fifth Amendment of the Constitution declares that no person shall "be deprived of life, liberty, or property without due process of law." The Fourteenth Amendment declares that no state shall "deprive any person of life, liberty, or property without due process of law." The Fifth Amendment is a limitation on the powers of Congress (the federal government); the Fourteenth Amendment is a limitation on the powers of the states. Due process has been defined in many ways and variously described by the Supreme Court as "those principles implicit in the concept of ordered liberty," "the principles of liberty and justice which lie at the base of all our civil and political institutions," and "the principles of justice so rooted in the traditions and conscience of our people as to be ranked fundamental."

The Supreme Court has never attempted to define with precision the words "due process of law," but, through its decisions, has made clear that the term *due process of law* asserts a fundamental principle of justice rather than a specific rule of law. The Supreme Court has said that the concept of due process is not to be frozen within the confines of historical facts or discredited attitudes. Rather, it is to be interpreted in the nature of a free society seeking to advance in its standards of what is deemed reasonable and right. Representing as it does a living principle, due process is not confined within permanent definitions of what may at a given time be deemed the limits or essentials of fundamental rights.

Flexibility of Constitution   The Constitution is not a lifeless, static instrument whose interpretation is confined to the conditions and outlook which prevailed at the time of its adoption. Nor is it a collection of dry, abstract rules. Rather, the Constitution is a flexible, vital, living document, drafted for the operation and perpetuation of American government and designed for an extended period, in war or in peace.

In determining whether a provision of the Constitution applies to a new area of law, it is of little significance that it is one with which the framers of the Constitution were not familiar. As explained by Supreme Court Justice Holmes:

> [W]hen we are dealing with words that also are a constituent act, like the Constitution of the United States, we must realize that they have called into life a being the development of which could not have been foreseen completely by the most gifted of its begetters. It was enough for them to realize or to hope that they had created an organism; it has taken a century and has cost their successors much sweat and blood to prove that they created a nation. The case before us must be considered in the light of our whole experience, and not merely in that of what was said a hundred years ago.[9]

---

[8]Constitutional protections in criminal cases are discussed in Chapter 4.
[9]*Missouri v Holland*, 252 US 416, 64 L Ed 641, 40 S Ct 382, *11 ALR 984* (1920).

1:5   Preventive Law in Business

To most people, the idea of "the law" is focused primarily on courtroom battles between attorneys representing disputing parties. Courts obviously play an important role in our society and system of government. However, the function of the law should be viewed as being much more than an avenue for the resolution of disputes: *The law should serve as a means for preventing disputes and avoiding court conflicts.*

If persons are aware of the legal consequences of their actions before they act, they may plan their conduct to minimize legal disputes and conflicts. This approach is termed *preventive law.*

Preventive law has the same basis as preventive medicine or preventive dentistry. It seeks to eliminate, or at least minimize, problems before they occur. Obviously, however, a person cannot avoid a problem unless he knows that a problem exists or could exist.

Business law is studied to gain sufficient familiarity with legal principles and the operation of the law so that the legal consequences of planned actions can be anticipated. If business plans can be seen to result in undesirable consequences, they can be modified to effect a desirable result. The focus of this book is on the preventive aspects of business law. Legal principles are set forth in a context enabling the legal consequences of actions to be anticipated and informed business decisions to be made.

Throughout this book we will use the symbol to highlight discussions aimed at cultivating a preventive outlook toward commercial law. Some of these discussions will be very direct: "Watch for this."; "Always seek legal counsel if. . . ."; other discussions will be historical or more reflective. The intent of these discussions, however, will be to alert you to areas in which, with a little forethought, you as a businessperson can anticipate a legal problem and prevent it.

1:6   The Attorney–Business Relationship

It is impossible to overestimate the importance of the attorney to modern business. As will be seen throughout this book, the complexity of the laws which regulate, control, and indeed permeate all business and industrial endeavors, indicates not only the need, but the absolute necessity, for legal advice and representation in many areas of business. Although courtroom litigation is the most visible, even spectacular, facet of the attorney's work, in business it is usually not legal counsel's most important duty. Quite the contrary. As mentioned in 1:5, it is the primary function of business law to minimize or prevent legal problems: This is the polestar which must guide any attorney representing a business client.

An attorney's advice should be sought whenever there is an intimation of possible legal complications. Counsel should be consulted when a businessperson receives any formal legal document, such as a subpoena (a court's demand to appear before it), governmental order or request, demand by another company or private person for a particular legal action, or notification that a lawsuit has been, or will be, filed against the businessperson personally or against the company or organization.

An increasing number of businesses (and their attorneys) have recognized the wisdom of periodic legal checkups. Just as a person should consult a physician periodically to be certain his medical condition is satisfactory and being taken care of, a business should undergo a periodic check on its legal condition. Laws, as well as individual conditions and circumstances, change from time to time. Unless such changes and their possible legal effects are analyzed on a regular basis, unanticipated legal difficulties could arise.

The business lawyer may be an attorney in a private law firm who is retained to perform legal services on a regular basis. Or, the business attorney may be "in-house" counsel, a full-time employee of the corporation. Some small companies have legal staffs consisting of one or two attorneys, while large corporations may have dozens of attorneys on their in-house staff.

Whether in-house or privately retained, the attorney performs a variety of functions for the businessperson. The attorney may, for example, advise and represent the client as to labor-management relations, antitrust law, patent or trademark law, or contract law. The attorney will review and prepare documents received and submitted by the business client, examine and evaluate the legal results which may flow from the client's numerous business activities, and, where necessary, represent the client in court or before governmental administrative agencies. Being itself a complex and specific specialty of law, trial work, even for a large corporate client which has in-house counsel, is frequently farmed out to private law firms specializing in trial litigation.

Selection of Attorney   There are half a million attorneys in the United States. Yet, selecting the right attorney for particular needs may not be an easy task. In selecting an attorney, a businessperson is a consumer and should "comparison shop" to find an attorney technically competent and psychologically dedicated to properly represent the client. Some studies indicate that many persons unfortunately select an attorney randomly or on the recommendation of someone who has not actually used that attorney.

In selecting an attorney, the businessperson should first determine the type of attorney he or she would need. For example, hiring an attorney whose practice is devoted to domestic relations cases as counsel in an antitrust matter would be equivalent to retaining a physician whose practice is limited to psychiatry to remove an appendix. If questions arise as to antitrust law, an antitrust attorney should be consulted. Questions involving labor law necessitate consultation with a labor attorney. If the questions involve criminal prosecution, consultation should be with a criminal lawyer. Some attorneys specialize in real estate matters, others in corporate law, still others in consumer law. There are many legal areas of concentration.

After determining what kind of lawyer is needed, the businessperson should speak with the attorney in person to find out how much experience and knowledge he or she has in that particular area of law. Besides being competent, the attorney selected should be committed to keeping the client informed at all stages of the case.

The Fee Arrangement   The fee should be discussed with the attorney at the initial meeting. The fee may be a so-called flat fee, a specific sum for performing a particular legal job, or the fee may be charged at an hourly rate. The flat fee or hourly rate will vary with the attorney's experience and degree of competence and the geographical area from which the attorney is selected. Another type of fee arrangement, called the contingency fee, is a percentage of the money, if any, recovered on behalf of the client. Generally, attorneys who represent plaintiffs suing for damages are paid on a contingency fee basis.

Some state and local bar associations publish suggested attorney fee schedules which, although not mandated, may in some cases be a guide as to the fee charged.

Attorney-Client Communication   Some attorneys have only cursory contact with their clients. This method of practicing law is not only insensitive, but is a violation of the attorney's duty to the client. Full, accurate, and frequent communication from the attorney to the client is a sign of a careful and competent attorney. It has been said that the primary cause of client dissatisfaction is the lack of communication by busy lawyers.

The businessperson should require from the attorney ongoing communication and status reports as to all work the attorney has undertaken. Furthermore, the attorney's communications should advise the businessperson of all legal rights and duties, recent legal developments affecting the client, and preventive legal measures applicable to the client's business. The attorney should explain these matters in a way which enables the client to understand the law and should not be presented in "legalese." In evaluating litigation, it is particularly important that the client understand the risks and costs involved, and the predictability of a successful outcome. The attorney should be requested to provide a brief written synopsis of the case, containing its strengths and weaknesses, and an estimate of the time, costs, and legal fees probably generated by the case.

If the client is suing another party, the attorney has the duty not only to advise the client as to progress of the case, but also as to all settlement offers made by the other party. While the client is wise to listen to the advice of a seasoned attorney as to reasonableness of any settlement offer, the final decision on making a settlement is the client's alone, not the attorney's.

Privileged Attorney-Client Communications   Under the so-called "attorney-client privilege," a client (including a corporate client) may be protected from having to disclose confidential communications to an attorney, made in seeking legal advice. The client's communications to the attorney are said to be privileged, although the attorney's advice to the client is not always similarly protected. The purpose of attorney-client privilege is to promote a full freedom of communication between counsel and client. In a 1981 decision, the United States Supreme Court held that communications between a corporation's employees and the corporation's general counsel (in-house counsel) were protected by the attorney-client privilege, and that, accordingly, disclosure of such communications could not be compelled by the Internal Revenue Service since such communications were made by the employees to the corporate counsel acting at the direction of corporate superiors.[10]

Key Concepts and Terms

- Law consists of the body of rules applied and enforced under the authority of established government.

- Law is a dynamic process, constantly changing, continually expanding. Law reflects the values which society deems important. Law plays a vital role in modern American business by providing stability in business transactions.

- The English system of common law, on which the American legal system is based, developed over the several hundred years following the Norman Conquest in the eleventh century. The common law was the body of rules which resulted from the case-by-case decisions of the Norman kings' judges, who relied on customs and traditions rather than legislation.

- The equity court system parallels the common-law system. In a court of equity, persons who administered relief (chancellors) fashioned a far greater range of remedies than did the common-law judges. The equity and common-law systems were essentially combined in the United States during the nineteenth century.

- The primary growth of law in the United States, particularly in the business area, has resulted from statutes enacted by state legislatures and by Congress, rather than by the courts.

- To obtain greater uniformity of state business laws, many state legislatures have enacted so-called "uniform laws" in certain fields, written and proposed by the National Conference of Commissioners on Uniform State Laws. Many states have also enacted the Model Business Corporation Act, written under the auspices of the American Bar Association.

- The United States Constitution establishes a federalist system, under which governmental powers are divided between the central government and the states.

- Under the delegated powers doctrine, the powers of Congress are specifically enumerated, and every federal law must have as its basis an enumerated power set forth in the Constitution. The specific powers of Congress may, however, be enlarged by the Constitution's Necessary and Proper Clause.

- Under the Constitution's Commerce Clause, Congress has broad powers to regulate the economics and business of the nation.

- The Constitution provides express and implied limitations on the exercise of federal and state power, the prime limitations being set forth in the Bill of Rights (the first ten amendments to the Constitution).

- The businessperson must learn the approach of preventive law, which is the

---

[10]*Upjohn Co. v United States*, 449 US 383, 66 L Ed 2d 584, 101 S Ct 677 (1981).

recognition and elimination of legal problems before they require the aid of legal counsel or court action.

- Bill of Rights
- Common Law
- Delegated Powers Doctrine
- Due Process of Law
- Equity
- Federalism
- Law

- Ordinance
- Preventive Law
- Restatement
- Statutory Law
- Uniform Laws
- United States Constitution

Questions and Case Problems

1. In what ways is law an instrument of business?

2. Under what types of business circumstances would it be wise to consult an attorney? Conversely, when would it probably be unnecessary to seek legal advice?

3. In what way is the system of justice that developed from the equity courts different from the system that developed from the common-law courts?

4. What are uniform laws, model laws, and the Restatement? Where do these "laws" come from? What is their significance to the business community?

5. In what ways does the American legal system protect the rights of individuals from arbitrary government action? In this regard, what is "due process of law" and how is it achieved under the United States Constitution?

6. What is the purpose of preventive law in business? Provide some specific examples.

2 Court System

*The judge is under a duty, within the limits of his power of innova-
tion, to maintain a relation between law and morals, between the
precepts of jurisprudence and those of reason and good conscience.*

B. Cardozo, *The Nature of the Judicial Process*

2:1 Judicial Functions

"Laws are a dead letter without courts to expound and define their true meaning
and operation," said Alexander Hamilton.[1] The function of courts has remained
basically the same since the days of Hamilton. That function is adjudication: The
settlement of legal controversies between opposing parties in a lawsuit. It is during
the trial that the judge or jury determines the facts in the case and applies the
applicable rules of law to those facts to reach a decision (see 2:4). Besides interpreting law, courts have the power to change existing law and to create new law (see
2:5).

Judicial Review Courts are sometimes called on to determine whether a statute
is constitutionally valid. This is usually referred to as judicial review of legislation.
The federal Constitution in Article III, § 2, gives the United States Supreme Court
the power to decide all cases and controversies that come from a lower court for
final review. This is called appellate jurisdiction. However, the Constitution does
not expressly give the Supreme Court power to determine the constitutionality of
acts of Congress or state statutes. The Supreme Court has gained these powers
through its own decisions. For example, in the famous case *Marbury v Madison*,[2]
the Supreme Court held that it has the power to review acts of Congress and
declare them void if they are inconsistent with the Constitution. Subsequently, the
Supreme Court established its power to review and invalidate state legislation that
the Court finds contrary to the Constitution or some treaty or act of Congress.

2:2 The Judicial Structure

The American judicial system consists of two parts: the court system of the federal
government and that of each of the 50 states. Figure 2-1 shows the structure and
relationship of the American judicial system.

---

[1] A. Hamilton, *The Federalist*, No. 22.
[2] 5 US (1 Cranch) 137, 2 L Ed 60 (1803).

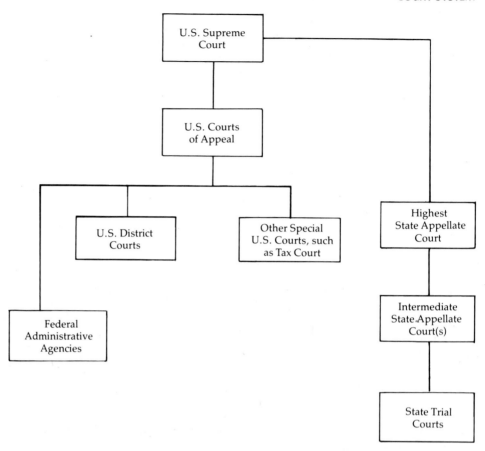

Figure 2-1
Diagram of basic appellate structure in federal and state court systems.

Federal Court System Article III, § 1, of the United States Constitution, states that the judicial power of the United States shall be vested in one Supreme Court and in those inferior courts (inferior to the Supreme Court) that Congress may establish. Congress, in the Judiciary Act of 1789, used this constitutional power to establish the federal judicial system. This system consists of several levels of federal courts. The United States District Courts are the federal trial courts. Every state has at least one United States District Court.

Federal cases tried and lost in the district courts may be appealed to the next level in the federal judicial system, which is the United States Court of Appeals. There are 12, one for each of the federal circuits, which are judicial districts located throughout the United States. The United States Court of Appeals for a particular federal circuit hears appeals from United States District Courts located in states within that circuit. For example, the United States Court of Appeals for the Ninth Circuit (located in San Francisco) hears appeals from United States District Courts within Guam and the states of Hawaii, Alaska, Idaho, Montana, Nevada, Arizona,

Oregon, California, and Washington, because these states are within the Ninth United States Circuit.

The highest level of the federal judicial system is the United States Supreme Court. The Supreme Court's primary function is to review decisions of the lower federal courts or, where federal questions are involved, of state courts. The Supreme Court also conducts trials in a few types of cases, including those affecting ambassadors, consuls and other public ministers, and cases in which a state is a party. The Supreme Court itself decides which cases it will hear. In one year it will not hear more than a few hundred of the thousands of requests for appeal that are made to it.

In addition to the federal courts just discussed, certain courts have been created by Congress to augment its legislative powers. These courts include the Court of Customs and Patent Appeals, the Court of Claims, the Tax Court, and the Court of Military Appeals. These courts have specific functions in dealing with only particular types of cases.

State Court Systems   State courts are generally independent from the federal courts, although in certain cases the United States Supreme Court has the power to review a decision rendered by the highest court of a state. A federal court will not ordinarily interfere with the administration of state law by a state court unless fundamental rights guaranteed by the federal Constitution are invaded or unless the enforcement of state law appears to violate the Constitution, federal laws, or treaties.

Although it may vary from state to state, most state court systems have three levels. On the first level—what might be termed the "battlefield" of the legal process—are the trial courts, in which the litigation actually takes place through presentation of evidence to a judge or jury (see 2:3). Trial courts are known by different names in different states. They may be called "superior court," "court of common pleas," or "county court."[3]

In addition to trial courts that have power to try most types of criminal or civil cases, most states have specialized courts, frequently called courts of limited jurisdiction. These courts have been given power by the state legislature to hear only particular types of cases. Examples of limited jurisdiction courts are traffic courts (which hear minor traffic violations), domestic relations courts (which hear matrimonial or family disputes), and probate courts (which hear matters pertaining to distribution of estates). Most litigation involving business law occurs in state general trial courts, because a business lawsuit usually does not involve the specialized subject matter of courts of limited jurisdiction.

At the next state court level are the *appellate courts*. As the name implies, this is the level to which persons who have lost at the trial level may appeal for review. Rather than retrying the case or reweighing the evidence, the appellate courts review the written trial records, known as transcripts, and make sure that the trial was fair, that procedural safeguards were duly followed, and that proper legal

---

[3]It should be noted that in New York the trial court is called the "supreme court" and the highest court of appeals is called the "court of appeals."

principles were applied by the trial judge. In some states, there are two levels of appellate courts: the intermediate appellate court at the first level of appellate review and the state supreme court at the second level. In other states, there are no intermediate appellate courts, but only a state supreme court which serves as the sole appellate judicial body.

Small Claims Courts   Another type of court system found in nearly all states is the small claims court or small debtors' court. The small claims court is usually a separate division of the general trial courts. If a lawsuit involves less than a particular amount of money, typically a few hundred dollars, the person bringing the suit may have the alternative of bringing the action in a small claims court rather than in the general trial court. Depending on the state, the persons involved in the suit may not be allowed to have an attorney, and may not appeal to a higher court.

Small claims litigation is a growing trend and provides a faster and less costly resolution for disputes involving small sums of money. Many procedural technicalities that may encumber an ordinary proceeding are dispensed with in a small claims proceeding.

2:3   Nature of a Lawsuit

A *lawsuit* is an adversary proceeding in which both the person bringing the action and the person defending it each seek to persuade the trier of fact—the jury, if there is one, or the judge—that under the facts of the case, the law entitles him to win. In a civil case, which involves a dispute between private parties, the person bringing the action is called the plaintiff, and the person defending the action is called the defendant. In a criminal case a person is charged with having committed an offense against society (see Chapter 4). That person is called the defendant, as in a civil case, but the "plaintiff" is a representative of the public, called the prosecuting attorney. The basic stages of a lawsuit are set forth below. Although the term "plaintiff" is used, these stages are essentially the same in a criminal case.

Pleadings and Service of Process   A lawsuit is initiated when counsel (the attorney) files a complaint for the plaintiff. The complaint states the cause of action, which means the grounds for the lawsuit. The defendant is then notified that a lawsuit has been filed against him. He is given a court-issued summons and a copy of the plaintiff's complaint. This procedure is called service of process and must occur within a specific period of time after the lawsuit is filed. Typically, process may be served by any person who is at least 18 years old and is not a party to the lawsuit. A marshal or sheriff or any private person may serve the process.

The defendant must file an answer or make some other appropriate response within a certain number of days, usually 30, from the date on which he is served the complaint. His failure to answer within this time may result in a default judgment against him.

 It is essential that any person, or company, served with notice of a lawsuit against him immediately determine how many days he has to answer the complaint, and then answer the complaint in time so a default is not taken against him.

In the answer, the defendant may make a general denial, in which he simply denies the facts stated in the complaint, or he may set forth an affirmative defense, which means that he alleges that although what the plaintiff's complaint says is true, there is a defense that will relieve the defendant of legal liability. After the answer is filed, the plaintiff may then file a reply, which is a response to the defendant's answer.

Rather than filing an answer, the defendant may file a demurrer, which is a formal pleading which, in effect, says "So what?" The defendant argues that even if everything the plaintiff says in the complaint is true, there is no legally recognizable cause of action. The defendant may also file a cross-complaint, in which the defendant brings an action against the plaintiff. When a cross-complaint has been filed, both plaintiff and defendant are in fact suing one another simultaneously.

The complaint, answer, reply, demurrer, and cross-complaint are called *pleadings*. After the pleadings are filed, the pleading stage is concluded and it is said that the "issue is joined."

Discovery   After the pleading stage comes the *discovery* stage. Discovery provides each party to a lawsuit with the opportunity to acquire information about the other party's case prior to trial. The theory is that trial may sometimes be avoided when all of the facts are laid out beforehand and that the parties may be more prone to settle the case without the time and expense of courtroom litigation. As stated by the United States Supreme Court, discovery rules make a trial less a game of blind man's bluff "and more a fair contest with the basic issues and facts disclosed to the fullest practicable extent."[4]

The primary discovery tools are depositions, which are statements taken by an official court reporter on one party's oral examination of the other under oath; interrogatories, which are written questions asked by one party of the other party which must be answered under oath; requests to a party to produce documents; and requests to a party for physical or mental examinations. For example, a person who has been sued for breach of contract may file a motion for discovery to require the plaintiff to submit a copy of the contract allegedly breached.

Pretrial Conference   Closely related to discovery procedures is the pretrial conference. In a pretrial conference the judge meets with the attorneys for both sides to encourage settlement of the case. If settlement cannot be achieved, then the pretrial conference will at least set the boundaries for the trial and attempt to remove elements of surprise from the trial. The trial judge wants to prevent the trial from becoming a spectacle or a contest between attorneys.

Settlement Negotiation   After extensive discovery procedures, both attorneys know fairly well what evidence will be produced in court. An experienced at-

---

[4]*United States v Procter & Gamble Co.*, 356 US 677 2 L Ed 2d 1077, 78 S Ct 983 (1958).

torney may even be able to predict what a jury is apt to award in a particular type of case. Thus, counsel will frequently negotiate a settlement prior to trial. Even cases that do proceed to trial are sometimes settled during the actual trial, when both counsel have an even better grasp on what the evidence is revealing.

Trial If a settlement is not reached, the case will go to trial. While the most common situation is a trial before a judge and jury, sometimes the trial judge acts as both judge and jury.

Before a jury trial actually begins, prospective jurors are questioned by counsel (and the judge) about their background and attitudes. This is called voir dire examination. If any prospective juror is thought to be prejudiced about the parties in the case or the particular type of case or in any other way seems nonqualified, he may be dismissed. After the jurors are selected, they are placed under oath to follow the law as instructed by the judge and not to consider any factors in their determination other than the evidence duly presented at trial.

After the jury is sworn, plaintiff's counsel makes an opening statement. The opening statement is a statement of what counsel intends to prove to the jury during trial. Then, defense counsel makes an opening statement. Following the opening statements, plaintiff's counsel presents his client's case to the jury. The case is presented through the introduction of evidence. Evidence may take the form of witnesses' testimony, documents, and physical items. All evidence must be reliable and relevant to the case to be legally admissible. After plaintiff's counsel examines a witness to establish a fact (direct examination), defendant's counsel may then cross-examine the witness to bring out additional facts or to test the reliability and honesty of the witness. After presentation of plaintiff's case, defense counsel presents his client's case.

After each party has presented its case, both counsel, in turn, may make closing arguments to the jury. At this point, either party may make a motion for a directed verdict. This motion is a request that the judge direct the jury to render a particular verdict. The judge then instructs the jury on the particular laws that can be applied in the case. It is the jury's role to determine the facts from the evidence, and then to apply the laws to those facts. On the basis of its findings, the jury renders a verdict. In a civil case, the jury will find for the plaintiff if there is "a preponderance of evidence," which means that there is more evidence in his favor than against him. In a criminal case, a preponderance of the evidence is not enough. The jury must be convinced of the defendant's guilt "beyond a reasonable doubt."

After presentation of the evidence and a jury verdict, the losing party may make a motion for what is called judgment notwithstanding the verdict. In this motion, the losing party argues that he is entitled to judgment under the law even though the verdict was rendered against him by the jury. The motion will be granted only if the trial judge determines that, under the law, the jury's verdict was improper.

Appeal Sometimes a losing party may appeal the case to a higher court, which means that the party requests the appellate court to review the case. For example, if the trial record indicates that the judge erred in admitting certain evidence that should not have been admitted, or refused to admit evidence that should have been permitted, or gave improper jury instructions, or acted prejudicially to one of the parties, the party harmed may appeal.

When an appellate court accepts a case, a certified record of the trial, which consists of a court reporter's and a clerk's transcript, is sent to the appellate court. The attorneys for both parties then file written briefs with the appellate court, arguing why the case should, or should not, be reversed, and setting forth citations to legal decisions or statutes supporting their positions. Sometimes, an appellate court will permit the attorneys to argue orally and answer questions from the court about their briefs.

The appellate court will only review the record of the lower court; it will not take testimony from witnesses. After analyzing the transcripts of the case, studying the attorneys' written briefs, and listening to any oral arguments, the appellate court will issue a written opinion that reverses, modifies, or affirms the trial court's judgment. These written opinions may then be published.

2:4   Anatomy of a Judicial Decision

Some published judicial decisions, or portions of them, will be used throughout this book to illustrate principles of law or to show how courts deal with particular types of business cases. The decisions create the "case law" that establishes *precedent* for future cases (see 2:5).

Usually, the highest court in a jurisdiction will have its opinions published. Decisions of the intermediate appellate courts may or may not be published, depending on the rules of the jurisdiction. Many jurisdictions will publish only those intermediate court opinions that establish a new rule of law, alter or modify an existing rule, or involve legal issues of continuing public interest.

The basic parts of a decision are identified in the following example of a brief but typical decision.

HEADING

Sharon Schwindt
v
Earl Tonglet and Ralph Delrio d/b/a A-1 Disposal Service, Samuel Duhon, Jr., and ABC Insurance Company
Court of Appeal of Louisiana
Fourth Circuit. 389 So2d 883
Oct. 9, 1980

Before Redmann, Schott and Garrison, JJ.

Garrison, Judge.

FACTS

This is an appeal from a judgment of the district court, granting to plaintiff damages in the amount of $3,500.00, plus $332.00 for medicals, and expert fees. The damages awarded were for an injury sustained by plaintiff on November 29, 1976, when the vehicle which she was driving was struck by a dumpster driven by the defendant's employee. The trial court apparently agreed with the plaintiff's evidence which tended to show that the defendant's truck, while in the process of backing up, collided with the driver's side door of plaintiff's stopped vehicle. From that decision, which we now affirm, the defendants appeal.

Defendant–appellant argues on appeal that the trial court erred in finding the defendant negligent, in failing to find the plaintiff negligent or contributorily negligent and abused its discretion by awarding $3,500.00 for personal injury. We disagree.

OPINION

Our independent review of the evidence and testimony presented convinces this court that the trial judge was not manifestly erroneous. This case involves *primarily* a credibility call on the part of the trial judge. Under the rule of *Canter v Koehring*, 283 So.2d 716 (1973) and *Arcenaux v Domingue*, 365 So.2d 1330 (1978), the trial judge's findings of fact will not be disturbed.

Plaintiff–appellee argues on appeal that the damages awarded should be increased. We disagree. Dr. Padua testified that the plaintiff suffered muscle spasms for which she received muscle relaxants, pain medication, and physical therapy. He further testified that she was asymptomatic as of January 11, 1977. Our review of the record coupled with a review of the scale and range of the case law on damages, as applied to this particular plaintiff in this particular case, convinces this court that the trial judge did not abuse his discretion in the damages awarded. *Reck v Stevens*, 373 So.2d 498 (1979).

JUDGMENT

For the reasons discussed, the judgment of the trial court is affirmed.

The *Schwindt* case heading sets forth the name of the parties, name of the court, page and volume number of the book in which the case is published, and date of the decision. In this case, Sharon Schwindt is suing, among others, Earl Tonglet and Ralph Delrio, who are doing business as the A-1 Disposal Service. The court is the Court of Appeal of Louisiana, which is an intermediate appellate court in Louisiana. The case has been appealed to this appellate court from a Louisiana trial court. If the case is further appealed, the appeal would be to the state court at the next highest level, the Louisiana State Supreme Court.

The names of the three judges who rendered the decision appear next. Usually, an intermediate appellate court is composed of three judges. In some states they are called justices. The court then sets forth the facts of the case and the reasons why the party who lost in the trial court appealed the decision. This statement may be very lengthy or very short, depending on the complexity of the case.

Technically, the entire judicial decision is the opinion. However, for purposes of dissecting a decision, the opinion is the portion of the decision in which the court states the rules of law and how it applied the rules to the facts of the case to reach its decision. Length of decisions ranges from one or two paragraphs to as many as several hundred pages. Obviously, very few decisions are as straightforward as the one presented in the example above. Decisions typically involve several legal questions and require a detailed discussion of the facts and law.

The judgment, the court's actual decision, is at the end. In the *Schwindt* case, the court affirms the trial court's judgment, which awarded to Sharon Schwindt a certain sum of money for damages caused by Earl Tonglet and Ralph Delrio's negligence. Had the appellate court agreed with the defendants' arguments, it could have reversed the trial judge's judgment. The appellate court might also have remanded the case, which means that the case would have been returned to the trial court with directions for the trial judge, for example, to retry the case or retry the case in compliance with particular procedures directed by the appellate court.

Case Citation   The reference to a published judicial decision is called its "citation" or "cite." The citation usually contains the name of the case, the volume and page number in the official (government-issued) case report, the volume and page number in unofficial, regional reports (published by a private publishing company), and the year in which the case was decided.

EXAMPLE (State case)
Combined Investment Co. v Board of County Commissioners, 227 Kan 17, 605 P2d 533 (1980). The names at the beginning identify the parties in the lawsuit; the case is published at page 17 of volume 227 of the official Kansas decisions (in this case, the Supreme Court of Kansas). The same case is also located at page 533 of volume 605 of the Pacific Reporter (2d series), published by a private publishing company. The case was decided in 1980.

EXAMPLE (Federal case)
Sheeran v General Electric Co., 593 F2d 93 (United States Court of Appeals, Ninth Circuit, 1979). The names are those of the parties to the suit. The case may be found at page 93 of volume 593 of the Federal Reporter (2d series). The abbreviation "CA9" means that the case was decided by the United States Court of Appeals for the Ninth Circuit. The case was decided in 1979.

2:5   Basic Judicial Concepts

To understand how courts operate, it is necessary to be aware of the basic judicial concepts that are set forth below.

Jurisdiction   Judicial jurisdiction is the power of a court to hear and decide the outcome of a lawsuit. A court obtains jurisdiction over a plaintiff when he brings a lawsuit, because in bringing the lawsuit he subjects himself to the court's power. Obtaining jurisdiction over a defendant is more complex. The court must meet three requirements: (1) the court must have a basis for the jurisdiction, which means that the defendant must have "sufficient contact" with the state for the court to be able to determine the defendant's legal interests; (2) the court must obtain service of process, which means that it must notify the person of the lawsuit in the statutorily prescribed manner; and (3) the court must be competent, which means that it must be authorized to decide this type of lawsuit. Due process of law, as guaranteed by the Fourteenth Amendment, requires that these three basic conditions be met before a court has jurisdiction over a defendant. A court judgment handed down without jurisdiction may be attacked and set aside as violating the Due Process Clause.

State statutes also set forth the various bases for a court's jurisdiction over a defendant. Typically, a court has jurisdiction over a defendant if he has one or more of the following sufficient contacts: residence in the state, presence in the state when served with notice of the lawsuit, employment in the state, ability to make personal appearance before the court, consent to be sued in this court, or acts done in the state.

Long Arm Legislation   A long arm statute is a statute that permits a court to acquire jurisdiction over a nonresident without service of process within the state, so long as there are "minimum contacts" between the defendant and the state. The theory is that jurisdiction is acquired if the defendant—whether an individual or a corporation—has enough of a connection with the state that traditional notions of fair play and justice are not jeopardized by the state's jurisdiction over the case. Examples of this kind of contact are doing business within the state when the cause of action arose, forming, within the state, a contract out of which the cause of action arose, and owning property in the state that caused injury to the plaintiff. The "minimum contacts" test will vary with the nature of the defendant's activity in the state to which the court belongs.

EXAMPLE
The Acme Trucking Corporation is incorporated and has its home office in New York. Acme Trucking performs a substantial amount of business nationwide, and its trucks travel in California several times a year. During one of its travels in California, an Acme truck collides with a car driven by Paul. Paul sues the Acme Trucking Corporation for negligence. Under the state long arm statute, the California courts have jurisdiction over the foreign (out-of-state) corporation on at least two tests: (1) It has engaged in a course of conduct or business within the state of California and (2) it has arguably committed a tort (civil wrong) within California. Under either test, Acme has a minimum contact with California that justifies its courts having jurisdiction over Acme. Clearly, this jurisdiction does not offend traditional notions of justice and fair play.

Standing to Sue   Courts are established to provide relief to persons whose rights have been invaded or are threatened with invasion. These persons have an interest on which to base a lawsuit. This capacity to bring a legal action is called *standing to sue*. A person must have standing to sue in order to maintain a lawsuit. A court will refuse to hear an action at the request of a person whose rights have not been invaded or infringed, such as a person who seeks a remedy on behalf of someone who is not himself seeking redress for grievances.

EXAMPLE
Kramer has breached a contract with Fowler. Kevin, a friend of Fowler, has nothing to do with the contract but wants to protect Fowler's legal rights. Kevin therefore attempts to bring a lawsuit against Kramer for breaching the Kramer–Fowler contract. A court will not permit Kevin to bring such a lawsuit because no legal interests of his have been violated. Fowler may or may not decide to sue Kramer, but that is Fowler's right, not Kevin's. Kevin has no standing to sue.

Class Action   A *class action* is a lawsuit filed by several persons on behalf of so many other persons that their voluntarily and unanimously joining in a suit is impracticable. Under federal and most state laws, one or more members of a class may sue or be sued as representatives of the class if (1) the class is so numerous that joinder of all members is impracticable, (2) there are questions of law or fact common to the class, (3) the claims or defenses of the representative parties are typical of those of the entire class, and (4) the representative parties will fairly and adequately protect the interests of the class. When the suit is filed, a notice that will reach all members of the class must be given.

One example of a class action is a suit by individuals against a city to prevent or limit a particular city appropriation of funds; if each person in the city who contested the distribution of funds brought a separate action, there would be a risk of inconsistent or varying judicial decisions. Defective products frequently are the subject of class actions, because it would be virtually impossible for all injured persons to bring individual lawsuits. For example, a few consumers injured by a defectively designed television set may file a class action on behalf of several thousand people across the country who are injured by the same defect in the same product.

Justiciable Controversy   Courts have the power and duty to hear only an actual controversy; that is, the parties must have actual adverse interests and conflicting claims. Such a controversy is said to be justiciable (capable of being decided by a judicial body). Courts will not hear "friendly" suits, which are suits that have been collusively arranged by persons wanting a judicial decision on a question but not having actual adverse interests.

EXAMPLE
The Clarion Corporation and the Blackmoor Construction Company want a judicial determination as to the precise location of the boundary between their two buildings. Therefore, both companies arrange for Clarion to bring a lawsuit against Blackmoor. If a court learns that this suit is collusive and fabricated, it would refuse to accept the case for decision.

Declaratory Judgments   A declaratory *judgment* is a judicial decision that is made to settle a dispute before there is an actual injury or a violation of legal rights. For example, a court may be asked to determine a question about the interpretation of a contract to prevent circumstances that would lead to a lawsuit. A declaratory judgment has the full effect of any final court judgment.

Res Judicata   The doctrine of *res judicata* is that a final court judgment is conclusive of all issues decided in that case. This judicially created doctrine exists out of fairness as well as practical necessity. It is based on the public policy that a controversy once litigated and decided on its merits should thereafter be "completely decided for all time," that subsequent judicial decisions should not be made on the same set of facts, and that judgments should have stability. If this doctrine did not exist, all litigation could be literally endless.

EXAMPLE
Fieldman Corporation successfully sues Willow Enterprises for breach of a particular contract. Subsequently, Willow Enterprises wants to sue Fieldman Corporation,

alleging that the same act that was involved in the first suit was a breach by Field-man. The court will not permit this lawsuit under the doctrine of res judicata. All questions relating to this particular contract's alleged breach were decided in the prior lawsuit. The doctrine is applicable because the subsequent attempted suit involved the same parties and essentially the same factual setting and was based on the same question.

Stare Decisis   *Stare decisis,* which in Latin means "let the decision stand," is the doctrine that judicial decisions should stand as precedents or guidance for similar future cases. Stemming from the development of the common law by court decisions (see 1:2), this doctrine reflects a strong judicial policy that the determination of legal questions—"points of law"—by a court will generally be followed by future courts, even though different parties are involved in the subsequent cases. This doctrine is intended to promote certainty, stability, and predictability of the law.

A *precedent* is a prior judicial decision that has factual patterns and legal principles similar to those in the case at hand. An attorney may research prior cases and locate precedents for his case. He may present these precedents to the court and argue that they are "controlling precedent" or "on point" for resolving his own case. Since precedents rarely control a given situation completely, it is usually necessary for the attorney to analyze in detail the facts of the cited cases, compare the facts to his own case, and argue that the prior cases are so similar to his own that they should control the outcome of his case.

Deviating from Precedent   Courts are not always bound to follow precedent. They may decide to "create new law" by reaching a decision which they believe will best fit the needs of the parties, or, on a larger scale, the public. In deciding to depart from the doctrine of stare decisis, and not to follow precedent in a particular case, courts may be influenced by the fact that following the rule might result in an injustice in the particular case or that a particular precedent is inconsistent with modern trends in law or is no longer valid public policy.[5]

An illustration of a court's refusal to follow precedent is the 1954 United States Supreme Court decision in *Brown v Board of Education.*[6] The Court in that decision decided that in the field of public education, the doctrine of "separate but equal" has no place; that separate educational facilities are inherently unequal; and that segregation was therefore a violation of the equal protection guaranteed by the Fourteenth Amendment of the Constitution. The court expressly reversed its 1896 decision of *Plessy v Ferguson,* which had held that school segregation did not violate the Constitution. In refusing to follow the *Plessy* decision as precedent, the Supreme Court, by the *Brown* decision, was creating "new precedent":

---

[5]In discussing judicial change in precedent, Justice Cardozo explained: "Little by little the old doctrine is undermined. Often the encroachments are so gradual that their significance is at first obscured. Finally we discover that the contour of the landscape has been changed, that the old maps must be cast aside, and the ground charted anew." B. Cardozo, *The Nature of the Judicial Process,* 178 (1921).
[6]347 US 483, 98 L Ed 873, 74 S Ct 686, 38 ALR2d 1180 (1954).

> In approaching this problem [school segregation], we cannot turn the clock back to 1868 when the [Fourteenth] Amendment was adopted, or even to 1896 when *Plessy v Ferguson* was written. We must consider public education in the light of its full development and its present place in American life throughout the nation. Only in this way can it be determined if segregation in public schools deprives these plaintiffs of the equal protection of the laws.

After examining evidence that racial segregation in public schools has a detrimental effect and fosters a sense of inferiority affecting the child's motivation to learn, the Court explained, "Whatever may have been the extent of psychological knowledge at the time of *Plessy v Ferguson*, this finding [the detrimental effect] is amply supported by modern authority."

2:6   Arbitration: The Growing Trend[7]

Arbitration is a process of dispute resolution between two parties through the efforts of an arbitrator, a person chosen to hear the case and settle the differences. Sometimes the parties agree on a particular arbitrator privately. In other situations, the arbitrator is appointed by the trial court. This is called judicial arbitration. The arbitrator's decision is enforceable under court order. As an alternative to court litigation, arbitration accomplishes much that the formal lawsuit does not, particularly in the commercial field.

In some states, either party may have the arbitrator's award set aside and may obtain a court trial. However, a party who loses at arbitration may not want to set aside the arbitrator's award since the arbitration is sometimes viewed as a "test run" for trial and the loser may have no reason to feel that a judge or jury would make a different award. Moreover, if the loser went into court and lost, he would have to pay attorney's fees and court costs.

Arbitration does have advantages over traditional courtroom litigation. One advantage is the amount of time arbitration takes as compared to litigation. In large cities like New York and Los Angeles, a five-year delay in getting a case to trial is not unusual. In Los Angeles, for example, there were 72,000 civil cases awaiting trial in 1981, with the figure increasing at the rate of 1,000 cases a month. Arbitration, on the other hand, may be concluded in a few months or even weeks.

Another advantage of arbitration is that it is a private proceeding. As a general matter, neither the government nor the public is alerted to the evidence presented in the arbitration. This factor may be important to businesspersons who do not want public access to information about particular trade practices or credit standings. A third advantage is that arbitration is less costly than litigation. It is not essential to retain an attorney for arbitration, since the rules of procedure are simpler than those in court proceedings.

 When negotiating a contract, it is sometimes to the advantage of both parties to include a provision that any disputes will be submitted to an arbitrator rather than to the courts. Even the name of the arbitrator may be set forth in

---

[7]Labor arbitration is discussed in Chapter 52.

the contract. Therefore, if there is dispute under the contract later, this provision may contribute to a quicker and less expensive resolution than can be obtained from a lawsuit.

Key Concepts and Terms

- Courts determine legal controversies between opposing parties in a lawsuit, create or change rules of law (in the absence of statutory law), and review legislation.
- The American judicial system consists of the courts of the federal government and the court systems of each of the 50 states. The federal judiciary is comprised of the United States District Courts, the 12 United States Courts of Appeals, and the United States Supreme Court.
- Court systems are comprised of trial courts and appellate courts.
- A lawsuit is an adversary proceeding in which the person bringing the action—the plaintiff—and the person defending the action—the defendant—each seek to persuade the trier of fact that under the facts of the case the law entitles him to win. The stages of a lawsuit are the filing of pleadings and service of process, discovery, pretrial conference, settlement negotiation, trial, and appeal.
- Judicial jurisdiction is the power of a court to hear and determine a lawsuit. Under long arm statutes, in certain circumstances a state court is permitted to acquire jurisdiction over a nonresident even though the nonresident is not personally served with process within the state, so long as there are certain "minimum contacts" between the defendant and the state.
- A court will refuse to hear a lawsuit unless the person seeking judicial relief has an actual interest in the case, or "standing to sue."
- Courts have the power and duty to hear only an actual controversy between parties who have adverse interests and conflicting claims. This is called a justiciable controversy.
- The doctrine of res judicata is that a court judgment is final and no issues litigated in that case can be relitigated between the same parties.
- Stare decisis is the doctrine that judicial decisions stand as precedents or guidance for similar future cases.
- Arbitration is a private proceeding for resolving a dispute between two parties. An arbitrator is a person who has been accepted by both parties, hears the case, and makes a decision.

- Appellate Court
- Arbitration
- Class Action
- Discovery
- Judgment
- Lawsuit

- Pleadings
- Precedent
- Res Judicata
- Standing to Sue
- Stare Decisis

Questions and Case Problems

1. What functions do courts perform?
2. What is the difference between the federal and state judicial systems? Explain the structure and function of each.
3. What is an appeal?
4. What is the doctrine of judicial review of legislation and how did it originate in the United States?
5. What does it mean to say that a court must have jurisdiction to hear a case? How does a court obtain jurisdiction?
6. What is long arm legislation? What is its relevancy to the transaction of modern business?
7. What is the doctrine of standing to sue? Give some examples of the operation of this doctrine.
8. What is a justiciable controversy? Provide some examples of controversies which are justiciable and some which are not.
9. What are the doctrines of res judicata and stare decisis? How do they differ?
10. What is arbitration? How does it relate to the judicial system?

3 Administrative Law

> *For many Americans, the influence of administrative officials seems
> far more pervasive than that of judges and legislators. Not only do
> these officials execute the laws; together they create more legal rules
> and try more cases than all the legislatures and all the courts.*
>
> George Spiro and James L. Houghteling,
> *The Dynamics of Law,* 2nd ed.

3:1 In General

In theory, American government consists of three branches: the legislative, to enact law; the executive, to administer and enforce law; and the judicial (the courts),
to interpret law. In reality, however, there is a "fourth branch" of government—
one consisting of administrative agencies. These agencies carry out certain investigatory, rule-making, or adjudicatory functions which are delegated by the legislative or executive branches of federal, state, or local government.

The quality of the food we eat, the means of transportation and communication
available to us, how we heat our homes and conduct our businesses, the houses we
build, and the companies we form, even the quality of the air we breathe are
controlled and regulated by these sometimes "invisible" administrative agencies.
As noted by the United States Supreme Court, "The rise of administrative bodies
probably has been the most significant legal trend of the last century and perhaps
more values today are affected by their decisions than by those of all the courts."[1]

Reasons for Development   *Administrative law* was born of necessity. Its growth as
a major force in the legal system began in the mid-nineteenth century as America
was transformed from an agricultural to an industrial nation. As industries grew
and social problems increased, numerous legal questions concerning the rights and
welfare of private persons and businesses arose. Legislative and executive branches
of government realized by the turn of the century that they were ill-equipped to
gain the practical experience and knowledge required to give day-to-day attention
to the complex, ever-changing problems that developed. This realization led to
adoption by Congress of the Interstate Commerce Act in 1887. This act established
the first federal administrative agency, the Interstate Commerce Commission. This
agency was responsible for day-to-day regulation of railroads. (The Interstate Commerce Commission presently regulates virtually all interstate commerce.) As the

---

[1]*Federal Trade Com. v Ruberoid Co.*, 343 US 470, 96 L Ed 1081, 72 S Ct 800 (1952).

Supreme Court, discussing reasons for establishment of the Interstate Commerce Commission, observed: "Congress has delegated the enforcement of transportation policy to a permanent expert body and has charged it with the duty of being responsive to the dynamic character of transportation problems."[2]

Since 1887, Congress has created so many agencies that today they form one of the largest bodies for government regulation in the world. Entire fields of human endeavor are controlled and regulated by specialized, complex agencies whose members have expertise in particular fields. At the federal level, for example, there are the Interstate Commerce Commission, National Labor Relations Board, Federal Communications Commission, Federal Trade Commission, Nuclear Regulatory Commission, Federal Power Commission, Securities and Exchange Commission, Occupational Safety and Health Administration, Bureau of Indian Affairs, Environmental Protection Agency, Civil Rights Commission, Federal Aviation Administration, Civil Aeronautics Board, Bureau of Land Management, and Social Security Administration, to name just a few. In some areas, the states have corresponding or additional administrative agencies to control such matters as workers' compensation, labor relations, civil rights, public utilities, and state unemployment compensation.

Federal Administrative Procedure Act   Dissatisfaction with arbitrariness in the operation of some administrative agencies resulted in the enactment of the *federal Administrative Procedure Act* of 1946 (APA) (5 USC §§ 1001 et seq.). Adoption of this act marked the beginning of a new era in administrative law, because finally there would be uniformity in the procedures of most federal administrative agencies. The APA covers nearly every phase of the administrative process in detail. The APA sets forth guidelines for uniform and impartial procedures. It guards against arbitrary official encroachment on private rights. Many states have laws, patterned after the APA, to govern the procedures of their administrative agencies.

Regulatory and Nonregulatory Agencies   Agencies are sometimes classified as regulatory or nonregulatory. Regulatory agencies have authority to regulate economic activities of individuals and businesses. They have licensing power, rate-making power, and power to regulate certain business practices. They also make rules, decide disputes, and impose fines. Examples of regulatory agencies are the Federal Trade Commission, which has power to prevent unfair or deceptive business practices in interstate commerce; Federal Communications Commission, which licenses and delicenses radio and television stations; and Interstate Commerce Commission, which has power to set rates for interstate carriers.

Nonregulatory agencies, on the other hand, are given authority to conduct investigations or administer benefits such as pensions, government insurance, and workers' compensation. Examples of nonregulatory agencies are the Social Security Administration, which administers benefits, and the Federal Bureau of Investigation, which investigates federal crimes.

---

[2]*Atchison, T. & S. F. R. Co. v Wichita Board of Trade,* 412 US 800, 37 L Ed 2d 350, 93 S Ct 2367 (1973).

3:2   Relation to Court System

While it is true that some administrative rulings are adjudicatory in nature (see 3:4), the purpose of all administrative action is to implement a particular legislative policy. In the administrative system, decisions are made through methods, for reasons, and by persons quite different from those in the judicial system. In the judicial system, the judge or jury makes decisions about the questions presented before it. In the administrative system, it is the members of the agency who set policy or make rules. Unlike judges and juries in the court system, agency members are experts in the particular field in which they are setting policy or making decisions. For example, administrators working for the National Labor Relations Board are experts and are sympathetic to the complex problems of collective bargaining and industrial relations. Members of the Federal Communications Commission have expertise in the electronic communications industry, while members of the Federal Trade Commission have expertise in the field of antitrust and trade practices. Only a few courts, such as the United States Tax Court and the federal Court of Patent Appeals, have specialized knowledge in a field.

Advantages and Disadvantages of the Administrative Process   There are many advantages in having a case heard before an administrative agency rather than a court. Some of these advantages lie in the very functions of an agency. Because courts generally do not have (1) the same power to initiate and control investigations, (2) the power to supervise the parties after a case has been decided, (3) the ability to provide expert knowledge in technical fields, or (4) procedures for easily obtaining decisions in advance of conduct that would lead to lawsuits, an administrative proceeding is more accessible to the parties, gives the parties closer attention, offers expert judgment in a specialized area, and can serve as preventive action against future litigation.

There is one disadvantage, though, in the lack of formality in administrative proceedings. This is that a person's constitutional rights are not as highly guarded as in court proceedings. The United States Supreme Court has repeatedly emphasized that there is more protection of individual rights in a judicial action than in an administrative action.

In regulating certain industries, some statutes have divided the duty of enforcement between courts and administrative agencies. Thus, it is possible for a case to be heard before both an administrative agency and a court. For example, federal antitrust legislation provides remedies against certain business activities detrimental to interstate competition, and these remedies may be sought in both a federal regulatory agency—the Federal Trade Commission—and the federal courts.

3:3   Limits on Agency Powers

As stated earlier, an administrative agency is created by legislation. The agency's powers are set forth in this legislation. In this sense, the legislature delegates power to the agencies. Consequently, the question whether the *doctrine of delegation* of power by the legislature is appropriate—that is, whether Congress or a state legislature has unconstitutionally "delegated away" its inherent legislative function—has arisen. Prior to 1935, most United States Supreme Court decisions upheld delegations of power to administrative agencies. The rationale usually was that agencies were simply "finding facts," "filling in administrative details," or effectuating "primary standards" already established by the legislative branch of government. Essentially, the Supreme Court recognized the impracticality of not permitting delegation of powers since it would clearly have been impossible for Congress to decide every detail as to each law it enacted. The court thus used various word formulas to do what was practical and necessary for the administration of government.

During the Depression the Supreme Court for the first time began to disapprove some delegations of congressional power. This disapproval resulted in striking down major sections of the National Industrial Recovery Act, which had granted extremely far-reaching powers to the President to control the economy. Theoretically, there may still be some constitutional limitations on the congressional delegation of powers to federal administrative agencies, but from a practical standpoint this issue is probably no longer viable. Recent rulings indicate that the current issue is simply whether, under all the circumstances, the delegation is "reasonable." If Congress has the constitutional power to regulate a field, and is as specific as possible under the circumstances, the delegation will usually be upheld.

Although the doctrine of nondelegability has lost most of its relevance in the federal government, it is still applied in some states. The following decision is an illustration of a state legislative delegation to an administrative agency of duties and powers for air pollution control.

Bortz Coal Co.
v
Air Pollution Commission
2 Pa Cmwlth 441, 279 A2d 388, 48 ALR 3d 311
(Pennsylvania Commonwealth Court, 1971)

[The Bortz Coal Company is appealing from an order of an administrative agency, the Air Pollution Commission, to cease operations for violating the state's air pollution control statute. The coal company has charged that the commission's duties were an unconstitutional delegation of legislative functions from the state legislature to the commission.]

Kramer, Judge.

*   *   *

Because of the fact that for all practical purposes this case represents the first venture of an appellate court of this Commonwealth into what in all probability will become a major development in the law, known generally as environmental law, we believe it would be beneficial to the bar and to the public, to the regulatory agencies, and to the courts, to make several preparatory comments.

Although one would be led to believe from the avalanche of recent publications on the subject of air pollution that it is something new, created by scientists and crusaded by modern youth, it should be pointed out that the law has been concerned with air pollution for centuries. As early as 1306, A.D., the use of "sea-coal" (as distinguished from charcoal) as fuel was forbidden on penalty of death.... During her reign, Queen Elizabeth of England forbade the burning of coal in London during sessions of Parliament, and in 1661 A.D., there was a plan to remove all industries in the city of London to its leeward side and to plant sweet-smelling flowers and trees on the windward side....

The point in citing these proofs of prior concern is merely to remind the reader that the law always provided for the protection against private nuisances. There is no doubt that because of the recent notoriety of the condition of the environment that there has been formed a new public policy in this State, as well as other States of this Nation, that there is need for protection of the public against public nuisances.

That new policy is found in Section 2 of the Air Pollution Control Act [which reads as follows:]

> "It is hereby declared to be the policy of the Commonwealth of Pennsylvania to protect the air resources of the Commonwealth to the degree necessary for the (i) protection of public health, safety and well-being of its citizens; (ii) prevention of injury to plant and animal life and to property; (iii) protection of the comfort and convenience of the public and the protection of the recreational resources of the Commonwealth; and (iv) development, attraction and expansion of industry, commerce, and agriculture."

In carrying out this public policy, the Legislature created the Air Pollution Commission ..., under the Department of Health. The Commission was directed by the Legislature to establish rules, regulations and standards for the enforcement of the Act. There can be no doubt from a reading of the Act that the legislative intent is to clean the air insofar as is reasonably possible under the police powers granted to the Commonwealth in both the State and Federal Constitutions.

It is well recognized as a principle of American jurisprudence that the Legislature may utilize the establishment of administrative agencies as a part of the legislative process in our tripartite system of government to regulate and control that segment of our society which the Legislature in its wisdom deems necessary of control.... The Legislature may not delegate its legislative function but it may authorize an agency to carry out the legislative intent described in general terms through rules, regulations and standards established by the agency.... There are certain constitutional tests to determine whether or not the Legislature has gone too far in its delegation.... The rules, regulations and standards of the regulatory agency must be reasonable, understandable, available, and must not violate the constitutional rights of any citizen.

Because of the well recognized problems involved in combining, in administrative agencies, all three functions of a tripartite form of government, viz., legislative, executive and judicial, the agencies and the courts must take care in carrying out their primary function of protecting the public, that they be vigilant to make certain that the individual citizen's rights in property and due process are not violated. Because it is common for the employees of the adjudicating regulatory agency to assume the role of prosecutor, witness and judge of the quasi-judicial functions of the agency, the courts must scrutinize the proceedings, the attitude and approach of the regulatory agency to assure that four centuries of well developed standards of fairness, procedure and substantive law are not washed away with the intense shower of exuberance and well meaning desires. Some environmental lawyers believe that the right to a decent environment may be within the penumbra of the unenumerated natural rights guaranteed by the Ninth Amendment of the United States Constitution.... Some lawyers believe that the protection of the environment comes within the public trust doctrine.... Only time will tell how far environmental control of the air will be developed, but no matter how it is developed, it must be done within the framework of the law. . . .

The basic premise, then, is that coke oven operators in this State may use their property so long as they do no injury to other citizens of the Commonwealth in violation of the law. It matters not under the law that these coke ovens in question have been in continuous use since 1898. There is no prescriptive right to cause injury to another, and this basic premise has existed every day of the operation of these coke ovens. They were always subject to that prohibition. In the Air Pollution Control Act, *supra*, the Legislature has established that certain air pollution is injurious to the public health, welfare and safety, and, now, it need only be determined whether or not those technical standards which were set by the Commission are reasonable, so as not to violate Bortz's constitutional rights. . . .

[Constitutionality of state's delegation upheld.]

Ultra Vires Acts   Under the *ultra vires* ("beyond the powers") *doctrine*, actions taken by an administrative agency must not be outside the scope of the power delegated to the agency by the legislature. When an agency acts outside the scope of its purposes and powers, the agency is unconstitutionally exercising legislative power and its actions are void. Most ultra vires acts are those that are in conflict with constitutionally protected civil liberties. In one case, for example, the Supreme Court invalidated agency regulations that permitted withdrawal of security clearances without giving the affected party opportunity for a hearing. The court declared that the regulations were unauthorized by Congress, and therefore were ultra vires and void.

Notice and Fair Hearing   Assuming an agency decides to take action against a private person or corporation, the agency must respect certain procedural safeguards imposed by the Constitution. If agency action would deprive a person of interests that are protected by due process, the agency must give the person notice and an opportunity to be heard. Constitutional due process, under the Fifth and Fourteenth Amendments, requires that federal and state governments provide *notice* and *fair hearing* before taking action that deprives an individual of "liberty" or "property." As a basic ingredient of administrative law, the right to notice and fair hearing provides vital protection against arbitrary governmental action. For example, if discharge from a governmental job would involve a stigma or in any other way would foreclose future employment opportunities, a "liberty" interest is involved, requiring an agency to give notice and hold a hearing before taking action. A person receiving welfare benefits under statutory and administrative standards defining eligibility has an interest in the continued receipt of the benefits where the statute provides a claim of entitlement to the benefits ("property") for anyone who qualifies. Hence, the issue of whether a person does qualify must be resolved by a full and fair hearing.

Other situations in which administrative agencies must provide notice and hearing before taking action include the expulsion or suspension of students from public schools, withholding of licenses, exclusion and deportation of aliens, revocation of parole or probation, denial of welfare or housing benefits, and injury to reputation.

Once it is established that the interest involved is protected by due process and that the type of issue requires a hearing, the form of notice and type of hearing must be determined. These vary depending on what is "appropriate to the nature of the case." The specific requirements of due process will be determined in each case by three factors: the nature of the private interest affected, the risk to that interest posed by existing procedures, and the burden on the government if other procedures are imposed.

Administrative hearings must be conducted in a fair, open, and impartial manner as to comply with due process of law. This kind of hearing is illustrated in the following decision. An administrative agency (a city's civil service commission) conducted a hearing to suspend a police chief without providing essential due process safeguards.

Adams
v
Marshall
212 Kan 595, 512 P2d 365
(Kansas Supreme Court, 1973)

[A suspended city police chief brought a suit to compel members of the city's civil service commission to follow certain due process procedures during the course of his suspension hearing. The police chief argued that the hearing was not conducted with due process of law because it was not open to the public and because his right to cross-examine was limited to five minutes. Agreeing that due process had been violated by the commission, the trial judge ordered the city civil service commission to open the hearing to the public and not to limit the cross-examination to five minutes. The agency appealed.]

Fontron, Justice.

*   *   *

The trial court was correct in its finding that the members of the Commission were acting in a quasi-judicial capacity in hearing the

Adams appeal. In *Thompson v Amis*, 208 Kan. 658, 493 P.2d 1259, we had under consideration the nature of an appeal conducted by the Kansas Civil Service Board in a case involving the dismissal of a state employee. We said in that case that quasi-judicial was "a term applied to administrative boards or officers empowered to investigate facts, weigh evidence, draw conclusions as a basis for official actions and exercise discretion of judicial nature." . . . We concluded in *Thompson* that the state board exercised quasi-judicial functions, and we are impelled to a similar conclusion with respect to the civil service commission in the present case.

Where an administrative body acts in a quasi-judicial capacity the requirements of due process will attach to the proceedings held before it. This principle was pointed out in *Neeley v Board of Trustees, Policemen's & Firemen's Retirement System*, 205 Kan. 780, 784, 473 P.2d 72, 75, where the court said:

"... The constitutional guaranty of due process of law applies to administrative as well as judicial proceedings where such proceedings are *quasi* judicial in nature." . . .

Two ground rules laid down by the Commission in this case are said by the plaintiff to violate basic due process demands: (1) the right to examine and cross-examine witnesses and (2) the right to an open or public hearing. We are inclined to agree.

The right to the cross-examination of witnesses in quasi-judicial or adjudicatory proceedings is one of fundamental importance and is generally, if not universally, recognized as an important requirement of due process. . . .

In speaking of due process requirements, the United States Supreme Court, in *Int. Com. Comm. v Louis. & Nash. R. R.*, 227 U.S. 88, 93, 33 S.Ct. 185, 187, 57 L.Ed. 431, said:

> ". . . All parties must be fully apprised of the evidence submitted or to be considered, and must be given opportunity to cross-examine witnesses, to inspect documents, and to offer evidence in explanation or rebuttal. In no other way can a party maintain its rights or make its defense. In no other way can it test the sufficiency of the facts to support the finding. . . ." . . .

It has somewhere been said, if our imperfect recollection can be trusted, that cross-examination is the anvil on which the truth may be forged. We have said many times that the extent of cross-examination lies largely within the sound judicial discretion of the court. . . . However, cross-examination may not be unduly curtailed in testing the soundness of a witness' testimony . . . , nor may it be so limited and circumscribed as to preclude a full disclosure of the facts. . . .

No administrative body, no matter how prescient its members, can foretell in advance of hearing the extent to which the testimony of witnesses may be limited without impinging upon the pursuit of truth. The five-minute limitation which the Commission, before trial, placed on the cross-examination of all witnesses was in our opinion an impermissible restriction on due process.

Passing to the question of public trial, we believe it may generally be said that proceedings of a judicial nature held behind closed doors and shielded from public scrutiny have long been repugnant to our system of justice. The concept that trials and judicatory hearings be open to the public gaze is inherent in our idea of due process. This view was voiced many years ago by the United States Supreme Court in *Morgan v United States*, 304 U.S. 1, 58 S.Ct. 773, 82 L.Ed. 1129, in the following words:

> ". . . The vast expansion of this field of administrative regulation in response to the pressure of social needs is made possible under our system by adherence to the basic principles that the legislature shall appropriately determine the standards of administrative action and that in administrative proceedings of a quasi-judicial character the liberty and property of the citizen shall be protected by the rudimentary requirements of fair play. These demand 'a fair and open hearing,' essential alike to the legal validity of the administrative regulation and to the maintenance of public confidence in the value and soundness of this important governmental process. Such a hearing has been described as an 'inexorable safeguard.' . . ." . . .

The requirements of an administrative hearing of a judicial or quasi-judicial character are phrased in this language in 2 Am.Jur.2d, Administrative Law, § 412, p. 222:

> ". . . A hearing before an administrative agency exercising judicial, quasi-judicial, or adjudicatory powers must be fair, open, and impartial, and if such a hearing has been denied, the administrative action is void. . . ."
> . . .

[Judgment affirmed.]

Legislative and Executive Control over Agencies   The legislative and executive branches of government have several means to control agencies. The legislative branch controls and limits agencies through budget appropriations, watchdog committees, investigations, appointment of agency personnel, and intercession in pending agency matters. The legislature can eliminate an agency simply by repealing the statute that created it. The legislature can also override administrative actions by statute. As to executive control over agencies, the President or a governor usually has power to select heads of agencies. With major federal posts, the Senate must approve the President's appointments. Executive control also extends to removing agency personnel and formulating fiscal policy and budgets.

3:4   Formulation of Agency Policy

An administrative agency may have broad discretion in implementing the statutory scheme for which the legislature has made it responsible. Administrative policy is formulated in any of the following ways: rule-making, adjudication (on a case-by-case basis), investigation, or informal action.

Rule-Making   Some agencies have the power to make, alter, or repeal laws or rules. Rule-making power is distinguished from adjudicative power in that usually the rules are general regulations that apply only to future, rather than past, transactions and circumstances, whereas adjudicative decisions are orders that apply to named persons or to specific situations that occurred in the past.

When a federal agency considers proposing a rule, it must first draft it and publish it in the *Federal Register*, which is a daily official federal publication of executive, legislative, and administrative regulations and actions. Then notice is given and a formal hearing is held to give interested parties the opportunity to respond. When the rule is adopted, it is published first in the *Federal Register* and then in the *Code of Federal Regulations*, a government publication of rules of federal administrative agencies.

 Once the draft of a rule is published in the *Federal Register*, the public has an opportunity to file comments on the proposal and, sometimes, to testify at hearings with regard to the desirability of the proposal. The public and the business community, at this stage, may also suggest redrafting the proposal. The businessperson should be alert for proposed administrative regulations that affect his industry, with a view toward submitting comments to the agency before it finalizes its rules.

In its rule-making capacity, the agency is a "mini-legislature" empowered by the state or federal legislature to promulgate rulings. In light of this, courts have broadly interpreted agency power to make rules that actually have the effect of substantive law. For example, the Supreme Court has held that the Federal Trade

Commission could substantively define "unfair methods of competition" by using its rule-making power, on the rationale that rule-making is essential to the regulatory process and in many ways superior to adjudication in making policy.

Adjudication   When an agency acts as an adjudicative body it is essentially performing court functions. Most adjudicative matters in federal agencies are heard by administrative law judges (formerly known as hearing officers). Administrative law judges preside at the hearing and render an initial decision, which can be appealed to the head of the agency. In some agencies, there is an intermediate review board which hears appeals, with limited right of appeal to the agency head. Policy on the following problems may be properly formulated by an agency on a case-by-case basis: problems that could not reasonably have been foreseen by the agency, problems as to which the agency has only a tentative judgment due to lack of experience in the particular area, and problems so specialized and varied that they cannot be resolved by general rules.

Investigation   Investigatory, or so-called "inquisitional," powers—such as the power to inspect or require disclosure of information—are conferred on many administrative agencies. Investigatory power is one of the distinctive functions which sets an agency apart from the courts. Some agencies are in fact solely investigatory or advisory bodies; they exist solely to secure and provide information, and in some cases, to make recommendations or to gather public opinion. So pervasive has the investigatory function of agencies become that there is now a considerable body of law relating to methods of individual and corporate protection from agency information-gathering functions (see 3:3 and 3:5).

3:5   Protection from Agency Information Gathering

Although administrative investigations are not criminal proceedings, they sometimes result in imposition of criminal penalties. Therefore, some of the constitutional safeguards which protect a defendant in criminal proceedings have been held applicable to administrative investigations and hearings. While most information sought by agencies is given voluntarily, individuals or corporations sometimes do not desire to provide an agency with requested information. In such cases, many agencies are authorized to use one or more methods to obtain information, including the subpoena power (obtaining testimony and documents under court order), periodic or special reports, and agency inspections of a company's records and business sites.

Agencies are frequently empowered to enforce their requests for information. For example, some agencies can revoke licenses or take other sanctions against a person or company not complying with an order for information.

Fourth Amendment Protection   Administrative officials sometimes desire to inspect homes and businesses in connection with health and fire laws. In these instances, the question may arise as to whether such "searches" violate the Fourth Amendment right to be secure against searches and seizures in the absence of a valid search warrant. The United States Supreme Court has held that a search warrant must be obtained, in the absence of an emergency situation that could be hazardous to a person's welfare, for most administrative inspections of commercial and residential premises pursuant to fire, health, and housing regulations, unless the occupant consents to the inspection.

The following decision is an example of such a holding. The Supreme Court, in this decision, makes clear, as it has in other cases, that "[t]he businessman, like the occupant of a residence, has a constitutional right to go about his business free from unreasonable official entries upon his private commercial property."

See
v
Seattle
387 US 541, 18 L Ed 2d 943, 87 S Ct 1737
(United States Supreme Court, 1967)

[A businessman was convicted for refusing to permit a representative of a city administrative agency (the Seattle Fire Department) to inspect his locked commercial warehouse without a warrant for probable cause to believe that a violation of any municipal ordinance existed. The inspection was conducted as part of a routine, periodic city-wide canvas to obtain compliance with the city's fire code. The businessman appealed the conviction.]

Justice White delivered the opinion of the Court.

*   *   *

In *Go-Bart Importing Co. v United States*, 282 US 344, 75 L ed 374, 51 S Ct 153; *Amos v United States*, 255 US 313, 65 L ed 654, 41 S Ct 266; and *Silverthorne Lumber Co. v United States*, 251 US 385, 64 L ed 319, 40 S Ct 182, 24 ALR 1426, this Court refused to uphold otherwise unreasonable criminal investigative searches merely because commercial rather than residential premises were the object of the police intrusions. Likewise, we see no justification for so relaxing Fourth Amendment safeguards where the official inspection is intended to aid enforcement of laws prescribing minimum

physical standards for commercial premises. As we explained in *Camara* [387 US 523], a search of private houses is presumptively unreasonable if conducted without a warrant. The businessman, like the occupant of a residence, has a constitutional right to go about his business free from unreasonable official entries upon his private commercial property. The businessman, too, has that right placed in jeopardy if the decision to enter and inspect for violation of regulatory laws can be made and enforced by the inspector in the field without official authority evidenced by a warrant.

As governmental regulation of business enterprise has mushroomed in recent years, the need for effective investigative techniques to achieve the aims of such regulation has been the subject of substantial comment and legislation. Official entry upon commercial property is a technique commonly adopted by administrative agencies at all levels of government to enforce a variety of regulatory laws; thus, entry may permit inspection of the structure in which a business is housed, as in this case, or inspection of business products, or a perusal of financial books and records. This Court has not had occasion to consider the Fourth Amendment's relation to this broad range of investigations. However, we have dealt with the Fourth Amendment issues raised by another common investigative technique, the administrative subpoena of corporate books and records. We find strong support in these subpoena cases for our conclusion that warrants are a necessary and a tolerable limitation on the right to enter upon and inspect commercial premises.

It is now settled that, when an administrative agency subpoenas corporate books or records, the Fourth Amendment requires that the subpoena be sufficiently limited in scope, relevant in purpose, and specific in directive so that compliance will not be unreasonably burdensome. The agency has the right to conduct all reasonable inspections of such documents which are contemplated by statute, but it must delimit the confines of a search by designating the needed documents in a formal subpoena. In addition, while the demand to inspect may be issued by the agency, in the form of an administrative subpoena, it may not be made and enforced by the inspector in the field, and the subpoenaed party may obtain judicial review of the reasonableness of the demand prior to suffering penalties for refusing to comply.

It is these rather minimal limitations on administrative action which we think are constitutionally required in the case of investigative entry upon commercial establishments. The agency's particular demand for access will of course be measured, in terms of probable cause to issue a warrant, against a flexible standard of reasonableness that takes into account the public need for effective enforcement of the particular regulation involved. But the decision to enter and inspect will not be the product of the unreviewed discretion of the enforcement officer in the field. Given the analogous investigative functions performed by the administrative subpoena and the demand for entry, we find untenable the proposition that the subpoena, which has been termed a "constructive" search . . . is subject to Fourth Amendment limitations which do not apply to actual searches and inspections of commercial premises.

We therefore conclude that administrative entry, without consent, upon the portions of commercial premises which are not open to the public may only be compelled through prosecution or physical force within the framework of a warrant procedure. We do not in any way imply that business premises may not reasonably be inspected in many more situations than private homes, nor do we question such accepted regulatory techniques as licensing programs which require inspections prior to operating a business or marketing a product. Any constitutional challenge to such programs can only be resolved, as many have been in the past, on a case-by-case basis under the general Fourth Amendment standard of reasonableness. We hold only that the basic component of a reasonable search under the Fourth Amendment—that it not be enforced without a suitable warrant procedure—is applicable in this context, as in others, to business as well as to residential premises. Therefore, appellant may not be prosecuted for exercising his constitutional right to insist that the fire inspector obtain a warrant authorizing entry upon appellant's locked warehouse.

[Conviction reversed.]

Although evidence seized in an unlawful search is inadmissible in a criminal proceeding, it has sometimes been admitted in administrative proceedings.

Fifth Amendment Protection   Witnesses called to testify in an agency investigation may assert the Fifth Amendment privilege against self-incrimination in refusing to answer specific questions if the information requested could supply a link in a chain leading to criminal conviction. The Fifth Amendment privilege is available only to an individual and may not be invoked by a corporation, union, or partnership. Thus, the record custodian of such an organization must produce requested *documents*, but he has a privilege to refuse to answer specific *questions*. The Fifth Amendment privilege against self-incrimination also protects the witness' private papers if they would incriminate the witness. However, the privilege does not extend to records required to be kept by statute.

Right to Counsel   A witness who must appear before an administrative investigatory hearing is entitled to be represented by an attorney.

 Some attorneys, many in the Washington, D.C., area, specialize in representing persons and corporations in dealings with and appearances before federal administrative agencies. Other attorneys specialize in particular agencies, such as the Federal Trade Commission, National Labor Relations Board, and Interstate Commerce Commission. Because of the complexity—and uniqueness—of each agency, a person dealing with or appearing before a particular agency is advised to consult an attorney who has experience with that particular agency.

3:6   Freedom of Information Act

As discussed earlier, most federal agencies have subpoena power to issue orders enforceable in federal court, to require a witness to testify and to hand over documents, subject to constitutional limitations. But does a private person or corporation have the right to require an administrative agency to turn over information to it? The *Freedom of Information Act* (FOIA) (5 USC § 552), contained in the Administrative Procedure Act, provides that records that have not been otherwise made available under the act must be disclosed if the request reasonably describes the record, and is made in accordance with published rules.

The act applies to *any* agency, broadly defined to include all executive and military departments, government-controlled corporations, and other divisions within the executive branch, even including the Office of the President. Specifically, the act requires that each agency make available for public inspection and copying its records, its opinions in decided cases, its statements of policy and interpretations, and any administrative staff manuals that affect the public. If an agency fails to disclose the requested information, the federal courts may compel production. An agency must respond to requests for records within 10 days, and if a refusal to produce can be appealed within the agency, the appeal must be decided within 20 days. Each federal agency is obligated to publish quarterly a current index of those matters required to be made available under the FOIA.

The FOIA sets forth a comprehensive statement of the rights of private persons and corporations to obtain information that is in the possession of the government and its administrative agencies. The purpose of the FOIA, in the words of the Supreme Court, is to "permit access to official information long shielded unnecessarily from public view and . . . to create a judicially enforceable public right to secure such information from possibly unwilling official hands."[3]

If a person or corporation who has submitted information to a federal agency wants to *prevent* disclosure of the information to persons who have requested it from the agency, a *reverse FOIA suit* may be filed. Although not expressly authorized by the FOIA, this kind of suit has been successful in preventing such disclosures.

Several states have enacted counterparts to the FOIA and laws that require agencies to conduct their discussions and hearings in public sessions.

Records   Federal regulations provide that the term "records," as used in the FOIA, means all books, papers, maps, photographs, or other documentary materials, regardless of their physical form or characteristics. The term "records" does not, however, include physical items in possession of the government, such as, for example, Lee Harvey Oswald's rifle.

Exceptions   The Administrative Procedure Act sets forth exceptions to the Freedom of Information Act. Federal courts may privately examine the requested records to determine whether any exceptions apply. The exceptions to the disclosure provisions are, broadly speaking, materials as to national defense, internal personnel rules, trade secrets, interagency or intra-agency memoranda, investigatory files compiled for law enforcement purposes, reports on financial institutions, and geological or geophysical information and data. These exceptions have all been litigated, and there is a body of law that applies to each.

3:7   Judicial Review

Judicial review is the review of administrative action by a court. A person or corporation suffering harm as a result of agency action may seek judicial review, but unless the case is "ripe" it will be denied judicial review. The ripeness doctrine is designed to avoid litigating in the abstract—that is, before the administrative rule has been definitely applied to the plaintiff. In deciding whether a case is ripe for review, the courts consider the extent of hardship on the parties that would result if the court denied review.

EXAMPLE
A Federal Drug Administration rule requires the brand name of drug labels to be accompanied by the generic name of the chemical. If a manufacturer fails to comply with the regulation, the Attorney General can confiscate its products and seek criminal prosecution. A drug manufacturer argues that this regulation exceeds the agency's powers and seeks to enjoin its enforcement in court. The issues are ripe for review since, if the court withheld review and the drug manufacturer engaged in the prohibited activity, the manufacturer would risk criminal prosecution.

---

[3]*Environmental Protection Agency v Mink*, 410 US 73, 35 L Ed 2d 119, 93 S Ct 827 (1973).

When reviewing agency action, courts are prohibited from second-guessing or changing rulings or findings of agencies. Courts are essentially limited to determining whether the agency ruling was reasonable and whether the agency exceeded its powers under the legislation that created the agency.

Primary Jurisdiction Doctrine   Under the *primary jurisdiction doctrine*, the agency rather than a court is empowered by statute to conduct the initial trial, or "first hearing," of the case. In two areas particularly, the courts have held that the legislative intent was for an administrative agency, not a court, to have primary jurisdiction in deciding a particular type of case. These two areas are antitrust, where the Federal Trade Commission has primary jurisdiction, and labor relations, where the National Labor Relations Board has primary jurisdiction. In these areas, as well as some others, the plaintiff must first seek relief through the agency, even though the agency's action will subsequently be subject to judicial review.

Exhaustion of Administrative Remedies   Generally, judicial review is not available until the party seeking it has exhausted all prescribed administrative remedies. The rationale for this rule is that it permits full development of the facts prior to judicial review. The agency is given the chance to use the discretion or expertise as expected of it by Congress. The rule recognizes the autonomy of the agency and its right to function without undue interruption.

 Of particular importance to the businessperson is the rule that a person who wishes to attack the granting of a license to a competitor must raise any objections at the hearing before the agency empowered to issue the license. If a businessperson fails to do so, he or she will be precluded from seeking judicial review.

Stays   Once a court has determined that an administrative decision is reviewable, it may grant a *stay* to postpone agency action pending outcome of its review. In deciding whether to grant a stay, the court will consider the following factors: whether the plaintiff is likely to prevail on the merits, whether the plaintiff has shown that without such a stay he would be irreparably injured, whether issuance of the stay would not substantially harm other parties in the proceedings, and whether the public interest will be harmed by granting the stay. If it does so, the court in effect is granting a judicial reversal of the agency order until the process of review is complete.

Key Concepts and Terms

- Administrative agencies are legal entities that are delegated certain functions by the legislative or executive branches of government. Administrative law deals with the operation of and limitations on these agencies.
- Administrative agencies usually have broad discretion in exercising their statutory powers. Agencies formulate policy in any of the following ways: adjudication (on a case-by-case basis), rule-making, investigation, or informal action. A

federal agency considering a rule must first publish a draft of it in the *Federal Register*. When the rule is adopted, it is published in the *Code of Federal Regulations*.

• The federal Administrative Procedure Act sets forth procedures that federal administrative agencies must establish to meet the requirements of uniformity, impartiality, and fairness. The act creates safeguards against arbitrary official encroachment on private rights. Several states have enacted similar legislation patterned after the federal model.

• The "delegation" of power from Congress to the agencies has been the subject of lawsuits. The federal courts usually hold that so long as Congress has constitutional power to regulate a field and is as specific as possible in such regulation, this delegation of power will be upheld. At the state level, however, courts still hold that legislative delegation of powers to state agencies is sometimes improper.

• Ultra vires, which means "beyond the powers," is the term used to describe acts that an agency performs outside the scope of its powers. Such actions are void.

• Due process, notice, and a fair hearing must be provided to a person or corporation whose liberty or property interests would be affected by an agency's action. The form of notice and type of hearing vary.

• Certain constitutional safeguards that protect a criminal defendant have been held applicable to administrative investigations and hearings. This is because some administrative investigations, while not criminal, may result in imposition of criminal penalties.

• The federal Freedom of Information Act provides that certain records must be disclosed by federal agencies after a person's request reasonably describing the record. The act sets forth exceptions from disclosure of materials relating to national defense, internal personnel rules, trade secrets, interagency memoranda, investigatory files, and some other types of records.

• A person or corporation that has suffered harm as a result of agency action may seek judicial review after all administrative remedies have been exhausted. When a court reviews an administrative agency's decision, it may grant a stay to postpone agency action pending the outcome of the judicial review.

• Administrative Law
• Delegation Doctrine
• Federal Administrative Procedure Act
• Freedom of Information Act
• Judicial Review
• Notice and Fair Hearing
• Primary Jurisdiction Doctrine
• Reverse Freedom of Information Act Suit
• Stays
• Ultra Vires Doctrine

Questions and Case Problems

Explanatory Note about Case Problems   Here, and at the end of all later chapters in this book, you will find both "questions" and "case problems." A question calls for a general type of response, and there is often only one "right" answer. For example, with respect to question 4 below, you either know what the Administrative Procedure Act is or you do not. You can usually prepare the answer to a question by stating in your own words information you learned when you studied the chapter.

A case problem, on the other hand, requires you to apply the general principles you have learned to a specific set of facts. Typically, you are asked to assume the role of a judge who must (1) resolve a particular legal dispute by answering the precise question or questions presented and (2) justify that resolution. Your answer to a question presented might be simply "yes" or "no," but your overall performance on the problem will be rated primarily on the basis of how you justify that answer. Indeed, two students might each prepare an adequate response to a case problem and yet arrive at entirely different answers.

As you can see, case problems require an approach that differs somewhat from the familiar one used in answering questions. To acquaint you with this approach, an analysis of a sample problem is presented below.

Many of the case problems in this book are based on actual cases. The *Adams* case (see 3:3) could be the source of the following case problem:

Pickle, the police chief of Plainsville, Kansas, is dissatisfied with the job performance of patrolman Adams. Pickle suspends Adams for two weeks, without pay, and Adams appeals his suspension to the Plainsville Civil Service Commission. The commission holds a hearing at which Adams is allowed to be heard. However, over Adams' objection, the commission closes the hearing to the public and allows only five minutes for the cross-examination of each witness. After the hearing the commission upholds the suspension and orders it to begin. Adams now seeks judicial review, arguing that his constitutional rights were violated. Should the court review the case? Why or why not? Assuming that the court does review the case, should it find any violation of Adams' constitutional rights? Discuss.

The first step in preparing a response to this problem is to read the problem carefully and, on a worksheet, note the important facts. Here, they are that (1) a public officer was suspended without pay, (2) an administrative agency upheld the suspension after a hearing, and (3) the agency ordered that the hearing be closed to the public and limited the officer's right to question witnesses who testified against him. Ignore any irrelevant facts. For example, Chief Pickle's name may be amusing, but it has nothing to do with how the court should decide the case.

The second step is to identify the legal issues and list them on the worksheet. The questions at the end of the problem can often help in this identification. Here, the first question makes it clear that reviewability of the agency's suspension order is an issue. The second question suggests issues concerning one's constitutional rights; what rights did the officer have with respect to the hearing, and how, if at all, were they violated?

The third step is to apply the appropriate legal principles to the issues. Recalling the discussion in 3:7, you conclude (and note on the worksheet) that Adams will suffer harm if the suspension is carried out, thus making the Commission's order both reviewable and ripe for review. Since nothing is said in the problem about the availability of further administrative review, you state as an assumption that

Adams has exhausted his administrative remedies. Therefore, you may conclude that the court should review the case.

Your analysis of the issues presented by the second question requires an understanding of what was discussed in 3:3. You recall that an individual is guaranteed the right to due process of law by the Fifth and Fourteenth Amendments to the United States Constitution, and that due process requires a fair hearing before an individual can be deprived of a property right. Given those principles, you must decide whether loss of pay for two weeks is a deprivation that requires a hearing, and if so, whether the hearing held by the Commission was "fair" within the meaning of the requirement. The fairness issue requires that you consider the importance of public hearings and the cross-examination of witnesses. In view of the circumstances of the case, you are apt to conclude, as the *Adams* court did, that the commission violated Adams' right to due process both by closing the hearing *and* by limiting the cross-examination.

Having concluded your analysis of the problem, you are prepared to write your response, using your worksheet as a guide. Answer the first question. Then, in a concise and orderly way, proceeding from general principles to their specific application to the facts, defend that answer by explaining how and why you reached it. You can then go on to the second question, which you handle in exactly the same manner.

1. A congressional statute gives the Department of the Interior power to allow or to curtail mining within national forests "as the best interests of all users of the national forest shall dictate." Is this an invalid delegation of legislative power? Discuss.

2. The Interstate Commerce Commission adopts a regulation that railroads that retain boxcars belonging to other railroads for an unreasonable time must pay a penalty of $100 per day. The Nevada Railroad seeks to enjoin the regulation on the theory that it is not authorized by statute. Will the court hear this attack now? Discuss.

3. The Nuclear Regulatory Commission operates a licensing scheme whereby certain laboratories having need for radioactive materials are permitted to use them under strictly limited conditions. The NRC reserves the right to make inspections of the premises where the materials are being used, without a search warrant, at any time. It makes such an inspection, discovers unauthorized uses of the material, and seeks to bar the laboratory from any further access from radioactive materials. Can the laboratory assert that the search was invalid? Discuss.

4. What is the Federal Administrative Procedure Act? What purposes does it serve?

5. Clyde wishes to inspect a report prepared by the Department of Defense concerning Middle East policy. This report has been classified "secret" under the government's classification procedure. Clyde asserts that the material should not be secret since there is nothing in it that would jeopardize foreign policy. If an action is brought to compel disclosure of the document, will Clyde win? Discuss.

6. What constitutional safeguards, if any, are applicable during an investigation by an administrative agency? Are the same constitutional protections available as in a criminal proceeding? Explain your answer.

7. The rules of the Small Business Administration require that anyone receiving an SBA loan preserve particular financial documents, in order that compliance with

the loan restrictions may be ascertained. Henry receives an SBA loan for use in his business. The SBA believes that Henry spent part of the money on a yacht for personal use. This conduct constitutes a violation of the SBA statute and would also be a criminal offense. The SBA orders Henry to produce particular financial records by which it can trace the use of the funds. Can Henry utilize his privilege against self-incrimination to avoid producing the record? Discuss.

8. Alice applies for a pilot's license. The license application remains with the Federal Aviation Administration for two years. The agency refuses to act on it, repeatedly stating that a hearing will be scheduled in the near future. The agency never does schedule a hearing. Can Alice go to court to force the FAA to act? Discuss.

9. Larry, a student at the Air Force Academy, is suspected of cheating. The applicable regulations of the academy provide that he could be given a hearing but that he is not entitled to confront the witnesses against him. Before the hearing begins, Larry goes into federal district court, seeking to enjoin continuation of the hearing. Should the court hear this case? Discuss.

10. What is the federal Freedom of Information Act? How may it benefit a businessperson? What is a "reverse Freedom of Information Act suit"?

4 Criminal Law

4:1 In General

A crime is an offense against society.[1] As the people's representative, government may seek redress for a crime by prosecuting the person accused of committing the crime. The redress may consist of fine, imprisonment, or execution. The harsh reality of criminal law is that, while in all other areas of law it is a person's property or economic interest that rests on the outcome of a case, in criminal law it is the liberty or life of the accused that is involved. Thus, it can be said that no field of law more directly affects the core of society.

Criminal law is a dynamic process, sometimes expanding, sometimes contracting. Decisions as to what types of conduct should be considered criminal reflect the changing mores and ethical precepts of the community. For example, the laws controlling abortion, prostitution, homosexual behavior, use or possession of marijuana, spousal battery, and rape have recently expanded or contracted, depending on what society deems criminal and what it deems noncriminal.

People who violate criminal laws are punished. Punishment is imposed on them to deter them from committing future crimes, to deter others from committing similar crimes, to rehabilitate the offender, and for the sake of retribution.

Classification of Crimes Traditionally, crimes were divided into two classes: *felonies* and *misdemeanors*. Felonies are more serious crimes than misdemeanors and generally involve harsher punishment. Some states classify felonies as offenses punishable by death or imprisonment for more than one year, while in other states a crime is a felony if it is punishable by death or incarceration in a state prison, as opposed to a county or city jail. Any crime that is not a felony is a misdemeanor.

In some states, certain acts are prohibited but made punishable by only a small fine. These offenses are sometimes referred to as violations or *infractions* and

---

[1]Crimes committed by and against business (so-called "white-collar crime") are discussed in Chapter 55.

should be distinguished from crimes. Illegal parking and littering are examples of this type of offense.

Role of Defense Counsel[2]   The role of the defense attorney cannot be overestimated in preserving the fundamental constitutional guaranties on which America was founded. The duty of a lawyer to both his client and to the legal system, according to the American Bar Association's Code of Professional Responsibility, is to represent the client zealously within the bounds of the law. Without a dedicated and competent defense lawyer to counterbalance the resources and authority of the prosecution, a criminal defendant's constitutional rights would be jeopardized.

4:2 Elements of a Crime

An act is a crime if the following elements are present: (1) the person who committed the act did so voluntarily and intentionally, and (2) the act was overt and unlawful. Under certain circumstances, a failure to act is a crime. If a person allowed something to happen that he could and should have prevented, or failed to do something that the law required him to do, he has committed a crime. This failure to act is called an omission. Examples of omission are a parent's failure to provide medical care to a child, a motorist's failure to stop at the scene of a traffic accident in which he is involved, and a taxpayer's failure to file tax returns.

While not technically considered part of the crime—that is, part of the act and intent—an essential element for criminal liability is causation. The defendant's act or conduct must have been the actual cause of the intended result or at least a material factor in bringing about harm.

EXAMPLE
A mugger observes Harry apparently asleep on a park bench, approaches, and shoots him five times to make sure that he has killed him in order to take his wallet. Unknown to the mugger, Harry had suffered a fatal heart attack an hour before and was already dead when the mugger shot him. Although he may have committed other crimes, the mugger is not guilty of murder since he did not in fact kill anyone, even though he had the intent.

A few criminal statutes dispense entirely with a state-of-mind requirement, giving rise to so-called "strict liability" crimes. A strict liability crime is one for which a person is guilty merely by committing the act. For example, the crime of selling narcotics does not usually require proof that the defendant knew the item sold was a narcotic; and the National Firearms Act, making it a crime to possess unregistered firearms, does not require proof that the defendant knew the firearm was unregistered.

It must be emphasized that the intent to commit a prohibited act, called *mens rea*—and not the *motive*—determines criminality. Thus, a person may have an arguably ethical motive or a "good reason" for committing an act and still be guilty of a crime.

---

[2]The constitutional right to counsel is discussed in 4:4.

EXAMPLE

A person enters the hospital room of a terminally ill patient who has only a few days to live. The person disconnects the life-support system to prevent the patient from experiencing the remaining days of excruciating pain. Under present concepts of criminal law, the person removing the life-support system is a criminal because he has committed an unlawful act—killing another human being—with the intent to take the other person's life. The intent is criminal because it is an intent to commit an unlawful act, even though the motive or reason is arguably ethically proper or even socially meritorious.

4:3   Particular Crimes

Crimes are broadly classified as crimes against persons, crimes against property, morals offenses, and crimes against government.

Crimes Against Persons   There are many crimes that are classified as crimes against persons. The following are a few of them:

(1) Murder: the intentional killing of a person without legal justification or excuse.
(2) Battery: the unlawful application of force to a person.
(3) Assault: an unlawful attempt to apply force to a person, also called attempted battery.
(4) Mayhem: the malicious disfiguring of a person.
(5) Rape: sexual intercourse with a female without her consent and usually by force.
(6) False imprisonment: intentional unlawful confinement of a person.

Crimes Against Property   The most common crime against property is the taking of another person's property. The modern trend is to consolidate many of these acquisition offenses into the statutory crime simply called theft. Crimes that constitute theft include the following:

(1) Larceny: a wrongful taking of personal property with an intent to permanently deprive the owner of it.
(2) Embezzlement: the fraudulent appropriation of property by a person to whom it has been entrusted.
(3) False pretenses: the obtaining of title to property by means of a false representation with intent to defraud the victim.
(4) Robbery: the taking of another's personal property, by means of force or fear, from his person or immediate presence and against his will.
(5) Extortion: the obtaining of property by means of threats but not necessarily to do violence to the person.
(6) Receiving stolen property: obtaining unauthorized possession of stolen property with the knowledge that it is stolen.

Most states have enacted bad-check legislation. While the statutes vary, typically the elements of the crime are the making, drawing, or delivering a check at a time when there are not sufficient funds in the account to cover the check, with the knowledge of the insufficiency.

Crimes against property may also involve a structure or dwelling place. They include burglary, the unauthorized entry into a structure with the intent to commit a theft or other felony, and arson, the malicious burning of a structure. Burning property with the intent to defraud an insurer is frequently made a separate crime.

Morals Offenses Historically, morals offenses were not common-law crimes but were punished by church authorities in early England. Today, such matters are frequently made criminal by statute. There is, however, a trend toward removing some of these offenses from the reach of criminal law. Included in the category of morals offenses are the following:

(1) Fornication: illicit sexual intercourse between persons not married to each other.
(2) Adultery: sexual intercourse by a married person with some person other than his or her spouse.
(3) Illicit cohabitation: living together in adultery or fornication.
(4) Bigamy: being married to more than one person at the same time.
(5) Incest: marriage, or sexual relations, between persons who are closely related by blood.

Crimes Against Government Most criminal statutes set forth particular offenses against the government or against the administration of justice. Such offenses include the following:

(1) Breach of the peace (or disorderly conduct): to unreasonably disturb the public peace.
(2) Riot: a tumultuous disturbance of the peace by three or more persons acting together to carry out a common enterprise.
(3) Treason: levying war against the United States, adhering to its enemies, or giving its enemies aid and comfort.
(4) Counterfeiting: falsely making, forging, or altering any obligation or other security of the government with intent to defraud.

Some offenses against the administration of justice, in addition to hindering the apprehension or prosecution of a felon, include the following:

(1) Misprision of felony: the failure to report or prosecute a person known to have committed a felony.
(2) Compounding a crime: agreeing for money not to prosecute another person for a felony.

(3) Perjury: the willful giving of a false statement under oath in a judicial proceeding.

(4) Subornation of perjury: the intentional causing of another person to commit perjury.

(5) Bribery: the giving of something of value to a person holding public office with the intent to influence the discharge of the person's legal duties.

4:4   Constitutional Safeguards

Constitutional protection for an accused person must be provided at all steps during the criminal process:

> A cardinal principle of the American legal system is that courts of justice act upon the belief that if guilty, the party will be so found after a *fair* trial; both the ends and the means of a trial must be fair, and no matter how abhorrent the offense charged or how evident the guilt, an accused has an absolute constitutional right to a fair trial before an impartial judge and an unprejudiced jury.[3]

Law enforcement officers use various methods to obtain evidence to be used in the trial of a criminal suspect. These are usually observation, surveillance, searches or seizures, and interrogations of the victim, witnesses, or the suspect. There are inherent dangers in some of these methods in that the evidence obtained may be false and may lead to conviction of an innocent person and that unrestrained police tactics may endanger fundamental individual rights and freedoms.

A person accused of crime has many constitutional protections. They are set forth in the *Bill of Rights*, the first ten amendments to the Constitution. These rights apply to all federal and state criminal prosecutions under the Due Process Clause of the Fourteenth Amendment. Some of these rights are the right to be free from unreasonable searches and seizures; the right that no search warrants may be issued without probable cause; the privilege against self-incrimination; the right to a speedy, public trial; the right to confront prosecution witnesses; the right to cross-examine; and the right to compel defense witnesses to appear in court.

Right to Counsel   A person accused of a crime has the right to assistance of counsel under the Sixth Amendment. This right literally affects an accused's ability to assert his other rights. Indeed, the Supreme Court of the United States has held this right to be so fundamental that state and federal courts are required to appoint legal counsel free of charge to persons who cannot otherwise afford a lawyer. Inherent in the concept of the right to counsel is that the representation be competent. Ineffective representation has been held to be worse than no representation at all.

Under the landmark case of *Miranda v Arizona*,[4] whenever state or federal law enforcement officers take a person into "custody" or otherwise deprive him of

---

[3]J. Purver and L. Taylor, *Handling Criminal Appeals*, 197 (1980).
[4]384 US 436, 16 L Ed 2d 694, 86 S Ct 1602, 10 ALR3d 974 (United States Supreme Court, 1966).

"freedom of action in any significant way," they are required to give the accused, prior to *any* questioning, the following five warnings which are now included under the constitutional privilege against self-incrimination: (1) that he has a right to remain silent; (2) that any statement he does make can and will be used as evidence against him in a court of law; (3) that he has the right to consult with counsel *before* answering any questions; (4) that he has the right to have counsel present with him during the interrogation; (5) that if he cannot afford an attorney, one will be appointed for him without cost, prior to the questioning, if he so desires. The giving of these warnings is an "absolute prerequisite" to any police interrogation and to the admissibility in evidence of any confession or statements made by the accused during in-custody interrogation.

Due Process Guarantees   The due process clauses of the federal and state constitutions protect the defendant's fundamental rights in a criminal prosecution. The due process guaranty of the Fifth Amendment (as to the federal government) and the Fourteenth Amendment (as to the states) insures that procedures leading to conviction cannot include methods that conflict with deeply rooted feelings of the community.

The following decision illustrates how the due process guaranty has been applied. The police methods used in securing the evidence on which the conviction was based offended a sense of justice and violated civilized notions of fairness and due process.

Rochin
v
California
342 US 165, 96 L Ed 183
72 S Ct 205, 25 ALR 2d 1396
(United States Supreme Court, 1952)

[Police officers had information that the defendant was selling narcotics. They illegally entered his dwelling, whereupon he swallowed two capsules containing morphine. The officers attempted to extract the capsules from his mouth by force. The defendent was handcuffed and taken to a hospital, where, at the direction of one of the officers, a doctor, against the defendant's will, forced an emetic solution through a tube into his stomach. On evidence of the capsules so obtained, the defendant was convicted in a state court of illegal possession of morphine.]

Justice Frankfurter delivered the opinion of the Court.

*   *   *

. . . Regard for the requirements of the Due Process Clause "inescapably imposes upon this Court an exercise of judgment upon the whole course of the proceedings [resulting in a conviction] in order to ascertain whether they offend those canons of decency and fairness which express the notions of justice of English-speaking peoples even toward those charged with the most heinous offenses." *Malinski v New York*, . . . (324 US at 416, 417, 89 L ed 1039, 65 S Ct 781). These standards of justice are not authoritatively formulated anywhere as though they were specifics. Due process of law is a summarized constitutional guarantee of respect for those personal immunities which, as Mr. Justice Cardozo twice wrote for the Court, are "so rooted in the traditions and conscience of our people as to be ranked as fundamental," . . . or are "implicit in the concept of ordered liberty." . . .

The Court's function in the observance of this settled conception of the Due Process Clause does not leave us without adequate guides in subjecting State criminal procedures to constitutional judgment. In dealing not with the machinery of government but with human rights, the absence of formal exactitude, or want of fixity of meaning, is not an unusual or even regrettable attribute of constitutional provisions. Words being symbols do not speak without a gloss. On the one hand the gloss may be the deposit of history, whereby a term gains technical content. Thus the requirements of the Sixth and Seventh Amendments for trial by jury in the Federal courts have a rigid meaning. No changes or chances can alter the content of the verbal symbol of "jury" —a body of twelve men who must reach a unanimous conclusion if the verdict is to go against the defendant. On the other hand, the gloss of some of the verbal symbols of the Constitution does not give them a fixed technical content. It exacts a continuing process of application.

When the gloss has thus not been fixed but is a function of the process of judgment, the judgment is bound to fall differently at different times and differently at the same time through different judges. Even more specific provisions, such as the guaranty of freedom of speech and the detailed protection against unreasonable searches and seizures, have inevitably evoked as sharp divisions in this Court as the least specific and most comprehensive protection of liberties, the Due Process Clause.

The vague contours of the Due Process Clause do not leave judges at large. We may not draw on our merely personal and private notions and disregard the limits that bind judges in their judicial function. Even though the concept of due process of law is not final and fixed, these limits are derived from considerations that are fused in the whole nature of

our judicial process. See Cardozo, The Nature of the Judicial Process; The Growth of the Law; The Paradoxes of Legal Science. These are considerations deeply rooted in reason and in the compelling traditions of the legal profession. The Due Process Clause places upon this Court the duty of exercising a judgment, within the narrow confines of judicial power in reviewing State convictions, upon interests of society pushing in opposite directions.

Due process of law thus conceived is not to be derided as resort to a revival of "natural law." To believe that this judicial exercise of judgment could be avoided by freezing "due process of law" at some fixed stage of time or thought is to suggest that the most important aspect of constitutional adjudication is a function for inanimate machines and not for judges, for whom the independence safeguarded by Article 3 of the Constitution was designed and who are presumably guided by established standards of judicial behavior. Even cybernetics has not yet made that haughty claim. To practice the requisite detachment and to achieve sufficient objectivity no doubt demands of judges the habit of self-discipline and self-criticism, incertitude that one's own views are incontestable and alert tolerance toward views not shared. But these are precisely the presuppositions of our judicial process. They are precisely the qualities society has a right to expect from those entrusted with ultimate judicial power.

Restraints on our jurisdiction are self imposed only in the sense that there is from our decisions no immediate appeal short of impeachment or constitutional amendment. But that does not make due process of law a matter of judicial caprice. The faculties of the Due Process Clause may be indefinite and vague, but the mode of their ascertainment is not self-willed. In each case "due process of law" requires an evaluation based on a disinterested inquiry pursued in the spirit of science, on a balanced order of facts exactly and fairly stated, on the detached consideration of conflicting claims. . . .

Applying these general considerations to the circumstances of the present case, we are compelled to conclude that the proceedings by which this conviction was obtained do more than offend some fastidious squeamishness or private sentimentalism about combatting crime too energetically. This is conduct that shocks the conscience. Illegally breaking into the privacy of the petitioner, the struggle to open his mouth and remove what was there, the forcible extraction of his stomach's contents—this course of proceeding by agents of government to obtain evidence is bound to offend even hardened sensibilities. They are methods too close to the rack and the screw to permit of constitutional differentiation. . . .

. . . Use of involuntary verbal confessions in State criminal trials is constitutionally obnoxious not only because of their unreliability. They are inadmissible under the Due Process Clause and even though statements contained in them may be independently established as true. Coerced confessions offend the community's sense of fair play and decency. So here, to sanction the brutal conduct which naturally enough was condemned by the court whose judgment is before us, would be to afford brutality the cloak of law. Nothing would be more calculated to discredit law and thereby to brutalize the temper of a society.

In deciding this case we do not heedlessly bring into question decisions in many States dealing with essentially different, even if related, problems. We therefore put to one side cases which have arisen in the State courts through use of modern methods and devices for discovering wrongdoers and bringing them to book. It does not fairly represent these decisions to suggest that they legalize force so brutal and so offensive to human dignity in securing evidence from a suspect as is revealed by this record. Indeed the California Supreme Court has not sanctioned this mode of securing a conviction. It merely exercised its discretion to decline a review of the conviction. All the California judges who have expressed themselves in this case have condemned the conduct in the strongest language.

We are not unmindful that hypothetical situations can be conjured up, shading imperceptibly from the circumstances of this case and by gradations producing practical differences despite seemingly logical extensions. But the Constitution is "intended to preserve practical and substantial rights, not to maintain theories." *Davis v Mills*, 194 US 451, 457, 48 L ed 1067, 1071, 24 S Ct 692.

[Judgment reversed.]

Constitutional Limits on Criminal Statutes   The Constitution, under the Sixth Amendment, requires that a criminal statute be reasonably precise in setting forth exactly what constitutes a crime and what constitutes the punishment for the crime.

Another constitutional limitation on criminal legislation is the Eighth Amendment, which prohibits cruel and unusual punishment. The scope of the Eighth Amendment has never been clearly defined but draws its meaning from evolving standards of decency. Thus, it is unconstitutional to use torture or to prolong death or to require forfeiture of citizenship. Penalties grossly disproportionate to the severity of the offense are cruel and unusual. In several sharply divided decisions, the United States Supreme Court has rejected the argument that the death penalty is inherently cruel and unusual.

4:5   Defenses to Criminal Charges

It is a basic tenet of the American judicial system that all individuals are presumed innocent of crime unless they are proven guilty beyond a *reasonable doubt* in a court of law after a fair trial with all constitutional safeguards. In many instances, there is no question that the person charged with a crime did commit the act. However, rather than admit to the crime and accept the punishment, the person claims he has a legitimate defense that justifies, excuses, or mitigates the acts to take away his criminal liability. The commonly asserted defenses in criminal cases are discussed below.

Infancy   At common law, a child under the age of 7 was presumed to be unable to form a criminal intent and therefore could not be convicted of a crime. A child between 7 and 14 years of age was also presumed to be incapable of forming criminal intent, although the presumption was rebuttable if the prosecution could establish that the child knew what he was doing and that it was wrong. At ages 14 and older, children are treated as adults.

Modern statutes vary in their treatment of the infancy defense. Some have made the common-law rules into statutes and others have modified them. In any case, all American jurisdictions have legistation that confers on juvenile courts jurisdiction over children of certain ages alleged to have committed a crime. In juvenile court proceedings, the child is not convicted but is adjudicated "delinquent." Most states permit juvenile court proceedings, and even criminal convictions of persons under certain ages, to be sealed from the public by court order.

Insanity   There is considerable disagreement as to what constitutes *insanity*. In some states, to be legally insane the defendant must prove that as a result of his mental illness he either did not know the nature of his act, or did not know that the act was wrong. This is the M'Naghten Test. In other states, insanity is found if a defendant's acts resulted from an "irresistible impulse." In still other states, the test is whether the defendant's act was the "product of" a mental illness. Finally, a few states consider whether a defendant "lacked substantial capacity" to appreciate the criminality of his conduct or to conform his conduct to the requirements of law.

Intoxication   Voluntary *intoxication* by alcohol or drugs is not normally a defense to crime. However, with certain crimes that require a specific state of mind, evidence of intoxication may be a defense.

Self-defense   Generally, a person may use that force which reasonably appears necessary to defend himself against an apparent threat of unlawful and immediate violence from another person. "Deadly force" may be used in self-defense only if the defendant reasonably believes that the other person is about to inflict death or great bodily injury on him and that deadly force would be necessary to prevent the harm.

At common law, the defendant was required to retreat before using deadly force. Today most American courts do not impose this requirement. If, for example, a person is being threatened with a gun, he is entitled to use deadly force, if necessary, to defend himself from the attacker. Under certain circumstances, a person is entitled to use force in defense of other persons. A person need not simply stand by and watch as another person is attacked. The bystander has as much right to protect another person from crime as he does to protect himself.

The right to use force to protect property is more limited than the right to use force in protecting persons. For example, a person cannot use deadly force simply to defend his property against unlawful interference. The rationale is that the interest in security of property does not justify jeopardizing the lives of others.

Consent Some crimes are defined in terms of the victim's lack of *consent*. If there is consent, it is a defense to a criminal charge. For example, rape requires the absence of the female's consent to intercourse, and proof of consent will be a bar to conviction.

Courts are more likely to recognize the defense of consent if the act did not involve serious bodily injury or the risk of such injury, or if there is a widespread acceptance of the risk, as in sporting events. For example, if during an ice hockey game one player grabs another player and breaks his nose with a hockey stick, the first player may not be criminally liable for battery because there is some degree of consent to roughness by the injured player.

Entrapment A defendant may claim that he was lured into committing the act by a law enforcement officer. This is the defense of *entrapment*. Entrapment exists only if the law enforcement officer's conduct, rather than the predisposition of the defendant, created the intent to commit the act. The test is subjective because a court's finding of entrapment depends on what subjectively stimulated the commission of the crime.

Key Concepts and Terms

- A crime is an offense against the people. As the people's representative, the government may seek redress for the crime by prosecuting the person who committed the crime. A crime is an act or a failure to act (omission) that is (1) unlawful and (2) committed with a criminal intent. Crimes are classified as felonies, misdemeanors, and infractions.

- Punishment for a crime is imposed to prevent and deter the offender from committing future crimes, to deter others from committing similar crimes, to rehabilitate the offender, and for retribution.

- The Constitution protects persons who are accused of crimes by granting them certain rights. These rights include the right to be free from unreasonable searches and seizures; the privilege against self-incrimination; the right to a speedy, public trial; the right to confront prosecution witnesses; the right to cross-examination; the right to compel defense witnesses to appear in court in their behalf; and the right to legal counsel, which includes the right to court-appointed counsel if they cannot afford to hire an attorney.

- Conviction of a crime requires that the person accused of committing the crime be proven guilty beyond a reasonable doubt in a court of law after a fair trial and with all constitutional safeguards.

- Commonly asserted defenses in criminal cases are infancy, insanity, intoxication, self-defense, consent, and entrapment.

- Bill of Rights
- Consent
- Constitutional Safeguards
- Entrapment
- Felony
- Infancy
- Infractions

- Insanity
- Intoxication
- *Mens Rea*
- Misdemeanor
- Motive
- Reasonable Doubt
- Self-defense

Questions and Case Problems

1. Kramer, a trained professional athlete and black belt in karate, is walking down the street when he hears a person scream. He turns around and sees a child being dragged into a dark alley by a man with a knife in his hand. Kramer decides to do nothing and walks away. Is Kramer guilty of any crime? Discuss. Assume Kramer recognized the child and did not like her, and was glad to witness her peril and intentionally decided not to intervene. If the child is killed, is Kramer guilty of any crime? Discuss. What if the person in the alley was not a child but was Kramer's wife and he chose not to intervene? Would the result be the same? Discuss.

2. Donald intends to kill Vance and buys a rifle for this purpose. While Donald is engaged in target practice in his own backyard, Vance unexpectedly runs by and is killed by a bullet that ricochets from the target. Is Donald guilty of murder? Discuss.

3. What are society's reasons for punishing criminal conduct? Discuss.

4. Why should a person who has "obviously committed a crime and is clearly guilty" be entitled to the time and expense of a trial? Discuss.

5. Frank forces John at gunpoint to drive him away from the scene of a robbery. He then forces John to drive into a roadblock, striking and killing a police officer. For what crimes may Frank be prosecuted? Discuss.

6. Henry is speeding down a highway at night when his car strikes and injures Sam. Because of the darkness, Henry is unaware of the accident and does not stop. Has Henry "acted" so as to be guilty of violating a hit-and-run statute? Discuss.

7. Jane is standing on a street corner. A stranger runs past and thrusts a package into her hand. A police officer immediately approaches and arrests Jane for possession of narcotics. Assuming the package contains heroin, can Jane be convicted of possession? Are any defenses applicable? Discuss.

8. John is arrested for engaging in illicit activities at a pool hall. On the way to the

police station, the police tell him that they will "treat him easy" if he admits to the activities. He confesses. Is the confession admissible against him at trial? Discuss.

9. Joe intentionally sets fire to his warehouse to collect insurance money. When he attempts to put out the fire, a firefighter has a heart attack and dies. For what possible crimes may Joe be prosecuted? Discuss.

10. Carolyn is charged with violating a statute that prohibits "any conduct infringing upon the public welfare." Is the statute constitutionally valid? Discuss.

PART TWO

Torts

Perhaps more than any other branch of the law, the law of torts is a battleground of social theory.

William L. Prosser, *The Law of Torts*

Introductory Comments

As this part of the book reveals, the law of torts seeks to maintain a balance between a person's right to exercise freedom of action and the rights of all other persons to live without unwarranted interference to their bodies and their property. The questions of how reasonable a person's conduct is and when a person can be held liable for acts that injure another person are questions that are confronted in tort law.

The word "tort," a French word introduced into the English language after the Norman Conquest, comes from the Latin "tortus," meaning "twisted," and translates to the English word "wrong." Broadly speaking, a tort is any civil (as opposed to criminal) wrong other than a breach of contract.

Individuals and corporations alike may be liable in tort for injuries—in some cases, injuries they did not intend to cause, particularly those that resulted from defective products or services and dangerous premises. Throughout the chapters in this part, potential (yet frequently hidden) areas of a businessperson's tort liability are examined, and ways to reduce or eliminate tort risks in modern business are suggested.

Oliver Wendell Holmes, the American judge who is often characterized as the greatest intellect in the history of the English-speaking judiciary, said that law is a seamless web. Nowhere is this seen more clearly than in the area of torts. While tort law has developed into specific subareas, such as negligence and strict liability (Chapter 6), products liability (Chapter 7), and premises liability (Chapter 8), the interrelationship of all areas of tort law is always present.

5 Introduction to the Law of Torts

5:1 In General

A *tort* is a civil wrong committed against an individual. When a person is a victim of a tort, he may claim and receive a cash award through a court action to compensate for the harm he suffered. This award is referred to as civil damages. A tort may be committed by individuals, corporations, or associations. A person or entity who commits a tort is called a tortfeasor. In tort law a person who commits an act, whether it is tortious or not, is called an actor.

Two distinctions must be made at this point. One is that a tort is a civil wrong that does not result from a breach of contract. A breach of contract is a failure of one person to act in a specific manner agreed to by both parties to the contract;[1] it is a breach of the parties' duty to be bound by their agreement. The tortfeasor, in contrast, breaches a more general duty—the duty to act in a manner that would not be harmful to others.

The other distinction is the distinction between a tort and a crime. A criminal act is intentionally harmful and is considered to be committed against society in general. Furthermore, a criminal act is punishable; the actor, if found guilty, is fined, imprisoned, or executed.[2] A tortious act, on the other hand, need not be intentional (although it can be). Also, as mentioned above, a tort is committed against an individual rather than against society, and the tortfeasor is ordered to pay damages to the victim rather than being fined, imprisoned, or executed. It should be noted, however, that a given act, such as striking another person without a legitimate excuse, can be both a crime and a tort.

Joint Tortfeasors Joint tortfeasors are two or more persons who unite in committing a tort or whose acts injure a third person. A person who joins others in committing a tort cannot escape liability by showing that the others are also liable. Neither is the fact that a third person cooperated in the wrong a justification for

---

[1]Mutual assent in contract law is discussed in Chapter 10.
[2]Crimes are discussed in Chapter 4. White-collar crime is discussed in Chapter 55.

the joint tortfeasor's misconduct. Joint tortfeasors are jointly and severally liable, which means that the recovery may come from one or all joint tortfeasors.

Intent   As used in tort law, the term *intent* means the intent to commit the wrongful act, but not necessarily the intent to do harm or injure anyone. Thus, to prove that an actor is liable for a tort, it need be shown only that his intent affects a legally protected interest in a way not permitted by law. In other words, the actor's intent need not be immoral, malicious, or hostile to constitute an intent to commit a tort. To prove intent it must also be shown that the actor knew or believed that certain results were substantially certain to follow from his conduct. This knowledge or belief is determined on what is called the objective basis—what the reasonable person can be expected to know or believe under the same circumstances. The objective basis must be distinguished from the subjective basis which would be attempting to determine what the actor was actually thinking at the time he committed the tort.

EXAMPLE
As a practical joke, the defendant pulls a chair out from under the plaintiff as she begins to sit, causing her to fall and sustain a hip fracture. Although the defendant actually meant the plaintiff no harm, a court could reasonably find that the defendant knew with substantial certainty that the plaintiff would attempt to sit down where the chair had been and could fall and injure herself. Hence, he did have the knowledge required to support a finding of intent for tort liability. His intent was to do an act that he could have reasonably foreseen would cause injury to another.

5:2   Invasion of Personal Rights

Some intentional torts take the form of interfering with or invading a person's right to be secure in his own body, physically and mentally, and the right simply "to be let alone." Invasion of these rights is not restricted to economic injury to the person, but concerns the integrity of his person, his being.

Battery   A *battery* is the intentional touching of, or harmful or offensive contact with a person's body or things closely attached to it without the person's consent. To constitute battery, the contact need not cause actual physical harm. It is sufficient that the contact be offensive or insulting, on the theory that a person's right not to be touched without consent is a legally protected interest.

Transferred Intent   If a person intends to commit a battery on a particular person, but through error commits the battery on a third person, he will be considered to be guilty of battery under the doctrine of *transferred intent*. For example, if an employer strikes at an employee and unintentionally hits another employee nearby, the employer will be guilty of battery on the injured employee. Under the doctrine of transferred intent, the employer's intent to commit a battery on *someone* will be "transferred" to the person actually battered.

Assault   An *assault* is an act—not mere words—that causes a person fear or apprehension of immediate harmful or offensive contact. The elements of assault are (1) the act, (2) the actor's intent, (3) the target party's fear or apprehension, and (4) the causal relation between the act and the target party's fear or apprehension. The actor's actual present ability to cause the threatened damage need not be shown to establish the tort of assault. Thus, if a person points an unloaded gun at another person, threatening to shoot, there is an assault, because the target party, unaware that the gun is unloaded, will be fearful or apprehensive. It should be noted that apprehension is not the same thing as fear; the target party can be confident of avoiding the actor's threatened force (not be afraid), but the latter will still be liable for assault simply for causing the target party's apprehension of the assault.

Defenses to Assault and Battery   The two significant defenses to the tort of assault and battery are *consent* and *privilege.* The plaintiff's consent to participate in certain acts that would otherwise give rise to assault or battery will relieve the defendant of liability. The consent may be expressed or implied, by words or conduct. If two persons, for example, engage in a fight, the injured party cannot sue for assault and battery because he consented to the fight. The other defense is privilege. One may be privileged, for example, to use force for self-defense, defense of others, or defense of property. The force must be reasonable under the circumstances and cannot go beyond the necessity of the situation. Force likely to cause death or serious bodily harm may be used in self-defense only if the user *reasonably* believes that the other person's conduct will result in either death or serious bodily harm to him. There is no right to retaliate, and when the danger has passed, the privilege of self-defense expires.

Malicious Prosecution   Malicious prosecution is the institution by one person of an unsuccessful, unwarranted legal proceeding against another person, with actual or implied malice, resulting in damage. According to most courts, the same principles govern regardless of whether the malicious prosecution was a criminal prosecution or a civil or administrative proceeding. Some states limit liability for the prosecution of civil suits to those actions in which the present plaintiff—the defendant in the malicious prosecution—was deprived of his personal liberty or suffered injury to his property or business. To recover for damages, the present plaintiff must show, in his suit against the person who instituted the malicious prosecution, that this person lacked probable cause for filing the original proceeding, whether criminal or civil. The question of probable cause depends on the honest and reasonable belief of the party commencing the prosecution or action.

A defense to a suit for malicious prosecution is the good faith reliance on the advice of counsel. In other words, the defendant in the malicious prosecution suit (who was the plaintiff in the original suit) can claim that his attorney advised him to file the original suit. Of course, the defendant must show that he fully and truthfully disclosed all facts of the case to his attorney. It should be noted that the attorney cannot be held liable for advising or prosecuting a proceeding for the client in good faith, regardless of whether the client may be liable.

Invasion of Privacy   The right to privacy has been defined as the right to be left alone, to be free from unwarranted publicity, and to live without unwarranted interference by the public or third persons in matters in which they are not concerned. The right of privacy is an independent legal right. The *Restatement of Torts* states that a person who unreasonably and seriously interferes with another's interest in not having his affairs known to others, or his likeness exhibited to the public, is liable to the party whose privacy he invaded.[3]

Through judicial decisions, the tort of *invasion of privacy* has come to include four kinds of interference with a person's right to be left alone: (1) intrusion on the plaintiff's solitude or into the plaintiff's private affairs; (2) public disclosure of embarassing private facts about the plaintiff; (3) publicity placing the plaintiff in a false light in the public eye; and (4) appropriation, for the defendant's advantage, of the plaintiff's name or likeness.

Development of the tort of invasion of privacy—as a separate and distinct tort— is a graphic example of how the courts and legislatures created a "new legal right." In the following decision, the court "creates" the tort of invasion of privacy in a state where there was no statute or previous decision. Note that the court discusses how courts in other jurisdictions have dealt with this new tort and explains why it is important, in terms of public policy, that this tort be recognized in its own jurisdiction.

Hamberger
v
Eastman
206 A2d 239
(New Hampshire Supreme Court, 1964)

[The plaintiffs, husband and wife, rented a home from the defendant. The defendant, who lived next door, placed an electronic listening device ("bug") in their bedroom "capable of transmitting and recording any sounds and voices originating in said bedroom." The listening device was connected to the defendant's house and was hooked up to a tape recorder. The plaintiffs brought suit for invasion of privacy. The defendant moved to dismiss the case on the ground that the facts stated no recognized cause of action. The trial judge transferred the case to the state supreme court for a ruling.]

Kenison, Chief Justice.

*   *   *

The question presented is whether the right of privacy is recognized in this state. There is no controlling statute and no previous decision in this jurisdiction which decides the question. Inasmuch as invasion of the right of privacy is not a single tort but consists of four distinct torts, it is probably more concrete and accurate to state the issue in the present case to be whether this state recognizes that intrusion upon one's physical and mental solitude or seclusion is a tort. . . .

In capsule summary the invasion of the right of privacy developed as an independent and distinct tort from the classic and famous article by Warren and Brandeis, The Right to Privacy, 4 Harv.L.Rev. 193 (1890), although Judge Cooley had discussed "the right to be let alone" some years previously. . . . In 1902 the New York Court of Appeals decided that the

---

[3]*Restatement (Second) of Torts* § 867 (1965).

right of privacy did not have "an abiding place in our jurisprudence." The following year the New York Legislature acted promptly to remedy this deficiency. Shortly thereafter in 1905 *Pavesich v New England Life Ins. Co.*, 122 Ga. 190, 50 S.E. 68 upheld the right of privacy and became the leading case on the subject. Since that time the right of privacy has been given protection in a majority of the jurisdictions in this country, generally without benefit of statute, and only a small minority have rejected the concept and some of these minority decisions are not recent. . . .

The four kinds of invasion comprising the law of privacy include: (1) intrusion upon the plaintiff's physical and mental solitude or seclusion; (2) public disclosure of private facts; (3) publicity which places the plaintiff in a false light in the public eye; (4) appropriation, for the defendant's benefit or advantage, of the plaintiff's name or likeness. In the present case, we are concerned only with the tort of intrusion upon the plaintiffs' solitude or seclusion. . . .

The tort of intrusion upon the plaintiff's solitude or seclusion is not limited to a physical invasion of his home or his room or his quarters. . . .

We have not searched for cases where the bedroom of husband and wife has been "bugged" but it should not be necessary—by way of understatement—to observe that this is the type of intrusion that would be offensive to any person of ordinary sensibilities. What married "people do in the privacy of their bedroom is their own business so long as they are not hurting anyone else." Ernst and Loth, For Better or Worse, 79 (1952). The Restatement, Torts s. 867 provides that "a person who unreasonably and seriously interferes with another's interest in not having his affairs known to others . . . is liable to the other." As is pointed out in *comment* d "liability exists only if the defendant's conduct was such that he should have realized that it would be offensive to persons of ordinary sensibilities. It is only where the intrusion has gone beyond the

limits of decency that liability accrues. These limits are exceeded where intimate details of the life of one who has never manifested a desire to have publicity are exposed to the public. . . ."

The defendant contends that the right of privacy should not be recognized on the facts of the present case as they appear in the pleadings because there are no allegations that anyone listened or overheard any sounds or voices originating from the plaintiffs' bedroom. The tort of intrusion on the plaintiffs' solitude or seclusion does not require publicity and communication to third persons although this would affect the amount of damages. . . . The defendant also contends that the right of privacy is not violated unless something has been published, written or printed and that oral publicity is not sufficient. Recent cases make it clear that this is not a requirement. . . .

If the peeping Tom, the big ear and the electronic eavesdropper (whether ingenious or ingenuous) have a place in the hierarchy of social values, it ought not to be at the expense of a married couple minding their own business in the seclusion of their bedroom who have never asked for or by their conduct deserved a potential projection of their private conversations and actions to their landlord or to others. Whether actual or potential such "publicity with respect to private matters of purely personal concern is an injury to personality. It impairs the mental peace and comfort of the individual and may produce suffering more acute than that produced by a mere bodily injury." III Pound, Jurisprudence 58 (1959). The use of parabolic microphones and sonic wave devices designed to pick up conversations in a room without entering it and at a considerable distance away makes the problem far from fanciful. Dash, Schwartz & Knowlton, The Eavesdroppers pp. 346–358 (1959). . . .

For the purposes of the present case it is sufficient to hold that the invasion of the plaintiffs' solitude or seclusion, as alleged in the pleadings, was a violation of their right of privacy and constituted a tort for which the plaintiffs may recover damages to the extent that they can prove them. "Certainly, no right deserves greater protection, for, as Emerson has well said, 'solitude, the safeguard of mediocrity, is to genius the stern friend.' " Ezer, In-

trusion on Solitude: Herein of Civil Rights and Civil Wrongs, 21 Law on Transition 63, 75 (1961).

[Motion denied.]

5:3   False Imprisonment

False imprisonment is the intentional detention of a person, with his knowledge and without his consent within boundaries for any length of time. The detention may be caused by the imposition of either actual or apparent physical boundaries. It is not necessary that there be confinement in a jail or a prison. The tort may be committed by acts or words, or both, or by merely operating on the individual's will, without personal violence. The confinement constituting false imprisonment has particular relevance to a businessperson since the tort may arise from a person's detention in a hospital, mental institution, restaurant, office, store, or even public street.

It is not necessary that the person be *totally* imprisoned to support the tort. False imprisonment will arise if there is no "reasonable avenue of exit" available; an exit is not reasonable if it is unknown to the restrained party or requires him to take risks to escape, is dangerous or is simply discomforting.

Shoplifter Detention   As pointed out by one court, "[t]here are few more horrifying experiences than that of being suddenly snatched from a peaceful and orderly existence and placed in the helpless position of having one's liberty restrained, under the accusation of a crime."[4] The most prevalent occasion of the tort of false imprisonment is the detention of a person who is wrongfully suspected to be a shoplifter. One reason that this tort arises so frequently is reflected in the statistics which show more than five billion dollars' worth of goods is shoplifted annually from the nation's retail stores, and approximately one person in 15 entering a retail store steals merchandise worth more than five dollars.

Defenses   A defense to an allegation of false imprisonment is the so-called *shopkeeper's privilege*. As the name suggests, this is a storekeeper's privilege to detain a person if he has a reasonable belief that the person shoplifted and to conduct an investigation in a reasonable manner. This reasonable belief is known as probable cause. In some states there is legislation that permits detention of customers reasonably suspected of shoplifting. Such legislation constitutes a justification for the merchant's actions. The following decision illustrates how the shopkeeper's privilege does *not* apply. Note the court's detailed discussion of the facts that demonstrate that there was no reasonable cause for believing the plaintiff had shoplifted.

---

[4]*Halliburton-Abbott Co. v Hodge*, 172 Okla 175, 44 P2d 122 (Oklahoma Supreme Court, 1935).

Great Atlantic and Pacific Tea Co.
v
Paul
261 A2d 731
(Maryland Supreme Court, 1979)

[Paul was shopping in an A & P supermarket when he was accosted and detained by Parker, the store's second assistant manager. Paul subsequently brought suit against the store for assault and battery, slander, and false imprisonment.]

Digges, Judge.

*   *   *

This case comes before us on appeal from an action for assault and battery, slander and false imprisonment. It involves as appellant The Great Atlantic and Pacific Tea Co., Inc., the owner of the nationally known chain of A & P food stores, and as appellee John Joseph Paul, a retired police officer suffering from a recent heart condition. On the charge that one of A & P's employees, John Parker, falsely accused the appellee of shoplifting, frisked him, and unlawfully detained him, Paul recovered $10,000 compensatory and $30,000 punitive damages.

Still in a convalescent stage Mr. Paul, in civilian garb, went shopping at his local A & P store in Hillcrest Heights, Maryland, on December 20, 1967. So recent had been his heart attack that this was one of the first times he had ventured out in his automobile. The Hillcrest Heights store was a typical supermarket with checkout counters in the front, many longitudinal rows of self-service aisles in the rear, and of course the usual fleet of shopping carts for the customers' convenience. There was no requirement that a customer must use a cart. On this occasion, due to heavy crowds in the store, Mr. Paul left his cart at the end of one aisle and slowly proceeded to examine carefully the labels of various articles of food to

make sure they complied with his strict post-cardiac diet. Having examined and selected a particular item he would then return to his cart, deposit the goods and go in search of other merchandise.

Mr. Parker, the second assistant manager, testified that he considered this method of shopping somewhat unusual, and his attention having been attracted, he observed Mr. Paul's shopping techniques for approximately twenty minutes. Although Mr. Paul was a regular shopper at this A & P and known to a number of employees there, Mr. Parker, a relatively new addition to the store, did not know him. Upon completion of his observation Parker came to the conclusion that Paul had taken a can of flea and tick spray and had placed it in his coat pocket with the apparent intention of shoplifting. The policy of A & P on shoplifting as testified to by the manager of the store in question was to let each employee "use his own judgment" as to what steps should be taken. He further testified that Parker was authorized to do what was done in this case.

The testimony conflicts widely at this point. Parker testified he merely questioned Paul about a can of flea and tick spray that had been in his cart earlier. He did not see Paul secrete this item anywhere, but assumed he had because it was no longer in the cart and in his opinion Paul had not had sufficient time to return the spray to its proper place on the shelf. He said appellee became nervous and defensive, demanding to see the manager. Parker said he never touched Paul, there was no commotion and there were few customers in the store. Paul testified that Parker accosted him in the middle of an aisle and demanded in a loud voice to know what he had done with the spray. When Paul said he did not have such an item Parker replied, "Don't tell me, you goddamn thief. You got it in your coat." Paul further testified that when this occurred some twenty-five to thirty customers in the immediate vicinity of the aisle turned and stared, and continued to watch as Parker roughly frisked him, knocking over a display of cans and loudly repeating his accusation of thievery. His testimony continues that Parker then grabbed him by the arm and forced him to march to the manager's office at the front of the store, attracting the attention of shoppers waiting at the check-out counters. No flea spray or any other item belonging to A & P was found on Paul's person. Appellee stated as a result of the experience he was severely upset and reached home in his automobile only with difficulty. . . .

Appellant . . . claims error was committed in the false imprisonment phase of the case. False imprisonment and false arrest are common law torts that apparently differ only in terminology. . . . The necessary elements of a case for false imprisonment are a deprivation of the liberty of another without his consent and without legal justification. . . .

The term legal justification has created some confusion in other courts. . . . This confusion arises because of the frequent statement that probable cause is not a defense to an action for false imprisonment but legal justification is. Probable cause, however, may be shown in mitigation of punitive damages. . . .

Appellant urges that Maryland should adopt the rule expressed in Restatement (Second) of Torts, Sec. 120 A (1965) "One who reasonably believes that another has tortiously taken a chattel [movable personal property] upon his premises, or has failed to make due cash payment for a chattel purchased or services rendered there, is privileged, without arresting the other, to detain him on the premises for the time necessary for a reasonable investigation of the facts." Appellant cites several jurisdictions which have adopted this qualified privilege. It offered an instruction substantially embodying the Restatement language at the trial level, and it is refusal to instruct the jury in accordance with this rule that it assigns as error. It urges strenuously that probable cause should be a defense in this lim-

ited situation, detailing the growing problem of shoplifting in this country. It states that the modern self-service style of retail selling makes the shopkeeper powerless to protect his goods unless Section 120 A is adopted in substance. Without being facetious we note that shoplifting may be regarded as the price merchants pay for the success of modern merchandising; goods alluringly displayed to stimulate "impulse buying" inevitably also stimulate "impulse taking." . . .

Whatever technical distinction there may be between an "arrest" and a "detention" the test whether legal justification existed in a particular case has been judged by the principles applicable to the law of arrest. A shopkeeper under these principles has only the rights of a private person. In Maryland a private person has authority to arrest without a warrant only when a) there is a felony being committed in his presence or when a felony has in fact been committed whether or not in his presence, and the arrester has reasonable ground (probable cause) to believe the person he arrests has committed it; or b) a misdemeanor is being committed in the presence or view of the arrester which amounts to a breach of the peace. . . . Breach of the peace signifies disorderly, dangerous conduct disruptive of public peace and it is clear that the usual shoplifting incident does not fit within this category. . . . Since most shoplifters steal inexpensive items, . . . the only crime they are generally guilty of is petit larceny, a misdemeanor. . . . Thus a private person has no power to arrest them, and probable cause to believe they committed the crime is in fact not a defense. . . .

There is a narrow exception to the general rules of arrest stated above. Any property owner, including a storekeeper, has a common law privilege to detain against his will any person he believes has tortiously taken his property. This privilege can be exercised only to prevent theft or to recapture property, and does not extend to detention for the purpose of punishment. This common law right is exercised at the shopkeeper's peril, however, and if the person detained does not unlawfully have any of the arrester's property in his possession, the arrester is liable for false imprisonment. . . .

As it now stands in this state arrest or detention without legal authority, with or without probable cause, will render the arresting person liable for such damages "as the jury may consider actual compensation for the unlawful invasion of his [the plaintiff's] rights and the injury to his person and feelings." In addition, if the act was "inflicted maliciously or wantonly, the jury are not restricted to an award of compensatory damages, but [in its discretion] may award . . . such punitive damages as the circumstances of the case may warrant as a punishment for the wrong done and as an example to others." *Dennis v Baltimore Transit Co.,* 189 Md. 610, 616, 56 A.2d 813, 816 (1948).

There was sufficient evidence for the jury to find that the manner and method of the detention here was not within the privilege "necessary for a reasonable investigation of the facts." See comments to Sec. 120 A, *Restatement (Second) of Torts.* But the reasonableness of the de-

tention does not become an issue unless it is first shown that the person invoking the privilege "reasonable believes that another has tortiously taken a chattel upon his premises." Parker testified he did not see Paul place any merchandise in his coat and did not check the shelf to see if the "missing" item had been returned, although if he had, these activities would not have necessarily constituted probable cause. He further testified he stopped Paul in an aisle before Paul had given any indication of leaving the store, even though customers could not pay for any item until they reached the check-out counters at the front of the store. In a self-service store we think no probable cause . . . for detention exists until the suspected person actually attempts to leave without paying, unless he manifests control over the property in such a way that his intention to steal is unequivocal. Construing all of the evidence in a light most favorable to the defendant, there is no showing of probable cause here. . . .

[Judgment affirmed.]

5:4   Intentional Infliction of Mental Distress

As early as 1899, a court recognized that "[w]ords in themselves may be harmless, while accent and manner may make them deadly."[5] The tort of mental distress is physical injury or severe mental suffering without physical impact, which results from an emotional disturbance caused by intentional highly aggravated or outrageous words or acts. The words or acts must be severe, exceeding all socially acceptable standards and must actually cause serious injury. Since people must occasionally "blow off steam," this tort is difficult to prove. Courts have been reluctant historically to find that an actual tort was committed; their viewpoint is that the tort of mental distress may lead to fictitious claims, and that the damages are of a subtle nature with psychic injuries more difficult to "see" than, for example, a broken arm. In spite of these objections, where the tortfeasor's conduct is sufficiently outrageous and exceeds all standards of propriety, recovery is allowed.

---

[5]*State v Kerns,* 47 W Va 266, 34 SE 734 (1899).

EXAMPLE
An association of rubbish collectors threatened to beat up the plaintiff, destroy his truck, and put him out of business unless he gave the association proceeds from a territory it had allocated to one of its members. The court held that the rubbish collectors were liable for causing "severe emotional distress" as an independent tort, even though there was no assault, only threats. The prime factor for recovery was their "extremely outrageous behaviour."[6]

In the modern business setting, unconscionable debt collection practices sometimes result in this tort.

EXAMPLE
A debt collector came to the home of the plaintiff, an eleven-year-old girl, knowing she was alone, to repossess a television set. After the girl refused to admit him, he went to another door and held up a note to the glass which stated that he would get the police and have her arrested if she did not admit him. She became extremely nervous, suffered great anxiety, and was unable to sleep at night. The plaintiff received damages for intentional infliction of mental distress on the basis of the debt collector's deliberate and malicious intent to frighten her.[7]

5:5 Defamation

The tort of *defamation* consists of injury to a person's reputation by the making of false statements. When the defamatory material is in the form of printing, writing, or pictures, the defamation is called libel. If the defamation is communicated orally or by acts or gestures, it is termed slander. Whether transmission of defamatory matter by radio or television is slander or libel is a question on which the courts have not agreed. Even an implication or insinuation against a person may be actionable if it has a clear defamatory meaning. Business partnerships and private corporations can maintain defamation suits respecting their business, integrity, solvency, or credit.

Defenses   There is a constitutional privilege that protects members of the press who publish otherwise defamatory material written about public officials, public figures, or persons of legitimate public interest. This privilege has been extended to cover even false reports of matters of public interest, unless it can be proven that they were published with knowledge of their falsity or in reckless disregard of the truth.

Two other privileges are absolute privilege and conditional privilege. Absolute privilege is a complete defense to defamation. Those who have this privilege are participants in a judicial proceeding, members of federal and state legislatures while in committee or legislative sessions, state and federal government executives at a policy-making level, and a spouse when communicating to the other spouse. A conditional privilege exempts a person from liability only when the defamation

---

[6]*State Rubbish Collectors Asso. v Siliznoff*, 38 Cal 2d 330, 240 P2d 282 (1952).
[7]*Delta Finance Co. v Ganakas*, 93 Ga App 297, 91 SE2d 383 (Georgia Court of Appeals, 1956).

was published in good faith and with proper motives. A defendant has a conditional privilege when he reasonably believes an important interest in person or property is being threatened or the defamation is necessary to protect a legitimate public interest, or when he is reporting the happenings in executive, legislative, or judicial proceedings. A conditional privilege is destroyed by publication for an improper purpose, publication not bearing on the interest to be protected, actual malice, or lack of belief in the truth of the statement. Most courts hold truth to be a complete defense to defamation, whatever the motive involved and even if the defendant thought the statement was false at the time he made it.

 A question regarding protected statements sometimes arises when unemployment agencies inquire of employers about an application for unemployment insurance by a former employee discharged for his conduct. Statutory provisions in several states provide that the employer's response to an unemployment agency's query is absolutely privileged. Most other states, even in the absence of statute, have reached the same result.

A creditor or credit agency has a privilege to report financial matters to those with a legitimate business interest. This privilege is conditioned on the inquirer's good faith and lack of malice; any conduct showing a reckless disregard for or conscious indifference to the rights of the debtor will destroy the privilege.[8]

Retraction   A retraction is the published withdrawal of defamatory material by the person who made it. At common law, retraction was not a complete defense, but it did remove the elements of malice and bad faith, thereby substantially reducing the damages. Today, several states have retraction statutes that generally relieve the media (television, radio, and newspapers) from some liability if they comply with the injured party's demand for a fair and prompt retraction.

 An employer who discharges an unsatisfactory employee should be alert to a possible defamation suit when responding to others with whom the discharged employee has applied for employment. If defamatory material is communicated to a prospective new employer and the employee can show that the prior employer did not make the communication in good faith or that statements were made with a reckless disregard for the truth, the employee may be able to sue for defamation. To prevent defamation litigation, an employer should consult an attorney as to the precise wording that should be used to communicate information about a prior or present employee.

5:6   Trespass and Conversion

Besides torts that involve invasion of an individual's right to be secure in person or reputation, there are torts that involve injury to the individual's property or property interest. These include trespass to land, trespass to chattels, conversion, and misrepresentation.

---

[8]Credit reporting is discussed further in 27:11.

Trespass to Land   The tort of *trespass to land* is the unauthorized entry of a person or thing on land belonging to another. The basis of the tort is the right to the exclusive possession of land. Possession sufficient to entitle the landowner to bring suit for trespass may be actual, as when the owner is actually on the land, or constructive, as when the land is possessed by someone responsible to the owner, such as an agent or employee. A person may sue for trespass even if the entry was made for or resulted in improvement to the land.

Under most decisions, if a person intends to be on another's land, he is liable for trespass even if his presence is based on a good faith mistake, such as ignorance as to the land's ownership or boundary lines, or other honest mistake causing him to go on the land.

EXAMPLE

A developer purchases certain land and believes in good faith that his neighbor's land is part of his purchase. He enters the neighbor's unposted, unenclosed land to survey it. The developer has committed the tort of trespass to land even though he did not intend to violate his neighbor's right to exclusive possession of the land. The crucial questions are whether the entry was unauthorized and whether the developer intended to enter the land. Since the answer is yes in both cases, the tort has been committed. However, if the developer were pushed onto the neighbor's land by a third person, and had no intention of entering the land, he would not be liable for trespass. In such a case, it would be the third person who would be liable.

Trespass to Chattels   A *chattel* is movable personal property, as distinguished from real property (land). *Trespass to chattels* is the intentional and harmful interference with possession of personal property without the owner's consent. The gist of the tort is physical interference with the exclusive right of another to use and possess a chattel. As with trespass to land, mistake is no defense to trespass to chattels. This tort is of diminishing importance because the courts are replacing it with the tort of conversion.

Conversion   *Conversion* is the intentional and wrongful acquiring, altering, damaging, transferring, using, or withholding of another person's property. The interest protected is that of possession of, control of, or right to control a chattel. The tort of conversion developed from the merging of several highly technical fifteenth-century English writs, with the result that today conversion has been said by some legal writers to defy a clear definition. The *Restatement (Second) of Torts* § 222A states that a conversion is an intentional exercise of dominion or control over a chattel which so seriously interferes with the right of another to control it that the one interfering is liable for its full value. Several factors are considered in determining whether the interference is serious enough to require full compensation: (1) the extent of dominion, (2) duration of interference, (3) harm to the chattel, and (4) inconvenience and expense to the owner. Neither good faith nor mistake constitute a defense to conversion. Hence, even though a person in good faith purchases converted goods, he will be liable to the true owner of the goods.

What May Be Converted   In the context of business, the question arises as to what may be converted. At common law, only property that could be "lost" was considered the subject of conversion; this limited the action to tangible personal property. Because of the need to protect intangible rights evidenced by checks, notes, bonds, stock certificates, and similar documents, the action for conversion was extended so that intangible rights were said to "merge with an instrument." Today, some states now permit recovery for conversion of an intangible right (if the type considered merged with an instrument), even though the instrument itself has not been converted. Recovery may be had, for example, for a corporation's refusal to transfer stock. Generally, intangible rights not considered merged with an instrument such as ideas and goodwill are not recognized as being convertible.

5:7   Misrepresentation

Misrepresentation is an all-embracing term. The ability of a person to devise fraudulent schemes is so great that courts have not defined misrepresentation, reserving to themselves the liberty to deal with it in whatever form it appears. It may broadly be said, however, that the tort of misrepresentation consists of the false representation of a material fact to a person who justifiably relies on it to his damage.

In the case of failure to disclose information, as opposed to an actual false statement, liability may be an open question. For example, if a person knows that his car's radiator is defective yet says nothing and sells the car to another person, who does not ask about the radiator, there would probably be no recovery for fraudulent concealment. A seller usually does not have to disclose a hidden defect, in the absence of a statutory or other duty to do so. On the other hand, if there has been an *active concealment* on the seller's part, such as attempts to conceal the radiator's defects, then the tort of misrepresentation in the form of fraud would probably be present. In this event, the courts say there is "more than mere failure to speak."

Liability for misrepresentation requires that the injured party's reliance on the misrepresentation be justifiable. To be the basis of liability, the misrepresentation must be of an existing fact, not just an expression of opinion. For example, if a buyer has ample opportunity to examine the goods to be purchased, general statements by the seller as to the performance or value of the goods ("performs well," "runs like a charm," "a great bargain"), which are false, will not usually give rise to a suit for misrepresentation. Courts permit a reasonable amount of "sales talk."

EXAMPLE
A used car salesman tells a potential car buyer "this little beauty is a great buy. It will take you wherever you want to go with no problems at all." After purchasing the car, the buyer discovers it has a leaky radiator and needs transmission work. The salesman is probably not guilty of the tort of misrepresentation since his statements were of a general "selling nature," not specific representations of facts or conditions of the automobile. If, on the other hand, the salesman had been specifically asked the condition of the radiator or transmission and had remained silent or had stated the condition to be good, then the purchaser would have a basis for suit.

5:8   Invasion of Civil Rights[9]

The phrase "civil rights" includes all private legal rights of individuals. The term is also used in a more restricted sense that refers to those rights created by state and federal constitutional and statutory provisions designed to prevent discrimination relating to race, color, sex, religion, or national origin. Many state and federal constitutional and statutory provisions prohibit discrimination on these grounds in connection with education, voting, transportation, employment, housing, and places of public accommodation or amusement, as well as other activities. Violation of these statutory rights has sometimes resulted in tort suits, as well as criminal prosecution.

Civil rights laws vary considerably in the type of relief permitted. While some give the individual a right to recover a statutory penalty in a specified amount, others give the right to recover both damages and penalties. Some statutes that provide no punishment or remedies at all have nevertheless been held to give an individual the right to recover damages from the violator in a civil action. The same result has been reached under some statutes expressly providing only criminal punishment.

Key Concepts and Terms

- A tort is a civil wrong other than breach of contract. While a crime is a wrong against society and punishable by the state, a tort is a wrong against an individual for which civil damages constitute the remedy. A person who commits a tort is called a tortfeasor. Joint tortfeasors are two or more persons who unite in committing a tort, or whose acts concur in producing an injury to a third person.

- Some intentional torts take the form of interfering with or invading a person's right to be secure in his own body and person. They include battery, assault, malicious prosecution, abuse of process, and invasion of privacy.

- False imprisonment is the wrongful obstruction or detention of a person within boundaries for any length of time, without his consent. The tort frequently arises in shoplifter detention cases. Under shopkeeper's privilege, followed in some but not all states, a storekeeper, who has a reasonable belief (probable cause) that a theft has been committed, may detain the suspect for a reasonable time and conduct an investigation in a reasonable manner without being liable for false imprisonment, even if the detained person was not a shoplifter.

- The tort of mental distress is characterized by injury to a person resulting from emotional disturbance without physical impact, caused by another's highly aggravated or outrageous words or acts, which exceed all socially acceptable standards. Unconscionable debt collection practices sometimes result in this tort.

- Defamation, which may be libel or slander, is injury to a person's reputation by

---

[9]Invasion of civil rights in employment discrimination is discussed in Chapter 52.

false statements. Certain defamatory statements, especially those about public persons, are privileged.

- Torts to property or property interests include trespass to land, trespass to chattels, and conversion.

- Misrepresentation is a broad term, referring generally to false representations of a material fact that a person relies on to his damage. Simple failure to disclose information, in the absence of a duty to do so, does not usually result in the tort of misrepresentation. However, active concealment of material information gives rise to the tort. In a sales situation, courts permit a reasonable amount of "sales talk."

- Some state and federal constitutional and statutory provisions prohibiting discrimination have been used as the base for tort suits.

- Assault
- Battery
- Chattel
- Consent
- Conversion
- Defamation
- False Imprisonment
- Intent
- Intentional Infliction of Mental Distress

- Invasion of Privacy
- Misrepresentation
- Privilege
- Shopkeeper's Privilege
- Shoplifter Detention
- Tort
- Transferred Intent
- Trespass to Chattels
- Trespass to Land

Questions and Case Problems

1. What are the differences between a tort, a crime, and a breach of contract?

2. Katie Valdez, while in a variety store owned by Michelle Whitney, notices a sign on the wall reading "FREE—PLEASE TAKE ONE," below which is a box of transistor radios. She puts one of the radios in her pocket and walks out of the store. Whitney rushes out of the store after Valdez, shouting, "Come back here with that radio, you thief!" The street is crowded, and Valdez, humiliated by the accusation, eludes Whitney and runs home. Later that day, Maria Garcia, a customer who resembles Valdez, enters the restroom of Whitney's store. Whitney, thinking Garcia is Valdez, locks the restroom door and calls the police. There is an open window in the restroom. Garcia decides to climb out the window and gets on a chair to reach the window. As she puts her weight on the back of the chair, it tips. Garcia falls to the floor and breaks her leg. Valdez learns later that the "FREE—PLEASE TAKE ONE" sign referred to advertising bulletins which were usually beneath the sign, and not to the transistor radios. Discuss the rights of Valdez and Whitney against each other and the rights of Garcia against Whitney.

3. As part of a nightclub act, Waldo hypnotizes volunteers from the audience. Horace volunteers and is hypnotized. Waldo directs Horace to pour a glass of water on Sharon, another member of the audience. Horace does so. Has Horace committed a battery on Sharon? Has Waldo committed a battery on Sharon? Discuss.

4. Explain the doctrine of transferred intent.

5. What are the differences between invasion of privacy and defamation?

6. Christopher purchases an expensive house from Dudley. Prior to signing the final papers, Christopher asks Dudley if the house is free of termites. Is there an actionable misrepresentation in any of the following responses by Dudley? (a) Dudley replies that he has recently obtained a termite report showing no visible infestation. In fact, no such report had been obtained, and unbeknown to Dudley, the house is full of termites. (b) Dudley replies that there are no termites, because he has never seen any, but afterwards, just to check, he crawls under the house and finds a large infestation. He decides not to tell Christopher about this, because he did not ask him to crawl under the house and report back to him. (c) Dudley makes no reply to Christopher's inquiry, but knows that there is extensive infestation. (d) Dudley's only reply to Christopher's inquiry is that the house was being sold "as is," while all along Dudley knows there is extensive infestation.

7. As part of the negotiations leading up to the sale of an apartment house, the seller makes the following representations to the buyer, each of which is false. Which of these representations, if any, would subject the seller to liability for misrepresentation if it is relied on by the buyer? (a) This property is worth at least $150,000, but I'll sell it to you for $120,000. (b) I have never previously offered this property for sale. (c) Nothing in the city building code prevents you from splitting the larger apartments into smaller ones, if you want to, thereby increasing the rents.

8. Fastbuck advertises lots for sale in Golden Years Subdivision, which consists of undeveloped desert acreage. Mr. Eager, a retiree, visits the subdivision, and asks what improvements are planned. Fastbuck tells him all about planned swimming pools, shopping areas, and an 18-hole golf course. Relying on Fastbuck's word, Eager buys one of the lots for $5,000. The swimming pools, shopping areas, and golf course are never built. Assume that Fastbuck never had the funds for this development and never had any reasonable prospects of being able to construct the promised amenities. Can Eager recover damages for misrepresentation?

9. Representatives of the Ajax Debt Collection Service come to the front door of Alice's home and in loud voices announce that Alice is four months behind in payments on her new sofa and that the debt collectors want to enter to repossess the sofa. The debt collectors refuse to leave the property and yell through the door that if Alice does not permit them to enter, they will break the door down. Alice then opens the door and the debt collectors enter and remove the sofa. All the while Alice is protesting. She throws a lamp at one of the debt collectors, and he sustains a concussion. Discuss the possible tort liabilities of all parties.

10. Mike's poodle runs away from home, and enters Mary's yard. Mary puts a leash on the dog. When Mike comes looking for his dog, Mary refuses to return it and locks the gate to her property. (a) Is Mike privileged to break down Mary's gate to enter her property to reclaim the dog? (b) If Mike is privileged to break Mary's gate, must he pay for any damage to the gate? (c) Is Mike privileged to break and enter Mary's front door if she has taken the dog inside her house?

6 Negligence and Strict Liability

Standards of prudent conduct are declared at times by courts, but they are taken over from the facts of life.

Justice Cardozo, *Pokora v Wabash R. Co.*
292 US 98, 78 L Ed 1149, 54 S Ct 480,
(United States Supreme Court, 1934)

6:1 In General

Over the course of time the courts have established the elements that constitute the tort of *negligence*. These elements must be shown to exist before an injured person can claim a right to recovery for negligence: (1) that the defendant had a duty to exercise reasonable care, (2) that there was a breach of that duty, (3) that a causal relationship exists between the defendant's conduct and the plaintiff's injury, and (4) that damages resulted. This chapter examines these elements and describes various defenses against the tort of negligence. The final section deals with the area of tort recovery called strict liability.

6:2 Duty to Exercise Reasonable Care

Every person has a duty to exercise the conduct that a reasonable person of ordinary prudence would follow under the same or similar circumstances. This stems from the fact that all persons are deemed to possess certain minimum levels of knowledge and skills, and, as a consequence, they are held to certain minimum standards of care in their activities.

EXAMPLE
The defendant fails to replace tread-bare tires on his car. Despite the fact that he had no actual knowledge of the danger of driving with poor tires, the defendant will be liable for negligence in not replacing the tires if, because of the tires, his car is in an accident that causes damage to another. Since it is supposed that a reasonable person would know that driving with poor tires is dangerous, the defendant has the duty to exercise reasonable care to maintain his tires in a safe condition.

The duty of care that the reasonable person is expected to exercise will vary according to the risk involved; more care must be used, for example, when handling explosives than when handling lumber.

Liability of Professionals   A professional, such as a physician, attorney, accountant, or other person whose occupation requires highly specialized knowledge, is obligated to have the same skill and learning as other members of his profession and to apply that skill and learning with the same care as generally exercised by other members of that profession.

EXAMPLE

In drafting a document, an attorney fails to take into consideration certain tax consequences. As a result, her client is required to pay more taxes than he would had the attorney prepared the document differently. The attorney will be liable in damages for professional malpractice if the client can show that the attorney failed to have, and to exercise, the same learning and skill as other members of her profession would have exercised.

Failure to Act   Generally, a person has no duty to come to the aid of others. Unless there is some special legal circumstance imposing a duty to rescue, the law does not enforce any moral obligation—one that should be observed out of common decency or humanity. Thus, failure to act, termed *nonfeasance,* does not create liability. However, if a person does render assistance and is thereafter negligent as a result of what he does or does not do, he will be liable. The courts recognize three ways in which a person can be negligent, or make another's situation worse: (1) by increasing the danger, (2) by depriving the person of other aid, and (3) by inducing the person to forgo other assistance because of reliance on his aid.

EXAMPLE

The defendant is driving down the highway and witnesses an automobile accident. She drives to the side of the road and observes that the plaintiff, whom she does not know, is trapped behind the steering wheel of his vehicle and apparently seriously injured. The defendant tries to extricate him from the vehicle, but after a moment gives up and leaves. She does not notify anyone of the accident. While the defendant did not have any *initial* duty to stop and render aid, once she did so, if it can be established that she acted negligently in rendering the aid (such as by not trying long enough or by not contacting other persons), then she may be liable for having left the plaintiff *worse* off than she found him. Other passersby, for example, who may have seen the defendant assisting the plaintiff, might otherwise have stopped to render better aid themselves.

The following decision exemplifies another instance in which a person who does not initially have a duty toward another voluntarily undertakes to perform some action as to the other and, in so doing, assumes a duty to perform with due care. Here it is shown that although an employer usually owes no duty to a prospective employee, once he assumes particular duties toward an employee, he is liable for failure to perform those duties with care.

Coffee
v
McDonnell-Douglas Corp.
8 Cal 3d 551, 105 Cal Rptr 358,
503 P2d 1366
(California Supreme Court, 1972)

[The plaintiff applied for a position as a pilot with the defendant corporation and, as an applicant, was required to undergo a preemployment physical examination to establish his physical fitness for the job. He was found to be physically fit and began employment. In the following case, the appellate court affirmed the plaintiff's judgment against the defendant employer for negligence in failing to bring the fact that the plaintiff had bone cancer to the plaintiff's attention. The court held that when the defendant employer undertook, although voluntarily, to examine the plaintiff so as to ascertain his physical fitness for duties as a pilot, such undertaking gave rise to a duty to perform the examination with care.]

Sullivan, Justice.

*   *   *

An employer generally owes no duty to his prospective employees to ascertain whether they are physically fit for the job they seek, but where he assumes such duty, he is liable if he performs it negligently. . . . The obligation assumed by an employer is derived from the general principle expressed in section 323 of the *Restatement (Second) of Torts*, that one who voluntarily undertakes to perform an action must do so with due care.

In the case at bench, defendant, in conformity with its policy that all prospective employees undergo a physical examination, required plaintiff to take such an examination in order to ascertain if he was physically fit to perform the duties of a test pilot. Having assumed the duty to examine plaintiff, defendant also assumed the duty to conduct and complete the examination with due care.

Defendant, however, contends that the duty of an employer, within the context of a preemployment physical examination, is a limited one; that defendant had no duty to *discover* diseased conditions in plaintiff; and, that even if it had the duty to *disclose known* results, defendant's conduct did not constitute a breach of such duty. More specifically, defendant argues, to impose on employers a "duty to discover" would "ignore the purposes" of preemployment physical examinations and would "place an undue and unreasonable burden on prospective employers screening possible employees."

We agree that defendant did not breach a duty "to disclose" known results of the examination. We have found no evidence in the record establishing that any of the doctor–employees had actual knowledge of the contents of the blood test report showing, among other things, an abnormally high sedimentation rate and thus indicating the presence of an inflammatory condition. Obviously, having no knowledge of the results of the blood test, defendant's doctor–employees who examined plaintiff were at no time under a duty to make a disclosure.

However, we think defendant has misconceived the issue crucial in this case when it asserts that it had no duty "to discover." The question presented here is not whether defendant has assumed the duty "to discover" diseased conditions; rather, the question is whether the relationship between the parties was such that plaintiff was entitled to legal protection against the wrongful conduct of the defendant. Such a relationship was formed here when defendant undertook, although voluntarily, to examine plaintiff so as to ascertain his physical fitness for duties as a pilot.

Defendant insists that the imposition of a duty "to discover" is an "undue burden." However, it has been said that an employer has failed to exercise due care when it fails "to disclose" diseased or dangerous conditions revealed in a physical examination.... Yet, defendant in effect argues that if an employer fails to perform an examination with due care and thereby fails "to discover" the presence of such a condition, he should not be held liable. In other words, defendant's liability would be limited by the commission of its negligent acts. We cannot approve of such a result.

At the same time we do not say that an employer once having required a prospective employee to submit to a physical examination in order to ascertain his fitness for the job, assumes an absolute obligation to discover any diseased conditions. In our view the proper test is this: whether the employer in such instance is liable for not discovering the disease depends upon whether or not in the light of all of the circumstances he conducted and completed the examination with due care. Included among the relevant circumstances is the purpose of the examination.

In the matter before us, the purpose of the physical examination was to determine plaintiff's physical fitness as a pilot. In order to examine prospective pilots properly, defendant decided it was essential to take a blood sample and subject it to analysis. The blood test report, indicating an inflammatory condition in plaintiff, was never seen by defendant's medical employees because of a corporate procedure allowing the report to be filed without evaluation. The question posed, already answered by the jury in the affirmative, was whether in the exercise of due care, defendant "should have known" of the results of the blood test.... Viewed in this context, the failure "to discover" the inflammatory condition in plaintiff was the consequence of defendant's own negligence....

The negligence of defendant corporation, ... independently of the conduct of the defendant doctors, consisted of its failure to establish a proper procedure for evaluation of blood test reports. Consequently, we think the jury could have reasonably concluded that although the doctors individually acted with due care, defendant corporation was negligent in failing to exercise due care in the handling of the blood test reports.

[Judgment affirmed.]

Degrees of Negligence   While some cases have talked about "degrees of negligence," most courts hold that there are not different degrees of negligence but rather circumstances that require more or less care. Statutes, however, sometimes speak in terms of "gross negligence" or "recklessness." Such statutory provisions are interpreted to mean a conscious and deliberate disregard of conditions that impose a high probability that someone will be injured.

Modification of Objective Standard of Care   The objective standard of care, or the care exercised by a reasonably prudent person, has been modified in the case of children. Several courts have expressed the view that the standard of a child's care is based on what may be expected of children of similar age, intelligence, and experience. A person with a mental incapacity, however, is held to the same standard of care as a person of ordinary intelligence because of the difficulties involved in determining the degree of disability. Likewise, the courts will not make allowances for voluntary intoxication when determining a defendant's duty to exercise reasonable care.

Clearly, the reasonable person confronted with an emergency may act differently than he would if there were no emergency. This does not mean there is a different standard applied; rather, it means that the emergency conditions become part of all the circumstances taken into consideration in determining how a reasonable person would act in that situation.

6:3   Defendant's Breach of Duty

Perfect conduct is humanly impossible. As such, the law does not exact an unreasonable amount of care from anyone. *Breach of duty* to exercise reasonable care means that a person fails to act as carefully as a reasonable person would have acted under the same or similar circumstances. The greater the danger that is known or that reasonably may be anticipated, the greater the degree of care the law requires one to observe.

The *"reasonable person" standard* is a rule. Yet, what it means in any particular case depends on how the court perceives a reasonable person would have acted. Thus, it is always dependent on proof of the circumstances that existed at the time. From such proof, the court determines what a "reasonable person" would have done and measures the defendant's conduct against this standard.

The following decision exemplifies how the court examines the facts and then applies those facts to the law to determine whether the defendant owed a duty of care to the plaintiff and whether it breached that duty of care. This decision is a typical negligence case in several respects; namely, it discusses separately, and in order, duty and breach, and it lays particular stress on the extent to which the defendant's activities require, in terms of public policy, particular procedures to protect the general public.

Williams
v
United States
450 F Supp 1040
(United States District Court, 1978)

[The administrator of a decedent's estate brought suit on behalf of the decedent, who was shot and killed by a mental patient who had been released from a Veterans' Administration Hospital the day before the shooting. The suit was based on negligence of the United States (through its agent, the Veterans' Administration Hospital) for failing to notify local authorities, as it had agreed to do, of the mental patient's discharge, particularly since the patient had known propensities for overtly violent conduct. The trial judge held the hospital negligent for failure to have notified the authorities.]

Bogue, District Judge.

*   *   *

On May 2, 1975, Alonzo Bush left the Veteran's Administration Hospital at Fort Meade. The Meade County Sheriff, John Eggar, testified that his office was not notified of Bush's release but that it had been his understanding that Bush was to be released to the sheriff's office. He testified that charges against Bush were pending. The Court finds on the basis of Sheriff Eggar's testimony that had notification been given, the Meade County Sheriff's office would have taken Alonzo Bush into custody on March 2, 1975, and would have held him for further court proceedings.

On May 3, the day following his release, Alonzo Bush approached three men who were standing outside of Bob's Sewing Center on Main Street in Rapid City, a business then owned and operated by Robert Williams. Bush was drunk, an altercation ensued, and one of the three men, Robert Williams, pushed Alonzo Bush away. Bush stumbled backwards and fell. He then got up, walked several feet away and told a woman passerby that "that white man over there is trying to kill me" and that he, Bush, was with the F.B.I. Bush then walked back toward the group of three men, pulled a revolver and shot Mr. Williams in the head. Mr. Williams died at a Rapid City hospital shortly thereafter.

NEGLIGENCE

The Court notes at the outset that a hospital cannot be charged with the responsibility of insuring the physical safety of the public from all harmful acts committed by patients who have been discharged. Such a course of action would place an unreasonable burden on treating institutions. The Court also recognizes that any claim of negligence against a hospital must be considered in light of the elusive qualities of mental disorders and the likelihood that honest errors in judgment will, from time to time, occur. . . .

Nonetheless, a hospital treating patients who have a history of behavior disorders is not, for that reason alone, shielded from liability in all instances when a patient it has released causes harm to others. VA hospitals have been held liable for negligent failure to properly inform a court of the potential danger to others posed by a patient the hospital has treated; . . . and for negligence in granting leave to a patient with a prior history of violent behavior without providing for proper supervision during that leave. . . . In *Homere v.*

State, 79 Misc. 2d 972, 361 N.Y.S.2d 820 (1974) a state hospital was held liable for failure to reconvene a discharge panel and to reevaluate the advisability of discharging a patient subsequent to the patient's display of violent behavior. In the present case, having agreed to notify the sheriff of the release of Alonzo Bush so that Bush, a man with a known propensity for violence, could be taken into custody, a duty was imposed upon the Fort Meade VA Hospital to exercise reasonable care under all the circumstances to see that such notification was provided. We find that the defendant hospital was negligent in that it failed to exercise such care.

Reasonable care is "that degree of care which a reasonably prudent person [or institution] would have used under the same or similar circumstances." . . . The circumstances of this case demanded a particular high degree of care. In addition to the sheriff's request to be notified of Bush's release which, in and of itself, should have alerted the hospital to the possibility that Bush might pose a danger to the public, the hospital knew that Bush had been arrested, that he had set fire to the jail, that authorities felt they could not control him and that Bush had been having "fits or something." Further, its own records (about which the hospital should have been informed) indicated that Bush had a strong propensity for hostile and violent behavior, that he had in the past made unprovoked attacks on an examining doctor and on a fellow patient, that he had been diagnosed as "psychotic," "paranoid" and "schizophrenic" at various times and that, only twelve days before, in the lobby of the very same hospital, had attacked a staff member and wrestled him to the ground.

Prosser has stated the standard of reasonable care under such circumstances:

". . . When the risk becomes a serious one, either because the threatened harm is great or because there is an especial likelihood that it will occur, reasonable care may demand precautions against 'that occasional negligence which is one of the ordinary incidents of human life and therefore to be anticipated.' " Prosser, *Law of Torts*, ch. 5, p. 171 (4th ed. 1971).

He has noted further that

"... The defendant's special responsibility may arise because he is in a position to control the criminal himself and so is held to be under an obligation to do so, extending to anyone who may be injured by his failure to exercise reasonable care." Prosser, *Law of Torts, supra*, p. 175.

It is difficult to glean from the record exactly why the hospital failed to notify the sheriff. The doctors who testified stated that notifying the sheriff was an administrative task and that physicians took no part in such procedures. On the other hand, Wayne Christenson, administrative assistant to the chief of staff, stated that notification was a "combined effort of the ward team and medical administration." The ward secretary on the alcohol ward stated in a deposition received into evidence that notification was the responsibility of the processing department, a division of the administrative branch of the hospital. She testified that, although she sat in on the discharge staff meeting, she knew nothing of Bush's past and did not know why the sheriff wanted to be called. She did, however, know that notification was to be made because a note card to that effect had been attached to Bush's file. She testified that she called the processing department but was told by a secretary in processing

that the instruction to notify the sheriff was probably related to an earlier admission. The secretary in processing, however, testified that no such note card was attached to Bush's file when she received it and that she had never been made aware of the sheriff's request.

Even without determining precisely what went wrong with the hospital's system for notification, it is apparent that the overall data dispensing procedures the hospital employed were faulty and that errors in patient care and discharge could easily occur. Old records were not adequately reviewed. Information about which the upper echelon of the administrative staff was aware, i.e. that Bush was "fairly dangerous" and had been "bouncing around the country hitting people," was not effectively reaching the medical staff in charge of releasing Bush. Nor was the information regarding the importance of notification of the authorities properly impressed upon the administrative staff members ultimately charged with calling the sheriff. Further, the hospital maintained no system of checks to insure that such notification had, in fact, been made. In short, hospital procedures were ineffective to protect against "that occasional negligence which is one of the ordinary incidents of human life and therefore to be anticipated," Prosser, *supra*, but which, in the exercise of reasonable care under the circumstances of this case, the hospital was bound to protect against. . . .

[Judgment affirmed.]

Res Ipsa Loquitur Doctrine   In certain cases, the very fact that a particular harm has occurred may itself tend to establish a breach of duty on the part of the defendant. Where the circumstances and type of accident strongly suggest that the plaintiff's injuries occurred through the defendant's negligence, the law may permit an inference that the defendant was at fault. This is the *doctrine of res ipsa loquitur*, which means literally "the act speaks for itself." There are three factors that must be established in order to invoke this doctrine: (1) the accident must be of a type that normally does not occur in the absence of someone's negligence, (2) the source of the negligence must be within the scope of a duty owned by the defendant to the plaintiff, and (3) neither the plaintiff nor any third person must have contributed to or caused the plaintiff's injuries. This doctrine is sometimes applied in airplane crash cases and medical malpractice suits in which the instrumentalities of the accident were completely within the defendant's knowledge and control and where the plaintiff had only limited access to the actual facts of the occurrence. It has also been applied in some cases involving exploding bottles and nonedible substances found in food.

Violation of Statute   If a person violates a criminal statute and in the process injures someone, he may be chargeable for negligence in addition to the crime. For the defendant's statutory violation to also constitute negligence, the statute must clearly define the conduct or duty required of the defendant and the types of individuals to whom it applies.

EXAMPLE
The defendant, a drugstore clerk, sold a poisonous substance without a "poison label," which was required by statute to be affixed to the container. The purchaser accidentally drank the poison and died. The defendant was liable in negligence since the statute created a duty to use reasonable care to protect customers from taking the wrong drug and the defendant failed to exercise this duty in the manner specified in the statute.

Similarly, many states have enacted statutes, commonly known as civil damage acts or dramshop acts, giving a right of action to persons injured by an intoxicated person against the individual who sold or furnished him the liquor. Although dramshop statutes generally provide for the recovery of damages from "any person" giving or selling intoxicating liquor, it is usually held that such statutes do not create a right of action against one who gives another the beverage as a mere act of hospitality or social courtesy without any connection to the business of selling liquor. Nevertheless, this is not always the case, and in some states a host, who at a social function serves liquor to a guest who subsequently injures another person, may be liable for damages.

6:4   Causation

For a defendant to have "caused" a plaintiff's injury and to be held negligent, the defendant's tortious acts must have been (1) the "cause in fact" and (2) the "proximate cause" of the plaintiff's injury.

Cause in Fact   *Cause in fact* means that the plaintiff's injury would not have happened "but for" the defendant's act or omission; therefore, the defendant's conduct is the cause in fact of the plaintiff's injury. For example, a defendant's failure to supply fire fighting equipment, which could not have been used anyway because there was no available water, cannot be considered the cause in fact of a plaintiff's loss of property from the fire. The reason is that it could not be shown that "but for" the failure to have the fire fighting equipment the plaintiff's building could have been saved.

Proximate Cause   Once actual causation (cause in fact) is established, the plaintiff must also establish *proximate cause*. Proximate cause is a concept developed by courts in an attempt to deal with the problem of liability for unforeseeable or unusual consequences following a defendant's act. "Proximate cause" is an unfortunate term, since closeness in time and space has nothing to do with the matter at issue. At issue is how far public policy will extend liability to a defendant for the consequences of his act. Proximate cause is established when there is not an intervening force between a defendant's negligent act and the harm to the plaintiff. For example, if while reaching for his cigarette lighter a driver crashes his car into a telephone pole, which falls onto a house, the driver's negligence is said to be the proximate cause of the damage to the house. Now, it also must be shown that the harm suffered by the plaintiff was a foreseeable consequence of the defendant's negligent act. This does not mean that the precise consequences could or should have been foreseen as they actually occurred; rather, it implies that the events were within the scope of a foreseeable risk. The following decision provides a further illustration.

George A. Hormel & Co.
v
Maez
92 Cal App 3d 963, 155 Cal Rptr 337
(California Court of Appeal, 1979)

[As a result of drunk driving, the defendant lost control of his vehicle and struck a power pole, causing power failure in the immediate area. When the pole went down, a power surge burned out and destroyed the motor on an ammonia compressor in the plaintiff's factory. All power in the factory was shut off for approximately two hours, resulting in monetary damages for wages paid to idled employees.]

Alarcon, Associate Justice.

*   *   *

In determining whether the injury suffered by the plaintiff here, economic loss as a result of a deprivation of power, was reasonably foreseeable, the test is not whether the defendant would have contemplated such injury at the time of his negligent conduct. In Commenting to the Restatement of Torts 2d, section 281, page 7, the authors explain: "In determining whether such events are within the risk, the courts have been compelled of necessity to resort to hindsight rather than foresight." Likewise, in *Dillon v. Legg*, . . . 68 Cal. 2d at page 741, 69 Cal. Rptr. at page 81, 441 P.2d at page 921, the [California] Supreme Court observed: "Such reasonable foreseeability does not turn on whether the particular defendant as an individual would have in actuality foreseen the exact accident and loss; it contemplates that courts, on a case-to-case basis, analyzing all the circumstances, will decide what the ordinary man under such circumstances should reasonably have foreseen. The courts thus mark out the areas of liability , excluding the remote and unexpected."

Certainly, the injury suffered by the plaintiff herein flowed directly from and was a direct and proximate result of the negligence of the defendant. Using hindsight, it is an easy matter to trace the injury back to the cause and to find it a reasonably likely result. However, the same result is reached by an application of foresight. The natural, logical, and foreseeable consequence of striking and destroying a power pole is the disruption of power service to those in the neighboring vicinity. This is not a freak result, nor one encumbered with unforeseeable intervening acts of others. . . . [T]here is no question that plaintiff suffered actual damage as a result of the surge and subsequent cessation of power; there is a close connection between defendant's conduct and plaintiff's damage. As previously noted, the damage to plaintiff is a direct result of the de-

fendant's negligent driving. No acts, foreseeable or otherwise, intervened between the act and the result. Appellant contends that the damages suffered here are highly unusual and unexpected. However, these same damages might have been suffered had defendant struck plaintiff's building, rather than the power pole. We see no reason why a different result should be reached here because of the fortuity that defendant struck a piece of property which did not belong to plaintiff. . . .

[Judgment affirmed.]

6:5 Defenses

There are several defenses that a defendant may assert against a plaintiff in a negligence suit. These are described below.

Contributory Negligence *Contributory negligence* refers to conduct on the part of a plaintiff that contributes to his own harm and that falls below the standard of reasonable care to which he must conform. Contributory negligence, which is a defense to a negligence suit, is much like negligence itself—the criteria are the same—but it involves a person's duty to exercise reasonable care for his own safety rather than for the safety of others. The standard of care, as in negligence, is determined by what the reasonable person would have done under the same or similar circumstances. In essence, even though he did not exercise due care, the defendant is not liable if the injury would have been avoided had the plaintiff himself exercised due care.

Last Clear Chance Doctrine The *doctrine of last clear chance*—sometimes referred to as the doctrine of discovered peril or the doctrine of supervening negligence or the humanitarian doctrine—states that if the plaintiff is also shown to be negligent, the negligent defendant is held liable for damages only if he was both aware of the plaintiff's peril and had a *later opportunity* than the plaintiff to avoid the accident.

EXAMPLE
The defendant negligently parks his automobile on the right side of a highway. The plaintiff, although she is able to see the defendant's car from several hundred feet away, collides with it. If the plaintiff sues the defendant to recover for her injuries, the defendant would be able to win by showing that the plaintiff had the last clear chance to avoid the collision.

Assumption of Risk   The defense of *assumption of risk* may apply when the plaintiff is shown to have voluntarily encountered a known danger (brought about by the defendant's negligence) and, by his own conduct, expressly or impliedly consented to take the risk of that danger. In such cases, the defendant will be relieved of responsibility for his negligence.

The essential elements of the defense of assumption of risk include the plaintiff's knowledge and appreciation of the danger and his voluntary exposure to that danger. Thus it is applicable only when the injured person might reasonably have elected to expose himself to the peril. It does not apply when the exposure was due to any inability to escape after the danger became known to him.

Immunities   *Immunity* as a defense to a negligence suit applies when the defendant's status or relationship to the plaintiff exempts him from liability. Applicability of this defense depends on the issue at trial and on the jurisdiction in which the tort occurred. For example, while husband and wife were once considered a single legal entity, some jurisdictions now allow either spouse to sue the other for torts to property but not for personal injuries. Still other states have rejected the doctrine of interspousal immunity entirely. Similarly, several jurisdictions have, by statute or case law, abolished the policy of immunity between parent and child. Under the historical doctrine "the king can do no wrong," some units of government still enjoy governmental immunity from tort suits. Nevertheless, under the Federal Tort Claims Act (26 USC §§ 1346, 2671 et seq.), the federal government, by its consent, has been stripped of some immunities with regard to negligence of government employees. State governments may claim immunity from suit in some jurisdictions.

   Most legislation that permits private individuals to sue a state, municipality, or other unit of government contains much shorter deadlines for filing claims than do laws specifying the conditions for initiating a lawsuit against a private party. Whenever suit against a governmental unit is contemplated, the matter should immediately be turned over to an attorney for evaluation and proper filing of the claim in a timely fashion.

Contract   Form contracts may be used by the issuer as a defense against negligence in some cases. These often provide *exculpatory clauses* (provisions that tend to relieve a party from liability) that set forth the specific limitations of the area of liability. However, since exculpation clauses are creatures of contract law, there must be agreement between the parties in order for them to be valid. "Fine print" or "boiler plate" contracts, which usually appear on the reverse side of tickets and receipts and typically deny any liability in an all-inclusive fashion, may be ineffective to the extent the attempted limitation was not conspicuous. Even if the limitations do become part of the agreement, they might not be enforced by the courts if they are unconscionable (unreasonably harsh). While some cases hold that persons may agree in advance that one of them shall not be liable to the other for negligence, the modern judicial trend is not to uphold such agreements if one of the parties, such as an employee, was clearly at a bargaining disadvantage.

Releases   A defense frequently raised is that the injured person gave a release of his rights to claim damages for the defendant's negligence. A *release* is a contract by which the releasor gives up or abandons a claim or right to the person against whom the claim exists. While the law favors and seeks to encourage private settlement of tort disputes and accords great weight to releases as a means of promoting out-of-court settlements, the law also favors just compensation of those who are injured by tortious acts. In many states courts permit the setting aside of a release that was not executed fairly and knowingly by the releasor. The need to protect those who literally sign away their rights of judicial recovery against others is particularly acute in view of the prevalence in modern business of insurance adjusters, who are often experienced business people, or attorneys motivated by a desire to settle claims as quickly and inexpensively as possible. As summarized by one commentator, "[a] relatively innocent plaintiff is often overwhelmed by the skilled negotiator."[1]

A release is of no legal effect as a defense to a tort suit if the release was forged, prohibited by law, given by one who was powerless to release the right, executed before any liability arose, or if the releasor was ignorant of the nature of the instrument he was signing, or—as in most cases—if the true nature of the plaintiff's injuries was not known at the time he signed the release. The last situation may occur when a seriously injured person signs a release in satisfaction "of all present and future claims," not knowing how serious the injuries are.

6:6   Comparative Negligence

At common law, a plaintiff's contributory negligence was a complete bar to his recovery against a negligent defendant. The doctrine of *comparative negligence* is an attempt to provide a system in which contributory negligence by the plaintiff is not a complete bar to recovery against a negligent defendant. In the absence of comparative negligence legislation, courts are very reluctant to apportion damages between a negligent plaintiff and a negligent defendant. A comparative negligence statute typically will apportion damages between negligent parties who injure one another in proportion to their fault. For example, if there are $10,000 in damages to the plaintiff, and the plaintiff is found by the court or jury to be 30 percent at fault, the plaintiff would be entitled to recover $7,000 from the defendant.

Under the rule of comparative negligence, even though the plaintiff was guilty of negligence that operated concurrently with the defendant's negligence as the cause of his injury, the plaintiff may recover if the degree of his negligence was less than that of the defendant. Under this doctrine, the plaintiff's negligence does not relieve the defendant entirely from liability, as under the old common-law rule of contributory negligence, but merely diminishes the damages recoverable.

No-fault insurance legislation has been enacted in several jurisdictions. The idea behind no-fault insurance is that regardless of legal fault, an insured motorist who suffers injury from an automobile accident shall receive recompense from his own insurer. Under some no-fault statutes, tort liability is abolished, although under

---

[1]Note, *Avoidance of Tort Releases*, 13 Western Reserve L Rev, 768 (1962).

other no-fault statutes, the exemption from tort liability does not apply when injuries of a serious nature are received as the result of an automobile accident. The purpose of no-fault insurance plans is to afford partial reparation for the objectively provable economic losses resulting from automobile accidents.[2]

6:7   Strict Liability

Strict liability is liability without fault. That is, under some circumstances a person can be liable for having caused an injury regardless of whether that person was negligent. Occasionally, a distinction is made between strict liability and so-called "absolute liability," which is liability under all circumstances. Today, however, both phrases are used interchangeably by most courts. Strict liability is based on a policy that an injured person must be given a right of recovery even though the person causing the injury did not act negligently.

Strict liability is applicable in situations in which social policy requires that the defendant make good the harm that results to others from abnormal risks inherent in those activities not considered blameworthy because they are reasonably incident to desirable industries or undertakings. The basis of liability in such cases is the intentional behavior of exposing a community to those abnormal risks. For example, strict liability has been found in cases where the use of chemical sprays, harmful gases, fumes, waste material, or other forms of pollution has resulted in the escape of those substances from one person's land onto the land or into the water supply of another.

Certain activities, which were undoubtedly dangerous when first begun as industries, sometimes over the course of time and through technological developments, have become "ordinary" and therefore no longer ultrahazardous. It has been held, for example, that flying is now so common that it is no longer ultrahazardous. Today, an airplane, when properly handled and cared for mechanically, is not inherently dangerous. Experimental planes, however, may still be considered dangerous; therefore, their owners or operators may be held strictly liable for damage. In some jurisdictions, blasting may or may not be subject to strict liability, depending on the location of the activity. If blasting occurs in an urban or highly populated area, it may be considered an ultrahazardous activity for which the defendant is subject to strict liability; if it is done in rural or unpopulated areas, the defendant's conduct may be judged by traditional negligence standards.

In strict liability suits, the defense of assumption of risk may be asserted against a plaintiff who voluntarily encounters a known danger and by his conduct expressly or impliedly consents to the risk of the danger. Contributory negligence, on the other hand, is no defense to strict liability.

The following decision is instructive in setting forth the policy considerations behind judicial acceptance of the strict liability doctrine. Tracing the historical development of the doctrine and the present-day policy considerations for its existence, the court expressly holds the strict liability doctrine to be applicable in its jurisdiction.

---

[2]No-fault insurance is discussed in Chapter 39.

Cities Service Co.
v
State
312 So 2d 799
(Florida Court of Appeals, 1975)

[The state of Florida brought suit against Cities Service, a mining company, seeking, among other things, damages caused by a dam break in one of the defendant's settling ponds, as a result of which one billion gallons of phosphate slime contained in the pond escaped into a state creek, killing countless fish and inflicting other damage. The trial court awarded damages against the defendant, holding it liable without regard to negligence or fault. The defendant appealed.]

Grimes, Judge.

*   *   *

The determination of this appeal necessarily requires the consideration of the doctrine of strict liability for the hazardous use of one's land which was first announced in *Rylands v Fletcher*, 1868, L.R. 3 H.L. 330. In that case the defendants, who were millowners, had constructed a reservoir upon their land. The water broke through into the shaft of an abandoned coal mine and flooded along connecting passages into the adjoining mine of the plaintiff. When the case reached the Exchequer Chamber, Justice Blackburn said:

> "We think that the true rule of law is that the person who for his own purposes brings on his land and collects and keeps there anything likely to do mischief if it escapes, must keep it at his peril, and if he does not do so he is prima facie answerable for all the damage which is the natural consequences of its escape."

This statement was limited in the House of Lords to the extent that Lord Cairns said that the principle applied only to a "nonnatural" use of the defendant's land as distinguished from "any purpose for which it might in the ordinary course of the enjoyment of land be used."

Since that time there have been countless decisions both in England and America construing the application of this doctrine. Most of the early American decisions rejected the doctrine. However, the pendulum has now decidedly swung toward its acceptance. W. Prosser, *The Law of Torts* § 78 (4th ed. 1971). According to Prosser, by 1971 the doctrine had been approved in principle by thirty jurisdictions with only seven states still rejecting the principle.

While the application of the doctrine has not been specifically passed upon by the appellate courts of Florida, an early Supreme Court case implies its acceptance. In *Pensacola Gas Co. v Pebbly* (1889) 25 Fla. 381, 5 So. 593, the plaintiff claimed damages which resulted when a neighboring landowner constructed a gas works and allowed refuse to spill out onto the land and sink through the sand into the common water thereby polluting the plaintiff's well. The trial court apparently charged the members of the jury that the plaintiff would be entitled to a verdict if they determined that the plaintiff's wells were rendered unfit for use by the defendant without regard to the question of negligence. . . .

In early days it was important to encourage persons to use their land by whatever means were available for the purpose of commercial and industrial development. In a frontier society there was little likelihood that a dangerous use of land could cause damage to one's neighbor. Today our life has become more complex. Many areas are overcrowded, and even the non-negligent use of one's land can cause extensive damages to a neighbor's property. Though there are still many hazardous activities which are socially desirable, it now seems reasonable that they pay their own way. It is too much to ask an innocent neighbor to bear the burden thrust upon him as a consequence of an abnormal use of the land next door. The doctrine of *Rylands v Fletcher* should be applied in Florida.

There remains, however, the serious question of whether the impounding of phosphate slime by Cities Service in connection with its mining operations is a nonnatural use of the land. In opposition to the State's motion, Cities Service filed an affidavit of the manager of the plant where the dam break occurred. The affidavit points out that the property is peculiarly suitable for the mining of phosphate and that the central Florida area of which Polk County is the hub is the largest producer of phosphate rock in Florida. It further appears that Florida produced over 80% of the nation's marketable phosphate rock and one-third of the world production thereof in 1973. The affidavit goes on to explain that the storing of phosphate slimes in diked settling ponds is an essential part of the traditional method of mining phosphate rock. Hence, Cities Service argues that its mining operations were a natural and intended use of this particular land. . . .

The American Law Institute has considered this question in §§ 519 and 520 of the *Restatement of the Law of Torts* (1938). These sections state:

"§ 519. MISCARRIAGE OF ULTRAHAZARDOUS ACTIVITIES CAREFULLY CARRIED ON.

Except as stated in §§ 521–4. one who carries on an ultrahazardous activity is liable to another whose person, land or chattels the actor should recognize as likely to be harmed by the unpreventable miscarriage of the activity for harm resulting thereto from that which makes the activity ultrahazardous, although the utmost care is exercised to prevent the harm.

§ 520. DEFINITION OF ULTRAHAZARDOUS ACTIVITY.

An activity is ultrahazardous if it
  (a) necessarily involves a risk of serious harm to the person, land or chattels of others which cannot be eliminated by the exercise of the utmost care, and

  (b) is not a matter of common usage."

Recognizing the evolving nature of the law in this area, the American Law Institute published Tentative Draft No. 10 in 1964 in which certain changes were recommended for §§ 519 and 520. Thus, in § 519 and § 520 the substitution of the words "abnormally dangerous" is suggested in place of the word "ultrahazardous." In § 520, the following factors are said to be pertinent in determining whether an activity is abnormally dangerous:

  "(a) Whether the activity involves a high degree of risk of some harm to the person, land or chattels of others;
  (b) Whether the harm which may result from it is likely to be great;
  (c) Whether the risk cannot be eliminated by the exercise of reasonable care;
  (d) Whether the activity is not a matter of common usage;
  (e) Whether the activity is inappropriate to the place where it is carried on; and
  (f) The value of the activity to the community."

Referring to these factors, F. James, *The Law of Torts*, Supp. to Vol. 2, § 14.4 (1968), states [in part]:

"The justification for strict liability, in other words, is that useful but dangerous activities must pay their own way. . . . There is nothing in this reasoning which would exempt *very* useful activities from the rule, as is shown by the granting of compensation even where the activity is of such paramount importance to society that it justifies the exercise of eminent domain. And if the law were to embrace wholly the principle of strict liability and its underlying rationale, there would be no place for the consideration of this factor. But this is not the present case. Tort law today contains two opposing strains or principles, strict liability and liability based on fault. It is not surprising, therefore, that any attempt to draw a line between them (which is being done in Section 520) should contain factors which would be irrelevant if one principle or the other alone were being consistently pursued. At any rate this factor will probably continue to influence courts in fact for some time to come." . . .

In the final analysis, we are impressed by the magnitude of the activity and the attendant risk of enormous damage. The impounding of billions of gallons of phosphatic slimes behind earthen walls which are subject to breaking even with the exercise of the best of care strikes us as being both "ultrahazardous" and "abnormally dangerous," as the case may be.

This is not clear water which is being impounded. Here, Cities Service introduced water into its mining operation which when combined with phosphatic wastes produced a phosphatic slime which had a high potential for damage to the environment. If a break occurred, it was to be expected that extensive damage would be visited upon property many miles away. In this case, the damage, in fact,

extended almost to the mouth of the Peace River, which is far beyond the phosphate mining area described in the Cities Service affidavit. We conclude that the Cities Service slime reservoir constituted a nonnatural use of the land such as to invoke the doctrine of strict liability.

. . . All of the assertions of Cities Service relative to the need to maintain settling ponds in its mining operations, the suitability of the land for this purpose and the importance of phosphate to the community as well as to the world at large may be accepted at face value. Admitting the desirability of phosphate and the necessity of mining in this manner, the rights of adjoining landowners and the interests of the public in our environment require the imposition of a doctrine which places the burden upon the parties whose activity made it possible for the damages to occur.

[Judgment affirmed.]

Key Concepts and Terms

- All persons have a duty to exercise reasonable care toward others. To recover for negligence, an injured person must show that (1) the defendant had a duty to exercise reasonable care, (2) there was a breach of that duty, (3) the defendant's conduct caused the plaintiff's injury, and (4) damages resulted.

- A person breaches his duty to exercise reasonable care toward others when he fails to exercise the degree of care that a reasonable person would have exercised under the same or similar circumstances. Under the res ipsa loquitur doctrine, the very fact that a particular injury has occurred may itself tend to establish a breach of duty on the part of the defendant.

- To recover in a negligence suit, the plaintiff must establish that the defendant's negligent act was both the cause in fact and the proximate cause of the injury. Thus, it must be shown that the injury would not have happened "but for" the defendant's conduct, and that there were no intervening forces between the negligent conduct and the plaintiff's injury. Furthermore, the plaintiff's injury must have been within the scope of a foreseeable risk.

- There are several defenses that a defendant may assert in a negligence suit; these include contributory negligence, the last clear chance doctrine, assumption of risk, immunity, contract, and release from liability.

- Comparative negligence legislation, which exists in some states, provides that even though the plaintiff was guilty of negligence that operated concurrently with the defendant's negligence as the cause of his injury, the plaintiff may nevertheless recover if the degree of his negligence was less than that of the defendant. Accordingly, damages are apportioned between the defendant and the plaintiff in proportion to each person's fault.

- Strict liability is liability without fault. It applies under circumstances in which public policy requires the defendant to make good the harm that resulted from an activity that, although socially necessary or desirable, involves an abnormal risk of harm to others.

- Assumption of Risk
- Breach of Duty
- Causation
- Comparative Negligence
- Contributory Negligence
- Cause in Fact
- Exculpatory Clause
- Immunities from Suit

- Last Clear Chance Doctrine
- Negligence
- Nonfeasance
- Proximate Cause
- "Reasonable Person" Standard
- Release
- *Res Ipsa Loquitur* Doctrine
- Strict Liability

Questions and Case Problems

1. Under what circumstances, if any, may a failure to act constitute negligence?

2. Discuss the various defenses that may be available to a negligence suit.

3. While operating his lawn mower in a careless manner, Andy strikes and seriously injures Bill's dog. In a frenzy, the dog runs into the house and bites Bill. Is Andy liable to Bill?

4. Amy is a passenger on a bus operated by Bus Company. She is injured when the bus collides with a car driven by Charlie. Both the bus driver and Charlie are negligent. Which, if either, driver's negligence is the "cause in fact" of Amy's injuries?

5. What is the rationale for strict liability? In your explanation indicate whether or not you agree with the rationale.

6. While driving her car in heavy traffic, Joan is distracted by a discussion she is having with her passenger, Peggy. As a result Joan strikes a truck driven by Felix. (a) Assume Felix's truck contained propane fuel and that the collision set off an explosion, injuring Phillip, a pedestrian on the street. Is Joan subject to liability for Phillip's injuries? (b) Assume that the same explosion knocked some bottles off a shelf in a medical laboratory nearby. The bottles shattered and a worker, Wilma, was cut by the flying glass. Is Joan subject to liability for Wilma's injury? (c) Assume that Joan herself was injured and rendered unconscious in the collision and that her car caught on fire. Assume further that a passerby, Sam, saw her predicament and rushed to her aid, but was injured himself in so doing. Is Joan subject to liability for Sam's injuries?

7. What is a release to a negligence claim? Are releases always upheld by the courts? Discuss.

8. A city ordinance prohibits the parking of cars so as to block driveways. In violation of this ordinance, Jones parks his car in front of Dr. Paul's office driveway. Mrs. Smith, a widow who resides in a nearby rural area, telephones Dr. Paul to come out right away to treat her son, Tom, who had just been bitten by a snake. Dr. Paul starts to go but is unable to back his car out of his driveway. Seeing no one around, Dr. Paul releases the brake on Jones's car and attempts to push it away. In so doing, he develops a hernia, suffers excruciating pain, and returns with difficulty to his office, where he makes several phone calls trying to get another doctor to go and see Tom but finds none available. It is agreed that had Dr. Paul been able to respond to Mrs. Smith's call, he would in all probability have been able to save Tom's arm, which had to be amputated because the snake bite was not treated quickly enough. Is Jones liable in negligence to Dr. Paul and/or to Tom? Discuss.

9. What are the elements of a negligence suit? What is the difference between the tort of negligence and an intentional tort?

10. A contractor is blasting rock at a remote desert quarry. Unexpectedly, the vibrations trigger an underground avalanche, which shifts subsurface formations miles away and knocks out a prospector's water well. Assuming no negligence, is the contractor liable for damages to the prospector's well?

7 Products Liability

The purpose of [products] liability is to insure that the costs of injuries resulting from defective products are borne by the manufacturers that put such products on the market rather than by the injured persons who are powerless to protect themselves.

Justice Traynor, *Greenman v Yuba Power Products, Inc.,*
59 Cal 2d 57, 27 Cal Rptr 697, 377 P2d 897, 13 ALR 3d 1049
(California Supreme Court, 1963)

7:1 In General

A scant 25 years ago there were few practicing attorneys who would even consider trying suits against a product manufacturer or distributor claiming that his client's injuries were due to faulty manufacturing, improper product design, or other product defect. There were numerous reasons for this reluctance to handle such cases. The consuming public had little understanding of the duties owed it by the manufacturing industry or product distributors. Newspapers seldom carried stories about civil actions and their results—even when a pioneering suit was successful. Members of the legal profession were reluctant to "take on" the huge corporate empires which usually produced the product. Also, the appellate courts had not yet imposed much liability for defectively designed or manufactured products. Today the situation has completely changed. Today's consumer can hope to successfully challenge the entire design concept of a product as complex as an automobile, airplane, or nuclear reactor.

Products liability is a phrase that has recently come into common use and that indicates the liability of the manufacturer, processor, or seller of a product for injury caused by a defect in or condition of the product. Some attorneys specialize entirely in products liability litigation. In fact, some attorneys devote their entire practices to products liability in a particular area, such as aviation products liability, automotive products liability, and medical products liability. Products liability applies to a broad spectrum of discipines—engineering, physics, chemistry, and even medicine. It has been said that no other area of the law is as difficult because product liability involves the relationship of man and machine and the extent to which as a matter of social policy the law will make producers and distributors of products liable to persons injured by those products.

Theories of Liability The manufacturer or seller of a defective product may be held liable for injuries resulting from the defect under three theories of liability: (1) negligence, (2) breach of warranty (see 7:2), and (3) strict liability (see 7:3). They are frequently applied in combination, and one, two, or all three theories may be found in a single case.

Negligence   In products liability suits based on *negligence*, the standard of care required is the same as in other cases based on negligence (see Chapter 6). That standard of care as applied to products liability is that a manufacturer, processor, or seller has a duty to use the care, skill, and diligence regarding the product that a reasonably careful, skillful, and prudent person would use in the same or similar circumstances. In negligence suits, the manufacturer or distributor is liable only where he fails to exercise the care that is reasonable under the circumstances. Absolute perfection and perfect safety are not required.

Duty to Warn of Danger   The manufacturer or seller has a duty to warn of a danger where (1) a product is dangerous when put to its normal and foreseeable use; (2) the danger in using the product is, or should be, known to the manufacturer or seller; and (3) the danger is not obvious, known to, or readily discoverable by the user. The basis of this duty is the manufacturer's superior knowledge of the dangerous characteristics of the product—that is, the manufacturer is considered to know everything about his own product and therefore is obligated to inform prospective users of any dangerous qualities in the product.

Multiple Defendants   A person injured by a defective product has a variety of potential defendants. These may include the manufacturer of the defective product, the designer, the manufacturer of a component part, the seller of the product, or the testing company that endorsed the product.

 If an employee is injured by a product in the course of employment, the employer may be a potential defendant because employers have an affirmative duty to furnish a reasonably safe place for their employees to work and to provide them with safe appliances and instrumentalities.[1]

7:2   Breach of Warranty[2]

Some courts have considered *breach of warranty* as a basis for the liability of a manufacturer or distributor of a product. The "warranty" on which the plaintiff (consumer) relies generally is a representation, either express or implied, made by the seller regarding the character, quality, function, performance, or reliability of the items sold. If the product suit is based on a warranty theory, the plaintiff must show (1) existence of the warranty, (2) breach of the warranty, and (3) injury caused by reason of the warranty defect in the product.

---

[1]The employer's duties in this regard in the employer–employee relationship are discussed in Chapter 51.

[2]Warranties in the law of sales generally are discussed in Chapter 21. Warranties under the Magnuson–Moss Warranty Act are discussed in 21:7. Warranties in leases of personal property are discussed in Chapter 33.

Express Warranties   An express warranty is an affirmation of fact or a promise made by the seller about the product that acts as an inducement for the purchaser to buy the product. The Uniform Commercial Code[3] § 2-313 states that *express warranties* by the seller are created as follows: (1) any affirmation of fact or promise made by the seller to the buyer which relates to the goods and becomes part of the basis of the transaction creates an express warranty that the goods conform to the affirmation or promise, (2) any description of the goods which is made part of the basis of the transaction creates an express warranty that the goods conform to the description, and (3) any sample or model which is made part of the basis of the transaction creates an express warranty that the whole of the goods conforms to the sample or model.

The words "guarantee" or "warrant" need not appear in the transaction for a warranty to exist. The affirmation of fact or promise may be written representation or oral statements made by the supplier, by a salesperson, or through advertising.

 Advertisements placed by the manufacturer or seller of products have sometimes been held to amount to an express warranty of the strength, condition, safety, or usefulness of the product.

EXAMPLE
A television commercial for a liquid drain cleaner described it as "safe" and showed a hand swishing water around in the sink. Subsequently, a child was burned by the spilled cleaner. The court held that the manufacturer had, through the television ad, breached an express warranty of safety for human conduct, and awarded the plaintiff $700,000 in damages.[4]

Until the Uniform Commercial Code was adopted, the principal statute giving buyers implied warranties was the Uniform Sales Act (USA), originally drafted in 1905. The USA provisions were designed to apply only between the seller and his immediate buyer. However, UCC § 2-318 attempts to create rights in remote purchasers and any "natural person who may reasonably be expected to use, consume, or be affected by the goods and who was injured in person by breach of the warranty."

Implied Warranties   When a manufacturer puts a new product on the market and promotes its purchase by the public, the manufacturer creates an *implied warranty* that the product is reasonably suitable for its intended uses.

7:3   Strict Liability

Suits against a manufacturer or seller to recover for product-caused harm are most often based on the theory of strict liability in tort.[5] Under the *Restatement (Second)*

---

[3]The Uniform Commercial Code (UCC), formulated through the joint efforts of the National Conference of Commissioners on Uniform State Laws and the American Law Institute, deals with most aspects of modern commercial transactions. The UCC has been adopted in practically all American jurisdictions. Additional background and philosophy of the UCC is discussed in Chapter 9.
[4]*Drayton v Jiffee Chemical Corp.*, 591 F2d 352 (United States Court of Appeals, Sixth Circuit, 1978).
[5]The tort theory of strict liability is discussed in Chapter 6.

of Torts § 402A (1965), the seller of any product that is in a defective condition "unreasonably dangerous to the user" is liable for injury to the ultimate user, even though the seller has exercised "all possible care" in the preparations and sale of the product. This liability remains with the seller even though the ultimate user of the product has not actually purchased the product from, or entered into a contractual relationship with, the seller. Although relatively new in its application in products liability cases, the doctrine has been favorably received and there is a strong trend toward its acceptance.

The first decision establishing strict liability in a products case was *Greenman v Yuba Power Products, Inc.*[6] In that case, the California Supreme Court expressly decided that a manufacturer was strictly liable in tort when a machine that it placed on the market, knowing it was to be used without inspection for defects, proved to have a defect that caused injury. The court ruled that it was not necessary for the plaintiff to establish an express warranty. The court observed that implicit in the product's presence on the market was a representation that it would safely do the job for which it was built. "Under these circumstances," said the court, "it should not be controlling whether plaintiff selected the machine because of the statements in the brochure, or because of the machine's own appearance of excellence that belied the defect lurking beneath the surface, or because he merely assumed that it would safely do the jobs it was built to do." Since 1963, the date of the *Greenman* decision, the doctrine of strict liability for products cases has been accepted in most states.

7:4   Consumer Product Safety Legislation

In several states warranties protecting consumer goods have been made to include more protection than the Uniform Commercial Code provides. These added protections, which are made a part of the implied warranty, might typically include guaranties that the goods are free from defects in workmanship and materials, are adequately contained, packaged, and labeled, and conform to representations on the label.

Consumer Product Safety Act of 1972   The federal *Consumer Product Safety Act* provides that the designer, manufacturer, and seller of a defective consumer product may be sued in federal court by an injured customer. Private individuals may bring suit to enforce consumer product safety rules that apply to substantial product hazards. The act also contains civil and criminal penalties, provisions for injunctions, and even a provision for seizure of the offending products. The act provides for inspections of the manufacturing site, the storage site, or the conveyance used for distribution of products. The act establishes record-keeping requirements for manufacturers, private labelers, and product distributors.

Consumer Product Safety Commission   To administer the Consumer Product Safety Act, Congress established an independent regulatory agency, the *Consumer*

---

[6] 59 Cal 2d 57, 27 Cal Rptr 697, 377 P2d 897 (1963).

Product Safety Commission, to establish consumer product safety standards. Any requirement of such a standard must be reasonably necessary to prevent or reduce an "unreasonable risk of injury" associated with the product. Acting in accordance with the rules governing administrative law generally, as discussed in Chapter 3, the commission sets standards for performance, composition, contents, design, construction, finish or packaging, and labeling of a consumer product. Labeling is especially important because it is visible to the consumer. The commission requires that a consumer product be marked with or accompanied by clear and adequate warnings or instructions.

 Manufacturers, distributors, or retailers who learn that a product does not comply with a safety rule, or that it has a defect that creates a substantial risk of injury must immediately notify the Consumer Product Safety Commission. The commission can then order the manufacturer, distributor, or retailer to notify all buyers, to offer repair, replacement, or refund, without charge, and to reimburse the consumer for any reasonable and foreseeable expenses incurred.

EXAMPLE
Blanco Automotive Company's engineers determine there is a danger in the design of the company's 1978 Turtle Car, of which 35,000 have been sold. After two years on the market, numerous accidents are occurring because of a defective braking mechanism. Blanco must immediately notify the Consumer Product Safety Commission, notify all Turtle purchasers, and arrange to repair the defect free of charge.

7:5   Proving Defective Product

To recover for injuries, a person must show that the product was defective. In deciding whether a product was unreasonably dangerous, or defective, courts have indicated the product may have been defective for at least one of three reasons: "(1) it may have been fabricated or constructed defectively in the sense that the specific product was not at the time of sale by the maker or other seller in the condition that the maker intended it to be; (2) it may have been improperly designed; and (3) purchasers and those who are likely to use the product may have been misinformed or inadequately informed, either about the risks and dangers involved in the use of the product or how to avoid or minimize the harmful consequences from such risks."[7]

The plaintiff must also prove that the product was defective when it left the control of the manufacturer or seller. The following decision is an illustration of proof that a product was defective. Particularly instructive is the court's comment that although there was no direct evidence tracing the defect in the product, a breast implant, to the manufacturer, the fact the product failed to function prop-

---

[7]Keeton, *Product Liability and the Meaning of Defect,* 5 St Marys L J 30, 33–34.

erly after it was implanted in the plaintiff's body could itself be considered as evidence that the product was defective when it left the manufacturer.

V. Mueller & Co.
v
Corley
570 SW2d 140, 1 ALR 4th 910
(Texas Court of Civil Appeals, 1978)

[A silicone prosthesis was implanted in the plaintiff, Mrs. Corley, and subsequently leaked material into her body, preventing proper healing of the surgical wound and causing severe damages. She brought suit against the manufacturer and distributor of the product, arguing that its rupture was caused by a defect that existed at the time it left the manufacturer. The trial court awarded Mrs. Corley $170,000 for damages due to the defective prosthesis, and the manufacturer appealed.]

Evans, Justice.

*   *   *

The jury was submitted issues under theories of both strict liability and negligence. In response to the strict liability issues, the jury found that "the form or material or performance of the prosthesis in question" rendered it defective as manufactured and that such defect was a producing cause of the occurrence. In response to the negligence issues, which were accompanied by an instruction on res ipsa loquitur, the jury found that the failure of the "form or material or performance" of the prosthesis was due to the negligence of the defendants and that such negligence was a proximate cause of the occurrence.

It was the plaintiff's burden under either theory of recovery to prove the defective condition of the product at the time it left the control of the manufacturer or seller.... It was not essential that the plaintiff identify the specific engineering or structural cause of the de-

fect.... However, the plaintiff was required to trace the defect to the manufacturer....

The evidence shows that the prosthesis reached the hospital in a sealed, sterilized container. There was testimony that the prosthesis was not damaged by the nurses or the physician from the time it was taken from the sealed container until it was placed in Mrs. Corley's body, and Dr. Leeves denied that he had cut or nicked the prosthesis during the suturing process. Dr. Leeves testified:

"Q. From the time it was removed from the sealed container by Nurse Welch to the time it was placed in the body of Mrs. Corley, did you see anyone mishandle the prosthesis in any way?

"A. No, Sir.

"Q. Was it nicked, cut or scraped or misused in any way?

"A. No, Sir.

"Q. Were your eyes on it the entire time?

"A. Yes, Sir.

"Q. From the time it was removed from its sealed container until it was placed in her body?

"A. Yes.

*   *   *

"Q. Did you at any time nick, touch or scratch the prosthesis with any surgical instrument?

"A. Not to my knowledge.

"Q. At any time?

"A. Not to my knowledge.

"Q. If you had done so, would it have come to your attention?

"A. Yes."

Dr. Leeves further testified that he carefully examined the prosthesis before inserting it in the body opening and that he turned it over and observed all sides. He saw no tear or holes in the envelope, and it was in good condition as far as he could ascertain. In order to thread the envelope into the opening, it was necessary that he "squeeze it down" because it was larger than the opening. If there were a defect in the envelope, it should have become apparent when the prosthesis was compressed, and he did not observe any imperfection.

The defendants contend that this testimony constitutes direct evidence that the prosthesis was free from defect at the time it was inserted in the body opening, and that the only reasonable inference which could be made from the evidence is that the tear had been caused by a nick or puncture during the surgical process.

The jury was at liberty to make this inference, as contended by the defendants, but it was not bound to do so. There was also testimony which indicated that after a prothesis had been implanted in a person's body, it was subject to a certain amount of pressure. If the person should sleep on her stomach or should bump into something, this might create sufficient pressure to bring about a rupture if there were some imperfection in the envelope. The degree of pressure required to rupture the envelope varied according to the nature of the imperfection and the type of pressure applied, and even though [the manufacturer's] testing procedures were designed to identify an imperfect prosthesis, its system was not foolproof.

It was for the jury to weigh the evidence and to accept that testimony which it found to be most credible. Although there was no direct evidence tracing the defect to the manufacturer, the fact that the product failed to function properly after being implanted in the plaintiff's body was a matter which the jury could consider as circumstantial proof of an original defect. . . . A product defect may be established by circumstantial evidence. . . .

The jury could have concluded from the evidence that the prosthesis was designed to maintain its integrity as a flexible, tissue-like "bubble" during the rigorous stresses of human activity. Based upon the testimony that the prosthesis left the manufacturer and passed from the distributor to the physician in a sealed and sterilized container and that it was handled with care and was not damaged during the surgical procedure, the jury could have concluded that the product underwent no change from the time it left the control of the manufacturer until the surgery was completed. Although the jury might have reached a different conclusion in its consideration of the evidence, it could reasonably have concluded from the circumstances before it that the tear in the envelope resulted from an imperfection in the product itself, rather than from the nature of its handling during the surgical process. Thus, the evidence supports the jury's inference that the product was defective at the time it left the hands of the manufacturer. . . . The defendants' points of error contending that there is no evidence and insufficient evidence to support the jury's findings are overruled. . . .

The trial court properly defined the term "defective," instructing the jury that a product was defective which exposed its user to an unreasonable risk of harm, making the product dangerous "to an extent beyond that which would be contemplated by the ordinary user." The defendants sought an instruction to the effect that the term defective meant a product which would be unreasonably dangerous to the user and that the term "unreasonably dangerous" meant the product was dangerous "to the extent beyond that which would be contemplated by the ordinary physician." The defendants argue that a prosthesis is a specialized medical product, requiring the exercise of a physician's skill and judgment in the determination of its use, and that the physician, rather than the user, would be required to determine whether the product exposed the user to an unreasonable risk of harm.

The defective condition in the prosthesis in question rendered it unreasonably dangerous to Mrs. Corley, not to her physician, Dr. Leeves. The appropriate question for the jury, therefore, was whether the defective condition was one which was not contemplated by the user, the "ultimate consumer." *Restatement (2d) of Torts* § 402 A (1965). The trial court properly keyed its instructions to the mind of the person who would be injured by the dangerous condition of the product. . . .

[Judgment affirmed.]

"Crashworthiness"   Courts do not agree whether a manufacturer is liable for failure to design its product to minimize foreseeable harm caused by *other* parties or conditions. For example, is an authomobile manufacturer liable for not designing cars that will safely withstand highway crashes caused by the negligence of other drivers? Is the car "crashworthy"? Many courts are beginning to decide that accidents and injuries are foreseeable risks involved in the operation of an automobile, and that the manufacturer owes a duty to protect against these risks. Manufacturers have been held liable for designing a gear shift lever that impaled the driver on collision; designing a fuel tank that caught fire following a rear-end collision; and designing a horn cap that came off the steering wheel, exposing sharp prongs that caused injuries greater than the driver otherwise would have received from the collision.

The issue in the following decision was whether an automobile manufacturer has a duty to design and manufacture a car so that the occupants will not be subjected to an unreasonable risk of injury if a collision occurs which is not itself caused by defects in the automobile's condition. In finding there is such duty, the court held that the failure of a gas tank to prevent leakage and explosion constituted a design defect because it was designed to prevent such leakage and explosion. The court stated that it was entirely "reasonable" and "foreseeable" that a vehicle might be struck by another with such force that its gas tank would need at least a reasonable degree of protection against rupturing.

Nanda
v
Ford Motor Co.
509 F2d 213
(United States Court of Appeals, Seventh Circuit, 1974)

[A motorist, Nanda, suffered permanently disfiguring and disabling burns because when his vehicle was struck in the rear by another car his gas tank exploded. Nanda brought a products liability suit against the manufacturer of his vehicle for failure to design the vehicle so that its occupants would not be subjected to an unreasonable risk of injury if a colli- *sion occurred. Nanda contended that absence of a fire wall or shield between the fuel tank and passenger compartment of his vehicle constituted an unreasonably dangerous defect in the product, and that this defect would be manifested in the event of a collision with another vehicle.]*

Tone, Circuit Judge.

*   *   *

Plaintiff contends that design defects in the Cortina caused his injury. The fuel tank in the 1967 Cortina, like that in at least some other models manufactured by defendant, was "dropped into" a hole in the floor of the trunk, the top of the fuel tank serving as a portion of the floor of the trunk. The only shield separating the fuel tank from the passenger compartment was a piece of cardboard. Other automobile manufacturers in the United States provided a trunk floor consisting of some kind of continuous metal panel which shielded the fuel tank from the passenger compartment, and after 1971 defendant itself abandoned the "drop-in" fuel tank installation. In addition, the fuel-filler pipe in the 1967 Cortina ran through the trunk compartment and was connected to the outer shell of the car by a rubber grommet and, the jury could have found, was so designed that it lacked flexibility, flexion at one end tending to pull the pipe loose. In at least some of the other types of cars defendant manufactured, it attached the flange of the fuel-filler pipe to the outer shell of the car by metal screws or bolts. . . .

Viewing the evidence in the light most favorable to the plaintiff, it does not appear to us to be "highly extraordinary" that the absence of a firewall or shield between the fuel tank and the passenger compartment and the condition of the filler-pipe assembly would bring about the harm for which plaintiff sues. The jury could have found that those conditions, . . . constituted an "unreasonable danger" and subjected the user of the product to "an unreasonable risk of injury." A rear-end collision is the most common of highway mishaps, and it is not "extraordinary," "bizarre," "unique," or "freakish and . . . fantastic" for such a collision to impel the victim vehicle into a collision with a third vehicle. We believe the law of Illinois to be that when an automobile is so constructed that its occupants are subjected to an unreasonable risk of being severely injured if it becomes involved in an accident that is not of a highly extraordinary kind, the manufacturer is liable for resulting injuries to occupants of the automobile.

In what amounts to an argument that the circumstances of plaintiff's injury were ex-traordinary . . . defendant assumes impact speeds of 20 or 25 miles per hour for the first impact and 40 or 45 for the second, applies the formula for determining kinetic energy to calculate the forces of the two impacts, and arrives at a total force which it says was approximately equivalent to the force that would have been received if the Cortina had been backed off the roof of the Marshall Field Building. The jury could have found, however, from testimony that the impact speeds were lower than defendant assumes and the evidence that the only major injuries suffered by anyone involved in the collision were plaintiff's burns, that lesser forces were involved. Indeed, it would be difficult for us to believe, if we were the trier of the facts, that a passenger in a car backed off the roof of the Marshall Field Building would suffer no major injury other than burns. Contrary to defendant's assertion, a holding of liability is not a holding that a manufacturer has a duty "to design and build a crash-proof vehicle." . . .

SUFFICIENCY OF THE EVIDENCE

Given the duty of defendant as we have defined it, the applicability of the strict-liability theory, and the absence of an issue as to whether the car was in the same condition as it was when it left defendant's control, there remain the unreasonably-dangerous-condition and probable-cause issues. If there was evidence from which the jury could find that an unreasonably dangerous condition existed in the Cortina by reason of its design, and that the fire that caused plaintiff's burns, or the instantaneous spread of that fire into the passenger compartment, resulted from that condition, plaintiff's prima facie case was complete, and the jury's verdict is supported by the evidence.

Plaintiff called two experts, whose combined testimony, viewed in the light most favorable to him, showed in substance that the fuel-filler neck of the 1967 Cortina tended to pull loose and be displaced into the trunk; that the fuel tank was "susceptible to distortion" because of its location in the frame; that the fuel tank, filler neck and cap were located in an extremely vulnerable position; and that these conditions created an unreasonable danger of fire in the event of collision. Their testimony also showed that there was no firewall between the fuel tank and the passenger compartment; and that this condition created an unreasonable danger that a fire in the area of the fuel tank resulting from a collision would spread into the passenger compartment before the occupants of the car could escape or be extricated. The causal relationship between one or both of these unreasonably dangerous conditions and plaintiff's injuries was shown prima facie by expert opinion testimony that the small fire after the first impact was caused by the design and location of the filler pipe; that this fire was spread by a gross leakage of fuel after the second impact; and, in the words of one of plaintiff's expert witnesses, that "the lack of isolation of the fuel-tank area from the passenger compartment allowed a very rapid spread of this fire in the interior of the car, thus preventing rescue personnel from evacuating the driver before he suffered serious burns."

The evidence of plaintiff's experts was confirmed by the deposition testimony of one of defendant's own engineers who had been assigned by defendant to investigate accidents involving 1967 Cortinas in England, one of which involved a fuel fire. In his report on this accident he referred to a similar occurrence in the United States and concluded that the bursting of the fuel tank and immediate conflagration in the latter accident "indicate that the floor mounted tank is hazardous and should be carefully reviewed and tested in each new model." . . .

[Judgment affirmed.]

The Expert Witness   In years past, attorneys facetiously referred to an expert as "anyone from out of town." While the definition may still hold in certain cases, it is the expert's testimony on which the modern products liability case will rise or fall. Such cases often involve a manufacturer's failure to design and equip the product with a safety device to protect the user from danger. Design negligence is a proper subject for expert testimony in products liability cases. The expert's training and background have equipped him to provide a reasoned opinion as to whether a particular product was safely designed in accordance with the way people generally think and would normally use the product. Products liability is concerned primarily with what is termed "safety engineering" or "human factors," and is a subject studied in many engineering schools and psychology departments. A "human factors expert" or "safety engineer" or "safety psychologist" is frequently used as an *expert witness* in products cases.

7:6 Defenses

The principles of contributory negligence and assumption of risk (see Chapter 6) may be applied in defending a products liability suit. Under the defense of contributory negligence, the manufacturer or seller of a defective product is not ordinarily liable to a person who, by his own negligent conduct, contributed to the injury.

Under the theory of assumption of risk, the person who voluntarily chooses to use a product with full knowledge of the risks and dangers involved assumes the risks.

Another defense is the consumer's failure to follow the manufacturer's instructions if the product requires assembly of component parts according to those instructions.

EXAMPLE

In a products liability suit for a death caused by the collapse of scaffolding purchased from a manufacturer, the manufacturer was not liable because the victim and others who assembled the scaffolding failed to follow the instructions and plans furnished by the manufacturer. The court noted that the scaffolding was not assembled according to the manufacturer's instructions, and as a result the scaffolding braces bent, causing the scaffolding to collapse.

Key Concepts and Terms

- Products liability refers to a type of tort litigation in which a plaintiff seeks recovery from a manufacturer, processor, or seller for injury resulting from a defective product. Liability may arise from any one, or a combination, of three theories of liability: (1) negligence, (2) breach of warranty, and (3) strict liability.

- Recovery for injuries is based on the theories of negligence, strict liability, and breach of warranty. When a negligence theory is asserted, the plaintiff must show that the manufacturer or seller failed to exercise reasonable care as to the product. Under a strict liability theory, liability may be proven simply on the plaintiff's showing that the product was "unreasonably dangerous to the user." Under a breach of warranty theory, the plaintiff must show existence of a warranty, breach, and injury.

- Defenses against a products liability lawsuit may be based on the general principles of contributory negligence and assumption of risk. Failure to follow instructions in the use or assembly of a product may also constitute a defense.

- The outcome of most products cases depends on the testimony of experts who examine the product and the industry standards, then render a reasoned opinion as to whether a particular product was properly manufactured or designed.

- Breach of Warranty
- Consumer Product Safety Act of 1972
- Consumer Product Safety Commission
- Expert Witness
- Express Warranty
- Implied Warranty
- Negligence
- Products Liability
- *Restatement* (*Second*) *of Torts* § 402A
- Strict Liability

Questions and Case Problems

1. The High Velocity Gun Shop sells a shotgun to Mr. Sport. The shotgun has a "hair trigger" (not common to this type of gun), but High Velocity neglects to warn Sport about this. While Mr. Sport is using the shotgun, it discharges prematurely

due to the "hair trigger," resulting in injuries to a child. Is the gun shop subject to liability for the child's injuries on any theory?

2. Alma buys a wrapped loaf of bread baked by Yummy Bakery. She takes it home, opens the sealed wrapper, eats a slice, and is injured by a piece of glass imbedded in the bread. Alma sues Yummy Bakery for her injuries. On what theories, if any, is Yummy Bakery liable to Alma? Discuss.

3. What are the theories of liability on which a seller or manufacturer of a defective product may be held liable for injuries?

4. Mr. Gonzo purchases a bicycle manufactured by Whizzo Company as a birthday present for his son, Gregory. Unknown to anyone, the bicycle has defective hand-brakes, which cause Gregory to lose control of the bicycle and injure a pedestrian who is crossing the street. If the pedestrian is unable to prove any negligence on Whizzo's part, can the pedestrian still recover from Whizzo for his injuries?

5. Bob is injured while driving his new sports car manufactured by Smith Motors. In which of the following cases, if any, could Bob most probably recover against Smith on either a negligence or strict products liability theory? (a) Bob's injuries are caused by his car going out of control while taking a highway curve at 120 miles per hour. (b) Bob's injuries are caused by his car rolling over when he slams on the brakes at 55 miles per hour to avoid a freeway crash ahead of him. (c) Bob's injuries are caused by the lack of any side braces or supports to shield him from the impact when his car is broadsided by another car.

6. No-Pest manufactures a garden insecticide packaged in a push–button spray can that is produced by Felton Container Company. George buys a can of the spray to use on his roses and is injured when he pushes the spray button and the insecticide sprays back into his face and eyes due to a defect in the spray mechanism. Can George recover on a strict products liability theory against both No-Pest and Felton?

7. Loveless Products markets a new hair dye that is safe when used on the scalp, but contains certain chemicals that could cause burns to the eyes. The label on the dye states that it is intended solely for use on the scalp, but no specific warning is made about the hazard to the eyes. Betty purchases the dye, uses it on her eyebrows and a drop gets into her eye, causing severe injury. Can Betty recover from Loveless on a strict liability theory?

8. What does it mean to say that a product is "defective"? In what ways may a product be "defective" so as to render the manufacturer or distributor liable? Discuss.

9. What is the Consumer Product Safety Act of 1972, and how does it affect manufacturers or distributors of consumer products? What type of enforcement procedures does the act contain? Whose responsibility is it to administer the act? Discuss.

10. What defenses are available against a products liability suit?

8 Premises Liability

8:1 Duties to Invitees

The traditional rule is that the liability of a landowner[1] for injuries to a third person entering his land depends on whether the third person was an invitee, a licensee, or a trespasser at the time of the accident. Today, the courts rely less on these classifications of the injured person. The modern view, which is based on the landowner's reasonable care to protect third persons from injury, is discussed in 8:4. First, the roles of an invitee, a licensee, and a trespasser must be examined.

An *invitee* is a person who is invited, directly or impliedly, by the landowner to enter the land for some purpose of interest or advantage to the owner. The *Restatement (Second) of Torts* § 332 (1965) defines an invitee as either a public invitee or a business visitor. A public invitee is a person who is invited to enter land as a member of the public for a purpose for which the land is held open to the public. A *business visitor* is a person invited to enter land for a purpose directly or indirectly connected with business dealings with the landowner. People who accompany invitees are usually held to have the same status as invitees. For example, a wife accompanying her husband, a nephew accompanying an uncle, or a friend accompanying another friend is usually considered to be an invitee so long as the prime person is an invitee.

A landowner owes to each invitee the duty to exercise ordinary and *reasonable care* to maintain the premises in a reasonably safe condition for its intended use. At a minimum, the landowner must warn the invitee of dangers that are not obvious and that are known to the owner, or that the landowner could have discovered with reasonable diligence. However, this duty does not extend to cleaning up "natural accumulations" of snow or ice. The invitee owes himself a duty to anticipate dangers caused by such conditions. Then again, if the landowner does undertake

---

[1]The duties of a landowner, land occupier, or person exercising direct control over land are generally the same. For convenience, the term "landowner" will usually be used in this chapter. A landlord's tort liability to his tenant for dangerous or defective premises is discussed in Chapter 36. An employer's tort liability for failure to provide his employee with a safe place to work is discussed in Chapter 51.

to clean away snow or ice accumulations and he acts negligently in his cleaning operations, such negligence may be deemed the legal cause of the injury, and he will be held liable. It should be noted that in some states there are statutes that require the removal of ice or snow.

Invitees to a store are owed a duty in the area in which the selling or business occurs, as well as at the entrances and exits of the store. Also, where a business is operated in connection with another store or parking lot, the duty to keep the premises reasonably safe extends to approaches connecting the store to the other store or its parking lot. This duty is well illustrated in the following decision. Note the evidence that an unsafe condition in the defendant's parking lot had existed for such a length of time that the defendant should reasonably have been aware of its danger and corrected the condition.

Stocking
v
Sunset Square, Inc.
504 P2d 100
(Oregon Supreme Court, 1972)

[The plaintiff brought suit against a shopping center for injuries sustained after she stepped into a depression in the shopping center's parking lot. She contended that the owner failed to exercise reasonable care to her, as an invitee, to render the premises reasonably safe from harm.]

Tongue, Justice.

*   *   *

This is an action for personal injuries sustained by plaintiff when she fell after stepping into a "depression" in the parking lot of defendant's shopping center. The jury returned a verdict for plaintiff. Defendant appeals from the judgment on that verdict. We affirm. . . .

Defendant concedes that the law controlling the disposition of this case is as stated in 2 *Restatement 215–16 Torts 2d* § 343, which provides that:

"A possessor of land is subject to liability for physical harm caused to his invitees by a condition on the land if, but only if, he

"(a) knows or by the exercise of reasonable care would discover the condition, and should realize that it involves an unreasonable risk of harm to such invitees, and

"(b) should expect that they will not discover or realize the danger, or will fail to protect themselves against it, and

"(c) fails to exercise reasonable care to protect them against the danger."

Defendant was the owner of the shopping center, including an asphalt paved parking lot, which was opened in August 1969. Defendant's manager testified that "depressions" sometimes appear in such parking lots when the soil under the asphalt paving erodes and "drops away." He also testified that in February 1970, after having "problems" with such "depressions," defendant had the lot patched, but that between then and the date of this accident more "depressions" appeared, at least some of which were "jagged and ragged."

By letter dated November 2, 1970, Safeway, as one of defendant's tenants, wrote a letter to defendant requesting that various items be "corrected," including "[r]epair deteriorating asphalt areas throughout parking lot."

After receiving that letter defendant, on November 10, 1970, wrote to the general contractor which had constructed the parking center, enclosing the Safeway letter and asking it to "make an inspection of these items for us and advise. . . ." No repairs were made, however, until after plaintiff's accident on December 19th.

Defendant's manager also testified that he had inspected the parking lot two days before the accident, but denied prior knowledge of "this particular depression" and said that such "depressions" are common to parking lots of this type and sometimes develop "overnight."

According to testimony offered by plaintiff, however, the "depression" which later caused plaintiff's fall was observed by an employee at one of the establishments in the shopping center at least one week prior to the accident.

Plaintiff testified that upon coming out of the laundromat in the shopping center with a large box of clothes, she balanced the box against the rear of her car and then stepped sideways into the "depression" and fell on her back. After she fell she observed the "depression" as being about the size of a soup plate, "the edges being ragged," and "tapering down" to a center about three inches deep. That same night her husband also examined it and testified that "the asphalt had been broken and had left a round, jagged hole" about "an inch-and-a-half at the outer edge and . . . deeper in the center." He also took a photograph of the "depression," which was offered in evidence.

Defendant offered evidence to the contrary and contended that:

> "The record is void of any evidence of the size and shape of the depression which preexisted plaintiff's fall. Thus a trier of facts could not conclude that the depression which existed for one week before the plaintiff's fall was unreasonably dangerous before the fall."

We hold, however, that based upon plaintiff's evidence, and giving plaintiff the benefit of all reasonable inferences from that evidence, as we are required to do in such a case, the jury could properly and reasonably infer and find that this and other "depressions" in defendant's parking lot existed a sufficient period of time prior to the accident, and were then of such a nature, that defendant, by the exercise of reasonable care should have "discover[ed] the condition [including this 'depression'], and should [have] realize[d] that it involve[d] an unreasonable risk of harm to . . . invitees," such as plaintiff, and that defendant also "fail[ed] to exercise reasonable care to protect them against the danger," within the meaning of 1 *Restatement 215–16, Torts 2d* § 343. . . .

[Judgment affirmed.]

A public employee—a policeman, fireman, or other public servant—is usually classified as an invitee on the theory that, in the scope of employment, he goes onto property to enforce and to look after a property owner's interests.

 A person who is *not* in direct or exclusive control of the land may be liable to invitees for the condition of the premises. For example, the operator of a market who rents space from an adjacent service station for parking is under a duty to exercise reasonable care to keep the parking lot in a safe condition.

8:2   Duties to Licensees and Adult Trespassers

Broadly defined, a *licensee* is a person who is invited or permitted by the landowner to enter the property for his own convenience, pleasure, or benefit, or for purposes that are not connected with the landowner's interests. Licensees, for example, may be business visitors who were initially invitees but who have strayed from that part of the premises to which they were invited or authorized to enter: door-to-door salespersons, process servers, social guests, and visiting relatives. A landowner is under no duty to inspect and prepare the premises so they will be safe for the licensee's reception. However, where (1) there is a known dangerous condition, (2) the landowner can reasonably anticipate that the licensee will not discover or realize the danger, and (3) the landowner invites or permits the licensee to enter or remain on the premises without exercising reasonable care either to give warning or to make the condition reasonably safe, the landowner can be liable for the licensee's injury.

Furthermore, the landowner owes a licensee, at least if his presence on the premises is known or reasonably should have been known, the duty to use reasonable care not to injure him by affirmative acts—the duty to refrain from unreasonably dangerous active conduct that might be harmful to the licensee.

Adult Trespassers   A *trespasser* is a person who enters another's premises without license, invitation, or other right to do so created by the landowner's consent. Traditionally, a landowner owes trespassers no duty to keep his premises in a safe condition for their use, and as a general proposition, he is not responsible for a trespasser's injury resulting from a defect of the premises. A landowner is obligated only to refrain from willfully or wantonly injuring a trespasser.

8:3   Child Trespassers and Attractive Nuisance

Most states today accept the view that under certain circumstances a landowner may be held responsible for injury caused by dangerous conditions on the premises to children who trespass, even though the landowner would not be liable if the injured person had been an adult trespasser. The expression *attractive nuisance* is the legal shorthand description used by courts to designate this type of case. The principle of liability has been known by other names, such as the "turntable" doctrine, the "infant trespasser," "dangerous instrumentality," "playground" rule, and "the trap" theory. Nonetheless, the basic principle is that one who has or creates on his own premises a condition that may reasonably be expected to be a source of danger to children is under a duty to take those precautions that a reasonably prudent person would take to prevent injury to young children whom he knows to be accustomed to be there, or who may be expected to be attracted to his land.

EXAMPLE
When a four-year-old boy drowned in an excavation ditch partially filled with muddy water, the court applied the doctrine of attractive nuisance, stating that there was a danger that a young child might suddenly come on the excavation and fall in without discovering it in time to avoid it, especially if the child was running.

The attractive nuisance doctrine has caused courts to struggle in arriving at a reasonable compromise between two conflicting interests: on the one hand, the interest of society in preserving the safety of its children, and on the other hand, the interest of landowners in using their land for their own purposes with reasonable freedom. The younger the child, the more likely will a condition be held to be an attractive nuisance. Unattended vehicles, swimming pools, pits, explosives, and machinery have all been held in particular cases to qualify as attractive nuisances. To be a child trespasser, the child must be so immature as to be unable to recognize the danger involved. In practice, children above the age of 14 years seldom qualify.

Some cases have expressed the viewpoint that the doctrine is applicable only if the injury is caused by an artificial condition on the land or by a structure that was placed on the land. This view is based on the idea that it is the responsibility of the parents or guardians to protect children from dangers posed by natural conditions.

8:4   Modern Viewpoint as to Landowner's Duties

There is a trend toward liberalizing the rules governing a person's recovery for injuries sustained on another's premises. Courts today are rejecting the principle that the standard of care owed by a landowner should be based on the status—as an invitee, a licensee, or a trespasser—of a person who comes on the premises. As stated by a legal writer in 1964: "The ideal development in [premises liability] would be to discard the classification system and substitute ordinary rules of negligence based upon foreseeability in its stead. In place of the continued using of such terms as the invitee, licensee and trespasser, the court should reconsider the basic issue of whether a duty of due care should, as a matter of policy, be imposed in the particular situation involved."[2]

An example of this modern viewpoint is the California Supreme Court case of *Rowland v Christian*, 69 Cal 2d 108, 70 Cal Rptr 97, 443 P2d 561, 32 ALR 3d 496 (1968). Here, the California Supreme Court abolished the status distinction governing the duties to licensees, invitees, and trespassers, and adopted a rule of "reasonable care" under all circumstances:

> Without attempting to labor all of the rules relating to the possessor's liability, it is apparent that the classifications of trespasser, licensee, and invitee, the immunities from liability predicated upon those classifications, and the exceptions to those immunities, often do not reflect the major factors which should determine whether immunity should be conferred upon the possessor of land. Some of those factors, including the closeness of the connection between the injury and the defendant's conduct, the moral blame attached to the defendant's conduct, the policy of preventing future harm, and the prevalence and availability of insurance, bear little, if any, relationship to the classifications of trespasser, licensee and invitee and the existing rules conferring immunity. . . . The proper test to be applied to the liability of the possessor of land . . . is whether in the management of his property he has acted as a reasonable man in view of the probability of injury to others, and, although the plaintiff's status as a trespasser, licensee, or invitee may in the light of the facts giving rise to such status have some bearing on the question of liability, the status is not determinative.

2Long, "Land Occupant's Liability to Invitees, Licensees, and Trespassers," 31 *Tenn L Rev*, 485 (1964).

In similar fashion, the Massachusetts Supreme Court announced, in *Mounsey v Ellard*, 363 Mass 693, 297 NE2d 43 (1973), that it would no longer follow the common-law distinction between licensees and invitees and, instead, created a "common duty of reasonable care which the occupier owes to all lawful visitors."

It should be pointed out that this liberal approach is being taken in only some jurisdictions, such as California and New York. Many courts in other jurisdictions show no inclination to abandon these status distinctions.

 Some state and local statutes, as well as government building codes and regulations, often have a direct bearing on the maintenance practices of land, particularly where businesses are conducted. While the violation of statutes or ordinances does not automatically amount to negligence, failure to follow legislative standards may be shown to amount to failure to have exercised reasonable care. Therefore, businesspersons should acquaint themselves with the pertinent codes and regulations.

8:5   Stores and Other Places of Business

Any person in possession of commercial premises—a store, office, bank, hospital, or public building—has a duty to exercise ordinary care to maintain the premises in a reasonably safe condition for customers and members of the general public who are properly on the premises. This duty applies to all parts of the store or business premises where the customer may properly go, such as entryways, doors, floors, aisles, and steps, and even extends to conditions such as lighting and displays. The rationale is that the customer has a right to consider himself safe from all dangers and defects while on commercial premises.

Self-service Marketing   Self-service marketing is widely practiced in a variety of commercial enterprises, particularly discount department stores and supermarkets. While it has economic advantages for the storekeeper and gives customers freedom to browse and to examine and select merchandise they desire, it has certain inherent problems that are usually not encountered in traditional merchandising, where customers are assisted individually by a salesperson. Customers in the self-service situation, for example, are usually not as careful in handling merchandise as are salespersons. A customer may drop and leave merchandise on the floor out of carelessness or because his attention is directed toward displayed merchandise and he is unaware that he dropped the merchandise. If the dropped merchandise does not immediately come to the attention of employees, it could present an opportunity for someone to slip and fall.

Merchants are under a duty to display goods so that they will not (1) fall and injure a customer, (2) topple if a customer using care attempts to take an item from the top of the display, or (3) generally be placed in a manner that would threaten to injure a store's visitors. Some conditions that have been identified as unreasonably dangerous are displays protruding into an aisle or passageway, falls of a display onto a customer, and hazards presented by floor debris.

The Slip-and-Fall Case   A frequent basis for premises liability of the operator of a store or other business is the presence of obstructions or slippery substances on the floor that the proprietor has notice of or that have been there long enough to charge the proprietor with knowledge of their presence. A person who owns commercial premises has a duty to exercise care to keep the floors free from litter or debris, even when the debris is brought into the store by customers. To fulfill this duty, the storekeeper must exercise reasonable care to inspect and clean the premises to make sure that fallen items do not remain on the floor. What constitutes "reasonable care" depends on the circumstances. Usually, the mere presence of debris on the store's floor and the fact a patron fell do not necessarily mean the storekeeper failed to exercise proper care. The key to liability is whether the storekeeper knew, or ought to have known, of the floor's condition. The storekeeper is deemed to have actual knowledge of a dangerous condition such as a floor spill, if he or his employee caused the condition or observed it.

To be liable, a storekeeper does not always need *actual* knowledge of the spill. A storekeeper may be deemed to have what is termed *constructive notice* of a condition. This means that he should have, or could have, discovered the dangerous condition if he had exercised reasonable care. For example, if a substance has remained on the floor for a long enough time that the storekeeper should have discovered it, he will be deemed to have constructive notice of its existence. This notice is sufficient to establish liability. In determining what constitutes a storekeeper's constructive notice, the courts have looked to several factors. Among these factors are (1) the number of customers who use the store, (2) the type of merchandise displayed, and (3) the location of the spill or other debris. For example, the operator of a busy supermarket should know that customers handling displayed produce often drop bits of produce on the floor of the area.

Where the method of doing business, as in the case of self-service supermarkets, tends to produce hazards because of large numbers of customers handling or dropping merchandise, the courts have sometimes said that constructive notice may exist even when the item was on the floor only a short time.

The following case is a typical slip-and-fall case. In this case the activities of the grocery store revealed a "pattern of conduct" that created a dangerously slippery floor that the defendant could have prevented by using a different type of display.

Garcia

v

Barber's Super Markets, Inc.
81 NM 92, 463 P2d 516
(New Mexico Supreme Court, 1969)

[Barbara Garcia was injured when she slipped and fell while shopping in a supermarket. She sued the

supermarket, and the court awarded her damages. The supermarket appealed.]

Hendley, Judge.

*   *   *

Plaintiff, Barbara Garcia suffered injuries when she slipped and fell on waterslick tile in defendant's store. Defendant had arranged an "Ice Cold Watermelons" tank display. When a customer would take a watermelon from the tank, water would drip on the floor. Barbara took one of the watermelons and placed it in her shopping basket. She then turned and started to walk toward a paper towel rack attached to an upright strut near the tank. She observed a puddle of water on the floor and stepped around it. There is evidence that this puddle of water did not come from her watermelon. She then took another step and looked up to get a towel when her right foot slipped and she fell. . . .

The defendant's store manager, assistant manager and produce manager testified that they had had a problem of water spilling on the floor for six or seven weeks; that the water spilling was inevitable and a continuing problem which they recognized as creating a hazard; that the tile became slippery when wet; there was a danger of someone falling because of the water, and this hazard could have been eliminated by a different display.

There is also evidence that even with water on the floor, the customer's attention would be diverted by the towel racks at the ends of the watermelon tank. The manager "absolutely" expected the racks to attract the customer's attention.

There is evidence that the water should be continually mopped. There is evidence of regular and close attention to the area to make sure that water was mopped up. Opposed to this, however, is testimony that, with knowledge of the hazard from a wet floor water was left for periods of time without mopping, that the hazard existed from hour to hour and there were periods of time when the water was allowed to remain for longer periods than at other times.

Defendant asserts that plaintiffs cannot recover unless they show either a specific act of negligence by defendant or the existence of a condition "so obviously dangerous" as to permit an inference of negligence. Defendant claims there is no such evidence.

The mere presence of a slick or slippery spot on a floor does not in and of itself establish negligence, for this condition may arise temporarily in any place of business. . . . Nor does proof of a slippery floor, without more, give rise to an inference that the proprietor had knowledge of the condition. . . . But we are not dealing with an isolated instance.

Plaintiffs were not required to prove either a specific act of conduct or an obvious dangerous condition. Such proof was not required once there was proof of a continuing messy condition—a pattern of conduct. . . .

The proof of the pattern of conduct does not, of course, establish the defendant's negligence . . . . Taking the evidence in the light most favorable to plaintiffs, not only was there proof of the pattern of conduct, there was evidence or inference of defendant's knowledge of a continuing hazard, that invitees might fail to protect themselves against that hazard and that defendant failed to exercise reasonable care to protect them from that hazard . . . . In the light of the evidence and inferences, it would have been error for the trial court to have sustained defendant's claim of "no negligence." . . . Barbara, in approaching the towel rack, observed some water on the floor. She attempted to go around this water. The only evidence in the record is that she slipped on something that she didn't see. The specific danger was not known to her. There is no evidence that whatever caused Barbara to slip was obvious. Accordingly, she cannot be presumed to know of this danger. . . .

[Judgment affirmed.]

Negligent Premises Design   An emerging basis of premises liability is the failure to exercise due care in the design of a building. This failure is illustrated in the following decision. Note that a psychologist's expert testimony helped establish the unsafeness of the defendant's premises.

Watt
v
United States
444 Fed Supp 1191
(United States District Court for the District of Columbia, 1978)

[A visitor who was injured on the steps of the Smithsonian Institution sued the federal government for negligent design of the stairs, which she contended caused her to fall. The federal trial court awarded her damages.]

Curran, District Judge.

*   *   *

This action against the United States under the Federal Tort Claims Act seeks to recover damages for personal injuries sustained by the plaintiff as a result of a fall on steps in the fountain area facing the north door of the Museum of History and Technology of the Smithsonian Institution, an entity of the United States Government. . . .

The plaintiff, Hazel D. Watt, a resident of New York, New York, had visited the Museum with her daughter and departed through the north door at about 2:45 p.m. on April 16, 1975, a sunny, clear and dry day. The two crossed a concrete sidewalk and curving asphalt driveway and entered the fountain area, descending two small steps. They were then standing on the uppermost of three levels of semicircular granite platform steps. The daughter, Ann Wiechmann, proceeded to the street to summon a taxicab while the plaintiff remained standing in the position just described. After waiting awhile, the plaintiff decided to join her daughter on the street and walked to the right a short distance when she

suddenly fell and fractured her right elbow. The plaintiff was wearing shoes with a 1½" heel, composition soles, rubber heels, and equipped with rubber preservers at the toe and heel.

The semi-circular platform steps around the circumference of the fountain are constructed of variegated granite. The riser of each step is approximately 5⅜ inches high and the tread is approximately 10 feet deep. On April 16, 1975, there were no cautionary signs warning pedestrians of the existence of the platform steps, nor were there stripes or other markings at the edge of the platform steps. The plaintiff's fall occurred at the edge of the top platform step.

The plaintiff alleges that the pedestrian walkway around the fountain was unreasonably dangerous because of the difficulty presented in visually detecting the presence of the platform steps. Additionally no warning was posted to alert pedestrians of the existence of the platform steps. The plaintiff's allegations include negligence in the design, construction and maintenance of the platform steps and a failure to exercise reasonable care.

The plaintiff testified that she did not see and was not aware of the presence of steps as she walked along the top platform step. She was looking ahead but not at the ground. She was aware that she was at a slightly higher elevation than the street, but it was not apparent to her that the downgrade was accomplished by steps rather than a ramp.

Expert testimony was presented by both parties. A psychologist and human factors specialist called by the plaintiff testified that the variegated granite presented a visual dilemma because of its texture and because the sharp edges of the rectangular platform blocks with grouting between them do not provide a contrast to the edge of the step. A person should be able to distinguish a step when three or four strides away, and at the area where the fall occurred, one does not receive a visual cue of the existence of a step until only one stride away.

An architect testified that the fountain area is designed so as to invite people to walk through but it is unsafe. A change in grade creates a hazard and unless steps are uniform and readily discernible, they are defectively designed. . . .

By a preponderance of the evidence, the plaintiff proved that the platform steps in the fountain area were designed so as to create a hazard for a pedestrian. It is difficult to distinguish that a step is present because of the sameness of color and inability to discern the edges. It is hazardous not to indicate different

levels. The platform steps were defectively designed because of the inability to detect their presence, and the government architects who approved the design showed a want of reasonable care. The architects' negligence is imputed to the defendant. . . .

It is the opinion of the Court that the negligence of the defendant's architects in approving a faulty design of platform steps was the proximate cause of the plaintiff's injury and that the architects knew and recognized the hazard at the time approval was given so that the defendant had actual notice of the defect. The plaintiff is entitled to recover damages. . . .

[Judgment affirmed.]

8:6 Defenses

Common defenses in a premises liability suit are (1) contributory negligence and (2) the geographical limitation of the landowner's duty. *Contributory negligence* is the failure of a person to exercise reasonable care for his own safety. Under ordinary circumstances, persons are obliged "to see what there is to see."

The extent to which the premises were used by the plaintiff before and at the time of his injury has a bearing on the question of his contributory negligence. A plaintiff is more likely to be found to be contributorily negligent if he conducts his movements in a manner that is unlike that of others who use the premises. For example, if a store patron ignores a safe, well-used route to his destination and uses an unlighted route, he may be contributorily negligent.

Geographical Extent of Duty Another factor examined by courts in considering the liability of a landowner is whether the injury occurred in a portion of the premises that was designated and prepared to accommodate customers and was an area in which the customer might reasonably be expected to be. The owner's duty of care extends only to portions of the premises where the customer might reasonably be expected to travel; the duty does not extend to premises reserved for use only by the storekeeper or his employees, such as shipping rooms and warerooms, and areas that are marked "private" or "employees only." Therefore, a business owner will not be liable if a customer is injured while on these premises.

 A businessperson who is in charge of premises that are open to the public should post "private" or "employees only" signs for all areas to which the general invitation to the public does not extend.

Key Concepts and Terms

- The common-law approach in determining a landowner's liability to persons injured on his land is to measure liability according to the status of the entrant at the time of the accident as an invitee, a licensee, or a trespasser. In some states, the status distinctions have been abolished and the courts have adopted a rule simply that a landowner must exercise "reasonable care" under all circumstances.

- An invitee is a person who has been directly or impliedly invited by the landowner to enter the land for a purpose of advantage to the owner. A landowner owes invitees the duty to exercise ordinary care to maintain the premises in a safe condition or at least to warn of dangers that are not obvious.

- A licensee is a person who is invited or permitted by the landowner to enter the property for his own convenience, pleasure, or benefit, or for purposes not connected with the landowner's interests. While a landowner has no duty to inspect or prepare the premises so they will be safe for a licensee, the landowner does have a duty to warn a licensee of a known dangerous condition.

- A trespasser is a person entering another's premises without invitation or permission. He is owed only a duty not to be willfully or wantonly injured by the landowner.

- Under the attractive nuisance doctrine, one who has or creates a condition on his premises that may be a source of danger to children is under a duty to take those precautions that a reasonably prudent person would take to prevent injury to young children who he knows go onto his land or who may be expected to be attracted by the condition.

- Merchants are under a duty to display their goods so they will not fall and injure a customer, so the merchandise will not topple if a customer using care attempts to take an item from the top of the display, and so that the merchandise is not placed in a manner that would threaten injury to those visiting the store.

- The owner of commercial premises has a duty to exercise reasonable care to keep the floors free from litter or debris, even when the debris is brought into the store by other customers.

• Attractive Nuisance	• Invitee
• Business Visitor	• Licensee
• Contributory Negligence	• Reasonable Care
• Constructive Notice	• Slip-and-Fall
• Geographical Extent of Duty	• Trespasser

Questions and Case Problems

1. One January evening, Larry steps out of his car in the parking lot of a supermarket. Although snow has not fallen for several days, the parking lot is still

covered with snow and ice. Larry slips and lands on his hip, sustaining severe injuries. He sues the supermarket for negligence. What is the result and why? Would the supermarket be liable if Larry was parking in the supermarket lot to attend a motion picture three blocks away? Discuss. How would liability be affected if Larry had parked in the supermarket lot because he intended to use the market's restroom, but not to purchase anything? Discuss.

2. What is the attractive nuisance doctrine?

3. One night a thief attempts to burglarize Margie's home. He falls into Margie's partially completed swimming pool and is severely injured. If Margie had failed to erect a fence or post any warning or lights around the pool, is she subject to liability for the thief's injuries?

4. What defenses may be raised in a premises liability suit?

5. Large piles of slag accumulate on Jack's mining property, which is unfenced. The neighborhood children play on the piles, although Jack has posted a "DANGER NO TRESPASSING" sign. One of these children, Jason, age seven, is injured when he cuts himself on the slag. Is Jack liable for Jason's injuries?

6. Allen sees Tim, a trespasser, on a part of his land previously free from trespassers, about to come in contact with dangerous machinery he maintains on his land. Allen has time to shut off the power but fails to do so and Tim is injured. Is Allen liable to Tim? Discuss.

7. Emily operates a gas station. One of her customers inadvertently spills water in the men's room, making the entrance very slippery. However, no one complains to Emily about the condition until several hours later, when John slips and falls, hurting his back. John was not a customer of the service station, but a 12-year-old child on his way home from school. Is Emily subject to liability for John's injuries?

8. Seymour, a door-to-door salesman, suffers a broken leg when he trips on a step of Carol's front porch. Carol was not at home at the time, but she knew that the step needed repair and that the danger was not readily visible. Is she liable for Seymour's injuries?

9. MacAdam Cement Company maintains large piles of sand on its premises for use in making concrete. The sand is impure and often contains sharp pebbles and bits of glass. Over the weekend, the premises are unattended. A fence and "NO TRESPASSING" signs have been erected. Several ten-year-olds climb through the fence one weekend and are cut while playing in the sand piles. Is the cement company subject to liability for their injuries?

10. Harry is walking on a city sidewalk adjoining Alison's property. (a) Assume that Harry is struck by a branch falling from a native tree located on Alison's property. If Alison has never inspected the tree to make sure it is safe, is she subject to liability for the injuries resulting to Harry? (b) If Harry is struck on the head by a baseball hit in a game being played on Alison's land, is she subject to liability for his injuries?

PART THREE

Contracts

Introductory Comments

Contracts are the basic tool of business. Yet businesspeople far too often enter contractual relationships in a casual way. Oral agreements are often used in situations calling for written ones, and written contracts frequently lack specificity on essential matters. The result is predictable: disagreements and lawsuits ensue, and good business relationships are destroyed in the process. A race car driver would never consider entering a race until the car was thoroughly inspected. By the same token, a businessperson should not enter a contract until all the ramifications of the contract have been thoroughly considered.

The material in Chapters 9 through 18 provides the information necessary to make an appraisal of a contract. These chapters discuss the basic elements necessary to create a contract, the various problems that may arise concerning the validity of a contract, and the performance or breach of contracts.

These chapters cover legal rules and include cases illustrating and applying various legal principles. It must be emphasized that the major reason for studying contract law is not to learn how to win court cases; judicial resolution of a contract dispute may take many years, and even the "winner" may in reality lose. The purpose of studying contract law is to learn how to *avoid* disputes and litigation. The one point to stress is that the contract should be negotiated, planned, and drafted with an eye to avoiding disputes. In addition to the specific suggestions given in the following chapters, it is hoped that students will come up with their own dispute-avoidance suggestions as they study the material.

While the subject of sales is covered in detail in Chapters 19 to 22, it should be noted that contract law is generally applicable to sales contracts. Contract law is also generally relevant to many of the more specific subjects covered later in this book. The study of contract law may therefore serve, in a sense, as a foundation for the study of all aspects of business law.

9 Nature and Classification of Contracts

9:1 Introduction; Definitions of Contract

Contracts are one of the basic tools employed in the everyday conduct of all types of business. Although contracts are often thought of as long and complex written documents, they may be oral as well as written, and may relate to relatively trivial matters. Potential examples of contracts abound; subscription to a magazine, purchase of an automobile, use of a credit card, and many other routine and not-so-routine activities all involve contracts.

There is no uniformly accepted definition of a contract. A contract has been simply defined as a legally enforceable agreement. Another frequently quoted definition is "a promise or a set of promises for the breach of which the law gives a remedy, or the performance of which the law in some way recognizes as a duty."[1] The *Uniform Commercial Code*[2] defines a contract as "the total legal obligation which results from the parties' agreement as affected by this Act and any other applicable rules of law" [UCC § 1–201(11)].

One reason for the difficulty in defining a contract is that a complete definition would require compressing the entire law relating to contracts into one sentence, an impossible task. Rather than attempting a comprehensive definition of contract, therefore, it is better to proceed to a study of the law of contracts. Although it will not offer a succinct definition of contract, a close examination of contract law will provide an understanding of what a contract is, and more importantly, how contracts may be used in the everyday conduct of business.

9:2 Nature of a Contract

As noted, a contract is a legally enforceable agreement. Agreement has been defined as "a manifestation of mutual assent on the part of two or more persons."[3] It

---

[1]*Restatement (Second) of Contracts* § 1 (1981).
[2]The UCC is discussed further in this chapter in section 9:4.
[3]*Restatement (Second) of Contracts* § 3 (1981).

is also "the bargain of the parties in fact as found in their language or by implication from other circumstances" [UCC § 1–201(3)]. Since some agreements are not legally enforceable, it cannot be said that all agreements are contracts. Agreement is, however, normally necessary to form a contract, and an agreement that includes the attributes making it legally enforceable is a contract. It is not surprising, therefore, that the terms "agreement" and "contract" are sometimes used interchangeably.

While various terms may be used to describe the parties to a contract, the words "offeror and offeree" and "promisor and promisee" are often used in discussing the formation of contracts and will be briefly defined at this point. An *offeror* is a party who makes an offer to another party to enter into an agreement; the party to whom the offer is made is the *offeree*. When a contract is entered into, there are usually promises of performance made by both parties. A person making a promise is a *promisor*; the person to whom a promise is made is a *promisee*. As will be shown, a party to a contract typically occupies a position as both a promisor and a promisee.

9:3   Elements and Classifications of Contracts

The essential elements of a legally enforceable contract are (1) two or more parties with the legal capacity to contract, (2) a manifestation of mutual assent by the parties to the contract and to its terms, (3) sufficient consideration, and (4) a purpose that is legal and not contrary to public policy. These elements are discussed in detail in later chapters in this part of the text.

Contracts may be classified in various ways, and the discussion that follows uses some commonly accepted classifications. It should be borne in mind, however, that the classifications are not mutually exclusive. Rather, they are descriptive of certain characteristics of contracts. For example, a bilateral contract may also be an express, valid, executory, and informal contract.

Bilateral and Unilateral Contracts   Most contracts involve an exchange of promises by the parties and are known as bilateral contracts. Typically, one party promises to perform some act in the future in exchange for the other party's promise to perform some other act in the future.

EXAMPLE
A university extends an offer in April to provide a student with a dormitory room in September, provided the student agrees to make specified payments beginning in August. Such a proposal is an offer of a bilateral contract. If the student accepts the offer and promises to make the payments specified, a bilateral contract is formed. Under this contract, the university's promise to provide a dormitory room in September serves as consideration[4] for the student's promise to pay money at the specified times.

It can be seen, therefore, that in a bilateral contract each party is both a promisor

---

[4]Consideration consists of the promises or performances that the parties to a contract exchange with each other. Consideration is discussed in Chapter 11.

and a promisee. In the example, the university as promisor is obligated to provide a dormitory room, and as promisee it has the right to payment from the student. The student as promisor has a duty to make the payments, and as promisee he has the right to a dormitory room.

In some contracts only one party makes a promise, with the consideration for the promise consisting of some action performed by the other party. Such contracts are called unilateral contracts. A promissory note, which is a written contract promising payment of a specified sum of money to a specified person, is a typical unilateral contract. The lending party actually loans money to the borrowing party in exchange for the borrowing party's promise to repay the money according to the conditions of the note. The act of lending the money is the consideration for the promise to repay. The act and the promise are exchanged simultaneously.

A unilateral contract also exists when one party makes a promise in exchange for a future act that the promisee has no obligation to perform but does perform. A typical example is the offer of a reward. If one person offers a reward for information leading to the apprehension of a named criminal, no one is obligated to provide the information. If someone does provide the information, a unilateral contract is created. Moreover, the only way to accept the promise is by providing the requested information. A mere promise to provide the information does not result in a contract.

A point that should be made about this second type of unilateral contract is that the offeror is ordinarily not obligated until the act is performed. A unilateral offer may be withdrawn at any time prior to performance. Thus, strictly speaking, the offer of a reward is not a contract at all, but merely an offer to make a contract that becomes a contract once the requested act is performed.

EXAMPLE

If Adam offers to pay Jennifer $5 to mow his lawn, no obligation exists to mow the lawn. If Jennifer mows the lawn, Adam is obligated to pay. Assume, however, that Jennifer does not mow the lawn immediately, but decides to do so the next day. If Adam then says he has changed his mind and will not pay to have the lawn mowed, there is no contract. If Jennifer proceeds to mow the lawn anyway, there is still no contract, because the offer was withdrawn prior to performance of the requested act.

An offer is sometimes unclear as to whether a return promise or actual performance is required to form a contract. In cases of doubt, a court will ordinarily presume that an offer was for a bilateral rather than a unilateral contract.

Express and Implied Contracts   A contract is express when the parties state its terms and show their assent by words, either oral or written. A contract is implied, or implied in fact, when the intent and assent of the parties are shown by their acts rather than by words. When a contract is express, its terms and conditions depend on the parties' words. When a contract is implied, the parties' conduct and the surrounding circumstances determine the terms and conditions. Stated another way, a contract implied in fact represents the presumed intent of the parties as indicated by their conduct.

Quasi-Contracts   Classification of contracts as express or implied is not based on any difference in the legal consequences of such contracts. Rather, the classification relates solely to the method by which the parties arrive at an agreement and the type of evidence which proves the contract's existence and its terms. *Quasi-contracts,* which are contracts implied in law, do have different legal consequences because quasi-contracts are not true contracts at all. Quasi-contracts are not based on the parties' intentions, real or presumed. Rather, they are creatures of law.

Quasi-contractual obligations are imposed when justice requires that one person pay for some benefit bestowed on him by another, even though the person receiving the benefit never agreed, either expressly or impliedly, to pay for the benefit. In fact, quasi-contractual obligations are frequently contrary to a party's intentions. The underlying principle is that a person should not be allowed to unjustly enrich himself at the expense of another. A classic example of a quasi-contract is the situation in which one person benefits another by mistake. If the person conferring the benefit reasonably believed that the recipient intended to pay for it, and the latter accepted the benefit knowing payment was expected, then fairness demands that payment be made.

EXAMPLE
Bentley's son, without Bentley's authorization, requests Neilsen to build a fence on Bentley's land. Neilsen proceeds to do so over a period of several days. Bentley knows that the fence is being built and that Neilsen expects payment, but he says nothing. When the fence is completed Bentley refuses to pay Neilsen, saying that there was no contract between them. A court may impose a quasi-contractual obligation on Bentley to pay the reasonable value of the benefit he received, since otherwise he would be unjustly enriched at Neilsen's expense.

One point should be made about the above example. Bentley knowingly accepted the benefit from Neilsen. Assume, however, that Neilsen built the fence while Bentley was away on vacation, and that Bentley did not find out about it until his return. Since Bentley had no knowledge that Neilsen was building the fence and expected payment, Bentley could not be held liable for payment, and quasi-contractual liability would not be imposed.

It should be noted that neither a quasi-contract nor an implied contract will be found when circumstances indicate that a service or other benefit was given gratuitously (free of charge).

Valid, Voidable, Void, and Unenforceable Contracts   A valid contract is one in which all the essential elements are present and, as such, the contract is legally binding on both parties and enforceable in court.

A voidable contract is one from which one or both parties have the power to withdraw, but which is otherwise valid and enforceable. Typically, in a voidable contract one party has the power either to ratify or reject, but the other party must perform unless the contract is rejected by the first party. A common example of a voidable contract is one between a minor and an adult. The minor may withdraw from (avoid) the contract, or he may affirm it and hold the adult to the contract.[5]

---

[5]The capacity of parties to enter a contract is discussed in Chapter 13.

Void contracts are different from voidable contracts in that they are legal nullities. A void contract is not binding, and it cannot be ratified and made enforceable by the parties. In legal effect a void contract is not a contract at all. For example, a contract requiring the commission of a crime is void and unenforceable, since it violates express statutory law.

An unenforceable contract is one that gives rise to contractual obligations, but for the breach of which there is no remedy available. Unenforceability usually results because the parties fail to comply with some rule of law. For example, some contracts are required by the statute of frauds[6] to be in writing, and non-compliance with the statute renders the contract unenforceable. As with a voidable contract, an unenforceable contract may become enforceable if the defect preventing its enforcement is cured or waived. Thus, if an oral contract is written to comply with the statute of frauds, it becomes enforceable.

Executory and Executed Contracts   Another classification of contracts depends on performance. An executory contract is one in which the parties have not yet performed all the terms and conditions. An executed contract is one that has been fully performed by all parties. A contract may be partly executory and partly executed, as when one party has performed completely but the other party has not.

Formal and Informal Contracts   The binding effect of certain contracts depends on their form. These are known as formal contracts. Formal contracts include (1) contracts under seal (sealed contracts), (2) recognizances (obligations entered into before a court of record), (3) negotiable instruments and documents (including commercial instruments such as bills of exchange and warehouse receipts), and (4) letters of credit (under the UCC).

All other contracts are known as informal or simple contracts. It should be noted that even informal contracts may be subject to formal requirements. The word "informal" merely indicates that a contract is not in one of the categories described above as formal.

9:4   Uniform Commercial Code

The Uniform Commercial Code (UCC), formulated through the joint efforts of the National Conference of Commissioners on Uniform State Laws and the American Law Institute, deals with most aspects of modern commercial transactions, although sometimes with amendments to the official text.[7]

The UCC was designed to bring the field of commercial law into line with contemporary business practices, to meet the needs of modern commercial society, and to promote fair dealing between parties to business transactions. The UCC is liberally interpreted by the courts and applied to promote uniformity and modernization of the laws relating to commercial transactions. The basic philosophy of the UCC is that practical businesspersons cannot govern all their actions by legal formalities.

---

[6]The statute of frauds is discussed in Chapter 15.
[7]The official text of the UCC is set forth in Appendix B.

The UCC is obviously of great importance in those commercial transactions, such as sales,[8] that it specifically covers. Moreover, the UCC is often applied by analogy even to transactions it does not regulate. The UCC is thus of great importance to the law of contracts. Its provisions will be discussed throughout this book, both generally and specifically with respect to certain types of transactions.

9:5   Realities of Standardized Contracts

The law of contracts developed on the assumption that a contract is the result of individual negotiations between the parties, and many principles of contract law are based on that assumption. In reality, however, many contracts today are standardized forms prepared by one of the parties, which require only the filling in of blanks to make them enforceable contracts. Sometimes only the signature of the parties is necessary.

There is nothing improper in the use of standardized forms. Indeed, use of such forms is often the most economical and efficient method of doing business. It must be recognized, however, that there are potential pitfalls. Failure to read a form contract carefully may result in a person's unwittingly agreeing to undesirable terms. Failure to make certain that the individualized portions of a form conform with the printed ones may also cause unnecessary problems and lead to litigation. It is unrealistic to suggest that such forms not be used, but it is important to stress that they be used with care. If a standardized contract does not accurately reflect the parties' intentions and desires, it either should not be used, or it should be used only after the necessary changes have been made to the form.

 A business that makes substantial use of standardized forms should have a regular schedule for reviewing them. Changes in the law, whether by new statutes or court decisions, may make a standardized form obsolete or even legally ineffective. Periodic review and redrafting of forms by an attorney will enable a business to keep its forms current with the law.

As the use of standardized form contracts has increased, the courts and legislative bodies have begun to develop rules of law designed to minimize or prevent some of the abuses resulting from their use. The law's response to oppressive, one-sided forms, discussed in Chapter 12 (see 12:13), is an example of the way the law changes to meet new needs and situations.

9:6   Government Contracts

Federal, state, and local governmental entities often enter into contracts with individuals or companies. These contracts relate to the entire range of government activities, including procurement of services and supplies, construction, and research and development. Government statutes and regulations contain thousands of provisions relating to the award and performance of government contracts. A

---

[8]Sales are discussed in Chapters 19–22.

businessperson who contracts with a government agency must comply with the appropriate rules and regulations. In addition to laws and regulations relating to the actual business relationship between the government and a private contractor, there are others that require compliance with certain social policies. For example, statutes and regulations prohibit certain types of discrimination by government contractors.

The laws relating to government contracting vary greatly from state to state. In the interest of uniformity and to simplify and modernize the law relating to government procurements, an American Bar Association committee drafted a proposed *Model Procurement Code* in 1978. The code would apply to all expenditures of public funds by state government units under contracts with nongovernmental bodies. If it is adopted by a substantial number of states, it would have a significant impact on government contract law. The code would govern the award of state contracts for supplies, services, and construction, would provide for resolution of disputes arising out of the award and performance of government contracts, and would set standards of ethical conduct for both government employees and public contractors.

Key Concepts and Terms

- A contract is a legally enforceable agreement between two or more parties. Contracts may be oral or written, simple or complex.
- The essential elements of a contract are parties who have the legal capacity to contract, mutual assent, consideration, and legality of purpose.
- Contracts may be classified as bilateral or unilateral; express or implied (implied in fact); valid, voidable, void, or unenforceable; executory or executed; and formal or informal. If no real contract exists, quasi-contractual obligations are sometimes imposed to prevent unjust enrichment.
- The Uniform Commercial Code (UCC), which has been adopted by most states, deals with most aspects of modern commercial transactions.
- Many contracts today actually consist of standardized forms, with or without blank spaces filled in. Use of such forms is legal and often desirable from a business standpoint, but care must be taken to avoid potential pitfalls.
- Persons or entities contracting with government agencies must comply with a wide variety of government statutes and regulations. The proposed Model Procurement Code, if adopted by a substantial number of states, would help to modernize and to create uniformity in government contract law.

- Government Contracts
- Model Procurement Code
- Offeree
- Offeror
- Promisee

- Promisor
- Quasi-Contract
- Standardized Contracts
- Uniform Commercial Code (UCC)

Questions and Case Problems

1. What is a contract? What are the essential elements of a contract?

2. What is the difference between a bilateral and a unilateral contract?

3. What is a quasi-contract, and how does it differ from a true contract?

4. Discuss the advantages and disadvantages of standardized contracts.

5. Lucas, a minor, told Sharon that if she would steal a set of stereo speakers, he would pay her $50 for them. Sharon stole the speakers and gave them to Lucas, who said he would pay her the following week. Classify the agreement between Lucas and Sharon in as many ways as you can.

6. What is the difference between an express and an implied contract?

7. Jacob asks Eva if she will pay him $5 if he washes her car. Eva says that she will. Jacob washes the car, but Eva refuses to pay, claiming that there is no contract since nothing was put in writing. Is she correct? If there is a contract, is it bilateral or unilateral?

8. What is the difference between voidable, void, and unenforceable contracts?

9. Miller drives into a service station and, with no intention of paying, has the attendant fill his car with gasoline. Does a contract exist? If so, how would you classify it?

10. Discuss the philosophy and the importance of the UCC.

10 Offer and Acceptance

10:1 Introduction

Formation of a contract requires an *offer* by one person (the *offeror*) to enter into a legally binding agreement and an *acceptance* by another person (the *offeree*). Each party must clearly express his intention to enter into a legally binding and enforceable agreement. When an offer has been made and an acceptance given, it is said that there is mutual assent—a meeting of the minds—and a contract exists.

An objective standard is used in determining whether there is mutual assent. Thus, in determining whether a particular communication is either an offer or an acceptance, the courts look to how a reasonable person would objectively view the language used. If it is reasonable to believe that one party intended to make a legally binding offer, and that the other party intended to make a legally binding acceptance, then a contract exists.

EXAMPLE
Mark tells Natasha, "I will sell you this vintage MG for $5,000." Natasha responds, "It's a deal. I accept your offer." Later that day, Mark refuses to complete the sale, claiming that he really intended to sell the car only if he could not get a better price for it. Mark's argument will be to no avail. His statement, objectively viewed, clearly and unequivocally expressed a present intention to sell the MG for a particular price, and Natasha's response, objectively viewed, was clearly an acceptance of the offer. Thus a contract was created, and Mark's subjective intent is irrelevant. The same would be true if it were Natasha who later attempted to renege on the deal.

The following case is a graphic illustration of the rule that a party's statements will be interpreted by comparison with an objective standard. The result in this particular case may appear harsh. Consider, however, the effect of a contrary ruling. Specifically, if one party can withdraw from a contract on the ground that he entered it in jest, of what value is a contract in the first place? When, if ever, should a party be permitted to avoid contractual obligations on the ground that the contract was entered as a mere joke?

Lucy

v

Zehmer
196 Va 493, 84 SE2d 516
(Virginia Supreme Court of Appeals, 1954)

[Mr. and Mrs. Zehmer owned some land known as the Ferguson Farm. On December 20, 1952, Lucy offered Mr. Zehmer $50,000 for the farm. Mr. Zehmer accepted and wrote an agreement stating: "We hereby agree to sell to W. O. Lucy the Ferguson Farm complete for $50,000.00, title satisfactory to buyer." Mr. and Mrs. Zehmer signed the agreement. Lucy took the agreement and offered $5 to bind the deal, but Mr. Zehmer refused the money. When the Zehmers refused to go through with the deal, Lucy sued to enforce the contract. The Zehmers defended on the ground that both men had been drinking and that the agreement had been written and signed as a joke. The trial court ruled in favor of the Zehmers, and Lucy appealed.]

Buchanan, Justice.

*   *   *

The defendants insist that the evidence was ample to support their contention that the writing sought to be enforced was prepared as a bluff or dare to force Lucy to admit that he did not have $50,000; that the whole matter was a joke; [and] that . . . no binding contract was ever made between the parties. . . .

In his testimony Zehmer claimed that he "was high as a Georgia pine," and that the transaction "was just a bunch of two doggoned drunks bluffing to see who could talk the biggest and say the most." That claim is inconsistent with his attempt to testify in great detail as to what was said and what was done. It is contradicted by other evidence as to the condition of both parties, and rendered of no weight by the testimony of his wife that when Lucy left the restaurant she suggested that Zehmer drive him home. The record is convincing that Zehmer was not intoxicated to the extent of being unable to comprehend the nature and consequences of the instrument he executed, and hence that instrument is not to be invalidated on that ground. . . .

The appearance of the contract, the fact that it was under discussion for forty minutes or more before it was signed; Lucy's objection to the first draft because it was written in the singular, and he wanted Mrs. Zehmer to sign it also; the rewriting to meet that objection and the signing by Mrs. Zehmer; the discussion of what was to be included in the sale, the provision for the examination of the title, the completeness of the instrument that was executed, the taking possession of it by Lucy with no request or suggestion by either of the defendants that he give it back, are facts which furnish persuasive evidence that the execution of the contract was a serious business transaction rather than a casual, jesting matter as defendants now contend. . . .

If it be assumed, contrary to what we think the evidence shows, that Zehmer was jesting about selling his farm to Lucy and that the transaction was intended by him to be a joke, nevertheless the evidence shows that Lucy did not so understand it but considered it to be a serious business transaction and the contract to be binding on the Zehmers as well as on himself. . . .

Not only did Lucy actually believe, but the evidence shows he was warranted in believing, that the contract represented a serious business transaction and a good faith sale and purchase of the farm.

In the field of contracts, as generally elsewhere, "We must look to the outward expression of a person as manifesting his intention rather than to his secret and unexpressed intention. 'The law imputes to a person an intention corresponding to the reasonable meaning of his words and acts.' "

First Nat. Exchange Bank of Roanoke v Roanoke Oil Co., 169 Va. 99, 114, 192 S.E. 764, 770.

At no time prior to the execution of the contract had Zehmer indicated to Lucy by word or act that he was not in earnest about selling the farm. They had argued about it and discussed its terms, as Zehmer admitted, for a long time. . . . [T]here had been what appeared to be a good faith offer and a good faith acceptance, followed by the execution and apparent delivery of a written contract. Both said that Lucy put the writing in his pocket and then offered Zehmer $5 to seal the bargain. Not until then, even under the defendants' evidence, was anything said or done to indicate that the matter was a joke. . . .

The mental assent of the parties is not requisite for the formation of a contract. If the words or other acts of one of the parties have but one reasonable meaning, his undisclosed intention is immaterial except when an unreasonable meaning which he attaches to his manifestations is known to the other party. . . .

An agreement or mutual assent is of course essential to a valid contract but the law imputes to a person an intention corresponding to the reasonable meaning of his words and acts. If his words and acts, judged by a reasonable standard, manifest an intention to agree, it is immaterial what may be the real but unexpressed state of his mind. . . .

So a person cannot set up that he was merely jesting when his conduct and words would warrant a reasonable person in believing that he intended a real agreement. . . .

Whether the writing signed by the defendants and now sought to be enforced by the complainants was the result of a serious offer by Lucy and a serious acceptance by the defendants, or was a serious offer by Lucy and an acceptance in secret jest by the defendants, in either event it constituted a binding contract of sale between the parties. . . .

[Judgment reversed.]

10:2   Intent to Make an Offer; Preliminary Negotiations

The expressed intent of the offeror viewed objectively determines whether an offer has been made. An offer must express the intent that, on acceptance by the other party—and nothing more—the offeror will be bound, and an enforceable contract will thereby be created. An expressed intention merely to do an act is not an offer to perform that act. Nor does a mere expression of intention or general willingness to do something on the happening of an event, or in return for something, amount to an offer. To illustrate, assume that Rubio writes to Kelly: "Are you interested in my property on Elm Street? I'm asking $100,000." This language would not indicate an offer. The first part is a mere inquiry, and the second part is mere information. There is no offer or promise by Rubio to sell the property to Kelly. If Kelly replies, making a commitment to purchase the property at the stated price, his communication would be the offer. Acceptance of that offer by Rubio would form a contract.

Frequently, one person will initiate preliminary or exploratory discussions concerning a possible contract with another person. The first person may suggest the general nature of the contract he would like to enter, and then wait for the second person to come forward with either a specific offer or some specific ideas. Such an invitation to negotiate does not constitute an offer, only the opening of discussions. For example, "Would you be interested in," "I might be willing to," "I hear you're looking for a," or similar words pave the way for an offer but do not constitute one.

Depending on the complexity of the contemplated contract, the negotiating process might continue for some time, with each party making suggestions or comments. For *mutual assent,* and thus a contract, to come into existence, the negotiations must come to an end with an actual offer and acceptance. A series of continuing negotiations does not constitute an offer.

 The complex language of modern commercial transactions sometimes makes it extremely difficult to determine whether particular words or acts were intended as a legally binding offer, as preliminary negotiations, or as an invitation to the other party to make an offer. Whenever a question exists as to whether a person is making an offer or just commencing negotiations, the person should clearly state his intent. If no offer is intended, that fact should be clearly and prominently stated. Such a statement may help to eliminate costly litigation. Equally important, such a statement may, by minimizing the possibility of any misunderstanding, help to preserve a valuable business relationship.

Advertisements; Catalogs   Advertising is a major facet of modern commercial life. While the average person may interpret an advertisement as an offer or promise to sell the goods advertised, the courts have generally held otherwise. Most courts have held that advertisements are only invitations to enter into a bargain or to patronize a store, and not actual offers, even if the advertisement specifies the article and the price. Some states, however, have statutes dealing with false and misleading advertising. These statutes impose liability on a merchant who refuses to accept offers for the advertised goods. Furthermore, as discussed later in this book, the Federal Trade Commission regulates many aspects of advertising by businesses involved in interstate commerce (see Chapter 53).

 As a practical matter, a merchant who advertises goods wishes to sell them. A merchant who persistently refuses to sell goods at the prices advertised will suffer adverse business consequences. On occasion, however, goods are advertised for sale at a mistaken price, sometimes through an error by the advertising media. Legally, a merchant usually is not obliged to sell the goods for the erroneously stated price. If the difference between the two prices is not great, a merchant may either decide to sell at the advertised price to maintain customer goodwill, or post a prominent notice explaining the erroneous advertisement. As a precautionary step, businesspersons should always check advertising copy before submitting it. If the advertisement is to be repeated, they should also make certain the first advertisement was accurate.

Catalogs and company price lists are generally considered advertisements, and not offers, even though they specify the items, terms, and prices of merchandise.

When a prospective customer orders a catalog item or writes a letter of purchase based on the price quotation, such conduct is generally considered the offer, and must be accepted by the sender of the catalog or price list before a contract exists.

Advertisements for rewards for information leading to the arrest or conviction of a criminal suspect are usually held to constitute offers rather than invitations to make offers. This rule is based on the public policy ground that it is to society's benefit that persons who have committed crimes be apprehended and brought to justice.

Auctions   An announcement of an *auction*, or an auction itself, is not an offer to sell which becomes binding on the owner when a bid is made. Rather, a notice to the public to sell property to the highest bidder is merely an invitation to make bids and a declaration of an intention to receive bids. Unless a sale is "without reserve," the seller of property at an auction, or the auctioneer, may withdraw the property from sale at any time before accepting a bid. When a bid is accepted, a contract is formed. If an auction is held "without reserve," the goods must be sold to the person making the highest bid (UCC § 2-328).

10:3   Reasonable Certainty of Terms

Generally, to be a legally binding contract, an agreement must be reasonably definite as to all material terms and must clearly set out all rights and duties. An offer must be reasonably definite since, for a court to enforce a contractual obligation or to award damages for a breach, it must be able to determine what the parties' obligations were. The time of performance, price to be paid, work to be performed, quantity of items involved, or other material terms must be definite.

Although the terms need to be definite, absolute certainty is not required; reasonable certainty is sufficient. A contract is not indefinite if the parties can reasonably determine their basic rights and duties. While the offer must be definite and certain in its terms, the offeror, for example, may make an offer which gives the other person a reasonable degree of discretion in performance. To illustrate, if a produce wholesaler offers to sell a grocery store as many apples as it needs at 25 cents per pound, such an offer is legally effective. If the store accepts the offer and names the number of apples it will take at the quoted price, a contract is formed and the parties are bound by its terms.

As the following case indicates, the requirement of certainty is to be applied in a practical way. Consider whether, if the defendant's position had prevailed, it would be possible to draft a sufficiently certain contract.

McMurray
v
Bateman
221 Ga 240, 144 SE2d 345
(Georgia Supreme Court, 1965)

[In 1962 Dr. Bateman, who had a medical practice in Atlanta and in nearby Forest Park, Georgia, employed Dr. McMurray as an associate. The employment contract was a three-page letter written by Bateman and signed by him and McMurray. In

1965 the association was terminated, and McMurray set up medical practice in Atlanta. Bateman sued to enforce a provision of the contract that prohibited McMurray, for a period of three years after termination of the association, from engaging in practice within a 50-mile radius of Forest Park. Among the defenses raised by McMurray was the claim that the contract was so indefinite and uncertain as to be invalid. The trial court, rejecting that defense, ruled in favor of Bateman. McMurray appealed.]

Quillian, Justice.

*   *   *

The defendant insists ... the contract between the parties ... is too incomplete and indefinite to be enforceable. The document was primarily an employment contract and possessed all of the requisites of a contract of that nature expressed in reasonably certain terms. It designated, as we construe it, the defendant's place of employment, the period for which he was employed, the nature of the services he was to render and the compensation he was to receive.

While the contract contains no express promise that the defendant's place of employment would be the Forest Park Clinic and the Georgia Professional Building, the contract is explicit that he was to come and practice with the plaintiff and that the latter's practice was conducted at the places mentioned. The contract stipulates services, those incident to the practice of medicine and surgery, and that his compensation is to be arrived at according to an understandable formula. ...

In reaching this conclusion we have considered the epitome of reasons the defendant contends the terms of the contract were incomplete and indefinite. He points out two provisions of the contract as indicative of its incompleteness: (1) "In the event anything arises not covered in this agreement nor already covered by precedent it shall be decided on the basis of the spirit herein contained and the Golden Rule, plus accepted Christian principles." (2) "Trips, vacations, outside study, time off, etc. to be arranged by mutual consent."

The former really has no legal significance. It is merely a statement that the contract may be altered by subsequent agreement of the parties. This is, as a matter of law, generally true of contracts, where the interest of a third party is not involved. The latter provision does not concern the essential elements of the contract, but simply provides that customary details concerning its performance will, from time to time, be determined by mutual consent of the parties. A contract is not usually incomplete because minor details incident to the performance of its terms are left to be agreed upon. ...

The defendant further contends that the contract is incomplete because it does not stipulate whether the plaintiff is to provide office space, secretarial services or other facilities for the practice of medicine, and did not define what was meant by "overhead" expenses. We think the letter embodying the contract and the terms of the contract made it clear that the defendant was to practice as the plaintiff's employee and associate at the Forest Park Clinic and this carries with it the inescapable conclusion that he was to have office space, and the use of the clinic's facilities. The term "overhead" is not defined. It was not necessary that the contract define words that are commonly used in the connection of the conduct of business or the practice of professions. "Overhead" has a connotation generally understood. It means those expenses incidental or incident to the practice of a profession. ... It is impossible to accurately stipulate in advance what will constitute such overhead expenses because from their very nature they depend upon contingencies occurring in the course of practice generally not predictable or certain. ...

[Judgment affirmed.]

The fact that an offer contains a choice of terms from which the accepting party may make a selection does not make the offer too indefinite. Acceptance of one of the alternatives will form a binding contract. For example, if a manufacturer offers to sell a customer a particular machine for $3,500 *or* a more complex machine for $7,500, and the customer notifies the manufacturer that he will buy the $3,500 machine, a contract is formed. If, on the other hand, the manufacturer offers to sell a machine for $7,500 *and* a service contract for the repair of that machinery, as a package deal, the customer would have to accept both items of the offer or neither. The precise wording used, and the conjunctions, such as "and" and "or," are of considerable importance.

Under the UCC, a contract for the sale of goods is not too indefinite even though one or more terms are left open, if the parties intended to make a contract and if there is a reasonably certain basis for giving an appropriate remedy (UCC § 2-204). The UCC provisions concerning open terms is considered in greater detail in Chapter 19.

10:4   Communication of Offer

An offer, to be legally effective, must be communicated by the offeror and received by the offeree. Unless an offer is communicated, no meeting of the minds—or mutual assent—can occur. If two parties make identical offers to each other which cross in the mail, no contract is created. For a contract to exist, one party must make and communicate an offer to the other party, who must accept the offer.

EXAMPLE
Acme Corporation writes a letter to the Maze Company stating, "We will sell you six turbojet engines for $300,000." Not knowing of this letter, the Maze Company at the same time writes to the Acme Corporation, "We would like to purchase six of your turbojet engines for $300,000." Each letter is subsequently received by the respective addressees. No contract is formed. Each party made an offer to the other, but neither offer was accepted.

A question sometimes arises, in connection with so-called "fine-print contracts," whether all of an offer was effectively communicated to another party. It is sometimes held, for example, that if particular provisions in a contract are not of a certain type size, they do not give the other party notice of their existence and the contract or the specific provisions will be held void. There is specific legislation that governs such matters where "consumers" are involved. For example, as discussed in Chapter 27, the federal Truth in Lending Act requires that certain important credit terms be printed conspicuously in a consumer credit contract.

10:5   Termination of Offer

An offer does not remain outstanding forever. If it is accepted, of course, the offer and the acceptance merge into the contract. If the offer is not accepted, there are various ways in which the offer may terminate. These ways include: (1) revocation by the offeror, (2) lapse of time, (3) rejection or counteroffer by the offeree, and (4) termination by operation of law.

Withdrawal or Revocation of Offer   Generally, an offer may be withdrawn at any time before it is accepted. This is so even if the offer states that it shall remain open for a designated time. The rationale for this is that if the offeror is not permitted to revoke the offer at any time before acceptance, he must give up flexibility with regard to his property or his services without receiving anything in return. To be effective, revocation of an offer must be communicated to the offeree before he accepts the offer. If the revocation is sent by mail or telegram, it becomes effective when it is received by the offeree and not when it is sent.

This general common-law rule covering revocation of offers has been modified by the UCC provision on "firm offers" (UCC § 2-205). Under the UCC, if a merchant, in a signed writing, offers to buy or sell goods and gives his assurance that the offer will be held open, he must abide by that assurance. Thus, a firm offer is not revocable during the time stated in the writing. If no time is stated, the offer must be held open for a reasonable time, not to exceed three months.

An *option contract* represents a second type of irrevocable offer. If the offeree gives something of value, called consideration, to the offeror to keep the offer open for a specified period of time, the offer is called an option, and the offeror (optionor) must hold the offer open for the specified time period. It should be understood that an option is a contract in itself. Thus, with an option there exists: (1) an offer, which does not become a contract unless and until accepted and (2) a completed contract to leave the offer open for the specified time. Option contracts are frequently used in connection with the sale of property. The owner grants a prospective purchaser the option to buy the property under certain terms within a specified time period. During that time the prospective purchaser may either exercise his option and contract to purchase the property, or he may let the option expire.

Lapse of Time   An offer may also expire as the result of a lapse of time. If the offer itself specifies the length of time that it will be held open, it will terminate after that time passes. When the offer does not specify how long it is to remain open, the courts have held that it will continue for a reasonable length of time. What is considered to be a reasonable time depends on the facts and circumstances of each situation. Among the factors that may be considered are the past business practices between the parties and the customs of the particular trade or industry. Such business practices or customs may even be relied on to interpret an expressly stated limitation on the length of time that the offer will remain open.

EXAMPLE

Gillian, an apple grower, has sold apples to Max's Market for many years. In each of the prior 20 contracts with Max, Gillian has given Max "two weeks" to accept the offer and has allowed Max 14 working days. Gillian again offers to sell Max apples and allows him two weeks to accept the offer. Max accepts the offer on the fourteenth working day (the eighteenth calendar day) after it was made. Max's acceptance is timely and effective, since the past practices between Gillian and Max have equated "two weeks" with 14 working days.

Rejection or Counteroffer   An offer will terminate if the offeree either rejects it or makes a counteroffer. If the offeree says or does anything to indicate that he declines the offer or to justify the offeror's belief that the offeree does not intend to accept it, the offer is rejected. Once the offeree has rejected an offer, he cannot later accept it. The rejection has the effect of terminating the offer.

If an intended acceptance is conditional, introduces new terms, or in any way varies from the terms of the offer, it is not an effective acceptance. The courts treat such conditional acceptances as *counteroffers*. A counteroffer is a rejection of the original offer, coupled with the offeree's submission of a new offer. As such, it terminates the original offer.

The offeree may ask the offeror questions about the offer and even ask whether he will alter its terms. Such questions do not necessarily constitute a rejection of the offer. Whether a rejection has occurred may depend on the specific words used. To illustrate, assume that A offers to sell B a car for $3,000. B responds that she will pay A $2,000 for the car. B has made a counteroffer that amounts to a rejection of A's initial offer. If, however, B says, "I'd like to buy the car, but can you lower the price a bit?" B has neither accepted nor rejected the offer. The offer remains open, unless it is revoked by A.

Termination by Operation of Law   Certain events terminate an offer as a matter of law. These events include (1) the death or insanity of either the offeror or the offeree, (2) destruction of the subject matter of the offer, and (3) the subject matter becoming illegal after the offer is made. Any of these events will automatically terminate the offer.

10:6   Acceptance of Offer

Acceptance of an offer converts it into a binding contract. To be effective, an acceptance must correspond with the terms of the offer. An acceptance must be unequivocal and unconditional, and it must not introduce additional terms or conditions. This does not mean, however, that the acceptance must be phrased in the identical language of the offer. Any form of expression that shows the offeree's intention to accept the offer is an effective acceptance.

The statement that an acceptance may not introduce new or additional terms must be qualified somewhat. For example, if an acceptance includes terms that would be implied as a matter of law anyway, it is a valid acceptance. Also, if an acceptance includes minor or immaterial matters not mentioned in the offer, the courts will generally consider it to be unconditional and effective acceptance. Likewise, an unconditional acceptance coupled with the offeree's requests to the offeror is effective to create a contract.

The following case discusses not only the requirement that an acceptance may not introduce any new and material terms, but also various other principles governing offer and acceptance that have been discussed in this chapter.

Apablasa

v

Merritt & Co.
176 Cal App 2d 719, 1 Cal Rptr 500
(California District Court of Appeal, 1959)

[Apablasa and Merritt exchanged a series of letters concerning the possibility that Merritt might produce and market an invention of Apablasa. The contents of the letters are discussed in the opinion. After nothing came of the correspondence, Apablasa sued Merritt, claiming breach of contract. The trial court concluded that there was no contract and entered judgment for Merritt. Apablasa appealed.]

Lillie, Justice.

*   *   *

[W]e conclude that no reasonable construction of the evidence will admit a binding contract between the parties; and that the correspondence amounts to nothing more than preliminary written discussions. . . .

The genesis of the controversy is found in a series of letters growing out of defendants' interest in a device invented by plaintiff. On August 24, 1955, the first letter (Ex. 1-A) was written by defendants to plaintiff:

> "I think you have a very fine invention. Undoubtedly with the right design worked out for the various models, proper sales brochures, and a concentrated direct-sales effort, the returns should be most gratifying. I feel confident that 50,000 units at $50.00 each could be sold within the first year. . . .
>
> "Should you decide to give us a try in merchandising and marketing the item, instead of the $50,000 cash you mentioned as your selling price, I should suggest $100,000 as a bonus payment to be paid from a fixed percentage of the earnings, and when this has been paid, that you should receive a continu-

ing graduated percentage of the profits thereafter. . . .

> "Trusting something like this would be acceptable to you, and looking forward to hearing from you quite soon, I am

> Sincerely yours,"

> "P.S.: As suggested percentage: 20% of the net until you have received $100,00(0), then 10% of the net thereafter. . . ."

It is this letter appellant claims constituted the offer [to manufacture and market the device].

An analysis of the writing fails to disclose the definitive terms necessary to constitute it an offer—to manufacture or have manufactured, merchandise and market plaintiff's invention—for an offer must be certain and definite, that the resulting contract may be enforceable. . . .

It is well settled that if the offer is so indefinite as to make it impossible for a court to decide just what it means, and to fix exactly the legal liability of the parties, its acceptance cannot result in an enforceable agreement. The letter, a definite rejection by defendants of the idea of an outright sale of the device and an invitation to consider their services in merchandising and marketing the same, omits any reference to manufacturing; indeed, nothing therein relates to how or by whom the article is to be produced; production cost and who shall bear the same; how raw materials, patterns, designs and samples will be supplied; in what manner plaintiff's invention and patent, if one exists, shall be transferred and to whom; and when production is to begin. Likewise, as to the marketing of the item, absent is any reference to territory, whether distribution is to be exclusive, who is to set the price, and the minimum amount to be sold in what period of time. Relative to the $50 figure mentioned, it appears to be only a suggested possible sales price used as a basis for speculation. . . . Nor is there mention of how much out of any established sales price defendants are to receive on each item for their services, and how much is to be paid plaintiff. The "suggested percentage" is exactly what it purports to be—a suggestion. . . . That this letter was by no means intended to constitute an offer is found in the last paragraph wherein defendants expressed their hopes that *something like* this" would be acceptable to plaintiff. [Court's emphasis]. . . .

On August 27, 1955, plaintiff, referring to defendants' letter of August 24, responded (Ex. 1-B) in part: . . .

> "After due consideration, and in view of my age and other circumstances I would like to sell the invention outright as I have already expressed to you, possibly taking less down payment—$5,000 instead of $10,000 and the balance on or before five years to make up the $50,000. . . ."

Herein plaintiff rejected consideration of any arrangement to market and merchandise his invention and professed interest only in its outright sale. Appellant does not dispute that defendants' August 24 letter relates only to marketing and merchandising; and it is obvious his reply actually proposes a plan altogether different than that suggested by defendants, revealing an absence of any meeting of the minds and a complete lack of interest in any program excluding outright sale. Had Exhibit 1-A constituted an offer of any kind, Exhibit 1-B completely negates plaintiff's claim he accepted it—for at most his letter of August 27 amounted to no more than a counterproposal by him rejecting any plan heretofore proposed by defendants and terminating any further discussions relative thereto. . . .

On September 20, 1955, plaintiff [wrote] Exhibit 1-D, which he contends constituted the acceptance of the offer he claims was contained in defendants' letter of August 24, 1955:

> "After careful consideration I have decided to accept your proposition as outlined in your letter to me of August 24th, 1955 with this proviso: that you agree to put this product in production within a definite period of time from the date of the signing of any agreement between us. . . ."

. . . Appellant's position that the September 20 letter constituted an acceptance resulting in a meeting of the minds is predicated on the false premise that defendants' letter of August 24 contained an offer which in spite of his intervening letter remained open. However, borrowing this premise solely for discussion, that the letter could not constitute an acceptance finds support in well-established authority and in the only reasonable interpretation that can be given to the writing itself.

It is fundamental that without consent of the parties, which must be mutual . . . , no contract can exist. . . . Consent cannot be mutual unless all parties agree upon the same thing in the same sense. . . . Hence, terms proposed in an order must be met exactly, precisely and unequivocally for its acceptance to result in the formation of a binding contract . . . ; and a qualified acceptance amounts to a new proposal or counteroffer putting an end to the original offer. . . . An offer "must be approved in the terms in which it is made. The addition of any condition or limitation is tantamount to a rejection of the original offer and the making of a counteroffer. . . . A counteroffer containing a condition different from that in the original offer is a new proposal and, if not accepted by the original offeror, amounts to nothing. . . ." [Citations omitted.]

To argue that the word "proviso" used by plaintiff in his alleged acceptance refers only to a "suggestion for better terms" and not to a new and different proposal varying with, and completely modifying, the terms of the original alleged offer (Ex. 1-A), is to ignore any reasonable construction of the latter writing. Nowhere mentioned therein (Ex. 1-A) was any proposal to manufacture or produce the machine—only a plan to merchandise and market it through an exclusive sales promotion.

Obviously production by defendants was not contemplated. Plaintiff's alleged acceptance (Ex. 1-D) contains the first mention that defendants are "to put this product in production," introducing a completely new proposal for their consideration. It is one thing to merchandise and market an item, quite another to assume the burden of producing it—requiring equipment, cost outlay, raw materials, designs, patterns, samples, etc. . . .

[The court concluded that no contract was ever entered between the parties and affirmed the judgment.]

The UCC sets forth an additional exception to the requirement that an acceptance cannot contain new and additional terms. Under the UCC, an acceptance containing new or additional terms is generally effective to create a contract for the sale of goods, and additional terms not materially altering the contract become a part of it (UCC § 2-207). This provision, and the reasons for it, are covered in greater detail in Chapter 19.

10:7 Communication of Acceptance

Just as an offer must be communicated, so must an acceptance. Depending on the terms of the offer, the offeree's acceptance may be communicated to the offeror by words, acts, or a combination of words and acts, so long as the communication is such that a reasonable person would understand that an acceptance has been made.

If the offer requires the acceptance to be communicated in a particular manner, such as in writing, then the acceptance must be communicated in the way specified or it will not be legally effective to create a contract. If the offer does not indicate any particular means of acceptance, then any reasonable means of acceptance communicated to the offeror will create the contract.

EXAMPLE
Wally offers to sell Irma a stereo set and states that the offer may only be accepted in writing. Irma telephones Wally and tells him that she accepts his offer. Since she failed to comply with an express term of the offer, her acceptance is not valid and no contract is created. If, on the other hand, Wally's offer is silent as to the manner of its acceptance, Irma's telephone call accepting the offer would be perfectly reasonable and would constitute a valid acceptance creating a contract.

If the offer specifies a time for acceptance, the acceptance must be communicated within that time. The language of the offer must, however, be reasonably interpreted. A requirement in an offer, for example, that it must be accepted "at once" or "immediately" will not be read to mean instantaneously, but will be read to require that an acceptance be communicated within a reasonably short time.

Use of Mail or Telegraph   If an offer is accepted in person or by telephone, the offeror learns of the acceptance at the same time it is made. When acceptance is made by mail or telegraph, however, there is a lapse of time involved. Moreover, the mail or the telegram may be lost and never delivered. The question then arises as to whether the acceptance was ever communicated, and if so, when.

Unless the offer provides otherwise, an acceptance may be made by the same medium through which the offer was made. If the offer was made by mail, the acceptance can be too. In such a situation, the acceptance is effective when the offeree deposits it with the Postal Service. This is so even if the acceptance never reaches the offeror, provided that the letter was properly addressed and had proper postage. Once a letter of acceptance has been properly mailed, the offer cannot be revoked, even if a letter of revocation was mailed, but not received, prior to the mailing of the letter of acceptance.

Contracts entered into by telegraph are governed by the same rules as contracts entered into by mail. If an offer is made by telegraph, then an acceptance by telegraph is effective when the offeree delivers it to the telegraph company.

Sometimes, an offer made in person or by telephone is accepted by mail or by telegraph. In such cases, the courts have generally agreed that such acceptance is proper, unless the circumstances indicate otherwise. The courts are not agreed as to when such an acceptance takes effect. Some courts, on the rationale that the offeror has not authorized the use of the mails or the telegraph, have held such an acceptance effective only when it is received by the offeror. Other courts, apparently reflecting a growing trend, make no distinction between cases in which the offer was communicated by mail or telegram and those in which it was not. In other words, if acceptance by mail is proper, the acceptance takes place on its deposit with the Postal Service, regardless of whether the offer was made by mail. Acceptance by telegram is treated similarly.

The offeror can, of course, specify the means of acceptance to be used. The offeror may also provide that any acceptance will not be effective until the offeror receives it. Moreover, past business practices or customs in an industry may indicate that acceptance by mail or by telegram is not permissible. For example, if personal acceptance is normal in a given industry, an acceptance by mail may be considered unauthorized. In such a situation, a letter of acceptance would be effective only when actually received, and not when mailed.

 To avoid problems regarding whether, and when, an acceptance was effectively communicated, the offeror should specify: (1) the manner of acceptance, (2) the time allowed for acceptance, and (3) the time when the acceptance will be effective. An offeree, for his part, should read an offer with care. If he decides to accept the offer, the offeree should make sure that he (1) complies with all terms and conditions of the offer, including any expressed manner and time of acceptance; (2) communicates his acceptance to the offeror in clear language; and (3) does not introduce any new or additional material terms or conditions.

Silence as Acceptance   Ordinarily, the offeree's silence cannot be interpreted as an acceptance of the offer. Under some circumstances, however, silence may be equivalent to acceptance. For example, if a seller on previous occasions has sent similar goods to the buyer and the buyer has always accepted and paid for them, the buyer's silence and retention of shipped goods on subsequent occasions will generally be considered an acceptance.

Acceptance of Offer to Enter Sales Contract (UCC § 2-206)   Under the UCC, an offer to enter a sales contract may be accepted in any manner and by any medium reasonable under the circumstances. This is true unless a specific manner or medium is clearly indicated by the language of the offer or the surrounding circumstances. The propriety of the manner of acceptance depends on whether it will be effective to reach the offeror in time to enable him to take the action contemplated by the parties.

Under the UCC, the offeree's commencement of performance of a contract is an effective acceptance only if, within a reasonable time after commencement, he notifies the offeror of his acceptance. For example, if Baker offers to purchase ball bearings manufactured to order by Carter, Carter may accept by beginning to manufacture the ball bearings. To avoid the possibility that Baker may later decide to revoke the offer, Carter must also notify Baker, within a reasonable time after he begins manufacturing, that he has accepted the offer. If Carter fails to do so, Baker may, after a reasonable time, treat the offer as having lapsed.

Under the UCC, an order or other offer to buy goods for current shipment invites acceptance either by a promise to ship or by actual shipment of the goods. Sometimes a seller may not have the exact goods ordered, but may have similar goods that he believes will be acceptable to the buyer. Shipment of such nonconforming goods also indicates acceptance, unless the seller notifies the buyer that the shipment is offered only as an accommodation to the buyer. (Such notification will protect the seller from a later claim that he breached the contract by sending the alternate goods.)

10:8   Acceptance of Unilateral Offers

As noted in Chapter 9, an offer for a unilateral contract is accepted by performance of the requested act, not by a promise to perform. The performance of the contract constitutes the acceptance. When performance can be completed quickly, no problems are likely to arise. Sometimes, however, performance may require a long time. The offeree may begin performance, only to have the offeror attempt to withdraw the offer prior to completion. Technically, the offeree has not accepted the offer, since he has not completed performance. At common law, the courts generally held that an offer of a unilateral contract could be revoked at any time until the requested act was completed. Thus, an offeree who had started performance could recover only the value of his services under a quasi-contract theory (see 9:3). The modern trend, however, grants more protection to the offeree. Courts now generally hold that, once the offeree has begun performance, the offeror's right to revoke the offer is suspended until the offeree has had a reasonable opportunity to complete performance. Once performance is completed, the offer is then said to have been accepted.

Key Concepts and Terms

- A contract requires mutual assent, which arises when one party (the offeror) makes an offer and the other party (the offeree) accepts it.

- The objective intention of the parties, expressed by their words or acts, determines whether an offer or an acceptance, and thus a contract, has been made.

- A valid offer must be reasonably definite and certain as to all material terms, and it must be communicated by the offeror and received by the offeree. A communication which merely initiates negotiations or solicits offers is not an offer. Advertisements, catalogs, and auctions are generally considered as only solicitations of offers. To create a contract, the person solicited must make an offer which must then be accepted.

- An offer may terminate by (1) revocation, (2) lapse of time, (3) rejection, (4) counteroffer, or (5) operation of law.

- Generally, an offer may be revoked at any time prior to acceptance. Exceptions to this general rule are (1) firm offers under the UCC, which must be kept open for the time stated or a reasonable time (not to exceed three months) and (2) options, which must be kept open for the time stated in the option contract.

- An acceptance, to be effective, must be unequivocal and unconditional. If an attempted acceptance contains material new terms or conditions, it is generally treated as a counteroffer.

- To be effective, acceptance of an offer must be communicated to the offeror. If the offer specifies a particular means or time for its acceptance, such requirements must be met. Otherwise, any reasonable means and time of acceptance is sufficient. The UCC generally permits acceptance in any manner and by any medium reasonable in the circumstances. Acceptance by mail or telegraph is ordinarily proper, becoming effective when the letter is deposited with the Postal Service or the telegram is delivered to the telegraph company. Acceptance by an unauthorized means is effective, if at all, only on its actual receipt by the offeror.

- An offer for a unilateral contract is accepted by performance of the requested act. When the requested act requires a period of time for performance, commencement of performance generally suspends the offeror's right of revocation, and the offeree is given a reasonable opportunity to complete performance.

- Acceptance
- Auction
- Counteroffer
- Firm Offer
- Mutual Assent

- Offer
- Offeror
- Offeree
- Option Contract
- Termination by Operation of Law

Questions and Case Problems

1. Is there an offer in each of the following situations? Why or why not? (a) A farmer says to the owner of a market chain, "I'll let you have as much corn as you need

next season. We'll hammer out the price next month." (b) A farmer says to the owner of a market chain, "I'll sell you all the corn I produce next season." (c) The farmer says, "I'll sell you all the corn I produce next season at $5 a bushel." (d) The farmer says, "I'll sell you 200 bushels of apples next season at $5 a bushel—as long as I'm able to produce that many." (e) The farmer says, "I'll sell you as many apples as you need next season as long as my kids don't get sick."

2. Sands says to Fraser, "I'll sell you my property over on Main Street for $25,000 cash." Fraser responds, "Sounds like a good deal. Will you give me a couple of weeks to see if I can come up with the money?" "Sure," says Sands. Five days later, Fraser comes to Sands with $25,000, and says, "I got the money, I want to buy your property." Sands responds, "I didn't think you would be able to get the money, so I sold the property to Wilson yesterday." What rights does Fraser have in this situation? Should Fraser have done anything differently? If so, what?

3. A written offer is made to Levin. At 10 a.m., Levin mails a letter of rejection, then changes his mind, and mails a letter of acceptance at 1 p.m. the same day. Is Levin's acceptance effective? Does it make any difference which of Levin's letters is received first by the offeror? What if the two letters are received at the same time, but one is opened and read before the other?

4. How does a court determine whether a contract has been formed?

5. Martin, offering in writing to pay Fong $2,000 to paint Martin's house, states, "This offer must be accepted in writing within 15 days from January 1." Fong does not respond in writing, but on January 2 he comes to Martin's house and begins painting it. He completes the job on January 8. Was there a contract? If there was not a contract, must Martin still pay Fong? Does it make any difference whether Martin was aware that Fong was painting the house?

6. Uhlman writes and signs a letter offering to sell Knapp 200 shares of Ace Corporation stock at $30 per share. The letter gives Knapp ten days in which to accept the offer. Through inadvertence, the letter is never mailed, but Knapp learns of its existence from Uhlman's secretary. Five days after the letter was written, Ace's stock doubles in value. Uhlman writes and mails a second letter revoking the previous offer. Before Knapp receives Uhlman's second letter he writes and mails a letter of acceptance to Uhlman. Is there a contract?

7. Collins orders a sleeping bag from Sparta's mail order catalog. Sparta delivers a different but comparable sleeping bag, together with a notice that the bag ordered was out of stock and that the bag delivered, although normally sold at a higher price, is being substituted at the lower price of the bag originally ordered. The notice states that if the substitution is unacceptable, the purchaser should return the bag to Sparta. Collins neither returns nor pays for the bag, and Sparta sues for breach of contract. Was there a valid contract?

8. Discuss the ways in which an offer may be terminated.

9. Draft an offer, a counteroffer, and an acceptance for the sale of a used car.

10. On May 1, State Bank offers a reward of $250 for information leading to the arrest and conviction of the person who had robbed the bank on the preceding day. On May 2, Lucas, unaware of the reward offer, informs the police that her sister is the robber. On May 3, Lucas learns of the reward offer and asks State Bank for the reward. The bank refuses, and Lucas sues. What is the result?

11 Consideration

11:1 Introduction to the Concept of Consideration

An agreement, to be an enforceable contract, must be supported by *consideration*. Consideration consists of the promises or performances that the parties to a contract exchange with each other. It is, in a sense, the "price" that one party to a contract pays for the promise or performance of the other party.

The concept of a *bargained-for exchange* is an important aspect of consideration; that is, the consideration given by one party to another must be what the latter has requested in exchange for his promise. The law normally will not enforce gratuitous promises. Rather, for a promise to constitute part of an enforceable contract, something must have been bargained for and given in exchange for that promise. The "something" is the element known as consideration.

In their everyday business dealings, people frequently honor the requirement of consideration without giving any thought to it as such. For example, if A offers to pay B $20 for a book, and B accepts the offer, each party has agreed, as part of the bargain, to provide consideration to the other party. A has promised to give B $20 as consideration for B's promise to give A the book, and B has promised to give A the book as consideration for A's promise to give B $20. On the other hand, if B merely offered to give A the book free of charge, and A immediately accepted the offer, there would be no enforceable contract, since A did not promise B any consideration in exchange for B's offer of the book.

The question whether consideration exists is frequently the subject of litigation. This question normally arises when one party to a contract (the promisee) seeks to enforce a promise made by another party (the promisor), because the promisor resists enforcement on the ground that his promise was not supported by consideration from the promisee. Various formulas have been advanced to determine the existence of consideration, with the most prominent formula focusing on the concepts of *legal detriment* and *legal benefit*. A detriment to the promisee exists when he does or promises to do something that he is not legally obligated to do, or when he refrains or promises to refrain from doing something that he otherwise legally could do. A benefit to the promisor exists when the promisor acquires some legal right to which he would not otherwise have been entitled. Thus, it has been said that consideration consists of some benefit to the promisor or some detriment to the promisee bargained for in exchange for the promisor's promise. It is important to remember that these terms are used in a legal sense and that they do not necessarily refer to actual financial or other material advantage or disadvantage to the parties.

The following case illustrates that there must be a detriment to the promisee at the request of the promisor for it to constitute consideration.

Fisher
v
Jackson
142 Conn 734, 118 A2d 316
(Connecticut Supreme Court of Errors, 1955)

[The plaintiff answered the defendant's advertisement offering a "permanent position" as a reporter and was hired in 1944. After his discharge in 1949, the plaintiff sued for breach of oral contract, claiming that, in exchange for the defendant's promise of lifetime employment, the plaintiff had given up a job with a bakery firm. A verdict was rendered for the plaintiff, and the defendant appealed.]

Wynne, Judge.

*   *   *

The substituted complaint alleged that the defendant, through his authorized agent, induced the plaintiff to give up his employment with a firm of bakers, where he was making $50 per week, under an oral contract that the employment would be for the life of the plaintiff or until he was physically disabled for work, with a yearly increase in salary of $5 per week. The defendant's contention is that there was no evidence that the parties had agreed upon such a contract. The defendant's claim is that the job under discussion was a permanent one rather than for a definite term and was terminable at will by either party.

In the absence of a consideration in addition to the rendering of services incident to the employment, an agreement for a permanent employment is no more than an indefinite general hiring, terminable at the will of either party without liability to the other. . . .

There is no occasion to discuss at length the claim advanced by the plaintiff that special consideration moved to the defendant because the plaintiff gave up his job with the bakery firm. The plaintiff did no more than give up other activities and interests in order to enter into the service of the defendant. The mere giving up of a job by one who decides to accept a contract for alleged life employment is but an incident necessary on his part to place himself in a position to accept and perform the contract; it is not consideration for a contract of life employment. . . .

The plaintiff argues that he suffered a detriment by giving up his job. To constitute sufficient consideration for a promise, an act or promise not only must be a detriment to the promisee but must be bargained for and given in exchange for the promise. . . . In the present case, the plaintiff's giving up of his job at the bakery was not something for which the defendant bargained in exchange for his promise of permanent employment. Nowhere in the plaintiff's testimony does it appear that the defendant's agent even suggested that the plaintiff give up the job he had with the bakery firm, much less that the agent induced him to do so. It would thus appear that there was not even a semblance of a claim that the giving up of the plaintiff's job was consideration for any promise that may have been made by the defendant's agent.

[Judgment reversed.]

Consideration may consist not only of a promise to take some action, but also of a promise to refrain from taking some specific action (*forbearance*). For example, assume that as a result of prior business dealings A owes B $1,000, that the date specified for payment of the debt has arrived, and that A has insufficient funds to make the payment. B intends to institute legal proceedings to collect the debt, and B so informs A. A requests B to refrain from taking legal action and to give A an additional six months in which to pay the debt. B agrees, on the condition that A agrees to pay an additional amount of money as interest on the original debt. A agrees. A's agreement to pay the additional sum is enforceable, since B's forbearance from filing a lawsuit during the specified period was consideration for A's promise.

11:2   Sufficiency and Adequacy of Consideration

In order for a binding contract to exist, the consideration bargained for must be legally sufficient. The courts tend to treat the terms "sufficient consideration" and "consideration" as synonymous, so that a promise or action that is legally insufficient is no consideration at all. It is nonetheless important to have some familiarity with the concept of sufficiency of consideration, particularly to avoid confusing *sufficiency* of consideration with *adequacy* of consideration.

To put the matter simply, if the consideration received by the promisor from the promisee is legally sufficient—that is, sufficient under contract law—the adequacy of the consideration is, under most circumstances, totally irrelevant. The courts have repeatedly emphasized that they will not inquire into the equality of the considerations exchanged between the parties to a contract, provided that each party in fact bargained for and accepted the consideration provided by the other party. For example, if A and B enter into a contract under which A agrees to sell to B a painting valued at $20,000 in exchange for B's promise to pay to A the sum of $1,000, the contract is supported by sufficient consideration from both parties, and a court asked to enforce the contract will not concern itself with the gross disparity between the value of the consideration being provided by each party.

 Although in theory the adequacy of consideration is irrelevant, in fact a court may be reluctant to enforce a contract when the consideration is clearly inadequate. This is particularly so when the party receiving the more valuable consideration is also the party who occupies the more powerful position in the negotiations leading to the contract. It is certainly permissible to drive a hard bargain, but one should always be wary of a bargain that is "too good," because a contract embodying such a bargain might be held invalid on a variety of grounds, such as fraud, mistake, or unconscionability.[1] Such a contract may also fail to meet specific statutory requirements designed to protect consumers or other unsuspecting persons. Thus, a prudent businessperson should not rely too heavily on the maxim that adequacy of consideration is irrelevant.

---

[1]The concepts of fraud, mistake, and unconscionability are discussed in Chapter 12.

The discussion in the following sections focuses on the legal sufficiency or insufficiency of various types of consideration.

11:3 Illusory Promises; Requirements and Output Contracts

A bilateral contract typically involves the exchange of promises by the parties to the contract, with each party's promise serving as consideration for that of the other party. To constitute consideration a promise must impose a binding obligation. The requirement that each party undertake some obligation has been expressed by the statement that there must be mutuality of obligation to have a valid contract. Sometimes, however, the promise of one party is only illusory in nature, in that the promise does not impose definite obligations on the party. For example, if A promises to sell B a used automobile for $2,000, and B promises to pay that price "if I decide I want the car," there is no mutuality of obligation, since B's promise to pay the money is not binding. Consequently, if B later decides that he wants the car and tenders the $2,000 to A, A is not obliged to sell the automobile for that amount, since B's illusory promise did not constitute consideration for A's promise.

Mutuality of obligation is necessary to what are known as *requirements* and *output contracts*. A requirements contract is one in which the seller agrees to supply all of a certain material required for the buyer's business over a specified time, in exchange for the buyer's promise to purchase all of such material from the seller. An output contract is one in which the buyer promises to purchase the seller's entire production, in exchange for the seller's promise to sell the entire production to the buyer. The main advantage of such contracts is that they provide a buyer with an assured source of supply and a seller with an assured market. Provided there is mutuality of obligation, such contracts are valid and enforceable.

Problems of *mutuality of obligation* arise, however, when one party, usually the buyer, inserts a "loophole" provision into the contract that has the effect of relieving the buyer from any obligation to purchase anything. Under this provision, if a seller agrees to supply all of a commodity that a buyer wants during a specified period, the buyer may, without violating the agreement, decide that he wants none of that commodity. Since the buyer under such an agreement has no obligation to purchase anything from the seller, the seller likewise is not obligated to sell anything to the buyer. On the other hand, if the seller agrees to supply and the buyer agrees to purchase all of a given commodity required in the buyer's business during a specified period, then there probably is a valid contract, since the buyer is obligated to purchase from the seller whatever he actually needs, not merely what he wants to purchase.

The UCC contains the following provision with respect to output and requirements contracts:

> A term which measures the quantity by the output of the seller or the requirements of the buyer means such actual output or requirements as may oc-

cur in good faith, except that no quantity unreasonably disproportionate to any stated estimate or in the absence of a stated estimate to any normal or otherwise comparable prior output or requirements may be tendered or demanded [UCC § 2-306(1)].

 As noted, requirements and output contracts can be extremely advantageous to both buyer and seller. When negotiating such a contract, therefore, a person should strive to ensure that there is true mutuality of obligation, so that the contract can be enforced.

If a buyer draws up the contract with such a loophole provision, the resulting one-sided contract may boomerang against him. For example, if a shortage of the particular commodity develops and the seller finds he can obtain a higher price elsewhere, the buyer will find that the assured supply has disappeared just at the time it is needed. The buyer should therefore be committed to buy all requirements in accordance with the provisions of the UCC, or at least to buy the minimum amount that will ensure that the contract is a meaningful one.

11:4   Performance or Promise to Perform Existing Obligation

Ordinarily, the performance of or a promise to perform an existing legal obligation does not constitute consideration for a contract, since a person suffers no legal detriment by doing or promising to do what he was already obligated to do. This principle has various applications. For example, a police officer has a legal duty to enforce the law and to apprehend violators. Thus, a law enforcement officer's apprehension of a suspected criminal cannot serve as consideration for a third party's offer of a reward for such apprehension; the officer was legally obligated to take such action before the reward was ever offered.

This principle also may be applied when a party attempts to modify a contract. Clearly, the parties to a contract can agree to modify its terms if each party provides consideration for the other's agreement to modify the contract. Sometimes, however, the modification is entirely one-sided. For example, assume A and B have entered into a contract whereby A has agreed to install a patio for B in exchange for B's promise to pay $2,000. Thereafter, A decides that the price is not sufficient, and informs B that she wants $2,500 instead. B agrees to pay the increased price. After completion of the patio, B refuses to pay A more than $2,000, claiming that the promise to pay the additional $500 was unsupported by any consideration. B's position would ordinarily prevail. Because A was already obligated to construct the patio at the time she sought the increased price and did not undertake any other obligations as consideration for B's additional promise to pay $500, the modified contract would not be valid.

Under some circumstances, a court might conclude that A was entitled to the additional $500, regardless of the existence of the previous obligation. The parties to a contract are free to cancel the contract if they so desire. If the court concluded that A and B had actually canceled their first contract, thereby releasing both parties from their obligations under that contract, and that they entered a new contract, then A's promise to construct the patio could constitute consideration for B's promise to pay $2,500. However, a court is likely to insist on very clear proof that there was actually a cancellation of the original contract, rather than an unsuccessful attempt by A to modify it and obtain a higher price.

A second possible situation in which A might prevail would be if A, after commencing work on the patio, discovered unforeseen problems which rendered the construction much more difficult, and hence more expensive, than anticipated when the contract was drafted. Under such circumstances some courts, using a variety of rationales, would enforce B's second promise to pay the higher price, even though technically A did not provide additional consideration for that promise. It is important to stress, however, that the unforeseen difficulties must be substantial. For example, the existence of soil conditions drastically different from those anticipated may constitute unforeseen difficulties in a contract that calls for excavation of land. On the other hand, the mere fact that the cost of materials used by a contractor increases or that there is a labor strike is not considered by the courts as an unforeseen difficulty sufficient to warrant a change in one party's obligations under the contract without consideration being provided by the other party.[2]

It should be noted that under UCC § 2-209(1) a contract for the sale of goods may be modified without consideration. There is a requirement of good faith, however, to prevent the extortion of modifications of sales contracts without legitimate commercial reasons.[3]

11:5 Past Consideration

It frequently happens that one person, without any request, performs services for another person, and that at some future date the benefited person promises to pay the first person for the services rendered. Here, the promise to pay generally is considered unenforceable, since the consideration for the promise is rendered before the promise is made. This consideration, called past consideration, is insufficient to support a promise.

Cases in which an attempt is made to enforce a promise on the basis of past consideration must be distinguished from cases in which the past services were rendered in exchange for an implied promise to pay for them. For example, if one person requests another to perform some act but makes no express promise to pay for that act, the courts often will first imply such a promise and find that an implied contract exists, and then view the subsequent promise as evidence of the reasonable value of such services.

[2]In some cases the existence of unforeseen problems might justify a court's cancellation of a contract on the ground of material mistake in the formation of the original contract. Mutual and unilateral mistakes are discussed in Chapter 12.
[3]UCC § 2-209, Comment 2; UCC § 1-203. UCC § 2-302, relating to unconscionability, might also be relied on to prevent extortionate modifications. Unconscionability is discussed in Chapter 12. Sales contracts are discussed in Chapter 19.

11:6   Moral Obligation

As stated previously, consideration may consist of either a legal detriment to the promisee or a legal benefit to the promisor. A mere moral obligation to do or to refrain from doing some act does not constitute consideration. For example, a promise made by a grandparent to a favorite grandchild to finance the child's college education, "in consideration of the love and affection" of the grandparent for the grandchild, is not enforceable because love and affection do not constitute a legally sufficient consideration. It should be noted, however, that if the grand-parent does pay for the grandchild's college education, then later sues for reim-bursement on the ground that there was no legal obligation to make such payments, the claim will be rejected because the payments will be considered a gift.

Application of the principle that past consideration or moral obligations do not constitute sufficient consideration could produce harsh results. The following case demonstrates how one court avoided a solution that, while in accord with the principle, would have been harsh.

Griffin

v

Louisville Trust Co.
312 Ky 145, 226 SW2d 786
(Kentucky Court of Appeals, 1950)

[Prior to his death William Mann had given Carrie Griffin, his housekeeper, a check for $6,000, but she was unable to cash the check due to insufficient funds in Mr. Mann's account. After his death she sought to recover the money from his estate, which was worth $130,000. To do so, it was necessary to prove that the check was given by Mr. Mann in exchange for consideration from Mrs. Griffin.]

Sims, Chief Justice.

*   *   *

... [I]t is admitted that if this check was given in payment for past services which Mrs. Griffin rendered deceased, she cannot recover. He had paid her in full by the week for the services as they were rendered, and even though her services were worth more than the wages she received under her contract with deceased, there would be no consideration for

this check since a moral obligation does not furnish a consideration for a new contract where there is no legal obligation. . . .

If there was any consideration to support this check, it was for services to be performed in the future for Mr. Mann by Mrs. Griffin. It will be necessary to give a brief picture of the Mann household, the services Mrs. Griffin ren-dered and then to turn to the evidence for a solution of this controversy.

Mrs. Griffin started working for Mr. Mann in 1938 as a housekeeper when she was 58 years of age. He had been totally blind for some fifteen years and lived in a large house in Louisville with two sisters, one of whom was deaf and dumb. The afflicted sister died soon after Mrs. Griffin entered Mr. Mann's ser-vice and the other sister lived only about a year. Mrs. Griffin's wages were $8 a week which were raised to $10 in about 1940. In De-cember 1945 her wages were increased to $25 per week at the suggestion of a nephew of Mr. Mann, and [he] gave her a $50 Christmas pres-ent that year.

Mr. Mann was a retired traveling salesman, whose chief interest was in flowers and he maintained a greenhouse on his premises. Although totally blind and a man advanced in years, Mr. Mann was quite active about his place and in caring for his flowers. Mrs. Griffin did everything for him: the housekeeping, the marketing, the cooking, the laundry, and the firing of the furnace. In addition to all this, she read to Mr. Mann and went about town with him and would go into his lockbox. She wrote all of his checks, which he signed. She was Mr. Mann's eyes and hands and cared for him 24 hours a day. Being unable to distinguish night from day, Mr. Mann would at times water and work his flowers in the middle of the night, and sometimes got lost in his garden and would have to call Mrs. Griffin to come and get him. She seems never to have lost patience with, nor tired from serving him.

. . . Oscar Nettleton, an employee of the Yellow Cab Company for 15 years and who often drove Mr. Mann, testified that Mrs. Griffin's health had failed under her strenuous duties. He stated Mr. Mann said, "Mrs. Griffin [was] a godsend to him"; and that he did not want her to die before him because, "I don't know what I would do without her." Deceased mentioned to him several times that he had drawn this $6,000 check and had given it to Mrs. Griffin.

Mrs. Julia Spellman, a next-door neighbor to deceased, testified that Mr. Mann regarded Mrs. Griffin very highly and appreciated her services to him and once told witness that he didn't think he could live very long without Mrs. Griffin.

Mr. C. B. Sims, a postal employee for 39 years whose home was next to deceased, stated that Mr. Mann's blindness made him peculiar

and "in later years he seemed to draw himself in more . . . and had great consolation having her [Mrs. Griffin] around, and depending upon her almost like a child."

Mrs. Marie L. Haury, a life-long friend of deceased and his family, testified that Mr. Mann told her of his great appreciation of Mrs. Griffin when witness visited his home. She expressed herself in these words: "He said he didn't know what he would do without her. In his later years, when his health became worse, he expressed to me that he was afraid she might die before him, or would have to leave him, and he said he did not know what he would do without her."

Here, we have an old, blind man with no relatives nearer than nephews, living alone in a large house with an old lady who had served him for more than seven years and to such an extent that she had become broken in health, which fact he knew. Mr. Mann appears to have been a gentleman of refinement and appreciation. He was worth something over $130,000 and was paying Mrs. Griffin but a meager wage for the service she was performing, and his great concern was that she might leave him before he died. It is clear to our minds from the competent testimony of the four witnesses to whom we have just referred that Mr. Mann executed this $6,000 check to Mrs. Griffin in consideration of her remaining with and caring for him until the end of his days, which she did, and not for services theretofore performed for which he had paid her in full.

[Judgment for Mrs. Griffin.]

11:7 Compromise or Settlement of Claim: Composition of Creditors

In the course of a business relationship between two persons, disputes may arise as to the parties' exact obligations. Of course, the parties may seek to settle their differences in court, but there are many advantages to seeking an out-of-court solution through a compromise and settlement agreement. A compromise agreement is a contract, and like any other contract it must be supported by consideration. The presence or absence of consideration normally depends on whether the compromise relates to a *liquidated* or to an *unliquidated debt*. A liquidated debt is one whose exact amount is not disputed by the parties. "Unliquidated" refers to the fact that the parties are in disagreement as to the amount owed.

A compromise agreement entered into to resolve an unliquidated claim is considered valid, while a compromise agreement entered into to dispose of a liquidated claim generally is considered unenforceable. The reason is simple. In the case of an unliquidated claim, the parties commonly split the difference in some manner, with the creditor agreeing to accept less than he believes is due, while the debtor agrees to pay more than he believes is due. Thus, the consideration for the creditor's agreement to accept less consists of the debtor's agreement to pay more, and vice versa. However, if a creditor holding a liquidated claim agrees to accept less than the full amount from the debtor, there is no consideration for the agreement, since the debtor admittedly had an obligation to pay that amount. For example, if A claims that B owes her $100, but B claims that he owes A only $50, each party incurs a legal detriment if they agree to compromise on $75. However, if A and B both agree that the amount due is $100, but A agrees to accept $75, A has incurred a legal detriment but B has not. If B proceeds to pay the $75, A can ordinarily insist that the additional $25 be paid as well, regardless of the agreement to accept $75.

Where there is a dispute as to the amount of a debt, and the debtor sends the creditor a check with words to the effect that the check is presented as payment in full of the indebtedness, the creditor's act of cashing the check will ordinarily be considered as acceptance of the debtor's compromise offer, and the debt will be considered discharged. In the case of liquidated claims, the effect of accepting such a check is less certain. Most courts have decided that acceptance of a check under such circumstances does not prevent the creditor from seeking the additional amount due. Under the UCC, however, accepting the check operates to discharge the debt (UCC § 3-408). However, most courts have held that a creditor under the UCC, by writing the words "without prejudice" or "under protest" on the check, may cash a full-payment check and later seek payment of the balance the creditor believes is still owed. This may also be done with unliquidated debts (UCC § 1-207).

Often, a debtor is unable to pay the liquidated claims of several creditors. Under such circumstances, an agreement called a *composition with creditors* is sometimes reached. Under a composition agreement, two or more creditors of the same debtor agree to accept payment of a specified percentage of their respective claims as full satisfaction of the debts. The significant factor in a composition agreement is that it involves an agreement not only between the debtor and his various creditors, but also among the creditors themselves.[4] Composition agreements are generally enforceable, and a creditor may not later seek payment of the balance of the claim. The rationale for sustaining such agreements varies. Some courts classify composi-

---

[4]Composition agreements are discussed more fully in 31:3.

tion agreements as an exception to the consideration requirement, while other courts stress that the consideration received by the creditors consists of the promises of their fellow creditors to forgo the opportunity to obtain full payment of their claims.

11:8 Exceptions to Requirement of Consideration

There are various exceptions to the rule that consideration is an essential part of a contract. The following exceptions are among the more important ones.

Promissory Estoppel   Under the doctrine of *promissory estoppel*, a promisor may not assert that his promise is unenforceable even though the promisee gave no consideration for the promise. The doctrine is applicable in a situation in which a promisor makes a promise and intends or should reasonably expect that the promisee rely on it, and the promisee in fact relies on it in some definite and substantial manner. The basis of the doctrine is that enforcement of the promise is the only way to avoid injustice under these circumstances. The following case illustrates one situation in which a court concluded that the doctrine was properly applied.

Hoffman

v

Red Owl Stores, Inc.
26 Wis 2d 683, 133 NW2d 267
(Wisconsin Supreme Court, 1965)

[Hoffman, the owner of a bakery in Wautoma, Wisconsin, entered into discussions with representatives of Red Owl Stores, a supermarket chain, about operating a Red Owl franchise store. Hoffman had $18,000 to invest, and Red Owl representatives assured him that amount would be sufficient to establish him in a store. Negotiations continued for about two years, during which time Hoffman, at Red Owl's suggestion, bought and operated a small grocery for three months, then sold it; paid $1,000 down on a store lot in Chilton, Wisconsin, where his Red Owl franchise was to be located; sold his bakery in Wautoma; and rented a house in anticipation of a move to Chilton. Red Owl representatives consistently assured Hoffman that he would obtain a Red Owl franchise. However, as time passed, Red Owl first told Hoffman that $24,100 would be necessary, then that $26,000 would be required, and finally that $34,000 would have to be invested. Hoffman

refused to invest $34,000, negotiations were terminated, and Hoffman sued Red Owl for breach of agreement. The trial court entered judgment for Hoffman, and Red Owl appealed.]

Currie, Chief Justice.

*   *   *

Recognition of a Cause of Action Grounded on Promissory Estoppel

Sec. 90 of *Restatement, 1 Contracts*, provides (at p. 110):

"A promise which the promisor should reasonably expect to induce action or forbearance of a definite and substantial character on the part of the promisee and which does induce such action or forbearance is binding if injustice can be avoided only by enforcement of the promise."

... Many courts of other jurisdictions have seen fit over the years to adopt the principle of promissory estoppel, and the tendency in that direction continues. As Mr. Justice McFaddin, speaking in behalf of the Arkansas court, well stated, that the development of the law of promissory estoppel "is an attempt by the courts to keep remedies abreast of increased moral consciousness of honesty and fair representations in all business dealings." . . .

Because we deem the doctrine of promissory estoppel, as stated in sec. 90 of *Restatement, 1 Contracts,* is one which supplies a needed tool which courts may employ in a proper case to prevent injustice, we endorse and adopt it.

Applicability of Doctrine to Facts of This Case

The record here discloses a number of promises and assurances given to Hoffman by Lukowitz in behalf of Red Owl upon which plaintiffs relied and acted upon to their detriment.

Foremost were the promises that for the sum of $18,000 Red Owl would establish Hoffman in a store. After Hoffman had sold his grocery store and paid the $1,000 on the Chilton lot, the $18,000 figure was changed to $24,100. Then in November, 1961, Hoffman was assured that if the $24,100 figure were increased by $2,000 the deal would go through. Hoffman was induced to sell his grocery store fixtures and inventory in June, 1961, on the promise that he would be in his new store by fall. In November, plaintiffs sold their bakery building on the urging of defendants and on the assurance that this was the last step necessary to have the deal with Red Owl go through.

. . .There remains for consideration the question of law raised by defendants that agreement was never reached on essential factors necessary to establish a contract between Hoffman and Red Owl. . . . This poses the question of whether the promise necessary to sustain a cause of action for promissory estoppel must embrace all essential details of a proposed transaction between promisor and promisee so as to be the equivalent of an offer that would result in a binding contract be-

tween the parties if the promisee were to accept the same.

Originally the doctrine of promissory estoppel was invoked as a substitute for consideration rendering a gratuitous promise enforceable as a contract. See Williston, *Contracts* (1st ed.), p. 307, sec. 139. In other words, the acts of reliance by the promisee to his detriment provided a substitute for consideration. If promissory estoppel were to be limited to only those situations where the promise giving rise to the cause of action must be so definite with respect to all details that a contract would result were the promise supported by consideration, then the defendants' instant promises to Hoffman would not meet this test. However, sec. 90 of *Restatement, 1 Contracts,* does not impose the requirement that the promise giving rise to the cause of action must be so comprehensive in scope as to meet the requirements of an offer that would ripen into a contract if accepted by the promisee. Rather the conditions imposed are:

(1) Was the promise one which the promisor should reasonably expect to induce action or forbearance of a definite and substantial character on the part of the promisee?

(2) Did the promise induce such action or forbearance?

(3) Can injustice be avoided only be enforcement of the promise?

We deem it would be a mistake to regard an action grounded on promissory estoppel as the equivalent of a breach of contract action. As Dean Boyer points out, it is desirable that fluidity in the application of the concept be maintained. . . .

We conclude that injustice would result here if plaintiffs were not granted some relief because of the failure of defendants to keep their promises which induced plaintiffs to act to their detriment.

[Judgment affirmed.]

Charitable Subscriptions   When a person pledges to donate money to a college, church, or similar charitable organization, consideration for the pledge—called a charitable subscription—ordinarily is lacking. Regardless of that fact, the courts tend to enforce charitable subscriptions. Various rationales have been offered in support of their enforceability. Some courts have held that the mutual promises of all the subscribers operate as consideration for the specific promises of each subscriber, while others have relied on a theory of promissory estoppel. The strong public policy of supporting charitable institutions has been the paramount factor in determining that charitable subscriptions may be enforced.

Promise to Pay Debt Rendered Unenforceable by Statute of Limitations or Discharge in Bankruptcy   If a debtor makes a promise to pay a debt rendered unenforceable by the *statute of limitations* or by a discharge in bankruptcy, most courts will hold the new promise enforceable, even though consideration is lacking for the promise. Each state has laws commonly known as statutes of limitations, which provide that various types of actions must be brought within specified time periods. The effect of failure to file an action within the appropriate time period is that the claim becomes unenforceable. Similarly, when a debtor receives a discharge in bankruptcy—that is, when all debts are discharged by the bankruptcy proceeding—they are unenforceable, even though the creditors received only a partial payment on such debts.

   If a debtor makes a new promise to pay a debt rendered unenforceable by the statute of limitations or by a discharge in bankruptcy, most courts will hold the new promise enforceable, even though consideration is lacking for the promise. Moreover, if the debtor in some way acknowledges the existence of the debt after passage of the period of limitations, most courts will hold such acknowledgment to be the equivalent of a new promise to pay and will enforce payment of the debt.

Contracts under Seal   At common law no consideration was necessary to support promises made in a contract under seal. Most states have, however, changed the common-law rule. The UCC provides that the law relating to sealed instruments does not apply to sealed writings with respect to the sale of goods (UCC § 2-203).

Key Concepts and Terms

- Consideration consists of the promises or acts that the parties to a contract, as part of their bargain, exchange with each other. Consideration may consist of legal benefit to the promisor or legal detriment to the promisee. An illusory promise cannot serve as consideration for the other party's promise.

- The consideration exchanged by the parties to a contract must be legally sufficient, but a court generally will not concern itself with the adequacy of the consideration.

- A promise to perform an already existing legal obligation does not, under most circumstances, constitute consideration. Thus, when an existing contract is modified, each party ordinarily must provide consideration. However, when a sales contract is modified, consideration is not necessary under the UCC.

- Past consideration is insufficient to support a promise.

- A moral obligation does not constitute consideration.

- A compromise and settlement agreement requires consideration from both parties. A compromise agreement is valid when a debt is unliquidated. Where a debt is liquidated a compromise agreement is invalid.

- A composition with creditors agreement is an agreement among the debtor and his creditors that each creditor will be paid only a percentage of the debt.

- The courts will enforce certain promises even in the absence of consideration. Such promises include (1) promises held enforceable under the doctrine of promissory estoppel, (2) charitable subscriptions, and (3) promises to pay debts rendered unenforceable by a statute of limitations or a discharge in bankruptcy.

- Bargained-for Exchange
- Composition with Creditors
- Compromise or Settlement of Claim
- Consideration
- Forbearance
- Legal Benefit
- Legal Detriment
- Liquidated Debt
- Mutuality of Obligation
- Output Contract
- Promissory Estoppel
- Requirements Contract
- Statute of Limitations
- Unliquidated Debt

Questions and Case Problems

1. A, having fallen off a cliff, is clinging by his fingernails to the edge. Unable to pull himself up, he asks B, who is standing nearby, to rescue him. B says, "I will save you if you promise to pay me $5,000." A promises to do so, and B then rescues A. Do A and B have an enforceable contract (is A's promise supported by consideration)?

2. Define and discuss the concept of consideration. Why do courts insist that a contract be supported by consideration?

3. "Plaintiff [Clausen] alleges that it had been a wholesale distributor of defendant's [Hamm Brewing Co.] products since 1911. Clausen states that in 1950 an oral contract was made with Hamm to become an exclusive Hamm's beer distributor for an area defined as Southern Minneapolis and contiguous suburbs. In reliance upon said contract Clausen alleges (1) they discontinued all competitors' products and (2) purchased and maintained inventories, sales, advertising, warehouse space, personnel, and facilities as a Hamm's exclusive distributor.... It is alleged that in April 1963 Hamm [illegally] terminated its oral agreement." Do the facts alleged show the existence of a contract supported by consideration? If not, might the plaintiff recover under some other theory?

4. Define and discuss requirements and output contracts. What are the advantages and disadvantages of such contracts?

5. Hunter was insolvent when he died; there was not enough money in his estate to pay his funeral expenses. Plaintiff bank holds Hunter's promissory note for $3,700, which represents a claim against Hunter's estate. Thereafter, Hunter's widow gives the bank her promissory note, "in consideration" of the bank's surrender to her of Hunter's note. Plaintiff bank brings an action against Mrs. Hunter to re-

cover on her promissory note. How should the case be decided?

6. Under what circumstances is consideration unnecessary to the formation of a contract?

7. Schwartzreich contracts in writing to work for Bauman-Basch for $90 per week for a period of one year. Prior to beginning work under the contract, Schwartzreich is offered $115 per week to work for a competitor of Bauman-Basch. Learning of this offer, Bauman-Basch offers to pay Schwartzreich $100 per week if Schwartzreich will stay. Schwartzreich accepts and a new contract, identical to the first one except for the weekly salary, is drafted. The signatures are torn off the original contract. Schwartzreich is subsequently discharged before expiration of the one-year employment period, and he brings a lawsuit for breach of the second contract. Can Schwartzreich recover on the second contract?

8. Levine leases a store to Blumenthal for two years, the rental to be $175 per month the first year and $200 per month the second year. Before the end of the first year, Blumenthal advises Levine that due to business difficulties it will be impossible to pay the increased rental during the second year. Levine thereupon agrees to continue accepting $175 per month. After the end of the lease, Levine sues Blumenthal to collect the additional $25 per month for the second year. Can Levine recover?

9. A requests his friend, B, an automobile mechanic, to repair A's automobile during B's spare time. B does so, and A, after driving the automobile, tells B that she did a fine job and promises to pay her $300. Is A's promise to pay B enforceable? Would your answer be any different if A had never requested B to repair the automobile?

10. Boehm is pregnant and believes that Fiege is the father. Prior to the child's birth, Fiege promises to pay child support if Boehm does not institute a paternity proceeding against him. Some time after the child's birth, Fiege learns that blood tests indicated that he could not possibly be the child's father, and he discontinues the support payments. Boehm files criminal paternity proceedings, but Fiege is found not guilty. Boehm then files an action to enforce Fiege's promise of support. Is she entitled to recover?

12 Reality of Consent

12:1 Introduction

Consent of the parties is an essential element of a contract. Under some circumstances a contract that appears to be valid is not enforceable because the consent is not a "real" consent, but a consent acquired through fraud, honest misrepresentation, mistake, duress, or undue influence. Contracts that are entered into in any of these ways, and other contracts that are totally or partially unenforceable for lack of consent—adhesion contracts and unconscionable contracts—are covered in this chapter.

12:2 Fraud

Fraud may assume so many different forms that the courts have declined to adopt any all-embracing definition of the term. Instead, the existence of fraud is determined by the facts and circumstances in a particular case. Indeed, it has been considered better not to define the term, so that the courts may retain the liberty to deal with fraud as it arises and in whatever form it takes. However, it may be said as a general rule that fraud comprises anything calculated to deceive and to take unfair advantage of another.

Fraud may exist in either the inducement or the execution of a contract. Fraud in the inducement of a contract exists when one party obtains the agreement of the other party by some fraudulent representation, such as by stating that the performance called for by the contract is other than as actually stated in the contract itself. A contract tainted by fraud in the inducement is generally considered voidable. Fraud in the execution of a contract consists of a surreptitious act that relates to the signing of the contract. For example, substituting one document for another at the time of signing would be fraud in the execution and would generally render a contract void. Such fraud is less common than fraud in the inducement and will not be further considered here.

The defrauded party has the option of seeking either monetary damages or annulment of the contract. Under the UCC the remedies available to a defrauded party to a sales contract include all remedies available for nonfraudulent breach of such a contract (UCC § 2-721).

To prove fraud, a person claiming to have been defrauded into entering a contract must establish the following elements: (1) that the other party misrepresented (or, under some circumstances, concealed or failed to disclose) a material fact, with knowledge of the falsity of the representation or with reckless disregard of its truth; (2) that the other party had the intent to deceive and to induce the person to act in reliance on such misrepresentation; (3) that he in fact reasonably relied on the misrepresentation; and (4) that he sustained some damage or injury. These elements are discussed individually in the sections that follow.

12:3   Misrepresentation of Fact

One element of fraud is a false representation about a present or past fact. Representations about nonfactual matters generally cannot form the basis of a charge of fraud, even though they may be false. A common method of determining whether a representation is one of fact is to inquire whether the matter asserted is capable of exact knowledge. If it is, then the representation is considered one of fact. Fraudulent representations may consist of words, acts, or a combination of words and acts.

EXAMPLE
While looking under the hood of a customer's car, a service station attendant squirts gasoline on the fuel pump. He then tells the customer to take a look at the fuel pump. The customer, seeing that the fuel pump appears to be defective, asks the attendant to replace it. Although the attendant never told the customer that the fuel pump was defective, the attendant, by his conduct and his request to look at the fuel pump, did represent that the fuel pump was defective.

Misrepresentation of Opinion   The expression of an opinion—even an erroneous one—does not normally constitute fraud. This is so because a matter of opinion is not capable of exact knowledge; reasonable people may have opinions that differ. The rule that fraud may not be based on a misrepresentation of opinion is frequently applied to situations in which one party to a transaction makes statements concerning the value, quality, or condition of property.

Value is considered largely a matter of judgment. When a person makes a statement concerning the value of some particular property, the statement is treated as only that person's opinion, not as a statement of fact. Even if the statement of value was erroneous, there is no fraud. For example, assume that the owner of a horse tells a prospective buyer that the horse is worth $1,000, and the buyer purchases the horse for that amount. Several other people subsequently tell the purchaser that the horse is not worth more than $800. The buyer cannot claim fraud, since the original owner's statement as to the horse's value was merely his personal estimate or opinion, not a statement of fact.

Statements of value should be distinguished from statements of cost. While a claim that some item has a certain value is only an opinion, a claim that the seller actually paid a certain amount for the item is in the realm of fact, since it is capable of knowledge. If a seller says, "This car is easily worth $1,000," it is only an opinion. However, if he says, "I paid $1,000 for this car," he has made an assertion of fact.

Representations as to the quality of products or other property are also considered statements of opinion rather than fact. Statements that a television set is well made and that a particular company produces high quality products, for example, generally are treated merely as expressions of the opinions of the persons making these statements.

The rule that fraud cannot be based on mere expressions of opinion is commonly applied in the area of so-called "trade talk" or dealer's puffing. It often occurs in sales situations and consists of the seller's describing the article to be sold in expansive or glowing terms. The courts generally have held that such "trade talk" does not constitute fraud because it is only an expression of the seller's opinion. Moreover, the courts have often expressed the view that no reasonable person would act in reliance on trade talk.

Misrepresentation Concerning Future Events or Intentions   Misrepresentations as to future events do not constitute fraud since they do not relate to some past or present fact. Statements as to probabilities, predictions of future business results, and expressions as to what a person intends to do in the future, even if ultimately false, are not classified as fraud. For example, assume that a furnace salesperson informs a potential customer that the customer's usage of natural gas should decrease 20 percent if an old furnace is replaced with a new one that the salesperson has to offer. The customer agrees, the new furnace is installed, and natural gas usage decreases only 5 percent. Since the salesperson's statements were only predictions of a future event, there is no fraud.

Misrepresentation of Law   Everyone is presumed to know the law and to have equal means of obtaining knowledge of the law. Therefore, a person is generally not considered to be deceived by misrepresentations of law. For example, a statement as to the legal effect of a particular written instrument, even if it is a false statement, does not constitute fraud.

Under some circumstances, a representation as to a matter of law might amount to a representation of a fact, and thus form the basis of fraud. For example, an assertion that a court has ruled a certain way in a particular case, although a representation as to a matter of law, might also be considered a fraudulent misrepresentation of fact if the court actually had not ruled at all or had clearly ruled to the contrary of what was stated.

Distinguishing Factual from Nonfactual Representations   The rules as to the types of misrepresentations that may be classified as fraudulent are fairly straightforward, but application of the rules is not always so simple. It is frequently difficult to distinguish between expressions of opinion and ones of fact, and the circumstances under which a statement was made often must be considered in determining whether it was intended as a factual statement or merely a statement of opinion. For example, assume that a contractor tells a homeowner that it will take one eight-hour day and ten sacks of cement to make a patio. On the basis of that representation the contractor charges, and the homeowner pays, a specified price for performance of the job. In fact, it takes only four hours and five sacks of cement to perform the job. Should the contractor's representations be viewed as statements of fact, based on his superior knowledge gained from past jobs, or merely as estimates (opinions) of the amount of labor and materials necessary?

A representation sometimes constitutes a mixture of fact and opinion. In such a situation, the representation may be fraudulent if it is false. For example, it is one thing to say that particular property is "good agricultural land." Such a statement merely expresses an opinion, since there may be differences of opinion as to what type of land is good agricultural land. It is quite another thing to say that property is "good agricultural land because it has low alkali soil"; the alkalinity of the soil may be measured, placing such a statement in the realm of fact. Thus, it is easy to move from statements of opinion to statements of fact, and the line between fact and opinion is neither clear nor distinct.

12:4   Exceptions to Misrepresentation of Fact Requirement

There are various exceptions to the rule that fraud may be based only on a misrepresentation of past or present fact. The major exceptions typically involve one or both of two types of misrepresentations: (1) a misrepresentation made in the context of a confidential relationship and (2) a misrepresentation made by a party who had or claimed to have superior knowledge about the subject under discussion. In these situations, misrepresentations of opinion or of law may be considered fraudulent. For example, as noted above, the courts traditionally have held puffing to be an expression of opinion and, as such, not fraudulent. However, if a seller who has superior knowledge or means of knowledge about the value or quality of a product misrepresents the value or quality to an ignorant buyer, the misrepresentation can be the basis of fraud. Similarly, if a party who has superior knowledge of the law misrepresents the law to another party, as an attorney might do to a client, the misrepresentation will constitute fraud. Today, the modern tendency is to view misrepresentations of opinion as fraud if they are made intentionally and with the purpose of inducing another person to rely on them. In addition, various statutes now protect the rights of purchasers and other consumers.

 When expressing an opinion, a businessperson should be sure that there is some factual basis that justifies the opinion. The businessperson should not unreasonably exaggerate the qualities or value of a product or service, especially when the businessperson has superior knowledge about that product or service. Being honest will not only help to avoid costly and time-consuming legal problems, it will also help to maintain goodwill with customers and other business contacts.

12:5   Concealment or Nondisclosure of Fact

Under most circumstances, one party to a contract has no obligation to disclose any fact to another. Silence does not constitute fraud, even though it may result in the other person's acting on the basis of erroneous assumptions. In other words, one party may take advantage of the other party's ignorance. This is particularly so when both parties have equal access to the facts. However, where one person, by words or conduct, actively and intentionally attempts to suppress material facts and to conceal them from another, fraud may be found. This is called active concealment and can be fraudulent because it can create in the other party a false impression of a fact.

In some situations, there is a duty to disclose information. This duty is typically found (1) when a relationship of confidence and trust exists between the parties to the contract, (2) when one party to a contract has superior knowledge or means of knowledge of the undisclosed facts, or (3) when one party makes a voluntary partial disclosure to the other party that is likely to result in creating a mistaken impression about some material fact. In this last situation, the duty is greater if the partial disclosure is accompanied by intentional concealment of other facts to mislead the other party.

EXAMPLE
A, a dealer in reptiles, has for sale several snakes that have been captured from the wild. He knows that these snakes will refuse to eat in captivity and will literally starve themselves to death. B comes into the store to purchase a snake and selects one of these wild snakes. Not having any experience with snakes, B asks A if the snake is healthy. A says that he has thoroughly examined the snake and that it appears to be free from disease, a true statement. A does not disclose to B that the snake has consistently refused to eat since its capture. Fraudulent concealment of the material fact that the snake has not eaten in captivity might be found on several grounds: (1) it might be found that A, by virtue of his superior knowledge concerning reptiles, had a duty of disclosure to B; or (2) it might be found that A, by his selective partial disclosure, intentionally misled B into thinking that the snake was a healthy specimen.

As should be obvious by now, the line between misrepresentation of fact and concealment of fact is not always a distinct one, and fraud may be based on a combination of misrepresentation of some facts and concealment of others.

12:6   Intent to Deceive

The essence of fraud is that one party has intentionally deceived and thereby taken unfair advantage of another. Proof of intent to deceive is, therefore, an essential element of a fraud action. Usually this intent is established by circumstantial evidence—that is, by reference to the other circumstances of the transaction. A showing that a representation was made either with knowledge of its falsity or with reckless disregard of its truth or falsity generally leads to the conclusion that the representation was made with intent to deceive and to induce the other party to rely on it.

12:7 Materiality and Reliance

To establish fraud, it must be shown that a misrepresentation was of a material fact and that the innocent party reasonably relied, to his detriment, on the misrepresentation. The test of materiality is whether the fact was of sufficient importance that it influenced the other party to enter into the contract. The test of reliance is whether the person would have entered into the contract but for the particular misrepresentation. These tests are tantamount to proof of fraud. If one party misrepresented a material fact, but the other party was not misled and did not rely on the misrepresentation, there would be no fraud. For example, assume that the owner of an apartment building tells a potential buyer that the building was constructed 10 years ago. The potential buyer, although she knows that the building was actually constructed 15 years ago, proceeds to enter a contract to purchase the apartment building. If the buyer should later bring suit against the original owner claiming fraud on the basis of the misrepresentation as to the building's age, no fraud should be found, since the buyer was not misled by and did not rely on the misrepresentation.

Under some circumstances, the reasonableness of a party's reliance on a particular misrepresentation is considered in determining fraud. The reasonableness is measured by the rule that one party to a contract cannot rely on a representation by the other party if no reasonable person under similar circumstances would do so. Thus, in some situations a party may have a duty to investigate whether certain representations are true or not.

12:8 Damage or Injury

To secure relief on the basis of fraud, the injured party must have suffered some damage or injury as a consequence of his reliance on the misrepresentation. He may ask for monetary damages or for termination, known as *rescission*, of the contract. Where monetary damages are sought, there must of course be a showing of a pecuniary loss. Where rescission of the contract is sought, a showing of monetary loss is usually not required; a showing that the party was induced by the misrepresentation to enter a contract that he would not otherwise have entered is sufficient. Remedies and damages for breach of contract are more fully discussed in Chapter 18.

The following case illustrates a number of the principles that have been discussed in the preceding pages, and also demonstrates the interrelationship of the various rules and their application in the context of a specific fact setting.

Holland
v
Lentz
239 Or 332, 397 P2d 787
(Oregon Supreme Court, 1964)

[Lentz, a real estate broker, contracted with the Hollands to sell them a new house in a real estate development for $23,500. The Hollands subsequently became dissatisfied with the house and sued for damages. They claimed that Lentz had induced them to purchase the house by means of false representations about the condition of the premises. They claimed that Lentz had represented that the house was "of good quality and that it was constructed in a good and workmanlike manner." They also alleged various specific misrepresentations, including the following: (1) that the east side of the house was insulated; (2) that the floor and walls of the basement had been underlaid with Visqueen; and (3) that damaged appliances would be repaired, as would wallboard defects. The jury returned a verdict for the Hollands, and Lentz appealed.]

Lusk, Justice.

*   *   *

Defendant moved for a directed verdict on the ground, among others, that none of the representations alleged is actionable. He contends that they are all mere expressions of opinion or promissory statements which do not afford a foundation for an action in deceit [fraud]. We have concluded that the motion was properly denied, although we agree with counsel for defendant that neither the representation that the house was "of good quality and that it was constructed in a good and workmanlike manner" nor the promissory statements alleged are actionable. We think, however, that the evidence concerning the representation as to insulation of the house was sufficient to carry the case to the jury, though the judgment must be reversed for errors committed upon the trial. . . .

At the time defendant showed the house to the plaintiffs they called his attention to a number of minor defects which, according to the plaintiffs, he assured them would be corrected. He also told them that it was a well-built house. Mrs. Holland testified: . . .

"Q Would you state to the Court what Mr. Lentz stated generally as to the quality of the house?

"A Yes. He said this was a fine house, it was very good. And I asked him who the builder was and he told me and I said, 'I've never heard of of him.' And he said, 'Well, I can vouch that he's a very good builder.' He said, 'We only let the finest builders build out here.' He said, 'You can look around and see the fine homes we have.' And he said, 'This is a good quality.' He said, 'The best.'

"Q Did he say it was a well-built house?

"A Yes, it was. He said it was.". . .

With respect to insulation Mrs. Holland testified:

"Q Now, did Mr. Lentz make any representations about how the house was insulated?

"A Yes.

"Q What did he say?

"A My husband asked him if the house was insulated.

"Q And what did he say?

"A He said, 'In the ceiling and on the East wall.' And my husband said, 'Just the East wall?' And he said, 'Yes.' He said, 'That's all you needed out here in this location.'

"Q Now, did Mr. Lentz make any representations whether there was insulation paper under the siding of the house?

"A Definitely.

"Q And where did he say this? That evening?

"A Yes, because my husband asked him if he had had the building paper on because he said he wasn't interested in a home without building paper at all because we've lived in that East wind for nine years and we know what a home is without building paper insulation. And he said it did contain it. He said, 'All the builders put the insulation paper on, or the building paper.'"

Upon the same subject Mr. Holland testified:

> "He stated to me that in the homes built out there, the East wall was the only section where the insulation should be, and I agreed with him, that would be fine. And the outside of the siding that—I asked him if they had the regular building paper under it and he said, 'Sure.'" Mr. Holland further testified that when the siding pulled away from the house he took off three or four more boards to see if there was paper there and there was no paper. . . ."

The defendant's representation that the east side of the house was insulated was material and false. It was material because, according to the plaintiffs' evidence, they told the defendant prior to executing the earnest money receipt that they would not buy a house which was not so insulated. It was not an insignificant matter, for, as above stated, an expert called as a witness by the plaintiffs testified that the cost of removing the siding, applying the insulating paper, putting back the siding, and repainting it would be $1,279. The representation was actionable, "An action of deceit will lie against one who makes a false representation of a material fact upon which another acts to his injury knowing it to be false, *or when he makes it recklessly as of his own knowledge, without knowing whether it is true* or not. . . ." [Court's emphasis.] . . .

The defendant made proper objection to the admission of evidence that he represented that the house was of good quality and well built. The objection was overruled and the ruling is assigned as error.

Generally, an action in deceit will lie only for false representations of matters of past or existing fact, and hence statements of opinion as, for example, expressions by a vendor commendatory of the thing which he is trying to sell are not actionable even though false. . . .

Such expressions are usually regarded as "dealer's talk" or "puffing." . . .

This rule is based on the universal practice of the seller to recommend the article or thing offered for sale and to employ more or less extravagant language in connection therewith. The law does not hold him to a strict accountability for those vague commendations of his wares which manifestly are open to difference of opinion, and which do not imply untrue assertions concerning matters of direct observation; nor has the buyer any right to rely on such statements. . . .

The matter was well put by Judge Learned Hand in *Vulcan Metals Co. v Simmons Mfg. Co.*, 248 F. 853, 856 (2d Cir., 1918):

> "The reason of the rule lies, we think, in this: There are some kinds of talk which no sensible man takes seriously, and if he does he suffers from his credulity. . . ."

It is recognized, however, that statements of opinion regarding quality, value, or the like, may be considered as misrepresentations of fact, that is, of the speaker's state of mind, if a fiduciary [confidential] relation exists between the parties as, for example, . . . where the parties are not on an equal footing and do not have equal knowledge or means of knowledge . . .

There are a number of cases in other jurisdictions, however, in which similar expressions have, under the particular circumstances, been found to be statements of fact and actionable if false, but in all these the representations were made by builders of the houses, and there were other circumstances from which it could be rightfully inferred that the person to whom the representation was made was justified in relying on it. . . . In the opinions in these cases emphasis was laid on the fact that the persons making the representations were builders and therefore had superior knowledge of the workmanship, quality of material, etc., that went into the house involved. . . .

Turning now to the evidence in the case at bar, it should first be observed that the defendant did not build the house he sold to the plaintiffs, that, although he had owned it for a month, he had never occupied it. He was a real estate broker, not a builder, and we are aware of no special competence possessed by one in that calling to discover hidden defects in the construction of a house. He is not shown to have been an expert in that art. While the plaintiffs may be persons of limited education, the evidence discloses that they are not lacking in common understanding or powers of observation and that they were unusually vigilant in their inspection of the house before they bought it. We think that there was no such disparity between the knowledge and means of knowledge of the respective parties as to take the case out of the general rule that expressions of opinion, and especially such vague generalities as we are dealing with here—a "well-built house," "good quality," "fine house"—are not actionable. . . .

The court erred in overruling the objection to the evidence just considered.

We think that the issue of fraud based on the alleged promises should not have been submitted to the jury. Such promises are not actionable unless made with the present intention not to perform them. . . .

> "A fraudulent intent not to perform a promise may not be inferred as existing at the time the promise is made from the mere fact of nonperformance. Other circumstances of a substantial character must be shown in addition to non-performance before such inference of wrongful intent may be drawn."

Our recent decision in *Reimann v Brent*, Or., 395 P.2d 284, holding that the plaintiff could not recover in deceit for failure of the vendor of a house to keep promises made by his agent to repair defects in the house is controlling on this question. . . .

The alleged representation that the basement slab and the walls of the basement had been underlaid with Visqueen should not have been submitted to the jury, as there is no evidence that the representation was false or that it was material. The only evidence as to what Visqueen is and what purpose it serves in a house was furnished by Mr. Holland, who testified: "Well, I don't know anything about building, but from what I understand, it's the stuff that they put under the slab before pourin'." This is not sufficient to support a finding that the representation, even though false, induced the plaintiffs to purchase the house. . . .

[Judgment reversed.]

Here ends the discussion of what constitutes fraud. As mentioned earlier, fraud is only one of several ways in which one party to a contract could wrongfully obtain the other party's consent. The others are honest misrepresentation, mistake, duress, or undue influence. Honest misrepresentation will be looked at next.

12:9   Honest Misrepresentation

Honest misrepresentation may be defined by contrasting it with fraudulent misrepresentation. There are two primary differences: An honest or innocent misrepresentation is one that is made with the belief, although mistaken, that it is true. Recall that a fraudulent misrepresentation is one made with knowledge that it is false or with reckless disregard of truth or falsity. The second difference lies in the remedies available to the injured party. While either monetary damages or rescission of the contract may be sought as a remedy for fraud, rescission is the only remedy available for honest misrepresentation.

12:10 Mistake

The consent of one or both parties to a contract may in some cases be made on the basis of a mistaken assumption or impression. Usually, these mistakes have no bearing on the validity of the contract. Under some circumstances, however, a mistake could lead to a contract's being set aside on the ground that there was no genuine consent to the contract. Several kinds of mistakes may affect the genuineness of a party's consent.

Mutual or Bilateral Mistake   A *mutual mistake,* as the name implies, is a mistake made by both parties. It is also known as a *bilateral mistake.* If both parties to a contract acted on the basis of a mistaken assumption about a material fact, the contract can be rescinded at the request of either party. The mistake must usually (1) relate to the essence of the bargain and (2) involve a fundamental assumption that caused the parties to act as they did. Mutual mistakes typically involve the existence, the identity, or the character of the subject matter of the contract or of some other person or thing essential to the contract.

Many cases have dealt with situations in which the contracting parties assumed the existence of the subject matter of the contract, only to discover later that it either had been destroyed or had never existed at all. Such a mistake usually justifies rescission of the contract. Examples of this kind of mistake are plentiful: a contract for the sale of a house, which unknown to either party had burned down prior to the contract; a contract to paint a portrait of a third person who, unknown to the parties, had died.

Two parties sometimes reach an apparent agreement, only to discover that each was operating under a different assumption as to the identity of the subject matter of the agreement. For example, assume that A, who has a brown horse and a black horse for sale, agrees to sell B a horse for $300. A believes that she has just sold the brown horse, while B believes she has just bought the black one. Under such circumstances there is no contract, since the parties never reached any true agreement.

Even if the subject matter of the contract exists, and the parties agree as to its identity, a mutual mistake that voids the contract could be made about some essential quality or characteristic of the subject matter. For example, assume that A sells B a bar believed by both of them to contain a substantial amount of silver, but the bar turns out to contain only base metal. The contract may be rescinded on the basis of mutual mistake, since the parties acted under an erroneous assumption concerning a basic fact that was fundamental to the agreement.

Under the UCC, certain contracts can be avoided under conditions similar to those recognized under the concept of mutual mistake. These conditions apply to avoiding contracts for the sale of identified goods before the risk of loss (see 20:5) has passed to the buyer. If the goods are totally destroyed, the contract *is* avoided. If the goods deteriorate to the extent that they fail to conform to contract conditions, the contract *can be* avoided; that is, the buyer has the option of avoiding it.

At this point, a distinction will be made between mistake and uncertainty to further clarify what a mutual mistake is. An uncertainty exists when the parties act in the hope that a certain fact exists but know that this fact may not exist. In uncertainty there is only hope that a fact will exist, whereas a mutual mistake involves a belief that a fact does exist.

EXAMPLE

A contracts to sell B a champion bull. Both parties know that B wishes to use the animal for breeding. It is subsequently determined that the bull is impotent. If both parties entered the contract on the assumption that the bull was capable of breeding, the buyer might be able to obtain rescission on the ground that the assumption was a mutual mistake. However, if both parties were aware that the bull might be impotent, the contract cannot be terminated on the ground of mistake, since B assumed the risk that the facts would be different than desired.

The following case illustrates the kind of mutual mistake of fact that may be held sufficient to justify rescission of a contract. Note that the three requirements of a mistake are present in this case.

Matanuska Valley Bank
v
Abernathy
445 P2d 235
(Alaska Supreme Court, 1968)

[In 1964 Abernathy contracted with the Matanuska Valley Bank for the purchase of the Copper Kettle Roadhouse, which consisted of a main building and related buildings located on land situated on both sides of the Glenn Highway in Alaska. Unknown to either party, six years earlier the United States had reserved an easement (right-of-way) 150 feet wide on each side of the Glenn Highway; use of the right-of-way area for other than highway, telegraph, or pipeline purposes was prohibited. In 1965 Abernathy learned that the right-of-way existed and that a substantial portion of the main building, as well as portions of related buildings, were within the right-of-way. She notified the bank that she was rescind-

ing the sale agreement, and in 1966 she brought an action for rescission. The trial court rendered a judgment for Abernathy, and the bank appealed.]

Nesbett, Chief Justice.

*   *   *

Appellant's main point questions the validity of the [trial] court's conclusion that the parties contracted under a mutual mistake of fact. Appellant's argument is that ignorance by both parties of the existence of the easement cannot legally support a finding that the parties acted under a mutual mistake of fact. The Bank relies upon the authority of *McNeely v Philadelphia National Bank* where the court defined mutual mistake of fact as:

. . . a clear impression in the minds of the parties as to the existence of a material fact, sufficient in importance to influence and govern a man of ordinary intelligence, and on which both parties relied and acted, which fact did not exist. The Bank contends that since the parties were acting in total ignorance of the fact that the easement existed, they were not acting under an erroneous impression concerning a material fact.

We are of the opinion that the trial court was correct in ordering rescission based on its finding that the parties had acted under a mutual mistake of fact. The evidence supports the conclusion that the Abernathys purchased the land and buildings for the sole purpose of engaging in the business of operating a roadhouse. The land and buildings were adapted to and had previously been used for this purpose. There can be no question but that both parties were of the belief, and acted in reliance upon their belief, that the buildings constituting the Copper Kettle, which were necessary

for the conduct of the roadhouse business, were located on land which would continue to be available for this purpose. Both parties were mistaken in this belief. A substantial portion of the roadhouse buildings were located on land under the permanent control of the United States. The terrain was such that the cost of moving the buildings was greater than their worth. . . .

. . . [There] was evidence of sufficient strength to support the court's finding that "the buildings were the principal consideration in the purchase" and its conclusion that the parties were mutually mistaken regarding the status of the buildings. . . .

The case is remanded to the trial court for the ascertainment of the facts necessary to the entry of an amended judgment consistent with the views expressed in [other portions of] this opinion.

Unilateral Mistake   If only one party to a contract acts on the basis of a mistaken assumption, it is a *unilateral mistake.* A unilateral mistake generally does not affect the validity of the contract, and the mistaken party must live with the bargain. However, under certain circumstances a unilateral mistake may justify rescission. These circumstances include the following: (1) if the other party either knew, or in the exercise of reasonable care should have known, of the mistake, such as a mistake that is so obvious that a reasonable person must know or suspect that a mistake was made; (2) if enforcement of the contract would result in such extreme hardship to the mistaken party that an injustice would occur, provided the parties can be returned to the position they held prior to the contract; and (3) if a mistake is made with respect to price bids by contractors for the performance of jobs, such as erroneous mathematical computations or omissions of certain items in computing the cost of the contract, the courts often grant rescission under such circumstances if the mistaken party notifies the other party of the mistake prior to any action by the other party to its detriment.

Mistake of Law   It is often broadly stated that a mistake of law—such as not knowing the legal effect of a particular document or language used in it—does not provide a basis for rescinding a contract. This statement is, however, subject to many qualifications and exceptions, and many courts now treat mistakes of law no differently than mistakes of fact. Therefore, it is probably more accurate to say that whether a mistake of law may affect the genuineness of consent to entering a contract, and thus provide a ground for rescission of the contract, depends on the nature of the mistake and the particular state in which it occurs.

12:11   Duress

A consent to a contract will be held invalid if it was obtained by means of *duress*. A contract is a result of duress if one party, by means of threats or actions, has instilled such fear and apprehension in the other party as to deny that party's exercise of free will, resulting in that party's consent not being truly voluntary.

Duress may take the form of threats by one party against the other, his family, his friends, or his property. A threat to do what one has a right to do cannot usually be the basis for a claim of duress unless, despite its being lawful, the threat is wrongful. For example, it is entirely lawful to report the commission of a crime to the appropriate authorities. It is, however, generally considered wrongful to use the threat of criminal prosecution to induce the consent of a person to a contract, and a contract obtained by means of such a threat may be rescinded on the ground of duress.

In negotiating a contract a party may generally take advantage of the precarious financial situation of another party to secure more favorable terms. Duress would exist only if the party with the advantage exerts extreme economic pressure through some wrongful action and leaves the threatened party with no real alternative but to comply with the threatening party's demands. This is known as the *business compulsion* or *economic duress* doctrine.

12:12   Undue Influence

If one party to a contract so dominates the other party as to deprive the latter of free will, the contract is said to be the result of *undue influence* and may be set aside at the option of the weaker party. Some courts consider undue influence to be a type of constructive fraud, while others have classified it as a type of duress. In any case, to establish undue influence it generally must be shown (1) that, under the circumstances, one party to a contract was particularly susceptible to the influence of the other party; (2) that because of this influence the weaker party lacked free will and was unable to act independent of the dominant party's desires; and (3) that as a result the parties entered a contract that was against the best interests of the weaker party.

In assessing a claim of undue influence, all the factors bearing on the weaker party's susceptibility to influence and the stronger party's position to exert such influence must be considered. The relationship of the parties is one of the most important of these factors. The relationship that is most often subject to such a claim is a confidential relationship. When a contract is entered into between persons in a confidential relationship, and the dominant party in the relationship is the beneficiary of the contract, it is presumed that the contract was the result of the dominant party's undue influence, and he has the burden of proving otherwise.

Other factors include the weaker party's advanced age, impaired physical or mental condition, lack of education, lack of independent and disinterested advice, or dependence for necessities on the dominant person, and the adequacy of consideration received by the weaker party. A fairly typical case might involve a contract between a very old person in poor physical health, with no access to outside advisers, and a private nurse. Since the nurse would be in a position to exert extraordinary influence, it is not unreasonable for the law to presume that a contract extremely favorable to the nurse and unfavorable to the other person would be the result of undue influence.

12:13   Contracts of Adhesion; Unconscionable Contracts

Standardized form contracts are often imposed by financially powerful businesses on smaller businesses or on consumers. These contracts frequently contain extremely one-sided provisions. Among the primary responses to the increased use of such contracts is the recognition of two types of standardized contracts for which relief can be given to the weaker party.

Adhesion Contracts   A *contract of adhesion* is a standardized contract that has been drafted by the dominant party and imposed on the weaker party without allowing the weaker party to bargain. The weaker party often is unable to obtain better terms elsewhere, either because the stronger party has a monopoly on the particular goods or services desired, or because all other businesses offering the same goods or services also use the same or similar types of contracts. The stronger party may therefore compel the weaker party to choose between acceptance of basically unfair contract provisions or forbearance of the desired goods and services. In recognition of this imbalance, the courts carefully scrutinize adhesion contracts and construe any ambiguities against the dominant party.

Modern insurance contracts are typical adhesion contracts. Virtually all insurance contracts contain standard provisions drafted by the insurance companies to restrict their liability and the coverage afforded by their policies. An applicant must fill out a standardized application form and accept a standardized policy, with no opportunity to negotiate particular terms and conditions. For this reason, the courts have construed insurance policies strictly against the insurers.

Unconscionable Contracts   "Unconscionable" cannot be precisely defined. Basically, it is the quality of being excessively unfair or unscrupulous. A court's statement that a contract is unconscionable reflects its conclusion that the contract or provision is so oppressive or unfair that the court should refuse to enforce it. Under the UCC the basic test of unconscionability is whether, in light of the general commercial background and the commercial needs of the particular trade or case, the clause or clauses involved are so one-sided as to be unconscionable under the circumstances that existed when the contract was made (UCC § 2-302, Comment 1).

The doctrine of unconscionability, under which a court grants relief from an unconscionable contract, is closely related to but broader than the doctrine of adhesion contracts. The doctrine of unconscionability may be applied to situations where the weaker party was oppressed or unfairly surprised, even though the weaker party might have obtained more favorable contract terms elsewhere. For example, a contract that contains many fine-print, one-sided provisions favorable to the drafter or a contract charging an excessive price might be considered unconscionable. Public policy considerations have led to reliance on the unconscionability doctrine as a means of protecting weak or ignorant parties from consenting to enter contracts with unscrupulous businesses. Cases in which contracts have been found unconscionable generally involve claims by consumers that they were unfairly taken advantage of; the consumers have often been poor, ignorant, or both.

The following case illustrates the application of the doctrine of unconscionability.

Williams

v

Walker-Thomas Furniture Co.
121 App DC 315, 350 2d 445, 18 ALR3d 1297
(United States Court of Appeals, District of Columbia Circuit, 1965)

[Walker-Thomas, a retail furniture store operator in the District of Columbia, sold household items on an installment basis. At the time of purchase, each customer signed a printed form contract, which provided that title would remain in Walker-Thomas until the item was fully paid off, and that Walker-Thomas could repossess the item in the event the customer failed to make any monthly payment. The contract also contained an obscure and complex provision that provided, in essence, that each new installment purchase was consolidated with all other outstanding accounts. The effect of the provision was that a customer always owed a balance on every item purchased, until all items were fully paid off. From 1957 to 1962 Williams, the appellant, made purchases totaling $1,800 from Walker-Thomas. Her last purchase, made when her balance was $164, was a $514 stereo set. At the time of that purchase, Walker-Thomas knew that Williams had seven children to support and that her monthly income consisted of a $218 government check. Williams defaulted soon thereafter, and, although

she had made payments totaling $1,400 over the years, Walker-Thomas sued to repossess all the items purchased since 1957. The trial court entered judgment for Walker-Thomas, and Williams appealed.]

J. Skeily Wright, Circuit Judge.

*   *   *

[Appellant's] principal contention, rejected . . . below, is that these contracts, or at least some of them, are unconscionable and, hence, not enforceable. . . .

We do not agree that the court lacked the power to refuse enforcement to contracts found to be unconscionable. In other jurisdictions, it has been held as a matter of common law that unconscionable contracts are not enforceable. . . . Since we have never adopted or rejected such a rule, the question here presented is actually one of first impression.

Congress has recently enacted the Uniform Commercial Code, which specifically provides that the court may refuse to enforce a contract which it finds to be unconscionable at the time it was made. [UCC § 2-302]. The enactment of this section, which occurred subsequent to the contracts here in suit, does not mean that the common law of the District of Columbia was otherwise at the time of enactment, nor does it preclude the court from adopting a similar rule in the exercise of its powers to develop the common law for the District of Columbia. . . .

Accordingly, we hold that where the element of unconscionability is present at the time a contract is made, the contract should not be enforced.

Unconscionability has generally been recognized to include an absence of meaningful choice on the part of one of the parties together with contract terms which are unreasonably favorable to the other party. Whether a meaningful choice is present in a particular case can only be determined by consideration of all the circumstances surrounding the transaction. In many cases the meaningfulness of the choice is negated by a gross inequality of bargaining power. The manner in which the contract was entered is also relevant to this consideration. Did each party to the contract, considering his obvious education or lack of it, have a reasonable opportunity to understand the terms of the contract, or were the important terms hidden in a maze of fine print and minimized by deceptive sales practices? Or-

dinarily, one who signs an agreement without full knowledge of its terms might be held to assume the risk that he has entered a one-sided bargain. But when a party of little bargaining power, and hence little real choice, signs a commercially unreasonable contract with little or no knowledge of its terms, it is hardly likely that his consent, or even an objective manifestation of his consent, was ever given to all the terms. In such a case the usual rule that the terms of the agreement are not to be questioned should be abandoned and the court should consider whether the terms of the contract are so unfair that enforcement should be withheld. . . .

Because the trial court and the appellate court did not feel that enforcement could be refused, no findings were made on the possible unconscionability of the contracts in these cases. Since the record is not sufficient for our deciding the issue as a matter of law, the cases must be remanded to the trial court for further proceedings.

So ordered.

As the *Williams* court pointed out, the UCC allows a court to refuse to enforce a contract containing one or more unconscionable clauses. The UCC also allows a court to enforce the remainder of the contract without the unconscionable clause, or to so limit the clause as to avoid any unconscionable result. The courts thus are given considerable leeway in dealing with unconscionable contracts.

Key Concepts and Terms

- Consent of the parties to a contract is not a genuine consent if it is acquired through fraud, honest misrepresentation, mistake, or undue influence.
- Fraud comprises anything calculated to deceive and to take unfair advantage of another. To establish fraud, the injured party must show (1) that the other party made a knowing or reckless misrepresentation of a material fact, (2) that the other party had an intent to deceive and to induce reliance, (3) that the injured party reasonably relied on the misrepresentation, and (4) that damage or injury resulted. The remedies for fraud are monetary damages or rescission of the contract.
- Fraud requires a misrepresentation, by words, acts, or both, of some present or past fact. A misrepresentation concerning opinion, value, quality, future events

or intentions, or law does not usually constitute fraud. A misrepresentation that relates to both factual and nonfactual matters may be fraudulent.

- Nonfactual assertions can be fraudulent where (1) a confidential relationship exists or (2) one party has superior knowledge.

- Nondisclosure ordinarily does not constitute fraud, but concealment of material facts does. Moreover, one party may have a duty of disclosure where a confidential relationship exists between the parties, where that party has superior knowledge, or where partial disclosure may result in a mistaken impression.

- Honest misrepresentation differs from fraud in that (1) the misrepresentation is based on the belief that it is true and (2) rescission is the only remedy.

- A mutual mistake is an erroneous assumption of both parties to the contract as to a material fact, such as the existence, the identity, or the character of some person or thing essential to the contract. Such a mistake is a ground for rescission of the contract.

- A unilateral mistake is a mistake made by one of the parties. It affords no grounds for relief, except when (1) the other party knew or should have known of the mistake, and the mistaken party would otherwise suffer extreme hardship; or (2) a contractor has made a mistake in computing a bid and has notified the other party before that party has taken any action.

- Duress exists where one party, by wrongful threats or actions, has instilled such fear in the other party that the other party involuntarily consents to enter a contract. Under the doctrine of "business compulsion" or "economic duress," a party is a victim of duress if he is forced to enter a contract as a result of business necessity and extreme economic pressure exerted by the other party. A contract may be rescinded by the threatened party on the ground of duress.

- Undue influence is the influence exerted by a dominant party on a weaker, more susceptible party to the extent that the weaker party lacked free will in consenting to enter the contract, resulting in a contract that is against the best interests of the weaker party.

- A contract of adhesion is a standardized contract drafted by a stronger party and imposed on a weaker one without allowing the weaker party to bargain and make a meaningful choice. Ambiguities in adhesion contracts are construed against the dominant party. Particular provisions may be held unenforceable as against the public's interests.

- An unconscionable contract is one that is so oppressive or unfair that a court either will refuse to enforce it or will limit its effect. The doctrine of unconscionability is often relied on to protect consumers.

- Business Compulsion (Economic Duress)
- Concealment or Nondisclosure
- Contract of Adhesion
- Dealer's Puffing
- Duress
- Fraud
- Honest Misrepresentation
- Mutual or Bilateral Mistake
- Rescission
- Unconscionable Contract
- Undue Influence
- Unilateral Mistake

Questions and Case Problems

1. A, having fallen off a cliff, is clinging by his fingernails to the edge. Unable to pull himself up, he asks B, who is standing nearby, to rescue him. B says, "I will save you if you promise to pay me $5,000." A promises to do so, and B then rescues A. Do A and B have an enforceable contract? Is A's consent to B's terms a genuine consent?

2. Sunderhaus purchases a diamond ring from a jeweler for $700. At the time of sale the jeweler's agent represents to Sunderhaus that the diamond is worth the amount paid. When Sunderhaus trades the ring in on another, one jeweler appraises its value at $300, and another jeweler values it at $350. Sunderhaus then sues the jeweler who sold her the ring, alleging fraudulent misrepresentation. What is the result?

3. Discuss the similarities and differences between misrepresentation of fact, concealment of fact, and nondisclosure of fact. What are the legal consequences of each?

4. Davis hires Gordon, a real estate broker, to inquire about the possibility of purchasing the Owens Office Building. Gordon knows the building well, since he is its managing agent, and he knows that there have been problems with the heating and cooling system, that the previous owner has spent $10,000 on repairs to the system, and that tenants continue to complain about the system despite the repairs. Before signing the contract for purchase of the building, Davis hears rumors that there are problems with the heating and cooling system. Davis asks Gordon whether there are any problems, and Gordon responds that there were some, but that $10,000 in repairs was made. Davis then buys the building. The tenants' complaints continue, and Davis learns that a complete overhaul of the system, costing $37,000, is required. After the repairs are made, Davis sues Gordon to recover the $37,000. What is the outcome?

5. Under what circumstances may a contract be set aside on the ground of mistake?

6. The Army sets out to obtain bids on the construction of a Pershing missile container. Packages of materials containing specifications, some 1,500 drawings, and parts lists are sent to prospective bidders, including Space Corporation. Space Corporation's chief estimator begins preparing a bid. The estimator realizes that a drawing of a particular monitoring system is missing. He consults his superiors. Based on their experience in building containers for earlier missiles, they tell him the cost of the monitoring system is $35 per unit. Some specifications are unclear, and there are meetings with government representatives to clarify ambiguities, but Space Corporation never mentions the missing drawing or the monitor. After being awarded the contract, Space Corporation receives additional copies of the drawings and realizes that the monitoring system will cost $410 per unit. Space Corporation performs the contract but applies for reimbursement, and the government refuses to pay. Space Corporation sues. How should the case be decided?

7. Loral Corporation is awarded a $6,000,000 Navy contract to produce radar sets. The contract contains a schedule of deliveries, a clause providing damages for late deliveries, and a cancellation clause for unsatisfactory performance. Loral solicits bids for a number of different component gears, and awards Austin Instruments a subcontract to supply most of them. After delivering for a few months, Austin threatens to stop deliveries unless Loral agress to substantial price increases, both retroactively on parts already delivered and prospectively on those to come. Austin soon stops deliveries as threatened. After contacting its entire list of approved

suppliers and finding none who could produce the parts in time for Loral to meet its contract schedules, Loral agrees to Austin's demands for higher prices. After the last delivery is received, Loral sues Austin for the money it has paid over the original price. Who should prevail?

8. Davidson, a musical concert promoter, contracts with Allen, a popular musician, to produce a concert by Allen. The contract calls for submission of any disputes to arbitration before the musicians' union to which Allen belongs. Davidson knows of the arbitration clause, but he also knows that the contract is a standard union form contract, that the union requires its members to use such contracts, and that the union refuses to allow any changes in such standard clauses. Because the union holds a monopoly over the musical services required by promoters, Davidson accepts the arbitration clause. The concert loses money, and a dispute arises as to who should bear the losses. Davidson sues for breach of contract, and Allen moves to compel arbitration by the musicians' union. Davidson objects to arbitration before a partial arbitrator. How should the case be resolved?

9. Cruz, who speaks only Spanish, goes to Al's Appliances to look at refrigerators. He is waited on by Ybarra, who converses with Cruz in Spanish. Cruz ultimately selects a refrigerator, and he and Ybarra orally negotiate. After they agree on a purchase price of $1,000, Ybarra prepares a retail installment contract written entirely in English and submits it to Cruz for signature. The contract provides for 36 monthly payments of $40, for total payments of $1,440. After making three monthly payments Cruz discovers that comparable refrigerators sell at other stores for no more than $500, and that the actual wholesale cost to Al's Appliances is $350. Cruz then refuses to make further payments on the refrigerator, claiming that the price is excessive. Al's Appliances sues for the balance remaining on the contract. Decide the case.

10. Describe contracts of adhesion and unconscionable contracts. Why do the courts look with disfavor on such contracts?

13 Legal Capacity of Parties

13:1 Introduction

The law presumes that most people are capable of deciding for themselves whether to enter a contract. It follows, then, that the law will ordinarily assume that the parties to a contract had the necessary legal capacity to enter into the agreement. The law is, however, particularly solicitous of classes of people who are especially susceptible to sharp business practices or other deceptions. These classes include *minors; insane, incompetent, or intoxicated persons;* and some *convicts*. To protect such people from their own immaturity, ignorance, or lack of judgment, the courts have held that they lack the necessary legal capacity to enter binding contracts. Thus, if a person who belongs to one of these classes enters a contractual arrangement, he generally has the right to *repudiate*, or avoid, the contract. If a person's legal capacity is questioned, the court determines whether the person belonged to one of the classes, not whether the particular person was actually capable of exercising judgment.

In this chapter the rules concerning the legal capacity of minors; insane, incompetent, or intoxicated persons; and convicts will be presented. In addition, as an example of the evolutionary nature of the law, there will be some discussion of past and current rules concerning the capacity of married women to enter contracts.

13:2 Minors

Legally, a minor or infant is any person under a specified age, known as the *age of majority*. While 21 was traditionally the age of majority under the common law, in most states the age of majority by statute is now 18. In the eyes of the law all minors lack the legal capacity to contract. Thus, any contract that a minor enters with a competent adult is not enforceable against the minor. In other words, the minor cannot legally be made to perform the contract. However, the minor has the option of enforcing the contract against the adult. Statutes in some states expressly permit minors to enter into certain types of agreements, and a minor has no right to avoid these agreements. Some states also have statutes prohibiting a minor from repudiating a contract that the other party was induced into entering by the minor's misrepresentation that he was of age.

13:3 Avoidance of Contract by a Minor

A minor has an absolute right to avoid a contract at any time during minority. Any unequivocal act by the minor indicating an intent to repudiate the contract is sufficient. For example, avoidance may be accomplished by notifying the other party in writing of the intent to repudiate the contract, by returning the property received by the minor from the other party, or by demanding from the other party the property given by the minor to the other party. A minor may even wait until the other party brings a lawsuit for enforcement of the contract, and then avoid the contract by asserting the fact of minority as a defense. A minor need not give any reason for the decision to avoid the contract.

If a minor repudiates an executory, or unperformed, contract, the minor's avoidance has the effect of terminating the contractual relationship, and no great hardship is worked on the other party. However, where the contract has actually been partly or wholly executed, a minor's repudiation may cause financial loss or other hardship to the other party. In that event, the minor has a duty to return any consideration that he received from the other party and still has. If the minor used, lost, or even destroyed the consideration received from the other party, most courts do not require the minor in any way to pay the other party the reasonable value of the consideration. The risk of such loss is squarely on the other party. The minor, on the other hand, has the right to full recovery of all consideration he has given to the other party. The potential inequity of these general rules is obvious. For example, assume that A, a minor, buys a car from B for $1,000. The very next day day A is in an accident and the car is totally destroyed. A then notifies B that she is exercising her right to avoid the contract and that she wants her $1,000 returned. A is entitled to the return of the consideration ($1,000) she gave to B. Since the consideration she received in return has been destroyed, she has no obligation to return anything to B.

Some states have therefore adopted a contrary view. In these states a minor who avoids a contract must either return the consideration received or account to the other party for the value of the consideration received. Going back to the example above, the minor A would be required to return to B the equivalent of the consideration received from B ($1,000, or whatever lesser amount represented the true value of the car at the time of the sale).

The following case shows one court's resolution of the competing policy interests involved in this area.

Pettit
v
Liston
97 Ore 464, 191 P 660, 11 ALR 487
(Oregon Supreme Court, 1920)

[Pettit, a minor, purchased a motorcycle from Liston, a motorcycle dealer. Pettit made a down payment of $125 on the $325 purchase price and agreed to make monthly payments of $25. After using the motorcycle for one month, Pettit returned it and demanded his money back from Liston. Liston refused, claiming that Pettit had caused damages of $156.65 to the motorcycle. Pettit sued. After a trial court judgment for Liston, Pettit appealed.]

Bennett, J.

*   *   *

The amount involved in this proceeding is not large, but the question of law presented is a very important one, and one which has been much disputed in the courts, and about which there is a great and irreconcilable conflict in the authorities, and we have therefore given the matter careful attention.

The courts, in an attempt to protect the minor upon the one hand, and to prevent wrong or injustice to persons who have dealt fairly and reasonably with such minor upon the other, have indulged in many fine distinctions and recognized various slight shades of difference.

In dealing with the right of the minor to rescind his contract and the conditions under which he may do so, the decisions of the courts in the different states have not only conflicted upon the main questions involved, but many of the decisions of the same court in the same state seem to be inconsistent with each other; and oftentimes one court has made its decision turn upon a distinction or difference not recognized by the courts of other states as a distinguishing feature.

The result has been that there are not only two general lines of decisions directly upon the question involved, but there are many others, which diverge more or less from the main line, and make particular cases turn upon real or fancied differences and distinctions, depending upon whether the contract was executory or partly or wholly executed, whether it was for necessaries, whether it was beneficial to the minor, whether it was fair and reasonable, whether the minor still had the property purchased in his possession, whether he had received any beneficial use of the same, etc.

Many courts have held broadly that a minor may so purchase property and keep it for an indefinite time, if he chooses, until it is worn out and destroyed, and then recover the payments made on the purchase price, without allowing the seller anything whatever for the use and depreciation of the property.

Many other authorities hold that where the transaction is fair and reasonable, and the minor was not overcharged or taken advantage of in any way, and he takes and keeps the property and uses or destroys it, he cannot recover the payments made on the purchase price, without allowing the seller for the wear and tear and depreciation of the article while in his hands. . . .

Some of the cyclopedias and some of the different series of selected cases state the rule contended for by plaintiff [Pettit], as supported by the strong weight of authority; but we find the decisions rather equally balanced, both in number and respectability. . . .

Our attention has not been called to any Oregon case bearing upon the question, and as far as our investigation has disclosed, there is none.

In this condition of the authorities, we feel that we are in a position to pass upon the question as one of first impression, and announce the rule which seems to us to be the better one, upon considerations of principle and public policy.

We think, where the minor has not been overreached in any way, and there has been no undue influence, and the contract is a fair and reasonable one, and the minor has actually paid money on the purchase price, and taken and used the article, that he ought not to be permitted to recover the amount actually paid, without allowing the vendor of the goods the reasonable compensation for the use and depreciation of the article, while in his hands.

Of course, if there has been any fraud or imposition on the part of the seller, or if the contract is unfair, or any unfair advantage has been taken of the minor in inducing him to make the purchase, then a different rule would apply. And whether there had been such an overreaching on the part of the seller would always, in case of a jury trial, be a question for the jury.

We think this rule will fully and fairly protect the minor against injustice or imposition, and at the same time it will be fair to the businessman who has dealt with such minor in good faith. . . .

Again, it will not exert any good moral influence upon boys and young men, and will not tend to encourage honesty and integrity, or lead them to a good and useful business future, if they are taught that they can make purchases with their own money, for their own benefit, and after paying for them in this way, and using them until they are worn out and destroyed, go back and compel the businessman to return to them what they have paid upon the purchase price. Such a doctrine, as it seems to us, can only lead to the corruption of young men's principles and encourage them in habits of trickery and dishonesty.

In view of all these considerations, we think that the rule we have indicated, and which is substantially the rule adopted in New York, is the better rule, and we adopt the same in this state.

We must not be understood as deciding at this time what would be the rule where the vendor is seeking to enforce an executory contract against the minor, which is a different question not necessarily involved in this case. . . .

[Judgment affirmed.]

Some states impose on the minor the obligation to return any property he has subsequently received in exchange for the consideration. For example, if a minor purchases a car from an adult, then trades the car to a third party in exchange for a motorcycle and money, and then seeks to avoid the original contract with the adult, the minor would be obligated to give the adult the motorcycle and the money received from the third party in exchange for the adult's payment of the purchase price to the minor.

At common law, a minor's right to recover the consideration paid by him ordinarily prevailed even when that consideration had been transferred to a third party. To illustrate, assume that A, a minor, agreed to and did sell a bicycle to B, who resold the bicycle to C. A then decided to avoid the original contract with B and sought to recover the bicycle from C. Under the common law the minor would be entitled to the bicycle. The result would be different, however, if the UCC applied. Under the UCC a good faith purchaser for value who purchases from a person with voidable title prevails [UCC § 2-403(1)]. Thus, C, as a good faith purchaser from B, would be entitled to retain the bicycle.

13:4   Ratification of Minor's Contract

A contract entered into by a minor may be ratified after the minor has achieved the age of majority. The right to ratify such a contract, like the right to repudiate, can only be exercised by the minor. *Ratification* may be explicit, as in a case where the minor, on attaining majority, specifically promises the other party that he will perform his obligations under the contract. Ratification may also be implied, as when a minor, after attaining majority, commences performance of the contract. If a minor's intent to ratify is not clearly indicated by his words or actions, all the circumstances must be considered. One important factor that the courts consider is the amount of time that has passed since the minor attained majority. Many courts have concluded that, if a minor fails to repudiate a contract within a reasonable time after reaching majority, it may be implied that the minor has ratified the contract. This rule has been applied more to executed contracts than to executory contracts.

13:5   Minor's Contracts for Necessaries

The term *necessaries* refers broadly to those items that are reasonably necessary for the proper and suitable maintenance of a person. These items include food, clothing, lodging, and education through high school. The courts have been flexible in determining what items are necessaries. They generally look at the circumstances of a particular case. It has often been noted that one's social position and situation in life are important in determining whether an item is a necessary. A purchase that might constitute a luxury for one person may be a necessary for another person. The courts have also stressed that the minor's actual need is the test. If the minor has a parent or guardian who is capable of or willing to supply certain items, these items will not be considered necessaries.

A minor may be held liable on a contract for the purchase of necessaries, but this liability is quasi-contractual. That is, the minor has a duty to pay only the reasonable value of necessaries actually furnished to him. Since the obligation is quasi-contractual in nature, the emphasis is on the minor's payment for value received; the specific terms are not binding.

EXAMPLE
A, a minor, contracts with B to buy clothing at a total price of $200. A takes delivery of and uses only some of the clothing. He delays delivery of the rest until a later date. Before the remaining clothing is delivered, A notifies B that he is disaffirming the contract. The value of the clothing A actually received and used is $50. A is liable to B for only $50 and is not obligated to accept or to pay for the remainder of the clothing.

While liability for necessaries traditionally has been limited to personal necessaries, some courts have extended the concept to permit liability for business necessaries. For example, under the general rule a car is not a necessary, but if a minor needs a car to conduct business, he will be liable for its purchase price.

The following case (1) demonstrates the manner in which the concept of necessaries may be expanded and (2) discusses, in both the majority and the dissenting opinions, the rationale underlying the rule that minors generally lack legal capacity to contract.

Gastonia Personnel Corp.
v
Rogers

276 NC 279, 172 SE2d 19, 41 ALR3d
1062
(North Carolina Supreme Court, 1970)

[Rogers, 19 years old, lived with his wife in a rented apartment. He needed one quarter's worth of schooling to complete the requirements for an A.S. degree in civil engineering at Gaston Tech. His wife became pregnant so he had to look for employment. Rogers visited the Gastonia Personnel Corporation office, and, following an interview, he signed a con-

tract to pay Gastonia $295 if it found him a job paying at least $4,680 a year to start. Gastonia soon placed him in a position paying $4,784, but Rogers never paid the fee. Gastonia sued, and Rogers defended on the ground that he was a minor at the time of the contract. The age of majority then was 21. Rogers' defense was upheld, and Gastonia appealed.]

Bobbitt, Chief Justice.

*   *   *

An early commentary on the common law, after the general statement that contracts made by persons (infants) before attaining the age of twenty-one "may be avoided," sets forth "some exceptions out of this generality," to wit: *"An infant may bind himself to pay for his necessary meat, drinke, apparell, necessary physicke, and such other necessaries, and likewise for his good teaching or instruction, whereby he may profit himselfe afterwards."* [Court's emphasis.] *Coke on Littleton*, 13th ed. (1788), p. 172. . . . If the infant married, "necessaries" included necessary food and clothing for his wife and child. . . .

In accordance with this ancient rule of the common law, this Court has held an infant's contract, unless for "necessaries" or unless authorized by statute, is voidable by the infant, at his election, and may be disaffirmed during infancy or upon attaining the age of twenty-one. . . .

This statement commands respect and approval:

"Society has a moral obligation to protect the interests of infants from overreaching adults. But this protection must not become a straightjacket, stifling the economic and social advancement of infants who have the need and maturity to contract. Nor should infants be allowed to turn that protective legal shield into a weapon to wield against fair-dealing adults. It is in the interest of society to have its members contribute actively to the general economic and social welfare, if this can be ac-complished consistently with the protection of those persons unable to protect themselves in the market place." . . .

In [a New Jersey case the Court said]:

"One of the great virtues of the common law is its dynamic nature that makes it adaptable to the requirements of society at the time of its application in court. There is not a rule of the common law in force today that has not evolved from some earlier rule of common law, gradually in some instances, more suddenly in others, leaving the common law of today when compared with the common law of centuries ago as different as day is from night. The nature of the common law requires that each time a rule of law is applied it be carefully scruntinized to make sure that the conditions and needs of the times have not so changed as to make further application of it the instrument of injustice."

In general, our prior decisions are to the effect that the "necessaries" of an infant, his wife and child, include only such necessities of life as food, clothing, shelter, medical attention, etc. In our view, the concept of "necessaries" should be enlarged to include such articles of property and such services as are reasonably necessary to enable the infant to earn the money required to provide the necessities of life for himself and those who are legally dependent upon him. . . .

The evidence before us tends to show that defendant, when he contracted with plaintiff, was nineteen years of age, emancipated, married, a high school graduate, within "a quarter of 22 hours" of obtaining his degree in applied science, and capable of holding a job at a starting annual salary of $4,784.00. To hold, as a matter of law, that such a person cannot obligate himself to pay for services rendered him in obtaining employment suitable to his ability, education and specialized training, enabling him to provide the necessities of life for himself, his wife and his expected child, would place him and others similarly situated under a serious economic handicap.

In the effort to protect "older minors" from improvident or unfair contracts, the law should not deny to them the opportunity and right to obligate themselves for articles of property or services which are reasonably necessary to enable them to provide for the proper support of themselves and their dependents. The minor should be held liable for the reasonable value of articles of property or services received pursuant to such contract. . . .

To establish liability, plaintiff must satisfy the jury by the greater weight of the evidence that defendant's contract with plaintiff was an appropriate and reasonable means for defendant to obtain suitable employment. If this issue is answered in plaintiff's favor, plaintiff must then establish by the greater weight of the evidence the reasonable value of the services received by defendant pursuant to the contract. Thus, plaintiff's recovery, if any, cannot exceed the reasonable value of its services to defendant.

[Judgment reversed and cause remanded.]

Lake, Justice (dissenting).

*   *   *

The defendant, a young man nineteen years old, with better than average education, has benefited from his use of the plaintiff's services for which he promised to pay an agreed amount. Now, having received the full benefit he desired, he refuses to pay for it. He does not contend, and there is nothing in the record before us to suggest, that the plaintiff overcharged him, or otherwise took any advantage of him. Nothing in this record arouses sympathy for the defendant. This is one of those hard cases which so frequently have turned out to be "quicksands of the law." In my view, the majority, in its proper desire to avoid an injustice to this plaintiff, has taken a step into quicksand.

As the majority opinion shows clearly, since a time prior to Columbus' discovery of Amer-ica, it has been the well settled rule of the common law, repeatedly stated by this Court, that an infant's contract may be disaffirmed by him without liability, unless it is a contract for what the law calls "necessaries." If the contract is one for necessaries, the infant is liable for the reasonable value of what he received.

The reason for this rule, in both its aspects, is the desire of the law to protect the infant. His liability to pay for necessaries is not imposed so as to protect an adult supplier against a shrewdly scheming infant. It is imposed solely because otherwise the infant, honest or not, might be unable to acquire that which he must have for the support of himself and his dependents. The rule permits the infant to refuse to carry out other contracts irrespective of the particular infant's intelligence, education or experience in business. It does not depend upon whether the particular contract was fair or unfair. It is immaterial, under this rule, that the application of it results in a loss to an adult who dealt in good faith with an unscrupulous infant. . . .

Stripped of emotional aspects, this case presents but one question, assuming the rule heretofore established is to be followed: Is an infant's contract for the services of an employment agency, under the circumstances disclosed in this record, a contract for necessaries? I do not think it is. . . . It is well settled that a "necessary" is something more urgently needed than a thing or a service which is merely a convenience or an assistance to the infant. This is the established rule both in America and England, apart from statute.

In *Pollock's Principles of Contracts*, pp. 49–50, it is said:

> "It is to be borne in mind . . . that the question is not whether the things are such that a person of the defendant's means may reasonably buy and pay for them, but whether they can reasonably be said to be so necessary for him that, though an infant, he must obtain them on credit rather than go without." [Court's emphasis.] . . .

That the services of the employment agency

in giving this defendant names of prospective employers was a convenience and an aid to him in getting a job with a minimum of inquiry and search from door to door is no doubt true. In the present eagerness of industry to find trained engineers, I cannot agree that such services are a "necessary" for an engineering student nearing graduation from Gaston Tech and seeking employment in the Charlotte area. . . . The authority of the people,

through their representatives in the State Government, to change the common law when conditions and needs have so changed as to render the law unjust or unwise is clear. They have, however, seen fit to vest this authority in the Legislature and not in us. . . . This power to change established law to meet changes in conditions is the essence of the legislative power. . . .

 A businessperson generally should not contract with a minor in the expectation that the contract can be enforced as one for necessaries. Such a course of dealing is fraught with danger. The businessperson has the burden of proving that the items purchased were in fact necessaries. This is a difficult proposition, since in fact most minors' necessaries are provided by their parents. Even if a businessperson were successful in showing that the items purchased were necessaries not provided by the minor's parents or guardian, the minor's liability may still be limited to an amount less than the purchase price, since reasonable value is the guide. Therefore, a businessperson must be extremely careful in determining whether to contract with a minor. Perhaps the most practical approach is to contract with the minor's parents, either in addition to or instead of with the minor. Then, in the event any dispute arises as to performance of the contract, liability may be imposed on the parents, without regard to whether the minor has affirmed or repudiated the contract, or whether the contract was one for necessaries.

13:6   Insane, Incompetent, or Intoxicated Persons

Attention often centers on insane persons as a class of persons who lack legal capacity to enter contracts. It is actually more appropriate to refer to "incompetent" persons because of the broad definition of the term. An incompetent person is one who is so lacking in mental capacity that he is unable to understand the nature and consequences of his acts and, in the case of a contract, of the agreement itself. A person may be classified as incompetent by virtue of insanity, severe mental retardation, or mental deterioration accompanying senility, as long as the person is incapable of understanding the character of the transaction in question.

An intoxicated person may be found to lack contractual capacity if he is so intoxicated that he has no knowledge of what he is doing.

The validity of a contract entered into by an incompetent person depends on the time of contract and the status of the person at the time. Contracts entered into by a person who has already been adjudicated insane or otherwise incompetent by a proper court are absolutely void, and such contracts cannot be ratified, even after the person regains sanity. If a person was insane or otherwise incompetent at the time a contract was entered into, but there had been no prior adjudication of such incompetence, the contract is voidable—that is, it may be ratified or repudiated by the person if he recovers, in much the same manner as a minor may repudiate or ratify a contract on attaining majority. Similarly, if a person was so intoxicated when he entered a contract that he was incapable of understanding what he was doing, generally he may, on recovery of sobriety, repudiate or ratify the contract.

Whether a contract is executory or executed also has an effect on repudiation. In the case of executory contracts, the courts generally grant incompetent and intoxicated persons the same right of avoidance as is possessed by minors. As for executed contracts, however, the rules are somewhat different. The courts permit avoidance only where the other party may be restored to the position he occupied prior to the contract. Thus, if the incompetent or intoxicated person has dissipated the consideration received and cannot give the other party equally valuable consideration, avoidance will not be permitted. This rule presupposes the good faith of the other party; if the other party in fact knew and intentionally took advantage of the incompetence or intoxication, then fraud is likely to be found and the insane or intoxicated person will be permitted to avoid the contract notwithstanding his inability to return the consideration.

Issues that must be determined when one party to a contract seeks to repudiate it on the ground of his insanity or intoxication include whether the person was in fact either insane or intoxicated, the degree of any such insanity or intoxication, and the effect that such insanity or intoxication had on the person's ability to comprehend what was happening. As the following case shows, the mere fact that a person suffers from mental disease, even one that is recognized as a serious impairment, does not necessarily lead to the conclusion that the person does not have the mental capacity to contract.

Smalley

v

Baker

262 Cal App 2d 824, 69 Cal Rptr 521
(California Court of Appeal, 1968)

[Smalley contracted with Baker for a license to market an axle puller and paid a $10,000 deposit as part of the agreement. Later, Smalley sued Baker to rescind the contract. The trial court found that Smalley was mentally incompetent to contract and entered judgment in his favor. The evidence as to Smalley's mental condition was (1) that he was a manic-depressive; (2) that he had been hospitalized in mental institutions prior to the agreement and was hospitalized for about a month after negotiations had begun but before the agreement was en-

tered; (3) that at the time of the contract Smalley was in a manic stage; and (4) that a manic-depressive in the manic stage feels invincible, is unable to realistically evaluate business transactions, and has grossly impaired judgment. Baker appealed from the judgment.]

Molinari, P. J.

*   *   *

In California, as in many states, a party is entitled to rescission of a contract if, when he entered into the contract, he was not mentally competent to deal with the subject before him with a full understanding of his rights, the test being, in each instance, whether he understood the nature, purpose and effect of what he did. . . . The test is aimed at cognitive capacity and specifically asks the question whether the party understood the transaction which he seeks to avoid. Some contracts require less competence than others, so that the test of understanding varies from one contract to the next. . . .

The traditional test of competence goes to understanding, that is, cognitive capacity, rather than to motivation. . . . Accordingly, cases in other jurisdictions have denied rescission to persons entering into contracts while afflicted by psychoses of the manic-depressive type because this particular illness impairs judgment but not understanding. . . . It should be here noted that the manic-depressive has alternating moods of euphoria and depression, and that during the euphoric cycle, or the excited phase of the illness the imprudent tendencies of the manic may motivate him to enter into ill-advised contracts and thus bring his contractual competence into question. . . .

One case has held that a party is entitled to rescission of a contract executed during the manic phase of a manic-depressive psychosis: *Faber v Sweet Style Mfg. Corp.* (1963) 40 Misc. 2d 212 [242 NYS2d 763]. In that case, the court acknowledged that the manic-depressive psychosis does not render a party incompetent under the traditional test of lack of understanding of the transaction, but stated that since this test was developed prior to the recognition of the manic-depressive psychosis as a distinct form of mental illness, it is now appropriate to broaden that test in light of recent psychiatric developments (*Faber, supra,* at p. 767.) Essentially, the court broadened the test of understanding to a motivational test which may be stated thusly: if, but for the mental illness, the contract would not have been entered into, then the contract is voidable. . . .

Our inquiry, therefore, is whether the *Faber* test is applicable in California. . . . There are, however, no California cases dealing with manic-depressive psychosis with respect to contractual incompetency.

Before proceeding to discuss the law of contractual incompetency applicable in this state to a contract entered into by a manic-depressive psychotic, we note that the Legislature has categorized incompetency due to weakness of mind as follows: (1) Total weakness of mind which leaves a person entirely without understanding and renders such person incapable of making a contract of any kind . . . ; (2) a lesser weakness of mind which does not leave a person entirely without understanding but destroys the capacity of the person to make a contract, thus rendering the contract subject to rescission . . . ; and (3) a still lesser weakness which provides sufficient grounds to rescind a contract because of undue influence. . . . [A California statute] provides that undue influence consists "In taking an unfair advantage of another's weakness of mind. . . ." In [an earlier California case] it is noted that the lesser weakness of mind referred to in section 1575 need not be long-lasting or wholly incapacitating, but may consist of such factors as lack of full vigor due to age, physical condition, emotional anguish, or a combination of such factors. . . . It would appear, therefore, that since the manic-depressive psychosis is a mental illness it is clearly a weakness of mind in the context of [the California statute].

The manic phase of the illness under discussion is not, however, a weakness of mind rendering a person incompetent to contract within the meaning of [California] Civil Code sections 38 and 39. These sections exclude the manic-depressive psychosis by their very language since they make specific reference to the person's *"understanding."* This language, as interpreted by the decisions, establishes the "understanding" or cognitive test as the prevailing standard of legal competency. As already pointed out, the cognitive test deals with the mental capacity to understand the nature and purpose and effect of the transaction and not with the motivation for entering into it. The manic phase of the manic-depressive psychosis does not impair such understanding, but only relates to the motivation. Notwithstanding the long-standing psychiatric recognition of such psychosis, the Legislature has not, in its wisdom, seen fit to broaden section 39 so as to include within its ambit the motivational standard of incompetency. We may not merely speculate that the Legislature has been oblivious of psychiatric developments. It should be apparent that the Legislature must be aware of the conflict posed by the desire to protect the manic, on the one hand, and on the other hand, the desire to safeguard the manic's right freely to contract and the stability and security of business transactions. An important consideration is that the motivational test may be used by both the manic and the person with whom he has contracted as a pretext to escape from a bad bargain or to avoid a bargain which has not come up to expectations.

In the present case all the evidence shows that Smalley did have the capacity to understand what he was doing. . . . In short, under the traditional test of competence set out in Civil Code section 39, Smalley was not incompetent to enter into a contract.

In this case the court found that there was no evidence of fraud. Not only is the record devoid of any evidence of fraud, but there is no evidence of unfairness, overreaching or undue influence. There is no claim or showing that Baker knew or was aware of Smalley's mental illness, or that he took advantage of such illness. . . . We, therefore, conclude that the finding that Smalley did not have the requisite mental capacity to enter into the agreements which are the subject of the action is not supported by the evidence.

[The court went on to find that Smalley had not consented to a substituted license modification agreement, and affirmed the judgment on that basis.]

Incompetent and intoxicated persons generally are liable on their contracts for necessaries in the same manner and to the same extent as are minors.

13:7   Convicts

In the absence of a statute to the contrary, a person convicted of and imprisoned for the commission of a felony generally has the right to enter into contracts. However, he may be denied access to the courts to enforce contracts. Some states have statutes restricting the right of a convicted felon to contract while in prison.

13:8   Married Women

The evolutionary nature of the law and the manner in which it responds to political and social changes and forces may be briefly illustrated by a discussion of the legal capacity of married women to contract. At common law a husband and wife became one person on marriage, and that person was the husband. A married woman was totally incapable of contracting, and her contracts were treated as absolutely void. In theory at least, the chief purpose behind a married woman's contractual incapacity was a desire to protect her. Blackstone, a noted eighteenth-century English jurist and commentator on the common law, thus stated "that even the disabilities which the wife lies under are for the most part intended for her protection and benefit: so great a favorite is the female sex of the laws of England."[1]

In response to demands for changes in the United States, each state gradually enacted constitutional provisions and statutes, commonly known as *Married Women's Property Acts*. This legislation removed the legal disabilities imposed on women under the common law. Today, a married woman—and a single woman, for that matter—may enter binding contracts.

Key Concepts and Terms

- Members of certain classes of people are presumed by the law to lack legal capacity to contract. These classes are minors, insane, incompetent, or intoxicated persons, and some convicts.
- Except as otherwise specified by statute, minors lack legal capacity to contract, and a minor's contract cannot be enforced against him.
- A minor may avoid a contract at any time during minority. When a minor repudiates a contract, he must return the consideration received from the other party. If that is impossible, most courts place the loss on the adult party. Other courts require the minor to account to the adult party for the value of the consideration received by the minor.
- A minor may ratify a contract after reaching the age of majority.
- A minor may be liable on a contract for the purchase of necessaries not supplied by a parent or guardian. Such liability is quasi-contractual in nature and is limited to the reasonable value of the necessaries received by the minor.
- A person who is so lacking in mental capacity or so intoxicated that he is incapable of understanding the nature or consequences of his acts lacks legal capacity to contract. Contracts entered into by incompetent or intoxicated persons may be either absolutely void or merely voidable, depending on whether there has been a previous judicial declaration of incompetence. Where the contract is voidable, the incompetent or intoxicated person may ratify or repudiate it in much the same manner as a minor.
- A convict generally has the right to enter contracts while in prison, unless provided otherwise by statute.
- At common law married women lacked legal capacity to contract. Today, married women have the same right to contract as married men.

- Age of Majority
- Convicts
- Insane, Incompetent, or Intoxicated Persons
- Married Women's Property Acts

- Minors (Infants)
- Necessaries
- Ratification
- Repudiation

---

[1]Blackstone, *Commentaries on the Laws of England*, 159 (G. Chase, ed., 1890).

Questions and Case Problems

1. A, a resident of a state where the age of majority is 18, leaves home and becomes self-supporting at age 16. An avid tennis player, he hopes someday to become a pro. In line with this goal, a year later he purchases tennis equipment worth $200 from B, a store owner, and signs a contract for tennis lessons with C, a tennis professional. A appears older than his years, and neither B nor C inquires about his age. After he completes the tennis lessons, C advises him that he is not good enough to play professionally. When A is 18 years three months old, he voluntarily commits himself to a mental institution, where he is determined to be incompetent. While he is institutionalized, all his tennis equipment is stolen. After two years of treatment A is released from the institution, his competency restored. He immediately notifies B and C that he is repudiating his contracts with them and demands that his money be refunded. Is A's demand justified?

2. Little enters an agreement with Turner, a minor, to assist Turner in financing a college education. Under the agreement Little agrees to loan Turner up to $30 per month, in exchange for Turner's execution of a promissory note when he receives each loan. The promissory notes provide for repayment of the amounts loaned, plus 6 percent interest. Of 23 promissory notes executed by Turner under the agreement, all but four are executed while he is a minor. When Little sues Turner on the 23 promissory notes, Turner pleads infancy as a defense to 19 of the notes. How should the case be decided?

3. What is the rationale behind the conclusion that some persons lack the legal capacity to contract?

4. Under what circumstances may a minor's contract be enforced?

5. In 1902 King, a 20-year-old minor, entered into an agreement with Welch, her guardian, which provided that certain property of King's should be held in trust by Welch. The agreement also provided that any income-producing property thereafter acquired by King be transferred to Welch to be included in the trust. Over the years King received and approved annual accounts from Welch and his successor trustees, but never had occasion to transfer any property to the trust. In 1931 King's husband gave her a $1,000 bond. Since the bond constituted income-producing property, the trustees demanded that King turn it over to the trust, but she refused. The trustees sued to recover the value of the bond, and King defended on the ground that she was a minor at the time the contract was entered. How should the case be decided?

6. Bowling, a 16-year-old high school student, goes to Sperry Ford with his grandmother, with whom he lives, and his aunt, and purchases an automobile for $140. He borrows $90 of the purchase price from his aunt, but the title is placed in his name. Bowling has a summer job at a restaurant some eight or nine miles from his home, and he normally drives to work. Sperry's manager understands that Bowling needs the car for transportation to that job. Within a week of the purchase one of the car's bearings burns out. Bowling returns the car to Sperry Ford. When he is informed that it will cost $45 to $95 to repair the car, he leaves it at Sperry, repudiates the contract, and demands the return of his money. Sperry claims that the bearing has burned out as a result of Bowling's improper operation of the car. When Sperry refuses to refund the money, Bowling sues. How should the case be decided?

7. A fervently believes that she is the Queen of England. On occasion she will don

royal regalia and perform her duties as monarch, issuing orders, signing contracts in the name of the Queen, and otherwise behaving as a queen might. On other occasions, however, she appears perfectly normal and owns and operates a small business. She enters a contract with B to have siding placed on her home. A couple of weeks later she has second thoughts and informs B that she wishes to cancel the contract. Is A entitled to repudiate the contract on the ground of lack of competence? Would your answer be any different if the contract had also called for the installation of a moat around her residence?

8. What facts should a court consider in determining whether a person lacked the mental competence to contract?

9. Beginning in 1965 or 1966, Grannen began experiencing memory loss. Other symptoms of organic mental disability later appeared, and by 1968 she was incapable of managing her own checking accounts. Physicians diagnosed her condition as a brain disorder involving gradual physical and mental deterioration, and in April 1972 she was declared incompetent. In 1970, Grannen had transferred certain property to Ey, her brother. After the declaration of incompetency, Grannen's guardian sued for the return of the property. Should he be permitted to recover the property?

10. Abrams purchases a new car for $10,000 from Murphy Motors on Friday. Over the weekend he drives the car 1,000 miles and is involved in an accident that causes $2,000 damage to the car. On Monday he returns the car to Murphy Motors and demands his money back, claiming that he had been on hallucinogenic drugs when he bought the car and had remained under their influence all through the weekend. Must Murphy Motors return Abrams' money? If Murphy does return his money, may it deduct any amount? If so, what amount?

14 Illegal Agreements

14:1 Introduction; Classification of Illegal Agreements

A competent person has wide latitude in exercising the right to enter contracts. This right is, however, not unlimited, and the courts are uniformly agreed that otherwise valid contracts may be held invalid if their formation or performance violates the law or public policy. The invalidity of such agreements, commonly referred to as illegal contracts or illegal bargains, is based on a regard for the public welfare and the effect that enforcement of illegal contracts would have on public health, morality, or welfare, rather than any defect in the actual bargaining process between the parties. Thus, a determination that a particular agreement or type of agreement is illegal is essentially a determination that it is in the public interest that such an agreement should not be recognized as a binding contract.

Illegal agreements are often classified as either (1) contrary to law (or to statute) or (2) contrary to *public policy*. While it is true that both types of agreements will be declared illegal, it is important to bear in mind that there is no clear-cut distinction between the two. For example, an agreement calling for the commission of a crime is often cited as the classic example of an agreement that is illegal and void because it violates express statutory law. Such an illustration is correct. It is obvious, however, that such an agreement would also be contrary to a state's public policy. As another example, an agreement calling for the commission of some act prohibited under common-law principles might be classified as illegal because it is contrary to law or because it is contrary to public policy, and either classification would be acceptable. The important point to remember is that a person's right to contract is subject to the paramount power of the state to protect the public good and welfare.

Illegal agreements are void and, with the exceptions noted later, are unenforceable in court.

14:2 Agreements Contrary to Law

An agreement that violates or that cannot be performed without violating some constitutional, statutory, or other rule of law is illegal and void. One should bear in mind that in order for an attempted contract to be declared void on this ground, the agreement itself must contemplate a violation of the law. The fact that some illegal act is actually committed during the performance of the contract does not mean the contract is illegal. If the formation of the contract violated no rule of law, and if the contract could have been performed without violating any law, then the contract is a legal and binding one. For example, assume that A contracts with B for the transportation and delivery of certain goods from one city to another. B loads all the goods into one truck, thereby violating a statutory provision as to the maximum weight that can be carried by the truck. The fact that B has violated the statute in the performance of the contract does not render the contract illegal, since B, by using two trucks, could easily have performed the contract without violating that statute. However, if the contract between A and B had called for the shipment of all the goods in the one truck, then the agreement would have been illegal, since it would have been impossible to perform the agreement without violating the law.

The discussion that follows focuses on several types of statutes that may be violated in the formation or performance of an agreement, thereby causing the agreement to be illegal.

Usury Laws   *Usury laws* specify the maximum rate of interest that may be charged on various types of loans. The interest rates allowed vary from state to state, and within a state the rates may vary depending on the type of loan involved, the lending institution, or the borrower. The common element of state usury statutes is that it is illegal for a lender to charge a rate of interest higher than that specified by the applicable statute.

Since the usury laws apply only to loans of money, and not to sales or leases, the parties to a contract may sometimes be tempted to characterize a loan as some other type of transaction. The courts have held that the character of the transaction determines whether it is usurious, and a court will look through a subterfuge to determine whether the transaction is actually a loan of money.

Whether installment sales involve loans of money is a question to which courts have found conflicting answers. The general rule is that a seller agreeing to a sale on credit may charge a higher price for a particular item than he would charge if the sale were for cash, and that no loan of money is involved in such a transaction. Some courts have held in accordance with this general rule; others have held that installment sales do indeed involve loans of money and are subject to the usury laws. Some states have adopted specific statutes governing the rates of interest permissible on installment sales.

The disposition of a loan contract that is found to be usurious varies from state to state. Under some statutes the contract is absolutely void and the lender can recover neither principal nor interest; other statutes permit the recovery of principal, but not interest; still other statutes permit recovery of principal and interest up to the legally permitted rate, but preclude recovery of any interest in excess of that permitted by law; and others contain variations on these basic approaches.

Gambling Statutes   Most states have adopted statutes that prohibit gambling agreements. The essential element of a gambling agreement is chance—the parties stand to gain or lose on the occurrence or nonoccurrence of some event in which they have no interest other than their gain or loss. Lotteries are also games of chance and are also generally prohibited, although some states now make certain lotteries, notably state lotteries, legal.

Gambling contracts must be distinguished from certain other contracts that also involve an element of speculation. Insurance contracts, for example, condition the right to recover on the occurrence of a contingency, but the insured has some insurable interest.[1] *Futures contracts,* under which the parties contract for the sale of personal property to be delivered at some future date, also involve speculation, but the courts have held such contracts to be valid if an actual delivery of the property is contemplated when the contract is formed. The contract would be an illegal gambling contract only if it involved nothing more than speculation on the future performance of the market, without any intent that the property ever be delivered.

Promotional schemes conducted by retail and other businesses that offer certain prizes as an inducement to customers are valid provided the customer does not pay for the opportunity to participate. If the right to participate is conditioned on the purchase of some product, then the customer is being required to give consideration for a chance at winning the prize. This is considered to be illegal gambling and is prohibited in most states.

Sunday Laws   Under the common law, contracts could be performed on any day of the week. Today most, if not all, states have statutes, commonly referred to as *Sunday laws,* or "Blue Laws," which regulate the business that may be performed on Sundays. The basic purpose of such statutes, whose provisions vary widely, is to prohibit the transaction of business on Sunday and to maintain that day as one of rest. The legality of a contract entered into or performed on Sunday depends on the particular Sunday law that a state has enacted. While some statutes expressly declare that particular contracts entered into or performed on Sunday are invalid, other states do not prohibit the making of contracts on Sunday.

Sunday laws are often honored more in their breach than in their observance. Nevertheless, it is always better to execute and perform the contract on some day other than Sunday to avoid any possibility of the Sunday law's being utilized to void an otherwise valid contract.

Regulatory and Licensing Statutes   Federal, state, and local governments have a variety of laws regulating the conduct of business and requiring that licenses be obtained by those practicing certain businesses. In determining the legality of contracts entered into by unlicensed persons or corporations, the courts generally distinguish between those licensing statutes that are regulatory in nature and those that are intended merely to produce revenue. For example, statutes that require professionals to be licensed are regulatory and are normally intended for the protection of the public, and a contract entered into by an unlicensed professional is illegal and void. Business license taxes, on the other hand, which are imposed by

---

[1]Insurable interests are discussed in Chapter 40.

statute, normally are designed as revenue-raising measures, and a contract entered into in violation of a business license law is generally considered enforceable, provided the business subsequently obtains the necessary license. In determining whether a particular licensing statute is a regulatory or a revenue law, the intent of the legislature or other enacting body governs.

14:3 Agreements Contrary to Public Policy

The underlying premise behind the rule that contracts contrary to public policy are illegal is that no person has a right to do something that is detrimental to the public good or welfare. Hence, the determination as to whether a particular agreement is contrary to public policy necessarily depends on an appraisal of the public good. The meaning of "public policy" is vague and variable, with no fixed definition applicable to all cases. Public policy is not static; it changes in response to the needs and interests of the times. Moreover, each state may have its own public policy, so that a contract illegal in one state as contrary to public policy may be legal and enforceable in another state.

Legislative bodies are primarily responsible for declaring the public policy and enacting statutes embodying such policy. Courts may also exercise authority in this area, and a contract may be declared illegal even though there is no statutory prohibition against such a contract.

The rationale behind the public policy concept, as well as the evolutionary nature of public policy, may be illustrated by a brief consideration of the law relating to agreements that promote sexual immorality. The traditionally accepted rule is that any agreement that has the direct effect of promoting sexual immorality is illegal and unenforceable. Hence, an agreement that involves the payment of consideration in exchange for the maintenance of a meretricious (immoral or illegal) sexual relationship has been held contrary to public policy and to the best interests of society. As the following case indicates, however, the courts are beginning to reconsider the law in this area in light of changes in contemporary social and sexual mores.

Marvin
v
Marvin
18 Cal 3d 660, 134 Cal Rptr 815, 557 P2d 106
(California Supreme Court, 1976)

[Plaintiff Michelle Marvin alleged that she and defendant Lee Marvin had entered an oral agreement in 1964 under which the parties agreed that, while they lived together, they would share equally all earnings and property acquired. The plaintiff agreed to give up her career as a singer and to devote her time exclusively to the defendant as a companion, homemaker, housekeeper, and cook, in exchange for the defendant's promise to support her financially. The parties lived together seven years, during which time substantial property was acquired, all in the defendant's name. After the parties separated, the plaintiff sued to enforce the alleged contract. After the trial court entered judgment for the defendant, the plaintiff appealed.]

Tobriner, J.

*   *   *

During the past 15 years, there has been a substantial increase in the number of couples living together without marrying. Such nonmarital relationships lead to legal controversy when one partner dies or the couple separates. . . . We take this opportunity to resolve that controversy and to declare the principles which should govern distribution of property acquired in a nonmarital relationship.

We [conclude that the] courts should enforce express contracts between nonmarital partners except to the extent that the contract is explicitly founded on the consideration of meretricious sexual services. . . .

Defendant first and principally relies on the contention that the alleged contract is so closely related to the supposed "immoral" character of the relationship between plaintiff and himself that the enforcement of the contract would violate public policy. He points to cases asserting that a contract between nonmarital partners is unenforceable if it is "involved in" an illicit relationship . . . , or made in "contemplation" of such a relationship. . . . A review of the numerous California decisions concerning contracts between nonmarital partners, however, reveals that the courts have not employed such broad and uncertain standards to strike down contracts. The decisions instead disclose a narrower and more precise standard: a contract between nonmarital partners is unenforceable only *to the extent* that it *explicitly* rests upon the immoral and illicit consideration of meretricious sexual services. [Court's emphasis.] . . .

Although the past decisions hover over the issue in the somewhat wispy form of the figures of a Chagall painting, we can abstract from those decisions a clear and simple rule. The fact that a man and woman live together without marriage, and engage in a sexual relationship, does not in itself invalidate agreements between them relating to their earnings, property, or expenses. Neither is such an agreement invalid merely because the parties may have contemplated the creation or continuation of a nonmarital relationship when they entered into it. Agreements between nonmarital partners fail only to the extent that they rest upon a consideration of meretricious sexual services. Thus the rule asserted by defendant, that a contract fails if it is "involved in" or made "in contemplation" of a nonmarital relationship, cannot be reconciled with the decisions. . . .

The decisions in [other California] cases thus demonstrate that a contract between nonmarital partners, even if expressly made in contemplation of a common living arrangement, is invalid only if sexual acts form an inseparable part of the consideration for the agreement. In sum, a court will not enforce a contract for the pooling of property and earnings if it is explicitly and inseparably based upon services as a paramour. . . . [E]ven if sexual services are part of the contractual consideration, any *severable* portion of the contract supported by independent consideration will still be enforced. [Court's emphasis.]

The principle that a contract between nonmarital partners will be enforced unless expressly and inseparably based upon an illicit consideration of sexual services not only represents the distillation of the decisional law, but also offers a far more precise and workable standard than that advocated by defendant. . . .

[A] standard which inquires whether an agreement is "involved" in or "contemplates" a nonmarital relationship is vague and unworkable. Virtually all agreements between nonmarital partners can be said to be "involved" in some sense in the fact of their sexual relationship, or to "contemplate" the existence of that relationship. Thus defendant's proposed standards, if taken literally, might invalidate all agreements between nonmarital partners, a result no one favors. . . .

In summary, we base our opinion on the principle that adults who voluntarily live together and engage in sexual relations are nonetheless as competent an any other persons to contract respecting their earnings and property rights. Of course, they cannot lawfully contract to pay for the performance of sexual services, for such a contract is, in essence, an agreement for prostitution and unlawful for that reason. But they may agree to pool their earnings and to hold all property acquired during the relationship in accord with the law governing community property; conversely they may agree that each partner's earnings and the property acquired from those earnings remains [*sic*] the separate property of the earning partner. So long as the agreement does not rest upon illicit meretricious consideration, the parties may order their economic affairs as they choose, and no policy precludes the courts from enforcing such agreements.

In the present instance, plaintiff alleges that the parties agreed to pool their earnings, that they contracted to share equally in all property acquired, and that defendant agreed to support plaintiff. The terms of the contract as alleged do not rest upon any unlawful consideration. . . .

In summary, we believe that the prevalence of nonmarital relationships in modern society and the social acceptance of them, marks this as a time when our courts should by no means apply the doctrine of the unlawfulness of the so-called meretricious relationship to the instant case. As we have explained, the nonen-forceability of agreements expressly providing for meretricious conduct rested upon the fact that such conduct, as the word suggests, pertained to and encompassed prostitution. To equate the nonmarital relationship of today to such a subject matter is to do violence to an accepted and wholly different practice. . . .

The mores of the society have indeed changed so radically in regard to cohabitation that we cannot impose a standard based on alleged moral considerations that have apparently been so widely abandoned by so many. Lest we be misunderstood, however, we take this occasion to point out that the structure of society itself largely depends upon the institution of marriage, and nothing we have said in this opinion should be taken to derogate from that institution. The joining of the man and woman in marriage is at once the most socially productive and individually fulfilling relationship that one can enjoy in the course of a lifetime.

We conclude that the judicial barriers that may stand in the way of a policy based upon the fulfillment of the reasonable expectations of the parties to a monmarital relationship should be removed. . . .

[Judgment reversed.]

The following is a discussion of some of the types of contracts that the courts have frequently held to be illegal on the ground that they are contrary to public policy.

Exculpatory Agreements   An *exculpatory agreement* relieves one party of liability for injury or damage caused by his own negligence or other wrong. Some states have adopted statutes that prohibit exculpatory clauses in certain circumstances. Where there is no statutory prohibition, exculpatory clauses are frequently held invalid as a matter of public policy.

Exculpatory clauses typically are included in contracts to enable a party to avoid responsibility that would otherwise be placed on that party by law for the public benefit. For example, a hotel might insert a clause in the registration agreement that it is not liable for any loss sustained by a guest as a result of any cause. The purpose of the clause is to relieve the hotel from any liability, even in the event of a loss caused by the hotel staff's negligence. Thus, exculpatory clauses are frequently objected to on the ground that they tend to induce a lack of care.

Two broad categories of exculpatory agreements have received particular attention in that regard: (1) employment contracts and (2) contracts between business people and members of the general public.

An employer has certain duties toward its employees.[2] Therefore, an employment contract that contains an exculpatory clause absolving an employer from any liability to its employees for injuries caused by the employer's negligence is usually held to be void. Similarly, a contract that contains a clause that exempts a businessperson from liability for injury or damage to customers caused by the businessperson's negligence is usually void.

An important factor in determining the validity of an exculpatory contract is the relative bargaining power of the parties. Where one person has a markedly inferior bargaining position, a contract that relieves the dominant party of liability for negligence will often be held invalid as contrary to public policy. For example, when contracting with an employer, an employee frequently must accept whatever terms the employer offers; similarly, a customer must ordinarily accept the terms proposed by a businessperson. In both these situations, the exculpatory clause would be considered invalid because of the dominant party's ability to take advantage of the weaker party's need for employment or for the particular goods or services offered. Where an exculpatory clause is included in a contract between parties of relatively equal bargaining power, the courts are more inclined to uphold it. For example, if two businesspersons of equal bargaining position negotiate a contract containing an exculpatory clause, the purpose of which is not the evasion of a legal duty but rather the allocation of the risk of loss, the courts generally will uphold the clause.

As the foregoing discussion suggests, the policy against exculpatory clauses is closely related to the policy against adhesion contracts and unconscionable contracts.[3] In fact, sometimes an invalid exculpatory clause will make the entire contract invalid on the ground that it is an adhesion contract or an unconscionable contract.

The following case illustrates the types of factors that the courts consider in determining whether a particular exculpatory clause should be enforced.

Crowell

v

Housing Authority of Dallas
495 SW2d 887
(Texas Supreme Court, 1973)

Walker, Justice.

*　　*　　*

Lewis Crowell *et al.*, petitioners, instituted this suit against Housing Authority of the City of Dallas, respondent. The suit was brought . . . to recover for medical expenses incurred and physical and mental pain suffered by peti-

---

[2]The employer–employee relationship is discussed in Chapter 51.
[3]Adhesion contracts and unconscionable contracts are discussed in Chapter 12.

tioners' father, who was alleged to have died as a result of carbon monoxide poisoning caused by a defective gas heater in an apartment leased by him from respondent. The trial court granted respondent's motion for summary judgment, and the Court of Civil Appeals affirmed. . . . We reverse the judgments of the courts below and remand the cause to the district court for trial.

Petitioners alleged that respondent had exclusive responsibility for maintenance and repair of the gas heater, and no attempt has been made to show that the heater was in proper condition or that respondent was not negligent. The summary judgment in respondent's favor is based on the following provision of the lease between respondent and the decedent:

> ". . . nor shall the Landlord nor any of its representatives or employees be liable for any damage to person or property of the Tenant, his family, or his visitors, which might result from the condition of these or other premises of the Landlord, from theft or from any cause whatsoever. . . ."

Agreements exempting a party from future liability for negligence are generally recognized as valid and effective except where, because of the relationship of the parties, the exculpatory provision is contrary to public policy or the public interest. If the contract is between private persons who bargain from positions of substantially equal strength, the agreement is ordinarily enforced by the courts. The exculpatory agreement will be declared void, however, where one party is at such disadvantage in bargaining power that he is practically compelled to submit to the stipulation. It is generally held, for example, that a contract exempting an employer from all liability for

negligent injury of his employees in the course of their employment is void as against public policy. The same rule applies to agreements exempting public utilities from liability for negligence in the performance of their duty of public service. . . .

The rules applicable to public utilities have been applied by some courts to innkeepers and public warehousemen. According to Professor Prosser, there is a definite tendency to extend the same rules to other professional bailees such as garagemen and owners of parking lots and parcel checkrooms. These bailees are under no public duty, but they deal with the public and the indispensable need for their services deprives the customer of any real bargaining power. . . .

The same considerations lead us to the conclusion that the exculpatory agreement in the present case is contrary to public policy. Respondent is a public body organized for the declared public purpose, among others, of providing safe and sanitary dwelling accommodations to persons of low income. It may lease accommodations only to families or persons who lack sufficient income to enable them, without financial assistance, to live in decent, safe and sanitary dwellings without overcrowding. . . . [T]he situation of respondent and its tenants presents a classic example of unequal bargaining power. The terms of the contract are dictated by respondent, and a prospective tenant has no choice but to accept them if he and his family are to enjoy decent housing accommodations not otherwise available to them. We hold that the exculpatory provision quoted above is contrary to public policy and void [insofar] as it purports to affect respondent's liability in the present case.

[Judgment reversed.]

Agreements in Restraint of Trade Agreements that tend to restrict competition or otherwise to interfere with the normal flow of goods may be held illegal on public policy grounds. Examples of this kind of agreement are covenants not to compete, price-fixing agreements, and monopoly agreements. Federal and state statutory and common law dealing with contracts in restraint of trade are treated in Chapter 54. It should be noted here, however, that the law has long frowned on various types of anticompetitive agreements and that public policy has often been used as a ground for declaring such agreements illegal.

Agreements Injurious to Public Service   Any agreement that deters a public servant from the proper performance of his duties is obviously contrary to the public interest. The courts have uniformly held such agreements to be invalid. Contracts that call for the use of corrupt or other improper means to secure favorable government service are unenforceable. For example, if A contracts with B to secure a government contract from C, and A authorizes B to offer C future employment in exchange for the award of the contract, the contract between A and B is void; B cannot recover the fee promised by A, even if B in fact secures the contract from C. Similarly, if A and B enter into a lobbying contract under which B is to use his personal influence with various legislators to secure favorable treatment on a particular bill, a court will hold the agreement to be an illegal and unenforceable lobbying contract. On the other hand, if the contract in either of the above situations calls only for the use of proper means to secure favorable governmental action, and proper means are in fact used, B can enforce the contracts against A.

 Procedures for the award of government contracts, as well as the propriety of various lobbying activities, are largely governed by federal and state statutes. A businessperson desiring to obtain a government contract or to otherwise influence the activities of government officials should always familiarize himself with the applicable statutes. The use of improper methods may result not only in an unenforceable contract, but in criminal liability as well.[4]

14:4   Effect of Illegality

Generally, illegal agreements are unenforceable; a court will leave the parties to the contract as it finds them. The fact that one party may have parted with consideration, while the other party has not, does not entitle the first party to any relief from a court. For example, assume that A agrees with B to act as a courier for an illegal gambling operation run by B and that A performs the services contracted for, but B refuses to pay A. If A were to sue B for the compensation promised by B, a court would ordinarily refuse to award A any money. The rule that illegal contracts are unenforceable is not based on any desire to punish one party or to reward another. Rather, the rule is based on the premise that it is in the public interest to refuse any assistance to illegal transactions.

Exceptions to the Rule of Unenforceability   In most illegal agreements, both parties are completely aware of the transaction and are considered by the courts to be *in pari delicto* (equally at fault). Under such circumstances, refusal to enforce the

---

4Potential criminal liability is discussed in Chapter 4.

agreement does not offend any sense of justice, even though one of the parties may suffer some detriment. Sometimes, however, only one party knows of the facts rendering the contract illegal, and the other party is innocent of any wrongdoing and may even be an innocent victim of the first party. When the facts reveal that the parties were not in pari delicto, a court will ordinarily grant relief to the innocent party and refuse any relief to the guilty party.

The rule that an innocent party may seek relief from a court is especially applicable to situations where the law rendering the agreement illegal was designed for the protection of one party against the other party's acts. Thus, where a law was passed to protect a class of persons from the unscrupulous activities of other persons, and a member of the protected class is victimized in precisely the manner that the law seeks to prevent, the fact that the transaction took the form of an illegal agreement will not deter a court from granting appropriate relief to the victimized party. This principle might be applied, for example, to award relief to a consumer who contracted with a seller in violation of a statute designed to protect consumers.[5]

Partial Illegality; Effect of Divisibility   The discussion thus far has proceeded on the assumption that an agreement is either legal or illegal in its entirety. It is possible, however, for a single agreement to contain both legal and illegal undertakings. Moreover, the same parties may enter into a number of separate and distinct agreements, some legal and some not. The question then arises as to whether any part of the agreement or agreements between the parties may be enforced, or whether the illegality of one agreement affects all agreements. In the case of multiple separate agreements, the answer is fairly simple. A contract between two parties entered into for legal purposes is valid and enforceable, even though the same parties may have also entered into an illegal agreement.

However, if an agreement contains both legal and illegal portions, the determination of the enforceability of the legal portions is more complicated. The courts generally look to whether the legal portions of the agreement are divisible or separable from the illegal portions. If the legal part of the agreement can be enforced without the illegal portion and without injustice to the parties, the courts normally will enforce the agreement, provided a statute does not declare the entire agreement void and the agreement itself does not indicate the parties' intent that the contract stand or fall as a whole. The question of *separability* necessarily depends on the circumstances of a given case. Generally, however, an agreement is more likely to be considered separable when the consideration involved is legal and only one of several promises is not legal, than when the consideration itself is illegal. Separability may also depend on whether the illegal portion of the agreement goes to the very essence of the parties' agreement, or whether it is ancillary or incidental to the transaction. If the legal portions cannot be separated from the illegal portions of the agreement, then the entire agreement will be considered void and unenforceable.

The court's inquiry in the *Marvin* case set out earlier demonstrates how a court may determine whether an agreement, or part of an agreement, that is based on

---

[5]Consumer credit protection, which is one type of consumer protection, is discussed in Chapter 27.

legal consideration may be enforced, despite the fact that the agreement also contains illegal undertakings or that the parties contracted for illegal matters in addition to legal ones. Adhesion contracts, unconscionable contracts, and contracts with exculpatory clauses are often held by the courts to be divisible. A court will frequently enforce the legal portions while refusing to enforce those portions that render the contract objectionable. For example, a court might enforce a contract between a health care provider, such as a hospital, and a patient, while refusing to enforce a particular provision of the contract that unfairly limited the health care provider's liability for its employees' negligence.

Key Concepts and Terms

- An agreement that violates or that cannot be performed without violating some rules of law is illegal. Agreements that violate usury laws, gambling laws, Sunday laws, or regulatory laws are illegal.

- An essential element of a gambling contract is chance. Although gambling agreements are illegal, other kinds of agreements involving speculation, such as insurance contracts and futures contracts, are valid and enforceable because they are entered into for legitimate interests. So are promotional schemes, provided the customer does not pay for the opportunity to participate.

- A contract entered into in violation of a regulatory licensing statute is illegal. However, a contract entered into in violation of a revenue-raising licensing measure may be enforced once the license has been obtained.

- Agreements contrary to public policy are invalid. These agreements include agreements in restraint of trade and agreements against the public service. What is considered "public policy" is variable; public policy is not static. It changes with the times.

- An exculpatory clause may be held illegal, particularly if it is used in an employment contract or a contract between a businessperson and a member of the general public. An exculpatory clause that is contained in a contract whose parties have equal bargaining power is likely to be considered legal.

- Agreements in restraint of trade may be held illegal on public policy or statutory grounds.

- Illegal contracts are generally void and unenforceable. However, where the parties are not equally knowledgeable about the contract and are not in pari delicto (equally at fault), the innocent party may be granted relief.

- An illegal portion of a contract does not make the entire contract illegal if it can be enforced without reference to the illegal portion and if the contract is separable. Where the same parties have entered two contracts, one legal and one illegal, the legal contract is enforceable and is not affected by the illegal one.

- Exculpatory Agreements
- Futures Contracts
- Gambling Contracts
- In Pari Delicto
- Public Policy
- Separability (Divisibility)
- Sunday Laws
- Usury Laws

Questions and Case Problems

1. As a promotion in connection with a golf tournament sponsored by the Elks, Marcel Motors, an automobile dealer, agrees to give a new car to any golfer who shoots a hole-in-one. Chenard registers for the tournament, pays the entrance fee of $10, and shoots a hole-in-one. Marcel Motors refuses to give Chenard the car. When Chenard sues, Marcel Motors argues that the promotional scheme was an illegal and unenforceable contract. How should the court rule?

2. In March 1962, Lee & Co. contracted to grade and fill land owned by Latipac, for a price of $740,000. Work began promptly. As required by law, Lee held a valid contractor's license. This license expired in June 1963, because Lee inadvertently failed to submit a renewal application and the $30 renewal fee. Lee completed the contracting job in April 1964 and renewed its license in June 1964. A state statute denied unlicensed contractors the right to bring actions in court to recover money owed for contracting work. Latipac still owed $432,000, but refused to pay. Lee sued. Should Lee be permitted to recover?

3. Discuss the factors that a court should consider in determining whether a contract is contrary to public policy.

4. When Tunkl entered the University of California Los Angeles Medical Center for treatment, he signed a document containing the following:

    "RELEASE: The hospital is a nonprofit, charitable institution. In consideration of the hospital and allied services to be rendered and the rates charged therefor, the patient or his legal representative agrees to and hereby releases The Regents of the University of California, and the hospital from any and all liability for the negligent or wrongful acts or omissions of its employees, if the hospital has used due care in selecting its employees."

   Tunkl subsequently suffered personal injuries, allegedly as a result of the negligence of Medical Center employees, and sued the Medical Center. Should the above release prevent him from recovering for any injuries?

5. Gabl leases commercial space in a multiple-unit residential–business building. A fire damages Gabl's property and Gabl sues the landlord, claiming that the landlord's negligence caused the fire. As a defense, the landlord claims that Gabl's action is barred by an exculpatory provision in the lease agreement exempting the landlord from liability for any damage to Gabl's property from any cause whatsoever. Should the landlord's position be upheld?

6. Prior to undergoing a tubal ligation, Bowman signed a consent form that absolved the attending physicians "from responsibility for any untoward or unfavorable results arising from this procedure." Due to the operating physician's negligence, the sterilization procedure is unsuccessful. Bowman becomes pregnant and suffers various damages as a result. Bowman sues the physician. Does the consent form protect the physician from liability?

7. Why do courts look with disfavor on exculpatory clauses? What factors do courts consider in determining whether to enforce an exculpatory clause?

8. Why do courts refuse to enforce illegal contracts? Under what circumstances will a court grant relief to a party to an illegal contract?

9. Karpinski is a dairyman whose economic survival depends on his ability to obtain a grade A milk contract in an area where such contracts are extremely scarce. Collins, the president of a local creamery, offers Karpinski a grade A contract if Karpinski will pay him a specified rebate. Unable to obtain any other grade A contracts, Karpinski accepts the offer. A formal contract is prepared between Karpinski and the creamery, and Karpinski sells his milk to the creamery for approximately two years. He gives Collins approximately $10,000 in rebate payments during that time. After termination of the contract Karpinski sues Collins for refund of the secret rebates. Collins defends on the ground that since such rebates are prohibited by statute, the agreement between him and Karpinski is an illegal contract. Should this defense be sustained?

10. Liebman, living in France in May 1941, wanted to get his family and himself to Portugal to escape the advancing German army. Rosenthal told Liebman that he, Rosenthal, was an intimate friend of the Portuguese Consul and could obtain visas to Portugal for Liebman and his family, but that it would be necessary to give the Consul $30,000. Liebman gave Rosenthal jewelry worth $28,000 to secure the visas, but Rosenthal absconded with the jewelry. Liebman subsequently met Rosenthal in New York and sued to recover the value of the jewelry. Rosenthal moved for a summary judgment on the ground that the agreement between him and Liebman was illegal. Should Rosenthal's motion be granted?

15 Formal Requisites; Statute of Frauds

15:1 Formal Requisites Generally; Oral Contracts

People may commonly perceive a contract to be a solemn and legalistic written document. This perception is erroneous. In the absence of a statute to the contrary, a contract may be oral as well as written, and no particular form is required. A complete contract may be gathered from several different documents. For example, a series of letters, writings, and telegrams may be connected with each other in such a way as to be considered one contract. Also, a contract may be partly oral and partly written. For example, a verbal acceptance of a written offer may result in the creation of an enforceable contract. A contract may even consist of an undated, unsigned, one-page handwritten document, provided all the required elements of a contract are present, and that no statute imposes more specific requirements.

 A businessperson should always be aware that oral communications may result in the formation of binding contracts. Frequently a telephone conversation that was intended merely as preliminary negotiation toward a contract has resulted in a claim that a contract actually was formed. It is therefore important to express oneself clearly, and to expressly state to the other party that there is to be no contract until an appropriate written document is drafted and signed by all parties. Also, where there is any chance of misunderstanding, an oral communication should immediately be followed up with a written one. Otherwise, if a court finds that the parties reached an oral agreement, which they intended to but never did put into writing, then the oral contract is enforceable.

Certain contracts, most notably those covered by the *statute of frauds*, must be in writing to be enforceable. In addition, if the parties indicate a definite intention not to be bound until a written agreement has been made, a writing is prerequisite to the formation of a contract. The form of some contracts, such as insurance contracts, is specified by statute, and a contract required to be in a particular form is unenforceable unless in that form.

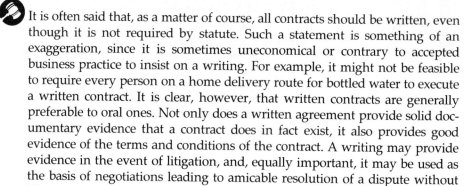 It is often said that, as a matter of course, all contracts should be written, even though it is not required by statute. Such a statement is something of an exaggeration, since it is sometimes uneconomical or contrary to accepted business practice to insist on a writing. For example, it might not be feasible to require every person on a home delivery route for bottled water to execute a written contract. It is clear, however, that written contracts are generally preferable to oral ones. Not only does a written agreement provide solid documentary evidence that a contract does in fact exist, it also provides good evidence of the terms and conditions of the contract. A writing may provide evidence in the event of litigation, and, equally important, it may be used as the basis of negotiations leading to amicable resolution of a dispute without litigation.

15:2   Statute of Frauds

In 1677 the English Parliament, concerned about various fraudulent practices, adopted "An Act For the Prevention of Frauds and Perjuries." This act required that certain specified types of contracts be evidenced by a signed writing. The act, commonly called the Statute of Frauds, subsequently became effective in the American colonies, and today each state, either as a matter of common law or by virtue of statutory enactment, now has its own statute of frauds.

The types of contracts that must be in writing, according to § 4 of the English statute, are (1) a promise of an executor or administrator to pay with his own funds a debt of the deceased, (2) a promise to answer for the debt of another, (3) an agreement made on consideration of marriage, (4) a contract for the sale of land or any interest therein, and (5) an agreement that is not to be performed within a year. Most state statutes of frauds have substantially retained the provisions of § 4.

Under § 17 of the English statute, contracts for the sale of goods for a price of 10 pounds or more were required to be in writing. Most states adopted statutes similar to § 17, but those statutes were supplanted first by the Uniform Sales Act, and then by the UCC, which contains its own statute of frauds with respect to the sale of goods (UCC § 2-201). This provision is discussed in detail in Chapter 19.

Most states, in addition to retaining the basic coverage of § 4 of the English statute, have adopted statutes requiring other particular classes of contracts to be in writing. Moreover, federal laws require that certain contracts be in writing. In determining whether a given contract must be written, therefore, it is essential to consider not only whether the contract falls within the provisions of the classic statute of frauds, but also whether some other statute requires that it be in writing.

Generally, if a contract is required by the statute of frauds to be in writing, any modification of the contract must also be in writing. However, an oral agreement to rescind an executory written contract is usually valid, even if the contract is one required by the statute of frauds to be in writing.

The remainder of this chapter will consider in greater detail some of the more important provisions of § 4 of the English statute and its modern state counterparts.

15:3   Agreements Not to Be Performed Within One Year

The English statute provided that "any agreement that is not to be performed within the space of one year from the making thereof" must be evidenced by a writing. Today, most state statutes have a similar provision. Although the provision appears simple and straightforward, it has given rise to a good deal of litigation. In most cases, the courts have held that the possibility that a contract may be performed within one year excludes it from the coverage of the statute. Note the statute's requirement that performance of the contract be possible within one year from the *making* of the contract, not the commencement of performance. In computing the one-year period, the day the contract is made is excluded, and the period expires at the close of the contract's anniversary date.

A contract that may be performed within one year need not be written, even though performance probably will, and in fact does, take more than a year. In short, to be within the coverage of the statute, it must appear from the terms and conditions of the contract itself that it cannot be fully performed within a year. To illustrate, if A enters into a contract to employ B for B's lifetime, the contract is not within the statute, since B may die within a year. On the other hand, if A employs B for a term of two years, the contract must be in writing. The fact that B might still die inside of a year does not remove the contract from the operation of the statute, since the statute requires full performance. The death of one person will excuse further performance, but that excuse is not the same as full performance.

The following case demonstrates some of the difficulties that may be encountered in determining whether a contract is one that is not to be performed within a year. Note particularly how the resolution of that issue depended on the court's determination as to exactly what the contract was.

Kiyose

v

Trustees of Indiana University
166 Ind App 34, 333 NE2d 886
(Indiana Court of Appeal, 1975)

[Kiyose sued Indiana University and various individual defendants for breach of an oral contract of lifetime employment. His complaint alleged that between 1966 and 1973 he was a lecturer at Indiana University while also pursuing his Ph.D. degree; that during that period he and the defendants orally agreed that, once Kiyose obtained his Ph.D., he would receive perpetual lifetime appointments at the University, commencing with a 3-year appoint-ment as assistant professor; that he received his Ph.D. degree in 1973 and was then appointed assistant professor; and that he was subsequently notified that he would not be reappointed for the 1974–75 year. The trial court granted the defendants' motion to dismiss the complaint, and Kiyose appealed.]

Lybrook, Judge.

*   *   *

. . . [P]laintiff's . . . complaint was dismissed on the ground that the action was barred by . . . the Indiana Statute of Frauds [provision concerning contracts not to be performed within one year]. . . .

... [The] complaint alleged that plaintiff and defendants agreed that if plaintiff would decline acceptance of positions being offered to him at other institutions and remain at Indiana University and obtain the degree of Doctor of Philosophy, the defendants would, upon plaintiff's attainment of such degree, appoint him to the position of Assistant Professor and thereafter continue to appoint him to teaching positions for the term of plaintiff's life.

Plaintiff advances several arguments in support of his position that the agreement alleged is not within the Statute of Frauds. . . . The first argument, which we find dispositive of the issue, is that the agreement alleged is a contract of lifetime employment and that to such contracts the statute has no application. . . .

The courts of this State have consistently held that the one year clause of the Statute of Frauds has no application to contracts which are *capable* of being performed within one year from the making thereof. . . . Thus, an oral agreement the performance of which is dependent upon the happening of a certain contingency is not encompassed by the Statute, provided the contingency is one which could possibly occur within one year. . . . In a contract of lifetime employment, death is the contingency which renders the agreement fully performed. Since the contingency is one which may occur at any time, such a contract *by its terms* is capable of being performed within one year and is therefore not within the Statute. [Court's emphasis.] . . .

The exact date upon which the alleged agreement between plaintiff and defendants was formed cannot be ascertained from an examination of the complaint. At the same time, however, it does not affirmatively appear that the alleged agreement could not have been performed within a year from its making. There is nothing to indicate that plaintiff could not have completed his required performance within a year, regardless of the formation date of the agreement and, of course, plaintiff could have upon the fulfillment of the conditions necessary to bind defendants immediately died, thereby rendering the agreement fully performed.

Defendants argue that the agreement alleged in the amended complaint is analogous to a contract of employment which was determined to be within the one year clause of the Statute of Frauds in [another Indiana case, in which], following discharge by his employer, the plaintiff brought an action seeking damages for breach of an alleged oral contract of employment providing for a *minimum term of eighteen months*. The contract was held to be within the statute on the ground that this alleged minimum term rendered it incapable of performance within one year.

Defendants in the instant case argue by attempted analogy that the claimed "lifetime" contract of employment was not to *commence* until the expiration of plaintiff's initial three year appointment to the rank of Assistant Professor. Thus, defendants envision their required performance under the contract to be a single appointment for the period of plaintiff's life which, due to an intervening three year appointment as Assistant Professor, could not have been made within one year of the formation of the contract. However, as we interpret plaintiff's allegations, the performance to which defendants were bound was that of making successive appointments for the period of plaintiff's life, *commencing* with a three year appointment as Assistant Professor. [Court's emphasis.] . . .

For the foregoing reasons, we conclude that plaintiff's action for damages for breach of the contractual agreement alleged is not barred by . . . the Indiana Statute of Frauds. . . .

[Judgment reversed.]

While the courts agree that the statute contemplates full performance and that partial performance within a year will not take a contract out of the statute, there is disagreement as to whether the possibility of full performance by one party is sufficient. The general rule is that a contract that is capable of full performance within one year by one party need not be in writing. For example, if A agrees to remodel B's store, in exchange for B's promise to make monthly payments to A over a three-year period, most courts would hold that the agreement was not within the statute of frauds, provided the remodeling was capable of being done within a year. Some courts, however, require the possibility of full performance by both parties within a year. A court following that rule would hold that A and B must have a written contract.

 A businessperson should make a point of learning whether the possibility of full performance of a contract by one party within a year takes the contract out of the statute of frauds under state law. A person who lacks this knowledge should assume that only the possibility of full performance by *both* parties will suffice for this purpose. The safest rule to follow is to use a written contract whenever either party will not be able to perform fully within a year.

15:4   Interests in Land

The English statute required that "any contract for sale of lands . . . or any interest in or concerning them" must be evidenced by a writing. This provision or a variation of it has been carried over into state statutes. The general effect of the provision is to require all contracts concerning real estate to be in writing. Thus, for example, mortgages and grants of easements, which are limited rights to use of another's land, must be in writing to be enforceable. Leases also are required to be in writing, unless the lease term does not exceed one year.

The phrase "interest in land" applies only to agreements that affect the title or right of possession to land; agreements that affect the land in other ways are not within the statute. Determining whether a particular contract affects an interest in land may sometimes be difficult. For example, it is agreed that improvements, such as buildings and other structures, are considered a part of the land and that a sale of the land normally includes the buildings on it. Thus, a contract for the sale or lease of a building ordinarily must be in writing. But the question has been raised as to whether a contract for the sale of a building that is to be removed from the land involves an interest in land. Most courts have held that it does not. Similarly, a contract to construct a building has been held not to involve an interest in land and not to require a writing.

Questions have also arisen as to whether contracts that involve growing crops, timber, minerals, and the like involve personal property and therefore need not be in writing, or involve interests in land and therefore need to be in writing. The courts generally have ruled that items such as growing crops are personal property, whereas items that spontaneously grow on or are an integral part of the land are real property. For example, it has been held that since grass and timber grow spontaneously, they are part of the land, and that contracts relating to grass and standing timber therefore must be in writing. However, once grass or timber has been cut, it is not an integral part of the land and is treated as personal property. A contract to sell downed trees, for example, does not need to be in writing.

A different rule regarding growing crops and timber is provided by the UCC. Under the UCC, a contract for the sale of growing crops or other things capable of severance from the land without material harm to the land, including timber to be cut, is considered a sale of goods, regardless of whether the subject matter is to be severed by the buyer or the seller [UCC § 2-107(2)]. This means, then, that the UCC regards growing crops and timber as personal property, and the contracts for the sale of these items need not be in writing. A contract for the sale of minerals or the like (including oil and gas) or a structure to be removed from the land is a contract for the sale of goods if severance is done by the seller, but until severance occurs such a contract is considered a transfer of an interest in land [UCC § 2-107(1)]. This means that a contract for the sale of minerals and like materials must be in writing unless the seller is going to remove them from the land. Once they are removed from the land, they are considered to be personal property that can be transferred by oral contract.

 Even if a contract for the sale of crops, timber, or minerals appears to be exempt from the statute of frauds because of the UCC classification of those items as personal property, other provisions of the statute might still apply. For example, if a contract is entered into in the spring of one year for the sale of crops to be harvested in the fall of the following year it would need to be in writing even though it is a contract for the sale of personal property. The reason is that the contract would be subject to the statute of frauds provision requiring that contracts not to be performed within a year be in writing. Moreover, if the price of the crops is $500 or more, the contract would also be subject to the UCC statute of frauds provision requiring a written contract for sale of goods worth $500 or more (UCC § 2-201). Thus, a conclusion that a particular contract affects land but does not involve transfer of an interest in the land does not necessarily mean that the contract is outside the coverage of the statute of frauds.

15:5 Promise to Answer for Debt of Another

Under the English statute, any "promise to answer for the debt, default or miscarriages of another person" was required to be evidenced by a writing. Most American jurisdictions have retained this requirement. The provision has primary application to *guaranty contracts*. These are contracts in which one person (guarantor) promises a second person (the creditor) to pay the debt of a third person (the debtor) in the event the debtor fails to do so. The key to the concept of guaranty is that the debtor is primarily liable on the debt; the guarantor becomes liable only after the debtor has failed to pay, and this liability is based on a related but separate promise. Thus, a person who assumes primary responsibility for a debt is not a guarantor—and the promise need not be in writing under this part of the statute of frauds—even though payment of the debt may benefit a third person.

The difficulties that can arise may be illustrated by considering the frequently encountered situation in which one person promises to pay a second person for goods or services delivered to a third person. If the goods or services are delivered on the third person's credit, then that person is liable, and the promisor's promise is an undertaking to pay the third person's debt if he fails to pay. This promise therefore comes under the statute of frauds and must be in writing. If, however, the goods or services were delivered solely on the promisor's credit, there is no promise to pay the debt of another and the promise is not within the statute and may be oral.

To illustrate another common situation, if goods are sold on the joint credit of two persons, each person's promise to pay for the goods is an original promise to the creditor even if the goods are to be delivered to and used by only one person. Thus, the promises are not within the statute and need not be in writing.

If the promisor has a personal interest in the transaction and will benefit by paying the other person's debt, the contract may not have to be in writing. This is because under the *main purpose* or *leading object rule*, no writing is required if the main purpose of the promise is to obtain some substantial benefit for the promisor, rather than to guarantee the third person's debt.

EXAMPLE
A hires B, a contractor, to construct a building. While the building is under construction, B fails to make timely payments to C, a supplier, and C notifies A and B that he will refuse to make further deliveries of supplies unless the outstanding debts are paid. A tells C that, if C will continue to make deliveries, A will pay for the supplies if B fails to do so. A's promise to C constitutes a promise to pay another's debt, but the main purpose of A's promise is not to guarantee B's debt, but rather to ensure the uninterrupted construction of the building. A's promise therefore need not be in writing.

A promise made to the debtor, as distinguished from the debtor's creditor, is uniformly held not to be within the statute. This promise may therefore be oral.

15:6 Nature of Writing Required

Section 4 of the English statute provided that a contract within the statute was unenforceable "unless the agreement . . . or some memorandum or note thereof, shall be in writing, and signed by the party to be charged therewith or some other person thereunto by him lawfully authorised." Similar requirements have been incorporated into the various state statutes. Thus, according to the statute it is not essential that the entire contract be in writing. An oral contract may be enforced as long as there is a *memorandum or note* to indicate that the contract exists. Moreover, the writing need not be signed by both parties. Only the party against whom the contract is being enforced ("the party to be charged") need sign.

Generally, a memorandum will be considered to comply with the statute if it contains the names of the parties, the terms and conditions of the contract, a reasonably certain description of the subject matter, and the signature of the party to be charged. Most statutes of frauds expressly allow the memorandum to be signed by an authorized agent. The agent generally need not have written authorization to act; oral authorization is sufficient. The writing, whether signed by the party to be charged or by an agent, need not be made and signed at the time the contract is made. It may be prepared at any time subsequent to the contract, and it may even be made prior to the actual formation of the contract.

EXAMPLE

A writes, signs, and mails a letter to B offering to maintain and repair all of B's office machines for a period of two years, in exchange for a specified monthly payment. After B receives the letter, she informs A by telephone that she accepts his offer. At that time the written offer, coupled with the oral acceptance, creates a contract. If A subsequently refuses to perform, B can rely on the written offer as a memorandum that is sufficient to comply with the statute of frauds. If, however, B refuses to perform, A would be unable to enforce the contract against her; the contract is within the statute of frauds (being a contract incapable of performance within a year), and no writing evidencing the contract was ever signed by B.

No particular form of writing or type of language is necessary to constitute a sufficient memorandum or note. Under appropriate circumstances, a canceled check, receipt, letter, or telegram might be held adequate. Even a request for relief from the obligations of the contract in question might be considered sufficient.

The memorandum may consist of several writings if, taken as a whole, they adequately evidence the agreement and, taken separately, they in some way indicate that they relate to the same transaction. The following case illustrates how one court determined the sufficiency of a writing and how it was influenced by the policies underlying the statute of frauds in coming to its decision.

Powers
v
Hastings
20 Wash App 837, 582 P2d 897
(Washington Court of Appeal, 1978)

[The Powers, plaintiffs, and the Hastings, defendants, entered into an oral lease and option to purchase agreement covering certain real estate. The Hastings subsequently breached the agreement, and the Powers sued for damages. The Hastings, both in their pleadings and in their trial testimony, admitted the existence of the agreement, but defended solely on the ground that the agreement was oral and not enforceable under the statute of frauds. The trial court granted judgment to the Hastings, and the Powers appealed.]

Dore, Judge.

*   *   *

ISSUES

Issue 1: Whether the trial court erred in granting a judgment . . . for defendants on the basis that enforcement of the oral lease and option to purchase agreement of the Hastings' farm was barred by the statute of frauds?

Issue 2: Whether the testimony of a defendant seller in open court as to the details of an oral lease with option to purchase constitutes sufficient "memoranda" or "writing" under the statute of frauds? . . .

DECISION

. . . *Corbin* has stated:

Let us proceed, therefore, with a general consideration of what constitutes a sufficient note or memorandum. We may well start with this one general doctrine: There are few, if any, specific and uniform requirements. The statute itself prescribes none; and a study of the existing thousands of cases does not justify us in asserting their existence. Some note or memorandum having substantial probative value in establishing the contract must exist; but its sufficiency in attaining the purpose of the statute depends in each case upon the setting in which it is found. A memorandum that is sufficient in one case may well be held insufficient in another. *A complete admission in court by the party to be charged should dispense with the necessity of any writing whatever.* [Court's emphasis.] . . .

Obviously the purpose of the statute of frauds is to prevent a fraud, not to perpetuate one, and in this regard the courts of this state are empowered to disregard the statute when necessary to prevent a gross fraud from being practiced. . . . The legislative intent in enacting the statute was to prevent fraud resulting from the uncertainty inherent in oral contracts of this nature. . . .

In examining the record in the subject case, we find that both parties agreed that the parties had entered into an oral lease with an option to purchase defendants' farm. . . . [T]he record . . . reveals that defendants on *six* differ-

ent occasions admitted the existence of the lease with option to purchase in *writing or in testifying in open court.* [Court's emphasis.] . . .

The statute of frauds was enacted to prevent frauds. Here both parties specifically testified as to the existence of an oral lease with an option to purchase defendants' farm and also to its particulars. The feared uncertainty and potential for fraud, inherent in such oral agreements and which is the basis for the statute of frauds' bar against enforcement, are clearly removed by their testimony.

Therefore, we hold that to apply the statute of frauds to bar enforcement of the option agreement in the subject case would constitute a gross fraud.

We further hold that the testimony of defendant Hastings in open court as to the details of the oral lease with option to purchase constitutes sufficient "memoranda" or "writings" to satisfy the statute of frauds, for we view recorded court testimony as equivalent to signed depositions.

We hold that in the subject case the statute of frauds is not a bar to enforcement of the parties' oral lease and option to purchase agreement. . . .

[Reversed and remanded.]

Generally, a written communication to a third person constitutes a sufficient memorandum, provided it adequately discloses the terms of and the parties to the contract. However, a minority of states require delivery of the memorandum to the other party.

15:7   Effect of Noncompliance with Statute

The original English statute provided that "no action shall be brought" on an agreement covered by the statute unless the agreement was in writing as required by the statute. Today, the statutes of most states contain similar provisions. Accordingly, the courts in most states have held that an oral contract within the scope of the statute is only voidable, rather than being entirely void. The distinction between a void contract and one that is simply voidable is that a void contract is invalid for all purposes, while a voidable one is valid between the parties unless and until one party sues on the contract. That is, the parties can perform a voidable contract, but neither party can sue either to recover damages for its breach or for a court order requiring the other party to perform. In some states, however, the statute of frauds declares that an agreement covered by the statute is void unless it is in writing.

Complete Performance of Oral Contract Full performance by both sides to an oral contract clearly removes the contract from the coverage of the statute of frauds. Where only one party has fully performed, the courts are in disagreement. Under the majority view, the lack of written evidence of the agreement does not preclude its enforcement in a court action by the party who fully performed. Under the minority view, that party cannot force the other party to perform, but can recover on the theory of quasi-contract, which is discussed below.

Part Performance of Oral Contract: Contract for Sale of Land Under the doctrine of *part performance*, an oral contract for the sale of land may be enforced if certain acts have been taken in reliance on the oral contract. For the doctrine to apply to a contract for the sale of land, the plaintiff must have so changed his position in reliance on the oral agreement that it is impossible to restore him to the status quo that existed prior to the agreement.

EXAMPLE
Norton wants to buy a farm, and he pays for and receives an option to purchase a farm owned by Johnson. Norton then finds a farm he likes better, owned by Williams. He and Williams orally agree to terms for sale of the farm. Relying on the agreement with Williams, Norton allows his option to purchase the Johnson farm to expire, and Johnson then sells it to someone else. Because of Norton's change in position in reliance on the oral agreement with Williams, the agreement is now enforceable by Norton.

The term "part performance" is in a sense a misnomer, since the doctrine may be applied even where certain acts have been performed in reliance on the contract but not in actual execution of it. While various acts may be shown in support of a claim of part performance, the actions most often shown are (1) the taking of possession by the purchaser, (2) the making of valuable permanent improvements on the land by the purchaser, and (3) the payment of money or rendition of services by the purchaser. If part performance is established, a court will grant *specific performance*, which is an order that the defendant deed the land if he is the seller, or pay the money if he is the buyer.

Most courts consider the taking of possession a necessary element of part performance, and a number of courts have even indicated that it is itself sufficient to warrant an order for specific performance. Most cases have involved the taking of possession in conjunction with other acts. The strongest and most unequivocal act of part performance is the making of permanent improvements to the land. Some courts have relied solely on this act in finding sufficient part performance. The payment of money or the performance of services, although almost universally considered insufficient part performance to warrant an order of specific performance, is nonetheless an important factor where there have been other acts as well.

Part Performance of Oral Contract: Other Contracts Within Scope of Statute
The courts have generally held that part performance of an oral contract that is required by the statute to be in writing, other than a contract for the sale of land, does not take the contract out of the scope of the statute. On rare occasions, however, where other remedies are clearly insufficient, specific performance may be ordered. Thus, if a person so changes his position in reliance on a contract that he would be substantially prejudiced by failure to enforce it, the contract may be enforced notwithstanding the lack of a writing.

EXAMPLE
A entered into an oral contract with B. Under this contract A was to be employed as an assistant sales manager in Hawaii for a period of three years. In reliance on the contract, A moved his family 2,200 miles, from Los Angeles to Hawaii. Since such a move was clearly foreseeable by B, and since injustice can be avoided only by enforcement of the contract, specific performance should be granted.

Even if a contract will not be enforced on the ground of part performance, a party who has taken some action in reliance on the contract may be entitled to recover money on a quasi-contract theory. The theory is that if one party, pursuant to a contract that is unenforceable under the statute of frauds, has rendered services to another party, made improvements on the other party's land, or paid money or parted with other consideration, the other party has made an implied promise to pay the reasonable value of such performance. Recovery in such a situation does not rest on the contract, but on the implied obligation to pay for benefits received.

Key Concepts and Terms

- Lacking a statute to the contrary, a contract may be either oral or written, and no particular form is required.

- Each state has a statute of frauds, which requires certain specified types of contracts to be evidenced by a signed writing. Other federal and state statutes also regulate the form of other particular classes of contracts.

- An agreement not to be performed within a year from the time it is made must be evidenced by a writing. The possibility of performance by both parties (or, in most states, by one party) within a year removes a contract from the statute's coverage, regardless of whether performance within a year is anticipated or occurs.

- Contracts for the sale of interests in land must be evidenced by a writing. The phrase "interest in land" applies only to agreements that affect title or right of possession. Whether a contract involving improvements, growing crops, timber, or minerals affects an interest in land depends on the particular factual circumstances.

- A promise to answer for another person's debt must be evidenced by a writing. This requirement applies primarily to guaranty contracts. If the main purpose of a contract to answer for another's debt is to benefit the promisor, it is not within the statute's coverage.

- The entire contract need not be written to satisfy the statute. Any memorandum or note is sufficient, provided it adequately identifies the parties, establishes the terms and conditions of the contract, and is signed by the party to be charged.

- A contract that is not in writing as required by the statute ordinarily is unenforceable in court. However, such a contract can be enforceable if there has been (1) complete performance by both parties (or, in most states, by one party); or (2) part performance of a contract for the sale of land. Part performance is most conclusively established by showing that the purchaser made permanent improvements to the land, although other relevant factors are that the purchaser took possession of the land, paid money, or rendered services. If the contract is not for the sale of land and has been partly performed, the performing party may recover on the theory of quasi-contract.

- Specific performance is a judicial remedy by which a court orders performance of a contract. In a suit based on a contract for the sale of land, the court will grant the plaintiff specific performance if he has established part performance. Therefore, the defendant would have to deed the land if he is the seller, or pay the money for the land if he is the buyer.

- Guaranty Contract
- Leading Object (Main Purpose) Rule
- Memorandum or Note

- Part Performance
- Specific Performance
- Statute of Frauds

Questions and Case Problems

1. Acme Company falls behind on premium payments to Jones, its insurance broker, and Jones notifies Acme that she intends to sue. Lopez contacts Jones and explains that his children have just purchased Acme, that they need at least a year to make the company profitable, that he has no financial interest in Acme but has assumed the title of chairman, and that he "will take care of the account" himself if Jones will refrain from suing Acme. Jones agrees. Another 18 months pass without payment. Jones then sues Lopez, seeking recovery of not only the amount due at the time of her meeting with Lopez, but also premium payments that had come due in the succeeding 18 months. Lopez raises the statute of frauds as a defense. How should the case be decided?

2. In May 1970, Fong was negligently injured by an employee of Baker Company. In June 1970, Fong and Baker entered an oral settlement agreement, whereby Fong promised not to bring suit for the injury in exchange for Baker's promise to pay Fong $100 per month for the next 20 years. Baker made payments to Fong for 5 years, then stopped. Fong sued, and Baker raised the statute of frauds as a defense. What is the result? Would the result be the same if the statute of limitations for personal injury actions was one year? If it was two years? If Baker had promised to pay Fong for the rest of Fong's life?

3. Casey holds a good position with ABC Company, but she periodically looks for better job opportunities. One year she receives two attractive job offers. After weighing her options, she accepts an oral offer of a 5-year contract from XYZ Corporation. Although Casey needs only two months to qualify for a pension at ABC, XYZ insists that she start immediately, and Casey reluctantly agrees to do so. Casey resigns from ABC and moves her family across the state to begin work for XYZ. After two years Casey is fired. She sues for breach of contract, and XYZ raises the statute of frauds. What is the decision?

4. Discuss the advantages and disadvantages of written contracts and oral contracts.

5. Roberts and Bryan orally agree that Bryan will purchase the entire output of railroad crossties from Roberts' sawmill for as long as Roberts owns the mill. Bryan buys the crossties for over a year, then refuses to make further purchases. Roberts is forced to close his mill, and he sues Bryan for damages. Bryan raises the statute of frauds as a defense. What is the result?

6. List the types of contracts that must be evidenced by a signed writing.

7. Crabtree orally agrees to become sales manager for Arden Corporation. An unsigned memorandum prepared by Arden indicates that Crabtree is to receive $20,000 to start, $25,000 after six months, and $30,000 after a year, and that he is to have "two years to make good." A payroll card, indicating Crabtree's starting salary and the agreed increases after six months and one year, is prepared and initialed by an Arden officer. Crabtree receives his 6-month increase, and after one year an Arden officer prepares and signs a new payroll card to reflect a salary increase to $30,000. Arden's president refuses to approve the increase. Crabtree quits and sues for breach of contract. What is the outcome?

8. Describe the doctrine of part performance and its application.

9. Brandenburger puts 880 acres of land up for sale at public auction. Klipfel is the successful bidder on 640 acres and Erlinbush on 240 acres. After the sale, the auctioneer prepares, dates, and signs the following memorandum: "Terms not over 20 percent down. Bal. 5 yr., 5 percent Int. Henry Brandenburger Auction. Land sold to Wilbur Erlinbush 240 acres at $44.00 per acre. Alvin Klipfel 640 acres at $39.00 per acre." When Brandenburger refuses to complete the sale to Klipfel, Klipfel sues for specific performance. What is the result?

10. Discuss the circumstances under which one person's promise to pay a debt, the payment of which benefits another person, must be in writing.

16 Construction and Interpretation of Contracts

16:1 Introduction

A contract, whether oral or written, should be clear and unambiguous so that there is no doubt as to its meaning. If a contract's terms are clear, interpretation by a court will be unnecessary. Also, if care is taken in wording a contract, both parties will understand their rights and obligations and will be less likely to make mistakes that can lead to litigation.

In the normal course of events, however, people do not always express their intentions clearly. Consequently, disputes frequently arise as to the exact meaning of a contract. When such disputes lead to legal actions, courts are called on to interpret the meaning of the contract. In so doing, a court will follow certain well-established rules of interpretation and evidence. These rules are discussed in the sections that follow.

16:2 Principles of Interpretation

The goal in interpreting a contract is to discover the parties' intent, as expressed in the language chosen by the parties and, where necessary, as revealed by the surrounding circumstances. In determining a contract's meaning, the court will look to what a reasonable person who is in the same position as the parties would understand it to mean. Once the parties' intent has been ascertained, the individual provisions of the contract will be interpreted to fit in with that intent. For example, if two interpretations of a contract are possible, one of which would make part of the contract unenforceable, the court will adopt the interpretation that enables the entire contract to be enforceable.

Contract as a Whole The meaning of a contract is gathered from the entire context; particular words or isolated portions are viewed in light of the whole contract. If a contract consists of two or more instruments, such as a series of letters, all the instruments will be construed together.

Meaning of Words   The words used in a contract will be given their ordinary meaning, unless the contract shows that they are used in some other sense. Words with an established legal meaning are presumed to have that meaning when used in a contract, unless a contrary intent clearly appears. Words of art or words connected with a particular trade are to be given the meaning attached to them by experts in such art or trade, even though it may differ from the usual meaning. Similarly, technical words are ordinarily to be interpreted as they are usually understood by persons in the profession or business involved.

Conflicting Provisions   If there are conflicting provisions in a contract, the court will first attempt to reconcile them. If the conflict is irreconcilable, the court will normally enforce the provision that ties in more closely with the contract's general purpose. If a contract contains conflicting general and special provisions relating to the same thing, the special provisions will control. Handwritten provisions prevail over contradictory typewritten ones, and typewritten provisions prevail over conflicting printed provisions. For example, when a contract consists of a standardized form with blanks filled in, those portions that have been filled in by the parties will be enforced over conflicting portions of the standardized form.

Interpretation Against Drafting Party   A contract that contains ambiguous language will be interpreted against the party who drafted the contract or who selected the particular language in issue. This rule is especially applicable to adhesion contracts.[1]

Implied Terms or Promises   Every contract carries an implied promise of good faith and fair dealing. Each party has an implied obligation not to do anything intentionally to prevent the other party from carrying out his part of the agreement. The UCC also imposes an obligation of good faith in the performance or enforcement of every contract, requiring that the parties act honestly with each other [UCC §§ 1-201(19), 1-203]. There may be other implied terms or promises that necessarily flow from the provisions of a contract. The court will also interpret these. For example, if a contract specified no time for performance, the allowance of a reasonable time will be implied.

Consideration of Surrounding Circumstances   In determining the meaning of uncertain provisions or clauses, the court may consider the surrounding circumstances at the time the contract was made. In placing itself in the positions occupied by the parties when the agreement was executed, the court will attempt to ascertain the parties' purpose and intention so that it can ascribe meaning to the ambiguous provisions.

Practical Construction by Parties   Often the parties will have performed under a contract for some time before a dispute arises. The court will give great weight to the practical construction placed on the contract as a result of the parties' course of

---

[1]Adhesion contracts are discussed in Chapter 12.

conduct. Under the UCC, a *course of performance* accepted or acquiesced in by the parties without objection is relevant in determining the meaning of a sales contract (UCC § 2-208).

EXAMPLE

A magazine publisher uses a standard form for its contract with the authors from whom it solicits articles. The form provides that the article contracted for will be "about _____ pages in length," and the blank is filled in each time a new contract is prepared. Robinson, an author, has contributed a number of articles to the publisher, each under a separate contract. In the past, the publisher has always accepted articles that varied in length by up to 20 percent from the length stated in the contract. Robinson's most recent submission was supposed to be "about 50 pages in length," but its actual length is 59 pages. The publisher rejects the article, claiming that "about" as used in the contract means plus or minus no more than 5 percent. If Robinson sues the publisher, the court will probably find that "about," as used in this contract, means plus or minus 20 percent.

Course of Dealing and Usage of Trade   Often the parties to a contract will have had earlier dealings with one another, and certain understandings will have been established between them. Under the UCC, "a course of dealing is a sequence of previous conduct between the parties to a particular transaction which is fairly to be regarded as establishing a common basis of understanding for interpreting their expressions and other conduct" [UCC § 1-205(1)]. Also, persons in a particular business may engage in certain practices with such repetition that these practices become known as *business or trade customs or usages*. Under the UCC, "a usage of trade is any practice or method of dealing having such regularity of observance in a place, vocation or trade as to justify an expectation that it will be observed with respect to the transaction in question" [UCC § 1-205(2)]. Parties entering into a specific contract often do so with such prior dealings or customs or usages in mind. Under the common law, evidence of prior dealings between the parties, or of trade customs or usages, could be utilized to determine the meaning of terms in the contract in issue. Likewise, under the UCC a *course of dealing* or a usage of trade gives particular meaning to and supplements or qualifies the terms of an agreement, provided there is no conflict between the express terms of the contract and the course of dealing or usage of trade [UCC § 1-205(3), (4)].

Under the UCC, express terms of a contract, course of performance, course of dealing, and usage of trade are to be interpreted as being consistent with each other whenever it is reasonable to do so. When there are irreconcilable conflicts, the order of priority is as follows: (1) express terms, (2) course of performance, (3) course of dealing, and (4) usage of trade [UCC §§ 1-205(4), 2-208(2)].

16:3   Parol Evidence Rule

Negotiation of a contract often takes a considerable period of time and may involve numerous written and oral communications. During the negotiations, various apparent promises may be made. Ultimately, the parties reach final agreement and reduce their contract to writing. Once the contract is in writing, that written contract embodies the parties' entire agreement. All prior negotiations, both oral and written, are presumed to have been integrated into the final written contract. All other verbal or written agreements or promises are superseded by the contract.

Once a contract has been reduced to writing, the *parol evidence rule* comes into play. This rule excludes from evidence any oral or other extrinsic proof of prior agreements or contemporaneous oral agreements that would vary with or contradict the written contract. The rule also excludes writings other than the final written contract.

EXAMPLE

Ayala enters into negotiations with Bauer, a longtime friend of and salesman for Chan, to purchase an airplane with custom features from Chan. During the negotiations Bauer orally assures Ayala that if Ayala changes her mind the order can be canceled and her $500 deposit returned. Bauer also sends Ayala a handwritten note reiterating that assurance. Ayala later signs a formal purchase contract, agreeing to purchase the plane for $40,000, and to be liable for any damages sustained by Chan in the event of a breach of the agreement. Subsequently, Ayala cancels the purchase order, and Chan retains the $500 deposit and sues for $4,000 in damages sustained by Ayala's breach. Chan should prevail in his suit over Ayala (unless Ayala can prove fraudulent misrepresentation), since the prior oral and written assurances were superseded by the written contract, which embodied the final agreement between the parties.

 It is not uncommon for people to rely on oral promises as qualifying written contracts, but under the parol evidence rule this reliance is usually misplaced. A person may protect himself from disappointment by asking that oral promises be put in writing at the time the deal is concluded. If the other party does not wish to place these promises in the body of the written contract, they may be attached to the contract and incorporated by reference. This makes them an integral part of the contract. Otherwise, a court will usually find them to have ben superseded by the signing of the written contract.

The parol evidence rule applies to all written contracts, whether or not they are required by the statute of frauds to be in writing. It applies, moreover, to all terms of a written contract, whether express or implied. Thus, for example, if a written contract specifies no time for performance, a reasonable time will be implied, and parol evidence will be inadmissible to establish some other specific time for performance, since that would amount to varying the contract.

The UCC has codified the parol evidence rule with respect to sales contracts, but has liberalized the rule somewhat. Unless the court finds the writing to have been intended as a complete and exclusive statement of the terms of the agreement, the UCC permits final written agreements to be explained or supplemented by evidence concerning course of dealing, usage of trade, or course of performance, as well as evidence of consistent additional terms (UCC § 2-202).

Partial Integration   The applicability of the parol evidence rule is based on the presumptions that the parties' final agreement has been entirely reduced to writing and that a written contract complete on its face integrates all prior dealings and constitutes the parties' final and entire agreement. When a written instrument is obviously not or is shown not to be the complete contract between the parties, it does not entirely supersede all prior negotiations. Rather, it supersedes prior negotiations only to the extent that they were integrated into the written portion of the contract. Unless the statute of frauds is applicable, the oral portion remains valid and enforceable. This kind of contract is called a *partially integrated contract*. Both the written and the oral portions of a partially integrated contract may be enforced, and parol evidence may be introduced to prove the oral portion and its terms, provided that such evidence does not conflict with the written terms.

 The parties to a contract often insert a clause to the effect that the writing contains the entire and final agreement of the parties and that all prior negotiations and agreements are merged in the writing. Such a clause might serve to alert both parties to the fact that they should not rely on any statements or assurances made during negotiations. Courts give great weight to this type of clause in determining whether there has been total or partial integration. It may be particularly important in any situation where there might otherwise be doubt.

The following case illustrates the type of analysis that often is necessary in interpreting a contract and determining the applicability of the parol evidence rule.

Brown

v

**Financial Service Corp., International
489 F2d 144
(United States Court of Appeals, Fifth
Circuit, 1974)**

[In November 1968, Brown was hired by Financial Service Corporation (FSC) as vice-president and director of a subsidiary. The compensation package included an agreement to sell Brown 4,000 shares of FSC's closely (nonpublicly) held stock at $5 per share. In May 1969, Branch, FSC's assistant secretary, wrote Brown a letter concerning the stock purchase. Enclosed was a stock purchase agreement, which contained a stock repurchase option providing that if Brown ceased working for FSC, "the Company shall have one year from the date of such

termination to repurchase any shares . . . for their fair market value." In response to the letter, Brown called Branch to discuss the stock purchase. In June 1969, Brown returned the signed stock purchase agreement, with a cover letter stating: "I wanted also to confirm the discussion you and I had yesterday on the phone on questions that I had raised. Referring to the termination of employment clause in the stock purchase agreement, while it is stated that the company shall have one year to repurchase any shares, we agreed that the company would repurchase almost immediately after termination." When FSC terminated Brown's employment in January 1970, FSC refused to repurchase the stock, despite Brown's desire to sell it. Brown sued, claiming breach of contract. The district court, applying Florida law, held that the parol evidence rule precluded consideration of discussions between Branch and Brown, as well as Brown's cover letter. The court *granted judgment to FSC, from which judgment Brown appealed.]*

Ingraham, Circuit Judge.

*   *   *

The flaw in the trial court's analysis is its implicit conclusion that the stock purchase agreement represented the complete agreement of the parties and that therefore Brown's cover letter had no legal significance according to the parol evidence rule. The parol evidence rule is a rule of the substantive law of contract, and its purpose is to preserve the sanctity of a written agreement once it is determined that the writing fully states the agreement of the parties. . . . Of necessity then the first question is whether the writing fulfills this function so as to be an integration of the [parties'] understanding. . . . To answer this question a court should consider the writing as well as the circumstances surrounding its execution, . . . and parol and extrinsic evidence may be used in making this determination. . . .

Without doubt a covering letter may constitute a part of the total agreement. . . . Here the cover letter itself clearly establishes that its purpose was to summarize in writing the content of a telephonic conversation concerning the purchase agreement; the cover letter specifically discusses terms of the stock purchase agreement. Moreover, the letter not only accompanied but was a cover to the signed stock purchase agreement when it was returned to Branch's office in Atlanta. And finally, Branch realized that at least to some extent the letter modified the terms of the purchase agreement. In short, the existence of the cover letter and the circumstances surrounding the execution of the stock purchase agreement preclude the conclusion that it was intended by the parties as the final memorial, the integration, of their understanding concerning the terms of the stock sale. Consideration of the cover letter would not, therefore, violate the parol evi-

dence rule because the cover letter was a part of the contract. . . .

The decision that the parties' contract is embodied in both the cover letter and the stock purchase agreement does not, of course, end the matter. For now there are arguably inconsistent contractual provisions dealing with the same subject matter—that is, the rights and duties of the parties on the purchaser's termination of employment. . . . [T]he cover letter says "we agree that the company would repurchase almost immediately after termination." Interpreting these words in the manner urged by Brown would lead to the conclusion that this language means that the company had an obligation to repurchase the stock and that this repurchase must occur immediately after termination. . . . Obviously this interpretation is in direct conflict with the interpretation of the agreement as giving the company an option to repurchase but imposing no affirmative duty.

There is, however, another interpretation which could be accorded to this language from the cover letter. . . . [I]t could be interpreted as imposing only a duty on the company to exercise its option immediately on termination. In the circumstances of this case it is this interpretation which we adopt as representing the intention of the parties at the time this contract was consummated. We reach this conclusion on the basis of the following analysis in which we apply several well established principles for the interpretation and construction of contracts.

The first principle is that in interpreting contractual language to determine the rights and obligations of the parties to the agreement the contract must be considered as a whole in an effort to give meaning to all of its provisions. . . . To interpret the language in Brown's letter as creating a duty in the company to repurchase his stock would render completely nugatory one of the crucial provisions of the document which he signed and returned to FSC. We would have to totally disregard the language in the purchase agreement conferring an option to the company to repurchase. By interpreting the disputed language in Brown's letter as going only to the time of repurchase rather than establishing such a duty, we afford meaning and significance to all parts of the contract. This interpretation also fulfills our duty to reconcile provisions which at first glance appear repugnant to each other. . . .

Another established rule of contract interpretation . . . is that courts may look to subsequent action of the parties to determine the interpretation that they themselves placed on the contractual language. . . . The conduct of both parties subsequent to Brown's termination leaves us convinced that neither FSC nor Brown believed that the company had an affirmative duty to repurchase shares.

The voluminous record . . . is replete with correspondence from Brown to FSC and vice versa. A good portion of these communications deal directly with the disposition of Brown's stock. . . . But none of his many letters exhorting the company to hurry up and repurchase his stock speak in terms of an affirmative obligation on the part of FSC. Likewise, when FSC offered to repurchase and hold the proceeds until the final accounting was completed, the offer spoke in terms of FSC's right to repurchase instead of a duty to do so. . . . The extensive correspondence between Brown and FSC simply does not support the interpretation now sought by Brown. Considering the contract as a whole, the circumstances surrounding its execution, and the conduct of the parties subsequent thereto, our conclusion is that this contract does not impose a duty on FSC to repurchase the 4,000 shares of stock issued to Brown.

[Judgment affirmed.]

16:4   Exceptions to Parol Evidence Rule

The courts have recognized a number of exceptions to the parol evidence rule. A discussion of some of the more important exceptions follows.

Prior or Contemporaneous Collateral Agreements   Parties often enter into several separate contracts. Parol evidence may be used to prove the existence of any prior or contemporaneous oral agreement that is independent of, collateral to, and not inconsistent with the written contract. In determining whether an oral agreement was indeed separate, the primary test is again the parties' intent. If it is reasonable to assume that both the oral and written agreements are intended to be included in the same contract, then it will usually be held that the oral agreement was integrated in the final written contract. However, if it is reasonable to assume that the parties might have executed the oral contract separate from the written contract, then parol evidence is permissible to prove the existence and terms of the oral agreement.

Subsequent Parol Agreements or Modifications   In the absence of a statute providing otherwise, the parties to a written contract may orally agree to modify or cancel that contract and to enter a new one. Parol evidence is admissible to show this modification or cancellation. Parties often insert in the contract a provision that requires any modification to be in writing. Even when this clause is included, however, the courts generally permit parol evidence to be introduced to prove that an oral modification was made.

Fraud and Related Matters   To show that there was no valid written contract, parol evidence is admissible in cases of fraud, misrepresentation, mutual or unilateral mistake, duress, or undue influence.[2]

 Parol evidence is often presented to prove that the failure to include an oral promise or guaranty in the final written contract was fraudulent. These claims are often favorably received, particularly with contracts between a consumer and a businessperson. It is always better, however, to read a contract carefully and to insist that it contain all the provisions agreed on prior to signing, than to seek a means of evading the parol evidence rule when a dispute arises after signing. Moreover, when the parties involved are both businesses of relatively equal bargaining power, claims of fraud are likely to be less well received, particularly if there is a clause in the written contract indicating that it is the final and entire agreement of the parties.

Contractual Interpretation   When a contract contains ambiguous or otherwise uncertain terms or provisions, parol evidence may be admitted to assist the court in determining the meaning of the uncertain provisions. However, if the ambiguity can be resolved from the instrument itself in accordance with the established rules of contractual interpretation, parol evidence may be held inadmissible. For example, in a case in which a typewritten provision conflicts with a printed one, reliance on the rule giving priority to the typewritten provision could resolve the conflict without resorting to parol evidence. Parol evidence is admissible to define and explain the meaning of technical words or phrases in a written contract (unless the contract itself defines them). Parol evidence may also be admitted to supply an obvious omission in a written contract.

Conditions Precedent   The existence of a contract may be, and frequently is, premised on the occurrence or performance of some prior act, which is called a condition precedent. Parol evidence may be introduced to prove the existence or nonexistence of the condition, and, therefore, of a valid contract.

Key Concepts and Terms

- In interpreting a contract, a court will seek to ascertain and give effect to the parties' intent. A contract is construed as a whole, and, where possible, conflicting provisions are reconciled. Ambiguous language is interpreted against the drafter. Certain obligations, such as those of good faith and fair dealing, are considered to be implied promises in a contract.
- Words in a contract are given their ordinary meaning, unless the contract shows

---

[2]These matters are discussed in Chapter 12.

that they are used in some other sense, or unless they have some established legal or technical meaning.

- Course of performance, course of dealing, and usage of trade may be considered in determining a contract's meaning.

- When an agreement has been reduced to writing, the writing becomes the contract, and all prior negotiations are integrated into the written contract.

- Under the parol evidence rule, oral and other extrinsic evidence cannot be used to prove the existence of prior agreements or contemporaneous oral agreements that vary or contradict the final written contract.

- Parol evidence can, however, be used to prove the existence of (1) prior or contemporaneous *collateral* agreements, (2) fraud, (3) a condition precedent, or (4) subsequent parol agreements or modifications. It can also be used to help interpret ambiguous provisions in a written contract.

- A partially integrated agreement is an agreement that is partially in writing and partially oral. Parol evidence is admissible to prove the existence of the nonwritten portion.

- Collateral Agreements
- Course of Dealing
- Course of Performance

- Custom or Usage of Trade
- Parol Evidence Rule
- Partial Integration

Questions and Case Problems

1. In 1951 Matula granted the gas company an easement to lay a pipeline through his property. Their agreement contained (1) a printed clause providing that an additional line could be laid in the future, parallel to and not more than 16 feet from the original one; and (2) a handwritten provision that stated: "line to be laid within 50' of the North Property Line." The first line was placed within the 50-foot limitation. In 1968, the gas company decided to lay the second pipeline within 16 feet of the first line, but more than 50 feet from the north boundary. When Matula raised the 50-foot limitation, the gas company replied that the limitation applied only to the first line. Matula sued. Who should prevail?

2. In 1960 Turski became an employee of Park Company and a member of Park's profit-sharing plan. Turski worked for Park until he was discharged in 1973, at which time he had vested rights in the plan worth over $15,000. When Turski went to work for a competing business, Park informed him that he was ineligible for plan benefits under a provision in the written plan disqualifying persons who "enter into a business competitive with the Company." Turski sued to recover the plan benefits. Park sought to prove that when it drafted the plan, it intended the above provision to include employment by a competing business. Should Turski recover?

3. Lane enters into a lease for office space. The lease provides that no rent will be due until the premises are modified to Lane's satisfaction. Lane then asks Specht, the landlord, to make alterations that are structurally impossible. Specht refuses to make the alterations, and Lane refuses to pay rent. Specht then sues Lane. Decide the case.

4. Bay Carpets obtains a job to install carpets in a motel. The carpets have to be ready for installation within 15 days. Bay asks Modern Carpets if it can supply the carpets. Modern replies that it can, but that the carpets will have to be specially dyed. Bay and Modern then execute a purchase order contract for the carpets. In the space for "date required" Bay's president writes "at once." It takes Modern a month to fill the order. By this time Bay has lost its installation contract, and therefore Bay refuses to accept the carpets. A lawsuit follows with Bay and Modern each claiming breach of contract. At trial Modern seeks, over Bay's objection, to present testimony that the phrase "at once" as used in the carpet industry means "as soon as possible," and that one month was a reasonable time for production. Should the testimony be admitted? Under the UCC?

5. Why are course of dealing, usage of trade, and course of performance considered in interpreting a contract?

6. Ross orally negotiates with Stinnett to have a house built on Ross's property. After reaching agreement on plans and specifications, the parties execute a written contract by which Stinnett is to build the house for $24,500. After the house is built at a cost to Stinnett of almost $24,000, he demands payment from Ross of cost plus 15 percent, in reliance on an alleged oral agreement entered prior to the written contract. Ross refuses. Stinnett sues, claiming that the recital of consideration in the written contract was a sham executed to enable Ross to obtain a loan and that the oral agreement was the true contract. Decide the case.

7. What is the distinction between a totally integrated and a partially integrated contract? Of what legal significance is the distinction?

8. List the principles that courts follow in interpreting contracts.

9. Fanning wants a new building for his automobile dealership. In preliminary negotiations with Stevens, an architect, Fanning tells him that the building must contain at least 40,000 square feet and cost no more than $250,000. A written contract is executed. One of its provisions states that Stevens is to design "a multiple-purpose building suitable to the needs of the Owner, at an approximate cost of $250,000." Stevens eventually submits two designs: one based on steel-frame construction at under $250,000, and one based on prestressed-concrete construction at $317,000. Fanning claims that subsequent to the written agreement the parties had orally agreed that the design was to be prestressed-concrete. Fanning terminates the contract for failure to perform, and Stevens sues Fanning for breach of contract. How should the provision as to estimated cost be interpreted? Should evidence of the parties' prior oral negotiations be admitted? Evidence of the alleged subsequent agreement?

10. Gans, a contractor, desires to subcontract a job requiring installation of a generator and accessories. She gives Wilson specifications for the equipment and asks if he can provide and install it. Wilson says that he can, and Gans orally places an order with Wilson for the specified equipment. A purchase order is later filled out; this order merely refers to the specified generator "with accessories." Wilson provides the generator specified and the accessories that normally come with it. The specifications, however, called for different accessories. New accessories have to be ordered, resulting in costly delays to Gans, and she sues Wilson for breach of contract. At trial, disputes arise as to the admissibility of the following evidence: (1) the oral order and oral negotiations preceding it and (2) the written specifications. Resolve those disputes.

17 Rights of Third Persons

17:1 Introduction

Ordinarily, the only persons with any legally enforceable rights in a contract are the parties to that contract. Under some circumstances, however, a third person may have such an interest in the contract, either as a third-party beneficiary or as an assignee of the contract, that it is proper to permit that person's enforcement of the contract. In addition, a third person may sometimes acquire rights by means of a contract of novation. Third-party beneficiary contracts, assignments of contracts, and contracts of novation will be discussed in this chapter.

17:2 Third-Party Beneficiary Contracts

When two persons enter a contract, their purposes ordinarily are to benefit themselves. On occasion, however, one or both parties execute a contract with the intent of benefiting a third person who is not a party to the contract. Such a contract is known as a third-party beneficiary contract, and the third person is known as a *third-party beneficiary.* This type of contract is employed in a variety of situations. It is frequently used when one party to a contract wishes to use the proceeds from the contract to pay a prior debt owed to a third person. For example, if Ben and Carol enter an agreement under which Ben is to perform services for Carol in exchange for Carol's payment of $500, and Ben owes Amy $500, the contract might be drafted to provide that Carol pay the $500 directly to Amy. Here, Amy would be a third-party beneficiary of the contract between Ben and Carol. As such, she would be entitled to enforce Carol's obligation to make the payment to her (provided Ben performed under the contract). Amy would be a type of third-party beneficiary known as a *creditor–beneficiary,* because Ben owed money to her.

Sometimes a contract provides for payment or other performance to a third party as a gift rather than as payment of a prior obligation. Using the same example, Ben might enter into the contract with Carol and not have a debt to Amy, but want to give Amy $500 as a gift. If Ben and Carol provide in the contract that Amy is to receive the $500, Amy would be a type of third-party beneficiary known as a *donee–beneficiary.* In the event that Carol does not give Amy the money, Amy would be entitled to enforce the contract against her because Amy was named in the contract as the donee.

The crucial factor in determining whether a third person is entitled to enforce a contract as a third-party beneficiary is whether the parties to the contract intended to benefit the third person. Thus, the third party is entitled to such enforcement when the parties clearly intended the contract to be for her benefit, as in the examples above. Enforcement by a third person will be denied when that person is only an *incidental beneficiary* of the contract. Contracts often provide unintended benefits to third persons, but the fact that a contract's performance will in some way benefit a third person is not by itself sufficient to confer a right of enforcement on that person. For example, if A promises to lend B money to pay her expenses, performance of the loan contract will obviously benefit the creditors of B. The intent of A and B was, however, to benefit themselves, and the benefit to B's creditors is merely incidental. B's creditors do not have the status of third-party beneficiaries and therefore are not entitled to enforce the contract.

The following classic case illustrates how public policy considerations influence a court in deciding whether a person is a third-party beneficiary.

H. R. Moch Co.
v
Rensselaer Water Co.
247 NY 160, 159 NE 896, 62 ALR 1199
(New York Court of Appeals, 1928)

[Rensselaer Water Company contracted with the city of Rensselaer to supply water, including water at fire hydrants. Moch's warehouse caught fire and was destroyed, due to the water company's failure to supply adequate water pressure at the hydrants. Moch sued for damages. He claimed that he was a third-party beneficiary and that there was a breach of the contract between the water company and the city. The trial court denied the water company's motion to dismiss the complaint, but the intermediate appellate court reversed the trial court and granted judgment to the water company. Moch appealed.]

Cardozo, C. J.

*   *   *

We think the action is not maintainable as one for breach of contract.

No legal duty rests upon a city to supply its inhabitants with protection against fire. . . . That being so, a member of the public may not maintain an action . . . against one contracting with the city to furnish water at the hydrants, unless an intention appears that the promisor is to be answerable to individual members of the public as well as to the city for any loss ensuing from the failure to fulfill the promise. No such intention is discernible here. On the contrary, the contract is significantly divided into two branches: One a promise to the city for the benefit of the city in its corporate capacity, in which branch is included the service at the hydrants; and the other a promise to the city for the benefit of private takers, in which branch is included the service at their homes and factories. In a broad sense it is true that every city contract, not improvident or wasteful, is for the benefit of the public. More than this, however, must be shown to give a right of action to a member of the public not formally a party. The benefit, as it is sometimes said, must be one that is not merely incidental and secondary. . . . It must be primary and immediate in such a sense and to such a degree as to bespeak the assumption of a duty to make reparation directly to the individual members of the public if the benefit is lost. The field of obligation would be expanded beyond reasonable limits if less than this were to be demanded as a condition of liability. A promisor undertakes to supply fuel for heating a public building. He is not liable for breach of contract to a visitor who finds the building without fuel, and thus contracts a cold. The list of illustrations can be indefinitely extended. The carrier of the mails under contract with the government is not answerable to the merchant who has lost the benefit of a bargain through negligent delay. The householder is without a remedy against manufacturers of hose and engines, though prompt performance of their contracts would have stayed the ravages of fire. . . .

So with the case at hand. By the vast preponderance of authority, a contract between a city and a water company to furnish water at the city hydrants has in view a benefit to the public that is incidental rather than immediate, an assumption of duty to the city and not to its inhabitants. . . . An intention to assume an obligation of indefinite extension to every member of the public is seen to be the more improbable when we recall the crushing burden that the obligation would impose. . . . If the plaintiff is to prevail, one who negligently omits to supply sufficient pressure to extinguish a fire started by another assumes an obligation to pay the ensuing damage, though the whole city is laid low. A promisor will not be deemed to have had in mind the assumption of a risk so overwhelming for any trivial reward. . . .

[Judgment affirmed.]

17:3   Assignment of Contract

Frequently one party to a contract transfers his rights under the contract to a third person. The transfer is known as an *assignment*, the party making the assignment is the *assignor*, and the person to whom the assignment is made is the *assignee*. The other party to the contract is referred to as an *obligor* or a debtor or by other designations, depending on the nature of the rights assigned. A party may also transfer his obligations under a contract to a third person. This type of transfer is not an assignment but is known as a delegation of duties and is discussed later in this chapter.

Most contractual rights are assignable. A party to a contract may assign all or part of his rights to an assignee, with or without the consent of the other party to the contract. Perhaps the most common type of assignment is the transfer of the right to receive money due or to become due under a contract. For example, in a contract for the sale of goods or services the seller often does not receive immediate payment, but he does not wish to wait to receive the money due. The seller may therefore enter into a contract with a third person, under which the seller assigns the right to the payment to the third person in exchange for the third person's payment of some lesser amount to the seller. In this way, the right to receive the money due under the original contract has been transferred by the seller (assignor) to the third person (assignee), to whom the original purchaser (obligor) now owes the duty of payment.

Form of Assignment   In the absence of statutory regulation, an assignment need not be made in any particular form. Any language that sufficiently indicates a party's intent to transfer his rights under a contract will suffice. An assignment may be oral or written, unless it is required by statute to be written.

Nonassignable Contracts   Various types of contracts or contractual rights are not assignable, unless the obligor consents to the assignment. Among the more important types of nonassignable contracts are the following:

(1) Contracts that involve a close personal relationship. They include contracts for personal services, contracts for professional services, and contracts that involve a relationship of confidence. For example, under an employment contract, the employer cannot ordinarily assign the right to the employee's services to a third person. Likewise, a person who is entitled to a lawyer's or doctor's services cannot assign these services to a third person. It should be noted, however, that a right to the payment that is to be received for services is assignable. For example, a physician may assign his right to payment from a patient.

 Rights under a personal services contract may be assigned if the contract explicitly so provides or if both parties to the contract consent to the assignment. For example, contracts with professional athletes often contain clauses that permit the team employing the athlete to assign the right to the athlete's services to another team.

(2) Contracts that contain a provision restricting or prohibiting assignment of the contract. The courts generally will enforce antiassignment provisions but interpret them narrowly and often insist that they be clear and explicit. For example, even though a contract contains a general provision stating that the contract is not assignable, a court will usually permit an assignment of the right to receive money due under the contract. The parties to a contract may waive an antiassignment provision.

(3) Contracts entered into in reliance by one party on the character or credit of the other party. In a contract of this type, the latter may not assign his rights under the contract. For example, if A agrees to loan B money in exchange for B's promise to make specified payments over a period of time, B may not assign his right under the contract to C, since A relied on B's credit in agreeing to the contract.

(4) Contracts whose assignability is limited by law. Many states have statutes that restrict or prohibit the assignment of certain interests, particularly wages. There are also statutes that specify certain formal requisites to the validity of these assignments.

17:4   Rights of Assignee

The assignee of a contract acquires all the rights possessed by the assignor, but no more than that. Any defenses that the other party to the contract might have asserted against the assignor can also be asserted against the assignee in the event of an action for enforcement. Some states have adopted statutes to this effect.

17:5   Notice of Assignment

The obligor does not need to be notified of an assignment. However, if he is not notified, he is free to continue making payment to his original creditor (the assignor). Once the obligor has received notice of the assignment, he must make payments on the contract to the assignee.

An assignor sometimes makes a second or even a third assignment of the same contractual right to successive assignees. When several assignees claim the same right, a court must determine which assignee should receive priority. If the first assignee in time also was the first to give notice to the debtor, then that assignee is clearly entitled to priority. When a later assignee in time is the first assignee to give notice, the courts are not in agreement as to the priority. Some states determine priority on the basis of the time of notice, granting priority to the first assignee to give the debtor notice. Other states base priority on the time of assignment, granting priority to the first assignee in time. If, however, a debtor pays a later assignee before receiving the first assignee's notice, the first assignee will not have priority.

 To protect his rights under an assignment, an assignee should always give prompt notice of the assignment to the debtor. This protects the assignee against both the possibility of further payments to the assignor and the risk that the assignor might make a second assignment of the same contract rights.

17:6   Delegation of Duties

An assignment of rights does not impose on the assignee any of the assignor's duties or liabilities to the other party to the contract. If the assignor wants to transfer these duties and liabilities, in addition to his rights, he may do so in a separate transaction. This transaction is called a *delegation of duties*, although it is often referred to merely as an assignment.

A party may delegate performance of his duties under a contract to a third person, provided that the third person's performance would be substantially the same as performance by the delegating party himself. For example, if a construction contract of a nonunique nature is involved, and if one contractor is equally as capable as another of performing the job, then the duty of performance can be delegated. However, if a party's personal acts and qualities are material ingredients of the contract, that party's duties may not be delegated to a third person without the other party's consent.

EXAMPLE
An opera association contracts with Mario, a charismatic operatic tenor, to give a recital. Mario can assign to anyone of his choice his right to receive the compensation agreed on for the recital. However, because of Mario's unique personality and skills, he cannot delegate to anyone else his duty to perform the recital, at least without the opera association's consent.

Assignor's Continuing Liability   The assignor of a contract remains liable for performance of the contract even though he has delegated duties to the assignee, unless the other party to the contract consents to relieve the assignor of all further responsibility for performance.

17:7   Assignments Under the UCC

The UCC favors the assignability of contracts. Under the UCC, all rights in sales contracts are assignable unless assignment would (1) materially change the duty of the other party, (2) materially increase the burden or risk imposed on the other party, or (3) materially impair the other party's chance of obtaining return performance [UCC § 2-210(2)]. Moreover, unless the circumstances indicate otherwise, a clause that prohibits assignment of "the contract" bars only delegation of duties, not assignment of rights [UCC § 2-210(3)]. The UCC also permits delegation of duties unless the parties agree not to delegate or unless the other party has a substantial interest in having his original promisor perform the contract [UCC § 2-210(1)]. Indeed, under the UCC both an assignment of rights and a delegation of duties have been made if the assignment is made using terms such as "assignment of the contract" or "assignment of all my rights under the contract," unless the circumstances indicate otherwise [UCC § 2-210(4)].

   The UCC provides that in a secured transaction,[1] a provision in a contract between an account debtor (the party obligated to pay on an account) and an assignor that prohibits assignment of the account is ineffective [UCC § 9-318(4)]. The UCC also provides that if the assignee must sue the account debtor to obtain payment, the account debtor may raise against the assignee all defenses that he has against the assignor [UCC § 9-318(1)]. The UCC also authorizes an account debtor to continue paying the assignor until he receives notice of the assignment [UCC § 9-318(3)].

17:8   Novation

A contract of *novation*, or simply novation, is an agreement among all parties concerned that (1) cancels an existing contract and (2) simultaneously creates a new one. If the new contract benefits a third party, it may have the same effect as either a third-party beneficiary contract (if the initial parties had used such a contract in the first place) or an assignment. For example, assume that Ellis owes Freed $1,000, and Ellis contracts with Mirza to perform certain services in exchange for Mirza's payment of $1,000. If Ellis wants to use that $1,000 to discharge his obligation to Freed, there are various methods by which he may do so: (1) he may simply wait until he receives the money from Mirza, then pay Freed; (2) Ellis and Mirza may provide in their contract that the $1,000 be paid directly to Freed, thereby making Freed a third-party beneficiary; (3) Ellis may assign his right to the $1,000 to Freed;

---

[1]Secured transactions are discussed in detail in Chapters 28 and 29. Briefly, such a transaction is one in which one party gives to another an interest in personal property or fixtures to secure payment of a debt or performance of some other obligation.

or (4) after Ellis has performed the services, the three may jointly agree that Mirza will pay the money to Freed and that Mirza' obligation to Ellis will be discharged immediately. The last alternative is a novation. As used in this situation, it creates a new contract between Freed and Mirza while extinguishing the original contract between Ellis and Mirza.

The following case illustrates how a single fact situation may create issues relating to assignments, delegations of duties, and novations.

Sisco
v
Empiregas, Inc. of Belle Mina
286 Ala 72, 237 So 2d 463
(Alabama Supreme Court, 1970)

[Sisco was employed as a salesman for Gas and Chemicals, Inc., a liquefied petroleum gas (LP gas) dealer, under a contract executed March 24, 1967. The contract contained a noncompetition provision, prohibiting Sisco from engaging in the LP gas business within a 50-mile radius of Jeff, Alabama, for five years after termination of employment. The employment relationship could be terminated by either party on 30 days' notice. Empiregas took over Gas and Chemical's LP gas business, and Sisco was a salesman for Empiregas from January 1969 until June 30, 1969, when he voluntarily terminated his employment and began working with another LP gas dealer in the same area. Empiregas sued to enforce the noncompetition clause. It claimed that Gas and Chemical had assigned Sisco's employment contract to Empiregas. Sisco claimed that the employment contract was a nonassignable personal service contract. The trial court rejected Sisco's claim and enjoined Sisco from violating the noncompetition clause. Sisco appealed.]

Bloodworth, Justice.

*   *   *

. . . Empiregas contends that the rule forbidding the assignment of personal services contracts means only that the "duty" of a party who has contracted to perform personally (the employee) cannot be performed by another (a delegate), that the rule does not prevent the party to whom the personal performance is due (the employer) from assigning his rights and delegating his duties. Under this view, it argues, the fact that Sisco had contracted to perform personally and could not delegate *his duties* did not prevent Gas and Chemicals from assigning *its rights* and delegating *its duties* under the contract. It is our view, hereinafter elaborated, that the performance owed by both Sisco and Gas and Chemicals was personal, and neither could delegate his (its) "duties."

We commence with the general proposition that personal service contracts are not assignable. . . . We think [the complaint] shows on its face that the contract here at issue involved a relationship of personal confidence between the parties. No other conclusion seems logical where the contract by its language permits the employer to discharge the employee on thirty days' notice and then to prevent him for five years from pursuing his livelihood over an area we judicially know to encompass some 7,850 square miles. . . . Surely, one would not be presumed to have intended to commit himself into the hands of a stranger so empowered, and the bill shows on its face that Gas and Chemicals was no stranger to Sisco, having been his employer for some two years and eight months prior to his execution of the contract at issue. These circumstances, we feel, demonstrate that Sisco relied upon the uniqueness of his corporate employer and their relationship of mutual confidence when he entered into this contract. . . .

Thus, it results that the assignee's (Empiregas') right to performance from Sisco (including performance of his covenant not to compete) is conditional upon personal performance of its duties by Gas and Chemicals. . . . The [complaint] does not allege that Gas and Chemicals has acted as Sisco's employer since the alleged assignment. On the contrary, it is clear that the alleged "assignment" of the contract was an attempt by Gas and Chemicals both to assign its "rights" and delegate its "duties." . . . Therefore, the conditions of Sisco's duty to perform having failed, the [complaint] shows that Empiregas, Inc. of Belle Mina has no right to performance from Sisco. . . .

Two additional situations are frequently cited as exceptions to the so-called rule against the assignment of personal services contracts. . . . First, it is said that the employee's "consent" to the assignment permits the attempted assignee to enforce the contract. Second, it is said that the employee's conduct in continuing in the employ of the assignee permits the assignee to enforce the contract, the theory being that the employee has thus "adopted" or "ratified" the contract. We think, however, that these two situations are improperly termed "exceptions." It appears to us that the effect of the employee's "consent" or of his continuing in the employment of the assignor ("adoption" or "ratification") is to create a new contract between employee and assignee rather than merely to permit the assignment of the old contract. . . .

To say that parties have adopted a contract, is . . . merely to say that they have entered into a new contract, referable to the old for its terms. The manifestation of assent required for the creation of this new contract must be as unambiguous and unequivocal as that required to create any other contract. . . .

Contractual obligations partake of a solemn character, and we should be zealous to ensure that no one is fettered who has not manifested his assent to be. The [complaint] did not expressly allege that Sisco and Empiregas entered into a new contract embracing all the terms of the contract between Sisco and Gas and Chemicals, nor did it allege conduct on the part of Sisco and Empiregas sufficiently unambiguous to constitute mutual assent to the terms of the Sisco-Gas and Chemicals contract. . . .

Reversed and remanded.

17:9   Combinations of Third-Party Rights

Although the various types of third-party rights have been discussed separately, it must be noted that a given situation may give rise to more than one of these rights. An assignment of rights may involve not only a delegation of duties, but also a third-party beneficiary contract or a novation. If the parties to a contract or potential contract want to benefit or involve a third person in some way, they may choose whatever method or combination of methods is best suited to the specific situation.

EXAMPLE
A, the owner of a catering business, and B enter a contract to sell the business to B. Under the contract, B receives the right to collect all outstanding accounts and agrees to assume all outstanding liabilities of the business. After the sale is completed, A and B conclude an agreement with C, the major supplier of the business.

Under the terms of this agreement, C agrees to release A from all further liability on outstanding debts and to accept B's promise to pay all these debts in the manner specified in the agreement. The three parties have created third-party rights in the following ways: (1) an assignment (B's right to collect the outstanding accounts due A); (2) a delegation of duties (B's assumption of the outstanding liabilities); (3) a third-party beneficiary contract (creditors of the business being third-party beneficiaries of A and B's contract); and (4) a novation (the agreement between A, B, and C).

Key Concepts and Terms

- A third-party beneficiary is a person who is intended by two parties to a contract to benefit from the performance of the contract. As such, the third-party beneficiary is entitled to enforce the contract. An incidental beneficiary is a person who is not specifically intended to, but does, benefit under a contract between two other persons. An incidental beneficiary cannot enforce the contract.

- An assignment is a transfer of rights under a contract. The person making the transfer is the assignor, and the person receiving the rights is the assignee. Most contract rights are assignable. Nonassignable contract rights include (1) those involving a close personal relationship (such as the right to personal services), (2) those containing antiassignment provisions, (3) those based on the character or credit of the party attempting assignment, and (4) those whose assignment is limited by law.

- An assignee acquires all the rights of the assignor, but any defenses available against the assignor are also available against the assignee.

- Notice to the obligor that an assignment has been made is not necessary. However, if the obligor is not notified he may continue to make payments to the assignor. When several assignments of the same rights are made in succession by the same assignor, the order in which the assignments are made may determine which assignment has priority. In some states, the time the notice is given to the obligor is the determining factor.

- A delegation of duties is a party's transfer of his obligations under a contract to a third person. A delegation of duties is permissible if (1) the third person's performance is substantially the same as performance by the party and (2) the party's personal acts or qualifications are not material to the contract. If the acts or qualities are material, the other party to the contract must consent to the transfer. Even though a party has delegated his obligations, he is still liable for performance of the contract.

- The UCC favors assignments and delegations of duties.

- A novation is an agreement among all parties concerned that cancels an existing contract and simultaneously creates a new one. Contracts of novation may be used in lieu of or in conjunction with third-party beneficiary contracts and assignments.

- Assignee
- Assignment
- Assignor
- Creditor–Beneficiary
- Delegation of Duties
- Donee–Beneficiary
- Incidental Beneficiary
- Novation
- Obligor
- Third-Party Beneficiary

Questions and Case Problems

1. Discuss the difference between a third-party beneficiary and an incidental beneficiary.

2. In 1959 Dooley, a stone quarry operator, contracted to sell stone to Rose at specified prices for a ten-year period. In 1960 Dooley sold his stone quarry to Vulcan. Vulcan wrote to Rose about the acquisition and stated that it "assumes all phases" of the contract between Rose and Dooley. Vulcan continued to sell stone to Rose, but at prices above those specified in the contract. Rose sued for breach of contract. Is Vulcan liable? Is Dooley liable?

3. What is the difference between an assignment of rights and a delegation of duties?

4. Chevron contracted with the New York State Thruway Authority to render emergency service to disabled vehicles on the authority's limited-access toll highway. The contract requires Chevron to provide service within 30 minutes after receiving a call. When Kornblut has a flat tire on the thruway, he calls Chevron. Chevron fails to respond. After waiting for two hours Kornblut changes the tire himself and suffers a heart attack. Kornblut dies, and his widow sues for damages on a third-party beneficiary theory. Should she recover?

5. A contracts to sell land to B for $150,000. The contract provides that B is to make a cash down payment of $30,000, with the balance to be paid by means of a mortgage loan to be secured by B. B assigns her rights under the contract to C. Must A complete the sale to C? If C refuses to purchase the land, may A recover from C for breach of contract?

6. List and discuss the types of contracts that are nonassignable.

7. As part of their divorce settlement, Bill and Jane agree that Bill will pay all costs of educating their minor child, Erin. Bill pays for Erin's undergraduate college education. When she enrolls in graduate school he refuses to make further payments. Erin sues, claiming Bill is obligated to pay under the divorce agreement. Result?

8. Roland, a real estate firm, opens a branch office. The branch manager orders furniture on credit from O'Brien for the new office. O'Brien then makes a verbal assignment of the Roland account to Woods, who gives written notice of the assignment to Roland at its main office. O'Brien later makes a written assignment of the Roland account to Brown, who telephones the branch office and informs the person who answers the telephone about the assignment. To whom should Roland make the next payment on the account?

9. Jeans, Incorporated, a clothing manufacturer, contracts with Kane Corporation, a small advertising agency, for promotional advertising of Jeans' products for a one-year period. Shortly afterward, Kane is purchased by and merged into Grimes Company, a larger advertising agency. Grimes assumes all of Kane's rights and liabilities, including Kane's obligations under its contract with Jeans. Jeans refuses to deal with Grimes, claiming that it has no contract with Grimes and prefers to do business with small agencies. Is Jeans' refusal justified?

10. Ross develops and obtains a patent on a new mousetrap. Ross sells the marketing rights to Feiner under a contract that provides for royalty payments to Ross based on sales and requires Feiner to use her best efforts to market the mousetrap over a five-year period. Feiner later sells all her rights under the contract to a third person, Drake. Ross consents to this sale and accepts royalty payments from Drake. Drake eventually abandons efforts to market the mousetrap, and Ross sues Feiner and Drake for breach of contract. Feiner claims that a novation had occurred. Drake claims that the contract between Feiner and him was an assignment of rights, not a delegation of duties. Decide the case.

18 Performance, Discharge, and Remedies

18:1 Introduction

A contract does not last forever; sooner or later it must come to an end. When the parties to a contract no longer have any obligations or duties to perform under the contract, the contract is said to be discharged. The normal, and usually preferable, method of discharging a contract is by *performance.* When both parties have performed all that the contract requires of them, the contract is totally executed and is discharged. When one or both parties do not fully perform, the parties' respective rights under the contract and the remedies available to them for the nonperformance must be determined. Resolution of these issues depends in part on whether a party's nonperformance was (1) legally excused or (2) consented to by the other party, and on whether it related to a trivial—as opposed to material—matter. If the nonperformance was not legally excused or consented to, and if it was related to a material matter, the nonperformance will constitute breach of contract, and the innocent party is entitled to a remedy designed to place him in the position he would have occupied except for the breach. This chapter considers these and other issues relating to the performance of contracts, their breach, and remedies for breach.

18:2 Conditions

A party's duty to perform under a contract is not always absolute. Contracts often condition a party's obligations on the occurrence or nonoccurrence of some event. Words and phrases such as "if," "when," or "provided that" are commonly used to indicate the existence of an express condition. Moreover, under some circumstances an implied condition may be found.

Conditions may be classified as precedent, subsequent, or concurrent. Sometimes a contract provides that a party's duty to perform some act arises only if or when some fact or event occurs; if that event never occurs, the duty to perform never arises. Such a provision is called a *condition precedent;* the occurrence of the event precedes and creates the imposition of the duty. Other times a contract provides that a party is obligated to perform some act, but further provides that the party will be relieved of that obligation if some fact or event occurs. Such a provision is called a *condition subsequent;* the occurrence of the event follows imposition of the duty and extinguishes it. Still other times, the performance of one party is conditioned on performance by the other party, and vice versa, as when the parties are to perform their promises simultaneously. This is a *concurrent condition.*

EXAMPLE

Granucci contracts with Rex Corporation to serve as its president for a period of five years. The contract provides that Granucci is to receive an annual salary of $200,000, with an increase in salary to $300,000 if Rex shows a specified net annual profit within two years. The contract also provides that, in the event Rex should move its corporate headquarters more than 25 miles from its present location, Granucci's obligation to act as president would cease and Rex would give Granucci severance pay of $100,000 if he decides to quit. There are two conditions precedent and one condition subsequent in this contract. The provision regarding a salary increase contains a condition precedent: Rex's obligation to pay the increased salary will arise only if its net profits increase to the level specified within the time specified. The provision regarding possible relocation of the corporate headquarters contains both a condition subsequent and a condition precedent: The relocation is a condition subsequent that will release Granucci from his obligation to serve, and Granucci's quitting is a condition precedent to Rex's obligation to provide the severance pay.

 It is extremely important that at the time a contract is being drafted the parties consider whether there are any possible contingencies that should affect the parties' obligations. If such contingencies can be anticipated, they should be provided for by means of conditions in the contract. As will become clear in the subsequent discussion in this chapter concerning performance and impossibility, failure to provide for contingencies may result in a party's being obligated to render a performance that is virtually, but not legally, impossible, or to pay damages for the failure to perform.

18:3   Sufficiency of Performance

When a contract is clear as to exactly what is required of each party, and each party renders exactly the performance specified, no issue can arise as to the sufficiency of performance. Frequently, however, a party's performance deviates in some way from what is required by the contract. Where there is a deviation, it must be determined whether the performance is sufficient to entitle the party who deviates to reciprocal performance from the other party. Some of the more important issues in determining sufficiency of performance will now be considered.

Substantial Performance   Some contracts contain such numerous and detailed requirements concerning performance that literal compliance is virtually impossible. Construction contracts present the prime example in this area. Construction contracts contain minute specifications, and almost invariably the completed project deviates in some way from the contractual requirements. When a contractor erects a building that is in essential compliance with the general plan, it is obviously unfair to permit the other party to refuse payment on the ground that there were some slight departures from contractual specifications. To prevent such unfairness, the doctrine of *substantial performance* was developed. This doctrine states that a party who substantially performs his obligations under a contract is entitled to performance by the other party, usually in the form of cash payment. To the extent that the other party has suffered some harm from the deviations, he may recover damages, but he may not refuse to perform his own obligations. The doctrine of substantial performance, although most often applied in cases involving building and construction contracts, may be applied to any kind of contract under appropriate circumstances.

The following case illustrates not only the type of situation in which substantial performance might be found, but also the methods used by courts in determining the damages resulting from minor deviations.

Plante

v

Jacobs

10 Wis 2d 567, 103 NW2d 296

(Wisconsin Supreme Court, 1960)

[Eugene Plante contracted to build a house for Frank and Carol Jacobs. Frank and Carol paid $20,000 on the contract price of $26,765, but refused to pay the balance. They claimed that Plante had not substantially performed the contract. Plante sued for the balance due. The trial court held that, although there were some deviations from the contractual specifications, Plante had substantially performed the contract. The trial court entered judgment for Plante, but deducted from his recovery the cost of correcting some of the defects. Note that no deduction was allowed for the misplacement of a wall between the living room and the kitchen. The Jacobses appealed.]

Hallows, Justice.

*　　　*　　　*

The defendants argue the plaintiff cannot recover any amount because he has failed to substantially perform the contract. . . . The defendants claim some 20 . . . items of in-

complete or faulty performance by the plaintiff and no substantial performance because the cost of completing the house in strict compliance with the plans and specifications would amount to 25 or 30 percent of the contract price. The defendants especially stress the misplacing of the wall between the living room and the kitchen, which narrowed the living room in excess of one foot. The cost of tearing down this wall and rebuilding it would be approximately $4,000. . . . Real estate experts testified that the smaller width of the living room would not affect the market price of the house.

. . . [T]here can be no recovery on the contract as distinguished from *quantum meruit* [quasi-contractual recovery] unless there is substantial performance. . . . The question here is whether there has been substantial performance. The test of what amounts to substantial performance seems to be whether the performance meets the essential purpose of the contract. . . .

Substantial performance as applied to construction of a house does not mean that every detail must be in strict compliance with the specifications and the plans. . . . There may be situations in which [there are] features or details of construction of special or of great personal importance, which if not performed, would prevent a finding of substantial performance of the contract. In this case the plan was a stock floor plan. No detailed construction of the house was shown on the plan. There were no blueprints. The specifications were standard printed forms with some modifications and additions written in by the parties. Many of the problems that arose during the construction had to be solved on the basis of practical experience. No mathematical rule relating to the percentage of the price, of cost of completion or of completeness can be laid down to determine substantial performance of a building contract. Although the defendants received a house with which they are dissatisfied in many respects, the trial court was not in error in finding the contract was substantially performed.

The next question is what is the amount of recovery when the plaintiff has substantially, but incompletely, performed. For substantial performance the plaintiff should recover the contract price less the damages caused the defendant by the incomplete performance.... [T]he correct rule for damages ... is the difference between the value of the house as it stands with faulty and incomplete construction and the value of the house if it had been constructed in strict accordance with the plans and specifications. This is the diminished-value rule. The cost of replacement or repair is not the measure of such damage, but is an element to take into consideration in arriving at value under some circumstances. The cost of replacement or the cost to make whole the omissions may equal or be less than the difference in value in some cases and, likewise, the cost to rectify a defect may greatly exceed the added value to the structure as corrected.

The trial court applied the cost-of-repair or replacement rule as to several items, relying on [a case] wherein it was stated that when there are a number of small items of defect or omission which can be remedied without the reconstruction of a substantial part of the

building or a great sacrifice of work or material already wrought in the building, the reasonable cost of correcting the defect should be allowed. ...

Of the defects claimed by the defendants, the court allowed the cost of replacement or repair except as to the misplacement of the living-room wall. Whether a defect should fall under the cost-of-replacement rule or be considered under the diminished-value rule depends upon the nature and magnitude of the defect.... Viewing the construction of the house as a whole and its cost we cannot say, however, that the trial court was in error in allowing the cost of repairing the plaster cracks in the ceilings, the cost of mud jacking and repairing the patio floor, and the cost of reconstructing the non-weight-bearing and nonstructural patio wall. Such reconstruction did not involve an unreasonable economic waste.

The item of misplacing the living room wall under the facts of this case was clearly under the diminished-value rule.... There is no evidence that defendants requested or demanded the replacement of the wall in the place called for by the specifications during the course of construction. To tear down the wall now and rebuild it in its proper place would involve a substantial destruction of the work, if not all of it, which was put into the wall and would cause additional damage to other parts of the house and require replastering and redecorating the walls and ceilings of at least two rooms. Such economic waste is unreasonable and unjustified. The rule of diminished value contemplates the wall is not going to be moved. Expert witnesses ... agreed that the misplacement of the wall had no effect on the market price. The trial court properly found that the defendants suffered no legal damage, although the defendants' particular desire for specified room size was not satisfied. ...

[Judgment affirmed.]

To entitle a party to payment on the basis of substantial performance, it is essential that the party have made an honest effort to perform in compliance with the contract. The doctrine cannot be applied where there are intentional omissions or departures from contractual specifications. For example, if a contractor inadvertently installed pipe different from, but of practically equal grade with, that specified in the contract, a court would find that there was substantial performance. But if the contractor intentionally installed a different type of pipe, the court would not find substantial performance.

Partial Performance Substantial performance is not the same as *partial performance*. Partial performance occurs where a party performs some of the obligations in a contract that contains multiple obligations. Generally, a party rendering partial performance is not entitled to reciprocal performance from the other party and need not be paid. Some courts, however, do permit recovery for the value of the benefit actually conferred by the partial performance.

To illustrate the difference between substantial and partial performance, assume that Jacobs had contracted to build an additional room on and to construct a carport adjacent to Miller's residence. If Jacobs constructs both the additional room and the carport, but deviates in some minor respects from the contract specifications, he has rendered substantial performance and is entitled to payment from Miller on the contract. However, if Jacobs builds only the additional room, and not the carport, he has rendered partial performance, and Miller is relieved of his contractual obligation to pay. Miller might, however, be required to pay for the value of the additional room since he has actually received that benefit.

Satisfaction Clauses Contracts often contain a requirement that the performance of one party be satisfactory to the other party. This requirement is called a satisfaction clause. Satisfaction clauses typically are inserted in contracts in which one party is to build for or provide some item to the other party. A satisfaction clause operates as a condition precedent to the obligation to pay for the item.

Disputes frequently arise as to whether compliance with a satisfaction clause is to be judged by subjective or objective standards. Generally, if a contract involves matters of personal taste, a party is the sole judge of his own satisfaction. For example, if A contracts to paint a satisfactory portrait of B, then B is the sole judge of whether the portrait is satisfactory. If B is genuinely dissatisfied with the portrait as painted, he has no obligation to pay A, even if everyone else who looks at the portrait considers it very good. This is the subjective standard. If, however, the satisfactory nature of a party's performance can be judged by objective standards, such as mechanical utility or fitness for the purpose intended, then the courts will apply a reasonable-person rule of satisfaction. For example, if A agrees to drill a well on B's land that will produce a satisfactory amount of water, and if the well as drilled produces sufficient water to satisfy a reasonable person, most courts will find that the satisfaction clause has been met and that B is obligated to pay for the drilling.

Obviously, there is a certain element of risk involved when one party agrees to render performance to the satisfaction of another party. Therefore, contracts often provide that performance must be satisfactory to some third person. In building contracts especially, the parties frequently include a contractual provision requiring that the work be done to the satisfaction of some third person, usually an architect or an engineer. The third person's approval constitutes a condition precedent to the contractor's right to payment from the other party.

A contract may also contain a clause providing that performance is to be judged by some specified test or by the ability of the completed item to perform some task. Failure to pass the test would prevent recovery. Such clauses are often inserted in contracts for the construction or supply of items whose physical characteristics or capacity is crucial.

Time of Performance   If a contract does not specify a time or times by which the parties are to complete performance, the contract will be interpreted to require performance within a reasonable time. What constitutes a reasonable time depends on all the facts and circumstances surrounding a given contract.

If a contract states specific times for performance by the parties, then a party's failure to perform by the time specified constitutes a breach of the contract. It does not necessarily follow, however, that the other party is relieved of his own duty to perform. Rather, failure to meet a contractual deadline ordinarily is remedied by permitting the other party to recover any damages caused by the delay.

The parties to a contract can expressly stipulate that performance by the time specified in the contract is essential. This is commonly done by stating in the contract that *time is of the essence.* When time is of the essence, failure to perform within the time specified relieves the other party from his own obligation to perform. Moreover, if the nature of the contract or its subject matter is such as to clearly indicate that time is a critical factor, some courts will find time to be of the essence even when it is not stated in the contract. For example, if a store enters an order with a manufacturer for winter coats to be delivered by September 1, and the coats do not arrive until March 1, the store would probably be permitted to refuse to accept the coats, with or without a time-is-of-the-essence clause in the contract. Some states, however, have statutes providing that time is never considered of the essence unless the contract so provides.

 If time is truly of the essence, the contract should so provide. It is inadvisable, however, to routinely insert such a clause in all contracts. Some courts will ignore a time-is-of-the-essence clause where the nature of the contract clearly reveals that performance by the specified time was not in fact essential. Moreover, a time-is-of-the-essence clause may be waived if a party fails to enforce it. For example, if late payments are accepted on an installment contract that provides that time is of the essence, most courts will hold that the clause has been waived. The best practice, therefore, is (1) to insert time-is-of-the-essence clauses only when performance by the specified time is critical and (2) to promptly enforce the clause when the other party fails to perform by the stated time.

18:4   Impossibility of Performance

A great deal can happen between the time a contract is formed and the time that performance is to occur. Frequently, intervening events make performance extremely difficult or even financially prohibitive. The occurrence of such events does not ordinarily constitute an excuse for nonperformance, unless the contract so provides. The fact that performance has been prevented by events such as a strike, an earthquake, a flood, or a war does not constitute legal justification for nonperformance. The theory of the courts is that, if the parties had so desired, such contingencies could have been expressly provided for in the contract.

There are some notable, but limited, exceptions to the above rule. Performance may be excused on the ground of impossibility if (1) an essential person has died, (2) some essential item or commodity has been destroyed, or (3) an intervening change of law has rendered performance of the contract illegal. Some courts also excuse nonperformance on the ground of commercial frustration or impracticability.

Death or Illness   Death of a party will terminate a contract if (1) the contract is one calling for the personal services of the deceased party or (2) the contract in other ways could only be performed by the deceased party. If performance of a contract depends on the continued existence of a particular person who is not a party, that person's death will also excuse performance. If a party is stricken by a disabling illness, the same general principles apply.

 Obviously, the parties to a contract do not normally anticipate each other's death. If a party's continued presence is essential to the contract, it should be written so that the entire agreement is null and void if that party dies or is disabled. Such a clause may be extremely important in a contract in which two or more people undertake joint obligations that neither would undertake if the other were to die. For example, if a husband and wife entered into a contract to purchase a house, the death of one spouse does not excuse nonperformance by the other, because the deceased spouse's personal representative can perform. Often, however, it will be practically impossible to proceed with the purchase, since the ability to make monthly mortgage payments may have been based on both spouses' income.

Destruction of Item   Where the contract relates to a specified item or piece of property and that item or property is destoyed prior to the time for performance, nonperformance is excused. If an equivalent item can be substituted, the contract usually must be performed.

Illegality   Nonperformance is excused when, prior to performance, a change in the law makes performance illegal or impossible. Not every change in the law will excuse nonperformance. For example, a law that makes performance more expensive does not create a legal impossibility or an illegal condition that excuses nonperformance.

Commercial frustration   The doctrine of *commercial frustration* states that nonperformance is excused where a contract cannot be performed without extreme and unreasonable difficulty, expense, or loss that is caused by some unanticipated and unforeseeable event. The doctrine cannot be applied if the hardship might have been foreseen. Generally, it can be relied on only when the change was so drastic that it simply could not have been anticipated. In most cases, therefore, the courts have rejected the defense of commercial frustration on the ground that the facts did not sufficiently show that the changed circumstances were unforeseeable. The doctrine of commercial frustration was developed to remedy the harsh rule that a party must perform unless it is absolutely impossible.

Impossibility of performance on the ground of commercial frustration is the claim made in the following case. The case is atypical in that the plaintiff, rather than the defendant, raised the claim. Note the reason for this reversal of roles. Observe also how the plaintiff's claim of impossibility was premised on the additional claim that the contract contained an implied condition.

American Trading & Production Corp.
v
Shell International Marine Ltd.
453 F2d 939
(United States Court of Appeals, Second Circuit, 1972)

[In March 1967 Shell International (charterer) hired the Washington Trader, a ship owned by the American Trading and Production Corporation (owner), to carry oil from Texas to India. The fee was based on the American Tanker Rate Schedule (ATRS) for the Texas-India trip, plus 75 percent, plus toll charges for the Suez Canal. The total fee came to $417,327.36. The ship left Texas in May 1967. On arrival at the entrance to the Mediterranean, the ship was warned of possible trouble in the Middle East. The ship continued into the Mediterranean toward the canal. When the ship had almost reached Port Said, the entrance to the canal, the canal was closed by the Arab–Israeli war. The ship was forced to proceed around the Cape of Good Hope to India at an additional cost of $131,978.44. American billed Shell for the additional cost, but Shell refused to pay. American then sued Shell. The district court entered judgment for Shell, and American appealed.]

Mulligan, Circuit Judge

*   *   *

On appeal and below the owner argues that transit of the Suez Canal was the agreed specific means of performance of the voyage charter and that the supervening destruction of this means rendered the contract legally impossible to perform and therefore discharged the owner's unperformed obligation (*Restatement of Contracts* § 460 (1932)). Consequently, when the WASHINGTON TRADER eventually delivered the oil after journeying around the Cape of Good Hope, a benefit was conferred upon the charterer for which it should respond in *quantum meruit*. The validity of this proposition depends upon a finding that the parties contemplated or agreed that the Suez passage was to be the exclusive method of performance, and indeed it was so argued on appeal. We cannot construe the agreement in such a fashion. The parties contracted for the shipment of the cargo from Texas to India at an agreed rate and the [agreement] makes absolutely no reference to any fixed route. It is urged that the Suez passage was a condition of performance because the ATRS rate was based on a Suez Canal passage, the invoice contained a specific Suez Canal toll charge and the vessel actually did proceed to a point 84 miles northwest of Port Said. In our view all that this establishes is that both parties contemplated that the Canal would be the probable route. It was the cheapest and shortest, and therefore it was in the interest of both that it be utilized. However, this is not at all equivalent to an agreement that it be the exclusive method of performance. The [agreement] does not so provide and it seems to have been well understood in the shipping industry that the Cape route is an acceptable alternative in voyages of this character. . . .

We hold that all that the ATRS rate establishes is that the parties obviously expected a Suez passage but there is no indication at all in the instrument or *dehors* [outside of it] that it was a condition of performance.

This leaves us with the question as to whether the owner was excused from performance on the theory of commercial impracticability (*Restatement of Contracts* § 454 (1932)). Even though the owner is not excused because of strict impossibility, it is urged that American law recognizes that performance is rendered impossible if it can only be accomplished with extreme and unreasonable difficulty, expense, injury or loss. There is no extreme or unreasonable difficulty apparent here. The alternate route taken was well recognized, and there is no claim that the vessel or the crew or the nature of the cargo made the route actually taken unreasonably difficult, dangerous or onerous. The owner's case here essentially rests upon the element of the additional expense involved—$131,978.44. This represents an increase of less than one third over the agreed upon $417,327.36. We find that this increase in expense is not sufficient to constitute commercial impracticability under either American or English authority.

Mere increase in cost alone is not a sufficient excuse for non-performance (*Restatement of Contracts* § 467 (1932)). It must be an "extreme and unreasonable" expense (*Restatement of Contracts* § 454 (1932)). . . .

Matters involving impossibility or impracticability of performance of contract are concededly vexing and difficult. One is even urged on the allocation of such risks to pray for the "wisdom of Solomon." 6 A. Corbin, *Contracts* § 1333, at 372 (1962). On the basis of all of the facts, the pertinent authority and a further belief in the efficacy of prayer, we affirm.

 Businesses have found it extremely difficult to prove commercial impracticability. Contingencies that might render performance of a contract economically prohibitive should be provided for when the contract is drafted. Businesspersons should ask themselves, "What would happen if?" about every contingency, and then provide for each contingency in the contract. This may not only prevent a substantial loss in the future, but might also help the parties to better understand which party assumes which risks. The possibility of a labor strike is a particularly important contingency, and many contracts now contain provisions specifically excusing performance in the event of a strike.

The UCC has a somewhat more lenient standard with respect to commercial impracticability. Under the UCC, performance of a sales contract is excused if performance "has been made impracticable by the occurrence of a contingency the nonoccurrence of which was a basic assumption on which the contract was made" (USS § 2-615).[1]

18:5   Discharge by Agreement

The parties to a contract may agree to modify it or to terminate the contract entirely. They can terminate the contract by either replacing it with a new contract or simply ending their contractual relationship. Discharge by agreement between the parties may take various forms. Among the more important ones are (1) *rescission*, (2) *novation*, and (3) *accord and satisfaction*. The parties may agree to modify a contract by waiver.

Rescission   Both parties may agree that their contractual relationship should be terminated without performance. This action is called rescission by agreement. It discharges the contract in its entirety; neither party has any obligation to perform under it. While consideration for the rescission is necessary, the courts will find that each party's agreement to discharge the other party from the performance of his contractual obligations constitutes sufficient consideration.

 Generally, rescission may be done orally, even if the original contract was required to be in writing. Only when the agreement involves a retransfer of land must the rescission be in writing. However, if one party should claim that an oral agreement was made to rescind a written contract, and the other party disputes that, a court will insist on clear proof of the rescission. For that reason, whenever a written contract is to be rescinded by agreement, as a matter of business practice the rescission should also be in writing.

A party's right to rescind a contract on the ground of fraud or for similar reasons has been discussed in Chapter 12. The use of rescission as a remedy for breach of contract will be discussed later in this chapter.

Novation   A contract of novation is an agreement among all the parties concerned that discharges the existing contract and simultaneously creates a new contract. The use of a novation as a means of substituting a third party in the place of one of the original parties was discussed in Section 17:8. In the present discussion, the original parties may utilize a novation to discharge their original contract and enter into a new agreement.

Accord and Satisfaction   An accord is an agreement by the parties to give and accept some performance different from that originally promised; a satisfaction is the actual performance of the substituted obligation. In order for an existing contract to be discharged by an accord and satisfaction, therefore, there must not only be a new agreement but also performance of that agreement.

---

[1]Performance of sales contracts generally is discussed in Chapter 22.

Waiver Either party to a contract may allow or accept from the other party performance that is not in full compliance with the contract. This allowance or acceptance is called a waiver. A waiver may be express or it may be implied from the acts of the parties. The concept of waiver is frequently applied to excuse a party's nonperformance of some act. For example, if an installment contract calls for payments to be made on the first of each month, and it further provides that time is of the essence, failure to make payments on time would ordinarily constitute a breach of contract. If, however, the creditor consistently accepts late payments, this acceptance may be interpreted as a waiver of the time-is-of-the-essence provision. If the creditor subsequently decides to insist on timely payments, he would probably have to give the debtor notice that in the future the provision is going to be enforced.

18:6 Discharge by Operation of Law

A contract can be discharged as a matter of law by the occurrence of certain events. Among the more important of these events are bankruptcy proceedings, passage of the period prescribed by the statute of limitations, and material alteration of the contract.

Bankruptcy A bankruptcy proceeding often culminates in an adjudication that a debtor is discharged from his contractual duties to most of his creditors. The subject of bankruptcy is covered in more detail in Chapter 31.

Statute of Limitations All states have statutes of limitations, which require that legal actions be brought within a specified time. State laws typically specify different limitations periods for different kinds of actions. For example, most states grant a longer period of time within which a party can bring an action on a written contract than they do for an oral contract. The limitations period begins to run when the right to sue arises (in most cases, when the contract was breached). If a party fails to bring suit within the period specified, the contract will be discharged.

Alteration A party's intentional and material alteration of a written contract will discharge the other party's obligations under the contract as a matter of law. To be material, an alteration must change the rights, obligations, or relations of the parties in some way.

18:7 Breach of Contract

A breach of contract is a party's failure to perform some contractual obligation without having a legal excuse for not performing. A material breach of contract has two interrelated consequences: (1) it relieves the other party from his obligation to perform under the contract, and (2) it entitles that party to seek damages or other appropriate relief as a remedy for the breach. A relatively minor or trivial breach of contract may not relieve the other party of his obligations, although he may be able to obtain damages. Remedies for breach of contract will be presented later in this chapter.

Anticipatory Breach of Contract   Prior to the time set for his performance, one party to a contract may inform the other party that he has no intention of performing the contract. This prospective failure to perform is called an *anticipatory breach* of contract. When an anticipatory breach occurs, the other party may treat the contract as broken, cease performance himself, and sue for breach of contract.

The rationale of the doctrine of anticipatory breach is that the innocent party may be able to minimize his losses if he is not forced to wait until an actual breach occurs. For example, assume that in September Yamada and Nance enter a contract under the terms of which Nance agrees to manufacture and provide a line of bathing suits to Yamada, to be delivered by February 28. In December, Nance informs Yamada that he no longer manufactures bathing suits and will be unable to fill Yamada's order. Yamada may treat Nance's statement as an anticipatory breach of contract and place an order elsewhere for the bathing suits without waiting for the actual breach (nondelivery by February 28) to occur. Yamada may also file a lawsuit for breach of contract at this time.

 A party's repudiation of the contract must be absolute and clear before the other party can treat it as an anticipatory breach. The fact that one party complains about his obligations under a contract or has a generally negative attitude toward the contract does not constitute an anticipatory breach, and the other party must continue to perform. Moreover, if a repudiation is withdrawn before the other party acts in reliance on it, the repudiation cannot be treated as an anticipatory breach.

The following case illustrates the importance of making certain that there has been an anticipatory breach before acting in reliance on it. In reading the case, consider whether the condition in the lease agreement was truly a condition subsequent, as stated by the parties, or a condition precedent.

STC, Inc.

v

Billings
168 Mont 364, 543 P2d 374
(Montana Supreme Court, 1975)

[In 1972, STC, Inc., a nonprofit corporation, purchased the Old Chamber Building in Billings, Montana, to renovate and preserve it. In June 1972, STC and the city of Billings entered a lease agreement that provided that STC would remodel the premises and the city would rent a portion of the

building for ten years at an agreed rental. The agreement was made subject to "the condition subsequent" that STC would obtain financing for remodeling and begin remodeling by the end of March 1973, or the lease would be null and void. STC had difficulty obtaining the necessary financing, but in November 1972 was notified that a lender would consider making a loan, provided, among other things, that STC would show firm ten-year leases for the building. On February 5, 1973, the Billings City Council voted "to not reaffirm the provisions of the original lease." STC made no further attempts to secure financing, and the remodel-

ing was never done. STC sued the city, claiming anticipatory breach of contract. The trial court entered judgment for the city, and STC appealed.]

Haswell, Justice.

*   *   *

Our decision in this appeal is bottomed squarely on one issue: Did the action of the city council on February 5, 1973 constitute a breach of the lease? . . .

An anticipatory breach of contract by the promisor is a repudiation of his contractual duty before the time fixed in the contract for his performance has arrived. . . .

The reasons supporting an action for anticipatory breach of contract have been variously stated to be: the uselessness and inequity of requiring the promisee to hold himself in readiness to perform his contractual obligation on the date performance is due where the promisor has already repudiated his reciprocal obligations under the contract; the present injury to the implied right of each of the contracting parties to refrain from impairing the ability or willingness of the other to perform when performance is due; the duty of the promisee to mitigate damages by withholding expenditures in preparation for carrying out his contractual obligations where the promisor will not perform in any event; the social and economic waste incident to prolonging a contractual status that is effectively at an end: and the necessity that the law recognize the commercial desirability of fixing legal rights, liabilities and damages as promptly as possible. . . .

The crux of the instant case is whether the action of the city council on February 5, 1973 constituted an anticipatory repudiation of the lease agreement. The city council voted to "not re-affirm provisions of the original lease." Plaintiff treats this as a repudiation or renunciation of the city's obligations under the lease. But was it?

It appears to us that the action of the city

council was subject to different interpretations. It might have meant the new mayor and council did not want to go on record as approving the original lease. It might have meant the new mayor and council refused to assist plaintiff corporation in its efforts to secure the necessary financing for remodeling by an affirmative expression of support. It might have meant the new mayor and council were repudiating the lease and refused to perform the city's obligations thereunder.

The language of the proposition on which the council voted is significant in our view. The council voted "not to re-affirm." The council did not vote "not to affirm." The council did not vote to repudiate, renounce, or cancel the lease, nor adopt any language manifesting an intention not to carry out its obligations under the lease. The language of the proposition on which the council voted was equivocal, ambiguous, and subject to conflicting interpretations.

The circumstances support a like conclusion. A city election intervened between the execution of the lease and the vote of the council on February 5, 1973. Some new aldermen and a new mayor had been elected who opposed the lease. STC, INC. had not secured the necessary financing despite some seven month's effort. Time was running out. Less than two months remained before the lease agreement would expire by its own terms if financing was not secured. No rational basis existed for the city to repudiate the lease at this time and under these circumstances, while a good reason did exist for the new mayor and council to refuse to go on record as approving the lease negotiated by their predecessors, or to refuse to assist STC, INC. in obtaining financing. At the very least the circumstances are equally consistent with this interpretation of the council's intention. The collective intention of the city council remains ambiguous and equivocal.

A repudiation or renunciation must be entire, absolute and unequivocal to support an action for anticipatory breach. . . .

Anticipatory breach must appear only in the clearest terms of repudiation of the contractual obligation. . . . An expression of intent not to perform, or not to be bound, standing alone, is not enough. . . . [N]or is a mere assertion that a party will be unable, or will refuse, to perform his contract an anticipatory renunciation. . . .

Applying these rules, we hold the action of the city council on February 5, 1973 to "not re-affirm provisions of the original lease" was not a positive, unequivocal, absolute expression of intention by the city not to perform its contractual obligations under the lease. Accordingly, it will not support an action for anticipatory breach and plaintiff's action must fail. . . .

The judgment of the district court is affirmed.

Most courts have held that the doctrine of anticipatory breach does not apply to promises to pay money. For example, assume that A lends B $1,000, in exchange for B's promise to repay the money two months later. One month later, B tells A that she will not repay the money. A may not treat B's statement as an anticipatory breach. In other words, A must wait until B actually fails to pay the money when due before A can sue B for breach of contract.

18:8   Remedies Generally[2]

When one party breaches a contract, the other party is entitled to a remedy. The purpose of the remedy is to place the innocent party in the position he would have occupied except for the breach. In other words, the law seeks to give the innocent party the benefit of the bargain contained in the contract. Usually the innocent party's injury can be gauged in monetary terms, so the most common remedy for the injury is money. This remedy is known as damages or money damages. To illustrate, assume that Karen contracted to buy Amina's car for $800, and then later refused to buy the car. If Amina then was able to sell her car to Walter, but for only $600, the injury to Amina as a result of Karen's breach of contract would be $200. A court would therefore award Amina that amount of money as damages.

If money damages are inadequate to redress the injury caused by a breach of contract, other remedies, such as specific performance and injunction, may be available. If money damages are adequate but the innocent party wants some other remedy, alternative types of monetary remedies, such as *restitution*, may be available. All these remedies will be discussed below. Where alternative remedies are available, a party must often make what is known as an election of remedies. For example, a party cannot seek both an order rescinding a contract and an order requiring specific performance of the same contract. Since the two remedies are inconsistent, he must select one.

---

[2]Remedies in sales cases are discussed in Chapter 22.

18:9 Damages

There are three basic kinds of damages: (1) compensatory, (2) nominal, and (3) punitive. *Compensatory damages* are awarded to reimburse the injured party for the loss actually caused by the breach of contract. Compensatory damages are always permitted in breach of contract actions. *Nominal damages* are awarded where a breach of contract is shown, but the innocent party is unable to prove any actual damages. The usual amount of a nominal damages award is one dollar. *Punitive damages* are damages designed to punish the wrongdoer and to set an example for others. Generally, punitive damages are not recoverable in a breach of contract action.

Compensatory Damages Compensatory damages may be classified as either general (direct) or special (consequential). General damages include those that naturally flow from breach of the kind of contract involved. Such damages are always recoverable. Special damages are those that result from the particular circumstances of the case, rather than from the nature of the contract. To illustrate the distinction, assume that Victor contracted to shoe Elaine's horse. Victor performed the job improperly, and a horseshoe fell off. General damages would certainly include the expense involved in having the horse properly shoed. General damages would also probably include the value of the horse if it broke its leg as a result of the improper shoeing. These types of damages might naturally be expected to result from a breach of the kind of contract involved. Now assume that the horse was Elaine's only means of transportation, that she had intended to ride the horse into town to complete a deal for the sale of cattle, that, because of the lost shoe, she was unable to reach town in time to complete the deal; and that as a result she lost $50,000. The $50,000 could be considered special, or consequential, damages. Is it fair, however, to award $50,000 as damages for breach of a contract to shoe a horse?

The foregoing example points up the problems posed by special damages. On the one hand, the innocent party has suffered certain damages as a result of the other party's contractual breach. On the other hand, as in many cases, there is no way that the breaching party could have anticipated such a loss. The courts have generally resolved the problem by permitting recovery of special damages only if they could have been resonably foreseen by the defaulting party. For example, if Victor knew that Elaine needed her horse in order to get to town to complete the deal, then it is reasonable to conclude that he knew or should have known that breach of the horseshoeing contract would probably result in Elaine's being unable to complete the transaction. In such a situation, Elaine could recover her special damages. If, however, Victor was totally unaware of Elaine's intended use of the horse, most courts would not permit recovery of the special damages.

 When one party is likely to suffer special damages if the other party breaches the contract, he should communicate this likelihood to the other party. Then, in the event of breach, he could probably recover special damages. More important, the other party, having knowledge of the special circumstances, might make a special effort to perform.

Liquidated Damages and Penalties   To recover damages, a party must show their existence with reasonable certainty. If it is very difficult, if not impossible, to calculate the loss caused by a breach of contract, a *liquidated damages* clause might be inserted in the contract, because a court will not permit recovery of wholly speculative damages. The purpose of a liquidated damages provision is to ensure that a resonable estimate of probable damages is available in case of a breach. A liquidated damages provision specifies a sum of money that the parties agree will be paid as compensatory damages. It may help to avoid not only the problem of calculating damages if a breach does occur, but also the likelihood of litigation over the amount of damages.

A liquidated damages provision must be enforceable if it is to be of any help. It is enforceable as long as the amount specified is a reasonable estimate of probable damages. If it appears to be designed to punish a party for default, it will be considered a penalty and will not be enforced. In that case, the nondefaulting party must prove actual damages to recover. The doctrine of unconscionability (see Chapter 12) figures prominently in denying enforcement of penalty provisions. While the parties are free to make a mutual good faith estimate of probable damages, one party is not free to oppress the other party by specifying an exorbitant amount and labeling it liquidated damages. A court will look to the circumstances of each case to determine whether a purported liquidated damages clause is one in fact, or whether it is a penalty.

Minimizing Damages   A party may not recover damages that reasonably could have been avoided. Rather, a party must take reasonable action to minimize the damages that result from a breach. For example, if A leases an apartment to B for one year, but B leaves after six months, A may not simply leave the apartment vacant and require full payment from B. A must take reasonable steps to rent the apartment to someone else to minimize the damages flowing from B's breach. Similarly, if an employer wrongfully discharges an employee, the employee must ordinarily seek other similar employment. A party's failure to seek to minimize damages will result in a reduction of the amount granted by the court.

Tort Remedies   The same set of facts may permit a party to sue under either a breach of contract or a tort theory. The damages recoverable in a tort action may be larger. For example, punitive damages may be recovered in a tort action. It may therefore be desirable in some cases to seek recovery on a tort theory, either in addition to or in lieu of a contract theory. For example, in the earlier horseshoeing illustration, Elaine might sue in tort on the ground that Victor negligently shoed the horse.[3]

---

[3]The subject of torts is covered in more detail in Chapters 5 and 6.

18:10   Other Remedies

A remedy other than damages may be appropriate in some cases. A party might seek specific performance, injunctive relief, rescission, restitution, or arbitration. Each of these possible remedies will be discussed briefly.

Specific Performance   Sometimes an award of damages, no matter how great, is simply inadequate to remedy the injury caused by a breach of contract. In such cases, a decree of *specific performance* may be sought. Specific performance is an equitable remedy, and it will be granted only when the remedy at law is inadequate. To be entitled to specific performance, the plaintiff must show that the subject matter of the contract was unique. Since a unique item cannot be replaced, an award of damages can never have the effect of giving the innocent party the benefit of the bargain. Specific performance is granted primarily in cases involving contracts for the sale of land. Each piece of land is considered unique and therefore irreplaceable. Personal property, in contrast, is ordinarily not considered unique. For example, if a seller breaches a contract for sale of an automobile, the buyer can always purchase a comparable automobile elsewhere. Therefore, if the contract involves personal property, the property must be shown to be truly unique before a court will order specific performance. A court might order specific performance of a contract for the sale of a Gutenberg Bible, for example, since it would probably be impossible for a buyer to purchase another copy.

Specific performance is not a remedy in cases involving personal service contracts. The primary reason for refusing specific performance is that it is impossible to coerce a person to render services.

Injunction   The equitable remedy of obtaining an injunction is closely related to, and in many cases has the same effect as, an award of specific performance. An injunction in contract actions is a court order to restrain a breach or a continuing breach of the contract. As with specific performance, injunctive relief is granted when the remedy at law is inadequate. In addition, there normally must be a showing that irreparable injury will result to the other party if the injunctive relief is not granted.

Injunctive relief may be utilized to effectively compel specific performance of a contract for personal services. When an employee possesses truly special, unique, or extraordinary qualifications, so that his services cannot be replaced, and the employee refuses to perform, a court might issue a kind of injunction called a negative injunction. This injunction prohibits the employee from performing services for any other person. For example, if an exceptional professional athlete or entertainer refused to honor his contractual obligation, a court might enjoin him from performing for any other person.

Injunctive relief is also often used to enforce anticompetition contracts. For example, assume that A sells his hamburger stand to B and that the contract prohibits A from operating another hamburger stand within a radius of five miles for a period of three years. If A immediately opens another hamburger stand across the street, B can seek an injunction ordering A to honor the anticompetition clause.

Rescission and Restitution   Rescission and restitution are closely related remedies by which an injured party seeks the return of whatever he parted with, or its monetary equivalent. The damages recoverable under either remedy are based on the value of the services performed by the injured party—which is the value of the benefit received by the other party—as opposed to the benefit of the injured party's original bargain.

Arbitration   Arbitration as a nonjudicial method of resolving disputes has been discussed in Chapter 2. Contracts often contain provisions that require disputes to be submitted to arbitration. Even without such a provision, the parties may, if they agree, submit any disputes to arbitration.

 Arbitration often provides a quicker and less costly resolution than a lawsuit can. When faced with a contract dispute, therefore, a businessperson is always well advised to consider the possibility of arbitration.

Key Concepts and Terms

- A contract is discharged when the parties no longer have any obligations under it. Performance is the normal method of discharge.
- A party's duty to perform may be contingent on the occurrence or nonoccurrence of certain conditions. A condition precedent involves an event, the occurrence of which precedes and creates imposition of the duty. A condition subsequent involves an event the occurrence of which follows and extinguishes the duty. A concurrent condition involves one party's performance being conditioned on performance by the other party, and vice versa.
- Substantial performance by a party is the performance of a contract with slight departures from contractual specification. Substantial performance entitles the performing party to performance by the other party. Partial performance is performance of some but not all of the contract's provisions. Partial performance does not generally entitle the performing party to performance by the other party.
- If a contract involves matters of personal taste, compliance with a clause requiring one party to render satisfactory performance is determined solely by the other party. In other situations, a reasonable-person rule of satisfaction is applied.
- When a contract specifies no time for performance, a reasonable time is allowed. If time is of the essence, failure to perform by the time specified relieves the other party from the obligation to perform. Otherwise, delay in performance merely entitles the other party to damages.
- The fact that intervening events render performance of a contract extremely difficult does not ordinarily excuse nonperformance. Acceptable excuses for

nonperformance include (1) death or illness of an essential person, (2) destruction of an essential item, (3) a change in law rendering performance illegal, and (4) commercial frustration.

- A contract may be discharged by agreement of the parties (rescission, novation, or accord and satisfaction) or by operation of law (discharge in bankruptcy, passage of the period prescribed by the statute of limitations, or material alteration). Performance of an obligation may also be waived.

- A breach of contract is a party's failure to perform a contractual obligation without having a legal excuse for not performing. An anticipatory breach, which also excuses performance by the innocent party, occurs when one party informs the other of his intention not to perform the contract, even though the time for performance has not yet arrived.

- The purpose of a remedy is to place an innocent party in the position he would have occupied were it not for a breach of contract. The usual remedy in a contract action is an award of compensatory damages, which are classified as either general (direct) or special (consequential).

- Liquidated damages are a kind of compensatory damages that are specified in a contract provision when it would be difficult or impossible to calculate the value of a loss caused by a breach of the contract.

- Specific performance and injunctions are court-ordered remedies granted to the injured party when damages are an insufficient remedy.

- Rescission, restitution, and arbitration are other remedies available for breach of contract.

- Accord and Satisfaction
- Anticipatory Breach
- Commercial Frustration
- Concurrent Conditions
- Condition Precedent
- Condition Subsequent
- Liquidated Damages
- Minimizing Damages

- Novation
- Partial Performance
- Performance
- Rescission
- Restitution
- Specific Performance
- Substantial Performance

Questions and Case Problems

1. What is the difference between substantial performance and partial performance?

2. Peters contracts to build a house for Jayo, a wheelchair-bound paraplegic. The house is generally constructed according to specifications. The only deviation from the contract is that the entrances and the bathrooms are not built for access by wheelchairs. This deviation does not affect the value of the house, but the cost of making the entrances and bathrooms accessible to wheelchairs would be $3,000. In making final payment to Peters, Jayo deducts $3,000 from the agreed price. Peters sues. What is the result?

3. In March, Schmidt contracted to supply eggs to the City College cafeteria for a year, beginning in September. During a heat wave in June, many of Schmidt's

chickens died, and on July 1 he informed the cafeteria manager that he would be unable to supply the eggs as agreed. On July 10, Schmidt informed the manager that he might be able to replace his hens faster than he thought; that if he did replace them he would be able to perform the contract; and that he would know for certain by July 31. On July 15, the manager, unwilling to wait, contracted with another egg supplier at a substantially higher price. On July 25, Schmidt informed the manager that he would perform the contract, but the manager told him that his eggs were no longer needed. Schmidt sued for damages due to loss of business, and the cafeteria counterclaimed for damages due to the increased price paid the second supplier. What is the result?

4. Mills contracts with Fauna Productions to serve as technical advisor on a movie concerning coyotes and to train a coyote named Alpha to perform in the movie. As partial compensation, Mills is to receive Alpha when the movie is completed. Fauna reneges on the promise to give Alpha to Mills, and she sues for specific performance. Although Mills admits that other coyotes could be trained as well as Alpha, she claims that Alpha is unique because her children had become attached to him during the filming. Should Mills be granted specific performance?

5. Johnson contracted with the Wallowa County School District to drive a bus for two years. The contract granted him an option to renew the contract for three additional years if his service proved to be satisfactory. Although there was no evidence of unsatisfactory service, the school board declined to renew the contract when it expired. Johnson sued for damages. Result?

6. Under what circumstances will a party's nonperformance of a contract be excused?

7. Under what circumstances can a party recover special damages for breach of contract?

8. Wafer sells his accounting business and equipment to Mullen. The contract of sale provides that Wafer will remain active in the business for two years to assist Mullen in making a satifactory transition. Less than a month after the sale, Wafer dies. Mullen sues to rescind the contract on the ground that Wafer's services were indispensable to the contract. What is the decision?

9. In December, Adam reserved a room at the Ras Hotel for the three days of the Memorial Day weekend; he made full advance payment of $315. In March, Adam canceled the reservation and asked for return of his advance payment. The Ras refused, and made no attempt to rent the room over the holiday. Adam sued. What amount, if any, should he recover? Would the answer be different if Adam had waited until the day before to cancel his reservation? If the reservation had been for a nonholiday period?

10. Cook contracted to sell his condominium to Dean, with a closing date of November 1. The contract provided that time was of the essence. On October 15, Dean informed Cook that she would not be able to close the sale on November 1, and that an additional month might be required. Cook told Dean not to worry and that the deal could be closed after November 1. On November 3, Cook received a better offer for the condominium. He immediately notified Dean that, unless the sale was closed within 15 days, he would consider the contract rescinded. When Dean was unable to close by November 18, Cook contracted to sell the condominium to the other buyer. On December 1, Dean sued for specific performance. Should specific performance be granted? Should the availability of identical condominium units in the same complex affect the result?

PART FOUR

Sales

Introductory Comments

Virtually every business engages in the sale of goods, often as both buyer and seller. A clothing manufacturer, for example, must buy raw materials to make the clothing he sells. It is therefore imperative that a businessperson have some knowledge of the legal rights and obligations of both buyer and seller.

The material in Chapters 19 through 22 focuses on the law of sales, with emphasis on the provisions of the UCC. These chapters discuss the formation of sales contracts, the actual transfer of goods and title to goods, the determination of which party bears the loss when goods are damaged, warranties relating to the quality and performance of goods, performance of sales contracts, and remedies for breach of these contracts.

Throughout this division, the practical aspects of sales transactions are considered because they are critical in determining the resolution of any sales dispute. The particular characteristics of an industry and the way in which it conducts its business must be taken into account. For example, the diamond industry conducts business differently than the aerospace industry, and it follows that the customary method of making a sale may also differ. As much as possible a buyer or seller should familiarize himself with and follow these customs.

At the heart of a sales transaction is the sales contract. Such a contract is just as binding as any other, and a businessperson should approach it with the same care as he approaches other contracts. Care should also be taken both in drafting and in using standardized forms.

In the same light, the value of cooperation should not be overlooked. Disagreements do arise in sales transactions. Often these disagreements may be settled amicably by the parties involved. A friendly settlement may prevent litigation, preserve a contract, and maintain a valuable business relationship. In other words, legal action is normally the last option to be pursued, not the first.

Finally, it should be noted that the area of sales does not constitute an island unto itself. General contract law, as discussed earlier in this book, is obviously relevant to sales contracts. The law of sales may also interact with the law of torts, the law of commercial paper, the law governing creditor–debtor relationships, and the law of insurance. For example, when a person is injured by a defective product, both tort law and sales law may be applicable. When a buyer pays for goods with a check or other commercial paper, the law governing commercial paper must be considered. When a buyer takes out a loan to finance a purchase, sales law and the law governing creditor–debtor relationships interact. And when insurance is taken out on goods, insurance law becomes relevant. Thus, although sales law is considered here as a separate subject, its relationship to other areas of law must always be borne in mind.

19 Introduction to the Law of Sales

19:1 Historical Background

Commerce as it is practiced today had its beginning in the latter part of the Middle Ages. It was virtually nonexistent in the centuries following the collapse of the Roman Empire, but began a gradual revival around the twelfth century. A significant contribution to this revival was the European fair. Held in different areas of the continent, these great fairs generated a tremendous amount of commercial activity as merchants from all parts of Europe gathered to exchange their goods. Out of necessity these merchants eventually developed a set of general rules to govern their commercial dealings. These rules, known as the *law merchant*, became recognized throughout Europe and England as the body of law that governed the resolution of commercial disputes.

In time the law merchant became a part of the English common law. The English common law of sales was codified into the English Sale of Goods Act. This act in turn served as the basis for the Uniform Sales Act, which was adopted by most American states. Finally, the Uniform Commercial Code (UCC) was proposed. It has been enacted by 49 states, the District of Columbia, and the Virgin Islands. (Louisiana has not adopted the UCC as a whole, but has adopted some portions of it dealing with matters other than sales.) Article 2 of the UCC deals with sales and has replaced the Uniform Sales Act as the basic law of sales.

As this brief survey indicates, the law of sales has developed literally over hundreds of years. In deciding controversies concerning sales, the courts therefore have a great body of legal tradition from which to draw. Indeed, the UCC itself recognizes that the law merchant may still be applied in appropriate situations (UCC § 1-103).

Portions of the UCC other than Article 2 also may be applicable to some sales contracts. These are Article 1, which contains general provisions applicable to all the remaining articles; Article 6, which relates to particular kinds of transfers of goods known as bulk transfers and is covered in Chapter 20 of this book; and Article 7, which deals with documents of title and is also covered in Chapter 20.

19:2   Subject Matter of Sales

Article 2 applies to "transactions in goods" (UCC § 2-102). While these transactions include more than sales, for practical purposes Article 2 deals with sales of goods. It becomes important, therefore, to determine what constitutes a sale, as well as what constitutes goods.

Sale   The basic feature of a *sale* is the passage of title from the seller to the buyer for a price [UCC § 2-106(1)]. This feature distinguishes a sale from various similar transactions. For example, in a lease of personal property, there is no transfer of title; the lessee is expected to return the property to the lessor at the conclusion of the lease.[1] In the case of a gift, there is passage of title, but no price is paid.

The payment in a sale need not be money. The price may be partially or wholly paid in other goods. For example, if Susan trades in her old car as down payment on a new car, the price paid by her for the new car consists in part of goods (her old car) rather than money.

 For various reasons, the parties to a contract sometimes wish to disguise its true nature. Installment sales, for example, are sometimes labeled leases. By calling a sale a lease, the parties may hope to avoid application not only of Article 2, but also of Article 9, which deals with secured transactions. This may lead to unforeseen difficulties because a court will look behind the name given a transaction to ascertain its true nature. In other words, a court might end up applying the UCC provisions that the parties were seeking to avoid. Therefore, it is normally better to structure the transaction in a straightforward way in the first place, so that the parties will know what to expect and will be aware of what law is applicable.

Goods   Under Article 2, *goods* includes all things that are movable at the time of identification to the contract [UCC § 2-105(1)].[2] Basically, this means that Article 2 governs all sales of tangible personal property of every variety. "Goods" includes the unborn young of animals, growing crops, timber to be cut, minerals, oil, gas, and structures that are attached to land if they are capable of being severed without material harm to the land, and are to be severed by the seller [UCC §§ 2-105(1), 2-107].

Land and intangible personal property are not "goods" under Article 2. For example, sales of intangible rights of action (such as one person's right to sue another for damages) or investment securities are not covered by Article 2 [UCC § 2-105(1)].

In order for a sale to actually occur, the goods must be both existing and identified. Where the goods are not existing and identified, the parties may enter into a contract for the sale of *future goods* [UCC § 2-105(2)]. Both a present sale and a contract for a future sale come within the coverage of Article 2, and the status of a transaction as a present sale or a contract to sell generally has no bearing on the

---

[1]Personal property leases and bailments, and the applicability of UCC principles to bailments, are discussed in Chapter 33.
[2]"Identification to the contract" is discussed in Chapter 20 (see 20:3).

rights of the parties. The UCC has specifically addressed some areas of previous difficulty. For example, Article 2 provides that "goods" includes specially manufactured items [UCC § 2-105(1)], and that the serving of food and drink is considered a sale [UCC § 2-314(1)].

Mixed Transactions   The general principles presented above are easy to apply in most instances to determine whether a transaction is a sale. If a person sells a desk, a suit, or a can of beans, he clearly has made a sale of goods. If a person sells a house, he clearly has not made a sale of goods. Similarly, a contract for legal or other professional services does not involve a sale of goods, and is therefore not within the scope of Article 2.

Often, however, a contract involves not only the rendition of services, but also the transfer of goods. A question then arises as to what part, if any, of the transaction should be governed by Article 2. To determine this, courts have generally looked to the primary focus of the contract. If it was essentially a contract for the rendition of services, with the transfer of goods being merely incidental to those services, Article 2 is inapplicable. However, if the transaction was primarily a sale, Article 2 is applicable to the entire transaction.

The following case illustrates how the courts approach the issue of whether a contract should be classified as a sales contract or a services contract.

Bonebrake
v
Cox
499 F2d 951, 14 UCCRS 1318
(United States Court of Appeals, Eighth Circuit, 1974)

[The Tamarack Bowl, a bowling alley, was owned by the Cox brothers. In February 1968 it was gutted by fire. The Coxes decided to rebuild and entered into two contracts with Simek for the purchase and installation of bowling equipment. The total cost was $55,000. Delivery and installation of the equipment began, but in September 1968 Simek died. The Coxes, who had paid $27,000 on the contracts, were forced to have the work completed by other persons. Simek's administratrix, Bonebrake, sued for the balance of the contract price, and the Coxes counterclaimed for damages from anticipatory breach. The district court granted judgment to Bonebrake for $27,000, and the Coxes appealed. One issue on appeal was the propriety of the trial court's ruling that, since the original contract was a mixed goods–

services one, it did not fall under Article 2 of the UCC.]

Talbot Smith, Senior District Judge.

*   *   *

We now consider whether the contract of April 17, 1968 comes under the Code. Its background we have noted. The fire suffered by defendant's bowling alley on February 5, 1968 had destroyed its equipment. This contract with Simek was to replace those goods. The "following used equipment" was purchased: lane beds, ball returns, chairs, bubble ball cleaning machine, lockers, house balls, storage racks, shoes, and foundation materials. The equipment was to be delivered and installed by Simek. He warranted that the lanes would be "free from defects in workmanship and materials," and that they would "meet all ABC specifications." The purchase price was stated to be "for the total price of $20,000.00." . . .

The language thus employed is that peculiar to goods, not services. It speaks of "equipment," and of lanes free from "defects in workmanship and materials." The rendition of services does not comport with such terminology.

The [district court], however, ruled that the above-described contract "is not the type of contract which falls within the statutory scheme of the U.C.C. It involved substantial amounts of labor, as well as goods, with a lump sum price. The Code was meant to cover contracts for the commercial sale of goods, not non-divisible mixed contracts of this type."

In such holding there is error. Article 2 of the Code, here involved, applies to "transactions in goods." [UCC § 2-102]. The definition of "goods" is found in [UCC § 2-105(1)]:

"Goods" means all things (including specially manufactured goods) which are movable at the time of identification to the contract for sale other than the money in which the price is to be paid, investment securities (Article 8) and things in action. "Goods" also includes the unborn young of animals and growing crops and other identified things attached to realty as described in the section on goods to be severed from realty [Section 2-107].

... [To constitute "goods"], the articles (the "things") must be movable, and the movability must occur at the time of identification to the contract. The applicability of the Code to the April contract is clear from and within its four corners. The "things" sold are all items of tangible property, normally in the flow of commerce, portable at the time of the contract. They are not the less "goods" within the definition of the act because service may play a role in their ultimate use. The Code contains no such exception. "Services," [states] Nordstrom [a legal commentator], ... "always play an important role in the use of goods, whether it is the service of transforming the raw materials into some usable product or the service of distributing the usable product to a point where it can be easily obtained by the consumer. The [UCC § 2-105(1)] definition should not be used to deny Code application simply because an added service is required to inject or apply the product." In short, the fact that the contract "involved substantial amounts of labor" does not remove it from inclusion under the Code on the ground, as the [district court] found that "The Code was [not] meant to cover ... non-divisible mixed contracts of this type." ...

Finally, on this phase of the case, we find a dearth of authority going to a point relied upon by the [district court], namely, that the Code was not meant to cover "non-divisible mixed [goods and services] contracts of this type." Rather, the cases presenting mixed contracts of this type are legion. The test for inclusion or exclusion is not whether they are mixed, but, granting that they are mixed, whether their predominant factor, their thrust, their purpose, reasonably stated, is the rendition of service, with goods incidentally involved (e.g., contract with artist for painting) or is a transaction of sale, with labor incidentally involved (e.g., installation of a water heater in a bathroom). The contract before us, construed in accordance with the applicable standards of the Code, is not excluded therefrom because it is "mixed," and, moreover, is clearly for the replacement of equipment destroyed by fire, i.e., "goods" as defined by the Code. ...

[Judgment reversed.]

Under Article 2, certain warranties come into existence when a sale of goods occurs.[3] Service contracts, since they do not come under Article 2, do not carry

---

[3]Warranties are discussed in Chapter 21.

similar warranties. Therefore, the determination of whether a transaction involves a sale of goods or merely a rendition of services may be extremely important. For example, assume that a water company provides contaminated water to its customers and that several of them become ill as a result. Does the provision of water constitute a sale, or is it merely a rendition of a service? There has been disagreement on the answer, with courts holding both ways.

The above discussion points up two additional important factors. First, while goods must be tangible and movable, they need not be solid. For example, a sale of electricity would constitute a sale of goods. Second, determination of whether a transaction involves a sale of goods or only a rendition of services may be extremely important in a products liability case.[4] For example, assume that a person goes to a physician, the physician gives the person a vaccination, and the person becomes ill because the serum was improperly constituted. May the physician be sued for breach of warranty for selling a defective product, or is he immune from suit on this theory because he was providing professional services?

19:3   General Principles Governing Sales Transactions

In studying the law of sales, it is worth bearing in mind that the UCC stresses the concept of fairness. The UCC specifically imposes an obligation of *good faith* in the performance or enforcement of every contract or duty that comes within the act (UCC § 1-203). The UCC also prohibits the parties from disclaiming the "obligations of good faith, diligence, reasonableness and care" imposed by the code [UCC § 1-102(3)]. The question of whether a party's actions were taken in good faith or were reasonable may therefore be crucial in resolving a sales dispute.

Merchants   The law prior to the UCC generally made no distinction between those transactions that involved *merchants* and those that did not. The UCC, however, makes a sharp distinction between transactions that involve a professional in a given field and those that involve amateurs or consumers. In keeping with the underlying premise that fairness should be an element of commercial transactions, several UCC provisions require higher standards of conduct by merchants as opposed to nonmerchants. In particular, merchants are held to a higher standard of good faith than are nonmerchants. The good-faith obligation requires simple honesty from nonmerchants [UCC § 1-201(19)], whereas for merchants good faith also requires the observance of reasonable commercial standards of fair dealing in the trade [UCC § 2-103(1)(b)]. Thus, merchants are held not only to a subjective standard of honesty, but also to an objective, reasonable person standard.

The rationale behind the imposition of higher standards on merchants is that a merchant is more knowledgeable or experienced in sales transactions. It is not surprising, therefore, that the definition of merchant revolves around the concepts of knowledge and experience. Under the UCC, a merchant is a person who (1) deals in goods of the kind involved in the transaction; or (2) otherwise holds himself out as having knowledge or skill peculiar to the practices or goods involved; or (3)

---

[4]Products liability is discussed in Chapter 7.

employs an agent, broker, or other intermediary who holds himself out as having such knowledge or skill [UCC § 2-104(1)].

It is important to note that a person may be considered a merchant even though he is not a dealer in the type of goods involved. Assume, for example, that a university music professor decides to sell his rare violin. Although he had never sold a violin before, the professor would probably be considered a merchant under the UCC definition because he has special knowledge and skill with respect to the goods for sale. It is also worth noting that a person may be a merchant for some purposes but not others. For example, a bank president would be a merchant with respect to banking transactions, but not with respect to a sale of fishing tackle.

Applicability of General Principles of Law   While the UCC, and specifically Article 2, contains the basic law of sales, it by no means contains the only law applicable to sales. General legal and equitable principles, including principles of contract law, may be applied in sales cases, unless they would conflict with the UCC (UCC § 1-103).

19:4   The Sales Contract

A sales contract is in many respects just like any other contract. There generally must be an offer and acceptance, consideration, competent parties, and legality of purpose. Therefore, general principles of contract law, discussed in detail previously (see Chapters 9–18), are frequently applied in disputes involving sales contracts. The UCC does, however, make significant changes in certain respects. Many changes, such as the UCC rules on firm offers and method of acceptance, have been covered in Chapter 10. Others will be touched on here.

The changes made by the UCC result largely from recognition of the fact that contracts, particularly sales contracts, often are not the result of careful negotiations. The parties may overlook or choose to ignore certain items, or not even make a specific offer or acceptance. The UCC disregards these defects as long as there is a true basis for agreement. Take § 2-204(1), for example. It provides that a sales contract may be made in any manner sufficient to show agreement, including conduct by both parties recognizing the existence of the contract. Moreover, under § 2-204(2), a sales contract may be found even though the time of its making cannot be determined.

Open Terms   All the material terms of an ordinary contract must be reasonably definite. In a sales agreement, however, certain terms may be left open without making the contract invalid for indefiniteness, provided the parties intended to make a contract [UCC § 2-204(3)]. The UCC provides generally that missing terms may be filled in by resort to course of performance, course of dealing, or usage of trade (UCC §§ 1-205, 2-208). These rules have been discussed previously, in Chapter 16.

If terms are left open, the UCC has provisions concerning specific ways in which the terms may be set. For example, the UCC permits parties to enter a sales contract with an open price. There are various ways in which the price might ultimately be set. The contract might specify that one party is to fix the price, in which case the UCC requires that the price be fixed in good faith. The contract might provide that the price is to be fixed by some third person or by reference to some set standard, or it might provide that it is to be agreed on later by the parties. Finally, the contract might provide no mechanism at all for setting the price. In this last instance, if the price is never set, a court will allow a reasonable price at the time of delivery (UCC § 2-305). For example, assume that Gaines, a retailer, orders some cloth from Lang, a wholesaler, but neither party mentions price. Lang delivers the cloth, and a dispute then develops as to what the price should be. A court might allow Lang a price based on the going wholesale rate at the time the delivery was made.

Additional Terms in Acceptance — The Battle of the Forms   There is often very little true bargaining involved in a sales transaction. A buyer will fill out a pre-printed form and send it to the seller. This constitutes the offer. The seller will in turn fill out his own preprinted form and return it to the buyer. This is the accep-tance. Since each party's form was drafted with that party's interests in mind, there are almost always discrepancies between the forms. A court applying tradi-tional contract law would conclude that no contract existed under such circum-stances. The UCC, in recognition of the reality of this battle of the forms in commercial transactions, has attempted to deal with the situation otherwise.

Under the UCC, an acceptance creates a contract, even though it includes addi-tional or different terms, unless the acceptance is expressly conditioned on the offeror's assent to the new terms [UCC § 2-207(1)]. The new terms do not, how-ever, automatically become part of the contract. New terms that are different from those contained in the offer become part of the contract only if the offeror assents. Additional terms are considered proposals for addition to the contract. If both par-ties are merchants, the additional terms become part of the contract unless (1) the offer expressly limits acceptance to the terms of the offer, (2) the additional terms materially alter the contract, or (3) the offeror gives notice of his objection to the additional terms within a reasonable time [UCC § 2-207(2)].

 Many sellers and buyers have their own forms drafted and periodically re-viewed by their attorneys. However, few sellers and buyers pay close atten-tion to the forms they receive from the other party. Purchase orders and confirmations are often received and filed unread by clerks, and discrepan-cies go unnoticed until a dispute arises. The final battleground in the battle of the forms is often the courts, where the results are unpredictable. These prob-lems may often be avoided if closer scrutiny is given to the other party's form. The major issue usually revolves around whether the additional terms contained in the seller's confirmation form materially alter the contract. If they do, then the buyer's consent is necessary to make such terms a part of the contract. If the seller considers the additional terms essential, he should make his acceptance conditional on the buyer's consent to the terms. If the additional terms do not materially alter the contract, they automatically be-come part of the contract unless the buyer objects. A buyer should therefore read the confirmation form with an eye to detecting any objectionable additional terms. Too often a buyer does not discover objectionable terms until a dispute has arisen, by which time it is too late to object.

The following case graphically illustrates the dangers of signing a form without reading it. Note how the court concluded that a contract existed despite the presence of open terms. Observe also how the court applied general principles of contract law to resolve the consent issue.

N&D Fashions, Inc.
v
DHJ Industries, Inc.
548 F2d 722, 20 UCCRS 847
(United States Court of Appeals, Eighth Circuit, 1976)

[N&D Fashions, a wholly owned subsidiary of Nelly Don, Inc., was a purchaser of fabric for apparel manufacturers. DHJ Industries made and sold this fabric to the apparel trade. In 1973 Shriber, an agent for N&D, met with DHJ representatives to arrange for the purchase of certain fabric. Shriber emphasized that the fabric had to have colorfast dye. The parties orally agreed on 75,000 yards of fabric and settled type, color, price, and delivery terms. A few days later, Shriber sent a Nelly Don purchase order form to DHJ. The bottom of the form said: "This Purchase Order shall become a binding contract when acknowledged by Seller, or upon whole or partial shipment by Seller." The purchase order contained no arbitration clause. In response, DHJ sent a confirmation consisting of four documents, one of which was a reply form. Just above the blanks provided for signatures was this statement:

THIS CONTRACT IS SUBJECT TO ALL THE TERMS AND CONDITIONS PRINTED ON THE REVERSE SIDE.

In fine print on the back were 16 terms and conditions, including a clause providing for arbitration of contract disputes. Shriber signed the reply form and returned it to DHJ. DHJ delivered the fabric, but it was not colorfast. N&D sued for misrepresentation and fraud, and DHJ requested the court to order ar-

bitration. The district court held that the arbitration provision was a material alteration to which N&D had not consented, and thus denied the motion for arbitration. DHJ appealed.]

Webster, Circuit Judge.

*   *   *

This litigation centers upon the effect to be given to a condition of sale requiring arbitration of disputes that was contained in the seller's acknowledgment of the buyer's written purchase order. It implicates the sometimes murky provisions of Section 2-207 of the Uniform Commercial Code, which was intended to put to rest uncertainty arising from the "battle of the forms." . . .

It is undisputed that the parties reached an agreement with respect to the nature and quantity of the merchandise to be sold and delivered by appellant DHJ, as well as the price to be paid by the buyers. The Uniform Commercial Code does not require that all of the terms of the agreement be decided provided "the parties have intended to make a contract and there is a reasonably certain basis for giving an appropriate remedy." Uniform Commercial Code § 2-204(3). A problem is presented, however, when an acceptance or confirmation contains terms which are "additional to or different from" an offer or prior agreement. Under Uniform Commercial Code § 2-207, if the dealings are between merchants, the additional terms become a part of the agreement provided (1) the original offer did not expressly preclude such additions (the offer here did not), (2) the additions do not materially alter the agreement, and (3) no seasonable notice is given of objections to the additions (none was given here). From this it follows that the provision for arbitration in this case, as a proposed additional term, became a part of the agreement unless, as the District Court found, it was a material alteration of the agreement. . . .

A clause will be held to "materially alter" a contract when it would "result in surprise or hardship if incorporated without express awareness by the other party." Uniform Commercial Code § 2-207, Comment 4. Official Comments 4 and 5 provide examples of terms which would and would not materially alter a contract, and an arbitration clause is listed under neither. While other cases have held that an arbitration clause would materially alter a contract under § 2-207, the better reasoned position is that the question whether an additional term in a written confirmation constitutes a "material alteration" is a question of fact to be resolved by the circumstances of each particular case. . . .

DHJ contends that the District Court's finding was clearly erroneous, as it disregarded the widespread use of arbitration clauses in the textile and garment industries, which gives a merchant reason to know that such clauses will be inserted in textile contracts. Nelly Don and N&D assert, and DHJ does not deny, that arbitration was never mentioned during the course of their negotiations. There was no arbitration provision in the Nelly Don purchase order, and there was no evidence regarding industry practices or the past experience, if any, of Nelly Don and N&D with such clauses. Shriber testified that he did not read the clause.

We do not think it was incumbent upon the District Court to take judicial notice of industry practice, nor can we fault its finding upon a bare record. While it is generally recognized that commercial arbitration has had its principal use and development as a means of resolving disputes in the garment and fabric industries, and from this it may be inferred that the buyers should not have been surprised or subjected to unnatural hardship upon finding the clause in the contract, we cannot say on this record that the District Court was clearly erroneous in holding that the arbitration provision in DHJ's acknowledgment form was a "material alteration." . . .

The effect of this holding is that we may not presume acceptance from mere failure to object; the arbitration clause in this case will not be considered a part of the agreement unless it was in fact [expressly] agreed to by N&D. . . .

The only mutually executed documents evidencing the agreement are the acknowledgments which DHJ sent to Nelly Don and which Shriber "accepted" and returned to DHJ. These contracts clearly stated, just above the parties' signatures, that they were "subject to all the terms and conditions printed on the reverse side." The arbitration clause was printed on the reverse side and it would thus appear that the clause, although a material alteration to the oral agreement, was "expressly agreed to" by Nelly Don. Appellees contend, however, as the District Court found, that Shriber's failure to read the contracts, coupled with the absence of the word "arbitration" on the front of the document to indicate the presence of an arbitration clause on the reverse, precluded actual consent to the inclusion of this clause in the final agreement. We disagree.

The holding of the District Court ignores the general rule of contract law that, in the absence of fraud, misrepresentation or deceit, one who executes a contract cannot avoid it on the ground that he did not read it or supposed it to be different in its terms. . . .

We . . . decline to impose in the case of arbitration provisions special and unique requirements which are concededly not applicable to other additional terms and conditions. While a party may not be subjected to a provision which materially alters the contract by failing to object to it, he cannot avoid the effect of his written acceptance of a contract which expressly, above his signature on the face of the contract, incorporates the provisions on the reverse side of the document. There being no evidence of fraud, misrepresentation or deceit in that execution of the acceptance, it follows that the agreement to arbitrate became a part of the agreement and must govern the resolution of the dispute between the parties which produced this litigation. . . .

[Order reversed.]

19:5   Statute of Frauds

Section 17 of the English Statute of Frauds required a contract for the sale of goods costing ten pounds or more to be evidenced by a written note or memorandum signed by the party to be charged. The Uniform Sales Act also contained a statute of frauds, and the UCC has its own statute of frauds in § 2-201. The UCC statute is, however, more liberal than the original English version.

Under the UCC, a contract for the sale of goods costing $500 or more must be evidenced by a writing to be enforceable. Unlike statutes of fraud generally, however, the UCC section provides that the writing need not contain all the essential terms of the contract. All that is required is "some writing sufficient to indicate" that a sales contract has been made. The only term that must be included is the quantity of goods to be sold.

The writing must ordinarily be signed by the party against whom enforcement is sought or by the party's authorized agent or broker [UCC § 2-201(1)]. The signature need not be handwritten. Rather, any authentication that identifies the party to be charged is considered a signature. For example, a letterhead might suffice if it represented the party's intention to authenticate the writing.

The UCC has a provision under which a writing signed by only one party is sometimes sufficient to be enforced against a nonsigning party. The essence of the provision is that a written confirmation of the contract that is signed by one party and sent to the other party may be used against the receiving party. The provision is applicable only to contracts between merchants, only if the confirmation is received within a reasonable time, and only if the party receiving it has reason to know its contents. If the nonsigning party objects, he must give written notice of such objection within ten days after receipt of the confirmation [UCC § 2-201(2)]. The purpose of this provision is to equalize the parties' position. Under prior law, a person who received a letter confirming a sale could bind the sender while remaining not bound himself. If there were a market with fluctuating prices, the nonsigning party could wait until the time for performance, check the market price, and then decide to perform or not perform without penalty. Under the UCC, such a waiting game is not possible.

 The confirmation or other writing evidencing the contract need not be the contract itself. Rather, it can be any evidence that satisfies the statute of frauds. In other words, the contract may be oral, provided there is a sufficient writing indicating the contract's existence. A written confirmation that specifies terms will, however, be given great weight by a court. A merchant who receives a confirmation of an oral agreement should therefore scrutinize it and object promptly if it departs from his understanding of the agreement.

Exceptions to Statute   There are three exceptions to the sales statute of frauds.

(1) A contract for the sale of goods that are to be specially manufactured for the buyer may be enforced without any writing if (a) the goods are not suitable for sale to others in the ordinary course of the seller's business and (b) the seller either has made a substantial beginning of the manufacture of the goods or has made commitments for their procurement before receiving notice of the buyer's repudiation [UCC § 2-201(3)(a)]. This exception might be applied not only to goods that are originally manufactured specially for the buyer, but also to standard products that are extensively modified at the buyer's request. To illustrate, assume that Sam orally agrees to buy a car for $10,000 from Mary, a dealer. A signed writing would be required to make the contract enforceable. However, if Sam requested that Mary make extensive modifications to the car, as a result of which it would no longer be suitable for sale to others in the ordinary course of her business, and if Mary actually made a substantial start on the modifications, then the contract would be enforceable despite the lack of a writing.

(2) The statute does not apply if the party against whom enforcement is sought admits in a legal proceeding the existence of a sales contract. In such a case, the contract is enforceable only for the quantity of goods admitted [UCC § 2-201(3)(b)].

(3) The statute does not apply to the sale of goods for which payment has been made and accepted or which have been received and accepted [UCC § 2-201(3)(c)]. The contract is, however, enforceable *only* to the extent of such payment or receipt of goods. For example, if a buyer orally contracts to purchase 100 typewriters and actually accepts delivery of 50, the seller can enforce the contract with respect to those 50, but not with respect to the rest. Similarly, if the seller accepts payment for 50 of the typewriters, the buyer can enforce the contract with respect to those 50, but not with respect to the remainder. Part payment on a single indivisible item may take the contract out of the statute of frauds, although some courts have held to the contrary.

  The fact that a contract is not required by the sales statute of frauds to be in writing does not mean that an oral contract is necessarily enforceable. Particularly with respect to consumer transactions, various statutes require not only that certain types of contracts be in writing, but also that the writing make certain disclosures or meet other specified requirements. Merchants should keep these statutes in mind when dealing with consumers.

Key Concepts and Terms

- Article 2 of the UCC deals with sales of goods and is the primary source of sales law. General legal and equitable principles, including principles of contract law and the law merchant, are also applicable.

- A sale consists of the passage of title from seller to buyer for a price, which may be payable either in money or in other goods.

- Goods include all things that are movable at the time of identification to the contract. Article 2 therefore is applicable to sales of tangible personal property, but not to rendition of services or sales of realty or intangible personal property. When a contract involves a mixed transaction, such as a transfer of goods and the rendition of services, the applicability of Article 2 depends on the focus of the contract.

- The UCC stresses the concept of fairness and imposes an obligation of good faith in the performance or enforcement of every contract or duty that comes within the act. The UCC often imposes higher standards on merchants than on nonmerchants. A party is classified as a merchant on the basis of his experience, knowledge, or skill with respect to the goods or practices involved.

- In most respects a sales contract must meet the requirements of contracts generally. Changes made by the UCC have tended toward more liberal recognition of the existence of contracts with the results that (1) a sales contract may contain open terms and still be enforceable; (2) an acceptance may create a contract even though it includes terms not contained in the offer, as long as they do not materially alter it and the offeror does not object; and (3) a sales contract is enforceable as long as there is a true basis for agreement.

- The UCC Statute of Frauds requires a contract for the sale of goods costing $500 or more to be evidenced by a signed writing. The writing must include the quantity of goods, but need not contain all essential terms. A writing signed by one party is sometimes sufficient to enforce a sales contract against the other party. A writing is not required if the goods are to be specially manufactured, if the party to be charged admits the contract's existence in a legal proceeding, or if partial payment or receipt of goods has occurred.

- Battle of the Forms
- Future Goods
- Good Faith
- Goods
- Law Merchant
- Merchant
- Open Terms
- Sale

Questions and Case Problems

1. Carroll goes to her dentist, Dr. Grabavoy, to have new dentures made. Grabavoy prepares a set of wax dentures, has Carroll try them on, and then prepares a set of dentures from the wax impressions. The dentures are too large and Carroll develops mouth sores, blisters, bloody gums, and mouth swellings. She returns the dentures to Grabavoy and demands a refund of the $775 that she had paid for them. Grabavoy refuses to give her a refund. Carroll sues, claiming breach of warranties

under Article 2 of the UCC. Grabavoy claims Article 2 is inapplicable, since there has been no sale of goods. What is the result?

2. Describe the historical evolution of the law of sales. Of what current significance is this history?

3. Ozark Airlines is a commercial air carrier. Ozark sells 40 used planes to Fairchild-Hiller, an aircraft manufacturer, as part of a deal for the purchase of planes from Fairchild-Hiller. Fairchild-Hiller later resells one of the planes to a third party. The plane is involved in a fatal crash, and suit is filed against various defendants, including Ozark. The claim against Ozark is premised on the contention that Ozark is in the business of selling airplanes and is therefore a merchant under the UCC. Should that contention be upheld?

4. The Denim Company orally agrees to purchase a specified amount of cotton from Western Farms. The parties do not discuss either price or arbitration. Denim sends Western a formal purchase order, and Western sends Denim a confirmation form. These forms pass in the mail. Later a dispute over price arises. Denim insists that the dispute be submitted to arbitration in Oregon, as provided in its purchase order form, while Western insists on arbitration in California, as provided in its confirmation form. How should the disputes as to arbitration on the price be resolved?

5. Eason, an attorney, decides to retire. He orally agrees to sell his law books to Duffy, another attorney, for $5,000. Duffy mails Eason a written confirmation of "our agreement for purchase of your books." Eason does not respond to the confirmation but later refuses to complete the sale. When Duffy sues for breach of contract, Eason claims in his answer that the contract was oral and therefore unenforceable. Should Eason's claim be upheld?

6. The Pioneer Company sustains extensive damage from a fire caused by escaping gas. Pioneer sues Northern Illinois Gas Company, the gas supplier, claiming breach of certain Article 2 warranties with respect to the gas company's meters and service lines. Is Article 2 properly applicable?

7. Wade orally agrees to sell Dalton a small plot of land and a new mobile home, which Wade intends to place on a foundation on the plot. The price of the purchase is $5,000 for the land and $25,000 for the mobile home. Dalton pays $2,000 down, and Wade gives him a receipt with the notation, "Down payment on lot and mobile home." Discuss (1) whether the parties contracted for a sale of goods subject to Article 2, (2) what statute of frauds should be applied in the event of a lawsuit, and (3) whether the applicable statute of frauds has been complied with. Would your answers differ if the contract had been for a sale of land and a mobile home that was already located on the land? If Dalton had bought the mobile home and had it installed on land he already owned?

8. How and why does the UCC impose higher standards on merchants than on nonmerchants?

9. Electro Flo Corporation wants to develop and market a portable electrified floor for carnivals. Alcoa agrees to design, produce, and deliver flooring material to Electro Flo for that purpose. The flooring material proves unsatisfactory, and Electro Flo claims breach of warranty under the UCC. Alcoa responds that the transaction involves the sale of professional engineering and design devices, not goods, and that the UCC is therefore inapplicable. Is Alcoa correct?

10. What is the battle of the forms, and how does the UCC deal with it?

20 Transfer of Title and Risk of Loss

20:1 Introduction

A transfer of title is the essence of a sale of goods. Usually, it is accompanied by a transfer of possession. The transfer of title and possession may occur immediately, as when goods are purchased at a retail store, or it may be delayed, as when goods are ordered for future delivery. Transfer of the goods can be made directly from the seller to the buyer or through a middleman, such as a public carrier. If all goes well, the buyer eventually receives the goods, the seller receives payment, and the transaction is concluded.

Sometimes, however, all does not go well. Goods may be lost, destroyed, or stolen in transit between seller and buyer. In such a situation, the obvious question is who bears the loss. While courts are commonly called on to resolve that question after a loss has actually occurred, the parties to a sales transaction can and should consider the question when the contract is entered. The method in which the parties structure the transaction may affect the allocation of risk of loss, and if the parties know the point at which the risk of loss passes from seller to buyer, they may take appropriate steps to insure the goods.

Prior to the UCC, the concept of title was all-important in determining the rights and responsibilities of the parties to a sales transaction. The risk of loss was placed on the party who had title. The UCC has drastically de-emphasized the importance of title, although it is still important under some circumstances. The UCC provisions concerning both passage of title and risk of loss will be considered in this chapter. Related subjects, such as documents of title and insurable interest, will also be examined. Finally, attention will be given to the specific provisions that govern (1) contracts permitting the return of goods and (2) the rights of third persons who have received goods from either the buyer or the seller.

20:2 Documents of Title

Bills of lading and *warehouse receipts*, collectively known as *documents of title*, are the subject of Article 7 of the UCC. When a seller ships goods to the buyer by means of a carrier, the carrier will give the seller a document known as a bill of lading. When the seller stores the goods in a warehouse and the buyer is to pick the goods up there, the warehouser will give the seller a document known as a warehouse receipt.

Typically, a document of title lists the goods received by the carrier or warehouser and contains the terms of the agreement for carriage or storage. As such, it is in the form of a combined receipt and carriage or storage contract, but it represents much more. A document of title is intended to take the place of and to represent the goods. If the document is a negotiable document of title, possession of it amounts to the right of possession of and title to the goods. For example, when goods have been delivered to a carrier for shipment and the carrier has issued a negotiable bill of lading, whoever has or obtains possession of the bill of lading has both title to the goods and the right to possess them.

A document of title is negotiable if by its terms (1) the goods are to be delivered to the bearer of the document; (2) the goods are to be delivered to the order of a named person; or (3) if negotiability of the document is recognized in overseas trade, the goods are to be delivered to a named person or his assigns. Any other document of title is nonnegotiable (UCC § 7-104). If a document provides for delivery "to" a named person instead of "to the order of" a named person, the document is nonnegotiable.

A negotiable document of title is much more easily transferred than a nonnegotiable one. For example, a negotiable document that provides for delivery to the bearer permits the goods to be delivered to any person presenting the document, and possession is tantamount to title to the goods. A negotiable document that provides for delivery to the order of a named person allows delivery to be made to that person or to any other person presenting the document after its proper indorsement by the named person (UCC §§ 7-403, 7-501, 7-502). In contrast, a nonnegotiable document transfers title only to the person named; the carrier or warehouser must deliver the goods in accordance with the instructions contained in the document.

20:3 Passage of Title

Title to goods is normally irrelevant in determining the rights of the parties to a sales contract under the UCC. There are, however, residual areas where solution of a problem may be influenced by the question of title. Such problems are most likely to arise in areas of law not covered by the UCC. For example, issues as to which party is liable for a property tax may be determined on the basis of which party held title to the goods on a given date. To cover such situations, the UCC has a catchall passage-of-title provision (UCC § 2-401).

Before title can pass under UCC § 2-401, the goods must be identified to the contract. This requirement is satisfied when the specific goods to be sold are in some way designated by the seller. To illustrate, assume that Wilson goes into Brown's retail camera store and places an order for a particular type of camera. Brown goes into the storeroom, where she has ten of these cameras, selects one of them, and sets it aside to give to Wilson when he returns to the store. The camera was identified as the subject matter of the contract when Brown singled it out from all the other cameras of the same type. Prior to that time, it was clear what type of camera Wilson wanted, but the specific camera to be sold to him was unknown.

If the goods have been identified, title can pass from the seller to the buyer in any manner explicitly agreed on by the parties. If none is agreed on, title passes when the seller physically delivers the goods. The time when that occurs depends on what is stated in the contract provisions concerning delivery. These provisions determine whether the contract should be classified as a *shipment contract*, a *destination contract*, or a contract that does not require the goods to be moved.

Shipment Contract   Under a shipment contract the seller must send the goods to the buyer but is not required to actually deliver them at the destination. In other words, the seller delivers the goods to a carrier for transportation to the buyer. Title passes to the buyer at the time and place of shipment, that is, when the goods are delivered to the carrier.

Destination Contract   A destination contract requires the seller to make actual delivery of the goods at a particular destination. Title passes to the buyer only when the goods are delivered at the specified destination.

Contracts Not Requiring Moving of Goods   Sometimes the seller makes delivery to the buyer without the goods actually being moved. This may occur, for example, in a situation in which a third person, called a bailee, has actual possession of the goods at all times. When delivery is to be made without moving the goods, title passes when the seller delivers the necessary document of title to the buyer. If, however, the goods are already identified, and if the contract does not call for delivery of any documents of title, then title passes at the time of contracting.

 Conditional sales contracts often provide that title shall remain in the seller until the buyer completes payment of all installments. Under the UCC, such a reservation of title is construed as a reservation of a security interest,[1] but it has no effect on the passing of title as provided by UCC § 2-401.

20:4   Insurable Interest[2]

A purchaser of insurance must have some legally recognized interest in the person or item being insured. A person, for example, cannot take out insurance on the life of a total stranger or purchase insurance on property in which he has no legal interest.

Under the UCC, a buyer obtains an *insurable interest* in existing goods once they have been identified to the contract, regardless of (1) whether title has passed or the risk of loss has been placed on the buyer, (2) whether the goods conform to the specifications of the contract, and (3) whether the buyer has an option to return or

[1]The reservation of security interests is discussed in Chapter 28.
[2]For a discussion of insurance law and insurable interest generally, see Chapter 40.

reject the goods. The seller has an insurable interest in goods so long as the title to or any security interest in the goods remains in the seller. In addition, a buyer or seller may have an insurable interest in goods if an insurable interest is recognized under any other statute or rule of law (UCC § 2-501). Under the UCC, therefore, the buyer and seller may have insurable interests in the same goods at the same time.

 It may sometimes be prudent for a buyer to insure goods that have been identified to the contract, even though the risk of loss has not yet passed to the buyer, and even if the contract calls for the seller to maintain insurance. For example, if the buyer has already made partial or full payment, and if the buyer doubts the seller's ability to pay any loss, the buyer might consider insuring the goods himself. The same principle applies to a seller. If full payment has not been received for goods already delivered, and if the seller retains a security interest, the seller should obviously either require proof of insurance from the buyer or insure the goods himself.

20:5   Risk of Loss

The basic UCC provisions dealing with *risk of loss* are §§ 2-509 and 2-510. There are other relevant provisions, and some of them will be discussed briefly here. The purpose of the UCC provisions is to provide clear guidelines to determine when the risk of loss passes from the seller to the buyer. In studying the specific risk of loss provisions, bear in mind that their application ordinarily results in the risk of loss being placed on that party who was in the best position to take steps to prevent the loss. For example, risk of loss will remain on a seller who has never parted with possession of the goods. Also bear in mind that the risk of loss often passes at the same time title does. Thus, the result in cases decided under the UCC is often the same as that in pre-code cases.

 The parties may agree to allocate the risk of loss in a manner different from that provided by UCC § 2-509. In addition, the parties may agree that the risk of loss shall be divided between them (UCC § 2-303). For example, where there is a substantial possibility that some loss may occur, the parties might seek an equitable sharing of the risk by means of such an agreement.

In allocating the risk of loss, the UCC distinguishes between three types of contracts: (1) contracts involving shipment of the goods by carrier; (2) contracts involving goods held by a bailee and delivered without moving; and (3) all other sales contracts. These will be considered in turn.

Contracts Involving Shipment by Carrier   When goods are to be shipped by carrier, the risk of loss normally passes at the same time as title, as already discussed. Thus, in shipment contracts, the risk of loss passes to the buyer when the seller has duly delivered the goods to the carrier. Due delivery occurs when the seller places the goods in the carrier's possession, makes a reasonable contract for their transportation, provides any document necessary to permit the buyer to obtain possession, and notifies the buyer of the shipment (UCC § 2-504). In destination contracts, the risk of loss passes to the buyer when the goods have reached the destination and have been duly tendered to the buyer.

Parties to sales contracts commonly use specific shipping terms to indicate whether a contract is a shipment or a destination contract and the precise point at which risk of loss passes. Probably the most common shipping term is "F.O.B." (free on board). When a contract requires "delivery F.O.B. the place of shipment," it is a shipment contract. A contract that requires "delivery F.O.B. the place of destination" is a destination contract [UCC § 2-319(1)].

Various other shipping terms may be used to denote specific types of shipment contracts. "F.A.S. vessel" (free alongside the vessel) denotes a shipment contract that requires the seller to deliver the goods alongside the vessel [UCC § 2-319(2)]. "C.I.F." (cost-insurance-freight) indicates a shipment contract under which the seller must put the goods in the carrier's possession, load the goods, and pay the cost of freight and insurance to the point of destination. "C.&F." or "C.F." imposes like obligations, except that the seller need not purchase insurance (UCC § 2-320).

A destination contract may be indicated by a term that requires "delivery F.O.B. the place of destination" or by a term that requires delivery of goods "ex-ship." The latter term requires delivery from a ship that has reached the port of destination (UCC § 2-322).

 All these terms are commonly used by businesspersons and should be included in contracts to clearly indicate the parties' obligations and the point at which risk of loss passes. A contract that requires shipment by carrier should therefore ordinarily include the appropriate term. The UCC itself regards the shipment contract as the normal one and the destination contract as the variant type. Unless the contract clearly indicates that it is a destination contract, a court will regard it as a shipment one.

Goods Held by Bailee   Situations in which delivery of the goods from the seller to the buyer is to be made without removal of the goods from the actual possession of a bailee, normally a warehouser, are governed by UCC § 2-509(2), in conjunction with UCC § 2-503(4). In general, under these provisions risk of loss passes to the buyer when he is given or acquires effective means of control of the goods. Thus, risk of loss will pass to the buyer on his receipt of a negotiable document of title or on the bailee's acknowledgment of the buyer's right to possess the goods. If the seller gives the buyer a nonnegotiable document of title, or if the seller simply gives the buyer a written direction to the bailee to deliver the goods, risk of loss does not pass to the buyer until he has had a reasonable time to present the document or direction. During this time, the buyer may make a timely objection to a nonnegotiable document of title or a written direction. If the buyer does object, risk of loss does not pass until the seller either delivers a negotiable document of title or obtains the requisite acknowledgment from the bailee of the buyer's right of possession. The bailee may refuse to honor a nonnegotiable document or to obey a written direction. If he does object, risk of loss does not pass to the buyer.

Other Transactions   Goods may be delivered in other ways, which are not covered by the foregoing rules. For example, the buyer may pick up the goods at the seller's place of business, or the seller may personally deliver the goods. In such cases, the time when risk of loss passes depends on whether the seller is a merchant. If he is a merchant, then risk of loss passes only on the buyer's actual receipt of the goods. Otherwise, the risk passes to the buyer when the seller tenders delivery of the goods, regardless of whether the buyer actually takes them. To illustrate the difference, assume that Hurvitz sells Ricolli a television set and makes the set available for Ricolli to take home. Ricolli requests Hurvitz to keep the set while Ricolli goes on vacation. During Ricolli's vacation the set is stolen. If Hurvitz is a merchant, the loss falls on him, since Ricolli never actually received the set. If Hurvitz is not a merchant, the loss falls on Ricolli, since tender of delivery was made.

The following case illustrates how one court determined risk of loss in a contract and what difficulties arose in making the determination.

Caudle

v

Sherrard Motor Co.
525 SW2d 238, 17 UCCRS 754
(Texas Court of Civil Appeals, 1975)

[In 1972 Caudle contracted to purchase a house trailer from Sherrard Motor Company in Denison, Texas. While the trailer was being readied, Caudle was called back to his Dallas office on business. Caudle told Sherrard he would return and take possession later. Two to four days later the trailer was stolen from Sherrard's place of business, and Caudle refused to pay. Sherrard sued for the contract price and won. Caudle appealed. The decisive issue on appeal was whether the risk of loss had passed from Sherrard to Caudle.]

Akin, Justice.

*   *   *

It is plaintiff's contention that the risk of loss had passed to the defendant before the trailer's disappearance under [UCC § 2-509 (2)(b)] which provides:

Where the goods are held by a bailee to be delivered without being moved, the risk of loss passes to the buyer ... [b] on acknowledgment by the bailee of the buyer's right to possession of the goods.

Plaintiff contends that it was acting as a bailee while the trailer remained on its premises and that by executing the contract, it had acknowledged the defendant's right to possession of the trailer. Plaintiff further argues that because it did not agree to deliver the trailer to Caudle in Dallas, the trailer was to be delivered to Caudle "without being moved." These arguments, however, erroneously assume that the plaintiff is a bailee under the Code. It is apparent that the drafters of the Code contemplated a common law commercial bailee, such as a warehouseman, when using the term "bailee" in [UCC § 2-509(2)]. . . . Implicit in [various UCC provisions] is the concept that the party who issues [documents of title] and acknowledges the buyer's right to possession of the goods be in the business of storing goods for hire—a commercial bailee. This is not true here. We conclude, therefore, that the plaintiff was not a bailee under the Code. Hence, [UCC

§ 2-509(2)] does not control the determination of whether the risk of loss had passed to the defendant.

Plaintiff contends further that if [UCC § 2-509(2)] is inapplicable then the risk of loss passed to the defendant pursuant to [UCC § 2-509(4)]. This section provides that a buyer and seller may specifically enter into a contract contrary to the other provisions [UCC § 2-509]. Plaintiff argues that such a contrary agreement was made because the terms of the contract for the sale of the trailer provided that the risk of loss passed to the defendant when the contract was signed by the parties.

The pertinent clause of the sales contract states:

> No transfer, renewal, extension or assignment of this agreement or any interest hereunder, and no loss, damage or destruction of said motor vehicle shall release buyer from his obligation hereunder.

We hold that this language is insufficient to constitute a "contrary agreement" between the parties pursuant to [UCC § 2-509(4)]. A contract which shifts the risk of loss to the buyer before he receives the merchandise is so unusual that a seller who desires to achieve this result must clearly communicate his intent to the buyer.... This clause was apparently intended to fix responsibility for loss *after the defendant had taken possession* of the trailer. [Court's emphasis.] This interpretation is consistent with other provisions of the contract. For example, the contract provides that the "buyer shall keep said motor vehicle in good order and repair...." It would indeed be difficult for the buyer to honor this responsibility without having acquired actual possession of the trailer.... Furthermore, since risk of loss is not specifically mentioned in the contract, we cannot say that an agreement to the contrary may be inferred from reading the document as a whole. We, therefore, conclude that it was not the intention of the parties to transfer risk

of loss of the trailer *prior to delivery of possession to the buyer.* [Court's emphasis.] To hold otherwise would be to set a trap for the unwary. If parties intend to shift the burden of the risk of loss from the seller to the buyer before delivery of the goods, then such must be done in clear and unequivocal language.

It is defendant's contention that pursuant to [UCC § 2-509(3)] the risk of loss remained with the plaintiff because he had not taken actual physical possession of the trailer. We agree. That section provides,

> In any case not within Subsection [1] or [2], the risk of loss passes to the buyer on his receipt of the goods if the seller is a merchant; otherwise the risk of loss passes to the buyer on tender of delivery.

To determine if this section applies, the following questions must be resolved: (1) was the plaintiff a merchant and (2) did the defendant receive the trailer? The plaintiff is a merchant under Article 2 of the Code as it "deals in goods of the kind ... involved in the transaction [UCC § 2-104(1)]. The language "receipt of the goods" is defined in the Code as "taking physical possession of them" [UCC § 2-103(1)(c)]. It is undisputed that the defendant never took physical possession of the trailer; therefore, he had not received the goods. Accordingly, we hold that the risk of loss did not pass to the buyer before the trailer was stolen....

Our holding is in accordance with the underlying principles of [UCC § 2-509] dealing with risk of loss. Under the Uniform Commercial Code, the risk of loss is no longer determined arbitrarily by which party had title to the goods at the time of the loss. Instead, as the drafters of the Code state: "The underlying theory of these sections on risk of loss is the adoption of the contractual approach...." Uniform Commercial Code, § 2-509, Comment 1.... Subject to the placement of a contractual approach at the analytic center of risk of loss problems is the policy that a party who had control over the handling of goods should bear their loss.... Strong policy reasons support this approach. The party in control is in the best position to handle properly the goods, to contract for shipment with a reliable carrier, and to insure the goods. This theory is particularly applicable when the buyer is not a merchant and is unfamiliar with the problems of handling the goods....

[A] merchant who is to make delivery at his own place of business continues to maintain control over the goods and can be expected to carry insurance to protect his interest in them. On the other hand, the buyer has no control over the goods and may not have had the foresight to obtain insurance on the undelivered merchandise....

[Judgment reversed.]

Effect of Breach   In situations in which either the buyer or seller is found to be in breach of the contract of sale at the time goods are lost, the risk of loss is on the breaching party (UCC § 2-510). Under this section the breaching party bears the risk of loss even if the other party would have borne it had there been no breach. Therefore, if the seller breaches the contract by tendering or delivering goods that do not conform to the contract requirements, so that the buyer has the right to reject the goods, the risk of loss remains on the seller until the defect is cured or until the buyer accepts the nonconforming goods. Similarly, if the buyer has the right to revoke his prior acceptance of goods and exercises that right, he may treat the risk of loss as having rested on the seller from the beginning. However, the buyer can pass the risk of loss back to the seller in this way only to the extent of any deficiency in the buyer's effective insurance coverage.[3] If the buyer repudiates or otherwise breaches the contract after conforming goods have been identified to the contract, the seller may treat the risk of loss as resting on the buyer for a commercially reasonable time, but, again, only to the extent of any deficiency in the seller's effective insurance coverage.

20:6   Sale on Approval; Sale or Return

Some sales contracts are contingent in nature. For example, a purchaser might buy an item on a trial basis with a right to return it if he is dissatisfied. This is called a *sale on approval*. Or a retailer might purchase goods for resale with the right to return any goods that he is unable to sell. This is called a *sale or return*. UCC §§ 2-326, 2-327 govern such sales.

Whether a contingent sale is (1) a sale on approval or (2) a sale or return depends on the purpose of the transaction. If the buyer purchases the goods for his own use, it is a sale on approval. For example, if a consumer purchases an item with the right to use it for a trial period and return it if dissatisfied, the transaction is a sale on approval. If the buyer purchases goods primarily for resale, the transaction is a sale or return. For example, if a record store ordered 100 copies of a partic-

---

[3]Performance and breach of sales contracts, including situations in which the buyer may reject goods or revoke a prior acceptance of goods, are discussed in Chapter 22.

ular record, with the right to return any copies unsold within a certain time, it would be a sale or return.

A third type of contingent transaction, known as a consignment, is not a sale at all. In a consignment transaction, one party, the consignor, delivers goods to another party, the consignee, and the consignee has a duty either to sell the goods on behalf of the consignor or return them to the consignor. The consignee is in effect a sales agent for the consignor. For all practical purposes, consignments are now treated as sale or return transactions under the UCC.

Sale on Approval   In a sale on approval, neither title nor risk of loss passes to the buyer until the goods are accepted by the buyer. The contract may provide a specified period within which the buyer must either accept or return the goods. If no period is specified, the buyer will be allowed a reasonable time within which to act. Failure to notify the seller of the decision to return the goods within a reasonable time constitutes acceptance. The buyer's actions or statements may indicate acceptance, but the fact that the buyer tries the goods does not constitute acceptance. If the buyer decides to return the goods, the return is at the seller's risk and expense. However, a merchant buyer must follow any reasonable instructions of the seller.

Sale or Return   In a sale or return transaction, title and risk of loss pass to the buyer in the same manner as they would in an outright sale. In other words, once proper delivery has been made, the risk of accidental loss or damage to the goods rests on the buyer, and any return of the goods is at the buyer's risk and expense. The time for return may be specified in the contract. If it is not, a reasonable time is allowed.

 The UCC provides that any "or return" term of a contract for sale is to be treated as a separate contract for sale that contradicts the sale aspect of the contract. This provision, read in conjunction with the statute of frauds and the parol evidence rule (UCC §§ 2-201, 2-202), requires that, if a written agreement is involved or if the price of the goods is $500 or more, the "or return" term must be contained in a written memorandum. Whenever anything is put in writing, therefore, even if it is only the purchase order, any right to return unsold goods must also be put in writing.

Creditors' Rights   The rights of the buyer's and seller's creditors are different for a sale on approval contract from those for a sale or return contract. Goods held on approval are subject to claims of the seller's creditors until the buyer accepts the goods. This is because until the buyer does so, the goods are still owned by the seller. After the buyer does accept the goods, however, they are subject to the claims of his creditors, the seller no longer having any interest in the goods. Because title to goods held on sale or return has passed to the buyer, subject only to his right to transfer title back to the seller later, goods of this type are subject to the claims of the buyer's creditors rather than those of the seller's creditors.[4]

---

[4]Creditors' rights and remedies are discussed in detail in Chapter 30.

Goods that a buyer purchases for resale at a place of business that does not bear the original seller's name are goods held on sale or return and are subject to the claims of the buyer's creditors. This is so regardless of the label the parties themselves put on the transaction. There are, however, certain exceptions to this rule. The goods are not subject to claims of the buyer's creditors if (1) a sign indicating the seller's interest is posted at the buyer's place of business, (2) the buyer's creditors generally know that the buyer is substantially engaged in selling the goods of others, or (3) the seller has complied with the filing provisions concerning secured transactions (see Chapter 28 for a discussion of such provisions).

Sellers often provide goods on consignment to retailers as a method of financing the retailer while retaining a security interest in the goods. Such consignments are treated as sale or return transactions, and the goods are thus subject to claims of the buyer's creditors unless the seller has taken one or more of the aforementioned protective steps. Since many retail businesses fail each year, a seller is well advised to protect himself. Practically speaking, the only effective way to do so is to comply with the provisions on secured transactions. Posting a sign is ordinarily an unrealistic alternative, and proof that the retailer's creditors knew he was selling the goods of others is likely to be extremely difficult.

20:7   Rights of Third Parties

The discussion so far has centered on situations in which there is a single seller and a single buyer. Sometimes third parties are involved and it must then be determined what their rights are as against those of the original seller or buyer. For example, an original buyer with defective title may resell the goods to a third person, or the seller may sell the same goods twice. These and similar situations will now be considered.

Rights of Bona Fide Purchasers   Ordinarily a person cannot transfer a better title to goods than he himself has. For example, if a thief sells stolen goods to a third person, the third person does not acquire title. The rightful owner can recover goods not only from the thief, but from any person to whom the thief has sold them.

An exception to the general rule is recognized in the case of a person having a voidable title. Under UCC § 2-403(1) a person with voidable title to goods may transfer good title to a good faith purchaser for value. This purchaser is called a *bona fide purchaser*.[5] Therefore, where a buyer acquires a voidable title from the seller, the buyer can, by making a resale to a bona fide purchaser, convey a good title to the third party. The reason that the original buyer's title was voidable does not matter. He may have deceived the original seller as to his identity, he may have written a bad check for the goods, or he may have obtained the goods

---

[5]Voidable contracts are discussed in Chapter 9. Factors that render a contract voidable are discussed in Chapter 12.

through fraudulent means. In all such cases, the original buyer can defeat the seller's right to recover the goods by selling them to a bona fide purchaser. To illustrate, assume that Cain sells a load of lumber to Wills, who pays for it by check. If the check is dishonored for insufficient funds, Cain has the right to rescind the contract and recover the lumber back from Wills. But if Wills has already resold the lumber to Kahn, and if Kahn was a good-faith purchaser for value, then Cain cannot recover the lumber from Kahn. Cain would still have a right of action against Wills for the purchase price, but title to the lumber would remain in Kahn.

A bona fide purchaser, by definition, must make a purchase for value in good faith. Value may consist of any consideration sufficient to support a simple contract [UCC § 1-201(44)(d)]. In most cases, therefore, there is no issue as to whether value has been given. There may, however, be an issue as to the purchaser's good faith. It will be recalled that the UCC imposes a different standard of good faith on merchants than it does on nonmerchants. In the case of an ordinary consumer, good faith merely requires simple honesty. Basically, this means that a consumer must not have been aware of the rights of the original seller to the goods. In the case of a merchant, good faith also requires the observance of reasonable commercial standards [UCC § 2-103(1)(b)]. Therefore, a merchant might be denied status as a good-faith purchaser in a case in which a nonmerchant would be accorded such status. For example, if a nonmerchant purchased a watch for $100 that normally would sell for $200, and if he had no notice or knowledge of the ordinary price, he might be classified as a good-faith purchaser for value. A jeweler, however, would probably not be so classified. While payment of $100 for a $200 watch does constitute value, it also indicates a lack of good faith on the jeweler's part.

Entrustment of Goods to or Retention of Goods by Merchant Seller   Any entrustment of the possession of goods to a merchant who deals in goods of that kind gives the merchant the power to transfer all rights of the entrustor to a buyer in the ordinary course of business [UCC § 2-403(2),(3)]. The classic illustration of this rule is the repair situation. Assume that Jake takes his radio to Carol's shop to have it repaired. Carol, whose business includes not only radio repair but also the sale of new and used radios, sells Jake's radio to Lee, a customer who entered the shop during normal hours to purchase a radio. Under the UCC, Lee has good title to the radio. This illustration also demonstrates the purpose behind the rule. A person who buys goods from a merchant whose business it is to sell those goods reasonably expects that the merchant had the right to sell them. If a buyer were required to investigate the merchant's title or authority to sell the goods, ordinary commercial intercourse would be seriously hampered.

This entrusting rule is also applied in situations in which a buyer of goods leaves them in the seller's possession. If Christina buys a bicycle from Barry's bicycle shop and pays cash, she obtains title to it. In the event of a dispute between Barry and Christina, she would recover. But assume that she asks him to keep the bicycle at his store until the following day, when she will pick it up. If, later that same day, Carl comes into the store and purchases the same bicycle in the ordinary course of business, Christina cannot recover the bicycle from him. Christina's allowing Barry to keep the bicycle permitted him to transfer good title to Carl.

In a similar vein, a buyer who, in the ordinary course of business, buys goods from a person engaged in selling such goods takes the goods free of any security interest held in the goods by third parties [UCC § 9-307(1)].

The following case, which involves a sale of entrusted goods, illustrates how one court determined whether a purchaser was a buyer in the ordinary course of business.

Mattek
v
Malofsky
42 Wis 2d 16, 165 NW2d 406, 6 UCCRS 277
(Wisconsin Supreme Court, 1969)

[Mattek authorized Frakes, a used-car dealer in Menasha, Wisconsin, to display her 1964 Plymouth automobile on Frakes' lot. Frakes placed his dealer's plate on the car and sold it to Malofsky, a used-car dealer in Appleton, Wisconsin, for $1,750. No certificate of title was delivered. Mattek sued Malofsky to recover the Plymouth. Mattek won, and Malofsky appealed.]

Hallows, Chief Justice.

*   *   *

Two issues are presented on this appeal: (1) Whether the provisions of [UCC § 2-403] are applicable to sales between merchants; and (2) whether an automobile dealer who buys a used car from another automobile dealer, who has lawful possession of the car, without obtaining or inquiring about the certificate of title to the used car is a "buyer in the ordinary course of business" within the meaning of [UCC § 2-403].

We think the provisions of [UCC § 2-403] are applicable to sales between merchants. We come to this conclusion because the purpose of [UCC § 2-403(2) and (3)] is to protect a person from a third-party interest in goods purchased from the general inventory of a merchant regardless of that merchant's actual authority to

sell those goods. This section does not expressly or by implication restrict such protection of a sale by a merchant to a member of the consumer public. If the policy of negotiability of goods held in the inventory of a merchant is to be promoted, it would seem to apply between merchants where merchants buy from one another in the ordinary course of business. The protection is afforded to "a buyer in the ordinary course of business," and by other provisions of the Uniform Commercial Code the term "buyer" includes a merchant.

In [UCC § 1-201(9)] a buyer in the ordinary course of business is defined as "a person who in good faith and without knowledge that the sale to him is in violation of the ownership rights or security interest of a third party in the goods buys in ordinary course from a person in the business of selling goods of that kind but does not include a pawn broker." Good faith is defined in [UCC § 1-201(19)] to mean "honesty in fact in the conduct or transaction concerned." This definition applies to a member of the consumer public only, because in [UCC § 2-103(1)(b)] " 'good faith' in the case of a merchant" is defined to mean "honesty in fact and the observance of reasonable commercial standards of fair dealing in the trade." In addition, [UCC § 2-104(3)], relating to the general standard applicable to transactions between merchants charges each merchant with the "knowledge or skill of merchants."

Consequently, a merchant may be a buyer in the ordinary course of business under [UCC § 2-403] from another merchant if he meets four elements: (1) Be honest in fact, (2) be without knowledge of any defects of title in the goods, (3) pay value, and (4) observe reasonable commercial standards. In the observance of reasonable commercial standards, however, a merchant is chargeable with the knowledge or skill of a merchant.

We think Malofsky was not the buyer in the ordinary course of business within the meaning of [UCC § 2-403]. Although the delivery of the automobile to Frakes, a used-car dealer, constituted an entrustment, Frakes could by subsequent sale pass title to a buyer in the ordinary course of business. However, Malofsky as a merchant was not a buyer in the ordinary course of business because he was chargeable with the knowledge that the registration law [required delivery of a certificate of title on sale of a used car]. Malofsky should have known the used automobile had a certificate of title outstanding and that Frakes was required to give him such certificate of title. Under the standards set forth in [UCC § 2-104(3)], applicable to transactions between merchants, Malofsky is chargeable with this knowledge

and his failure to procure a certificate of title or some evidence of title was unreasonable as a matter of law. Evidence of custom or usage of automobile dealers contrary to the statute cannot be used to defeat the rights of a third party whatever the value of such evidence may be in adjusting disputes between dealers. . . .

This is the first [Wisconsin] case interpreting the impact of [UCC § 2-403]. . . . But it should be noted that while a seller under this section has power to pass a better title than he possesses, nevertheless, the buyer must meet certain requirements to be entitled to the protection of that section.

. . . We think . . . the Motor Vehicle Code must be construed with the [UCC] and it is proper to refer to the Motor Vehicle Code to determine what a used-automobile dealer is supposed to know or what knowledge he is chargeable with when he claims to be a buyer in the ordinary course of business.

[Judgment affirmed.]

Rights of Seller's Creditors   The discussion here concerns the rights of the creditors of a seller who sells goods but retains possession of them and then becomes insolvent or is otherwise in financial difficulty. If a creditor has seen the goods in the seller's possession after the sale and perhaps even extended credit to the seller on the supposition that the seller owned the goods, the question is whether the buyer or the seller's creditors have priority. Under the UCC, a seller's creditor may treat a sale or an identification of goods to the contract as void if the seller's continued possession of the goods is fraudulent (against the creditor) under any rule of law of the state where the goods are located. However, a merchant-seller's retention of possession of goods in good faith and current course of trade for a commercially reasonable time after a sale or identification is not fraudulent (UCC § 2-402). For example, it would not be fraudulent for a buyer to leave goods in the seller's possession until a contract for delivery can be arranged. In such a situation, the buyer would have priority over any of the seller's creditors.

20:8   Fraudulent Conveyances and Bulk Transfers

A *fraudulent conveyance* is a transaction by which a property owner attempts to hinder or defraud his creditors by placing the property beyond the creditors' reach. He does so by conveying (transferring) the property to someone else.

EXAMPLE
Art owns goods worth over $15,000, and he is indebted to Jake and Tom in amounts totaling $10,000. To avoid paying these debts, Art agrees with Bob, his brother-in-law, that he will sell the goods to Bob for $10,000 and then depart. The sale is made, and Art leaves town with the money. Jake and Tom are victims of a fraudulent conveyance.

All states have enacted statutes intended to protect creditors like Jake and Tom. Under these laws, creditors can obtain relief from a fraudulent conveyance by suing the transferor (the original debtor, who made the conveyance). In connection with that lawsuit the creditors can either (1) have the conveyance set aside entirely or (2) have the property taken from the transferee (the person who received it) and held under the court's control until all parties' rights have been decided.[6]

A creditor's right to relief depends primarily on whether the transaction in question constitutes a fraudulent conveyance. The most important factor in making this determination is whether the parties had fraudulent intent, which is the intent to hinder or defraud the transferor's creditors. It is hard to prove actual fraudulent intent, so the law recognizes what are known as *badges of fraud*. The existence of several of the badges in a given transaction leads to the presumption that the parties acted with fraudulent intent. These badges of fraud include the following:

- Transferor's indebtedness when the conveyance was made
- Lack of fair consideration for the conveyance
- Family or other close relationship between the transferor and transferee
- Transferor's retention of possession of the property
- Litigation involving the transferor that is pending or threatened at the time of the conveyance
- Secrecy or concealment in connection with the conveyance

Bulk Transfers   From the viewpoint of a merchant's creditors, a particularly worrisome type of transaction is one in which the merchant quietly sells his business (the major asset of which is often the stock in trade) and then disappears without paying the creditors. A transaction of this type is often not a fraudulent conveyance as previously discussed because the buyer has frequently paid a fair consideration and is innocent of any fraudulent intent. Article 6 of the UCC is intended to give creditors some protection in this situation by regulating the conduct of what are known as *bulk transfers*.

A bulk transfer is a transfer that meets all the following criteria:

- Transfer is made in a single transaction

---

[6]Creditors' rights and remedies are discussed in detail in Chapter 30.

- Property transferred is a major part of the transferor's materials, supplies, merchandise, or other inventory
- Transfer is not made in the ordinary course of the transferor's business
- Transferor's principal business is the sale of merchandise from stock

Farming activities are not covered by Article 6. This means that a farmer's sale of his crop to a single buyer (a common occurrence) is not a bulk transfer. If a business sells goods but also provides services, as might be true of an air conditioning business, for example, the applicability of Article 6 depends on whether the business is primarily sales-oriented; if it is, Article 6 applies to a sale of all or most of the business's inventory or other goods.

Article 6 Requirements   The Article 6 requirements are fairly simple. When a bulk transfer is going to be made, the transferor must first prepare a list of his creditors, showing names, addresses, and (if known) the amounts owed or claimed to be owed to each one (UCC § 6-104). The list is given to the transferee. Also given to the transferee is a schedule that describes all the property being transferred. The transferee must keep the list and schedule for six months after the transfer or file them in a public office.

The heart of Article 6 is the requirement that before a bulk transfer takes place, all known creditors of the transferor must receive a written notice about the transfer. For most transfers the transferee gives the notice, which must be either delivered personally or sent by registered or certified mail. The notice has to be given at least ten days before either the transferee's taking possession of or his paying for the transferred goods, whichever occurs first (UCC § 6-105). The content of the notice is prescribed (see UCC § 6-107), and either a short form or a long form can be used. The long form is required if all the transferor's debts will not or may not be paid in full as they become due. As a practical matter, the short form is rarely used; since the form states that all debts *will* be paid as they fall due, it can be interpreted as the transferee's independent promise to pay the transferor's creditors.

 Any businessperson involved in a bulk transfer should try to make sure that all pertinent requirements are complied with. Qualified legal counsel should be consulted as to any doubts about the requirements or, for that matter, about whether the contemplated transaction falls within the scope of Article 6 at all.

Effect of Noncompliance   If a bulk transfer is made without compliance with the requirements of Article 6, the transfer is "ineffective" against any creditor of the transferor [UCC § 6-104(1)]. This means that the creditor has the same remedies that exist under the fraudulent conveyance statutes, discussed previously. Some states have enacted an optional section of Article 6 (§ 6-106), which requires a bulk transferee to see that the consideration received by the transferor is properly applied to payment of the transferor's creditors. Courts in a few of these states have interpreted § 6-106 to mean that if the consideration received in a bulk transfer is *not* properly applied to the transferor's debts, the transferee can be held personally liable for up to the fair market value of the property.

Key Concepts and Terms

- Article 7 of the UCC deals with documents of title (bills of lading and warehouse receipts) issued by carriers and warehousers. A document of title may be negotiable or nonnegotiable; if negotiable, it represents a right of possession and title to goods.

- Title to goods that have been identified to the contract can pass in any manner explicitly agreed on by the parties. In the absence of such an agreement, title passes when the seller completes his performance with respect to physical delivery of the goods. The time when this occurs depends on whether the contract is a shipment contract, a destination contract, or a contract not requiring moving of goods.

- A buyer obtains an insurable interest in existing goods once they have been identified to the contract. A seller has an insurable interest so long as he has title to or any security interest in the goods.

- Risk of loss is normally borne by the party who is in the best position to prevent the loss. It is determined by the type of contract involved. These types are (1) contracts involving shipment by carrier, (2) contracts involving goods held by a bailee and delivered without moving, and (3) all other sales contracts. In contracts involving shipment by carrier, the risk of loss passes to the buyer either when the seller delivers the goods to the carrier or when the goods have reached their destination, depending on whether the contract is a shipment contract or a destination contract. In contracts involving goods being held by a bailee and delivered without moving, risk of loss passes when the buyer acquires effective means of control of the goods. In other transactions, risk of loss passes on the buyer's actual receipt of the goods from a merchant seller, or on a nonmerchant seller's tender of delivery to the buyer.

- When one party breaches the contract, the risk of loss is on that party, at least to the extent of any deficiency in the other party's insurance.

- In some sales contracts the buyer has the right to return the goods. If goods are purchased under a contract of this type primarily for the buyer's own use, it is a sale on approval. If goods are delivered primarily for resale, it is a sale or return. A sale's status as a sale on approval or a sale or return affects the time when title and risk of loss pass, as well as the right of the buyer's and seller's creditors to reach the goods.

- A bona fide purchaser is a person who makes a purchase in good faith and gives valuable consideration for the goods. A person with voidable title may transfer good title to a bona fide purchaser.

- If the owner of goods entrusts them to, or leaves them in the possession of, a merchant who deals in goods of that kind, the merchant may transfer the entrustor's rights in the goods to a buyer in the ordinary course of business.

- If a seller retains possession of goods that have been sold, the seller's creditor can ignore the sale, giving the creditor priority over the buyer, if the seller's retention is fraudulent against the creditor.

- A fraudulent conveyance is a conveyance of property intended to hinder or defraud the transferor's creditors. State statutes have been enacted to protect creditors against fraudulent conveyances.

- A bulk transfer is the transfer, in a single transaction and not in the ordinary course of business, of a major part of the inventory or other goods of a transferor whose principal business is the sale of merchandise from stock. Bulk transfers are governed by Article 6 of the UCC, which requires (1) preparation of a list of the transferor's creditors, (2) preparation of a schedule of the property being transferred, and (3) advance notice to creditors about the transfer.

- Bill of Lading
- Bona Fide Purchaser
- Bulk Transfer
- Destination Contract
- Document of Title
- Fraudulent Conveyance

- Insurable Interest
- Risk of Loss
- Sale on Approval
- Sale or Return
- Shipment Contract
- Warehouse Receipt

Questions and Case Problems

1. Finch contracted to purchase a helicopter from Ace Aviation, a helicopter manufacturer and seller, with a delivery date of July 1. On June 15, Ace notified Finch that she could pick up the helicopter at Ace's plant on July 1. Finch responded that she would be unable to do so and asked Ace to hold it until August 1. Ace replied that it did not have available storage facilities, but that the helicopter could be stored in a hangar at a nearby airport if Finch agreed and paid the storage charge. Finch agreed, and the helicopter was delivered to the airport on July 1, with the instructions to deliver it to Finch on demand. On July 2, the airport notified Finch that the helicopter was in its possession pending further instructions from her. On July 3, the helicopter was destroyed in a fire. Who should bear the loss?

2. Roth telephones Jenkins and places a purchase order for 20 calculators at a total price of $1,000. Roth requests that the calculators be shipped from New York, where Jenkins maintains his business, to Roth's business address in Boston. Jenkins packs the calculators in a carton, places a label indicating the carton's contents on its side, and mails the carton by fourth-class mail. He takes out no insurance, and he places an incorrect zip code on the carton. The carton does not arrive, and Roth refuses to make payment. Jenkins sues for the purchase price. What is the decision?

3. What are documents of title and what purpose do they serve?

4. What is the difference between a sale on approval and a sale or return?

5. Clay buys a car from Akins, a used car dealer, for $750, but leaves the car on the lot while she goes to have lunch. While she is gone, Akins agrees to sell the car to Dahl for $700 cash, and Dahl leaves in the car to obtain the cash. Dahl never

returns. He resells the car to Gomez for $600. Clay sues to recover the car. How should the case be decided?

6. Multiplastics agrees to specially manufacture and sell 40,000 plastic pellets to Arch Industries. Arch breaches the contract by failing to accept delivery when the pellets are tendered, and Multiplastics stores the pellets in its plant. The plant burns down one month later. Multiplastics does not have insurance on the pellets, and it sues Arch for the contract price. What is the result?

7. Chamberlin, a mobile home dealer, sells Crowder a new camper unit for $1,757.74. Crowder pays by check and loads the camper onto his pickup truck, even though the camper is too large for a proper fit. The next day Crowder sells the camper unit to Hollis, another mobile home dealer, for $500. Hollis does not ask why the camper does not fit the truck and does not ask Crowder for any evidence of title. Crowder's check to Chamberlin is not honored by the bank. Chamberlin sues Hollis to recover possession of the camper unit. What is the outcome?

8. Sanchez, an interior decorator, agrees to decorate and furnish McClure's home. Under the agreement, Sanchez places various items of furniture in McClure's home on a trial basis. The parties agree that once the entire decorating plan is completed to McClure's satisfaction, a sales contract will be executed for those items of furniture McClure wishes to keep, and the rest will be returned. After the furniture has been in McClure's house for two months, he obtains a loan from State Bank, using the furniture as collateral. McClure and Sanchez then sign a sales contract for the furniture, under which McClure agrees to pay in installments. Again the furniture is used as collateral. McClure defaults on both the loan and the installment payments, and both State Bank and Sanchez claim the right to levy on the furniture. Whose claim should be upheld?

9. Selma Hayes stores her refrigerator at Warren's Warehouse, and she receives a warehouse receipt that provides for "delivery to Selma Hayes." Hayes later sells the refrigerator to Gary Cobb. She endorses the warehouse receipt with the notation, "deliver to Gary Cobb." Cobb accepts the warehouse receipt, but he makes no attempt to take possession of the refrigerator. One week later the warehouse burns down and the refrigerator is destroyed. Cobb demands that Hayes refund his money. Should she do so?

10. During divorce proceedings, Menyhart buys the Continental Coiffures Beauty Salon from Rogers, his wife, giving Rogers a promissory note for $7,000 as part of the purchase price. Later, while the bulk of the debt is still unpaid, Menyhart sells the salon business to Yarbrough, and neither party attempts to comply with the requirements of UCC Article 6. Menyhart disappears with the sale proceeds. Rogers seeks to have the sale invalidated on the ground that it violated Article 6. Does Article 6 apply? Why or why not? What would be the significance, if any, of detailed evidence as to the type of business carried on at the salon?

21 Warranties

21:1 Introduction

All of us have been recipients or beneficiaries of warranties at one time or another. Purchase of an automobile, an appliance, or even a hamburger is typically accompanied by one or more warranties. If a person buys a new toaster, and it turns out that the toaster does not work, he can return it to the seller and demand a refund or replacement. The seller will usually comply without argument. Although the parties may not ever have mentioned the word "warranty," such a situation would probably involve warranties that are both express and implied.

A sales warranty is a promise that the object sold has certain qualities or conditions. The basic distinction between an express and an implied warranty is the manner of creation. An express warranty arises from some representation made by the seller. In the case of the toaster, the seller may have said that the toaster was free of defects in workmanship. This representation may be enforced as an express warranty. An implied warranty is one that has been imposed on the seller by law. In the case of the toaster, there would be an implied warranty of merchantability, which means suitability for the ordinary uses for which the toaster was manufactured. Various express and implied warranties are treated in more detail later in this chapter.

The rise of warranties, and particularly of implied warranties, has largely displaced the ancient doctrine of caveat emptor, which means "let the buyer beware." The doctrine of caveat emptor expresses the rule that a buyer purchases at his peril and that it is incumbent on him to ascertain beforehand any defects in the purchased goods. This doctrine has been eroded not only by the development of implied warranties, but also by the development of related concepts such as unconscionability (see Chapter 12).

The UCC contains several sections dealing with warranties. In addition, other state legislation and the federal Magnuson–Moss Warranty Act deal with warranties. All of these will be considered in this chapter. At this point, the discussion will briefly touch on the law of warranties and its relation to other rules dealing with products liability, and on the relatively minor warranty of title.

Related Areas of Law: Negligence and Strict Liability   This chapter deals primarily with breach of warranty and the loss that results in the value of the product itself. Using the example of the toaster again, a new toaster that does not work obviously is not worth very much. The breach of warranty with respect to the toaster has left the purchaser with a product considerably less valuable than that for which he bargained. Assume, however, that the defect in the toaster resulted in an electrical malfunction that caused a fire that, in turn, injured the purchaser and damaged his home. The purchaser would then demand not only a refund or replacement for the toaster, but also monetary damages for the personal injury and property damage. Here, the law of negligence and strict liability may be applied along with the law of warranties. The purchaser may claim damages in any of these three areas. He might bring a breach of warranty action. He might also bring a negligence action, claiming that the toaster was not manufactured with reasonable care. Or, the purchaser may seek to recover from the manufacturer under the theory of strict liability, which relieves the purchaser of the need to show negligence.[1]

Warranty of Title (UCC § 2-312)   A contract for the sale of goods includes a seller's warranty that he has good title, the transfer is rightful, and the goods shall be delivered free of any security interest (see Chapters 28 and 29) or other encumbrance of which the buyer, at the time of contracting, has no knowledge. The purpose of these warranties is clear. A buyer has the right to expect that the seller can convey a good title. If the seller cannot do so, the *warranty of title* has been breached. For example, a seller of stolen goods cannot convey a good title, and a buyer could claim breach of the warranty of title and recover the money he paid to the seller.

The warranty of title may be excluded or modified by specific language. For example, if the seller notifies the buyer that the property being sold has a lien on it, the warranty of title will not apply to that lien, but it would apply to all other liens of which the seller does not notify the buyer. The warranty of title may also be excluded or modified by circumstances that give the buyer reason to know that the seller does not claim title or is selling only the right or title that he may have. For example, the circumstances of a foreclosure sale (a resale of property after the initial buyer has defaulted and the seller has retaken possession of the property) might indicate to the buyer that the person making the sale did not warrant the title to the goods or their freedom from encumbrances.

21:2   Express Warranties (UCC § 2-313)

An express warranty may be oral or written and may be created in various ways. The seller need not use the word "warranty" or any other formal word. If his words or conduct amount to an express warranty, he is bound by that warranty, even if he never intended to make a warranty.

Under pre-code law, it was held that a representation constituted an express

---

[1]Negligence and strict liability are discussed in more detail in Chapter 6. Products liability is discussed in Chapter 7.

warranty only if the buyer actually relied on the representation. The UCC changed this rule, and the buyer's reliance on any representation is generally not essential. Instead, the UCC requires that the representations be "part of the basis of the bargain." Under this approach, the mere fact that certain representations were made is generally sufficient to lead to the conclusion that they were part of the basis of the bargain, unless the seller can prove otherwise.

A representation, in order to constitute an express warranty, need not be made simultaneously with the conclusion of the bargain. It may be made during the course of negotiations. Moreover, under some circumstances representations that are made after the sale, without further consideration from the buyer, may be considered express warranties. Under the UCC, a sales contract can be modified without consideration (UCC § 2-209). A representation made subsequent to the sale may therefore be treated as a modification of the contract. However, not every such representation will be considered a warranty. To be a warranty, the representation must still be part of the basis of the bargain, and most postsale representations are unlikely to be so classified, the bargain having already been made.

Affirmation of Fact or Promise   Any affirmation of fact or promise made by the seller to the buyer that relates to the goods and is part of the basis of the bargain creates an express warranty that the goods shall conform to the affirmation or promise. Such an affirmation or promise may be made in various ways. For example, statements made in a newspaper advertisement, if read by the buyer, might amount to an express warranty.

Statements concerning the value of the goods or concerning a seller's opinion or recommendation of them are considered to be only puffing and not express warranties.[2] Considerable problems may be encountered in determining whether a particular representation is one of fact or of opinion. Such factors as the specificity of the statement, the buyer's reliance on it, and the buyer's knowledge or lack of knowledge concerning the product all may bear on a court's determination.

 It is always risky for a seller to make statements that he cannot back up. The clear trend is toward considering borderline statements as affirmations of fact and therefore as express warranties. Even if a seller is ultimately vindicated in his contention that a statement was mere puffing, it may be only after years of expensive litigation and at the expense of a specific customer and the seller's good will.

Description of Goods   Any description of the goods that is made part of the basis of the bargain creates an express warranty that the goods shall conform to that description. A description need not be by words. Technical specifications and blueprints, for example, provide a more exact description than language. A warranty based on description is an important one, because goods are often offered for sale or ordered by reference to descriptive or generic names. For example, an agreement to sell "portland cement" carries a warranty that the cement delivered shall

---

[2]Statements of fact and statements of opinion, including dealers' puffing, are discussed in Chapter 12.

conform to the requirements for portland cement. The warranty arises when the seller makes a statement descriptive of the goods sold or when the buyer orders goods of a specific kind.

The following case illustrates how a court determined whether a description of goods in an advertisement was a warranty.

Interco Inc.

v

Randustrial Corp.
533 SW2d 257, 19 UCCRS 464
(Missouri Court of Appeals, 1976)

[Interco's shoe division occupied 21 buildings in St. Louis. In Building No. 3 the first floor was extremely rough, making it difficult to move merchandise. In 1971, a Randustrial representative recommended application of Sylox, a Randustrial product, because of its flexibility. Sylox was applied and proved satisfactory. In 1972, Interco experienced a similar roughness problem on the second floor of Building No. 1. Interco applied Sylox to the floor without consulting Randustrial. Due to floor movement ("give"), Sylox proved ineffective. Sylox had worked on the other building's floor because that floor had less movement. Interco filed suit against Randustrial. Interco claimed breach of an express warranty created by the following catalog description of Sylox: "Sylox is a hard yet malleable material which bonds firm to wood floors for smooth and easy hand-trucking. Sylox will absorb considerable flex without cracking and is not softened by spillage of oil, grease or solvents." A jury returned a verdict for Randustrial, and Interco appealed.]

Gunn, Judge.

*   *   *

Both parties agree that [UCC § 2-313] is applicable to the facts of this case. . . .

We have noted that Interco claims the existence of a warranty as to Sylox, and Randustrial argues the absence of a warranty. We disagree with Randustrial's contentions in this

regard. Although Randustrial contends its reference to Sylox in its sales catalogue did not constitute an express warranty, if the words used in the catalogue constitute a description or an affirmation of fact or promise about Sylox and became a part of the basis of the bargain, an express warranty was created. . . .

Randustrial also asserts that there could be no breach of warranty because Interco had failed to test the material before applying it to Building No. 1 and had failed to seek advice from Randustrial on its application. The uncontradicted evidence was that the cause of the breakup of the Sylox was the movement in the floor. There was nothing vague in Interco's evidence as to the intended use of Sylox. The evidence was palpable that Interco wanted something to withstand flex without breaking. The catalogue stated that "Sylox will absorb considerable flex." Thus, there was a description or affirmation of fact or "warranty" regarding Sylox giving rise to the purpose for which it was purchased by Interco. This was not mere puffing of a product. Interco was entitled to take the catalogue description of Sylox at its face value and plain meaning. There was no need to consult Randustrial or seek its advice regarding the use of Sylox. Any suggestion that Interco was at fault for not having tested the product or sought consultation is fatuous, for the catalogue description made no such requirement. "All the buyers are required to establish is that the express warranties were made and that they were false, thereby establishing a breach of the contract." . . . Interco had no obligation to establish a defect in Sylox as Randustrial suggests. . . .

Randustrial's argument that Interco failed to prove reliance on any warranty is also not felicitous. There is no mention of reliance in

[UCC § 2-313]. And the comments to that section of the U.C.C. reveal that the concept of reliance as required in pre-U.C.C. warranty cases was purposefully abandoned:

> "In actual practice affirmations of fact made by the seller about the goods during a bargain are regarded as part of the description of those goods; hence *no particular reliance on such statements need be shown in order to weave them into the fabric of the agreement. Rather, any fact which is to take such affirmations, once made, out of the agreement requires clear affirmative proof.* The issue normally is one of fact." Official Comment 3, [UCC § 2-313]. [Court's emphasis.]

The unchallenged evidence was that Interco's Manager of Facilities Engineering read the catalogue description which stated that Sylox would "absorb considerable flex"; that his testimony was that "the literature says that it [Sylox] absorbs considerable flex. Based on that I was assuming that it would do the job." The U.C.C. requires no more than what took place here. The statement "absorbs considerable flex" became "part of the basis of the bargain." The fact that Interco relied to some extent on its past experience with Sylox in Building No. 3 is not determinative of any issue, as no particular reliance on an express warranty is necessary. . . .

The fact that the language read by Interco was contained in a catalogue and was basically an advertisement does not preclude a finding that it is a warranty. A brochure, catalogue or advertisement may constitute an express warranty. . . . However, the catalogue advertisement or brochure must have at least been read, . . . as the U.C.C. requires the proposed express warranty be part of the basis of the bargain. . . . Randustrial does not dispute the fact that Interco had read the catalogue.

Randustrial [argues] that the statement that Sylox "will absorb considerable flex" merely reflects the seller's opinion of the goods and creates no warranty. . . . [UCC § 2-313] specifically excludes a seller's mere opinion or com-

mendation from being interpreted as an express warranty. . . . [However,] the language chosen by the seller in his advertising must be interpreted in favor of the buyer in order to restrict "untruthful puffing of wares." We believe that this is the same type of approach desired by the draftsmen of the U.C.C. In Official Comment 8, the draftsmen explain the difference between the "mere opinion" exclusion of [UCC § 2-313(2)] and the requirement that the language be "part of the basis of the bargain":

> "Concerning affirmations of value or a seller's opinion or commendation under subsection (2), the basic question remains the same: What statements of the seller have in the circumstances and in objective judgment become part of the basis of the bargain? As indicated above [i.e. in previous Comments], *all of the statements of the seller do so unless good reason is shown to the contrary.* The provisions of subsection (2) are included, however, since common experience discloses that some statements or predictions cannot fairly be viewed as entering into the bargain." Official Comment 8, [UCC § 2-313]. [Court's emphasis.]

An important factor is whether the seller assumes to assert a fact of which the buyer is ignorant or whether the seller merely expresses an opinion on which the buyer may be expected to have an opinion and be able to express his own judgment. . . .

Although Randustrial is pertinacious in its contention that the catalogue content regarding absorbability of considerable flex is merely a reflection of opinion, we must disagree. It is manifest that the words so used were meant to induce purchases through the assurance that considerable flex would be absorbed and were not mere opinion. The words were an affirmation of fact within the meaning of [UCC § 2-313]. . . .

[The court concluded, however, that the warranty was not breached, and the judgment was affirmed.]

A *warranty of conformity* to description does not arise if a sale of specific items is involved. For example, assume that Robin offers to sell Charles "a Stradivarius violin" but does not show Charles any particular violin. Here, a warranty of conformity to description would arise. However, if Robin shows Charles a violin, states that it is a Stradivarius, and offers to sell it to Charles, there is no warranty of conformity to description. If the violin is not in fact a Stradivarius, Charles may not claim breach of warranty (although he might be able to obtain rescission of the contract on grounds of fraud, misrepresentation or mutual mistake; see Chapter 12).

Sample or Model   Any sample or model that is made part of the basis of the bargain creates an express warranty that the whole of the goods shall conform to that sample or model. To illustrate, a potato seller opens a bag, shows some of the potatoes to a potential buyer, and then states that the rest of the potatoes are as good as those examined. The seller has made a warranty of conformity to sample.

The point must be made here that a sample is different from a model. The difference is that a sample is drawn from the bulk of the goods to be sold, while a model is individually constructed and is generally used when the goods are not available for inspection. The potatoes in the example above are a sample. A model might be used when a very large object is not readily available. The courts generally permit greater variation from a model than they do from a sample.

21:3 Implied Warranties

Implied warranties are imposed by operation of law to promote high business standards and to discourage sharp dealings. The UCC imposes two types of implied warranties: a warranty of *merchantability,* and a warranty of *fitness for a particular purpose.* These warranties reflect the fact that, as noted in an old English case, a "purchaser has the right to expect a saleable article answering the description in the contract."[3]

Implied Warranty of Merchantability (UCC § 2-314)   A sale of goods by a merchant who deals in goods of that kind usually carries with it a warranty that the goods are suitable for the ordinary purpose for which they are to be used. This is the implied warranty of merchantability. Goods do not have to be perfect to be merchantable. The warranty is essentially one of general fitness. For example, some goods are merchantable if they are of fair, average quality. The warranty is applied to merchant sellers only. It does not apply to a casual seller such as a vendor at a garage sale. The warranty is also inapplicable if the seller has disclaimed it, as discussed later in this chapter.

The UCC specifically provides that the sale of food or drink, whether for consumption on the premises or elsewhere, is subject to the implied warranty of merchantability. As applied to food, the warranty generally requires that the food be

---

[3]*Gardiner v Gray,* 171 Eng Rep 46, 47, 4 Camp 144 (King's Bench, 1815).

wholesome and not contain foreign objects. Some courts have held that the presence of natural objects in food does not constitute a breach of warranty. This distinction has sometimes resulted in unjust decisions.

EXAMPLE

Amy breaks her tooth on a hard object in a walnut–cream cheese sandwich. If the object were a piece of glass, a court would find the warranty of merchantability has been breached, and Amy would probably be able to recover damages. However, if a piece of walnut shell were in the sandwich, a court may find that the warranty of merchantability has not been breached, and Amy would not be able to recover damages.

Many courts, however, have discarded the distinction between foreign and natural objects. These courts focus instead on what a consumer should reasonably expect to find in the particular food.

The warranty of merchantability also applies to goods sold in the manufacturer's original package, even though they may not have been inspected by the retailer. A can of beans, for example, cannot be inspected by the seller, but if it contains insects, the seller will have breached the warranty of merchantability. It should be noted that the wholesaler who sold the beans to the retailer will have breached the warranty to the retailer, and the manufacturer will have breached the warranty to the wholesaler.

Fitness for Particular Purpose (UCC § 2-315)   An implied warranty of fitness of goods for a particular purpose arises when the seller has reason to know that there is a particular purpose for which the goods are required and that the buyer is relying on the seller's skill or judgment to select suitable goods. This warranty applies to sales by nonmerchants as well as merchants. In practice, however, the warranty usually involves a merchant seller, since a buyer normally does not rely on a nonmerchant seller's knowledge.

The warranty of fitness for a particular purpose involves two conditions: (1) that the seller has reason to know that the buyer intends a particular use, as distinguished from an ordinary use, for the goods; and (2) that the seller knows that the buyer is relying on the seller's skill and judgment in selecting the goods. The essence of the warranty is the buyer's reliance on the seller's expertise in selecting the right product for the buyer's intended use. A major factor in determining whether a warranty of fitness for a particular purpose should be implied is therefore the knowledge possessed by the respective parties. Where the seller is clearly much more knowledgeable than the buyer, the warranty is likely to be implied. Where the buyer's knowledge is equal or superior to the seller's, there probably is no such warranty.

EXAMPLE

A purchased bricks from B to build a fireplace, and the bricks proved unsatisfactory for that purpose. If A were a homeowner inexperienced in building fireplaces, and B were a merchant familiar with bricks and their uses, and A had told B of the intended purpose and asked B to recommend a suitable brick, then a court would find an implied warranty of fitness of the bricks for the intended purpose. If, however, A were in the business of building fireplaces and A had specifically requested the type of brick involved, then a court would not find any implied warranty of fitness for the particular purpose. In other words, if the buyer provides his own specifications, he cannot later claim that he relied on the seller's expertise.

 Most people tend to think of warranties in terms of new products, but warranties may also exist with respect to used goods. A seller of used goods should therefore be aware that a court may find an implied warranty of merchantability or fitness for a particular purpose. If the seller does not want to warrant the goods, he should take clear steps to disclaim these warranties, as discussed in Section 21:4.

Two cases follow. The first case illustrates that compliance with the warranty of merchantability does not always ensure the buyer's satisfaction. Consider whether the result would have been different if the purchaser had informed the seller that she intended to eat the pork without cooking it. Note how the court treats the breach of warranty and strict liability theories together. The second case illustrates the not uncommon situation in which one set of facts gives rise to claims of both express and implied warranties.

Hollinger
v
Shoppers Paradise of New Jersey, Inc.
134 NJ Super 328, 340 A2d 687
(New Jersey Superior Court, Law
Division, 1975)

[Mrs. Hollinger and some of her children contracted trichinosis from some pork chops she had cooked. Mrs. Hollinger filed suit against Shoppers Paradise, the seller, seeking recovery on theories of strict liability in tort and breach of warranty of merchantability. At the trial there was evidence that trichinosis is caused by parasitic worms called trichinae and that proper cooking is the only way to ensure that pork is completely free of trichinae. The trial court ruled in favor of the seller and wrote this opinion explaining its reasons. (The decision was affirmed on appeal; see 142 NJ Super 356, 361 A2d 578.)]

Rosenberg, J.S.C.

*   *   *

... [R]ecovery for [either] strict liability [or] breach of implied warranty of merchantability [does not require] proof of negligence by the defendant. Liability is established if the evidence shows that the product was not reasonably fit for the ordinary purposes for which it was sold and such defect proximately caused injury to the ultimate consumer. . . . It seems clear that these principles are applicable to the retail sale of food products. . . . Thus, in the instant case, if plaintiffs show that the pork was not reasonably fit for eating when it was sold and that the defect therein caused their injuries, they may recover by reason of either breach of warranty or strict liability theories, which are considered together for purposes of analysis. . . .

Two reasonable inferences which could be drawn from the sale of the pork chops to Mrs. Hollinger and the subsequent illness of her and her family are that the meat was unfit for consumption and that this unfitness proximately caused plaintiffs' injuries. However, to infer that the product was unfit upon reviewing the consequences of its use is not to say that it was not *reasonably* fit at the time of sale for its ordinary and intended purpose. [Court's emphasis.] Raw pork is a unique product in that it may contain an inherent defect (trichinae) which is undetectable by the seller but curable through preparation by the consumer. The fact that there is a danger of illness as a consequence of eating uncooked or underdone pork is a matter of common knowledge which courts in other jurisdictions have recognized and of which this court takes notice. . . . It follows that the ordinary and intended purpose for raw pork is consumption after *proper cooking by the consumer* and that if the chops in question were reasonably fit at the time of sale for such use Shoppers Paradise may avoid a finding of strict liability or breach of warranty. [Court's emphasis.] . . .

. . . New Jersey has been in the forefront of jurisdictions extending protection to consumers by imposing strict liability in tort. . . . Recovery is based on considerations of policy rather than actionable conduct by the defendant. These considerations are identified in [*Cintrone v Hertz Truck Leasing*]:

. . . Warranties of fitness are regarded by law as an incident of a transaction because *one party to the relationship is in a better position than the other to know and control the condition* of the chattel transferred. . . . [This factor makes] it likely that the party acquiring possession of the article will assume it is in a safe condition for use and therefore refrain from taking precautionary measures himself. [Court's emphasis.] . . .

In the case of raw pork the factual premise upon which [this] policy consideration rests is not present. Because of the character of the product it is impossible for the seller to detect the presence of the latent defect. . . .

. . . Since the presence of trichinae in raw pork can be cured *but only by the consumer*, the rationale for absolving the helpless seller from strict liability for damages caused by the parasite is [compelling]. [Court's emphasis.] . . .

For the foregoing reasons it is the opinion of the court that the policies compelling application of strict liability are not applicable in the case of a consumer contracting trichinosis from pork chops. This is consistent with the holding that Mrs. Hollinger failed to properly cook the meat served on October 10, 1971 and leads to the conclusion that plaintiffs have failed to prove as a matter of law that defendant sold a product not reasonably fit for its ordinary and intended purpose. For these reasons the motion of Shoppers Paradise for dismissal of the complaint is granted.

Kopper Glo Fuel, Inc.
v
Island Lake Co.
436 F Supp 91, 22 UCCRS 1117
(United States District Court, E.D. Tennessee, 1977)

[In 1975 Kopper Glo agreed to sell coal to Island Lake, a company owned by Jackson. Kopper Glo knew that Island Lake needed the coal to fulfill a supply agreement it had with General Motors. Sales were made between November 1975 and May 1976. When Island Lake failed to make payment, Kopper Glo sued. Island Lake counterclaimed for breach of warranties, claiming that Kopper Glo had delivered inferior quality coal containing excessive ash, sulfur, and slate. The trial court rendered judgment for Kopper Glo. The portion of its opinion dealing with the existence of warranties follows.]

Robert L. Taylor, District Judge.

*   *   *

The facts material to this issue are sharply in dispute. . . .

Island Lake contends that Kopper Glo expressly warranted that its coal would meet General Motor's specifications. Express warranties were created under UCC § 2-313, according to Island Lake, because Kopper Glo: (1) showed Jackson coal samples and laboratory analyses that met the specifications during the course of their negotiations, (2) made affirmations of fact to the effect that its coal reserves met the specifications, and (3) shipped coal pursuant to purchase orders which listed the specifications.

Kopper Glo denies that it made an express warranty, and contends that the samples and laboratory analyses were shown solely to illustrate the quality of coal that had been mined in the past. It asserts that it is difficult, if not impossible, to predict the quality of unmined coal, and any statements made to Jackson did not purport to represent that all coal mined in the future would be identical to that mined in the past. Kopper Glo contends that Jackson, who has an M.D. and a degree in chemical engineering, was provided with this information so that he could make his own judgment on the quality of Kopper Glo's reserves. As to the purchase orders, it is apparently Kopper Glo's position that they are merely written confirmations of the oral agreement, and, as such, cannot materially alter the terms of the oral agreement.

Island Lake further contends that Kopper Glo breached an implied warranty of merchantability under UCC § 2-314 and an implied warranty of fitness for a particular purpose under UCC § 2-315. Kopper Glo denies that such warranties were created or breached. . . .

Having considered the sharply conflicting evidence, the Court is of the opinion, and finds, that Kopper Glo agreed only to furnish the best coal it had available. The preponderance of the evidence shows that this was done. It is true, as defendants contend, that the purchase orders issued by Island Lake specified, among other things, the ash, sulfur and slate content of the coal it desired to obtain for its customers. By their own terms, these forms merely confirmed oral orders placed by Jackson over the telephone. Under certain circumstances a seller's acquiescence to the terms of a purchase order operates to make those terms part of an oral agreement. *See* UCC § 2-207. When merchants are involved, however, such terms cannot become part of the agreement when, as here, they materially alter it. *Id.* (2)(b).

Whether an express warranty was created by the coal samples and laboratory analyses presents a close question about which there is much disagreement. The exhibition of a sample does not necessarily create an express warranty; the agreement must evidence an intention to contract by sample. . . . The preponderance of the evidence shows that the samples and laboratory analyses were provided solely for what they were worth to Jackson, who was a highly educated man well-versed in the chemistry of coal. Plaintiff did not represent that all coal mined in the future to fill Island Lake's needs would conform to the sample or analyses because the quality of coal varies significantly within a given mine. The Court finds that, under these circumstances, no express warranty was created by the samples or analyses.

As to the alleged breach of implied warranty, the Court finds that the coal shipped by Kopper Glo was fit for the ordinary purpose for which it was used. All coal shipped by Kopper Glo was burned as fuel by Island Lake's customers. Since Kopper Glo agreed only to ship the best coal it had available, the coal otherwise conformed with UCC § 2-314 by meeting the contract description, being within the variations permitted by the agreement, being of fair and average quality within the description agreed upon, and being of even kind, quality and quantity within the variations permitted by the agreement.

Whether an implied warranty of fitness for a particular purpose was created under UCC §

2-315 turns upon whether Kopper Glo knew that Island Lake was relying on Kopper Glo's skill and judgment to furnish appropriate coal, and whether Island Lake, in fact, relied on such skill or judgment. Although it cannot be disputed that Kopper Glo knew the particular purpose for which Island Lake was ordering the coal, Jackson, as previously indicated, was quite knowledgeable of coal. He personally inspected Kopper Glo's coal and was quite capable of making his own independent judgment of whether Kopper Glo's reserves would be of sufficient quality to meet Island Lake's needs. Under these circumstances, the Court is of the opinion that an implied warranty of fitness for a particular purpose was not created. . . .

21:4   Exclusion or Modification of Warranties (UCC § 2-316)

Express and implied warranties may be excluded or modified by the seller's disclaiming them. The courts look with disfavor on *disclaimers of warranty,* especially in cases involving consumers. The UCC to some extent reflects that disfavor. The UCC seeks to protect buyers from unexpected language in contracts that excludes or modifies warranties.

The rules governing warranty disclaimers in UCC § 2-316 are neither designed nor interpreted as loopholes for evasion of a seller's warranty obligations. The courts insist that sellers comply strictly with the methods of disclaimer specified in these rules. Even when a seller has complied, under certain circumstances courts have held that disclaimer provisions are unconscionable under UCC § 2-302.[4] In addition, a warranty disclaimer that would be effective under the UCC might be unenforceable because of other applicable state or federal legislation, as discussed in Section 21:7. Furthermore, a buyer who is prevented by a disclaimer from claiming breach of warranty may sue on tort theories of negligence or strict liability.

Disclaimer of Express Warranties [UCC § 2-316(1)]   The UCC makes express warranties much more difficult to disclaim than implied warranties. Under the UCC, a seller's words or conduct indicating that there is an express warranty are interpreted as being consistent with other words or conduct indicating that the warranty does not exist or is limited, as long as this interpretation is reasonable. If this interpretation is not reasonable, then the exclusion or limitation of the express warranty is totally ineffective unless the parol evidence rule (UCC § 2-202) compels a different conclusion.

The above provision typically comes into play when the seller has allegedly made oral warranties, but the written contract disclaims all warranties. The parol evidence rule protects a seller when a buyer falsely claims that the seller made oral warranties. If the written contract was intended by the parties as the final expression of their agreement, the buyer cannot offer evidence of the oral warranties to prove that they were breached. This rule would seem to indicate that a written disclaimer of express warranties would prevail over prior oral express warranties.

---

[4]Unconscionability is discussed in Chapter 12.

In practice, however, prior oral express warranties are often accepted as evidence in court. For example, a court may find that the written contract was not intended as the final expression of the parties' agreement, that the oral warranty is consistent with the written disclaimer, that the disclaimer is unconscionable, or that its inclusion in the contract was fraudulent.

The effect of UCC § 2-316 as it has been interpreted is that a seller is indeed protected against claims of oral warranties if the seller can convince the court that they are false. If, on the other hand, the court believes the buyer's testimony concerning oral warranties, it can find a way to refuse to give effect to the seller's written disclaimer.

Disclaimer of Implied Warranties [UCC § 2-316(2), (3)]   Implied warranties are easier to disclaim than express warranties, but the UCC does specify procedures designed to ensure that the buyer is aware of such a disclaimer. Under the UCC, the implied warranty of merchantability may be excluded or modified in whole or in part only by language that mentions "merchantability." A disclaimer of the warranty of merchantability need not be in writing, but if it is, the disclaimer must be conspicuous. To exclude or modify any implied warranty of fitness, the exclusion must be in writing *and* conspicuous. For example, all implied warranties of fitness may be disclaimed by the conspicuous statement, "There are no warranties which extend beyond the description on the face hereof."

The UCC provides alternative methods of excluding *all* implied warranties. One method is the use of expressions like "as is" or "with all faults." Another method is the use of other language which in common understanding calls the buyer's attention to the exclusion of warranties and makes plain that there is no implied warranty. Most courts have held that "as is" disclaimers must be conspicuous, although the UCC does not specifically so require. The UCC also permits implied warranties to be excluded or modified by course of dealing, course of performance, or usage of trade.

To be conspicuous, a disclaimer must be so written that a reasonable person against whom it is to operate ought to notice it [UCC § 1-201(10)]. Many warranty disclaimers have been held ineffective because they were not conspicuous. In assessing conspicuousness, courts have considered such factors as the disclaimer's location in the document and the size and color of the type. For example, a printed heading (1) in capital letters, (2) in contrasting type or color, and (3) placed on the front of a form contract is considered conspicuous. The same heading might not be considered conspicuous if placed on the back of the form, since a customer is unlikely to look there. Similarly, a misleading heading will not be effective even though capital letters are used. For example, a reasonable person would not expect to find a disclaimer of warranty under the heading "WARRANTY," and that disclaimer would be ineffective.

 The courts are clearly concerned that unscrupulous sellers may use disclaimer provisions to evade responsibility for the proper functioning of the products they sell. With that fact in mind, a seller who desires to limit warranties should do so by means of a carefully worded, prominently placed, and fair provision. The seller might also have the buyer sign a statement certifying that the buyer has read the warranty disclaimer provision. Such an approach helps to eliminate the reasons for distrusting disclaimers.

The following case demonstrates the antipathy that courts often express toward disclaimer provisions, and is indicative of the close scrutiny that such provisions receive.

Dorman

v

International Harvester Co.
46 Cal Ap 3d 11, 120 Cal Rptr 516, 16 UCCRS 952
(California Court of Appeal, 1975)

[Dorman bought a tractor and backhoe from International Harvester. The tractor suffered numerous breakdowns, and Dorman sued International Harvester for breach of express and implied warranties. International Harvester countered that implied warranties had been disclaimed. At issue were two disclaimer provisions. The first disclaimer was in the purchase contract and stated that the tractor was "sold subject only to the applicable manufacturer's standard printed warranty . . . and no other warranties, express or implied, including without limitation, the implied warranties of merchantability and fitness for a particular purpose shall apply." The second disclaimer was contained in the manufacturer's standard printed warranty, which was apparently never delivered to Dorman. The trial court held that the purchase contract disclaimer was valid, and it awarded Dorman damages (equal to the amount paid on the contract) for breach of express warranty only. Both parties appealed.]

Stephens, J.

*   *   *

[UCC § 2-316(2)] provides that an exclusion of the implied warranty of merchantability "in case of a writing must be conspicuous," and that an exclusion of the implied warranty of fitness for particular purpose "must be by a writing and conspicuous." The code defines "conspicuous" as "so written that a reasonable person against whom it is to operate ought to have noticed it. . . .

. . . The official comment to [UCC § 1-201(10)] states that the test [of conspicuousness] is whether attention can reasonably be called to [the disclaimer provision]. . . . We must examine this comment in the light of the official comment to [UCC § 2-316], which states:

> "This section is designed principally to deal with those frequent clauses in sales contracts which seek to exclude 'all warranties, express or implied.' It seeks to protect a buyer from *unexpected* and unbargained language of disclaimer by denying effect to such language when inconsistent with language of express warranty and permitting the exclusion of implied warranties only by conspicuous language or other circumstances which protect the buyer from surprise." [Court's emphasis.]

In other words, [UCC § 2-316] seeks to protect the buyer from the situation where the salesman's "pitch," advertising brochures, or large print in the contract, giveth, and the disclaimer clause—in fine print—taketh away.

Here, the disclaimer provision appears in close proximity to where Dorman signed the contract, but emphasized (italicized) the implied-warranties wording *"merchantability and fitness for particular prupose shall apply."* [Court's emphasis.] Although the disclaimer provision was printed in a slightly larger type face than was the preceding paragraph of the contract, it was not in bold face type, and we are of the opinion that it was not sufficiently conspicuous to have negated the implied warranties, particularly where no "standard printed warranty" was in fact given to Dorman at the time of execution of the contract. . . . It thus violated the underlying rationale of [UCC § 2-316] as set forth in the official comment of protecting the buyer from an unbargained for limitation in the purchase of a product. In order to have a valid disclaimer provision, it must be in clear and distinct language and prominently set forth in large, bold print in such position as to compel notice. [UCC § 1-201(10).] . . . The contract here also failed to have an adequate heading at the beginning of the disclaimer provision, such as "DISCLAIMER OF WARRANTIES," to call the buyer's attention to the disclaimer clause.

The attempted disclaimer of implied warranties in the instant case is ineffective for another reason. Construing the language of the provision strictly . . . , construction of the wording is ambiguous and could easily be misleading. A purchaser glancing at the provision would reasonably observe the *italicized* language, which reads: *"merchantability and fitness*

for the particular purpose shall apply," and would be lulled into a sense of security. [Court's emphasis.] This is directly contrary to the actual intent of the provision. . . .

Moreover, the manufacturer's standard printed warranty (which also endeavored to limit the warranties . . .) was not included in the contract which Dorman signed on November 3, 1968. It was on the reverse side of the purchase order, a separate document not shown to have been signed by Dorman or delivered to him at any time. A disclaimer of warranties must be specifically bargained for so that a disclaimer in a warranty given to the buyer *after* he signs the contract is *not* binding. [Court's emphasis.] . . . The disclaimer of consequential damages which was included in the manufacturer's standard warranty is also not binding. . . .

We conclude that the disclaimer was insufficiently conspicuous to inform a reasonable buyer that he was waiving his right to have a quality product. . . .

[Judgment reversed.]

Limitation of Remedy for Breach of Warranty (UCC § 2-719)   As an alternative to disclaiming warranties, some sellers prefer to limit the remedies available in the event of a breach of warranty. In other words, a buyer may be allowed only certain remedies for the breach. The UCC permits a seller to limit his responsibility only to repairing or replacing defective goods or parts. The UCC also provides that a seller may limit the damages that the buyer can claim, or exclude consequential damages. However, such a limitation is invalid if it is unconscionable, and limitation of consequential damages for personal injuries caused by consumer goods is presumed to be unconscionable. In addition, if circumstances cause a limited remedy to fail in its essential purpose, the buyer may have recourse to any other remedy provided by the UCC. For example, if repeated repair attempts are unsuccessful, a court may find that the warranty fails in its essential purpose. In such a case, a consumer may demand and be granted a refund.

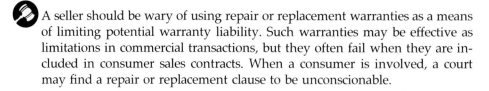 A seller should be wary of using repair or replacement warranties as a means of limiting potential warranty liability. Such warranties may be effective as limitations in commercial transactions, but they often fail when they are included in consumer sales contracts. When a consumer is involved, a court may find a repair or replacement clause to be unconscionable.

Effect of Opportunity to Examine Goods   If the buyer, before entering the contract, examined the goods or a sample or model of them to his satisfaction, or if he refused to examine the goods, there is no implied warranty with regard to defects that an examination ought to have revealed—that is, open or visible defects. This rule does not apply if the seller has merely offered to let the buyer examine the goods. Rather, the buyer must actually examine the goods, or the seller must demand that the buyer examine them. The provision concerning examination does not apply to express warranties.

21:5   Cumulation and Conflict of Warranties (UCC § 2-317)

A sale of goods may be accompanied by several warranties, both express and implied. Under the UCC these warranties are interpreted as being consistent with each other and cumulative wherever possible. When the warranties cannot be interpreted as being consistent, the intention of the parties determines which warranty is dominant. The UCC sets forth rules to assist a court in determining the parties' intention. The essence of these rules is that the more specific warranty generally prevails over the less specific. For example, technical specifications prevail over an inconsistent sample, model, or description; a sample prevails over an inconsistent general description; and express warranties prevail over inconsistent implied warranties, except for the implied warranty of fitness for a particular purpose.

 The rules for determining priority between inconsistent warranties are designed for situations in which the seller has in good faith made warranties that turn out to be inconsistent. If the seller has led the buyer to believe that all the warranties can be performed, he will be prevented from relying on inconsistency as a defense to a breach of warranty action.

21:6   Privity Requirements

Under what is known as the doctrine of *privity of contract*, a buyer can sue only the immediate seller for breach of warranty. This doctrine is being rejected in many courts. Most states now permit a buyer to bring a breach of warranty action not only against the immediate seller, but also against intermediate sellers and the manufacturer. For example, a defective bicycle purchased by an adult may cause injury to a child, and the purchaser may be able to hold the manufacturer liable for the defect.

Rights of Third Persons (UCC § 2-318)   Consumers other than the purchaser are generally permitted to sue sellers and manufacturers. The UCC has three alternative provisions on warranty actions by third persons. Each state chooses one of the alternatives when it adopts Article 2 of the code.

   Alternative A extends warranty protection to family members and guests of the buyer who may reasonably be expected to use, consume, or be affected by the goods. Alternative B extends warranty protection to *all* persons who may reasonably be expected to use, consume, or be affected by the goods. Alternatives A and B are limited to personal injury. Alternative C extends warranty protection to the same persons as Alternative B, but includes *any* injury caused by the breach of warranty. To the extent the UCC alternative adopted by a state does not expressly give warranty protection to a person other than the buyer, the UCC remains neutral on extension of sellers' warranties to nonbuyers.

21:7 Other Warranty Legislation

The UCC is not the sole source of warranty law. In 1975 Congress passed the *Magnuson–Moss Warranty Act,* which regulates warranties of consumer products. In addition, various states have enacted laws dealing with consumer product warranties. These state statutes often provide consumers greater protection than is provided by either the UCC or the federal act.

Magnuson-Moss Warranty Act   The Magnuson–Moss Warranty Act (15 USC §§ 2301–2312) was Congress' response to a general belief that consumer warranties were often misleading, difficult to understand, and even more difficult to enforce. The act establishes certain requirements that must be met whenever a written warranty is given in connection with a sale of a consumer product (any tangible personal property normally used for personal, family, or household purposes) that costs $15 or more.

Under the act, a written warranty is (1) any written affirmation of fact or promise, made in connection with the sale of a consumer product, that the material or workmanship is defect-free or will meet a specified level of performance over a specified period of time; or (2) any written undertaking, made in connection with the sale of a consumer product, to refund, repair, replace, or take other remedial action if the product fails to meet the specifications set forth in the undertaking.

The act does not require that any warranty be given on a consumer product. If, however, a warranty is given, (1) it must be phrased in simple and readily understandable language, (2) it must be made available for the purchaser's inspection prior to the sale, and (3) it must be clearly and conspicuously designated as either a *full* or a *limited warranty.* A full warranty must meet the following minimum standards: (1) the warrantor must remedy any defects or malfunctions of the product within a reasonable time, and without charge; (2) the warrantor may not impose any limitation on the duration of any implied warranty; (3) the warrantor may not exclude or limit consequential damages for breach of any warranty, unless such exclusion or limitation conspicuously appears on the face of the warranty; and (4) if the warrantor is unable, after a reasonable number of attempts, to remedy a defect or malfunction in the product or one of its parts, the warrantor must give the consumer the option of a refund or replacement of the product or part. All other written warranties under the act are considered limited warranties.

A seller may not disclaim or modify any implied warranties on a consumer product (1) if a written warranty is given on the product or (2) if, within 90 days of the sale, the seller and consumer enter into a service contract for the product.

However, if a written warranty is limited to a reasonable duration, then implied warranties may be similarly limited, provided the limitation is conscionable and is clearly and prominently stated on the face of the warranty.

The act encourages the use of informal dispute settlement procedures and also provides for its enforcement by judicial proceedings.

Key Concepts and Terms

- A sales warranty is a promise that the object sold has certain qualities or conditions. A warranty may be express or implied and may exist with respect to new and used goods alike.

- The warranty of title is a warranty that the seller has good title and the goods are rightfully transferred free of encumbrances of which the buyer is unaware. This warranty may be excluded or modified by specific language or under certain circumstances.

- An express warranty is an oral or written representation that is part of the basis of the bargain. An express warranty may be created by the seller's affirmation of fact or promise, description of goods, or exhibition of a sample or model of the goods. Statements of the product's value or the seller's opinion do not create express warranties.

- The implied warranty of merchantability is a warranty that goods sold are suitable for their ordinary purposes. Every sale of goods, including the sale of food or drink, by a merchant who deals in goods of that kind generally includes this warranty.

- An implied warranty of fitness arises if the seller has reason to know that the buyer is relying on the seller's skill or judgment to select goods suitable for the buyer's particular purpose.

- Any disclaimer of a warranty must be made in strict compliance with the UCC requirements. If a seller has made an express warranty *and* a disclaimer, the warranty and disclaimer will both be given effect unless it is unreasonable to do so, in which event the disclaimer is inoperative.

- An implied warranty of merchantability may be disclaimed only by language that mentions merchantability. If the disclaimer is written, it must be conspicuous. A disclaimer of an implied warranty of fitness must be written and conspicuous. Alternatively, all implied warranties may be excluded by a sale of goods in which the term "as is" or "with all faults" is used.

- A seller may limit a buyer's remedy for breach of warranty by being responsible only for repairing or replacing defective parts and by excluding consequential damages. These limited remedies are invalid if they are found to be unconscionable or to fail in their essential purpose.

- A buyer's examination of, or refusal to examine, the goods prior to entering into a contract prevents the existence of any implied warranty with respect to defects that an examination ought to have revealed.

- Multiple warranties are interpreted as being consistent and cumulative whenever possible. When they are not consistent, the parties' intent determines which warranty applies, with the more specific warranty generally prevailing over the less specific.

- The UCC has alternative provisions concerning warranty rights of third persons, but it generally remains neutral concerning such rights. Many courts have rejected or limited the doctrine of privity of contract, and have extended warranty rights to nonbuyers.

- The Magnuson–Moss Warranty Act contains requirements of disclosure and content with respect to written warranties on consumer products. Some states have statutes that also deal with warranties on consumer products.

- Disclaimer of Warranty
- Fitness for a Particular Purpose
- Full Warranty
- Limited Warranty
- Magnuson–Moss Warranty Act

- Merchantability
- Privity of Contract
- Warranty of Conformity
- Warranty of Title

Questions and Case Problems

1. Bundy, an experienced printer, needs a new press. He visits Quality Presses, which specializes in the sale of printing presses. Bundy sees two machines there, an Alpha and an Omega, but he does not see either one print. Quality's president advises Bundy that the Alpha would best suit Bundy's printing needs. Bundy reads a brochure, put out by the Alpha's manufacturer, which states that the Alpha can do up to "7,000 impressions an hour" and has a "superior inking system and precise inking controls." Bundy eventually buys an Alpha press from Quality. The purchase contract contains a disclaimer, in boldfaced capital letters, which states that the seller makes no express or implied warranties and expressly excludes any implied warranties of merchantability or fitness. Bundy's Alpha turns out to be a "lemon." It cannot do more than 5,000 impressions an hour, its printing quality is inconsistent, and it breaks down frequently. Finally, Bundy sues Quality for breach of express and implied warranties. What is the result?

2. In March 1973, Kavanaugh read a newspaper advertisement for a secondhand 1956 Cessna airplane. He met with Keenan, the owner, to discuss buying it. Keenan gave Kavanaugh an engine and propeller logbook detailing the mechanical repair and flight history. Kavanaugh carefully perused the logbook; it stated that on May 16, 1972, the engine had a major overhaul in which new mechanical parts were placed in it in conformity with the manufacturer's engine overhaul manual. Based on this information Kavanaugh bought the plane. On December 5, 1973, the engine lost power and began to shake violently in flight, and Kavanaugh made an emergency landing. The engine had to be completely overhauled. In the process, it was discovered that the 1972 overhaul had not included new parts and had been performed in a defective manner. Kavanaugh sued Keenan for the cost of the overhaul, claiming breach of express warranty. Was there a breach of express warranty?

3. What is the difference between a warranty of merchantability and a warranty of fitness for a particular purpose?

4. Sowards buys a used coal truck from Childers & Venters. The seller knows that the buyer intends to use the truck to haul coal. The sales contract is a printed form, the first paragraph of which states that the sale is subject to the terms and conditions "set forth below and upon the reverse side hereof." The words, "and upon the reverse side hereof," are in bolder print than the rest. The back of the form is headed "PROVISIONS," under which are eleven numbered paragraphs. All except the eighth paragraph are in identical type. The eighth paragraph is in larger, bolder type, and disclaims any implied warranty of merchantablility and any implied warranty of fitness for a particular purpose. The truck turns out to be unsuitable for hauling coal, and Sowards refuses to pay for it. Childers & Venters sues Sowards for the purchase price. How should the case be decided?

5. Nathan goes to Debs' Department Store, tries on a pair of slacks, and decides to purchase them. Before taking the slacks off, he puts his hand into a pocket and is bitten by a venomous spider hidden in the pocket. Nathan sues Debs' for breach of the warranty of merchantability. Is Debs' liable?

6. Why do courts look with disfavor on warranty disclaimers? How does the UCC reflect this disfavor?

7. Luke goes to Bill's Hardware to purchase some drill bits for drilling steel. Not knowing a great deal about such bits, Luke asks a clerk for assistance and explains his needs. Luke also shows the clerk an old wood-drilling bit that he has used for other drilling jobs. The clerk shows Luke a drill bit set and says that "this will probably do the job for you." When Luke tries to use the new bits, they break. Luke seeks a refund from Bill's, but the manager points out that the set's label clearly states that the bits are for drilling wood only and explicitly warns that the bits should not be used to drill steel. The manager also points out that the set came with a written warranty against defects in materials or workmanship when used properly. Luke admits that the bits would work on wood but still demands a refund. Is he entitled to one?

8. Discuss the relationship among breach of warranty, negligence, and strict liability.

9. Mays buys a new Ford pickup truck from a Ford dealer. Ford's warranty provides for free repair of any parts found defective within the earlier occurrence of 12 months or 12,000 miles. The warranty excludes any other express warranty and limits any implied warranty of merchantability or fitness to the 12-month/12,000-miles duration. About five weeks after the purchase, Mays notices unusual noise and vibration. During the next five months the dealer makes seven or eight repair attempts and replaces various parts, but nothing eliminates the problem. Finally, it is discovered that the truck's frame is bent. Since a distorted frame can cause excessive wear to all moving parts, Mays returns the truck. Ford refuses to do anything other than repair the truck, and Mays sues. Should he be awarded a refund of the purchase price?

10. Tam sees a picture of a pair of gray hiking boots in Nance's mail order catalog and orders the boots. When they arrive, the boots are not the same color as illustrated in the catalog; they are slightly darker. Has Nance breached any warranties? What if the product involved were paint, or the catalog had stated that actual colors might differ slightly from the illustration?

22 Performance; Remedies for Breach

22:1 Introduction

A contract of sale imposes basic obligations on both seller and buyer. The seller's basic obligation is to deliver goods that conform to the contract, and the buyer's basic obligation is to accept and pay for those goods (UCC § 2-301). The UCC provides specific rules for determining when the performance of these obligations is sufficient. Those rules are discussed in this chapter. Various rules discussed in preceding chapters also relate to the subject of performance. For example, the subject of delivery was considered to some extent in connection with transfer of title and risk of loss (Chapter 20), as was the seller's obligation to deliver goods that conform to any warranties (Chapter 21).

The parties' respective obligations sometimes are not clearly established in the contract. Some terms may be left open; the parties may intentionally leave some particulars of performance to be specified later by one or the other party (UCC § 2-311). Or, the contract may be silent as to obligations. When the contract is silent, general contract principles, as well as principles of interpretation set forth in the UCC, are used to determine the parties' respective obligations. Again, some of these rules of interpretation, such as the rules with respect to course of performance, course of dealing, and usage of trade, have been considered earlier (Chapter 16).

The most important factor to consider in determining what the parties' obligations are—and therefore whether the parties have performed those obligations—is the contract itself. Bear in mind that the parties may alter by agreement most obligations that would otherwise be imposed under the code, except for the obligation of good faith that the code imposes in the performance or enforcement of all contracts. For merchants, the obligation of good faith includes the observance of reasonable commercial standards of fair dealing.

Sales contracts, like all other kinds of contracts, are sometimes breached. When one party fails to perform, the other party is entitled to one or more of the various remedies permitted by the UCC. Along with performance, these remedies will be discussed in this chapter.

22:2   Seller's Obligation

The seller's primary obligation consists of (1) a proper tender, or offer, of delivery of (2) *conforming goods* to the buyer. A *tender of delivery* is proper when it is made in accordance with the provisions of the contract and with the applicable provisions of the UCC. Goods are conforming when they comply with the obligations under the contract [UCC § 2-106(2)].

The seller must deliver the goods at the time and place specified in the contract. If the contract is silent as to the time and place for delivery, delivery must be made within a reasonable time [UCC § 2-309(1)] and ordinarily at the seller's place of business (UCC § 2-308). The seller must tender delivery of the goods at a reasonable hour, must give the buyer reasonable notice of the tender, and must keep the goods available for the period reasonably necessary to enable the buyer to take possession [UCC § 2-503(1)].

As discussed earlier (see Chapter 20), the place and manner of delivery often are indicated by the use of shipping terms. To make a proper tender under a shipment contract, the seller must (1) put the goods in the carrier's possession, (2) make a reasonable contract for their transportation, (3) deliver to the buyer any document necessary to enable him to take possession, and (4) promptly notify him of the shipment (UCC § 2-504). In the case of a destination contract, as well as a contract involving goods held by a bailee, delivery may take place in one of the following ways: (1) the seller's giving the buyer a negotiable document of title; (2) the seller's receiving the bailee's acknowledgment of the buyer's right to possession; or (3) the seller's giving the buyer a nonnegotiable document of title or a written direction to the bailee to deliver the goods, unless the buyer seasonably objects (objects within a reasonable time), to such a tender [UCC § 2-503(3)–(5)].

Sufficiency of Seller's Performance   At common law, the *perfect tender* rule required the seller to make a tender of delivery that conformed in all respects to the contract requirements. In theory the UCC retains the perfect tender rule as a basic standard of performance, granting the buyer the right of rejection "if the goods or the tender of delivery fail in any respect to conform to the contract" (UCC § 2-601). However, in actual practice the UCC generally requires only substantial performance by the seller (see Chapter 18). The UCC also contains several exceptions to the basic rule.

One exception, perhaps the most important one, permits a seller to *cure* a nonconforming delivery under some circumstances (UCC § 2-508). In other words, if the seller, prior to the time set for performance, makes a delivery of nonconforming goods, he is permitted to rectify the improper tender by delivering conforming goods before the time for performance expires. To exercise this right, the seller must seasonably notify the buyer of his intention to do so. Another situation to which this exception would apply is the buyer's making a surprise rejection of goods for nonconformity. If the buyer rejects a nonconforming tender that the seller had reasonable grounds to believe would be acceptable, the seller may, with notice, have reasonable additional time to make a conforming delivery.

EXAMPLE

The seller of a hearing aid delivers a modified and improved version of the one ordered, thinking the buyer will accept this newer model. The buyer rejects it. Therefore, the seller has the right to then cure the improper tender by delivering the hearing aid specified in the contract.

The following case illustrates how the courts apply the doctrine of cure in a practical manner. Note how the court's decision effectively prevented the buyer from rejecting the goods on the basis of a minor nonconformity.

<hr />

Wilson
v
Scampoli
228 A2d 848, 4 UCCRS 178
(District of Columbia Court of Appeals 1967)

[Scampoli purchased a television set from Wilson. When the set was delivered, Mrs. Kolley, Scampoli's daughter, noted the picture had a reddish tinge. A service representative examined the set and told Mrs. Kolley that it would be necessary to take the chassis into the shop to determine the cause of the problem. Mrs. Kolley refused to allow him to take it, stating that she wanted a "brand new" set, not a "repaired" one. She later demanded a refund of the purchase price. Wilson refused, and Scampoli sued for a refund of the purchase price. The trial court ordered the contract rescinded and the purchase price refunded. Wilson appealed.]

Myers, Associate Judge.

*   *   *

Appellant does not contest the jurisdiction of the trial court to order rescission in a proper case, but contends the trial judge erred in holding that rescission here was appropriate. He argues that he was always willing to comply with the terms of the sale either by correcting the malfunction by minor repairs or, in the event the set could not be made thereby prop-

erly operative, by replacement; that as he was denied the opportunity to try to correct the difficulty, he did not breach the contract of sale or any warranty thereunder, expressed or implied.

[UCC § 2-508] provides:

(1) Where any tender or delivery by the seller is rejected because non-conforming and the time for performance has not yet expired, the seller may seasonably notify the buyer of his intention to cure and may then within the contract time make a conforming delivery.

(2) Where the buyer rejects a nonconforming tender which the seller had reasonable grounds to believe would be acceptable with or without money allowance the seller may if he seasonably notifies the buyer have a further reasonable time to substitute a conforming tender.

A retail dealer would certainly expect and have reasonable grounds to believe that merchandise like color television sets, new and delivered as crated at the factory, would be acceptable as delivered and that, if defective in some way, he would have the right to substitute a conforming tender. The question then resolves itself to whether the dealer may conform his tender by adjustment or minor repair or whether he must conform by substituting brand new merchandise. . . .

Although the Official Code Comments do not reach this precise issue, there are cases and comments under other provisions of the Code which indicate that under certain circumstances repairs and adjustments are contemplated as remedies under implied warranties. . . .

While these cases provide no mandate to require the buyer to accept patchwork goods or substantially repaired articles in lieu of flawless merchandise, they do indicate that minor repairs or reasonable adjustments are frequently the means by which an imperfect tender may be cured. In discussing the analogous question of defective title, it has been stated that:

> The seller, then, should be able to cure [the defect] under subsection 2-508(2) in those cases in which he can do so without subjecting the buyer to any great inconvenience, risk or loss. Hawkland, Curing an Improper Tender of Title to Chattels: Past, Present and Commercial Code, 46 Minn.L.Rev. 697, 724 (1962). . . .

Removal of a television chassis for a short period of time in order to determine the cause of color malfunction and ascertain the extent of adjustment or correction needed to effect full operational efficiency presents no great inconvenience to the buyer. In the instant case, appellant's expert witness testified that this was not infrequently necessary with new televisions. Should the set be defective in workmanship or parts, the loss would be upon the manufacturer who warranted it free from mechanical defect. Here the adamant refusal of Mrs. Kolley, acting on behalf of appellee, to allow inspection essential to the determination of the cause of the excessive red tinge to the picture defeated any effort by the seller to provide timely repair or even replacement of the set if the difficulty could not be corrected. The cause of the defect might have been minor and easily adjusted or it may have been substantial and required replacement by another new set—but the seller was never given an adequate opportunity to make a determination.

[Judgment reversed.]

A second exception to the perfect tender rule applies to *installment contracts* (UCC § 2-612). Under the UCC, an installment contract is one that requires or authorizes the delivery of goods in separate lots to be accepted separately. The buyer may reject an installment only if the nonconformity substantially impairs the value of that installment and cannot be cured. Otherwise, the buyer must accept the installment, provided the seller gives adequate assurance that the nonconformity will be cured. Moreover, a nonconforming delivery of one or more installments will not be considered a breach of the entire contract unless the nonconformity substantially impairs the value of the whole contract. In other words, the UCC in essence adopts a standard of substantial performance with respect to installment contracts.

The UCC also adopts the substantial performance standard with respect to the third exception, which concerns deviations in shipping and delivery arrangements. Therefore, in a shipment contract, the buyer cannot reject a tender of delivery for such deviations unless he will suffer a material delay or loss on account of them (UCC § 2-504). Where the agreed means or manner of delivery becomes unavailable or commercially impracticable, the seller may use a commercially reasonable substitute (UCC § 2-614).

Commercial Impracticability; Impossibility   The UCC recognizes the fact that under some circumstances a party may find it impossible or commercially impracticable to perform a sales contract. Thus, a party need not perform the contract if performance "has been made impracticable by the occurrence of a contingency the nonoccurrence of which was a basic assumption on which the contract was made" (UCC § 2-615). This is the doctrine of commercial impracticability. Despite the UCC's recognition of the doctrine, courts are reluctant to use it to relieve a seller of his obligation to perform. For example, most courts have rejected claims that increased costs excuse a seller from his obligation to deliver in accordance with the contract. One instance in which commercial impracticability *has* been recognized as an excuse for nonperformance is unanticipated failure of the source of supply if the contract called for the use of only a particular source. For example, under a contract to sell a crop growing on designated land, failure of the crop would excuse the seller's performance.

The destruction, before risk of loss passes to the buyer, of identified goods essential to the contract also excuses performance by the seller. If the loss is total, the contract is avoided; if the loss is partial, or if the goods have so deteriorated that they are no longer conforming, the buyer may either avoid the contract or accept the goods with an allowance in price (UCC § 2-613).

If commercial impracticability affects only a part of the seller's capacity to perform, he must perform to the extent possible. If the seller has more than one customer, he must adopt some fair and reasonable manner of allocating the available goods among his customers (UCC § 2-615).

22:3   Buyer's Obligations

The buyer's basic obligations are to accept and to pay for the goods (UCC § 2-301). Before doing so, however, the buyer ordinarily has the right to inspect the goods.

Inspection of Goods (UCC § 2-513)   The buyer generally has the right to inspect the goods, prior to acceptance or payment, at any reasonable place and time and in any reasonable manner. The parties may specify in the contract the place, time, or manner of inspection. The buyer must pay the expenses of the *inspection,* but he may recover the expenses from the seller if the goods are nonconforming and are rejected.

The parties may provide in their contract that payment must precede inspection. In any event, the code lists specific circumstances in which the buyer must pay before inspecting the goods, unless the parties have agreed otherwise. Thus, advance payment for inspection is normally required (1) if the contract provides for delivery C.O.D. (collect on delivery) or on other like terms, or (2) if the contract calls for payment against documents of title before the buyer actually receives the goods.

 The inclusion of a provision requiring payment prior to inspection obligates the buyer to pay even though the goods do not conform to the contract, unless the nonconformity appears without inspection [UCC § 2-512(1)(a)].

The buyer's payment does not, however, mean that the buyer has accepted the goods. The buyer still retains the basic right to inspect the goods before acceptance and retains all remedies, such as rejection, that the code provides for nonconforming goods [UCC §§ 2-512(2), 2-606(1)(a)].

Acceptance of Goods (UCC § 2-606) If the goods delivered by the seller conform to the contract, the buyer must accept them. If they do not conform, the buyer generally can reject them. *Acceptance* may be manifested by words, conduct, or both. The UCC specifies three methods: (1) if the buyer, after a reasonable opportunity for inspection, signifies to the seller that the goods are conforming or that they will be accepted despite some nonconformity; (2) if the buyer fails to make a timely rejection or to give the seller timely notice of rejection of the goods; or (3) if the buyer performs any act that indicates his ownership (such as reselling or consuming the goods).

When both conforming and nonconforming goods are delivered under a single contract, the buyer may wish to accept only those goods that conform. He may make such a partial acceptance, but is limited to acceptance of a commercial unit or units. A *commercial unit* is a single whole, the division of which would materially impair its character or value [UCC § 2-105(6)].

EXAMPLE
Valdez orders 100 cases of canned goods. If the cans are customarily sold by the case, Valdez could reject any cases that were nonconforming and accept those cases that were conforming. Valdez could not, however, break open a case and accept only a portion of its contents.

If the buyer accepts goods that are defective in some manner, he must notify the seller within a reasonable time after he discovers or should have discovered the defect. Failure to notify the seller will bar the buyer from later pursuing any remedy.

Rejection or Revocation of Acceptance [UCC §§ 2-601-2-605, 2-608, 2-612, 2-711(3)] When nonconforming goods are delivered, the buyer may accept the entire delivery and seek damages (see 22:7); he may make a partial acceptance under certain circumstances; or he may reject the entire delivery. In addition, under some circumstances the buyer may revoke an acceptance already made.

The buyer may revoke an acceptance if it was made on the reasonable assumption that the nonconformity would be cured by the seller and it has not been seasonably cured, or if the buyer accepted delivery without discovering the nonconformity and the acceptance was reasonably induced either by the difficulty of discovering the nonconformity before acceptance or by the seller's assurances.

Theoretically, the buyer can reject delivery if the goods are nonconforming in any respect, but he may revoke acceptance only if the nonconformity substantially impairs the value of the goods to him. In practice, however, the absolute right of rejection is in many respects virtually indistinguishable from the right to revoke acceptance. Perhaps the major practical distinction is that sometimes acceptance with knowledge of a substantial nonconformity amounts to a waiver of that nonconformity and disallows the buyer from later revoking the acceptance.

As a practical matter, there are several reasons why a buyer ordinarily should not reject goods on the basis of a minor or technical nonconformity. First, the buyer usually needs the goods. Second, a court is not likely to look favorably on a rejection based on some minor deficiency. A court may, for example, hold the buyer's rejection improper on the ground that the buyer failed to permit the seller to cure. Finally, a buyer should always consider his business reputation. If he acquires a reputation for rejecting goods without substantial reason, other businesspersons will be leery of dealing with him.

The buyer must give the seller timely notice of a rejection or revocation of acceptance. When rejection is based on a defect that is ascertainable by reasonable inspection, the buyer under certain circumstances must notify the seller of that defect. If he does not, he cannot later rely on that defect to justify rejection (1) if the seller could have cured the defect or (2) when both parties are merchants, if the seller, after rejection, made a written request for a statement of defects from the buyer.

When a buyer finds himself still in possession of the goods after he has rejected them or revoked his acceptance of them, he must hold them for a reasonable time and follow the seller's reasonable instructions concerning their disposition. If the seller gives no instructions, the buyer may store the goods for the seller, reship them to the seller, or resell them. The buyer may also resell the goods if the seller does not pay the buyer's expenses for inspection, receipt, transportation, care, and custody of the goods. If the buyer is a merchant, and if the seller has no agent or place of business at the market where the goods were delivered and rejected, the buyer must, in the absence of instructions from the seller, sell goods that are perishable or that may quickly decline in value. The manner in which a resale must be conducted is discussed in 22:6 and 22:7.

The following case exemplifies the importance of examining all the facts in deciding the related questions of whether a buyer has accepted or rejected goods, whether he has revoked a prior acceptance, and whether his actions were timely. Note how the court, in reaching its conclusion, gave consideration both to industry practices and to the practicalities involved in making an inspection.

La Villa Fair

v

Lewis Carpet Mills, Inc.
219 Kan 395, 548 P2d 825, 19 UCCRS 120
(Kansas Supreme Court, 1976)

[La Villa Fair, a carpet wholesaler and retailer specializing in large buildings, placed an order with Lewis Carpet Mills for approximately "12,000 square yards of carpet, 25 ounce face weight, 100 percent acrylic cut pile of first quality (no seconds)." When Lewis shipped the last portion of the order, La Villa's customer was not ready to take the carpeting. La Villa arranged to have Lewis deliver it to a warehouse until it was needed. Over eight months passed before La Villa's customer was ready to install the carpeting. There were 21 100-foot rolls of the carpeting, and the installers examined and cut into three or four of the rolls without finding enough carpet that matched to finish even a 23-foot area in a display apartment. The carpeting was ex-

tensively patched, of varying texture and color, delaminated in places, not 25 ounce face weight, and nylon instead of acrylic. La Villa's customer rejected the carpeting, and La Villa informed Lewis that it also rejected the carpet. La Villa then sued Lewis for the purchase price. At trial, Lewis claimed that La Villa had waited too long to inspect and had therefore accepted the goods. La Villa claimed that it was a common industry practice to defer inspection of carpeting until it was ready for use. The trial court ruled in favor of La Villa, and Lewis appealed.]

Miller, Justice.

*   *   *

[The issue on appeal] is: Notwithstanding the carpet's nonconformity, was plaintiff's rejection, or revocation of its acceptance of the same, timely?

[Defendant claims] that plaintiff's delayed inspection was unreasonable as a matter of law. . . .

Defendant contends that a failure by plaintiff to inspect is only justified where such inspection is wholly impracticable, not just inconvenient or time-consuming and thus it argues that the plaintiff had a reasonable opportunity to inspect and that its failure to do so amounts to acceptance under [UCC § 2-606]. . . .

. . . [I]t would seem that it cannot be said that plaintiff's nine-month delay in inspecting and accepting or rejecting the carpet is itself an acceptance as a matter of law, but rather should be left to the trier of fact. . . . [T]here was evidence in the instant case that the defendant was aware that plaintiff's purchaser was not ready to use the goods it shipped . . . and that it was aware that the goods were to be shipped to a warehouse for storage. There was also evidence that no set time for inspection exists but that the industry practice is not to inspect until a purchaser is found and is

ready to use the goods. There was further evidence that the carpet, when received in a large order such as this one, is stocked until ready for use rather than unrolled for inspection of concealed defects. Under all the evidence the carpet was timely and reasonably inspected and the trial court's finding to that effect is supported by substantial competent evidence.

There is a further question, however, whether or not the acts of the carpet installer for plaintiff's purchaser, Lay-Rite, were so inconsistent with the seller's ownership as to amount to the exercise of ownership and dominion by the plaintiff thereby constituting acceptance.

. . . [I]t would appear that the actions of the installer for plaintiff's purchaser were not inconsistent with seller's ownership and could not be said to amount to acceptance as a matter of law. . . . In the instant case there would appear to be evidence that it was necessary to unroll and cut into three of four rolls of carpet in order to determine that the carpet was extensively patched, was delaminated in places, that it varied in width and in hue, and that it was not 25 oz. face weight. . . . After unrolling three or four rolls of carpet it became obvious that the carpet was defective since Lay-Rite could not find 23 feet in the several hundred feet of carpet that would match for installation in a "show" apartment. Had Lay-Rite installed the carpet in the "show" apartment or other apartments before rejecting it, [such action might have been inconsistent with the seller's ownership]. Here, however, the deficiencies complained of were readily apparent upon inspection after the carpet was unrolled, and rejection preceded installation. It cannot be said that the unrolling and cutting of the carpet in an attempt to match portions for installation was inconsistent with the seller's ownership as a matter of law so as to constitute an acceptance of the carpet. . . .

[Judgment affirmed.]

Payment   The parties may of course specify the time and terms of payment, but unless otherwise specified payment ordinarily is due at the time of delivery [UCC §§ 2-310(a), 2-507(1), 2-511(1)]. The buyer may pay in any manner currently in the ordinary course of business. Payment by check is a common and acceptable practice. The seller may demand payment in legal tender (actual cash) but must give the buyer any time reasonably necessary to procure the money. Dishonor of a check by the bank defeats the payment. In other words, the buyer is obligated to pay again if his check is not good [UCC § 2-511(2), (3)]. If the parties agree, the buyer need not pay with money (UCC § 2-304). For example, the purchaser of a new car frequently trades in a used car as partial payment.

22:4   Anticipatory Repudiation and Assurance of Performance

The UCC provision (UCC § 2-610) on *anticipatory repudiation,* which is rejection of contractual obligations before the time for performance, follows the basic common-law concept. This concept is that if one party, by words or actions, repudiates a performance due in the future (states or shows by his actions that he will not perform), as a result of which the value of the contract to the other party is substantially impaired, the innocent party can treat the repudiation as a breach and choose among various courses of action: (1) he may, for a commercially reasonable time, await performance by the repudiating party, although if he waits longer than a commercially reasonable time, he cannot recover any damages that he should have avoided; (2) he may resort to any remedy for breach of contract (see 22:5–22:7), even if he has notified the repudiating party that he would wait for performance; or (3) regardless of whether the innocent party awaits performance or treats the repudiation as a breach, he may suspend his own performance until the matter is clarified one way or the other.

As noted in Chapter 18, an anticipatory breach must be unequivocal. Mere hesitation or ambivalence concerning performance does not constitute an anticipatory breach. It is difficult to determine when a party's words or actions in fact constitute an anticipatory breach of a contract. If one party ceases performance because he incorrectly concluded that the other party has committed an anticipatory breach, the first party may himself be found in breach of contract.

The UCC includes a provision designed to eliminate much of the uncertainty that surrounds anticipatory breach. This provision (UCC § 2-609) permits one party, when in doubt as to the other party's intention or ability to perform as promised, to demand adequate *assurance of performance.* Under this provision, when one party has reasonable grounds to be insecure about the other party's performance, the first party may demand in writing that the other party give adequate assurance of performance. Pending the receipt of this assurance, the demanding party may, if commercially reasonable, suspend his own performance. If his performance includes preparatory action, he may also suspend that action. For example, if a seller of specially manufactured goods had reason to doubt the buyer's ability to pay, the seller might make a written demand for assurance and stop manufacturing until the assurance was forthcoming.

UCC § 2-609 is used primarily in transactions between merchants. Between merchants, the reasonableness of grounds for insecurity and the adequacy of any assurance offered are determined according to commercial standards. Naturally, the reasonableness of both the demand and the assurance received will depend on the particular facts involved. The grounds for insecurity are often based on one party's apparently precarious financial situation. For example, if the buyer is behind in payments on the contract, the seller might demand an assurance of performance. Similarly, if the seller appeared to be on the brink of failure, the buyer might demand assurance of the seller's ability to deliver.

The ground for insecurity need not be related to the contract itself. For example, if the seller learned that the buyer was behind in payments to other creditors, it might be reasonable for the seller to demand an assurance of the ability to pay. If the goods involved were precision parts, and if the buyer learned that the seller was delivering defective precision parts to other buyers, the buyer might be justified in demanding assurance from the seller.

The adequacy of the assurance offered will also depend on the circumstances. In some situations a mere promise by the buyer or seller might be adequate. In other situations more might be demanded. For example, it might sometimes be reasonable to demand that the buyer deposit all or part of the purchase price in escrow. When the seller's ability to manufacture the goods is at issue, a demand for some proof of ability might be reasonable. The party on whom a justified demand has been made must give the assurance of performance within a reasonable time, not to exceed 30 days after receipt of the demand. Failure to provide the assurance within such time constitutes a repudiation of the contract.

The following case sets forth factors that a court considers in determining both the reasonableness of a demand for assurance of performance and the adequacy of the assurance given.

AMF, Inc.
v
McDonald's Corp.
536 F2d 1167, 19 UCCRS 801
(United States Court of Appeals, Seventh Circuit, 1976)

[In 1967 AMF and McDonald's agreed that AMF would install a model 72C computerized cash register in a McDonald's restaurant to evaluate it. In April 1968, a prototype 72C unit was installed in McDonald's busiest restaurant, located in Elk Grove, Illinois. In December 1968 and January 1969, McDonald's agreed to purchase 23 additional

72C's to be placed in McDonald's restaurants, with delivery to be made between February and June 1969. AMF had problems developing a reliable 72C. In February 1969, AMF revised the delivery schedule to between July 1969 and January 1970. The revised schedule was contingent on AMF's completion and satisfactory testing of a test unit being built at its Vandalia, Ohio, plant. On March 18, 1969, representatives of McDonald's and AMF met to discuss various problems, including the poor performance of the Elk Grove prototype 72C. At that meeting McDonald's suggested, and AMF agreed, that production of the other 23 units be suspended pending agreement on performance and reliability *standards. In April 1969, the Elk Grove prototype was removed from McDonald's due to its poor performance. On May 1, 1969, representatives of McDonald's and AMF again met. At that time AMF did not have a working 72C, and, due to the inexperience of its Vandalia personnel, could not produce one within a reasonable time. The parties were unable to agree on reliability and performance standards, and McDonald's canceled the contract. The formal cancellation came on July 29, 1969. The reasons for cancellation were the poor performance of the prototype, the lack of assurances that a workable machine was available, and the unsatisfactory conditions at the Vandalia plant. AMF sued McDonald's for breach of contract. The trial court ruled in favor of McDonald's, and AMF appealed.]*

Cummings, Circuit Judge.

*   *   *

Whether in a specific case a buyer has reasonable grounds for insecurity is a question of fact. Comment 3 to UCC § 2-609. . . . On this record, McDonald's clearly had "reasonable grounds for insecurity" with respect to AMF's performance. At the time of the March 18, 1969, meeting, the prototype unit had performed unsatisfactorily ever since its April 1968 installation. Although AMF had projected delivery of all twenty-three units by the first half of 1969, AMF later scheduled delivery from the end of July 1969 until January 1970. When McDonald's personnel visited AMF's Vandalia, Ohio, plant on March 4, 1969, they saw that none of the 72C systems was being assembled and learned that a pilot unit would not be ready until the end of July of that year. They were informed that the engineer assigned to the project was not to commence work until March 17th. AMF's own personnel were also troubled about the design of the 72C, causing them to attempt to reduce McDonald's order to five units. Therefore, under [UCC § 2-609] McDonald's was entitled to demand adequate assurance of performance by AMF.

However, AMF urges that [UCC § 2-609] is inapplicable because McDonald's did not make a written demand of adequate assurance of due performance. In [a prior case] we noted that the Code should be liberally construed and therefore rejected such "a formalistic approach" to Section 2-609. McDonald's failure to make a written demand was excusable because AMF's [representative's] testimony and his April 2 and 18, 1969, memoranda about the March 18th meeting showed AMF's clear understanding that McDonald's had suspended performance until it should receive adequate assurance of due performance from AMF. . . .

After the March 18th demand, AMF never repaired the Elk Grove unit satisfactorily nor replaced it. Similarly, it was unable to satisfy McDonald's that the twenty-three machines on order would work. At the May 1st meeting, AMF offered unsatisfactory assurances for only five units instead of twenty-three. The performance standards AMF tendered to McDonald's were unacceptable because they would have permitted the 72C's not to function properly for 90 hours per year, permitting as much as one failure in every fifteen days in a busy McDonald's restaurant. Also, as the district court found, AMF's Vandalia, Ohio, personnel were too inexperienced to produce a proper machine. Since AMF did not provide adequate assurance of performance after McDonald's March 18th demand, [UCC § 2-609(1)] permitted McDonald's to suspend performance. When AMF did not furnish adequate assurance of due performance at the May 1st meeting, it thereby repudiated the contract under [UCC § 2-609(4)]. At that point, [UCC § 2-610(b)] permitted McDonald's to cancel the orders . . . , as it finally did on July 29, 1969. . . .

[Judgment affirmed.]

UCC § 2-609 is designed for use in situations in which one party begins to have reasonable doubts concerning the other party's ability or intent to perform as promised. The section is designed to eliminate the necessity of having to guess, perhaps incorrectly. Any assurance that removes the uncertainty should be sufficient. A doubting party should, therefore, not be oppressive in the demands he makes. If the assurance demanded is out of proportion to the grounds for insecurity, a court might well find the demanding party's suspension of performance to constitute a breach of the contract.

Retraction of Anticipatory Repudiation   As with contracts generally, a repudiating party may retract the repudiation at any time before performance is due. If, however, the aggrieved party has canceled the contract or otherwise materially changed position in reliance on the repudiation, the repudiation may not be retracted. The retraction must include any assurance of performance justifiably demanded by the aggrieved party (UCC § 2-611).

22:5 Remedies Generally

When one party to a sales contract breaches the contract, the other party is entitled to a remedy. The UCC specifies in detail various remedies available to the seller and the buyer. Before studying these remedies, it is important to take note of the underlying philosophy of the UCC: The remedies specified are to be liberally interpreted to the end that the innocent party is put in as good a position as if the other party had performed (UCC § 1-106). Thus, the remedial provisions are not to be narrowly or technically interpreted. In addition, the code's provision of remedies is not meant to be exclusive. Unless the UCC otherwise provides, a party to a sales contract may pursue any general remedy available to him.

If the parties wish to do so, they can limit or modify the remedies that would otherwise be available under the UCC by including the limitations or modifications in the contract. The parties may also expressly agree that a remedy specified in a contract will be the exclusive remedy available. If they do not, the remedy will be considered optional. In addition, any limitation will not be given effect if it fails in its essential purpose, and any limitation or modification of remedies that is unconscionable is void (UCC § 2-719). In other words, the UCC leaves the parties free to shape their remedies according to their particular requirements, but insists that they be reasonable.

The inclusion of a liquidated damages provision is a common way in which remedies are limited (see Chapter 20 for a discussion of liquidated damages provisions). Again, reasonableness is the key concern. The UCC permits the parties to a sales contract to agree to reasonable liquidated damages, but a provision for unreasonably large liquidated damages is void as a penalty [UCC § 2-718(1)].

Statute of Limitations (UCC § 2-725)   Under the UCC, an action for breach of a sales contract must be brought within four years after the cause of action has accrued. A cause of action normally accrues when a breach occurs, regardless of the innocent party's knowledge of the breach. For example, if the seller delivers nonconforming goods, a breach has occurred, a cause of action has arisen, and the four-year period begins to run. By agreement, the parties may reduce the period of limitations to not less than one year, but they may not extend the period. In most cases it is easy to apply the statute of limitations.

In a breach of warranty case, a cause of action accrues when tender of delivery is made, except when the warranty explicitly extends to future performance of the goods. Application of this rule may sometimes result in harsh decisions. Assume, for example, that a purchaser is injured by a defective product five years after the purchase. Because this is after the statute of limitations period, a personal injury action based on a theory of breach of warranty would be barred, even though the defect was unknown and undiscoverable prior to the injury. In light of that fact, injured persons often seek recovery in a tort action. Tort statutes of limitations are typically less than four years, but the period of limitations does not begin to run until the injury occurs. Thus, if a defective product caused an injury five years after its purchase, the buyer or other user would still have a potential tort action.

Not all courts have accepted such reasoning, however. Some courts have held that all actions, even personal injury actions, that arise out of a breach of warranty are governed by the UCC's four-year limitations period. Other courts have disagreed and have applied the tort statute of limitations. Still other courts have been influenced by the precise nature of the pleadings in the case. In other words, if the plaintiff classifies his action as one for breach of warranty, the UCC provision might be applied; if the plaintiff classifies his action as one in tort, the tort statute of limitations might be applied.

22:6   Seller's Remedies

The UCC provides the seller with a wide variety of remedies. The primary remedies to a buyer's breach are set forth in UCC § 2-703 and are discussed here. If a buyer breaches a contract, the seller may (1) withhold delivery of the goods; (2) stop delivery of the goods; (3) identify to the contract finished goods that were not previously identified to it, and finish or salvage unfinished goods; (4) resell the goods and recover damages; (5) recover damages for nonacceptance or repudiation; (6) recover the price; or (7) cancel the contract. In addition, the UCC provides the seller with various remedies in the event of the buyer's insolvency.

The availability or desirability of any particular remedy will, of course, depend on the particular facts involved and the nature of the breach. For example, if the buyer's breach consists of an improper rejection of the goods, the seller cannot be expected to withhold delivery of the goods as a remedy. Or, if the buyer's breach consists of nonpayment for goods already delivered, several of the remedies provided by the code are simply inapplicable. This is not to say, however, that the seller must select only one remedy. The seller may pursue as many remedies as are appropriate and desirable in a given case.

Specific remedies will now be considered in greater detail.

Withholding or Stoppage of Delivery; Effect of Buyer's Insolvency (UCC §§ 2-702, 2-705)   The seller's right to withhold or stop delivery of goods is available as a remedy for various breaches by the buyer. These include (1) the buyer's repudiation of the contract, (2) the buyer's failure to make a payment when due, and (3) the buyer's insolvency.

The seller's right to stop delivery basically extends until such time as the buyer has either received the goods or obtained effective control of them. To stop delivery, the seller must notify the carrier or other bailee so that he can, by reasonable diligence, prevent delivery, and must surrender any negotiable document of title that has been issued for the goods. The seller cannot stop delivery if the buyer's right to possession has been acknowledged by a bailee other than a carrier, or if the buyer has a negotiable document of title. The seller cannot stop delivery of small shipments for any reason other than the buyer's insolvency.

A buyer's insolvency affects the seller's remedy in different ways, depending on the circumstances. The seller may demand cash payment on future delivery and payment for all goods previously delivered under the contract, even though the contract includes credit terms. If the goods have already been delivered to a carrier or other bailee for ultimate delivery to the buyer, the seller may stop delivery, provided he complies with certain requirements. If a seller discovers a buyer's insolvency after the goods have actually been delivered, the seller has a right to reclaim them within ten days after the buyer receives them. However, if the buyer made a written misrepresentation of solvency to the seller within three months prior to delivery, the ten-day limitation does not apply. If the buyer refuses to return the goods, the seller has no right to forcibly retake them. Note also that insolvency is often a prelude to bankruptcy proceedings. If the buyer does become involved in bankruptcy proceedings, the provisions of the bankruptcy act would take precedence over any provisions of the UCC, and the seller's right to reclaim the goods might be defeated.[1]

Resale and Recovery of Damages (UCC § 2-706)   Resale and recovery of damages is the seller's primary remedy when the buyer's breach leaves the seller in possession of the goods. This remedy is available, for example, when the buyer's breach consists of repudiation of the contract or nonacceptance of the goods. If the seller resells the goods in a commercially reasonable manner, he may recover the difference between the resale price and the contract price, together with any incidental damages incurred, but less any expenses saved. Incidental damages might include expenses incurred in stopping delivery and returning the goods to the seller, and resale expenses (UCC § 2-710).

The goods may be resold at either a public or a private sale. If the resale is private, the seller must give the buyer reasonable notice of his intention to resell. If

---

[1]Bankruptcy is discussed in Chapter 31.

the resale is public, the seller must notify the buyer of the time and place, unless the goods are perishable or may quickly decline in value.

Recovery of Damages for Nonacceptance or Repudiation (UCC § 2-708)   When the buyer's breach consists of nonacceptance or repudiation, the seller may resell the goods, but he is not obligated to do so. The seller has the option of seeking damages based on the difference between the market price of the goods at the time and place of tender and the unpaid contract price. The seller may also recover any incidental damages, but expenses saved as a result of the buyer's breach must be deducted. If the damages as computed under this contract–market price formula are inadequate to put the seller in as good a position as performance would have, then the seller may recover as damages the profit lost as a result of the buyer's breach, plus incidental expenses. This alternative measure of damages is designed for use in cases involving readily available standard-priced goods.

EXAMPLE
Lane sells encyclopedias at $500 per set. He makes a profit of $200 on each sale. He contracts to sell a set to Orloff, who wrongfully repudiates the contract. Lane then sells the set to a third person who intended to buy a set anyway. Lane will recover nothing if damages are based on the difference between resale price and contract price, or if damages are based on the difference between market price and contract price. Yet Lane clearly has lost $200, since the result of Orloff's breach is that Lane has made only one sale—and a profit of $200—whereas he would have made two sales—and a profit of $400—had Orloff not breached. In such circumstances, Lane would obviously seek recovery of damages measured by lost profits.

Recovery of Contract Price (UCC § 2-709)   If the buyer accepts the goods but fails to pay the purchase price, the seller may recover the price, together with any incidental damages caused by the breach. The seller may also recover the contract price in two other situations: (1) when the goods were lost or damaged within a commercially reasonable time after the risk of loss had passed to the buyer[2] and (2) when goods have been identified to the contract and the seller, after reasonable effort, is unable to resell them or the circumstances reasonably indicate an attempt to resell would be unsuccessful. These are the only three instances in which the seller may recover the purchase price as a remedy.

Unidentified or Unfinished Goods (UCC § 2-704)   The discussion of a seller's remedies thus far has proceeded on the premise that the goods involved have been finished and identified to the contract. Frequently, however, a buyer repudiates or otherwise breaches the contract before the goods have been identified to the contract. In this case the seller may identify the goods to the contract if they are in his possession and then seek appropriate remedies. To illustrate, assume that Johnson contracts to sell Kenny 500 pairs of socks of the 1,000 pairs he has in storage. If Kenny repudiates the contract, Johnson can designate 500 pairs as the subject of

---

2Risk of loss is discussed in Chapter 20.

the contract. Johnson may then proceed to resell them or seek any other appropriate remedy under the UCC for Kenny's breach.

If the goods are unfinished when the seller learns of the buyer's breach, the seller has several options. He may resell any unfinished goods that were intended for the contract. Or, if it is commercially reasonable to do so, he may either (1) finish the goods and identify them to the contract or (2) stop manufacturing and resell the unfinished goods for their salvage value. The theory is that when unfinished goods are involved, the seller should act in such a manner as to lessen any damages flowing from the buyer's breach. Thus, the seller should choose whichever option is likely to result in the least damages.

Cancellation of Contract   Cancellation occurs when one party puts an end to the contract because of the other party's breach. A party may cancel the contract and still pursue any other available remedy, such as damages [UCC §§ 2-106(4), 2-720]. Thus on the buyer's breach, the seller may cancel the contract and pursue any other remedy that may be appropriate under the circumstances.

The UCC distinguishes between cancellation and termination of a contract. Termination occurs when a party legally puts an end to the contract for some reason other than its breach by the other party. Termination has the effect of discharging all unperformed obligations that remain, although any rights based on prior breach or performance survive [UCC § 2-106(3)].

22:7   Buyer's Remedies

The buyer's remedies for a seller's breach are cataloged and described in several sections of the UCC. These remedies include (1) rejecting or revoking acceptance of goods when they are nonconforming (which is discussed in 22:3); (2) reselling the goods under certain circumstances and in the same manner as the seller, as described in 22:6; (3) obtaining substitute goods, called *cover*; (4) recovering damages under various circumstances; (5) requesting an order for *specific performance* or *replevin*; and (6) cancelling the contract. In addition, the buyer may always recover any part of the purchase price that has already been paid. Because the first two remedies have been treated elsewhere, only the last four will be discussed here.

Cover (UCC § 2-712)   Cover, or the right to obtain substitute goods, is the principal remedy under the UCC when the seller's breach deprives the buyer of the goods for which he has contracted. The buyer's right to cover is the counterpart of the seller's right to resell, and both remedies are widely used. The buyer may cover by purchasing substitute goods from another source. The buyer's purchase must be made in good faith, without unreasonable delay, and in a reasonable manner. The buyer may then recover from the seller damages equal to the difference between the cost of cover and the contract price, plus incidental or consequential damages, less expenses saved by virtue of the seller's breach.

Cover is an optional remedy, and if the buyer elects not to cover he can later recover any consequential damages that could have been prevented by cover.

However, cover is normally a desirable remedy, since it permits the buyer to obtain a substitute for the performance promised in the original contract.

Damages (UCC §§ 2-713-2-715)   As an alternative to cover, a buyer may merely seek damages for nondelivery or repudiation. If the buyer receives the goods and they are defective, he may accept them and seek to recover damages based on the nonconformity. The measure of damages depends on the alternative selected by the buyer. In all situations, the buyer may recover appropriate incidental or consequential damages.

The measure of damages for nondelivery or repudiation is the difference between the market price when the buyer learned of the breach and the contract price. When the buyer accepts the goods and seeks damages based on their nonconformity, the measure of damages is the loss resulting in the ordinary course of events from the seller's breach. Any reasonable manner of determining such damages may be used, but the most common measure is the difference between the value of the goods as accepted and the value they would have had if they had conformed to the contract. This measure is specifically prescribed for breach of warranty cases.

 While the discussion here is couched in terms of recovering damages, it is obviously preferable for the buyer and seller to reach an agreement on a reduced purchase price when defective goods are delivered and accepted. As a practical matter, it is sometimes difficult for the buyer to obtain a partial refund from the seller. The UCC, however, authorizes a buyer, on giving the seller notice of his intention to do so, to deduct the damages resulting from the breach from any part of the purchase price not yet paid (UCC § 2-717). Therefore, a buyer who has accepted defective goods but has not yet paid the full price should consider exercising his right to deduct the damages when he makes his final payment.

The incidental damages that a buyer may recover include expenses reasonably incurred in inspection, receipt, transportation, and care and custody of goods rightfully rejected; any commercially reasonable expenses incurred in effecting cover; and any other reasonable expenses caused by the breach. Consequential damages are recoverable if the seller at the time of contracting had reason to know of the buyer's general or particular requirements and needs. In other words, consequential damages are recoverable if they are foreseeable, but are not recoverable if the buyer could have prevented them. Thus, the buyer must seek to minimize his damages, either by cover or other means.[3]

The following case illustrates the use of alternative methods of computing damages and how they sometimes lead to the same dollar figure. Note the court's emphasis on the buyer's failure to act in a commercially reasonable manner after the seller's anticipatory repudiation.

---

[3]Consequential damages and the duty to minimize damages are discussed in Chapter 18.

Oloffson
v
Coomer
11 Ill App 3d 918, 296 NE2d 871
(Illinois Appellate Court, 1973)

[Oloffson, a grain dealer, contracted in April 1970 to purchase 40,000 bushels of corn from Coomer, an Illinois farmer. The corn was to be delivered in October and December at an average price of $1.12½ per bushel. On June 3, Coomer informed Oloffson that he was not going to plant corn because the season had been too wet. He told Oloffson to arrange to get the corn elsewhere if he already had a commitment to deliver to a third party. On that date corn futures were selling at $1.16 per bushel. In September Oloffson asked Coomer about the corn delivery, and Coomer again said he would be unable to deliver. Oloffson persisted, mailing Coomer a confirmation of the April contract. When no shipments were received on the delivery dates, Oloffson finally bought elsewhere to fulfill his commitments, paying an average of $1.42 per bushel. Oloffson sued, and the trial court awarded him damages of $1,500, based on the difference between the minimum contract price of $1.12¼ and the market price on June 3. Oloffson appealed on the issue of damages.]

Alloy, Presiding Justice.

*   *   *

Oloffson argues on this appeal that the proper measure of his damages was the difference between the contract price and the market price on the dates the corn should have been delivered in accordance with the April 16 agreement. . . .

It is clear that on June 3, 1970, Coomer repudiated the contract "with respect to performance not yet due." Under the terms of the Uniform Commercial Code the loss would impair the value of the contract to the remaining

party in the amount as indicated. [UCC § 2-610.] As a consequence, on June 3, 1970, Oloffson, as the "aggrieved party," could then:

> "(a) for a commercially reasonable time await performance by the repudiating party; or
>
> (b) resort to any remedy for breach (Section 2-703 or Section 2-711), even though he has notified the repudiating party that he would await the latter's performance and has urged retraction;"

If Oloffson chose to proceed under subparagraph (a) referred to, he could have awaited Coomer's performance for a "commercially reasonable time." As we indicate in the course of this opinion, that "commercially reasonable time" expired on June 3, 1970. The Uniform Commercial Code made a change in existing Illinois law in this respect, in that, prior to the adoption of the Code, a buyer in a position as Oloffson was privileged to await a seller's performance until the date that, according to the agreement, such performance was scheduled. To the extent that a "commercially reasonable time" is less than such date of performance, the Code now conditions the buyer's right to await performance. . . .

If, alternatively, Oloffson had proceeded under subparagraph (b) by treating the repudiation as a breach, the remedies to which he would have been entitled were set forth in [UCC § 2-711]:

> "(1) Where the seller fails to make delivery or repudiates or the buyer rightfully rejects or justifiably revokes acceptance then with respect to any goods involved, and with respect to the whole if the breach goes to the whole contract (Section 2-612), the buyer may cancel and whether or not he has done so may in addition to recovering so much of the price as has been paid

(a) 'cover' and have damages under the next section as to all the goods affected whether or not they have been identified to the contract; or

(b) recover damages for non-delivery as provided in this Article (Section 2-713). . . ."

Plaintiff, therefore, was privileged under [UCC § 2-610] to proceed either under subparagraph (a) or under subparagraph (b). At the expiration of the "commercially reasonable time" specified in subparagraph (a), he in effect would have a duty to proceed under subparagraph (b) since subparagraph (b) directs reference to remedies generally available to a buyer upon a seller's breach.

Oloffson's right to await Coomer's performance under [UCC § 2-610(a)] was conditioned upon his:

(i) waiting no longer than a "commercially reasonable time." . . .

Since Coomer's statement to Oloffson on June 3, 1970, was unequivocal and since "cover" easily and immediately was available to Oloffson in the well-organized and easily accessible market for purchases of grain to be delivered in the future, it would be unreasonable for Oloffson on June 3, 1970, to have awaited Coomer's performance rather than to have proceeded under [UCC § 2-610(b)] and, thereunder, to elect then to treat the repudiation as a breach. Therefore, if Oloffson were relying on his right to effect cover under [UCC § 2-711(a)], June 3, 1970, might for the foregoing reason alone have been the day on which he acquired cover. . . .

. . . Oloffson knew or should have known on June 3, 1970, the limit of damages he probably could recover. If he were obligated to deliver grain to a third party, he knew or should have known that unless he covered on June 3, 1970, his own capital would be at risk with respect to his obligation to his own vendee. Therefore, on June 3, 1970, Oloffson, in effect, had a duty to proceed under [UCC §§ 2-610(b) and 2-711(1)(a), (b)]. If Oloffson had so proceeded under [UCC § 2-711(1)(a)], he should have effected cover and would have been entitled to recover damages all as provided in [UCC § 2-712], which requires that he would have had to cover in good faith without unreasonable delay. Since he would have had to effect cover on June 3, 1970, according to [UCC § 2-712(2)], he would have been entitled to exactly the damages which the trial court awarded him in this cause.

Assuming that Oloffson had proceeded under [UCC § 2-711(1)(b)], he would have been entitled to recover from Coomer under [UCC §§ 2-713 and 2-723] the difference between the contract price and the market price on June 3, 1970, which is the date upon which he learned of the breach. This would produce precisely the same amount of damages which the trial court awarded him. . . .

[Judgment affirmed.]

Specific Performance or Replevin (UCC § 2-716)   Specific performance of a sales contract may be ordered if the goods involved are unique or "in other proper circumstances."[4] The UCC contains no specific requirement that the remedy at law be inadequate, although in most instances where specific performance is proper the remedy at law will be inadequate. Uniqueness is to be determined in light of

---

[4]The circumstances under which specific performance will ordinarily be ordered are discussed in Chapter 18.

the total situation. For example, output and requirements contracts that involve a particular or peculiarly available source or market may be the subject of an order of specific performance.

The UCC also grants the buyer the right to obtain possession of the goods under certain circumstances. This is called the right of replevin. The remedy of replevin is available only if the goods have been identified to the contract and only if cover is not reasonably obtainable.[5]

Cancellation of Contract   The buyer's right to cancel the contract for a breach is the same as the seller's right in that regard. Thus, a buyer may cancel the contract and pursue other appropriate remedies.

Key Concepts and Terms

- The seller's basic obligation is to deliver conforming goods. Under the perfect tender rule, the buyer has the right to reject a tender of delivery that is nonconforming in any respect. In practice, however, substantial performance by the seller is generally sufficient, and the seller has the right to cure an improper delivery under certain circumstances. The doctrine of substantial performance is also applicable to deviations from shipping and delivery arrangements.

- A seller may be excused from performance of the contract if it is commercially impracticable to perform or if goods essential to the contract were destroyed.

- The buyer's basic obligations are to accept and pay for conforming goods. The UCC specifies three methods by which acceptance may occur. These are: (1) informing the seller that the goods are conforming or are acceptable despite some nonconformity; (2) failing to reject or give the seller notice of rejection within a reasonable time; or (3) performing any act that indicates ownership of the goods.

- The buyer generally may inspect the goods prior to acceptance or payment. Certain contracts require payment before inspection, but the buyer still has the right to inspect the goods before accepting them.

- Under the UCC a party, when in doubt as to the other party's intention or ability to perform, may demand adequate assurance of performance. The demanding party may suspend performance pending receipt of such assurance. Failure to provide the assurance constitutes repudiation of the contract.

- An action for breach of a sales contract must be brought within four years after the cause of action has accrued.

- The remedial philosophy of the UCC is that an innocent party should be put in as good a position as if the breaching party had performed. Therefore, in addition to remedies provided by the UCC, an aggrieved party may pursue any other available remedies.

- When a buyer breaches, the seller may pursue one or more of the following

---

[5]Replevin is discussed in more detail in Chapter 30.

remedies: (1) withholding of delivery; (2) stoppage of delivery; (3) identification of goods to the contract, finishing of unfinished goods, or salvage of unfinished goods; (4) resale of goods and recovery of damages; (5) recovery of damages for nonacceptance or repudiation; (6) recovery of the price of the goods; or (7) cancellation of the contract. If the buyer is insolvent, the seller may also reclaim the goods under certain circumstances.

- The measure of damages recoverable by the seller varies depending on the remedy selected. Damages may be based on the difference between resale price and contract price, or the difference between market price and contract price, or on lost profits. Incidental damages are also recoverable.

- When a seller breaches, the buyer may pursue one or more of the following remedies: (1) rejection or revocation of acceptance; (2) resale; (3) cover (procurement of substitute goods); (4) recovery of damages; (5) specific performance or replevin; or (6) cancellation of the contract. The buyer may also recover any part of the purchase price that has been paid.

- The measure of damages recoverable by a buyer depends on the remedy selected. Damages may be based on the difference between the cost of cover and the contract price, the difference between the value of accepted nonconforming goods and the value of conforming goods, or on some other reasonable basis. Incidental damages are also recoverable, as are consequential damages that could not have been prevented.

- Acceptance
- Anticipatory Repudiation
- Commercial Unit
- Conforming Goods
- Cover
- Cure

- Incidental or Consequential Damages
- Inspection
- Installment Contract
- Perfect Tender
- Specific Performance or Replevin
- Tender of Delivery

Questions and Case Problems

1. Barrett orders carpeting from Venture on the following discount terms: five percent off the price of the order if paid within 60 days; four percent off if paid within 90 days. Venture ships carpeting that conforms to the order, but Venture's invoice sets out different discount terms: five percent off if paid within 60 days; no discount if paid within 90 days. Barrett objects and requests that Venture correct the nonconforming terms. When Venture refuses, Barrett rejects the carpeting. Barrett keeps the carpeting in its warehouse, where it is destroyed by fire three months later. Was there a contract? If so, was Barrett's rejection justified? On whom should the risk of loss fall?

2. Discuss the perfect tender rule and its applicability to performance of sales contracts.

3. In 1967 Chapman, a plumbing contractor, purchased four kitchen units from Cervitor for installation in a university dormitory. The kitchen units were delivered in shipping crates on May 4, 1967. As was the custom in the construction industry, the units were stored on the job site until the time for installation. On August 5,

1967, Chapman removed the units from the crates and installed them. The university's engineer inspected the units, noted several readily observable defects, and notified Chapman of his disapproval. Chapman then notified Cervitor that he was rejecting the units. Chapman reshipped the units to Cervitor, who refused to accept them. They were ultimately sold for storage charges. Cervitor sued Chapman for the purchase price. Who should win the case?

4. Moss contracts to supply plumbing equipment to Devine for use in a building Devine is constructing. The contract requires payment to be made within 15 days of each delivery. Devine's payments are frequently late, and his indebtedness to Moss gradually increases to $25,000. Moss writes Devine a letter stating that further deliveries will be made only if: (1) the past due amount is paid in full and (2) Devine deposits sufficient cash ($50,000) in escrow to guarantee payment for supplies yet to be delivered. Devine immediately sends Moss a check for $25,000, and informs Moss that he will not put $50,000 in escrow, but will make future payments on time. Moss refuses to make further deliveries, and Devine sues for breach of contract. What is the result?

5. In January, Reed contracted to purchase 1,000 hula hoops from Barry at a price of $3,000. Delivery was scheduled for June. In March, the bottom fell out of the hula hoop market, and Reed notified Barry that he was repudiating the contract. At that time Barry had spent $750 on production of the hoops, which were unfinished. Their salvage value was $500. In the hope that the hula hoop market would revive, Barry finished manufacturing the hoops, at an additional cost of $750. In May, the hula hoop market was still sinking, and Barry resold the order to another purchaser for $250. Barry then sued Reed for breach of contract. What damages should Barry recover?

6. Discuss the relationship between assurance of performance and anticipatory repudiation.

7. McCoy contracts to buy ball bearings from Kemp. Delivery is to be made in nine equal shipments over a three-month period. The contract specifies that a delivery is satisfactory if no more than five percent of the ball bearings are defective. When the first shipment arrives, McCoy finds that eight percent of the ball bearings are defective, and he so notifies Kemp. Kemp offers to cure the nonconforming delivery by granting McCoy a five percent price reduction, but McCoy refuses. McCoy tells Kemp that "you are obviously unable to meet our specifications" and cancels the contract immediately. Kemp sues McCoy for breach of contract. How should the case be decided? What if a defective rate greater than five percent seriously impaired McCoy's ability to meet his contractual obligations to others? What, if anything, should McCoy have done differently?

8. Pasquale wants to purchase an airplane from L & H International, an aircraft dealer. L & H informs Pasquale that its credit situation requires a quick sale and therefore it is willing to sell the plane for $75,000, with $10,000 down. Pasquale agrees, a contract is signed, and a down payment is made by check. The contract states that if the buyer breaches, the seller may keep the down payment as liquidated damages. Pasquale reneges on the contract and stops payment on its $10,000 check. Within a month, L & H sells the airplane to someone else for $89,000. L & H then sues Pasquale for the $10,000. What is the outcome of the case?

9. What is the primary remedy available to a seller in the event of a buyer's breach? To a buyer in the event of a seller's breach? Describe the requirements that must be met by the seller and buyer in pursuing these remedies.

10. Taylor buys a used heater. He becomes dissatisfied with the way it works and tells the seller so. He continues to use it for a while. Still dissatisfied, he decides to disconnect it and set it aside in a safe place. He also stops making payments. When the seller sues for the balance, Taylor claims he had never fully accepted the goods. Should his claim be upheld?

PART FIVE

Commercial Paper

Introductory Comments

Commercial paper is the lifeblood of business: promissory notes, checks, drafts and other kinds of negotiable instruments are indispensable to commercial transactions. Virtually everyone uses commercial paper countless times during the course of a lifetime. For example, a person who signs a check or a promissory note is using commercial paper. Indeed, most people use commercial paper without being aware of what the term means.

This can even be said of businesspersons. Commercial paper, and particularly negotiable commercial paper, is of tremendous significance to businesspersons. The proper use of commercial paper can be extremely advantageous, while improper or careless use can have disastrous consequences. Yet, many businesspersons really know very little about the legal aspects of commercial paper.

The material in Chapters 23 through 26 pro-

vides the information necessary to make intelligent use of commercial paper. These chapters discuss the various types of commercial paper, the concept and the requirements of negotiability, the actual negotiation of commercial paper, the concept and rights of a holder in due course, and the liability of the various parties to commercial paper. The specific rights and liabilities arising out of the bank–customer relationship are also discussed.

An important point to make about negotiable instruments is that they should be treated with the same care as cash. Businesspersons do not leave money lying around the office; they take precautions in handling money. All too often, however, similar care is not taken with respect to negotiable instruments. Negotiable instruments are easily transferred and are in many respects the functional equivalent of cash. A businessperson should therefore adopt procedures designed to ensure that negotiable instruments are safeguarded in the same manner as cash.

Although commercial paper is treated as a distinct subject in these chapters, it is clear that commercial paper is not used in a vacuum. Checks, promissory notes, and other forms of commercial paper are used in connection with numerous types of transactions discussed in the other parts of this book. For example, commercial paper may be issued in connection with a contract, the sale of goods, the sale of real property, or the extension of credit. In such situations, a person must have knowledge not only of the law that governs the underlying transaction, but also of the law that governs the use of commercial paper. An understanding of commercial paper, therefore, will enhance understanding of other aspects of business law.

23 Negotiable Instruments

23:1 Introduction

Commercial paper is the term used to describe the various types of paper that represent cash value in commercial transactions. Commercial paper is used for two purposes: as a substitute for money and as a means of obtaining credit. For example, when a person makes a purchase and pays for it by *check*, he has used commercial paper—the check—for one of its two purposes: as a substitute for money. When a person makes a purchase and executes a *promissory note* in lieu of immediate payment, he has used commercial paper—the promissory note—for the second purpose: as a means of obtaining credit. Using commercial paper is extremely important to the conduct of business because major transactions may be consummated without the danger and inconvenience involved in using large sums of cash.

Commercial paper is not a recent innovation. Indeed, it has been used for centuries. The law merchant, which was the medieval body of law governing business dealings, included rules governing the issuance of commercial paper.[1] These rules eventually became part of English common law, and today they are codified as Article 3 of the UCC. The UCC has changed the prior law in some respects; it has been said, however, that it has made no radical changes in the law of commercial paper as that law has developed over the centuries. Thus, many of the rules embodied in Article 3 can be traced to the law merchant, and the principles of the law merchant may still be applied except where they are inconsistent with the UCC (UCC § 1-103).

However, it is likely that the law of commercial paper will change over the next few decades. As the electronic age progresses, there is a possibility that tangible commercial paper will disappear. It costs money to process and store commercial paper. One way to eliminate tangible paper is to transfer funds electronically (see Chapter 26). Undoubtedly, rules of commercial paper will be adapted to meet the problems posed by electronic commercial paper.

---

[1]The law merchant is discussed in Chapter 19.

23:2 Types of Commercial Paper

Commercial paper includes (1) orders to pay money and (2) promises to pay money. Under the UCC, an order to pay money may be classified as either a *draft* or a check, and a promise to pay money may be classified as either a note or a *certificate of deposit* [UCC § 3-104(2)].

Drafts A draft, also known as a bill of exchange, is a written order by one person (the *drawer*) directing another person (the *drawee*) to pay money to a third person (the *payee*). A typical draft is illustrated in Figure 23-1. Here, the drawer is Jane Rowe, the drawee is John Doe, and the payee is Crocker Bank.

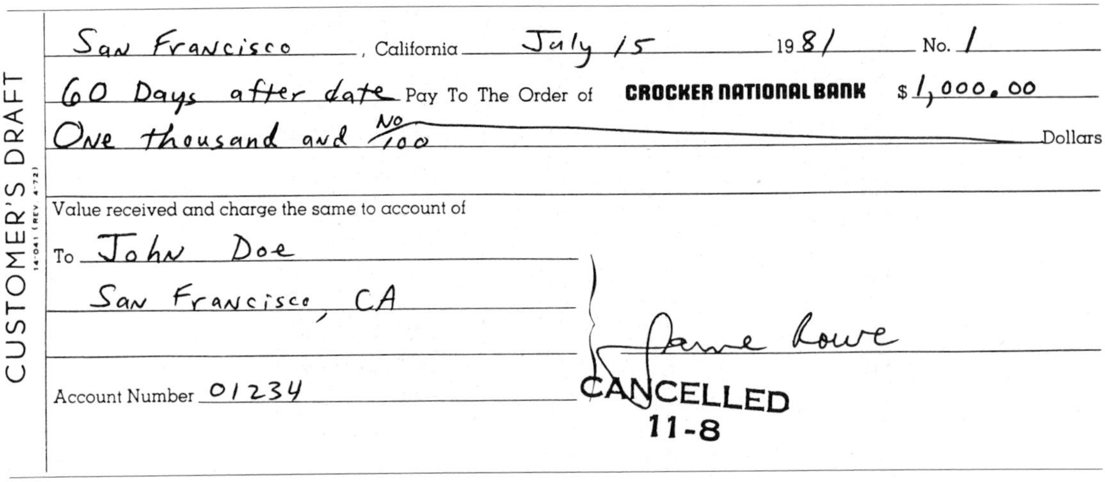
CUSTOMER'S DRAFT
14-041 (REV 4-72)

San Francisco, California July 15 1981 No. 1

60 Days after date Pay To The Order of CROCKER NATIONAL BANK $1,000.00

One thousand and No/100 Dollars

Value received and charge the same to account of

To John Doe

San Francisco, CA

Jane Rowe

Account Number 01234

CANCELLED
11-8

Figure 23-1*

Obviously, there must be some relationship between the drawer and the drawee, or the drawee would simply ignore the order. Often the drawee has funds belonging to the drawer, and the draft is used as a means of transferring those funds to the payee. In this regard, banks may be the greatest users of drafts, and they sell them to persons who want to transmit funds. If a person residing in one city wishes to make a payment in another city, he may do so by means of a bank draft. In exchange for his payment of money, the bank in the city of residence (the drawer bank) draws a draft on a bank in the city of payment (the drawee bank) directing that funds be paid to a specific party (the payee).

Another frequently used draft is the *trade acceptance.* It is used in connection with a sale of goods. A trade acceptance is a draft that enables the seller to extend credit to a buyer and yet receive immediate payment. In a trade acceptance, the seller draws a draft directing the buyer to pay the seller at some future time. The buyer then accepts the draft by signing it, thereby obligating himself to make the payment ordered. The seller then turns the trade acceptance into cash by negotiating it to a third party at a discount. Negotiation is discussed later in this chapter.

*The documents reproduced in Figures 23-1 through 23-4 were supplied through the courtesy of Crocker National Bank, San Francisco, California.

The drawee is not obligated to honor a draft until he accepts it by signing it. Once he has done so, the drawee is known as the *acceptor*.

Checks A check is a specific form of draft. Its distinctive characteristics are that (1) it is always drawn on a bank and (2) it is always payable on demand. Checks are widely used and are of enormous importance. An example of a check is shown in Figure 23-2.

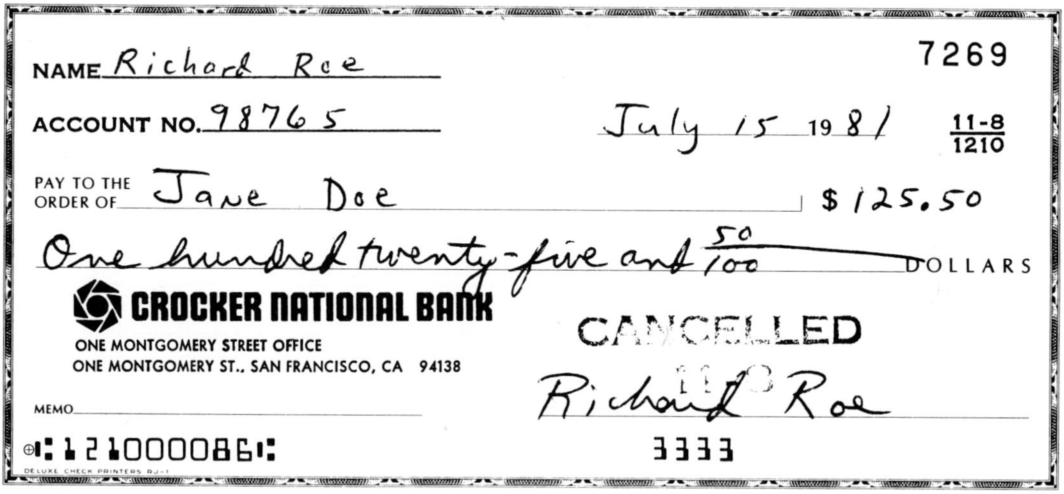

NAME Richard Roe 7269

ACCOUNT NO. 98765 July 15 1981 11-8/1210

PAY TO THE ORDER OF Jane Doe $ 125.50

One hundred twenty-five and 50/100 DOLLARS

CROCKER NATIONAL BANK

ONE MONTGOMERY STREET OFFICE

ONE MONTGOMERY ST., SAN FRANCISCO, CA 94138

CANCELLED

MEMO Richard Roe

⑆121000086⑆ 3333

DELUXE CHECK PRINTERS RJ-1

Figure 23-2

The various types of checks, and the duties of banks with respect to checks, are covered in detail in Chapter 26.

Notes A note, known also as a promissory note, is an unconditional promise by one party (the *maker*) to pay money to a second party (the payee). The basic distinction between a note and a draft is that in a note the maker promises to make payment himself, while in a draft the drawer orders another person—the drawee—to make payment. Thus, a note involves only two parties, the maker and the payee, while a draft involves three parties, the drawer, the drawee, and the payee. Promissory notes are used primarily in conjunction with credit transactions. Often the note is secured by some property of the maker. For example, the sale of real property may involve a real estate mortgage note secured by a mortgage on the property; the installment sale of personal property may involve an installment note secured by the property sold; and other transactions may involve collateral notes secured by the maker's personal property. A simple note is illustrated in Figure 23-3.

Certificates of Deposit A certificate of deposit is a specific type of note. It is an acknowledgement by a bank of the receipt of money, with the bank's promise to repay the money. Figure 23-4 is an example of a certificate of deposit.

LOAN NO. _1_ | _R.R._ INITIALS | | _1/15/82_ MATURITY DATE |

NOTE—SINGLE PAYMENT—INTEREST PAYABLE SEPARATELY

$2,500.00 _____ _San Francisco_ ,California, _July 15_ , 198_1_

_Six months a~~fter~~ CANCELLED _____ after date

for value received, the undersigned _Jane Doe 11-8_ _____ promise(s) to pay to **CROCKER NATIONAL BANK**,

or order, at its _Main_ _____ Office in _San Francisco_ , California, in lawful money

of the United States of America, the principal sum of

Two thousand five hundred and $\overset{XX}{/}$ _00_ _____Dollars,

plus interest, payable _monthly_ _____ , on the unpaid balance of said principal sum at the rate equal to 1/ _20_ th of _one_ percent

per day from date hereof until paid. /

Upon default in payment of any interest hereon when due, the whole of said principal sum then remaining unpaid and all interest accrued hereon, at the option of the holder hereof, shall become immediately due and payable without demand or notice. Should any payment hereof not be made when due, the undersigned further promises to pay all costs of collection and a reasonable attorney's fee. If the undersigned is more than one, their covenants and obligations hereunder are joint and several and each hereby waives demand, diligence, presentment, protest and notice of every kind.

0 Main Street ADDRESS   _Jane Doe_ _____

San Francisco CA STATE _94000_ ZIP CODE _____

_111-1112_ TELEPHONE _____   **CANCELLED** _____

.11-8

50-9208 (REV. 10-77)

Figure 23-3

Parties to Commercial Paper In discussing the four types of commercial paper reference has already been made to the essential parties—the drawer, drawee, maker, and payee. A person cannot understand the law of commercial paper without understanding the positions occupied by these parties. Special attention to the distinguishing characteristics of these parties is therefore warranted at this point, and definitions of these original parties to commercial paper follow. It should also be noted at this point that other parties may become involved in commercial paper, and these parties will be discussed at the appropriate places in the text.

Drawer: The person who creates a draft or a check by issuing a written order directing another person to pay money to a third person.

Drawee: The person upon whom a draft or check is drawn and who is directed by the draft or check to make payment.

Maker: The person who creates a note or a certificate of deposit by making a promise to pay money to another party.

Payee: The person to whom a commercial instrument directs the payment of money.

Negotiable and Nonnegotiable Commercial Paper The terms "commercial paper" and "negotiable instruments" often are used interchangeably. It is important to note, however, that commercial paper can be nonnegotiable. Article 3 of the

| FIXED TIME CERTIFICATE OF DEPOSIT | Nᵒ 10216803 |

Main Office   San Francisco , California   July 15 ,19 81
Issued At (Office Name)   City   Date

This certifies that there has been deposited in this bank the sum of

Five thousand and no~~CANCELLED~~   Dollars $ 5,000.00

payable to Jane Roe 11-8 , depositor

or order, at maturity on July 15 , 19 83 , upon presentation and surrender of this certificate, properly endorsed, at the office named above.

This deposit earns simple interest at the rate of 14 % per annum, payable (select one) [ ] Monthly, [X] Quarterly, [ ] Semi-Annually, or [ ] at Maturity, and computed for the actual number of days in each interest payment period on a 360-day year basis. This deposit earns no interest after maturity. If this certificate is transferred, both parties to the transfer must notify in writing the branch office listed above. This Fixed Time Certificate of Deposit is subject to all present and future applicable laws and regulations.

CROCKER NATIONAL BANK

NO INTEREST PAID AFTER MATURITY DATE

CANCELLED 11-8   John Doe
AUTHORIZED SIGNATURE

Read the rules on the back of this Certificate. They contain important information on your deposit.

02-6013 (Rev. 02-81) Type 41

Figure 23-4

UCC applies to negotiable commercial paper. As a result, negotiable commercial paper is easily transferable, and holders in due course of such paper acquire certain special rights (see Chapter 24). Article 3 generally does *not* apply to nonnegotiable commercial paper; rather, such paper is treated as only a contract and is governed by the rules of contract law. As a result, nonnegotiable commercial paper is not easily transferred, and the holder in due course rules are not applicable. The utility of commercial paper lies in its ability to be transferred. Therefore, to serve as a substitute for money and a credit device, commercial paper must be negotiable. The rest of this chapter and the next three chapters will focus on negotiable instruments.

An instrument may create rights and obligations even though it is not negotiable. Also, the rights of the parties to a negotiable instrument may be affected by a separate agreement between them (UCC § 3-119). (Such an agreement does not affect the rights of persons with no notice of it.) The resolution of a dispute as to the negotiability of an instrument does not necessarily have any bearing on the resolution of a dispute as to the rights of the parties under a separate agreement. In other words, a party may be unable to recover on an instrument while still recovering on the contract that gave rise to the instrument.

23:3   Requirements of Negotiability

The negotiability of commercial paper depends on its form. The instrument itself must contain all the essential elements of negotiability. Compliance with the statutory requirements is mandatory, and the parties may not alter these requirements by agreement. To be negotiable, an instrument must (1) be in writing and signed by the maker or drawer, (2) contain an unconditional promise or order to pay a *sum certain* in money, (3) be payable on demand or at a definite time, and (4) be payable to order or to bearer [UCC § 3-104(1)].

The requirements of negotiability will now be considered in detail.

In Writing and Signed   A negotiable instrument must be in writing and signed. The term "writing" includes printing, typewriting, or any other intentional reduction to tangible form [UCC § 1-201(46)]. Note, for example, that the negotiable instruments in Figures 23-1 through 23-4 contain both printed and handwritten matter. The requirement of a signature may be met in various ways. The signature may be handwritten, typed, printed, or made in some other manner. A person may sign his own name, use a trade or assumed name, or even use a symbol or mark, provided that he does so with the intention of authenticating the writing [UCC §§ 1-201(39), 3-401]. A signature may also be made by an agent or other duly authorized representative [UCC § 3-403(1)].[2]

Unconditional Promise or Order to Pay (UCC § 3-105)   To be negotiable, an instrument must also contain an unconditional promise or order to pay. A promise must be a definite undertaking to pay; mere acknowledgment of a debt does not constitute a promise. For example, an I.O.U. is not a promise. An order is a direction to pay. A simple authorization or request does not constitute an order. Nor do words such as "I wish you would pay." However, words of courtesy, such as "please," do not reduce an order to a simple request. Figures 23-3 and 23-4 are examples of promises to pay, while Figures 23-1 and 23-2 are examples of orders to pay.

The promise or order must be unconditional. That is, the promise or order to pay cannot be made contingent on the happening of some event. To be acceptable as a substitute for money or a credit device, a draft or promissory note must contain a definite and clear obligation to pay. A person must be able to tell from the instrument itself what obligations and rights it creates.

When an instrument is issued in conjunction with some other transaction, as when a promissory note is given as payment for a purchase, the instrument must not state that it is being issued on some condition related to the transaction. In the case of the promissory note given for payment, the note may refer to the sales agreement, but it may not state that it is subject to or governed by the underlying agreement. Such a statement would constitute a condition and render the note nonnegotiable.

Similarly, when a note or draft is drawn on an account that is maintained for a specific purpose, it is permissible to refer to the particular account to be debited, provided the reference does not amount to a condition. For example, the note or draft cannot state that it is to be paid only out of the particular fund. This statement is conditional, since the obligation to pay depends on the continued existence of the fund. The UCC makes an exception with respect to instruments issued by government entities. They are permitted to limit payment of an instrument out of a particular fund without destroying the instrument's negotiability.

 All these rules may appear highly technical, but their purpose is simple: The instrument itself must contain an unconditional obligation to make payment. With that in mind, a person drafting the instrument should ask himself two

---

questions: (1) Is the obligation to pay absolute? (2) Can the obligation to pay be determined from the instrument itself, or must some other document be consulted? If the answer to either question is "no," the instrument is not negotiable. Any reference to the underlying transaction or to the fund out of which the instrument is to be paid must be phrased in such a way that it will not affect the unconditional nature of the obligation contained in the instrument.

Sum Certain in Money (UCC §§ 3-106, 3-107)   This requirement of negotiability can be explained by defining "sum certain" and "money." "Sum certain" refers to the amount to be paid and must be an amount that can be mathematically computed from the instrument itself. The amount may vary depending on the time of payment and still be considered to be certain. An example of this is the payment of interest at a stated rate. The instrument may provide for different rates of interest before and after default, or it may provide for a stated discount or addition depending on the time payment is made, and still be negotiable. However, an instrument that called for interest payable "at the current rate" would be nonnegotiable, since the amount to be paid could not be determined from the instrument itself. The note in Figure 23-3 and the certificate of deposit in Figure 23-4 both provide for payment of interest at a stated rate.

There is one exception to the requirement that the sum certain be computable from the instrument itself. This exception is payment of costs of collection or an attorney's fee on default. The basic obligation (the principal and interest) must still be computable from the instrument, but the collection costs and attorney's fee may be determined from other sources. The note in Figure 23-3 contains a provision for payment of collection costs and attorney's fees in the event of default.

The UCC provides that "money" means a medium of exchange authorized or adopted by a domestic or foreign government as part of its currency [UCC § 1-201(24)]. Thus, an instrument that states the sum to be paid in a foreign currency is negotiable. Such an instrument may be paid either in the foreign currency or in dollars measured by the foreign currency, unless the instrument specifies that payment is to be made in the foreign currency.

Payable on Demand or at Definite Time (UCC §§ 3-108, 3-109)   The requirement that a negotiable instrument be payable on demand or at a definite time is a clear-cut requirement. Instruments payable on demand, commonly known as *demand instruments* or sight instruments, contain a provision that the instrument is payable on demand, payable at sight, or payable on presentation. (Instruments that contain no time for payment are also payable on demand.) Instruments that provide for payment at a definite time—known as *time instruments*—provide for payment on or before a stated date, at a fixed period after a stated date, or at a fixed period after sight. The instruments in Figures 23-1, 23-3, and 23-4 are time instruments; the check in Figure 23-2 is a demand instrument.

Under the UCC, an instrument that contains an acceleration clause meets the definite time requirement and is negotiable. An acceleration clause typically provides that on the happening of a certain event, such as the obligor's default, the obligation is immediately payable. The note in Figure 23-3 contains an acceleration clause. In some instances an instrument that contains an extension clause is also negotiable. An extension clause typically provides that on the occurrence of some event the time for payment is extended. To meet the definite time requirement, the extension clause must be exercisable only by the holder. An instrument that contains an extension clause exercisable by the maker or acceptor does not meet the definite time requirement unless the extension includes a definite time limit. Otherwise, the maker or acceptor would have the right to extend the time for payment indefinitely, making the instrument not payable at a definite time and thus nonnegotiable.

If an instrument is payable only on the happening of an act or event uncertain as to time of occurrence, it clearly does not meet the definite time requirement and is nonnegotiable.

Payable to Order or to Bearer (UCC §§ 3-110, 3-111)   To be negotiable, commercial paper must contain words that indicate that the original payee may transfer the paper to third parties. Such words are commonly called words of negotiability. Under the UCC, the words "order" and "bearer" are used to denote negotiability. Thus, to be negotiable, an instrument must be made payable to order or to bearer.

An instrument is payable to order if it is payable to the order of a specific person, to the order or assigns of a specific person, to a specific person or his order, or to the order of an unnamed person who is specified in the instrument with reasonable certainty. An example of this last condition is a draft payable to the order of "the mayor" of a particular city; the person is unnamed, but the person's identity is reasonably certain. The instruments in Figures 23-1 through 23-4 are all payable to order.

The term "bearer" means the person in possession of an instrument [UCC § 1-201(5)]. An instrument is payable to bearer if by its terms it is payable to bearer, to the order of bearer, to a specified person or bearer, to cash, or to the order of cash. An instrument is also payable to bearer when it uses any other words that do not purport to designate a specific payee.

On occasion an instrument is made payable "to order or to bearer." Under the UCC, such an instrument is payable to order, unless the bearer words are handwritten or typewritten. The presumption is that if the bearer words are printed, the maker or drawer of the instrument merely forgot to delete them when he inserted the name of the specific payee.

 The words "order" and "bearer" have clearly defined meanings and are intended to indicate that commercial paper is negotiable. An *order instrument* provides more protection than a *bearer instrument*, because the latter can be transferred from one person to another without *indorsement*. Since the rules are so clear in this regard, there is really no excuse for a mistake. Unless there is some compelling reason for not doing so, a drafter of commercial paper that is intended to be negotiable should always use the word "order" or the word "bearer."

The following case illustrates the basic requirement that the negotiability of an instrument must appear on the face of the instrument itself. The case is also noteworthy for its discussion of the reasons underlying this rule. In addition, the case exemplifies a situation in which the obligor successfully argued that the instrument was not negotiable, but still lost the case.

First State Bank
v
Clark
91 NM 117, 570 P2d 1144, 22 UCCRS 1186
(New Mexico Supreme Court, 1977)

[M.S. Horne executed a $100,000 promissory note payable to R.C. Clark. The note provided that it could not be transferred, pledged, or assigned without Horne's written consent. At the same time Horne gave Clark a letter authorizing Clark to pledge the note as collateral for a $50,000 loan that Clark intended to obtain from First State Bank. Clark obtained the loan and pledged the note, which was accompanied by Horne's letter of authorization. First State called Horne to verify his agreement to use of the note as collateral. When First State attempted to collect on the note from Horne, Horne refused to pay, and First State sued him. The trial court granted summary judgment for First State, and Horne appealed.]

Easley, Justice.

*   *   *

The issues raised on appeal include (1) whether the note was a negotiable instrument for purposes of Article 3 of the Uniform Commercial Code (U.C.C.) . . . ; (3) whether, if Article 3 does not apply to the instrument, the note was nevertheless negotiable as between the parties under ordinary contract principles; and (4) whether, under ordinary contract law, Horne is estopped to deny the note's validity. . . .

Article 3 of the U.C.C. defines a certain type of readily transferable instrument and lays down certain rules for the treatment of that instrument and rules concerning the rights, remedies and defenses of persons dealing with it.

In order to be a "negotiable instrument" for Article 3 purposes the paper must precisely meet the definition set out in § 3-104, since § 3-104 itself states that, to be a negotiable instrument, a writing "must" meet the definition therein set out. Moreover, it is clear that in order to determine whether an instrument meets that definition *only the instrument itself* may be looked to, *not* other documents, even when other documents are referred to in the instrument. [Court's emphasis.] . . .

Section 3-104 thus requires that, in order to be a negotiable instrument for Article 3 purposes, one must be able to ascertain without reference to other documents that the instrument:

> (a) [is] signed by the maker or drawer; and (b) contain[s] an unconditional promise or order to pay a sum certain in money and no other promise, order, obligation or power given by the maker or drawer except as authorized by [Article 3]; and (c) [is] payable on demand or at a definite time; and (d) [is] payable to order or to bearer.

The note in question here failed to meet the requirements of § 3-104, since the promise to pay contained in the note was not unconditional. Moreover, the note was expressly drafted to be non-negotiable since it stated:

> This note may not be transferred, pledged, or otherwise assigned without the written consent of M.S. Horne.

These words, even though they appeared on the back of the note, effectively cancelled any implication of negotiability provided by the words "Pay to the order of" on the face of the note. Notations and terms on the back of a note, made contemporaneously with the execution of the note and intended to be part of the note's contract of payment, constitute as much a part of the note as if they were incorporated on its face. . . .

Counsel argue that § 3-119 applies and allows incorporating other documents to remove the defects on the face of the instrument. They argue that Horne's separate letter to Clark authorizing the pledging of the note to First State removed the conditions in the note and the express prohibition therein against its negotiability and rendered the note negotiable for Article 3 purposes. This is incorrect. An instrument which in and of itself does not meet the requirements of § 3-104 cannot be made negotiable for Article 3 purposes by reference to another document which purports to cure the defects in the note's negotiability. . . .

Section 3-119 and the Official Comments thereto go only to clarifying what the effect is of referring to other documents which may affect negotiability where such reference is on the face of *an otherwise negotiable instrument.* [Court's emphasis.] See U.C.C. § 3-119, Official Comment, Purposes. Neither § 3-119 nor any other U.C.C. section applies to allow the use of other documents to correct defects in otherwise *non-negotiable* instruments. [Court's emphasis.]

The whole purpose of the concept of a negotiable instrument under Article 3 is to declare that transferees in the ordinary course of business are only to be held liable for information appearing in the instrument itself and will not be expected to know of any limitations on negotiability or changes in terms, etc., contained in any separate documents. The whole idea of the facilitation of easy transfer of notes and instruments requires that a transferee be able to trust what the instrument says, and be able to determine the validity of the note and its negotiability from the language in the note itself. . . . Section 3-119 in no way implies or states, and neither do any comments

thereunder, that an instrument non-negotiable on its face can be cured by reference to a document removing the defect which renders the instrument non-negotiable. . . .

Even though a note or instrument is not a "negotiable instrument" for Article 3 purposes, it may nevertheless be negotiable between the parties involved under ordinary contract law. . . . The Official Comments to § 3-119 which counsel have cited recognize this principle. E.G., U.C.C. § 3-119, Official Comment 3. The comments assert that even where an instrument *is* negotiable for Article 3 purposes the parties in any transaction are always bound by the totality of documents which are intended to form a contract between them, not just the terms set forth in one which happens to be a negotiable instrument. The same is true when the instrument does not meet Article 3 requirements. . . .

As between Clark and Horne, Clark had a contract right to pledge Horne's note to Clark as security. Clark had a contract right to negotiate the note. Thus the note was negotiable for Clark's limited purposes even though it was not an Article 3 negotiable instrument. Before accepting Clark's pledge, First State verified by direct conversation with Horne that Clark had Horne's authority to pledge the note as the letter permitted. Horne in no way suggested that he had any offsetting defense to the validity of the note. . . .

U.C.C. § 3-104, Official Comment 2 states in part:

> While a writing cannot be made a negotiable instrument within this Article by contract or by conduct, nothing in this section is intended to mean that in a particular case a court may not arrive at a result similar to that of negotiability by finding that the obligor is estopped by his conduct from asserting a defense against a bona fide purchaser. Such an estoppel rests upon ordinary principles of the law of simple contract.

We have long recognized the possibility of estoppel in appropriate cases. . . . These cases clarify that equitable estoppel results from a course of conduct which precludes one from asserting rights he otherwise might assert against one who has in good faith relied upon such conduct to his detriment.

In the instant case the evidence clearly indicates that First State relied on the validity of Horne's note to Clark as a pledge to secure Clark's obligation to First State.... Horne knew he had an offsetting note from Clark which would in effect invalidate or cancel his obligation under the pledged note, but he failed to tell First State the true state of affairs.

First State relied in good faith on Horne's conduct—his failure to reveal material facts—to First State's detriment. As a matter of law Horne cannot assert any defenses he has against First State arising from the material facts he failed to reveal.... [Since] there is no genuine issue as to any material fact regarding the genuineness of Horne's note and letter, summary judgment for First State against Horne was proper....

[Judgment affirmed.]

23:4 Effect on Negotiability of Omissions or Additional Terms; Ambiguities in Instrument

A note or draft is negotiable if it contains all the basic elements discussed in the preceding section. The omission of customary but nonessential matters does not effect its negotiability. For example, commercial paper often includes statements indicating where it was drafted and where it is payable, but the omission of such statements does not affect negotiability [UCC § 3-112(1)(a)].

The omission of the date generally does not affect negotiability. An undated instrument is not negotiable only when it is payable at a fixed period "after date," since it is neither payable on demand nor at a definite time. It can be made negotiable by insertion of the date (UCC § 3-115). Antedated or postdated instruments are also usually negotiable. The time when an antedated or postdated instrument is payable is determined by the stated date if the instrument is payable either on demand or at a fixed period "after date" (UCC § 3-114).

An instrument is obviously incomplete if it fails to state the name of the payee or the amount to be paid. If an instrument is otherwise complete, and if there are blank spaces for the insertion of such omitted items, it may be completed by a person with proper authority. Once completed, the instrument is then negotiable (UCC § 3-115). For example, a signed but otherwise blank check may be filled in by any person authorized to do so.

 The danger involved in signing a blank check cannot be overstated. The possibility always exists that the person to whom the check is given will insert an unauthorized amount and then promptly cash the check. Of course, the drawer (signer) of the check can always assert that he did not authorize the person to complete the check. The drawer may not, however, assert such lack of authorization against subsequent holders in due course (see 24:2 for definition of holder in due course). In other words, a holder in due course may enforce the check as completed [UCC § 3-407(3)]. While the drawer may seek recourse against the person who inserted the figure, that person often will be unable to repay the money.

Additional Terms in Instrument   An instrument, to be negotiable, generally may not contain any promise or order other than the promise or order to pay money [UCC § 3-104(1)(b)]. There are certain limited exceptions to this prohibition, however. The more important exceptions are: (1) a negotiable instrument can contain a provision granting the holder of the instrument the power to sell the collateral securing the obligation in the event of default; (2) a negotiable instrument may include a promise or power to maintain or protect the collateral or to give additional collateral under specified circumstances; and (3) a draft may include a provision stating that the payee's indorsement or cashing of the instrument acknowledges full satisfaction of the drawer's obligation [UCC § 3-112(1)].

Ambiguities in Instrument (UCC § 3-118)   The UCC provides specific rules for the resolution of certain ambiguities. Among the more important rules are the following: (1) when there is doubt whether an instrument is a draft or a note, the holder may treat it as either one; (2) in the event of a conflict, handwritten terms control typewritten and printed ones, and typewritten terms control printed ones; and (3) unambiguous words control figures, and figures control ambiguous words.

23:5   Methods of Transferring Commercial Paper

There are two basic methods of transferring commercial paper: (1) *negotiation*, which ordinarily involves indorsement, and (2) assignment. By its very nature a nonnegotiable instrument cannot be negotiated, but it may be assigned. Negotiable instruments can be transferred by either method.

The usual method of transferring negotiable instruments is by negotiation. This involves delivery of the instrument to the transferee, who is the person to whom the instrument is being transferred. The instrument is now negotiated, and the transferee becomes a holder and may qualify for the rights accorded a holder in due course. In this way, the transferee can actually acquire greater rights in the instrument than the transferor had.

A negotiable instrument may also be transferred by assignment. In an assignment, the transferee acquires only those rights that the transferor had. As discussed in Chapter 17, this means that any defenses that could have been asserted against the transferor may also be asserted against the transferee. Although the subject of defenses to negotiable instruments is covered in Chapter 24, an example now may help to illustrate the significance of the distinction between negotiation and assignment.

EXAMPLE
Barnes contracts to purchase a typewriter from McCoy and gives McCoy a promissory note as payment. McCoy never delivers the typewriter. If McCoy were to sue Barnes for payment of the promissory note, Barnes would have a good defense. If McCoy assigned the promissory note to a third party, who then sued Barnes, Barnes would still have a good defense. But if McCoy negotiated the promissory

note to a holder in due course, who then sued Barnes for payment, Barnes would *not* have a good defense against that person.

Negotiation is obviously the preferable way to transfer a negotiable instrument. It will now be examined more closely.

23:6   Negotiation

Negotiation is the transfer of an instrument in such form that the transferee qualifies as a *holder*. The term "holder" is a technical one in the law of negotiable instruments. Under the UCC, a holder is a person who is in possession of an instrument drawn, issued, or indorsed to him, to his order, to bearer, or in blank [UCC § 1-201(20)]. An instrument payable to order is negotiated by delivery of the instrument with any necessary indorsement, which is the transferor's signature. An instrument payable to bearer is negotiated simply by delivery of the instrument to a holder; no indorsement is required [UCC § 3-202(1)]. As a practical matter, however, the transferee of a bearer instrument often requires that the transferor indorse it. There are important practical reasons for requiring indorsement of a bearer instrument. First, indorsement is a means of identification of the transferor. Second, indorsement under some circumstances obligates the indorser to pay the instrument if it is subsequently dishonored. (These circumstances are considered at length in Chapter 25.)

To allow an effective negotiation, an indorsement must be written on the instrument itself or on a paper so firmly affixed to the instrument that it becomes a part of the instrument. This paper is called an allonge. The indorsement must also convey the entire instrument. An indorsement that attempts to convey a portion of the instrument operates only as a partial assignment, and the transferee does not become a holder [UCC § 3-202(2), (3)].

Instruments Containing Incorrect Name (UCC § 3-203)   If an instrument is made payable to a person under a misspelled name or under a name other than his own, he may indorse it in the incorrect name, in his own name, or in both names. The preferable procedure is to sign both names, and any person paying or giving value for the instrument may require indorsement in both names.

Multiple Payees (UCC § 3-116)   Checks and other negotiable instruments are often made payable to more than one person. If an instrument is made payable to A *or* B, it can be negotiated by either payee; only one payee's indorsement is necessary. If an instrument is made payable to A *and* B, it can be negotiated by both parties; both payees' indorsements are required. An instrument made payable to A *and/or* B is treated as the equivalent of A *or* B.

Transfer of Order Instrument Without Indorsement   As noted earlier, negotiation of an order instrument normally requires indorsement. An attempted negotiation of an order instrument without indorsement is ineffective, and the transferee does not qualify as a holder. However, if the transferee has given value for the instrument, he has the right, enforceable by an action for specific performance, to have the unqualified indorsement of the transferor [UCC § 3-201(3)].

When a customer has deposited an instrument with a bank but neglected to indorse it, the bank may supply the customer's indorsement. The bank may also place a notation on the instrument that it was deposited by the customer or credited to his account. This notation is effective as the customer's indorsement. However, if the instrument contains words such as "payee's indorsement required," the bank may not supply a missing indorsement [UCC § 4-205(1)].

Rescission of Negotiation (UCC § 3-207)   Negotiation of a negotiable instrument may be rescinded on much the same grounds as those on which a contract generally may be rescinded. Thus, negotiation may be rescinded on the grounds of infancy or other incapacity, fraud, duress, mistake, or illegality. However, a negotiation may not be rescinded if the instrument has subsequently been transferred to a holder in due course. As a practical matter, therefore, the right of rescission is of little real value.

23:7   Types of Indorsements

There are four basic kinds of indorsement: (1) special, (2) blank, (3) restrictive, and (4) qualified. Each type of indorsement has the effect of transferring title to the instrument. Each type also has the effect of creating certain warranties. And, with the exception of qualified indorsements, each type has the effect of guaranteeing payment under certain circumstances.

The choice of indorsement has important consequences. Use of a particular type of indorsement may transform an order instrument into a bearer one, and vice versa. The indorsement may condition the right of the indorsee (person to whom the instrument is negotiated) to receive payment on the instrument. Also, the type of indorsement used always determines the method in which the indorsee may further negotiate the instrument. The various kinds of indorsements will now be considered in detail.

Special Indorsements [UCC § 3-204(1)]   A special indorsement specifies the person to whom or to whose order it makes the instrument payable. For example, "Pay to John Doe," followed by the indorser's signature, is a special indorsement. Further negotiation of the instrument therefore requires the indorsement of the special indorsee. A special indorsement thus has the effect of maintaining the order character of the instrument. If the instrument was originally a bearer instrument, a special indorsement transforms it into an order instrument.

Unlike the instrument itself, indorsements need not have words of negotiability. "Pay to John Doe" has the same effect as "pay to the order of John Doe." In either case, the instrument can be negotiated further only with the indorsement of John Doe.

Blank Indorsements [UCC § 3-204(2), (3)]   A blank indorsement is one that specifies no particular indorsee. A blank indorsement of an order instrument has the effect of transforming it into a bearer instrument. A bearer instrument that is indorsed in blank remains a bearer instrument. The effect in either case is the same: The instrument may thereafter be negotiated by delivery without indorsement by any person who has possession of it. For example, a check made payable to the order of John Doe is an order instrument. If John Doe simply signs his name on the back, his signature is a blank indorsement. The check becomes a bearer instrument; no additional indorsement is needed to negotiate the check again.

 A negotiable instrument with a blank indorsement is as easily transferred as cash. Blank indorsements should therefore be used with extreme caution. When one is making a bank deposit, for example, a check should be indorsed in blank only in the teller's presence. Under no circumstances should a check intended for deposit be indorsed in blank prior to entering the bank, unless the words "for deposit only" are included in the indorsement. For example, if a payee writes a blank indorsement on a check and goes to the bank to deposit it, but the check is blown out of his hand and found by someone else, the finder can then cash the check.

The holder of an instrument may convert a blank indorsement into a special indorsement by writing the name of a new payee over the signature of the indorser in blank. This has the effect of making the instrument an order instrument. For example, if a check payable to Jane Roe is indorsed "Jane Roe" and delivered to John Doe, it has been transformed from an order instrument to a bearer one. John Doe may reconvert it into an order instrument by writing "pay to John Doe" above Jane Roe's signature.

The following case illustrates the effect of a blank indorsement on future negotiation of a promissory note. The court was also presented with an issue as to the completion of an instrument containing blank spaces. Note the court's resolution of this issue.

Westerly Hospital
v
Higgins
106 RI 155, 256 A2d 506, 6 UCCRS 1072
(Rhode Island Supreme Court, 1969)

[In consideration of services rendered in connection with the birth of their child, Clyde Higgins and his wife executed a promissory note payable to the order of Westerly Hospital. The note was for $527.58 and was payable in 18 monthly installments of $29.31. An agent of Westerly Hospital indorsed the note in blank and delivered it to the Industrial National Bank at a discount. The in-dorsement guaranteed payment if the maker defaulted. Higgins defaulted after making three payments. Under the terms of the note, the entire balance became immediately payable on the default. On demand by Industrial, Westerly Hospital paid Industrial the balance due. Industrial then re-delivered the note to Westerly, which sued Higgins for the balance due. The trial court granted summary judgment to the hospital, and Higgins appealed.]

Roberts, Chief Justice.

*   *   *

The defendant contends that the trial justice's ruling granting summary judgment to plaintiff was error because a genuine issue existed as to whether Westerly Hospital or Industrial was in fact the proper party to bring the instant action on the note. We cannot agree with this contention. In our opinion, the face of the instrument discloses as a matter of law that Westerly Hospital is the holder of the note in question and, therefore, a proper party to bring this action. The face of the instrument reveals that Westerly Hospital was the payee of the note made by defendant and his wife as co-makers. It further discloses that an indorsement of guarantee was executed in blank by an authorized representative of plaintiff hospital. The note was then delivered to Industrial. The pertinent provisions of the [UCC] provide that where, as in the instant case, there has been a blank indorsement, mere delivery is sufficient to constitute the transferee a holder thereof and is sufficient to make the transfer a valid negotiation. [UCC §§ 3-202, 3-204.] Thereafter, when defendant defaulted, Industrial delivered the note to plaintiff in return for the payment of the remaining amount of defendant's obligation that had been guaranteed by plaintiff hospital.

The defendant argues that this delivery of the note back to plaintiff was not sufficient to constitute a valid negotiation. He argues that the attempted special indorsement by Industrial to Westerly Hospital was invalid for the lack of the signature of a duly authorized representative of Industrial and thereby Westerly Hospital was precluded from becoming a holder of the instrument. Thus, according to defendant, Industrial was the proper party to bring the action on this note. It seems rather obvious that had the transfer of the note from Westerly Hospital to Industrial been other than in blank, this argument would have merit, it being true that an authorized signature of an agent of Industrial would be necessary to negotiate the instrument.

However, [UCC § 3-204(2)] states, in pertinent part, that "An instrument payable to order and indorsed in blank becomes payable to bearer and may be negotiated by delivery alone until specially indorsed." Here Westerly Hospital as payee of the note caused its indorsement to appear thereon without specifying to whom or to whose order the instrument was payable. Instead, a blank indorsement, one specifying no particular indorsee, was made. The legal effect of such an indorsement and delivery was to authorize Industrial as the transferee and holder of the note to further negotiate the note without indorsement but by mere delivery alone. It is clear that any attempt on its part to achieve negotiation by indorsing the note to plaintiff would have been mere surplusage.

In our opinion, then, the redelivery of the note in question by Industrial to Westerly Hospital accomplished a negotiation of the instrument, and the fact that a purported special indorsement to Westerly Hospital was not legally executed is of no consequence and does not affect plaintiff's status as the holder of the note. . . .

Similarly, defendant's further charge that the instrument which was signed contained blank spaces which were subsequently filled in by plaintiff is not a sufficient defense to a motion for summary judgment on a promissory note. Well-settled authority establishes the rule that one signing an instrument containing blanks is said to have conferred upon the transferee of the instrument the implied authority to complete the instrument in accordance with the understanding of the parties. Once so completed, the instrument will be in force as if it had been completed prior to the signature of the objecting party. . . .

Statutory authority for a similar result is provided for by [UCC § 3-115(1)]. That section states that "When a paper whose contents at the time of signing show that it is intended to become an instrument is signed while still incomplete in any necessary respect it cannot be enforced until completed, but when it is completed in accordance with authority given it is effective as completed." It is our view that since defendant does not allege that plaintiff acted in excess of his implied authority in filling in the blanks on the note in question, plaintiff would be entitled to judgment as a matter of law on the facts stated and, therefore, summary judgment was properly granted.

[Judgment affirmed.]

Restrictive Indorsements (UCC §§ 3-205, 3-206)   A restrictive indorsement is one that in some way limits the purpose of the indorsement. It may limit the use that the indorsee may make of the instrument or it may specify the circumstances under which the indorsee is entitled to payment. The UCC recognizes four different kinds of restrictive indorsements: (1) indorsements "for deposit" or "for collection," (2) conditional indorsements, (3) indorsements for the benefit or use of the indorser or another, and (4) indorsements prohibiting further transfer.

Indorsements "for deposit" or "for collection" are by far the most common restrictive indorsements. "For deposit" indorsements are commonly used when depositing checks in bank accounts. They have the effect of ensuring that the funds from the instrument will be used as directed, that is, credited to the indorser's account. An indorsement "for collection" is similar; it directs the indorsee (usually a bank) to collect on the instrument for the indorser. "Pay any bank" is a form of indorsement used by banks in the collection process and has the same effect as a "for collection" indorsement.

A conditional indorsement is simply an indorsement that conditions the order to pay on the occurrence of some act or event. Conditional indorsements are used in situations in which the indorser negotiates the instrument to the indorsee as payment for some act to be performed by the indorsee. If the indorsee fails to perform that act, then he has no right to recover on the instrument. Recall that the instrument itself may not make the obligation to pay conditional; if it does, the instrument is not negotiable. An indorser, however, may condition the obligation to pay without affecting the instrument's negotiability.

Indorsements for the benefit or use of the indorser or another are commonly known as trust or agency indorsements. As the name implies, these indorsements are used where an instrument is negotiated to one person, but is intended for the use of another person. For example, a check might be indorsed to a guardian for the use of his ward. In a trust indorsement, the transferee must apply the funds as directed by the indorsement. Any subsequent transferees of the instrument need not do so, unless they have knowledge that the original transferee in some way breached the restrictive indorsement.

An indorsement that prohibits further transfer of the instrument really imposes no restriction at all, because the attempted limitation on further negotiation is given no effect. An indorsement "pay to John Doe only" is treated as the equivalent of the indorsement "pay to John Doe."

The various kinds of restrictive indorsements have certain common consequences. First, a restrictive indorsement cannot prevent further negotiation of the instrument. Second, with some exceptions noted later, the indorsee and any subsequent transferee must apply any funds paid for the instrument to the purpose or in accordance with the condition stated in the indorsement. Third, if the indorsee and any subsequent transferees do abide by the terms of the restrictive indorsement, they may qualify as holders or holders in due course of the instrument.

Banks handle negotiable instruments, especially checks, in large numbers, and it is impractical for them to check the effect of all restrictive indorsements. In recognition of that fact, the UCC sets out special rules governing banks' handling of restrictively indorsed instruments. A bank may disregard any restrictive indorsement except that of the bank's immediate transferor. As a practical matter, this means that a "for deposit only" indorsement needs to be honored only by the bank in which the check is deposited. Other banks involved in the process of collecting on the check need not honor the restrictive indorsement.

Qualified Indorsements [UCC § 3-414(1)]   A qualified indorsement is one that contains the words "without recourse." The effect of this indorsement is that the indorser is not liable for payment of the instrument in the event that the party primarily responsible for it defaults. A qualified indorsement is used when the indorser wants to transfer a check to the indorsee, but does not want to guarantee that there are sufficient funds in the drawer's account to pay the check. For example, if an attorney receives a child-support check from one parent to be forwarded to the other parent, who is the attorney's client, the attorney may make a qualified indorsement of the check to the client. If the check is ultimately dishonored by the bank, the client of course may seek recourse against the other parent, but the attorney cannot be held liable on the check.

Key Concepts and Terms

• Commercial paper is paper that represents cash value in commercial transactions. It is used as a substitute for money and as a credit device. Examples of commercial paper are orders to pay money (drafts and checks) and promises to pay money (notes and certificates of deposit). Commercial paper may be either negotiable or nonnegotiable, but only negotiable instruments are easily transferable.

• An order is a direction to pay. A promise is a definite undertaking to pay.

• A draft is a written order by one person (the drawer) directing another person (the drawee) to pay money to a third person (the payee). Bank drafts and trade acceptances are examples of commonly used drafts.

• A check is a specific form of draft. It is always drawn on a bank and is always payable on demand.

• A note, also known as a promissory note, is an unconditional promise by one party (the maker) to pay money to a second party (the payee). Real estate mortgage notes, installment notes, and collateral notes are examples of commonly used notes.

• A certificate of deposit is a specific type of note. It is an acknowledgment by a bank of the receipt of money, with the bank's promise to repay the money.

• To be negotiable, an instrument must (1) be in writing and signed by the maker or drawer, (2) contain an unconditional promise or order to pay a sum certain in money, (3) be payable on demand or at a definite time, and (4) be payable to order or to bearer.

• Omission of customary but nonessential terms does not affect the negotiability of an instrument. Under some circumstances, an incomplete instrument may be completed, after which it becomes negotiable.

• Commercial paper may be transferred by negotiation and by assignment. Negotiation is the usual and preferable method. Negotiation is the transfer of an instrument in such form that the transferee qualifies as a holder. An order instrument is negotiated by delivery of the instrument with any necessary indorsement. A bearer instrument is negotiated by delivery alone.

• An indorsement is the signing over of an instrument. There are four basic kinds of indorsement: (1) special, (2) blank, (3) restrictive, and (4) qualified.

• A special indorsement specifies the person to whom or to whose order it makes the instrument payable. A specially indorsed instrument remains or becomes an order instrument.

• A blank indorsement is one that specifies no particular indorsee. An instrument indorsed in blank remains or becomes a bearer instrument. A blank indorsement may be converted into a special indorsement by writing the name of a new payee over the blank indorsement.

• A restrictive indorsement is one that in some way limits the purpose of the indorsement. There are four different kinds of restrictive indorsements: (1) indorsements "for collection" or "for deposit," (2) conditional indorsements, (3) indorsements for the benefit or use of the indorser or another, and (4) indorsements prohibiting further transfer.

• A qualified indorsement is one that contains the words "without recourse." This indorsement relieves the indorser from any liability for payment of the instrument in the event of default.

- Acceptor
- Bearer Instrument
- Certificate of Deposit
- Check
- Demand (Sight) Instrument
- Draft (Bill of Exchange)
- Drawee
- Drawer
- Holder

- Indorsement
- Maker
- Negotiation
- Note (Promissory Note)
- Order Instrument
- Payee
- Sum Certain
- Time Instrument
- Trade Acceptance

Questions and Case Problems

1. In connection with a divorce proceeding, Kathy and Joel Fox enter a property settlement agreement that calls for Kathy to pay Joel $100,000. Kathy executes an installment note promising to pay Joel "$100,000, at the rate of $5,000 per month, in accordance with the property settlement entered into by the parties, the terms of which settlement are incorporated herein by reference." Joel promptly writes

the following on the back of the note: "I hereby authorize Carl Ross, my attorney, to make all collections on this note, and I assign a one-third interest in this note to Carl Ross. /s/ Joel Fox." Is the installment note a negotiable instrument? Does Joel's writing constitute an indorsement? If so, what kind?

2. What is the difference between a negotiable and a nonnegotiable instrument? What are the advantages of negotiability?

3. Berger writes out a check to "cash" and delivers it to Macias. Macias signs the check on the reverse side and gives it to Deborah Bonds. Bonds writes "Pay to Deborah Bonds" above Macias' name, then signs her name below that of Macias and gives the check to Aiso. Aiso loses the check, and Art Rubin finds it. Rubin writes, on a separate piece of paper, "For deposit only to account of Art Rubin. /s/ A. Rubin," and staples the paper to the check. Describe the effect of these various transactions.

4. Distinguish between negotiation and assignment of commercial paper. Why is negotiation considered the preferable method of transfer?

5. Distinguish between restrictive indorsements and qualified indorsements. Under what circumstances might restrictive or qualified indorsements be used?

6. Leroux signs the following document:

    May 3, 1979

    To whom it may concern:

    I have this day borrowed $5,000 from: Helen Keyes $5,000 to be paid on demand.

    Is the document a negotiable instrument?

7. Thomas gave Dozier a $20,000 promissory note. The note, when delivered, provided for "interest at the annual rate of _____ percent." The note also provided for payment of "attorney's fees of $_____ in the event of default." The parties orally agreed that Dozier could use the note as collateral for a bank loan and could enter the rate of interest charged by the bank as the rate of interest on the note. Dozier obtained a loan from State Bank at an annual rate of interest of 12 percent. She then wrote "12" in the blank space provided for interest in the note. The blank space provided for attorney's fees was never completed. Is the note a negotiable instrument?

8. Kelly contracts to purchase some wheat from Bonnelli, with delivery to be made within three months. Kelly wishes to pay by means of a negotiable instrument. He wants to deliver the negotiable instrument to Bonnelli now, but wants it to become payable only at the time when actual delivery of the wheat is made. What options are available to Kelly?

9. What is a trade acceptance?

10. Knight writes a check naming Wolfe as payee. Wolfe indorses the check "without recourse" and delivers it to Sims, who pays Wolfe cash. The check is subsequently dishonored by the bank. Sims demands her money back from Wolfe. Must Wolfe repay the money? What if Wolfe and Sims had orally agreed that Wolfe would repay the money in the event of dishonor?

24 Holder in Due Course

24:1 Introduction

The holder in due course doctrine is an essential part of the law of negotiable instruments. Under the doctrine, a transferee of an instrument who qualifies as a *holder in due course (HDC)* takes the instrument free of most traditional contract defenses. The doctrine facilitates orderly commercial transactions. Its purpose and importance are best illustrated by applying it to a fact situation. Assume that Martin contracts to sell a load of plywood to Lucy. Lucy pays Martin with a promissory note. Martin never delivers the plywood, but he still demands that Lucy pay the promissory note. Obviously, Lucy need not do so. If Martin sues her, she has a valid defense based on Martin's breach of the underlying contract. Assume, however, that Martin has sold the note to Nicole, who is an HDC. Nicole can demand that Lucy pay the note. Lucy cannot assert Martin's breach of contract as a defense against Nicole.

From the example, it can be seen that the holder in due course doctrine facilitates the easy transferability of negotiable instruments. A transferee of a negotiable instrument wants to be assured of payment, regardless of any disputes between the obligor and the original payee. The holder in due course doctrine, by limiting the defenses that can be raised against an HDC, effectively assures the HDC's right to payment. The position of an HDC can be contrasted with that of an assignee under ordinary contract law. An assignee has no greater rights than his assignor had. Any defenses that could be raised against the assignor can also be raised against the assignee. By contrast, an HDC *does* acquire greater rights than his transferor had. Certain defenses that can be raised against the transferor cannot be raised against the HDC.

It is important to bear in mind that commercial paper is used widely in commercial transactions, and that a negotiable instrument often changes hands several times before it is ultimately paid. For example, a farmer may wish to purchase supplies on credit, to be paid for several months later out of the proceeds of the season's crop. The retailer selling the supplies may be unable to extend credit for that long. To solve the problem, either a trade acceptance (discussed in Chaper 23) or a note may be used. The farmer, by accepting the trade acceptance or executing the note, becomes obligated to make payment to the retailer several months in the future. However, neither party expects payment actually to be made to the retailer. Rather, both parties expect that the retailer will in turn sell the instrument to a third party, such as a bank or other lending institution. Typically, this third party purchases the instrument from the retailer at a discount; that is, the third party pays the retailer an amount less than the amount payable on maturity. In the same manner, the purchaser of this instrument may also purchase other instruments at a discount from other parties. Naturally, the purchaser of these instruments expects to be paid when they are due, and does not want to become embroiled in controversies between the original parties to the various instruments it has purchased. The HDC doctrine in most cases permits the purchaser to do exactly what all parties intended: to collect on the instrument when due, regardless of any breakdown in the relationship between the original parties to the instrument.

Classes of Holders   Under the UCC, there are three classes of holders of negotiable instruments: (1) simple holders, (2) holders for value, and (3) holders in due course. A simple holder is a person who possesses a negotiable instrument drawn, issued, or indorsed to him, to his order, to bearer, or in blank. In other words, a simple holder is one who has possession and good title to the instrument. A holder for value is, as the name implies, one who has given value for the instrument. What constitutes *value* is discussed in 24:3. A holder in due course is one who has given value *and* who meets the other requirements for HDC status; all of these requirements are discussed later. Only an HDC is accorded special protection under the UCC. Other holders take the instrument subject to any defenses that could be asserted by the drawer or maker of the instrument[1] against the initial payee.

Since many legal disputes have arisen as to whether a particular person qualifies as an HDC, the bulk of this chapter is devoted to a discussion of the requirements for HDC status. Consideration will also be given to the rights acquired by an HDC.

Consumer Credit Transactions   The holder in due course doctrine is generally inapplicable to consumer credit transactions as a result of state and federal rules. These rules are discussed at the end of this chapter. For present purposes, simply bear in mind that the holder in due course doctrine applies primarily to commercial transactions not involving consumers.

24:2   Requirements for Holder in Due Course Status

A holder must meet each of the following requirements to qualify for the status and protections accorded to a holder in due course: He must take the instrument (1) for value, (2) in *good faith*, (3) without notice that it is overdue or has been dishonored, and (4) without notice of any defense against or claim to it [UCC §

---

[1]The term "drawer" refers to one who draws a check or other draft. A "maker" is one who signs a note as the party primarily liable on it. The term "obligor" refers to the party who must actually pay an instrument. Therefore, the maker of a promissory note is an obligor. However, the drawee is ordinarily the obligor on a check or other draft, rather than the drawer. This is so because after the instrument has been drawn and accepted, it is the drawee who is primarily liable on it.

3-302(1)]. Although easily stated, these requirements, which will be considered in detail in the following sections, have been the subject of much litigation.

A holder's status as an HDC is determined either at the time the instrument is negotiated to him or at the time he gives value for it, whichever occurs later. Once a holder qualifies as an HDC he remains an HDC, even though he later acquires knowledge of some defense or claim or learns that the instrument is overdue or has been dishonored. To illustrate, assume that Adam Attorney has purchased a word processing system from Computers Incorporated and has executed a promissory note payable to Computers Incorporated as payment. Computers Incorporated has in turn negotiated the promissory note to Office Financiers, which has not yet given value for the note. Adam Attorney later rescinds the purchase contract on the ground that the word processing system is defective. If Office Financiers learns of Adam's repudiation before giving value, Office Financiers can no longer qualify as an HDC because it learned of a defense to the note prior to giving value. It is not enough that Office Financiers had agreed to give Computers Incorporated value for the note before learning of the defense; the value must actually have been given. If, on the other hand, Office Financiers gives value before receiving any notice of Adam's rescission of the contract, Office Financiers does qualify as an HDC.

Holder Through Holder in Due Course   Under some circumstances the holder of an instrument may obtain the rights accorded to an HDC without meeting the requirements for HDC status. A provision of UCC Article 3 known as the "shelter provision" provides that the transferee of an instrument acquires the rights the transferor had in the instrument [UCC § 3-201(1)]. Therefore, if the transferor is an HDC, the transferee automatically acquires the rights of an HDC. For example, if an HDC of a promissory note gives the note to another person, that person is not an HDC, since he did not give value for the note. The person does, however, have the rights of an HDC because the transferor had such rights. Through this transfer, the transferee becomes what is known as a *holder through holder in due course*. The rights of an HDC may be transferred in succession this way. That is, a holder through holder in due course can in turn make a transfer to another person, and that person will acquire the rights of an HDC.

There are two situations to which the shelter provision does not apply. It does not apply to a transferee (1) who was a prior holder and, while a holder, had notice of a defense or claim against the instrument; or (2) who was a party to any fraud or illegality affecting the instrument. These exceptions are designed to prevent a holder from improving his position by first transferring the instrument to an HDC and then reacquiring the instrument.

EXAMPLE
Machine Corporation contracts to sell machinery to Factory Company, with delivery to be made in 30 days. Unknown to Factory Company, Machine Corporation has no intention of delivering the machinery. Factory Company executes a promissory note payable in 45 days as payment. Machine Corporation sells the note at a discount to an HDC, then later repurchases the note from the HDC. Although Machine Corporation's transferor was an HDC, Machine Corporation does not ac-

quire the rights of an HDC, since Machine Corporation was a party to a fraud affecting the instrument.

Payee as Holder in Due Course [UCC § 3-302(2)]   Prior to the UCC, the courts disagreed as to whether the original payee of a negotiable instrument could be an HDC. The UCC specifically provides that a payee can be an HDC. This rule is of limited practical importance because (1) if the drawer or maker of an instrument has some defense against enforcement of the instrument, the payee will almost always have notice of that defense and thus will not qualify as an HDC; and (2) if the obligor has no defense against the instrument, the payee will ordinarily be entitled to recover on it whether he is an HDC or not. In some circumstances, however, the original payee may take the instrument without knowing that a defense or claim exists. It is in this situation that the payee's HDC status is important. To illustrate, assume that Aaron defrauds Michael into signing a check payable to Peter. Peter, in good faith and without notice, pays Aaron for the check. In such a situation Peter, the payee, would qualify as an HDC, even though Michael had a good defense against Aaron.

24:3   Value

A requirement for holder in due course status is the giving of value in exchange for the instrument. A holder has given value if (1) the act (payment or other performance) that constitutes the consideration has been performed, (2) the holder has acquired a security interest in or a lien on the instrument (other than by legal process), (3) the holder has taken the instrument in payment of or as security for a prior debt, (4) the holder has given a negotiable instrument for the instrument taken, or (5) the holder has made an irrevocable commitment to a third person (UCC § 3-303).

The important thing to remember about the value requirement is that the value must actually have been given. Value is thus quite distinct from consideration. A promise to perform some act may constitute consideration for the negotiation of a negotiable instrument, but it does not constitute value for purposes of qualifying as an HDC. Value has been given only when the promised action is actually taken.

EXAMPLE
Berk negotiates a promissory note to Fowler in exchange for Fowler's promise to rewire Berk's house. Fowler never rewires the house. Fowler's promise to rewire constitutes consideration. However, he has not given value because he did not rewire the house.

The rationale for the value requirement is that the holder who has not given value may avoid any loss by simply rescinding the contract. In the above example, Fowler may simply rescind the contract and not rewire the house.

Partial Performance of Consideration   A holder may perform the act that constitutes consideration in stages. Where a holder has only partially performed the agreed consideration, he has given value only to the extent of his performance. For example, Duran promises to pay $5,000 for a note, with the money to be paid in five equal monthly installments. After making two payments, Duran learns of a defense against the instrument. Duran has given value for 40 percent of the note. Therefore, he may qualify as an HDC of a 40 percent interest but cannot qualify as an HDC with respect to the remaining 60 percent.

Prior Debt as Value   A holder takes for value when he takes the instrument as payment of or security for a prior debt. This is so even if the debt is not yet due and even if the debt is that of a third person. For example, if A gives B a promissory note as security for C's debt to B, then B takes the instrument for value.

The following case emphasizes the point that the holder must actually give value to qualify for HDC status. Note how the holder argued that he had given value under two theories and that both of these theories were rejected.

Bennett

v

United States Fidelity & Guaranty Co.
19 NC App 66, 198 SE2d 33, 13 UCCRS 288
(North Carolina Court of Appeals, 1973)

[Stephen Bennett's grandparents purchased a 1971 Datsun for his use. Title to the car was held by Mabel Bennett, Stephen's mother. Stephen loaned the car to Wilbur Prince, who wrecked it in an accident. United States Fidelity & Guaranty Company, Prince's insurer, issued a $4,400 draft payable jointly to Prince and to Mabel Bennett as settlement. Both payees indorsed the draft to Stephen Bennett, who deposited it in his bank account. United States Fidelity issued a stop payment order when it discovered that Prince did not have collision coverage for vehicles other than his own. Stephen Bennett sued United States Fidelity to recover on the draft. The trial court granted summary judgment for United States Fidelity, and Stephen Bennett appealed.]

Morris, Judge.

*   *   *

Plaintiff contends that he is entitled, under [UCC § 3-302], to the amount of the draft. [UCC § 3-302] defines a holder in due course as

one who takes an instrument for value, and in good faith, and without notice that it is overdue or has been dishonored or of any defense against or claim to it on the part of any person.

The undisputed evidence discloses that plaintiff was without notice of the defense of the issuer and that he took the instrument in good faith and for the purpose of purchasing an automobile to replace the one wrecked by defendant's insured. The only question about which the parties disagree is whether plaintiff took the check for value.

[UCC § 3-303] defines taking for value as follows:

"A holder takes the instrument for value

(a) to the extent that the agreed consideration has been performed or that he acquires a security interest in or a lien on the instrument otherwise than by legal process; or

(b) when he takes the instrument in payment of or as security for an antecedent claim against any person whether or not the claim is due; or

(c) when he gives a negotiable instrument for it or makes an irrevocable commitment to a third person."

Plaintiff earnestly contends that he comes within the purview of the definition for two reasons.

He first contends that the evidence discloses

that he took the check in payment of an antecedent claim against Wilbur Lee Prince and, therefore, he took the check for value. There is no dispute about the fact that the car was registered in the name of plaintiff's mother. Plaintiff, therefore, had no claim against Prince for the damage to the car. . . .

On appeal he says, however, that he had a claim against Prince for damage to personal property in the car at the time of the wreck. A close examination of the record, and particularly the deposition and affidavit of plaintiff, reveals absolutely no evidence of whether plaintiff had any property in the car and if so, what it was. . . . Plaintiff has failed to present any evidence which would tend to show any legal claim against either payee, which plaintiff had and relinquished.

He also contends that he gave value by virtue of the provisions of [UCC § 3-303(c)] in that he made an irrevocable commitment to a third person. Plaintiff contends and the evidence reveals that he intended to use the amount of the check for the purchase of a new car. He stated in his deposition that the insurance draft was delivered to him; that he carried it to his mother and to Prince for endorsement and then deposited it in his checking account at Wachovia Bank and Trust Company; that he was told at the time he made the deposit that it would take "a couple of days to clear"; that he then called the insurance agent who suggested that he postdate the

check he was to give in payment for the car he was buying; that he then went to the dealer and followed this suggestion.

The official comment to [UCC § 3-303(c)] is as follows:

"Paragraph (c) is new, but states generally recognized exceptions to the rule that an executory promise is not value. A negotiable instrument is value because it carries the possibility of negotiation to a holder in due course, after which the party who gives it cannot refuse to pay. The same reasoning applies to any irrevocable commitment to a third person, such as a letter of credit issued when an instrument is taken."

We are of the opinion that the wording of the statute contemplates a simultaneous transaction—a commitment to a third person made when the holder takes the instrument. We do not construe it to include a commitment made subsequent to the taking of the instrument. We hold, therefore, that plaintiff's subsequent reliance on the payment of the draft does not constitute a taking for value necessary to put plaintiff in the position of holder in due course.

The undisputed facts establish that plaintiff is not a holder in due course. The court properly granted defendant's motion for summary judgment.

[Affirmed.]

Bank Deposits (UCC §§ 4-208, 4-209)   A bank may qualify as an HDC on the basis of a bank deposit if the bank has given value for the deposit. This rule can be clarified by the following situation. When a customer of one bank deposits a check drawn on another bank, the customer's bank, which is the depositary bank, commonly credits the customer's account and places the check in the collection process. The check ultimately reaches the drawee bank and, in most cases, is paid. If the drawee bank finds that the check is not payable for some reason—such as the drawer's having insufficient funds in his account or having issued a stop payment order—the bank will not pay the check. Rather, it will send the check back to the depositary bank. The question then arises as to whether the depositary bank qualifies as an HDC and is entitled to insist on payment.

Under the UCC, if the depositary bank's customer has withdrawn the funds represented by the check, the bank qualifies as an HDC (assuming it meets the other HDC requirements). It has given value for the deposit. However, the mere crediting of a customer's account does not constitute the giving of value. If the check is dishonored, the bank can always debit the customer's account, therefore sustaining no loss.

EXAMPLE
Green maintains an account in State Bank. On June 1 the balance is $500. On June 2 Green deposits a check for $400 drawn on County Bank, increasing his balance to $900. On June 3 Green withdraws $425 from his account, lowering his balance to $475. On June 4 State Bank is notified that there are insufficient funds in the drawer's County Bank account to pay the $400 check. State Bank has not given value on that check. Since Green still has $475 in his account, the bank can debit his account for the $400 represented by the County Bank check, and it loses nothing in the transaction.

To determine whether funds have been withdrawn, the principle of first-in, first-out (FIFO) is applied. Under this rule, it is presumed that money is withdrawn from an account in the same order in which it is deposited.

24:4   Good Faith

The requirement of good faith that permeates the UCC has been discussed in previous chapters. To qualify as an HDC, a holder of an instrument must meet the same basic test of honesty. The good-faith requirement is a subjective one in that it focuses on the holder's actual state of mind. The fact that a reasonable person might have been suspicious under similar circumstances does not prevent a finding of good faith if the holder in fact was not suspicious. The determination of good faith always depends on the particular facts and circumstances in a given case.

Although good faith is a separate requirement for HDC status, the courts usually consider good faith in connection with claims that the holder had knowledge or notice of some defense to or defect in the instrument. If a holder had notice of a defense, it will generally be found that he acted in bad faith.

24:5   Lack of Notice That Instrument Is Overdue or Dishonored

Another qualification for HDC status is that the holder must take the instrument without notice that it is overdue or has been dishonored. Under the UCC, a person has notice not only when he has actual knowledge or notice, but also when the facts and circumstances known to him give him reason to know [UCC § 1-201(25)]. In other words, the issue of whether a holder has notice is determined by an objective standard (what a reasonable person would know under the circumstances), rather than a subjective standard (what the holder actually knew).

Under the UCC, a holder has notice that an instrument is overdue if at the time he purchases it or otherwise acquires it he has reason to know (1) that any part of the principal amount is overdue, (2) that there is an uncured default in payment of another instrument of the same series, (3) that acceleration of the instrument has been made, (4) that he is taking a demand instrument after demand has been made, or (5) that he is taking a demand instrument more than a reasonable length of time after its issue [UCC § 3-304(3)].

The notice provided by some of the above circumstances is largely self-explanatory. If an instrument is payable on May 31, and a holder purchases it on June 1, he clearly has notice that the instrument is overdue. If an instrument is payable in installments, the fact of default on a prior installment should also put a prospective purchaser on notice that the instrument is overdue. It should be noted, however, that knowledge of a default in the payment of interest does not constitute notice that an instrument is overdue, since such defaults are fairly common and are often tolerated in commercial transactions [UCC § 3-304(4)(f)].

For most time instruments it is clear when they are overdue. A demand instrument, though, has no stated time for payment, and for this reason it is often more difficult to determine whether a purchaser had notice that a demand instrument was overdue. If a purchaser knows that payment has been demanded but has not been made, he of course has notice. In other situations, it is presumed that a demand instrument is overdue after a reasonable amount of time has passed. With respect to checks, for example, a reasonable time is presumed to be 30 days. With other instruments, the determination of a reasonable time depends on the nature of the instrument, the usage of the trade or business, and the facts of the particular situation.

 If a prospective purchaser has any doubt as to whether a demand instrument is overdue, the prudent course of action is to investigate the matter before making the purchase. In this regard, it is often possible for the prospective purchaser to contact the obligor on the instrument and clarify any doubts that may exist.

24:6 Lack of Notice of Defense or Claim

A holder must take the instrument without notice of any defense against or claim to the instrument to qualify as an HDC. A defense exists if the maker or drawer of the instrument has a valid reason for refusing to pay the initial payee. A claim exists if a third party asserts ownership of the instrument. An objective standard is used in determining whether the holder had notice, although the subjective element of good faith also figures prominently.

The UCC lists several factors that either do or do not constitute notice (UCC § 3-304). Sometimes the notice appears from the instrument itself. For example, if the amount payable has obviously been altered, a prospective purchaser should be suspicious and is put on notice that a defense probably exists. In other cases knowledge of the underlying transaction may put the purchaser on notice. For example, if the purchaser of an instrument knows that the original payee has breached his contract with the obligor, the purchaser has notice. Regardless of the nature of the notice provided, the basic issue remains the same: In light of all the facts and circumstances known to the holder at the time of purchase, did he know or have reason to know that a defense or claim existed? Consideration will now be given to some of the specific factors that the courts consider in determining what constitutes notice of a defense or claim. These are (1) the existence of irregularities in the instrument, (2) knowledge that an obligation is voidable or discharged, (3) knowledge of an extremely large discount in the purchase price of the instrument, (4) knowledge of the transferor's past business practices, and (5) knowledge of a close connection between the holder and the transferor.

Incomplete or Irregular Instruments   A purchaser has notice if an instrument is incomplete or otherwise irregular and the irregularity creates doubt as to the instrument's validity, terms, or ownership. To create such a doubt, an irregularity must relate to a material factor in the instrument. For example, visible evidence of forgery or failure to fill in the amount payable would constitute notice. Whether an irregularity constitutes notice depends on how material the irregularity is.

EXAMPLE
Brock purchases a promissory note. The original date of January 1, 1981, has been crossed out and January 1, 1982, has been inserted. The note originally specified interest at eight percent, but the figure "8" has been lined out and the figure "15" inserted. The instrument states that the obligation is "payable _____ days after sight," and that payment is to be made in the "city of New York, state of _____." This note contains both material and immaterial omissions and irregularities. The change in date does not put Brock on notice of a potential defense, since mistakes in date are common, particularly at the start of a new year. The change in interest rate, however, does put him on notice because the change constitutes a material change in the obligation evidenced by the note. Similarly, the failure to fill in the blank as to time of payment is material because it makes the instrument non-negotiable, the instrument not being payable on demand or at a definite time. The failure to fill in the blank concerning the state is not material because specifying the place of payment is nonessential. It is reasonable to assume, anyway, that the state of New York was intended because the city of New York is specified.

Obligation Voidable or Discharged   The purchaser of an instrument may not qualify as an HDC if he takes the instrument with notice that the obligation of any party is voidable or that all parties have been discharged. For example, if the original payee fraudulently induced the execution of the instrument, the obligation is voidable. If a purchaser has knowledge or notice of facts indicating such fraud, he cannot qualify as an HDC. Here, good faith figures prominently in determining whether such notice existed. A purchaser ordinarily does not have to inquire, but he may not ignore the obvious. If the purchaser knows facts that should alert him to the possibility that the obligation is voidable, he must inquire or be found guilty of bad faith.

Discounted Instruments   Negotiable instruments are commonly purchased at less than the face price. Thus, the mere fact that an instrument is offered for sale at a discount does not constitute notice. It is the purchase of an instrument at an extremely large discount that might indicate both a lack of good faith and notice of a defense. This is particularly true if other suspicious circumstances are also present.

Knowledge of Transferor's Past Business Practices   A prospective purchaser of a negotiable instrument generally has no obligation to ask about the reputation or past business practices of the transferor. The fact that the transferor may have engaged in some questionable dealings in the past does not necessarily indicate that there is anything wrong with the instrument in question. However, the transferor's past business practices may constitute one factor that should be considered in conjunction with all the other factors in determining whether the purchaser took the instrument without notice of defenses and in good faith.

 A prospective purchaser of a negotiable instrument should never ignore indications of defects in the instrument. Failure to make reasonable inquiry may lead to difficulty in obtaining payment on the instrument and possibly to a lawsuit. If the purchaser can prove his good faith and lack of notice, he may win the lawsuit. However, he might be able to avoid the entire problem by inquiring about the transferor's prior dealings before buying the instrument.

Close Connection Between Transferor and Holder   The existence of a close business relationship between the transferor and the purchaser is one factor that the courts consider on the issues of notice and good faith. Notice exists if the relationship is so close that the purchaser must have known of the facts giving rise to the defense.

The following case illustrates a close and continuing relationship between the transferor and the purchaser. Note how the issues of good faith and lack of notice are jointly discussed as one basic element to be met by an HDC.

Slaughter
v
Jefferson Federal Savings & Loan Association
361 F Supp 590, 13 UCCRS 89
(United States District Court, District of Columbia, 1973)

[Monarch Construction Corporation engaged in a scheme to defraud homeowners in the District of Columbia. Monarch representatives, by misrepre-sentations and high-pressure sales tactics, induced owners of deteriorating inner-city houses to sign home improvement contracts. The prices charged were excessive, usually double or more than double the fair value. Lapin, a previous employee of Monarch, obtained first trust deed financing for the contracts from either Jefferson Federal Savings & Loan Association (Jefferson) or Montgomery Federal Savings & Loan Association (Montgomery). The home-owners, some illiterate and many of limited education, were hurried through settlement pro-ceedings and often signed papers without reading them.

Between 1964 and 1965, Jefferson made 171 loans to Monarch customers. Jefferson received the loan applications and the underlying home improvement contracts from Lapin, who was ostensibly acting as the homeowners' agent. Jefferson's appraisal committee, consisting of experienced real estate men familiar with values and financing, viewed the homes. The settlement sheets sent to Jefferson frequently contained indications of irregularity or inconsistency with the underlying contract. Montgomery made loans to Monarch customers in much the same manner, making 31 loans in 1964. Montgomery's president knew home improvement costs, inspected many of the homes, and reviewed the settlement sheets. Despite the indications of irregularities, neither Jefferson nor Montgomery ever investigated or inquired about Monarch or Lapin.

A number of homeowners sued Jefferson and Montgomery, seeking rescission and restitution of money paid. The trial court concluded that the home improvement contracts were unconscionable and that the contracts and notes had been fraudulently induced. The court then turned to the issue of whether Jefferson and Montgomery were holders in due course entitled to take, free of the defenses asserted.]

Gesell, District Judge.

*   *   *

Neither Jefferson nor Montgomery ... was, however, a party to the fraud practiced on these homeowners nor did they have direct knowledge of its existence. Accordingly, as a defense against plaintiffs' claims the defendants have each interposed that they hold plaintiffs' notes in due course. If the claim of holder in due course prevails, defendants are, of course, immune from [plaintiffs'] defenses to the notes. ... The burden of proof rests always on the one claiming to be a holder in due course. ... A holder, to sustain this burden, must demonstrate that he meets the standards

set forth in [UCC § 3-302], which provides in pertinent part:

Holder in Due Course

(1) A holder in due course is a holder who takes the instrument
    (a) for value; and
    (b) in good faith; and
    (c) without notice ... of any defense against ... it on the part of any person.

In dispute here is whether the instruments were taken in good faith and without notice of any defense to them. Good faith is defined as "honesty in fact in the conduct or transaction concerned." [UCC § 1-201(19)]. Willful ignorance or failure to inquire may negate good faith. ... A person has "notice" of a fact when (a) he has actual knowledge of it; or (b) he has received a notice or notification of it; or (c) from all the facts and circumstances known to him at the time in question he has reason to know that it exists. [UCC § 1-201(25)].

The cases are sparse and uninstructive as to the duty of a first trust lender such as Jefferson or Montgomery. From the briefs and arguments, the issue here boils down to the following query: Where the holder is himself the original lender, as in these instances, can he insulate himself from the underlying transaction and thus, because he knows nothing and makes no inquiry, claim the good-faith status that is at the foundation of a holder in due course's immunity from defenses that are otherwise available to the borrower? While payees such as Jefferson and Montgomery may be holders in due course, [UCC § 3-302(2)], they must meet all of the requirements of 3-302. The inquiry must turn to an analysis of the case in the light of modern commercial realities.

It is necessary to avoid the obvious tendency to view this question in the light of hindsight. ... The record is, moreover, devoid of proof that either Montgomery or Jefferson followed procedures that diverged from other responsible first trust lenders refinancing to aid home improvement purchases. Each case must rest on its own facts to determine whether or not the holder holds the note in due course. There is no rule of thumb to be automatically applied.

In concluding that Jefferson and Montgomery were not holders in due course, the Court has weighed the totality of the circumstances shown by the proof. It must be borne in mind that neither of these concerns stand in the same position they could readily urge if, as part of their general business, they had occasionally written a first trust loan generated by Monarch. Their volume of Monarch business was in each case continuous and substantial. Their representatives knew that Monarch's contracts were being written on marginal properties in the ghetto areas of the city; that many of Monarch's customers were of limited intelligence and as a class, were apt to be heavily burdened with consumer and other debt measured by their apparent income levels; and that many were being refinanced out of other satisfactory notes of reputable financial institutions having lower interests rates and lower monthly payments. Their trained real estate men saw the properties and the work being done and had access to the contract charges they were helping to finance.

Rather than make obvious inquiry into Lapin's bona fides and the contract requirements and settlement adjustments, they chose to be ignorant by trying to insulate themselves from the realities of their activity. The contracts and settlement sheets were at their disposal and revealed both internal irregularities and contradictions between the two documents. They were on notice that Lapin had ties with Monarch as he repetitively peddled loans to them. They were thus chargeable with a heavy duty to be assured that his purported representation of the borrower was aboveboard, for he was obviously acting for two principals whose interest could well be in conflict. . . . Given their superior knowledge of building costs and financial matters and the

opportunity they had to observe and to question, plus the obvious need to inquire which the circumstances presented, they cannot rely on their self-induced ignorance to put themselves into a position of holders in due course. In short, there were many warnings of irregularity which even limited inquiry would have readily disclosed.

Jefferson and Montgomery may not in the light of these irregularities and indicia of fraud be heard to suggest that the proof as to a particular plaintiff does not put them on precise notice of misrepresentation and unconscionable dealing. All of the plaintiffs were targets of the fraud. The education, understanding, recollection and details of each borrower's dealings vary, but the pattern is overwhelmingly apparent, and had either of these associations taken appropriate precautions, under the circumstances presented they would have ceased facilitating Monarch's scheme, and none of the plaintiffs would have been serviced regardless of the particular course of their individual dealings with Monarch. Of course, if there is notice as to one defense or good faith is not shown, all defenses to the transaction are valid. [UCC § 3-306]. . . .

This is an equitable proceeding and the Court must consider the obvious commercial realities presented by the record before it. Indeed the Uniform Commercial Code itself recognizes something less than actual notice may suffice to destroy the holder in due course defense. The Court finds the commercial realities persuasive in determining that Jefferson and Montgomery did not act in good faith, and were on notice because they "should have known." These sophisticated financial institutions were concerned solely with the sufficiency of their security. But they were not dealing with comparably sophisticated borrowers experienced in commercial matters. The borrowers, many of whom were semi-literate, had no clout. They were threatened with loss of their homes if they raised any question and went forward, sometimes with enormous sacrifice, resigned in their ignorance to pay off unjustifiable charges to keep a roof over their heads. Where lenders facilitate consumer credit financing they must be held to a high standard of inquiry to make certain their ser-vices are not being misused by unscrupulous merchandisers such as Monarch. . . .

[The court ordered judgment for the plain-tiffs.]

 The judgment in the above case was reversed on appeal in *Slaughter v Jeffer-son Federal Savings & Loan Association*, 538 F2d 397 (United States Court of Appeals, District of Columbia Circuit, 1976). The appellate court agreed that Monarch and its agents were guilty of fraud, but concluded that Jefferson and Montgomery acted in good faith and without notice. Note, however, that Jefferson and Montgomery were tied up in litigation for over five years (from January 1971, when the action was originally brought, to mid-1976, when the appeal was decided). Consider also the possible damage to Jefferson's and Montgomery's reputations as a result of the protracted litigation. All this might have been avoided if they had made some investigation into the na-ture of Monarch's and Lapin's dealings.

24:7   Rights of Holder in Due Course

When a holder seeks payment from the obligor of a negotiable instrument, there are two categories of defenses that may be used: (1) *personal (limited) defenses* and (2) *real (universal) defenses*. When a person qualifies as an HDC, only real defenses may be asserted against him by the obligor. Personal defenses, which consist of most of the traditional defenses to contract actions, may not be asserted against an HDC unless the person asserting one of them has personally dealt with the HDC.

Real Defenses (UCC § 3-305)   As a matter of public policy, the drafters of the UCC (and the states enacting it) decided that certain defenses should be univer-sally available. These are called real defenses. Real defenses include minority status (under legal age) to the extent it is a defense to a contract (see Chapter 13), dis-charge in bankruptcy or other insolvency proceedings (see Chapter 31), and any other discharge of which the holder has notice when he takes the instrument (see Chapter 25).

Forgery of the obligor's name and material alteration of the instrument are also real defenses. Therefore, the obligor can claim that the signature on the instrument was not his or that a material part of the instrument was altered. In the case of material alteration an HDC may enforce the instrument according to its original terms, but not as altered (UCC §§ 3-404, 3-407).

Certain other traditional contract defenses are classified as real defenses if they make the obligation entirely void, as opposed to merely voidable. These defenses are incapacity (other than minority), duress, and illegality. The drafters of the UCC felt that the extent to which these defenses should be assertible against an HDC was largely a matter of local policy. Therefore, the law of the particular state must be checked to determine when, if ever, these defenses make a contract absolutely void, and thus when they may be asserted against an HDC.

There is a similar UCC provision with respect to fraud.[2] Fraud in the inducement is considered a personal defense not available against an HDC. This means that most types of fraud, such as misrepresentation, are unavailable as a defense. Fraud in the execution of a contract may, however, be asserted as a defense against an HDC. This means that the obligor can contend that he was tricked into signing the instrument. To prevail on such a claim, the obligor must show that he was induced to sign the instrument without knowing and without reasonable opportunity to know its character or essential terms. In other words, the test is that of excusable ignorance of the writing's contents.

Personal Defenses (UCC § 3-306)   Personal defenses may not be raised against an HDC, but they may be raised against any person who is not an HDC and takes the instrument. For example, if the holder of the instrument fails to meet the requirements for HDC status, the obligor on the instrument may assert both real and personal defenses against the holder. Personal defenses include all defenses other than those classified as real defenses. They consist largely of traditional contract defenses, such as lack of consideration, nondelivery, breach of warranty, and unconscionability. Lack of capacity, duress, illegality, and fraud are also personal defenses except to the extent that they qualify as real defenses, as discussed earlier.

Rights of Holder Not Qualifying as Holder in Due Course   The rights of an ordinary holder of a negotiable instrument are generally determined according to basic contract law. Where the holder is not the original payee, the holder has the rights of an assignee. Both real and personal defenses may be asserted against a holder. If there are no defenses available, then the holder can, of course, recover on the instrument.

24:8   Limitation of Holder in Due Course Doctrine in Consumer Credit Transactions[3]

The holder in due course doctrine functions well in business transactions. It permits negotiable instruments to be freely and quickly transferred among holders. In consumer transactions, however, the doctrine has frequently been used unscrupulously.

EXAMPLE
Karen buys a refrigerator from Ace Appliances on credit and signs a promissory note payable to Ace. Ace immediately negotiates the note to a bank at a discount. Shortly afterward, the refrigerator breaks down. When Karen goes to Ace to complain and demand repair of the refrigerator, she learns that Ace has gone out of business. She then stops making payments on the note. The bank sues her, and

---

[2]Fraud as a defense to a contract action is discussed in Chapter 12.
[3]Consumer credit and credit protection generally are discussed in Chapter 27.

she asserts breach of warranty as a defense. Because the bank is an HDC of the note and Karen's defense is a personal one, the defense will be disallowed against the bank. In other words, Karen must continue paying on the note. She has a potential breach of warranty action against Ace, but the action is worthless because Ace is no longer in business. In short, Karen is left with a malfunctioning refrigerator and the obligation to continue paying for it.

Abuses such as that described above led to demands for legislation to protect consumers in these transactions. In response, most states passed laws limiting the application of the holder in due course doctrine in consumer transactions. These laws vary widely in their effect. Some laws prohibit the use of negotiable instruments in consumer financing, requiring instead the use of instruments labeled "consumer paper." Other laws eliminate the holder in due course doctrine in consumer transactions. Still other laws provide varying measures of lesser protection for consumers.

In 1975 the Federal Trade Commission (FTC) promulgated a trade regulation rule that effectively abolished the holder in due course doctrine in most consumer credit transactions (16 CFR §§ 433.1, 433.2). The FTC rule requires that any consumer credit contract contain a prominent notice stating that any holder of the contract is subject to all claims and defenses that the consumer could assert against the seller. The net effect of the rule is the abolition of the holder in due course doctrine in such transactions. The FTC rule also has the effect of prohibiting "waiver of defenses" clauses. Under a waiver of defenses clause a consumer agrees not to assert against an assignee any claims or defenses he could have asserted against the original seller.

The FTC rule applies to two kinds of transactions: (1) consumer transactions in which the purchaser signs a promissory note payable to the seller, which the seller then negotiates to a third party; and (2) consumer transactions in which the seller arranges for a direct loan from a third party to the consumer, with the proceeds of the loan being used to pay for the purchase. The rule has national application. Thus, the holder in due course doctrine is inapplicable to most consumer credit transactions. It must be remembered, however, that the FTC rule does not apply to business transactions, to real property transactions, or when payment is made by check. The holder in due course doctrine remains in full effect with respect to these transactions.

Key Concepts and Terms

- There are three classes of holders of negotiable instruments: (1) simple holders, (2) holders for value, and (3) holders in due course (HDCs). Only HDCs are accorded special protection under the UCC.
- To qualify for HDC status, a holder must take the instrument (1) for value, (2) in good faith, (3) without notice that it is overdue or has been dishonored, and (4) without notice of any defense against or claim to it. A holder through holder in due course usually obtains the rights accorded an HDC. The payee of an instrument may be an HDC.

- Value must actually be given to qualify for HDC status. A mere promise does not constitute value. A holder may give value in several ways, the primary way being by performance of the agreed consideration.

- A transferee must take the instrument in good faith to qualify as an HDC. The good-faith test is a subjective one and requires honesty. The good-faith requirement is generally considered in conjunction with the requirements concerning notice.

- A holder has notice (1) when he has actual knowledge or notice or (2) when the facts and circumstances known to him give him reason to know. The existence of notice is thus determined by an objective standard.

- Another requirement for HDC status is that the transferee must take the instrument without notice that it is overdue or has been dishonored. The UCC specifies several situations that constitute this notice. Notice exists if the purchaser has reason to know (1) that any part of the principal amount is overdue, (2) that there is an uncured default in payment of another instrument of the same series, (3) that acceleration of the instrument has been made, (4) that he is taking a demand instrument after demand has been made, or (5) that he is taking a demand instrument more than a reasonable length of time after its issue.

- The last requirement of HDC status is that the transferee take the instrument without notice that there is a defense or claim against it. Notice is based on whether, in light of all the facts and circumstances known to the purchaser at the time of purchase, he knew or had reason to know that a defense or claim existed. Among the factors considered are the existence of irregularities or omissions in the instrument, knowledge of the transferor's past business practices, and the existence of a close relationship between the transferor and the holder.

- Two kinds of defenses may be raised against a holder by the obligor of a negotiable instrument: real defenses and personal defenses. Real defenses include minority, discharge in insolvency proceedings, any other discharge of which the holder has notice, forgery, material alteration, certain forms of incapacity, duress, illegality, and fraud in the execution. All other defenses are personal. Real defenses may be raised against an HDC, but personal defenses may be raised against an HDC only if the obligor has personally dealt with the HDC. A holder *not* qualifying as an HDC has the rights of an assignee and takes the instrument subject to both personal and real defenses.

- Most states have passed laws limiting application of the holder in due course doctrine in consumer transactions. These laws vary widely in their effect. The FTC has promulgated a rule that effectively abolishes the holder in due course doctrine in most consumer credit transactions involving sale of goods or services. The FTC rule does not apply to business transactions, to real property transactions, or when payment is made by check.

- FTC Rule
- Good Faith
- Holder in Due Course (HDC)
- Holder Through Holder in Due Course
- Notice
- Personal (Limited) Defenses
- Real (Universal) Defenses
- Value

Questions and Case Problems

1. Why does the law afford special status and protections to a holder in due course?

2. Akins agrees to sell his corn crop to Sweeney. As payment, Sweeney executes a promissory note payable to Akins. Akins pledges the note to Rogers as security for a loan. Akins defaults on the loan, and Rogers demands payment on the note from Sweeney. Sweeney responds that Akins has not delivered the corn. Rogers has Akins indorse the note, then sues Sweeney for payment. What is result of the lawsuit?

3. On March 9, 1981, Peter deCoote executed a promissory note payable to Ginny Dorg. The note provided that it was to be paid in 36 equal installments, "payable monthly after date beginning _____ 1, 1981, and on the first day of each month thereafter." Dorg sold the note to a bank. Does the bank qualify as a holder in due course?

4. Stereo Sales, Inc., sells equipment to Holmes for making stereo tapes from master tapes. Holmes pays $3,000 down and executes a $3,000 promissory note for the balance due. Stereo sells the note to National Bank for $500. Stereo's contract with Holmes requires it to furnish him master tapes weekly, from which Holmes is to produce individual tapes for resale to Stereo. Stereo never furnishes any master tapes and eventually goes out of business. Holmes refuses to pay the note and National Bank sues. At trial Holmes raises the defense of fraud, and National Bank claims it is a holder in due course. Holmes proves that Stereo has sold National Bank 30 other notes at similar discounts and that the makers of 25 of those notes have defaulted and claimed breach of contract by Stereo. How should the case be decided?

5. Describe the "shelter provision" and its exceptions.

6. Egan signs two blank checks. Irving steals the checks and fills in the blanks. Irving cashes one check at his bank on Friday. The bank is notified the following Tuesday that Egan's bank has dishonored the check. Irving cashes the second check at his bank on Wednesday. That check is also dishonored. Irving's bank sues Egan for payment of the checks. Must Egan pay? Does Egan have any defenses?

7. Warren executes a $3,000 promissory note payable to Yvonne as payment for roofing his house. Yvonne gives the note to her son Ben as a birthday present. Ben negotiates the note to Owen, his bookie, as payment of a $2,000 gambling debt. Owen gives the note to his friend Jennifer as a wedding present. Jennifer sells the note to Marie for $2,500. Marie negotiates the note to Bill as payment for furniture, which he fails to deliver. Which of the parties qualify for the rights of a holder in due course? Which parties do not? Why?

8. Max executes a note payable on demand to Pat. One month later Pat demands payment, but Max refuses to pay. Two weeks after that, Pat sells the note to Wally at a 30 percent discount. Wally is unaware of the prior demand and does not know Max. One week later, Wally sells the note to Ann at a 25 percent discount. Ann is unaware of the prior demand, but she does know that Max has frequently defaulted on similar notes. Are Wally and Ann holders in due course? Would the time within which demand is generally made on similar notes have any bearing on the decision?

9. Payne, a college-educated businessperson, signs a promissory note payable to Industrial Supplies, Inc. and State Bank. Payne delivers the note to Industrial, which indorses the note and sells it to State Bank at a 20 percent discount. Payne refuses

to pay the note and is then sued by State Bank. At trial Payne claims that State Bank is not a holder in due course. Payne also claims that Industrial tricked him into signing the note by misrepresenting it as an order for supplies and that he did not read the note before signing it. The trial court enters judgment for State Bank. Payne appeals. Should the judgment be affirmed or reversed on appeal?

10. Describe the FTC rule concerning holders in due course and the reasons for its promulgation.

25 Liability of Parties

25:1 Introduction

A negotiable instrument may be transferred many times before it must be paid. Ordinarily, the obligor, who is the drawee or maker of the instrument, pays the ultimate holder according to the terms of the instrument, and the instrument is *discharged*. Sometimes, however, the obligor fails to make payment. The holder must then determine from which of the various parties to demand payment.

The liability of a party is classified on two levels: primary and secondary. A person is primarily liable if the instrument absolutely requires him to make payment. Since the maker of a note and the acceptor of a draft are absolutely required to make payment, they have primary liability. A person is secondarily liable when the person's liability arises only if whoever is primarily liable fails to make payment. Since drawers and indorsers, *the secondary parties,* must pay when the *primary parties* do not, drawers and indorsers have secondary liability.

Within each level, the liability of the parties is based either on contract or warranty. The parties do not, however, actually draft a contract or a warranty agreement; rather, the UCC specifies the contract and warranty terms. In other words, each party enters a contract that is implied in law, the exact terms of which are determined by reference to the applicable UCC provisions. The rules governing the liability of primary and secondary parties, including both contractual and warranty liability, will be discussed in detail in the succeeding sections. The liability of certain special types of parties and the liability on instruments containing forged signatures will also be examined. In addition, the various ways in which the parties to a negotiable instrument may be discharged from liability will be considered here.

Before proceeding to a discussion of the specific rules governing liability and discharge of parties, it is important to stress the complexity of transferring a negotiable instrument several times.

EXAMPLE
East Electronics as drawer executes a draft drawn on Creative Credit as drawee, with South Suppliers named as payee. South indorses and sells the draft to Money

Company, which in turn indorses and sells the draft to North Bank. North presents the draft to Creative for payment, but Creative refuses to pay. North obviously does not want to sustain the loss, so it will look to one of the other parties for payment. Should North demand payment from Money Company, its immediate transferor; from South, the original payee; or from East, the drawer? If North demands and receives payment from Money Company, can Money Company in turn demand payment from either South or East? What if North presented the draft for payment after the due date? What if North never notified Money Company, South, or East of Creative's refusal to pay? The answers to all these questions have a bearing on which party, if any, must make payment to North, and which party must suffer the loss caused by Creative's nonpayment.

In studying the rules that follow, therefore, bear in mind that the rules are often applied to extremely complex transactions, and that the rules themselves are complex. It is suggested that after reading this chapter the student return to the preceding example to determine the liability of the various parties involved.

25:2 Contractual Liability of Primary Parties

The term "primary party" is used to refer to the maker of a note and the acceptor of a draft. Makers and acceptors have the same liability in an action based on contract. However, a point must be made about the acceptor's liability. Recall that an acceptor is not designated as such until he accepts the draft—that is, until he puts his signature on the face of the draft. Prior to acceptance, he is a drawee and has no obligation to the payee or to any subsequent holder to honor the instrument [UCC §§ 3-409(1), 3-410(1)]. It is important to bear this in mind during the discussion of the liability of primary parties.

The maker or acceptor of a negotiable instrument has an absolute obligation to pay according to the terms of the instrument. If the instrument is incomplete when signed, the maker or acceptor undertakes to pay it when it is completed as authorized. Moreover, the maker or acceptor conclusively admits the payee's existence and capacity to indorse. The maker or acceptor cannot, for example, later assert that the payee was a minor incapable of negotiating the instrument (UCC § 3-413).

The primary party's obligation continues until payment is actually made or until such time as the statute of limitations has run. Recall that a statute of limitations is a law that specifies the period of time within which a person can bring an action. Thus, the primary party remains liable until he pays the holder or until the holder can no longer bring a lawsuit to compel payment. There is one exception to this rule. A maker or acceptor of an instrument payable at a specific bank is discharged from liability if (1) the instrument is not presented for payment when due, (2) the bank becomes insolvent during the delay in presentment, and (3) the maker or acceptor is thereby deprived of funds maintained in the bank [UCC § 3-502(1)]. This exception is rarely, if ever, of any practical importance.

EXAMPLE
Lake executes a draft directing Carter as drawee to pay $1,000 to Watson. The draft is payable at State Bank. Carter accepts the draft by signing it. Watson does not present the draft for payment until six months after the due date. Unless the bank has become insolvent during the delay, Carter as acceptor is still obligated to make payment.

25:3   Contractual Liability of Secondary Parties

Secondary parties to negotiable instruments include drawers and indorsers [UCC § 3-102(1)(d)]. Their contractual liability is secondary in the sense that they are obligated to make payment only if the primary parties fail to do so. There is, however, a marked difference between the potential liability of drawers and that of indorsers. If a drawee refuses to accept the draft or if he accepts it but later refuses to pay it, the drawer is as liable as a primary party. An indorser, however, is liable only if there has been compliance with the rules governing presentment and notice of *dishonor*. These rules generally require the holder to present an instrument to the primary party for payment when due. This is called *presentment*. Sometimes, presentment of a draft to the drawee with a request that he accept it is also required. If the instrument is not accepted or payment is refused, the instrument is considered dishonored, and the holder or indorser must notify secondary parties of that fact. The rules governing presentment and notice of dishonor are discussed more fully in 25:4. Noncompliance with these rules discharges the indorser's liability.

Drawer's Liability [UCC § 3-413(2)]   The drawer is liable for payment of a draft if the drawee–acceptor refuses to make payment. This rule stems from the fact that most drafts call for disbursement of the drawer's funds held by the drawee. Usually, the drawer's liability continues until payment is made or until the statute of limitations has run. In other words, if the drawee–acceptor refuses to pay, the drawer is, for practical purposes, treated the same as a primary party. Like the primary party, the drawer conclusively admits the payee's existence and capacity to indorse [UCC § 3-413(3)].

Although the drawer is in many respects treated like a primary party, the UCC does make distinctions between a primary party's liability and a drawer's liability. The most important distinction is that the drawer is liable only if the primary party—the drawee–acceptor—fails to pay. A second distinction, which has little practical effect, is that the drawer's liability is technically conditioned on due presentment and notice of dishonor. However, delay in presentment or notice of dishonor will discharge the drawer only if the drawee becomes insolvent during the delay [UCC § 3-502(1)]. Most drafts are drawn on banks, so a drawer is discharged from liability under the same circumstances as a maker or acceptor—that is, if the bank fails during the delay.

A drawer does have a more practical way of avoiding secondary liability. The drawer may disclaim liability by drawing the draft "without recourse."

Indorser's Liability (UCC § 3-414)   An indorser (other than a qualified indorser) is liable on the instrument if the party primarily obligated to make payment fails to do so. The indorser's liability, like the drawer's, is conditioned on the holder's due presentment, the primary party's dishonor, and notice of dishonor by either the holder or an indorser. For an indorser, unlike the drawer, these requirements have real meaning. Failure to meet the requirements will discharge the indorser from the contractual obligation to make payment.

EXAMPLE
Tamura executes a draft directing County Savings to pay $500 to Global Products. County Savings accepts the draft. Global then indorses the draft to Fast Financing. When Fast Financing seeks payment from County Savings, County refuses to pay. Fast Financing may turn either to Global as indorser or to Tamura as drawer for payment. However, while Fast Financing must comply with the requirements concerning presentment and notice of dishonor to hold Global liable, it does not need to comply to hold Tamura liable because she is the drawer.

When an instrument is dishonored by the primary obligor, every indorser is directly liable to the holder of the instrument. The holder may therefore demand payment from any indorser. Indorsers are generally liable to one another in the order in which they indorse, which is presumed to be the order in which their signatures appear on the instrument. In other words, the first indorser is liable to all subsequent indorsers, the second indorser is liable to all indorsers except the first, and so on.

25:4   Requirements of Presentment, Dishonor, and Notice of Dishonor

An indorser's contractual liability is strictly conditioned on the holder's compliance with the UCC requirements concerning presentment, dishonor, and notice of dishonor. This means that the holder must demand payment or acceptance by the primary party in a timely manner and, on the primary party's refusal to pay or accept, the holder must give timely notice of the refusal to secondary parties. The following discussion deals with these matters.

Necessity of Presentment [UCC § 3-501(1)]   Presentment consists of a demand for acceptance or payment made by the holder on the maker, acceptor, or drawee. Only drafts can be presented for acceptance, but all negotiable instruments must ultimately be presented for payment.

The purpose of presenting a draft for acceptance is simply to obtain the drawee's agreement to pay the draft and thus to insure his primary liability. For example, if the holder of a time draft has any doubts as to the drawee's willingness to pay it when due, he can allay these doubts by presenting the draft for acceptance at any time prior to the due date.

Some drafts *must* be presented for acceptance. *Presentment for acceptance* is required (1) if the draft so provides, (2) if the draft is payable elsewhere than at the drawee's residence or place of business, or (3) if the draft's date of payment depends on such presentment. The holder has the option of presenting any other time draft for acceptance, but he may not present other demand drafts for acceptance.

Time of Presentment (UCC § 3-503)   The time when an instrument must be presented for either acceptance or payment depends on whether it is a time or a demand instrument.

Presentment for acceptance of a time instrument, if it is required, must be made on or before the due date. *Presentment for payment* must be made on the due date. If the time for payment is accelerated, the instrument must be presented for payment within a reasonable time after the acceleration. A demand instrument must be presented for acceptance or payment within a reasonable time unless it is payable after sight. In that case it must be either presented for acceptance or negotiated within a reasonable time after date or issue, whichever is later.

The UCC provides guidelines for determining what is a reasonable time. The nature of the instrument, any usage of banking or trade, and the facts of the particular case are all relevant. The code states that certain time periods are presumed to be reasonable in the case of uncertified checks, which are basically all checks except what are known as certified checks (see Chapter 26 for a discussion of the various types of checks). To hold a drawer liable, a holder should present the check for payment or initiate bank collection within 30 days. To hold an indorser liable, a holder should present the check for payment or initiate bank collection within seven days after the indorsement.

 The UCC provisions concerning the time for presentment are detailed and complex. A holder of an instrument should remember three basic rules. First, a time instrument should be presented for payment on the date due. Second, a demand instrument should be presented for payment or negotiated to another party as quickly as is reasonably possible. Third, failure to make a timely presentment for acceptance or payment will discharge all indorsers from liability on the instrument. Therefore, a businessperson handling a large volume of negotiable instruments should adopt internal procedures designed to avoid delay in the negotiation and presentment of those instruments.

Manner of Presentment (UCC § 3-504)   Presentment may be made in various ways. It may be made in person, by mail, through a clearinghouse, or through a collecting bank. When presentment is not made in person, the time when the demand for acceptance or payment is actually received is considered the date the presentment is made. Presentment must be made at the place specified for acceptance or payment. If the instrument does not specify any place, then presentment may be made at the place of business or residence of the party from whom payment or acceptance is demanded. When two or more obligors are involved, presentment may be made to any one of them.

Dishonor of Instrument (UCC § 3-507)   Dishonor of a negotiable instrument (except a draft) consists of nonpayment by the primary party after due presentment. A draft is dishonored either by nonacceptance or by nonpayment (UCC §§ 3-505, 3-506). This is not to say that the maker or acceptor must make payment immediately after being presented with the instrument. Reasonable examination to ensure that the instrument is properly payable is permissible, and the primary party may take certain steps, such as requiring reasonable identification from the holder, to ensure that payment will be made to the right person.

Notice of Dishonor (UCC § 3-508)   When an instrument has been dishonored, notice of such dishonor may be given by the holder to any party potentially liable on the instrument.

EXAMPLE

Laura executes a promissory note payable to Adam. Adam indorses the note to Karen, who indorses the note to Craig. Craig presents the note to Laura for payment, but she refuses to pay. Craig gives timely notice of the dishonor to Karen, who in turn gives timely notice to Adam. Since both indorsers of the instrument have been given notice, both remain liable for payment.

Such notice may also be given by a potentially liable party to any other potentially liable party. Notice must be given to all indorsers of the instrument or they are discharged from liability for payment, although it need not be given in order of indorsement. If the holder or indorser is a bank, it must give notice before its midnight deadline (see Chapter 26). Any other holder or indorser must give notice before midnight of the third business day after dishonor or receipt of notice of dishonor from another party. The notice may be oral or written, and it may be given in any reasonable manner. Written notice is given when it is sent and will be considered given even if it is not received.

 A holder should give written notice to all potentially liable parties whenever it is feasible to do so. In that way the holder has the most assurance of being able to prove that notice was given and of ultimately receiving payment. If the holder gives notice only to his immediate transferor, he runs the risk that other indorsers will not receive timely notice and will be discharged. If the holder gives oral notice, he runs the risk of being unable to satisfactorily prove that notice was ever given.

Situations Excusing Compliance with Presentment and Notice Requirements (UCC § 3-511)   Under some circumstances a failure to comply or a delay in complying with the presentment and notice of dishonor requirements is excused. The holder may then hold indorsers liable on the instrument despite lack of presentment or notice. These circumstances include the following:

Waiver of presentment or notice. An indorser may waive the right to require presentment or notice of dishonor. Such a waiver may be expressed or implied, oral or written. Negotiable instruments often contain a waiver provision excusing presentment or notice.

Inability to make presentment or give notice. Circumstances beyond his control may make it impossible for a holder to present the instrument to the primary party or to give the indorser notice of the primary party's dishonor of the instrument. In such a case, the presentment or notice is entirely excused. To avail himself of this excuse, a holder must (1) use reasonable diligence to make presentment or give notice or (2) show that reasonable diligence would have been unsuccessful. Moreover, where presentment or notice is still possible after a delay caused by circumstances beyond the holder's control, such presentment or notice must be made or given. The delay is then excused, but a complete failure to make presentment or give notice would not be.

Actions of indorser. A party who, as a result of his own conduct, has no right to require or reason to expect that the instrument will be honored is not entitled to presentment or notice. For example, if the party has himself dishonored the instrument or has countermanded payment, presentment or notice is excused.

Death or insolvency. The death or insolvency of the maker, acceptor, or drawee excuses the holder from making a presentment. It does not, however, excuse him from giving notice of dishonor to the indorser.

Refusal of acceptance or payment. If payment or acceptance has been refused for some reason other than the lack of proper presentment, presentment is excused. For example, an anticipatory repudiation by the maker or acceptor would excuse formal presentment. Again, however, the holder is not excused from giving notice of dishonor.

The following case illustrates how a court first determined whether presentment and notice of dishonor were timely and then whether presentment and notice were excused under the circumstances.

Hane
v
Exten
255 Md 668, 259 A2d 290, 7 UCCRS 35
(Maryland Court of Appeals, 1969)

[*Theta Electronics Laboratories executed a promissory note for $15,377.07, payable in monthly installments beginning January 1965. The note, indorsed by Gerald Exten and his wife, contained an acceleration clause making the entire amount due 30 days after failure to make payment. In November 1965 the original payees, George and Marguerite Thomson, assigned the note without recourse to John Hane. Although the note was apparently overdue at that time, Hane made no demand for payment until April 1967. In June 1967 Hane sued the Extens on the note. The Extens won, and Hane appealed.*]

Singley, Judge.

*   *   *

This case raises the familiar question: Must Hane show that the Extens were given notice of presentment and dishonor before he can hold them on their endorsement?

The court below, in finding for the Extens, relied on the provisions of [the UCC]. § 3-414(1) of the U.C.C. provides:

"Unless the indorsement otherwise specifies (as by such words as 'without recourse')
every indorser engages that upon dishonor
and any necessary notice of dishonor and
protest he will pay the instrument according
to its tenor at the time of his indorsement to
the holder or to any subsequent indorser who
takes it up, even though the indorser who
takes it up was not obligated to do so."

§ 3-501(1)(b) provides that "Presentment for
payment is necessary to charge any indorser"
and § 3-501(2)(a) that "Notice of any dishonor
is necessary to charge any indorser," in each
case subject, however, to the provisions of §
3-511, which recite the circumstances under
which notice of dishonor may be waived or
excused, none of which is here present. §
3-502(1)(a) makes it clear that unless presentment or notice of dishonor is waived or excused, unreasonable delay will discharge an
indorser. . . .

There was testimony from which the trier
of facts could find as he did that presentment
and notice of dishonor were unduly delayed.

It is clear that Hane held the note from
November, 1965, until some time in April
1967 before he made demand for payment.
U.C.C. § 3-503(1)(d) provides that "Where an
instrument is accelerated presentment for payment is due within a reasonable time after the
acceleration." "Reasonable time" is not defined
in § 3-503, except that § 3-503(2) provides, "A
reasonable time for presentment is determined
by the nature of the instrument, any usage of
banking or trade and the facts of the particular
case." But § 1-204(2) characterizes it: "What is a
reasonble time for taking any action depends
on the nature, purpose and circumstances of
such action."

Reasonableness is primarily a question for
the fact finder. . . . We see no reason to disturb
the lower court's finding that Hane's delay of
almost 18 months in presenting the note "was
unreasonable from any viewpoint." . . .

As regards notice of dishonor, § 3-508(2) requires that notice be given by persons other
than banks "before midnight of the third business day after dishonor or receipt of notice of
dishonor." Exten . . . testified that his first
notice that the note had not been paid was . . .
on 7 June 1967. Hane's brother testified that
demand had been made about 15 April 1967.
He was uncertain as to when he had given Exten notice of dishonor, but finally conceded
that it was "within a week." The lower court
found that the ambiguity of this testimony,
coupled with Exten's denial that he had received *any* notice before 7 June fell short of
meeting the three day notice requirement of
the U.C.C. The date of giving notice of dishonor is a question of fact, solely for determination by the trier of facts. . . . We cannot
say that the court erred in its finding.

In the absence of evidence that presentment
and notice of dishonor were waived or excused, Hane's unreasonable delay discharged
the Extens, § 3-502(1)(a).

Hane would have us hold that presentment
and notice of dishonor were impliedly excused
under § 3-511(2)(b) because Exten himself had
dishonored the note or had no reason to expect
that the note would be paid. Hane finds support for this theory in testimony that payment
had been demanded of Theta, the obligor, in
behalf of the Thomsons, the payees, in February or March of 1965, at a time when Exten
was president of Theta, an office from which
he was removed in April or May of 1965. The
court below rejected this contention on the
ground that there was no evidence that Exten
dishonored the note in his individual capacity.

There is an even more persuasive reason
which negates the contention that Exten had
reason to expect that the note would not be
paid. Hane's brother [testified] that on 26
November 1965, the balance due on the note
was $13,154.94. While the manner in which
$2,222.13 had been paid was unexplained, it
would appear that at least six monthly payments of $320.47 had been met, with the result
that payments were current for the period
when Exten was president. . . . In the face of
this Hane offered no proof that Exten, in his

capacity as president of Theta, knew or should have known that the note would not be paid. An indorser's knowledge of the maker's insolvency, standing alone, will not excuse the giving of notice of dishonor. . . .

Hane makes much of the fact that he is a holder in due course. We doubt that he was, since there is some evidence that he took the note with notice that it was overdue, § 3-302(1)(c). . . . Whether Hane was or was not a holder in due course has no relevance to the issue here presented. In either case timely presentment and notice of dishonor were required to hold the Extens. . . .

[Judgment affirmed.]

25:5   Warranty Liability

The holder of a negotiable instrument may seek payment from a secondary party by claiming that there was a breach of warranty. Two types of warranties exist with respect to negotiable instruments: *transfer warranties* and *presentment warranties*. Transfer warranties arise whenever an instrument is transferred for consideration. Presentment warranties arise whenever an instrument is paid or accepted. Liability based on warranty is often discussed as an aspect of indorsers' liability. This is somewhat misleading because both transfer and presentment warranties arise even in the absence of an indorsement. Therefore, a person who, without indorsement, transfers or obtains payment on an instrument that is payable to bearer may be held liable for breach of warranty, although such a person could not be held liable as an indorser. The possibility of obtaining payment from a person who has not indorsed the instrument is one advantage of seeking recovery on a breach of warranty theory. A second advantage is that the requirements concerning presentment, dishonor, and notice of dishonor do not apply to actions for breach of warranty. Thus, a holder may be able to recover from an indorser without meeting those requirements.

EXAMPLE

Nelson, an HDC of a check, presents it for payment, but the drawee bank refuses to pay because the original payee's signature is forged. Nelson fails to give Oakes, who indorsed the check over to Nelson, notice of the dishonor. Nelson cannot obtain payment from Oakes based on an indorser's contractual liability, since failure to give notice of dishonor discharges that liability. As will be seen, however, Nelson could obtain payment from Oakes based on Oakes' breach of transfer warranties.

Claims of breach of warranty most often arise in cases involving forged, stolen, or altered instruments. For example, a businessperson who frequently uses promissory notes may maintain a supply of preprinted notes. Someone could steal one of the notes, fill it in and forge the businessperson's name as maker, and negotiate it to another person. The note may be negotiated several times before finally being presented to the ostensible maker for payment. The ostensible maker may pay it and later discover that it was a forgery, or may note the forgery immediately and refuse payment. In either case, litigation is likely to result, and the courts must determine which of the various parties who handled the instrument must suffer the loss. The warranty rules are utilized in resolving such cases.

Similar allocation of loss problems arise in the case of stolen or altered instruments. If A writes a check payable to B, but C steals and cashes the check, who should bear the loss? What if the check passes through several hands before it is finally presented for payment at the bank where A maintains his account? What if a person alters a check and obtains payment of a greater amount than the check was written for? Again, the warranty rules are relied on to determine which of the various parties handling a stolen or altered instrument must ultimately bear the loss.

In theory, the person who forged, stole, or altered an instrument should ultimately bear the loss, but that person is seldom, if ever, available. The loss must therefore be placed on some innocent party. As discussed below, the protections accorded to the holder of such an instrument are substantially greater than those accorded to a party who makes payment on the instrument. The reason that a maker or drawee has less protection is that a maker or drawee is more likely to know that an instrument has been forged, stolen, or altered than is a holder in the chain of possession. In other words, among innocent parties the maker or drawee is in the best position to have avoided the loss.

UCC warranty provisions are contained in Articles 3 and 4 (UCC §§ 3-417, 4-207). In the event of a conflict between the provisions, those of Article 4 govern.

Transfer Warranties [UCC §§ 3-417(2), 4-207(2)]   When a transferor transfers a negotiable instrument for consideration, he makes five warranties to his immediate transferee. These warranties are (1) that he has good title to the instrument and the transfer is rightful; (2) that all signatures are genuine or authorized; (3) that the instrument has not been materially altered; (4) that no defense of any party is good against him (or, in the case of a qualified indorser, that he has no knowledge of such a defense); and (5) that he has no knowledge of any insolvency proceeding involving the maker, acceptor, or drawer. In addition, if the transfer is by indorsement, the transferor makes the same warranties to any subsequent holder who takes the instrument in good faith.

The most important of the transferor's warranties are the warranties of good title, genuine signatures, and lack of *material alteration*. Taken together, they amount to a guaranty that the instrument itself is not a forgery, that the signatures of the indorsers are not forgeries, that there have been no material changes made in the instrument, and that the transferor is a rightful holder of the instrument. If, for example, it should turn out that the maker's signature on a note was forged, the warranty of genuine signatures would be violated. Consequently, any transferee of this note could recover for breach of warranty from his immediate transferor, as well as from any previous transferors who indorsed the instrument.

Presentment Warranties [UCC §§ 3-417(1), 4-207(1)]   Each person who obtains payment or acceptance of a negotiable instrument, as well as any prior transferor of the instrument, makes three warranties to the person who in good faith pays or accepts the instrument. These warranties are (1) that the holder has good title, (2) that he has no knowledge that the maker's or drawer's signature is unauthorized, and (3) that the instrument has not been materially altered. These warranties are considerably narrower than the warranties made on transfer.

There are exceptions to the second and third warranties that benefit an HDC. Because these exceptions are complex, they will not be discussed here. Suffice it to say that their basic effect is to eliminate the warranties when payment or acceptance is obtained by an HDC from the maker, drawer, or acceptor.

The presentment warranties do not guarantee that all signatures are genuine. The warranty of good title is basically a warranty that only indorsements are genuine, since a forged indorsement cannot transfer title. The warranty of good title does not, however, guarantee that the instrument itself is not a forgery. The obligor's signature may be forged without violating the warranty of good title. Furthermore, the person presenting the instrument for payment only warrants that he has no knowledge that the obligor's signature was forged. Without proof that the holder had this knowledge, an obligor who pays a forged instrument cannot recover for breach of warranty from the person receiving payment. The reason for this rule is quite simple: As between two innocent parties, the one in the best position to have avoided the loss should bear the loss. A maker or drawer should know his signature; similarly, a drawee should ordinarily know the signature of his drawer. Those parties are therefore in a better position to detect a forged instrument than is a transferee of the instrument.

EXAMPLE

Abraham maintains a checking account at State Bank. Louise steals one of Abraham's checks, makes it out for $100 payable to herself, and forges Abraham's signature. Nicole, with no knowledge of the forgery, cashes the check, then obtains payment on the check from State Bank. On discovering the forgery, State Bank cannot seek repayment from Nicole. State Bank has Abraham's signature on file and could have verified the signature and detected the forgery before it made payment to Nicole. Nicole, on the other hand, had no way to verify the signature.

25:6   Liability of Agents, Accommodation Parties, and Guarantors

The UCC contains various rules concerning the liability of certain special types of parties, known as *agents, accommodation parties,* and *guarantors.* These parties are special in that they sign the instrument either on behalf of or to lend support to some other party to the instrument.

Agents (UCC § 3-403)   Under the UCC, no person is liable on a negotiable instrument unless his signature appears on the instrument. A signature may, however, be made by an agent or other authorized representative. An agent is a person who is authorized to act for another; the person for whom an agent acts is known as the principal (see Chapter 48).

When an agent names the principal and clearly signs in a representative capacity, there is no question as to who is liable on the instrument. It is clear that the principal is liable and the agent is not. Problems do arise, however, when an agent fails to clearly disclose that he is signing in a representative capacity. In such a situation, the agent generally is personally liable on the instrument.

To avoid personal liability, the agent must disclose two facts in the instrument: (1) the name of the principal and (2) the fact that the agent has signed in a representative capacity. All subsequent holders are then put on notice that the principal, and not the agent, is liable for payment. If the instrument discloses neither fact, the agent is personally obligated to all holders of the instrument. If the instrument shows one of the facts, the agent is liable to all parties except those who dealt directly with the agent. For example, if the original payee dealt with the agent and knew that the agent was acting only on behalf of the principal, the agent is not liable to the payee, but the agent is liable to all subsequent holders of the instrument.

 The UCC sets forth two methods of clearly indicating that an agent has signed in a representative capacity only. An agent for an individual should sign in this manner: "Peter Pringle by Arthur Adams, Agent." When signing on behalf of a corporation or other organization, an agent should name the organization and both the name and office of the agent. For example, "Ace Corporation by Arthur Adams, Treasurer," would be sufficient.

If the instrument does not contain the principal's name, the principal is not liable on it even though the agent intended to execute the instrument on behalf of the principal.

Accommodation Parties (UCC § 3-415)   An accommodation party is one who signs a negotiable instrument in any capacity for the purpose of lending his name to another party to the instrument. To illustrate, assume that Kirk wants to purchase a television set on time, but the retailer will not extend credit to him. Helen, Kirk's mother, agrees to help out by signing a promissory note. The retailer then agrees to make the sale and accept the note. Helen is the accommodation party, and Kirk is the accommodated party. Although the retailer expects payment from Kirk, she now knows that she can look to Helen for payment if Kirk defaults.

An accommodation party is generally liable in the capacity in which he signed the instrument. For instance, Helen, as an accommodation maker of the note in the example just given, has basically the same liability as any other maker of a negotiable instrument. This rule is subject to certain exceptions, however. The accommodation party is discharged from liability to the holder (1) if the holder releases the accommodated party from liability or grants an extension of time to make payment (assuming that the holder knew of the accommodation party's status), or (2) if he unjustifiably impairs any collateral given to secure payment of the instrument. If the holder wishes to take either of these actions without discharging the accommodation party, he must either obtain the accommodation party's consent or else expressly reserve his rights against the accommodation party (UCC § 3-606). To return to our illustration, this means that if the retailer wants to grant Kirk an extension of time to pay the note without discharging Helen, the retailer must either obtain Helen's consent to the extension or must expressly reserve his right to obtain payment from Helen.

Accommodation parties, like agents, do not always clearly disclose their status. When the instrument does not disclose a party's status as an accommodation party and the instrument is being held by an HDC who took the instrument without notice of the accommodation, the accommodation party cannot take advantage of the exceptions to liability just discussed. In other cases, an accommodation party who proves his status may take advantage of the exceptions; accommodation status may be proved by oral proof.

The UCC specifically provides that an indorsement that is not in the chain of title (an indorsement by someone with no apparent interest in the instrument) is notice of its accommodation character. For example, if a check is made out to Jones as payee, but is indorsed first by Wilson, then by Jones, all subsequent takers of the instrument are on notice that Wilson signed as an accommodation party. In addition, certain words of guaranty are, as will be discussed, clear indication that a party has signed an instrument as an accommodation party rather than as the party primarily liable for payment.

The following case discusses two issues: (1) whether the accommodation parties were properly permitted to prove their status as such and (2) whether the payee's actions toward the accommodated party had the effect of releasing the accommodation parties from liability. Consider what steps the payee might have taken to avoid the result in the case.

Lee Federal Credit Union

v

Gussie

542 F2d 887, 19 UCCRS 630
(United States Court of Appeals, Fourth Circuit, 1976)

[As consideration for a $30,000 loan, Ernest Lee executed a promissory note payable to Lee Federal Credit Union (Credit). At Credit's request, Warnetta Gussie and Kwang Rowe signed the note as comakers. The loan, granted in 1971, became delinquent in June 1972. In August 1972, Lee gave Credit a check for $4,900, which was postdated to October. Credit deposited the check in October, but it was dishonored for insufficient funds. Credit never informed the co-makers of its acceptance of the postdated check or of the delinquency on the note. After the check was dishonored, Credit made attempts to collect from Lee. In August 1973, after learning that Lee had filed for bankruptcy, Credit notified Gussie of the delinquency and demanded payment. Gussie refused, and Credit sued Gussie,
who in turn sued Rowe. The trial court concluded that both Gussie and Rowe were accommodation makers whose liability had been discharged and it entered judgment in their favor. Credit appealed.]

Widener, Circuit Judge.

*   *   *

It is clear from the evidence that both Gussie and Rowe signed the note in question "for the purpose of lending [their] name[s] to another party to it," namely Ernest Lee. As such, they were accommodation parties within the meaning of [UCC § 3-415(1)]. Credit contends that the oral evidence as to the accommodation status of the co-makers should have been excluded since the face of the note reveals that they signed it as makers without any reservation of rights. Therefore, according to Credit, they are liable in the same manner and to the same extent as Ernest Lee. Section

[3-415(3)] provides to the contrary, however. It reads:

> "As against a holder in due course and without notice of the accommodation oral proof of the accommodation is not admissible to give the accommodation party the benefit of discharges dependent on his character as such. In other cases the accommodation character may be shown by oral proof."

While Credit may have been a holder in due course, the district court found as a fact, which is not clearly erroneous, that Credit knew that the co-makers on the note were in fact accommodation parties, so Credit could not have been a holder in due course "without notice of the accommodation." This is one of the "other cases" mentioned in § [3-415(3)] in which "the accommodation character may be shown by oral proof." Thus, the oral evidence as to the status of the parties was properly admitted.

The question then becomes whether the actions of Credit in relation to the note were sufficient to discharge Rowe and Gussie from any further liability. We are of opinion they were. [UCC § 3-606] provides that:

> "(1) The holder discharges any party to the instrument to the extent that without such party's consent the holder
>
> (a) without express reservation of rights releases or agrees not to sue any person against whom the party has to the knowledge of the holder a right of recourse or agrees to suspend the right to enforce against such person the instrument or collateral or otherwise discharges such person, except that

failure or delay in effecting any required presentment, protest or notice of dishonor with respect to any such person does not discharge any party as to whom presentment, protest or notice of dishonor is effective or unnecessary . . ."

In the instant case, Credit accepted Ernest Lee's post-dated check and, without notice or reservation of rights, extended the time of payment from the date the note had become delinquent until October when the check became payable. Such extension of time was granted without the consent of the accommodation parties and they were thus relieved of further liability upon the note. Credit, by its extension of time, at the very least, had "agree[d] to suspend the right to enforce against" Ernest Lee. § [3-606(1)(a)].

We recognize it is at least arguable that the agreed extension of time may not have been binding upon Credit and that it may have been able to institute proceedings against Lee prior to the date the check became payable. Yet, under the UCC in Virginia, it is the agreement which is controlling and not whether that agreement is necessarily binding. . . . The evidence clearly indicates that Credit agreed to extend additional time for payment on the note to Ernest Lee in exchange for the post-dated check which he tendered in August. This agreement, having been reached without the consent of either Rowe or Gussie, was sufficient to relieve them from further liability. . . .

[Judgment affirmed.]

An accommodation party is not liable to the accommodated party. Moreover, if an accommodation party pays the instrument, he may sue the accommodated party for reimbursement.

Guarantors (UCC § 3-416) A guarantor is a particular kind of accommodation party. When there are two or more makers or acceptors, the use by one of words of guaranty indicates that that party is an accommodation party. The words "payment guaranteed" subject the signer to primary liability. A payment guarantor promises that if the instrument is not paid when due, he will pay it. The words "collection guaranteed" mean that the signer will pay an overdue note, but only after the holder has obtained and unsuccessfully attempted to collect on a judgment against the primary obligor, or has proved that such a proceeding would be useless. Words of guaranty which do not specify payment or collection are interpreted as a payment guaranty. The liability of a guarantor is primary in nature. This is so even when the guaranty is given on behalf of a secondary party.

25:7   Liability on Instruments Containing Forged Signatures[1]

Any person whose signature has been forged on a negotiable instrument is not liable for payment of that instrument (UCC § 3-404). A person whose name has been forged to an instrument can, however, later ratify (approve) it and thereby become liable on it, although such ratification is a rare occurrence.

Under the UCC, a forged signature operates as the signature of the forger. Thus, a forged instrument can still be negotiated. For example, assume that A executes a promissory note and forges B's name as maker. B is not liable on the note, but A is. The note can be negotiated from one party to another, and a holder in due course may acquire good title. When the time comes to seek payment, however, B is obviously not going to pay, and A is probably going to be impossible to find.

The above example deals with forgery of the obligor's signature. Forgery of a necessary indorsement has different consequences. Order paper (any negotiable instrument payable to order) requires an indorsement to be negotiated. A forged indorsement is, for purposes of negotiating the instrument and transferring title, no indorsement at all. Because a forged indorsement does not transfer title, the person acquiring under a forged indorsement cannot become a holder or an HDC. Thus, he in turn is incapable of transferring good title to the instrument.

There are certain exceptions to the rule that a forged indorsement is ineffective. Two noteworthy exceptions are known as the *impostor rule* and the *fictitious payee rule*. These exceptions will now be discussed.

Impostor Rule [UCC § 3-405(1)(a)]   An impostor is a person who pretends to be someone he is not. For instance, if Adams pretends to be Murphy, he is an impostor. A person who impersonates another frequently does so for dishonest purposes. One purpose might be to obtain possession of a negotiable instrument made payable to the person impersonated. Expanding on the example above, assume that Quincy owes money to Murphy, whom he has never met. Adams, knowing this, pretends to be Murphy and induces Quincy to issue a note (payable to Murphy) and give it to Adams. Adams now has the note and obviously intends to negotiate it to some innocent party. To do so, he must forge Murphy's name. This would ordinarily render the negotiation invalid and relieve Quincy of the obliga-

---

[1]A bank's liability for payment of a forged check is discussed in Chapter 26.

tion to pay on presentment. The UCC, however, recognizes that a person in Quincy's position has only himself to blame for issuing the note to an impostor and provides that in such circumstances an indorsement by any person in the name of the named payee is effective. If Adams indorses Murphy's name and negotiates the note to Wilson, Wilson can demand payment from Quincy (assuming that Wilson is not a party to the scheme). Moreover, if Adams should lose the note, any person who finds it can forge Murphy's indorsement and demand payment from Quincy. Thus, the UCC places the risk of loss on the person who permitted the impostor to obtain the instrument.

The following case illustrates application of the impostor rule to negotiation of a draft that named two payees. Note the policy reasons relied on by the court in making its decision.

Fair Park National Bank

v

Southwestern Investment Co.
541 SW2d 266, 20 UCCRS 454, 92 ALR
3d 600
(Texas Court of Civil Appeals, 1976)

[Southwestern Investment Company agreed to finance James Impson's purchase of a front-loader machine from J. L. Williams and James L. Wilson, who were doing business as Universal Constructors. Impson gave Southwestern a note, and Southwestern prepared a draft for $12,000, payable to J. L. Williams and James L. Wilson. Southwestern gave the draft to a man representing himself as J. L. Williams. This man gave Southwestern a bill of sale for the machine purportedly signed by Williams and Wilson. Impson somehow obtained the draft, and he deposited the draft, containing both payees' indorsements, in his account at Fair Park National Bank. The draft was paid by Southwestern's bank. Impson defaulted on his note. Southwestern then discovered that the machine had been stolen, rather than purchased from Williams and Wilson, and that the indorsements of Williams and Wilson were forgeries. No trace could be found of Williams, Wilson, or Universal Constructors. Southwestern sued Impson and Fair Park Bank for breach of warranty. The trial court entered judgment for Southwestern, and Fair Park Bank appealed.]

Guittard, Justice.

*   *   *

The "impostor rule" of the Uniform Commercial Code fixes the loss resulting from the fraud of an impostor on the drawer of a check or draft who delivers it to the impostor rather than on a subsequent holder, regardless of the lack of a genuine endorsement by the nominal payee. This case involves applicability of this rule to a draft delivered to one impostor but payable to two payees. We hold that the impostor rule applies so that the drawer cannot recover against the collecting bank on the ground of the lack of genuineness of the endorsement of either of the joint payees....

[Fair Park Bank contends] that under the impostor rule, the endorsements on the draft were effective, whether or not they were the genuine signatures of J. L. Williams and James L. Wilson. Southwestern responds that even though the man representing himself to be Williams may have been an impostor, so that the endorsement was effective as respects his purported signature, nevertheless there was no effective endorsement by or on behalf of the other payee, James L. Wilson, because no person representing himself as Wilson had any connection with the issuance of the draft. Southwestern argues that under § [3-116(b)] of the Code, when an instrument is payable to two or more persons and not in the alternative, it must be negotiated by both. Consequently, Southwestern asserts that Fair Park Bank is liable for breach of warranty of the Wilson endorsement.

We conclude that Fair Park Bank is not liable for breach of warranty for two reasons. In the first place, the impostor rule applies to the person who signed the bill of sale as James L. Wilson as well as to the person who signed as J. L. Williams. The jury found that Wilson as well as Williams was an impostor. . . . Apparently, Southwestern's position is that there was no imposture with respect to James L. Wilson because no one pretending to bear that name appeared before Southwestern's representative and joined with the purported J. L. Williams in inducing Southwestern to deliver the draft.

This argument erroneously assumes that an "impostor" under § [3-405(1)(a)] must meet his victim face to face. That section does not so provide. Rather, it states the rule as follows:

[1] An endorsement by any person in the name of a named payee is effective if
[a] an imposter [sic] by use of the mails or otherwise has induced the maker or drawer to issue the instrument to him or his confederate in the name of the payee. . . .

One of the purposes of drafting the rule in this language was to eliminate the requirement of a face-to-face meeting, which had been imposed by some of the pre-Code cases. Uniform Commercial Code, § 3-405, Comment 2. . . .

Here the evidence and the verdict established that the person who signed the bill of sale as "James L. Wilson," as well as the person who signed as "J. L. Williams," was an impostor. . . . Although an impostor cannot be a fictitious person, since there must be a real person who impersonates someone else, an impostor may impersonate a fictitious person. Both of the persons who signed the bill of sale induced Southwestern to issue the draft, since, presumably, Southwestern would not have issued it without a bill of sale bearing both signatures. Consequently, § [3-405(1)(a)] makes both endorsements effective to relieve Fair Park Bank of liability for breach of warranty, regardless of who wrote them.

In the second place, we conclude that the impostor rule applies even if the "James L. Wilson" named in the bill of sale, or the person who signed the bill in his name, was not an impostor. Southwestern does not challenge the finding that the man who represented himself as J. L. Williams was an impostor. In effect, it concedes that the endorsement of this name on the draft was effective under § [3-405(1)(a)], but it contends that unless Wilson also is shown to be an impostor, the bank is liable for breach of its warranty of his endorsement. We cannot agree. Section [3-405(1)(a)] is not limited to situations in which impostors have impersonated all the joint payees. If an impostor "has induced the maker or drawer to issue the instrument to him or his confederate in the name of the payee," the endorsement of any person "in the name of a named payee is effective." We interpret this language to mean that if an instrument is payable to A and B, and X, by impersonating A, induces the drawer to deliver the instrument to him, then X, or anyone else, can make effective endorsements in the names of both A and B. This interpretation is consistent with the policy of the impostor rule, which is to throw the loss resulting from dealing with an impostor on the person who dealt with the impostor, and, presumably, had the best opportunity to take precautions that would have detected the fraud, rather than on a subsequent holder, who had no similar opportunity. . . . A drawer who deals with a person impersonating one of several payees has as good an opportunity to detect the fraud as one who deals with the impersonator of a single payee. Consequently, on this ground also we hold that the endorsement in the name of James L. Wilson was as effective under § [3-405(1)(a)] as was the endorsement in the name of J. L. Williams. . . .

[Judgment reversed.]

Fictitious Payee Rule [UCC § 3-405(1)(b), (c)]   The fictitious payee rule is that an indorsement by any person in the name of the named payee is effective. This rule applies when a negotiable instrument is made out to a payee with the intention that the payee have no interest in the instrument. The maker or drawer may himself intend that the payee have no interest; or an agent or employee of the maker or drawer, intending that the payee have no interest, may supply the name to the maker or drawer.

The fictitious payee rule is usually applied to situations involving business fraud. In a typical situation the obligor, or his employee, intends to pocket the money. He draws a check made payable to a fictitious payee with the intention of forging the payee's name and pocketing the proceeds. For obvious reasons the UCC places the risk of loss in such situations on the maker or drawer. If the obligor himself perpetrated the fraud, he can scarcely complain about being forced to pay. If the obligor's employee perpetrated the scheme, the obligor must pay because his carelessness permitted the employee to carry out the scheme.

25:8   Discharge of Parties

The UCC lists various ways in which parties may be discharged from liability on an instrument. A discharge may relieve one or more individual parties from further liability, or it may relieve all parties from liability. Certain methods of discharge (such as discharge of an indorser for noncompliance with the presentment and notice requirements) have already been discussed. Other important methods of discharge will be discussed here.

Payment (UCC § 3-603)   The normal method of discharge is by payment. When the party primarily liable on the instrument (the maker or the drawee–acceptor) pays the holder of the instrument, all parties are discharged from further liability on the instrument. If a secondary party makes payment, that party is discharged. Other parties who may be liable to the party making payment are not discharged.

EXAMPLE
Arnold executes a promissory note payable to Brenda. Brenda indorses the note to Carl, who in turn indorses it to Dana. If Arnold pays Dana, all parties are discharged. If Brenda pays Dana, Brenda and Carl are discharged, but Arnold remains liable. If Carl pays Dana, he is discharged, but Arnold and Brenda remain liable.

When only partial payment is made, the party doing so is discharged only to the extent of the payment.

A party who pays an instrument in full may require that the instrument be given to him. This should always be done, since a negotiable instrument retains its negotiable character even after all parties have been discharged. No discharge is effective against a subsequent holder in due course who takes the instrument without notice of the discharge. The way to prevent an instrument from being fraudulently renegotiated is to take possession of the instrument when making payment on it.

Cancellation or Renunciation (UCC § 3-605)   The holder may discharge liability by canceling the instrument in several ways. The holder may cancel the instrument in its entirety. This discharges all parties from liability. The holder may also discharge an individual party by canceling the party's liability or by giving the instrument to the party. Cancellation may be accomplished in any manner that is apparent on the face of the instrument or in the indorsement. For example, the holder's striking out an indorser's signature discharges that indorser. The holder may also renounce his rights in writing, which means that he may state in writing that he gives up his right to receive payment from a party or parties.

Impairment of Right of Recourse or of Collateral (UCC § 3-606)   As just noted, the holder might discharge an individual indorser from liability by striking that indorser's signature. According to the UCC, a party is discharged from liability if the holder of the instrument releases any other party against whom the first party has a right of recourse. Therefore, the holder's discharge of an indorser has the effect of discharging any indorsers subsequent to that indorser. The provision may apply to other parties to the instrument as well. For example, assume that a note is issued payable to Shani. Shani indorses the note to Brad, who in turn indorses it to Alyssa. At this point Shani and Brad are both secondarily liable to Alyssa, and Shani is secondarily liable to Brad. If Alyssa releases Shani from liability, that release also has the effect of discharging Brad. This is because Brad had a right of recourse against Shani.

 A businessperson might want to prevent the above result for various reasons. For example, Alyssa's release of Shani might be part of a larger business transaction between the two. Brad not being a part of that transaction, Alyssa would have no reason to release him. There are two ways in which a holder may release an individual indorser from liability without also discharging subsequent indorsers. The holder may obtain the consent of the subsequent indorsers, or the holder may expressly reserve his rights against the subsequent indorsers. Therefore, Alyssa can either secure Brad's consent to the release of Shani, or Alyssa can release Shani with an express reservation of rights against Brad. Brad then remains potentially liable to Alyssa, and Shani remains potentially liable to Brad. The only liability that has then been discharged is Shani's potential liability to Alyssa, which was Alyssa's intent.

The holder also discharges any party if he unjustifiably impairs any collateral given for that party's benefit. Such a discharge usually involves an accommodation party. If an accommodated party has given the obligor collateral to insure payment, the obligor's return of the collateral to the accommodated party would be an *unjustifiable impairment* and would discharge the accommodation party. To prevent such a discharge, the obligor can either secure the accommodation party's consent or can make an express reservation of rights.

Material Alteration (UCC § 3-407)   A material alteration of the instrument by the holder discharges from liability to the holder any party whose contract is thereby changed. That party, however, remains liable to a subsequent holder in due course. The subsequent HDC may still enforce the instrument against any party according to its original terms.

Key Concepts and Terms

- A primary party is the person who has an absolute obligation to pay the instrument. Primary parties include makers of notes and acceptors of drafts. A drawee is obligated to honor the instrument only after he has accepted it.

- A secondary party is a person who is obligated to pay the instrument if the primary party fails to do so. Secondary parties include drawers and indorsers.

- Generally, the holder of an instrument must present it to the primary party for payment when due; sometimes, the holder of a draft must also present the draft to the drawee with a request that he accept it. If the instrument is not accepted or payment is refused, the instrument is considered dishonored, and the holder or potentially liable indorsers must notify secondary parties of that fact.

- The act of presenting an instrument and demanding acceptance or payment is called presentment. All negotiable instruments must be presented for payment; some drafts must be presented for acceptance. Generally, presentment must be made no later than the due date on a time instrument and within a reasonable time on a demand instrument.

- Dishonor consists of the obligor's nonacceptance or nonpayment after due presentment. Notice of dishonor may be given by the holder to any potentially liable party, and by any potentially liable party to any other potentially liable party. A bank must give notice before its midnight deadline. Other holders or indorsers must give notice before midnight of the third business day after dishonor or receipt of notice of dishonor.

- Compliance with the presentment and notice requirements is not required if (1) the indorser has waived compliance; (2) the holder is unable to comply; or (3) the indorser, as a result of his own conduct, has no right to require or reason to expect that the instrument will be paid. Presentment is not required if the obligor is dead or insolvent, or if payment or acceptance has been refused for some reason other than lack of proper presentment.

- Negotiable instruments carry five transfer warranties and three presentment warranties. The more important transfer warranties are the warranties of good title, genuine signatures, and lack of material alteration. The most important presentment warranty is the warranty of good title. These warranties arise even in the absence of indorsement, and noncompliance with presentment and notice requirements does not discharge warranty liability. Transfer warranties provide greater protection than presentment warranties.

- An agent is a person who is authorized to act for another; the person for whom an agent acts is known as the principal. An agent may sign an instrument on behalf of the principal, thereby obligating the principal. To avoid personal liability, the agent must disclose (1) the name of the principal and (2) that the agent has signed in a representative capacity.

- An accommodation party is a person who signs a negotiable instrument in any capacity for the purpose of lending his name to another party to the instrument. An accommodation party who uses words of guaranty such as "payment guaranteed" or "collection guaranteed" is a guarantor. An accommodation party is generally liable in the capacity in which he signed the instrument. He is discharged from liability if the holder takes certain actions that have the effect of increasing the risk to the accommodation party. To avoid discharging an accommodation party, the holder must either secure the accommodation party's consent or make an express reservation of rights.

- A person whose signature has been forged is not liable for payment of a negotiable instrument, but the forger himself is liable. A forged instrument can be negotiated, but an instrument bearing a forged indorsement generally cannot be negotiated. A forged indorsement of a payee's name is effective if (1) the instrument was issued to an impostor (impostor rule) or (2) the instrument was issued with the intention that the payee have no interest in the instrument (fictitious payee rule).

- A discharge may relieve individual parties from further liability, or it may relieve all parties from liability. The usual method of discharge is by payment. Other methods of discharge include cancellation or renunciation, impairment of right of recourse or of collateral, and material alteration. No discharge is effective against a subsequent holder in due course who takes the instrument without notice of the discharge.

- Accommodation Party
- Agent
- Discharge
- Dishonor
- Fictitious Payee Rule
- Guarantor
- Impostor Rule
- Material Alteration

- Presentment
- Presentment for Acceptance
- Presentment for Payment
- Presentment Warranties
- Primary Parties
- Secondary Parties
- Transfer Warranties
- Unjustifiable Impairment

Questions and Case Problems

1. Why is a drawer's liability more closely akin to that of a primary party than to that of other secondary parties?

2. Pamela forges Milt's name as maker of a promissory note payable to Pamela. Pamela indorses the note and sells it to Trudy. Trudy indorses the note and makes a gift of it to David. David presents the note to Milt for payment. Milt refuses to pay. One week later David tells Trudy of the dishonor. Is either Pamela or Trudy liable to David? If Milt had paid David, would any of the parties have been liable to Milt?

3. Young and Angelo, partners in a bakery, borrow $15,000 from State Bank and execute a 90-day promissory note for the debt. May also signs the note under the words, "Collection guaranteed." One week before the note is due Angelo informs the bank that she and Young have terminated their partnership, that Young has

assumed all liabilities of the business, that Angelo does not want the note extended, and that Angelo will not sign a renewal note. The bank president gives Young an informal 60-day extension to pay the note. Young never pays, and State Bank sues Angelo and May on the note. Is either one liable? Discuss.

4. Can the holder of an instrument who has failed to comply with the presentment and notice requirements ever recover from an indorser of the instrument? Explain your answer.

5. Sally buys some sheep from Omar and pays him with a check for $500. She asks him to hold the check for two weeks, so that she can place sufficient funds in her bank account. Omar holds the check three weeks, then indorses it to Gennet as payment for work that Gennet performed on Omar's ranch. Gennet intends to deposit the check in her savings account the next day, but there is a blizzard and she is snowed in for two weeks. When she finally deposits the check, it is dishonored for insufficient funds. She seeks reimbursement from both Omar and Sally, but they claim that Gennet's delay in presenting the check absolved them of all liability. Are they correct?

6. Lambert sells supplies to City Hardware and accepts a promissory note as payment. The note states, "We promise to pay...." Immediately above the signature the makers are identified as, "City Hardware and/or Robert Schwartz, Owner." The note is signed, "Robert Schwartz, President." The note is not paid when due, and Lambert sues Schwartz. Schwartz denies liability, claiming that he signed as an agent only. Is Schwartz in fact liable?

7. McCoy is the bookkeeper for Sam's Market. Knowing that she has insufficient funds in her bank account, McCoy writes a $2,000 check payable to Sam's Market and cashes it from the current day's receipts. She places Sam's Market's indorsement on the check as she is authorized to do. The check is given to Sano as payment for supplies. The check is dishonored by the bank, and Sano sues Sam's for the $2,000. Sam's denies liability on the ground that Sano failed to give the market notice of dishonor. How should the case be decided?

8. List and discuss five ways in which parties may be discharged from liability on a negotiable instrument.

9. Magee, an employee of Snug Harbor Realty Company, is responsible for examining and initialing for payment invoices submitted to the company. The initialed invoices are forwarded to the company's bookkeeper for preparation of checks payable to the company's creditors. The checks are sometimes given to Magee for delivery to the payees. Magee forges the payees' indorsements on some checks, and the checks are paid by the drawee bank and charged against Snug Harbor's account. When Snug Harbor learns of the forged indorsements, it sues the bank. The bank argues that the fictitious payee rule relieves it of liability. Should the bank's position be sustained?

10. Bragg as maker and Sands as accommodation maker execute a promissory note payable to Cruz. The face of the note contains the following provision: "Presentment for payment and notice of dishonor are hereby waived." Cruz indorses the note and negotiates it to Elliott, who in turn indorses the note and negotiates it to Quoc. When the note is due, Bragg requests and receives a one-month extension from Quoc. Bragg eventually defaults and Quoc sues Sands, Cruz, and Elliott. The defendants claim that they have been discharged from liability as a result of (1) the extension of time and (2) the failure to give them notice of dishonor. How should the case be decided?

26 Bank Deposits and Collections

26:1 Introduction

Banks serve individuals and the business community by making loans and by providing a safe place in which to keep cash assets. Equally important, by offering checking services banks provide a means by which their customers can pay debts conveniently by *check* and obtain payment on checks received by them.

The preceding three chapters have dealt generally with commercial paper, as governed by Article 3 of the UCC. This chapter focuses primarily on the check, which is a specific type of commercial paper. The emphasis here is on the rights, duties, and liabilities of banks with respect to what is known as the check collection process (see Section 26:4).

Definitions (UCC §§ 3-104, 4-104, 4-105) Most people are familiar with checks and use them regularly, but perhaps without an accurate understanding of what checks really are. By definition, a check is a "draft" that is payable by a bank on demand. A draft is a negotiable instrument (see Chapter 23) that is an "order." An order is a written direction (as opposed to a request or authorization) that a designated person or entity pay a stated amount of money. Thus, a check is a written direction to a bank to pay someone a stated amount of money.

For purposes of this chapter, a "customer" is a person or an entity that has an account with a bank or for whom a bank has agreed to obtain payment on checks. A customer is said to draw a check by writing it out, after which that customer is referred to as the drawer of the check. The bank on which the check is drawn and which must ultimately pay the check is known as the payor bank, while the bank with which the check is initially deposited by a customer is the depositary bank. The party in whose favor a check is drawn is the payee. When the payee deposits the check—that is, when he delivers it to a bank with instructions that the amount of the check be credited to his account—he becomes a depositor.

Governing Law Checks are governed to a large extent by Article 3 of the UCC (see Chapters 23–25). However, the collection of checks is governed by Article 4 of the UCC, which has been enacted in all the states. Article 4 establishes (1) a time schedule for collecting and paying checks and (2) the framework of the relationship between banks and their customers. These generally can be varied by agreement between a bank and its customer. Bear in mind, though, that the bank's duty to act in good faith and to use ordinary care in its processing of checks cannot be eliminated by agreement.

26:2 Deposits; Relationship Between Bank and Depositor

A deposit can be of cash, of a check, or of certain other drafts and orders. Depending on the mutual intent of the bank and its customer, any given deposit can be general or specific.[1]

Most deposits are general. A general deposit is, in effect, a loan by the depositor to the bank, and it is payable on demand. As soon as a general deposit of money is made, title to that money passes from the depositor to the bank. If the customer deposits a check, however, the deposit is of a *right* to money rather than of money itself. The deposit does not become one of money—so that title passes to the bank—until the check has been accepted and paid by the payor bank. Thus, for example, if a check is returned unpaid due to lack of sufficient funds in the drawer's account, the check is still the depositor's property. Therefore, the depositor (rather than the bank) will then proceed against the drawer to obtain the amount of money represented by the check.

Every deposit is regarded as being general unless it is made special by agreement between the parties. The distinctive feature of a special deposit used to be that when the depositor demanded it, the bank had to return exactly what had been deposited, rather than its equivalent. Since this requirement is illogical with respect to money deposits, it no longer exists under most circumstances. Today, a special deposit is one made for a special purpose that, in effect, prevents the bank's use of the deposited money. For example, a corporation might make a special deposit to establish a fund for the redemption (buying back) of some of its outstanding stock.[2]

Relationship Between Bank and Depositor   The relationship between a bank and its depositor is voluntary and based on contract. With respect to a general deposit, the relationship is one of creditor and debtor, which is consistent with the bank's acquisition of title to a general deposit. With respect to a special deposit, the relationship is more like one of bailment[3] because the deposited money does not become part of the bank's general assets.

---

[1]The discussion in this chapter focuses on deposits in checking accounts. Bear in mind, however, that deposits can also be made in other types of accounts. For example, depositors often deposit money in savings accounts. The traditional form of savings account is the passbook account, which pays a low rate of interest but allows withdrawals at any time. Money can also be deposited for fixed terms ranging from 30 days to a number of years. A typical example is the treasury bill account, which has a 26-week term. Term accounts pay higher rates of interest than passbook accounts, but depositors incur a substantial penalty if they have to withdraw their money before the end of the term.

[2]A corporation's redemption of its stock is discussed in Chapter 43.

[3]A bailment arises when one person has temporary possession of, but not title to, another person's property. Bailments are discussed in Chapter 33.

In certain transactions there is an agency relationship (see Chapter 48) between a bank and its depositor. For example, the depositary bank acts as the depositor's collection agent when the depositor deposits a check that is drawn on a different bank. Moreover, a bailment relationship exists even as to what will become a general deposit when, for example, a merchant places a sack containing his business receipts for the day in a bank's night deposit box.

 Some banks attempt to limit their liability with respect to night deposits by requiring that the depositor agree to accept the full risk of any loss until the deposit has been verified by a bank employee the next day. Courts in a number of states have held that these agreements violate public policy, and so have refused to enforce them.

26:3   Checks and Checklike Drafts

When a person buys goods or services, there may or may not be an immediate assignment of the person's money to the seller, depending on how the person pays for the goods or services. If he pays in cash, there is an immediate assignment to the seller. If, however, the buyer pays by check, there is *not* an immediate assignment to the seller of money that the buyer has on deposit with the payor bank. Instead, and as discussed in more detail in Section 26:4, the seller receives only a provisional credit to his account when he deposits the check. Thus, the credit becomes final—and an actual transfer of money has occurred—only after the payor bank has received and paid the check. For this reason, the seller holding the check has no rights against the payor bank if that bank refuses to pay the check; the seller's only recourse is against the drawer.

Types of Checks   The check that an individual or business usually draws is an ordinary check. This is simply a draft drawn on a bank and to be paid on demand out of the drawer's personal or business account with that bank. An ordinary check that bears a date later than the date on which the check was drawn is a postdated check. A postdated check is valid, and it is payable on or after the date indicated on it. Among the reasons why a drawer would use a postdated check is the drawer's knowledge that although he currently has insufficient funds in his account to cover the check, there will be sufficient funds on the indicated date.

At times, a party being paid by check is unwilling to accept the risk that an ordinary check will not be paid. Special types of checks are available to meet this need. These include certified checks, cashier's checks, banker's checks, and traveler's checks.

A certified check is one that the payor bank has agreed in advance to pay, so that the check must ordinarily be paid even if there are insufficient funds in the drawer's account. The check is presented to the payor bank by either the drawer or the payee. After satisfying itself that the check is valid and that the drawer has sufficient funds in his account to cover it, the bank stamps the check "certified" or "accepted." The object of having a check certified is to make the check the equivalent of money.

A cashier's check is a check drawn by a bank on itself. Its strength lies in the fact that it is the obligation of the bank rather than of a bank customer. A banker's check is similar to a cashier's check except that the check is drawn on another bank rather than on the drawer bank.

A traveler's check is purchased for later use by a customer who does not want to carry cash. It is similar to a cashier's check in that it is drawn on the payor bank (or other issuing organization, such as American Express). It differs from a cashier's check in that (1) the name of the payee is left blank, to be filled in later when the customer uses the check and (2) the customer signs the check twice—once when he purchases it and again when he uses it. The customer's second signature makes the check both negotiable and the equivalent of money.

Checklike Drafts   At one time so-called "thrift institutions" such as savings and loan associations and credit unions could offer a higher rate of return on money deposited with them than banks could. At the same time, banks were not permitted to pay interest on money deposited in checking accounts. The result was that people turned to banks for checking account services, but they often deposited their savings with thrift institutions. Much of that has changed in recent years. Today banks are permitted to offer interest-bearing checking accounts, while the thrift institutions are allowed to offer checklike services to their depositors. The result is that some people who once relied exclusively on conventional checks now use drafts drawn on thrift institutions instead.

A checklike draft drawn on a savings and loan association is called a *negotiable order of withdrawal (NOW)*. This instrument is much like a check except that it is not drawn on a bank. A draft drawn on a credit union is known as a share draft. Since credit unions do not have direct access to the Federal Reserve collection system (see 26:4), share drafts are payable through commercial banks that do have access to the system. As a result, a share draft indicates on it not only the credit union that is ultimately responsible for payment, but also the bank through which the draft is payable.

NOWs and share drafts fall within the scope of instruments governed by Articles 3 and 4 of the UCC. It is likely that the courts will decide that the checklike drafts that money market funds are currently allowing their depositors to write are also governed by Articles 3 and 4.

26:4   The Collection Process

The holder of a check is the party (1) having possession of a filled-out check and (2) having the right to payment on the check. The payee, who is the initial holder, first indorses the check.[4] The payee can then (1) attempt to cash the check, usually by presenting it to the payor bank and requesting payment; or (2) deposit it in his account; or (3) give it to somebody else, who becomes the new holder. At some

---

[4]The payee indorses the check by signing his name on the back. A depositary bank will not ordinarily accept an unindorsed check for deposit although, to avoid delay, Article 4 allows the bank to add any needed indorsement. Indorsements are discussed in more detail in Chapter 23.

point a holder usually deposits the check, and the depositary bank then attempts to obtain payment on the check from the payor bank.

In essence, the *collection process* is the means by which a check deposited in one bank but drawn on another is paid. Thus, if a drawer and payee are both customers of the same bank, collection does not occur if the payee deposits the check with that bank. The bank simply deducts the amount of the check from the drawer's account and adds it to the payee's account.

The holder of a check usually deposits the check in a bank other than the payor bank. The check must then be physically transferred back to the payor bank, which is accomplished through one or more interbank transfers. Because it is possible that the payor bank will *dishonor* the check when it receives it, the depositary bank accepts the deposit "subject to collection." The bank, acting as the depositor's agent, then begins the collection process. Meanwhile, the bank makes a *provisional settlement* of the check. This means that the bank gives the depositor's account a provisional credit for the amount of the check. A provisional credit is a credit that can be reversed later if the check is not paid. The provisional credit that the bank gives does not become final until enough time has passed for the depositary bank to have received either a notice of dishonor or return of the unpaid check (see Section 26:6).

 Generally, a depositary bank will neither allow its customer to withdraw money that has been only provisionally credited to his account nor pay checks drawn against the credit. Exceptions are often made, however, for valued customers whose credit is known to be good.

A depositary bank can send a check directly to the payor bank for payment. However, the route is usually less direct. If the depositary and payor banks are in different parts of the country, the check is apt to pass through two of the 13 Federal Reserve Banks (FRBs) located across the country.

EXAMPLE
Williams, a resident of Show Low, Arizona, draws a check on her account at the Show Low branch of First Arizona Bank. The payee named in the check is Zebco, a Pennsylvania company. Zebco deposits the check in its account at Colonists Bank in Philadelphia. The route then taken by the check might be as follows: Colonists sends the check to the FRB serving Philadelphia, which sends it to the FRB serving Phoenix, Arizona, which sends it to First Arizona's headquarters bank in Phoenix, which sends it to the First Arizona Show Low branch.

Banks in the collection chain other than the depositary and payor banks are called intermediary banks. The term "collecting bank" refers to any bank in the collection chain other than the payor bank. Thus, Colonists Bank and all the intermediary banks in the above example are collecting banks. Just as the customer who deposits a check receives a provisional credit for it from the depositary bank, each collecting bank receives a provisional credit from the bank to which it transfers the check.

Clearinghouses   Because of the large flow of checks in major urban areas, banks in many cities have formed what are known as *clearinghouses*. Each day, every bank that is a member of a clearinghouse (1) sends to the clearinghouse all checks received by it and drawn on other member banks and (2) receives from the clearinghouse, in a single package, all checks that are drawn on that member bank and received by the clearinghouse from other member banks. The clearinghouse makes a single daily settlement with each member bank for checks handled by the clearinghouse that day. If the total amount of all checks sent by a member is more than the total of the checks received by it, the clearinghouse pays the member the difference. In the opposite situation, the member bank makes a payment to the clearinghouse.

26:5   Rights and Duties of Collecting Bank

Whenever a check is deposited with other than the payor bank, there will be at least one collecting bank, and often there will be more than one. Article 4 imposes certain requirements on each collecting bank and, for that matter, on the customer who deposits the check in the first place.

General Duty of Ordinary Care; Midnight Deadline (UCC §§ 4-104, 4-107, 4-202)   Article 4 lists five specific collection tasks that each collecting bank must perform with ordinary care. For example, the bank must use ordinary care in sending a check to the next bank in the collection chain, whether the check is moving toward the payor bank or, if the payor bank has refused to pay the check, toward the collecting bank's transferor. This ordinary care requirement applies to such matters as the method by which a check is physically transferred and the choice of intermediary banks or other agents, if such a choice exists.

Each collecting bank must also accomplish its processing of a check within a reasonable time. Generally speaking, the bank satisfies this requirement if it meets its *midnight deadline*. The midnight deadline is midnight of the banking day following the banking day on which a bank receives a check. To allow a more uniform work flow, Article 4 permits each bank to set an afternoon hour of 2 p.m. or later as a cutoff hour for the processing of checks on any given day.

EXAMPLE
Valley Bank, which is open for business between 9 a.m. and 5 p.m. on weekdays, has set 3 p.m. as its cutoff hour. At 2:30 p.m. on Friday, June 6, Valley receives for collection check #501 drawn on Prairie Bank. At 3:30 p.m. on the same day it receives check #703, also drawn on Prairie. Valley has until midnight on Monday, June 9, to send check #501 to Prairie or to another collecting bank, but it has until midnight on June 10 to complete its processing of check #703.

Warranties of Customer and Collecting Bank (UCC § 4-207)   Article 4 lists a number of warranties that collecting banks and customers are deemed to make whenever they transfer a check and receive provisional credit for it. A collecting bank warrants, among other things, (1) that its title to the check is good, (2) that all indorsements on the check are genuine or authorized, and (3) that the check has not been materially altered (see 26:8). These warranties are in favor of the transferee collecting bank and each collecting bank that comes later in the collection chain. Warranties of a similar type, but in favor of the payor bank, are deemed to be given by each customer or collecting bank that obtains payment of a check.[5]

The distinction between the two types of warranties is, in essence, that warranties of the first type operate as a check moves from the depository bank to the payor bank, while those of the second type operate as the "payment" moves back along the chain to the depository bank. In practice, instead of there being any actual transfer of payment for every individual check, each collecting bank simply allows its provisional settlement of the check to become final. This occurs automatically with the passage of time unless the payor bank revokes the settlement.

The article 4 warranty provision has the effect of placing on the depository bank the burden of making sure that all indorsements on a check are valid. This policy if logical since the depository bank can investigate the validity of indorsements more easily than intermediary banks or the payor bank can. Thus, if a payor bank has paid a check that has a forged indorsement, the bank is usually liable to the drawer if the drawer has given timely notice about the error (see Section 26:8). The payor bank will then seek recourse from the collecting bank from which it received the check, claiming breach of warranty. This process will be repeated back along the collection chain until it reaches the depository bank. That bank's only recourse is against the customer who deposited the check.

 Any claim for breach of one of these warranties must be made within a reasonable time after the claimant's discovery of the breach. If a claimant delays beyond a reasonable time, the party who would otherwise be liable is discharged to the extent of any loss suffered by that party because of the delay.

EXAMPLE
On August 1, State Bank learned that a $1,000 check it paid had carried an unauthorized indorsement. The check had been indorsed by Tom Horn and deposited by him in his account with First Federal Bank. During the month of August, Horn maintained more than $1,000 in his First Federal account, but on September 2, he closed the account and left for parts unknown. If State does not assert a breach of warranty claim against First Federal until September 15, First Federal will probably not be liable for the $1,000. State will have failed to act within a reasonable time, and First Federal will have suffered potential loss as a result. Had the claim come during August, First Federal could have recovered from Horn, but now it cannot do so.

Charge-Back or Refund (UCC § 4-212)   If a collecting bank that has given a provisional credit on a check fails to receive a final settlement of the check, the bank has the right to *charge-back* (reverse) the credit given to its customer or to obtain a

---

[5]Bear in mind that both types of warranties discussed here are the same warranties that exist with respect to the transfer or obtaining of payment or acceptance of *any* negotiable instrument. The warranties are discussed in greater detail in Chapter 25.

refund from its customer. For example, if a depositary bank has provisionally credited its customer's account and the check is returned due to insufficiency of funds in the drawer's account, the bank can deduct the amount of the check from the customer's account. The following case illustrates how the midnight deadline rule applies to a bank's exercise of the charge-back right.

Manufacturers Hanover Trust Co.
v
Akpan
91 Misc 2d 622, 398 NYS2d 477, 22 UCCRS 1009
(New York City Civil Court, 1977)

[On Monday, August 18, Akpan, the defendant, deposited a $2,500 check drawn by Lawrence on her account with Branch 102 of the plaintiff, Manufacturers Hanover Trust Company. On August 19, the check was received by the payor bank, and it was not paid due to insufficient funds in Lawrence's account. The payor bank returned the check to Manufacturers' headquarters bank that day. On August 22, Akpan drew a check for $2,490 on her account at Branch 102 and received cash for it. On Monday, August 25, Branch 102 first received notice from Manufacturers' headquarters bank that the $2,500 check had been returned. Branch 102 notified Akpan at once and informed her that her account had been charged for that amount. Apparently because there was little or no money left in the account, Manufacturers then sued Akpan to obtain the refund allegedly due it.]

Imperato, Judge.

*   *   *

Plaintiff's first theory of liability is based on [UCC § 4-212], which gives a collecting bank (plaintiff) a remedy of charge-back if it has made a provisional settlement with its customer which fails by reason of dishonor. But this remedy is conditioned on the requirement that the bank, by its midnight deadline or within a longer reasonable time after it learns of the facts, [return] the item or sends notification of the facts. . . .

Thus, applying the midnight deadline rule in the instant case, plaintiff would have had to have given notice to Mrs. Akpan by midnight of Wednesday, August 20, . . . in order to exercise its right of charge-back. Notice was not actually given until Monday August 25, . . .

Plaintiff relies on [UCC § 4-106], which states that a separate office of a bank is considered a separate bank for the purpose of determining time limits under Articles 3 and 4 of the U.C.C. But even considering Branch 102 as a separate bank and not bound by information of the check's dishonor had by [Manufacturers's headquarters bank], this cannot be construed to mean that the midnight deadline rule first began to run on Monday August 25, . . . when Branch 102 first received notice of the dishonor.

The official comment #4 to [UCC § 4-106] seems to deal with a situation such as in the instant case.

"Similarly, the receipt of a stop payment order at one branch should not be notice to another branch . . . , *although in circumstances in which ordinary care requires the communication of a notice or order to the proper branch of a bank, such notice or order would be effective at such proper branch from the time it was or should have been received.*"[Court's emphasis.]

Ordinary care required in the instant case that notice be sent to Branch 102 by the midnight deadline of [Manufacturers's headquarters bank] on midnight Wednesday. Such notice would be effective at the time Branch 102 *should have received notice;* thus the midnight deadline for Branch 102, was midnight Thursday. [Court's emphasis.] Since notice of dishonor was not sent to defendant within the midnight deadline, the remedy of charge-back is unavailable. . . .

[Judgment for defendant.]

26:6   Duties of Payor Bank

A payor bank has the general duty of paying a valid check drawn on it if the drawer has sufficient funds in his account at the time the bank receives the check. UCC § 4-302 provides, in essence, that a payor bank must make a provisional settlement of a check before midnight of the day of receipt. The bank then has until its midnight deadline to (1) pay the check; (2) return the check; or (3) if the check is not being either paid or returned, send a notice of dishonor. A returned check or notice of dishonor is sent to the collecting bank from which the payor bank received the check. If the payor bank fails to take the required action in time, it is liable for the amount of the check unless it has a valid defense, such as breach of a warranty (see Section 26:5).

Final Payment of Checks; Posting (UCC §§ 4-109, 4-213)   The term "final payment" refers to the time when the settlement of a check by the payor bank becomes final, rather than being merely provisional. Article 4 lists various events, the occurrence of any one of which constitutes final payment. For example, final payment occurs (1) when the payor bank pays a check in cash, (2) when it has completed the *posting process,* or (3) when it fails to revoke a provisional settlement made by it earlier.

The term "posting process" refers to the usual procedure by which the payor bank (1) decides to pay a check and (2) records the payment. Examples of steps, one or more of which can constitute posting, are (1) verifying any signature, (2) determining whether the drawer has sufficient funds in his account to cover the check, and (3) stamping the check "Paid."

Charging Customer's Account; Order of Payment (UCC §§ 4-303, 4-401)   When a payor bank receives and pays a check drawn by its customer, the bank charges the customer's account for the amount of the check. As is discussed in more detail below, the bank has the right (1) to pay a check even though the customer has insufficient funds in his account to cover the check, (2) to pay an altered check, (3) to pay a check that has been completed by someone other than the drawer, and (4) to pay in any order convenient to it checks from the same account that it receives at the same time.

A payor bank's payment of a check drawn on insufficient funds in the drawer's account creates an overdraft, which is a negative amount in the drawer's account. Bear in mind that the bank is under no obligation to pay a check if the payment will create an overdraft. The bank's *right* to pay the check exists because the check is deemed to carry the drawer's promise to reimburse the bank.

If a check has been altered as, for example, by having the amount of the check increased, the bank can charge the customer's account for the original amount of the check. The bank can also pay and charge the customer's account for a check that was completed by other than the drawer, as long as the bank has not been notified that the completion is improper.

EXAMPLE

Axel gives Katrinka a check to cover the cost of groceries that Katrinka is going to buy. Axel dates and signs the check, and he writes in the name of the local supermarket as payee, but he leaves the amount blank. After completing her shopping, Katrinka completes the check by filling in the amount of her shopping bill. Unless Axel's bank has notice that Katrinka's completion of the check is improper, it can and probably will pay the check as written.

A payor bank does not necessarily receive checks in the same order in which the checks were drawn. Also, and particularly with respect to a high-activity account, the bank might receive at the same time a number of checks drawn on the same account. Article 4 gives the bank the right to pay the checks in any order convenient to the bank.

Wrongful Dishonor (UCC § 4-402)   A bank that wrongfully dishonors a customer's check is liable to the customer for damages proximately caused by the wrongful dishonor. The term "proximate cause" means a primary cause from which a particular loss followed as a natural and direct consequence, and without which the loss would not have occurred. If a dishonor occurs because of a mistake, the customer can recover only the actual damages sustained. If dishonor occurs for a reason other than mistake, such as if the bank acted intentionally and without a good reason, the customer can also recover punitive damages.[6]

Whether particular loss suffered by a customer is proximately caused by a wrongful dishonor is a question of fact that must be determined in each case. That question, as well as the related problem of computing the amount of money that the customer should be awarded, can be troublesome, as the following case illustrates.

American Fletcher National Bank & Trust Co.
v
Flick
146 Ind App 122 252 NE2d 839, 7 UCCRS 224
(Indiana Appellate Court, 1969)

[Flick sued American Fletcher Bank for damages arising from American Fletcher's dishonor of checks drawn by Flick. Flick had operated a used-car business, and the checks were drawn on his business account. He sought $125,000 for damages to his credit and business standing, for loss of business income, and for mental suffering. The trial court awarded Flick $18,000, and American Fletcher appealed.]

Sullivan, Judge.

*   *   *

---

[6]Punitive damages are awarded to a person not as compensation for actual loss suffered, but as a civil penalty against a wrongdoer and to deter similar wrongful acts by others.

We are here faced with two questions. First, how much evidence is sufficient to allow reasonable men to differ as to whether a particular loss, injury, or harm was proximately caused by a wrongful dishonor? Second, once a particular harm is deemed compensable (proximately caused) how much evidence is sufficient to establish the amount of money which should be awarded for such harm? It must be kept in mind that both questions primarily involve determinations of fact according to the evidence adduced in the particular case. As a matter of law, however, certain minimum standards must be met before the questions of fact may be considered. . . .

As to the first question posed, we hold that when a bank wrongfully dishonors its customer's business check there arises a presumption that the customer's credit and business standing is thereby harmed. . . . The primary reason for the recognition of this presumption is that a wrongful dishonor renders the existence of *some* harm to the customer's credit and business standing so probable that it makes legal sense as well as common sense to assume the existence of such harm unless and until the adversary comes forward with some evidence to the contrary. [Court's emphasis.] Although we are not prepared to go as far as did [the court in a Pennsylvania case], the following statement from that opinion is a recognition of the high probability of such harm:

> In the modern world the financial credit of a man, particularly of one engaged in commercial pursuits, is a much prized and valuable asset. Although laboriously built it is easily destroyed. The banks of the country, through which the great volume of our commercial business is transacted, have a deserved reputation for accuracy and care in the conduct of their affairs. Hence when a check of a depositor is refused at the counter of his bank, that portion of the commercial world, greater or less, that comes within the sphere of his transactions, promptly imputes the blame to him rather than to the bank. . . .

The rationale of the [above case], however, does not hold true as to such other "consequential" losses or injuries as may be conceivably sustained as a proximate result of wrongful dishonor. Additional harms, injuries or losses, such as those alleged by Flick, are susceptible of evidentiary proof, both as to their actual existence and as to their extent. Flick here has failed to bring forth sufficient evidence to show that loss of income or other expense, harm or injury, if any, was proximately caused by the wrongful dishonor. He, therefore, cannot recover for such alleged loss, expense, harm or injury. He is . . . restricted to recovery for the harm to his credit and business standing, which harm is established by way of the unrebutted presumption heretofore discussed. . . .

Having found only the harm to credit and business standing compensable in this case the question which remains is whether there was sufficient evidence to justify any more than nominal damages. We think not and therefore plaintiff may only recover nominal damages. . . .

The law presumes that at least nominal damages result from a harm. . . . Therefore, plaintiff is entitled to at least nominal damages for the harm to his credit and business standing. We are not unmindful that there must be drawn a clear distinction between the measure of proof necessary to establish the fact that the plaintiff sustained some harm and the measure of proof necessary to enable the trier of fact to fix the amount to compensate for such harm. And we do not preclude recovery for other than nominal damages . . . merely because plaintiff is unable to fix the exact amount. We recognize that the amount of damages appropriate for harm to credit and business standing is difficult to prove. When it is found that a harm has been caused and the only uncertainty is as to the dollar value of the harm, there can rarely be good reason for refusing, on account of such uncertainty, any damages whatever. . . . However, there must be some evidence on which to base an award of *substantial* damages. [Court's emphasis.] . . .

In [one case] there was evidence that ten checks were dishonored; that one [creditor] thereafter refused to accept a [check drawn by the plaintiff in the case], and that [the plaintiff] was required to go to the bank, cash the check, then take the cash to the [creditor]. There was further evidence that some persons who had previously accepted the [plaintiff's] checks now refused to accept them; that other places of business denied the [plaintiff] credit after the dishonors; and that a salesman, who had sold the [plaintiff] a map and for which he was paid by one of the dishonored checks, came to the [plaintiff's] place of business, and ripped the map off the wall because he had been given "a bad check for it." The . . . court held this evidence sufficient to raise a question of fact to be determined by the jury as to whether the [plaintiff's] credit had been substantially damaged as a proximate result of the dishonors.

In our case, Flick completely failed to present any evidence that the wrongful dishonor proximately caused the substantial damages which were alleged. The evidence is undisputed that shortly after April 15, 1965, the bank returned three of Flick's checks because of insufficient funds in Flick's account. It is also undisputed that some time after April 15, 1965, Flick's business at Morris Street Auto Sales declined, he sold fewer autos, his income declined, he eventually began to lose money, and that his used car lot was closed in the fall of 1966. There is nothing in the record, however, linking these undisputed facts with the dishonor of the checks. There is nothing in the record which indicates that anyone other than the payees on the checks and Flick had knowledge of the dishonored checks or *could* have had any knowledge of said checks. [Court's emphasis.] There is nothing in the record to indicate that the checks caused any action or inaction by any other party. To the contrary, there is affirmative evidence in the record indicating that there were reasons other than the dishonor for the decline of Flick's business. We hold that appellee Flick is entitled to recover only nominal damages. . . .

[Judgment reversed.]

Stale Checks (UCC § 4-404)   A check is regarded as being stale six months after the date of the check. A payor bank is not required to pay a stale check (other than a certified check), although it can do so as long as it acts in good faith. In practice, most banks will not pay a stale check without first consulting the drawer, but exceptions are made under some circumstances. For example, a bank receiving a stale dividend check drawn by its corporate customer will ordinarily pay it at once, realizing that the corporation wants payment to be made.

26:7   Stop-Payment Orders

A *stop-payment order* is an order directing that a payor bank not pay a particular check. UCC § 4-403 gives each customer the right to stop payment on a check drawn by him. To be effective, the order must be received by the payor bank early enough to give the bank a reasonable time to act on it. An order is too late if the bank has taken any one of various actions listed in § 4-303 before receiving and having a chance to act on the order. For example, the order is too late if the bank has already paid or certified the check, or if it has completed the posting process.

What constitutes a reasonable time if none of the events listed in § 4-303 has occurred depends on the circumstances. For example, if a customer gives his bank a stop-payment order, but the bank cashes the check when the payee presents it at that bank 90 minutes later, the bank has probably had sufficient time for processing and acting on the order. The same would not be true if the check were presented for payment only several minutes after the bank's receipt of the stop-payment order.

A person who fears that a stop-payment order might not be processed in time to stop a particular check can create an overdraft situation by withdrawing most of the money from his account, thus leaving insufficient funds to cover the check in question. This procedure is risky in view of the bank's right to pay a check drawn on insufficient funds (see 26:6). The safer practice is to close the account by withdrawing everything from it, although the customer must then make other arrangements for outstanding checks that *are* to be paid.

A stop-payment order can be oral or in writing. An oral stop-payment order is effective for only 14 calendar days unless the order is confirmed in writing within that period. A written order is effective for six months, but it can be renewed at the end of that period, and again following subsequent six-month periods if the drawer believes that the check might still be in circulation. In this regard, recall that a payor bank has the right to pay a stale check, although it is not required to do so (see 26:6).

A bank that pays a check despite having received a timely stop-payment order is liable to the customer for any damages that the customer suffered as a result. Article 4 states that the customer must prove both the existence and the amount of his damages, although some courts say that the measure of damages is automatically the amount of the check unless the bank shows that the customer suffered a lesser loss.

Payment generally cannot be stopped on a cashier's check, although an exception can be made under unusual circumstances.

26:8   Bank's Liability as to Forged or Altered Check

A forged check is one on which what appears to be the signature of the drawer or indorser has actually been written by someone else, acting without authorization. Forged drawer signatures usually occur after an unauthorized person has obtained possession of one or more blank checks belonging to somebody else. Since checks that have already been drawn are often accessible to more people than blank checks are, forged indorsements are more common than forged drawer signatures. At times, however, the signatures of both the drawer and the indorser can be forgeries. For example, a person can obtain someone else's blank check and draw the check payable to a legitimate payee, forge the drawer's signature and the payee's indorsement, and then attempt to cash the check at the payee's bank.

An altered check is one on which the words or numbers written by the drawer have been changed by someone else. For example, what was drawn as a $100 check might be altered to call for the payment of $1,000, or the drawer's intent in postdating a check might be frustrated by someone else's alteration of the date.

The payor bank is under no duty to pay a forged or altered check. Indeed, the bank can be liable to its customer, the drawer, if it does so (UCC § 4-406). This liability is not automatic, however, and it might not exist at all if the customer has failed to perform the duties imposed on him. Assuming that the payor bank has paid a check and charged the drawer's account, the check will eventually be returned to the drawer, usually with a periodic statement showing the activity in the drawer's account during the period covered by the statement. Most banks send out statements and canceled checks to their customers monthly. If a statement and the checks are not sent to the customer, they are at least made available for the customer's inspection. The customer is required to use reasonable care and promptness to examine the statement and checks, discover any forgery of his signature or alteration of a check, and notify the bank.

If the bank can show that the customer failed to perform this duty and that the bank suffered loss as a result, it is not liable to the customer with respect to the forgery or alteration. Also, if the customer fails to notify the bank about a forgery or alteration within 14 days after having access to the check and statement, the bank is not liable with respect to its later good-faith payment of any checks that are forged or altered in the same way by the same person.

EXAMPLE

Althea works for Gibson Co. in the accounting department. She has access to Gibson's blank checks. Each month Althea writes a check naming herself as payee and forges the drawer signature authorized for the Gibson account. Gibson receives its statement and canceled checks each month, but Althea's unlawful activity goes undiscovered for eleven months. Because of the 14-day rule, the bank is liable on only the first two forged checks at most, and it could be liable on only the first one, depending on the timing.

The above rules by which the payor bank can escape liability on a forged or altered check do not apply if the customer can show that the bank failed to use ordinary care in paying the check. Lack of ordinary care can be established by proof that the bank's procedures are below standard or that the bank's employees failed to exercise reasonable care in processing the check. For example, a bank receiving a check for payment is generally expected to verify the drawer's signature. It does so by comparing the signature on the check with the drawer's signature on the bank's signature card. If the check appears to have been altered, the bank should contact the drawer before paying it. A bank can also violate the ordinary care requirement by paying a check bearing a facsimile drawer signature if the bank has authority only to pay checks on which the drawer signature is handwritten.[7]

---

[7]A facsimile signature is placed on a document with a stamp or signature plate. Businesspeople often use facsimile signatures on routine correspondence, and sometimes they also use them on checks.

Even if a bank failed to use ordinary care, it is not liable on a forged drawer signature or an alteration if the customer does not discover and report the forgery or alteration within one year after the check and statement are made available to him. In the case of a forged indorsement, the customer has three years in which to discover and report it. The reason for the longer period is that the customer himself is apt to be unaware that an indorsement is a forgery until the matter is brought to his attention by the party who was supposed to have received payment on the check.

Under some circumstances, a payor bank that has paid a forged or altered check can also escape liability because of a provision of UCC Article 3. UCC § 3-406 prevents the drawer from recovering against the bank if the drawer's negligence was a substantial contributing factor in allowing the forgery or alteration to occur. For example, an employer who leaves blank checks in an unlocked drawer that is easily accessible to employees who are not authorized to handle checks is apt to find it difficult to recover from the bank for payment of a check forged by an employee.

 Employee dishonesty is a chronic problem for many businesses. If possible, duties connected with keeping a business checking account should be divided among several employees. One employee might be made responsible for blank checks, while another is made responsible for inspecting bank statements and canceled checks. If facsimile signatures are used on checks, a third employee should be responsible for the stamp or signature plate.

26:9 Customer's Death or Incompetence

The drawer of a check might die or be declared by a court to be mentally incompetent after he has drawn the check, but before it is paid by the payor bank. With one exception discussed below, UCC § 4-405 provides that a bank loses its authority to accept, collect, or pay a check only when the bank (1) becomes aware of the death or adjudication of incompetence of its customer and (2) has a reasonable chance to act on that knowledge. Until those conditions are met, any collecting or payor bank can process the check in the usual manner.

The exception to the above rule is that regardless of a bank's knowledge of its customer's death, during the ten-day period following the date of death the bank can pay or certify checks drawn by the customer. The reason for this exception is that holders of recent checks should be permitted to obtain payment without having to assert their claims (for the amounts of the checks) against the deceased drawer's estate.[8] The only limit on this ten-day rule is that any person claiming an interest in the estate, such as a relative or creditor, can order the bank to stop payment on all the deceased drawer's checks or on one or more specific checks.

EXAMPLE
Jake was of limited means, and he owed $10,000 to Smoot and $15,000 to Hawley. On January 10, Jake drew a check for $10,000 payable to Smoot, and he sent Smoot

---

[8]The liability of a decedent's estate for the decedent's debts is discussed in Chapter 38.

the check. Jake died on January 12, and it is apparent to Hawley that the value of Jake's estate is less than $15,000. Hawley can order the payor bank to stop payment on Smoot's check, even though the bank could otherwise have paid it until at least January 22. By so doing, Hawley can increase the value of Jake's estate, which constitutes the fund available for paying Jake's creditors.

26:10   Customer's Right to Privacy

The financial records that banks compile and maintain on their customers are confidential by nature, and most customers would prefer that the records not be publicly disclosed. Accordingly, banks have the general duty not to disclose financial information about their customers without the customers' authorization or consent. This authorization or consent, when given, usually arises from a customer's naming a bank as a credit reference. As the following case illustrates, however, there can be circumstances under which a bank *should* disclose confidential information about one of its customers.

Richfield Bank & Trust Co.
v
Sjogren
309 Minn 362, 244 NW2d 648
(Minnesota Supreme Court, 1976)

[Mr. and Mrs. Sjogren, the respondents, borrowed money from Richfield Bank & Trust Company, the appellant. The loan, which was to be repaid in 90 days, was obtained so that the Sjogrens could buy air purification units from National Pollution Eliminators, Inc., which had a checking account with Richfield. The loan was handled exclusively by Michael Thompson, Richfield's loan officer. Thompson was the only bank officer who handled National Pollution's account, and he was an active member in National Pollution's business affairs. He also knew that National Pollution was insolvent and would be unable to supply the purification units (which it intended to buy using the money received from the Sjogrens), but he did not disclose this information to the Sjogrens. The Sjogrens failed to repay the loan, and Richfield sued them. The Sjogrens' defense was that the transaction had been induced by Richfield's fraudulent concealment of material information. The jury found for the Sjogrens, Richfield moved

for judgment notwithstanding the verdict, and the motion was denied. Richfield appealed.]

MacLaughlin, Justice.

*   *   *

The determination of whether the facts of this case fall within a category of "special circumstances" which would jusitfy imposing on the bank the duty to disclose the financial condition of its depositor, National Pollution, is complicated by the principle that a bank is generally under a duty not to disclose the financial condition of its depositors. . . .

In the [cases supporting this principle], however, the banks did not have actual knowledge of any fraudulent activities. . . . The clear implication is that if the bank actually knew that its depositor was insolvent and engaged in fraudulent activity at the time of the transaction, then it would have been under a duty to disclose this fact, since, . . .

[t]here is a moral duty of banks to the community in which they do business to use reasonable care in seeing that their depositors are not committing a fraud upon the public.

Thus, the instant case can be distinguished from those cases holding that a bank may not disclose the financial condition of its depositors if it can be shown that Richfield Bank had *actual knowledge* of the fraudulent activities of its depositor, National Pollution. [Court's emphasis.]

In determining whether Richfield Bank had actual knowledge of fraudulent activity, it should be noted that knowledge of insolvency is not necessarily equivalent to knowledge of fraud. It is well settled that an insolvent purchaser, buying on credit, is not bound to disclose his financial condition to the seller if he has a reasonable expectation of being able to pay for the goods. . . . If, on the other hand, a party is so insolvent that he has no reasonable expectation of fulfilling his contract obligations, then it is fraud for that party to fail to disclose his insolvency before entering the contract. . . .

Applying this principle to the instant case, the determinative question is whether Richfield Bank, through its loan officer, Michael Thompson, actually knew that National Pollution was so irretrievably insolvent that it had no reasonable expectation of fulfilling its obligations under the contract with respondents. If Richfield Bank knew only that National Pollution was insolvent, it would not have actual knowledge of fraud and thus would not be under a duty to disclose the financial condition of its depositor to respondents.

The jury specifically found (1) that National Pollution's officers knew that they could not fulfill their contractual obligation to respondents; and (2) that Michael Thompson knew of the pertinent financial condition of National Pollution and of the actions, concealment, and representations of the officers of National Pollution in the conduct of their business in relation to the respondents. These findings are adequately supported by the record, which included substantial evidence as set forth herein, clearly demonstrating Thompson's extensive personal participation in an intimate knowledge of the affairs of National Pollution. Based on this evidence, the conclusion that Thompson actually knew that National Pollution had no reasonable expectation of fulfilling its contractual obligations is compelling.

Therefore, we hold that under the unique and narrow "special circumstances" of this case, in which the bank had *actual knowledge* of the fraudulent activities of one of its depositors, it had an affirmative duty to disclosure those facts to the respondents before it engaged in making the loan to respondents which furthered the fraud. [Court's emphasis.] . . .

[Affirmed.]

Federal Legislation In 1970 Congress enacted legislation requiring all insured banks (banks insured by the Federal Deposit Insurance Corporation) to maintain on their customers certain financial records that Congress viewed as having "a high degree of usefulness in criminal, tax, and regulatory investigations and proceedings" (12 USC § 1829b). This legislation did not limit the federal government's access to the records so maintained, and the result was that federal agencies could often obtain financial records on any customer by merely requesting them. This situation was alleviated somewhat when, in 1978, Congress enacted the *Right to Financial Privacy Act* (RFPA) (12 USC §§ 3401 et seq.).

The RFPA does not prevent federal access to the financial records maintained by banks. It does, however, specify alternative procedures that a government agency must follow, and it limits the use of any information that an agency obtains. Some of the procedures give the customer the right to advance notice and an opportunity to be heard before records concerning him are disclosed. Note, however, that most customer rights in this regard are bypassed if the requesting agency determines that a delay in gaining access would create (1) a danger of physical injury to a person, (2) serious property damage, or (3) a person's flight to avoid prosecution. Another important exception to customers' rights under the RFPA is that nothing in the act prevents the disclosure of financial records in accordance with the procedures authorized by the Internal Revenue Code.

26:11   Electronic Fund Transfers

An *electronic fund transfer* (EFT) is a transfer of money that is made by using an electronic terminal, a telephone, a computer, or magnetic tape—in other words, without either a physical transfer of cash or the use of checks or other negotiable paper.

A common form of EFT is the service available from the automated teller machine (ATM) found at many banks. Another EFT is the automated clearinghouse (ACH) transaction, by which, for example, wages or social security benefits are automatically deposited in the payee's bank account. Still another type of EFT occurs through use of a point-of-sale (POS) computer terminal. The POS terminal is located in the store or office where goods or services are bought. By making a proper entry on the terminal, the seller directs a computer to deduct the sales price from the customer's account and to credit that amount to the seller's account. Unlike the situation in a check transaction, the seller receives final payment at once.

Federal Legislation   The use of EFTs has much to recommend it to businesses and individuals. When an EFT system works properly, a money transaction can be completed easily, safely, and rapidly. However, everything does not always work as intended. For example, a bank customer might lose the card and related code that gives access to an ATM, and before the customer even discovers the loss, someone may find the card and code, and then clean out the customer's account. Because of potential losses of this sort, as well as the possibility that individuals would be treated unfairly with respect to their use of EFTs, Congress enacted the Electronic Fund Transfer Act (EFTA) (15 USC §§ 1693 et seq.). The act became effective in 1980.

The EFTA offers individuals much the same sort of protection that the federal consumer credit protection legislation (discussed in Chapter 27) gives consumers. Thus, the act requires that (1) when an individual contracts for EFT services, prescribed terms and conditions relating to the services must be disclosed in advance; (2) the individual must be furnished both with written documentation of each EFT involving his account and, in most circumstances, with periodic statements covering account activity; and (3) any preauthorized EFT from an individual's account must be authorized in writing in advance.

One EFTA provision limits an individual's liability for unauthorized withdrawals from or charges to his EFT account. Other provisions prohibit (1) distributing unsolicited cards or other means of access to EFT systems; and (2) requiring that, before receiving credit an individual preauthorize EFTs for payment to the creditor. In addition, the EFTA provides for (1) a detailed procedure for resolving errors with respect to an individual's EFT account, (2) stopping payment on pre-authorized EFTs, and (3) recovering damages from a bank or other financial institution that fails to comply with the act.

Key Concepts and Terms

- A draft is a negotiable instrument that is a written direction to pay a stated amount of money. A check is a draft payable by a bank on demand.

- Most bank deposits are general. A special deposit arises only by special agreement between the bank and its depositor.

- The relationship between a bank and its depositor is usually one of creditor and debtor, although the bank acts as the depositor's agent in such activities as obtaining payment on deposited checks.

- The collection process is the means by which payment on a check deposited in a collecting bank is obtained from the payor bank. It is governed by Article 4 of the UCC. The depositor receives only a provisional credit until final payment has been made.

- A collecting bank has a duty of ordinary care in its processing of a check. Generally, the bank must meet its midnight deadline. This means that the bank must process the check before midnight of the banking day following the banking day on which it received the check.

- "Charge-back" refers to the right a collecting bank has to charge its customer's account for the amount of a check that was deposited by the customer and was dishonored by the payor bank.

- A payor bank has the general duty of paying valid checks drawn on its customer's account. It, too, must process checks within prescribed time limits.

- A payor bank that wrongfully dishonors a check can be liable to its customer for damages.

- The drawer of a check can, in effect, cancel that check by issuing a stop-payment order. A stop-payment order directs the payor bank not to pay the check in question.

- A payor bank that pays a forged or altered check can be liable to its customer for the amount of the check. Depending on the circumstances, the bank might then have recourse against the collecting bank from which it received the check.

- If a bank's customer dies or is declared incompetent, the bank's authority to pay checks drawn by the customer ordinarily ceases when the bank learns of the event. However, checks of a deceased customer can usually be paid for ten days after the death, regardless of the bank's knowledge.

- A bank cannot ordinarily disclose financial records about a customer without the customer's consent. The federal Right to Financial Privacy Act limits the federal government's access to such records.

- An electronic fund transfer (EFT) is a transfer of money that is made by using an electronic terminal, a telephone, a computer, or magnetic tape. Consumer EFT accounts are regulated by the federal Electronic Fund Transfer Act.

- Charge-Back
- Check
- Clearinghouse
- Collection Process
- Dishonor
- Electronic Fund Transfer
- Midnight Deadline

- Negotiable Order of Withdrawal (NOW)
- Posting Process
- Provisional Settlement
- Right to Financial Privacy Act
- Stop-Payment Order

Questions and Case Problems

1. What are the differences among an ordinary check, a certified check, and a cashier's check? If you were accepting payment for goods or services by check, which type of check would you prefer to receive? Why?

2. Define and distinguish the terms "depositary bank," "collecting bank," and "payor bank." What difference, if any, does it make that in a particular transaction a given bank's status is that of collecting bank rather than payor bank?

3. What is the check collection process? Briefly, how does it operate? In your answer, discuss the significance of a bank's midnight deadline.

4. To what does the term "EFT" refer? Discuss the advantages and disadvantages of EFT systems from the viewpoint of (a) the businessperson and (b) the consumer.

5. A $13.50 check payable to a welfare recipient is drawn by Nassau County on its welfare account with Franklin Bank. The check is altered to increase the amount payable to $313.50, and it is then presented to Westbury Bank for payment. The alteration is not obvious from the face of the check, and Westbury cashes it. Westbury then sends the check to Franklin, which pays it. A Nassau County employee notices the alteration on receipt of the canceled check, and Franklin is notified promptly. How much, if anything, must Franklin recredit to Nassau County's account? Why? How much, if anything, can Franklin recover from Westbury? Why?

6. Marvel has a checking account with Pacific bank, and Fikes, a forger, obtains several of Marvel's blank checks. Fikes fills out one of the checks naming Palmer as the payee, and she forges Marvel's signature and Palmer's indorsement. Fikes then presents the check for payment at North Shore Bank, at which Palmer has a checking account. North Shore pays the check, but five days later the check is returned, unpaid, to North Shore by Pacific due to the forgeries. At this time, Palmer has $150 in his North Shore account. North Shore charges Palmer's account for $275, the amount of the check, and advises Palmer by phone about the situation. Palmer comes to the bank and states that he does not know Marvel and that the indorsement is a forgery. The North Shore officer with whom Palmer talks does not believe him, and she calls over an armed guard to escort Palmer from the building. Palmer then reports the matter to the police. Over the next few days, North Shore, claiming insufficiency of funds, refuses to pay three checks drawn earlier by Palmer to pay creditors. The bank charges Palmer's account $5 for each returned check, and it then places in the hands of a collection agency the $140 debt it claims to be owed by Palmer. Palmer sues North Shore for wrongful dishonor of his three checks. Discuss the damages, if any, that Palmer should recover.

7. Granite Corporation draws a check payable to Overseas Corporation on its account with Hempstead Bank, to pay a business debt. Five days later Granite learns that Overseas has not received the check, so Granite issues a new check. Granite then writes to Hempstead, ordering it to stop payment on the first check. Thirteen months later a collecting bank presents the original check to Hempstead for payment. Although Granite does not have sufficient funds in its account to cover the check, Hempstead pays it anyway, and charges Granite's account. When Granite's president discovers the charge she is outraged, claiming that Hempstead should not have paid the check. Discuss the rights and liabilities of Granite and Hempstead with respect to the check.

8. In May of 1976, Industrial Corp. hired Julie as its new bookkeeper. Julie's responsibilities included keeping track of and paying Industrial's bills, and examining all bank statements and canceled checks. She paid Industrial's bills by preparing checks drawn on its account and adding a facsimile signature using a signature plate. All outgoing checks were supposed to be inspected and approved by Victor, Industrial's president, but Victor's usual examination was cursory at best. Often he did not look at the checks at all. On June 15, Julie prepared a check for $500, payable to a fictitious payee. She forged the payee's indorsement and deposited the check into her own account. The check was paid and returned to Industrial with the statement it received on July 1. On July 15, Julie forged another $500 check and, growing bolder due to the success of her scheme, between July 15 and December 20, she forged ten more checks for increasingly large amounts. The proceeds from all these checks found their way into Julie's account. On December 24, Julie resigned without notice and left the area. Industrial learned about what had happened as a result of its year-end audit. It sued its bank for $25,000, the total amount paid from its account on the twelve checks forged by Julie. How much, if anything, can Industrial recover from its bank? Why?

9. Vincent, who had a checking account with Highland Bank, died on June 24. On June 28, and before Highland was aware of its customer's death, Vincent's sister, Annette, appeared at Highland with one of Vincent's checks. The check was blank except that Vincent's signature was written on it, as drawer. Annette stated that Vincent wished to close his account, asked about the current balance in the account, learned that it was $1,500, and then wrote that amount on the check. She then added the date and her own name as payee, and indorsed the check. After verifying Vincent's signature on the check and Annette's identity, Highland cashed the check. It later appeared that Annette had acted without proper authority. Drake, the executor (legal representative) of Vincent's estate sued Highland to recover the $1,500 paid to Annette. How much, if anything, can Drake recover for the estate? Why?

10. Johnson had a checking account with Trans-World Bank, but on September 20, 1982, he closed the account by withdrawing all funds from it. On July 19, 1983, Johnson, who still had blank checks from his old Trans-World account, used one of those checks to pay a grocery store bill. When the check was returned unpaid, marked "account closed," the supermarket notified the police department, which began an investigation. You are the manager of the Trans-World branch at which Johnson formerly had his account. A representative from the state district attorney's office visits you and states that Johnson will soon be arrested for having passed a bad check. She then asks you for information concerning the past and present existence and status of Johnson's account. Should you disclose this information? Why or why not?

PART SIX

Creditor–Debtor Relationship

Introductory Comments

The creditor–debtor relationship is fundamental to American business. The relationship exists between two parties if one of them, the creditor, is owed money by the other, the debtor. A creditor or debtor can be an individual or a partnership, corporation, or other entity.

Some businesses are primarily debt-oriented. A good example is a bank. As a debtor, a bank attracts deposits from customers and then, as a creditor, loans those deposits to others who, the bank hopes, will pay more interest than the bank must pay to its depositors. For most other enterprises, the continual creation and paying off of debts is a common and necessary part of doing business. The business with enough cash to pay for all its needs is rare, as is the business that can survive without extending credit to its customers. Also rare is the individual who does not rely on credit.

The American life-style would be greatly altered—for the better, some would say—were we all to return to the quaint practice of saving for desired goods and services before buying them.

To stay in business, a creditor must collect most of the debts owed to him. Therefore, his first concern is that these debts satisfy all legal requirements when they are created. Usually a debt owed by a business debtor is valid and enforceable. However, debts owed by "consumers"—individuals who buy for personal, family, or household purposes—may be a different matter. Consumer debts might not be as secure as business debts. For this reason, creditors may have a tendency to manipulate credit terms in their favor. To protect consumers from unfair and abusive credit practices, consumer credit protection laws have been enacted. These laws are discussed in Chapter 27,

429

and the creditor who ignores them does so at his peril.

Another major concern of a creditor is whether the debts owed to him will actually be paid. Chapters 28 and 29 discuss how the creditor can reduce the risk somewhat by obtaining an interest, known as a security interest, in some of the debtor's property. The idea is that if the debtor fails to pay, the creditor can take the property covered by the security interest, sell it, and use the sale proceeds to pay off the debt.

A creditor who lacks a security interest can still look to the debtor's property for payment of the debt. As discussed in Chapter 30, the creditor can sue the debtor, win a judgment, and then force the sale of some of the debtor's property so that the judgment can be satisfied. Before the judgment is obtained, the creditor might be able to tie up the debtor's property temporarily, regardless of who has possession of that property.

Clearly, creditors have many rights under the law, but debtors also have rights of their own. Chapter 30 points out that some of a debtor's property cannot be reached by creditors at all; other property cannot be taken before the debtor has the chance to present his side of the matter in court. If a creditor violates a debtor's rights, the debtor can sue the creditor. The debtor might also recover an award of money damages.

Finally, what of the debtor who simply cannot pay all his debts? Chapter 31 covers the major options that are available to this debtor. One option is an agreement with creditors by which each creditor will accept less than what is actually owed. The debtor can also give his property to a neutral person, who sells it and pays off the creditors to the extent possible. If all else fails, the debtor can file for bankruptcy. The debtor's creditors may or may not be paid, but if the debtor is discharged in bankruptcy, most of his debts are extinguished, and he has the chance to make a fresh start in life.

27 Consumer Credit and Credit Protection

27:1 Introduction to Consumer Credit

Credit is the quality that attracts trust. In particular, it attracts trust in a person's intent and ability to pay money. As popularly used, the term "credit" involves the loan of money.

A person is a "consumer" if he buys an item (or a service) primarily for personal, family, or household purposes. The goods or services he buys for those purposes are known as *consumer goods* or *consumer services*. For example, a new family car is "consumer goods," while that same car bought for business use is not. The credit extended for the purchase of consumer goods or services is called consumer credit, and the transaction in which the extension of credit is made is a consumer credit transaction. The party extending credit is the *creditor*. The consumer or borrower party is the *debtor*.

The traditional source of borrowed money is the bank. Had banks remained the major source of consumer credit, extended on a transaction-by-transaction basis, it is possible that modern consumer credit law would never have developed. However, major banks now extend to consumers lines of credit that, through the magic of the bank credit card, can be used for any purpose whatsoever. Also, credit is routinely offered by many other entities, such as finance companies, retailers, and contractors that offer consumer-related services.

This widespread extension of credit has been referred to as the "consumer credit revolution." Its development was not without problems and abuses. One major problem was that credit terms could be worded or explained in many ways. For example, one lender might quote the interest rate on a loan to be "$10 per $100 per year," another might offer a "10 percent add-on" rate, and a third might offer "10 percent simple interest per year." These three offers may seem to be the same, but they actually differ in terms of the real cost of credit to the borrower. As a result, consumers found it difficult to shop intelligently for credit.

State Legislation Some problems relating to consumer credit were addressed in state statutes. These statutes, when they were enacted at all, tended to be spotty and inconsistent. For example, the requirements applying to small loans were often not the same as those applicable to installment sales (credit sales in which the buyer makes a series of periodic installment payments).

The first state-oriented, comprehensive statutory scheme involving consumer credit was the Uniform Consumer Credit Code (U3C). The U3C was first proposed in 1968 and was revised in 1974. It covers all the important areas of consumer credit, including disclosures of true credit terms, rate ceilings for interest and other charges, and creditors' rights. Similar to the U3C, but of somewhat broader scope and designed to be more in the consumer's favor, is the National Consumer Act (NCA). The NCA was proposed in 1970.

Neither the U3C nor the NCA is a state statute as such. The idea was that states would enact one or the other of the acts in entirety or at least in large part. What in fact happened was that only a few states enacted the U3C, and none at all enacted the NCA. A number of states have, however, extracted bits and pieces from both the U3C and the NCA for inclusion in their other statutes. The result is that even now, few states have comprehensive consumer credit codes.

Federal Legislation, Generally States would likely have acted with greater authority in the consumer credit area had Congress not acted. In 1968, based on its constitutional authority to regulate commerce between the states, Congress enacted the *Consumer Credit Protection Act (CCPA)* (15 USC §§ 1601 et seq.). The major focus of the CCPA as it was originally enacted was on disclosing the true cost of consumer credit. This coverage is part of Title I of the act, which is also known as the *Truth in Lending Act (TILA)*. Also included within the CCPA are provisions regulating equal credit opportunity, credit billing, and credit reporting.

Conflicts Between Federal and State Law As a general rule, the CCPA "preempts the field" of consumer credit. This means that any state statute conflicting with a CCPA provision is ineffective, although only to the extent of the inconsistency. Some parts of the CCPA provide that a state statute is "inconsistent" only if it gives the consumer *less* protection than the federal statute does.

27:2 Truth in Lending Act, Generally

Congress' broad purpose in enacting the TILA in 1968 was to promote the informed use of consumer credit by requiring the clear disclosure of credit terms to consumers in a consistent way. Key features of the act are (1) the disclosure requirements and (2) consumers' right to sue and recover damages from noncomplying creditors. These matters are discussed in detail later in this chapter (see 27:4 and 27:5). First, however, it is appropriate to discuss the interpretation, coverage, and enforcement of the TILA, and to define some of the important terms used in the act.

Administrative Interpretation of TILA (15 USC § 1604) The TILA is basically just a framework of consumer credit protection law. This framework is filled out by regulations issued by the Board of Governors of the Federal Reserve System (the Board). These regulations are published first in the Federal Register and later in the Code of Federal Regulations (CFR).

The Board's TILA regulations are known as *Regulation Z* (12 CFR §§ 226.1 et seq.). Regulation Z offers an authoritative interpretation of the TILA. For this reason, business people (or their attorneys) must often look to Regulation Z for answers to specific TILA questions.

Both the TILA and Regulation Z impose many duties on creditors, and these duties can change somewhat each time the act or regulation is amended. Regulation Z is amended frequently. Although most large retailers and lenders keep up with the changes and are aware of and comply with the requirements that apply to them, the same is not true of many small businesses, such as "mom and pop" stores. Many operators of small businesses are still violating the TILA in various ways, often without even being aware that they are doing so. To aid these people and the consumer credit industry overall, Congress attempted to simplify some of the truth in lending requirements when it enacted the Truth in Lending Simplification and Reform Act in 1980. One significant change was that the effective dates of new Board regulations requiring new or different credit disclosures are no longer scattered throughout any given year. Instead, all regulations of this type issued between April 1 of one year and March 31 of the next become effective on October 1 of the second year.

EXAMPLE
During 1983, the Board issued three new disclosure requirements to be added to Regulation Z. The first requirement was issued on February 15, the second on March 28, and the third on June 11. The effective date of the first and second new requirements is October 1, 1983. The effective date of the third is October 1, 1984.

Transactions Covered (15 USC § 1603)   Generally speaking, the TILA and Regulation Z apply to all consumer credit transactions. Rather than stating its applicability in this way, however, the TILA sets forth the transactions to which it does *not* apply. These include (1) transactions involving extensions of credit primarily for business, commercial, or agricultural purposes; and (2) transactions in which the total amount financed is more than $25,000, unless a security interest is given in real property or a mobile home used as the consumer's main home.[1]

Administrative Enforcement (15 USC § 1607)   The TILA is enforced by several different federal administrative agencies. The proper agency in a given case depends on the type of creditor involved. For example, an airline creditor's compliance with the TILA is the responsibility of the Civil Aeronautics Board. Generally, however, the TILA is enforced by the Federal Trade Commission (FTC). Under some circumstances, the FTC and other agencies can also require a creditor to reimburse a consumer for excess credit charges if the charges imposed were higher than the charges disclosed earlier by the creditor.

---

[1]A security interest is an interest in property given to a lender to secure repayment of a debt. Security interests in real property are discussed in Chapter 35. Security interests in personal property are discussed in Chapter 28. Note that if a security interest is given in residential real property, the requirements of the Real Estate Settlement Procedures Act of 1974 (RESPA) might also apply. RESPA is discussed in Chapter 34 (see 34:7).

27:3 Truth in Lending Definitions

If the TILA and other parts of the CCPA are to make sense, certain key terms in addition to those defined in 27:1 must be understood. These terms will now be defined.

Creditor (15 USC § 1602):   Generally speaking, a creditor under the TILA is an individual or firm satisfying two criteria. First, the individual or firm must regularly extend consumer credit (1) that is payable in more than four installments or (2) for which a finance charge (defined below) will or may be required. Second, the individual or firm must be the one to whom the sale or loan contract initially requires payment of the debt arising from the transaction. For example, if Dobbs buys a new washing machine on credit from Ace Appliance Company and signs a promissory note in which he agrees to pay Ace for the machine, plus credit charges, in 12 monthly installments, Ace is a creditor under the TILA.

Also within the scope of "creditor" is a person who regularly arranges with others for extending consumer credit if (1) the credit is payable in more than four installments or a finance charge will or may be imposed and (2) the person actually extending credit is not himself a "creditor." In addition, most issuers of credit cards are creditors for purposes of the TILA.

Debtor: Neither the TILA nor Regulation Z uses the term "debtor." Instead, they use either "consumer" or "obligor" to describe the person taking out a loan or buying goods or services on credit. For purposes of this chapter, "debtor" refers to a consumer who has entered into a consumer credit transaction, or intends to do so, and is the person obligated to pay the creditor later on.

Finance charge (15 USC § 1605):   Perhaps the most important TILA concept is that of the *finance charge*. The term "finance charge" refers to the cost of credit. Generally, the finance charge for a consumer credit transaction is the sum of all charges (1) payable by the consumer and (2) imposed directly or indirectly by the creditor in connection with the extension of credit. Specific types of charges that would be included in a finance charge are

- Interest
- Time–price differential (difference between cash price of item and total amount paid if item bought on credit)
- Charges payable under a point system (system requiring payment of a fee equal to a percentage of the loan being offered)
- Service or carrying charges
- Finders' fees
- Fees for most credit reports
- Premiums for some insurance protecting creditor in connection with the debt

Open-end credit; closed-end credit (15 USC § 1602):   Consumer credit as regulated by the TILA is either "open end" or "other than open end." *Open end* refers to a continuing credit arrangement, such as a charge account with a department store. Specifically, an "open-end credit plan" is a plan in which (1) the creditor reasonably expects repeated transactions; (2) the consumer can pay the balance on his account in full at any time without penalty; (3) the creditor can impose a finance charge from time to time on the outstanding unpaid balance; and (4) the creditor sets a credit limit, and the amount of credit available to the consumer at any time is the difference between that limit and the unpaid balance on the account. The typical bank or department store credit card is issued under an open-end credit plan.

Credit that is "other than open end" is, obviously, consumer credit that does not qualify as open end. Regulation Z uses "closed end" to describe this sort of credit arrangement. In essence, *closed-end credit* involves a single extension of credit. For example, if a person arranges to buy furniture under a credit arrangement made with the furniture dealer only for that specific transaction, the credit offered by the dealer would be closed end.

Annual percentage rate (15 USC § 1606):   For a consumer to be able to compare different types of credit arrangements effectively, the cost of credit under each type of plan must be expressed in the form of some common term. The common term used in the TILA is the *annual percentage rate* (*APR*). The APR is the cost of credit for one year, expressed as a percentage. It is usually simple to compute for an open-end plan. For example, a credit card plan might provide for a finance charge at the rate of 1.8 percent per month on the unpaid balance. This translates into an APR of 21.6 percent (12 times 1.8 percent).

For credit other than open end, computation of the APR is more complicated. As a practical matter, tables compiled by the Board are usually used for computing it with respect to a given transaction. The difference between the APR and what might appear to be the interest rate in a closed-end transaction can be illustrated as follows. A bank offers a loan at "$10 per $100 per year." This might appear to be a loan at 10 percent interest. However, assume that a consumer borrows $100 under these terms and repays it, with interest, in 12 equal monthly installments. The consumer has the use of the full $100 for only one month; the average amount of the bank's money he has during the year is about $50. The APR as determined under the TILA and Regulation Z is close to 20 percent.

27:4   Truth in Lending Disclosures

When consumer credit is extended, the creditor must make a number of disclosures to the consumer about the credit arrangement. This is a significant feature of the TILA. The specific disclosures required depend on whether the credit is open end or closed end, but certain general requirements apply to all disclosures.

General Rules Governing Disclosures (15 USC §§ 1631, 1632)   All information required to be disclosed by the TILA or Regulation Z must be disclosed clearly and conspicuously. The terms "finance charge" and "annual percentage rate" have to be more conspicuous than other terms or information. The purpose of these requirements is to prevent the creditor from using fine print, which most consumers will not read, and from burying the finance charge and APR information among other terms that might be more favorable. Numerical amounts must be expressed in figures, not words.

Open-End Credit Disclosures (15 USC § 1637)   In an open-end consumer credit arrangement, there are two types of required disclosures. First, the creditor must disclose a number of facts to the debtor before an open-end account is opened. These disclosures cover the basic rights and duties of both the debtor and the creditor. They inform the debtor about when a finance charge will be imposed and how the charge will be computed (which includes a statement of the APR). Second, the creditor must make additional disclosures at the end of each billing cycle (usually a 30-day period) if money is owed on the account. The periodic disclosures inform the debtor about activity in the account during the billing period, the total outstanding balance on the account (including a separate showing of the finance charge), and when payment must be made to avoid additional finance charges.

Reproduced on pages 438–39 are illustrative forms showing for an open-end account the required initial disclosures (Figure 27-1) and periodic disclosures (Figure 27-2).

Closed-End Credit Disclosures (15 USC § 1638)   The disclosures required to be given to the debtor by the creditor in connection with closed-end consumer credit are longer and more complex than those connected with open-end credit. In fact, some creditors used to draw up what were really one-time credit arrangements in the form of open-end plans to avoid the tougher requirements. This practice was halted when Congress added to the definition of open-end credit the requirement that the creditor expect repeated transactions.

As with open-end disclosures, the required closed-end disclosures are intended to advise the debtor about the significant financial and legal aspects of the credit arrangement. Generally, they are made before credit is extended, and they must be segregated from other information. In practice, a separate disclosure form is usually used. The form is slightly different depending on whether the closed-end credit transaction is a loan (Figure 27-3, p. 440) or a credit sale (Figure 27-4, p. 441).

Since 1968, when the TILA was enacted, the courts have been called on to settle many disputes arising under the act. A number of these cases have involved interpretation of the disclosure requirements. The following case, only the second truth in lending case to reach the United States Supreme Court, illustrates the judicial approach to truth in lending problems. Note how much emphasis the Court places on the Board's opinion about the disputed disclosure.

Ford Motor Credit Co.
v
Milhollin
444 US 555, 63 L Ed 2d 22, 100 S Ct 790
(United States Supreme Court, 1980)

[Milhollin and several others, the respondents, bought cars from various Ford dealers on credit. The sales contracts were assigned to the petitioner, Ford

Motor Credit Company (FMCC). Thus, FMCC, rather than the dealers, became the creditor. The front page of each contract contained the TILA closed-end disclosures. Not mentioned in the disclosures was the creditor's right to accelerate payment if the debtor defaulted. The respondents later sued the petitioner, claiming a violation of the TILA and Regulation Z. The district court held that a violation had occurred, and the Court of Appeals for the Ninth Circuit affirmed, although on the basis of somewhat different reasoning than the district court *had used. The Supreme Court accepted the case for review because courts of appeals in other circuits had reached different conclusions on questions concerning the need to disclose acceleration rights.]*

Justice Brennan delivered the opinion of the Court.

*   *   *

The Truth in Lending Act has the broad purpose of promoting "the informed use of credit" by assuring "meaningful disclosure of credit terms" to consumers. . . . Because of their complexity and variety, however, credit transactions defy exhaustive regulation by a single statute. Congress therefore delegated expansive authority to the Federal Reserve Board to elaborate and expand the legal framework governing commerce in credit. . . . The Board executed its responsibility by promulgating Regulation Z, . . . which at least partly fills the statutory gaps. Even Regulation Z, however, cannot speak explicitly to every credit disclosure issue. At the threshold, therefore, interpretation of TILA and Regulation Z demands an examination of their express language; absent a clear expression, it becomes necessary to consider the implicit character of the statutory scheme. . . .

Respondents have advanced two theories to buttress their claim that [the TILA and Regulation Z] expressly mandate disclosure of acceleration clauses. In the district court, they contended that acceleration clauses were comprehended by the general statutory prescription that a creditor shall disclose "default, delinquency, or similar charges payable in the event of late payments," . . . and were included within the provision of Regulation Z requiring disclosure of the "amount, or method of computing the amount, of any default, delinquency, or similar charges payable in the event of late payments." . . . Before this Court, respondents follow the court of appeals in arguing that [Regulation Z] may be the source of an obligation to disclose procedures governing the rebate of unearned finance charges that accrue under acceleration. . . .

A fair reading of the pertinent provisions does not sustain respondents' contention that acceleration clauses are within their terms.

An acceleration clause cannot be equated with a "default, delinquency, or similar charg[e]." . . . In itself, acceleration entails no monetary penalty. . . . A "default, delinquency, or similar *charg[e]*," on the other hand, self-evidently refers to a specific assessable sum. Thus, within the trade, delinquency charges are understood to be "the *compensation* a creditor receives on a precomputed contract for the debtor's delay in making timely instalment payments," . . . [Court's emphasis.] Acceleration is not compensatory; a creditor accelerates to avoid further delay by demanding immediate payment of the outstanding debt. . . .

The prepayment rebate disclosure regulation . . . also fails to afford direct support for an invariable specific acceleration disclosure rule. To be sure, payment by the debtor in response to acceleration might be deemed a prepayment within the ambit of that regulation. But so long as the creditor's rebate practice under acceleration is identical to its policy with respect to voluntary prepayments, *separate* disclosure of the acceleration policy does not seem obligatory under a literal reading of the regulation. [Court's emphasis.] [The regulation], therefore, squares with the position of the Federal Reserve Board staff that specific disclosure of acceleration rebate policy is only necessary when that policy varies from the custom with respect to voluntary prepayment rebates. . . .

It is a commonplace that courts will further legislative goals by filling the interstitial silences within a statute or a regulation. . . . But legislative silence . . . may . . . betoken permission or, perhaps, considered abstention from regulation. In that event, judges are not accredited to supersede Congress or the appropriate agency by embellishing upon the regulatory scheme. Accordingly, caution must temper judicial creativity in the face of legislative or regulatory silence.

Cardholder agrees to pay Creditor the full amount of the New Balance on receipt of the monthly statement for the account. If not so paid, a **FINANCE CHARGE** will be added as explained below.

FINANCE CHARGE: A **FINANCE CHARGE** will be computed on the New Balance of your account as of the closing date shown on the statement by applying the PERIODIC RATE shown below (after first subtracting any unpaid **FINANCE CHARGES**).

ANNUAL PERCENTAGE RATE		PERIODIC RATE
Under $1,000	19.2%	1.60%
Over $1,000	12.0%	1.00%

If we receive full payment of your New Balance within 30 days after the statement closing date, no additional **FINANCE CHARGE** will be imposed on the New Balance.

New Balance: We compute the "New Balance" of your account by taking the balance you owed at the end of the previous billing cycle and subtracting any payments and credits received or credited during the present billing cycle.

Minimum Payment: You must make at least the Minimum Payment shown on your statement, computed as follows:

NEW BALANCE	MINIMUM PAYMENT
Less than $20	The amount of your New Balance
$20 to $500	$20 plus any amount past due
Over $500	4% of your New Balance plus any amount past due

Liability for Unauthorized Use: You may be liable for the unauthorized use of your credit card. You will not be liable for unauthorized use that occurs after you notify us at our address listed above, orally or in writing, of the loss, theft, or possible unauthorized use. In no event will your liability exceed $50.

In Case of Errors or Questions about Your Bill

If you think your bill is wrong, or if you need more information about a transaction on your bill, write us on a separate sheet at the address shown on your bill as soon as possible. We must hear from you no later than 60 days after we sent you the first bill on which the error or problem appeared. You can telephone us, but doing so will not preserve your rights.

In your letter, give us the following information:

- Your name and account number.
- The dollar amount of the suspected error.
- Describe the error and explain, if you can, why you believe there is an error. If you need more information, describe the item you are unsure about.

You do not have to pay any amount in question while we are investigating, but you are still obligated to pay the parts of your bill that are not in question. While we investigate your question, we cannot report you as delinquent or take any action to collect the amount you question.

Special Rule for Credit Card Purchases

If you have a problem with the quality of goods or services that you purchased with a credit card, and you have tried in good faith to correct the problem with the merchant, you may not have to pay the remaining amount due on the goods or services. You have this protection only when the purchase price was more than $50 and the purchase was made in your home state or within 100 miles of your mailing address. If we own or operate the merchant, or if we mailed you the advertisement for the property or services, all purchases are covered regardless of amount or location of purchase.

Figure 27-1

At the very least, that caution requires attentiveness to the views of the administrative entity appointed to apply and enforce a statute. . . . Unless demonstrably irrational, Federal Reserve Board staff opinions construing the Act or Regulation should be dispositive. . . .

Finally, wholly apart from jurisprudential considerations or congressional intent, deference to the Federal Reserve is compelled by necessity; a court that tries to chart a true course to the Act's purpose embarks upon a voyage without a compass when it disregards the agency's views. The concept of "meaningful disclosure" that animates TILA . . . cannot be applied in the abstract. *Meaningful* disclosure does not mean *more* disclosure. [Court's emphasis.] Rather, it describes a balance between "competing considerations of complete disclosure . . . and the need to avoid . . . 'informational overload.' ". . .

The Federal Reserve Board staff treatment of acceleration disclosure rationally accommodates the conflicting demands for completeness and for simplicity. In determining that acceleration rebate practices need be disclosed only when they diverge from other prepayment rebate practices, the Federal Reserve has adopted what may be termed a "bottom-line" approach: that the most important information in a credit purchase is that which explains differing net charges and rates. . . . [The] court of appeals had no ground for displacing the Federal Reserve staff's expert judgment. . . .

[Reversed and remanded.]

Account No.:		Statement No.:		
Cardholder:		Creditor:		

PREVIOUS BALANCE	**CHARGES**	**FINANCE CHARGE**	**PAYMENTS AND CREDITS**	**NEW BALANCE**
$ _____	$ _____	$ _____	$ _____	$ _____

Minimum Payment Due: $

Closing Date:

To avoid all additional **FINANCE CHARGES,** pay the entire New Balance so that we receive it within 30 days after the above closing date.

Date	Transaction No.	Store	Description	Charges	Credits

FINANCE CHARGE is assessed on: $_____, which amount was the New Balance of your account as of _____, the closing date shown on your last statement (after first subtracting unpaid **FINANCE CHARGES**).

ANNUAL PERCENTAGE RATE		PERIODIC RATE
Under $1,000	19.2%	1.60%
Over $1,000	12.0%	1.00%

Send any Billing Inquiry, with account number, to:

Figure 27-2

ANNUAL PERCENTAGE RATE The cost of your credit as a yearly rate.	FINANCE CHARGE The dollar amount the credit will cost you.	Amount Financed The amount of credit provided to you or on your behalf.	Total of Payments The amount you will have paid after you have made all payments as scheduled.
%	$	$	$

You have the right to receive at this time an itemization of the Amount Financed.

☐ I want an itemization.   ☐ I do not want an itemization.

Your payment schedule will be:

Number of Payments	Amount of Payments	When Payments Are Due

Insurance

Credit life insurance and credit disability insurance are not required to obtain credit, and will not be provided unless you sign and agree to pay the additional cost.

Type	Premium	Signature
Credit Life		I want credit life insurance. _____ Signature
Credit Disability		I want credit disability insurance. _____ Signature
Credit Life and Disability		I want credit life and disability insurance. _____ Signature

You may obtain property insurance from anyone you want that is acceptable to (creditor). If you get the insurance from (creditor), you will pay $ _____.

Security: You are giving a security interest in:

☐ the goods or property being purchased.

☐ (brief description of other property).

Filing fees $ _____   Non-filing insurance $ _____

Late Charge: If a payment is late, you will be charged $ _____/_____ % of the payment.

Prepayment: If you pay off early, you

☐ may   ☐ will not   have to pay a penalty.

☐ may   ☐ will not   be entitled to a refund of part of the finance charge.

See your contract documents for any additional information about nonpayment, default, any required repayment in full before the scheduled date, and prepayment refunds and penalties.

_____

e means an estimate

Figure 27-3

ANNUAL PERCENTAGE RATE The cost of your credit as a yearly rate.	FINANCE CHARGE The dollar amount the credit will cost you.	Amount Financed The amount of credit provided to you or on your behalf.	Total of Payments The amount you will have paid after you have made all payments as scheduled.	Total Sale Price The total cost of your purchase on credit, including your downpayment of $ _____.
%	$	$	$	$

You have the right to receive at this time an itemization of the Amount Financed.

    ☐ I want an itemization.   ☐ I do not want an itemization.

Your payment schedule will be:

Number of Payments	Amount of Payments	When Payments Are Due

Insurance

Credit life insurance and credit disability insurance are not required to obtain credit, and will not be provided unless you sign and agree to pay the additional cost.

Type	Premium	Signature	
Credit Life		I want credit life insurance.	_____ Signature
Credit Disability		I want credit disability insurance.	_____ Signature
Credit Life and Disability		I want credit life and disability insurance.	_____ Signature

You may obtain property insurance from anyone you want that is acceptable to (creditor). If you get the insurance from (creditor), you will pay $ _____.

Security: You are giving a security interest in:

    ☐ the goods or property being purchased.

    ☐ (brief description of other property).

Filing fees $ _____   **Non-filing insurance $ _____**

Late Charge: If a payment is late, you will be charged $ _____/_____ % of the payment.

Prepayment: If you pay off early, you

    ☐ may ☐ will not have to pay a penalty.

    ☐ may ☐ will not be entitled to a refund of part of the finance charge.

See your contract documents for any additional information about nonpayment, default, any required repayment in full before the scheduled date, and prepayment refunds and penalties.

_____

e means an estimate

Figure 27-4

The Board is required to prepare and publish model disclosure forms for common consumer credit transactions. Figures 27-3 and 27-4 are examples. Any creditor who uses one of the Board's forms, even with certain minor variations, will be considered to have complied with the disclosure requirements except as to any numerical disclosures. Most businesses should seriously consider using the Board's forms.

27:5   Civil Liability for Truth in Lending Violation

As was pointed out in 27:2, the FTC and various other administrative agencies are responsible for enforcing the TILA. While administrative enforcement benefits the public at large, it often does little to help the individual consumer who is the victim of a violation of the act. For this reason, Congress included in the TILA a provision allowing consumers to sue and recover damages from noncomplying creditors.

Nature of Violation; Amount of Liability (15 USC § 1640)   A creditor can be sued for a violation of the TILA itself or for a violation of Regulation Z. Among the types of violations that can and do occur are a creditor's failure to (1) make the required disclosures at all; (2) make accurate disclosures; (3) make disclosures at the proper time; or (4) furnish the debtor with other required information, such as the debtor's right to cancel certain credit transactions (see 27:7). It should be noted that the right to sue exists only for violations as to the more important disclosures.

An individual debtor who succeeds in a lawsuit against a creditor for violation of the TILA can recover (1) the amount of any actual damages or loss suffered; and (2) twice the amount of any finance charge imposed, but not less than $100 or more than $1,000; and (3) legal expenses, including reasonable attorney's fees. The effect of the TILA is that even if the finance charge involved is only several dollars, the successful debtor can recover at least $100. That is bad enough from the creditor's viewpoint, but the damages can be far higher in a class action. Recall that a class action is one begun by one or more debtors for the benefit of themselves and all others who have been harmed in the same way by the defendant's act, here, the creditor's violation. In a successful class action under the TILA, the damages recoverable are decided by the court. There is no minimum, but the total amount of damages awarded can be up to $500,000 or 1 percent of the creditor's net worth, whichever is less. Thus, any creditor having a net worth of $50,000,000 or more who violates the TILA can be liable for $500,000 in a class action.

Liability of Assignee (15 USC § 1641)   A creditor who enters into a consumer credit transaction often assigns the contract with the debtor to another party, such as a bank or credit company, before the debtor has paid off the debt. If the creditor does so, the assignee has the right to receive the debtor's future payments. The assignee also gains all the creditor's other rights with respect to the contract, such as any security interest taken or retained in the debtor's property.

The effect of an assignment is to put the assignee in the original creditor's place.

The TILA recognizes this fact and allows the debtor to sue the assignee for some violations of the act, even though the violation was actually made by the original creditor. The violations for which an assignee can be sued are those that are apparent from the disclosure statement. An example of an apparent violation is the failure to use such terms as "finance charge" and "annual percentage rate" as required in a disclosure statement.

Defenses Available to Creditors (15 USC § 1640)   If a creditor (or assignee) is sued for a TILA violation, proof of any one of three different defenses offered by the creditor will succeed (cause the debtor to lose the lawsuit) even if a violation actually did occur. The first of these defenses is that the creditor acted to correct the error. This defense is available if (1) the correction is timely, (2) the debtor is notified about the error, and (3) adjustments are made to make sure that the debtor will not pay more than the finance charge (or dollar equivalent of APR) actually disclosed. A correction is timely if it is made within 60 days after the creditor discovers the error, before the debtor sues the creditor based on the error, and before the creditor receives written notice about the error from the debtor.

The second defense a creditor can assert is that he acted (or failed to act) because he relied on a Board rule or regulation, and that he did so in good faith. This right of reliance extends to the Board's interpretations of its rules and regulations, and also to any interpretation or approval given by an authorized Federal Reserve System employee. An authorized employee is one to whom the Board has given the authority to issue interpretations of regulations or approvals of particular conduct.

Finally, a creditor can successfully defend himself against a suing debtor by proving that the violation was (1) unintentional and (2) caused by a bona fide error that occurred even though the creditor followed procedures that should have avoided the error. Examples of bona fide errors are clerical, printing, and computer errors. An error that does *not* qualify is a mistake of law. For example, a creditor might fail to include a given fee in a disclosed finance charge because his attorney, after studying the TILA and Regulation Z, had incorrectly concluded that the fee need not be included. That omission is not an excusable bona fide error.

27:6   Consumer Leases

The TILA as originally enacted covered installment sales of consumer goods, but it did not cover leases of those goods. Abuses were thought to have developed in the consumer products leasing industry. For this reason, Congress in 1976 enacted the Consumer Leasing Act (CLA) (15 USC §§ 1667 et seq.), which became part of the TILA.

Definitions (15 USC § 1667)   A lease is a consumer lease under the CLA if (1) the subject of the lease is personal property; (2) the property is to be used by an individual mainly for personal, family, or household purposes; (3) the lease term is more than four months; and (4) the total amount that the lessee is to pay under the lease is $25,000 or less. "Lessor" under the act refers to an individual or firm regularly engaged in the consumer leasing business, either by making consumer leases or by offering or arranging for them. "Lessee" refers to a person who is offered a consumer lease or becomes obligated to pay under one.

 If a consumer goods item is rented on a weekly basis, the fact that the lease term can extend for longer than four months if the lessee renews it each week does not make the lease a consumer lease.

Requirements as to Consumer Leases (15 USC §§ 1667a-1667c)   The CLA requires that the lessee be given a number of disclosures before signing a consumer lease. These disclosures advise the lessee about important terms of the lease. They cover such matters as periodic payments, other payments the lessee must make, warranties on and maintenance of the leased property, and termination of the lease.

In what is known as an open-end lease, the lease states that the property will have a given value at the end of the term. This is called the depreciated value. If the actual value of the property at the later date is less than the estimated depreciated value, the lessee must pay the difference. This difference can be substantial if, for example, the lessor originally sets an unrealistically high depreciated value. Since a lessor who does so can then count on receiving a large payment at the end of the lease term, he can offer deceptively low monthly rental payments. To curb abuses of this nature, the CLA limits the amount that the lessee can be obligated to pay at the end of the lease term.

Civil Liability (15 USC § 1667d)   A lessor who violates the CLA also violates the TILA. He can be sued by the lessee who was affected by the violation, just as a debtor can sue a creditor under the TILA (see 27:5).

27:7   Rescission of Credit Transactions

A consumer has a limited right to rescind certain credit transactions even if his only reason for doing so is that he changed his mind. The right applies (1) to some transactions in which the creditor receives a security interest in the consumer's home and (2) to some *home-solicitation sales*. These two classes of transactions are discussed below.

Security Interest Covering Dwelling (15 USC § 1635)   The creditor in a consumer credit transaction often requires some sort of security for the credit extended. The creditor can retain a security interest in property being bought by the debtor. Or, and perhaps in addition, the creditor can demand a security interest in other property owned by the debtor. The debt would then be secured in the sense that if the debtor defaults later on, the creditor can enforce the security interest. Typically, enforcement consists of the property being taken from the debtor and then sold so that the creditor can be paid. If the property in which a creditor takes a security interest is the debtor's main dwelling (which can be a mobile home), enforcement of the interest can result in the debtor's loss of the dwelling.

Because consumers sometimes rush into credit purchases without giving sufficient thought to possible consequences, Congress included in the TILA a cooling-off period with respect to certain transactions. Essentially, in most consumer credit transactions in which the creditor will get a security interest in the debtor's main dwelling, the debtor has three days in which he can rescind the transaction. The three-day period begins either when the transaction takes place or when the creditor has delivered the material (more important) truth in lending disclosures and other required documents, whichever is later. Thus, for example, if a home improvement contract that grants the contractor a security interest in the house is signed on March 1, but the contractor does not deliver all the material disclosures until June 6, the homeowner has until midnight of the third business day after June 6 to rescind the contract. Even if the truth in lending disclosures have not been made, however, a debtor who waits too long will lose the right to rescind. In most cases the right expires when the dwelling is sold or three years after the contract is signed, whichever occurs first.

The major exception to the three-day rescission rule is that no right to rescind exists in the typical home mortgage situation, as where a bank's security interest in a dwelling secures repayment of money that the debtor borrowed to buy that dwelling.

Home-Solicitation Sales   Often, in what are known as home-solicitation sales, a consumer is emotionally overwhelmed by a door-to-door salesperson. The consumer signs a contract for the credit sale of goods or services that he may not really require or, more important, that he cannot really afford.

Many states addressed the problem of abuses in the home-solicitation sales business. For all practical purposes, these state statutes were preempted by the federal government when, in 1974, the FTC adopted a trade regulation rule governing home-solicitation sales (16 CFR § 429.1). The FTC rule allows a consumer to cancel most home-solicitation sales contracts any time within three business days after the contract is signed.

The FTC rule applies only to sales (1) to a consumer and (2) of consumer goods or services costing $25 or more. A sale need not actually be made in the consumer's home to qualify as a home-solicitation sale. Essentially, it is only required that (1) the seller or its representative personally sought the sale on a face-to-face basis and (2) the consumer's agreement or offer to purchase was made at a place other than the seller's place of business.

EXAMPLE
Brady is a salesman with AAA Home Insulation Company. He makes an unannounced visit to Lester's home, where he tries to interest Lester in insulation for Lester's house. Lester wants to think it over, and Brady leaves, promising to call later in the week. Several days later, Brady phones Lester and invites him to a local coffee shop. Lester accepts, and he signs a contract for insulation while at the coffee shop. This sale is a home-solicitation sale under the FTC rule.

The sale to Lester in the above example would also be a home-solicitation sale if, instead of having come unannounced, Lester had invited Brady to his house to make a sales presentation. However, it would not be a home-solicitation sale if, for example, Lester's initial contact with Brady had occurred when Lester stopped at AAA's sales office and inquired about insulation.

If the FTC rule applies to a sale, the consumer has certain rights and the seller has certain duties. The contract must conspicuously disclose the consumer's right to cancel the contract. The seller must also furnish a properly filled-out notice of cancellation. If the consumer elects to cancel, he merely signs and dates the notice and mails it to the seller. The seller must then return any payment made by the consumer and any promissory note signed by the consumer. The consumer must, of course, offer to return any goods delivered by the seller, although the consumer can keep the goods if the seller waits too long to pick them up.

 If the FTC rule applies, most sellers will not deliver any goods or services until the rescission period has ended. If the consumer needs the goods or services at once, he can sign a separate, *handwritten* statement waiving his rescission right.

27:8   Claims and Defenses Against Assignees

A credit sale of goods or services to a consumer can be handled entirely by the seller. This occurs when a consumer and seller enter into a retail installment contract, and the consumer then makes payments to the seller over the term of the contract. Frequently, however, the seller discounts the contract to a bank or other third party; that is, he assigns the contract to someone else. For example, if a contract requires the consumer to pay $1,000 over 12 months, the seller might assign the contract to a bank immediately and receive a smaller amount, say $900, from the bank. The consumer then would make his payments to the bank.

In the traditional installment contract there is a *waiver of defenses* clause, which applies if the contract is assigned. The effect of this clause is that the consumer cannot assert against the assignee certain claims and defenses he could have asserted against the original seller. As a result, the consumer can be left with little or no recourse.

EXAMPLE
Harold buys a new car on credit, and Harold's contract includes a waiver of defenses clause. The dealer assigns the contract to a bank. The car turns out to be a lemon, but the dealer refuses to repair it properly or replace it. Having waived his defenses, Harold cannot withhold payment from the bank, even though the car may be entirely unsatisfactory.

In 1975 the FTC acted to protect consumers like Harold by issuing a trade regulation rule (16 CFR §§ 433.1, 433.2). The rule does not prohibit the use of waiver of defenses clauses in installment contracts for the sale of consumer goods or services to consumers. Instead, it requires that any such contract include a prominent notice to the effect that anyone holding the contract is subject to all claims and defenses that the consumer could assert against the seller. The same requirement exists for a purchase money loan (loan for purchase of consumer goods or services) if the seller either refers the consumer to the lender or is related in some way to the lender. Thus, for example, if a seller routinely refers his credit customers to a particular finance company, the required notice must appear in the loan contract even though no actual assignment of the contract will occur.

Under the FTC rule, the maximum amount the consumer can recover from the assignee or purchase money lender is the amount already paid by the consumer on the assigned contract.

27:9   Equal Credit Opportunity

In past years, the availability of credit to some persons depended on factors other than the persons' ability to repay. For example, a married woman often found it difficult to obtain credit of her own when she wanted it for reasons unrelated to her husband's credit rating. The lack of a credit history sometimes caused serious problems for a woman who was later widowed or divorced. The *Equal Credit Opportunity Act (ECOA)* (15 USC §§ 1691 et seq.) was added to the CCPA in 1974 in an effort to alleviate this problem and to allow aggrieved persons to recover damages for discriminatory credit practices. The ECOA is interpreted and expanded somewhat in Regulation B (12 CFR §§ 202.1 et seq.). The act's scope is not limited to applications for *consumer* credit. For example, a denial of credit to a business because key people in that business are women violates the act.

Prohibited Conduct (15 USC § 1691)   The ECOA prohibitions come into play at the time a person applies for credit. A creditor is forbidden to discriminate against any credit applicant on the basis of the applicant's race, color, religion, national origin, sex, marital status, or age (as long as the applicant is old enough to enter into a valid contract). Nor can a person be discriminated against because (1) all or part of his income comes from welfare, or (2) he has, in the past, exercised any right under the CCPA in good faith.

These statutory prohibitions have been expanded in Regulation B, which lists information that a creditor cannot request from an applicant. For example, a creditor cannot require an applicant to disclose income from alimony or child support unless the applicant wants the creditor to consider that income in deciding on the applicant's creditworthiness. Nor can a creditor inquire about birth control practices, intentions about childbearing, or childbearing capability.

No listing of "do's and don'ts" covers all situations. The following case illustrates how the question whether particular conduct of a creditor violates the ECOA is apt to be decided by a court.

Markham

v

Colonial Mortgage Service Co.
Associates, Inc.
196 App DC 50, 605 F2d 566

(United States Court of Appeals, District
of Columbia Circuit, 1979)

[*The issue in this case is whether the ECOA prevents creditors from refusing to combine the incomes of two unmarried people who, together, apply for a loan. The plaintiffs, Jerry and Marcia Markham, found a house they wanted to buy. Although unmarried at the time, they applied for a loan to be made to them jointly. The significance of the joint loan was that although the debtors intended to repay the loan together, each of them would have been responsible for the full amount if the other did not pay. The application found its way into the hands of Illinois Federal, a lending institution and one of the defendants. Just before the planned signing of all papers to complete the transaction, Illinois Federal advised the plaintiffs that their application had been denied because they were not married. The plaintiffs then sued Illinois Federal under the ECOA, and the district court granted Illinois Federal's motion for summary judgment. The plaintiffs then appealed.]*

Swygert, Circuit Judge.

*   *   *

The district court concluded . . . that plaintiffs could not state a claim under the [ECOA] even if they showed that Illinois Federal's refusal to aggregate their incomes resulted, in whole or in part, in the denial of their loan application. This conclusion was based on the premise that creditors need not ignore the "special legal ties created between two people by the marital bond." . . .

We fail to see the relevance of any special legal ties created by marriage with respect to the legal obligations of joint debtors. This was not an instance where a single person is applying for credit individually and claiming income from a third party for purposes of determining creditworthiness. In such an instance, the absence of a legal obligation requiring continuance of the income claimed by the applicant from the third party would reflect on the credit applicant's creditworthiness. Inasmuch as the Markhams applied for their mortgage jointly, they would have been jointly and severally liable on the debt. Each joint

debtor would be bound to pay the full amount of the debt. . . . Illinois Federal would have had no greater rights against the Markhams had they been married, nor would the Markhams have had greater rights against each other on this particular obligation. . . .

We turn to a consideration of whether the [ECOA's] prohibition of discrimination on the basis of sex or marital status makes illegal Illinois Federal's refusal to aggregate plaintiffs' income when determining their creditworthiness. Illinois Federal contends that neither the purpose nor the language of the Act requires it to combine the incomes of unmarried joint applicants when making that determination.

We start, as we must, with the language of the statute itself. . . . This language is simple, and its meaning is not difficult to comprehend. . . . The Act forbids discrimination "on the basis of a person's marital status, that is, to treat persons differently, all other facts being the same, because of their marital status." . . . Illinois Federal does not contend that they would not have aggregated plaintiffs' income had they been married at the time. . . . Thus, it is plain that Illinois Federal treated plaintiffs differently—that is, refused to aggregate their incomes—solely because of their marital status, which is precisely the sort of discrimination prohibited by [the ECOA]. . . .

Illinois Federal expresses the fear that a holding such as we reach today will require it to aggregate the incomes of all persons who apply for credit as a group. Lest it be misinterpreted, we note that our holding is not itself that far-reaching. It does no more than require Illinois Federal to treat plaintiffs—a couple jointly applying for credit—the same as they would be treated if married. . . .

[Judgment reversed.]

After setting forth the prohibited conduct, the ECOA lists creditor acts that do not amount to discrimination under the act. In essence, a creditor can:

- Inquire about marital status if the creditor's purpose is to find out its rights with respect to particular extension of credit

- Inquire about age or welfare source of income if the creditor's purpose is to find out the amount and likely continuation of applicant's income level

- Use a credit system that considers age, if the system is valid

- Inquire about or consider age of an elderly applicant if age is to be used by the creditor in favor of the applicant

After credit has been applied for, the creditor must notify the applicant within 30 days as to the action taken on the application. If the action is adverse, the applicant is entitled to be told why. Adverse action includes a denial or revocation of credit and a refusal to grant credit substantially as requested by the applicant. If the applicant is already delinquent under an existing credit arrangement, however, the creditor's refusal to extend additional credit under that arrangement is not an adverse action under the act.

EXAMPLE
Doris holds a MasterCard credit card issued by the Ajax Bank, and she is behind on her payments to Ajax on the account. Doris requests Ajax to raise her credit limit. She also applies to the Bradley Bank for a Visa card. Both Ajax and Bradley deny Doris' requests. Bradley's denial is an adverse action under the ECOA, but Ajax's is not.

 Although the ECOA itself does not say so, the legislative history of the act shows that Congress intends that the courts and the FTC, in enforcing the act, should look to the *effects* of creditor practices, not just to the creditors' motives or actual conduct.

Enforcement; Civil Liability (15 USC §§ 1691c, 1691e)   Various federal agencies enforce the ECOA. The primary enforcing agency is the FTC.

The ECOA allows a credit applicant who has been discriminated against to sue the creditor for damages. If the applicant is successful he can recover both the amount of his actual loss and punitive damages (damages awarded as a penalty against the wrongdoer rather than to compensate the victim for the actual loss suffered). The court can award up to $10,000 in punitive damages to a plaintiff who sues on his own behalf. Far more is recoverable in a class action. A successful plaintiff is also entitled to recover the amount of the legal expenses in bringing the lawsuit, including reasonable attorney's fees.

 A creditor who acts (1) in good faith and (2) in accordance with instructions from the Board cannot be liable for violating the ECOA. An "instruction from the Board" can be in the form of a Board rule, regulation, or official interpretation. It can also be an interpretation or approval by an authorized Board employee.

27:10   Credit Cards and Credit Billing

It is commonplace to use a credit card instead of cash or a check to pay for goods or services. Predictably, this increased use of credit cards has been accompanied by various abuses. These abuses were addressed by Congress in 1970 when it added several sections (15 USC §§ 1642–1644) to the TILA, and again in 1974 when it enacted the Fair Credit Billing Act (FCBA) (15 USC §§ 1666 et seq.).

Issuance of Cards; Unauthorized or Fraudulent Use (15 USC §§ 1642–1644)   Under the TILA, a credit card (other than a renewal card) can be isued *only* in response to a request or application for it. If a properly issued card is lost or stolen, the maximum amount the cardholder can be required to pay for unauthorized use of the card is $50. Unless the card issuer has taken a number of prescribed steps, the holder is not even liable for that amount. In no event is the cardholder liable for charges made *after* the issuer has been notified about the loss. As interpreted by Regulation Z the $50 limit on a cardholder's liability for unauthorized use of a card extends to most business credit cards.

The following case illustrates how the TILA makes it a crime to use a credit card that was fraudulently obtained, although the act does not cover all fraudulent uses of a card. The case also sheds some light on when use of a card is unauthorized.

United States

v

Kasper

483 F Supp 1208

(United States District Court, E.D. Pennsylvania, 1980)

[The use of a credit card obtained by fraud is prohibited by 15 USC § 1644, which sets forth criminal sanctions for violation of the section. In this case, the defendants, Kasper and Gray, were charged in an eleven-count indictment (written accusation of commission of a crime) with having violated § 1644. In this action the defendants have moved for dismissal of all but one of the counts. They argue that the acts they committed were not offenses under the statute.]

Shapiro, District Judge.

*   *   *

The gravamen [essence] of the facts stipulated for purposes of the motions is that credit cards were obtained by the original cardholders without the intent to defraud the issuing companies, sold or given to Kasper and Gray with the knowledge of the persons to whom the cards were originally issued that Kasper and Gray would use the cards to make charges without paying for them, and then reported as lost or stolen by the original cardholders. The government claims that the schemes [violate § 1644] because the cards, bought or received with the fraudulent intent to make charges without paying for them, were "fraudulently obtained" within the scope of the statute. In opposition, the defendants claim that the cards were neither fraudulently obtained from the issuer by the original cardholder nor fraudulently obtained from the cardholders by defendants and, since the cards were given or sold by the cardholders rather than stolen from them, the credit cards were not "fraudulently obtained." . . .

The *fraudulent intent* of the defendants on these facts is not at issue; they obtained credit cards intending to use them to obtain goods and/or services without paying for them. [Court's emphasis.] The issue is whether or not the cards were also *obtained by fraud*. [Court's emphasis.] The government presumably concedes that defendants did not fraudulently obtain the cards from the *cardholders*; the defendants bought or received the cards from cardholders who were not deceived as to the plan to charge goods and not pay for them. . . . [Court's emphasis.] The government argues that the cards were fraudulently obtained from the card issuers, the holders being bailees [people in temporary possession of another's property] of the issuers because the issuers required the original holders to agree to each instance that the cards remained the property of the issuer to be returned on demand.

A credit card gives the holder the privilege of charging items at establishments associated with the issuer. . . . The statute contemplates that a holder may authorize another to use a card. . . . The defendants obtained from the cardholders what they had—the privilege of charging items [using credit cards that] remained the property of the issuer to be returned on demand. The card issuer's right to demand a card's surrender does not convert an obtaining with fraudulent intent from an assenting cardholder to a fraudulent obtaining from a nonassenting issuer. The credit cards were not fraudulently obtained from the issuers because they were not obtained from the issuers at all. On the facts as stipulated, defendants have not "fraudulently obtained" credit cards within the meaning of [the statute].

The fallacy of the government's argument is that it confuses or equates "fraudulently ob-

tained" and obtaining with "fraudulent intent." Fraudulent obtaining and fraudulent intent are two separate and distinct elements of this offense. . . .

Courts which have examined the meaning of "fraudulently obtained" in § 1644 have uniformly found some deceitful or false action by the obtainer with regard to the one from whom the card was actually obtained. . . .

In cases where the card was obtained by third parties from the original cardholder, some deception of or theft from the original cardholder has been deemed necessary for conviction. . . .

. . . [The] government claims that § 1644 must be construed to provide protection to card issuers rather than cardholders. . . .

The government's argument fails for [several] reasons. First, the legislative history of the 1974 amendments to the [TILA] manifests a clear Congressional intent to protect cardholders, yet is completely silent as to card issuers. . . .

Second, by limiting the protection of cardholders in certain ways, the [TILA] amendments provide greater protection for card issuers than the government concedes. Section 1643 limits cardholders' liability only for "unauthorized use." . . . Where purchases are authorized by a cardholder, the holder having sold or given another the card with knowledge that the other intended to use it without making payment, the issuer may seek full payment from the holder. . . .

[The court expressed its intention to enter an order granting the defendants' motion.]

Offsets (15 USC § 1666h)   A holder of a bank-issued credit card often has money deposited in a checking or savings account with the issuing bank. If the cardholder is late in making payments on the card account, the bank may be tempted to deduct the amount owed to it on the card from the funds that the cardholder has in his checking or savings account. This procedure, known as an *offset*, is forbidden by the TILA unless the cardholder has given advance written consent to it.

EXAMPLE

Jasper holds a Visa card issued by the Argo Bank. The total amount he owes on the Visa account is $1,200. Jasper also has $500 deposited with Argo in a savings account. Argo requires that at least $100 be paid each month on any Visa account having an outstanding balance of over $1,000. If Jasper fails to make the required monthly payment, it would be a simple matter for Argo to withdraw $100 from Jasper's savings account and apply it to the Visa account. However, unless Jasper has consented to an offset, his account is protected under the TILA provision.

Claims and Defenses Arising Out of Transaction (15 USC § 1666i)   Another potential problem of a customer's using a credit card issued by other than the seller is illustrated in the following scenario: Mason, a consumer, goes to a hardware store and buys a new power saw. He pays for it with his MasterCard, which was issued by Valley Bank. Two weeks later the saw proves to be defective, and Mason takes it back to the store. The dealer, who has already turned in the credit-card slip and been credited for the sale, refuses to take the saw back or do anything else to help Mason. Indeed, he claims that Mason's problems with the saw were caused by misuse. At this point, Mason has a useless saw that he has not yet even paid for. Valley Bank is equally unsympathetic to Mason's plight. It was not directly involved in the sale, having merely extended credit, and it wants to be paid.

The TILA eases the difficulties faced by cardholders like Mason in the above example. As to most transactions exceeding $50, the card issuer is subject to all claims and defenses (other than tort claims) arising out of the original transaction, up to the amount owed to the issuer on that transaction. The purpose of this TILA provision is not necessarily to "stick it" to banks and other card issuers. Rather, the provision was included on the theory that the issuers can often force retailers and others honoring credit cards to do what is right, while the typical consumer cannot.

Credit Billing (15 USC §§ 1666-1666d)   As many holders of credit cards learn, mistakes can and do occur when the card issuer bills for credit extended. When that happens, a cardholder can find himself in an endless battle with a computer. The TILA includes provisions intended to offer some relief in this situation. Note that these provisions apply to billing in connection with *all* open-end credit, not just to credit-card accounts.

If the debtor under an open-end credit plan finds what he believes to be an error in a statement of his account sent by the creditor, the debtor has 60 days in which to notify the creditor about it, in writing. Assuming that the notice contains sufficient information, the creditor must then investigate the matter and either correct the error or advise the debtor why the disputed charge is correct. A creditor who fails to carry out these duties forfeits up to $50 of the amount owed by the debtor.

Other aspects of billing under open-end plans are also regulated by the TILA. These include (1) the length of time during which the amount due under a plan can be paid without further finance charge (the "free ride" period), (2) the prompt crediting of payments, and (3) the treatment of excess payments (people actually pay too much on occasion). A debtor who is affected by a creditor's violation of the credit billing requirements can sue and recover damages, as discussed in 27:5.

27:11   Credit Reporting

The most significant security that a consumer can offer when he seeks credit is the likelihood that he will repay the debt. A prospective creditor asks two key questions: Can the consumer repay? If so, will he repay? Many businesses do not have the means to obtain credit information on their own. Instead, they usually turn to a credit reporting agency, also known as a credit bureau, to acquire the needed data. For a fee, the agency prepares a report outlining the credit history of the prospective debtor.

Because one's credit rating is so important, the consumer wants to be sure that information contained in a credit report is accurate. The consumer also wants to preserve his privacy as much as possible. These considerations, among others, have been the subject of abuses and problems that developed in the credit-reporting industry over the years. As a result, in 1970 Congress enacted the *Fair Credit Reporting Act* (*FCRA*) (15 USC §§ 1681 et seq.). The major purpose of the FCRA is to require credit-reporting agencies to obtain and distribute credit information in a way that is fair to consumers. Specific problems covered by the act include (1) the consumer's privacy; (2) the accuracy, relevance, and proper use of credit information; and (3) the consumer's access to and right to correct credit information concerning him.

The FCRA regulates credit-reporting activities concerning applications for employment and consumer-related insurance as well as applications for consumer credit. However, the primary focus of the discussion here is on the consumer credit aspect of the act.

Definitions (15 USC § 1681a)   For purposes of the FCRA, a credit-reporting agency is a *consumer-reporting agency*. This term refers to any person or firm that regularly gathers and evaluates credit information on consumers for the purpose of furnishing reports to others.

Perhaps at the heart of the FCRA is its definition of the term *consumer report.* Essentially, a consumer report is any communication (written or oral) that (1) is made by a consumer-reporting agency; (2) concerns specific matters listed in the FCRA; and (3) is or likely will be used as a factor in determining a consumer's eligibility for consumer credit, insurance, or employment. The "specific matters" referred to above are creditworthiness, credit standing, credit capacity, character and general reputation, personal characteristics, and mode of living. Among types of reports that are *not* consumer reports are reports containing information *only* about transactions between the consumer and the person making the report.

EXAMPLE
Clarence applies to Secaucus Bank for a loan, and he lists Williams, his landlord, as a credit reference. Secaucus contacts Williams. The only information Williams provides is that although Clarence has been a quiet tenant, he has often been late in paying his rent. This information given by Williams affects Clarence's credit rating, but it is not a consumer report within the scope of the FCRA.

Obsolete Information (15 USC § 1681c)   As a general rule, a consumer report must not contain obsolete adverse information. Under the FCRA, most adverse information is obsolete if it is more than seven years old. Examples of information to which the seven-year limit applies are criminal records, unpaid bills, and lawsuits against the consumer. The only exception to the seven-year limit concerns a consumer's bankruptcy; bankruptcy information is obsolete after ten years.

The restriction on obsolete information does not apply if a consumer report is to be used in connection with a credit transaction involving $50,000 or more. Thus, for example, a consumer report used by a bank in deciding whether to loan a consumer $75,000 to buy a new house can state the fact that the consumer was convicted of embezzlement 20 years earlier and that he was imprisoned for five years for that offense.

Distribution of Consumer Reports (15 USC § 1681b)   The FCRA limits the right of consumer-reporting agencies to furnish consumer reports to other persons. A report can be furnished as the consumer involved instructs in writing, or as a court may order. Otherwise, and excluding the furnishing of reports with respect to insurance, employment, and several other purposes listed in the act, a credit reporting agency can furnish a consumer report only under limited circumstances. This is illustrated in the following case.

Greenway

v

Information Dynamics, Ltd.
399 F Supp 1092
(United States District Court, Arizona, 1974)

[The plaintiffs, Greenway and others, sued the defendant, IDL, for violation of the FCRA. IDL provided merchants who subscribed to its services with information about the check-cashing histories of potential customers. As is described in the court's opinion, it was the manner in which IDL conducted this business that led to the lawsuit. The plaintiffs seek, among other relief, that the court issue a preliminary injunction. In the context of this case, the injunction is a court order forbidding IDL from continuing the conduct complained of until the legality of the conduct is determined. That determination will be made at a later stage of the lawsuit.]

Copple, District Judge.

*   *   *

The IDL "data base" is gathered through reports from merchants who subscribe to IDL's services. These merchants report to IDL the names of those individuals from whom they have received checks which have, for whatever reason, not been honored by the bank upon which they were drawn. Other information, such as the individual's checking account number, his or her driver's license number, and the reason for return of the check is also furnished to IDL. IDL then compiles all the information garnered from each individual subscribing merchant, and regularly disseminates it to *all* its subscribing merchants. [Court's emphasis.] This dissemination is accomplished by distributing to subscribing merchants microfilm or microfiche lists. . . . Each subscribing merchant is given a machine which permits him to "read" the information set forth on these lists. Once in possession of these lists, each IDL subscriber can ascertain the name, driver's license number and checking account number of every individual who has had a check returned to *any* of IDL's subscribers during the period covered by the report. [Court's emphasis.] The merchant can also ascertain the number of checks that returned, and, in many cases, the reasons for their return. The ostensible purpose of this service is to enable a merchant who is presented with a check from a customer to ascertain whether that particular customer has had check cashing difficulties with any of IDL's subscribing merchants in the past. However, as should be apparent, each merchant is provided with the names and check cashing histories of thousands of individuals with whom they will never transact business. It is this systematic over-dissemination of credit information that lies at the heart of this controversy.

... The primary question presented is whether the activities of IDL fall within the scope of the FCRA....

As stated by [§ 1681b of the FCRA], one of the purposes for which disclosure of consumer information is authorized is to a person whom the disseminator has reason to believe:

> (E) otherwise has a legitimate need for the information *in connection with a business transaction involving the consumer.* [Court's emphasis.] ...

[The court concluded that the microfiche lists sent out by IDL constitute consumer reports within the meaning of the FCRA.]

The FCRA is quite clear on the scope of dissemination permissible for consumer reports. Thus, ... § 1681b provides in pertinent part:

> A consumer reporting agency may furnish a consumer report under the following circumstances *and no other*:
>
> *   *   *   *   *   *
>
> (3) To a person which it has reason to believe—
> (A) intends to use the information in connection with a credit transaction involving the consumer on whom the information is to be furnished and involving the extension of credit to or review or collection of an account of, the consumer; or

*   *   *   *   *   *

> (E) otherwise has a legitimate business need for the information in connection with a business transaction involving *the* consumer. [Court's emphasis.]

The limitation on distribution is quite explicit. Information on a particular consumer may only be provided to a third party who requires it in connection with a specific transaction between that party and *that particular consumer.* IDL's information dissemination practices clearly fail to comply. [Court's emphasis.]

Periodically, each IDL subscriber receives a microfiche list which contains check cashing information about hundreds, if not thousands, of individuals. While it is obviously anticipated that the merchant will become involved in business transactions with some of the individuals on this list, it is conceivable that the merchant will never do business with any of the individuals listed. In any event, it is totally inconceivable that any subscriber could ever have transactions with everyone listed. Clearly, then, each subscribing merchant receives a wealth of information on individual consumers for which that merchant will *never* have a legitimate business need. [Court's emphasis.]

Dissemination practices such as IDL's have been condemned in the strongest terms by the FTC. In regulations dealing with so-called "credit guides," which listed consumers and gave them credit ratings, and were disseminated to all members of credit bureaus, the Commission indicated ... [that] *the permissible purpose for furnishing the consumer report must exist at the time the request for the report is made; it is not enough to obtain the consumer report in anticipation that a permissible purpose will arise subsequently.* [Court's emphasis.] ...

[The court ordered that a preliminary injunction be issued.]

Disclosures to Consumers (15 USC §§ 1681g, 1681h, 1681m)   The FCRA requires that both users of consumer reports and consumer reporting agencies make certain disclosures to consumers. Most consumers are quite aware of their own credit history in general terms, but they may be unaware of particular facts that creditors look to before extending credit. Often, the first clue a consumer receives that something is "wrong" with his credit history is a potential creditor's either denying credit or offering credit at a higher charge than the consumer had expected. Whenever either event occurs and the action was based on information in a consumer report, the user of the report (the potential creditor) must inform the consumer of that fact and provide the name and address of the consumer reporting agency that made the report. If consumer credit is denied or made more costly because of information obtained from *other than* a consumer-reporting agency, the consumer has only the right to learn the nature of the information. He is not entitled to learn its source.

Regardless of whether a consumer knows that a given consumer-reporting agency has prepared a consumer report on him or has information concerning him in its files, the consumer is entitled to a disclosure of certain information from the agency, on request. This information is (1) the nature and substance of all nonmedical information that the agency has on the consumer in its files, (2) the sources of that information, and (3) the identification of those to whom the agency has furnished any consumer report on the consumer (other than for employment purposes) within the last six months. These disclosures must be made during normal business hours. They can be given over the phone or to the consumer in person. A consumer visiting the consumer-reporting agency can bring along one other person, such as an attorney.

Disputed Accuracy of Information (15 USC § 1681i)   A consumer may dispute the accuracy of an item of information in a consumer-reporting agency's file on him. If so, and if the consumer advises the consumer-reporting agency about it, the agency must generally investigate the matter. Information found to be inaccurate must be deleted promptly. Information that can no longer be verified must also be deleted.

If the agency's investigation fails to resolve the dispute, the consumer can file a brief statement presenting his side of the matter. The dispute must then be noted by the agency in any later consumer report it prepares on the consumer. The consumer's statement, or a summary of it, must also be included with each later report. If the consumer requests it, the agency must also notify recent recipients of consumer reports about deleted or disputed items of information.

Compliance Procedures (15 USC § 1681e)   Consumer-reporting agencies are required to follow reasonable procedures (1) to avoid including obsolete information in any consumer report and (2) to furnish consumer reports only to those entitled to receive them. As a general matter, agencies must also follow reasonable procedures to assure the maximum possible accuracy of all information in reports prepared by them.

EXAMPLE

A bank requests a consumer-reporting agency to prepare a consumer report on Hansen, who has applied for a loan. The agency phones the local branch of a major retailer, states Hansen's name and address, and asks the retailer for whatever information on Hansen it has in its files. The retailer indicates that Hansen's credit rating is bad. Without any further information or investigation, the agency prepares a report stating that Hansen is a bad credit risk. The agency has violated the FCRA because it has not followed a reasonable procedure to maximize the accuracy of its information.

Enforcement; Civil Liability for Violation (15 USC §§ 1681n, 1681o, 1681s)   The FTC is charged with enforcement of the requirements of the FCRA in most situations, just as it is the primary enforcement agency for other parts of the CCPA.

If a consumer-reporting agency or user of a consumer report fails to comply with any requirement of the FCRA, the affected consumer can sue and recover damages from that agency or user. The affected consumer can recover the amount of his legal expenses (including reasonable attorney's fees), as well as damages for actual injury to his individual credit.

If a consumer-reporting agency or user of a consumer report intentionally fails to comply with the FCRA, the consumer can also recover punitive damages in an amount that the court determines. Thus, there is no limit on the damages recoverable for intentional misconduct. In this respect, the FCRA differs from parts of the CCPA which do limit the damages recoverable. If the situation warrants it, the consumer may also be entitled to equitable relief, as was granted in *Greenway v Information Dynamics, Ltd.*, above, in the form of an injunction.

 If a user of a consumer report or other consumer credit information is sued for violating the user-oriented requirements, discussed earlier, the user is not necessarily liable even if the alleged violation is proven. The FCRA provides that no user will be liable if it proves that when the alleged violation occurred, it maintained reasonable procedures to assure compliance with the FCRA requirements.

Civil Liability for Defamation and Related Torts (15 USC § 1681h)   Before the FCRA (or any similar state legislation) was enacted, the usual approach taken by a consumer who had been wronged by incorrect information supplied by a credit-reporting agency was to sue for defamation,[2] invasion of privacy, or negligent reporting of information. A consumer-reporting agency, user of consumer credit information, or person furnishing information to a consumer-reporting agency can still be sued for these torts under the FCRA. Generally, however, the basis of the lawsuit is limited to false information furnished with malice of willful intent to

---

[2]Defamation is the publication of false information that injures the name or reputation of another person. In this context, publication means disclosure to other than the person involved. For example, a credit agency publishes defamatory information about a consumer when it includes in a report given to a retailer the untrue statement that the consumer was recently convicted of a crime.

injure the consumer. Thus, the plaintiff must prove more than just a willful violation of the FCRA. Essentially, the plaintiff must show that the person or entity sued acted in bad faith and that this bad faith was intentionally directed at the plaintiff.

 The FCRA does not cover the tort of commercial defamation. Essentially, this tort involves injury to one's business or business credit caused by the publication of inaccurate credit information. A lawsuit based on commercial defamation can still be brought, but the plaintiff's right to recover damages is based entirely on state law.

Key Concepts and Terms

- The federal government has enacted comprehensive legislation intended to protect consumers in their credit transactions. Statutes in some states provide similar protection, but usually on a less comprehensive basis.

- The federal Truth in Lending Act (TILA) helps consumers shop intelligently for credit by requiring that credit terms be disclosed in advance and in a consistent way.

- The nature of the required TILA disclosures depends somewhat on whether the credit involved is open end or closed end. More detailed disclosures must be made for closed-end credit than for open-end credit.

- A creditor who violates the TILA requirements can be liable to the consumer who was affected by the violation. If the consumer sues and wins, he recovers at least $100 plus his legal expenses. The consumer also recovers the amount of any actual damages he suffered.

- Certain leases of consumer goods are governed by requirements similar to those governing consumer credit transactions.

- A consumer has a three-day cooling off period in which to cancel a credit transaction if (1) the creditor acquires a security interest in the consumer's dwelling as part of the transaction and (2) the loan is for a purpose other than buying the dwelling. The same right applies to many home-solicitation sales.

- The assignee of an installment contract for the sale of consumer goods or services to a consumer is subject to the claims and defenses that the consumer could assert against the original seller. The same is true for some purchase money lenders.

- A person cannot be denied credit on the basis of sex, marital status, age, or race. A creditor who discriminates on this basis can be liable for substantial damages.

- Numerous requirements exist as to the issuance to and use of credit cards by consumers. A cardholder has limited liability for unauthorized use of his card, and a card issuer is not immune from liability with respect to transactions in which its card was used.

- A consumer can question an item that appears on the periodic bill of the consumer's open-end credit account. If he does so, the creditor must investigate the matter.

- There are limits on the adverse information that can be included in credit reports on consumers, and the distribution of the reports is restricted. Consumers are entitled to learn about adverse information in credit files on them and to have inaccurate information corrected.

- A credit reporting agency that violates the statutory requirements can be liable to the affected consumer. The extent of liability depends on whether the violation was intentional. It can also depend on whether the agency acted maliciously toward the consumer.

- Annual Percentage Rate (APR)
- Closed-End Credit
- Consumer Credit Protection Act (CCPA)
- Consumer Goods and Services
- Consumer Report
- Consumer-Reporting Agency
- Creditor
- Debtor

- Equal Credit Opportunity Act (ECOA)
- Fair Credit Reporting Act (FCRA)
- Finance Charge
- Home-Solicitation Sale
- Offset
- Open-End Credit
- Regulation Z
- Truth in Lending Act (TILA)
- Waiver of Defenses

Questions and Case Problems

1. Why was the TILA and related consumer protection legislation considered necessary? In your opinion, does this legislation serve its intended purpose effectively? Why or why not?

2. Define "consumer," "creditor," "finance charge," and "annual percentage rate" according to your understanding of those terms as they are used in this chapter.

3. What is the difference between open-end credit and closed-end credit? State a simple example of each type of credit arrangement.

4. Sapenter owns two pieces of property. One is her home, on which she owes only a small amount to a bank. The other property is a six-unit apartment building on which Sapenter owes a large amount to Dreyco, a lender. Sapenter falls behind in her payments to Dreyco, and Dreyco threatens to enforce his security interest in the apartment building. To avoid having to enforce the security interest, Dreyco agrees to loan Sapenter additional money and to take a security interest in Sapenter's home. Sapenter soon falls behind once again, and Dreyco seeks to enforce his security interest in the home. Sapenter argues that since Dreyco never gave her any of the required TILA disclosures concerning the final loan, she can and wishes to rescind that transaction. Sapenter also sues Dreyco for damages for having violated the TILA. Can Sapenter rescind the loan transaction? Is she entitled to damages? Discuss the reasons for your answers.

5. On Thursday, Fred visited Vacuums Unlimited, where he talked with Kirby, a salesman. Kirby demonstrated a new Superflo machine and its attachments. Not entirely convinced, Fred left the store. The next day, Friday, Kirby visited Fred's home and demonstrated the machine there. Fred was won over. He paid Kirby $100 as a down payment and signed a contract for payment of the $900 balance,

plus a finance charge, over the next 24 months. Not having read the contract carefully before signing it, Fred was unaware that it contained a printed waiver of any right Fred might have to rescind the contract. Kirby departed with the signed contract, leaving the machine and attachments with Fred. On Saturday, a friend advised Fred that Superflo products are overpriced and of poor quality. Vacuums Unlimited was closed on Sunday, but on the following Monday Fred called Kirby and said that he wanted to cancel the contract. Kirby declared that Fred had no right to do so. Fred failed to make any payments on the machine, and Vacuums Unlimited is now suing him. Fred defends on the basis that he should have been allowed to rescind the contract and get his $100 back. Is Fred correct? Why or why not?

6. Ken buys a new mobile home costing $15,000. He gives the dealer a $3,000 down payment and finances the $12,000 balance by signing an installment contract. The dealer immediately assigns the contract to a bank. After Ken has paid $500 to the bank on the contract, the mobile home turns out to have many design and manufacturing defects. Among other problems, the roof develops a bad leak, and Ken's uninsured $10,000 stamp collection is destroyed. Both the dealer and the mobile home manufacturer have gone out of business, so Ken turns to the bank. He (a) refuses to make further payments on the contract, (b) sues the bank for breach of warranty, and (c) also sues the bank for the value of the ruined stamp collection. What rights does Ken in fact have against the bank?

7. Helen Harbaugh, a teacher, is married to John Harbaugh. Helen fills out an application for a Visa card to be issued by Continental Bank. In the application she states her name as "Mrs. John Harbaugh," and she also signs the application that way. Continental feeds the information into its computer for a credit check. The computer system used by Continental is such that courtesy titles such as Mr., Mrs., and Ms are suppressed. Therefore, the name entered into the computer is John Harbaugh. The computer is unable to verify that John is employed as a teacher. Continental so advises Helen, who supplies the necessary information. Helen's employment is confirmed, and Continental issues two Visa cards, but in the name of John Harbaugh. Helen complains to Continental, but without success. Several months later, Continental advises John that the cards will be reissued and asks him to correct erroneous information. Helen and John send back a new application indicating that the applicant is "Helen Harbaugh." Again, two Visa cards are issued in the name of John Harbaugh. Helen sues Continental, claiming that it violated the Equal Credit Opportunity Act. Should she prevail? Why or why not?

8. Cody receives a Visa card in the mail from Tri-State Bank. Having been discharged in bankruptcy only a year before, Cody is happy to get the card, although he had not applied for it. The letter accompanying the card states that Cody's credit limit is $1,100, and that his use of the card will constitute his acceptance of it. All the terms of Tri-State's credit arrangement are properly disclosed, but there are no instructions about what to do if the card is lost or stolen. Cody uses the card to pay a $100 car-repair bill. He then loses the card, and he does not notify Tri-State. Somebody else finds the card and runs up charges of $2,000 with it. A month later Cody receives a bill from Tri-State for $2,100. Cody fails to pay, and Tri-State sues him for $2,100. Discuss whether Cody is liable to Tri-State and, if he is, the extent of his liability.

9. Retail Credit Company, a consumer-reporting agency, prepares an investigative consumer report on Mrs. Rasor. The report is done in connection with Rasor's application for health insurance that she needs to obtain a loan from the Small

Business Administration (SBA). Retail Credit's agent spends about four hours investigating Rasor and ten other people. The report falsely states that Rasor has a reputation of "living with more than one man out of wedlock," that her reputation has suffered because of this fact, and that she drinks to excess. As a result of the report, Rasor is denied insurance by one company and is offered insurance by another only at an above-average premium rate. Rasor's SBA loan is also delayed. At Rasor's insistence, Retail Credit eventually conducts a second, more thorough investigation, which reveals that much of the initial report is incorrect. Rasor sues Retail Credit for damages. How should the case be decided?

10. Ackerley applies for credit with several retailers, but he is turned down each time. The first retailer, Atlas Lumber Company, refuses to explain why it is denying credit. The second retailer, Hercules Hardware Supplies, discloses that the reason for its action is an adverse consumer report that it has received from CBS Credit Bureau. Ackerley visits CBS, which refuses to show him anything in its file on him or even to discuss the matter. Ackerley sues Atlas, Hercules, and CBS for $200 in actual damages for lost wages. Each defendant moves for dismissal (asks the court to throw out the complaint against that defendant). Atlas, which had in fact relied on the adverse consumer report from CBS, argues that it was unaware of any requirements under the Fair Credit Reporting Act. Hercules argues that it complied with the law. CBS argues that it did not violate the law. CBS also argues that since Ackerley was unemployed, he suffered no actual damages. You are the judge. How will you rule on each defendant's motion? Why?

28 Introduction to Secured Transactions

28:1 Introductory Comments

Obtaining and extending credit are at the hub of most transactions that involve more than a minor sum of money. This is as true for an ordinary consumer as it is for a multibillion-dollar corporation. People who extend credit, whether they are merchants, bankers, or others, can do so on the bare strength of the debtor's promise to pay or repay in the future. Transactions between friends or closely related parties are often handled this way. Commercial transactions, however, often are not. For his own protection, the commercial creditor requires more than a mere promise to pay.

The added protection the creditor seeks is the acquisition of some kind of interest in property owned by the debtor. That interest is known as a security interest if a creditor receives it to secure the payment of a debt. The interest can be in any kind of property or right that the debtor has. Here, however, and for reasons that will soon be apparent, the discussion concerns only security interests in the debtor's personal property or fixtures.[1] Thus, the essence of what is known as a secured transaction is the use of personal property or fixtures, known as the *collateral*, to secure the performance of an obligation. The obligation is usually one to pay money.

In the past, creditors used a number of different devices to obtain security interests. These included the following:

- Pledge (debtor's temporary transfer of possession of collateral to creditor)
- Chattel mortgage (mortgage on personal property)
- Conditional sale (credit sale by which seller retains title to goods sold until entire price has been paid)

---

[1]"Personal property" consists of almost all property that is not real property. "Real property" refers to land and improvements (houses or other buildings) erected on land. "Fixtures" are items of personal property that have been attached to real property. For example, a new furnace is personal property when it is delivered to a building, but it becomes a fixture when it is installed. Security interests in real property are discussed in Chapter 35.

- Trust receipt (device by which lender retains title to a merchant's inventory items until they are sold)
- Factor's lien (statutory lien on inventory acquired by lender under a state factor's act)
- Assignment of accounts receivable (creditor's transfer of right to receive payments from debtors)

A problem with these devices was that the law governing them was inconsistent and confusing. Legal requirements varied somewhat from state to state. Even worse, the requirements varied for different devices within the same state.

Today, the governing law in all states other than Louisiana is Article 9 of the UCC. Article 9 is a comprehensive scheme for regulating security interests. With several exceptions, which are discussed in 28:5, it applies to *any* transaction that is intended to create a security interest in personal property or fixtures. Article 9 provides a relatively simple and unified system by which the large variety of modern secured transactions can take place with less cost and greater certainty than under the earlier law. In another sense, Article 9 balances the often conflicting goals of debtors and creditors. It seeks to protect the debtor from a creditor who demands too much control over the collateral or the right to seize the collateral at will, but it also protects the creditor from debtor wrongdoing.

 Article 9, originally made available to the state legislatures in 1962, was substantially revised in 1972. The revised article is printed in Appendix B, and it should be referred to during the study of this chapter. Bear in mind that although many states have adopted the 1972 revision, some states have not. Also, some states have altered the official version of Article 9 by adding, modifying, or deleting particular provisions.

28:2   Relationship with Other Transactions

A few comments about how Article 9 relates to other areas of business law may make it easier to understand the concept of secured transactions.

Contracts   A contract can be defined as an agreement between parties by which each party receives something and gives up something else.[2] Any agreement by which a security interest is created usually qualifies as a contract. Obviously, the opposite is not true; many contracts have nothing at all to do with secured transactions.

Sales   Sales are governed by Article 2 of the UCC, and most security interests arise in connection with sales on credit. "Credit" is the key to the distinction between the scope of Articles 2 and 9. Article 2 covers the pure sales aspects of a transaction (see Chapters 19 through 22), while Article 9 governs to the extent that, as security for the buyer's payment of the purchase price, the seller retains an interest in the goods sold. On those sales that do not involve credit, Article 9 does

---

[2]The concept of what constitutes a contract is thoroughly discussed in Chapters 9 through 15.

not apply at all. If a transaction cast in the form of a sale is actually intended to operate only as a secured transaction, Article 9 applies.

EXAMPLE
Bradley requires a short-term loan of $1,000 and is prepared to offer a security interest in his car as collateral. McDuff is willing to make the loan, but she knows nothing about security interests and distrusts them. Because of McDuff's attitude, Bradley sells the car to McDuff for $1,000, but the parties agree that Bradley can repurchase the car later on for the same amount plus interest. The "sale" is a secured transaction, and Article 9 governs the parties' rights and liabilities.

Commercial Paper   Article 3 of the UCC deals with the rights and relationship of parties to checks, promissory notes, and other commercial paper (see Chapters 23 through 25). Article 9 applies to these negotiable instruments to the extent that they are collateral in a transaction, such as where a negotiable document of title is pledged as security. If Article 3 conflicts with Article 9 in a particular situation, Article 9 governs.

Leases   A lease of personal property (see Chapter 33) is usually not a secured transaction. The parties to a lease normally intend that the lessee possess and use the leased property during the lease term and then return it to the lessor. However, Article 9 applies if a lease is intended as security. A lease that includes an option to purchase the leased property is not necessarily a lease intended for security. If, however, the lessee can become the owner of the property for little or no additional consideration after he has complied with the mandatory lease terms, the lease *will* be considered to be one intended for security and will be governed by Article 9.

EXAMPLE
Johnson leases a vehicle valued at $20,000 from Smith Leasing Company. The sum of the required monthly payments during the lease term is $21,000, and Johnson can acquire title to the vehicle at the end of the term by paying an additional $100. Article 9 governs the parties' rights and liabilities because the transaction is deemed to be one intended for security.

28:3   Definitions

The study of secured transactions requires familiarity with a number of terms, all of which are defined or used in Article 9. "Secured transaction" and "security interest" were defined earlier in this chapter. Other important terms are explained below. Except as indicated, the official definitions appear in UCC § 9-105.

   Collateral: The property in which a security interest exists.

   Security agreement: Any contract or agreement that creates or provides for a security interest.

   Debtor: The party who must pay or otherwise perform the obligation that is secured.

   Secured party: The seller, lender, or other party in whose favor a security interest exists.

   Purchase money security interest (UCC § 9-107):   Primarily, a security interest that secures payment of the purchase price of the collateral in which that interest exists. The interest can be retained by the seller who sold the collateral to the debtor on credit, or it can be granted to a lender who loaned the debtor the money to buy the collateral.

Attachment of security interest (UCC § 9-203):   The process by which a security interest becomes enforceable against the debtor, though not necessarily against other persons.

Perfection of security interest: The process by which a secured party acquires the maximum rights obtainable under Article 9 with respect to the collateral. "Perfection" is not defined in the UCC, but essentially, once a secured party has "perfected" his security interest, he has done everything to secure his rights. These rights are then superior to the rights of many other persons who may lay claim to the collateral.

Goods: Most things that are fixtures or are movable when a security interest in them attaches. Excluded from the scope of "goods" are such things as money, commercial paper, accounts (see 28:4), and minerals that have not yet been extracted from the ground.

Consumer goods (UCC § 9-109):   Goods that are used or bought for use primarily for personal, family, or household purposes.

EXAMPLE

Willard decides to buy a new car for personal use. The price of the car is $10,000, and since Willard has only $2,000, he visits his local bank. The bank agrees to lend Willard $8,000, and Willard agrees that, to secure the loan, the bank shall receive a security interest in the new car. This loan arrangement is a secured transaction in which Willard is the debtor and the bank is the secured party. The agreement between Willard and the bank is the security agreement, while the car qualifies as consumer goods and constitutes the collateral. The security interest in the car that the bank receives is a purchase money one because the loan is used for buying that car. The bank can then perfect its interest as discussed later in this chapter.

28:4   Types of Collateral

Most security interests cover "personal property," a term that includes many different types of collateral within its scope. It is helpful to classify personal property as being tangible, quasi-tangible, or intangible. Each of these categories is then further subdivided under Article 9.

Tangible Collateral (UCC § 9-109)   Literally, property is "tangible" if it is capable of being touched. Tangible collateral is property that has material substance, such as a piece of fruit, a book, or a car. For purposes of Article 9, tangible collateral is "goods," which is divided into four categories. The first is consumer goods, defined in 28:3. The second is equipment—goods used or bought for use primarily in business, including farming or the practice of a profession. The third category is farm products—crops, livestock, or supplies used or produced in farming operations. The last category is inventory—goods held for sale or lease, or to be furnished under service contracts.

The actual or intended use of tangible collateral, rather than the nature of the collateral itself, determines its status under this scheme. For example, a new car bought for family use is "consumer goods," but if the car is bought by a traveling salesman for business purposes, it is "equipment." That same car is "inventory" while it is in the dealer's showroom or, for that matter, if it is bought by another dealer who intends to resell it.

Quasi-Tangible Collateral (UCC 9-105)   "Quasi" means "as if," and collateral is quasi-tangible if it is represented by a piece of paper rather than by the property itself. Under Article 9 there are three categories of quasi-tangible collateral: (1) chattel paper, (2) documents, and (3) instruments. "Chattel paper" refers to one or more writings that are evidence of both a money obligation and a security interest in specific goods. A "document" is a document of title, which is any piece of paper commonly treated as adequate evidence that the person in possession of it has the right to hold and dispose of both the document and the goods it covers. An example is a warehouse receipt [see discussion in Chapters 20 (20:2) and 33 (33:5)]. "Instruments" refers to commercial paper, such as checks, promissory notes, and certificates of deposit (see Chapter 23).

EXAMPLE
Drew agrees to buy a new refrigerator for $600, and he makes a down payment of $100. If Drew simply signs a promissory note in favor of the appliance dealer for $500 plus interest, the note is an "instrument." If, however, Drew also signs an agreement giving the dealer a purchase money security interest in the refrigerator, the note and agreement together constitute "chattel paper."

Intangible Collateral (UCC § 9-106)   Collateral is intangible if it has no physical form. Intangible collateral is divided into the categories of accounts and general intangibles. An "account" is any right to payment for goods sold or services rendered if the right is not evidenced by either an instrument or chattel paper.

EXAMPLE
Wilson owns a hardware store, and she needs to buy additional inventory. She orders 20 gallons of paint from a paint company. The company ships the order and sends Wilson a bill. Wilson also orders a variety of power tools from a tool manufacturer. Before shipping the tools, the manufacturer requires Wilson to sign a promissory note and security agreement in its favor. Wilson also signs a promissory note in favor of a local contractor who has done some remodeling of the store. In this situation, the paint company holds an "account," the tool manufacturer holds "chattel paper," and the contractor holds an "instrument."

"General intangibles" is a catchall category for all personal property other than goods, accounts, chattel paper, documents, instruments, and money. Examples of general intangibles are the goodwill of a business and literary rights.

28:5   Excluded Transactions

Certain types of transactions are not governed by Article 9 even though they might appear to fall within its scope. The reason for many of the exclusions is that bodies of law outside the UCC adequately regulate these transactions.

Real Property (UCC § 9-104)   Article 9 applies if the collateral subject to a security interest is a fixture, but it does not apply to the creation or transfer of an interest in real property. Thus, Article 9 is inapplicable in the common situation where a person decides to buy a new house, obtains a loan to pay the purchase price, and signs a mortgage or similar instrument covering the property by way of security for the loan (see Chapter 35). Also outside the scope of Article 9 are leases of real property (see Chapter 36), transfers of the right to receive rent under leases, and statutory liens on real property. An example of a statutory lien on real property is a landlord's interest in the personal property of a tenant who has not paid his rent.

Accounts (UCC §§ 9-102, 9-104)   Many businesses must maintain inventories and replenish them as goods are sold. Sales are often on open account, leaving the businesses with accounts rather than cash. A common method by which these businesses obtain needed operating capital is through what is known as *accounts receivable financing*. One way a business does this is by assigning its accounts to its creditor as security for existing loans or future advances. Article 9 clearly applies to this type of transaction because a security interest would be created. However, Article 9 also applies to most *sales* of accounts or chattel paper. As a result, Article 9 also governs a second method of accounts receivable financing, by which a business needing capital sells its accounts outright to someone else.

It may be clear in a given situation that an assignment or sale of accounts is not made to obtain or secure financing. Article 9 recognizes this possibility by listing four types of transfers of accounts to which it does not apply: (1) a sale made as part of a sale of the business out of which the accounts arose, (2) an assignment for purposes of collection only, (3) a transfer of a right to payment under a contract if the transferee is the person who is also to perform the contract, and (4) a transfer of a single account to satisfy a prior debt.

Other Exclusions (UCC § 9-104)   Article 9 does not apply to transfers by government agencies. Other transactions to which it does not apply include any transfer of (1) a claim for employee compensation, (2) a claim under an insurance policy, (3) a tort claim, and (4) an interest in most types of bank accounts.

Creation and Perfection of Security Interest

28:6   Attachment of Security Interest

A security interest is created when it attaches. *Attachment* occurs when the following three events have taken place, in any order: (1) the secured party has possession of either the collateral (see discussion below) or a written security agreement (see 28:7), (2) the secured party has given value (see 28:8), and (3) the debtor has acquired rights with respect to the collateral (see 28:9). Obviously, the debtor must also have incurred some sort of debt or other obligation. This requirement is implicit in, for example, the definition of "security interest" as an interest-securing payment or performance of an obligation.

Possessory Security Interests (UCC § 9-203)   In most secured transactions the parties intend that the debtor will retain possession of the collateral, at least prior to any default by the debtor. However, that is not always true. Sometimes, the debtor transfers possession of the collateral to the secured party, who holds it until the secured debt has been paid. The secured party is then said to have a *possessory security interest.* Most possessory security interests arise from pledge transactions. For example, a person might pledge shares of corporate stock as collateral for a loan. A possessory interest can attach without a written security agreement, although some sort of written agreement is often used. The debtor must, however, deliver the collateral to someone else. Delivery can be either to the secured party or to some third person who, by arrangement, is to have possession. Ordinarily, the debtor is entitled to regain possession only after the secured debt or obligation has been satisfied.

Rights and Duties of Secured Party in Possession (UCC § 9-207)   A secured party who has the collateral in his possession has certain rights. He can (1) re-pledge the collateral on terms that do not impair the debtor's right to redeem it (see Chapter 29); (2) use or operate the collateral to preserve it or its value; and (3) unless the collateral is consumer goods, use or operate the collateral to the extent allowed by the terms of the security agreement. A secured party in possession also has certain duties. He must take reasonable care of the collateral. Ordinarily, he must also keep it identifiable, although fungible collateral (such as grain) can be mixed with other property of the same kind. If the secured party fails to carry out these duties he is liable for any resulting loss.

Even though collateral is in the secured party's possession, the debtor must bear the risk of its being damaged or destroyed. This means that the secured party can charge the debtor with reasonable insurance expenses. The debtor can also be charged with taxes and other reasonable payments required in connection with the secured party's possession, preservation, or use of the collateral.

 The rights and duties noted above also apply when a secured party has re-possessed collateral after the debtor's default, as discussed in Chapter 29 (see 29:11).

28:7   Security Agreement (UCC § 9-203)

In the case of a security interest other than a possessory one, the debtor and se-cured party must enter into a written *security agreement* before the interest can attach. In most cases the agreement must contain only (1) a description of the collateral and (2) the debtor's signature. If the collateral is either crops that will be or are being grown or timber that is to be cut, a description of the land involved must also be included in the agreement. However, most security agreements, such as the one illustrated on pages 472 and 473, also contain other provisions.

Description of Collateral   The description of the collateral in a security agreement must be reasonably specific. Generally, a description is sufficient if it makes it possible to identify the property intended as security. As the following case illustrates, however, other potential collateral that the secured party may have intended to include will not be covered unless it is adequately described. Note how the parties' use of a preprinted agreement form contributed to their problem.

Mitchell
v
Shepherd Mall State Bank
324 F Supp 1029, 9 UCCRS 165
(United States District Court, W.D.
Oklahoma, Bankruptcy Division, 1971)

[Mitchell and his partner, the debtor, filed a petition in bankruptcy, and the bankruptcy judge in that proceeding found that a security interest held by Shepherd Mall State Bank covered equipment, inventory, accounts receivable, contract rights, and proceeds in the debtors' stores. The trustee in bankruptcy now seeks review of the correctness of that finding.]

Daugherty, District Judge.

*   *   *

The relevant portions of the Security Agreement are set out below: ([italicized] portions indicate typewritten insertions on the form agreement) . . .

D. COLLATERAL
1. The security interest is granted in the following collateral:
   a. Describe collateral. . . . (4) If insufficient space to list all collateral, continue on separate sheets affixed hereto and signed for purposes of identification.
   See EQUIPMENT LIST *attached hereto and made a part hereof, describing equipment, fur-*

niture and fixtures located at Moore and Edmond stores. (Description continued on 2 pages attached hereto).
2. Classify goods under (one or more of) the following Uniform Commercial Code categories:
   ☐ Consumer Goods
   ☒ Equipment (business use)
   ☒ Inventory
   ☒ Accounts Receivable
   ☒ Contract Rights

As can be seen from the material quoted above the collateral described ("equipment, furniture and fixtures") is not the same as the collateral classified. The list describing the "equipment, furniture and fixtures" makes no reference to either "Inventory," "Accounts Receivable," or "Contract Rights."

. . . [The court discusses financing statements (discussed in 28:11) filed by the bank. These statements described the collateral as including inventory and proceeds, accounts receivable, and contract rights. The court concludes that it is the security agreement, not the financing statement, that creates a security interest.]

Paragraph D1 of the security agreement quoted above which purports to describe the collateral is unambiguous. . . . However, it is not the sufficiency of the description which is questioned. The language of this paragraph is clear as to what is described.

It is the statement contained in Paragraph D2 of the security agreement which it is contended extends the security interest to the inventory, accounts receivable, and contract rights. . . . This printed paragraph attempts the impossible under the Code. It purports to classify accounts receivable and contract rights as goods. Goods, however, include only "consumer goods," "equipment," "farm products," and "inventory." . . . Accounts receivable and contract rights are otherwise defined in [UCC § 9-106].

Classifications under the Code are important to determine such questions as the place of filing, etc. . . . It is, however, not among the purposes of classification to describe or create the security interest. . . .

The printed form invited a misclassification, but should this error be permitted to render an otherwise unambiguous description of collateral uncertain? We think not. . . .

It could as well be said in the instant case that a third party would only be interested in the collateral as clearly designated by the form itself. He would not be concerned with the classification made by the parties, and should

not be required to read and interpret the paragraph which purports to deal only with classification.

. . . [The court discusses the bankruptcy trustee's having received parol (oral) evidence (here, testimony of a bank officer) as to what the bank had *intended* to be covered in the agreement, even if the agreement was unclear. Parol evidence about the meaning of a contract provision is permitted to explain an ambiguous provision.]

We conclude that the [bankruptcy judge] in this case should not have received the parol evidence in determining the collateral encompassed by the Security Agreement. Therefore, the [Judge must be held to have erred]. The Security Agreement given to Shepherd Mall State Bank covered only the equipment specifically enumerated in the attached list, and the security interest did not extend to the accounts receivable, inventory, and contract rights.

[The court held that the bankruptcy judge erred.]

After-acquired Property (UCC § 9-204)   *After-acquired property* is property that might or will come into the debtor's possession after the security agreement is signed. The parties to a secured transaction often want the collateral to include after-acquired property. For example, one holding a security interest in inventory wants that interest to cover new goods bought by the debtor to replace goods that are sold. Otherwise, the collateral might eventually disappear altogether.

As to collateral other than consumer goods, the security agreement can provide that the security interest created extends to after-acquired collateral. The description of the collateral must be reasonably adequate, although the law in some states is that a specific reference to after-acquired property is unnecessary if the nature of the collateral is such that it will necessarily change, as is true of inventory. On the other hand, vagueness in an after-acquired property clause can lead to problems.

EXAMPLE
A security agreement covers "all farm equipment" owned by the debtor, as well as "all property similar to that listed above" that the debtor acquires later. Since the latter clause can include anything from a screwdriver or garden hoe to the largest of farm machinery, the secured party's security interest might not include a farm tractor that the debtor acquires later.

SECURITY AGREEMENT

Agreement Number: Account Number:

Buyer: Seller:

    Buyer hereby grants to Seller a security interest in the Collateral described below. Said interest is given to secure the performance and payment of a promissory note of even date herewith in the principal amount of $_____, with interest at the rate of __% per annum on the unpaid balance, which note is given to Seller and is payable as therein provided.

    Description of Collateral:

    The above Collateral is classified as (check one or more):
- ☐ Consumer goods
- ☐ Equipment (business use)
- ☐ Inventory
- ☐ Accounts Receivable
- ☐ Contract Rights

    The security interest herein granted also covers property of the same character as that described above which Buyer may hereafter acquire at any time until the termination of this security agreement, such after-acquired property being more specifically described as follows:

    The names and addresses of all persons to whom notices required or permitted by law are to be sent are set forth below.

    Buyer acknowledges that (1) Buyer has read both sides of this agreement and (2) Buyer has received a legible, completely filled-in copy of this agreement.

    SEE OTHER SIDE FOR ADDITIONAL TERMS AND CONDITIONS

IN WITNESS WHEREOF, Buyer and Seller have executed this agreement on the _____ day of _____, 19__.

BUYER   SELLER

_____ By_____

_____   _____

_____   _____

TERMS AND CONDITIONS

1. Payment.   Buyer shall pay to Seller the sum evidenced by the above-mentioned promissory note or any renewals or extensions thereof.

2. Buyer's Covenant.   Buyer covenants that except for the security interest hereby granted, Buyer has, or on acquisition will have, full title to the collateral free from any lien, security interest, or claim. Buyer will, at Buyer's expense, defend any action that may affect Seller's security interest in, or Buyer's title to, the collateral.

3. Proceeds.   Buyer hereby grants to Seller a security interest in and to all proceeds of the collateral, as defined by Article 9 of the Uniform Commercial Code as enacted in the State of _____. This provision shall not be construed to mean that Buyer is authorized to sell, lease, or dispose of the collateral without Seller's consent.

4. Financing Statements.   At the request of Seller, Buyer will join in executing, or will execute as appropriate, all necessary financing statements in a form satisfactory to Seller, and will pay the cost of filing such statements.

5. Location of Collateral.   Buyer will keep the collateral separate and identifiable at the address of Buyer shown herein, and Buyer will not remove the collateral from such address without the written consent of Seller.

6. Alienation of Collateral.   Buyer will not, without the written consent of Seller, sell, contract to sell, lease, encumber, or otherwise dispose of the collateral or any interest therein until this security agreement and all debts secured hereby have been fully satisfied.

7. Protection of Collateral.   Buyer shall keep the collateral in good order and repair, and Buyer shall not use the collateral in violation of any statute or ordinance.

8. Insurance.   Buyer shall insure the collateral with an insurer acceptable to Seller against such casualties and in such amounts as Seller may require. Said insurance shall be for the benefit of Buyer and Seller as their interests may appear.

9. Taxes and Assessments.   Buyer shall pay promptly when due all taxes and assessments levied on the collateral or on its use or operation.

10. Default.   If Buyer fails to pay when due any amount payable on the above-mentioned note or on any other indebtedness secured hereby, or shall fail to observe or perform any of the provisions of this agreement, Buyer shall be in default.

11. Remedies.   On any default, and at any time thereafter:

(a) Seller may declare all obligations secured hereby immediately due and payable and may proceed to enforce payment of the same and exercise any and all of the rights and remedies provided by law.

(b) Seller shall have the right to remove the collateral from Buyer's premises. Seller may require Buyer to assemble the collateral and make it available to Seller at any place to be designated by Seller that is reasonably convenient to both parties. For purposes of removal and possession of the collateral, Seller or its representative may enter any premises of Buyer without legal process, and Buyer hereby waives and releases Seller of and from any and all claims in connection therewith or arising therefrom.

12. Effect of Seller's Waiver.   Failure of Seller to exercise any right or remedy, including but not limited to the acceptance of partial or delinquent payments, shall not be a waiver of any obligation of Buyer or right of Seller; nor shall it constitute a waiver of any other similar default subsequently occurring.

13. Time as of Essence.   Time is of the essence of this agreement.

14. Waiver of Defenses.   Buyer hereby waives as against any assignee of the security interest granted hereby any claim or defense which Buyer may have against Seller to the full extent permitted by law.

15. Governing Law.   This agreement shall be construed according to the law of the State of _____ .

The rule about after-acquired property is somewhat more limited if the collateral is consumer goods. After-acquired consumer goods are not subject to the secured party's security interest unless the debtor acquires the additional goods *within ten days* after the secured party "gives value" (see 28:8).

Other Optional Provisions   Most security agreements include far more than just a description of the collateral and perhaps an after-acquired property clause. Some types of optional coverage are expressly provided for in Article 9. Other types, while not mentioned in Article 9, are included in agreements simply as a matter of common sense, past practice, or convenience. Some of the various matters likely to be included or covered in a security agreement are listed below. As a practical matter, the secured party usually has superior bargaining power and is thus able to dictate the form and content of the agreement.

- Identification of parties
- Description of value given by secured party
- Grant of security interest
- Debtor's rights in collateral
- Secured party's rights in collateral
- Accelerated payment of secured debt
- Protection of collateral; risk of loss or damage
- Time and manner of satisfying secured obligation
- Debtor's waiver of rights and defenses
- Events of default
- Secured party's rights and remedies on debtor's default

Debtor's Waiver of Defenses (UCC § 9-206)   A security agreement that covers a debtor's credit purchase of goods often includes what is known as a *waiver of defenses* clause. The purpose of the clause is to prevent the debtor from asserting certain claims or defenses against one to whom the secured party assigns the security interest (see Chapter 29). Bear in mind that a seller who takes a security interest in goods he has sold on credit often wants to be paid at once. He is also happy to pass on to someone else the risk and administrative cost involved in collecting the debt. The seller can achieve these goals by assigning the chattel paper (here, the security agreement and the buyer's promissory note) to a third party (the assignee). However, under general sales law a buyer can assert certain claims or defenses against the seller if there are problems under the sales contract.[3] For example, a buyer might claim failure of consideration or breach of warranty (see Chapters 21 and 22).

If the seller assigns the chattel paper, the assignee would prefer not to be placed in the same position as the seller with regard to liability for performance of the

---

[3] A "claim" becomes a "defense" if it is asserted by the buyer in a lawsuit brought by the seller, rather than being directed to the seller informally.

contract. Often, the assignee will not have had anything to do with the original contract—he has only the buyer's promise to pay a given amount and a security interest in the collateral. This is why the waiver of defenses clause is desirable from the assignee's viewpoint. Without it, the assignee would be left open to a lawsuit by the buyer and might hesitate to accept the assignment from the seller in the first place.

Article 9 takes the position that a waiver of defenses clause is enforceable by certain assignees. The assignee must have paid value for the assignment and have taken it in good faith. As the following case illustrates, the assignee must also have been unaware of the particular claim or defense that the buyer later asserts.

Massey-Ferguson Credit Corp.
v
Brown
547 P2d 846
(Montana Supreme Court, 1976)

[Brown, the appellant, bought a harvesting machine from Dan Morrison & Sons, and as part of the transaction he traded in his old harvesting machine. Brown signed a security agreement in the form of a retail installment contract covering the transaction. Morrison immediately assigned the contract to Massey-Ferguson Credit Corporation, the respondent. The new machine turned out to be defective, and Morrison failed to repair it despite its agreement to do so. Morrison later went out of business, and Brown stopped making payments on the machine. Massey-Ferguson then enforced its security interest by taking the machine back and selling it to someone else for less than Brown had owed on it (this procedure is discussed in Chapter 30). Massey-Ferguson sued Brown for the amount still owed to it on the contract, and Brown counterclaimed for the value of his trade-in. The trial court entered judgment for Massey-Ferguson, and Brown appealed.]

Harrison, Justice.

*   *   *

[The court first determines that Morrison's breach of the agreement to repair was a valid

defense in Massey-Ferguson's action on the retail installment contract.]

[We] now consider whether [the breach of the repair agreement] defense can be applied to respondent, seller's assignee. Respondent asserts the seller's breach is not an applicable defense against the assignee of this retail installment contract. Undeniably, appellant's signature appears on a contract which states:

> "... buyer(s) will not set up any claim, or defense which he may have against the seller as a defense ... in any action ... by the seller's assignee."

The enforceability of covenants of this type is governed by [UCC § 9-206(1)], which provides in pertinent part:

> "... an agreement by a buyer or lessee that he will not assert against an assignee any claim or defense which he may have against the seller or lessor is enforceable by an assignee who takes his assignment for value, in good faith and without notice of a claim or defense...."

In our view, respondent Massey-Ferguson Credit Corporation cannot be considered among those whose protection is contemplated by [§ 9-206(1)]. The evidence shows that respondent's representative participated, at least to some degree, in making the sale by orally affirming the seller's promises to appellant buyer. It is clear from the exhibits that the contract was executed and assigned at about the same time and upon the same instrument, and the blank form sales contract employed was in this case furnished by respondent corporation. Under these circumstances, it has been held the assignee does not take the assignment "without notice of a claim or defense" and is therefore not entitled to the enforcement protection provided by [UCC § 9-206(1)]. We find [this rule to be] in strict accord with the purpose and policy behind this section of the Uniform Commercial Code, as explained in [a Kentucky case]:

"We consider it to be the policy of the Uniform Commercial Code to encourage the supplying of credit for the buying of goods by insulating the lender from lawsuits over the quality of the goods. But we conceive that the insulation was intended primarily for *financial institutions* rather than the manufacturer who finances his own sales. He needs no inducement to supply credit for the purchase of his goods because the whole object of his business is to sell his goods." . . .

[Judgment reversed.]

A waiver of defenses clause is *not* effective with respect to the so-called "real defenses," which are the defenses that can be asserted against the holder in due course of a negotiable instrument. As discussed in Chapter 24, the real defenses include infancy, illegality of the transaction, certain misrepresentations, and discharge in bankruptcy.

 A waiver of *any* defenses might be unenforceable by an assignee if the collateral is consumer goods. This is so because the Article 9 rule is subject to any statute or court decision that establishes a different rule for buyers of consumer goods. Statutes in some states invalidate waivers of defenses in consumer transactions. In other states, court-made law has the same effect. Moreover, as discussed in Chapter 27 (see 27:8), a rule issued by the Federal Trade Commission requires that any sales contract for a credit sale of consumer goods conspicuously advise the debtor that, in effect, any assignee of the contract is subject to *all* claims and defenses that the debtor could assert against the seller. The only exception to this requirement concerns consumer goods bought with a credit card. As also discussed in Chapter 27, the liability of a credit-card issuer, such as a bank, is governed by the federal Fair Credit Billing Act.

28:8   Secured Party's Giving of Value (UCC § 9-203)

A security interest cannot attach until "value has been given." This requirement concerns a duty of the potential secured party. Essentially, it means that in exchange for granting the security interest, the debtor must receive from the secured party consideration sufficient to support a simple contract. The value given can be a present extension of credit or a commitment to extend credit in the future. This is the value given in most secured transactions. In others, one might "give value" for rights acquired either (1) in exchange for partial or total satisfaction of a preexisting claim or (2) as security for a preexisting claim.

EXAMPLE

John owes Bill $1,000, but the debt is unsecured; that is, Bill has only John's promise to pay. John now signs a security agreement granting Bill an interest in certain property owned by John, as security for the debt. Bill now has a valid security interest. He has given value because the interest was granted as security for a preexisting claim.

28:9   Debtor's Acquisition of Rights in Collateral

The requirement that a debtor have "rights" in collateral before a security interest in that collateral can attach is logical; a debtor can hardly grant a security interest unless he himself has some rights in the property. Unfortunately, Article 9 does not define exactly what rights the debtor must have. This means that the courts must interpret the requirement.

A debtor has sufficient rights to grant a security interest if he has both title to and possession of the property, as where the debtor buys goods on credit and takes them home with him. However, the nature and extent of the debtor's rights need not be so obvious. Instead, it is generally enough that the debtor has some ownership interest in the property or some right to obtain possession of it.

EXAMPLE

Farmers Bank loans farmer Jones money to buy a new harvesting machine, and the parties sign a security agreement to cover the new machine. Jones then places an order for the machine with Acme Equipment Company, which has several, identical harvesting machines in stock. Since Farmers Bank has a signed security agreement and has given value, its security interest attaches as soon as Acme identifies a machine to the contract—in other words, as soon as Acme determines the particular machine that will be delivered to Jones. Attachment is not postponed until the time when Jones actually acquires possession of the machine.

28:10   Perfection of Security Interest, Generally

The attachment of a security interest gives the secured party only limited rights with respect to the collateral. Attachment does not protect the secured party against many other people who may acquire or claim some sort of interest in that collateral. As a result, the secured party ordinarily wants to maximize his rights by perfecting his interest. If he does so, his interest becomes superior (1) to unperfected interests arising earlier and (2) to some interests of others arising subsequently.

A security interest is perfected when (1) it has attached and (2) any required additional steps for perfection have been taken. *Perfection of security interest* occurs automatically at the time of attachment for some types of interests, but it usually requires something more. That "something more" consists of either the secured party's taking possession of the collateral, or the secured party's filing a financing statement. These requirements are discussed in the remainder of this chapter.

Perfection on Attachment (UCC § 9-302)   Article 9 lists several types of security interests that are, in effect, automatically perfected when they attach; that is, the secured party need not do anything more. The most important type of security interest that is perfected when it attaches is a *purchase money security interest* in consumer goods other than motor vehicles or fixtures. This exception to the usual requirement (that a financing statement be filed, as discussed in 28:11) is significant because more secured transactions involve purchase money security interests than any other type of interest.

The automatic perfection rule may worry a secured party since a given item bought by the debtor may or may not qualify as "consumer goods," depending on its use. For example, an armchair qualifies if it is bought for use in the debtor's home, but it does not qualify if it is bought for use in the debtor's office. The answer to this problem is that the secured party can take the debtor's word about the intended use of the goods, even if the debtor is lying.

 Although the secured party need not file to perfect a purchase money security interest in consumer goods, it is to its advantage to do so. As discussed in Chapter 29 (see 29:8), filing can save an interest that would otherwise be lost if the debtor sells the goods to another consumer.

Perfection Through Possession (UCC §§ 9-302, 9-304, 9-305)   A secured party can perfect a security interest in certain types of collateral, including goods, money, instruments, and chattel paper, by taking possession of the collateral. Indeed, perfection of a security interest in money or most instruments other than those constituting part of chattel paper can be done *only* in this way. Perfection by possession is simple, but is not practicable in most cases. The result is that if some act of perfection is required, filing is the method generally used.

28:11   Perfection by Filing (UCC §§ 9-302, 9-304, 9-403)

Under Article 9, *filing* usually consists of the secured party's presenting a "financing statement" to the appropriate public official (filing officer) and offering the required filing fee. The filing officer then indexes the financing statement so that it can be located, and he holds the statement for public inspection. The purpose of filing is to give people other than the parties to a secured transaction a way to learn about the secured party's interest. For most types of collateral, filing either is mandatory to perfect a security interest or is optional in the sense that it can be done even though it is not necessary.

Financing Statement (UCC § 9-402)   Article 9 specifies the information that must be included in a *financing statement* if the statement is to be effective. For most types of collateral, the minimum required information is as follows:

- Names of debtor and secured party
- Addresses of debtor and secured party
- Statements showing types of collateral or describing collateral
- Description of land, if collateral is crops growing or to be grown
- Debtor's signature

A financing statement that substantially complies with the Article 9 requirements is effective even though it contains minor errors, as long as the errors are not seriously misleading to those reading the statement. An example of a financing statement is set forth below.

FINANCING STATEMENT

This financing statement is presented to a filing officer for filing pursuant to provisions of Article 9 of the Uniform Commercial Code of ___20_____ *[jurisdiction]*.

Debtor (or assignor)   Name: ___21_____
                                         Address: ___22_____
                                                  ___23_____

Secured party (or assignee)   Name: ___24_____
                                         Address: ___25_____
                                                  ___26_____

1. This financing statement covers the following types (or items) of property: ___27_____ *[brief description of security]*.
                    (Check Applicable Items)

2. (If collateral consists of goods which are or are to become fixtures) The above-described goods are affixed or are to be affixed to property located at:

Street & No.	Section	Known As	Block No.	City	County	State	Name of Record Owner of Premises
___28___	___29__	___30___	___31__	___32__	___33__	___34__	___35__

3. ☐ Proceeds of the collateral are also covered.

4. ☐ Products of the collateral are also covered.
                    Debtor (or assignor): ___36_____ *[Signature]*

The description of the collateral in a financing statement need not be detailed, but if the description is too general and vague, the statement will be ineffective to perfect the secured party's security interest. Examples of descriptions that are suspect because they are too general are "all personal property," "all assets, regardless of type or description, now owned or to be bought in the future," and even "all equipment now owned or hereafter acquired." If an error is to be made, it is better from the secured party's viewpoint that the collateral be described in too much detail, rather than in too little.

Place of Filing (UCC § 9-401)   The place where a financing statement is to be filed depends on the nature of the collateral described in the statement. For collateral of a given type, the proper place of filing varies among the states because Article 9 provides for three alternative schemes to govern the matter. Each scheme involves the use of local and state filing. "Local filing" means filing with a designated county officer, such as the county recorder. "State filing" means filing with the secretary of state. It should be noted, however, that under each of the three alternative schemes, financing statements covering most nonfarm business secured transactions are filed in a single place, the office of the secretary of state.

Outlined below are the requirements under the scheme adopted by a majority of the states:

Collateral	Place of Filing
• Consumer goods, farm equipment, or farm products	Generally, local filing in county of debtor's residence; if debtor is nonresident of state, local filing in county where collateral located
• Crops growing or to be grown	Local filing in county where land located, *in addition to* local filing in county of debtor's residence, if different
• Timber, minerals, or fixtures	Local filing in county where land located
• All other collateral	State filing

The scheme adopted in a substantial minority of the states is similar to the one outlined above except that all state filing must be accompanied by local filing, usually in the county where the debtor's place of business is located.

If filing is done either in the wrong place or in not all the required places, but in good faith, it is effective for any collateral as to which the filing is proper. It is also effective against anyone who has actual knowledge about the contents of the financing statement.

Duration of Filing (UCC § 9-403)   A filed financing statement is usually effective to perfect the secured party's security interest for five years after the date of filing. Before that five-year period ends, the secured party can file a *continuation statement* to extend the effectiveness of his financing statement.

If a secured party fails to file a timely continuation statement, his security interest becomes unperfected and is not perfected again until he files a new financing statement. "Timely" means within six months before the financing or continuation statement then in force expires. In any period during which the security interest is unperfected, it becomes subordinate to the interests of all other parties who have perfected interests in the collateral.[4]

---

[4]The priority of conflicting interests in the same collateral is discussed in Chapter 29 (see 29:2–29:4).

EXAMPLE

On January 1, 1978, Able filed a financing statement covering a debtor's inventory. He failed to file a continuation statement during the last half of 1982 but, on June 1, 1983, he realizes his error and files a new financing statement. Meanwhile, Baker perfected a security interest in the debtor's inventory on January 1, 1980, while Charlie perfected an interest in the same inventory on April 1, 1983. Able's interest is now subordinate to those of both Baker and Charlie.

Key Concepts and Terms

- A secured transaction is a transaction in which payment of a debt or performance of some other obligation is secured, and the security is an interest in the debtor's personal property or fixtures. Secured transactions are governed by Article 9 of the UCC.

- A security interest is created when it attaches. Attachment occurs when (1) the secured party has given value, (2) the debtor has acquired rights in the collateral, and (3) the secured party is in possession of either the collateral or a security agreement.

- The minimum requirements for a security agreement are that it be in writing, describe the collateral, and be signed by the debtor. Most security agreements cover many other aspects of the transaction.

- To maximize his rights in the collateral, the secured party must perfect his security interest. Filing a financing statement is the usual method of perfection.

- A filed financing statement perfects the secured party's security interest for five years. The secured party can extend the perfected status of his interest by filing a continuation statement.

- Accounts Receivable Financing
- After-acquired Property
- Attachment of Security Interest
- Collateral
- Consumer Goods
- Continuation Statement
- Filing
- Financing Statement
- Perfection of Security Interest
- Possessory Security Interest
- Purchase Money Security Interest
- Security Agreement
- Waiver of Defenses

Questions and Case Problems

1. Define "security interest" as that term is used in UCC Article 9. Give an example of a simple secured transaction governed by Article 9.

2. What is the significance of the "attachment" of a security interest?

3. What does the holder of a security interest gain by perfecting that interest? How is perfection accomplished?

4. The collateral described in a security agreement is "all inventory, equipment, and other goods now owned or hereafter acquired" by Antenna Systems, the debtor. Antenna Systems later goes bankrupt, and a dispute arises between the secured

party and the trustee in bankruptcy as to their rights in the following property of Antenna Systems: (a) confidential blueprints and technical data produced by the engineering staff in designing products for customers; (b) information in the form of bids, proposals, and cost estimates, all of which would be of value to other firms in the same business; (c) tooling (jigs, patterns, templates, and the like) used to reproduce parts of antenna systems; and (d) a supply of standard replacement parts. How much, if any, of the property listed in categories (a) through (d) is covered by the security interest? As to each class of items, why should those items be included or excluded?

5. On May 1, Sullivan signed a security agreement giving Wald a security interest in Sullivan's business equipment. Wald agreed to lend Sullivan $15,000, which Sullivan received on May 10. Wald also agreed to lend Sullivan an additional $25,000, to be secured by Sullivan's inventory and a new car that Sullivan intended to buy. Sullivan received the $25,000 on June 1, and he bought the new car on June 15. What was the date of attachment of Wald's security interest in (a) Sullivan's equipment, (b) Sullivan's inventory, and (c) the car?

6. What is a "financing statement," and what is it used for?

7. Wong obtains a loan from a finance company and uses the money to buy a car for personal use. As part of the transaction, Wong signs a security agreement that grants the finance company a security interest in the car. One month later the car is destroyed in an accident, and Wong's insurer sends her a check covering the loss. With the finance company's consent, Wong uses the insurance money to buy another car, but no new security agreement is signed. The finance company now claims that it has a security interest in the replacement car. Is its claim valid?

8. Lopes owes Garvey $1,500, and the debt is unsecured. Garvey learns that Lopes' business is doing poorly, and he wishes to protect himself by obtaining a security interest covering the debt. Lopes signs an agreement that grants Garvey a security interest in Lopes' car in exchange for Garvey's agreement to reduce the debt to $1,000. Later, a dispute arises as to whether Garvey has a valid security interest in the car; Lopes claims that he does not. Is Lopes correct?

9. Harrison grants to the local bank a security interest covering certain equipment and fixtures. The bank files an appropriate financing statement with the secretary of state, but it fails to file locally. Later, Harrison becomes indebted to both Starr and McCartney, each of whom made a search to determine the extent of existing security interests in Harrison's property before they extended credit and took security interests in the same equipment and fixtures covered by the bank's security interest. Starr searched locally and at the secretary of state's office, where he discovered the bank's financing statement. McCartney only checked in the county where Harrison lived and carried on his business; therefore, he did not find the financing statement. To what extent is the bank's security interest perfected as against Starr? To what extent is it perfected as against McCartney?

10. Jones, who operates his own machinist's shop, buys a new milling machine from Morton on credit. Jones signs a promissory note for the unpaid part of the purchase price. He also signs a security agreement that grants Morton a security interest in the new machine, and the agreement includes a waiver of defenses clause. One week later Morton assigns Jones' promissory note and the security interest to Chandler and receives a sum of money from Chandler in exchange. Two months after that the milling machine turns out to be defective, and Morton refuses to correct the defect or accept a return of the machine. Jones then stops making pay-

ments on the note held by Chandler, and Chandler sues Jones to recover the amount due. Jones argues that he should not have to pay because warranties covering the machine were breached. How should the court decide the case?

29 Rights of Parties to Secured Transactions

29:1 Introduction

Chapter 28 covers the concept of what a secured transaction is, as well as the manner in which a security interest in personal property or fixtures is created. It is now time to consider certain rights of both secured parties and debtors that are also governed by Article 9 of the UCC. For example, Article 9 establishes a system of priorities by which the relative rights of several secured parties, each of whom holds a security interest in the same collateral, can be determined (see 29:2 through 29:4). It allows a secured party to transfer his interest to someone else (see 29:5). It also sets forth detailed rules as to how a security interest can be enforced if the debtor defaults by failing to satisfy the secured obligation (see 29:9 through 29:13). As for the rights of the debtor, Article 9 allows him to transfer collateral that is covered by a security interest (see 29:7 and 29:8), and it permits the debtor to reobtain possession of collateral that has been taken from him after a default (see 29:14). Article 9 also provides for recovering damages from a secured party who has acted improperly (see 29:16).

Priorities

29:2 Priorities, Generally

Priority refers to the superiority of one claimant's rights or interests over those of another. It involves the problem of resolving conflicting interests of different claimants who are all asserting rights in the same *collateral*.

The simplest method of determining priority would be to do so according to the order in which the interests in particular collateral arose. The UCC rejects this approach, however. Instead, the UCC favors certain claimants over others. The Article 9 priority rules are complex and riddled with exceptions. However, the basic factors used in determining priority are (1) the status of a particular claimant (who may or may not be a secured party) and (2) the time when a secured party claimant's security interest attached or was perfected. These factors are discussed in detail in 29:3 and 29:4.

29:3   Priorities Among Different Classes of Claimants

A number of different types or classes of claimants (in addition to the debtor) might claim rights in particular collateral. They include (1) unsecured creditors, (2) unperfected secured parties, (3) perfected secured parties, (4) subsequent buyers, (5) judicial lien creditors, and (6) statutory lien creditors. By way of definition, an unsecured creditor is one who holds a personal claim against the debtor. He has no security interest in the collateral, unlike a secured party. Whether a secured party's interest is perfected depends on whether the party took the required action (if any) to perfect the interest, as discussed in Chapter 28. A subsequent buyer is a person to whom the debtor sells the collateral. A judicial lien creditor is a creditor who has acquired a *lien* on the collateral through the judicial process, such as by attachment or execution.[1] A statutory lien creditor, on the other hand, is a creditor whose lien arose automatically under state law other than the UCC.

EXAMPLE
Linda has her car repaired at Blake's garage, and a state statute gives Blake a possessory lien (lien that requires continued possession to be effective) on the car for the cost of work done on it. If Linda does not pay Blake's repair bill and Blake refuses to release the car to Linda, Blake is a statutory lien creditor. If, on the other hand, Blake does release the car to Linda, Blake becomes an unsecured creditor. If Blake later sues Linda, is awarded judgment, and has the car seized under a writ of execution, Blake becomes a judicial lien creditor. And in the unlikely event that, after relinquishing possession, Blake persuades Linda to enter into a security agreement covering the car, Blake becomes a secured party, and he can then perfect his security interest.

Unsecured Creditors   As to particular collateral, the interest of an unsecured creditor is generally subordinate or junior to the interests of all the other classes of claimants listed above.

Unperfected Secured Creditors (UCC § 9-301)   Generally speaking, an unperfected secured party's interest is junior to that of (1) any perfected secured party, (2) any judicial or statutory lien creditor, and (3) many subsequent buyers.[2]

Perfected Secured Creditors (UCC §§ 9-301, 9-307, 9-310)   As already noted, the interest of a perfected secured party in collateral is superior to that of both an unsecured creditor and an unperfected secured party. It is also usually superior to that of a judicial lien creditor. The priority of most statutory liens is governed by

---

[1]A lien is any interest in property claimed by someone other than the owner. Attachment and execution are discussed in Chapter 30.
[2]The rights of subsequent buyers are discussed in 29:8.

state or federal law outside the UCC. However, a *possessory* lien arising under state law in favor of a person who furnishes services or materials with respect to goods that are covered by a perfected security interest has priority over the perfected security interest.

EXAMPLE
Friendly Finance Company has a perfected security interest in Victor's expensive wristwatch. Victor leaves the watch with Jake for repair, and under the law Jake has a possessory lien on the watch for the value of the work he does on it. If Victor does not pay for the repairs and Jake retains possession of the watch in accordance with his statutory right, Jake's lien is superior to Friendly's security interest. If, on the other hand, state law does not require Jake to retain possession of the watch to retain his lien, state law other than the UCC will govern the question of priority between Friendly and Jake.

In some circumstances a subsequent buyer has priority over perfected secured parties, as discussed in 29:8. Therefore, even though a secured party has done all he can to maximize his rights in collateral, he can lose his right to priority if the collateral finds its way into the hands of a subsequent buyer.

29:4   Priorities Among Members of Same Class

More than one security interest of the same type can exist in the same collateral. For example, two different creditors can hold unperfected security interests in the same property owned by the debtor. In that event, priority is given to the secured party whose interest attached first.

 Disputes between unperfected secured parties should never go to court. If creditor A is junior to creditor B under the above rule, A need simply file to perfect his interest before proceeding further against the debtor or the collateral. By so doing, A achieves priority over B.

Perfected Secured Parties (UCC § 9-312)   The rule for determining the priority among two or more perfected secured parties is not quite so simple. One might think that priority should be determined according to the order in which the parties perfected their interests. This was the rule under the original (1962) version of Article 9, but that rule can lead to injustice.

EXAMPLE
On January 1, Penny arranges with a bank for a loan, which is to be secured by Penny's jewelry. Penny signs a security agreement and financing statement, and the bank files the statement on January 2. However, the bank does not advance the loan proceeds until January 10, so that its security interest neither attaches nor is perfected until that date (date of giving value). Meanwhile, on January 5, Penny obtains a loan from a finance company, and on that date she gives the finance company possession of the jewelry as security. As a result, the finance company's interest is perfected on January 5, and the finance company has priority over the

bank. This is so even though, before January 1, the bank may have made a careful search of the records in the proper office to learn whether Penny's jewelry was the subject of any existing security interest.

The rule as to the priority of perfected secured parties was changed in the 1972 revision of Article 9. Today, the general rule is that priority is given to the secured party who is the first to *either* file or perfect his interest. Hence, in the above example the bank has priority over the finance company because the bank filed first, even though the finance company was the first to perfect its interest.

An important exception to the general rule as to priority among perfected secured parties involves *purchase money security interests.* The priority of a creditor holding such an interest, who is known as a purchase money secured party, depends on whether the collateral is inventory. If (1) the collateral is *not* inventory; and (2) the purchase money secured party perfects the interest within ten days *after* the debtor takes possession of the collateral, the purchase money security interest has priority over other security interests in the same collateral, even if those other interests are perfected.

EXAMPLE
First National Bank has a perfected security interest in all of Brown's equipment, including after-acquired equipment. On January 1, Goldberg loans Brown money to buy a new machine and receives a security interest in the machine. Brown buys the machine and takes possession of it on January 3. On January 5, Hassad makes a loan to Brown. Hassad also takes a security interest in the new machine, and she perfects her interest on January 6. As long as Goldberg perfects his interest in the machine on or before January 12, he will have priority over both First National Bank and Hassad as to the machine.

A security agreement that covers *inventory* usually includes an after-acquired property clause because of the expected changes in the inventory. Since one holding a perfected security interest in inventory ordinarily expects to have top priority as to new inventory, the rule of "super-priority" for purchase money security interests discussed above is slightly different if the collateral is inventory. The purchase money secured party can still achieve priority over earlier perfected interests, but the requirements are stricter. First, the purchase money security interest must be perfected *before* the debtor receives possession of the new inventory to be covered. Thus, there is no ten-day grace period as there is for noninventory collateral. Second, the purchase money secured party must give a written notice containing prescribed information to every other secured party who has previously filed a financing statement covering inventory of the same type. The other secured parties must receive this notice before the debtor receives possession of the new inventory.

EXAMPLE
Reed holds a perfected security interest in Sam's inventory, and the security agreement contains an after-acquired property clause. Sam orders new inventory items from suppliers Jackson and Winfield, both of whom want purchase money security interests covering what they deliver. On August 1, Jackson files a financing

statement covering his interest, and Jackson also sends a notice to Reed. The notice states that Jackson intends to acquire a purchase money security interest in described goods that will be delivered to Sam. Reed receives the notice on August 3. On August 10, Sam receives the shipments from both Jackson and Winfield. On August 15, Winfield files to perfect his interest, and he sends Reed an appropriate notice. Jackson's interest has priority over Reed's interest as to the goods Jackson shipped. However, Winfield's interest does not have priority over Reed's as to the goods Winfield shipped because Winfield filed and gave notice too late.

Transfer of Interests

29:5   Transfer of Security Interest

A secured party can transfer, or assign, the security interest to someone else, who is the assignee. Any assignment of a security interest involves three parties: (1) the original debtor; (2) the original secured party, who is the assignor; and (3) the assignee. An assignment gives the assignee all the rights that the assignor had before the assignment. The assignee in effect becomes the new secured party, and the original secured party is out of the picture concerning the collateral to which the assigned interest relates. Whether a given assignment of a security interest is valid and will serve its intended purpose is left to law outside the UCC. The assignment must satisfy the requirements of a valid contract (see Chapters 10 through 15), and there must be some sort of delivery to and acceptance by the assignee.

The underlying reason for the assignment of a security interest is often the assignor's need to secure his own financing. The assignor assigns his right to payment or performance of the secured obligation, and the assignment carries with it the security interest in the collateral that constitutes the security. The security interest cannot be assigned alone; that is, without the secured obligation.

Perfected Status of Assigned Security Interest [UCC §§ 9-302(2), 9-405]   If a security interest was perfected by the assignor before the assignment, the assignee need not file to continue the perfected status against creditors of the original debtor. Article 9 does, however, allow a *statement of assignment* to be filed, and it requires such filing under several circumstances that are not directly related to the assignment itself.

From the assignor's viewpoint, a reason for filing the statement is to have inquiries concerning the initial secured transaction addressed to the assignee, rather than to himself. Recognizing the fact that an assignment of a security interest often occurs at or near the beginning of a secured transaction, Article 9 allows an assignment to be disclosed in the original financing statement.

 The optional aspect of filing with respect to an assignment applies only between the debtor and the assignor (the original secured party). If, as is often true, the assignment itself is a new secured transaction, the assignee must take whatever steps are required to perfect his interest. The manner in which this is accomplished depends on the nature of the collateral. The usual method is filing, as discussed in Chapter 28 (see 28:11).

29:6   Assignment of Account (UCC § 9-318)

Recall that Article 9 governs most *assignments of accounts.* To be considered at this point are the relative rights of the account debtor and the assignee when an account is assigned. The account debtor is the party who is obligated to pay the account, and he may or may not be the debtor in a secured transaction.

EXAMPLE
Allen owes money on an open account he has with Moss, a merchant from whom Allen buys business supplies and equipment from time to time. Since there is no security agreement in force between Allen and Moss, Moss is an unsecured creditor. Moss needs financing, so she assigns most of her accounts, including Allen's, to a lender as security for a loan. In this situation, Allen is the account debtor regardless of what, if anything, Moss does with the account. However, since only Moss and the lender entered into a secured transaction, only Moss is the "debtor" in that transaction.

The contract between an account debtor and his creditor might prohibit any assignment of the account. This contract term cannot be enforced against an assignee. On the other hand, the assignee's rights against the account debtor are subject to all the terms of the contract and to any claim or defense arising from that contract. His rights are also subject to any other claim or defense the account debtor has against the assignor if the claim or defense arose before the account debtor was notified about the assignment. The only limit on the account debtor's rights in this regard arises if and to the extent that the account debtor has agreed to waive certain defenses, as discussed in 28:7.

After the assignment of an account, the account debtor and assignor may find it necessary or desirable to change the terms of the contract between them. As long as any change is made in good faith and in accord with reasonable commercial standards, the assignee is also bound by the change. A major exception to this rule is that no change can alter the assignee's right to payment that has already become due. Note also that such a modification can constitute a breach of the contract between the assignor and the assignee.

EXAMPLE
Gray, a general contractor, was the successful bidder on a government construction contract. Gray entered into a subcontract with Stuart, a plumber, to do the plumbing work on the project. Before Stuart even began work, he assigned his right to payment under the subcontract to EZ Finance Company as security for a loan. After Stuart has completed ten percent of his work under the subcontract, the government agency that contracted for the project is ordered to cut its expenses as part of an effort to balance the federal budget. The agency modifies the project by

reducing its scope, one result being that the need for plumbing work is cut in half. Gray and Stuart can modify the subcontract as reasonably required without EZ's participation or consent. EZ will be bound by the terms as modified except to the extent that the modification attempts to affect EZ's right to payment for the ten percent of the plumbing work already done. However, depending on the terms of the assignment agreement between Stuart and EZ, Stuart may be liable to EZ for breach of contract.

Article 9 recognizes the plight of an account debtor who pays the assignor because he is unaware or merely suspects that an assignment has been made. If the account has, in fact, been assigned, must the account debtor pay again, this time to the assignee? The answer is that until he is properly notified about the assignment, the account debtor can continue making payments to the assignor, regardless of the assignment.

29:7   Transfer of Collateral (UCC §§ 9-205, 9-311)

Article 9 states that a debtor's rights in collateral can be transferred voluntarily or involuntarily. Examples of voluntary transfers are sales or grants of security interests. Attachment of the property is an example of an involuntary transfer. Article 9 also states that a security interest is not invalid or fraudulent against other creditors (see Chapter 20) simply because the security agreement allows the debtor to sell all or part of the collateral, or requires him neither to replace sold collateral nor to account for the sale proceeds. Article 9 takes this approach to validate and offer some flexibility as to what are known as floating liens on changing inventory.[3]

The Article 9 provisions referred to above do not mean that a debtor and secured party cannot include coverage about the debtor's transfer rights in the security agreement. Most security agreements do cover the matter. For example, the agreement can forbid any sale or other transfer of the collateral. Any such prohibition is effective between the debtor and secured party.

EXAMPLE
Gustav buys a new bulldozer for business use with funds advanced by Rotkopf for that purpose. Gustav grants Rotkopf a security interest in the bulldozer, and the agreement states that Gustav cannot sell the machine until the secured obligation has been discharged. The agreement also makes any sale in violation of this restriction an "event of default." While Rotkopf's security interest still exists, Gustav sells the machine without notice to or the consent of Rotkopf. Rotkopf can now declare Gustav to be in default and can pursue any of the available remedies, as discussed in 29:9 through 29:13.

On the other hand, the security agreement can *permit* sale of the collateral, and

---

[3]A "floating lien" covers new inventory as the debtor acquires it, but the lien is lost as old inventory is sold. Thus, at any given time the lien covers whatever inventory the debtor has at that time.

most merchant debtors would be unable to remain in business without that permission. The permission to sell can be expressed in broad terms, or the agreement can require that specific consent be obtained for each planned sale. The agreement can also require the debtor to notify the secured party about each sale.

Continuation of Security Interest [UCC § 9-306(2)]   The general rule, subject to various exceptions, is that a security interest continues in collateral after its sale by the debtor unless the sale was authorized (agreed to) by the secured party. The secured party also acquires a security interest in the identifiable proceeds from the sale regardless of whether the sale was authorized. A critical issue is apt to be whether a particular sale was authorized. Problems arise when authorization was not express but, arguably, could be implied from the parties' past dealings. The following case illustrates this situation. It also shows that if the debtor makes an unauthorized sale, the secured party may be able to sue the buyer for conversion (wrongful taking) of the collateral.

Hedrick Savings Bank
v
Myers
229 NW2d 252 16 UCCRS 1412
(Iowa Supreme Court, 1975)

[Hedrick Savings Bank, the plaintiff, had loaned money to Eckley, a rancher, from time to time. The loans were secured by a security interest covering all of Eckley's livestock, and the security agreement stated that Eckley would not sell any of the livestock without the plaintiff's written consent. Despite this provision, Eckley frequently did sell livestock without the plaintiff's consent. During 1968 and 1969 he sold 96 animals to Myers, the defendant. Hedrick sued Myers for conversion of those animals. The trial court held for Myers, and the plaintiff appealed.]

LeGrand, Justice.

*   *   *

Plaintiff ... asserts the trial court erred in finding ... plaintiff had authorized the sale of the livestock....

The question whether plaintiff's lien was waived by authorizing Eckley's various sales to

defendants raises controversial issues under Article 9 of the [UCC]....

The controlling statute [UCC § 9-306(2)] contains this:

> "Except where this Article otherwise provides, a security interest continues in collateral notwithstanding sale ... by the debtor *unless his action was authorized by the secured party in the security agreement or otherwise,* and also continues in any identifiable proceeds including collections received by the debtor." [Court's emphasis.]

... [The] sole issue is whether plaintiff ... impliedly consented to the sale of the [96] animals.

Since such authorization was not given in the security instrument, the implied consent must be found, if at all, in the "or otherwise" provision of the statute. The trial court found such authorization in the course of dealing between plaintiff and Eckley. The crucial question is whether a course of dealing may constitute authority to sell in violation of the express prohibition of the security agreement....

We hold there is substantial evidence to support the trial court's finding that, from the very beginning of plaintiff's relationship with Eckley, sales of livestock pledged as collateral were made to various dealers. Plaintiff had knowledge of this, raised no objection, accepted checks from these sales for credit to Eckley's account, and clearly relied on Eckley's honesty to properly account for the proceeds. This established a course of dealing from which the trial court could find, as it did, implied authority to sell to defendants in the challenged transactions.

[The court discusses UCC § 1-205(4), which concerns the interrelationship between the written terms of an agreement and a course of dealing that is inconsistent with those terms.]

We rely on [an earlier Iowa case] for the principle that evidence of a course of dealing has relevance in interpreting agreements under the [UCC]. . . . Taking [that case] one step further, we now hold a prior course of dealing may, upon proper proof, constitute authority to sell pledged collateral under [UCC § 9-306(2)]. As used in the statute, "otherwise" should be construed to include a prior course of dealing. . . .

Affirmed.

29:8   Rights of Purchaser of Collateral

As discussed above, a secured party who authorizes the debtor's sale of collateral loses the security interest in that collateral when the sale is made. Even if a sale is *not* authorized, the secured party can still lose either the security interest or the right to priority, depending on the buyer's status.

Buyers Taking Free of Perfected Security Interest: Buyers in Ordinary Course of Business (UCC § 9-307)   *Buyers in the ordinary course of business* (other than those buying farm products from farmers) are the major class of subsequent buyers who take free of security interests, whether or not those interests are perfected. The following case illustrates the requirements that one must meet to qualify as a "buyer in the ordinary course of business." Note that, for all practical purposes, a sale must be from inventory if the buyer is to qualify.

Bank of Utica
v
Castle Ford, Inc.
36 AD2d 6, 317 NYS2d 542, 8 UCCRS 910
(New York Supreme Court, Appellate Division, 1971)

[Worden ran a car sales business. He obtained financing from the plaintiff, Bank of Utica, which was granted security interests covering all of Worden's cars. Under the financing arrangement, a separate "chattel mortgage" (which is the same as a security agreement) was signed for each car as Worden obtained it. In 1967 Worden bought a 1965 Oldsmobile to offer for sale in his business, and he signed a chattel mortgage covering the car. The mortgage forbade Worden to part with possession of the car or to use it except for display for sale to a buyer in the ordinary course of business. Worden later sold the car to Castle Ford, the defendant, which was another car dealer. Castle asked Worden

*if he had any "floor plan financing arrangement,"
and Worden said that he did not and that the car
was fully paid for. Worden later went bankrupt,
leaving the Bank of Utica unpaid. The bank then
sued Castle to recover the Oldsmobile or its value.
Judgment was for the bank, and Castle appealed.]*

Witmer, Justice.

*   *   *

Uniform Commercial Code, section 1-201(9)
provides " 'Buyer in ordinary course of business' means a person who in good faith and
without knowledge that the sale to him is in
violation of the ownership rights or security
interest of a third party in the goods buys in
ordinary course from a person in the business
of selling goods of that kind but does not include a pawnbroker." Section 9-307(1) thereof
provides "A buyer in ordinary course of business . . . takes free of a security interest created
by his seller even though the security interest
is perfected and even though the buyer knows
of its existence." . . .

[The trial court] held that since Castle is an
automobile dealer, it was not a buyer in ordinary course of business within the meaning of
the above quoted sections, and hence that
plaintiff's security interest in said vehicle gave
it prior rights therein as against Castle. The
court reasoned that . . . another dealer in motor
vehicles was not a purchaser in ordinary
course of trade when it bought a vehicle from
a fellow dealer. With this conclusion we cannot agree. . . .

. . . The nature of Castle's business is immaterial under present law, so long as it was not a
pawnbroker. As to Castle, the question is
merely, did it buy the vehicle in good faith
and without knowledge of the violation of
plaintiff's security interest therein? . . .

"Good faith" is defined in the statute in general as "honesty in fact in the conduct or transaction concerned" [UCC, §1-201(19)], and "in
the case of a merchant [it] means honesty in
fact and the observance of reasonable commercial standards of fair dealing in the trade"
[UCC, § 2-103(1)(b)]. It may be argued that as a
dealer Castle should have been aware that vehicles of other dealers are often under financing plans and that it should not have taken
Worden's word that none existed with respect
to the vehicle in question, but that it should
have investigated the official records of financing statements and lien filings concerning the
existence of such security agreement. The answer to such argument, however, is that even
if Castle searched the records of such filings
and learned that plaintiff had a lien interest in
this vehicle, it would not have been warned
against buying or forbidden to buy, for by the
express terms of the statute. . . . Castle could
buy the vehicle free of plaintiff's lien interest
provided that he otherwise acted in good
faith, that is, without knowledge that Worden
was not authorized to sell the vehicle. . . .
There is nothing in the record to show that the
details of the particular loan from plaintiff to
Worden upon this vehicle were filed, as opposed to the general financing statement filed
by plaintiff in 1965. Failure of Castle to search
the official records does not constitute bad
faith nor charge it under these circumstances
with notice that Worden lacked authority to
make the sale. . . .

Upon this record, therefore, we hold that
Castle was a buyer in the ordinary course of
business and purchased the vehicle in question free of plaintiff's validly perfected security
interest. . . .

[Judgment reversed]

**Buyers Taking Free of Perfected Security Interest: Buyers of Consumer Goods
(UCC § 9-307)**   A buyer of consumer goods can also take free of a security inter-

est, even though it is perfected. This occurs if (1) the buyer gives value; (2) the goods are bought for the buyer's personal, family, or household purposes; and (3) the buyer is unaware of the security interest. However, this rule does *not* apply if, before the sale, the secured party filed a financing statement covering the goods. This exception might seem to wipe out the "general rule," but recall from Chapter 28 (see 28:10) that filing is not required to perfect a purchase money security interest in most consumer goods.

EXAMPLE
Baldwin, a consumer, buys a refrigerator from appliance dealer Godsey, and he grants Godsey a purchase money security interest. While Godsey's interest still exists, Baldwin sells the appliance to Walton, another consumer, for a fair price. If Walton does not know about Godsey's security interest, she takes the appliance free of that interest unless Godsey has taken the unusual step of filing.

Buyers Taking Free of Unperfected Interest (UCC § 9-301)   Any subsequent buyer of collateral who takes the collateral free of perfected interests, as discussed above, also takes free of unperfected interests. However, Article 9 also gives many other buyers priority over unperfected secured parties. A buyer of farm products in the ordinary course of business qualifies for this priority. Also qualifying are most buyers *not* in the ordinary course of business, as long as any such buyer (1) gives value, (2) is unaware of the security interest, and (3) receives delivery of the collateral (assuming that delivery is possible).

EXAMPLE
Rose operates a machine shop and owns various machines used in his business. Gosnell holds an unperfected security interest in all of Rose's machines. Rose sells a machine to Spencer for a fair price and delivers the machine the same day. Unless Spencer knows about Gosnell's interest, that interest is junior to Spencer's rights in the machine.

Default; Enforcement of Security Interest

29:9   What Constitutes Debtor's Default; Secured Party's Remedies

Article 9 does not specify what constitutes a debtor's *default.* Instead, the matter is usually covered in the security agreement. A typical agreement lists various events, the occurrence of any one of which will be treated as an event of default. The most usual event of default is the debtor's failure to discharge the secured debt by paying it. Examples of other common events of default are (1) the debtor's having misrepresented an important fact in his credit application, (2) the debtor's being a party in a bankruptcy proceeding, (3) damage to or destruction of the collateral, and (4) the death of the debtor or a key person in the debtor's business.

Secured Party's Remedies on Default (UCC § 9-501)   The occurrence of a default does not necessarily mean that the secured party will take any action adverse to the debtor. Rather, it gives the secured party the *right* to act if desired. When a default has occurred, the secured party is apt to consider the nature and extent of the default and the nature of the underlying transaction itself before deciding what, if anything, to do. For example, a business debtor's failure to pay an installment on time can signal the debtor's approaching bankruptcy. The same default by an individual debtor who signed a security agreement covering consumer goods may reflect no more than an oversight on the debtor's part.

Assuming that a secured party wishes to act after a default, Article 9 provides certain remedies. Within prescribed limits, the security agreement can also provide for other remedies. Essentially, there are three approaches the secured party can take: (1) he can sue the debtor for the amount owed on the debt, just as he could do if the debt were unsecured; (2) he can foreclose on the collateral; or (3) he can obtain possession of the collateral and then take one or more of several available actions. The first of these three options is not governed by Article 9, and the second is referred to only in a general way (see 29:10). However, the third option is covered in detail (see 29:11).

29:10   Foreclosure (UCC § 9-501)

Foreclosure is a process by which a debtor's rights in collateral are extinguished. A secured party who desires to exercise the right to foreclose frequently does so under an acceleration clause in the security agreement. An acceleration clause provides that on the debtor's default, the secured party can declare the entire debt to be due.

The most common method of foreclosure following a debtor's default under a security agreement consists of the secured party's commencing a suit for foreclosure in an appropriate court. If the secured party wins the suit, the collateral is ordinarily disposed of in a judicial sale, which is a sale carried out under the court's supervision.[4] The secured party might want to buy the collateral at the judicial sale. Article 9 appears to give the secured party this right, but it does not clearly say so.

29:11   Repossession of Collateral (UCC § 9-503)

A key feature of Article 9 is what is known as the *self-help* provision. Unless the security agreement provides otherwise, the secured party has the right to *repossess* the collateral (take possession of it) following the debtor's default. The secured party does not have to seek a court's assistance. Instead, he can repossess privately if it can be done without a *breach of the peace*. The following excerpt from a New York court's opinion[5] illustrates what constitutes a "breach of the peace."

---

[4]Under what is sometimes referred to as strict foreclosure, the secured party obtains possession of the collateral and simply retains it in satisfaction of the secured obligation. The secured party's retention of the collateral is discussed in 29:13.

[5]*Cherno v Bank of Babylon*, 54 Misc 2d 277, 282 NYS2d 114, 4 UCCRS 505, (New York Supreme Court, Special Term, 1967).

... The Uniform Code "makes no attempt to articulate the standards for determining whether the repossession can be accomplished without breach of the peace." ... The classic definition of breach of the peace is "a disturbance of public order by an act of violence, or by an act likely to produce violence, or which, by causing consternation and alarm, disturbs the peace and quiet of the community." ... Thus, when in the course of repossession, the conditional vendee received a black eye, it was a question for the jury whether a breach of the peace had occurred, ... and when padlocks on a building are broken there is such force and violence as to constitute a violation of [a criminal statute] ... and, presumably, a breach of the peace. Here, however, the bank's employees entered by use of a key, unauthorizedly obtained. Such an entry, the [debtor's] consent aside, would constitute a breaking. ... But, breaking or not, there was nothing in what they did that disturbed public order by any act of violence, caused consternation or alarm, or disturbed the peace and quiet of the community. Nor was the use of a key to open the door an act likely to produce violence; indeed, it produced from the landlord only (1) a call for the police and (2) a request to the bank employees that they leave the key when they were through. Under the circumstances that existed during the times the bank's employees entered the premises, there was as a matter of law no breach of the peace. ...

A secured party who intends to repossess collateral would prefer not to give the debtor advance notice of the intention. Given notice, the debtor might hide the collateral or otherwise attempt to put it beyond the secured party's reach. Article 9 does not include a notice requirement, and most courts have not imposed such a requirement either. As the following case illustrates, however, notice is required under some circumstances.

Nevada National Bank
v
Huff
582 P2d 364
(Nevada Supreme Court, 1978)

[Huff leased a truck from Nevada National Bank (NNB) in January 1973. Lease payments were to be made for a 36-month period, and the terms of the lease were such that it was, in effect, a security agreement. In earlier transactions between Huff and NNB, Huff had consistently been behind in his payments. This pattern of behavior continued with respect to the truck. Between January 1973 and March 1975 NNB tried to keep the transaction going, rather than repossessing the truck. However, after further events that are described in the opinion, NNB did repossess the truck. Huff sued NNB for wrongful repossession, and he won in the trial court. NNB appealed.]

Per curiam:

*   *   *

Huff was late with his payments every month after March 1975. ... On July 17, when he was technically one payment behind again, Huff made another double payment, bringing him current through September 1. Huff made this last payment in an attempt to get ahead of schedule so that he could take an extended vacation. He apparently thought, erroneously, that the July 17 double payment would bring him current through October 1, 1975.

On October 15, 1975, Huff's insurer notified

him that the insurance on the truck was about to be cancelled. On this same date, the insurer mailed official notification of the impending cancellation to NNB as "owner" of the vehicle. This notice stated that coverage . . . would expire on October 31. . . .

On October 16, Huff personally visited the insurer's Reno office, where he paid his past-due premium and averted the impending cancellation of his insurance coverage. . . .

On October 21, five days after Huff had forestalled cancellation of the insurance policy, NNB Assistant Branch Manager Sharp received the cancellation notice sent on October 15 by the insurer. . . . Disregarding the Bank's entire course of dealing with Huff, Sharp (1) did not telephone or otherwise contact either Huff or the insurer to ascertain whether the past-due premiums had been paid and cancellation averted (it had); (2) did not telephone or otherwise contact Huff regarding his arrearages on his monthly payments, and (3) did not inform Huff that strict compliance with the terms of the lease agreement would henceforth be required to avert repossession. Rather, Sharp and another NNB employee went on Huff's property at 1 a.m. on Saturday, October 25, and repossessed the truck. . . .

Clearly there is nothing unconscionable in a contract clause authorizing the repossession of a chattel upon default. . . . Further, an established course of dealing under which the debtor . . . makes continual late payments and the secured party . . . accepts them does not result in a waiver of the secured party's right to rely upon a clause in the agreement authorizing him to declare a default and repossess the chattel. . . .

However, it is clear that even though no outright waiver of a secured party's right to rely upon such a clause occurs through a course of dealing involving the acceptance of late payments, a secured party who has not insisted upon strict compliance in the past, who has accepted late payments as a matter of course, *must*, before he may validly rely upon such a clause to declare a default and effect repossession, *give notice* to the debtor . . . that strict compliance with the terms of the contract will be demanded henceforth if repossession is to be avoided. [Court's emphasis.] . . .

Assessing NNB's conduct in this case, it must be noted at the outset that . . . the only ground upon which the Bank could have declared a default under the contract was Huff's one and one-half month arrearage in his payments: on October 21, Huff had paid only through September 1, instead of through November 1 as required under the contract. This delinquency clearly would constitute valid grounds for the declaration of a default under the contract.

However, analysis of the course of dealing between Huff and NNB, both with respect to the specific transaction in question and with respect to the two similar transactions during the same time period, reveals that it was a common occurrence for Huff to be behind in his monthly payments. In fact, Huff had been late with every single payment under the truck lease. . . . In spite of these delinquencies, NNB had never declared a default or invoked its right to repossess. . . . Rather, written and oral demands for payment had always been made upon him, and payment had always quickly followed.

This course of conduct established between Huff and NNB imposed upon NNB the duty, before it could properly rely upon the default and repossession clauses in the lease agreement, to give notice to Huff that strict compliance with the terms of the long-ignored contract would henceforth be required in order to avert repossession of the vehicle. Upon NNB's failure to give such notice, the jury could properly have concluded that NNB's repossession of the truck was wrongful. . . .

Affirmed.

Article 9's lack of a notice requirement offers the potential for a constitutional challenge. As discussed in Chapter 30, other types of proceedings by which property can be taken from a person without notice or the person having a chance to present his side of the case have been held to violate that person's constitutional rights. Indeed, several federal courts have declared that the Article 9 self-help provision is unconstitutional.

Consumer Goods   Article 9 makes no distinction between self-help repossession of consumer goods and self-help repossession of other types of collateral. However, the repossession of consumer goods may also be governed—and limited—by other state law concerning consumer credit protection or retail installment sales.

Resort to Judicial Process   If the debtor resists an attempted repossession of collateral after default (so that the repossession cannot be done without a breach of the peace), the secured party can seek judicial assistance. The procedure that the creditor should follow depends on state law other than the UCC. For example, the secured party might commence an action under a claim and delivery statute in one state, a replevin action in another.[6]

29:12   Disposal of Collateral after Default (UCC § 9-504)

If a debtor has defaulted and the secured party has repossessed the collateral, the secured party has the right to dispose of the collateral. In some instances, the secured party *must* dispose of it (see 29:13). The most common disposition method is sale of the collateral.

Article 9 imposes only two requirements with respect to how a sale of repossessed collateral is carried out. First, the secured party must generally give the debtor "reasonable notification" about the sale. Notice to the debtor is not required only if (1) after the default, the debtor waived his right to notice; or (2) the collateral (a) is perishable, (b) threatens to decline rapidly in value, or (c) is of a type normally sold on a recognized market. Unless the collateral is consumer goods, if the notice requirement applies, the secured party must also notify any other secured party who claims an interest in the collateral.

The second requirement for a sale of repossessed collateral is that all terms of the sale must be *commercially reasonable*. The price received for the collateral is the sale term most apt to be challenged, but the focus of Article 9 is on the overall procedure used, rather than merely on the price. For example, in one case,[7] the court held that the procedure followed in a sale was commercially reasonable even though inventory with an estimated retail value of over $3,000,000 was sold for $300,000. Interestingly, $300,000 was the exact amount owed to the secured creditors!

6"Claim and delivery" refers to a statutory legal action by which the plaintiff, a person who has rights in specific property, seeks to recover that property or its value from someone else who has possession of it. A "replevin action" is essentially the same, except that the plaintiff seeks only possession of the property. These types of actions are discussed in Chapter 30 (see 30:9).
7Re Zsa Zsa Ltd., 352 F Supp 665, 11 UCCRS 1116 (United States District Court, S.D. New York, 1972).

UCC § 9-501(3) provides, in effect, that although a security agreement cannot include the debtor's waiver of his right to a commercially reasonable sale after default, the agreement *can* set forth reasonable standards for measuring the secured party's actions in carrying out a sale. If the collateral can be easily classified and is generally treated in a uniform way, it may be to the secured party's advantage to include standards for disposition in the agreement. That simple act might avoid a lawsuit later in which the debtor claims that the disposition made was not commercially reasonable.

Repossessed collateral can be sold at either a private sale or a public sale. The distinction between the two types of sales is that a public sale is advertised to the public, while a private sale follows private negotiations between the secured party (who repossessed the collateral) and the buyer. A public sale is usually required if the secured party wants to buy the collateral (which he often wants to do since nobody else will pay an adequate price for it). This is because in a private sale the secured party is allowed to buy only limited types of collateral. Regardless of the type of sale and who the purchaser is, the purchaser acquires all the debtor's rights in the collateral. The purchase also has the effect of ending the secured party's security interest and any subordinate security interest or lien.

29:13   Secured Party's Retention of Collateral [UCC § 9-505(2)]

Experience has shown that the parties are often better off if a resale of repossessed collateral can be avoided. Recognizing this fact, Article 9 allows the secured party to retain collateral other than certain consumer goods, in full satisfaction of the secured debt. A secured party who wants to retain the collateral instead of sell it must generally notify the debtor of that intent. If the collateral is other than consumer goods, the secured party must also notify any other secured party claiming an interest in the collateral. If anyone to whom a notice must be sent objects within 21 days to the secured party's retention of the collateral, the secured party must sell the collateral instead of retaining it.

Consumer Goods [UCC § 9-505(1)]   Article 9 gives added protection to a debtor who has acquired a substantial equity in repossessed consumer goods. The secured party must sell or otherwise dispose of the goods within 90 days unless, after default, the debtor waives this requirement. The extent of the debtor's protection depends on whether a purchase money security interest is involved. If so, the mandatory disposal rule applies if the debtor has paid 60 percent or more of the cash price of the goods. In the case of other security interests, the rule applies if the debtor has paid 60 percent or more of the loan.

EXAMPLE
Edward buys a new car for $8,000, paying $2,000 down and borrowing $6,000 from a bank. The bank has a purchase money security interest in the car. Edward

later defaults, and the bank repossesses the car. If Edward has reduced the debt by at least $2,800, the bank cannot retain the car in satisfaction of the debt without Edward's consent ($2,800 plus $2,000 down payment equals $4,800, which is 60 percent of $8,000). If, however, Edward had paid cash for the car and later obtained a $6,000 loan from the bank using the car as collateral, the bank would have a security interest in the car, but not a purchase money security interest. Edward would then need to have paid at least $3,600 on the debt (60 percent of $6,000) before he would have the right to automatic sale or other disposal of the car after repossession.

29:14   Debtor's Redemption Right (UCC § 9-506)

Just because collateral has been repossessed after the debtor's default does not mean that the debtor will never see the collateral again. On the contrary, unless the debtor has signed a written waiver after the default, he can redeem the collateral (regain possession of it). To do so, the debtor must offer (1) to fulfill all obligations secured by the collateral, and (2) to pay the expenses reasonably incurred by the secured party in connection with the repossession.

"All obligations secured by the collateral" can consist of only the amount past due, which might be a single installment payment. However, if the security agreement contains an acceleration clause that the secured party elects to enforce, the debtor has to come up with the entire outstanding balance plus interest. As a result, the *redemption* right is often of little relief to the debtor; a person who cannot make a single payment often lacks sufficient resources to pay off the entire debt.

While there is rarely much doubt about the amount of the secured obligation, there may be a question about repossession expenses. A dispute can involve not only whether a given expense is reasonable, but also whether that expense is even one incurred in connection with the repossession. A secured party who demands more than he should from a redeeming debtor can be liable for conversion of the collateral.

EXAMPLE
Boris bought a car with money loaned by a bank, and he gave the bank a security interest in the car. Boris later moved to a neighboring state, and still later he became delinquent in his payments to the bank. The bank then arranged with Ajax, an automobile recovery bureau, to repossess the car. Instead of repossessing the car, Ajax merely located Boris, arranged for him to make the back payments, and allowed him to keep the car. Ajax then billed the bank $130 for its services. Later, Boris was again in default, Ajax was again ordered to repossess the car, and this time Ajax did so, at an expense of $90. In an attempt to redeem the car from Ajax, Boris offered to pay $350 ($90 plus the principal and interest due on the loan). On the bank's orders, Ajax demanded $480 ($350 plus the $130 billed to the bank earlier), which Boris refused to pay. The bank is liable to Boris for conversion of the car because the $130 is not an amount incurred in connection with the repossession.

The redemption right continues to exist until the secured party (1) disposes of the collateral, (2) enters into a contract for its disposition, or (3) has discharged the debt by retaining the collateral. The last of these three events cutting off the redemption right raises the question of whether a creditor can block redemption by simply deciding to retain the property. For the answer, recall that even if the 60 percent rule for consumer goods does not apply, the secured party must notify the debtor of his intent to retain repossessed collateral, and that the debtor then has 21 days in which to object. Thus, the debtor's right to redeem cannot be blocked in this way unless the debtor fails to object in time to the secured party's proposed retention of the collateral.

29:15 Distribution of Proceeds; Deficiency Judgment (UCC § 9-504)

Article 9 establishes the order by which the proceeds received by a secured party from a nonjudicial sale of repossessed collateral are to be distributed. The proceeds are applied first to the reasonable expenses that the secured party incurred in connection with the repossession. Any surplus is then applied to satisfaction of the secured debt. After that, any remaining surplus is applied to satisfy debts secured by any subordinate security interest in the collateral that was sold, but only if the holder of the subordinate interest makes a written demand for payment. In the unlikely event that there is still a surplus after payment according to the above schedule, the debtor is entitled to it, and the debtor cannot waive this right.

Article 9 does not apply to disposition of the proceeds from a judicial sale of the collateral. However, under general state law, the result is usually about the same as for nonjudicial sales.

Deficiency Judgment (UCC § 9-504)   Although the debtor *can* receive some of the proceeds from a sale of repossessed collateral, he rarely does so. A more likely situation is that the proceeds are insufficient even to pay off the secured debt. The debtor is then liable to the secured party for the deficiency unless the parties have agreed to the contrary. Rare indeed is the debtor who has sufficient bargaining power to persuade a potential secured party to abandon his right to a *deficiency judgment*.

EXAMPLE
Rossi buys a business machine from Mangione, incurring a secured debt. The machine is later repossessed and sold by Mangione at a time when the amount of the debt, plus interest, is $5,000. Mangione incurs reasonable repossession expenses of $500. The parties' rights to the sale proceeds depend on the price received. If the price exceeds $5,500, Rossi is entitled to the excess. If it is less than $5,500, Mangione can sue Rossi to recover the difference between $5,500 and the actual sale price.

Right to Deficiency Judgment if Secured Party Retains Collateral (UCC § 9-505)   Since retention of repossessed collateral constitutes satisfaction of the debt in full, the retaining secured party loses any right he otherwise would have had to recover a deficiency judgment. This fact may be significant if the value of the collateral is less than the amount outstanding on the debt, a common situation in the case of some types of collateral.

 The secured party can also lose the right to a deficiency judgment or, indeed, the right to sue on the secured obligation, by holding repossessed collateral for an unreasonable time. Note that unless the 60 percent rule for consumer goods applies, Article 9 does not specify *when* a notice of proposed retention of collateral must be sent.

EXAMPLE
Ahab was in default on his car loan after paying off less than 60 percent of the debt. Lawrence, the lender, repossessed the car, held it for four months, and then sued Ahab on the promissory note. The case was not tried until 27 months after the repossession. During that 27-month period Lawrence had possession of the car but neither gave notice of intent to retain it nor attempted to sell it. Due to Lawrence's inaction, Ahab's debt probably would be discharged. In effect, Lawrence would be deemed to have elected to retain the collateral even though he never gave the required notice.

29:16   Secured Party's Liability to Debtor [UCC § 9-507(1)]

Article 9 offers some protection to a debtor who will be or has been harmed by a repossessing secured party's failure to carry out his duties. For example, the debtor can apply to a court for an order preventing the secured party from disposing of the collateral in a commercially unreasonable manner. If an improper disposition has already been made, the debtor can recover damages from the secured party. The measure of damages set forth in Article 9 is generally the loss suffered by the debtor due to the improper disposition. This loss is the difference between the proceeds received by the secured party and the proceeds that should have been received. If the secured party cannot show that the proceeds received reflected the proper value of the collateral, the proper value will be presumed to be at least the amount of the debt secured by that collateral. This presumption has the effect of preventing the secured party from obtaining a deficiency judgment.

EXAMPLE
Union Bank repossesses collateral and sells it for $10,000 without notifying Andrews, the debtor, of the sale. The outstanding balance on the secured debt is $15,000. Union then commences an action to recover the $5,000 deficiency. Unless Union can prove that only $10,000 would have been received, even if Andrews had been notified about the sale, the value of the property will be presumed to be $15,000. Andrews is thus entitled to recover $5,000 in damages, which cancels Union's deficiency.

State law other than the UCC may allow the recovery of damages other than simply those based on the debtor's "loss." For example, the debtor might be able to sue the secured party for *conversion*, which is the wrongful taking of property. The measure of damages for conversion is the value of the property at the time of the conversion, less the unpaid balance of the purchase price. Obviously, these damages can be significantly greater than the debtor's provable loss.

Consumer Goods [UCC § 9-507(1)]   If the collateral is consumer goods, the damages recoverable by the debtor are not limited to the loss suffered because of the secured party's noncompliance with the Article 9 requirements. Instead, the *minimum* amount that the debtor is entitled to recover is, depending on the nature of the transaction (1) the credit service charge plus ten percent of the debt or (2) the time price differential plus ten percent of the cash price.

EXAMPLE

Mildred agrees to buy a new car for personal use from Valley VW. The price is $5,000. Mildred pays $1,000 down and agrees to pay off the balance in 36 monthly payments of $150. The deferred payment price is hence $6,400 (36 times $150 plus the $1,000 down payment), and the time-price differential is $1,400. Mildred defaults and Valley VW repossesses the car and sells it without notifying Mildred. Mildred can recover at least $1,900 ($1,400 plus ten percent of $5,000) in damages from Valley VW.

Punitive damages   Punitive (or exemplary) damages are awarded to a victim as a civil penalty (a penalty paid to a private individual rather than to a governmental subdivision) for a wrongful act, rather than to compensate the victim for his losses. Article 9 does not specifically provide for punitive damages. However, they may be recoverable under other state law if a secured party acted with malice or reckless disregard of the debtor's rights, as is illustrated in the following case.

Davidson

v

First State Bank & Trust Co.
609 P2d 1259
(Oklahoma Supreme Court, 1976)

[*Davidson sued the First State Bank and Trust Company of Yale, Oklahoma (Bank). Davidson sought punitive damages in connection with Bank's repossession of certain marble-making equipment. The actions of Bank supporting Davidson's claim are outlined below in the opinion. The jury awarded Davidson $20,000 in punitive damages and the intermediate appellate court affirmed. Bank appealed to the state supreme court.*]

Doolin, Justice.

*   *   *

A debtor–creditor relationship existed between Davidson . . . and Bank for a number of years prior to this action. At the suggestion of Bank, Davidson contacted a man named Sneed to work with him to enable his marble-making business to operate in a profitable manner. At this time Davidson executed a promissory note and security agreement in favor of Bank which provided for monthly payments with a final balloon payment at the end of the year.

Testimony indicated that in November of 1972, Bank, because of differences between Davidson and Sneed, attempted to foreclose before the note was in default. The problems were resolved however, and Bank refinanced the note in a similar manner, payable by Davidson only.

The situation between Davidson and Sneed did not improve and they had a falling out in the early fall of 1973. Sneed removed a portion of the marble-making equipment from Davidson's shop, some of which he claimed to own, and opened a competitive marble-manufacturing business across the street. The volume of equipment taken is in dispute, but Sneed admits "borrowing" with Bank's permission, the two major pieces of equipment owned by Davidson. Because of the loss of this equipment, Davidson was effectively put out of business and he defaulted on the last balloon payment due November 15, 1973.

Bank obtained entry to the shop through Sneed and on November 21, 1973 took possession of the remaining property secured by the agreement. On November 21, 1973, Bank executed its "Notice of Sale under Security" listing items to be sold at public auction on December 6, 1973 at 10:00 A.M. The notice did not cover all items of property listed on the security agreement. Although the secured items were unique and there was no ready market for marble-making equipment in Yale, Bank posted only three notices of sale in Yale. This was the extent of its commercially reasonable advertisement. At the time of the sale, the front door of the building remained locked and when no prospective buyers appeared, Bank's employees left the store. Bank did not credit Davidson's account on date of sale; it retained the repossessed equipment until after Davidson filed his original petition. The items were eventually sold to Sneed privately some four months later without notice to the public or to Davidson. Sneed paid Bank $1,000 for the equipment, less than ¼ of the stipulated value at time of sale.

On December 20, 1973 Davidson initiated the present suit against . . . Bank for conversion of property by means of a wrongful taking of the equipment. . . .

Trial was had to a jury. Davidson went to the jury on the theory that Bank had converted the property because it "was not sold in a commercially reasonable manner." It was stipulated by the parties [that] the value of the property equaled the balance remaining unpaid on the note in the amount of $4,285. The jury was instructed that if it found conversion by commercially unreasonable sale, the court would determine the actual damages and if it found such conversion by Bank was malicious and with wilful intent to deprive Davidson of his property, punitive damages would be proper. The jury found the issues in favor of Davidson. . . .

Bank appealed the award of punitive damages, specifically claiming it was error to instruct the jury that punitive damages are allowed for failure to sell in a commercially reasonable manner. . . .

We agree with the opinion and result of the [intermediate appellate court] holding the jury was properly instructed as to punitive damages. If repossessed property is sold in a commercially unreasonable manner there is a conversion, the actual damages being the difference between the value of the property and the proceeds of the sale. If there is a conversion, and the actions are malicious or wilful, punitive damages may be awarded by the jury under existing statutory and case law. . . .

Numerous cases, not decided under the U.C.C. have awarded punitive damages for actions involved in repossession of collateral where aspects of malice, fraud, or oppression are shown. Although the U.C.C. does not favor punitive damages, these jurisdictions have applied rules of damages, including punitive, in proper cases under aggravated circumstances. See [a Colorado case] where punitive damages were permitted against a bank who refused to return plaintiff's tools that had been wrongfully repossessed. [A federal case] allowed punitive damages for unlawful repossession of a car where plaintiff was given no notice of repossession and was not in default. [A Texas case] allowed punitive damages five times that of actual damages where defendant had sold plaintiff's furniture before actual repossession. [A Washington, D.C. case] allowed punitive damages for wrongful repossession under the U.C.C. . . .

. . . Bank's cavalier manner in its dealings

with Davidson is sufficient evidence to send the question of punitive damages to the jury. As pointed out in Davidson's brief, the entire sequence of events involved in the sale was improper. The Bank did not give proper notice of the items to be sold. The only justification Bank gave for its failure to pursue a likely market for sale of the equipment is that it did not want to spend the money. On the sale date Bank's officer did not open the front door or even attempt a sale. Bank permitted Sneed to borrow items belonging to Davidson prior to default on the note in order that Sneed could open a competing business. Bank retained the collateral after default for several months without crediting it against Davidson's note. The final sale was made to Sneed for a price less than ¼ the stipulated value of property at time of sale. These facts are evidence of the tortious conduct upon which the jury based its award of punitive damages. . . .

[Judgment affirmed.]

Key Concepts and Terms

- The priority of conflicting interests in collateral depends on the status of the claimants. As between two perfected secured parties, the first either to file or to perfect his interest usually has priority over the other.

- A secured party can assign the secured obligation to someone else, and such an assignment carries the security interest with it. Similarly, one holding an account can sell or assign that account.

- A debtor can sell collateral that is subject to a security interest, although the sale may be a breach of the contract with the secured party.

- A secured party who authorizes sale of the collateral loses his security interest in it. A seller's security interest, even if perfected, is also often lost if the collateral is sold to a consumer or buyer in the ordinary course of business.

- A debtor defaults when he acts in violation of the security agreement. Failure to discharge the secured debt or to make timely payment on it is the most common default.

- After default, the secured party can (1) sue on the debt, (2) foreclose on the collateral, or (3) repossess the collateral.

- Repossessed collateral must generally be sold or otherwise disposed of in a commercially reasonable manner. At times, the secured party can retain the collateral in satisfaction of the debt. The debtor has the right to redeem repossessed collateral within a limited period.

- If repossessed collateral is sold, the sale proceeds are applied first to the repossession expenses and then to the secured debt. The debtor is entitled to any surplus. The secured party can recover a deficiency judgment if the sale's proceeds are insufficient to discharge the debt.

- A secured party who fails to carry out the duties imposed on him can be liable to the debtor for damages, which may include punitive damages.

- In a number of ways, Article 9 gives credit buyers of consumer goods protection that is not enjoyed by other classes of debtors.

- Assignment of Account
- Breach of the Peace
- Buyer in Ordinary Course of Business
- Collateral
- Commercially Reasonable
- Conversion
- Default
- Deficiency Judgment
- Foreclosure

- Inventory
- Lien
- Priority
- Purchase Money Security Interest
- Redemption
- Repossession
- Self-help Repossession
- Statement of Assignment

Questions and Case Problems

1. What is the general rule governing the priority of two or more secured parties, each of whom holds a perfected security interest in the same collateral? In your opinion, is this rule fair? Why?

2. Discuss the rights and duties of a secured party who has repossessed collateral after the debtor's default.

3. How can a debtor reobtain possession of collateral that has been repossessed? Discuss.

4. What is a deficiency judgment? Under what circumstances does a secured party who has repossessed collateral lose the right to obtain a deficiency judgment?

5. Delta's truck, which Delta bought and used for business purposes, is in Able's garage for repairs. The repairs are completed, but Delta cannot pay the repair bill. Able elects to retain possession of the truck until the bill is paid, as state law allows him to do. Meanwhile, several others are also asserting interests in the truck. Those claimants, listed in the order in which their claims against Delta arose, are as follows: Baker, who loaned Delta money to start her business and who holds a promissory note signed by Delta; Charlie, who also loaned Delta money and took a security interest covering all of Delta's equipment, including after-acquired equipment, but did not perfect his interest; and Eagle, who sold Delta the truck on credit and perfected a security interest in it. Discuss the relative priority of the claims of Able, Baker, Charlie, and Eagle.

6. PCA held an unperfected security interest in all of farmer York's farm equipment, and the security agreement contained an after-acquired property clause. On April 1, Carson sold York a new tractor on credit, retaining a security interest in it. York took delivery of the tractor on April 2. On April 5, PCA filed to perfect its security interest, and Carson filed on April 10. As between PCA and Carson, who has priority with respect to the tractor? How would your answer differ, if at all, if York were a merchant rather than a farmer, and Carson had sold York inventory items instead of a tractor?

7. Builder Bob has an open account with Mitchell, a merchant. At Bob's insistence, the contract between Bob and Mitchell provides that Mitchell cannot assign his right to receive payment from Bob. Hard times befall Mitchell, however, and to secure needed financing he assigns all his accounts to Anderson. At that time, Bob owes Mitchell $10,000. Bob is not advised about the assignment, and he pays Mitchell $8,000 on the account. Mitchell then departs, leaving many unpaid creditors in his wake. Anderson now informs Bob about the assignment, directs that payments be made to him (Anderson), and advises Bob that he currently owes $10,000 plus interest. Is Bob liable to Anderson? If so, for how much?

8. White, a full-time car salesman, sells yachts on the side from an office in her home. White does not have a merchant's license as is required by state law. She does have business cards bearing an appropriate firm name, White's home phone number, and the name of a yacht manufacturer. White had sold several yachts in the past. A bank loans White money to purchase a new yacht, takes a security interest in the boat, and perfects that interest. White displays the boat at a boat show and later moors it at a nearby lake. Stanley sees the boat at the lake and buys it from White for personal use. White defaults on her loan from the bank, and the bank sues Stanley for conversion of the yacht. Should the bank prevail? Why or why not?

9. Donald buys a new car from BMC Motors, and BMC retains a security interest in the car. Donald is often late in his payments. Several times he phones BMC to ask for more time to make particular payments, and on each occasion he withholds payment until he receives written notice that an extension has been granted. Once again Donald is behind on a payment, and once again he phones BMC for an extension. Donald is told that he will be notified by letter as to the pattern of payment expected in the future. While awaiting the notification, Donald takes the car to a garage for an oil change and leaves it there. BMC's employee goes to the garage; lies to the attendant, saying that Donald consented to repossession; and starts to drive off in the car. Donald walks up at that moment, guesses what is happening, shouts at the driver to stop, and hurries toward the car. However, BMC's employee "floors it" and leaves with haste. As she does so, the left rear wheel of the car passes over Donald's foot, crushing it. Donald sues BMC for damages. Should he prevail? Why or why not? In your answer, discuss the propriety of the repossession and the nature of any damages to which Donald is entitled.

10. Well-Bilt, a furniture manufacturer, repossesses certain furniture from Morton, a dealer, after Morton's default under the agreement between them. At the time the unpaid balance of the secured debt is $50,000. The wholesale value of the repossessed furniture is $60,000, and its retail value is about $100,000. Well-Bilt gives Morton eight days' advance notice that the furniture will be sold privately. Before the sale date, Well-Bilt contacts one possible buyer for the furniture, and the prospect expresses some interest. On the sale date, Well-Bilt buys the furniture for $35,000. Well-Bilt sues Morton for the $15,000 deficiency, and Morton counterclaims (sues Well-Bilt) for damages, alleging that the sale was improper. How should the court decide the case? Why?

30 Creditors' Remedies; Debtors' Corresponding Rights

30:1 Introduction

A debt is satisfied, and the debtor is discharged, when the debt no longer exists. A creditor usually intends that the debtor will pay off the debt voluntarily, and most debts are satisfied this way. Depending on the nature of the debt, payment can be either in a lump sum or in installments over a period of time. All is well as long as the debtor pays on time. Sometimes he does not, however, and the creditor must then look for a way to collect the debt. The creditor's available remedies can be classified as being either nonjudicial or judicial. A nonjudicial remedy is one that the creditor can use on his own, while a judicial remedy involves some sort of participation by a court.

Nonjudicial Remedies, Generally   The most common nonjudicial remedy is the use of what are known as dunning letters. Strictly speaking, a dun is no more than a persistent demand for payment. In practice, however, dunning letters reflect an attempt to shame or coerce the debtor into paying up. Under the federal Fair Debt Collection Practices Act (15 USC §§ 1692 et seq.), there are limits on the allowable use of dunning letters.

If a creditor's collection efforts fail, the creditor himself may be able to seize certain of the debtor's property. This nonjudicial remedy is usually available only to a creditor who has a security interest in the property to be seized, as discussed in Chapter 29 (see 29:11). If this remedy is not available, the creditor must turn to a judicial remedy.

Judicial Remedies, Generally   A creditor's basic judicial remedy is a lawsuit on the debt. In the complaint filed against the debtor, the creditor alleges that the debtor owes him a specific amount of money, and he requests that the court issue a judgment in his favor ordering the debtor to pay him that amount. If the creditor loses, the alleged debt is discharged in the sense that a court has found that no enforceable debt exists. If the creditor wins, he obtains a judgment against the debtor for a specific amount. That amount becomes a new debt, replacing the old one.

The court proceeding and judgment against him may cause the debtor to pay up. Often, however, the debtor does not. In a sense, the creditor is then in the same position he occupied before, except that now there is no question about the validity or amount of the debt. There is a more significant difference, however. The creditor now has the status of a *judgment creditor,* which gives him rights with respect to some property owned by the debtor (see 30:4 and 30:5). The problem with a creditor's waiting until he has been awarded a judgment on a debt is that the judgment is often not issued until long after the lawsuit begins. To avoid this problem, the creditor can obtain rights in some of the debtor's property at once, using what is known as a prejudgment remedy (see 30:6 and 30:9).

The judicial remedies referred to above are available only with respect to the debtor's property that is nonexempt (see 30:3). If a creditor misuses a remedy, the debtor might be able to recover damages from the creditor (see 30:12 and 30:13). Also, creditors' rights against debtors have been limited in recent years by federal statutes (see 30:10) and by court decisions that have liberally interpreted debtors' constitutional rights (see 30:11).

30:2   Definitions

Certain terms occur frequently in a discussion of creditors' remedies. A familiarity with these terms at the outset will make discussion in the rest of this chapter easier to understand.

Bond: A written contract between one person (the principal) and a surety company (the surety) for the benefit of a third person (the obligee). A *bond* is basically a promise that the principal will perform a stated duty owed to the obligee, and that if he fails to do so, the surety will pay the obligee up to a stated amount of money. The language of the bond is often quite specific as to exactly how and when the surety will be liable. One "posts" a bond by obtaining it from a surety company (for a fee) and filing it with the proper person, who, in the law of creditors' remedies, is usually the clerk of a court.

Default: The failure to perform a duty or obligation. With respect to the creditor–debtor relationship, the most common default is a debtor's failure to pay a debt at all or in the proper manner. For example, if a person buys new furniture on credit and obligates himself to pay the furniture dealer in monthly installments over the next two years, the person is in default if he fails to pay an installment on time.

Unsecured creditor: A creditor who has only the debtor's promise to pay. An unsecured creditor has no present rights with respect to any specific property owned by the debtor. The debtor can promise to pay in a signed, written document such as a promissory note. Alternatively, the debt may exist only on the creditor's books, such as when goods are sold on open account (buyer orders goods or services; seller delivers them and later bills buyer).

Secured creditor: A creditor who has, in addition to the debtor's promise to pay, certain rights in specific property owned by the debtor. These rights are known as a security interest in the property. Ordinarily, the security interest is created when the debt is created.[1]

Lien: An interest in certain property, usually arising in connection with a debt of the property owner. The debt often involves the property on which the *lien* is claimed, but it does not have to. A lien can be consensual, statutory, or judicial. A mortgage securing repayment of the loan used to buy a home is an example of a consensual lien (the buyer consented to the mortgage). A statutory lien is one granted by statute, such as the lien on a car granted to a mechanic who worked on the car but was not paid. A judgment lien, defined below, is an example of a judicial lien. The priority of one lien over another depends on the status of the lienholder. One lien is said to be junior to a second lien if the second lienholder's rights in the property are superior to those of the first lienholder. For example, a judicial lien is usually junior to a statutory lien.

Money judgment: A court's judgment by which the loser of a lawsuit is ordered to pay a stated amount of money to the winner.

Judgment debtor: A person against whom a money judgment has been issued.

Judgment lien: A lien on the property of one against whom a money judgment has been issued. The lien is in favor of the person who successfully sued the property owner. In most states it covers only the debtor's real property, but its coverage includes real property that the debtor acquires after the judgment is issued.

Encumbrance: A right or interest in real property held by someone other than the property owner. A person encumbers his property when he creates or allows the creation of an *encumbrance* on it. The most common example of an encumbrance is a mortgage.

Insolvency: The situation in which the value of a person's assets other than exempt property (see 30:3) is less than the total amount of his debts.

Consumer: An individual who buys goods or services primarily for personal, family, or household purposes.

Retail installment contract: A contract for the credit sale of goods or services to a consumer. The contract requires payment of the price of the goods or services, plus the credit charges, in periodic installments.

30:3 Exempt Property

A defaulting debtor could be left with nothing if a creditor could look to all the debtor's property for satisfaction of the debt. To protect some debtors, statutes in every state provide that certain property is not subject to the claims of the property owner's creditors. This property is known as *exempt property*. The rationale for the exemption statutes is that if a debtor is left with something, he will continue to be able to support himself and his family and hence not burden society by going on welfare.

---

[1]Security interests in personal property are discussed in Chapter 28. Security interests in real property are discussed in Chapter 35.

Exemption statutes do not apply to a creditor's claim to property on which the creditor holds a security interest. The grant of a security interest is a voluntary act in that the debtor can encumber exempt property with a security interest if he chooses to do so. As a practical matter, the grant of a security interest is often required if the debtor is to obtain desired credit. Thus, the only real voluntary aspect of the transaction is apt to be the debtor's decision to buy on credit rather than wait until he can pay cash for desired goods or services.

Persons Protected   Only a debtor who falls within the class of debtors described in an exemption statute can take advantage of the statute. Typically, the debtor must be an individual, rather than a corporation, partnership, or other business. Some exemption statutes apply to individuals in their capacity as consumers. Others apply to people working in particular trades or occupations.

Homestead Exemption   For a person who owns his home, that home can constitute a major part of his exempt property under what is known as the *homestead exemption*. A homestead exemption statute usually states the maximum dollar amount of the exemption. Bear in mind, though, that many homestead exemption statutes have not kept pace with inflation. For example, a debtor might have paid $35,000 for a home in 1975, but by 1983 the home is worth $100,000; if $40,000 is the maximum amount of the exemption under the applicable statute, the statute protects less than half the value of the home in 1983, although it protected it fully in 1975. On the other hand, the exemption is generally applied only to the value of the property in excess of outstanding loans secured by the property. Thus, a $40,000 exemption fully covers a debtor's interest in a $100,000 home if the home is encumbered by a $20,000 first mortgage and a $40,000 second mortgage.

If the value of homestead property exceeds the exempt amount, the rights of creditors to reach that excess value depend on state law. In some states, the creditor can do nothing as long as the debtor continues to use the property as his home. In other states, the property can be split, if possible, and creditors can force a sale of the part not covered by the exemption, to satisfy debts. In still other states, creditors can force a sale of the entire homestead, as long as the debtor receives the exemption amount out of the sale proceeds.

EXAMPLE

Haller's home is worth $100,000, and the homestead exemption amount in her state is $30,000. Haller owes $20,000 on a loan secured by the home. She is in default on unsecured debts totaling $80,000. If Haller's unsecured creditors can force a sale of the home, only the sale proceeds in excess of $50,000 (homestead exemption amount plus amount of mortgage lien) can be subjected to the creditor's claims.

Other Exempt Property   The exemption statutes in most states also cover some personal property, up to stated value limits. Types of personal property apt to be listed in such statutes include (1) wages or salary; (2) tools and equipment used in the debtor's trade or occupation; (3) the debtor's automobile; (4) household goods and furniture; (5) food and clothing; and (6) some insurance proceeds, pensions, and related benefits. In addition, many exemption statutes allow the debtor to exempt other property of his choice, as long as the total value of the property he selects does not exceed the amount specified in the statute.

Claim of Exemption   Some exemptions must be claimed by the debtor, while others take effect automatically. The governing statute states what, if anything, the debtor must do to claim a particular exemption. For example, the homestead exemption statutes in some states require the homeowner to claim the exemption by filing a "declaration of homestead" in the office of the local county recorder. Generally, the exemption is automatic if a statute does not specifically require the debtor to do anything.

30:4   Execution

Execution is a remedy that is available only to a creditor who has already obtained a money judgment. Its purpose is to assist the creditor in obtaining satisfaction of the judgment debt. In essence, nonexempt property is taken from the debtor and sold, and the sale proceeds are paid to the judgment creditor.

Procedure   The procedure followed in an execution is closely governed by state statute, but the usual procedure is along the following lines. First, the creditor obtains a writ of execution, which is a court order directed to the county sheriff and ordering him to "levy on" property belonging to the judgment debtor. The writ states the dollar amount of the judgment against the debtor. In theory, the sheriff "executes the writ" by locating nonexempt property owned by the debtor and in the debtor's possession, and then levying on enough of the property so that when the property is later sold, the debt can be satisfied. In practice, the creditor locates the property and, in effect, leads the sheriff to it. Generally, the sheriff must look first to the debtor's personal property. If he cannot find enough personal property, then he can levy on real property.

What constitutes an effective levy on property depends on the nature of the property. Strictly speaking, a *levy* is an interference with an owner's possession of his property. The traditional form of levy for personal property that is easily moved is a seizure of the property. In the case of other property, a levy can consist of the sheriff's taking control of the property in some other manner. For example, the sheriff might order the debtor not to either use or move a large machine. Similarly, a physical seizure is usually not required for a levy on real property. Property that has been levied on is considered to be in the sheriff's custody even if the property has not actually been moved. The debtor can get the property released from the sheriff's custody by posting a bond in which the debtor, as principal, promises to preserve the property and deliver it as and when ordered by the court to do so.

The next step in the typical execution process is the execution sale. The property levied on is sold to the highest bidder at a public auction held for that purpose. Advance public notice of the sale must be given, and a personal notice to the debtor may be required as well. The judgment creditor is often the buyer at the sale although, in some states, he is not a legitimate buyer at an execution sale.

The proceeds from the sale are applied first to payment of the expenses incurred in carrying out the execution and sale. The judgment creditor can be paid next under some circumstances, but if the property sold was subject to a prior lien that, under state law, must be satisfied out of the sale proceeds, the judgment creditor will be paid after that lien is satisfied. Also, it is not uncommon for several different judgment creditors to have caused writs of execution to be issued, so that the property sold was levied on under more than one writ. In that event, the priority of the judgment creditors is generally determined according to the order in which the creditors obtained their writs. In the rare event that any sale proceeds are left over after all judgment creditors have been paid, the balance is paid to the judgment debtor.

The final step in the execution process involves what is known as the return of execution. The return is a report prepared by the sheriff in which the sheriff outlines exactly what he did to obey the original writ.

Property Subject to Execution   The particular types of property that can be levied on under a writ of execution depend on state exemption statutes (see 30:3) and other statutes relating specifically to execution. Generally speaking, all nonexempt real and tangible personal property can be levied on. Intangible property or property interests that usually *cannot* be levied on include (1) contract rights; (2) tort claims; (3) promissory notes (a note itself is tangible, but the right to its payment is not); (4) rights to the cash value of life insurance policies; and (5) patents, copyrights, and licenses.

Effect of Execution Sale; Debtor's Redemption Right   A valid execution sale operates to satisfy the judgment debt to the extent of the amount that the judgment creditor actually receives. If, as is often true, the sale proceeds are insufficient to satisfy the debt fully, the balance of the debt remains.

A debtor can redeem (regain possession of) his property that was sold at an execution sale if the applicable execution statute provides for redemption. Generally, if the redemption right exists, the debtor exercises it by offering to pay the amount received by the sheriff at the execution sale, plus interest and expenses related to the sale. The governing statute specifies (1) the person to whom the offer is submitted, 2) how the purchaser at the execution sale recovers whatever he paid, and (3) the time period during which redemption is permitted.

Relief from Execution   Irregularities (mistakes) can and do occur in the process of carrying out an execution. For example, the creditor who sought execution might not have had a final judgment in his favor, so that he had no right to a writ of execution; or the sheriff might have levied on the wrong kind of property; or an execution sale might have been held without proper notice or at an improper place.

A debtor who has been wronged by an irregularity can often recover damages, as discussed in 30:12. If the right to sue for damages does not exist or could not compensate the debtor adequately, the debtor might be able to apply for other appropriate relief from the court that issued the writ of execution. Depending on how far the execution proceeding has gone and on the governing state law, the debtor may be able to persuade the court to grant relief, such as (1) canceling the writ, (2) temporarily enjoining execution (forbidding execution until the debtor presents his argument against it in court), (3) compelling a resale of the property levied on, or (4) ordering that the property be returned to the debtor.

30:5   Postjudgment Garnishment

A judgment creditor must find a remedy other than execution if the writ of execution is returned unsatisfied. That is, the sheriff might not have been able to levy on any of the debtor's property, or the proceeds from the sale of what property was levied on might have been insufficient to satisfy the judgment debt. Money is still owed to the judgment creditor in either case. To alleviate this problem, statutes in most states provide an additional remedy that becomes available if execution has proved to be ineffective. This remedy is known by different names in different states, but for present purposes it is referred to as *postjudgment garnishment*.

As discussed in 30:6, garnishment is ordinarily a prejudgment remedy in that a creditor uses it *before* obtaining a judgment against the debtor. The distinctive feature of garnishment is that it applies to the debtor's property that is in somebody else's possession. Postjudgment garnishment is thus a means by which a creditor can obtain satisfaction of a judgment debt through property that, although owned by or owed to the debtor, is in the hands of a third person. The third person might be a bank or similar institution in which the debtor has money on deposit, or it might be the debtor's employer who holds wages or salary owed to the debtor but not yet paid to him. Other property that might be subject to postjudgment garnishment includes insurance proceeds payable to the debtor and money or other property due the debtor under a deceased person's will.

30:6   Attachment and Garnishment, Generally

A defaulting debtor might have nonexempt property at the time the creditor sues him on the debt, but the creditor has no guaranty that the debtor will have that or other nonexempt property later, when the creditor obtains a judgment. Thus, a prudent creditor wants to do something to tie up the debtor's property *before* he obtains a judgment against the debtor. The processes by which the creditor can do so are known as *prejudgment remedies*. The remedies are so called because they are available before judgment. Two of the most common prejudgment remedies are *attachment* and *garnishment*. These remedies are available in most states and are governed by state statutes.

Attachment and garnishment are distinguishable, although in some states "attachment" is used in such a way as to include garnishment within its scope. For present purposes, the differences between the two remedies are that (1) attachment affects property owned by the debtor and in his possession, while garnishment affects property owned by *or owed to* the debtor and in the possession of someone else (known as the garnishee); (2) attachment involves a levy on the property while garnishment does not; and (3) attachment creates an attachment lien on the property while, in at least some states, garnishment does not create a lien.

Purposes   Attachment and garnishment have several purposes. The primary purpose of each remedy is to allow an unsecured creditor to obtain an immediate lien on or interest in some of the debtor's property. The nature of that lien or interest is such that it prevents the disposal or dissipation of property that can ultimately be sold on execution to satisfy the debt. Also, the lien or interest is superior to some other liens or interests covering the same property.

EXAMPLE

Hood is in default on unsecured debts owed to both Scarlett and Tuck. Tuck sues Hood in 1980, but, believing Hood to be an honorable fellow, he does not attach any of Hood's property. Scarlett sues in 1981, and he immediately attaches Hood's forest retreat. If Tuck obtains a judgment against Hood in 1983, his judgment lien on the forest retreat is junior to Scarlett's earlier attachment lien.

Another reason a creditor attaches or garnishes the debtor's property is to try to pressure the debtor into paying up. Litigation is expensive, and both parties will save money if the legal action on the debt (the principal action) can be dropped at an early stage. Also, since the debtor is often deprived of the use of attached or garnished property, the debtor's desire to get the property back might force him to pay.

Finally, attachment or garnishment of property within a state can serve as the only practical means by which a court of that state can acquire jurisdiction over the principal action. This situation arises when the debtor has property in the state where the action is filed but is, himself, outside the state.[2]

 Some attorneys believe that attaching or garnishing an individual debtor's property is not always wise. Their theory is that the attachment or garnishment may irritate the debtor and cause him to defend himself in the principal action, thus making it impossible for the creditor to obtain a default judgment.[3]

---

[2]A debtor being sued on a debt must be served with process. In essense, this means that the debtor must be personally served with a copy of the creditor's complaint in the principal action. Also, the debtor must be served within the court's jurisdiction if the court is to have the power to order the debtor to do anything. Typically, the court has jurisdiction only in its own state. Thus, for example, if the creditor sues in California but the debtor lives in Oregon and remains there, the debtor cannot be effectively served with process or made to appear before the California court. However, if the debtor has property in California, the California court has jurisdiction over that property, can authorize attachment of it, and can later order its sale or transfer to someone other than the debtor. This power of the court can have the effect of forcing the debtor to appear in California to defend his interest in the property. Jurisdiction acquired in this way is known as *quasi in rem jurisdiction*.

[3]A default judgment is a judgment for the plaintiff that is issued when the defendant fails to answer the complaint or otherwise defend himself. Creditors favor default judgments because they can be obtained quickly and with little expense.

Procedure, Generally   The procedure to be followed for both attachment and garnishment varies somewhat from state to state. Outlined below is the procedure under typical statutes of the *traditional* type. Bear in mind, though, that the discussion of debtors' constitutional right to notice and a hearing (see 30:11) must also be read for a complete picture.

Attachment Procedure   The first step taken by a creditor who wants to attach the debtor's property is to prepare an attachment affidavit. An *affidavit* is a written statement of facts, the truth of which is sworn to by the person signing the affidavit, called the affiant. An attachment affidavit identifies the debtor, describes the nature and amount of the debt, and states one or more of the grounds for attachment that are set forth in the statute. A common ground is the affiant's belief that the debtor is about to dispose of his nonexempt property or to move it outside the court's jurisdiction. In most states, the creditor must also obtain an attachment bond. The purpose of the bond is to give the debtor some protection if the attachment turns out to have been improper.

The affidavit and bond are filed with the clerk of the court. If the creditor has already begun the principal action (or is filing a complaint against the debtor at the same time), the clerk issues a writ of attachment. The writ is similar to a writ of execution in that it directs the sheriff to levy on the debtor's nonexempt property. The writ usually describes the particular property to be levied on.

The sheriff then "executes the attachment," which means that he levies on the property. The levy is accomplished in the same way as a levy of execution. Thus, for example, the sheriff need not necessarily physically seize and remove bulky property, and under some statutes he need not remove the property at all, no matter how movable it is. In most jurisdictions the debtor must be personally served with a written notice about the levy, even if the debtor was present when the levy was made. Finally, the sheriff prepares a return of the writ, describing exactly what he did.

Once property has been attached, the attachment continues until further order of the court. If the creditor ultimately wins in his lawsuit against the debtor, the attached property is then subject to execution and sale to satisfy the judgment debt.

 An attachment lien on the debtor's property might be canceled if the debtor later files a petition for bankruptcy. This cancellation is likely to occur if (1) the lien was obtained 90 days or less before the bankruptcy petition was filed and (2) the debtor was insolvent when the lien was obtained.[4]

Garnishment Procedure   Garnishment is similar to attachment in that it is begun by the creditor's preparing an affidavit and, in most states, obtaining a garnishment bond. The garnishment affidavit differs from an attachment affidavit in that it identifies the garnishee and states the creditor's belief that the garnishee is hold-

---

[4]The bankruptcy law tries to treat creditors equally. An attachment lien in favor of one creditor gives that creditor rights superior to those of other creditors. As a result, the attachment constitutes what is known as voidable preference in favor of the attaching creditor. Preferences under the bankruptcy law are discussed in Chapter 31.

ing some of the debtor's nonexempt property (which includes money owed to the debtor).

The creditor files the affidavit and bond with the clerk of the court, and the clerk issues a writ of garnishment. The writ has the effect of bringing the garnishee into the proceeding as an additional defendant. It is served on the garnishee, and that service establishes the court's jurisdiction over the garnishee. The garnishee then must answer the writ; in effect, he admits or denies that he possesses any of the debtor's property. Assuming that the garnishee has some of the debtor's property, the creditor can use various means to discover the nature and extent of that property. In the meantime, the garnishee must hold and preserve the property until the court's further order; the garnishee cannot give the property to the debtor. As with attachment, if the creditor later obtains a judgment against the debtor, the garnished property (or the proceeds from its sale) can eventually be applied toward payment of the debt.

30:7   Property Subject to Attachment or Garnishment

Property can generally be attached or garnished if that property is subject to execution. In some states, though, a creditor can also attach or garnish property that is *not* subject to execution. The fact that the property is already encumbered by one or more liens held by others is not a bar to attachment or garnishment.

Real Property   Real property can be and often is attached. The debtor need not necessarily own the property outright. For example, he might have only a life estate, which means that the ownership of the property will automatically pass to someone else when the debtor dies. Real property is usually not, however, subject to garnishment.

Personal Property   As pointed out in 30:4, personal property can be tangible or intangible. A car is an example of tangible personal property, while a *chose in action*[5] is not. Virtually all nonexempt tangible personal property can be attached or garnished. Also subject to attachment and garnishment under some statutes are many types of intangible personal property, such as shares of stock in a corporation.

If the intangible property to be garnished is a debt, the debt must have present, rather than future, existence. For example, if a debtor owns rental property, the creditor can garnish currently owed rent and past due rent, but he cannot garnish rent that is not yet due. Under most statutes, the debt must also be for a fixed amount. Thus, for example, a tort claim on which the victim has not yet obtained a money judgment is usually not subject to garnishment because the amount of the damages payable to the victim is unknown.

---

[5] A chose in action is a right that can be reduced to possession in a lawsuit. Examples of choses in action are (1) a creditor's right to be paid by one to whom he has sold goods on an open account and (2) a tort victim's right to recover damages from the wrongdoer.

Money   Money found in the debtor's possession can be attached, although the right of attachment does not usually extend to money that the debtor has in his pockets at the time of the levy. Most people do not keep any sizable amount of money lying around, however. If a debtor has money, it is apt to be either deposited in a bank or owed to him by his employer. Both bank deposits and unpaid wages are subject to garnishment. Indeed, most garnishees are either banks in which debtors have checking or savings accounts, or employers. The law of some states allows a continuing garnishment of unpaid wages, thus making it unnecessary for the creditor to obtain and serve a new writ of garnishment each time the debtor is due to be paid.

30:8   Relief from Attachment or Garnishment

Just as irregularities can occur in connection with an execution (30:4), they can also occur in an attachment or garnishment. Examples of irregularities are the creditor's making a false statement in his affidavit or the creditor's not stating an adequate ground for the attachment or garnishment. Another irregularity is excess attachment. For example, the sheriff might have levied on exempt property or on property having a value far exceeding the amount of the debt.

   If a writ of attachment or garnishment has already been issued and the debtor's property has been attached (or the garnishee had been served with the writ), the debtor can apply to the court in the principal action for relief from an irregularity. For example, if there has been an excessive attachment, he might ask the court to dissolve the attachment as to part of the property. Depending on the circumstances, the debtor may also be able to recover damages for wrongful attachment or garnishment, as discussed in 30:12.

Bond to Release Property   The debtor usually has the right to post a bond to obtain the temporary release of his property, even if there has been no irregularity in an attachment or garnishment. Most bonds of this type provide that, in effect, the debtor will produce the property if the judgment in the principal action is against him. If the debtor does not produce the property, the surety is liable for the value of that property. Some bonds operate as a full release of the property, however. Under a bond of this type the debtor promises to pay any judgment against him, and if he fails to do so, the surety pays.

Other Occurrences that Release Property   Various possible occurrences after property has been attached or a writ of garnishment has been served on the garnishee have the effect of dissolving the attachment or garnishment and releasing the property. The most obvious of these occurrences is a judgment against the creditor in the principal action. Other occurrences that can result in releasing the debtor's property include (1) in some states, the debtor's claiming a homestead exemption on attached real property; and (2) the creditor's abandonment of the action against the debtor.

30:9   Repossession

Attachment and garnishment are not the only prejudgment remedies available to some creditors. A creditor who has some interest in particular personal property can attempt to repossess that property through use of a somewhat different remedy. The name of this additional remedy varies, depending on the governing state statute. For example, it is called replevin in some states, claim and delivery in others. For present purposes, *replevin* is used to describe all these remedies.

Replevin is a legal remedy by which the creditor seeks a judgment that specific property must be returned to the creditor, rather than a money judgment. It is also a prejudgment remedy in that the creditor can reobtain possession of the property at once, rather than having to wait until the case is decided.

The interest in particular property that gives rise to a creditor's resort to replevin is usually based on a credit sale of goods. The creditor sells goods to the debtor under a contract that lists various events, the occurrence of any one of which constitutes a default by the debtor. A common default is the debtor's failure to pay on time. The typical contract then provides that if a default occurs, the creditor is entitled to repossess the property.

Under Article 9 of the UCC, an interest retained by a seller of goods on credit is a security interest. As discussed in Chapter 29, Article 9 provides for self-help repossession. In essence, the creditor can repossess goods using his own private means if the repossession can be carried out peacefully. Motor vehicles are often repossessed in this way. However, self-help repossession of goods that are in the debtor's home or place of business is often difficult; peaceful repossession is impossible if the debtor refuses to allow the creditor entry. It is at this point that the creditor turns to replevin.

Traditional Replevin Procedure   The typical replevin procedure was quite simple before 1969 when, as a result of a series of important cases (see 30:11), the procedure became more complex. The traditional procedure is similar to attachment in many ways. The creditor prepares an affidavit in which he describes the basis of his claim, the particular property in which he has an interest, and the nature of that interest. He presents this affidavit and an appropriate bond to the clerk of the court. The clerk then issues the writ, which directs the sheriff to levy on the specific property described in the writ. The sheriff executes the writ by seizing the property. He retains custody of the property for several days, and during that period the debtor can reobtain possession of it by posting a bond. If the debtor fails to post a bond, the sheriff delivers the property to the creditor. The sheriff then prepares and files his return of the writ. Meanwhile, the creditor retains the property until a court hears the case and issues a judgment stating to whom the property should go.

Today, the replevin procedure in most states includes the above steps. However, it also provides for advance notice to the debtor and for the debtor's opportunity to be heard. The discussion in 30:11 must be read for a complete picture of replevin under modern practice.

The general rule is that replevin is available only to a creditor who has a security interest in the property sought to be replevied. However, this rule does not always apply. The following case illustrates how state law can make the remedy available to an unsecured creditor as well.

National Steel Products Co.
v
Donald L. Myrick and Associates, Inc.
353 So2d 657
(Florida District Court of Appeal, 1977)

[National Steel Products, the appellant, had delivered building materials to Myrick, the appellee. The materials were to have been used for construction of a skating rink, but they were not actually used at all. Myrick was to pay the cost of the materials in three installments, but he defaulted after making two payments. Although National Steel had not retained a security interest in the building materials, it filed a replevin action against Myrick. National Steel stated in its complaint that the present value of the materials was less than the amount still owed on the debt. The trial court dismissed National Steel's complaint, and National Steel appealed.]

Ryder, Judge.

*   *   *

We are of the view that the allegations of appellant's [complaint] state a cause of action for the replevin of the building materials, founded on [a Florida statute] which provides:

> If for any reason the completion of an improvement is abandoned or though the improvement is completed, materials delivered are not used therefor a person who has delivered materials for the improvement which have not been incorporated therein and for which he has not received payment may peaceably repossess and remove such materials or replevy the same. . . .

Only two of the various arguments ad-

vanced by the appellees below and in this court to sustain the dismissal of the complaint merit discussion. First, the appellees contend that [the above statute] does not give appellant an independent right to replevy the materials, but rather appellant as vendor of the materials must first allege the replevin statute . . . by way of its retention of some right, title or security interest. Only then, it is argued, could appellant look to the [statute] providing for repossession and removal or replevin of the materials. Since appellant has not alleged that it retained any security interest in the materials in question, but rather that it sold and delivered them to appellee Myrick, appellees conclude that the allegations of the . . . complaint were insufficient to state a cause of action for replevin.

We cannot agree with this argument of appellees. A close reading of the clear terms of the statute resolves this point in favor of appellant's argument that it grants an independent right to replevin when allegations are made . . . of facts coming within the ambit of the statute. At this juncture we emphasize the first sentence of the statute. . . .

[The statute] gives the person who delivered the materials two distinct courses of action, peaceable repossession and removal of the materials (i.e., through self-help) *or* replevin (i.e., through the judicial process). The person who delivered the materials may elect to pursue either course of action. If he elects to institute a legal action for replevin, as did appellant here, this statute itself confers the right to maintain such an action whether or not he may also have a security interest in the materials. . . .

[Judgment reversed.]

30:10   Restrictions on Garnishment of Wages

Compensation for personal services owed to but not yet paid to an employee by his employer has long been a favorite target of garnishing creditors. This is because the typical employer is easily identified and found, and the amount of compensation due is easily determined. Also, many debtors have little or no other nonexempt property that the creditor can turn to.

As noted in 30:3, "wages" (including salary and any other form of money compensation for personal services) is exempt to some extent in virtually all states. The need for this exemption arose because garnishment of all or a major part of a debtor's wages often led to the debtor's bankruptcy. The state exemption statutes are far from uniform, however, with the result that they serve their purpose effectively in only some states.

Federal Legislation, Generally (15 USC §§ 1671, 1675, 1677)   The federal government entered the picture in 1968 when Congress enacted the Consumer Credit Protection Act (CCPA). Most of the CCPA directly concerns credit offered to individuals for personal, family, or household purposes, as discussed in Chapter 27. However, Title III of the CCPA (15 USC §§ 1671 et seq.) imposes restrictions on the garnishment of wages.

The Title III restrictions apply to wages paid to all employees throughout the United States. These restrictions have no effect on any state statute that prohibits garnishment of wages altogether or restricts garnishment more than the federal law does, but state statutes that provide less protection are, in effect, superseded by the federal law.

Restriction on Amount Garnished (15 USC §§ 1672, 1673)   With several exceptions, the maximum amount of a person's weekly wages that can be garnished is the lesser of (1) 25 percent of the person's disposable earnings for that week or (2) the amount by which the person's disposable earnings for that week exceed 30 times the federal minimum hourly wage. If an employee is paid other than by the week, the wages are translated into a weekly wage to determine the limits on garnishment.

For purposes of the CCPA, "disposable earnings" is compensation for personal services minus any amount that the employer is required to withhold.

EXAMPLE
Alfred takes home $150 per week (his gross earnings, less deductions for social security and federal and state income taxes). Wilfred takes home $260 per week. Assuming that the federal minimum wage is $4 per hour, the maximum amount of Alfred's weekly wages that can be garnished is $30 ($150 minus 30 times the minimum wage, which is less than 25 percent of $150). The maximum amount of Wilfred's weekly wages that can be garnished is $65 (25 percent of $260, which is less than $260 minus 30 times the minimum wage).

As the following case illustrates, disposable earnings can, in effect, be reduced by an amount deducted by the employer under an earlier voluntary agreement between the employer and employee. The case also shows how different judges interpreting the same law can reach entirely different conclusions.

Sears, Roebuck & Co.

v

A.T. & G. Co.
66 Mich App 359, 239 NW2d 614
(Michigan Court of Appeals, 1976)

[Sears, the garnishor, obtained a money judgment against Phillips, the debtor. Sears then served a writ of garnishment on Phillips' employer, A.T. & G. Company, as garnishee. As state law required it to do, A.T. & G. disclosed to Sears that Phillips' gross weekly earnings were $189.88 and that mandatory deductions were $26.30, leaving a disposable income of $163.58. Of that amount, A.T. & G. had been withholding $40.89 (25 percent of $163.58) under an agreement between Phillips and A.T. & G. for payment of A.T. & G. loans made earlier to Phillips. Since A.T. & G. was already deducting 25 percent of Phillips' disposable income, it refused to withhold anything more under the writ of garnishment. Sears then sued A.T. & G. in the Michigan District Court. Dissatisfied with the ruling of that court, which is described below in the opinion, Sears appealed to the Michigan Circuit Court. Sears then appealed the circuit court's order to the Michigan Court of Appeals.

In this opinion, the court discusses the right of setoff. In essence, a setoff is a reduction or discharge of one person's claim against another by a different claim that the second person has against the first.]

Cavanagh, Judge.

*   *   *

It is clear that, in the present case, there was a "garnishment proceeding" that brings into consideration the congressional restrictions; it is equally clear that the disposable income sub-ject to the garnishment formula is $163.58. The loan payment deduction by the garnishee cannot serve to reduce disposable income for purpose of the act, for the loan payment is not a deduction "required by law to be withheld."

Were it not for the loan payment deduction by the garnishee, there is no doubt that the garnishor could, under the act, garnish 25% of $163.58, or $40.89. . . . The question to be resolved is whether the garnishor can claim any or all of that 25% of disposable income when the garnishee has a valid deduction. The presence of the loan agreement requires us to turn to the state law for a determination of priorities in payments.

Under [a Michigan District Court rule], a garnishee is required to file a disclosure statement. This court rule does more than merely require disclosure: the rule establishes a priority in favor of the garnishee:

> "Disclosure. The garnishee shall file with the clerk of court a disclosure under oath within 6 days after the date of the service of the writ upon him. The *disclosure* shall reveal any liability to the principal defendant [the employee] . . . and, except as to claims for unliquidated damages for wrongs or injuries, *may claim any setoff of which the garnishee could have availed himself against the principal defendant if he had not been garnisheed*. [Court's emphasis]
> . . .

The issue in the present case is how the setoff rights given to the garnishee by [the above court rule] affect the garnishor's claim to 25% of the debtor's disposable income. We must determine if either the Federal act or the state court rule requires a particular order of preference.

In so doing, it is helpful to realize that the respective Federal and state enactments here involved do not conflict with each other. . . .

The number of possible interpretations of how the Federal statute and the court rule interact in this particular case is considerable. The two courts below, the parties, and even the judges of this panel are divided in construction.

The district court ruled that Federal law was inapplicable to the garnishee's claim, as the loan payment deduction was not itself a garnishment. The court further determined that the priority given in [the state court rule] allowed the garnishee to deduct from disposable income whatever sum the debtor had consented to be deducted. The garnishor was then entitled to 25% of the balance, if any, that remained after deduction of the loan payment from disposable income. In this case, the garnishee, by agreement with the debtor, could take $40.89 of the $163.58 disposable income; the garnishor could take 25% of the $122.69 balance, or $30.67.

The [circuit court] determined that the court rule did not establish any priority in favor of the garnishee, because the garnishee, unlike the garnishor, was not a judgment creditor. Therefore, the garnishor could take its 25% claim from the disposable income. Once the garnishor had taken its full 25% claim, the garnishee could take nothing. . . .

The dissent of Judge Bashara [dissenting court of appeals judge] would allow the garnishee to deduct whatever sum agreed to by the debtor, with no limitations, and then allow the garnishor to take 25% of the original disposable income out of the balance, if any, remaining after garnishee's deduction. In this case, the garnishee would take $40.89 and the garnishor would take $40.89.

Our conclusion draws upon all of the above interpretations and yet differs from them all. We hold that a garnishee is entitled to deduct from disposable income whatever sum agreed upon by the debtor, with no limitation. The garnishor can then claim the difference, if any, between 25% of disposable income and the garnishee deduction. If the garnishee deduction is more than 25% of disposable income, the garnishor will recover nothing. In this case, the garnishee is entitled to $40.89, the garnishor nothing.

Our primary support for this conclusion is the interpretation we give to [the court rule]. . . .

We think that the [proper] interpretation of the court rule is that the garnishee's claim against the debtor be set off against the claim made by the garnishor. . . .

This interpretation . . . is additionally buttressed by doctrines of construction that serve to protect the principal debtor. Because garnishment is a harsh remedy, its application will be limited whenever possible by reasonable construction of court rules and statutes. . . .

[Judgment reversed, one judge dissenting.]

The federal restrictions apply separately to each person. Thus, for example, if both husband and wife work, but a debt is owed only by the husband, only his disposable income determines the maximum permissible garnishment of his wages. On the other hand, if an employee has two jobs, the earnings of both jobs are combined in determining the disposable income to which the federal restriction applies. A question that has not yet been settled is whether the garnishment restrictions also apply to a checking account if the sole source of money for the account is wages. At least one court has held that the restrictions do not apply to this situation.

The garnishment limits do not apply at all to any order of a bankruptcy court or to any debt for state or federal taxes. Also, the limits are considerably higher if the debt involved is a support order issued by a court. For example, up to 65 percent of the disposable earnings of a divorced person can be garnished for payment of overdue alimony and child support.

Discharge of Employee [15 USC § 1674(a)]   Since garnishment generates administrative expenses that must be paid by the garnishee, employers do not like to have the wages of their employees garnished. Indeed, garnishment often used to lead to the employee's being fired. The CCPA limits this practice by prohibiting the discharge of an employee due to garnishment of wages for any *one* debt.

 A businessperson should be aware that the federal discharge prohibition has been interpreted to mean that if the maximum allowable amount of an employee's wages has already been garnished for one debt, service of a writ of garnishment on the employer in connection with a second debt is not a second garnishment within the meaning of the discharge rule. The rationale for this interpretation is that since the employee no longer has any disposable earnings subject to garnishment, the employer could not comply with the second writ, even if it wanted to.

Enforcement; Civil Liability [15 USC §§ 1674(b), 1676]   The Wage and Hour Division of the Department of Labor enforces the federal restrictions on garnishment of wages. An employer who wrongfully discharges an employee because of a garnishment can be fined, imprisoned, or both. However, the CCPA is silent on the question whether that employer can also be sued for damages by the discharged employee. Different courts have reached contrary results on this question.

 The CCPA should not be viewed as giving an employer the *right* to discharge an employee whose wages are garnished for more than one debt. For example, the discharge might violate the employee's rights under other federal law (such as the civil rights legislation forbidding discrimination in employment), and the employee might be able to recover damages under that law.

30:11   Debtors' Constitutional Rights

The Fourteenth Amendment to the United States Constitution, as interpreted by the courts, is the source of a vast body of law. Much of the litigation based on the amendment has stemmed from its *due process clause,* which provides that no state shall "deprive any person of . . . property, without due process of law."

Until 1969, the creditors' remedies discussed earlier in this chapter were thought not to violate due process requirements; the legal atmosphere was favorable to creditors. This favorable atmosphere collapsed abruptly in 1969 when the United States Supreme Court issued the following landmark decision.

Sniadach

v

Family Finance Corp.
395 US 337, 23 L Ed 2d 349,
89 S Ct 1820
(United States Supreme Court, 1969)

[Family Finance Corporation, the respondent, sought to garnish the wages of Sniadach, the petitioner, in connection with a $420 debt. Sniadach received no advance notice about the garnishment, and none was required under the governing Wisconsin statute. Sniadach's employer stated that it had under its control wages of $63.18 owed to Sniadach but not yet paid to her. The employer agreed to hold one-half of the unpaid wages subject to the court's order. Sniadach moved for dismissal of the garnishment proceeding on the ground that her right to due process had been violated. The trial court denied the motion, and the Wisconsin Supreme Court affirmed, in effect holding that the statute was not unconstitutional. The United States Supreme Court accepted the case for review.]

Justice Douglas delivered the opinion of the Court.

*   *   *

The Wisconsin statute gives a plaintiff 10 days in which to serve the summons and complaint on the defendant after service on the garnishee. In this case petitioner was served the same day as the garnishee. She nonetheless claims that the Wisconsin garnishment procedure violates that due process required by the Fourteenth Amendment, in that notice and an opportunity to be heard are not given before the . . . seizure of the wages. What happens in Wisconsin is that the clerk of the court issues the summons at the request of the creditor's lawyer; and it is the latter who by serving the garnishee sets in motion the machinery whereby the wages are frozen. They may, it is true, be unfrozen if the trial of the main suit is ever had and the wage earner wins on the merits. But in the interim the wage earner is deprived of his enjoyment of earned wages without any opportunity to be heard and to tender any defense he may have, whether it be fraud or otherwise.

Such summary procedure may well meet the requirements of due process in extraordinary situations. . . . But in the present case no situation requiring special protection to a state or creditor interest is presented by the facts; nor is the Wisconsin statute narrowly drawn to meet any such unusual condition. Petitioner was a resident of this Wisconsin community and [personal] jurisdiction was readily obtainable. . . .

In this case the sole question is whether there has been a taking of property without that procedural due process that is required by the Fourteenth Amendment. . . . [The] right to be heard has little reality or worth unless one is informed that the matter is pending and can choose for himself whether to appear or default, acquiesce or contest. . . . In the context of this case the question is whether the interim freezing of the wages without a chance to be heard violates procedural due process.

A procedural rule that may satisfy due process for attachments in general . . . does not necessarily satisfy procedural due process in every case. . . . We deal here with wages—a specialized type of property presenting distinct problems in our economic system. We turn then to the nature of that property and problems of procedural due process.

A prejudgment garnishment of the Wisconsin type is a taking which may impose tremendous hardship on wage earners with families to support. Until [enactment of the CCPA], which forbids discharge of employees on the ground that their wages have been garnished, garnishment often meant the loss of a job. Over and beyond that was the great drain on family income. . . .

Recent investigations of the problem have disclosed the grave injustices made possible by prejudgment garnishment whereby the sole opportunity to be heard comes after the taking. . . .

The leverage of the creditor on the wage earner is enormous. The creditor tenders not only the original debt but the "collection fees" incurred by his attorneys in the garnishment proceedings. . . .

Apart from those collateral consequences, it appears that in Wisconsin the statutory exemption granted the wage earner is generally insufficient to support the debtor for any one week.

The result is that a prejudgment garnishment of the Wisconsin type may as a practical matter drive a wage-earning family to the wall. Where the taking of one's property is so obvious, it needs no extended argument to conclude that absent notice and a prior hearing . . . this prejudgment garnishment procedure violates the fundamental principles of due process.

Reversed.

The *Sniadach* decision is limited to garnishment of the wages of an individual over whom the court could acquire personal jurisdiction—that is, Sniadach could have been personally served with process. More significant to creditors was the underlying legal theory, known as the *Sniadach* doctrine, that a debtor is entitled to notice and an opportunity to be heard before his property can be taken, even if the taking is not necessarily permanent and will ultimately be judged by a court.

Developments since *Sniadach* It did not take the courts long to extend the *Sniadach* doctrine to garnishment of a consumer's bank account. Later, the Supreme Court extended the doctrine to cover garnishment of a corporate debtor's bank account. This decision made it clear that businesses also have due process rights that must be observed. Other courts extended the *Sniadach* doctrine to cover attachments. And in the case of *Fuentes v Shevin*[6] the Supreme Court declared unconstitutional the taking of consumer goods under a writ of replevin issued without the debtor's having been given advance notice or an opportunity to be heard.

Creditors have not lost all the battles, however. For example, the remedy of postjudgment garnishment without advance notice and a hearing has withstood constitutional attack. The reason is that a postjudgment garnishment order is based on a court's judgment that itself was issued in a proceeding during which the debtor's due process rights were observed. Execution without advance notice and a hearing can be defended on the same basis. And in another Supreme Court case,[7] the Court suggested that a statute allowing a debtor's property to be seized before judgment without advance notice and a hearing is not unconstitutional if the statute (1) requires the creditor to post a bond, (2) requires the creditor to file an affidavit alleging personal knowledge of specific facts forming a basis for the seizure, (3) requires a judge to decide whether the writ should be issued, (4) allows the debtor

---

[6]407 US 67, 32 L Ed 2d 556, 92 S Ct 1983, 10 UCCRS 913 (1972).
[7]*Mitchell v W.T. Grant Co.*, 416 US 600, 40 L Ed 2d 406, 94 S Ct 1895 (1974).

to recover the property by posting a bond, and (5) gives the debtor the right to a hearing immediately after the seizure.

The constitutional questions relating to creditors' remedies have not all been answered yet. However, it seems that the following criteria (discussed below) determine whether a particular creditor prejudgment remedy is unconstitutional under given circumstances: (1) the debtor's status, (2) the extent of the debtor's deprivation of his property, (3) the extent of any compelling state interest, and (4) the presence of "state action."

Status of Debtor   If the debtor is a consumer, the notice and hearing requirement generally exists. Moreover, it is unlikely that a consumer will be found to have waived the right. For example, a retail installment contract might include a provision to the effect that, on default, the debtor consents to seizure of the property and waives his right to prior notice and hearing. This waiver is apt to be disregarded by a court because it was imposed by the creditor in an adhesion contract (see Chapter 12), not mutually agreed to by the creditor and debtor. On the other hand, a business debtor's waiver of its rights can be upheld. The theory is that a business' waiver results from bargaining between two relatively equal parties although, in practice, a small business often has little more bargaining power over its creditors than a consumer has over his.

Deprivation of Property   The physical seizure of a debtor's property clearly deprives the debtor of a substantial interest in that property, so that the notice and hearing requirement apply. Other creditor actions lead to less substantial deprivations. For example, an attachment can be nonpossessory, that is, the debtor might be allowed to retain possession of the property. Another example of a less substantial deprivation is a creditor's filing a statutory lien on real property. The courts have reached different conclusions as to whether prior notice and a hearing are required in connection with nonpossessory attachment. In view of the current liberal judicial trend in the area of debtors' rights, the question is likely to be resolved against creditors. On the other hand, the mere filing of a statutory lien does not generally require notice and a hearing.

Compelling State Interest   Most rights that each individual has are subject to exceptions based on what is known as compelling state interest. In essence, a compelling state interest is a public interest that is so strong that the individual's rights must give way to it. Both the *Sniadach* case and *Fuentes v Shevin*, mentioned earlier, suggest that the acquisition of quasi in rem jurisdiction over a debtor is a compelling state interest. Hence, it appears that attachment of the property of a nonresident debtor without prior notice or a hearing is not unconstitutional. However, the general interest of creditors in collecting debts with a minimum of red tape is not a compelling state interest that eliminates the need for notice and a hearing.

State Action   A common factor in all the cases in which state statutes have been declared unconstitutional under the *Sniadach* doctrine is state action. Recall that the Fourteenth Amendment due process requirement is imposed on the states. State action occurs when the state participates in a taking of property. Examples of state participation include a state court clerk's issuing a writ of attachment, garnishment, or replevin, and a county sheriff's levy on property; both the clerk and the sheriff are public officers.

Apparently, a state's enactment of a statute that allows a taking of property without notice and hearing is not, itself, enough to constitute impermissible state action. This principle is suggested by the fact that, so far at least, the self-help repossession provision of UCC Article 9 has withstood most constitutional challenges.[8] The reason is that no public officer is involved in self-help repossession.

Nature of Due Process Required   Obviously, a full trial is not required before a debtor's property can be attached, garnished, or replevied. The requirement of a full trial would have the effect of eliminating the prejudgment remedies altogether. In an effort to comply with due process requirements, most states have amended their attachment, garnishment, and replevin statutes to include what is known as a "show cause" procedure. In essence, the creditor obtains from the court an order addressed to the debtor and directing the debtor to show why a writ of attachment, garnishment, or replevin should not be issued. The debtor then has a specified time in which to answer the order. He or his attorney can appear before the court for this purpose, and if the debtor makes a sufficient showing, the writ is not issued. As a practical matter, it should be noted that this sort of procedure can weaken the creditor's position substantially because it gives the debtor time to put his property beyond the creditor's reach in any number of different ways. Some state statutes address this problem by allowing a debtor's property to be seized without notice under limited circumstances and providing for a hearing very soon afterward. The courts have reached different conclusions about whether statutes of this last type are constitutional.

 Not all state statutes have been amended or replaced to comply with the constitutional principles discussed above. Any creditor who seeks to attach, garnish, or replevy property under a statute not providing for advance notice to the debtor and some sort of hearing must realize that the action might be challenged on constitutional grounds, and that the challenge might succeed.

30:12   Wrongful Attachment, Garnishment, or Execution

An attachment, garnishment, or execution and sale can be wrongful in a number of different ways. For example, the creditor might have used the remedy for an improper purpose or have made a false statement in his affidavit; the sheriff might have levied on exempt property or property having a value far exceeding the amount of the debt; or an execution sale might have been held without proper notice to the debtor.

If a wrongful act has occurred, the debtor can recover damages from whoever was responsible for or carried out the act. The proper defendant is often the credi-

---

[8]Self-help repossession is discussed briefly in 30:9. It is discussed in detail in Chapter 29.

tor, sometimes the sheriff, and at times both the creditor and the sheriff. The debtor's right to damages for wrongful attachment or garnishment does not require him having prevailed in the principal action. Indeed, his right to damages can arise before a judgment is even issued in that action.

Measure of Damages   If there has been a wrongful attachment, garnishment, or execution, the debtor is generally entitled to be compensated for his loss. Naturally, the debtor has the right to have his property returned to him (or, in a garnishment, to have the garnishment dissolved). If the property cannot be returned, the debtor receives its value, determined as of the time of the seizure.

The recovery of the property or its value only returns the debtor to his original position, rather than compensating him for any loss he suffered. Depending on the circumstances, the debtor might also be able to recover damages for such factors as (1) the debtor's loss of use of the property; (2) damage to or depreciation of the property; (3) lost business profits, including a lost opportunity for an advantageous sale of the property; (4) injury to the debtor's credit rating, and (5) the debtor's mental suffering and humiliation.

If the creditor (or, rarely, the sheriff) is found to have acted with malice, the debtor may also be able to recover punitive damages. Malice in this context generally means that the wrongdoer intentionally acted against the debtor and with an evil purpose. For example, an attaching creditor, whose primary purpose is supposed to be obtaining security for his debt, acts maliciously if his real purpose is to drive the debtor out of business by tying up the debtor's inventory.

Nature of Legal Action, Generally   Several approaches may be available to a debtor who is the victim of a wrongful attachment, garnishment, or execution. First, the debtor may be able to sue the surety named in a bond. Second, he may be able to file an action for wrongful attachment, garnishment, or execution. Finally, he may be able to sue for the tort of either *malicious prosecution* or *abuse of process*. These three approaches are discussed below.

Action on Bond   There may be a bond covering whatever wrongful act occurred in an attachment, garnishment, or execution. "Covering" in this context means that the wrongful act falls within the scope of the protection afforded by the bond. For example, a creditor might have obtained a writ of attachment without having ever sued the debtor on the debt. The attachment bond filed by the creditor with the attachment affidavit would normally cover this impropriety. Note that the maximum amount that the surety can be required to pay under a bond will rarely be enough to cover an award of punitive damages.

The surety might pay up based on an informal showing of its liability under the bond. If not, a debtor who is looking to a bond for the satisfaction of his claim will have to sue the surety. In practice, the debtor often sues the wrongdoing party, such as the creditor, and it is the latter who turns to the surety, just as a motorist who is sued for an automobile accident turns to his insurer.

Action for Wrongful Attachment, Garnishment, or Execution   Under the law of most states, the debtor can sue the creditor or sheriff directly in connection with a wrongful attachment, garnishment, or execution. The showing that the debtor must make if he is to prevail depends on the governing state law and on the nature of the wrongful act. In some states the debtor must show that the defendant acted with malice, while in others the debtor must show only that an impropriety occurred. In an action against the creditor, the debtor may have to show that the creditor lacked probable cause for obtaining the writ; probable cause will have existed if, when the writ was issued, the creditor reasonably believed the truth of all facts required for its issuance.

Malicious Prosecution; Abuse of Process   Malicious prosecution and abuse of process are separate torts that are recognized in most states. Both torts require a showing that the defendant acted with malice. In the present context, the basis of malicious prosecution is that the creditor should never have sued the debtor in the first place, so that the creditor never had the right to attach or garnish any of the debtor's property. Before the debtor can sue for malicious prosecution, the creditor's lawsuit on the debt must have ended in the debtor's favor.

The basis of a debtor's action for abuse of process is that the creditor intentionally used a proper legal procedure for an improper purpose. For example, the creditor may have had the right to sue on the debt and to obtain a writ of attachment against the debtor's property, but he is liable for abuse of process if his purpose in attaching the property was to vex and harass the debtor, rather than to obtain security for the debt. The following case illustrates abuse of process in that a creditor attached property having a value far exceeding the amount of the debt. Note the court's discussion about different types of wrongful attachment, and the debtor's proper course of action for each one.

White Lighting Co.
v
Wolfson
68 Cal 2d 336, 66 Cal Rptr 697, 438 P2d 345
(California Supreme Court, 1968)

[White Lighting Company sued Wolfson on an $850 debt. White then attached 5,000 shares of stock, claimed by Wolfson to be worth $15,000, and an automobile, claimed to be worth $4,500. White also tried to garnish Wolfson's $250 bank account and threatened to garnish his wages. As part of the principal action, Wolfson filed against White a claim in which he sought damages for abuse of process. The trial court upheld a demurrer to this claim on the ground that the claim was premature, and Wolfson appealed.

A demurrer is a procedural device (permitted in only some states) by which one against whom a claim is asserted says that, in effect, even if all the alleged facts are true, the claimant has no right to relief. Sustaining a demurrer has the effect of dismissing the claim. The trial judge had reasoned that Wolfson's claim should have been based on the tort of malicious prosecution, and that the tort could not exist unless and until a judgment for Wolfson was issued in the principal action. According to this reasoning, Wolfson could recover damages only by filing a separate legal action against White at some future time.]

Tobriner, Justice.

*   *   *

The trial court erred in sustaining [the demurrer] on the asserted ground of the prematurity of the cause of action. A claim based on excessive attachment constitutes in essence a cause of action for abuse of process rather than a cause of action for malicious prosecution. Consequently it is unnecessary for Wolfson to prove that the proceeding in which the attachment was issued has terminated in his favor, or that the process was obtained without probable cause or in the course of a proceeding begun without probable cause. . . . The claim may therefore be brought in the [principal action].

The case law on wrongful attachment presents a complicated and confused picture. Most of the California opinions have treated actions for wrongful attachment as actions for malicious prosecution rather than for abuse of process. Much of the confusion in the characterization of these actions for wrongful attachment results from the courts' failure to distinguish the following four different types of wrongful attachment: (1) levying attachment in an action prosecuted maliciously and without probable cause; (2) maliciously procuring attachment in a properly instituted action in which the creditor is not entitled to the writ; (3) attaching property which is exempt from attachment or possesses a value greatly in excess of the amount of the legitimate claim; (4) using regularly issued attachment for an improper purpose.

The courts generally and correctly treat the above-mentioned first type of wrongful attachment as constituting part of an action for malicious prosecution. . . . In those cases in which the courts have articulated the reasons for the alleged wrongfulness, they have in most instances properly treated the fourth type of wrongful attachment—wrongful use of properly procured attachment—as creating an action for abuse of process. . . . Thus the problem of proper characterization mainly arises in the second and third types of wrongful attachment cases: those cases in which the underlying action is proper but the creditor either is

not entitled to a writ of attachment or attaches property which is exempt or possesses a value greatly in excess of the amount of the legitimate claim. . . .

Although the courts in [two California cases] *described* an action based on an excessive claim and attachment as an action for malicious prosecution . . . they both allowed recovery in the absence of two essential elements of malicious prosecution: lack of probable cause in prosecution of the action in which the attachment issued and termination of that action in favor of the attachment defendant. [Court's emphasis.] The sole basis for the recovery stemmed from the excessiveness of the claim and attachment. . . .

We believe that in view of the reasons stated below excessive attachments should be treated as giving rise to a cause of action for abuse of process rather than for malicious prosecution. First, in the case of an excessive attachment action, two requirements of the malicious prosecution action may very well be lacking: absence of probable cause to institute the proceedings in which the attachment issued and termination of that action in favor of the attachment defendant. The attaching creditor typically prevails on his claim, but for a much smaller amount than the value of the property attached. Second, the wrongfulness in the excessive attachment lies, not in the institution of the suit or the procurement of the attachment, but in the illegitimate use of the attachment process to tie up more property than is reasonably necessary to secure the attaching creditor's claim. Third, the attachment defendant should not be forced to wait until final termination of the attaching creditor's action to sue for wrongful attachment: The attachment defendant should be able to assert the damages caused by the excessive attachment in the attaching creditor's primary action.

In cases such as the instant one in which the alleged wrongfulness of the attachment does not depend upon an alleged lack of probable cause and malice in instituting the action in which the attachment issued—i.e., in cases in which the alleged wrongful attachment falls under categories (2), (3), and (4)—a termination of that action in favor of the attachment defendant has no bearing upon the determination of whether the attachment writ was maliciously procured or improperly used. The attachment defendant should therefore not be forced to wait until the termination of the creditor's primary action to seek damages for the alleged wrongful attachment. It would, indeed, be extraordinary, if the attachment defendant was denied the right in the same action, not only to defend against it, but to claim redress for the wrongs inflicted upon him by the attachment plaintiff. . . .

[Judgment reversed.]

30:13   Wrongful Repossession

A creditor who repossessed a debtor's property will often have acted under the self-help provision of UCC Article 9 (see 30:9 and Chapter 29). If, however, the creditor had the debtor's property seized under a writ of replevin and the replevin was wrongful, the debtor can recover damages from the creditor.

Recall that replevin is a complete remedy. The creditor can obtain possession of the debtor's property before the court issues a judgment, but that judgment, when issued, will determine the party to whom the property is to go (rather than merely awarding or denying the creditor a money judgment). If the judgment is in the creditor's favor, the debtor will not ordinarily have suffered any loss for which he is entitled to compensation. If the debtor wins, however, the replevin judgment will usually attempt to serve at least two functions. The first function is to return the parties to their positions before the replevin proceeding was begun. The second function is to compensate the debtor for his loss.

To serve its first function, the typical replevin judgment in favor of the debtor requires the creditor to return the replevied property or, if the property cannot be returned, to pay the debtor the value of the property. That value is determined as of the time when the property was seized. As to the second function, the debtor can have suffered the same types of loss that can occur with wrongful attachment or garnishment (see 30:12). All aspects of the loss that the debtor has proved are added up, and the total is listed in the judgment as the damages that the creditor must pay. In addition, if the creditor is found to have acted maliciously, the judgment can include an award of punitive damages against the creditor. For example, the creditor might have obtained the writ of replevin even though he knew that he had no actual right to do so. Or, having innocently replevied property, the creditor might have refused to return the property after having discovered that it belonged to someone else.

Key Concepts and Terms

- A debt is satisfied when it has been paid off or otherwise ceases to exist.
- A debtor who fails to make a payment is in default. The creditor can then sue on the debt and obtain a money judgment. The creditor can then obtain satisfaction

of the judgment by execution, postjudgment garnishment, or both. Before the judgment is issued, the creditor might be able to attach or garnish the debtor's property.

- Certain property of individuals is exempt from the claims of creditors. Exempt property cannot be subjected to attachment, garnishment, or execution.

- Execution involves a seizure of a judgment debtor's nonexempt property, the sale of that property, and the application of the sale proceeds toward satisfaction of the debt.

- If execution is ineffective to satisfy a money judgment, the creditor can use postjudgment garnishment to obtain property or money that, although owned by or owed to the debtor, is in someone else's possession.

- After a creditor has sued on a debt, but before he has recovered a judgment, the creditor can attach nonexempt property in the debtor's possession or garnish the debtor's nonexempt property in the possession of somebody else. Both attachment and garnishment deprive the debtor from using the property and can lead to execution on the property later, when the creditor has obtained a judgment against the debtor.

- A creditor who has an interest in particular property owned by a defaulting debtor can sue the debtor in replevin to obtain title to that property. A creditor suing in replevin can obtain possession of the property before a final judgment is issued.

- Federal law limits the amount of an employee's wages that can be garnished. It also protects the employee against being discharged by his employer due to a single garnishment of wages.

- Many debtors have the constitutional right to be notified in advance and to be able to present their side of disputes with creditors before their property can be taken from them in connection with their debts.

- A debtor can usually reobtain possession of property that has been levied on, garnished, or replevied by posting a bond. If an attachment, garnishment, replevin, or execution is improper, the debtor may be able to apply to the court for appropriate relief. He may also be able to recover damages from whoever committed the impropriety.

- Abuse of Process
- Affidavit
- Attachment
- Bond
- Chose in Action
- Due Process Clause
- Encumbrance
- Execution
- Exempt Property
- Garnishment
- Homestead Exemption
- Judgment Creditor
- Levy
- Lien
- Malicious Prosecution
- Postjudgment Garnishment
- Prejudgment Remedy
- Quasi in Rem Jurisdiction
- Replevin

Questions and Case Problems

1. What is the difference between a judicial remedy and a nonjudicial remedy? State an example of both a judicial and a nonjudicial remedy that a creditor might use against a defaulting debtor.

2. Define and distinguish execution, attachment, garnishment, and replevin according to your understanding of those terms as they are used in this chapter.

3. From a creditor's viewpoint, for what purposes are the prejudgment remedies intended? How effectively do the remedies serve those purposes, in your opinion? Why?

4. What is the purpose of the bond posted by a creditor who is seeking the issuance of a writ of attachment or execution? To what extent does the bond effectively serve that purpose?

5. Plunkett is injured, and his new car is slightly damaged, when Fouts runs a red light and hits Plunkett's car. Fouts carries no automobile liability insurance. It appears that his only asset of any value is his car, which was not damaged in the accident. Plunkett sues Fouts for damages and wins a $2,000 default judgment when Fouts fails to appear in court. Plunkett now seeks to levy execution on Fouts' car so that it can be sold to satisfy the judgment. Discuss the likelihood of Plunkett's success in this effort.

6. Johnson obtains a $5,000 money judgment against Roberts, and Roberts fails to pay it. Roberts owns relatively little property. Indeed, her only nonexempt property currently in her possession is an oil painting that has an appraised value of $2,000. However, Roberts does have $10,000 deposited in a savings account at a local bank. How can Johnson obtain satisfaction of his judgment against Roberts?

7. Lorenzo works for Metropolitan Opera Association. His gross wages are $300 per week, and Metropolitan deducts $80 per week for Social Security and state and federal income taxes, as it is required to do by state and federal law. On April 1, 1982, Metropolitan was served with a court order requiring it to withhold $100 per week from Lorenzo's wages and to pay the $100 to Lorenzo's former wife as overdue alimony and child support. These payments are to continue until Metropolitan receives a further order from the court. Meanwhile, GMAC, one of Lorenzo's creditors, has sued Lorenzo on a debt and been awarded a judgment for $300. Execution turned out to be ineffective, so GMAC proceeded under the state postjudgment garnishment statute. On June 1, 1982, a writ of garnishment was served on Metropolitan, but Metropolitan refused to withhold any of Lorenzo's wages for GMAC, claiming that federal law forbids any additional withholding. GMAC now seeks a court order requiring Metropolitan to withhold $55 from Lorenzo's wages each week and to pay it to GMAC until the $300 judgment has been satisfied. Assume that the federal minimum wage is $4 per hour. Is GMAC entitled to garnish $55 per week from Lorenzo's wages? Why or why not? If not, how much can GMAC garnish? Why?

8. Peebles sues Clement for $4,000 on an overdue debt, and she seeks to attach some of Clement's property without advance notice or a hearing. In accordance with the state attachment statute, Peebles (a) signs an affidavit in which she states her belief that Clement is about to remove his property from the state, (b) obtains an attachment bond in double the amount claimed in the legal action, and (c) files the affidavit and bond with the clerk of the court. The clerk then issues a writ of

attachment, and the sheriff levies on some of Clement's nonexempt property. The state statute provides that Clement can (a) recover the property by filing his own bond in double the amount of Peebles' claim; or (b) ask the court to dissolve the attachment, at which point he is entitled to a hearing on the matter. Instead of taking either of these two steps, however, Clement asks the court to dismiss the attachment altogether, claiming that the procedure followed by Peebles violated his constitutional rights. You are the judge. How do you rule on Clement's request? Why? If you find that the statute is unconstitutional, how, if at all, could it be amended to satisfy debtors' right to due process, yet protect creditors' rights as well?

9. Overmyer Company, a warehouse firm, contracts with Frick Company for the installation of refrigeration equipment, and Overmyer signs a promissory note covering the cost of the work. Frick completes its work, but Overmyer fails to make required payments on the note. Frick then files statutory liens covering some of Overmyer's property. Overmyer wants the liens to be removed and its time for payment on the promissory note to be extended. Attorneys for Overmyer and Frick meet and agree to a new promissory note that includes a clause whereby Overmyer waives its right to notice and a hearing before its property can be attached if it defaults on the new note and is sued by Frick. After the note is signed, Frick releases the liens it had filed. Overmyer defaults on the new note, and Frick sues Overmyer on the note and obtains a writ of attachment against Overmyer's property without advance notice or a hearing. Overmyer applies to the court for relief from the attachment, claiming that its right to due process was violated. How should the court rule? Why?

10. CFI holds two promissory notes signed by Mr. and Mrs. Howard in connection with the Howards' purchase of new furniture. The Howards default on the notes, and CFI repossesses the furniture, sells it, and applies the sale proceeds to the debt. The receipt given to the Howards when their furniture was repossessed has "paid in full" written across the bottom, although CFI and the Howards disagree as to whether that phrase was there when CFI's agent signed the receipt. CFI sues the Howards on the balance it claims to be still due on the notes, and it is granted a default judgment. The next day, CFI obtains a writ of execution, and the sheriff seizes the Howards' car, after being directed to it by CFI's agent. At the time, Mrs. Howard protested vigorously and produced the "paid in full" receipt, but to no avail. The Howards later have the default judgment set aside, answer CFI's complaint for the balance due on the notes, and claim damages from CFI for the wrongful taking of the car. At the trial, the judge rules that the notes had been satisfied before the default judgment was obtained; that is, he finds that the "paid in full" term on the receipt was valid. The judge also awards the Howards a total of $3,000 for wrongful attachment, broken down as follows: $240 for lost use of the car, $760 for Mrs. Howard's mental suffering, and $2,000 as punitive damages. CFI then appeals. The judge assigned to write the court's opinion asks for your written advice. What advice do you give the judge about the following questions: (a) Did the seizure of the car constitute wrongful attachment? If not, what, if any, tort was committed? (b) Was the damages award for mental suffering justified? Why or why not? (c) Was the punitive damages award justified? Why or why not?

31 Debtor Relief

31:1 Introduction

"Debtor relief" has many different meanings. It can refer to the rights of a debtor (1) who is billed incorrectly for credit extended to him in the past (see Chapter 27) or (2) whose property has been seized by or for the benefit of his creditors (see Chapters 29 and 30). Debtor relief also involves the options available to a debtor who cannot pay his debts. The more important of these options are discussed in this chapter.

A person who needs debtor relief in the sense the term is used here is often *insolvent*. This means that the value of all the debtor's assets, other than exempt property (property that is not subject to the claims of the debtor's creditors, as discussed in Chapter 30) is less than the total amount of his debts. As an insolvent debtor defaults on his debts (fails to pay the debts on time) he finds himself under increasing pressure from his creditors. The debtor looks for a way to escape his indebtedness, and as discussed in the rest of this chapter, there are various approaches available to him.

Relief Short of Bankruptcy

31:2 Simple Forms of Debtor Relief

Relatively simple methods by which debtors might be able to find relief include informal agreements with creditors, debt consolidation loans, and professional debt counseling.

Informal Agreements A debtor who cannot make current payments on his debts can contact his creditors, inform them of his problems, and attempt to work out an acceptable solution. For example, a creditor might allow the payment period to be extended or even reduce the amount of the debt. Although any agreement of this nature is apt to be unenforceable due to lack of consideration (see Chapter 11), many creditors will accept and perform the agreement if the debtor seems honest and it appears likely that payment will be made eventually.

Debt Consolidation Loans   A debt consolidation loan is a new loan obtained by a debtor and intended to provide him with money to pay off all or the most pressing of his creditors. In essence, the debtor substitutes a single new debt for a number of old ones. The new loan is repayable over a long enough term so that, in theory, the debtor can make the required payments out of his regular income.

The major problem with consolidation loans is that many debtors who require the loans are unable to qualify for them. Moreover, even if a debtor can qualify, the rate of interest might be so high that the debtor only postpones his predicament until the time he defaults on the new loan.

Professional Debt Counseling   In some states a debtor can seek help from a professional debt counselor in preparing a plan for paying his debts. The counselor might contact some of the creditors in the course of working out the plan, and he might be able to obtain concessions from them as to time of payment and perhaps even the amount to be paid. The plan sometimes provides for the debtor to make periodic large payments to the counselor, who then makes payments to the creditors.

If debt counseling is to work, the debtor must have enough regular income, property that can be sold, or both so that he can make the payments suggested by the counselor or required by the payment plan. Also, most debt counselors charge a fee. Therefore, unless one or more creditors can be persuaded to reduce the size of their claims, the debtor ends up paying more than he was obligated to pay before visiting the counselor. It is for this reason that a majority of the states prohibit the offering of certain debt-counseling services on a fee basis.

31:3   Composition with Creditors

The term *composition with creditors* refers to a contractual arrangement between a debtor and at least two of his creditors. The parties enter into an agreement under which the creditors agree to accept less than is actually due, as full satisfaction of the debts owed to them. A single agreement includes both a composition and an extension if it provides for the debtor to pay less than was originally due over a longer period than was originally planned.

Advantages and Disadvantages of Composition   From a debtor's viewpoint, the major advantage of a composition with creditors is that the debtor can retain his property rather than having to give it up at once, as is required under most other debtor relief arrangements. Other advantages are that by not declaring bankruptcy (which is the main alternative to composition), the debtor (1) leaves the bankruptcy option open for possible use at a later time and (2) avoids the stigma associated with bankruptcy.

To creditors, the main advantage of a composition is that because the procedure is relatively simple and does not generate court costs, trustees' fees, and other administrative expenses, more money is available for payment of debts than is available under other arrangements. This advantage is especially important to unsecured creditors since, as discussed later in this chapter, they often receive little or nothing in a bankruptcy proceeding.

The major disadvantage of a composition arrangement is that unless all the debtor's creditors accept and sign the agreement, nonassenting creditors can cause problems. For example, nonassenting unsecured creditors might be able to force the debtor into bankruptcy (see 31:7). In addition, although composition is theoretically available to any debtor, creditors are more receptive to it if the debtor is a business that can be expected to continue as the creditors' customer.

Validity and Effect of Composition Agreement   At least two creditors must sign a composition agreement since the creditors' promise to each other that each will abide by the agreement (for their mutual benefit) constitutes the consideration for it. Perhaps the most important requirement of a valid composition agreement is that all the parties must act in good faith. All signing creditors need not be treated equally, but the treatment of each one must be disclosed and agreed to by all. Thus, for example, if the debtor secretly agrees to give a special advantage to one creditor, the agreement cannot be enforced against the other creditors.

A valid composition agreement is binding (1) on all the signing creditors, between themselves, and (2) between the debtor and each of those creditors. The debts covered by the agreement are discharged as soon as the agreement has been performed, and any new promise by the debtor to pay more on one of those debts requires new consideration. A composition agreement can also be binding on a creditor who, while not having signed the agreement, accepted his share of payments made under it.

EXAMPLE
Pierce, Lynch, and Fenner are Bean's creditors. All four parties prepare a composition agreement that provides for the satisfaction of the debts owed to Pierce, Lynch, and Fenner at the rate of 75 cents on the dollar. At the last minute Fenner decides not to sign the agreement, but Bean pays him in accordance with the agreement anyway, and Fenner keeps that payment. The debt owed to Fenner is now considered to be fully satisfied, and Fenner cannot sue to recover the unpaid part (25 percent) of the original debt owed to him.

31:4   Assignment for Creditors

An insolvent debtor might wish to avoid bankruptcy even though he is not able to persuade enough of his creditors to agree to a workable composition arrangement. An option that might be available to this debtor is an *assignment for creditors*, also known as an assignment for the benefit of creditors. In essence, a debtor wishing to make an assignment for creditors transfers all or much of his property to another person, who is called the *trustee*. The trustee then liquidates the property (converts it to cash by selling it) and distributes the cash among the debtor's creditors.

Comparison with Composition Arrangement   An assignment for creditors is similar to a composition arrangement in that it usually allows creditors to receive more than they would in a bankruptcy case. However, it differs from a composition in a number of ways. Significant distinctions are that (1) the assent of all or most creditors is not required, (2) an assignment is a sufficient ground for the debtor's involuntary bankruptcy (see 31:7), and (3) debts are usually satisfied only to the extent of the payments actually made to creditors.

Governing Law   Assignments for creditors developed under the English common law. They are now governed by statute in a number of states, although common-law assignments are also permitted in some of those states. Where a choice exists, most assignments are of the common-law type because they are usually simpler, quicker, and cheaper than statutory assignments. Common-law assignments also impose fewer restrictions on the debtor. For example, a typical state statute (1) requires a detailed disclosure of the debtor's assets and business dealings, (2) limits the choice of the trustee, (3) states how creditors are to be notified and must present their claims, and (4) governs the distributions to the creditors.

Procedure   A debtor who wishes to make an assignment for creditors prepares a written instrument. Among other things, this instrument (1) designates the trustee; (2) describes the property being assigned; (3) identifies the creditors and debts; and (4) within any applicable statutory limits, instructs the trustee as to how distributions to creditors are to be made.

In practice, the trustee is often one of the debtor's creditors. The property that the debtor can assign to the trustee is any property that the debtor could legally sell or give away. Ordinarily, the debtor assigns all of his nonexempt property, although he can assign exempt property as well. The debtor can, of course, assign only whatever interest he has in his property. If, for example, a creditor holds a lien covering some of the property, that lien is usually not affected by the assignment.

 UCC § 9-301 provides a major exception to the above rule concerning lienholders. A perfected security interest under Article 9 is enforceable against the trustee, consistent with the rule. However, the trustee's rights, in his capacity as trustee, are superior to those of someone holding an unperfected interest.[1]

EXAMPLE
Jean operates a beauty salon, and Zenith Corporation is one of her creditors. Jean grants Zenith a security interest covering some of her equipment, and Zenith does not take the steps required to perfect its interest. Jean then makes an assignment for creditors, and the property transferred to the trustee includes the equipment

---

[1]The perfection of security interests under UCC Article 9 is discussed in Chapter 28. The priority or ranking of different claims to the same property is discussed in Chapter 29.

covered by the security interest. If Zenith had perfected its interest, the trustee would take the equipment subject to that interest. Since Zenith did not perfect, however, its rights in the equipment are now subordinate to the trustee's rights. For all practical purposes, Zenith has lost its lien.

Once an assignment has been made, the trustee ordinarily liquidates the property and distributes the cash. Administrative expenses (including the trustee's fee) are paid first, and claims against the debtor for taxes are paid next. The remaining cash is available for distribution to the creditors. Secured creditors must normally be paid first. In a common-law assignment, the assignment document can specify the order and extent of each unsecured creditor's participation in the distribution. All unsecured creditors must be treated equally under a typical assignment for creditors statute.

Validity of Assignment   An assignment for creditors generally does not take effect until the trustee and at least some of the debtor's creditors have consented to it. Trustee consent is rarely a problem since the debtor usually obtains it before making the assignment. As for creditors, they are presumed to have consented to the assignment. This means that if an assignment is otherwise valid, it will take effect unless all or at least most of the creditors object to it.

The basic requirement of a valid assignment for creditors is that the debtor act in good faith. In particular, the debtor must not act with intent to hinder or defraud his creditors.

EXAMPLE
Dawes, an insolvent debtor, indicates to his creditors that he is assigning all his nonexempt property to a trustee, for the creditors' benefit. In fact, Dawes only assigns some of that property, and he conceals the remainder of it. Dawes has acted fraudulently, and the assignment can be set aside by a court if one of the creditors applies for that relief.

Effect of Assignment   After an assignment for creditors becomes effective, the debtor cannot revoke it, and he has no further interest in the assigned property. Because of this lack of interest, creditors cannot levy on or garnish the property; as discussed in Chapter 30, attachment, garnishment, and execution are available only with respect to property owned by or owed to the debtor.

Unfortunately for the debtor, an assignment for creditors discharges only those debts that are paid in full by the trustee. Thus, the debtor can emerge with some of his debts untouched and others merely reduced in amount. It is for this reason that assignments for creditors are used primarily by corporations; after all its property has been assigned, a corporation is an empty shell, and its remaining debts are uncollectible.[2]

---

[2]The immunity of shareholders from corporate debts is discussed in Chapter 45.

Bankruptcy

31:5 Introduction to Bankruptcy

The term *bankruptcy* is commonly used to describe what is actually insolvency. However, it is more accurate to define bankruptcy as a statutory procedure by which (1) a debtor places his assets under a court's control, after which (2) either the assets are sold for the benefit of creditors or a plan for the debtor's financial rehabilitation is prepared and executed, and (3) the debtor can be discharged from liability on all or some of his unpaid debts.

Governing Law   The United States Constitution (Article I, § 8) grants to Congress the power "to establish . . . uniform laws on the subject of Bankruptcies throughout the United States." The first modern federal bankruptcy act was enacted in 1898. The 1898 act was amended from time to time, and it remains the law today as to bankruptcy cases commenced before October 1, 1979. In 1978 the 1898 act was replaced by the current Bankruptcy Code (11 USC §§ 101 et seq.).

Overview of Bankruptcy Code   The Bankruptcy Code is divided into eight chapters, numbered 1 through 15 (odd numbers only). Chapters 1, 3, and 5 contain general provisions, most of which apply to all bankruptcy cases. Of the remaining five chapters, the important ones for present purposes are Chapters 7, 11, and 13, each of which concerns a different type of bankruptcy case. The distinction between the coverage of these three chapters is discussed throughout the remainder of this part of the book. However, a brief description of the three different types of bankruptcy cases here will make the later discussion easier to understand.

Chapter 7 (liquidation):   Chapter 7 covers what is known as straight bankruptcy. Distinctive features of a Chapter 7 case are that (1) the debtor in effect washes his hands of his financial problems by turning them over to a court and (2) creditors seek payment of their claims primarily from assets that the debtor already has, rather than from the debtor's future earnings. In a Chapter 7 case, the debtor's nonexempt assets are taken from him and liquidated, after which the creditors are paid to the extent possible from the fund created by the *liquidation*. The bankruptcy court can then order that many of the debtor's debts are discharged, even if all the creditors have not been paid. The large majority of all bankruptcy cases are Chapter 7 ones.

Chapter 11 (reorganization):   Chapter 11 involves the reorganization and financial rehabilitation of business debtors. It is intended to be attractive to a financially troubled business at a time when effective reorganization of the business is still possible. The business debtor in a Chapter 11 case usually retains possession of its assets. A key feature of a Chapter 11 case is the preparation of a *rehabilitation plan*, which is done under the court's supervision. The plan provides for the continued operation of the business and the payment of all or at least some of its debts over an extended period. Thus, the primary source of payments to creditors is the debtor's future income.

Chapter 13 (adjustment of debts of individual with regular income):   Chapter 13 is somewhat the same as Chapter 11. However, it applies only to individual debtors who have limited debts and a regular source of income, and its focus is on getting an individual back on his financial feet rather than salvaging a business. As in a Chapter 11 case, a key feature of a Chapter 13 case is the preparation of a rehabilitation plan by which all or some of the debtor's creditors will be paid, primarily out of the debtor's future income. From the debtor's viewpoint, an attractive feature of Chapter 13 is that if the debtor makes all the payments required under the plan, the court can order the discharge of more of his debts than can be ordered discharged in a Chapter 7 case.

31:6   Bankruptcy Courts and Officers; Creditors and Other Interested Parties

A bankruptcy case is heard by and carried through under the supervision of a bankruptcy judge. Each federal judicial district has a separate bankruptcy court, just as each district has its own federal district court.

 During the course of a bankruptcy case, the court (judge) issues many orders that affect one or more persons who are interested in the case. The Bankruptcy Code provides for the issuance of many of these orders "after notice and a hearing," but the hearing requirement is somewhat misleading. While advance notice to the parties must be given before any such order can be issued, an actual hearing generally need not be held unless a party requests it.

Trustees   A trustee carries out much of the actual administration of most bankruptcy cases. A trustee, who is the representative of the bankruptcy estate (see 31:9), is required in Chapter 7 and Chapter 13 cases. A trustee is not required in a Chapter 11 case, although one can be appointed. If there is no trustee in a Chapter 11 case, the debtor remains in possession of the estate and is referred to as a *debtor in possession.*

The trustee (or a debtor in possession) has many powers. For example, he can sue and be sued and, with the court's approval, can hire attorneys, accountants, and other professionals to assist him as needed. The trustee's fee and the fees of others hired by the trustee in that capacity are paid out of the estate. Since these payments are made before any creditors can be paid (see 31:14), the fees reduce the amount that the creditors will eventually receive.

Creditors   Under the Bankruptcy Code a creditor is a person or entity (including a government entity such as the Internal Revenue Service) holding against the debtor a claim that arose before what is known in a bankruptcy case as the "order for relief" (see 31:7). Persons not falling within this definition are not "creditors" under the Bankruptcy Code, even though they have valid claims against the estate. An example of a "noncreditor" is a person who sells goods or services to the trustee after the order for relief; his claim falls within the category of administrative expenses which, as discussed in 31:14, are paid before many other claims.

Committees In a Chapter 7 case the creditors can (although they need not) elect a committee of three to eleven unsecured creditors to consult with and make recommendations to the trustee. The purpose of the committee is to ease communications between the debtor, the trustee, and the creditors. In a Chapter 11 case there must be at least one committee of unsecured creditors, and the court appoints it. Additional committees are also permitted, to represent various creditor interests.

Custodians Another class of persons recognized in the Bankruptcy Code is referred to collectively as *custodians*. A custodian is someone (other than the debtor) who has possession of all or most of the debtor's property. An example is the trustee under an assignment for creditors (see 31:4). A custodian must usually deliver the property to the bankruptcy trustee, although the court can allow the custodian to remain in possession if that would better serve the creditors' interests.

Parties in Interest The term *party in interest* refers to any person, group, or entity having an interest in a bankruptcy case. The debtor, the trustee, all creditors, and creditors' committees are all parties in interest.

31:7 Commencement of Bankruptcy Case

A bankruptcy case is commenced by filing a petition with the bankruptcy court, specifying the particular chapter (Chapter 7, 11, or 13) under which relief is requested. The case can be commenced either voluntarily or involuntarily. A voluntary case is one in which the debtor files the petition. In an involuntary case, the petition is filed by one or more creditors.

In a voluntary case, the filing of the petition constitutes the order for relief. In an involuntary case the order for relief, if any, comes later on, after the court has decided not to dismiss the case (see 31:8).

Eligible Debtors Whether relief under a particular chapter of the Bankruptcy Code is available to a given debtor depends on that debtor's status. With the exception of insurance companies, banks, and several other specific businesses, any person can be a debtor under Chapters 7 or 11. The term "person" in this sense means an individual, a partnership, or a corporation. Thus, for example, a sole proprietorship (unincorporated business conducted by an individual) cannot file under either chapter, although the proprietor can file as an individual.

Eligibility for Chapter 13 relief is more restricted. The relief is available only to individuals other than stockbrokers or commodity brokers. The individual (or couple, if a husband and wife file together) must have less than $100,000 in unsecured debts and less than $350,000 in secured debts. In addition, the individual must have a regular source of income that is large enough to allow a meaningful payment to creditors under a Chapter 13 plan.

EXAMPLE
Until recently, John earned $125,000 per year as a business executive. He is currently unemployed, however, and the prospects for a new job comparable to his old one are poor. Mary, his wife, has never worked outside their home and has no marketable skills. John and Mary's unsecured debt is $75,000 and their secured debt is $357,000. John and Mary cannot file under Chapter 13. Not only is their secured indebtedness too high, but they also lack a regular source of income. Instead, John and Mary must file under Chapter 7.

Involuntary Cases An involuntary bankruptcy case can be commenced only under Chapter 7 or 11, and against an eligible debtor. There are, however, several restrictions as to allowable debtors in addition to those discussed above. For example, due to the cyclical nature of the farming industry, an involuntary petition cannot be filed against a farmer. There are also restrictions as to the creditors who can file an involuntary petition. If the debtor has 12 or more different creditors, any three or more creditors who together hold unsecured claims of at least $5,000 can file. If there are less than 12 creditors, any one creditor who has an unsecured claim of at least $5,000 can file. In determining whether there are fewer than 12 creditors, creditors who are the debtor's employees or are insiders (persons or entities closely related to the debtor) are not counted.

EXAMPLE
Washington Corporation is indebted to Adams, Jefferson, Madison, and nine others, one of whom, Polk, is the president of Washington Corporation. Since Polk is an insider, he would not be counted as a creditor for filing purposes. Therefore, an involuntary petition can be filed by less than three of the creditors. The unsecured debts owed to the named creditors other than Polk are as follows: Adams is owed $6,000, Jefferson $4,000, and Madison $2,000. Adams can file alone, and Jefferson and Madison can file together. If it is only Jefferson who wants to force Washington into bankruptcy, Jefferson must persuade one or more other creditors holding at least $1,000 in unsecured claims to join him on the petition.

 Even though a petition for involuntary bankruptcy has been filed, the debtor can continue to use, acquire, and dispose of his property until the court orders otherwise. The court can, however, appoint a temporary trustee if that is necessary to preserve the debtor's property.

As mentioned earlier, the order for relief in an involuntary case comes after the filing of the petition. The debtor can oppose the petition by filing an answer to it. If no answer is filed, the court orders relief under Chapter 7 or 11, as requested in the petition. If the debtor does file an answer, the court must hold a hearing to determine whether either of two prescribed grounds for involuntary bankruptcy exists. The first ground is that the debtor is "generally not paying" his debts as they become due. The other ground is that, within 120 days before the petition was filed, a custodian was appointed or took charge of all or most of the debtor's property. For example, if an involuntary petition is filed on July 1, 1983, and it is shown that on April 16, 1983, the debtor made an assignment for creditors (see 31:4), the court can order relief.

 If neither ground for involuntary bankruptcy is shown to exist in the hearing on an involuntary petition, the court can order the petitioning creditors to pay the debtor for legal expenses and a reasonable attorney's fee. In addition, any petitioner who is found to have acted in bad faith (with evil intent toward the debtor) can be ordered to pay damages to the debtor.

31:8   Dismissal of Bankrupcy Case; Conversion to Different Chapter

The bankruptcy court has jurisdiction over all matters arising in or related to bankrupcy cases. The court is not required to accept that jurisdiction in any given case, however. Instead, it can dismiss the petition. For example, if a debtor is negotiating an out-of-court settlement with most of his creditors and there are only several dissenting creditors who have filed a petition, the court might dismiss the petition on the ground that the parties' interests would be better served in that way. A bankruptcy case can also be dismissed "for cause." For example, the court can dismiss a Chapter 13 or voluntary Chapter 7 case because of the debtor's unreasonable delays or because the debtor failed to pay required legal fees. Among the prescribed grounds for dismissal of a Chapter 11 case is a continuing loss to or reduction of the estate (see 31:9), coupled with no reasonable likelihood that the business debtor can be financially rehabilitated.

Generally, the dismissal of a case operates to return everything to its status before the case was commenced. For example, if a custodian has delivered property to the trustee and the case is dismissed, that property is returned to the custodian. If the trustee has avoided a creditor's lien or prepetition transfer (see 31:12), the lien or transfer is reinstated.

Conversion to Different Chapter   A case filed under one chapter of the Bankruptcy Code can often be converted to a case under a different chapter. Possible conversions are discussed below. Note that some conversions are voluntary while others are involuntary.

Chapter 13 case: The debtor has the right to convert a Chapter 13 case to a Chapter 7 case. Generally, the court can order conversion to Chapter 11 on request by a party in interest, after notice and a hearing. Also, the court has the right to order conversion to Chapter 7 if that would be in the best interest of the creditors and the estate.

Chapter 11 case: The debtor can convert a Chapter 11 case to a Chapter 7 one if two requirements are met. First, the debtor must be a debtor in possession. Second, if the case was originally begun under Chapter 11, it must be a voluntary case; if it was converted to Chapter 11, that conversion must have been at the debtor's request. The court can order conversion to Chapter 7 if that would be in the best interest of the creditors and the estate.

Chapter 7 case: If a Chapter 7 case was originally filed under that chapter, the debtor has the right to convert it to a Chapter 11 or 13 case. On request of a party in interest, and after notice and a hearing, the court can convert a Chapter 7 case to Chapter 11, but not to Chapter 13 unless the debtor requests it.

 A debtor cannot waive his right to convert a Chapter 7 case to one under Chapter 11 or 13, and any waiver he attempts or is persuaded to make cannot be enforced.

31:9   The Bankruptcy Estate; Exemptions

The bankruptcy estate is automatically created on the commencement of a bankruptcy case. It consists of all property and property interests that the debtor owned at the time of commencement. Among the many types of property or property interests included in the estate are (1) real property, and liens on real property, such as a mortgage held by the debtor as mortgagor; (2) unpaid wages; (3) tangible personal property; (4) rights to sue other people; (5) interests in patents or trademarks; and (6) the right to a tax refund.

It is immaterial that a specific property item is covered by a lien or is only partly owned by the debtor. For example, if a debtor and his brother are equal co-owners of a house on which there is a mortgage (see Chapter 35), the debtor's half-interest in the house is included in the estate. Also included is any property that the estate, rather than the debtor, acquires after the case commences. For example, if a bankruptcy petition is filed on August 1 and the estate includes corporate stock, dividends paid on the stock after August 1 go to the estate. In addition, the estate includes (1) all property that is delivered to the trustee by a custodian, (2) all property that the trustee obtains through exercise of his power to avoid prepetition transfers (see 31:12), and (3) some property that the debtor acquires after filing the petition.

Exemptions   A basic purpose of the Bankruptcy Code is to give debtors a fresh start. An individual debtor can retain basic necessities by filing a list of them that he claims to be exempt. Each listed item automatically becomes exempt unless a party in interest objects, in which event the court determines the exempt status of that item. Once property is exempt, it is not subject to creditors' claims with respect to most debts arising before the case was commenced.

Any individual debtor can claim available exemptions under *both* general state law (see Chapter 30) and federal law other than the Bankruptcy Code. Examples of property that is exempt under federal nonbankruptcy law are Social Security benefits and veterans' benefits. Some debtors have the option of claiming instead the exemptions set forth in the Bankruptcy Code itself. These exemptions include the following:

- Up to $7,500 for debtor's equity (value, less total amount of liens) in homestead (main residence)
- Up to $1,200 for motor vehicle

- Up to $200 per item for household furnishings and goods, clothing, appliances, books, and many other consumer goods (property held for personal, family, or household use)
- Up to $400, plus unused portion of homestead exemption, for *any* property
- Up to $750 for professional books or tools of trade
- Reasonable alimony or child-support payments received by debtor

For purposes of the federal exemption scheme, the value of any property item is that item's fair market value.

The Bankruptcy Code's $7,500 homestead exemption is low by current standards. Other parts of the federal exemption scheme, notably the $200-per-item exemption for many consumer goods, are quite generous. Obviously, a debtor who has a choice will select the exemption scheme that benefits him the most. To give the states some control over exemptions claimed by their citizens, the Bankruptcy Code provides that each state can forbid its citizens from selecting the federal scheme. A number of states have enacted or are considering enacting this prohibition.

If a husband and wife file a bankruptcy petition together, *each* spouse can exercise the exemption right as to his or her property. Unless state law bars selection of the Bankruptcy Code exemption scheme, one spouse can select the Bankruptcy Code scheme while the other claims exemptions under state law and federal non-bankruptcy law.

Debtor's Power to Avoid Certain Liens   An individual debtor might own property that he could claim to be exempt if the property were not covered by a lien. For example, before the bankruptcy case was commenced, a creditor might have sued the debtor and obtained a judicial lien[3] on property that, while not exempt under state law, could be claimed as exempt under the Bankruptcy Code. The debtor can avoid (have set aside) any judicial lien on that property. He can also avoid any nonpossessory, non-purchase-money security interest[4] covering certain items if the lien of the security interest prevents the property from being claimed as exempt. This right applies to professional books, tools of trade, and prescribed health aids. As the following case illustrates, the right also applies to many (but not all) types of consumer goods.

---

[3]A judicial lien is an interest in property arising from judicial process. An example is an attachment lien, discussed in Chapter 30.

[4]A security interest is nonpossessory if the debtor, rather than the creditor, is in possession of the property. The interest is a non-purchase-money one if it was *not* acquired (1) in connection with the sale of the property covered by the interest and (2) by either (a) the lender whose loan was used to buy the property or (b) the seller. For example, if a person buying a new car on credit is required to give the car dealer one security interest covering the car and another covering the person's household furniture and appliances, both security interests are nonpossessory, but only the interest covering the furniture and appliances is a non-purchase-money one.

Re Ruppe
3 BR 60, 1 CBC2d 479, 5 BCD 1404
(United States Bankruptcy Court, Colorado, 1980)

[Ruppe, the debtor, filed a petition under Chapter 7. Ruppe's property included a movie camera, a slide projector, and a movie projector, all of which was part of the property covered by a nonpossessory, non-purchase-money security interest held by GFC, a creditor. Ruppe has sought to avoid GFC's lien.]

Keller, Bankruptcy Judge.

*   *   *

There is, in fact, a genuine dispute as to whether the camera and two projectors constitute household furnishings or appliances within the meaning of [the Bankruptcy Code]. The new Bankruptcy Code does not contain any definitions of any of these items which is helpful to the Court. The [code language] is significant in that it provides the debtor may avoid the fixing of lien on an interest of the debtor in:

"household furnishings, household goods, wearing apparel, appliances, books, animals, crops, musical instruments, or jewelry that are held primarily for the personal, family, or household use of the debtor or a dependent of the debtor." . . .

It seems clear to the Court that household goods and household furnishings would not include a camera or a projector within the definitions there set forth if taken in the context of the list of goods which are held to be exempt. Certainly, under many definitions of household furnishings and goods, appliances would be considered to be included. They have been specifically set forth in this statute, indicating a narrow definition for household goods and household furnishings as therein used. The same might be true of musical instruments under some modern, liberal definitions of exempt household goods. . . .

The Court can only conclude that the definition of household goods must be given a narrow construction here. The construction most properly applied would be those items necessary to the functioning of the household. . . .

[Avoidance of lien denied.]

An additional important right that an individual debtor has in a Chapter 7 case is what is known as the redemption right. In essence, if consumer goods have been (1) exempted or (2) abandoned by the trustee (see 31:14), the debtor can avoid a lien on the property by paying the lienholder the value of the property. Thus, for example, in the *Ruppe* case, above, the court determined the value of the camera and projectors to be $305 and ordered that Ruppe could redeem those items by paying that amount to GFC.

 A debtor's waiver of his right to avoid a lien or security interest, or to redeem property, is unenforceable in a bankruptcy case. Also unenforceable under some circumstances is a debtor's waiver of his right to claim an allowable exemption.

31:10   Administration of Bankruptcy Estate

After a bankruptcy case has commenced, the debtor must file a list of his creditors with the court. Usually, he must also file a schedule showing his assets and debts, and a statement about his financial affairs. The list and schedule are used as the basis for a notice concerning the case. The notice is sent to each creditor. After notice has been given, the trustee schedules a meeting that each creditor can attend in person or by sending an agent, such as an attorney. There are frequently other meetings as well. For example, an unsecured creditors' committee in a Chapter 7 case might meet informally with the trustee to discuss the administration of the estate.

The debtor is required to cooperate with the trustee in all respects. Thus, the debtor must surrender to the trustee all estate property and related documents, and he must appear at the meeting of creditors. At the meeting, the debtor must answer relevant questions directed to him by the trustee or by any creditor. If an individual debtor fails to cooperate as required, the court can deny granting him a discharge (see 31:18).

Duties of Trustee   The trustee or debtor in possession must disclose any information about the estate and its administration that a party in interest requests, unless the court orders otherwise. The trustee (but not a debtor in possession) must also investigate certain aspects of the debtor's affairs. The scope of this investigation is limited to financial affairs in Chapter 7 and most Chapter 13 cases, but it is broader in a Chapter 11 case and a Chapter 13 case in which the debtor conducts a business.

One of the trustee's primary duties in a Chapter 7 case is to collect all the estate property and liquidate it. The debtor's duty to give up property in his possession has already been mentioned. To assist the trustee in obtaining other property, the Bankruptcy Code requires that most estate property in someone else's possession when the petition is filed be delivered to the trustee. If the property cannot be delivered, then its value must be. This requirement extends not only to custodians (who hold all or most of the debtor's property), but also to others holding any property of value. Generally, any debt owed to the estate must also be paid to the trustee. The trustee also has two years after the filing of the petition in which to exercise any right to sue that has passed to the estate. In addition, the court can order an attorney or accountant who has information about the debtor's property or financial affairs to disclose certain of that information to the trustee.

In a Chapter 11 or 13 case the trustee does not usually liquidate the estate property; the purpose of the proceeding is to rehabilitate the debtor. However, the trustee must obtain possession of the property in the manner discussed above if he is to assess and administer the estate properly.

Trustee's Use of Estate Property   The court can authorize the temporary continuation of the debtor's business in a Chapter 7 case. In contrast, in a Chapter 11 or 13 case the debtor's business can be continued *unless* the court orders otherwise. A trustee or debtor in possession who is continuing a business has the right to use, sell, or lease most estate property in the ordinary course of that business. This right is superior to any provision in a contract or lease that would cause a debtor's interest in property to be terminated or modified because of the debtor's being the subject of a bankruptcy proceeding. This means that a contract or lease provision of this type is unenforceable against a trustee or debtor in possession.

31:11   Automatic Stay; Relief from Stay

A basic debtor protection device provided for in the Bankruptcy Code is that as soon as a bankruptcy petition is filed, a number of acts and proceedings involving the debtor or his property are automatically stayed.[5]

Acts and Proceedings Stayed   Included among the acts and proceedings that are stayed by the filing of a bankruptcy petition are:

- Commencement or continuation of any civil action against the debtor
- Enforcement against the debtor or estate property of any judgment obtained before the bankruptcy petition was filed
- Any act to obtain possession of estate property
- Any act to create, perfect (see Chapter 28), or enforce any lien against estate property
- Any act to collect a claim against the debtor if the claim arose before the petition was filed
- In a Chapter 13 case, most efforts to collect on any debt for consumer goods from a codebtor (other person, often a family member, who is also liable on the debt)

The purpose of the *automatic stay* is to give the debtor a breathing spell from his creditors by stopping all their efforts to collect from or harass him. Bear in mind, though, that some acts or proceedings are *not* covered by the automatic stay. These include (1) the commencement or continuation of a criminal prosecution against the debtor, (2) the collection of alimony or child support from other than estate property (such as from the debtor's wages), and (3) the perfection of certain security interests within the ten-day grace period provided by UCC § 9-301 (see 29:4).

Relief from Stay   An automatic stay is terminated by dismissal of the bankruptcy case. Also, any party in interest can request the court to grant relief from a stay. The court has 30 days in which to act on the request, and it can hold a hearing on the matter. If, within that 30-day period, the court does not order the stay to be continued, the stay terminates as to the requesting party.

The following case illustrates that termination of the stay is not the only relief

---

[5]A stay is a postponement of an action or proceeding. Used as a verb the word means putting a stop to further proceedings, usually temporarily. For example, if a criminal defendant is sentenced to death and his execution is stayed, the state is temporarily barred from carrying out the sentence.

available to a party in interest. Note especially the court's power to grant relief with respect to a secured claim that is found to be inadequately protected.

Re A.L.S., Inc.
3 BR 107, 1 CBC2d 516, 6 BCD 4
(United States Bankruptcy Court, E.D. Pennsylvania, 1980)

[A.L.S., the debtor, failed to pay the rent on the leased premises where it conducted its business. Because of that default, City Stores, the landlord, declared the lease to be terminated as of November 20, 1979. However, A.L.S. filed a petition under Chapter 11 of the Bankruptcy Code on that date, thus staying City Stores' efforts to obtain possession of the premises. City Stores seeks termination of the stay.]

Goldhaber, Bankruptcy Judge.

*   *   *

This case involves relief from the automatic stay and is governed by [a section of the Bankruptcy Code that] provides that:

"(d) On request of a party in interest and after notice and a hearing, the court shall grant relief from the stay . . . , such as by terminating, annulling, modifying, or conditioning such stay—

"(1) for cause, including the lack of adequate protection of an interest in property of such party in interest; or

"(2) with respect to a stay of an act against property, if—

"(A) the debtor does not have an equity in such property; and

"(B) such property is not necessary to an effective reorganization."

Because we find that the leased premises are necessary to an effective reorganization of the debtor and because we will provide for the adequate protection of City Stores' interest in the premises, we will deny the request for relief.

In the instant case, the debtor has only one place of business (those premises which City Stores seeks to repossess), and the debtor's [Chapter 11 plan] apparently contemplates the continuation of the debtor's business at that site. Consequently, we find that the success of the plan depends upon the debtor's possession of the premises and that the premises are necessary to an effective reorganization of the debtor. Therefore, since subsection [(d)(2)(B) of the above statute] is not present in this case, City Stores' complaint seeking relief from the stay cannot be predicated on that subsection.

To obtain relief from the stay under subsection [(d)(1)], some cause must be shown why relief from the stay should be granted. Such cause may be established by proof that the party seeking relief from the stay does not have adequate protection of its interest in the property. This is the position of City Stores and is based on evidence that the debtor has failed to pay any rent or other charges since July of 1979 and that the security deposit, which has been applied to the unpaid rent and charges, is almost, if not completely, depleted. Consequently, City Stores argues, it is without any protection for its interest in the property.

We believe, however, that the instant case is an appropriate case for the provision of adequate protection by the court [under the Bankruptcy Code provision that] provides in part:

"When adequate protection is required . . . of an interest of an entity in property, such adequate protection may be provided by

"(1) requiring the trustee to make periodic payments to such entity, to the extent that the stay . . . results in a decrease in the value of such entity's interest in such property."

Pursuant to that section, we will order the debtor to pay all rent and charges as they may hereafter become due according to the lease. We will further order the debtor to deposit with City Stores the sum of $6,250 (representing approximately three months' rent) to provide City Stores with some security in the event that the debtor defaults in the payment of the above rent and charges. In addition, our denial of City Stores' request for relief from the stay will be without prejudice to its right to renew its request should the debtor default at any time in paying the above rent and charges. We conclude that these orders will provide .City Stores with adequate protection of its interest in the premises. . . .

 The court decides whether a particular proposal for modifying a stay or providing other relief will give the party in interest adequate protection. However, although it was not pointed out in the *A.L.S.* case, it is the trustee (or debtor in possession) who actually submits the proposal to the court. A failure to submit a proposal can result in the court's granting broader relief to the petitioning creditor than it might otherwise have done.

31:12   Bankruptcy Trustee's Avoidance Powers

One of the most significant powers held by the trustee in a bankruptcy case is the power to avoid several types of prepetition transactions (transactions that occurred before the bankruptcy petition was filed) that affect the debtor's property. The *avoidance powers* extend to transactions that were both voluntary and involuntary from the debtor's viewpoint. The powers exist to allow the trustee to nullify the effect of transactions that, on the eve of bankruptcy, operated to dissipate the estate. Among the general types of transactions that the trustee can avoid are (1) transactions that certain other creditors could avoid and (2) *preferential transfers.* Note that the trustee does not exercise his avoidance power by merely declaring that he is avoiding a given transaction. Instead, he must commence a separate proceeding by filing a complaint for that purpose with the bankruptcy court.

Transactions Avoidable by Other Creditors   11 USC § 544(a) is known as the strong-arm clause. Under it, the trustee is given the rights of several types of creditors, the most important being a creditor who has a judicial lien (such as an attachment lien, as discussed in 30:6) on the debtor's property on the date the bankruptcy petition was filed. There does not have to be an *actual* creditor or an actual lien in the case; the trustee's status is that of a hypothetical creditor. He is simply given whatever rights and powers a judicial lienholder would have under the governing state law. The strong-arm power is primarily intended to avoid prepetition transfers of unperfected security interests.

EXAMPLE

On September 1, Acme Corporation granted to Delta, one of Acme's creditors, a security interest covering Acme's inventory. On October 1, Acme filed a bankruptcy petition, and as of that date Delta had made no attempt to perfect its security interest. Since a judicial lien has priority over an unperfected security interest under state law, which is UCC Article 9 (see 29:3), the trustee can avoid the security interest, meaning that the interest is invalid against the trustee. The result would be the same if Delta had attempted to perfect its interest but had done so improperly.

Preferential Transfers (11 USC § 547)   In essence, a prepetition transfer is preferential if it gives the transferee an advantage over other creditors. The Bankruptcy Code gives the trustee the power to avoid certain prepetition transfers even if they were legally valid. This power, when exercised, promotes the equal treatment of creditors. Its existence is intended to discourage creditors from racing to the courthouse to dismember a debtor during his slide into bankruptcy. For example, a creditor is less likely to obtain an attachment lien against a debtor who is about to file a bankruptcy petition if the creditor knows that the trustee can avoid the attachment as a preferential transfer.

As the following case indicates, a transfer is avoidable as being preferential only if prescribed requirements are met. Note the court's discussion about (1) a debtor's persumed insolvency before a bankruptcy petition is filed and (2) the question of whether the act of perfecting a security interest is an avoidable transfer.

Re Butler
3 BR 182, 1 CBC2d 533, 6 BCD 32, 28 UCCRS 596
(United States Bankruptcy Court, E.D. Tennessee, 1980)

[Butler, the debtor, filed a bankruptcy petition on November 19, 1979. Earlier, Butler had granted a security interest in a bulldozer he owned to a creditor, the defendant. The creditor perfected its interest on November 1, 1979. The trustee, wishing to sell the bulldozer free of the creditor's lien, commenced a proceeding to avoid that lien.]

Kelly, Bankruptcy Judge.

*   *   *

It is the trustee's contention that defendant's perfection of its security interest just eighteen days before the filing of the bankruptcy case constitutes a preferential transfer and is voidable under [the Bankruptcy Code].

The code allows the trustee to recover transfers, either securing or paying antecedent debt, within a prescribed period of time before the bankruptcy case. It replaces [complex provisions of the 1898 act].

The six elements of a preference under [the Bankruptcy Code] are:

(1) a transfer of property of the debtor;
(2) to or for the benefit of a creditor;
(3) for or on account of an antecedent debt;
(4) made while the debtor was insolvent;
(5) made within 90 days before the date of the filing of a petition; and
(6) that enables the creditor to receive more than he would have received if the transfer had not been made and the case were a liquidation case under Chapter 7.

There was a requirement [in the 1898 act] that the creditor receiving the preference have reasonable cause to believe that the debtor was insolvent.

Congress in its wisdom has chosen to eliminate the reasonable-case-to-believe test from the ordinary preference situation. The goal of equality of distribution among creditors becomes paramount. Whether or not a preferred creditor had knowledge of the debtor's insolvency, with one exception which is not relevant in this proceeding, will no longer be relevant in a proceeding to avoid a preference.

Congress has simplified the trustee's burden in preference actions in another way. [The Bankruptcy Code] grants the trustee a presumption of insolvency during the 90 days before bankruptcy. Under [the 1898 act], proof of insolvency was always difficult. Reconstructing the debtor's books and records was never an easy matter. Yet it was unusual when a debtor was not insolvent for the 90 days before bankruptcy.

The presumption of insolvency in the Code recognizes this, but permits the creditor against whom the action is pending to come forward with evidence of solvency. . . .

Under [the Bankruptcy Code] a transfer is deemed to be made when it takes effect between the parties, if it is perfected no more than 10 days after it takes effect. If it is perfected more than 10 days after it takes effect, the transfer is deemed made when it is perfected. . . .

In the present proceeding the court finds that "transfer" of property of the debtor occurred within 90 days of the filing of the petition. It was for the benefit of defendant and involved an antecedent debt.

The creditor put on no proof to overcome the presumption of debtor's insolvency. The proof indicated, in fact, that debtor was insolvent. The proof further showed that in a Chapter 7 case the only asset for creditors will be the proceeds from the sale of the dozer. Defendant will receive a pro rata share. The "transfer" would enable the defendant to get all of the proceeds. This would be "more" than he would receive in a liquidation case under chapter 7.

From the proof and the entire record the court finds all six elements of a preference. The transfer will be *Avoided* and the trustee may sell the dozer free and clear of any claimed lien. [Court's emphasis.]

The Bankruptcy Code also lists various transfers that the trustee *cannot* avoid as being preferential. Several of these exceptions involve situations in which, because the debtor received something of value at the time of transfer, the estate suffered no net loss. Other exceptions exist because of the importance of certain creditor interests. For example, the debtor's payment of a debt incurred in the ordinary course of business is often not an avoidable preference if the debt was incurred no more than 45 days before the date of payment.

Limits on Avoidance Powers   The Bankruptcy Code includes some limits on the trustee's avoidance powers. First, the trustee must commence any proceeding to avoid a prepetition transaction (1) within two years after his appointment as trustee or (2) before the bankruptcy case is closed or dismissed, whichever is earlier. If the avoidance action succeeds and a second proceeding is needed to recover the property, the trustee has one year from that time, or until the bankruptcy case is closed or dismissed, in which to begin that proceeding.

A second limit on certain of the trustee's avoidance powers is that the powers are subject to any state law that, in effect, allows a grace period for the perfection of interests in property.

EXAMPLE

Abbott Corporation sells a piece of equipment to Costello Company on credit and reserves a security interest in the equipment. The equipment is delivered to Costello on July 10. UCC Article 9 provides that if Abbott perfects its interest by July 20, Abbott's interest is superior to that of a lien creditor whose lien arose between July 10 and the date of perfection (see 29:4). If Costello files a bankruptcy petition on July 13 and Abbott perfects its interest on July 19, the trustee cannot use the strong-arm clause to avoid the interest.

A third important limit on the trustee's avoidance powers concerns the right of one who sells goods to a debtor on credit to reclaim those goods if the debtor was insolvent when he received the goods. For example, UCC Article 2 gives the seller the right to reclaim under this circumstance, as long as he does so within ten days after the debtor received the goods. If, in addition to complying with the ten-day requirement, the seller demands reclamation in writing, the Bankruptcy Code allows the seller to reclaim the goods even though a bankruptcy petition concerning the debtor has been filed in the meantime.

Finally, although the trustee can generally recover the property involved after a transfer has been avoided, he cannot do so if the property has passed from the original transferee to one who, in essence, paid for the transfer to him and was unaware that the prior transfer could have been avoided by the trustee.

31:13 Creditors' Claims Under Bankruptcy Code

The Bankruptcy Code classifies creditors' claims as being either secured or unsecured. A claim can be secured only if the creditor holds a lien on property of the bankruptcy estate (see 31:9). Here, "lien" means a judicial lien, a statutory lien, or a security interest.[6] A given claim is considered to be secured *only* to the extent of the value of the property covered by the lien when the bankruptcy petition was filed.

EXAMPLE

A secured creditor is owed $100,000 by the debtor, but the value of the estate property covered by the security interest was only $60,000 when the debtor's bankruptcy petition was filed. As far as the bankruptcy case is concerned, the creditor has a secured claim for $60,000. The remaining $40,000 of the debt is treated as an unsecured claim.

It is possible for a lienholder's *entire* claim to be treated as an unsecured claim in a bankruptcy case. This situation occurs if the lien has been avoided. Recall that

---

[6]Judicial and statutory liens are discussed in Chapter 30. Security interests are discussed in Chapters 28 and 29 (personal property) and 35 (real property).

both the debtor (see 31:9) and the trustee (see 31:12) have the power to avoid certain liens.

Presentation and Allowance of Claims   After a bankruptcy proceeding has commenced, each creditor can present his claim against the estate by filing a document, known as a *proof of claim*, in which the claim is described. In a Chapter 11 case, the list of creditors filed by the debtor (see 31:10) is treated as a proof of claim covering most claims. If a creditor fails to file a proof of claim, the debtor can file one on the creditor's behalf; the debtor's reason for doing so is that otherwise the claim might not be discharged (see 31:18).

 In a Chapter 7 case there can be no distribution to a creditor who has not filed a proof of claim (or had one filed on his behalf). While filing is not required, a creditor should usually file in a Chapter 7 case unless there is no prospect of receiving a distribution from the estate.

Generally, only the holders of *allowed* claims can participate in distributions from the bankruptcy estate. An allowed claim is one that the court recognizes as being valid. Filing a proof of claim (or listing a claim in a Chapter 11 case) automatically leads to that claim being allowed unless a party in interest objects. Ordinarily, if there is an objection, the court holds a hearing on the matter. At the hearing the court determines the amount of the claim and allows or disallows the claim in whole or in part.

In deciding the allowability of a claim, the court is bound by a number of requirements. For example, the court must disallow most claims that are unforceable against the debtor, such as claims that are barred by the state statute of limitations. A claim must also be disallowed to the extent that it can be offset against a debt owed by the creditor to the debtor. Thus, for example, if Williams, the debtor in a bankruptcy case, owes Jensen $500, but Jensen owes Williams $100, Jensen's claim for $500 will be reduced to $400 before being allowed. Note that the allowance of a creditor's claim does not necessarily mean that the creditor will receive *any* payment, let alone payment of his entire claim. The allowance merely means that the creditor might receive something and, in effect, sets an upper limit on what he can receive.

31:14   Distributions Under Chapter 7

The stated policy of the Bankruptcy Code is to treat creditors equally, but examination of the rules governing distributions to creditors reveals the Orwellian nature of the equality: some creditors are clearly more equal than others. In a Chapter 7 case, secured claims must be satisfied first. Whatever remains in the estate is paid to unsecured creditors, but some types of unsecured claims must be paid before others.

Secured Claims   Recall that under bankruptcy law a claim is secured only to the extent of the value of the property covered by the lien (see 31:13). A secured claim—or the secured part of a claim—is fully satisfied in a bankruptcy case if the property covered by the lien is released to the lienholder or if the lienholder is allowed to pursue the nonbankruptcy remedies available to him under state law. The result is that a secured claim can have been satisfied before the distribution phase of a Chapter 7 case. For example, property of little value to the estate might have been abandoned to the lienholder.[7] Or, as discussed in 31:11, the lienholder might have been permitted to enforce his lien by way of relief from the automatic stay.

To the extent that the secured claims have not already been disposed of in the above or other, related ways, the first step in the Chapter 7 distribution process is settlement of those claims. Ordinarily, the trustee either delivers the property covered by the liens to the lienholding creditors or, more often, he sells the property and distributes the sale proceeds, less costs of the sale, to those creditors. When the trustee sells the property, he usually sells it free of the creditor's liens; the Bankruptcy Code allows him to do this under prescribed circumstances.

Unsecured Claims   The distribution to creditors holding unsecured claims would be simple if the assets remaining in the estate after the satisfaction of secured claims were merely divided among the unsecured creditors pro rata (in proportion to the amount of the creditors' claims). However, the Bankruptcy Code recognizes special circumstances that warrant exceptions to this policy. The exceptions are achieved primarily by means of a system of priorities. Under this system *all* higher ranking claims must be paid in full before anything can be paid on lower ranking claims.

The six types of priority claims, listed in their order of rank, are briefly described as follows:

- Administrative expenses
- Debts incurred after an involuntary petition was filed, but before the order for relief (see 31:7)
- Certain wages owed to the debtor's employees, up to $2,000 per employee
- Certain contributions to the debtor's employee benefit plans
- Prepetition deposits of money for the purchase or lease of undelivered consumer goods or services
- Federal, state, and local taxes

Another set of priorities governs the distribution of the money, if any, that is left in the estate after all priority unsecured claims have paid in full. Again, higher ranking claims are paid in full before lower ranking claims receive anything, and

---

[7]An example of property having little value to the estate is a machine that, although worth $1,500, is covered by a lien to secure a $2,000 debt. As discussed in the next paragraph of the text, since the lienholder would get the machine or the proceeds from its sale in any event, the trustee saves time and administrative expense by merely abandoning the machine (giving up the estate's interest in it), which allows the creditor to enforce its lien.

distributions are made pro rata for claims of a given rank if full payment cannot be made. The ranking under this final set of priorities is as follows, in the order listed:

- Allowed unsecured claims for which the creditors filed proofs of claim in time, or had acceptable excuses for filing late
- Allowed unsecured claims for which proofs of claim were filed late and without acceptable excuse
- Interest on claims already paid, for the period between the filing of the petition and the date of payment of the claims

The debtor is entitled to any money left over after all the above claims have been paid. As a practical matter, unsecured creditors whose claims are not entitled to priority usually receive little or nothing on their claims in a Chapter 7 case. Thus, there is almost never anything for the debtor.

31:15   Rehabilitation Plans Under Chapters 11 and 13, Generally

In a Chapter 11 or 13 case there can be a liquidation and distribution of estate assets as occurs in a Chapter 7 case. Usually, however, the intent in a Chapter 11 or 13 case is a restructuring of the debtor's finances so that creditors can be paid in full, or at least in part, over an extended period. The restructuring is done through a plan that governs the creditors' rights with respect to the debtor and his property. The goal in both a Chapter 11 and a Chapter 13 case is the creation of a plan that the court will confirm.

One of the purposes of a Chapter 11 plan is to allow the debtor to remain in business. The plan thus serves much the same function as a composition with creditors (see 31:3). While a composition arrangement requires the consent of almost all the creditors to be effective, a Chapter 11 plan can be confirmed even though a substantial number of creditors object to it.

Once a plan is confirmed, its terms bind all the creditors, not just the creditors who accepted the plan. Thus, the debtor is protected from harassment by the creditors. Unless the plan or confirmation order provides otherwise, the debtor gets all the estate property back at the time of confirmation. A Chapter 11 plan is executed by the debtor and by any entity (such as a new corporation) organized for the purpose of executing it. A Chapter 13 plan is usually executed by the trustee, with the debtor's cooperation. The court can order the debtor's employer to pay all or part of the debtor's wages to the trustee; the trustee then distributes the money in accordance with the plan. Under some circumstances, a confirmed plan under either Chapter 11 or Chapter 13 can be modified at a later time.

31:16   Chapter 11 Plans

During the 120 days after the order for relief in a Chapter 11 case, the debtor ordinarily has the exclusive right to propose a plan, which it does by filing the proposed plan with the court. However, *any* party in interest can file a plan under some circumstances, such as if a trustee has been appointed or if the debtor has not filed a plan within the 120-day period. After a plan is filed, its terms are disclosed to all the creditors, and their acceptance of the plan is then solicited.

Plan Requirements   A Chapter 11 plan must divide all the creditors' claims into classes, each class consisting of substantially similar claims. In a case involving many creditors, there can be many claims in some classes, but few claims, or perhaps only one claim, in other classes. On the other hand, in a case involving only a few creditors, there can be as many classes as there are claims if none of the claims are substantially similar.

The plan must specify which of the classes are "impaired" and which ones are not. In essence, a class is impaired unless the plan provides that the creditors holding the claims in that class will (1) be paid in full on their claims or (2) emerge from the bankruptcy proceeding with their legal and contractual rights unchanged.

A Chapter 11 plan is required to satisfy a number of requirements. It must, among other things:

- Specify how each impaired class will be treated
- Provide for equal treatment of all claims in each class (except as to any particular creditor who agrees to less favorable treatment)
- Provide adequate means for its execution
- Provide suitable treatment of priority claims (see 31:14), except as to a holder of a priority claim who agrees otherwise

Examples of adequate means by which a plan can provide for its execution are (1) the debtor's retention of all or part of the estate property, (2) the debtor's merger with another business entity, (3) sale of part of the estate property, and (4) distribution of estate property to persons holding liens on that property.

In addition to satisfying the mandatory Bankruptcy Code requirements, a Chapter 11 plan can include any provision that is appropriate under the facts of the case and is not inconsistent with the code. For example, the plan can impair or leave unimpaired *any* class of secured or unsecured claims.

Acceptance and Confirmation of Plan   If a Chapter 11 plan meets all the prescribed requirements and is accepted by all the creditors, the court will ordinarily confirm it, after notice and a hearing. However, it is rare that all creditors will accept the plan. Therefore, the Bankruptcy Code allows confirmation despite some creditors' nonacceptance of it if the plan meets two additional requirements. The first requirement concerns the plan's treatment of each nonaccepting creditor, and the second concerns the treatment of each nonaccepting impaired class.

To satisfy the first requirement mentioned above, the plan must satisfy what is known as the *best interest of creditors* test: each nonaccepting creditor must receive *no less* under the plan than he would receive in a Chapter 7 case involving the same debtor. Because of this requirement, a calculation of what the distributions under Chapter 7 would be (see 31:14) is almost always required.

As to the second requirement, it must first be pointed out that a class is treated as having accepted a plan if, of the creditors who vote at all, those holding at least two-thirds in amount and more than one-half in number of the allowed claims in that class vote for acceptance.

EXAMPLE

The claims in a given class, and the creditors holding those claims, are as follows: $600 (Groucho), $400 (Chico), $300 (Harpo), and $200 (Zeppo). If Groucho and Zeppo vote to accept a proposed Chapter 11 plan, Chico votes to reject it, and Harpo does not vote, the class has accepted the plan (two out of three voting claims voted to accept; $800 is two-thirds of $1,200).

The general rule is that a plan cannot be confirmed unless each class either accepts the plan or is unimpaired. There must always be acceptance by at least one class, but the Bankruptcy Code includes an exception to the general rule by providing for the "cram-down" of a plan (enforcement against unwilling creditors) that meets two additional requirements: (1) the plan must not "discriminate unfairly" against any nonaccepting impaired class and (2) it must be "fair and equitable" in its treatment of nonaccepting classes. The code includes various requirements that must be satisfied to meet the "fair and equitable" standard. As to a class of unsecured claims, for example, the plan can merely provide that no holders of claims junior to the claims of that class will receive anything. As to a class of secured claims, a plan can, in essence, allow the creditors to retain their liens and receive payments later on.

31:17   Chapter 13 Plans

A Chapter 13 case differs from a Chapter 11 case in a number of ways. For example, the focus is on getting an individual debtor back on his financial feet, rather than on salvaging a business that is in financial difficulty. The debtor files the proposed payment and rehabilitation plan; under no circumstances can creditors file a plan. There is no requirement that claims be divided into classes, and the consent of unsecured creditors is not required for confirmation of a plan.

Plan Requirements   If a Chapter 13 plan is to be confirmed, it must satisfy a number of requirements. Among the provisions that must be made in the plan are the following:

- Submission to the trustee's supervision and control of all or part of the debtor's future income, as necessary to execute the plan
- Full payment, by means of later cash payments, of all priority claims (see 31:14), except as any holder of a priority claim otherwise agrees
- If the plan classifies claims, equal treatment for each claim within a given class

- Repayment over not more than a three-year period, although the court can approve up to a five-year period

The Bankruptcy Code lists additional types of provisions that can, if desired, be included in a Chapter 13 plan. Thus, a plan can:

- Modify the rights of holders of all secured claims except those secured *only* by the debtor's principal residence
- Modify the rights of holders of all unsecured claims
- Provide for curing of a default and continuation of payments on a debt, such as a home mortgage, on which the last payment is due after termination of the plan
- Reject any executory contract or unexpired lease
- Provide for the payment of any claim from exempt property
- Provide for the redelivery of estate property to the debtor, either when the plan is confirmed or at a later time

Confirmation of Plan   Although there is no solicitation of acceptances of a Chapter 13 plan, unlike the procedure under Chapter 11, the court must hold a confirmation hearing. At the hearing any party in interest can object to confirmation, although it is only the secured creditors holding allowed claims who must accept the plan (or receive other treatment, as discussed below). The major requirements for confirmation of a plan are, briefly, that (1) the debtor pay all required legal fees; (2) the plan have been proposed in good faith; (3) the plan be such that, consistent with his duty to support dependents, the debtor should be able to make payments under and otherwise comply with the plan; and (4) the planned distributions to unsecured creditors are not less than what those creditors would receive under Chapter 7.

Requirement 4, above, suggests that unsecured creditors who would receive nothing under a Chapter 7 liquidation can be allotted nothing under a Chapter 13 plan. As the following case illustrates, however, a number of courts have interpreted the good-faith requirement (number 2, above) to require that a plan provide more than that. The case also points out the danger of a debtor's using Chapter 13 primarily as a vehicle for restructuring his secured debts.

Re Anderson
3 BR 160, 2 CBC2d 594, 6 BCD 73
(United States Bankruptcy Court, S.D.
California, 1980)

[Gordon Anderson and his wife filed for relief under Chapter 13. They owe over $10,000 on unsecured debts and $2,805 on secured debts, although the

property on which the secured creditors have liens (two cars, a television set, and a stereo) is worth only $2,125. Currently, out of Gordon's net monthly earnings of $1,016, the Andersons are obligated to pay about $200 per month on the secured debts. According to the Andersons' proposed rehabilitation plan, the secured debts will be restructured by lowering monthly payments and interest *rates, and by lowering the total amount due (because of the property's value being less than the indebtedness). The plan calls for the Andersons to pay the trustee $150 per month for about 15 months; the trustee is then to pay the creditors. Unsecured creditors will be paid only 1 cent on the dollar under the plan. At the confirmation hearing, the Andersons stated that their purpose in filing the plan was to restructure the secured debts.]*

Pyle, Bankruptcy Judge.

*   *   *

This court does not agree that the proper sole purpose of a Chapter 13 plan is to rewrite a debtor's contracts with secured creditors. To the extent that a Chapter 13 plan rewrites a secured creditor's contract *incidental* to the carrying out of a plan, some alteration of contractual obligations is permissible. [Court's emphasis.] . . .

What makes this plan impermissible is that the effect of the 1% treatment of unsecured claims creates a plan which has the single purpose of restructuring the debtors' contracts to purchase the two automobiles, the television and the stereo.

What the debtors are attempting to do is to take advantage of the Chapter 13 provisions to rewrite their secured contracts and yet avoid proceeding under the straight bankruptcy provisions of Chapter 7. . . .

The debtors comply with the requirement of Chapter 13 in most respects. . . .

The only question then remaining is whether the plan has been proposed in good faith. . . .

The proposed plan treats unsecured creditors and the allowed unsecured portion of the secured claims on a [minimal] basis. The only reason *anything* is offered is so that they can . . . qualify for Chapter 13 to rewrite their secured contracts. . . .

This does not forward the basic purpose of Chapter 13 which is that an individual pay his debts in a reasonable fashion under a plan,

which, in the debtor's circumstances, is fair to his creditors. Where a debtor can afford to pay reasonable amounts for a reasonable length of time but elects to make only token payments on his unsecured debts, the plan is unfair and should not be confirmed. . . .

The plan proposed in the case at bar is not a fair and reasonable treatment of the debtors' unsecured creditors in that the payments extend for the relatively short period of 15 months, well within the debtors' financial ability to pay creditors. . . .

If creditors claims are to be totally abrogated despite the debtors ability to pay, Chapter 7 is the appropriate choice within the contemplation of the Bankruptcy Code. If such a debtor is to avoid bankruptcy and gain the benefits of Chapter 13, . . . he should pay according to his ability and circumstances, thereby providing fairly and responsibly for his creditors within the spirit of Chapter 13. That is what the "good faith" requirement demands. That element is one which the court must consider on a case by case basis since the circumstances and abilities of each debtor will differ. . . .

Several bankruptcy judges who have considered Chapter 13 plans being proposed at the 1%, or nominal level have concluded that such plans were not contemplated by Congress when it enacted the new code. . . .

The conclusion reached in the case at bar does not mean that, in a Chapter 13 plan proposed in good faith which fairly treats creditors within the circumstances and means of the debtor, secured contracts cannot be rewritten or restructured as an incident to and to properly implement such a plan. . . . Nor does this ruling mean that a debtor cannot propose to pay only a modest amount to creditors in an appropriate case. Denial of confirmation in the case at bar means simply that the facts and circumstances here presented fail to demonstrate to the satisfaction of this court that this plan was proposed in good faith. . . .

[Confirmation denied.]

If one or more secured creditors refuse to accept a Chapter 13 plan, the plan can still be confirmed, but only if the interest of each nonaccepting secured creditor is satisfied in one of two ways. The first of these "cram-down" alternatives is that the debtor can simply surrender the property covered by each nonaccepting secured creditor's lien to that creditor. The second option available to the debtor is that the plan can provide that the nonaccepting secured creditor (1) retains his lien and (2) will receive property having a present value (value as of the effective date of the plan) not less than the allowed amount of his claim.

EXAMPLE

Brown, the debtor in a Chapter 13 case, conducts business as a sole proprietor. Brown owes $5,000 to Curb Corporation, which holds a security interest in a machine that, although worth only $2,000, is essential to the continuation of Brown's business. Curb refuses to accept Brown's Chapter 13 plan. The plan can be confirmed if it provides that Curb will (1) keep its security interest in the machine and (2) receive either (a) later periodic payments or (b) other property, such as Brown's old car, as long as the present value of the deferred payments or other property is at least $2,000.

31:18   Discharge of Debtor; Reaffirmation of Debts

A *discharge* in a bankruptcy case means that the debtor is free from further liability on certain debts. For an individual debtor, the object of *any* bankruptcy proceeding is to obtain a discharge. A corporate or partnership debtor can receive a discharge only in a Chapter 11 case. Bear in mind, however, that some debts *cannot* be discharged, and other debts *will not* be discharged under certain circumstances. Debts that cannot or might not be discharged are discussed below. To be considered first, though, are the circumstances under which any type of discharge can be granted.

Grant of Discharge   The Court grants a discharge in a Chapter 7 case unless the trustee or a creditor objects. If an objection if made, the discharge will not be granted if any one or more of a number of specific facts are found to exist. Among the listed facts are the following:

- Debtor is not an individual
- Within one year before the petition was filed, debtor transferred or concealed property with intent to hinder or delay a creditor
- Debtor concealed, destroyed, falsified, or failed to keep or preserve adequate records as to his financial condition or business affairs
- Debtor failed to explain any loss of assets satisfactorily
- Debtor refused to obey a lawful order of the bankruptcy court
- Debtor was granted a discharge under Chapter 7 or 11 (or Chapter 13 under some circumstances) in a case commenced within six years before the petition in the present case was filed

Generally, confirmation of the rehabilitation plan in a Chapter 11 case discharges the debtor, although there are exceptions to this rule. In a Chapter 13 case, the court ordinarily grants a discharge after the debtor has completed all payments under the Chapter 13 plan. If the debtor failed to make all payments under the plan, the court can still grant what is known as a hardship discharge. The requirements for a hardship discharge are that (1) the debtor failed to complete payments under the plan due to a reason beyond his control, (2) unsecured creditors received at least as much as they would have received in a Chapter 7 case, and (3) modification of the plan is impracticable.

EXAMPLE
A confirmed Chapter 13 plan requires the debtor to pay the trustee $150 per month for 36 months, for the benefit of the creditors. Thus, the total amount to be paid by the debtor is $5,400. After the debtor has made payments for 20 months, he is disabled in an accident and forced to leave his job. His income is reduced to half of what it was before and, for the indefinite future, will consist only of disability compensation and related benefits. As a result, the debtor pays the trustee only $75 per month for the last eight months of the plan. The court can grant a hardship discharge if unsecured creditors have received what they would have received under Chapter 7.

If the debtor has not paid at least 70 percent of the unsecured claims when a Chapter 13 hardship discharge is granted, the debtor cannot receive a discharge in a later Chapter 7 case commenced within six years after commencement of the earlier Chapter 13 case.

Debts Not Discharged in Chapter 7 Case   The Bankruptcy Code lists various types of debts that are not discharged in a Chapter 7 case. Examples of such debts are fines or penalties imposed by government entities, most unpaid taxes, most unpaid student loans, and unpaid alimony or child support.

Other types of debts will not be discharged if, and only if, the creditors involved object to discharge and make an adequate showing that one of the Bankruptcy Code's grounds for exception from discharge exists. The most significant debt of this type is one that the debtor incurred by using a written statement that (1) was false in one or more important respects, (2) concerned the debtor's financial condition, (3) was reasonably relied on by the creditor, *and* (4) was intended to deceive the creditor. A typical example of a statement of this type is an application for a loan or other credit. Of the four listed requirements, the one that often determines the dischargeability of the debt is the creditor's reasonable reliance on the statement. Thus, for example, a creditor's failure to convince the court that his reliance on a false financial statement was reasonable under the circumstances will lead to the debt's being discharged.

 If a creditor challenges the discharge of a consumer debt (debt incurred by individual for personal, family, or household purposes), but the court discharges the debt anyway, the creditor must usually pay the debtor's legal expenses for the dischargeability proceeding.

Exceptions to Discharge in Chapter 11 and 13 Cases   In a Chapter 11 case involving an individual debtor, the Chapter 7 exceptions to discharge apply. Regardless of who the debtor is, the Chapter 11 plan can limit the scope of the discharge by adding additional exceptions.

If the debtor has completed his payments under a Chapter 13 plan, the only allowed debts provided for by the plan that are not discharged are (1) debts for alimony or child support and (2) certain long-term obligations (such as a loan secured by a home mortgage), the last payment of which is due after the last payment under the plan. However, if the debtor is granted a Chapter 13 hardship discharge, *all* the Chapter 7 exceptions apply.

Reaffirmation of Debt   A debtor reaffirms a debt if, after a bankruptcy case has commenced, the debtor agrees to pay a creditor on a debt that is dischargeable in the case. Because the existence of *reaffirmation* agreements can hinder or even prevent a debtor's fresh start after a bankruptcy proceeding, the Bankruptcy Code imposes several requirements as to these agreements. For example, the agreement must be made before any discharge is granted, and the debtor can cancel the agreement within 30 days after making it. If the debtor is an individual, the court must inform the debtor about his right not to make the agreement. Also, the court must approve any reaffirmation of a consumer debt that is not secured by real property. This approval generally requires a finding that the reaffirmation does not impose an undue hardship on the debtor or a dependent and that it is in the debtor's best interest.

Key Concepts and Terms

- Insolvency is the situation in which the total amount of a debtor's debts exceeds the total value of those of the debtor's assets that can be reached by creditors.
- An individual debtor can sometimes relieve his financial difficulties by obtaining a debt consolidation loan or using the services of a debt counselor.
- A business debtor can be relieved from some of its indebtedness if it can persuade all or most of its creditors to agree to a composition arrangement, which reduces the debtor's total indebtedness and, if performed, discharges the debts. Otherwise, the debtor might still avoid bankruptcy by making an assignment for creditors, which discharges debts to the extent that they are paid.
- Bankruptcy is a form of debtor relief by which the debtor places his assets under judicial control, after which either the assets are liquidated and sold for the benefit of creditors by the trustee, or a plan for the debtor's financial rehabilitation is prepared. Bankruptcy is governed by the federal Bankruptcy Code.
- A bankruptcy case is commenced by filing a petition with the bankruptcy court. The debtor files the petition in a voluntary case, while one or more creditors file in an involuntary case. A voluntary petition can be filed under Chapter 7 (liquidation of assets), Chapter 11 (reorganization and financial rehabilitation of business debtor), or Chapter 13 (financial rehabilitation of certain individual debtors). An involuntary petition can be filed only under Chapters 7 or 11.

- The court can dismiss any bankruptcy case for cause, and it must dismiss an involuntary case if either of the two statutory grounds for involuntary bankruptcy does not exist.

- The bankruptcy estate consists of all the debtor's property and property interests. It is usually administered by the trustee. Individual debtors can exempt certain property from the estate.

- When a bankruptcy petition is filed, creditors' efforts to collect on debts owed by the debtor are automatically stayed. The court can terminate or modify the stay as to a particular creditor on request.

- The trustee has the power to avoid certain prepetition transfers involving the debtor's property, including (1) transfers that some actual or hypothetical creditors could avoid under state law, and (2) preferential transfers. A preferential transfer is one that gives a creditor greater benefits than the creditor would receive if the transfer had not been made.

- Creditors' claims are secured or unsecured. A claim is secured if the creditor has a lien on property of the bankruptcy estate, and the claim is secured only to the extent of the value of that property. Claims are presented by the filing of proofs of claim in most cases.

- The right and extent to which a given creditor shares in the distributions in a Chapter 7 case depends on the status of the creditor's claim as secured or unsecured and, as to an unsecured claim, the ranking of the claim in the statutory scheme of priorities.

- A Chapter 11 plan is intended to allow the debtor to remain in business. A Chapter 13 plan is intended to give the individual debtor a fresh start while, at the same time, making it possible for him to pay at least some of his debts.

- A Chapter 11 or 13 plan must be confirmed by the court before it can be executed, and confirmation will be withheld unless the plan meets detailed statutory requirements.

- An individual debtor will usually receive a discharge from most of his debts. Some debts cannot be discharged, however, and others will not be discharged under certain circumstances.

- A debtor can, but need not, reaffirm a debt that will be discharged. Strict requirements apply to any reaffirmation by an individual debtor, especially as to consumer debts.

- Assignment for Creditors
- Automatic Stay
- Avoidance Power
- Bankruptcy
- Best Interest of Creditors
- Composition with Creditors
- Custodian
- Debtor in Possession
- Discharge of Debtor

- Insolvency
- Liquidation
- Parties in Interest
- Preferential Transfer
- Proof of Claim
- Reaffirmation of Debt
- Rehabilitation Plan
- Trustee

Questions and Case Problems

1. Compare and contrast compositions with creditors and assignments for creditors. What factors would influence a debtor in choosing one remedy over the other?

2. What are the advantages and disadvantages of bankruptcy, as compared against other forms of debtor relief from the viewpoint of (a) creditors and (b) debtors?

3. Discuss the basic differences between the relief available under Bankruptcy Code Chapter 7 and the relief available under Chapters 11 or 13. Why might an insolvent debtor who has the choice of filing under either Chapter 7 or Chapter 13 prefer to file under Chapter 13?

4. The Bankruptcy Code has been criticized as providing a loophole for deadbeats because it allows people to avoid debts that they are capable of paying. Do you agree with this criticism? Why or why not?

5. Define "secured claim" and "unsecured claim" as those terms are used in the Bankruptcy Code. What, if any, advantages does the holder of a secured claim have over the holder of an unsecured claim? What is the significance of a claim's being allowed?

6. Meyers files a voluntary bankruptcy petition, and among his assets he lists a pickup truck that is worth $1,650, but which is covered by a nonpossessory, non-purchase-money security interest in Credithrift's favor, securing a debt of $2,500. Meyers works as a forklift operator at a factory, and he uses the truck for commuting to and from work. Credithrift applies to the court for relief from the automatic stay so that it can enforce its lien on the truck; it has evidence that the truck is depreciating at the rate of $75 per month. In response, Meyers claims that the truck is a tool of his trade and that Credithrift's lien should be set aside. (a) What, if any, relief from the automatic stay should be granted to Credithrift? Why? (b) Is Credithrift's lien avoidable by Meyers? Why or why not? (c) If the court decides, rightly or wrongly, that Meyers' argument lacks merit, how else, if at all, can Meyers obtain the release of the lien on his truck?

7. On June 1, Scopes gave up on his cabinet-making business and filed a bankrtupcy petition under Chapter 7 of the Bankruptcy Code. Earlier the same year Scopes had bought some new equipment on credit, as follows. On January 1, he bought a radial arm saw from Bryan and gave Bryan a security interest covering the saw. Bryan perfected that interest on January 5. On February 1, Scopes bought a lathe from Darrow. Darrow was granted a security interest in the lathe but did not perfect that interest until March 15. Scopes defaulted on his payments to Bryan and Darrow, and both creditors acted to protect their interests. On April 1, Bryan repossessed the saw, as he had the right to do under his contract. On April 15, Darrow repossessed the lathe. The bankruptcy trustee now seeks to recover both the saw and the lathe for the bankruptcy estate. She argues that both Bryan and Darrow received the benefit of preferential transfers that she, the trustee, has the power to avoid. Discuss what, if any, rights the trustee has with respect to the two pieces of equipment.

8. Curtis and his wife, the debtors in a Chapter 13 case, file a proposed payment plan in which they divide their unsecured debts into two classes: (1) unpaid child support owed to Curtis' former wife and (2) all other unsecured debts. Under the Curtis plan, the unpaid child support will be paid in full, but the other unsecured creditors will receive only 10 cents on the dollar. For payment of these debts, the plan calls for Curtis' employer to make direct payment to the trustee, at the rate of

$75 per month out of Curtis' wages, for 18 months. Curtis' net earnings are $787 per month, and he estimates that the total of his recurring monthly expenses is $700. At the confirmation hearing Curtis states that his wife is pregnant and that he will have to pay some, if not all, of the costs of childbirth; that he had no prospect of a wage increase; and that his employer is unsympathetic and is apt to fire him if payments under the plan extend beyond 18 months. The trustee objects to the Curtis plan, claiming that it was not proposed in good faith and that the 10 percent payment to the second class of unsecured creditors is too low. She proposes to file an alternate plan for the court to consider. (a) Should the court allow the trustee to file an alternate plan? Why or why not? (b) Should the Curtis plan be confirmed? Why or why not?

9. In 1981 Jones applied for a $1,700 loan from Merchants Bank. In the space on the loan application provided for the listing of existing debts, Jones stated the following: (1) "auto loan from United Bank," with no amount stated, (2) "F&M," with no amount stated, (3) "Am Cr?—$250," and (4) "MasterCard," with no amount stated. Merchants checked with a local credit bureau about Jones' credit rating, and it then made the loan. In 1982 Jones applied to Merchants for a second loan, for $1,000, and this time he left the space for listing existing debts blank. In early 1983 Jones applied to Merchants for a $4,000 loan to pay off the earlier two loans and provide Jones with needed capital. Again, Jones left blank the space on the application provided for the listing of debts, although he was indebted to Merchants and several other creditors at the time. Later in 1983 Jones filed for bankruptcy under Chapter 7. The case has proceeded to the point where the court is ready to grant Jones a discharge. Merchants Bank argues that because of Jones' failure to list his debts on the 1983 loan application, the $4,000 debt owed to it should not be discharged. Should the $4,000 debt be discharged? Why or why not?

10. Stephens files a petition for relief under Chapter 7. Among Stephens' debts is a debt of $550 owed to BFC, a loan company. The debt is secured by a non-possessory, non-purchase-money security interest in certain of Stephens' household goods, worth $500. After the meeting of creditors, Stephens visits BFC seeking a new loan of $1,000. BFC agrees to make the loan, but only if Stephens reaffirms the $550 debt. Stephens does so and obtains the new loan. At no time did the court approve the reaffirmation or even receive a copy of the loan agreement in which it was made. Discuss any ways in which, under these facts, BFC has or might have violated requirements of the Bankruptcy Code. Can BFC enforce Stephens' reaffirmation? Why or why not?

PART SEVEN

Property

Introductory Comments

Property is one of the most important areas of business law. The reason for its significance is readily apparent. All businesses buy, sell, and lease property, and otherwise engage in a host of property transactions in the course of their daily activities. Property is the measure of success in our society, and its acquisition is the means by which businesses grow and prosper.

There are two basic classes of property: land and buildings, which are called real property; and movable things and intangibles, which are known as personal property. While most of the other chapters in this book involve property or property rights, the material in the following chapters analyzes the law applicable specifically to these classes of property. The basic concepts of property law are introduced in Chapter 32. Succeeding chapters discuss bailments and personal property leases (Chapter 33); the purchase and sale of real property

(Chapter 34); mortgages and deeds of trust (Chapter 35); the landlord–tenant relationship (Chapter 36); zoning and land use planning (Chapter 37); and trusts, wills, and estate administration (Chapter 38).

There are few broadly applicable or unifying doctrines in property law, and at times property law appears to bear little relation to modern economic or social conditions. The principal reason for this state of affairs is that property law has its origin in feudal England, with its peculiar system of land tenure dating back hundreds of years. This is not to say, however, that property law is totally of English origin; laws affecting property in many states reflect other historical antecedents. For example, community property laws in several western states can be traced to the laws of Spain and Mexico.

Perhaps another reason why property law is

not based on broadly applicable doctrines is that the law has been adapted over the years to meet changing economic, political, and social conditions in the United States, and it continues to be refined by the courts today. For example, the courts are now frequently using contract principles in deciding property cases, whereas in the past property law and contract law were considered quite distinct—each with its own peculiar doctrines and rules. As older property law doctrines fail to meet the needs of modern times, new rules are being fashioned and adopted.

Despite the complexities of property law, it remains one of the most fascinating and important areas of business law: it incorporates and reflects history, economics, and politics. For this reason, studying property law is vital not only in terms of its usefulness in guiding the conduct of business, but also in terms of understanding the most important underpinning of the nation's economy.

32 Introduction to the Law of Property

32:1 General Comments

The meaning of "property" depends on how the term is used. What is property in one situation might not be considered property in another. In one sense, the term refers to the right of possessing, enjoying, and disposing of a thing, ordinarily to the exclusion of others. In another sense, it refers to a thing that can be owned. The meaning of "property" can also depend on the particular circumstance in which it is used. For example, it is sometimes used to mean land rather than buildings or other improvements on that land.

Property, a property right, or an interest in property can be tangible or intangible. Property can consist of land, buildings, or articles of personal use. The term includes all animate objects that are capable of appropriation or manual delivery. It also includes obligations, debts, products of labor or skill, and all other things of value.

There are two fundamental classes of property: (1) land and that which is attached to land, all of which is called *real property*, and (2) movable or intangible things, which are called personal property.

Constitutional Protection of Property Rights   Property is specifically protected by the Constitution of the United States. Indeed, some historians have asserted that the fundamental impetus for the adoption of our constitution and the failure of the initial form of government after independence, under the Articles of Confederation, was precisely the lack of suitable protection to property owners. The Fifth Amendment to the Constitution provides, "No person shall be . . . deprived of life, liberty, or property, without due process of law; nor shall private property be taken for public use, without just compensation."[1] The Fourteenth Amendment to the United States Constitution prohibits the states from denying any person the due process of law or the equal protection of the laws.

---

[1]The power of government to take property for public use by eminent domain or other similar proceedings is discussed in Chapter 37. The Constitution is reprinted in Appendix A.

32:2   Ownership of Property

All property has an owner, whether public or private. Ownership and property are interrelated concepts. Ownership of something is the right of one or more persons to possess and use it to the exclusion of others, and property is the "something" that can be owned, including what is known as the "bundle of rights" incident to ownership. For example, one can own an idea (which is intangible personal property) just as one can own a parcel of land (real property).

Incidents of Ownership   The ownership of property is either absolute or qualified. It is absolute when a single person (sole owner) has absolute control over the property and can use or dispose of it according to his pleasure, subject only to the general laws in force. Ownership is qualified when property is shared with one or more persons, when the time of its enjoyment is deferred, or when its use is restricted.

Special Rights Based on Ownership   In the absence of statute or case law to the contrary, the owner of real property has the right to its surface and to everything permanently situated beneath or above it.[2] Every property owner is entitled to what is called lateral and subjacent support, which is what his land receives from adjoining property. This right is subject to the right of the adjoining property owner to make excavations on the land for construction or other improvements, as long as the walls of the excavations are properly braced.

The occupants of property have rights to the natural condition, level, and purity of all streams, lakes, and ponds which their property adjoins. If rights to the use of waters are based on ownership of property bordering a natural body of water, they are called riparian rights. Riparian owners are usually entitled to the reasonable use of water from such bordering or adjacent bodies of water. In some western states, however, a riparian owner's use of the water may be limited under what is called the prior appropriation doctrine. The effect of the doctrine is that a riparian owner located downstream can, because of his prior use of a given quantity of water, have acquired the right to continue receiving that amount of water.

Under the common law, a property owner was deemed to own the land and the property under it to the center of the earth and above it to infinity in space. Violation of the airspace above an owner's property was deemed to be as much a trespass as entry on the land without the owner's permission. Obviously, the needs of commercial, military, and private air traffic have made inroads on the strict common-law theory. However, property owners may still have remedies available to protect against unreasonable interferences with their use and quiet enjoyment of the airspace above their property.

Owners of property also enjoy rights to air, light, and a view unobstructed by neighboring property. If a proposed or new building on adjoining property blocks any of these rights, the affected property owner might be able to obtain an injunction, or even damages under certain circumstances.

---

[2]Not all countries view ownership in a similar fashion. In Mexico, for example, ownership of property does not extend to subsurface minerals; they belong to the state.

Fixtures   When property becomes permanently attached to land, it is called a fixture. Under the common law, fixtures could not be removed from the land by a tenant or other temporary occupant; rather, the fixtures became part of the property owned by the landlord. An early exception to the rule of fixtures was recognized to allow a tenant to remove trade fixtures, those installed to carry on a trade or business. This exception encouraged economic investment for trade. The tenant remained liable, however, for material damage caused by removing trade fixtures. Today, most states have liberalized the rules governing fixtures. A person can generally remove from leased premises any property, whether or not used in a trade or business, so long as the removal does not cause substantial damage.

32:3   Possessory Interests in Property

There is an often-repeated adage to the effect that possession is nine-tenths of the law. There is much truth to this statement because the law does protect the possessor of property for many different purposes. However, possession is distinguishable from ownership. Both terms denote dominion and control over property, but ownership denotes title to the property while possession denotes the right to use the property for a specific period of time. For example, a landlord owns property, while a tenant enjoys its possession.

Possession generally requires both physical control of property and the intent to control it. When the law deems a person to be in possession and in fact he is not, the person is said to be in constructive possession of the property. For example, an owner of a mountain cabin who uses the cabin only during the winter is in constructive possession of it during the rest of the year.

A person who possesses property usually prevails against all claimants but the true owner. The following classic case illustrates the distinction between possession and ownership, and how this distinction affects property rights. Note that the party seeking damages was not the owner but was only in possession of the property. Indeed, while the question of ownership was raised, it was not dispositive of the issues in the case. Rather, the inquiry focused on the property rights of two parties neither of whom owned the disputed property.

Anderson

v

Gouldberg
51 Minn 294, 53 NW 636
(Minnesota Supreme Court, 1892)

[Anderson sued to recover possession of 93 pine logs or their fair market value. Anderson claimed he cut the logs and hauled them to a mill, where they were taken by the defendants. The defendants contended that Anderson did not own the logs and had no authority from the owners to cut them. At trial, the court instructed the jury that even if Anderson had obtained possession of the logs as a trespasser, his title would be good against anyone except the true owner or someone who had authority from the owner to take them. The jury found for Anderson, and the defendants appealed.]

Mitchell, J.

*   *   *

It is settled by the verdict of the jury that the logs in controversy were not cut upon the land of the defendants, and consequently that they were entire strangers to the property. For the purposes of this appeal, we must also assume the fact to be ... that the plaintiffs obtained possession of the logs in the first instance by trespassing upon the land of some third party. Therefore the only question is whether bare possession of property, though wrongfully obtained, is sufficient title to enable the party enjoying it to maintain replevin [a legal action in which the plaintiff seeks the return of specific property rather than damages] against a mere stranger, who takes it from him. ... When it is said that to maintain replevin the plaintiff's possession must have been lawful, it means merely that it must have been lawful as against the person who deprived him of it; and possession is good title against all the world except those having a better title. Counsel says that possession only raises a presumption of title, which, however, may be rebutted. Rightly understood, this is correct; but counsel misapplies it. One who takes property from the possession of another can only rebut this presumption by showing a superior title in himself, or in some way connecting himself with one who has. One who has acquired the possession of property, whether by finding, bailment, or by mere tort, has a right to retain that possession as against a mere wrongdoer who is a stranger to the property. Any other rule would lead to an endless series of unlawful seizures and reprisals in every case where property had once passed out of the possession of the rightful owner.

Order affirmed.

Interests and Estates in Property   The concept of property is based on the legal concept of estates in property. Both of these concepts developed at a time when land was the only property of substantial value. Thus, interests in property were historically referred to as estates in land. As personal property was accumulated and became more important, the system of estates or interests in land was applied to personal property as well. Although the types of estates and the terms used to distinguish among the classes of property apply primarily to real property or land, they have general applicability to personal property for purposes of the discussion in this chapter.

An *estate* is an interest in property that is of a given duration or time. An interest can be a present or a future interest. The owner of a present interest has the right to the immediate possession of property, while the owner of a future interest has the right to the possession of property at some future time. Only the transfer of present interests is recognized by the law. Thus, if one were to deed to another his expectancy of a future inheritance, the conveyance would be void.

Fee Simple   The term *fee simple* refers to an estate or interest in property of potentially infinite duration with no restrictions. Under the common-law system of land-holding, the fee simple ownership was the closest to absolute ownership that could exist. When one normally speaks of ownership of property, without qualification or restriction, it is the fee simple to which reference is being made.

Life Estate   A *life estate* is an interest in property limited in duration to the lifetime of a particular person or persons. This limitation distinguishes the life estate from the other estates. A life estate is usually limited to the lifetime of the holder of the estate, but it can be limited to someone else's life.

The holder of a life estate, who is known as a life tenant, is entitled to all income from the property during the life tenancy. If the tenancy is in real property, the life tenant can exploit the natural resources so long as the exploitation does not permanently damage the interests of those who will enjoy the property on termination of the life estate. The life tenant must preserve the property, maintain it, and keep structures in good repair, but he is under no obligation to improve it. The life tenant must pay all ordinary taxes on the land during the existence of the life estate. When a life tenant dies, the property reverts to the owner or his heirs, or passes to a third person as designated by the grantor of the life estate.

Future Interests   A *future interest* is a property interest that will come into existence at some time in the future. The term is somewhat misleading in that the *interest* must have present existence, even though *possession* is postponed to some future time. If the property owner has disposed of less than his entire estate for a period of time, his remaining interest is called a *reversion*. For example, if an owner conveys a life estate, his future interest on termination of the life estate is the reversion. The owner has not fully conveyed the estate and is entitled to its return. If, instead, a person granting a life estate *has* disposed of his entire interest in the property, he has given a third person the right of possession and ownership on termination of the life estate. This interest is known as a *remainder.*

Nonfreehold Estates   The common law developed certain estates that conveyed possession and use but retained ownership in the grantor. These estates were known as *nonfreehold estates;* today they are called leaseholds. Leaseholds, and the rights and duties of the grantor (landlord) and grantee (tenant) are discussed in detail in Chapter 36.

32:4   Concurrent Ownership of Property

Any of the estates in property discussed above may be held by a single individual or concurrently by two or more persons. For example, a fee simple, life estate, or other type of estate may be owned by two or more people. The major forms of concurrent ownership are (1) tenancy in common; (2) joint tenancy; (3) partnership ownership;[3] (4) condominium or cooperative ownership; and (5) forms of marital ownership, such as tenancy by the entireties.

Tenancy in Common   A *tenancy in common* is a cotenancy in which each tenant is considered to be an owner of a separate and distinct share of the property. The property itself is not physically divided, but the interest of each tenant in common

---

[3]Partnerships are discussed in Chapter 41.

is transferable. Statutes in many states provide that an interest created in favor of several persons is an interest in common unless it is acquired by them as partners or is declared in its creation to be a joint interest.

Each tenant in common has the right to possession and enjoyment of all of the property, with the other tenants. When one tenant in common dies, his interest passes as he wishes to the beneficiary of his estate or to his heirs. The surviving tenants in common have no right of survivorship—that is, they do not automatically acquire the deceased tenant's interest.

Joint Tenancy   *Joint tenants* are in effect owners of undivided shares in property. That is, each joint tenant owns the entire property, subject to the interests of the other joint tenants. This kind of estate, as distinguished from the tenancy in common, has survivorship as one of its incidents. Under the doctrine of *survivorship*, the death of one joint tenant causes his interest to pass automatically and immediately to the remaining joint tenants without ever becoming a part of his probate estate.

A joint tenancy can be created between or among two or more persons. In fact, there can be an unlimited number of joint tenants. On the death of each one, the estate belongs to the survivors until only one is left; the tenant who lives the longest takes the estate as the absolute owner. Since joint tenants possess undivided property as one fictitious entity, most states require that their interests in the property be equal in all respects. They must take the property at the same time, by the same instrument, with identical interests, and with an undivided right to possess the whole property, and not merely a portion of it. If these four unities of time, title, interest, and possession are not present, a joint tenancy cannot be created. The joint tenancy can be severed at any time by one joint tenant destroying one of the four unities as, for example, by conveying his interest in the property or by giving up possession. When a joint tenancy is severed, it becomes a tenancy in common and the right of survivorship is destroyed.

The absence of the right to survivorship is the principal feature distinguishing a tenancy in common from a joint tenancy. Tenants in common are each presumed to own an equal share, but equal shares are not required. Thus, for example, Lewis may convey a one-fourth undivided interest in certain property to Nicholas and a three-fourths undivided interest in the same property to Melissa, as tenants in common. Both Nicholas and Melissa have the right to possession of the whole property. Any rental income from the property goes one-fourth to Nicholas and three-fourths to Melissa. On the sale of the property, the proceeds are divided in the same fashion.

Rights and Duties of Cotenants   Each tenant in common or joint tenant is equally entitled to the possession and enjoyment of the entire cotenancy property. A cotenant may not exclude another cotenant from any part of the property. As long as a tenant in possession does not exclude another cotenant, he is entitled to use and occupy every part of the property without paying any amount to the other cotenant. However, in some states one cotenant must account to other cotenants for the reasonable rental value of the property and for profits derived from the use of property that permanently reduces its value.

A tenant in common or a joint tenant may convey his interest in the property to a third party or may agree with the other cotenants to a voluntary partition or division of the land among themselves. The tenants may also seek what is known as judicial partition, by which a court either divides or sells the property through court order and then adjusts all the parties' claims. A joint tenant cannot convey his interest by will since his interest ceases on his death.

The rights of cotenants are discussed further in the following case. Consider the parties' rights to the value of the minerals extracted from the property, to profits, and to partition. Note the amount of damages and the reasoning of the dissent that the award was improperly calculated in the majority opinion.

White
v
Smyth
147 Tex 272, 214 SW2d 967, 5 ALR2d 1348
(Texas Supreme Court, 1948)

[White, the owner of an undivided one-ninth interest in two tracts of land totaling 30,200 acres, mined and removed from the property a large quantity of rock asphalt, valued at $99,000. The net profit realized by White in the conduct of his rock asphalt business was $250,000. The other joint owners sued White, claiming that he failed to account to them for their portion of the rock asphalt mined, and they sought a division of the proceeds among them. White contended that (1) he owed no duty to account to the other owners because he had not taken more than his fair share of the rock asphalt in place; (2) he did not exclude the other owners from mining on the property; (3) if he were to account to the other owners, he should be liable only for eight-ninths of the value in the ground of the rock asphalt mined and not for the profits he made in his business; and (4) the property should be physically partitioned among the parties according to their respective interests. The trial court ruled against White. It held that the property could not be partitioned among the owners and ordered it sold with the proceeds to be distributed among all of them. The court further ordered White to pay eight-*

ninths of his net profits to the other owners. White appealed.]

Smedley, J.

*   *   *

... In our opinion the facts in evidence ... bring the case well within the general rule that known mineral lands, because of elements of uncertainty, not resolvable at reasonable cost, are not susceptible of fair division ... and should be partitioned by sale and distribution of the proceeds. ...

It seems that there are no decisions in this state as to the duty of a co-owner who takes solid minerals from the property to account to his cotenant. It is held, however, as in most of the other states, that one who takes oil without the consent of his cotenants must account to them for their share of the proceeds of the oil less the necessary and reasonable cost of producing and marketing it. ...

[White] contends that the rule above stated does not apply to this case, and that he need not account to his cotenants, because he has mined no more than his fair share of the rock asphalt in place and has not excluded them from the premises. ...

The facts of this case attest the obvious soundness of the rule that a cotenant cannot select and take for himself part of the property jointly owned and thus make partition. . . . White selected the site for and developed the present pit, making extensive improvements, including the construction of roads, excavations and grading for private tracks, other excavations and grading, all at great cost and of very substantial value. The location of the plant site was favorable and valuable. The rock asphalt in the pit was both rich rock and lean rock, both of which were necessary to meet market demands and specifications. . . .

. . . The rock asphalt estate in all of the lands belonged to all of the cotenants, as did also the added advantages and values to the entire mineral estate created and existing by reason of the developed pit and mine site; but White, taking advantage for himself of the added values, . . . mined from the pit about four hundred thousand tons of the rich, valuable and readily accessible rock asphalt. . . .

It is argued by petitioner that his receipts have been from sales of a manufactured product, and that [the cotenants] should not be permitted, by sharing in the profits, to obtain the benefits of his personal skill and industry and of the flux oil and water used and the machinery, apparatus and equipment belonging to [him]. We believe that the preparation of the rock asphalt for market, as described by [White's] testimony and by that of other witnesses, is a processing rather than a manufacturing. The rock asphalt is rock asphalt in the ground, that is, limestone rock impregnated with asphalt. To make it ready for the market and for use in the building of roads it is mixed and crushed, and oil is mixed with it to give the small particles of rock a film of oil, and water is put in the mixture so that it will not become solid in transit. It is rock asphalt when it is sold and when it is used on the roads. The producing tenant is required to account to his cotenants for net profits realized from mining, smelting, crushing, processing or marketing solid minerals taken from the land. . . .

The rock asphalt was owned in undivided interests by all of the cotenants. Their owner-

ship extended to all of the rock asphalt and to all of the advantages and peculiar conditions and stages of development of the property. . . . This ownership extended to the developed pit with its great wall of easily accessible rock asphalt and to the valuable mining site. It extended to the use value of the rock asphalt and to its profit possibilities. To limit the accounting to the value in place of the rock asphalt mined by [White], would be to permit him to use for his own profit the property owned in common and the advantages and opportunities for profit inherent in that ownership and to deprive [the cotenants] of a substantial part of its value and benefits. In our opinion, the trial court's judgment, requiring [White] to account to his co-owners according to their interests for the profits realized from the common property after crediting him with all expenses and with the compensation above mentioned, assures to all of the co-owners the benefits and values of their ownership, is correct in principle and, as has been said, is supported by the decided weight of authority.

[Judgment affirmed.]

Simpson, J., dissenting.

*   *   *

It is respectfully submitted that the measure of recovery allowed the [cotenants] by the majority ruling is wrong, and is contrary to the applicable precedents under the established facts. It results in what is earnestly urged to be an unjust exaction of . . . White, who should have been required to account for $99,334.53, the value in place of the rock asphalt taken, and not $222,382.72, its net manufactured value. . . .

What the complaining cotenants are entitled to get is the value of that which was taken, that is, crude rock asphalt. Any higher figure would no longer be compensatory but punitive. And this is the measure of recovery fixed by the authorities. . .

The rule in Texas as elsewhere in oil and gas cases is that a cotenant producing oil must account to his co-owners for the value of the crude oil produced less the reasonable cost of producing and marketing. . . . None would say that if a joint owner produced crude oil and then refined it, his cotenants would be entitled to an accounting on the basis of the value of the refined products. Yet that is the very result the majority has reached here. The raw rock asphalt when first mined is no doubt as little suited for paving as crude oil when first produced is suitable for automobile fuel. Just as it takes refining to prepare crude oil for motor fuel, so does it take manufacturing and processing, including the addition and blending of other products more valuable than the crude rock asphalt itself, coupled with an experienced skill and knowledge of the business,

to ready the raw rock asphalt for paving. The nonmining cotenant is entitled only to the net value of the crude oil in the one case, and certainly to no more than the net value of the crude rock asphalt in the other.

The [cotenants] ought not to be allowed to share in the capital investment, the experience, enterprise and personal business acumen of [White]. To allow this sharing puts a grim penalty upon freedom of enterprise and the risk of one's own capital in a highly hazardous and competitive business. The [cotenants] can be made whole by awarding them the value of their share in place of the crude rock asphalt which was mined. This is fair and just. It allows full compensation for what was taken. [They] are entitled to this, but certainly not to more.

Marital Estates   A form of concurrent ownership limited to property owned by husband and wife is called a *tenancy by the entireties*. It is similar to joint tenancy in that it includes the right of survivorship. It is distinguishable from joint tenancy in that neither husband nor wife can destroy or sever the tenancy without the other's consent. Many states do not recognize this type of estate, and others restrict its use. The tenancy by the entireties usually takes the form of a transfer to husband and wife. Thus, where a conveyance is made to a husband and wife and a third person, the husband and wife would take their interest in tenancy by the entireties, and the third party would take his interest in the property as a tenant in common. This follows from the common-law view of the husband and wife as one person. A tenancy by the entireties can be terminated only (1) if one spouse conveys his or her interest to the other, (2) if both spouses convey their interests to a third party, (3) on the death of one spouse, or (4) on divorce.

Another type of marital estate is that of *community property*. Community property has been adopted by eight states: Arizona, California, Idaho, Louisiana, Nevada, New Mexico, Texas, and Washington. The law of community property is derived from the civil law of Spain, France, and Mexico, whose laws were applied in the eight community property states before they joined the United States. Although modern community property law varies from state to state, the central idea is that a community interest of husband and wife exists in most property acquired during marriage regardless of which spouse actually acquired the property.

Community property is similar to both joint tenancy and tenancy in common. As with joint tenancy, each spouse owns an undivided interest in community property, and the interest of each spouse in the property is equal. As in a tenancy in common, there is no right of survivorship; a spouse may dispose of his or her interest in community property by will. However, most states have enacted statutes by which the community property interest of one spouse who dies without a will passes in whole or at least in part to the surviving spouse. Finally, it should be noted that community property does not extend to property owned by one spouse before marriage or acquired after marriage by gift or inheritance. Unless such property is commingled with or treated as community property, it remains the separate property of the particular spouse.

32:5 Nonpossessory Interests in Property

Certain relationships between owners of property and others can create interests in property that are not possessory. The basic types of nonpossessory interests are (1) easements, (2) profits, and (3) licenses.

Easements   An *easement* is a person's interest in somebody else's land which gives the person the right to use the land in some fashion. An easement is always distinct from the possession of the land itself, for it does not convey title to the land.

EXAMPLE
A utility company has an easement to run power lines over another's property. The utility only enjoys a limited right to use the land for a specific purpose. It has no right to possession of the property.

An easement can be created (1) voluntarily, (2) by necessity, (3) by implication, or (4) by prescription. Creation by the first three is discussed below; prescriptive easements are discussed in 32:7.
　　A property owner can voluntarily convey an easement to another person. In such a case, the owner must grant the easement by means of a deed that meets the formal requirements of the statute of frauds (see Chapter 15). An easement can also be created voluntarily by reservation. For example, an owner of property might convey part of it to another but keep an easement for himself to benefit his remaining property.
　　An easement by necessity is created when, for example, one parcel is divided into two lots and access to one lot can be had only by crossing the other. An easement by necessity can arise only if (1) the boundaries of the property over which the easement is claimed are fixed and certain; (2) the original parcel was owned at some time by a common owner; (3) there is a strict necessity for the easement's existence, such as no other access to a public road; and (4) the necessity arose when one parcel of land was severed from another. An easement by necessity terminates as soon as the necessity terminates.
　　An easement can also arise by implication under certain circumstances. For example, if a person owns two adjacent pieces of property and uses one as a roadway to benefit the other, an implied easement will arise if the parcel benefited is later conveyed. The deed does not have to convey the easement; it will arise by implication due to the former owner's use over a continuous period of time.

Another type of easement is an easement appurtenant. An easement appurtenant is created when the owner of land grants to another some right to use the land, for the benefit of the grantee's land. The land benefited is called the dominant estate, while the land to which the easement is attached is the servient estate.

EXAMPLE

Henry owns a lot on Georgian Bay and has divided it into two parcels for sale. He conveys one to Clara and retains the other. At the time Henry conveys the land to Clara by deed, he also grants her an easement for access over his remaining parcel. The grant is an easement appurtenant since Clara owns the land benefited by the easement. Clara's parcel is the dominant estate; Henry's, the servient estate.

An easement that is not appurtenant is called an easement in gross. Easements in gross are said to be of personal benefit to the easement holder.

EXAMPLE

Con Edison obtains an easement from Farmer Dittle to run high-voltage power lines across Dittle's land to utility consumers in New York. Because this easement will benefit Con Edison itself rather than its real property (Con Edison acquires only the right to build and maintain power lines across Dittle's property), the interest is an easement in gross.

The periods of potential duration of an easement are the same as those of estates in lands. Therefore, an easement can be in fee simple, for life, or for a period of years, or it can terminate on the occurrence of a specified event. An easement in gross, being personal, is good only for the life of the easement holder.

Scope and Termination of Easements   The scope of an easement created by express grant is determined by the terms of the grant. The right to an easement includes the right to do what is necessary for its full enjoyment, but no more than that. For example, one holding a road easement may repair the road when necessary, but he is not permitted to go beyond making repairs to making improvements (such as widening and paving what was a gravel road) unless the owner of the servient estate consents.

Whenever circumstances may appear to terminate an easement, termination will occur only if the parties intended those circumstances to result in termination. Otherwise, the easement will continue to exist. If an owner of an easement discontinues its use and intends to abandon it, the easement will be extinguished. Mere nonuse, without acts indicating an intent to abandon, is insufficient to extinguish an easement by grant, but may extinguish a prescriptive easement (see 32:7) if nonuse extends for a certain statutorily prescribed period of time. Adverse use by the owner of a servient estate can also extinguish an easement. For example, if a servient estate owner constructs a fence blocking an old road used for access to another's property, such adverse use over an extended period of time might extinguish the easement. In addition, an easement can be terminated by (1) the owner's acquisition of the servient estate, or (2) a written release signed by the easement holder and the owner of the servient estate.

Profits A *profit* is the right to take off or from another's land something that is part of the property, such as minerals, crops, timber, or even wild animals living on the land. A profit is thus one person's nonpossessory interest to acquire possessory rights in something on another's property. When a profit is granted, an easement will be implied to aid in taking the profit. For example, if Wellesley, the owner of 1,000 acres of prime timber land, sells the timber to McAvoy, the latter has a profit, together with an easement to go on the timber land and remove the timber.

Licenses A *license* is a privilege to go on another's property and to do acts that otherwise would constitute trespass. The license is different from an easement because a license is revocable by the grantor. For example, if Zadok tells Brodie that he may hunt and fish on his property, Brodie has a license. If Brodie shows up to fish and Zadok obstructs his passage, this act revokes the license and Brodie has no claim against Zadok. A license is usually presumed to be personal and nonassignable. However, if the parties so intend, it may be made transferable.

32:6   Transfer of Property by Deed

A *deed* is an instrument by which a property owner, called the grantor, conveys property to a purchaser or other transferee, called the grantee. The deed has the legal effect of transferring to the grantee title to an interest in land and buildings or other structures situated on the property. Deeds are generally classified on the basis of different title covenants or guaranties undertaken by the grantor. These covenants protect the grantee against problems that might occur after title has been transferred.

Originally, under feudal law, conveyances occurred in a ceremonial, physical transfer of property called livery of seisin, with both parties on the land. No written instrument was required in the ceremony. In 1536, the Statute of Uses was enacted in England by which a conveyor of property could transfer title by document. In 1677, the Statute of Frauds was enacted in England. It provided, among other things, that no estate could be created or transferred except by an instrument in writing signed by the grantor. This statute caused documentary transfers to be absolutely necessary and in this way established the foundation for our modern system of deeds and conveyances.[4]

To satisfy the modern statute of frauds, which has been codified by every state, a deed must be in writing and signed by the grantor. A deed must sufficiently identify the parties to the transaction and identify the property conveyed with reasonable certainty.

Title to property passes on actual or constructive delivery of a valid deed describing that property. Actual delivery occurs on the physical delivery of the instrument to the grantee by the grantor with the intent to pass title. Constructive delivery occurs if it is evident that, by his words and conduct, a grantor intends to relinquish all control and ownership of a deed or property, even though the deed

---

[4]The statute of frauds as it pertains to contracts is discussed in Chapter 15.

or property might still be in his possession. The recording of a deed by a grantor in the appropriate county registry of deeds raises a presumption that the deed was delivered. However, recording is not considered delivery under the law; the grantee's subsequent acceptance of a deed after recording will ordinarily be considered legal delivery. Therefore, when a grantor has delivered a deed with intent to transfer title and the grantee has accepted delivery, title to the property becomes vested in the grantee. A simple redelivery or cancellation of the deed at this time does not restore the property to the grantor.

A deed cannot be delivered conditionally to a grantee. However, a deed can be given to a third party to be held pending the happening of a certain event, after which it is to be delivered unconditionally to the grantee. In such a case, the instrument becomes effective as a conveyance on the second delivery, when title actually passes.

EXAMPLE
A typical residential sale entails the conditional delivery into escrow of a deed to the property to be sold, contingent on the purchaser's performance of various acts, including payment of the purchase price. When these conditions have been performed and the purchase price is paid "into escrow" (see Chapter 34), title to the property is delivered to the purchaser out of escrow and the purchase price is transferred to the seller.

 Under the law, a deed is simply an evidence of title. Its loss, destruction, assignment, redelivery, or other disposition has no effect on the title or ownership of the property conveyed.

Description of Property   No particular method of land description is required to convey property by deed. To be effective, any description used must identify the property with reasonable certainty. If a description is ambiguous, the general rule is that the grantor did not intend to convey anything and that no property was actually transferred. Although property is sometimes described by street and number, reference to adjacent property, or the historical name of property, there are four methods of land description that are primarily used. They are (1) rectangular coordinates, (2) parcel maps, (3) metes and bounds, and (4) courses and distances.

Under the system of rectangular coordinates as used in federal surveys, particularly in the western United States, land is divided into square townships that are six miles on each side, and identified by reference to a principal meridian, which runs longitudinally, and a principal base line, which runs latitudinally. Each township is composed of 36 sections, each containing one square mile, or 640 acres. Each township is further subdivided into quarter-quarter sections, each containing 40 acres. Thus, for example, a boundary line might be described in part, using rectangular coordinates, as "running in a north–south direction and being 150 feet east of the northwest corner of the northeast quarter" of a particular section in a particular township.

When a tract of land is subdivided, the subdivider ordinarily files a parcel map in the appropriate public office. The parcel map becomes a public record in which each parcel in the subdivision is identified by number. When a parcel is sold, the description in a deed will refer to the parcel map and be identified by its number.

Property can also be described by the location or identity of natural or artificial monuments, such as rocks, trees, fence posts, and stakes located on the periphery of affected property. The distance along the peripheral lines of property between two monuments is described in feet, yards, or meters. Such a description in a deed giving distances is called a description by metes and bounds.

Property can also be described by reference to directions on a compass and distances in such directions. For example, a deed may describe a particular piece of property, beginning with "monument A, then north 150 feet, then west 150 feet, then south 150 feet, then east 150 feet, then back to the place of beginning." Such directions, based on the points of the compass, are called courses and distances.

General Warranty Deed   The type of deed that gives the grantee the most protection is called the general *warranty deed*. By a general warranty deed, the grantor warrants (guarantees) the title against defects arising both before and during his ownership of the property. The grantor warrants that he has the estate he purports to convey and the authority to convey it, and that there are no physical or title encumbrances outstanding against the property.

The law has developed various guaranties of the grantor's title and ownership to protect the purchaser of property. These guaranties are commonly referred to as covenants for title and are incorporated into the general warranty deed. They include (1) the covenant for seisin, which is a guaranty that the grantor owns the property to be conveyed; (2) the covenant of the right to convey, which is a guaranty that the grantor has a right to convey the property; (3) the covenant against encumbrances, which is a guaranty that there are no mortgages, tax liens, easements, or other encumbrances outstanding against the property to be conveyed; (4) the covenant of quiet enjoyment, which is a guaranty that the purchaser will not be disturbed in the future by the grantor or others who may claim an interest in the property; and (5) the covenant for future assurances, which is a guaranty that the grantor will do all acts within his power necessary to make the purchaser's title good. Breach of any of these covenants may entitle the grantee to damages for losses arising from the breach.

Special Warranty Deed   The special warranty deed is more limited in the number of covenants that the grantor gives. Under the special warranty deed, the grantor warrants (1) that the title is free of defects that arose during his ownership of the property, (2) that he has the estate that he purports to convey, and (3) that the estate is free from physical or title encumbrances that may have been created by him.

 In the past, most deeds of conveyance were general warranty deeds. In recent years, there has been a steady trend against the use of such deeds, particularly in large cities. Banks and lending institutions almost invariably refuse to give any warranties, and well-advised businesspersons will do the same. A deed without guaranties requires the purchaser to satisfy himself about the sufficiency of title before the transaction is completed, and it precludes future claims that could arise against the grantor, except in case of fraud. The grantee ordinarily protects himself by obtaining "title insurance."[5]

Quitclaim Deed   A grantor who conveys property by a *quitclaim deed* does not make any warranties with respect to title. The effect of a quitclaim deed is limited to transferring to the grantee whatever interest, if any, that the grantor has in the land. In some states, so-called bargain and sale deeds are used in lieu of quitclaim deeds, but there is no real difference between them.

Recording of Deeds   In some circumstances, the same interest in property will be conveyed to more than one person. If a dispute develops between or among conflicting interests, the law must have a fair and predictable method of deciding who will win. Today, the recording acts adopted in every state establish priorities among multiple grantees of the same interest in property. Recording acts are designed to protect innocent purchasers, while affording grantors a procedure to protect title to their property and to provide a permanent record of land transactions.

Under the recording acts, which vary significantly from state to state, any instrument evidencing an interest in property can be recorded. The grantee presents the instrument at a clerk's office or registry of deeds in the county where the land is located. A permanent copy of the instrument is made, and it is thereafter filed according to the date and time of presentation. The original deed is returned to the grantee. A reference to the deed is also usually made in some sort of index, arranged either alphabetically by name (grantor–grantee and grantee–grantor indexes) or according to the location of the property (tract index). These indexes are keyed by date and page number to the volumes of copied instruments so that a deed can be located if the name of either party or the property's location is known.

The act of recording gives notice to the entire world of the existence and contents of a recorded deed or instrument. Obviously, not everyone has actual notice of a deed or its recordation. The primary significance of recording acts is that they are the basis of constructive notice. This means that although a person might not actually know of a deed's existence, the opportunity to learn about it exists, and the person can be charged with knowledge of its contents.

32:7   Other Methods of Acquiring or Transferring Property

Property can be acquired through occupancy, transfer, gift, will, or purchase. All these methods imply voluntary acts by owners to part with their property. Other methods of acquiring property also exist by which ownership is transferred through use, either adverse or in opposition to the rights of the true property owner. Title to property so acquired is gained through *adverse possession*. Lesser rights to the use of property can be acquired through prescriptive easements.

---

[5]Title insurance is discussed in Chapters 34 and 40.

Adverse Possession Public policy protects established interests in property, but it also favors the productive use of property. Adverse possession is a method of acquiring title to property based on possession. To establish title by adverse possession, a claimant must show possession that (1) is actual, (2) is open, (3) is either hostile to the true owner's rights or based on a claimed right, (4) is exclusive, and (5) lasts during the period of time required by statute.

The basic theory of adverse possession is simple. If after a specific number of years a property owner has not taken legal action to eject one who has been occupying his property without consent, the owner is prevented from bringing an action, and title passes to the person in possession. Bear in mind, however, that the statutes governing adverse possession vary considerably from state to state.

The elements of adverse possession are discussed and analyzed in the following case. Note how, under the facts of the case, the requirements of adverse possession were met as to one of the parcels in question, but not as to the other.

Teson

v

Vasquez
561 SW2d 119
(Missouri Court of Appeals, 1977)

[Teson filed suit in 1969 seeking to quiet title to certain property, allegedly acquired by adverse possession. This means that he sought a court order to the effect that he was now the true owner of the property. Teson claimed one parcel through acquisition of title by quitclaim deed in 1925, continuous farming of it since 1941, and the payment of taxes. As to a second parcel, Teson claimed that he had begun clearing the property approximately 25 years before commencing the lawsuit, but he admitted that he had begun farming this tract only a few years prior to trial. The trial court held that Teson established the elements of adverse possession to both tracts, and the owner appealed.]

Gunn, Presiding Judge.

*   *   *

Before detailing and examining claimant's acts of possession which allegedly vested title in [him] to the land in controversy, we [state] the well settled precepts of the law of adverse

possession. The claimant has the burden of proving by the preponderance of the evidence the existence for the entire statutory period of each and every element of adverse possession. He must show actual, hostile, i.e., under a claim of right, open and notorious, exclusive and continuous possession of the property for [the statutory period, which is ten years in Missouri]. Failure to prove any one element prevents the ripening of title by adverse possession. . . .

The essential requirement of adverse possession is that the possessor's occupancy be truly adverse and in opposition to the title of the record owner. . . . The claimant must occupy the particular piece of property intending to possess it as his own. His occupancy must be in defiance of, not in subordination to, the rights of others. . . . An adverse possessor does not recognize the authority of the record titleholder to permit or to prevent his continued use of the property claimed. . . . Such adversity is shown by satisfaction by the five elements of adverse possession.

The first element is actual possession. Two concepts are relevant in determining whether a claimant has established his actual possession of the land claimed. They are his present ability to control the land and his intent to exclude others from such control. . . . Where the claimant occupies land without color of title, in order to prevail, he must show physical possession of the entire area claimed. . . . A mere mental enclosure of land does not constitute the requisite actual possession. . . . Rather, there must be continual acts of occupying, clearing, cultivating, pasturing, erecting fences or other improvements and paying taxes on the land. The performance of all or any combination of these acts of occupancy serves as evidence of actual possession but is not conclusive. . . .

Where the claimant occupies land under color of title the requirement of actual possession of the entire area claimed is relaxed. By statute, one who occupies land under color of title is required only to physically possess a part of the tract claimed in the name of the whole, if during the period of possession he exercises the usual acts of ownership over the whole. . . . Thus, color of title is not an element of adverse possession, but it serves to extend actual possession of some portion of the land claimed to constructive possession of the whole tract described in the instrument providing the basis for color of title. . . . The instrument relied upon as color of title must be bona fide and must purport on its face to convey title to the land. . . . It need not actually convey legal title so long as it pretends to make the claimant the apparent owner. Even a void deed is sufficient to constitute color of title if it includes within its description the land claimed. . . .

The second element which must be proved to establish adverse possession is that the possession be hostile or under a claim of right. Naked possession asserted for any period of time, no matter how lengthy, is insufficient to ripen into adverse possession. . . . For possession to be hostile it is neither required that the true owner have knowledge of the hostile claim of right nor that the claimant intend to deprive him of title. . . . The possession must be opposed and antagonistic to the claims of all others, i.e., the claimant must occupy the land with the intent to possess it as his own and not in subservience to a recognized, superior claim of another. . . . Furthermore, the claim of right or ownership must be unequivocal. . . .

The third element of adverse possession is that the possession be open and notorious. To satisfy this element it is necessary to prove that the claimant's occupancy was conspicuous, widely recognized, and commonly known. . . . One may not acquire title by adverse possession if his occupancy has been so covert that it is unknown to the persons who deal regularly with and around the land claimed. The reason the law requires open and notorious possession for title to ripen by adverse possession is to give the owner cause to know of the adverse claim of ownership by another. Thus, if the true owner has actual knowledge that another claims in defiance of and in opposition to his title, the openness and notoriety requirement is satisfied. It is not the mere knowledge of occupation of his land by another which will prejudice the true owner's rights under his title. Rather, it is the adverse and hostile character of the occupation which must be known. . . . If actual knowledge is not proved then the claimant must show an occupancy so obvious and well recognized as to be inconsistent with and injurious to the real owner's rights that the law will authorize a presumption from the facts that he had such knowledge. . . .

The fourth element of adverse possession, that of exclusivity of possession, only requires that the claimant occupy the land for his own use and not for that of another. . . . Generally, one may not be vicariously vested with title by adverse possession as a result of possession by another, though where there is the requisite relationship between the parties, tacking of possession [adding the period of one person's possession to that of another person] is allowed. . . .

The final element of adverse possession is that the occupancy be continuous, i.e., without lapse, for the entire statutory period. Temporary absence from the land without an intention to abandon possession will not break the continuity of possession; intermittent and sporadic occupancy will. . . . In judging the continuity of possession, the character and use to which the land is adaptable must be taken into account. For instance, under the facts of this case, the periodic flooding which made access to and use of the property impossible for entire growing seasons would not interrupt the continuity of possession unless there was an intent to abandon possession after the waters receded.

One overriding requirement to establish adverse possession to a particular piece of property is that the precise location of the land claimed be identified in such a way that the boundaries may be ascertained and recognized. . . . Absent proof by claimant of the exact location of lands claimed, any judgment would be void, because it would rest entirely on speculation and conjecture. . . .

The trial court held that Teson's 1925 deed did not constitute color of title. Nevertheless, it held that Teson had established the elements of adverse possession to a tract of approximately twenty acres adjacent to Aubuchon Road extending north of Cowmire Creek to a small tarn known as "Round Pond." Title to a second parcel of almost forty acres near the [Missouri River] was also vested in Teson. . . .

Under the . . . facts we affirm the trial court's judgment as to the parcel near Aubuchon Road and reverse as to the parcel near the river. . . . Teson's proof failed to establish that he had continuously and actually possessed any specific portion of the property near the river. There was testimony of sporadic clearing and cultivation of land somewhere near the river over the years by various persons, including defendant [the record owner] and his relatives. There was little credible evidence of any sustained and permanent clearing until the mid 1960's. Teson admitted in his deposition that he had not farmed the . . . land claimed until the last few years before the trial, because it was covered with timber.

Though there is sufficient proof that Teson and his sons did engage in some farming activities on the land near the river, the evidence completely failed to establish the precise boundaries of any tract Teson used for the statutory period. As such, the trial court had no basis to conclude that Teson actually and continuously possessed the 40 acre tract it awarded him.

Furthermore, title by adverse possession to land near the river could not vest in Teson, because his possession was not open and notorious for the entire statutory period. There is no evidence that defendant had actual knowledge of Teson's possession. Nor does the record reveal sufficient facts from which we could presume constructive knowledge on the part of defendant. Teson's presence on the land was only sporadic and until the mid 1960's was confined to small areas which he could clear with hand equipment. The land was densely thicketed with trees, brush and vines which served to obscure any progress made. Moreover, there were no fences or other readily observable boundaries. Thus, the trial court's finding of title by adverse possession to the northern 40 acres in Teson was in error, because actual, open and notorious possession was not proved. Nor were exact boundaries established to any smaller parcel for which the elements of adverse possession may have been satisfied. Therefore, the trial court's designation of title to the northern 40 acres in Teson was speculative and conjectural and cannot stand.

As to the southern portion near Aubuchon Road, it cannot be said that the trial court erred in finding title by adverse possession in Teson. It is clear that Teson had acquired title to the tract between Aubuchon Road and Cowmire Creek by adverse possession. . . . The land in question is only that which lies between Cowmire Creek and Round Pond.

The testimony was conflicting, but there was competent evidence that Teson had farmed the 20 acres between Aubuchon Road and Round Pond continuously for a time well beyond the statutory period. This parcel, unlike that near the river, was in plain sight from Aubuchon Road. The cultivation must have been clearly visible from the public thoroughfare and open and notorious.

[Judgment affirmed in part and reversed in part.]

Prescriptive Easements   Just as title to property can be acquired by adverse possession, an easement can be acquired by what is known as prescription through adverse use. The elements required for obtaining easement rights by prescription are similar to those involved in adverse possession. The scope of a *prescriptive easement*, however, is measured by the extent of the actual, adverse use of the property over which the easement is acquired. For example, if a pathway is acquired by prescription, the easement is generally limited to foot traffic, or at most bicycle traffic; certainly, the easement holder may not drive a dump truck along the pathway. This limit on prescriptive easements is quite different from the permissible uses of property acquired by adverse possession, where no such restrictions apply. For example, if title to property is gained through adverse possession by the possessor's herding cattle for the required number of years, his rights are absolute. He can stop herding cattle and build condominiums on the land or use it for any other lawful purpose.

 An owner can protect his rights in a variety of ways to prevent prescriptive easements from arising. He can block off his land from time to time, thereby breaking the continuity of use. He can also give users written permission to use the property for a stated purpose at stated times. This permission negates one of the elements required to establish a prescriptive easement. Finally, the owner can go to court to stop the use by injunction within the time limit specified by law.

Key Concepts and Terms

- The ways by which property can be acquired include occupancy, transfer, gift, will, and purchase.
- Property can be tangible or intangible and can constitute land, buildings, or articles of personal use. "Property" includes animate objects, obligations, debts, products of labor or skill, and all other things of value.
- The two basic classes of property are (1) land and that which is attached to land, called real property; and (2) movable things or articles, called personal property.
- All property has an owner, either public or private. Ownership carries with it the right to dispose of and create lesser interests in property.
- The ownership of property is either absolute or qualified. It is absolute when a single person has absolute dominion and control over the property and can use or dispose of it according to his pleasure, subject only to general laws in force.

The ownership of property is qualified when it is shared with one or more persons, when the time of enjoyment is deferred, or when its use is restricted in some fashion.

- Property rights are specifically protected by the United States Constitution and by the laws of every state. The Fifth Amendment to the United States Constitution prohibits the deprivation of property without due process of law or the taking of property for public use without just compensation. The Fourteenth Amendment provides in part that a person may not be deprived of property without due process of law.

- An estate in land is an interest in property of a given duration or time. The principal types of estates that exist are (1) fee simple, (2) life estate, and (3) non-freehold estate. A future interest is a property interest that comes into existence at some time in the future.

- An estate in property can be held by a single individual or concurrently by two or more persons. The major forms of concurrent ownership are (1) tenancy in common; (2) joint tenancy; (3) partnership ownership; (4) condominium or co-operative ownership; and (5) forms of marital ownership, such as tenancy by the entireties.

- A cotenancy is a property interest in which ownership interests are shared. Types of cotenancy include (1) a joint tenancy, (2) a tenancy in common, (3) a tenancy by the entireties, and (4) the community interests of husband and wife.

- Property is usually transferred by deed. A deed is an instrument made by a grantor of property in favor of the grantee, the person to whom the property is conveyed. Deeds are generally classified on the basis of different title covenants or guaranties undertaken by the grantor. The most common deeds are the general warranty deed, the special warranty deed, and the quitclaim or bargain and sale deed.

- A deed must be in writing and signed by the grantor. The deed must sufficiently identify the parties to the transaction and the land conveyed, and it is not effective until it is delivered.

- Land is usually described by one of the following methods: (1) rectangular coordinates, (2) parcel maps, (3) metes and bounds, and (4) courses and distances.

- A property owner can also grant to someone else a nonpossessory interest in the property. The basic types of nonpossessory interests are (1) easements, (2) licenses, and (3) profits.

- Adverse possession is a method of acquiring title to property based on possession. To establish title by adverse possession a claimant must show possession that (1) is actual, (2) is open and notorious, (3) is either hostile to the record owner's rights or is based on a claim of right, (4) is exclusive, and (5) lasts during the period of time prescribed by statute.

- An easement, which is a person's interest in somebody else's land that gives the person the right to use the land, can be acquired by prescription or adverse use.

- Adverse Possession
- Community Property
- Deed
- Easement
- Estate
- Fee Simple
- Future Interest
- Joint Tenants
- License
- Life Estate
- Nonfreehold Estate

- Prescriptive Easement
- Profit
- Quitclaim Deed
- Real Property
- Remainder
- Reversion
- Survivorship
- Tenancy by the Entireties
- Tenancy in Common
- Warranty Deed

Questions and Case Problems

1. Delamirie finds a ring with a valuable stone and takes it to Armory for appraisal. Armory retains the ring, and takes the stone from the setting. When Delamirie demands the ring's return, she is offered the setting minus the stone. Delamirie sues Armory for the return of the stone. How should the case be decided? Why?

2. Lewis sells Lester the Boca Grande Residential Hotel for $100,000 in cash. The terms of sale do not mention fixtures, such as stoves, refrigerators, rugs, curtain rods, and bathroom and light fixtures, which Lewis placed on the property during his ownership. Lewis wants to remove these from the hotel but Lester objects, claiming that the items are fixtures which pass with the real estate under the conveyance. To whom do the items belong?

3. Truax and Ajax purchase a dairy and hold title to the property as tenants in common. Ajax takes possession of the farm, while Truax continues to reside in a distant city. The dairy becomes very profitable under Ajax. Is Truax entitled to share in the proceeds? If so, to what degree? If Ajax leases the land to Cardax for $1,000 per month, is Truax entitled to a portion of the rental? If Ajax commences a farming operation on the property, growing corn and other grains, is Truax entitled to share in the proceeds of sale? If Ajax constructs new buildings on the property to maintain the dairy and farming operations, must Truax contribute to the cost of construction? If Ajax wants to leave the dairy and farming business, may he sell the property on his own, or must he obtain the consent of Truax? Suppose that Truax objects to the sale of the dairy; what can Ajax do?

4. Analyze the various possessory interests in property and the characteristics of each.

5. Compare and contrast ownership with possession of property.

6. Buller prepares a deed conveying her ranch to Roberts and instructs a friend, Powell, to give the deed to Roberts. Can Buller recall the deed before it is given to Roberts? Is it possible for Roberts to take title before the deed has been handed over to him?

7. Why is an easement called a nonpossessory interest in property?

8. Franks builds a fence on property she thinks she owns, but it is actually 15 feet within her neighbor Nunes' lot. After the prescribed statutory period has expired, does Franks acquire the strip by adverse possession? If Franks and Nunes both

INTRODUCTION TO THE LAW OF PROPERTY

agree on the location of the fence, but each erroneously thinks it is built on the property line, when in fact it is entirely on Nunes' property, does Franks acquire title after expiration of the applicable statutory period?

9. RKO Theater and a bank are neighbors. A public sidewalk runs in front of the two buildings. The bank owns the land under the sidewalk, but since the theater had been built its employees have used the sidewalk to maintain and change the marquee. For 21 years the theater has used the sidewalk for this purpose. Has the theater acquired an easement? If so, what kind? Can a court order the bank not to interfere with the theater's use of the sidewalk?

10. Discuss the elements of adverse possession. How does property acquired by adverse possession differ from a prescriptive easement?

33 Bailments and Leases of Personal Property

Bailments

33:1 Introduction

A *bailment* is a legally recognized relationship that arises when one person delivers personal property to another on condition that the property be returned. The person who owns the property and turns over possession of it is called the bailor. The person to whom possession is given is the bailee. The principal elements of every bailment are (1) the bailor's delivery of property into the bailee's lawful custody or possession, (2) the bailee's acceptance of the property, and (3) the bailee's obligation to restore it to the bailor. Examples of particular bailment transactions include lending or leasing personal property for cleaning, repair, or the performance of services; delivering goods on commission for sale; and pledging personal property as security for a debt. A bailment also arises when goods are stored in a warehouse or transported by a common carrier.

Most bailments are created by express agreement. A bailment agreement can be oral or written, and it may or may not be supported by consideration. A bailment can also be implied by the parties' acts, however. For example, an implied bailment is created when a person deposits clothes with a dry cleaner. A written contract in such a situation is not ordinarily signed by the parties, it being understood that the clothes will be returned to the owner after they are cleaned. In addition, the law implies a bailment in certain situations. These bailments are known as involuntary or constructive bailments.

EXAMPLE
The captain of a fishing vessel unintentionally hauls in traps belonging to a commercial lobsterman and keeps them on board until the boat's return to port rather than throwing them back into the water. The captain is an involuntary bailee of the lobster traps. If, instead, the captain obtained possession of the traps through fraud or trickery, the bailment would be a constructive one.

Classes of Bailments   Bailments are generally classified according to the duties and liabilities of the parties. The three classes of bailments are (1) those for the sole benefit of the bailor, (2) those for the sole benefit of the bailee, and (3) those for the mutual benefit of both parties. By way of example, a bailment for the sole benefit of the bailor is created when the owner of a trailer stores it free of charge on a truck dealer's lot near his home. A bailment for the sole benefit of the bailee is created when a used-car dealer parks another's antique car in a display area of his car lot to attract customers. A *bailment for the mutual benefit* of both parties is created when one person leases a car from another. Bailments for the sole benefit of either the bailor or bailee are generally gratuitous, while bailments for the mutual benefit of both parties involve compensation and are known as bailments for hire.

The various elements of a bailment are discussed in the following case. Consider why the court held that a bailment contract did not arise here.

Collins

v

Boeing Co.
4 Wash App 705, 483 P2d 1282, 46 ALR3d 1294
(Washington Court of Appeals, 1971)

[Collins sued his employer, Boeing, for the loss of tools that had been stolen after he had left them overnight for his own convenience. When Collins had first begun to work for Boeing, the company had informed him that it would not be responsible for the loss of personal tools. At work Boeing did not provide lockable receptacles or the means to secure tool boxes to work benches, but it did maintain an internal security system that included guards on duty 24 hours a day. Collins contended that a bailment relationship arose, imposing on Boeing a duty of ordinary care with respect to his tools. Judgment was for Boeing in the trial court, and Collins appealed.]

Horowitz, Ch. J.

*   *   *

Plaintiff . . . contends that the defendant is under a contractual duty to protect his toolbox containing his tools against theft by third persons on contract principles predicated upon the existence of a bailment relationship between the parties. Under the evidence here, we find no bailment. Except in the so-called constructive or involuntary bailment cases in which a duty of care is recognized, e.g., possession taken by a finder, or possession taken by mistake, or because involuntarily thrust upon another, bailment normally is a consensual transaction. . . .

The bailor intentionally delivers possession of his goods to the bailee and the latter accepts the same with a real or a presumed knowledge of the responsibility entailed thereby. . . . Resort to the concept of constructive or involuntary bailment on which to base a duty of care is unnecessary here. There is sufficient evidence from which the court could find that the mutual intention of the parties, manifested by their conduct, prevented a consensual bailment from arising. We know of no public policy that requires us to substitute a constructive or involuntary bailment responsibility which the parties by mutual manifest intention have rejected.

Before a consensual bailment of personal property may be said to arise, there must be a change of possession and an assumption or acceptance of possession by the person claimed to be a bailee. . . . Whether there is a change or acceptance of possession depends on whether there is a change or acceptance of actual or potential control in fact over the subject matter. Such control may be actual or physical, or it may be constructive—recognized by law as the equivalent of actual control. In determining whether control exists, it is relevant to consider the subject matter's amenability to control, steps taken to effect control, the existence of power over the subject matter, the existence of power to exclude others from control, and the intention with which the acts in relation to the subject matter are performed. Thus one who pays a fee to a parking lot operator, parks his car himself on the parking operator's lot and retains his own keys, does not thereby change possession of his car to the parking lot operator so as to create a bailment. . . . If, however, the parking lot operator gives the person parking his car a claim check and receives a key to the car, thus giving him control over it, then there is both change and assumption of possession and a bailment is thereby created.

In addition to physical control over the thing possessed, there must be a manifested intention to exercise that control. . . .

In the instant case, the trial court could draw more than one inference concerning the existence of the constitutive elements of bailment. Defendant's security provisions, including ingress and egress requirements, might suggest change of control by plaintiff and assumption of control of the toolbox by defendant with resulting imposition upon defendant of a duty of care to prevent its theft by third persons. There is other evidence, however, that the security measures were adopted to protect defendant's plant and defendant's own personal property therein—measures which might also serve to protect plaintiff's toolbox and tools as a matter of accommodation. That this was so is confirmed by the fact that from the inception of the employment relationship and without objection by the plaintiff, and consistent with industry practice, defendant had disclaimed any responsibility for theft by third persons. Accordingly, as plaintiff at all times knew, defendant provided no receptacles, lockable enclosures, chains or other lines affixed to benches or posts to which the toolbox containing the plaintiff's tools could be tied to prevent wrongful removal. . . . The trial court could find that plaintiff, by manifest intention and for his own convenience and without defendant's request and at his own risk, left his toolbox containing all his tools, both required and not required, at the plant at the close of the working day without changing their possession to the defendant; and that the defendant took neither custody, control, nor possession of the toolbox and tools in the sense required by the law of bailment. We know of no public policy that requires us to fail to give effect to the manifest intentions of the parties here. . . .

[Judgment affirmed.]

33:2   Termination of Bailments

A bailment can be terminated in a number of ways. For example, the parties can terminate a bailment by mutual agreement at any time, or one party might be able to rescind the bailment contract. A bailment for a stated period terminates at the end of that period; one for a specific purpose terminates when that purpose is accomplished. Destruction of the property may also terminate a bailment. Further, if a bailee acts improperly with respect to bailed property, the bailment may be terminated by operation of law, and any attempt by a bailee to sell or substantially abuse or misuse the bailed property automatically terminates the bailment in most states and entitles the owner to recover the property.

33:3 Rights and Liabilities of Bailor and Bailee

The rights, duties, and liabilities of a bailor and a bailee between one another are generally fixed by state statute or common law unless modified by the terms of a valid contract between them. As a rule, the bailment contract determines the parties' rights and duties.

Title to Property and Right of Possession On the creation of a bailment, title to the property remains in the bailor. Unauthorized acts by the bailee, such as a sale of bailed property to an innocent purchaser, do not affect the bailor's title. During the bailment, the bailee controls the property and can prevent others from possessing it. So long as the bailee acts within the purpose of a bailment, the bailor has no right to retake possession of the property without the bailee's consent.

Return of Bailed Property On termination of a bailment, the bailee must return bailed property or account for it according to the terms of the bailment. A bailee who refuses to return property, disposes of it in an unauthorized manner, or uses it for purposes not contemplated in the bailment can be held liable to the bailor for damages. In most cases, the bailee must return the identical goods bailed. However, in the case of fungible goods, such as wheat, coffee, barrels of oil, or canned goods, a return of the same quantity as originally bailed is sufficient; each unit of the bailed property is the same as every other. Some bailment agreements include an option to purchase the bailed property. These options are often used in lease transactions. If the bailee exercises the option, the transaction becomes a sale and the bailee does not have to return the bailed property.

Bailee's Duty of Care The degree of care required of a bailee depends on the class or type of bailment. When the bailment is for the bailor's sole benefit, without any compensation to the bailee, the bailee is answerable for loss or damage only if he is grossly negligent. When a bailment is mutually beneficial to both parties, the bailee is held responsible for ordinary negligence. When it is for the bailee's sole benefit, as in the case of a simple loan of property without compensation, the bailee must exercise the highest degree of care and will be held liable for even slight negligence resulting in loss or damage to the property. Distinctions in the duty of care among the three classes of bailments have been abolished in some states. There, all bailees must exercise ordinary care over bailed property depending on its nature, value, and quality; the circumstances under which it was deposited; and the terms of the bailment agreement. A few types of bailees, such as common carriers and innkeepers, are held strictly liable for loss or damage of bailed property on the grounds of public policy (see 33:4 through 33:7).

Burden of Proof To recover for loss or damage to bailed property, the bailor must generally prove that the bailee breached his duty of care. In most states, the bailee's negligence is presumed if the bailee either is unable to redeliver bailed property at all or redelivers the property in a damaged condition. In these states, the bailor need only establish that a bailment was created, that bailed property was delivered in good condition, and that the bailee failed to return the property in the same condition at the end of the bailment. The bailee must then prove otherwise if he is to avoid liability for the loss or damage. The rationale behind this rule is that the bailee is always in a better position to offer proof of his own care for bailed property than is the bailor to offer proof of the bailee's negligence.[1]

The following case illustrates the bailor's burden of proof and why bailment is considered a special relationship in the law. Consider the burden of proof and the presumption of negligence, and compare these with the requirements of proof in normal negligence cases.

Jones

v

Warner

57 Wash 2d 647, 359 P2d 160, 92 ALR2d 1404

(Washington Supreme Court, 1961)

[Jones bought a new set of tires from Warner and left his car to have them mounted. At the same time, he requested Warner to adjust the valves. Later in the day, Jones returned and was informed that the car was inoperative. On examination, it was revealed that one of the valves had broken, causing severe damage to a cylinder and to the pistons of four other cylinders. Jones sued to recover the cost of installing a new engine. Judgment was for Jones, and Warner appealed.]

Rosellini, J.

*   *   *

The appellant contends ... that the evidence is insufficient to support the court's finding that the appellant was negligent.

A bailee is not an insurer of property placed in his charge, but is only required to exercise ordinary care.... But where property not per-

ishable in nature is delivered to a bailee in good condition, and is not returned or is returned damaged, a presumption arises of negligence on the part of the bailee and casts upon him the burden of showing the exercise of ordinary care.... However, the presumption does not arise unless it appears that the subject of the bailment is of such a nature that loss or injury could not ordinarily have occurred without negligence on the part of the bailee....

The appellant's evidence showed that there was a possibility that the damage was caused by crystallization of the metal, and his [employees] testified that they performed their work in a careful and proper manner. The respondent's evidence, on the other hand, tended to show that the damage occurred one of three ways, each of which would have been the result of negligence, and that the damage was of a kind which cannot occur, ordinarily, without negligence. The court was not obliged to accept the appellant's evidence and reject that of the respondent.

The evidence of the respondent, which was believed by the trier of the facts, was sufficient to raise a presumption of negligence on the part of the appellant, and we cannot say that,

---

[1]Negligence and the burden of proof are discussed generally in Chapter 6.

as a matter of law, the evidence offered by the appellant rebutted that presumption.

It is not the law, as contended by the appellant, that he has sustained his burden of proof when he has produced evidence that the damage possibly could have resulted from some cause other than his negligence. In order to make a prima facie case, a plaintiff is not required to show that a cause other than negligence could not possibly have produced the damage; consequently, if the plaintiff's evidence has shown to the satisfaction of the court that the damage could not ordinarily occur without negligence, a defendant cannot rebut the presumption by merely introducing evidence of some other possible cause.

[Judgment affirmed.]

Limits on Liability   Frequently, bailees insert provisions in bailment agreements limiting their liability to specified amounts. Generally, if the terms of the contract are clearly called to the bailor's attention, or if the facts are such that the bailor is chargeable with notice of the terms (as, for example, by a large sign posted at a parking lot and limiting its liability), the limit on liability set forth in the bailment contract will be upheld, at least as to claims based on negligence or breach of contract. However, provisions that excuse or limit a bailee's liability for willful injury to bailed goods are usually held to violate public policy, and they are rarely enforced by the courts. In some states, liability-limiting provisions are declared unlawful by statute.

Bailee's Lien   A bailee who has worked on an article or performed some other act in reference to it by which its value has been enhanced has a lien on the property for the value of his reasonable services. This lien allows the bailee to keep the property until he is reimbursed for his labor and expenses.

EXAMPLE

A film editor edits 39,000 feet of exposed film to make a finished product of approximately 5,000 feet for the bailor. The bailor then fails to pay the editor the agreed amount for his services. The editor has a bailee's lien covering the film footage remaining in his possession.

A *bailee's lien* traditionally has been limited to keeping bailed property until payment of the lien. Most states provide by statute for the public sale of bailed property after notice to the bailor that the property will be put up for sale due to nonpayment. A bailee who fails to follow any of the statutory requirements in enforcing the lien can be liable to the bailor for conversion of the property.

Bailor's Duty of Care   The extent of a bailor's obligation depends primarily on the class of the particular bailment. In every bailment the bailor has a minimum obligation to refrain from knowingly delivering property that is likely to imperil the bailee's life or property. Where a bailment is purely gratuitous and for the bailee's exclusive benefit, as where articles are loaned without compensation, a bailor's only duty is to inform the bailee of any known defects. In a bailment for hire or for the mutual benefit of both parties, the bailor is held to a higher degree of responsibility. Although a bailor of this type is not ordinarily an insurer against injuries to the bailee for defects, he is held to a high degree of care to examine the property before it is bailed. Frequently he is regarded by the courts as impliedly warranting the reasonable suitability of the property for its intended use (see 33:9). If injury results from defective bailed property, the bailor can be liable for breach of this implied warranty. The bailor can also be liable for injuries caused by a defective condition in bailed property if the defect was known or was discoverable through the exercise of due care.

Rights and Liabilities as to Third Persons If a third person damages or unlawfully obtains possession of bailed property, either the bailor or the bailee can maintain a damages action against the third person. If the bailor sues and recovers damages, the bailee is prevented from doing so, and vice versa.

Because the bailee has possession and control of bailed property, liability for injuries resulting to a third person normally falls on the bailee rather than the bailor, whose responsibility terminates with his relinquishment of control over the property. Thus, if a bailee tries to repair bailed property but does so negligently, he can be held liable for resulting injury or damage to third persons. However, the bailor will be held liable for injuries to a third person if the bailor has been negligent in entrusting a dangerous article to a person who he knows is unfamiliar with its dangerous character or is incompetent to operate it safely. For example, if a leased machine or motor vehicle is likely to cause injury to third persons unless operated with care and skill, the lessor (bailor) can be liable in damages for injuries inflicted by the bailee if he knows the bailee is incompetent or reckless. Likewise, a bailor who negligently furnishes a bailee with property that is not reasonably fit and proper for its known or intended use can be answerable to a third person injured from the use of the property. If, however, a third person is contributorily negligent, or if the third person's injuries result from obvious defects in the bailed article or defects that are unknown to the bailor, the bailor is not liable.

33:4 Special Bailments, Generally

Bailments are sometimes classified as being either ordinary or special. Ordinary bailments include those previously discussed in this chapter. Special bailments include those involving warehousers, common carriers, and innkeepers. These bailments are for the mutual benefit of both parties and in many respects are subject to the same rules that govern ordinary bailments. However, special bailments affect the public interest in such a way that, for reasons of public policy, the law has imposed on the special bailee a somewhat different liability from that imposed on the ordinary bailee. It should be noted that special bailees may and frequently do act as ordinary bailees and are treated as such whenever the reasons for their exceptional liability do not exist.

Consignors and Factors A consignment is a transaction in which goods are delivered by their owner to another who is an agent to sell the goods. It is also called a bailment for sale and a bailment coupled with an agency to sell and, as such, is a special bailment. Delivery under a consignment is made with the understanding that the recipient (consignee) will either sell the property for the supplier (consignor) and remit the proceeds, or return the goods if a sale has not been made. The *consignor* retains title to the goods until a sale is made to a third party. The consignee never becomes personally liable for the purchase price except in the sense that he must account for the proceeds of any of his sales. When a consignee makes a sale, title to the goods flows immediately to the purchaser from the owner. By their nature, consignment transactions thus allow a supplier to sell goods through a merchant who is unwilling to risk finding a market and accept title. In a consignment, risk of loss is ordinarily placed on the consignor until the goods are sold to a third party, unless, of course, the consignment contains a provision to the contrary.

If a consignee is engaged in the business of selling goods, he is called a *factor* or commission merchant. A factor is an agent who is employed by another to sell property for him. The factor is vested by the owner with the possession or control of the property or with authority to receive payment from the purchaser for the property sold. In most states, the conduct of factors and other consignees is regulated by statutes known as Factors' Acts or Traders' Acts. These acts govern the sale of consigned goods and the rights of purchasers. The UCC also governs the rights of purchasers of goods entrusted to a merchant who deals in goods of a particular kind.

Finders of Lost Property   Many states have enacted statutes that set forth procedures, usually involving advertising and the posting of notices, by which a finder of lost property can acquire title to it. Ordinarily, a person who finds lost property does not become its owner. Rather, the finder is a bailee who must exercise the same degree of care required of any other bailee. A person cannot claim to be a finder if goods are not in fact lost.

A finder of lost property is not entitled to compensation for his services, but he may be entitled to reimbursement from the owner for any expenses incurred in protecting or preserving the property or in advertising for the owner. The finder has a duty to restore the goods to the owner if known, and if unknown, to make reasonable efforts to locate the owner. The finder also has a duty to exercise reasonable care in ascertaining the right or identity of any person claiming to be the true owner. Thus, a finder can be liable to the owner if he carelessly gives found property to someone claiming to be the owner without making reasonable inquiries to determine the validity of the claim.

33:5 Warehousers

A *warehouser* stores bailed goods and merchandise for compensation. State and federal regulations have been enacted to regulate the warehouse business. In the states, the warehousing business is governed by common-law rules involving bailments and by statute, particularly Article 7 of the UCC. The federal government has enacted the United States Warehouse Act (7 USC §§ 241–273), which regulates the storage of agricultural products.

Warehouse Receipts   Under the UCC, a warehouser must issue and deliver a warehouse receipt for goods received for storage. The warehouse receipt acknowledges that the warehouser has received certain described property from the owner or depositor; it creates the bailment contract. Transfer of property stored in a warehouse can be made by a transfer of the warehouse receipt rather than by a physical transfer of the goods. This is so because in ordinary commercial transactions, a warehouse receipt is regarded as a symbolic representation of the property stored. The receipt can also modify the ordinary rules of liability that the law imposes on warehousers.

Warehouser Liability and Standard of Care   UCC § 7-204 provides that a warehouser is liable in damages for loss of or injury to goods caused by the failure to exercise reasonable care. What constitutes reasonable care depends on the circumstances, including the nature and value of the goods stored, their exposure to injury or loss, and the means taken to prevent the injury or loss. All warehousers are generally obligated to store goods in a place that is reasonably safe from dangers, both inside and outside the premises, and reasonably fit for goods of the type accepted. A warehouser's obligation with respect to the safekeeping of goods begins when control of them is assumed, and it terminates on their delivery to the proper person. In case of theft, the warehouser must show that the loss was caused by an event beyond his control, giving proof of the circumstances of the theft and some evidence of due care on his part.

 Not being an insurer of stored goods, the warehouser is not automatically liable for loss of bailed property. The UCC requires a warehouser to exercise the degree of care in relation to stored goods that a reasonably careful person would exercise under like circumstances.

Measure of Damages   The measure of damages in an action by an owner or depositor of warehoused goods against the warehouser is full compensation for the loss. If all the goods have been lost, recoverable damages are measured by the market value of the merchandise as reflected in the warehouse receipt. If goods have been damaged, the amount recoverable is the difference in value between the goods in the condition delivered to the warehouser and their value in the damaged condition on redelivery.

Limit on Liability   Warehouse receipts frequently contain clauses limiting the warehouser's liability in case of injury to or loss of stored goods. Unless a state statute governs the matter, courts usually uphold provisions limiting liability to an agreed valuation of the property. However, a limit on liability does *not* apply if the warehouser has willfully or intentionally damaged or injured the goods, or if the warehouser has converted them to his own use.

 Despite their general tendency to uphold liability-limiting provisions in storage contracts or warehouse receipts, as mentioned above, courts have ruled that stipulations totally relieving the warehouser from the consequences of his own negligence are invalid. The UCC provides that damages for loss of or damage to stored goods can be limited by the terms of the warehouse receipt or storage agreement. The receipt or agreement can set forth a specific liability per article, item, or unit of freight. However, any such receipt or storage agreement must provide the bailor an opportunity to request an increased valuation with a corresponding increase in rates. The UCC further permits reasonable conditions as to the time and manner of presenting claims to be included in the warehouse receipt or tariff.

33:6 Common Carriers

A *common carrier* engages in the business of transporting persons or property from place to place for compensation. It is a bailee with respect to property entrusted for delivery. Common carriers are extensively governed and controlled by federal and state statutes, as well as by the UCC. Since 1887, carriers engaged in interstate commerce have been regulated and controlled by the Interstate Commerce Act (49 USC §§ 1 et seq.). The *Carmack Amendment* of 1916 is a portion of the Interstate Commerce Act. It codifies the common-law rule that a common carrier, although not an absolute insurer of goods transported, is liable for damage or loss to the goods unless the carrier can show that damage was caused by (1) an act of God, (2) a criminal act, (3) an act of the shipper, (4) action by a public authority, or (5) the inherent nature of the goods themselves [49 USC § 20(11)].

Under the Carmack Amendment, the initiating carrier is liable for the full amount of any damage to goods when they are in the care of the initiating carrier, any of the connecting carriers, or the delivering carrier. The initiating carrier's liability as an insurer ends when the final carrier ceases to act as a carrier and either assumes the role of warehouser or delivers the goods to the consignee.

The federal Bills of Lading Act of 1916 (49 USC §§ 81–124) governs bills of lading issued by common carriers for the transportation of goods in interstate or foreign commerce. Intrastate shipments and bills of lading are regulated by Article 7 of the UCC.

Carrier Liability and Duty of Care A common carrier's liability for loss, damage, or destruction of goods in transit is that of an insurer. That is, the carrier is strictly liable for loss, and no showing of its negligence is necessary unless one of the statutory or common-law exceptions applies. This rule of *strict liability* generally pertains regardless of whether a shipment is interstate (and thus subject to federal law) or intrastate (and thus subject to state law). However, limits on liability are common, and the parties can agree to reasonable limits as long as they do not violate public policy.

Freight Forwarders The *freight forwarder* is a person or firm in the business of assembling or consolidating goods that are consigned by shippers and are smaller than a carload, and then arranging for their shipment by a carrier for ultimate delivery to the intended consignees. The freight forwarder does not generally transport the goods, but acts as an agent or broker working with a carrier, which does the actual transporting. In receiving goods from shippers and in turn delivering them to a carrier, the freight forwarder is both consignee and consignor. Unless a freight forwarder also offers carrier services, it is not aware of the identity of the original consignors whose goods have been consolidated or of the ultimate consignees to whom the goods are being shipped. When the carload of consolidated goods arrives at its destination, it is broken up into the original shipments by the carrier and then delivered to the intended consignees.

33:7   Innkeepers

The business of innkeeping is as old as civilization and has a law of its own. As has been the case with other branches of the law, the rules governing innkeepers have necessarily been broadened in their application by the ever-changing conditions of modern life. The number of persons living in places other than the traditional home, either temporarily for business or pleasure, or indefinitely, has made the hotel business one of the country's largest industries.

The relationship between an innkeeper and a guest is a mutual one involving reciprocal rights and obligations. In most states many duties and obligations of both innkeepers and their guests are regulated by statute. Under a typical statute the innkeeper must furnish accommodations and exercise proper care for the safety and tranquility of the guest. In turn, a guest must observe recognized proprieties and refrain from conduct that would be offensive to other guests or bring the hotel into disrepute. Although an innkeeper's rates and charges can be fixed by contract between the parties, they are generally the same for all guests and must be just and reasonable.

Innkeeper Liability and Duty of Care   Under the common law, an innkeeper was practically an insurer of his guests' property. Today, most states have reduced the innkeeper's liability to that of an ordinary bailee. Most states also limit the extent of an innkeeper's liability, either to a stated amount for each piece of luggage or to a stated total for all other property, unless the innkeeper contractually agress to assume a greater liability. If a guest desires to impose on an innkeeper liability in excess of the limit imposed by statute, the guest must notify the innkeeper of the nature and value of the property sought to be protected.

 As a general rule, most state statutes that limit liability apply to money, jewelry, or other valuables that are to be kept within a hotel's safe or the guest's room. Under these statutes, unless the guest deposits articles of value in a hotel's safe or gives notice as to their value and existence, the innkeeper is usually absolved of any liability for loss.

Innkeepers' Liens   Under the common law, innkeepers were given a lien on their guests' property for the amount of reasonable charges furnished. That is, if a guest failed to pay, the innkeeper could assert a lien over the guest's property. In most states, the common-law lien has been codified, and innkeepers have the power to enforce their liens by court action or by sale of the property after a prescribed length of time. If a statutory lien enforcement procedure is prescribed, it is ordinarily exclusive and must be followed. Despite the increasing due process protections given owners of property before it may be taken or sold (as discussed in Chapter 30, for example, the constitutionality of these lien statutes has been upheld against contentions that they permit the taking of property without due process of law or without just compensation.

Leases of Personal Property

33:8   Introduction

The *leasing of personal property* plays a prominent and vital role in the American economy. Billions of dollars' worth of new and used goods and equipment are under lease today. It has been estimated that 70 percent of all computers, 30 percent of all passenger cars, 60 percent of all office equipment, 50 percent of all railroad cars, 25 percent of all aircraft, 15 percent of all ships, and 10 percent of all machinery and furniture are under lease.

A personal property lease entails the temporary transfer of possession and use of one's property for compensation to another, who agrees to return the property at a future time. The lease is a type of bailment and is generally governed by the rules of law applicable to bailments. The parties to a personal property lease used to be referred to as the lessor and the hirer, but today they are more commonly referred to as the lessor and the lessee.

Various types of leases are commonly used by the business community. The lease that is ultimately chosen depends, of course, on the circumstances of the leasing transaction and the parties' needs. Leases offer many advantages to a business. Since leasing does not require a large outlay of cash, working capital remains free for other uses. This freed working capital can improve the appearance of the lessee's short-term financial position as indicated on its balance sheet. Leasing is also preferable when permanent ownership is not desired, such as when a product is in a high technology field and is likely to become rapidly obsolete. Leases are also attractive to businesses that are subject to frequently changing government regulations or when property is likely to wear out or need constant repair. Leasing may be particularly attractive to a business experiencing a cash shortage. In this situation, leasing offers the additional advantages of conserving credit; the business can maintain its cash position by not having to pay a down payment in a purchase that is financed by a loan. Another financial benefit is more favorable tax treatment in that the business can often deduct larger sums for rentals than it could deduct for depreciation on a purchase. Finally, leasing can also be advantageous if the lessor provides other services such as accounting, maintenance, or repair. Bookkeeping is simplified in this situation, since the lessee's only expense is rent.

Regulation of Leases   The leasing of personal property is generally governed by the rules of law applicable to bailments. It is not ordinarily deemed to be within the scope of Article 2 of the UCC, which governs sales transactions. The applicability of the UCC to lease transactions, however, is undergoing rapid change, particularly through decisional law. As discussed in 33:9, many states now apply the sales provisions of the UCC to leases, either directly or by analogy. Leases that are actually secured transactions continue to be regulated by Article 9 of the UCC (see Chapter 28). In addition, various states and the federal government have enacted statutes that regulate the leasing of personal property, particularly the leasing of motor vehicles. For example, in 1976 the federal government enacted the Consumer Leasing Act (15 USC §§ 1667a–1667e), which protects any lessee who has entered a "consumer lease" for a period exceeding four months for a total contractual obligation not exceeding $25,000.[2]

33:9   Rights and Liabilities of Lessee and Lessor

A lessee of personal property has a duty to use ordinary care to preserve the leased property safely and in good condition. This duty can be expanded or diminished by contract. Except to the extent that the duty has been modified by contract, a lessee who fails to exercise ordinary care must repair all damage to the property caused by this failure. The lessee must also bear all expenses naturally arising in the use of the property, such as the cost of diesel fuel for a leased bulldozer. As for the lessor, unless his duties have been modified by contract, he is obligated to repair all deterioration of and damage to the property not caused by the lessee. He may also be responsible for reimbursing the lessee for any expenses that the lessee incurred for repair work after having given the lessor sufficient notice that the work was necessary.

Liability for Defects in Leased Property   A lessor is obligated to put leased property into a condition fit for the purpose for which it is leased. If the lessor fails to do this, the lessee can pay for the work necessary to repair the defects after giving proper notice, and then recover his expenses. The lessor can be liable to the lessee for personal injuries, as well as property damage, resulting from the lessor's negligence. A lessor can also be liable to third persons injured by leased property that was defective at the time of delivery to the lessee.

A lessee or third party injured due to a defect in a leased article is confronted with many theories of liability on which an action against the lessor can be based. Negligence, discussed in Chapter 6, is the traditional remedy, but problems of actually proving negligence impair its effectiveness. In addition, defenses, such as assumption of the risk or contributory negligence, may bar or limit recovery in an action based on negligence. For these reasons, the modern trend is to hold purchasers or suppliers of products or other goods strictly accountable to intended users. As discussed below, one avenue open to an injured lessee or third party is recovery on an implied warranty theory, the basis of which is that a leased product must be (1) fit for the purpose for which it is intended and (2) of merchantable quality. Another avenue has been the imposition of strict liability in tort by which

---

[2]Consumer leases and the Consumer Leasing Act are discussed in Chapter 27 (see 27:6).

sellers and manufacturers of products are held strictly liable for injuries caused to users of these products regardless of fault.

Breach of Warranty   Traditionally, warranty protections extended only to sales transactions. Increasingly, however, warranties have been extended to bailments and leases. Since nearly every state has adopted the UCC, cases now arise in which the express and implied warranty protections of the UCC are also sought to be applied. As discussed in Chapter 21, the warranties imposed by the UCC are both express and implied. UCC § 2-314 imposes on sellers certain implied warranties independent of the contract between the parties. UCC § 2-315 provides a warranty of fitness when a buyer relies on a seller's skill or judgment in selecting suitable goods. UCC § 2-316 provides that disclaimers inconsistent with express warranties will not be given legal effect. Finally, UCC § 2-318 lists those persons who receive warranty protection in personal injury cases.

The difficulty of applying the UCC warranty protections directly to leased trans-actions is that the UCC applies expressly to sales and not leases. Under Article 2 of the UCC, a buyer from a merchant seller is entitled to a warranty of merchan-tability, including a warranty that goods are fit for the ordinary purposes for which they are used. In contrast, in a lease situation there is no express warranty of merchantability under the UCC. The following case illustrates the situation in which an injured person argued that the Article 2 warranty provisions should apply to a lease transaction or bailment for hire. Consider whether the court's reasoning is persuasive.

Bona

v

Graefe

264 Md 69, 285 A2d 607, 10 UCCRS 47, 48 ALR3d 660 (Maryland Court of Appeals, 1972)

[Bona was injured when the brakes of a power golf cart failed during its use on a golf course. Bona sued Royce, the owner–lessor of the cart, and Graefe, the golf course manager–sublessor, alleging breach of warranty. The trial court entered a directed verdict in favor of Royce and Graefe, and Bona appealed.]

Singley, J.

*   *   *

Perhaps no uniform act was the subject of more extensive study and debate prior to its

adoption than the Uniform Commercial Code (the UCC). . . . The express warranty provi-sions of § 2-313 and the warranty of fitness im-plied by § 2-315 are parts of Article 2 of the UCC, which is clearly limited to sales of goods. Bona would have us read the sections as being also applicable to bailments for hire. Perhaps one answer to this contention, like A. P. Her-bert's Lord Mildew's, is that if the draftsmen had intended the sections to apply to leases of goods as well as to sales, they should have said so. . . .

It seems anomalous to us that many authors of the texts and commentaries seem to take the stance that there should be no differentiation between sales and bailments under Article 2 of the UCC, reasoning either by analogy or by interpretation. . . .

For us to accept Bona's contention would take us beyond the limits of judicial restraint and into the area of judicial legislation. . . .

Concededly, a few courts have read UCC § 2-315 as being applicable to cases where a chattel is the subject of a lease rather than a sale.... Most frequently these are instances where the arrangements are equivalent to the purchase price plus interest, or a purchase is contemplated at the end of the lease period, and the lessee assumes obligations more consistent with ownership than with bailment....

Another class of bailor–bailee cases is bottomed on strict liability in tort, ... although on occasion, passing reference may be made to the implied warranties of the UCC....

There is a third type of case in which one who leases goods has been held to have impliedly warranted either under common law concepts or by analogy to the UCC the suitability of the chattel leased....

Other cases may give lip service to breach of warranty but usually require proof coextensive with that required in a negligence action....

Another case to which we have been referred which applied UCC thinking to the lease of a chattel ... also involved an injury suffered by the lessee of a golf cart when there was a brake failure. There the court struck down a disclaimer contained in a lease, analogizing the lease to a sale, by applying UCC § 2-316 and § 2-719....

Maryland seems never to have adopted what has been the general rule elsewhere: that the bailor of a chattel to be used by the bailee for a particular purpose known to the bailor impliedly warrants the reasonable suitability of the chattel for the bailee's intended use of it....

Consequently, the liability of the lessor of a chattel, as distinguished from that of a vendor, if it is to be imposed at all in Maryland, must be imposed in a tort action for negligence. It is not enough for a plaintiff to prove that a lessor failed to make proper inspections; he must prove either that the lessor knew of the defect or that a reasonable inspection, if made, would have disclosed the defect....

[Judgments affirmed.]

Strict Liability in Tort   The doctrine of strict tort liability imposes on sellers and manufacturers strict liability for injuries caused to a user of products regardless of fault.[3] The doctrine of strict liability often offers an injured bailee the most convenient path for recovering damages for injuries caused in the lease of a product. Strict liability in tort is particularly useful in situations in which parties have contractually eliminated warranties of fitness or merchantability; in these cases it may offer an injured lessee or third party the only path for recovery of damages. Under the doctrine of strict liability in tort, one who, as lessor, leases a product that is (1) defective and (2) dangerous to the user is liable for harm if the lessor is engaged in the business of leasing such products and if the product is expected to and does reach the consumer without substantial change in its condition. The injured person must prove that (1) the leased article was the cause of the injury, (2) the defect existed at the time the product left the lessor's possession and control, and (3) the defect made the article unreasonably dangerous.

The following case illustrates a lessor's liability under the doctrine of strict liability in tort for defects causing personal injuries. Note the difference between the expansive opinion and reasoning of the California Supreme Court in this case and

---

[3]Products liability is discussed in Chapter 7.

the more narrow, strict constructionist opinion of the Maryland Court of Appeals in the previous case, *Bona v Graefe,* concerning the applicability of the UCC warranty protections to lease transactions. Consider whether the Maryland court would have been as receptive as the California court to a contention that strict liability applies to leases as well as sales.

Price
v
Shell Oil Co.
2 Cal 3d 245, 85 Cal Rptr 178, 466 P2d 722
(California Supreme Court, 1970)

[Price, an airline mechanic, sustained injuries when a ladder on a tank truck he was climbing split into segments. The ladder was part of a truck leased to his employer by Shell Oil Company. A suit was brought against Shell, and Price's case was submitted to the jury on the theory of strict liability in tort. The jury returned a verdict against Shell Oil, which appealed. Shell contended that the doctrine of strict liability in tort was not applicable to lessors and bailors of personal property.]

Sullivan, J.

*   *   *

We hold in this case that the doctrine strict liability in tort which we have heretofore made applicable to sellers of personal property is also applicable to bailors and lessors of such property. . . .

Shell contends that the trial court erred in submitting the case to the jury on the issue of strict liability. It argues that it is not a manufacturer, distributor or retailer of gasoline trucks. On the contrary, Shell asserts that in the present circumstances it was a bailor or lessor [with] . . . no greater duty than that of exercising ordinary care. In support of this contention Shell notes that section 408 of the *Restatement Second of Torts* "continues to hold" *lessors* of personal property liable only for negligence although section 402A now imposes strict liability upon sellers of such property. From this premise Shell argues that the *Restatement* did not intend to apply strict liability to lessors.

The rule is now settled in California that "A manufacturer is strictly liable in tort when an article he places on the market, knowing that it is to be used without inspection for defects, proves to have a defect that causes injury to a human being." . . . A retail dealer, being an "integral part of the overall producing and marketing enterprise" . . . is similarly liable. . . . We have given this rule of strict liability a broad application. . . .

Such a broad philosophy evolves naturally from the purpose of imposing strict liability which "is to insure that the costs of injuries resulting from defective products are borne by the manufacturers that put such products on the market rather than by the injured persons who are powerless to protect themselves." . . . Essentially the paramount policy to be promoted by the rule is the protection of otherwise defenseless victims of manufacturing defects and the spreading throughout society of the cost of compensating them. . . .

[W]e can perceive no substantial difference between *sellers* of personal property and *nonsellers,* such as bailors and lessors. [Court's emphasis.] In each instance, the seller or nonseller "places [an article] on the market, knowing that it is to be used without inspection for defects. . . ." In the light of the policy to be subserved, it should make no difference that the party distributing the article has retained title to it. Nor can we see how the risk of harm associated with the use of the chattel can vary with the legal form under which it is held. Having in mind the market realities and the widespread use of the lease of personalty in today's business world, we think it makes good sense to impose on the lessors of chattels the same liability for physical harm which has been imposed on the manufacturers and retailers. The former, like the latter, are able to bear the cost of compensating for injuries resulting from defects by spreading the loss through an adjustment of the rental.

Two recent decisions support this view. In *Cintrone v Hertz Truck Leasing & Rental Service* (1965 45 N.J. 434 [212 A2d 769]), the court held that a lessor of trucks is liable upon the basis of strict liability in tort because "A bailor for hire, such as a person in the U-drive-it business, puts motor vehicles in the stream of commerce in a fashion not unlike a manufacturer or retailer," subjects such a leased vehicle "to more sustained use on the highways than most ordinary car purchasers," and by the very nature of his business, exposes "the bailee, his employees, passengers and the traveling public . . . to a greater *quantum* of potential danger of harm from defective vehicles than usually arises out of sales by the manufacturer." . . .

A similar result was reached in this state in [an earlier case in which] a bailor of maintenance equipment was held strictly liable when a leased stepladder collapsed, resulting in the death of the bailee. The court reasoned:

> "Lessors of personal property, like the manufacturers or retailers thereof, 'are engaged in the business of distributing goods to the public. They are an integral part of the overall . . . marketing enterprise that should bear the cost of injuries resulting from defective products.' . . . In some cases the lessor 'may be the only member of that enterprise reasonably available to the injured plaintiff' . . . , and the imposition of strict liability upon

him serves, as in the case of the retailer, as an incentive to safety. . . . This will afford maximum protection to the injured plaintiff while working no injustice upon the lessor: the latter can recover the cost of the protection by charging for it in his business. . . ."

[We are not] dissuaded from our above conclusion by Shell's somewhat oblique argument that the *Restatement Second of Torts* in section 408 imposes on *lessors* of personal property liability only for negligence while in section 402A it imposes strict liability only on *sellers* of such property. [Court's emphasis.] This is no more than saying what is obvious—that the doctrine of strict liability as articulated in the *Restatement* was not made applicable against lessors or bailors. As we have explained, we think it should be, . . . even though the authors of the *Restatement* refrained from expressing such a view.

For the above reasons, we are of the opinion that the doctrine of strict liability in tort should be made applicable to bailors and lessors of personal property in the same manner as we have held it applicable to sellers of such property. . . .

However, since we reason by analogy, we make clear that the doctrine should be made applicable to lessors in the same way as we have made it applicable to sellers. . . .

Our anaysis of these authorities leads to the conclusion that for the doctrine of strict liability in tort to apply to a lessor of personalty, the lessor should be found to be in the business of leasing, in the same general sense as the seller of personalty is found to be in the business of manufacturing or retailing. . . . There is ample evidence in the record indicating that Shell was engaged in more than a single lease transaction. . . .

[Judgment affirmed.]

Key Concepts and Terms

- A bailment is the relationship that is created when one person deposits his property with another person. The person who owns the property and turns over possession of it is the bailor. The person to whom possession is given is the bailee.

- The principal elements of every bailment are (1) the bailor's delivery of property into the bailee's lawful custody or possession, (2) the bailee's acceptance of the property, and (3) the bailee's obligation to restore it to the bailor.

- A bailment does not involve any change in title to or ownership of the bailed property, but only a change in regard to possession.

- On termination of bailment, the bailee must return bailed property or account for it according to the terms of the bailment.

- Exceptions to the rule requiring the bailee to return bailed property arise in bailments of fungible goods and in those coupled with an option to purchase.

- Bailments are generally classified as (1) those for the sole benefit of the bailor, (2) those for the sole benefit of the bailee, and (3) those for the mutual benefit of both parties.

- To recover for loss of bailed property under a bailment for the mutual benefit of both parties, the bailor need only establish (1) that a bailment was created, (2) that the bailed property was delivered in good condition, and (3) that the bailee failed to return the property in the same condition at the end of the bailment. The bailee is presumed to have been negligent and must prove otherwise.

- Special bailments are for the mutual benefit of both parties and affect the public interest in such a way that the law has imposed on the bailee somewhat greater liability than that imposed on the ordinary bailee. Examples of special bailees are warehousers, carriers, and innkeepers.

- A common carrier transports property (and people) from place to place for compensation. Common carriers are generally strictly liable for loss or damage to property delivered to them unless they can show that the loss or damage was caused by means beyond their control.

- The personal property lease is a type of bailment and is generally governed by the rules of law applicable to bailments. The parties to a personal property lease are commonly referred to as the lessor and the lessee.

- A personal property lessor is obligated to put leased property into a condition fit for the purpose for which it is leased. The lessor's liability for defects in leased property may be based on negligence, breach of warranty, or strict liability in

- A lessee has the duty to use ordinary care to preserve leased property safely and in good condition.

• Bailee's Lien	• Breach of Warranty
• Bailment	• Carmack Amendment
• Bailment for Mutual Benefit	• Common Carrier

- Consignor
- Factor
- Freight Forwarder

- Lease
- Strict Liability
- Warehouser

Questions and Case Problems

1. Mrs. Brown brings her drapes in good condition to Howard's Laundry for cleaning. When she picks them up, they have shrunk. The laundry's efforts to stretch the drapes are unsuccessful. Was a bailment created? If so, what must Mrs. Brown prove to recover for damages sustained to her drapes?

2. Weinberg holds a "Parkard" issued by the Wayco Petroleum Company, entitling him to park his automobile in the company's five-story garage. The card states that the holder is licensed to park one automobile at his own risk, that he should lock his car, and that Wayco will not be responsible for the car or its contents. Entrance to the self-park garage is gained by placing the "Parkard" in a mechanical device that opens the entrance gate. No specific space is assigned to Weinberg, and he can park anywhere in the garage. One night, after Weinberg parks his car, the car is broken into and personal property is stolen. Was a bailment created? Is Wayco liable to Weinberg? Would the result be different if an attendant were on duty who retained ignition keys and parked the vehicles?

3. What are the principal characteristics of every bailment? Is the bailor always entitled to the return of the bailed property?

4. Southeastern Steel hires Luttrell to weld the engine of an air compressor which was damaged when water froze in the cooling system. Before delivering the compressor to Luttrell, employees of Southeastern remove various parts, but they leave oil, and possibly gasoline and ether, in the compressor. Following the custom of the welding trade, Luttrell makes no examination of the engine before welding. The contents ignite, causing an explosion with resulting injuries to Luttrell, who sues Southeastern Steel for damages. Was a bailment created? If so, what duty did Southeastern Steel owe to Luttrell? How should the case be decided?

5. Compare and contrast ordinary bailments with special bailments.

6. Does the duty of care applicable to ordinary bailments govern the conduct of warehousers and common carriers? If not, how does it differ as to each?

7. On the eve of an extended trip to Europe, Kraut, a collector of rare Russian enamels, places approximately 300 of her acquisitions, valued at $731,000, in storage with Morgan, a commercial storage company. The enamels are later stolen from Morgan's warehouse. After advertising that she will pay a reward for their return, Kraut recoups most of the stolen items by paying an unidentified intermediary $71,000. Can Kraut recover from Morgan the ransom and other expenses paid to recover the stolen art? Why?

8. Mrs. Caranas leaves her purse containing $5 in cash, credit cards, and ten pieces of jewelry worth $13,000 in the restaurant of the Hilton Hotel, where she and her husband are lodging. A busboy finds the purse and gives it to the hotel cashier, who later gives it to a man who came to claim it. The claimant was not Mr. Caranas. The Caranases sue the hotel for their loss. Was a bailment created? What is the extent of the hotel's liability?

9. Discuss the extent to which the doctrine of strict liability in tort applies to bailments and personal property leases.

10. Sister Stang is killed in an automobile accident when the tire on a leased car in which she is riding blows out, causing the accident and her death. Should her representatives be permitted to recover against the lessor under the doctrine of strict liability in tort? Would it make any difference if the lessor were not in the business of leasing vehicles on a regular, continuous basis? Would it make a difference if the driver of the car rented it for one day rather than for a longer term?

34 Purchase and Sale of Real Property

34:1 Introduction

The purchase of real property—and buildings—either by businesses or by individuals usually involves the investment of substantial sums of money for relatively long periods of time and the transfer of valuable assets. Indeed, the purchase of a home ordinarily represents the average American's largest single purchase.

The purchase and sale of real property is governed primarily by state law. However, federal laws also apply to some extent. These laws are limited to specific national problems for which individual state remedies have been inadequate. For example, the Real Estate Settlement Procedures Act (12 USC §§ 2601 et seq.) standardizes the disclosure of financial information required in connection with a sale of residential property. This act is discussed in 34:7. The Interstate Land Sales Full Disclosure Act (15 USC §§ 1701–1720) governs the sale or lease of subdivision lots by developers throughout the country. It requires subdivisions to be registered and detailed records and property reports to be filed.

The procedures involved in selling residential property are basically the same as those involved in the sale of commercial real estate, which is property purchased by a business or for business purposes. In most states, the typical home purchase or simple commercial real estate transaction involves (1) a brokerage contract, (2) preliminary negotiations with a prospective purchaser, (3) the deposit receipt, (4) a contract of sale, (5) a mortgage or other security instrument, (6) a survey or other investigation of the property, (7) title insurance, (8) drafting of documents, and (9) the closing in escrow. Except for mortgages, which are discussed in Chapter 35, these matters are discussed in this chapter. Additional considerations in commercial real estate transactions include the type of financing to be used, tax problems, and the structure of the entity that is to acquire title to the property.

If property is to be acquired by individuals or by a married couple, all parties must consider how title to the property will be held. For example in states where the law of community property applies, a husband and wife may acquire the property as the separate property of either spouse, as community property, or in joint tenancy. For both individuals and businesses, therefore, the choice of the purchasing entity, or how title will be held, is a vital concern. This decision may affect the degree to which property will be taxed, the liability of owners, and the ease of transferability. The form of ownership which is ultimately chosen depends on the purchaser's needs, the reasons for acquiring the property, and the advantages one form of ownership offers over the others.

 The form of ownership (how title to the property being acquired will be held) should be determined during the initial stages of a purchase. For a business, how title is held can vitally affect its liability, taxation, or the ease with which it can undertake future property transactions. Property can be purchased by one or more individuals, a partnership, a joint venture, a corporation, or a trust. Convenience and simplicity of ownership, as well as the ease of transfer, may dictate that the name of an individual be used to acquire property. In other situations, the limited liability of corporations or their more favorable tax structure might favor acquisition by a corporation. Occasionally, it may be desirable to use a third person otherwise unconnected with the purchase as the purchasing entity. For example, if several tracts of land are being acquired for development, confidentiality may be most important, requiring the purchase of property in this fashion.

34:2   The Brokerage Contract

Most sales of residential and commercial property are handled through brokers. A real estate broker is an agent of the buyer or the seller and is ordinarily compensated by that party.[1] The broker may neither acquire an interest adverse to the principal nor make a profit other than the commission to which he is entitled, unless, of course, the principal acquiesces or consents to a different arrangement.

 Most sellers of residential property are well aware that the broker is entitled to a commission on completion of the sale. In most states, however, a broker is said to earn his commission when a buyer "ready, willing, and able to buy on the seller's terms" is found. Therefore, in these states it is possible for a broker to legally earn his commission even though a sale was never actually closed. Sellers are thus advised to obtain a written agreement from the broker that provides for payment of the broker's commission only "if, as, and when" title passes to the purchaser.

The Listing Agreement   The rights and obligations of the seller and the real estate broker are ordinarily set forth in a *listing agreement*. This is a contract of employment that gives the broker limited authority to act on the owner's behalf to sell the property. In return, the broker is entitled to a commission contingent on the performance of the services within the terms of the listing agreement.

There are five basic types of listing agreements in general use in the real estate brokerage business. The *exclusive authorization and right to sell contract* gives the

---

[1]The agency relationship is discussed in Chapter 48.

broker the sole right to sell property listed. Even if the owner sells the property himself, the broker is still entitled to the agreed commission. An *exclusive agency contract* gives the broker taking the listing the exclusive right to act as an agent to sell the owner's property. The owner promises the broker that the property will not be listed with any other agent during the period of time the exclusive agency contract is in effect. However, since the owner is not an agent, he may sell the property without being obligated to pay the broker a commission on the sale. In certain situations, a *nonexclusive agency contract* is used with specific commencement and termination dates stated. As the name implies, the broker under contract does not have the exclusive right to represent the owner. If specific dates are included in the contract, the agency begins and ends at a certain time. In contrast, an *open listing*, which is very similar to the nonexclusive agency contract, requires no termination date. An open listing may be terminated at any time before sale of the property without the owner incurring any liability to the broker. Finally, the *net listing* is used occasionally for an owner who has determined the selling price of his property but is willing to let the broker make what he can on the sale by trying to sell it for more. In other words, the seller fixes a price for his property and the broker may sell it for more money. The price differential becomes the broker's commission. This type of listing assumes, of course, that the seller knows the market, knows how much the property is worth, and has full faith in the broker selected. If not, there is a potential for fraud; for this reason the net listing is used less often than the other types of agreements.

A somewhat related type of contract used by real estate brokers is known as a *multiple listing agency contract*. This is a device used by a group of brokers to obtain a wider market for the sale of property. Property is listed, usually on a weekly basis, among the subscribing brokers, all of whom thus have a quick and easy reference to most of the property being sold in any given area. The multiple listing usually entails an exclusive agency contract with the broker.

34:3 Preliminary Negotiations

When a potential buyer indicates to a broker or directly to the seller an interest in purchasing property offered for sale, negotiations usually begin between the parties, particularly in the more complicated residential and commercial transactions. Normally, the broker acts as an intermediary. In some cases, the broker conducts all of the negotiations, while the seller merely ratifies the agreement reached with the purchaser. In other cases, attorneys representing the parties conduct the negotiations and draft all of the pertinent documents involved in the sale. During negotiations, the parties must agree on all of the terms of the purchase and sale. They must consider such problems as the mode of paying the purchase price, tax consequences, the status of fixtures or personal property, the time in which possession is to be transferred, and who must pay for repairs or bear the burden of loss prior to closing. Important questions should be anticipated by the parties. The purchaser and seller should thoroughly discuss and agree on all of the pertinent details of the contract of sale, thus preventing future disputes as to the meaning of terms, and even litigation in case the sale falls through.

Representations and Warranties   Representations and warranties play an important role in the sale of real property. A major purpose of representations and warranties is to furnish information about the property that will help the purchaser decide whether to buy the property and to protect the purchaser from future surprise as to what has actually been purchased. A *representation* is a statement of fact or opinion during negotiations that induces one of the parties to enter into the contract of sale. A warranty is basically a promise made by the seller that a certain fact relating to the property or the contract of sale is or will be as it is stated or promised to be.

If there is a breach of a representation, the affected party may be able to void the contract, unless the breach has been waived. In contrast, if there is a breach of a warranty, the contract remains binding and the injured party is entitled only to damages.

Seller's Considerations   There are a variety of factors that the seller should consider in negotiating a contract of sale. During negotiations, the seller must be assured that once the terms of the contract have been reached and the contract is signed, it will be binding on the parties. In addition, if representations and warranties are to be made, the seller should limit their scope and restrict the time period during which they will be effective. If the purchaser is deferring payment of a portion of the purchase price, the seller should set forth the specific provisions of the financing agreement and the parties' obligations.

A seller should also take into account the tax consequences of a real estate transaction. For income tax purposes, a gain or loss is not recognized until there is a sale, exchange, or other disposition of property. A gain or loss is measured as the difference between (1) the amount realized, such as cash and other property received; and (2) the adjusted basis of the property, including the seller's cost, acquisition expenses, and certain other expenses such as the cost of constructing a building that the seller erected on the property. If a seller can postpone a gain (or sometimes a loss), he might obtain substantial tax savings.

The most commonly used methods of deferring gain or loss are installment sales and "like kind" exchanges of property between a purchaser and seller. For example, a seller can elect to postpone reporting income, and thus defer taxes, when the transaction is structured so that installment payments are received from the purchaser beyond the year of sale. In this fashion, gain is spread out over several tax years, and tax liability is reduced.

Sellers of residential housing commonly take advantage of a federal tax law that permits them to defer income and hence reduce taxes. If a seller purchases and uses a new principal residence within a prescribed period (currently 24 months) after the date of sale, gain is recognized only to the extent that the sale price of the old residence exceeds the cost of the new one. Taxation of the rest of the gain is deferred, even though a profit has been made by the seller within the particular taxable year.

Purchaser's Considerations   In buying a particular piece of property, the purchaser should be concerned with the price, how and to what extent it will be financed, the amount of debt to be incurred, and the costs of financing.[2] In negotiating the purchase of real property, the purchaser, unlike the seller, will want as many conditions in the contract as possible to assure that the property will meet his requirements in every respect. The purchaser should insist that (1) the property not be threatened or adversely affected by eminent domain or natural disaster on the closing date; (2) the seller's representation and warranties, if any, be true on the closing date; (3) the seller comply with all of his agreements on or before the closing date; and (4) that the property be properly zoned and that no proposed zoning change occur before the date set for closing. A purchaser should condition the sale on the receipt of satisfactory evidence that adequate utilities, including water and sewer, are available to service the property. The purchaser might also want to include a condition that any necessary easements be obtained. Obviously, the matters covered by some of these conditions may appear to be remote, but no one would like to be the purchaser of a piece of property, for example, that is under water on the closing date as a result of an unexpected flood, without being protected by appropriate conditions in the contract of sale. In negotiating the contract of sale, the purchaser should remain flexible, always bearing in mind the principal objectives in purchasing the property. If these objectives are met the sale should be concluded; if not, the purchaser should not enter into a contract of sale or should withdraw from negotiations.

34:4   Purchase Price and Deposit Receipt

Perhaps the most important aspect of any sale is the purchase price and how it will be determined. A total dollar amount ordinarily forms the basis of most residential and commercial transactions. Price may be determined by the total area of the property to be sold, calculated on a per-acre or per-square-foot basis. If area is used as the means of determining price, the contract of sale should include the total number of acres of square feet to be included within the purchase. In other transactions, portions of property to be sold may be more valuable than other portions. For example, different zoning classifications may apply to different portions of property to be sold. In such cases, it may be advantageous for the purchaser to allocate the purchase price among the various portions of the property according to their relative value. Such an allocation can affect subsequent taxation of the property or may even affect the profits to be made when the various portions are sold in the future.

Deposit Receipt   In most residential and commercial real estate transactions handled by a broker, the prospective purchaser makes the seller a firm offer, accompanied by a deposit, also known as earnest money, that is later credited to the purchase price. The document by which the offer is made, and which shows the amount of the deposit, is called a *deposit receipt*. After the prospective purchaser

---

[2]Mortgages and deeds of trust used in financing the purchase of land and buildings are discussed in Chapter 35.

signs the deposit receipt, the seller can accept or reject the offer. If the offer is accepted, a contract is ordinarily prepared and signed (see 34:5), and the transaction is then concluded in escrow (see 34:7) It should be noted, however, that in some states the deposit receipt is the only contract between the parties. It becomes a contract in these states when the seller signs it, thus showing his acceptance of the offer.

In the purchaser's offer there should be no material variance between the terms and conditions set forth in the listing agreement by which the property is offered for sale and those contained in the deposit receipt. Because the owner in most cases will already have indicated the terms of sale, the purchaser will not usually vary his offer significantly from the terms and conditions of the listing, except perhaps for the purchase price. These procedures as to offers, of course, are more applicable to the ordinary sale of residential housing than to more complicated commercial transactions in which extensive negotiations between the parties usually precede an offer or deposit receipt.

In the ordinary, uncomplicated real estate transaction in which the broker acts as an intermediary between the parties, the deposit receipt used in a given locality is a standard form. The form often provides that if a purchaser fails to pay the balance of the purchase price or to complete the purchase as provided in the receipt, any amounts paid on deposit by the purchaser can be retained by the seller as liquidated damages. Some deposit receipts also provide that the broker retain as a commission a portion of the forfeited deposit. Note, however, that in some states the seller must return to the buyer any amount over the actual damages suffered by the seller and caused by the buyer's breach. Of course, if the seller either refuses or fails to perform, the purchaser is entitled to the return of his deposit.

The following case illustrates the legal effect of the deposit receipt in a state where a valid deposit receipt constitutes a binding contract between the purchaser and seller. Note that the breach of a deposit receipt can subject the offending party either to damages or specific performance of the contract.

Meyer
v
Benko
55 Cal App 3d 937, 127 Cal Rptr 846
(California Court of Appeal, 1976)

[The Meyers wanted to purchase the Benkos' home. The parties executed a signed deposit receipt that named the sellers and buyers, identified the property being sold, specified a price of $23,500, detailed the method of financing, and allocated various incidental costs and duties. The deposit receipt also required the seller to do any necessary work at his expense. The purchase price was apparently somewhat below the market value. As a condition to guaranteeing the Meyers' loan, the Federal Home Administration (FHA) required that a new roof be installed. Both parties refused to pay for the cost of the roof, and the loan commitment lapsed. The Meyers then filed suit seeking specific performance of the contract and alleging that despite the fact that they had performed all of the conditions precedent to the conveyance of the property, the Benkos' refused to convey the property. The trial court held that no contract existed between the parties. It found that the deposit receipt merely constituted an offer subject to various unsatisfied contingencies. The Meyers appealed.]

Stephens, J.

*   *   *

Every contract requires the mutual assent or consent of the parties. . . . The existence of mutual consent is determined by objective rather than subjective criteria, the test being what the outward manifestations of consent would lead a reasonable person to believe. . . . Accordingly, the primary focus in determining the existence of mutual consent is upon the acts of the parties involved. In the case at bar, this focus is directed toward the Deposit Receipt and related documents, and the actions of the parties during the period of time encompassing the execution of these documents.

The utilization of the objective test of mutual consent demonstrates that the Deposit Receipt is in fact a contract. The fact that this document was signed by *both* parties indicates that the parties entered into an enforceable agreement. [Court's emphasis.] . . . Although the parties introduced conflicting testimony as to whether or not the terms of the Deposit Receipt were explained to the defendants before they signed that document, this evidence was not sufficient to establish a lack of mutual consent. "The general rule is that when a person with the capacity of reading and understanding an instrument signs it, he is, in the absence of fraud and imposition, bound by its contents, and is estopped from saying that its explicit provisions are contrary to his intentions or understanding." . . . In addition, the material factors common to a contract for the sale of real property are contained within the terms of the Deposit Receipt. The Deposit Receipt named the sellers, named the buyers, identified the property being sold, and specified the price for which that property was being sold. Further, it detailed the method of financing the transaction, as well as providing an allocation of various incidental costs and duties. The presence of these material factors upon the face of the document raises two inferences, both of which indicate the existence of mutual consent. First, these factors indicate that the parties had proceeded beyond the stage of mere preliminary negotiations and into the stage of actual contract formation. Moreover, the presence of this material in the document gave notice to the subscribing parties, notably the defendants, that they were entering into a binding contract by subscribing their signatures upon that document. The evidence introduced by the defendants relating to their lack of knowledge about the implications of the terms contained in the Deposit Receipt fails to rebut these inferences. Finally, the execution of the escrow instructions, whose terms substantially mirrored those found in the Deposit Receipt, further demonstrates the mutual consent of the parties to those terms as a binding commitment.

In toto, the various facts discussed above lead to the inescapable conclusion that, based upon an objective test of contract formation, the parties mutually assented to the formation of a contract on the terms and conditions set forth in the Deposit Receipt. Accordingly, pursuant to the term obligating the seller "to pay for . . . FHA appraisal and . . . to do any necessary work at his expense," the defendants were bound to pay for the new roof.

We take note of the fact that our resolution of this case is consistent with the general view that such deposit receipts constitute binding and enforceable contracts. . . .

. . . [T]he Deposit Receipt constitutes a valid enforceable contract. . . .

[Judgment reversed.]

34:5 The Contract of Sale

After the terms of sale have been negotiated, the purchaser and seller must enter into a formal contract unless the deposit receipt serves as a contract, as discussed above. The importance of this document cannot be overstated. Because each sale is unique, a special contract is ordinarily required, particularly in commercial transactions. The contract is usually prepared by an attorney, and it is signed by all parties concerned.

Land Contract   The most common type of sale contract used is the *land contract*. Under it, one party agrees to convey title to real property to the other party on the satisfaction of specified conditions set forth in the contract. While the form of the land contract varies from state to state, many of the basic provisions are similar.

The land contract is ordinarily executory in nature. That is, the terms and conditions specified in the contract must be performed by either or both of the parties in the future. These obligations generally include (1) the seller's delivery of a deed on his receipt of all the purchaser's payments and (2) the seller's turning over possession of the property to the purchaser. Usually the purchaser is allowed to take possession after the contract has been signed, but before delivery of the deed. At times, however, the purchaser receives possession only after title has been transferred and all the conditions of sale have been performed. In this event, the land contract will often provide for such matters as the use of the property during the pendency of the sale and the right to rents or profits generated by the property during that period.

Land contracts often include basic representations and warranties covering such matters as the marketability of title and the absence of pending condemnation proceedings. These representations and warranties are usually made by the seller. In certain circumstances, a seller might make representations or warranties as to the existence of leases and tenants, pending litigation, special assessments, building permits, or the assessed valuation of the property.

Many contracts include provisions for the award of damages in case of breach, and a fixed (or liquidated) damages clause is often used for this purpose. This clause provides that in the event of breach or default by one party, a specific sum is to be awarded to or retained by the other. In some states, liquidated damages clauses of this type will be enforced as written. In other states, where statutory provisions against forfeitures are strictly enforced, damages on breach will be awarded only to the extent that they have been actually incurred, regardless of what a liquidated damages clause might provide.

Description of Property   A precise description of the property to be sold is ordinarily included in every land contract. Note, however, that if a survey or other independent determination of the boundaries has not been made, a purchaser should not necessarily rely on a description furnished by the seller. In this regard, many land contracts provide that the purchaser is buying a specified number of acres, "more or less." If the purchaser requires a certain minimum acreage and is found to be getting less than that, he should be given the right to terminate the contract or to receive a pro rata deduction in the purchase price.

 If an accurate description of the property is not available, or if the parties agree that a survey will be made before the closing, it is wise to provide in the contract of sale that the description used at the closing will be based on the survey.

Time of the Essence   In many land contracts, time is "of the essence." This means that one party's performance at or within the time specified in the contract is essential to the performance required of the other party. Therefore, the purchaser must comply strictly with the provisions regarding the time of payment. If he does not, he can forfeit all rights, and the seller can be relieved of his obligation to perform.

Time-of-the-essence provisions are ordinarily created either by express stipulation of the parties in the contract of sale or by implication, depending on the circumstances of the transaction. Even when time is not made expressly or impliedly of the essence, a contract can be rescinded if one party fails or refuses to perform within a reasonable time. This rule governs the time fixed both for paying the purchase money and for conveying title to the property. Thus, for example, if parties have agreed to the payment of the purchase price and delivery of the deed on a particular day, they will be bound by the agreement, and time will be of the essence in that agreement.

Risk of Loss   In many states, once a contract has been signed, the risk of loss passes to the purchaser unless there is an agreement to the contrary. Thus, for example, damage to property from flood, hurricane, or even condemnation passes to the purchaser after the land contract has been signed. To avoid assuming this risk, a purchaser can (1) include a provision that all risk of loss before closing will be borne by the seller; (2) include specific covenants to limit the seller's use of the property before closing, thereby decreasing the risk of loss; and (3) require the seller to repair or restore the property if it is damaged before the closing.

In other states, the *Uniform Vendor and Purchaser Risk Act* has been enacted. The act provides that during the pendency of a sale the purchaser in possession bears the risk of loss of improvements, buildings, or other structures, as well as loss of land by eminent domain. Under the act, therefore, it is the purchaser's *possession* of the property, rather than his having simply signed the contract, that shifts the risk of loss to him.

Distinction Between Land Contract, Deed, and Option to Purchase   A land contract for particular property gives the purchaser what is called equitable ownership of the property. In contrast, a deed gives the purchaser legal title to the property. An option to purchase is simply an owner's continuing offer to sell property on his stipulated terms. An option ripens into a contract of sale if and when it is exercised by the purchaser on the terms and within the time stipulated.

Doctrine of Merger   A purchaser's acceptance of the seller's deed in accordance with a land contract constitutes completion of the contract and all its terms, unless the contract provides otherwise. Consistent with this principle, when the purchaser accepts a deed, the land contract and deed are said to merge. The effect of this merger is that the seller is discharged of all contractual duties to the purchaser except those contained in the deed itself. Thus, for example, a purchaser who has bargained for some right in the contract of sale may learn to his dismay that the right has been lost by default on acceptance of the deed. To avoid this result, the parties must see to it that all warranties, representations, or conditions contained in a contract of sale are fully performed before the deed is accepted.

The following case illustrates a common application of the *merger doctrine*. Consider the parties' contentions, and note the exceptions to the merger doctrine stated by the court.

Fraser
v
Schoenfeld
364 So 2d 533
(Florida District Court of Appeal, 1976)

[Fraser purchased an apartment house on Miami Beach from the Schoenfelds. In the contract of sale, the Schoenfelds guaranteed that there were no building code violations in the premises. After the closing of the sale and the delivery of the deed, building code violations were uncovered, and repairs had to be made. Fraser sued the Schoenfelds for violation of the contract of sale. The trial court awarded Fraser only partial recovery for the cost of repairs, and Fraser appealed.]

Pearson, Judge.

*   *   *

The appellant, Thomas J. Fraser, contracted to purchase a fifty year old apartment house on Miami Beach from the appellees, Irving Schoenfeld and Ruth Schoenfeld, his wife. Before closing, Fraser discovered what he believed to be violations of the building and zoning regulations of the City of Miami Beach. He wrote a letter declining to close. Thereafter, upon the statement of the Schoenfelds that they would sue him if he did not close, the purchase and sale were completed and the deed and possession delivered. Shortly after the closing of the sale, the City of Miami Beach building inspectors uncovered substantial and numerous defects in the building. The appellant, Fraser, sued for damages alleging a violation of a covenant in the contract of sale. The covenant reads as follows:

> "8. Seller further states that there are no code violations of the City of Miami Beach or the County of Dade."

The trial judge, after a trial before the court without jury, allowed recovery to Fraser for certain incidental repairs necessary to correct plumbing defects but denied recovery for the alleged structural violations.

This appeal urges error by the trial court in failing to allow the purchaser, Fraser, recovery for the substantial defects that existed in the building prior to the sale but which the City of Miami Beach had not inspected until after the sale. . . .

We hold that where, as here, the purchaser has knowledge of claimed violations and, thereafter, closes the deal, he is precluded by the doctrine of merger from a subsequent suit on a covenant contained in the contract of sale. . . .

. . . As stated in [an earlier Florida case]:

> "It is a general rule that preliminary agreements and understandings relative to the sale of property usually merge in the deed executed pursuant thereto. . . . However, there are exceptions to the merger rule. The rule that acceptance of a deed tendered in performance of a contract to convey land merges or extinguishes the covenants and stipulations

contained in the contract does not apply to those provisions of the antecedent contract which the parties do not intend to be incorporated in the deed, or which are not necessarily performed or satisfied by the execution and delivery of the stipulated conveyance."

... In the present case, it is apparent that the nature and wording of paragraph 8 of the preliminary agreement ... do not bring that paragraph within the exception.... Unquestionably, the agreement was fully merged into the completed deed. ...

[Affirmed.]

34:6   Establishing Title

An agreement to sell and convey property is in effect a legal agreement to sell a title to the land. Unless there is a provision in a land contract indicating the specific type of title to be provided, the law ordinarily implies that the seller will convey a good or *marketable title* to the purchaser. As a general rule, "good title" is synonymous with "marketable title."

What constitutes a marketable title may sometimes be difficult to determine. The basic requirements are (1) that there be no doubt about the true ownership or status of the property; (2) that the title be free of any reasonable objection of a reasonable purchaser; and (3) that the title be free of encumbrances, liens, or other charges on the property unless these are accepted by the purchaser.

 The purchaser of real property should not blindly rely on the seller's representation or warranty that he has a good, marketable, or even an insurable title to the property. As soon as possible after the parties have signed the contract of sale, the purchaser should have the title searched and should obtain a preliminary title report of the seller's title.

Title Search   The product of a title search is a title report containing an *abstract of title*. The abstract of title contains (1) a brief description of the land and structures to be conveyed, (2) a list of the various grantors who have conveyed the property in the past, (3) the essential elements of each instrument or deed affecting the land, and (4) a conclusion about the present status of the title.

 Purchasers of property are generally unaware that a title company does not guarantee that its search is accurate. Only by asking (and paying) for title insurance (discussed below) does a purchaser get this guaranty. Without title insurance, the purchaser must bear the risk of loss from problems such as the title searcher's overlooking a lien on the property or making an honest mistake in describing the boundaries.

Title Insurance   Title insurance insures the purchaser against loss or damage due to defects, liens, and other encumbrances on his title that are not specifically excepted from or excluded by the policy. Title insurance differs from other forms of insurance in that it insures title as of the date of the policy against loss due to existing or past occurrences. Most other types of insurance insure against loss resulting from future events.[3] Every policy of title insurance basically contains (1) a description of the property, (2) the name of the insured, (3) the amount of loss insured, (4) the extent of coverage, (5) the exclusions from coverage, (6) general exceptions, and (7) conditions and stipulations.

 It must be stressed that a title insurance company does not *cure* a defective or unmarketable title. Nor in most states is a title insurance company under a duty to point out title defects or encumbrances to the purchaser. A title insurance company is only bound to protect the purchaser against loss as a result of defects and encumbrances. It is therefore of utmost importance for the purchaser to have complete confidence in the title insurance company selected, to understand fully the type of title policy issued, and to review, when appropriate, the status of the property with either an attorney or title insurance company personnel.

34:7   Closing

The sale of property involves many details. Just as the seller should not be required to deliver a deed until payment is received, the buyer should not risk payment until he receives the deed to the property or some obligation to deliver it. A purchaser must either be assured in the contract of receiving marketable title, or obtain title insurance. Liens, encumbrances, and other charges against property must be settled as agreed between the parties. Prorations of rents, taxes, assessments, insurance premiums, and interest charges must be made. Documents must be drafted and signed by the parties. Carrying out all these steps takes time. During the time required to carry them out—and to make sure that they *are* carried out—the property is put "in escrow." This means that the seller in effect places the property in the hands of a third party, who delivers the property to the purchaser when all the conditions of sale have been performed.

Escrow   The deposit of an instrument or document in *escrow* is usually referred to as the opening of the escrow, although it is also called the "beginning of the escrow" or "going into escrow." The term "close of escrow" is used when the escrow conditions have been performed by all of the parties so that the third party must deliver the deed to the purchaser and the purchase money to the seller.

Creation of an escrow requires (1) an agreement as to the subject matter, (2) an escrow agent, (3) delivery of documents to the escrow agent, (4) performance of the required acts by the seller and purchaser, and (5) transfer of title and payment of the purchase price out of escrow.

Escrow Agent   The third party in an escrow arrangement is called the *escrow agent*. The agent is both an agent of and a trustee for the parties, with limited

---

[3]The various types of insurance are discussed in Chapter 39.

powers. Before the close of escrow, the escrow agent is no more than a depositary for the property. The agent must strictly comply with the terms of his instructions. When the agent has done so, he becomes a trustee of both the party for whom the various instruments or funds are held and the party to whom they are to be delivered.

Escrow Instructions   The duties of the escrow agent are usually set forth in escrow instructions. In some states there is only one set of instructions governing the agent's conduct. In other states there can be two sets of instructions, one prepared and signed by the purchaser, the other by the seller. Often, printed instructions are prepared by corporate escrow agents or title companies who handle escrows and other real estate transactions for purchasers and sellers. Since the escrow agent is bound by the instructions, it is imperative that they be clearly drafted, to avoid confusion or misunderstanding.

Performance of Escrow Conditions   The parties to an escrow must strictly comply with the terms and conditions of the escrow. The doctrine of substantial performance (see Chapter 18) does not apply. This means that title to the property being sold will not pass until there has been full performance of the escrow agreement terms. If escrow instructions specify the time for performance, the escrow agent has no authority to accept performance after that prescribed time limit. In short, if either party fails to perform according to the terms of the sales contract and the escrow instructions, the escrow will not be closed and title to the property will not be transferred. When the time fixed for performance expires, a party who *has* fully performed can withdraw from the agreement and terminate the escrow if the other party has failed to perform as agreed.

Title and Right of Possession to Deposits in Escrow   The escrow agent obtains no title to the subject of the escrow. Legal title to the property to be sold, for example, remains in the seller until the escrow conditions are performed. Similarly, the deposit of a deed in escrow does not pass title to the purchaser until all the escrow agreement terms have been performed. However, at the time the contract of sale is signed and a deed deposited in escrow, the purchaser acquires an equitable interest in the property. In such a case, if a purchaser has fully performed all of the obligations under the contract of sale, as well as all of the escrow terms, but the seller dies before the escrow is actually closed, the law resorts to a legal fiction known as the doctrine of relation-back. The theory is that the delivery of legal title to the purchaser relates back to the time the equitable title was acquired. This allows the transfer of the property to be made. The doctrine of relation-back is an exception to the general rule that escrow does not convey title before all of the conditions have been performed.

Termination of Escrow Before Closing   A party to an escrow has no right to withdraw from the escrow before expiration of the time period fixed for performance of the conditions unless (1) the other party consents or (2) the escrow agreement provides otherwise. If an escrow is terminated in this way, the delivery of the deed in escrow is ineffectual.

Closing Statement   When all of the terms and conditions of the contract of sale have been completed, the escrow is closed by the escrow agent. At this time, a *closing* statement is prepared in which the details of the transaction are listed. These details include (1) the purchase price of the property, (2) obligations chargeable to each party, (3) proration of taxes, (4) charges or payments to be shared by the seller and purchaser, (5) the title company's charges, (6) real estate broker's commission, (7) insurance, and (8) loan payments.

Real Estate Settlement Procedures Act   The federal *Real Estate Settlement Procedures Act* (12 USC §§ 2601 et seq.) governs some aspects of residential real estate sales throughout the United States. The act is intended to make sure that sellers and purchasers of residential housing that is designed for occupancy by one to four families will receive disclosures showing all the costs of the transaction. These disclosures cover such matters as the cost of financing the transaction, the cost of title insurance, prepayment rights and penalties, and the proration of insurance and taxes on the property. At the same time, the act protects the parties from unnecessarily high charges caused by abusive practices, especially by lenders. A standard form must be used for the disclosures. The form clearly itemizes all charges imposed on the parties in connection with the transaction.

34:8   Remedies

The purchaser of property under a land contract has several remedies against a seller who wrongfully fails or refuses to perform the contract or to convey the kind of title required to be conveyed. If the seller is able but unwilling, or refuses, to convey title to the property sold, the purchaser can seek specific performance of the contract. In other cases, the purchaser can bring an action for damages. A damages action is particularly appropriate if the seller is unable to convey the property according to the terms of the contract because of a defect in or lack of title to the property. If a seller defaults under an executory contract, if the contract is invalid, or even if property has been destroyed or so materially damaged as to relieve the purchaser from the contract, the purchaser can ordinarily recover the payments or deposits he made on the contract (but not damages) so long as he himself is not in default.

The damages that a purchaser can recover for the seller's breach of a land contract are only those that, in fairness, can be considered to have either arisen from the breach or been contemplated by both parties when the contract was made. In other words, if a seller wrongfully breaches the contract, the measure of the purchaser's damage is the loss that he has sustained as a result of the breach. The burden is on the purchaser to show the amount of damages caused by the seller's breach. A purchaser who cannot do so is limited to a recovery of nominal damages. In some states, the purchaser is entitled, as general damages for the seller's wrongful failure or refusal to convey, to recover the difference between the actual value of the property and the agreed price, plus any payments that may have been made.

Seller's Remedies   The seller has a variety of remedies if the purchaser has breached the provisions of a land contract. If the contract has been signed and then breached by the purchaser the seller can seek (1) damages for the contract price or (2) specific performance to require the purchaser to pay the amount due under the contract. If the purchaser has been allowed possession under the terms of the contract, the seller can elect to declare the contract at an end and bring an action to recover possession.

Rescission   A contract of sale can be rescinded at any time before closing on the consent of all the parties to the agreement. However, one party's neglect, refusal, or failure to perform permits the other party to rescind the contract, as long as he does so within a reasonable time after the other party's default. In other circumstances, a contract for the sale of property can provide that the obligations of both parties depend on the happening of certain events; if the events do not occur, neither party is obligated to perform and the contract stands rescinded.

The purchaser under a land contract may be entitled to rescind the agreement for (1) the seller's material default in performing his obligations, (2) fraud, (3) mistake in inducing the signing of the contract, or (4) a defect in the seller's title. In some states, the purchaser can also rescind if improvements on the property are accidentally destroyed or an eminent domain proceeding (see Chapter 37) commences before the property is conveyed.

Rescission must be evidenced by some positive act or words. The right to rescind can be lost by unreasonable delay. Furthermore, rescission can be waived if what is actually an invalid contract is treated by the parties as being valid and enforceable.

"As Is" Sales   In the past, most real estate transactions were "as is." That is, no implied warranties of condition or fitness were imposed, and the doctrine of caveat emptor ("let the buyer beware") prevailed. Any representations and warranties contained in the contract of sale terminated at the closing with the conveyance of the deed. Today, only a minority of states still apply the caveat emptor doctrine in the sale of residential housing. The modern trend is to hold the seller liable for damages or injuries that are caused by defects and arise after title has been conveyed and possession transferred.

The following case illustrates what one court considers to be the implied warranties in the sale of residential housing. Consider the court's rationale for imposing these warranties and why the traditional doctrine of caveat emptor is no longer appropriate to residential housing.

McDonald

v

Mianecki

79 NJ 275, 398 A2d 1283

(New Jersey Supreme Court, 1979)

[The McDonalds purchased a new home built by Mianecki. The well water used in the home failed to meet state standards of potability. The water had a bad odor and taste, and it caused clothes, dishware, and utensils to become stained when washed. A de-

vice installed by Mianecki to remove impurities after the McDonalds had moved in proved inadequate. Eventually, the McDonalds sued Mianecki for damages, alleging breach of an implied warranty of habitability because of the impure well water.]

Pashman, J.

*   *   *

Prior to the mid-1950's the ancient maxim of *caveat emptor* ("let the buyer beware") long ruled the law relating to the sale of real property. Thought to have originated in late sixteenth-century English trade society, the doctrine was especially prevalent during the early 1800's when judges looked upon purchasing land as a "game of chance." . . . The maxim, derived from the then contemporary political philosophy of *laissez faire*, held that a "buyer deserved whatever he got if he relied on his own inspection of the merchandise and did not extract an express warranty from the seller." . . .

According to one commentator . . . [:]

> After World War II . . . the building industry underwent a revolution. It became common for the builder to sell the house and land together in a package deal. Indeed, the building industry outgrew the old notion that the builder was an artisan and took on all the color of a manufacturing enterprise, with acres of land being cleared by heavy machinery and prefabricated houses being put up almost overnight. Having learned their law by rote, however, the lawyers tended to insist that *caveat emptor* nonetheless applied to these sales.

In light of this modern day change in home buying practices, it is not surprising that increased pressure developed to abandon or modify the ancient doctrine. . . .

The reasoning underlying the abandonment of *caveat emptor* in the area of home construction is not difficult to fathom. Tribunals have come to recognize that "[t]he purchase of

a new home is not an everyday transaction for the average family[;] . . . in many instances [it] is the most important transaction of a lifetime." . . . Courts have also come to realize that the two parties involved in this important transaction generally do not bargain as equals. The average buyer lacks the skill and expertise necessary to make an adequate inspection. . . . Furthermore, most defects are undetectable to even the most observant layman and the expense of expert advice is often prohibitive. . . . The purchaser therefore ordinarily relies heavily upon the greater expertise of the vendor to ensure a suitable product, . . . and this reliance is recognized by the building trade. . . .

Aside from superior knowledge, the builder-vendor is also in a better position to prevent the *occurrence* of major problems. [Court's emphasis.] . . . As one court has stated, "[i]f there is a comparative standard of innocence, as well as of culpability, the defendants who built and sold the house were less innocent and more culpable than the wholly innocent and unsuspecting buyer." . . .

It is not in expertise alone that the builder-vendor is generally superior. In the vast majority of cases the vendor also enjoys superior bargaining position. . . . Standard form contracts are generally utilized and "[e]xpress warranties are rarely given, expensive, and impractical for most buyers to negotiate. Inevitably the buyer is forced to rely on the skills of the seller." . . .

The application of an implied warranty of habitability to sellers of new homes is further supported by the expectations of the [parties]. Clearly every builder-vendor holds himself out, expressly or impliedly, as having the expertise necessary to construct a livable dwelling. It is equally as obvious that almost every buyer acts upon these representations and expects that the new house he is buying, whether already constructed or not yet built, will be suitable for use as a home. . . .

For the reasons set forth herein, we conclude that (1) the doctrine of implied warranty of habitability applies to the construction of new homes by builder-vendors whether or not they are mass-developers, and (2) potability of the water supply is included within the items encompassed by the implied warranty. *Caveat emptor* is an outmoded concept and is hereby replaced by rules which reflect the needs, policies and practices of modern day living. It is our conclusion that in today's society it is necessary that consumers be able to purchase new homes without fear of being "stuck" with an uninhabitable "lemon." *Caveat emptor* no longer accords with modern day practice and should therefore be relegated to its rightful place in the pages of history.

[Judgment affirmed.]

The implied warranties of *habitability*, condition, or fitness do not apply to commercial transactions. Here, the traditional rule is still applied, and the purchaser takes the property "as is."

 The purchaser of commercial property should either order a careful inspection by qualified experts before a contract is signed, or insist that a satisfactory inspection be made a condition of the sale. For example, a contract might require that before closing, the seller of a commercial building remedy all defects, including any fire, health, or building code violations. If this is done, there should be no question as to the parties' obligations if defects are discovered during the pendency of a sale or after the sale has been concluded.

Key Concepts and Terms

- The purchase and sale of real property is governed primarily by state law. However, certain federal laws have been enacted to govern specific national problems for which individual state's remedies are inadequate. These laws include the Real Estate Settlement Procedures Act and the Interstate Land Sales Full Disclosure Act.

- In most states the typical residential purchase or simple commercial transaction involves (1) a brokerage contract, (2) preliminary negotiations, (3) the deposit receipt, (4) a contract of sale (unless the deposit receipt serves as the contract), (5) a mortgage or other security arrangement, (6) a survey or other investigation of the property, (7) title insurance, (8) drafting of documents, and (9) the closing in escrow.

- The sale of residential and commercial property is handled exclusively through brokers in most states. The contract between a broker and a property owner is governed by the laws of agency.

- The rights and obligations of the seller and real estate broker are ordinarily set forth in a listing agreement. This is an agency contract of employment giving the broker limited authority to act on behalf of the owner to sell the property.

- The purchaser's written offer, accompanied by a deposit to be credited to the purchase price, is generally called the deposit receipt. The deposit receipt is a firm offer that the seller can accept or reject.

- Except in states where the deposit receipt serves as the contract after the seller's acceptance, the land contract is the most common type of contract used for a sale of real property. Under the land contract, one party agrees to convey title to real property to the other on the satisfaction of specified conditions set forth in the contract.

- The deposit of an instrument or document with a third party for the purpose of exchanging papers, documents, deeds, or other instruments, as well as money, is called an escrow. The deposit of these instruments in escrow is usually referred to as the opening of the escrow. When all the conditions have been performed by all the parties, so that the escrow agent is required to deliver the deed to the purchaser and the purchase money to the seller, the escrow is closed.

- The duties of the escrow agent are normally set forth in escrow instructions. The escrow agent must act specifically in accordance with the instructions given. The instructions should be clearly drafted to avoid confusion or misunderstanding as to what is required before the escrow will be closed.

- The purchaser of property under a land contract has several different remedies against a seller for the wrongful failure or refusal to perform the contract or to convey the appropriate title. These remedies include (1) specific performance of the contract, (2) reformation or rescission of the contract, and (3) the recovery of damages.

- Remedies of a seller of property when provisions of a land contract have been breached by the purchaser include (1) the recovery of damages; (2) specific performance of the contract; and (3) if the purchaser has been allowed possession of the property under the terms of the contract, recovery of possession of the property.

- Traditionally, real estate was bought and sold "as is." Today, many states hold sellers of residential property liable for damages and injuries that are caused by defects and arise after title has been conveyed and possession transferred. These implied warranties of habitability, condition, or fitness do not apply to commercial transactions; the traditional rule still applies to those transactions.

- Abstract of Title
- Closing
- Deposit Receipt
- Escrow
- Escrow Agent
- Land Contract
- Listing Agreement
- Marketable Title

- Merger Doctrine
- Real Estate Settlement Procedures Act
- Representation
- Time Is of the Essence
- Uniform Vendor and Purchaser Risk Act
- Warranty of Habitability

Questions and Case Problems

1. Discuss the stages in a typical commercial sale of real property.
2. Ziminski lists property that he wishes to sell with Trade Properties, a real estate

company, at a selling price of $100,000. Zwas, a salesman for Trade Properties, advertises the property and shows it to potential buyers. Zwas introduces Falk, a potential buyer, to Ziminski. A binder is drafted, and both Falk and Ziminski sign it. Ziminski insists that a clause be inserted in the binder that his acceptance is subject to the approval of his attorney. The broker agrees, and the clause is inserted. Later, Ziminski's attorney disapproves of the deal, and the whole thing falls through. Trade Properties sues Ziminski for its commission. How should the case be decided?

3. The Brewers list their home with Lewis Real Estate. Lewis finds Myers, a suitable prospective broker who is willing to meet the Brewers' terms. The parties sign a "binder deposit" and Myers puts $200 in escrow with Lewis. The binder provides that if Myers fails to enter into a formal sales contract, the Brewers have the right to retain the deposit as liquidated damages. Thereafter, Myers changes her mind and refuses to enter into a contract of sale. Because they cannot find another buyer who will pay the same price that was offered by Myers, the Brewers sue her for the difference between what she offered and the ultimate selling price. The Brewers contend that Myers gave them the option of either accepting the $200 deposit as liquidated damages or suing the buyer for actual damages. Is Myers liable for the seller's actual damages? Why?

4. Which representations or warranties should sellers and buyers consider in negotiating a contract of sale?

5. The Brooks sell their house to the Rouses. In the "Acceptance of Purchase Offer" the sellers represent and warrant to the broker and to any subsequent purchaser that the property and its improvements, equipment, and facilities are "in good, proper, satisfactory, and functional working order and condition." After the sale, the purchasers discover that the septic tank leaks, the air conditioning equipment is defective, and the swimming pool and basement leak. The Rouses sue the sellers for breach of express warranties and contract. The trial court dismisses the suit, finding that the clause in the sales contract merged with and was extinguished by the deed, which contained no such warranties. Was the trial court correct in its decision? Why?

6. Smith enters into a written contract to sell his house to Jones, with title to pass on the closing of escrow in 45 days. The contract calls for Jones to pay the purchase price into escrow on or before December 31. Jones offers the money on January 1, one day late. On Smith's refusal to perform, can Jones now enforce the contract?

7. Convey purchases a cold storage plant from Capitol Savings under an installment land contract. Under the terms of the contract, Convey is not given legal title to the property until the final installments are paid, but he is given possession and use of the plant. After he acquires possession, the plant collapses, and it will take $15,000 to rebuild it. Who bears the risk of loss?

8. Discuss and distinguish a land contract, option to purchase, and deed.

9. On September 15, Mallen gave A-1 Escrow Company a deed naming Dube as grantee of Mallen's river property. Mallen orally instructed A-1 to give the deed to Dube if Dube pays $5,000 on or before December 15. On October 1, Mallen decides to cancel the transaction and recall the deed from A-1 because she no longer wants to sell to Dube. Is she legally entitled to do this? If Dube had given A-1 $5,000 on September 30, would the result be different?

10. Ern-Roc Homes builds a house and sells it to the Sanjs. The contract of sale provides the usual guaranties, including a guaranty against roof leakage "due to de-

fective materials and/or installation." The guaranty is for one year from the time of closing of title. A few months after buying the home, the Sanjs sell it to Gomes, and they assign Ern-Roc's guaranties along with it. When the house develops roof trouble within the one-year period, Gomes contacts Ern-Roc and asks it to do the repair work. Ern-Roc refuses, claiming that guaranties made to the first purchaser were not meant for subsequent purchasers. Ern-Roc also points to a provision in the original contract with Sanj, which states: "It is expressly understood and agreed that the purchaser will in no event assign this contract without the written consent of the seller." If Gomes were to sue Ern-Roc, who would win the case? Why?

35 Mortgages and Deeds of Trust

A client came into a lawyer's office and said:
"Is this a lawyer's place?"
"Yes, I am a lawyer."
"Well, Mr. Lawyer, I need a paper made."
"What kind of paper?"
"Well, I think I want a mortgage. Why, you see, I bought some land from Angus McPherson and I want a mortgage on it."
"Oh no, you don't want a mortgage; what you want is a deed."
"No, Mr. Lawyer, I want a mortgage. Why, you see, I bought two pieces of land before and I got a deed for both of them and another fellow came along with a mortgage and took the land; so I think I'd better get a mortgage this time."[1]

35:1 Nature, Form and Elements of the Mortgage

Real property has long been considered the primary security for the payment of debts. The *mortgage* is the instrument that, traditionally, has been used to create a security interest in real property.

In early English law, the mortgage took the form of an absolute conveyance of land. A debtor, the *mortgagor*, conveyed land to a creditor, the *mortgagee*, on the condition that the mortgage would become void—and the creditor would reconvey the land to the debtor—on performance of the obligation. The date of maturity was called the "law day." By a provision in the mortgage known as the defeasance clause, payment of the debt on law day defeated the mortgage and put ownership back in the mortgagor. However, if the debtor did not pay the debt before the law day, the creditor became the absolute owner of the mortgaged property. The mortgagor's failure to pay the mortgage indebtedness when due automatically extinguished all his interest in the property; legal title to the mortgaged property then passed to the creditor. It was not unusual for a mortgagor to fail to pay the mortgage debt, especially since execution of the mortgage gave the creditor the right to possession of the land and to the profits generated from its use. The land was "dead" in the sense that it gave no return to the debtor. In fact, in England, the word "mortgage" meant "dead pledge" (mort = dead, gage = pledge).

As discussed in more detail later in this chapter, the hardships resulting from the forfeiture or loss of mortgaged property prompted courts of equity to give protections to the mortgagor so that he could regain or redeem the property. Accordingly, a body of law developed by which the debtor could do so by repaying

---

[1] Adapted from M. Brown, *Wit and Humor of Bench and Bar*, 352 (1899), quoted in Henkel & Seltzer, "Acceleration Clauses in Mortgages: Misuse During Periods of Tight Money," 17 *Am Bus L J* 441 (Winter 1980).

the debt within a reasonable time after breach of any of the mortgage conditions. This right to save property after its forfeiture was called *equity of redemption*. With the adoption of the debtor's right to redeem the mortgaged property after forfeiture, creditors were placed at a disadvantage. They could no longer count on receiving payment or obtaining the security by a certain time. To remedy this situation, a procedure evolved for *foreclosure* of (cutting off) debtors' rights. The creditor would petition a court of equity to foreclose on mortgaged property, seeking a decree that required the debtor to repay the debt by a fixed date. If the debt was not paid, the debtor's equity of redemption would be barred forever.

Title Versus Lien Theory of Mortgages   Because the law of mortgages developed in courts of both law and equity, modern mortgages have a dual character: the mortgage is a conveyance, yet it is also a lien to secure the payment of debt.

EXAMPLE

D owns property worth $20,000. He wants to borrow $10,000 from C. In turn, C wants some security for the money he is about to loan. D executes a promissory note to C by which he promises to pay $10,000 to C with interest. At the same time, D gives to C a mortgage on the land to secure the obligation of the note. The mortgage gives C a claim against D's land for repayment of the loan. The mortgage will be recorded in the appropriate public office where the property is located. The note will not be recorded since it does not create any interest in land; it is not a document of title but merely a promise. Thus, in a broad sense the mortgage encompasses two documents. The first is a promissory note by which D becomes obligated to pay C a sum of money. The second, the actual mortgage, gives C a security interest in the property to ensure D's performance of the obligation. D is said to hold the equity in the property now, whereas before the mortgage he held title.

Although most states have adopted the English theory of mortgage law, they have modified the strict, legal *title theory*, which views the mortgage as a conveyance. Most states follow the equitable or *lien theory*, which holds that a mortgage does not convey the legal title to land but simply creates a lien to secure payment of the mortgage debt. In most states, a mortgage vests title in the mortgagee only to protect his interest and give him the full benefit of the security, but for no other purpose. The mortgagor retains title until foreclosure and ordinarily is entitled to possession and use of the mortgaged premises, as well as to the rents and profits generated by the property. However, the mortgage may also permit possession by the mortgagee.

Form and Elements of the Mortgage   A mortgage must be in writing, and it must bear the signature of the mortgagor. It must also be based on a legal and valid consideration.[2] Any interest in real estate can be made the subject of a mortgage, so long as the interest is sufficiently described. A mortgage on land generally covers

---

[2]Consideration is discussed in Chapter 11.

all of its structures and improvements, including those made after the conveyance of the mortgage.

Under the modern view of mortgages, the debt secured by a mortgage is the primary obligation between the parties. The mortgage is merely incidental to the indebtedness. Hence, the existence of a valid obligation is an essential element of a mortgage. If an obligation purported to be secured is invalid, the mortgage is of no effect.

EXAMPLE
Morton gives a mortgage to Crabbe to secure payment of a gambling debt that Morton previously incurred. Later, the debt is declared invalid. Because the underlying debt is invalid, the mortgage—given to secure that debt—is also invalid.

In some states, every transfer of an interest in real property (other than in trust) made only as security for the performance of another act is considered to be a mortgage. If the purpose of an instrument is to secure a debt, it does not matter what particular form the transaction takes. In these states, therefore, a deed intended as security is treated as a mortgage.

35:2   Types of Mortgages and Security Transactions; Mechanic's Liens

A security transaction in real property creates an interest in the property to secure the performance of an obligation. Deeds of trust (or trust deeds) and mortgages are the most common types of instruments used in these transactions.

Deeds of Trust   *Deeds of trust* are used in many states exclusively in lieu of mortgages, but they are functionally identical. Deeds of trust may be given as security for the performance of an obligation, and they are generally regarded as containing the elements of a valid mortgage. The distinctive feature of a deed of trust is that the property that is to stand as security is conveyed by the debtor to a trustee for the creditor's benefit, rather than directly to the creditor as is done in a mortgage. Thus, there are three parties to a deed of trust: (1) the trustor (debtor; also known as the trust deed mortgagor), (2) the trustee, and (3) the beneficiary (creditor). The trustee's powers and duties are fixed by the trust deed, and the trustee occupies a fiduciary relationship to both the beneficiary and the trustor. What the trustee eventually does with the property depends on whether the trustor pays off the secured debt.

EXAMPLE
D (trustor) conveys title to his property to T (trustee) to secure a debt owed by D to B (beneficiary). If D performs his obligation, T reconveys the property to D. However, if D defaults in performance, T can sell the property and apply the sale proceeds to satisfy the debt owed to B.

A formal difference between a trust deed and a mortgage is that with a mortgage, title remains in the mortgagor (the debtor) subject to a lien in the mortgagee's favor until title is divested by foreclosure sale, whereas with a trust deed, legal title actually passes to the trustee and remains there until either the debt is paid or the trustee transfers title to a purchaser after a sale following default (as discussed in 35:6). However, in many states, although the trust deed actually transfers title, it is *regarded* as simply a mortgage with the *power of sale*. The trustee has only the title necessary to fulfill the terms of the trust. Until a sale becomes necessary, the trustee's title lies dormant. In the meantime, the trustor is entitled to possession and can convey or encumber the property subject to the trust deed. On payment of the debt, the trustee's interest in the property ceases even though no reconveyance of the title is made.

The deed of trust ordinarily contains a default clause providing that all sums secured by the deed shall immediately become due and payable at the beneficiary's option if the trustor defaults in payment of the underlying debt. On demand of the beneficiary, the trustee is obligated to sell the property under the power of sale contained in the deed of trust. After the property is sold the trustee must apply the proceeds of the sale first to pay off the loan or debt; the balance, if any, is given to the trustor. The trustee then delivers a trustee's deed to the purchaser of the property.

Equitable Mortgages   An *equitable mortgage* is a mortgage that, although technically invalid as a mortgage because it fails to satisfy one or more legal requirements, is treated as a mortgage by the courts. This means that if a mortgage is defective for some reason, the courts can, in effect, cure the defect. The result is that almost every express written agreement by which one party clearly indicates an intention to make particular property a security for a debt creates an equitable, enforceable lien on the property.

EXAMPLE
Jim and Rose, a married couple, gave Gene a mortgage to secure a debt for $10,000. The mortgage was carelessly prepared: (1) it was signed by Jim but not by Rose, although they jointly owned the property; (2) it inaccurately described the property as being located in a neighboring state, although the location of the property was obvious from the terms of the mortgage; and (3) it was never recorded. Despite these defects, the instrument will be enforced against Jim and Rose as an equitable lien or mortgage.

Various remedies exist to enforce equitable mortgages. In some states a legal proceeding can be brought to establish and foreclose an equitable mortgage. Another remedy is a proceeding to reform and enforce a defective mortgage. A proceeding to obtain specific performance is also possible.

Purchase Money Mortgages   A *purchase money mortgage* is usually one given by a purchaser to the seller of property simultaneously with the delivery of the seller's deed to secure payment of the purchase price of the property conveyed.

EXAMPLE
Doris purchases a piece of property from Blake for $20,000. She gives Blake $10,000 in cash and, at the same time, a promissory note and mortgage for the balance.

Because the mortgage is given to secure the purchase of the property being bought, it is a purchase money mortgage.

A mortgage need not be given to a seller to make it a purchase money mortgage. In some states it can be given to anyone—such as a bank—advancing the purchase money.

Open-End Mortgages   An open-end mortgage permits a debtor to borrow money at will in the future with certain real estate as security, and normally without any expense or delay. In other words, the open-end mortgage is a mortgage given to secure a present loan or debt as well as future loans by or debts due to the same lender; it is a mortgage to secure both present and future advances of money. These mortgages have been frequently used to secure building or construction loans.

 The use of an open-end mortgage for future advances is relatively common in real estate financing to provide working capital for business enterprises. Financing the construction of a shopping center, a commercial housing project, or a manufacturing plant are typical examples of transactions involving such a loan. Under an open-end mortgage the lender may agree, for example, to lend $1 million to the borrower. The borrower in turn agrees to use the loan proceeds to construct the facility in question. To provide security for repayment of the loan, the borrower executes and delivers to the lender a mortgage deed covering the land on which the facility is to be constructed. The lender then advances installments of the loan to the borrower as the work progresses on the facility. In this manner, the lender minimizes the risk of his investment by insuring that the loan is in fact used to increase the value of the mortgaged land; it also relieves the borrower of having to invest funds until they are needed. The borrower is also assured of a continuing supply of capital and avoids the expense and inconvenience of obtaining a new loan when additional sums are needed. Moreover, the borrower pays interest not on the face amount of the mortgage loan but, rather, only on the amount of the loan outstanding. The use of future advance financing also benefits the lender. It promotes additional borrowing since it minimizes the bother and cost of frequent individual loans. It permits the lender to retain the right to disburse the loan in installments as the value of the mortgaged property increases rather than requiring the lender initially to disburse the entire amount of the loan at a time when the value of the land securing the loan might be less than the amount to be disbursed.

Second Mortgages   A property owner who has previously granted a mortgage to secure a debt can give another, or second, mortgage on the same property to the extent of his remaining interest. Indeed, there can be a second, a third, and a fourth mortgage all covering the same property.

EXAMPLE
Bill buys a piece of property from Clarence for $20,000. Bill pays Clarence $10,000 in cash and gives him a purchase money mortgage for the balance. Later, Bill

wants to build an addition to his home. He borrows $5,000 from Hope and gives her a second mortgage on the property. This second mortgage is inferior in terms of rights and priorities to the first mortgage. If Bill needs still more money for another project and can arrange for another loan secured by his property, the third lender will receive a third mortgage. The third mortgage will be inferior in terms of rights and priorities to both the first and the second mortgages.

Second mortgages are relatively common in real estate sales, financing, and business construction. They are used by banks to secure homeowner loans and by other financial institutions that extend credit. In building construction, they play a prominent role in the financing or refinancing of multimillion-dollar projects. Although first mortgages take priority over second mortgages, in practice all mortgages are paid off simultaneously. Only in the event of a sale of the property, causing the mortgages to become due, or on default and foreclosure, do the priorities come into play, entitling the first mortgage to be satisfied first, out of the proceeds of sale.

Wraparound Mortgages   In recent years, there has been a renewed use of a real estate financing device, first used in the 1930s, known as the *wraparound mortgage.* The use of this type of mortgage has been prompted by relatively high interest rates on real property loans and by a tight money market. The wraparound mortgage is a second mortgage (or trust deed) securing a promissory note, the face amount of which is the sum of the existing first mortgage liability *plus* the cash advanced by the second mortgagee. The wraparound borrower must make payments on the first mortgage debt to the wraparound lender, who in turn makes payments on the first mortgage debt to the first mortgagee. The interest rate on the wraparound note is normally higher than the interest rate on the underlying debt, since a wraparound mortgage is used generally in a high-interest period. The economic advantage of a wraparound mortgage is that interest accrues to the lender on the full amount of the wraparound note instead of the amount of additional funds or credit loaned. This is so despite the fact that the lender has actually loaned (or extended credit on) only the amount of the additional funds.

Disguised Security Transactions   Security transactions involving real property that are not evidenced by a mortgage or deed of trust are a long-standing problem in mortgage law. In most states, the law is that a disguised security transaction, understood by the parties to secure a debt, will be given the effect of a mortgage. For example, a creditor might require a debtor to grant him land by absolute deed under an oral agreement or tacit understanding that the land will be reconveyed only if the debtor pays the debt when it is due. Or, a creditor might obtain from a debtor an absolute deed to real property and give him some sort of unrecorded agreement to reconvey the property on receiving payment of the debt. The written agreement to reconvey could take the form of (1) an option to repurchase, (2) an unconditional contract obligating the grantee to reconvey and the grantor to repurchase, or (3) a lease-back to the grantor with an option to repurchase at or before the end of the lease term. Some contracts or options provide for the deposit in escrow of a deed of reconveyance.

The above transactions are all designed to eliminate the equity of redemption and the necessity of foreclosure in case the debtor defaults. Besides avoiding the expense and delay involved in foreclosure, the creditor often expects to gain other advantages that cannot be obtained with a regular mortgage. These include a right to possession of the property before default, the ability to prevent the debtor from further encumbering the property, and the possibility of enlarging the creditor's security interest to cover future advances to the debtor without the execution of a new security instrument.

All of these transactions, which are absolute conveyances on their face but are intended only to be security for debt, will be regarded by the courts as mortgages. The reason is that if the purpose of a conveyance is security, it should be treated by the parties and the courts as a mortgage even though the parties might have agreed or understood that the debtor should have no right to redeem. The right to redeem after default is an inseparable incident of the mortgage relationship.

Mechanic's Liens   A *mechanic's lien* is a lien on real property given by statute to a person who has performed labor or furnished materials or equipment contributing to the improvement of property at the owner's request. A mechanic's lien is thus a type of security interest in real property that is based on statute rather than on a mortgage. A mechanic's lien provides a means by which the payment of certain debts incurred by a property owner can be enforced. The right to the lien depends on the specific terms of the appropriate statute; that is, a mechanic's lien cannot exist unless it is expressly created by statute. A lien claimant acquires a lien superior to the rights of the property owner and any subsequent purchaser, among others. A mechanic's lien is similar to a mortgage in being a a lien on real property. It differs from a mortgage in that it is not given as security for a debt but, rather, arises because of the performance of labor or the furnishing of material to benefit the property.

A mechanic's lien is not enforceable in most states unless the claim of lien has been perfected within the statutory period and in the manner provided by law. The initial step in perfecting a claim is to give preliminary notice to the owner, stating in general terms the kind of labor or materials furnished, the value, and the name of the person to whom the items were furnished. The claim is then recorded in a prescribed public office in the locality where the property is situated. If the debt is not paid, the lien can be foreclosed. The lien foreclosure procedure follows the procedure used in foreclosing a mortgage, as discussed in 35:6. In most states, a mechanic's lien has priority over all liens that attach after the mechanic's lien claimant first performed work or furnished materials. A mechanic's lien can be waived by failing to perfect it in the proper manner.

Although no two state mechanic's lien statutes are identical, most statutes are similar to either the New York statute or the Pennsylvania statute. Under the New York system, a lien of a subcontractor or materialman is based on and subordinate to the contractor's rights. This means that the lien is dependent on and limited by (1) the amount that remains due the contractor at the time the subcontractor or materialman serves notice on the owner (that he has furnished or is about to furnish labor or material) or (2) the amount that may become due the contractor after this time. Under the Pennsylvania system, the lien of the subcontractor or materialman is a direct lien and does not depend on the existence of any indebtedness due from the owner to the contractor.

The following case illustrates how strictly the notice requirement under a state mechanic's lien statute is generally construed. It also illustrates the nature of mechanic's liens and how they can be perfected, and it reviews the important distinction in the law of mortgages between the lien theory and the title theory.

R.L. Sweet Lumber Co.
v
E.L. Lane, Inc.
513 SW2d 365, 76 ALR3d 596
(Missouri Supreme Court, 1974)

[Subcontractors filed an action to enforce mechanic's liens for labor and materials furnished in the construction of an apartment building on which there was a mortgage. Before filing mechanic's lien statements, as required by state statute, each of the subcontractors personally served statements on the registered agent of the property on which the building was being constructed. However, the subcontractors failed to give advance notice to the mortgagees and to a title company. The trial court ruled that the subcontractors were not entitled to a lien because of their failure to give ten days' notice to the mortgagees and to the title company claiming a security interest in the real property. The subcontractors appealed. They argued that under the lien theory of mortgages, mortgagees were not owners, and thus the subcontractors were under no duty to give them notice before the filing of a lien statement.]

Holman, Judge

*   *   *

In this . . . mechanic's lien suit the trial court held that the sub-contractor lien claimants were not entitled to a lien for the sole reason that they had failed to give ten days' notice to the mortgagees and the title company (which claimed a security interest) before the filing of their lien statement. . . .

We are in general agreement with the opinion of the court of appeals and adopt the following portion thereof:

"The single issue presented is whether appellants, who were subcontractors in the construction of an apartment building complex . . . must, to enforce their claims for mechanic's liens, give to respondents, First National Bank of Wellston, Johnson County National Bank and Trust Company (mortgagees), and Chicago Title Insurance Company (the disburser of construction funds), the 10 day notice of intention to file mechanic's liens under [Revised Statutes of Missouri] § 429.100. It is claimed by respondents that they are 'owners' within the meaning of § 429.100 by reason of the definitions in § 429.150: 'Every person, including all cestui que trust [beneficiaries], for whose immediate use, enjoyment or benefit any building, erection or improvement shall be made, shall be included by the words "owner or proprietor" therefor under sections 429.010 to 429.340, ...' In short, respondents claim that by reason of being named as beneficiaries or mortgagees in certain security agreement instruments executed by the owner, . . . they are 'cestui que trust' parties under § 429.150. Appellants' basic contention is that respondents are not owners or cestui que trust parties because they, as security holders only, do not have the *'immediate* use, enjoyment or benefit' of the property involved as would an ordinary beneficiary . . . and thus appellants were not required to give the 10 day notice to respondents. [Court's emphasis.] . . .

"It is not controverted that appellants fully performed and that all labor and materials were actually furnished by them and incorporated into the improvements on [the] real estate; that the lien statements filed contained just and true statements of the accounts; or that the lien statements were in conformity with the statutory requirements for their filings. . . .

'. . . A deed of trust in the nature of a mortgage given on land to secure the payment of a debt is held to be "a lien and nothing more. . . . So viewed, it is neither an estate in land, nor a right to any beneficial interest therein. . . . It is merely the right to have the debt, if not otherwise paid, satisfied out of the land. The debt is the essence of the mortgage, the lien a mere incident that follows it as a shadow." . . .' We must hold, therefore, that appellant's ownership of the deed of trust on the property did not constitute him the owner of the title to the property. He had 'a lien and nothing more' which gave him only 'the right to have the debt, if not otherwise paid, satisfied out of the land.' . . .

"Under the foregoing cases and authority, . . . which [set] forth the 'lien theory' of mortgages as the law of this state, it is clear that respondents are not owners . . . for whose *immediate* use, enjoyment or benefit any building, erection or improvement shall be made. . . . [Court's emphasis.] Respondents have merely a security interest by which all they can expect is the possibility *in the future* that the debts of the owner . . . will be paid from the proceeds of the sale of the premises if default occurs. [Court's emphasis.] . . .

"The purpose of the 10 day notice of intention to file mechanic's liens . . . is to warn the *owner* of the property against paying the original contractor while outstanding claims exist in favor of laborers and materialmen; and to give him the opportunity to discharge the debt before the lien is filed. [Court's emphasis.] The notice is for the benefit of the *owner* alone. [Court's emphasis.] . . . It is the *owner* who has the obligation to pay the debt and prevent the lien from being perfected. [Court's emphasis.] In the ordinary situation a mortgagee–security holder would have no such obligation.

"It is apparent from the foregoing that a mortgagee–security holder is not a beneficiary of a trust who has the *immediate* use, enjoyment or benefit of any building, erection or improvement upon lands, and thus is not entitled to the 10 day notice. [Court's emphasis.] . . ."

[Judgment reversed.]

35:3   Rights of Parties; Use and Enjoyment of Property

The interests of the mortgagee and mortgagor in property are for many purposes considered separate and distinct. Under the law, the mortgagee has no control over mortgaged property. However, the mortgagee has the right to protect his separate interest and to this end may obtain insurance or pay off prior liens that affect his interest. As for the mortgagor, he must preserve the mortgaged property for the purpose of the security for which it was originally pledged, and it is customarily his duty to pay taxes and assessments levied on the property. If the mortgagee pays these taxes or assessments to protect his interest, he is entitled to be reimbursed for the amounts so paid, which means that he can add the amounts to the mortgage debt.

Acceleration Clauses   Mortgages, deeds of trusts, and the underlying promissory notes commonly provide for acceleration of the indebtedness on any failure to pay a required installment of principal or interest. In addition to acceleration for failure to pay installments, the instruments might permit acceleration at the option of the mortgagee or trust deed beneficiary if the borrower sells the property or further encumbers it. Some acceleration clauses provide that on certain conditions or the happening of specified events, the entire balance due on the debt "shall immediately become due and payable," but most clauses provide that in that event, the holder of the note or the mortgagee "may, at his option, declare," the entire unpaid balance immediately due and payable.

A *due-on-sale clause* is an acceleration clause that authorizes a mortgagee or trust deed beneficiary to accelerate the entire loan balance if and when the owner (mortgagor or trustor) sells or conveys the property. These clauses have been used by lenders as a means of increasing the interest rates on loans that are below current rates. Frequently, a lender will offer to waive enforcement of the clause only if the interest rates on the loan are increased. The practical effect of a lender declaring the balance of a loan due is to restrict the owner's ability to sell the property securing the loan. Consequently, in some states the due-on-sale clause has been voided by judicial decisions.[3] In other states acceleration clauses have been upheld by courts against attacks that they constitute unreasonable restraints on the sale of property. On the whole, however, courts are often reluctant to enforce the terms of an acceleration clause if enforcement will work a hardship on the mortgagor.

Rights to Possession of Mortgaged Property   In lien theory states, the mortgagee is not entitled to possession of the mortgaged property except through foreclosure and purchase or on agreement of the parties. The same is true of the trustee or beneficiary under a deed of trust. A mortgage can, however, contain an express provision giving the mortgagee certain rights, such as the right to take possession of or manage the property, to pay expenses, and to collect rents and profits. A mortgagee can also take possession with the mortgagor's implied consent. The mortgagee (or trustee under a deed of trust) in all these situations is known as a mortgagee in possession and is subject to certain rules governing his duties and conduct toward the mortgagor.

Ordinarily, the mortgagor remains in possession of mortgaged property. As legal owner, the mortgagor can use it as he pleases. Still, in most states, if the mortgagor's use of the property is so excessive or unreasonable as to be wasteful, the mortgagee can recover damages, obtain an injunction, or initiate other legal proceedings.

"Waste" is a special term in law that refers to conduct that causes physical damage to or destruction of property. It includes both "voluntary waste," such as excessive cutting of timber or removal of minerals or permanent structures, and "permissive waste," such as not keeping the property repaired properly. A mortgagor might also engage in "financial waste" by failing to pay taxes or to pay off other liens, thus impairing the mortgagee's security.

---

[3]See, for example, *Wellenkamp v Bank of America*, 21 Cal 3d 943, 148 Cal Rptr 379, 582 P2d 970 (California Supreme Court, 1978).

35:4   Priorities

The general principle expressed in the maxim "first in time, first in right" applies to mortgages. Under this rule, any lien or encumbrance that attaches to mortgaged property after the execution of a mortgage is subject to the mortgage. For example, a mortgage on property given to secure a loan for the construction of a building on the property is superior to the liens of laborers and materialmen who later enter into contracts with the property owner and furnish labor and materials used in the construction. It is beyond the power of the mortgagor to disturb this priority. On the other hand, a mortgagee's interests and rights are subject to any outstanding interest in the mortgaged property acquired before the execution of the mortgage. In determining the priority of several mortgages on the same property, they are generally ranked in order of their creation, the first in time standing first in order. The question of priority is, however, almost entirely regulated by state recording laws, discussed below.

Recording Laws   Mortgages, like deeds to property, can be and usually are recorded in the appropriate public office. In most states, the right to record a mortgage is purely statutory and must be exercised in accordance with the terms of the statute.

Most state recording systems give priority to the person whose mortgage is first recorded. Thus, mortgage priorities are similar to the rules governing deeds, discussed in Chapter 32. In other words, if an owner mortgages his property twice, the first mortgage recorded will be given priority over all other mortgages or liens, unless the mortgagee knew of these other mortgages or liens at the time of recording. In a minority of the states, the mortgage takes effect when executed, not when recorded. Thus, where two mortgages are executed on the same day, the fact that one is recorded before the other does not necessarily give it priority in these states. In the absence of other facts, both claims would be equal.

An exception to the general rule of priorities is applied to purchase money mortgages (see 35:2), which are generally entitled to preference over all other claims or liens arising through the mortgagor. The reason frequently advanced for this rule is that the execution of the deed and the mortgage are regarded as simultaneous acts, so that no claim or lien arising through the mortgagor can attach before the mortgage.

35:5   Payment and Discharge; Equity of Redemption

Payment of the indebtedness secured by real estate must be made at the time and in the manner provided in the mortgage or other security instrument. Usually, all or most of the debt is paid in periodic installments, but the instrument can also call for payment in a lump sum on the maturity date. A payment or offer of payment of all that remains owing on the maturity date extinguishes the mortgage lien and discharges the debt. When the debt is paid, the mortgagee customarily signs—and in some states records—a release, acknowledging payment and satisfaction of the debt. Bear in mind, however, that although the mortgagor must pay the debt *by* the maturity date, he generally has no right to pay the entire debt *before* it is due unless a mortgage provision or an agreement between the parties authorizes such payment. Indeed, there is often a penalty for prepayment because of the loss of interest that the mortgagee may suffer.

Equity of Redemption   Under the common law, a mortgagor's failure to pay the mortgage debt on the exact date on which it matured—the law day—extinguished the mortgagor's right and title to the mortgaged property and made the mortgagee's title absolute. This harsh rule not only became a common theme of melodrama, but it also received the early attention of courts of equity, which soon came up with more equitable rules. They first developed the equitable or lien theory of mortgages, as discussed in 35:1. The courts then developed what is known as the "equity of redemption." It offered a defaulting debtor a way to avoid forfeiting his title by allowing him to pay the debt at any time before actual foreclosure of the mortgage. Today, this right exists in all states.

EXAMPLE
Don purchased a mountain lot. To finance the purchase, he obtained a loan from his local bank and gave in return a promissory note and mortgage for $10,000. He subsequently defaulted on payments. At the time of default, Don owed $2,500. Before the bank initiates foreclosure proceedings to terminate his interest in the property, Don can pay—or offer to pay—the bank the total amount then due under the mortgage, thereby redeeming the property.

It is important to note that for reasons of public policy, the right of redemption cannot be waived or relinquished by agreement. Any agreement that is made to waive or relinquish this right is void.

35:6   Foreclosure

A mortgagor's failure to pay off the mortgage debt or to perform any of his other contractual duties can result in sale of the mortgaged property and the mortgagor's loss of his equity of redemption. The process by which this is done is called foreclosure. As discussed in detail below, two kinds of foreclosure procedures are in general use: (1) foreclosure by sale pursuant to judicial decree and (2) foreclosure by private sale without judicial intervention. The latter procedure is customarily referred to as power of sale or nonjudicial foreclosure. In most states, mortgages and deeds of trust contain a clause providing that on default, the mortgagee or trustee can sell the property to satisfy the debt. In other states, foreclosure is commonly accomplished only through judicial action.

Foreclosure by Judicial Action   Foreclosure by judicial action begins with a proceeding to foreclose brought against the mortgagor. At the proceeding, the mortgagor is given the opportunity to raise defenses that might prevent foreclosure. If the court determines that there has been a default and that the mortgagee has a right to foreclose, a decree or judgment is entered stating the amount due the lender and specifying a period in which the borrower can redeem the property by paying off the whole obligation. The decree provides that a specified period of notice be given to the public that the property is to be sold at public auction. This notice, which is published in a newspaper, must include a description of the property and the time, place, and terms of sale, as well as the officer named to conduct the sale.

The mortgagee is customarily permitted to bid at the auction, and in practice the mortgagee is often the only or the highest bidder. A mortgagee who successfully bids no more than the unpaid amount of the obligation secured by the mortgage need not pay anything at all, the bid price is merely applied to the mortgage debt. If the court approves the propriety of the sale, the officer who conducts it must execute a deed to the purchaser.

The following opinion sets forth the circumstances in which a foreclosure can arise. Note that the mortgagee in the case used an acceleration clause as the basis for foreclosure. Compare the foreclosure process with the more easily accomplished power of sale under a deed of trust, as discussed following this case.

Federal Home Loan Mortgage Corp.
v
Taylor
318 So 2d 203
(Florida District Court of Appeal, 1975)

[George Taylor and his wife owned a home in Florida. When they bought the home, they had executed a promissory note and mortgage, and the debt was to be paid in monthly installments of $104.58. Taylor was a noncommissioned officer in the United States Air Force, and from September 1972 until 1974 he was on active duty in the Philippine Islands. Until April 1973 the Taylors made monthly payments to the Federal Home Loan Mortgage Corp., the mortgagee. The May 1973 payment was over one month late but was accepted by the mortgagee. Three installments were made on September 10, 1973. These were accepted and applied to the installments due on the first of June, July and August 1973. Mail deliveries to and from the Philippines and the United States required 7 to 18 days. On September 29, 1973, Taylor and his wife mailed two money orders totaling $121.38, which was the correct amount for the monthly payment due September 1, 1973. The payment included the $104.58

installment as specified in the note, $14.42 for accrued taxes and insurance as provided in the mortgage, and a late charge of $2.38. This payment was returned with a covering form letter dated October 4, 1973, stating that the remittance was not sufficient to reinstate the delinquent account and that $240.38 was required to eliminate the delinquency; this larger amount included the regular installment due on October 1 and an additional late charge. After that the Taylors mailed payments each month for several months. Had these payments been received within the current month, they would have been sufficient to pay the accruals, but each one was received after the succeeding month's installment came due. In each instance the mortgagee mailed back the payment because it was insufficient to cover the current installment due. This pattern continued until March 1974, with remittances and returns often crossing in the mail. In April 1974 the Taylors discontinued payments, believing it to be likely that the payments would be returned or even misplaced in the mails. However, they set aside money in an escrow account, to be available for payments on the debt. On April 6, 1974, the mortgagee filed a complaint in court seeking foreclosure of the mortgage, alleging the Taylors' default by *their failure to make the payment due September 1, 1973, and all subsequent payments. The trial court refused to foreclose the mortgage, and the mortgagee appealed.]*

Willis, Ben C., Associate Judge.

*   *   *

The appellant was plaintiff in the trial court in a suit to foreclose a real estate mortgage given by appellees to secure an installment promissory note by them. Appellant is the owner and holder of the note and mortgage. The parties will be referred to as the mortgagors and mortgagee. . . .

The complaint seeking foreclosure . . . alleged default by failing to pay payments due September 1, 1973 and all subsequent payments. . . .

It is apparent that the cause was heard primarily on the issue of whether or not the acceleration of the due date of future mortgage installments with resultant foreclosure would be unconscionable and an inequitable result. . . .

The mortgagor, George Taylor, testified that the reason for the late payment in September was the necessity of having his daughter flown back to the mainland to a hospital in Texas. He further testified that in October and November he was still having financial problems as he had to pay rent for his wife in Texas, presumably in connection with the child's hospitalization, also pay for his living quarters in the Philippines, and pay the installment on the mortgage in Florida.

The mortgagee contends that the trial court abused its discretion in refusing to honor acceleration of the due date of the debt and accord a foreclosure for the full amount of the unpaid principal and accrued interest. It is fully established in . . . this state that an acceleration clause or promise in an installment note or mortgage confers a contract right upon the note or mortgage holder which he may elect to invoke upon default and to seek enforce-

ment. . . . It is essential that valid contracts be safeguarded and the right of enforcement in the event of breach be accorded. A mere offer or willingness of a mortgagor to cure a default, after a valid election to accelerate, is not deemed a sufficient ground to deny acceleration and foreclosure. . . . The obligation of a mortgagor to pay and the right of a mortgagee to foreclosure in accordance with the terms of the note and mortgage are absolute and are not contingent on the mortgagor's health, good fortune, ill fortune, or other personal circumstances affecting his ability to pay.

However, it is equally well established in our law that a court of equity may refuse to foreclose a mortgage when an acceleration of the due date of the debt would be an inequitable or unjust result and the circumstances would render the acceleration unconscionable. . . .

In the case [before the court] the mortgagor had not prior to the return of his tendered payment received by the mortgagee subsequent to October 1, 1973, been aware of any purpose or inclination of the mortgagee to be uneasy about this account. After nearly three years of regular payments, there was one lapse of a month plus 20 days in making a payment followed by a three month lapse but immediately afterwards there were paid three installments with late charges. The September 10, 1973 payment did not include the installment which fell due September 1. However, prior to October 4 this installment was paid, but mortgagee refused to accept it because the October 1 installment was not included. The lag in mail deliveries was obviously a circumstance which contributed to much of the lack of communication and misunderstanding. It is to be noticed here that the mortgagors were not in the [Philippines] by mere choice but due to a military assignment. Though the personal hardship arising from the daughter's need of stateside hospitalization is not a circumstance to excuse payment of a debt when due, the distance between the mortgagors and mortgagee's agent because of military obligations of the mortgagor is not to be ignored as a factor impairing the ability of the parties to communicate demands and responses thereto. The total evidence indicates a good faith effort on the part of mortgagors to meet the mortgagee's conditions of bringing the account current. Perhaps the mortgagee would have been less adamant in returning tendered payments were it not for the fear that continued acceptance may have worked a waiver or estoppel to assert an accelerated default.... Here, the trial judge was well within his discretion in concluding that it would be unconscionable to precipitate the maturity of the entire balance of over $14,000 which could only result in the loss of the mortgaged property through foreclosure, all because of a technical default of one month's installment which well could arise from excusable misunderstanding and lack of effective and timely communication. We find no error in that portion of the judgment declining foreclosure and effecting reinstatement of the note and mortgage.

The Final Judgment recites at the outset a finding that "this action is the result of both parties' conduct".... As the court found, and the evidence shows, more provident conduct on the part of each side would have made the action unnecessary. The mortgagors might have sent an extra month's payment to be sure of meeting the requirements of reinstatement. The mortgagee might well have been less inflexible and adamant in pursuing its strict policy in view of the serviceman's station on the other side of the world. Symbolically, the mortgagee resorted to a bulldozer when a garden spade might well have sufficed....

[Affirmed.]

Foreclosure Through Power of Sale   Sale under a power contained in a mortgage or deed of trust is the other established mode of mortgage foreclosure. In states where such foreclosures are recognized, the sale is made without recourse to the courts, although statutes generally prescribe the manner of advertising and conducting the sale. The sale must be made strictly in accordance with the power conferred and with the terms of the mortgage or deed of trust. The advantage of the power of sale to the creditor derives from the right to choose between the alternatives of foreclosure by court action or the trustee's sale. In this manner, a creditor can avoid the delay and expense accompanying a judicial foreclosure proceeding which, as the previous case illustrates, may last for several years. While the mortgagor generally has a statutory right to redeem his property after judicial foreclosure and sale, he has no such right of redemption once the property is sold pursuant to a power of sale.

Power of sale foreclosures afford mortgagees greater efficiency and substantial savings in comparison with judicial foreclosure. At the same time, important rights of the mortgagor are sacrificed. The mortgagor is forced to give up substantial judicial protection where the only recourse is a personal action against the mortgagee to enjoin a sale, to undo it, or to seek damages after its completion.

A nonjudicial foreclosure sale is open to many abuses. For example, a mortgagee might not make a good faith effort to realize from the sale any more than the amount of the debt, despite the fact that the mortgagor might have considerable equity in the property. The mortgagee might also foreclose through the power of sale only for a technical default, based on conduct that the court in a judicial foreclosure might overlook. Finally, a mortgagee might sell the property after a default with respect to fraudulent or usurious terms in the mortgage contract, terms that a court would refuse to enforce in a judicial foreclosure.

The general rule is that in the absence of fraud, mistake, or unfairness, the fact that the sale price received in a foreclosure sale was low is not a sufficient ground to invalidate the sale unless (1) the price was grossly inadequate and unconscionable or (2) additional circumstances affected the regularity of the sale.

EXAMPLE

A mortgagor sues to have a foreclosure sale set aside. He alleges that the mortgagee, who successfully bid on the property, was unjustly enriched due to the low price bid. However, the mortgagor fails to allege any fraud or irregularity surrounding the sale. The court will probably refuse to set the sale aside.

Consider in the following case how easily the power of sale was accomplished as compared to judicial foreclosure requiring court approval.

Outpost Cafe, Inc.

v

Fairhaven Savings Bank
3 Mass App 1, 322 NE2d 183
(Massachusetts Appeals Court, 1975)

[In 1972 Outpost Cafe, Inc., was in breach of one or more of the conditions contained in a mortgage of certain premises. Outpost Cafe had given the mortgage to the Fairhaven Savings Bank in 1970. On January 16, 1973, the bank, pursuant to a power of sale contained in the mortgage, conducted a duly advertised sale and sold the premises to the highest bidder. The purchaser put down a deposit in accordance with the terms of the sale and entered into a memorandum of sale with the attorney for the bank. Six days later, on January 22, 1973, Outpost Cafe tendered to the bank an amount in excess of the amount then due under the terms of the mortgage. The bank refused to accept the tender. Outpost Cafe then sued to redeem. By this time the bank had executed but had not yet delivered a deed of the premises to the purchaser at the foreclosure sale. The pertinent state statute provided that a mortgagor could redeem mortgaged property after a breach of condition unless the land had been sold pursuant to a power of sale contained in the mortgage deed. The

court dismissed the redemption suit on the ground that the tender came too late because the equity of redemption had already been foreclosed. Outpost Cafe appealed.]

Grant, Justice.

*   *   *

The disposition of this case turns on when "the land has been *sold* pursuant to a power of sale contained in the mortgage deed" . . . and on when a "*sale* [occurs] pursuant to a power contained in the mortgage" . . . [Court's emphasis.] The defendant and the purchaser contend that the premises were "sold" within the meaning of those sections at least as early as the time when they executed the memorandum of sale at the foreclosure sale; the plaintiff contends that a "sale" is not complete until a deed is delivered to the purchaser at the foreclosure sale and that it may redeem the premises at any time prior to the delivery of such a deed.

An auction sale is complete, in the generally understood sense, when the auctioneer signifies his acceptance of the highest bid. . . .

If we were to be guided solely by the ordinary principles of statutory construction, we would unhesitatingly conclude that the premises in this case were "sold" within the meaning of [the statute] on the date of the foreclosure sale and that the plaintiff's tender came too late because not made until after the equity of redemption had been barred by virtue of the concluding provision of [the statute]. We believe that a careful analysis of the pertinent cases leads to the same conclusion. . . .

. . . [W]e hold that the plaintiff's equity of redemption was barred . . . at least as early as the point in time when the memorandum of sale was executed with the purchaser at the foreclosure sale. It follows that the plaintiff's tender and bill came too late under [the statute]. . . . The tender was properly refused, and the bill was properly dismissed.

[Decree affirmed.]

Single-Action Rule   Under what is known as the single-action rule, when a mortgagor defaults, the mortgagee usually institutes a single action for the collection of the mortgage debt and foreclosure of the mortgage. This is required by statute in some states, and in these states, a separate action for either kind of relief bars the other kind.

Deficiency Judgments   A mortgage foreclosure sale reduces the mortgage debt by an amount equal to the sale price, minus the expenses of the foreclosure and sale. For example, if a mortgagee is owed $25,000 on the mortgage, the foreclosure sale raises $22,000, and the cost of the foreclosure and sale is $2,000, the mortgage debt is reduced by only $20,000, leaving a deficiency of $5,000. Because the mortgagor is personally liable for the mortgage debt due to the promissory note that accompanies the mortgage, the mortgagee is at least theoretically entitled to a personal judgment against the mortgagor for the amount of the deficiency. In some states, a mortgagee can obtain a personal judgment for the debt in the foreclosure judgment itself; the amount raised by the foreclosure sale is applied to satisfy this personal judgment. In other states, no personal judgment is entered until the sale reveals the shortfall.

During the Depression, mortgage foreclosure sales routinely failed to raise enough money to cover the mortgagors' debts. As a result, mortgagees in great numbers obtained personal judgments against debtors seeking to recoup deficiencies. In response to this, many states enacted antideficiency judgment statutes that prohibit to some degree a mortgagee's ability to obtain a personal judgment against the mortgage debtor after foreclosure and sale. Most antideficiency judgment statutes do not absolutely bar mortgagees from obtaining a *deficiency judgment*. For example, some statutes place substantial burdens of proof on mortgagees seeking deficiency judgment. Whatever their provisions, antideficiency judgment statutes have the effect of making deficiency judgments after mortgage foreclosure relatively rare today.

Rights of Purchasers and Other Lienholders   The doctrine of caveat emptor ("let the buyer beware") applies to both kinds of foreclosure sales discussed above. A purchaser at a foreclosure sale must determine the validity of the title that is acquired, although he can be entitled to relief if he has been misled by fraud or mistake and was not contributorily negligent. If a foreclosure sale is invalid for any reason for which the purchaser is not responsible, he generally stands in the position of a mortgagee and can institute another foreclosure proceeding.

In the absence of any binding stipulation in the mortgage or deed of trust regarding the distribution or application of the proceeds of a foreclosure sale, a court having jurisdiction of the proceeding can determine the order of priority of various liens on the property and give specific directions as to the distribution and application of the proceeds. Generally, the proceeds must first be applied to the mortgage debt. Any surplus that remains after the discharge of the mortgage debt and other liens on the property must be paid to the mortgagor.

35:7   Redemption from Sale

After foreclosure of a mortgage by public sale, the *equitable* right of redemption ends, as discussed previously. However, in approximately 25 states, a *statutory* right of redemption exists. The statutes granting this right vary greatly from state to state, but they all prescribe a period after a foreclosure sale during which a mortgagor can reacquire his property by paying a sum computed in accordance with the statutory formula. Statutes in a few states also provide that the mortgagor can remain in possession during the statutory redemption period. Note that this right of redemption, called the redemption from sale, is quite distinct from the equity of redemption that is entirely cut off by a foreclosure. Because the right to redeem after a foreclosure sale is purely statutory, it can be exercised only in the manner prescribed by statute. Exercise of the right generally defeats any rights acquired by a purchaser at the foreclosure sale and restores the title to the property as though no sale had been attempted. That is, the purchaser at a foreclosure sale buys the property subject to any statutory right of redemption.

35:8   Receivers

In most states a receiver can be appointed to take charge of mortgaged property at the request of the mortgagee, to protect the mortgagee's interest. In practice, receiverships are usually requested only during foreclosure proceedings, and the court does not always grant the request. For example, the inadequacy of security for the mortgage debt is not, without more, a ground for appointing a receiver unless a statute provides otherwise. In some states the mortgagee can claim the rents, income, and profits of the mortgaged property after the mortgagor defaults and the mortgagee is given a right to the appointment of a receiver to take charge. In other states the mortgagor's insolvency, combined with the insufficiency of the security to pay the debt, can be the ground for appointing a receiver, at least when the mortgagor is in default. Appointment of a receiver is especially appropriate if these factors are combined with a danger of loss, waste, destruction, or serious impairment of the property.

A court has the power to appoint a receiver to manage a mortgagor's business. Here, too, the circumstances of each case will determine whether the appointment is proper and should be made.

35:9 Transfer of Mortgaged Property and Mortgage Debt

A mortgagor's interest in mortgaged property can be sold and conveyed at any time. When a mortgagor sells mortgaged property, he loses all control over it, but his liability under the mortgage continues. If the purchaser actually assumes and agrees to pay the mortgage debt, he becomes liable for the debt not only to the mortgagor but also to the mortgagee.

Most sellers of real property take it for granted that if there is a debt still owing on the property, the purchaser takes complete responsibility for payment of that debt. This is not always true. Liability on the debt depends on whether the buyer takes the property "subject to" the mortgage or "assumes" it. In the "subject to" approach the property alone stands as security for the debt; the buyer undertakes no personal liability. When a buyer "assumes" a mortgage, however, he agrees to make the payments and becomes personally liable to the mortgagee for the mortgage debt.

Transfer of Mortgage and Debt Just as a mortgagor can convey his interest in mortgaged property, the mortgagee can transfer or assign the mortgage and secured debt. When a valid transfer or assignment is made, the transferee receives the mortgagee's rights and powers just as though he had been named in the mortgage. For example, the transferee can foreclose the mortgage on the mortgagor's default. In lien theory states, where a mortgagee's interest is a lien and for security purposes only, a transfer of the mortgage debt automatically operates as a transfer of the lien securing it. This is so because under the lien theory a mortgage has no independent existence. That is, it only reflects the debt, and cannot be separated from it.

Key Concepts and Terms

- The modern mortgage is both a conveyance and a lien to secure the payment of debt.

- Most states have adopted the equitable or lien theory of mortgages. This is the theory that a mortgage does not convey legal title to land but only creates a lien to secure payment of the mortgage debt.

- A security transaction in real property creates an interest in the property to secure the performance of an obligation. Mortgages and deeds of trust are the instruments used in most security transactions. A security transaction that is not evidenced by a mortgage or deed of trust but is understood by the parties to secure a debt will be given the effect of a mortgage.

- Any kind of interest in real property can be made the subject of a mortgage. A mortgage on land generally covers all structures and improvements on the land, including those made after the mortgage transaction.

- The owner of property who was previously granted a mortgage to secure a debt can give one or more junior mortgages on the same property to the extent of his remaining interest.

- The interests of the mortgagee and mortgagor in property are separate and distinct. The mortgagee has no control over mortgaged property and is not entitled to possession either before or after the mortgagor defaults, unless authorized by the mortgage. The mortgagor must preserve the mortgaged property to protect the mortgagee's security interest.

- The equity of redemption gives a defaulting mortgagor the right to pay the mortgage debt at any time before foreclosure. This right cannot be waived or relinquished by agreement because of the strong public policy favoring it.

- Foreclosure of a mortgage entails the sale of the mortgaged property and termination of the mortgagor's equity of redemption. It can occur when the mortgagor fails either to pay the secured debt or to perform other duties imposed on him by the terms of the mortgage. The basic foreclosure procedures are (1) sale pursuant to a judicial decree and (2) private sale without judicial intervention.

- Statutes in about half the states provide for redemption from sale. These statutes allow a mortgagor to redeem his property after a foreclosure sale by paying a sum computed according to the statutory formula within a prescribed time after the sale.

- A receiver is a person or entity appointed by the court to protect the rights of a mortgagee whose security in mortgaged property is threatened. A receiver can be appointed to manage a mortgagor's business.

- A mortgagor can convey his interest in the mortgaged property at any time. If he does so he loses all control over the property, but his liability under the mortgage continues. A purchaser who actually assumes and agrees to pay a mortgage debt becomes liable for the debt not only to the mortgagor but also to the mortgagee.

- A mortgagee can assign the mortgage and mortgage debt.

- Assumption of Mortgage
- Deed of Trust
- Deficiency Judgment
- Due-on-Sale Clause
- Equitable Mortgage
- Equity of Redemption
- Foreclosure
- Lien Theory
- Mechanic's Lien

- Mortgage
- Mortgagee
- Mortgagor
- Open-End Mortgage
- Power of Sale
- Purchase Money Mortgage
- Title Theory
- Wraparound Mortgage

Questions and Case Problems

1. Compare and contrast the title and lien theories of mortgages. Determine whether your state is a title theory or a lien theory state.

2. Boardwalk Corporation proposes to erect a five-story building in New York City, and hopes to seek financing from its regular construction financier, Builders Bank.

Boardwalk estimates that the total cost of the project will be $10 million. It would prefer to receive only $2 million initially and to draw the balance of the loan in subsequent installments as dictated by the progress of the project. Since cost over-runs are almost inevitable, Boardwalk wants to ensure that the financing is suffi-ciently flexible to permit the extension of credit beyond the initial $10 million without undue cost or delay. Builders Bank is prepared to deal with Boardwalk if the firm can provide sufficient security of real property to cover not only the $10 million primary indebtedness, but also an unsecured note in the amount of $100,000 executed previously by Boardwalk in favor of the bank on a previous construction job. How can this transaction best be structured?

3. Why are certain land security transactions considered under certain circumstances to be mortgages or deeds of trust?

4. Is a mechanic's lien a mortgage? If not, how does it differ?

5. Wisconsin Wire Works conveys mortgaged premises to Megao Development Corp. without the consent of the mortgagee, Mutual Federal. The mortgage provides for acceleration of the balance due if the mortgagor "shall convey away" the mort-gaged premises. Mutual Federal initiates a proceeding to foreclose the mortgage, seeking to enforce the due-on-sale acceleration clause. How should the court de-cide the case?

6. Compare and contrast the equity of redemption and the statutory right of redemp-tion from sale.

7. A law that would govern due-on-sale clauses has been proposed. It would provide that a due-on-sale clause would be enforceable as long as the original borrower was provided with a choice between a loan with a due-on-sale clause and one at a higher rate of interest without such a provision. The choice offered by the pro-posed law is shown by the following notice that would have to be given to the buyer:

Notice

You have a choice of mortgage contracts to finance your home. Before you sign one of the contracts you should understand the following differences in terms between them:

Contract "A" has an interest rate of [13] percent and is repayable over _____ years. Unless otherwise agreed to by _____ [lender] the loan must be repaid in full on transfer of the real property. Contract "B" has an interest rate of [16] percent and is repayable over _____ years. The loan need not be repaid in full on a transfer of the real property and the buyer may continue to make the payment without any change in the interest rate or other terms of the contract. To have your loan remain outstanding on a transfer of your property may be of value if the interest rates on mortgage loans are higher when you transfer your property than present rates.

Please indicate by checking the appropriate box and signing below whether you want Contract "A" ☐ or Contract "B" ☐

Does this proposed legislation offer borrowers a real choice or is it merely an-other type of "Hobson's choice" in which the result will always be predictable, although alternatives are seemingly given? Would not most borrowers choose only Contract A because of the lower interest rate? Does this legislation lessen any of the problems associated with due-on-sale clauses?

8. First Federal forecloses and sells real property owned by Molds. It later seeks a deficiency judgment and the appointment of a receiver for the property during the period of redemption. First Federal alleges that the property will depreciate in value during the period of redemption and for that reason a receiver is required. Does depreciation in value constitute waste and a sufficient basis on which the appointment of a receiver may be made?

9. Potwin State Bank agreed to finance the construction of houses by Warrant. The mortgage expressly stated that it was given to include security for future advances. During the construction of various houses by Warrant, labor and materials were furnished by contractors. Mechanic's liens attached after the mortgage was recorded but before various advances were made under the mortgage. Ultimately, the bank foreclosed on the mortgage, seeking priority over the mechanic's lien claimants. Do the mechanic's liens take priority over the mortgage advances?

10. Compare and contrast judicial foreclosure and foreclosure through a power of sale.

36 Landlord and Tenant

36:1   Introduction; Types of Tenancies

Many people rent the real property on which they live rather than owning it. This has traditionally been true for young people during their early years away from their parents' home. As real estate prices have skyrocketed in recent years, however, it has become increasingly true for many older, established people as well. This chapter discusses the relationship that exists when a person who owns real property rents that property to someone else.

The renting of real property is based on a form of contract that is most commonly referred to as a *lease* or a rental agreement. This is true whether the contract is oral or in writing. The person who gives possession and use of real property to the other is known as the landlord, or lessor. The person who receives possession of the property and has use of the premises during the term of the lease is the tenant, or lessee.

If a landlord–tenant relationship exists, the tenant's interest or estate is called a leasehold. Leaseholds are generally classified according to their duration as (1) a tenancy for years, (2) a periodic tenancy or tenancy from year to year, (3) a tenancy at will, or (4) a tenancy at sufferance. These types of tenancies will now be discussed.

Tenancy for Years   A *tenancy for years* is one in which the beginning and end are fixed in advance. The term is a misnomer because the tenancy can be for a certain number of days, weeks, months, or years. The chief difference between a tenancy for years and other tenancies is that it expires at the end of a stated period without the need for either party to give notice of its expiration or termination. A lease can be created for as long a period as desired unless there is a statute that limits the maximum years of a particular lease.

Periodic Tenancy   A *periodic tenancy* continues for successive periods of the same length of time—weekly, monthly, or yearly, as long as the beginning of the tenancy is certain. It is terminated by notice at the end of one of the periods. Frequently, a periodic tenancy arises by implication. This occurs if property is leased with no specific termination date, but provision is made for periodic payments of rent. In such a case, the tenant has a periodic tenancy measured by the rental periods. For example, if a tenant rents an apartment beginning January 1 and pays rent monthly, a periodic tenancy (month-to-month) has been created.

Tenancy at Will   In a *tenancy at will* the tenant has a right to possession of premises for an indefinite period. A tenancy at will terminates at the will of either the landlord or the tenant.

Tenancy at Sufferance   A *tenancy at sufferance* is an unlawful possession of property. For example, a tenant who occupies the premises without the landlord's consent after the stated period of tenancy has expired is a tenant at sufferance. One who obtains possession of property without the owner's permission is also considered to be a tenant at sufferance. A tenancy at sufferance lasts only until the landlord takes steps to evict the tenant or seeks to regain possession. If a landlord gives either express or implied consent to a tenant's holding over after the expiration of a lease, this consent may be sufficient to transform the tenancy at sufferance into a tenancy at will or, under certain circumstances, into a periodic tenancy.

36:2   The Lease Agreement

A lease transfers a right to possession of property from the property owner to a tenant who, in turn, gives some consideration (usually rent) to the owner. Thus, a lease is both a conveyance and a contract for the possession of property. Leases are generally governed by the same principles that govern other contracts. There must be a delivery and acceptance of the lease, and the lease must contain the names of the contracting parties and a description of the leased premises. A lease must also be supported by consideration. Fraud or mutual mistake, or other illegality, can invalidate a lease.

While no particular legal terminology is required to make a lease, the document must (1) express an intention to establish the relationship of landlord and tenant; (2) include provisions for the transfer of use and possession of the property and its reversion to the landlord at the end of the term; and (3) state the boundaries of the property, the term of the leasehold, the agreed rent, and how and when the rent is to be paid.

Oral Leases   A landlord–tenant relationship can be created orally in most states. However, if the term of an oral lease exceeds the period set forth in the state statute of frauds, which affects oral contracts (see Chapter 15), the lease is unenforceable and might even be invalid, depending on state law.

Other Relationships Distinguished   The leasehold is the only interest in real property that confers a right to possession. Other interests, such as easements and licenses, entitle the holder to use another's land but do not entail the transfer of possession. For example, a typical billboard agreement gives the advertiser the right only to erect a billboard on another's property; since it does not entail possession, a landlord–tenant relationship is not created.

Covenants and Conditions   A *covenant* is an undertaking by one of the parties to a lease to do or not to do a particular act, and most leases include express covenants. For example, a lease is liable to include covenants by which the tenant promises to use the property only for a specific purpose and the landlord promises to make needed repairs and to ensure the tenant's quiet enjoyment of the property. As discussed further in 36:3, "quiet enjoyment" refers to the tenant's right to possess and use the property without interference by the landlord.

Covenants are classified as independent or dependent. An independent covenant is one that can be enforced or performed despite the other party's failure to perform his own covenant or obligation. For example, assume that L covenants under a lease to paint a house and T covenants to pay rent for the right to occupy that house. If L fails to paint the house, T must still continue to pay rent. L's breach of his covenant does not excuse T from paying rent since the covenants are independent. T's remedy is to sue L for damages for failing to paint the house.

A dependent covenant is an obligation that constitutes consideration for another obligation undertaken by the other party. If one party fails to perform, the other party is relieved of the obligation under his covenant. For example, a tenant's covenant to pay rent is dependent on a landlord's performance of the covenant for quiet enjoyment; an act by the landlord that interferes with the tenant's enjoyment or possession of the property can suspend the tenant's obligation to pay rent.

Most leases also include "conditions," which are qualifications or restrictions. For example, a lease provision that premises are to be used for "bakery and associated purposes and traffic in food and beverages and for no other purposes" is a *condition.* If the tenant changes the use of the premises from a bakery to a nightclub featuring topless dancers, the condition is breached and the landlord can forfeit the lease or obtain a court order prohibiting the tenant from violating it.

The most significant difference between covenants and conditions lies in the remedies available to either party in case of breach. The remedy for breach of a covenant is usually an action for damages. In contrast, a party usually cannot recover damages for breach of a condition. Instead, the breach can result in forfeiture of the lease.

36:3   Possession of Premises

Some states follow what is usually termed the English rule as to the possession of leased premises. Under this rule the landlord must provide the tenant with possession of premises at the beginning of the agreed term, even to the extent of ousting anyone who may already be in possession. Other states follow the so-called "American rule." This rule is that unless a provision to the contrary is included in the lease, a landlord must give the tenant only the legal right to possession at the beginning of the term, not necessarily actual possession. In these states, the landlord does not have to put the tenant in possession as against an intruder or other party. The realities of modern leasing, however, are such that most tenants are actually put in possession of leased property at the inception of the agreed term. Moreover, both the Model Residential Landlord–Tenant Code and the *Restatement (Second) of Property, Landlord and Tenant,* recognize that a landlord is obligated to provide the tenant with actual possession except to the extent that the parties agree otherwise. A landlord breaches this obligation if a third party is in possession on the date the tenant is entitled to possession of the leased property.

Peaceful and Quiet Enjoyment   The essence of the landlord–tenant relationship is the tenant's right to have the peaceful and quiet use of real property throughout the duration of the tenancy. This right, based on the *covenant for quiet enjoyment*, is contained in most written leases and rental agreements. The covenant for quiet enjoyment protects the tenant against physical expulsion, interference by the landlord, or other acts threatening the tenant's beneficial enjoyment of the premises. In short, the covenant operates to guarantee that the tenant will have possession of the property throughout the lease term.

Landlord's Reversionary Interest   For all practical purposes, the tenant is the absolute owner of the leased premises during the lease term. The landlord's rights are confined to his reversionary interest in the premises. At the end of the term, the tenant must vacate and surrender the premises to the landlord unless the tenant has an option to purchase and exercises it in a timely fashion. The landlord does not have to request that the tenant vacate. However, a tenant can remain in possession after the original term ends if (1) he pays rent to the landlord and (2) the landlord accepts the rent. The tenant will then be considered either a periodic tenant or a tenant at will.

Eviction   An *eviction* is any act by a landlord that deprives the tenant of possession, expels him from the premises, or deprives him of enjoyment of the premises. The wrongful eviction of a tenant will terminate the tenant's obligations under the lease and entitle him to recover damages. Eviction can be actual, as where it occurs because of the landlord's affirmative act. As discussed below, however, eviction can also be constructive.

Constructive Eviction   A *constructive eviction* is the landlord's substantial interference with the tenant's possession that (1) renders the premises unfit for the purposes for which they were leased or (2) deprives the tenant of the enjoyment of the premises. To establish a constructive eviction, there must be (1) a substantial interference and (2) abandonment of the premises by the tenant. For example, if a landlord fails to furnish heat, light, or other utilities, the tenant is constructively evicted if he is forced to abandon the property as a result. In certain cases, constructive eviction has also occurred because of a landlord's failure to make repairs or alterations required by the terms of the lease or by public authorities.

EXAMPLE
Dr. Peters, a psychotherapist, rents an office from Rockrose Associates for professional use. Under the lease, the landlord is required to soundproof the office. He fails to do so, and over a period of three months, neighboring tenants' noise interferes with the doctor's sessions with her patients. Under the doctrine of constructive eviction, Dr. Peters is relieved of paying rent if she abandons the premises.

Retaliatory Eviction   A landlord is prohibited from evicting a tenant as retaliation for the tenant's complaints to a governmental agency as to the condition of a dwelling, its habitability, or housing code violations. If a retaliatory motive can be imputed to the landlord, the tenant cannot be evicted; if he is, he may be entitled to damages. Retaliation is difficult to prove, particularly if a landlord waits several months after a tenant's complaint before initiating eviction. To lighten the burden of proof, some states have enacted statutes that provide for a presumption of retaliatory motive if the landlord commences an eviction proceeding within a specified period of time after the tenant has complained to a governmental agency. If the landlord's dominant purpose is retaliation for the tenant's exercise of his lawful rights, however, a *retaliatory eviction* will be found regardless of the time period involved.

36:4   Use and Enjoyment of Premises

During the term of a lease, the tenant has the sole and exclusive right to occupy and control the premises. A tenant may use leased property in the same manner as the owner might have done and for any lawful purpose or business that does not injure the landlord's interest. As discussed above, however, parties to a lease can restrict the uses to which leased property can be put, so long as these restrictions are not contrary to law or public policy. A tenant does not have the right to remove, destroy, or even alter buildings or make other improvements without the landlord's consent.

A lease usually covers all the property and fixtures that are essential or reasonably necessary to the full use and enjoyment of the property. Thus, if use of a portion of a building not included in the lease is necessary to the enjoyment of the leased portion, an easement or privilege passes to the tenant. A right-of-way for access to leased property, including the right to use steps, halls, stairways, and elevators, is ordinarily implied. A landlord may or may not be required to furnish water, lights, heat, and other utilities, depending on the terms of the lease.

Tenant's Use of Premises   A tenant must take care not to damage leased premises. The tenant is responsible to the landlord for all property damages that the tenant causes intentionally or negligently. A tenant is not responsible for depreciation in value of the property as a result of ordinary wear and tear, in the absence of an agreement to the contrary.

If a tenant creates a nuisance that affects other tenants or third parties on leased premises, or if he uses property unlawfully, he may be subject to an eviction even though there is no specific agreement between the parties dealing with these subjects. A nuisance occurs if the tenant's conduct substantially interferes with the enjoyment by other tenants or third persons of their own property. In rental apartments, for example, the most common instances creating a nuisance are noise during the usual hours of sleep and harassment of cotenants. A nuisance does not arise if conduct only annoys an apartment manager. For example, if a tenant fails to make prompt rental payments, argues with a manager, demands repairs of property, or complains about other things, his conduct might not be a legal nuisance, even though it would certainly be aggravating to the parties involved.

Change of Use   It is not uncommon for the landlord to insist on inserting a clause in the lease restricting a tenant's use of the premises. Landlords do this because they have the right to control the uses to which leased property may be put. The violation of a lease clause limiting the use of property can result in a forfeiture of the lease, constitute grounds for an injunction, or be the basis of an award of monetary damages.

Improvements and Alterations   Unless a lease provides to the contrary, neither the landlord nor the tenant has the obligation of making specific improvements or alterations to leased property. Either party can make minor improvements or alterations that do not materially change the condition of the premises. Leases frequently provide that improvements, alterations, or additions made by one of the parties shall be the property of the landlord and shall remain on the property at the termination of the lease.

 At times, a tenant's right to remove improvements or additions is expressly authorized or prohibited by the lease. Some leases cover this matter by use of broad terms, such as "improvements" and "additions." Whether or not a particular improvement or addition will in fact be covered depends on the specific language used. To avoid future problems, any lease—and especially a lease of business property—should specify as precisely as possible exactly what improvements or additions the tenant will (or will not) be permitted to remove.

36:5   Condition of Premises; Repairs

Under the common law a landlord was generally not responsible for the condition of leased premises at the beginning of a lease. The tenant took the premises as they were, with all their faults. This rule developed from the view that a lease is a conveyance—a sale for a term—to which the principle of "let the buyer beware" applied. It was perhaps best typified by the language of one court, which stated that "fraud apart, there is no law against letting [leasing] a tumbled-down house, and the tenant's remedy is upon his contract, if any."[1] Clearly, in the absence of express warranty, statute, fraud, or misrepresentation by a landlord, the tenant traditionally has been required to take property as he finds it, with all known defects or those that can be ascertained by reasonable inspection.

Landlord's Obligation to Repair   In the absence of statute or an agreement to the contrary by parties to a lease, there is generally no implied covenant by a landlord to repair leased property during the lease term. In some states, statutes have changed the landlord's obligations to undertake repairs of rented or leased premises, however. Under these statutes, a residential landlord must put premises into a condition fit for human occupancy and must repair subsequent dilapidations other than those attributable to the tenant. If a landlord fails to make repairs within a

---

[1]*Robbins v Jones*, 15 CB [NS] 221, 240 (1803).

reasonable time after notice, a tenant can either make the repairs himself or vacate, thereby discharging himself from further obligations under the lease.

Implied Warranty of Habitability   In many states, the common-law rule that a landlord is under no obligation to maintain premises in a reasonable state of repair is giving way to other legal doctrines that impose affirmative duties on landlords to furnish habitable premises at the commencement of a lease or rental agreement. This duty is based on what is called the implied *warranty of habitability*. The warranty extends primarily to premises used for residential rather than commercial purposes, and it applies during the entire term of the lease rather than only at its inception.

If a landlord breaches the implied warranty of habitability, a tenant can rescind the lease, vacate the premises, offset the costs of repair against the rent due, or seek money damages. In many states, a tenant's remedy of offsetting repair costs against rent is regulated by statute. In determining whether a landlord has breached the implied warranty of habitability, several criteria are used by courts. These include:

- Whether the defect is a violation of any applicable housing code or building or sanitary regulations
- Whether the defect affects a vital facility
- Potential effect of the defect on safety and sanitation
- Length of time the defect has persisted
- Age of the structure
- Amount of the rent
- Whether the tenant has waived the defect
- Whether the tenant was in any way responsible for the defect

The following case discusses the implied warranty of habitability. Consider the court's reasoning and why it held that the common-law rule must give way to the modern approach that imposes on the landlord a duty to place premises in a habitable condition.

Green

v

Superior Court of San Francisco
10 Cal 3d 616, 111 Cal Rptr 704, 517 P2d 1168
(California Supreme Court, 1974)

[Sumski, the landlord, commenced an eviction action against his tenant Green, seeking possession of leased premises and $300 in back rent. Green admitted that he had not paid the rent, but he defended the action on the ground that Sumski had failed to maintain the leased premises in a habitable condition. Some of the more serious defects described by Green include (1) the collapse and nonrepair of a bathroom ceiling; (2) the continued presence of rats, mice, and cockroaches on the premises; (3) the lack of any heat in four of the apartment's rooms; (4)

plumbing blockages; (5) exposed and faulty wiring; and (6) an illegally installed and unsafe stove. At trial, the court rejected Green's defense that the landlord breached an implied warranty of habitability. Green appealed.]

Tobriner, J.

*   *   *

At common law, the real estate lease developed in the field of real property law, not contract law. Under property law concepts, a lease was considered a conveyance or sale of the premises for a term of years, subject to the ancient doctrine of caveat emptor. Thus, under traditional common-law rules, the landlord owed no duty to place leased premises in a habitable condition and no obligation to repair the premises. . . . These original common-law precepts perhaps suited the agrarianism of the early Middle Ages which was their matrix; at such time, the primary value of a lease lay in the land itself and whatever simple living structures may have been included in the leasehold were of secondary importance and were readily repairable by the typical "jack-of-all-trades" lessee farmer. Furthermore, because the law of property crystallized before the development of mutually dependent covenants in contract law, a lessee's covenant to pay rent was considered at common law as independent of the lessor's covenants. Thus even when a lessor expressly covenanted to make repairs, the lessor's breach did not justify the lessee's withholding of the rent. . . .

In recent years, however, a growing number of courts have begun to re-examine these "settled" common-law rules in light of contemporary conditions, and, after thorough analysis, all of these courts have discarded the traditional doctrine as incompatible with contemporary social conditions and modern legal values. This emerging line of decisions, along with a veritable flood of academic commentaries, demonstrates the obsolescence of the traditional common-law rule absolving a land-

lord of any duty to maintain leased premises in a habitable condition during the term of the lease.

The recent decisions recognize initially that the geographic and economic conditions that characterized the agrarian lessor–lessee transaction have been entirely transformed in the modern urban landlord–tenant relationship. We have suggested that in the Middle Ages, and, indeed, until the urbanization of the industrial revolution, the land itself was by far the most important element of a lease transaction; this predominance explained the law's treatment of such leases as conveyances of interests in land. In today's urban residential leases, however, land as such plays no comparable role. The typical city dweller, who frequently leases an apartment several stories above the actual plot of land on which an apartment building rests, cannot realistically be viewed as acquiring an interest in land; rather, he has contracted for a place to live. . . .

Modern urbanization has not only undermined the validity of utilizing general property concepts in analyzing landlord–tenant relations, but it has also significantly altered the factual setting directly relevant to the more specific duty of maintaining leased premises. . . . Contemporary urban housing and the contemporary urban tenant stand in marked contrast to this agrarian model.

First, the increasing complexity of modern apartment buildings not only renders them much more difficult and expensive to repair than the living quarters of earlier days, but also makes adequate inspection of the premises by a prospective tenant a virtual impossibility; complex heating, electrical and plumbing systems are hidden from view, and the landlord, who has had experience with the building, is certainly in a much better position to discover and to cure dilapidations in the premises. Moreover, in a multiple-unit dwelling repair will frequently require access to equipment and areas solely in the control of the landlord.

Second, unlike the multi-skilled lessee of

old, today's city dweller generally has a single, specialized skill unrelated to maintenance work. Furthermore, whereas an agrarian lessee frequently remained on a single plot of land for his entire life, today's urban tenant is more mobile than ever; a tenant's limited tenure in a specific apartment will frequently not justify efforts at extensive repairs. Finally, the expense of needed repairs will often be outside the reach of many tenants for "[l]ow and middle income tenants, even if they were interested in making repairs, would be unable to obtain any financing for major repairs since they have no long-term interest in the property." . . .

In addition to these significant changes, urbanization and population growth have wrought an enormous transformation in the contemporary housing market, creating a scarcity of adequate low cost housing in virtually every urban setting. This current state of the housing market is by no means unrelated to the common-law duty to maintain habitable premises. For one thing, the severe shortage of low and moderate cost housing has left tenants with little bargaining power through which they might gain express warranties of habitability from landlords, and thus the mechanism of the "free market" no longer serves as a viable means for fairly allocating the duty to repair leased premises between landlord and tenant. For another, the scarcity of adequate housing has limited further the adequacy of the tenant's right to inspect the premises; even when defects are apparent the low income tenant frequently has no realistic alternative but to accept such housing with the expecta-

tion that the landlord will make the necessary repairs. Finally, the shortage of available low cost housing has rendered inadequate the few remedies that common-law courts previously have developed to ameliorate the harsh consequences of the traditional "no duty to repair" rule.

In most significant respects, the modern urban tenant is in the same position as any other normal consumer of goods. . . . Through a residential lease, a tenant seeks to purchase "housing" from his landlord for a specified period of time. The landlord "sells" housing, enjoying a much greater opportunity, incentive and capacity than a tenant to inspect and maintain the condition of his apartment building. A tenant may reasonably expect that the product he is purchasing is fit for the purpose for which it is obtained, that is, a living unit. Moreover, since a lease contract specifies a designated period of time during which the tenant has a right to inhabit the premises, the tenant may legitimately expect that the premises will be fit for such habitation for the duration of the term of the lease. It is just such reasonable expectations of consumers which the modern "implied warranty" decisions endow with formal, legal protection. . . .

For the reasons discussed at length above, we believe that the traditional common-law rule has outlived its usefulness; . . . modern conditions compel the recognition of a common-law implied warranty of habitability in residential leases. . . .

[Judgment vacated.]

Tenant's Obligation to Repair   Under the common law, a tenant was obligated to make certain repairs that were necessary to prevent waste or decay of the premises. Today, under the terms of most long-term leases, it is customary for the tenant to make *all* necessary repairs and to restore or reconstruct the premises after damage by fire or other causes. Beyond this, a tenant, particularly a residential tenant, is not obligated to make repairs in the absence of an agreement to do so in the lease. In any event, a tenant is not bound to make substantial or lasting repairs or improvements, such as putting on a new roof or constructing buildings on the property.

36:6 Rent

Rent is the consideration paid by a tenant to a landlord for the use and occupation of the leased property. The amount and terms of rent payment are usually stipulated in the lease. If the lease does not contain a provision as to rent, the law implies a promise by the tenant to pay the reasonable value of his use and occupation of the property.

As long as a lease is in existence, rent must be paid. This is true even if the lessee refuses to take possession of the leased property or takes possession but later abandons the premises. Unless the abandonment is justified, as in the case of damage or destruction of the property or a constructive eviction, the landlord can even leave the property vacant in some states and recover rent periodically during the remainder of the term. Under this view, which is contrary to the general rule that damages be mitigated (see 36:11), a landlord is not obligated to find a new tenant or relet property so long as the lease continues and the tenant has unjustifiably abandoned the property.

 Leases are usually drafted in favor of the landlord. Often, they place heavy burdens on a tenant who does not fulfill his terms of the bargain. For example, in some states a lease can provide that the tenant's failure to pay rent on time permits the landlord to accelerate the entire rent due for the rest of the term, even under a multiyear lease. A business tenant often has greater bargaining power than an individual who is trying to rent residential premises. The tenant should use that power to persuade the landlord to delete or alter provisions that are unduly burdensome.

The following case illustrates that the rule imposing on the tenant an absolute obligation to pay rent regardless of the landlord's conduct or the condition of the premises is giving way in many states.

Albert M. Greenfield & Co.

v

Kolea

**475 Pa 351, 380 A2d 758, 99 ALR3d 731
(Pennsylvania Supreme Court, 1977)**

[Kolea leased a garage to store automobiles. One year after he occupied the premises, the building was completely destroyed by an accidental fire.

Kolea later refused to pay rent, contending that the fire excused him from continuing to perform his obligations under the lease. Although the lease did not contain a provision as to the tenant's obligations in the event of the building's destruction, the landlord sought to hold Kolea liable for rent after the building's destruction. At trial, the court held Kolea liable for the unpaid rent. Kolea appealed.]

Mandarino, Justice.

*   *   *

The general rule has been stated that in the absence of a lease provision to the contrary, a tenant is not relieved from the obligation to pay rent despite the total destruction of the leased premises. . . .

The reason for the rule has been said to be that although a building may be an important element of consideration for the payment of rent, the interest in the soil remains to support the lease despite destruction of the building. It has also been said that since destruction of the building is usually by accident, it is only equitable to divide the loss; the lessor loses the property and the lessee loses the term. . . .

Two exceptions designed to afford relief to the tenant from the harshness of the common-law principle have been created. These exceptions reflect the influence of modern contract principles as applied in the landlord–tenant relationship.

The first exception provides that where only a portion of a building is leased, total destruction of the building relieves the tenant of the obligation to pay rent. . . . This exception recognizes that in the leasing of a part of a building there is no implication that any estate in land is granted. This Court, in other words, has recognized that in a landlord–tenant relationship with respect to an apartment, the parties have *bargained for* a part of a building and not the land beneath. [Court's emphasis.]

The influence of contract principles of bargained for exchange is also apparent in the second exception to the general common-law rule. The second exception is based on the doctrine of *impossibility of performance.* [Court's emphasis.] . . .

. . . [W]here a contract relates to specific property the existence or maintenance of which is necessary to the carrying out of the purpose of the agreement, the condition is implied by law, just as though it were written into the agreement, that the impossibility of performance or the frustration of purpose arising from the destruction of the property or interference with its use, without the fault of either party, ends all contractual obligations relating to the property. Moreover, impossibility in that connection means not only strict impossibility but impracticability because of extreme and unreasonable difficulty, expense, or loss involved. . . .

In the instant case, it is apparent that when the building was destroyed by fire it became impossible for the [lessor] to furnish the agreed consideration— "[an entire] one story garage building. . . ." Nothing in the first lease implies that any interest in the land itself was intended to be conveyed . It is also obvious that the purpose of the lease . . . was thereby frustrated. As noted in the lease, the parties contemplated that [the lessee] would use the building for the repair and sale of used motor vehicles. Without a building [the lessee] could no longer carry on a used-car business as contemplated by the parties at the time they entered into the lease agreement. It became extremely impracticable for the [lessee] to continue using the adjoining lot when his business office and repair stations were destroyed by the fire. Additionally, because of the dangerous condition created by the fire, the city required [the lessor] to barricade the property covered by both leases, thus preventing [the lessee] from entering the property. . . .

The trial court's decision to bind the lessee to the lease was simply an application of an outdated common-law presumption. That presumption developed in a society very different from ours today; one where the land was always more valuable than the buildings erected on it. Buildings are critical to the functioning of modern society. When the parties bargain for the use of a building, the soil beneath is generally of little consequence. Our laws should develop to reflect these changes. . . .

. . . It is no longer reasonable to *assume* that in the absence of a lease provision to the contrary the lessee should bear the risk of loss in the event of total destruction of the building. [Court's emphasis.] Where the parties do not expressly provide for such a catastrophe, the court should analyze the facts and the lease agreement as any other contract would be analyzed. Following such an analysis, if it is evident to the court that the parties bargained for the existence of a building, and no provision is made as to who bears the risk of loss if the building is destroyed, the court should relieve the parties of their respective obligations when the building no longer exists.

[Judgment reversed.]

Late Charges   Under most commercial and residential leases, late charges can be imposed when the tenant fails to pay the rent when due. Unquestionably, the imposition of a late charge induces the tenant to pay rent on time. Although interest can be added to any payment that is late, late charges might not be valid if an arbitrary sum is set for the late payment with little or no regard to the amount or duration of the delinquency. A sum that fairly compensates the landlord and at the same time is not excessive is usually considered to be valid.

Security Deposits   Under most leases, before the lease term commences the tenant is required to deposit some form of security for use in the event the tenant fails to perform any of the obligations under the lease. Security deposits are commonly used, since other, older common-law remedies, such as the landlord's physical taking of the tenant's personal property in the event of default, have been abolished or restricted by statute. There are several forms of security, the most common of which is cash.

Taxes and Other Payments   In most states, a tenant is not obligated to pay real estate taxes assessed against leased property. Unless this duty is transferred by the terms of the lease, it must be met by the landlord.

36:7   Liability for Injury on Premises

In most states, landlords are not liable for injury sustained by a tenant on leased premises. However, there are exceptions to this general rule. Liability can be imposed if (1) a landlord knew of a dangerous condition or should have known of it and failed to inform the tenant; (2) the landlord concealed a dangerous condition; (3) the landlord made repairs in such a negligent fashion that the tenant was injured; (4) the injury occurred in a common area or an area in the landlord's possession; or (5) the lease or rental agreement specifically provided that the landlord would make a designated repair, and he failed to do so, resulting in a tenant's injury.[2]

If the landlord leases part of the property to different tenants, and reserves other parts, such as common entrances, halls, stairways, and utility or service rooms for the common use of all the tenants, the landlord must exercise reasonable care to

---

[2]A property owner's liability for injuries resulting from the defective or dangerous condition of the property is discussed in detail in Chapter 8.

keep these reserved areas safe. As the following case illustrates, a landlord can be liable to a tenant, members of a tenant's family, or third persons for injuries resulting from the landlord's negligence.

Macke Laundry Service Co.
v
Weber
267 Md 426, 298 A2d 27, 66 ALR3d 365
(Maryland Court of Appeals, 1972)

[Bruce Weber, about 3 ½ years old, wandered alone into the laundry room of an apartment building where he lived with his parents and was severely injured when he placed his left hand in the drive mechanism of a clothes dryer. The dryer was owned by Macke Laundry Service, which operated and serviced the equipment in the laundry room. Bruce's mother sued both the landlord and Macke, and she was awarded $9,000 in damages. Macke, which had to pay the entire judgment because of separate indemnity agreement with the landlord, then appealed.]

Singley, J.

*   *   *

There is substantial authority for the proposition that when a landlord sets aside areas for the use of his tenants in common, he owes the duty of reasonable and ordinary care to keep the premises safe for his invitees. . . .

. . . The duty stems from the responsibility engendered in the landlord by his having extended an invitation, express or implied, to use the portions of the property retained by him. . . . Such an invitation extended to a tenant includes the members of his family, his guests, his invitees and others on the land in the right of the tenant. . . . It has been held that a child on the land at the invitation of the child of the tenant is entitled to the benefit of the landlord's obligation in this respect. . . . There is an

important qualification to the rule as to the duty of the landlord. His responsibility for the reasonably safe condition of premises retained under his control is limited to the confines of his invitation to use them, express or implied. It does not extend to the use of such premises for an unintended purpose. . . .

Our decisions have consistently held a landlord liable for improper maintenance of facilities or for failure to remedy defects in equipment over which he retains control and furnishes for common use by his tenants. . . .

Although a landlord owes no greater duty of care to a child than to an adult, . . . [the landlord] knew or should have known that the laundry room was readily accessible to children, a circumstance which made what might otherwise have been a theoretical hazard an actual danger to a person unable to comprehend it. . . .

Here, it is clear that the facilities installed in the laundry room were provided for the use of tenants, who were invitees. There is no evidence that such use was restricted to adults, or that entry was in [any way] restricted to adults and children accompanied by adults. On the contrary, there was testimony that the door was always open, and was usually propped open by one of the trash cans which were customarily stored there.

On these facts, Bruce was neither a trespasser nor a bare licensee: he was an invitee, to whom a duty of reasonable care was owed. This duty was breached when the guard which normally shielded the drive mechanism on the back of the clothes dryer fell off, or was taken off and never replaced, despite the fact that Mrs. Weber and two of her neighbors testified that they had reported the condition by calling the "service number" which appeared on the dryer. It was the breach of this duty which was the sole cause of Bruce's injury. . . .

Macke urges on us the argument that when Bruce chose to go behind the dryer, he became a trespasser or mere licensee. . . .

We do not see it quite that way. There was uncontroverted testimony that the laundry room in Building No. 2 was used for the collection of trash, for the storage of certain of the tenants' effects, that the door was always open, and was frequently propped open, and that there had been a problem with children playing there. There was testimony that if clothing dropped behind the dryer, it was necessary to go behind the dryer to retrieve it. Although Mrs. Weber's testimony may have been wanting in explicit technical terminology, there was enough for the jury to conclude that she did her laundry in Building No. 1 because she was apprehensive about the manner in which laundry equipment had been installed in Building No. 2. Even apart from the testimony as regards the telephone calls about the ab-

sence of the guard from the drive mechanism—and the existence of such calls was denied by Macke—there was certainly enough for the jury to conclude that the defendants failed to meet the standards of care required to make the premises safe for the tenants.

We think *Restatement (Second, Torts* § 360, at 250 states the rule:

> "A possessor of land who leases a part thereof and retains in his own control any other part which the lessee is entitled to use as appurtenant to the part leased to him, is subject to liability to his lessee and others lawfully upon the land with the consent of the lessee or a sublessee for physical harm caused by a dangerous condition upon that part of the land retained in the lessor's control, if the lessor by the exercise of reasonable care could have discovered the condition and the unreasonable risk involved therein and could have made the condition safe." . . .

[Judgment affirmed.]

Liability for Crimes of Third Persons   The general rule is that the landlord–tenant relationship does not impose a duty on a landlord to protect a tenant from criminal activities of third persons. Under this rule the landlord is not an insurer of a tenant's safety against crime. For a landlord to be liable for injuries that result from criminal activities, it must be shown that he breached contractual or statutory obligations or was negligent in keeping the premises safe. In some states, statutes and regulations requiring a landlord to maintain "safe premises" have been interpreted to mean that the landlord has a duty to keep the premises safe only in the sense of being free from physical defects likely to cause injury, but not to require the landlord to take security measures against criminal activities. Bear in mind, though, that some courts *have* imposed on landlords the duty to protect tenants against criminal activities of third persons. Their decisions have been based largely on the unique facts and circumstances presented in each case.

EXAMPLE
A landlord rented space in his building to a state mental clinic. The landlord was advised that clinic patients might assault other tenants in the building, but he took no security measures. If a clinic patient does in fact assault one of the other tenants, a court might find that the landlord was negligent for not having (1) foreseen the assault and (2) protected the other tenants accordingly.

Landlord's Liability to Third Persons   In most states, landlords are not liable to third persons for injury caused by the condition or use of leased premises if the premises are under a tenant's full control and were in good condition when leased. However, the fact that a tenant occupies leased premises when an accident occurs does not automatically relieve the landlord of liability for injury or damage to third persons that results from his own negligent maintenance of the premises. Indeed, there are many circumstances under which a landlord can be held liable to third persons injured as a result of the condition or use of the leased premises. If the landlord has authorized his property to be used in such a manner as to endanger and injure a third person, the landlord is answerable for the consequences. Liability can even extend to owners or occupants of adjoining or neighboring property or to users of an adjacent public highway injured through some act or omission attributable to the landlord.

A landlord's duties and liabilities to persons who are on leased property with the tenant's consent are the same as those owed to the tenant himself. An important exception, frequently termed the public purpose rule, applies when there is a lease involving the use of premises by the public: A business patron's rights to recover for injuries from defects in leased property are not necessarily limited to the rights of the tenant. Courts in many states have held that where property leased for a public purpose is not safe for the purpose intended, and the owner knew or should have known of the unsafe conditions through the exercise of reasonable diligence, the owner is liable to patrons on the premises for injury that results from these conditions.

Exculpation Clauses   Many leases contain provisions that excuse the landlord from liability for injury or damage, even when the injury or damage is caused by the landlord's own negligence. These provisions are called exculpatory or exculpation clauses. In most states this type of limit on a landlord's liability is generally permitted in commercial leases, but it is invalid and cannot be enforced in residential leases.

 If a landlord's negligence involves a failure to fulfill a statutory duty, an exculpation clause will often not be enforceable to avoid liability even under a commercial lease.

Tenant's Liability to Third Persons   When property is leased in a condition suitable for its ordinary and contemplated use by the tenants, it is the tenant—and not the landlord—who is liable to a third person on or off the property for injuries caused by a condition or use that is under the tenant's control. The tenant's liability to third persons or the public continues to exist even though the landlord has agreed to keep the premises in repair.

If a business patron or customer is injured on leased premises, the tenant is usually liable for injuries caused by a negligent act or the tenant's failure to correct a defect or dangerous condition on the premises. A proprietor of a public place of business is bound to keep such premises in a safe condition and to use ordinary care to avoid accident or injury to those entering the premises on business. The fact that the proprietor is a tenant does not lessen his duty to keep the premises reasonably safe for customers.

36:8   Assignment and Subletting

An *assignment* of a lease is the lessee's transfer of his entire interest in the leased premises for the entire unexpired term of the original lease. In the absence of a statutory provision or a restriction in the lease, a tenant for a definite term has the right to assign his interest without the landlord's consent. When a valid assignment is made, the assignee succeeds to all the tenant's interests and to the benefit of all covenants and agreements made by the landlord. In turn, the assignee must perform all of the original tenant's duties. That is, the assignee must pay rent, taxes, or other sums of money to the original landlord as required under the terms of the original lease. The assignee's duties terminate when the lease expires or when the assignee reassigns the lease to a third party.

Subletting   A tenant under a lease for a definite period has the right to sublet the premises (lease the premises to someone else) in the absence of statutory prohibitions or restrictions imposed by the lease itself. The relation between the sublessor (original tenant) and sublessee is that of landlord and tenant, and their rights are governed by the terms of the sublease. The only limit on the right to sublet is that premises may not be sublet for a use that is either inconsistent with the terms of the original lease or injurious to the premises. For example, a tenancy at will cannot be sublet to another without the landlord's consent since the landlord can terminate the original lease at any time. When property is sublet, the sublessee acquires no greater rights in the use and enjoyment of the premises than were enjoyed by the original lessee.

 A subletting does not remove the tenant's liability to the landlord for the payment of rent or the performance of the agreements or covenants contained in the original lease. In addition, the tenant is liable to the landlord for damage to the premises caused by the sublessee's negligence or wrongful acts.

Limits on Assignment and Subletting   Leases often prohibit the tenant from assigning or subletting without the landlord's consent. In the absence of other provisions in the lease, a landlord may well refuse to grant his consent to a sublease or assignment. Therefore, some leases also contain provisions that the landlord's consent will not be arbitrarily or unreasonably withheld. In determining whether a particular refusal by a landlord is unreasonable or arbitrary, a key factor is whether the landlord will be assured that the principal terms of the lease, particularly those as to the payment of rent, will be met if the premises are assigned or sublet.

EXAMPLE
A tenant requests the landlord to consent to a sublease of the leased premises. The landlord refuses, although he does not object to the nature of the proposed sub-

lessee's business. In fact, his refusal to consent is based on his desire to rent directly to the proposed sublessee under a new lease, at a higher rent. If the original tenant agrees to guarantee all the proposed sublessee's obligations, a court will probably find that the landlord's refusal to consent is unreasonable.

36:9   Termination of the Lease

A lease can be terminated for several reasons. The most common is the expiration of the agreed term. However, a lease can also end by (1) forfeiture, as where a tenant fails to meet his obligations under the lease in breach of a condition; (2) rescission by one party; or (3) agreement between the parties. A lease can also terminate if the premises are destroyed or rendered uninhabitable. Ordinarily, the death of either the tenant or the landlord does not terminate a lease.

Whether the breach of a condition in a lease will terminate the lease or give one party the right to rescind or cancel the lease depends on the provisions of the lease itself and how vital or essential the breached provision is. For example, late payment of rent is not ordinarily a ground for the termination of a lease unless it is expressly made so by a provision in the lease.

A tenant loses all his interests in the property when he surrenders the leased property. A surrender generally occurs only if the lease is terminated by agreement of the parties.

Termination by Notice   Most states have enacted statutes that explicitly set forth the procedural steps by which a leasehold tenancy can be lawfully terminated. Under a typical statute, the landlord must give what is called a notice to quit in order to terminate a periodic tenancy—one from year to year or month to month—if the term of the tenancy is not definitely fixed. The same rule is applied to tenancies at will. A notice to quit is not necessary in the case of any lease that fixes the time of its termination since the lease terminates automatically on expiration of the lease term.

36:10   Renewal of Lease; Holding Over

A landlord is not bound to renew a lease unless there is an express agreement in the lease to do so. Similarly, the tenant is not bound to accept a renewal. This is not to say, however, that the terms of a lease cannot be renewed or extended after the lease expires. Provision for renewal or extension is frequently in the form of an option, which the tenant can exercise by giving the landlord proper notice, as discussed below. If the renewal provision in the lease does not set forth the terms of the renewal, the terms of the original agreement will generally govern.

The purpose of the requirement that the tenant give the landlord notice of his intention to exercise a renewal option is to enable the landlord to rent the property to someone else if the present tenant does not renew. Therefore, the tenant must give the notice before the expiration of the present lease term. A tenant's renewal notice need not be in writing; it can be oral or it can be implied by a tenant's holding over. However, the notice must accept the renewal privilege as offered.

The landlord can treat any attempt to change the lease terms offered by the option to renew as a rejection of the option. For example, a notice from a tenant that he will remain one year after expiration, when he has an option to renew for four years, can be treated as an invalid notice, which terminates the lease on its original expiration.

Holding Over by Tenant A tenant has no right to "hold over" (remain in possession of the leased premises after the termination of the lease, without the landlord's consent). A landlord can choose either to waive a holdover or to treat the tenant who holds over as a trespasser. If the landlord does allow the tenant to remain, the tenant can be a tenant at sufferance, a tenant at will, a periodic tenant, or a tenant for a definite term, depending on both the circumstances of the case and the statutes in effect.

When a landlord neither assents to the tenant's holding over nor agrees to an extended or renewal term, the tenant is liable to the landlord for his unlawful occupancy of the premises. The measure of damages that the landlord can recover is generally the rental value of the property for the period of the tenant's wrongful possession, although some states permit the recovery of greater damages or the imposition of penalties.

36:11 Landlord's Remedies; Damages

There are a variety of remedies by which a landlord can regain possession of leased premises or obtain money damages after a lease is forfeited, a condition is breached, or the lease expires. Some state statutes permit the landlord to reenter the property if the tenant has vacated and abandoned it; other states require that the landlord take court action first. The landlord can also seek to evict a tenant who, for example, breaches a condition by holding over after the expiration of a lease or rental agreement or by failing to pay rent.

Every state provides for a summary eviction procedure by which the landlord can recover possession of leased property quickly and at low cost. This procedure is often called *unlawful detainer*, which is so named because the tenant remains in possession contrary to the lease. In a summary proceeding, the landlord must prove that the lease has expired or that the tenant has breached a condition or covenant. The tenant is usually permitted few defenses, although in some states the tenant can raise any breaches by the landlord, particularly the breach of the implied warranty of habitability.

A landlord can also sue to have the tenant ejected to regain possession of leased property. Unlike the eviction procedure, ejectment does not take precedence over all other civil litigation and might not come to trial for some time. During the pendency of an ejectment action, the tenant is entitled to possession. For these reasons, most landlords prefer the summary eviction procedure to a suit in ejectment.

Landlord's Lien Many states have statutes that allow a lien on a tenant's personal property that is located on leased premises. This lien is referred to as a landlord's lien. In some states there is a general landlord's lien on all the tenant's personal property, giving the landlord priority over other creditors. Because no right of possession is conferred, however, the landlord must usually institute judicial proceedings to foreclose the lien if the rent is unpaid. In other states, the landlord is authorized to enter premises peaceably and seize certain types of property that belong to the tenant, and to hold them as security for the unpaid rent. If a statute of this type permits seizure of a tenant's property without prior notice or the tenant's right to be heard at a judicial hearing, it is apt to violate the tenant's constitutional right to due process of law.[3] In fact, some states have extensively rewritten landlord lien statutes in an attempt to satisfy due process requirements. Where the statutes authorize a hearing and court order before a landlord can seize property, and the landlord is authorized only to hold, but not dispose of, a tenant's property until court order, they satisfy due process requirements.

Landlord's Duty to Mitigate Damages   Under the common law, if a tenant abandoned possession of property without legal justification, the tenant's obligations under the lease continued without change. Indeed, since the most important obligation of the tenant was the payment of rent, the common law did not impose on the landlord the duty of reletting the premises. On the contrary, the landlord could permit the premises to remain vacant and sue the tenant for the unpaid rent as it accrued. A landlord could even arbitrarily refuse to accept a new tenant, even one suitable and responsible in every way.

The privilege enjoyed by landlords not to minimize damages has given way in many states to a more modern view similar to that in the law of contracts. In these states, a landlord has the duty to make reasonable efforts to reduce his damages by reletting leased premises after a tenant's abandonment. This view conforms to contract principles in which a party to a contract must mitigate damages following a breach of the other party (see Chapter 18). It is also based on the modern theory that a lease of real property is more in the nature of a commercial contract than a conveyance of an estate or interest in land. Therefore, if a landlord is allowed to reenter premises after they are abandoned by a tenant, the landlord must usually use reasonable efforts to procure a new tenant. If the landlord does not do this, the tenant might be relieved of his obligation under the lease as well as his duty to indemnify the landlord for loss of rent.

EXAMPLE
The Lamberts rented an apartment in Lefrak City. When they were unable to pay rent, they vacated the apartment and requested that the landlord apply their security deposit to the rent owed. The apartment remained vacant for 17 months. Finally, the landlord filed suit, claiming rent due during the remaining rental term under the lease until the apartment was rerented. If the landlord fails to establish that he acted in good faith to rerent their apartment, a court is apt to find that the landlord is entitled only to three months' rent; three months being a reasonable period of time in which to rerent.

---

[3]The constitutionality of statutes that allow seizure of property without notice and a hearing is discussed in more detail in Chapter 30 (see 30:11).

Key Concepts and Terms

- The rental of real property is based on a form of contract that is most commonly referred to as a lease or rental agreement. The person who owns real property and leases it to someone else is known as the landlord or lessor. The person who receives possession and has use of the premises during the term of a lease is the tenant or lessee.

- A leasehold is generally classified according to its duration as (1) a tenancy for years, (2) a periodic tenancy, (3) a tenancy at will, or (4) a tenancy at sufferance.

- A lease is usually in writing, but it can also be oral in most states. If the term of an oral lease violates a state's statute of frauds, however, the lease is unenforceable.

- In most states, the landlord must actually put the tenant in possession of leased property at the beginning of the agreed term. The very essence of the landlord–tenant relationship is the right to have the peaceful and quiet use of property throughout the duration of a tenancy. This right is guaranteed by the landlord's covenant for quiet enjoyment, which is contained in most written leases and rental agreements.

- During the term of a lease, the tenant is the absolute owner of the leased premises for all practical purposes. The landlord's rights are confined to his reversionary interests in the premises. At the end of the tenancy, the tenant must vacate and surrender the premises to the landlord.

- An eviction consists of any act by a landlord that (1) deprives the tenant of possession, (2) expels him from the property, or (3) deprives him of its enjoyment. The wrongful eviction of a tenant by the landlord not only terminates the tenant's obligations under a lease, but it also entitles the tenant to recover damages.

- A landlord is generally not responsible for the condition of leased premises at the beginning of a lease period. The tenant takes the premises as they are, with all their faults. However, in some states, a residential landlord must, under what is called the implied warranty of habitability, put premises into a condition fit for human occupancy and repair all subsequent dilapidations other than those attributable to the tenant.

- Rent is the consideration paid by a tenant to a landlord for the use and occupation of real property under a lease. As long as a lease is in existence, rent must be paid. In some states, even if leased property is damaged or destroyed, the obligation to pay rent continues.

- Liability can be imposed on a landlord for injuries to a tenant if (1) the landlord knew of a dangerous condition or should have known of it and failed to inform the tenant; (2) the landlord concealed a dangerous condition; (3) the landlord made repairs in a negligent manner, causing injury to the tenant; (4) an injury occurred in a common area or one in possession of the landlord; or (5) the lease or rental agreement specifically provided that the landlord would make a designated repair, and he failed to do so, later causing a tenant to be injured.

- When property is leased in a condition suitable for its ordinary and contemplated use by the tenant, the tenant—and not the landlord—is usually liable to a third person on or off the property for injuries caused by a condition or use of the property under the tenant's control.

- An assignment of a lease is the transfer of a tenant's entire interest in leased premises to a third person for the entire unexpired term of the original lease. In the absence of a statutory prohibition or restriction in a lease, a tenant has the right to assign or sublet his interest without the landlord's consent.

- A sublease is a leasing of premises by the original tenant to someone else. It differs from an assignment in that the original tenant (the sublessor) retains an interest in the property.

- A lease can be terminated (1) through forfeiture on the tenant's failure to meet his obligations under a lease, (2) by recission or agreement between the parties, and (3) under some circumstances by an occurrence that causes the premises to be destroyed or otherwise made uninhabitable. Ordinarily, the death of a lessee or lessor does not terminate a lease

- A lease can usually be renewed or extended after the expiration of the original time set forth in the lease agreement.

- A tenant has no right to hold over (remain in possession of leased premises after the termination of a lease) without the landlord's consent.

- In many states, statutes grant to a landlord a lien on the tenant's personal property located on leased premises. However, the statute does not give the landlord the right to possession of the tenant's property. The landlord must institute judicial proceedings to foreclose the lien in cases of unpaid rent.

- The major remedy that a landlord has to regain possession of leased property is a summary eviction procedure, known in most states as unlawful detainer.

- Under the common law, if a tenant abandoned possession of the leased property, the tenant's obligations continued under the lease, and the landlord was not required to mitigate damages. Today, most states require a landlord to minimize damages by making a reasonable effort to relet premises after a tenant's abandonment.

- Assignment
- Condition
- Constructive Eviction
- Covenant
- Covenant for Quiet Enjoyment
- Eviction
- Lease
- Mitigation of Damages

- Periodic Tenancy
- Rent
- Retaliatory Eviction
- Tenancy at Sufferance
- Tenancy at Will
- Tenancy for Years
- Unlawful Detainer
- Warranty of Habitability

Questions and Case Problems

1. Analyze the various types of leaseholds and the distinguishing characteristics of each.

2. Klingensmith leases an office to Burke under a year-to-year lease. At the end of the second year, Burke moves out without giving Klingensmith any notice. Is Burke liable for another year's rent?

3. Chris Whitney rents a warehouse for storage of high explosives. Shortly after the lease is signed, most of the warehouse is destroyed by a hurricane. Is the lease terminated by this event?

4. Discuss the circumstances that may give rise to an implied warranty of habitability.

5. The Isaacsons lease farmland from the Richards under a lease that provides that they will be granted the "first right of refusal to purchase the premises." Later, the Richards convey the property, valued at more than $60,000, to their son for $20,000 and the son's promise that he will care for his mother after his father's death and keep the farm in the family. The Isaacsons then bring an action against the Richards for specific performance of the right to purchase under the "first refusal" provision in the farm lease. What is the result?

6. Tappa leases store space in a shopping center from Linke for a rental of $6,000 per year. Eight months after occupying the space, Tappa's retail permit is revoked by the city. As a result, Tappa is forced to vacate the store. Is Tappa entitled to stop paying rent for the remaining period of the lease? Discuss.

7. Duvall rents an apartment on a month-to-month basis. She complains to the landlord about a broken lock, a leaky roof, lack of hot water, a leaking toilet and pipes, cockroach infestation, and hazardous floors and steps. The landlord does nothing. Duvall repairs some of the malfunctions on her own and deducts the cost from her rent. Eventually she stops paying rent because the other repairs are not made. The landlord then sues her for the back rent and for possession of the premises. What is the outcome?

8. Brenda rented an apartment from Reicher Enterprises in Baltimore. Before renting the apartment, she made an inspection of it and noticed chipped and cracked paint throughout. The landlord promised to paint and fix up the apartment after she moved into it, but he never did so. Later, one of Brenda's daughters became seriously ill from eating the chipped and cracked paint, which was lead-based. The child suffered blindness, retardation, and other neurological handicaps. Brenda sued the landlord for the injuries to her child. How should the case be decided?

9. Weber rents a berth at the dock of John's Pass Seafood Company to moor his fishing boat. Under the lease, Weber agrees to indemnify John's Pass from all liability occasioned by the use of the dock, even if the injury is caused by John's Pass' negligence. One night, a fire on a nearby vessel moored to the same dock spreads to Weber's boat. Weber sues John's Pass for the damage to his boat, charging it with negligence in failing to provide fire extinguishers and other firefighting equipment required by a local ordinance. John's Pass points to the exculpation clause by way of defense to the lawsuit. Is John's Pass liable to Weber? Why or why not?

10. Sommer rented an apartment to Kridel for a two-year term. Before she even moved in, Kridel notified Sommer that she would be unable to take possession of the apartment. Later, Sommer told a third party who was interested in renting the apartment that it was unavailable. Sommer then sued Kridel for the total amount due under the lease. Who should win the lawsuit? Why?

37 Regulation and Control of Land Use

[T]he general rule at least is, that while property may be regulated to a certain extent, if regulation goes too far it will be recognized as a taking.

Justice Oliver Wendell Holmes,
Pennsylvania Coal Co. v. Mahon, 260 US 393, 415 (1922)

37:1   Introductory Comments

Traditionally, the regulation of land use in the United States has been left to the individual property owner. This stems in part from the history of the country as well as from a recognition that some land-use decisions can best be made by individual property owners without governmental intervention. Today, with the increase in both the scarcity and value of land and the recognition that individual land-use decisions vitally affect the entire community, there is a growing need for state and federal land-use regulations.

Police Power   A state generally regulates the use of land under the authority of what is known as its police power. The United States Constitution does not specifically provide for the exercise of this power by the states; rather, it is one of the unspecified powers reserved to the states or the people by Article X of the Constitution. The police power of states is quite distinct from other constitutional provisions, such as the Fifth and Fourteenth Amendments, which require compensation for private property taken for *public use*. When property is reasonably regulated pursuant to the police power and the property owners are not actually deprived of its use, the payment of compensation is not required. The reason is that no taking has occurred.

Nuisance   Before the advent of zoning laws and other laws aimed particularly at the use of land, application of the nuisance doctrine was the primary means by which property use was regulated. A *nuisance* in this context is an invasion of another person's interest in the use and enjoyment of his property. A nuisance is termed a private nuisance when it interferes with the private use of property. For example, a property owner who constructs a 400-foot tower, installs a loudspeaker on top of it, and then plays loud music at night has created a private nuisance. A nuisance is a public nuisance when it interferes with a right enjoyed by the general public. An example of a public nuisance is a property owner's pollution of a stream used by an entire community, so that it is no longer fit for drinking or swimming. The right to relief from a nuisance is based on the idea that one must use one's property so as not to injure that of another. An individual who is harmed by a private nuisance can sue for relief from the nuisance. The appropriate relief is often a court order requiring the nuisance to be eliminated. The general rule is that only a government entity can sue for relief from a public nuisance.

37:2   Eminent Domain

The state's right to take private property for public use is known as the right of *eminent domain*. The procedure involved is variously called an eminent domain action, an appropriation action, or a condemnation proceeding. The power of eminent domain is based on the concept that privately owned property is held subject to the state's right to take it if the public would benefit more by its public use than by its private use. The power of eminent domain is not granted by the United States Constitution. Instead, it is an inherent power of the states. It is limited only by the Fifth Amendment, which requires that property owners be compensated for property taken for public use. Every state has a statute that gives the right of eminent domain to a variety of public and semipublic authorities and organizations. The specific procedure for taking property varies from state to state.

Public Use   Since eminent domain is the right to take property for public use, a taking for private purposes violates the constitutional rights of the owner. A public use is one that promotes the general interests of the community as a whole and furthers a legitimate purpose of government. Once the taking of property is deemed to be for a public use, however, the fact that private persons can or will receive benefit from it is not sufficient to take away the characteristics of a public use.

   The following case illustrates the situation in which property was to be taken under the power of eminent domain and then used or managed by private entities. Consider the property owner's argument that the proposed taking was unconstitutional.

Berman
v
Parker
348 US 26, 99 L Ed 27, 75 S Ct 98
(United States Supreme Court, 1954)

[*The District of Columbia Redevelopment Act of 1945 was enacted for the purpose of redeveloping substandard housing and blighted areas in the District of Columbia. The District of Columbia Redevelopment Land Agency was empowered to acquire real property by eminent domain. An owner of property that was used as a department store* claimed that because his property was commercial property, rather than unsafe or unhealthy slum housing, the property could not be taken in connection with the redevelopment of the area. He also contended that his property was being illegally taken since, under the terms of the statute, the property would be redeveloped by a private agency rather than by a public one. The trial court upheld the validity of the taking, and the property owner appealed.*]

Justice Douglas delivered the opinion of the Court.

*   *   *

... Miserable and disreputable housing conditions may do more than spread disease and crime and immorality. They may also suffocate the spirit by reducing the people who live there to the status of cattle. They may indeed make living an almost insufferable burden. They may also be an ugly sore, a blight on the community which robs it of charm, which makes it a place from which men turn. The misery of housing may despoil a community as an open sewer may ruin a river.

We do not sit to determine whether a particular housing project is or is not desirable. The concept of the public welfare is broad and inclusive. . . . The values it represents are spiritual as well as physical, aesthetic as well as monetary. It is within the power of the legislature to determine that the community should be beautiful as well as healthy, spacious as well as clean, well-balanced as well as carefully patrolled. In the present case, the Congress and its authorized agencies have made determinations that take into account a wide variety of values. It is not for us to reappraise them. If those who govern the District of Columbia decide that the Nation's Capitol should be beautiful as well as sanitary, there is nothing in the Fifth Amendment that stands in the way.

Once the object is within the authority of Congress, the right to realize it through the exercise of eminent domain is clear. For the power of eminent domain is merely the means to the end. . . . Once the object is within the authority of Congress, the means by which it will be attained is also for Congress to determine. Here one of the means chosen is the use of private enterprise for redevelopment of the area. Appellants argue that this makes the project a taking from one businessman for the benefit of another businessman. But the means of executing the project are for Congress and Congress alone to determine, once the public purpose has been established. . . . The public end may be as well or better served through an agency of private enterprise than through a department of government—or so the Congress might conclude. We cannot say that public ownership is the sole method of promoting the public purposes of community redevelopment projects. What we have said also disposes of any contention concerning the fact that certain property owners in the area may be permitted to repurchase their properties for redevelopment in harmony with the overall plan. That, too, is a legitimate means which Congress and its agencies may adopt, if they choose.

In the present case, Congress and its authorized agencies attack the problem of the blighted parts of the community on an area rather than on a structure-by-structure basis. That, too, is opposed by appellants. They maintain that since their building does not imperil health or safety nor contribute to the making of a slum or a blighted area, it cannot be swept into a redevelopment plan by the mere dictum of the Planning Commission or the Commissioners. The particular uses to be made of the land in the project were determined with regard to the needs of the particular community. The experts concluded that if the community were to be healthy, if it were not to revert again to a blighted or slum area, as though possessed of a congenital disease, the area must be planned as a whole. It was not enough, they believed, to remove existing buildings that were insanitary or unsightly. It was important to redesign the whole area so as to eliminate the conditions that cause slums—the overcrowding of dwellings, the lack of parks, the lack of adequate streets and alleys, the absence of recreational areas, the lack of light and air, the presence of outmoded street patterns. It was believed that the piecemeal approach, the removal of individual structures that were offensive, would be only a palliative. The entire area needed redesigning so that a balanced, integrated plan could be developed for the region, including not only new homes but also schools, churches, parks, streets, and shopping centers. In this way it was hoped that the cycle of decay of the area could be controlled and the birth of new slums prevented. . . . Such diversification in future use is plainly relevant to the maintenance of the desired housing standards and therefore within congressional power. . . . Property may of course be taken for this redevelopment which, standing by itself, is innocuous and unoffending. . . . If owner after owner were permitted to resist these redevelopment programs on the ground that his particular property was not being used against the public interest, integrated plans for redevelopment would suffer greatly. . . . But as we have already stated, community redevelopment programs need not, by force of the Constitution, be on a piecemeal basis—lot by lot, building by building.

It is not for the courts to oversee the choice of the boundary line nor to sit in review on the size of a particular project area. Once the question of the public purpose has been decided, the amount and character of land to be taken for the project and the need for a particular tract to complete the integrated plan rests in the discretion of the legislative branch. . . .

The rights of these property owners are satisfied when they receive that just compensation which the Fifth Amendment exacts as the price of the taking. . . .

[Affirmed.]

Persons and Interests Entitled to Compensation To be entitled to compensation in an eminent domain proceeding, a property owner must show a taking of property or a property interest that he owned. For example, a leasehold is a property interest that cannot be taken or damaged for public use without compensation. A lienholder and the owner of an unexercised option to purchase land also possess property rights which cannot be taken by the government without compensation.

The only compensation allowable in most states is the value of property actually taken, plus the amount, if any, by which the value of the owner's adjacent property is decreased. "Adjacent property" as used here refers to that which remains after a taking of less than all the owner's property, as where a strip of land running through a farm is condemned for highway purposes. The compensation for damage to adjacent property is known as severance damages. No compensation is allowed for consequential losses, such as lost business opportunities, inconvenience, or the mere frustration of a landowner's plans. Nor is compensation allowed for the operating equipment or merchandise of a business, even though the taking terminates a successful commercial enterprise on the premises. However, in some states the owner of a business can be compensated for the loss of goodwill, which consists of the benefits accruing to the business as the result of its location or reputation.

Valuation of Property The measure for valuing condemned property in most states is its fair market value. An important rule in this process is that the property be measured by the value of its *highest and best use*. In urban areas, the highest and best use of a home is obviously use as a dwelling. As to other types of property, the highest and best use is not so easily determined. Consequently, an appraiser is ordinarily employed to determine the value of property and its highest and best use. The use ultimately determined can make a tremendous difference in valuation and the payment of compensation.

The rule in most states is that the highest and best use of property encompasses not only its present use but also any other use to which it could be put to make it more valuable. Thus, the potential use of property can be considered even though the land is vacant at the time of the taking.

37:3   Zoning

Zoning is a relatively recent concept in the regulation of land use. The earliest zoning laws, enacted in 1914 in New York, were intended to protect the public against nuisances and land uses that were dangerous to the public's health. The United States Supreme Court upheld the states' right to enact zoning laws in 1926.[1] Today, the state is still the only entity with authority to impose and enforce zoning restrictions, either directly or through local or municipal authorities to which the power has been delegated.

Zoning Ordinances   A zoning ordinance generally consists of two parts: (1) a map showing the location of the various zones or districts and (2) a text setting out the rules applicable to each zone with general information about the rules and their administration. The term "zone" does not necessarily mean that only one area is set aside for each use. Rather, several widely separated areas covered by a zoning ordinance can have the same general use. Most zoning ordinances include structures, use, or area regulations that govern such matters as the height, location, setback (the minimum permissible distance for a building to be located from the boundary of the property), and minimum floor space of buildings, as well as lot sizes and parking requirements.

Spot Zoning   Spot zoning designates relatively small parcels of land for a use different from that governing the surrounding area, even though all of the land is of the same character. Spot zoning is generally invalid because it violates the requirement that a particular zoning ordinance apply to all property within a particular zone. Where spot zoning is valid, it can result in either economic hardship to the affected property owner (by decreasing the value of the property) or economic advantage (by granting the owner a special privilege not given to others similarly situated).

Contract Zoning   Contract, or conditional, zoning is zoning that is done on the condition that the owner of the affected land execute a contract or covenant restricting the use of the land in certain ways specified in the contract. Contract zoning is thus a method of land-use control whereby a locality can tailor land use to particular tracts of land, permitting an owner to develop land in ways that do not harm the surrounding district or zone as a whole, without the need for spot zoning.

EXAMPLE
A landowner wishes to build a light manufacturing plant on a lot zoned for resi-

---

[1] *Euclid v Ambler Realty Co.* 272 US 365, 71 L Ed 303, 47 S Ct 114, 4 Ohio L Abs 816, 54 ALR 1016 (1926).

dential use. If the owner agrees to provide a park surrounding the plant to protect nearby houses, the locality may agree to rezone the land for light industrial use. The owner would execute the covenant in favor of the locality, which in turn would agree to rezone the land.

Floating Zones   Another method of achieving flexibility in land-use planning is use of the "floating zone." A floating zone is a zone that, when created, exists only in the abstract. That is, the land to be included in the zone is neither described in the zoning ordinance nor shown on the zoning map. Particular land is included in the new zone later, by amendment to the general zoning ordinance, after a land-owner has made a request for it.

EXAMPLE
A zoning ordinance creates a limited industrial district, setting forth the requirements, conditions, and uses permitted. No land in the affected locality is placed within this limited industrial district. Later, a property owner whose tract is in a residential district applies for rezoning to this limited industrial use. Because the limited industrial district can be located anywhere within the locality, it is a floating zone, and the owner's application can be approved.

Adoption of Zoning Ordinances   Zoning ordinances are normally enacted by municipalities and other local government entities. Various boards or commissions are usually created by these ordinances and are given the power to establish administrative rules and regulations governing the procedure to be followed in zoning cases. The zoning board can also recommend the adoption of district boundaries and appropriate regulations to be enforced in these districts.

Enforcement of the zoning ordinances can be entrusted to a zoning board or commission or to a specified administrative official, such as a zoning officer or building inspector who also may be given the power to issue building permits. If proposed construction, submitted to the zoning officer or building inspector for review, meets the requirements of a particular zoning ordinance, the permit is usually granted. If the requirements of the zoning ordinance are not met, the permit is usually denied and the applicant permitted to make suitable modifications. An applicant can also seek judicial relief or appeal the denial of an application for a building permit to the zoning board or board of review.

The following case demonstrates the scope of the zoning power. Note the extent to which social and moral values can be regulated by zoning ordinances, and consider the views expressed in the dissent.

Belle Terre
v
Boraas
416 US 1, 39 L Ed 2d 797, 94 S Ct 1536
(United States Supreme Court, 1974)

[Belle Terre, a village of 220 homes inhabited by 700 people on Long Island's north shore, adopted a zoning ordinance that prohibited more than two unrelated persons from occupying a "one-family" house. Six unmarried university students, three male and

three female, leased a home for their own use and claimed to be "one family." The owners of the house and the students were served by the village with an order to remedy the violation of the zoning ordinance. The students then brought an action in court, challenging the constitutionality of the zoning ordinance. They contended that it violated equal protection of the law and their rights of association, travel, and privacy. At trial, the district court upheld the validity of the ordinance, but the court of appeals reversed the decision, declaring the law to be unconstitutional. The case was then appealed to the United States Supreme Court.]

Justice Douglas delivered the opinion of the Court.

*   *   *

The present ordinance is challenged on several grounds: that it interferes with a person's right to travel; that it interferes with the right to migrate to and settle within a State; that it bars people who are uncongenial to the present residents; that it expresses the social preferences of the residents for groups that will be congenial to them; that social homogeneity is not a legitimate interest of government; that the restriction of those whom the neighbors do not like trenches on the newcomers' rights of privacy; that it is of no rightful concern to villagers whether the residents are married or unmarried; that the ordinance is antithetical to the Nation's experience, ideology, and self-perception as an open, egalitarian, and integrated society.

We find none of these reasons in the record before us. It is not aimed at transients. . . . It involves no procedural disparity inflicted on some but not on others. . . . It involves no "fundamental" right guaranteed by the Constitution, such as . . . the right of association, . . . the right of access to the courts, . . . or any rights of privacy. . . . We deal with economic and social legislation where legislatures have historically drawn lines which we respect against the charge of violation of the Equal

Protection Clause if the law be "reasonable, not arbitrary' " . . . and bears "a rational relationship to a [permissible] state objection". . . .

It is said, however, that if two unmarried people can constitute a "family," there is no reason why three or four may not. But every line drawn by a legislature leaves some out that might well have been included. . . .

A quiet place where yards are wide, people few, and motor vehicles restricted are legitimate guidelines in a land-use project addressed to family needs. This goal is a permissible one. . . . The police power is not confined to elimination of filth, stench, and unhealthy places. It is ample to lay out zones where family values, youth values, and the blessings of quiet seclusion and clean air make the area a sanctuary for people. . . .

[Judgment reversed.]

Justice Marshall, dissenting.

*   *   *

I am in full agreement with the majority that zoning is a complex and important function of the State. It may indeed be the most essential function performed by local government, for it is one of the primary means by which we protect that sometimes difficult to define concept of quality of life. I therefore continue to adhere to the principle . . . that deference should be given to governmental judgments concerning proper land-use allocation. . . .

I would also agree with the majority that local zoning authorities may properly act in furtherance of the objectives asserted to be served by the ordinance at issue here: restricting uncontrolled growth, solving traffic problems, keeping rental costs at a reasonable level, and making the community attractive to families. The police power which provides the justification for zoning is not narrowly confined. . . . And, it is appropriate that we afford zoning authorities considerable latitude in choosing the means by which to implement such purposes. But deference does not mean abdication. This Court has an obligation to ensure that zoning ordinances, even when adopted in furtherance of such legitimate aims, do not infringe upon fundamental constitutional rights. . . .

My disagreement with the Court today is based upon my view that the ordinance in this case unnecessarily burdens appellees' First Amendment freedom of association and their constitutionally guaranteed right to privacy. Our decisions established that the First and Fourteenth Amendments protect the freedom to choose one's associates. . . . Constitutional protection is extended, not only to modes of association that are political in the usual sense, but also to those that pertain to the social and economic benefit of the members. . . . The selection of one's living companions involves similar choices as to the emotional, social, or economic benefits to be derived from alternative living arrangements. . . . The choice of household companions—of whether a person's "intellectual and emotional needs" are best met by living with family, friends, professional associates or others—involves deeply personal considerations as to the kind and quality of intimate relationships within the home. That decision surely falls within the ambit of the right to privacy protected by the Constitution. . . .

The instant ordinance discriminates on the basis of just such a personal lifestyle choice as to household companions. It permits any number of persons related by blood or marriage, be it two or twenty, to live in a single household, but it limits to two the number of unrelated persons bound by profession, love, friendship, religious or political affiliation, or mere economics who can occupy a single home. Belle Terre imposes upon those who deviate from the community norm in their choice of living companions significantly greater restrictions than are applied to residential groups who are related by blood or marriage, and compose the established order within the community. The town has, in effect, acted to fence out those individuals whose choice of lifestyle differs from that of its current residents. . . .

A variety of justifications have been proffered in support of the village's ordinance. It is claimed that the ordinance controls population density, prevents noise, traffic and parking problems, and preserves the rent structure of the community and its attractiveness to families. As I noted earlier, these are all legitimate and substantial interests of government. But I think it clear that the means chosen to accomplish these purposes are both overinclusive and underinclusive, and that the asserted goals could be as effectively achieved by means of an ordinance that did not discriminate on the basis of constitutionally protected choices of lifestyle. The ordinance imposes no restriction whatsoever on the number of persons who may live in a house, as long as they are related by marital or sanguinary bonds—presumably no matter how distant their relationship. Nor does the ordinance restrict the number of income earners who may contribute to rent in such a household, or the number of automobiles that may be maintained by its occupants. In that sense the ordinance is underinclusive. On the other hand, the statute restricts the number of unrelated persons who may live in a home to no more than two. It would therefore prevent three unrelated people from occupying a dwelling even if among them they had but one income and no vehicles. While an extended family of a dozen or more might live in a small bungalow, three elderly and retired persons could not occupy the large manor house next door. Thus the statute is also grossly overinclusive to accomplish its intended purposes. . . .

By limiting unrelated households to two persons while placing no limitation on households of related individuals, the village has embarked upon its commendable course in a constitutionally faulty vessel. . . . I would find the challenged ordinance unconstitutional. But I would not ask the village to abandon its goal of providing quiet streets, little traffic, and a pleasant and reasonably priced environment in which families might raise their children. Rather, I would commend the town to con- tinue to pursue those purposes but by means of more carefully drawn and even-handed leg- islation. . . .

Variances   It is difficult to draft a general zoning ordinance that takes into ac- count all the existing shapes, sizes, and peculiar conditions of every lot in a city or other locality. For this reason, most zoning ordinances provide for relief to affected property owners by way of a *variance* from a general zoning ordinance. The crite- rion for granting a variance is usually a hardship imposed on the property owner due to a unique or peculiar aspect of his lot. A variance must not result in substan- tial detriment to the public health, safety, or welfare, and it must not depart sub- stantially from the comprehensive plan.

EXAMPLE
A zoning ordinance requires a 20-foot building setback from the street. Because of the shallowness of a particular lot, which was laid out before the enactment of the zoning ordinance, it is not practicable for the owner to set back a new building 20 feet. This is a proper case for a variance. However, if the shallow lot had been created *after* the enactment of the zoning ordinance, the difficulty would be self- created, and a variance would probably not be granted.

Nonconforming Uses   A *nonconforming use* is a use of property that (1) exists at the time a particular zoning ordinance is enacted and (2) is not permitted in the newly created zone. Nonconforming uses are recognized and allowed to continue both to facilitate the adoption of comprehensive zoning plans (by eliminating non- conforming users' need to challenge the zoning) and to protect the nonconforming users' property rights. A zoning ordinance can, however, provide that a given nonconforming use must terminate after a specific period of time. For example, a period of years may be granted a property owner for the removal of a junkyard located in an area newly zoned for residential use.

Discrimination and Exclusionary Zoning   The control and restriction of land through zoning is a legitimate use of the police power to provide for the general health and welfare of the community. Obviously, this power can be abused. Land- use controls, such as minimum lot sizes, minimum floor space, bans on apart- ments, limits on the number of bedrooms, and building moratoriums can discrimi- nate against minorities or low-income groups, or even exclude them from entire neighborhoods. For example, limits on the number of bedrooms can tend to dis- criminate against and exclude families with children. Land-use controls that are discriminatory and exclude specific individuals or groups from communities are invalid. On the other hand, if a zoning scheme is not aimed at specific groups but is reasonably related to community needs, it will usually be upheld.

EXAMPLE
A locality adopts a system of land-use planning that permits only high-priced sin-

gle-family dwellings to be built and requires that they be built on large lots. The stated purpose of the zoning is to keep property taxes at a low level. However, since the effect of the zoning will be to exclude low-income and middle-income families, the zoning will probably be declared to be invalid if it is challenged in court.

37:4 Inverse Condemnation

In certain circumstances, property can be damaged or taken for public use by government action without a formal taking or eminent domain proceeding. For example, a particular zoning ordinance might so restrict an owner's use of property as to render it of no value for any purpose, or noise from a municipally owned airport might so interfere with an owner's use and enjoyment of property that the property could be considered taken by the municipality. This inadvertent taking is called *inverse condemnation*—the owner is deprived of use of his property to the extent that it may as well be condemned. A property owner can seek compensation by filing an inverse condemnation action. An action of this type is also known as a reverse condemnation proceeding since it is the same as an eminent domain proceeding, except that it is initiated by the property owner rather than by a governmental entity.

The following case illustrates inverse condemnation. Note the scope of the court's ruling and the types of government action that may or may not constitute a taking of property.

Agins

v

Tiburon

447 US 255, 65 L Ed 2d 106, 100 S Ct 2138

(United States Supreme Court, 1980)

[The Agins, who owned a five-acre parcel of unimproved land in the city of Tiburon, California, sued the city after the city adopted a zoning ordinance that placed the land in a residential planned development and open-space zone, permitting the Agins to build no more than five single-family residences on the tract. The Agins sued for damages in state court, alleging inverse condemnation. They asserted that the city had taken their property without just compensation and sought a declaration that the zoning ordinance was unconstitutional. The trial court upheld the validity of the ordinance, and the

California Supreme Court affirmed. The Agins then sought review by the United States Supreme Court.]

Justice Powell delivered the opinion of the Court.

*   *   *

The Fifth Amendment guarantees that private property shall not "be taken for public use, without just compensation." . . .

The application of a general zoning law to particular property effects a taking if the ordinance does not substantially advance legitimate state interests . . . or denies an owner economically viable use of his land. . . . The determination that governmental action constitutes a taking is, in essence, a determination that the public at large, rather than a single owner, must bear the burden of an exercise of state power in public interest. Although no precise rule determines when property has been taken, ... the question necessarily requires a weighing of private and public interests. The seminal decision in *Euclid v Ambler Co.* 272 US 365, 71 L Ed 303, 47 S Ct 114, 4 Ohio L Abs 816, 54 ALR 1016 (1926), is illustrative. In that case, the landowner challenged the constitutionality of a municipal ordinance that restricted commercial development of his property. Despite alleged diminution in value of the owner's land, the Court held that the zoning laws were facially constitutional. They bore a substantial relationship to the public welfare, and their enactment inflicted no irreparable injury upon the landowner....

In this case, the zoning ordinances substantially advance legitimate governmental goals. The State of California has determined that the development of local open-space plans will discourage the "premature and unnecessary conversion of open-space land to urban uses." ... The specific zoning regulations at issue are exercises of the city's police power to protect the residents of Tiburon from the ill-effects of urbanization. Such governmental purposes long have been recognized as legitimate....

The ordinances place [the Agins'] land in a zone limited to single-family dwellings, accessory buildings, and open-space uses. Construction is not permitted until the builder submits a plan compatible with "adjoining patterns of development and open space." ... In passing upon a plan, the city also will consider how well the proposed development would preserve the surrounding environment and whether the density of new construction will be offset by adjoining open spaces.... The zoning ordinances benefit the [Agins] as well as the public by serving the city's interest in assuring careful and orderly development of residential property with provision for open-space areas. There is no indication that the [Agins'] five-acre tract is the only property affected by the ordinances. [The Agins] therefore will share with other owners the benefits and burdens of the city's exercise of its police power. In assessing the fairness of the zoning ordinance, these benefits must be considered along with any diminution in market value that the appellants might suffer.

Although the ordinances limit development, they neither prevent the best use of [the Agins'] land, ... nor extinguish a fundamental attribute of ownership.... [The Agins] have alleged that they wish to develop the land for residential purposes, that the land is the most expensive suburban property in the State, and that the best possible use of the land is residential.... The California Supreme Court has decided, as a matter of state law, that [the Agins] may be permitted to build as many as five houses on their five acres of prime residential property. At this juncture, [the Agins] are free to pursue their reasonable investment expectations by submitting a development plan to local officials. Thus it cannot be said that the impact of general land-use regulations has denied [the Agins] the "justice and fairness" guaranteed by the Fifth and Fourteenth Amendments....

[Judgment affirmed.]

37:5 Landmarks and Historic Buildings

The preservation of the nation's cultural resources has been a public concern almost since the founding of the Republic. For example, in 1816 the City of Philadelphia prohibited private development in the Independence Square area, and later in the century, to preserve the Gettysburg battlefield, the federal government declared it a national monument. Today, there is government action at all levels to preserve landmarks and historic buildings.

The preservation of historic structures generally is accomplished by one of two methods. The first is direct governmental intervention through the power of eminent domain, which establishes public ownership of historic buildings. Landmarks and structures taken in this fashion require compensation to the affected landowner. The second method involves indirect action through zoning regulations, requiring private owners to preserve their property in a specific fashion; it does not necessarily involve the taking of property.

The principal question involved in governmental regulation of landmarks through zoning is whether the restrictions imposed constitute a taking for which compensation must be paid. If a regulation deprives an owner of all reasonable uses of his property, then it can be said that a taking has occurred for which compensation is required. In contrast, if an ordinance permits some uses, the property has not been taken and the owner need not be compensated.

Most state and local preservation statutes empower a "preservation commission" to designate a geographical area or an individual building as a historic site. The owner is then denied the right to demolish or renovate any buildings involved, especially their facades. While most ordinances of this type permit an owner of a historic structure to apply for a permit to demolish or alter the building, this permission is usually denied as inconsistent with the preservation agency's basic function.

Federal Landmark Preservation   Early in this century, Congress enacted the Antiquities Act of 1906 (16 USC §§ 431–33). This act empowered the President to declare historic landmarks, structures, and other objects of historic or scientific interest located on federal land to be national monuments. Landmarks such as the Statue of Liberty and the Edison Laboratory were designated national monuments pursuant to this act. In 1935, the Historic Sites, Buildings, and Antiquities Act (16 USC §§ 461 et seq.) was adopted to identify and preserve cultural resources in the United States. Today, the preservation of landmarks and historic buildings is governed by the National Historic Preservation Act of 1966 (16 USC §§ 470 et seq.). This act establishes a review process that federal agencies must follow in assessing the effect of their programs on districts, sites, buildings, or other structures that are included in a listing prepared by the Secretary of the Interior. This listing, known as the National Register of Historic Places, serves as a guide for implementing national historic preservation policy. Any property that has national historical significance or commemorative value is eligible for the registry. The Advisory Council on Historic Preservation coordinates the national historic preservation program and regulates the impact of federal agency actions on National Register properties.

37:6   Federal Regulation of Land Use

The role of the federal government in land-use control has been primarily to provide financial aid to cities and states for development and urban renewal.

Obviously, many other types of federal legislation designed to preserve clean air, eliminate water pollution, or regulate noise, for example, vitally affect the uses to which land can be put. Moreover, legislation enacted by the federal government often parallels similar legislation adopted by the states. Indeed, it is not uncommon for a particular project to be the subject of regulation by several government entities, ranging from the localities themselves to federal agencies. For example, an *environmental impact statement* may be required at all levels of government before a project may be approved. Different aspects of federal regulation of land use will now be discussed.

National Environmental Policy Act (NEPA)   A major piece of federal legislation that vitally affects the use of land throughout the United States is the *National Environmental Policy Act* of 1969 (*NEPA*) (42 USC §§ 4321 et seq.). The purpose of NEPA is to establish procedures by which environmental concerns that are created by proposed government projects are identified and then thoroughly analyzed. Accordingly, whenever a federal agency proposes "legislation and other major federal actions significantly affecting the quality of the human environment," it must prepare an environmental impact statement and file it with the proposal. No particular federal agency has the power to enforce the act. Instead, because the act provides that the impact statements must be made available to the public, the public at large has the right of enforcement.

NEPA is specifically directed at projects that involve a major federal action. Examples of "major federal actions" are government construction projects, the granting of federal permits for private projects (even if no federal funds are involved), and the issuance of federal mortgage insurance and loans.

Coastal Zone Management Act   The Coastal Zone Management Act of 1972 (16 USC §§ 1451 et seq.) authorizes a national program for the management, use, protection, and development of natural resources along the nation's coasts. The program establishes standards for public and private uses of land and waters in the coastal zone, and it provides funds to coastal states to develop and implement their own coastal management programs. These state programs must consider ecological, cultural, historic, and aesthetic values, as well as the need for economic development of the lands in question.

Federal Land Policy and Management Act   In 1976, Congress enacted the Federal Land Policy and Management Act (43 USC §§ 1701 et seq.). The act repealed many outdated and archaic public-land laws. The law now requires that the Secretary of the Interior prepare and maintain an inventory of all public lands, including their resources and uses.

Wilderness and Open-Space Preservation   Every year at least two to three million acres of open space or farmland in the United States are developed to accommodate the growth of industry and expanding urban areas. About one-third of the land lost is prime agricultural land. It is only in recent years that the federal government has begun to respond to this situation. For example, before 1964 there were no statutorily designated wilderness areas. Any areas that did receive protection for their wilderness qualifications were protected by the federal government only pursuant to administrative action within a particular federal agency or, less formally, on a regional basis by the Department of the Interior. The Wilderness Act of 1964 (16 USC §§ 1131 et seq.) created the national wilderness preservation system and established several wilderness areas as components of that system. The act also requires the Department of the Interior to review areas previously set aside by administrative action to determine whether they should also be included in the wilderness system.

37:7   Private Land-Use Restrictions

There is a long history of regulation of land through private restrictions. One of the earliest forms of land-use control was the *restrictive covenant.* Sellers of property used restrictive covenants to impose limits on purchasers as to the type of improvements that could be built on land sold, to restrict the use of land to specific purposes, and even to specify to whom property could or could not be sold. A restrictive covenant is usually imposed directly by the seller on a purchaser of property. In this way, there can be no question that the purchaser is aware of the restriction and is bound by it.

Another type of private restriction is called an equitable servitude. Although just as binding on property owners as a restrictive covenant, the equitable servitude differs in that the restriction is not necessarily mentioned in a particular deed. For example, a developer of a residential tract might file in the appropriate public office a subdivision map, plat, or other document containing all the pertinent data about the development, as well as specific restrictions. The owner of a lot in the subdivision—and all future owners—are bound by the restrictions. They are considered to have constructive notice of the restrictions so long as their deed refers to the existence of the map or plat. In fact, however, an owner often does not realize that the use of his property is restricted until he has attempted to use his property in a way that is contrary to the restriction imposed and is then restrained in court by other property owners.

Creation of Restrictive Covenants   Any landowner can impose restrictions on the use of land that he conveys to others so long as the restrictions are not unlawful or against public policy. Restrictive covenants are generally treated as covenants running with the land. This means that the duty to perform the covenants—as well as any right to take advantage of them—passes to those who may purchase the property in the future.

Restrictive covenants are primarily used to maintain a general scheme, plan of design, or purpose on the land on which the restrictions are placed. They are most frequently imposed on residential property. The object of restricting the type of building to be built and the use to which the land is put is to ensure purchasers of lots within a subdivision, for example, that the use and enjoyment of their land for residential purposes will not be affected by the development of commercial activities in the neighborhood. Likewise, a person who buys or builds a home will be assured through the use of restrictive covenants that his property will not be depreciated by subsequent construction of inferior structures on adjoining lots.

Frequently, restrictive covenants are imposed on land to protect a seller from competition by the purchaser. The owner of a tract of land on which a business is maintained may want to sell a part of the land and yet prevent the new owner or subsequent purchasers from engaging in a competing business on the property. Restrictions of this type are valid and, as long as they are not unreasonable and do not amount to an undue restraint of trade, they are enforced. They are normally limited to a period of years, however.

Extinguishment of Restrictions   Restrictive covenants can be extinguished by mutual agreement, abandonment, waiver and acceptance, or changes in the character of a neighborhood that would make enforcement of the restrictions unjust.

Enforcement of Covenants   Restrictive covenants are special forms of contract, and damages for their breach are governed by the general law of damages in contract actions (see Chapter 18). They can also be enforced through injunctive relief. Moreover, an owner of land on which restrictions have been imposed can seek declaratory relief to determine whether or not a proposed use of land violates the restrictions or whether the restrictions have been extinguished.

The following case illustrates the use of restrictive covenants as a private land-use control. Note the defenses raised in the case and the court's general attitude toward restrictive covenants.

Gaskin
v
Harris
82 NM 336, 481 P2d 698, 47 ALR3d 1227
(New Mexico Supreme Court, 1971)

[The owners of lots within a subdivision sued to enjoin the defendants from completing the construction of a swimming pool enclosure on their lot. The plaintiffs alleged that the design of the enclosure violated covenants restricting the architectural style of buildings in the subdivision to "old Santa Fe or Pueblo-Spanish" style. The pool enclosure was in a modern style described as "oriental" or "pagoda." The defendants contended that there was enough deviation from the permissible style in the existing buildings that the covenant should be extinguished in their case. The evidence indicated that although none of the buildings in the subdivision exactly conformed to the definition of "old Santa Fe or Pueblo-Spanish" architecture, all

except the defendants' proposed structure were in conformity with one another. The trial court ordered the defendants to remove the offending structure, and the defendants appealed.]

McManus, J.

*   *   *

Plaintiffs brought suit in the District Court of Santa Fe County to enjoin the defendants from [completing] on their residential property a structure alleged to be in violation of an architectural restriction applicable to the property. . . .

The plaintiffs . . . are the owners of lots within . . . a residential development in Santa Fe. The defendants are the owners of a lot within the same subdivision, on which lot they constructed the swimming pool cover in question. It is likewise undisputed that all of the property in the subdivision is subject to certain restrictive covenants containing building restrictions, the material parts of which provide:

"FIRST: That no building whatever except a private dwelling house with the necessary outbuildings, including a private garage, shall be erected, placed or permitted on said premises or any part thereof, and said dwelling house permitted on said premises shall be used as a private residence only . . . ; and said dwelling house and necessary outbuildings shall be in the style or form or appearance known as the Old Santa Fe or Pueblo-Spanish style of architecture; . . .

"IT IS UNDERSTOOD AND AGREED that said covenants on the part of the grantee herein, shall attach to and run with the land hereby conveyed, and the party of the first part (the Company) or any owner of adjacent or abutting premises, shall have the right to enforce compliance with said covenants by injunction, or other legal proceedings. . . ."

The defendants were in the process of constructing a swimming pool enclosure on their property which was visible from outside their property, and from the plaintiffs' lots. The plaintiffs complained that this structure violated the restrictive covenants of the deeds to the subdivision as it did not in any manner conform to the "Old Santa Fe or Pueblo-Spanish" style of architecture required by the covenants. Instead, the pool enclosure was in a modern style variously described as being of an oriental or pagoda style, but certainly in no

way resembling the adobe style known to Santa Fe.

. . . [T]he defendants refer to change of condition as to architectural styles in their subdivision and the relative hardships that would be imposed upon them if they should be ordered to remove the structure in question. Yet, as to the alleged change of conditions, even the defendants' own architect . . . conceded that the homes within the subdivision, even if not complying exactly with the definition of "Old Santa Fe or Pueblo-Spanish style of architecture," were of a consistent and uniform type of construction. . . .

In their briefs and arguments before this court, the defendants emphasized that they were not asking the court to extinguish the architectural restriction contained in the covenants but only not to enforce it in this case. . . . [T]he defendant would have the architectural restriction removed from his lot, while leaving the restriction on the rest of the subdivision. This cannot be done.

Finally, the defendants would argue relative hardship in that they had no actual notice of the restrictive covenants from the time they bought their lot, until after the swimming pool cover was substantially erected. . . . In this case, the restrictive covenant does exist, and because of the aims and purposes of such covenants, as discussed above, the relative hardship to the defendants is far outweighed by the benefits to the community affected.

[Judgment affirmed.]

Key Concepts and Terms

- The regulation of land use is performed by most states or localities pursuant to their police power.
- The right to take property for public use is known as the right of eminent domain. This right is inherent in government and is based on the concept that privately owned property can be taken for public purposes for the public's benefit.

- If property is taken for public use or is damaged by governmental action, either with or without a formal taking or eminent domain proceeding, the owner is entitled to compensation. The procedure by which a property owner tries to obtain just compensation in a case not involving a formal taking is commonly referred to as inverse condemnation.

- The measure of damages for property taken in eminent domain is its fair market value. In determining fair market value, the highest and best use of the property is considered.

- Zoning is an important technique in regulating land use. Zoning regulations may fix the height of buildings, the character of materials, methods of construction, and the separation of residential districts from industrial and commercial areas.

- A zoning ordinance generally consists of (1) a map showing the location of the various zones and (2) a text setting out the rules applicable to each zone and information about their administration.

- The federal government regulates the use of land indirectly through agencies. The federal government has also enacted legislation such as the National Environmental Policy Act, the Coastal Zone Management Act, and the Federal Land Policy and Management Act, which vitally affect all public lands and resources.

- Restrictive covenants are private land-use restrictions that impose limits on purchasers of property to protect the seller or neighboring landowners.

- Eminent Domain
- Environmental Impact Statement
- Highest and Best Use
- Inverse Condemnation
- National Environmental Policy Act (NEPA)

- Nonconforming Use
- Nuisance
- Public Use
- Restrictive Covenant
- Variance
- Zoning

Questions and Case Problems

1. How is the regulation of land reconciled with the constitutional guaranties of due process, equal protection, and just compensation for property taken for public purposes?

2. Analyze the following statements:

    a. "It is time that we apply the clear and unmistakable lesson of the past 50 years: Zoning has been a failure and should be eliminated! Governmental control over land use through zoning has been unworkable, inequitable, and a serious impediment to the operation of the real estate market and the satisfaction of its consumers."

    b. "It's absurd and tragic that the national goals of stimulating more and better housing in a desirable housing environment are being frustrated by local goals of limiting housing. It is equally inexcusable that federal policies to encourage business and development and competition are being impeded by local policies that operate to discourage them."

3. Sundell owns land on the shore of a lake. The town of New London operates a sewage treatment plant that discharges nutrient-laden effluent into a brook upstream from Sundell. Ample evidence indicates that algae bloom in the lake, causing it to emit foul odors and to become less capable of supporting fish life. There is also ample evidence to show that the algae are the result of the town's activities. Is this a nuisance? Can the city be enjoined? Has Sundell's property been taken? Can he bring a successful action in inverse condemnation for the taking of his rights to enjoy the lake and lakeshore?

4. How does eminent domain differ from inverse condemnation? How does zoning differ from eminent domain?

5. Compare and contrast the federal and state regulation of land use.

6. The Stovers, as a protest against high taxes, hung tattered clothing, old uniforms, underwear, rags, and scarecrows in their front yard. After several years, a city ordinance was enacted prohibiting the erection and maintenance of clotheslines or devices for hanging clothes or other fabrics in a front or side yard abutting a street. Provisions were included for the issuance of a permit in certain circumstances. The Stovers were refused a permit on the grounds that they had sufficient other property for the maintenance of a clothesline. When they continued to maintain the clothesline, they were arrested, tried, and convicted of violating the ordinance. Should their conviction be upheld? Is the ordinance a proper exercise of municipal power?

7. The city of Petaluma, California, responding to a 25 percent growth rate over a period of two years, instituted a comprehensive five-year housing and zoning plan that fixed the housing development growth rate at 500 dwelling units per year. The plan also directed that building permits be divided evenly between the east and west sections of the city, and positioned a 200-foot-wide "green belt" around Petaluma to serve as the boundary for urban expansion during the plan's term. Two property owners sue the city. They attack the plan as an unconstitutional infringement of their freedom to travel and a violation of their right to due process of law. The city defends its plan as a reasonable exercise of its police power in preserving the rural character of Petaluma and pacing its growth at an orderly rate. How should the case be decided?

8. Penn Central wanted to lease air rights above its Grand Central Terminal in New York City to UGP Properties, Inc. UGP planned to construct a 55-story office tower above the site. Plans drawn up by a noted architect complied with the city's zoning requirements. Since Grand Central Terminal had previously been designated as a landmark and the city block a "landmark site" under New York City's landmarks preservation law, the property owner was required to apply to the Landmarks Preservation Committee for administrative approval. After a hearing, the necessary certificates were denied by the Commission. Penn Central sued New York City claiming that the application of the landmarks law had (1) resulted in a taking of its property without just compensation in violation of the Fifth and Fourteenth Amendments to the United States Constitution and (2) arbitrarily deprived them of property without due process of law. Should New York's landmarks preservation law be upheld?

9. Shady Acres is a small, unincorporated community 15 miles from a large city. All

the residences in Shady Acres are ranch and split-level homes. A social action group from the city purchases five acres of land for construction of low-income housing units in Shady Acres. The local citizens become apprehensive about overcrowded schools and an increase in the crime rate. Eventually they force a revision of the local zoning ordinance. Local land, formerly zoned for multiple dwellings, is rezoned to permit only single-family dwellings. The owner of the land on which the low-income housing units were to be built sues to have the law declared unconstitutional. Decide the case.

10. The Cottonwood subdivision includes restrictive covenants in deeds for residential property prohibiting (1) the erection of any structure other than a detached single-family dwelling and a private garage and (2) the keeping of livestock and fowl, with the exception of small birds or animals kept as pets. Bagley constructs a home in Cottonwood and then wants to build a three-horse stable and tack room on an adjoining lot. Her plan calls for a one-story concrete block structure. What are the rights of Bagley's neighbors? Can Bagley build her stable and tack room?

38 Trusts, Wills, and Estate Administration

38:1 Estates and Estate Planning

Most people acquire property during their life. The property a person owns at any given time comprises his "estate." This estate will vary in nature and amount until the person dies. Part of one's estate is consumed or destroyed in the normal course of events. For example, a person's estate is reduced slightly when he spends money on groceries and then eats them. The part of a person's estate that is not consumed or destroyed must be passed on to some other person or entity. This passing on *can* occur during the property owner's lifetime; otherwise, it *will* occur after his death.

The simplest means by which a living person can dispose of property is by outright gift, and property is often transferred in this way. A person who gives a gift is a donor. A recipient of a gift is a donee. From the donor's viewpoint, the major objection to disposition by gift is that a gift is absolute. That is, the donor gives up not only the right to receive any benefits from the property, but also all power to control the property or its use in the donee's hands. Another potential shortcoming of making a gift is that due to age, health, or extravagant spending habits the donee might be incapable of using the gift in the manner intended by the donor.

In recognition of these and other problems, the legal system provides a device, known as a *trust*, by which a living donor can dispose of property and still retain some control over it. The legal system also allows a property owner to make a will, by which he can decide who is to receive his property after his death. Gifts, trusts, and wills are the basic tools used in what is called *estate planning*, as discussed below. If a person dies leaving property that he has not disposed of by will or one of the other means available to him, the property is distributed to the persons and in the manner provided by state statute.

Estate Planning Estate planning is an activity by which one's estate is identified, increased if possible, and later disposed of according to the owner's wishes, all with minimum loss through taxation. These goals are pursued through a comprehensive plan that requires a carefully drafted will and can also include the use of such devices as gifts, life insurance, and trusts.

Because of its tax-limiting function, estate planning is often thought to be of concern primarily to the wealthy, but this view ignores the property-disposition function of the planning. It also ignores the ways in which estate planning can serve people of only moderate means. For example, an estate plan that calls for the purchase of life insurance might create an estate where none would otherwise exist, due to the enforced-savings nature of some life insurance; or a plan might help a person prepare for retirement by providing for an individual retirement account. An estate plan can also make adequate provision for the continuation or orderly transfer of a business after the owner's death.

Trusts

38:2   Introduction to Trusts

A trust is a three-party agreement concerning certain property, which is the subject of the trust. The three parties are (1) the trustor (sometimes called settlor), who is the original owner of the trust property and is the creator of the trust; (2) the *trustee*, to whom legal title to the property is transferred; and (3) the beneficiary, who receives certain benefits from the property. The trustee can be either a private person or an institutional trustee, such as a bank. Ordinarily, the trustee receives a fee, which is paid out of the trust income, although a trustee who is a friend or family member will often agree to serve without compensation. The "benefits from the property" that the beneficiary receives is usually the income, such as interest or dividends, generated by the property.

As discussed in 38:5, most trusts cannot continue indefinitely. When a trust terminates, the property held in trust must pass to somebody, and that person is known as the remainderman. The remainderman can be the beneficiary. If so, the beneficiary/remainderman acquires full title to the property when the trust terminates, instead of only the benefits from the property that he received during the duration of the trust. However, the remainderman is often someone else.

EXAMPLE
Brown creates a trust under which the local bank is the trustee, Brown's wife is the income beneficiary, and Brown's son is the remainderman. Brown's wife will receive the income generated by the trust property during the duration of the trust. When the trust terminates, the trustee will transfer the trust property to Brown's son, who will then hold it free of any trust.

The distinctive feature of a trust is its separation of what is known as the equitable ownership of property from the legal title to that property. Equitable ownership means, in essence, the right to benefit from the property. Thus, for example, Rudolfo might create a simple trust by transferring 1,000 shares of stock to Mario for the benefit of Alfonso. Mario, as the trustee, will receive the dividends paid on the stock, but he will then pay those dividends—the benefit from the property—to Alfonso.

A trust can be created by more than one person, as where a husband and wife are the trustors, and there can be more than one trustee, as where an individual and bank are made joint trustees. There are often multiple beneficiaries and remaindermen. Moreover, the same person can assume more than one role under a trust. For example, Brown in the above example might have named his son as trustee, himself and his wife as beneficiaries, and his son as remainderman.

If the same person is the only trustee, beneficiary, and remainderman there can be no trust; the equitable and legal ownership of the trust property has merged in that person.

Purposes   Trusts are used for various purposes. Many trusts are created to reduce the trustor's income tax, the estate tax payable by the trustor's estate after his death, or both (see 38:14). Other purposes include avoiding probate (see 38:13), providing income to people who would be unsuitable recipients of outright gifts, and obtaining the services of a trustee who is an expert at managing property of the type that is the subject of the trust.

Types of Trusts, Generally   Trusts can be classified in many different ways. For example, a given trust can be express or implied, private or charitable, or revocable or irrevocable. It can have been created either while the trustor was living or after his death.

Express and Implied Trusts   An express trust is created intentionally by the trustor. Most trusts are of this type. The trust is a private express trust if the beneficiaries are private persons, usually relatives or close friends of the trustor. It is a charitable trust if the beneficiary is a charitable organization such as a church, a school, or the Red Cross.

An implied trust is one created by operation of law to correct what would otherwise be an unfair situation. It can be either a resulting trust or a constructive trust. A resulting trust is one in which title to property is acquired by someone other than the person who gave the consideration for the property, for the latter's benefit but without an express trust or intent that there be a gift. For example, if Benny buys a piece of land, but he has Rochester, his valet, named as the new owner in the deed, a court is apt to charge Rochester with the duties of a trustee with respect to the land since Benny is entitled to the beneficial interest in it.

A constructive trust arises when a party has obtained money or other property by fraud or similar wrongdoing, such as violation of a confidential relationship. If, for example, Benny in the above example had directed Wilson, his attorney, to handle the real estate transaction and to have title to the property placed in Benny's name but, in fact, Wilson had arranged to have title placed in his own name, a court would probably find that Wilson holds the property in a constructive trust, with Benny as the beneficiary.

The basic duties of the trustee, discussed in 38:4, are essentially the same whether a trust is express or implied, except to the extent that additional duties are provided for in the document creating an express trust (see 38:3).

Revocable and Irrevocable Trusts; Living and Testamentary Trusts   The distinction between revocable and irrevocable trusts is obvious—a trust of the former type can be canceled by the trustor, while one of the latter type cannot. As discussed in 38:5, the trustor's right to revoke a trust can have adverse income tax consequences. A trust can be classified as living or testamentary. A *living trust*, also called an *inter vivos* trust, is one created while the trustor is alive. A *testamentary trust* is one created after the trustor's death.

Spendthrift Trusts   At times a trustor wants to provide for a beneficiary who, because of his many creditors, his unwise spending habits, or both, should not be given even the limited rights of a beneficiary under a normal express trust. This problem can be solved by including in the terms of the trust what is known as a spendthrift provision. The distinctive feature of a trust containing such a provision is that the beneficiary's interest in the trust cannot be assigned, voluntarily or involuntarily, to someone other than the beneficiary. For example, the beneficiary cannot assign to a creditor his right to receive income from the trust, and the creditor is powerless to reach that income by judicial means (such as execution, as discussed in Chapter 30) until the income has been paid to the beneficiary. Once the income has been paid, the beneficiary can, of course, do whatever he wants to with it. Note in this regard that if a spendthrift provision is *not* included in a trust, a beneficiary generally can assign his interest in the trust, and creditors can reach that interest, although statutes in some states limit the creditors' right somewhat.

38:3   Creation of Express Trust

No particular formal words or acts are required to create a valid express trust. There are, however, a number of general requirements. First, the trustor must intend to create the trust, and he must be legally capable of doing so. For example, neither a child nor a person who has been declared to be mentally incompetent can create a valid trust. Second, there must be both a legally capable trustee who is willing to act in that capacity and at least one beneficiary. However, the fact that the person who is named as trustee by the trustor turns out to be unwilling to serve or incapable of serving does not invalidate an otherwise valid trust; a court has the power to appoint a new trustee.

The third requirement of a valid trust is that there be some kind of trust property, the property transferred to the trustee by the trustor. It can be money, other personal property, real property, or any combination of different types of property. Some states recognize what are known as life insurance trusts, under which the trustee is the beneficiary named in one or more insurance policies on the trustor's life, and there is no actual trust property until the insurance proceeds are paid after the trustor's death.

A fourth requirement is that the beneficiaries be described clearly enough to be identified with reasonable certainty. Although any person or entity capable of owning property can be a trust beneficiary, the trust instrument must at least guide the trustee as to the identity of the intended beneficiaries. Finally, the trust must have a legal purpose and not violate public policy. For example, if a trustor names his daughter as the beneficiary of a trust but requires that she divorce and cease living with her husband before she can receive trust income, the trust is invalid as being contrary to the public policy favoring marriage.

Trust Agreement   Although a trustor can create a living trust orally, the usual and better practice is for him to use a written instrument for that purpose. In the instrument, known as the trust agreement for a living trust, the trustor sets forth all the desired terms concerning the trust. A typical trust agreement covers such matters as:

- Identification of trustor, trustee, beneficiaries, and remaindermen
- Purpose of trust
- Description of trust property
- Trustee's powers and duties in managing trust (see 38:4)
- Trustor's retained powers with respect to trust property, including power to modify or revoke trust (see 38:5)
- Distributions of trust income to beneficiaries
- Duration of trust; terminating events

The trust agreement is signed by the trustor, and the trustee's written acceptance of the trust is often attached. Other formalities are required only to the extent dictated by the type of property being transferred to the trust. For example, if real property is being transferred, the agreement might have to satisfy certain formal requirements so that it can be recorded in the county recorder's office.

Testamentary Trusts   Rather than being set forth in a separate trust agreement, the terms of a testamentary trust are included as part of the trustor's will. Most of the terms are along the same lines as those used in trust agreements. Since the trustor will have died when a testamentary trust begins, the trustor cannot, of course, retain any powers concerning the trust property.

38:4   Trustee's Role

By definition, the trustee's basic duty is one of trust. A fiduciary relationship exists between the trustee and the beneficiaries, which means that the trustee is held to a high level of honesty and good faith in managing the trust property.

State statutes give trustees certain powers and impose on them certain duties and responsibilities, but for the most part, these statutes apply only to the extent that they do not conflict with the terms of the trust instrument. That is, when the trustor creates the trust he has the right to vary the trustee's required performance in most respects from what it would be under state law.

Trustee's Powers   The trustee's primary responsibility is to manage the trust property. To do so, he must have certain powers with respect to the property. Powers typically granted by law or the trust instrument include the power to:

- Invest trust property
- Sell, exchange, or least trust property
- Enter into other contracts with respect to trust property
- Mortgage trust property
- Distribute trust income to beneficiaries.

Trustee's Duty to Account and Pay Taxes   After a trust has been created and the trustee has acquired the trust property, the trustee is required to account for that property for as long as he serves as trustee. The trustee should have records of all receipts of money and other property, all transactions involving the trust property, and all distributions and other disbursements from the trust.

Trust property will ordinarily generate income, which is subject to state and federal income taxation. A trust is treated as a separate entity for tax purposes, and state and federal statutes include specific provisions governing the taxation of its income. The trust can deduct expenses in managing the trust and trust income that is distributed to beneficiaries. The trustee is responsible for preparing and filing needed tax returns and paying any tax due.

Allocations Between Principal and Income   Under the terms of the typical trust, the trustee must distribute trust income to the beneficiaries. The trustee might also receive money or other property that, although received because of the trustee's legal ownership of the trust property, does not really constitute income. Receipts of this type are credited to principal rather than income, and they are frequently required to be retained by the trustee and added to the trust property. The result is that the trustee must decide how each receipt is to be allocated between principal and income; depending on the nature of the trust property, this can be a major duty. Trusts also have expenses, and the trustee must make a similar allocation for each expense. Note that the beneficiaries benefit to the extent that a given receipt is allocated to income or an expense to principal. Conversely, allocating a receipt to principal or an expense to income benefits the remaindermen by increasing the property that they will receive when the trust terminates.

The manner in which the trustee carries out the allocation duty is governed by any instructions set forth in the trust instrument. To the extent that there are no instructions, the trustee must act in accordance with state statutory and case law. State law varies on this subject, although over half the states have enacted the Uniform Principal and Income Act in either its original (1931) or revised (1962) version.

In most states, a trustee is permitted to allocate between principal and income at his own discretion if the trustor has given the trustee that power. Some allocation decisions faced by a trustee holding this power are simple. For example, if the trust property consists of money that the trustee has invested in a certificate of deposit, the periodic interest payments received obviously constitute income. However, a large portion of the property currently being held in trusts in the United States is corporate stock. As the following case illustrates, a corporation's declaration of a stock dividend (dividend paid in form of corporation's stock, not cash) can lead to an allocation problem for the trustee.

Re Warner's Trust
263 Minn 449, 117 NW2d 224
(Minnesota Supreme Court, 1962)

[The property in a trust consisted in part of common stock in Northern Pacific Railway Company. The trustee (respondent) received 220 additional shares of Pacific stock as a stock dividend and, in his accounting, credited the dividend to principal. Later, the trustee petitioned the court for approval of his account for the preceding year. The court issued an approval order, and one of the trust beneficiaries (appellant) appealed.]

Knutson, Chief Justice.

*   *   *

Appellant contends that this stock dividend constitutes income and belongs at least in part to the income beneficiaries. Respondent contends, and the trial court held, that it belongs to principal.

Throughout the country there are two principal rules followed in the absence of an expression by the creator of the trust. Under the so-called Massachusetts rule, cash dividends are treated as income and all stock dividends as principal. Under the so-called Pennsylvania rule, the source of the dividend rather than its form determines whether and to what extent it is income or principal. Under this rule, such dividends are income if declared out of the earnings accruing to the corporation during the period of the trust but are principal if declared out of earnings accruing prior to the creation of the trust.

In [an earlier case] we adopted the Pennsylvania rule. . . .

The growing complexities of corporate accounting and the difficulties of determining whether a stock dividend comes from earnings and, if so, when it was earned, have led many courts that had followed the Pennsylvania rule, including Pennsylvania itself, . . . and

others who had not adopted any rule, to now follow the Massachusetts rule. It is apparent that a majority of the courts now follow the Massachusetts rule. Like many other states, Minnesota, in 1951, enacted substantially the Uniform Principal and Income Act . . . , which adopts the Massachusetts rule. . . .

The trust in this case was established prior to 1951, so [the Uniform Act does not apply]. Appellant argues that to now repudiate the Pennsylvania rule would unconstitutionally deprive the income beneficiaries of property without due process of law. [Cases from two other states] hold to the contrary. . . . The unworkability of the Pennsylvania rule, under modern conditions, is aptly described by the Pennsylvania court in its latest decision. We think that as far as the constitutional question is concerned these two decisions should be followed.

However, the trial court did not base its decision on the rejection of the Pennsylvania rule. Nor need we do so. The trust instrument provides, among other things:

> "The Trustees are authorized to treat as principal or income any receipt or any part thereof from the Trust Property . . . as they may in their judgment deem fair and reasonable in the circumstances in such case as it may arise, having due regard to any applicable rules of law."

While the discretion granted to the trustee may not be arbitrarily exercised for the benefit of the remaindermen and at the expense of the income beneficiaries, it does have some meaning. . . . In construing such clauses, we should try to determine the purpose the settlor had in including them in the light of the instrument as a whole and to give effect to such purpose. . . .

The settlor could have expressly provided that stock dividends should be considered income or principal under [state law]. What he could do himself he could empower his trustee to do. . . .

From the language of the clause quoted above it would seem quite clear that the settlor had in mind the possibility of a change in our law. It is not unreasonable to assume that the settlor intended to give the trustee power to determine, from time to time, based upon existing law, where these stock dividends should go. The complexity of corporate accounting and the almost impossibility of applying the Pennsylvania rule to the stock dividends here is sufficient reason for construing the language of the trust so as to give the trustee authority to apply our present statutory rule. . . .

[Affirmed.]

Level of Skill Required   Some trustees lack special property management skills, while others are property management specialists. A trustor's intentions often can best be met by his naming two trustees. One trustee would be a friend or relative who is aware of personal relationships between the trustor and the beneficiaries and remaindermen, the other a professional person.

 An unskilled trustee must use the same degree of care and skill that a reasonably prudent person would use in managing his own property and affairs. A trustee who has special qualifications is held to the standard set by others having similar qualifications. For example, if the trust property consists of a stock portfolio, a professional stock advisor named as trustee would be held to a higher standard of skill in managing the portfolio than would a trustee not having those credentials.

Conflicts of Interest   The trustee's duty of good faith requires that he keep trust property and affairs separate from his other property and affairs. In particular, the trustee must avoid self-dealing, and the prudent trustee avoids even an appearance of self-dealing. For example, it is unwise for a trustee to purchase trust property for himself or another client, even if the price is fair. The trustee violates his trust if he purchases that property at less than a fair price.

38:5   Duration of Trust; Modification or Revocation

A trust continues to exist until its purpose has been accomplished or until the terminating event specified in the trust instrument occurs. Many trusts are structured so that they terminate after a set period of time or after the death of the beneficiaries.

A charitable trust can continue indefinitely, but a private trust cannot. Specifically, a private trust cannot violate what is known as the rule against perpetuities. In essence, the rule is that the trust must terminate—so that the trust property must pass to the remaindermen—not later than 21 years after the death of one or more designated people who were alive when the trust was first created.

EXAMPLE
Evert creates a trust in which her son, Connors, is the initial beneficiary. Connors is to receive the trust income until he dies, after which the trust property is to be divided among Connors' children. The share of any minor child will be held in the trust until that child reaches the age of 21. This arrangement will not violate the rule against perpetuities, even though it is not presently possible to know how many children Connors will have at the time of his death. However, the trust *would* violate the rule if Evert's great-grandchildren, rather than her grandchildren, were the remaindermen. This is so because property ultimately intended to pass to the child of a currently unborn grandchild could pass later than 21 years after the death of any currently living person.

There are limits on who can be the "designated persons" for purposes of the rule against perpetuities. These persons should be reasonably easy to identify. For practical purposes, the broadest designation a trustor can use is "all my heirs, currently living" or words to that effect.

Modification or Revocation   Once a trust has been created, the trustor can neither modify the trust terms nor revoke the trust unless he has reserved those rights in the trust agreement. The power to modify which, for practical purposes, includes the power to revoke, is attractive to the trustor because it allows him to reacquire all or part of the trust property whenever he wishes.

Not so attractive are the adverse tax consequences of these powers. If the trustor retains the power either to modify or to revoke the trust (1) the trustor will probably be taxed on trust income, thus negating possible income tax savings and (2) even if the power is not exercised, the mere existence of the power means that the trust property will probably be included in the trustor's estate for estate and inheritance tax purposes when he dies (see 38:14). These results can be prevented by making the trust irrevocable. However, many people lack enough financial security to dispose of their property irrevocably.

A partial solution to the above problem is use of what is known as a Clifford trust, which is a short-term irrevocable trust. A Clifford trust takes advantage of the fact that under federal law and the law of many states the trustor is not taxed on the income of an irrevocable trust having a term of over ten years even if, after the trust terminates, the trustor will reacquire the trust property as remainderman. The same tax advantage results if, instead of setting a period longer than ten years, the trust agreement provides that the trust will terminate on the death of the beneficiary.

EXAMPLE
Hunt, who is in a high income tax bracket, signs a trust agreement under which he transfers $50,000 to himself as trustee for the benefit of his elderly parents. Trust income is to be paid to Hunt's parents. On the second parent's death, the trust terminates and the trust property is transferred back to Hunt. For as long as the trust exists, Hunt will not be taxed on the trust income.

Wills

38:6   Introduction to Wills

A *will* is a statement, usually written (see 38:7) by which a person indicates how his property is to be disposed of after his death. Making a will is a voluntary act; nobody can be forced either to make one at all, or to make one providing for any particular scheme of distribution.

The person making a will is referred to as the testator (male) or testatrix (female). Persons to whom property is to pass under the will are the beneficiaries. The person who has the duty of actually making the distributions of property according to the will is commonly referred to as the *personal representative*.[1] A person who dies without having made a valid will is said to have died intestate. His property is distributed according to a fixed statutory scheme (see 38:11).

Purposes of Will   Although the primary purpose of a will is to allow the testator to declare the intended distribution of his property, a will can also serve other purposes. For example, the testator can use his will to create a testamentary trust if he does not wish property to pass to beneficiaries outright soon after his death. He can designate the personal representative of his choice and perhaps one or more alternate representatives as well. He can also indicate his desires as to who should be appointed guardian of his minor children.

Types of Gifts   A gift provided for in a will is referred to as a devise if the gift is real property. The terms "bequest" and "legacy" refer to gifts of personal property. The beneficiary receiving a devise is known as a devisee, while a legatee is one receiving a legacy or bequest.

A legacy can be specific, general, or residuary. A specific legacy is one of particular property that is identified in the will, such as "Aunt Matilda's ivory brooch." A general gift is one that is not described specifically; an example is "the sum of $10,000 to Hobbs, my faithful butler." A residuary gift is one of all or part of the residue of the estate, which is the property left over after all priority claims against the estate have been paid (see 38:12) and distribution of all specific and general gifts has been made.

 Every will should include a clause disposing of the residuary estate. Otherwise, the residuary property will pass as if the testator had died intestate, which can result in distributions that the testator did not intend.

---

[1]The traditional title of a personal representative designated by the testator in his will is executor (male) or executrix (female). A person appointed by the court, either because the testator failed to designate anyone or because of intestacy (see 38:11) was traditionally known as the administrator (male) or administratrix (female). "Personal representative" is commonly used today in place of the traditional terms.

Will Beneficiary's Death   If the beneficiary named in a will does not survive the testator, the gift can lapse (be canceled). Whether a particular gift will lapse depends in part on the testator's stated intent, if included in the will, and on the language used by the testator.

EXAMPLE
In his will, Jacob left his summer cottage to "my beloved daughter Melinda or her estate" and his vintage MG sports car to "my son Jack." The will contains no specific language as to the lapse of either gift. Jacob, Melinda, and Jack die together in a plane crash. According to the general rule, the gift to Jack has lapsed; the MG will be retained by Jacob's personal representative and added to the residuary estate. However, because of the words "or her estate," the summer cottage will pass to Melinda's estate.

The rule as to lapsed gifts has been modified in many states by what are known as antilapse statutes. The scope of these statutes varies, but in essence the statutes prevent lapses by specifying to whom property left to a deceased beneficiary is to go.

38:7   Requirements of Valid Will

The key requirements of a valid will are that (1) the testator have testamentary intent and testamentary capacity when he makes the will, (2) all required formalities be observed, and (3) the will not be made as a result of undue influence. These and related requirements concerning wills are governed by state statutes, and the statutes vary somewhat among the states. There is some uniformity in that over one-fourth of the states have enacted the Uniform Probate Code.

Testamentary Intent   Testamentary intent is simply the intent to provide for the distribution of one's property after death. It is normally stated in a will. Otherwise, it can sometimes be presumed, either from the language used in a document that is offered as a will or from the testator's acts or statements at the time he signed the document.

Testamentary Capacity   *Testamentary capacity* is the power to make a valid will, and not everybody has it. First, a person must be of at least the age specified by statute; a child lacks testamentary capacity. Second, the person must be "of sound mind," meaning that he must be mentally competent. While one's age is a fact that can be determined objectively, one's mental competence is not. A person can have testamentary capacity even though lacking sufficient mental competence to operate a business or even to sign a valid deed. Generally speaking, testamentary capacity exists if a testator is aware of the following basic facts:

• Nature and extent of his property
• Effect of making a will
• Instrument being signed is his will

- Manner of disposition provided for in will
- Natural objects of his bounty and their relationship to him

The term "natural objects of his bounty" refers to those persons who, because of their close relationship to the testator, would reasonably be expected to share in the estate.

The required level of mental competence must exist only at the time the testator signs the will. For example, a will is not invalidated if the testator becomes senile later on. Nor is a will invalid because the testator was mentally disordered at some time before (but not when) he signed the will.

Formal Requirements   Some states recognize a nuncupative (oral) will if (1) it is later reduced to writing by a witness and (2) the testator declared it during his last illness. Generally, however, a will must be in writing and signed by the testator.

Most wills are prepared by someone other than the testator, often an attorney. A will of this type, often referred to as a formal will, must always be signed by the testator or at his direction. Some states require that while signing, the testator declare aloud that he is signing his will. This act is known as publication of the will.

One or more attesting witnesses must also sign a formal will in most states. The number of witnesses required depends on state law, as does the exact procedure to be followed. For example, in some states the witnesses must observe the testator signing the will, while in other states the testator need only declare that the document is his will and that he has signed it. The main purpose for requiring attesting witnesses is that later, after the testator's death, the witnesses can state that the testator actually signed the will and that he did so voluntarily. The witnesses are also expected to satisfy themselves that the testator is mentally competent to make a will. They are not expected to read the will, and under the law of many states, they cannot be beneficiaries under the will.

The simplest type of written will is a holographic, or handwritten, will. It is recognized in most states and must be entirely handwritten and signed by the testator. A handwritten date is also required in some states. Any typing on the document invalidates the will, as does any writing by a person other than the testator. The advantage of a holographic will is that no witnesses are required. The requirement is dispensed with because forgery of an entire document is far more difficult than forgery of only a signature.

Undue Influence   The term *undue influence* refers to influence or pressure that substitutes the wishes of another for those of a testator regarding the disposition of his property. Undue influence invalidates a will. Requiring a testator to sign a will at gunpoint is an obvious example of undue influence, but usually the influence is more subtle. The following case indicates the required elements of undue influence and presents a classic example of facts leading to the presumption of its existence.

Re Estate of Nelson
274 NW2d 584
(South Dakota Supreme Court, 1978)

[Nelson died leaving as his only heirs a brother, a sister, and a nephew. In wills signed before October 1953, Nelson had left most of his estate to his three heirs. Through a series of three later wills, however, the provision made for the heirs was decreased, ever-increasing amounts of the estate going instead to Theodosen, Nelson's attorney. Nelson's final will, signed in 1956, made Theodosen the sole beneficiary, completely disinheriting the heirs. The probate court accepted the 1956 will as being valid, and the heirs appealed. In its opinion, the court uses the term "proponents." As is discussed in 38:10, the proponent is the person claiming that a given document is the testator's valid will.]

Zastrow, Justice.

*   *   *

Influence, to be undue, must be such as to destroy the free agency of the testator and substitute the will of the person exercising it for that of the testator. . . . Its essential elements are (1) susceptibility of the testator to undue influence; (2) opportunity for the exercise of undue influence; (3) disposition to exert undue influence; and (4) a result in the will showing the effect of such undue influence. . . .

Where a confidential relationship exists between a testator and a beneficiary, the beneficiary actively participates in the preparation and execution of the will, and the beneficiary unduly profits in the will, a presumption of undue influence arises. . . . The establishment of facts giving rise to the presumption also establishes a prima facie case which can sustain a finding of undue influence. . . . The presumption of undue influence remains even though the beneficiary introduces evidence rebutting the presumption. . . .

The proponents argue that the presumption of undue influence does not exist in the present case. We do not agree. Theodosen and Nelson were not social friends. Their only relationship was that of attorney–client. That relationship is a confidential relationship. . . . Theodosen admits that he drafted the January 24, 1956 will and was present when it was executed. This will devises and bequeaths all of Nelson's property "to my friend, John M. Theodosen . . . , and leaves "nothing to any of my relatives." [Personal instructions accompanying the will] give Theodosen the discretion to turn over the property he [receives under the will] to a charitable corporation. These facts give rise to a presumption of undue influence and, in this case, sustain a finding of undue influence.

The proponents argue, however, that the presumption was conclusively rebutted at trial. They claim that two of the essential elements of undue influence, susceptibility and opportunity, are lacking. Again we disagree.

Although Nelson was mentally astute until his death, Theodosen, by virtue of his legal training and confidential relationship, held the dominant position. He allowed Nelson to give him [broad discretionary powers as a trustee] in the first will. In 1955 after office hours on New Year's Eve, Theodosen drafted another will giving himself all the property. . . . Finally, in 1956, Nelson gave Theodosen all of his property . . . with personal instructions involving broad discretion. . . . Theodosen encouraged complete confidence in his legal advice by never refusing to write himself into the will and never insisting that Nelson seek independent legal advice if he (Nelson), in fact, did want to make such a disposition.

Added to this is the fact that pre-Theodosen wills provided for Nelson's sister, brother, and nephew. Within four years of Nelson's first dealing with Theodosen they were totally disinherited. While these relatives are not considered the natural objects of the testator's bounty, ... their gradual disinheritance by Nelson in wills drafted by Theodosen demands close judicial scrutiny. ... The pattern of the wills indicates an inability by Nelson to resist Theodosen's influence. ...

There are additional facts pointing to undue influence by Theodosen. Theodosen was the attorney for Nelson's sister Fern when each will was drafted and while Fern was disinherited. Theodosen was named executor in all the Nelson wills; a practice that was apparently standard in Theodosen wills for many other decedents. Theodosen was present at the execution of all the wills, and was alone in his office with Nelson before the witnesses arrived

to execute the final will. The will remained in Theodosen's safe and was under his control until admitted to probate.

While the presence of any of these facts standing alone may not have been enough to establish undue influence, taken together they clearly create a presumption of undue influence. The evidence presented was insufficient to rebut the presumption. No evidence was presented indicating that Theodosen took no unfair advantage of his dominant position. A prima facie case of undue influence was established and it required a finding of undue influence. ...

[Judgment reversed.]

38:8   Modification or Revocation of Will

Unlike most legal documents, a will can be modified or revoked at any time by the testator. There are also certain events, the occurrence of any of which can operate as an entire or partial revocation.

Testator's Voluntary Acts   Most wills include a clause to the effect that the testator is revoking all prior wills. Whether or not this clause is included, a new will, if valid, automatically revokes all prior wills made by the testator, at least to the extent that the prior wills are inconsistent with the new one. If a new will is invalid, however, the next preceding valid will remains in effect.

EXAMPLE
On June 15, 1975, Tom signed a will, and all required formalities were observed. Eight years later, in July of 1983, Tom directs his attorney to prepare a new will since he has decided to make major changes in the distribution of his estate. Tom signs the new will on July 29, 1983, but, due to an oversight, only one attesting witness signs the will, although state law requires two. Tom dies in September 1984. The 1983 will is invalid, and Tom's estate will pass under the 1975 will.

A testator can revoke a will by destroying or obliterating it. He can make a partial revocation by obliterating the provisions desired to be revoked. In many states, the testator can also revoke his will by using a separate instrument as to which the formalities required for the will itself are observed. For example, if three attesting witnesses are required to sign a formal will, three witnesses must also sign a separate document revoking that will.

The usual and safest method of modifying a will is use of a *codicil*. A codicil is a separate instrument, executed with the same formalities as the will, in which the testator states the desired changes. The changes can consist of additions, deletions, altered language, or any combination of these. The advantage of the codicil procedure is that it saves the time and expense required for preparation of a new will, although execution of a new will is recommended if changes are numerous or substantial. There is no limit on the number of codicils a testator can execute.

Revocation by Operation of Law   Certain events are so closely related to the likely intended disposition of a person's property that if one of them occurs, the disposition provided for in an existing will is automatically altered. Events of this type include the testator's marriage or divorce, and the birth of his child. The exact effect of such an event varies, depending on state law. The testator's marriage revokes his existing will in some states. In most states, the testator's divorce operates to delete any devise or legacy to the former wife. A child born after the execution of a will that omits any reference to that child is generally entitled to the share of the parent's estate that the child would take if the parent had died intestate, that is, without a valid will.

38:9   Disclaimers; Spouse's Right to Take Against Will

A beneficiary is not required to accept the property that would otherwise pass to him under a will. For example, the beneficiary might prefer that the subject of a specific legacy pass to the residuary beneficiary rather than to himself. A more common situation is that unnecessary adverse tax consequences would result from the beneficiary's acceptance of property as specified in the will.

EXAMPLE
Harry's will establishes a testamentary trust under which Sam, Harry's son, is the life beneficiary and Gloria, Sam's daughter, is the remainderman. If Sam disclaims (refuses to accept) his interest in the trust, the trust property will pass directly to Gloria and so will not be subject to estate tax as part of Sam's estate (see 38:14) when Sam dies.

State law and, in many instances, federal tax law govern both the timing and the manner of making an effective disclaimer of an interest under a will.

Election to Take Against Will   A testator can disinherit most of the natural objects of his bounty. He can leave nothing or only a token gift to children, parents, siblings, or other relatives. The only practical requirement in this regard is that the intent to disinherit a close relative should be stated in the will. Otherwise, the relative might be able to successfully claim that he was pretermitted, which means that he was unintentionally overlooked by the testator, in which event the relative will receive an intestate share of the estate.

The person one cannot effectively disinherit under the law of most states is one's spouse. Under a typical statute, the surviving spouse has the right to accept the provision made for her or him in the will (which might be no provision at all) or, instead, to elect to take a share of the estate, as prescribed in the statute. For example, the statute might give the survivor the right to one-third of the estate. An election to take against the will must be made within the time limits specified by state law.

 There can be legitimate estate planning reasons for disinheriting a spouse. Potential tax savings is the major one. A spouse who is disinherited as part of an estate plan should be aware of and in agreement with the plan and, presumably, can be relied on not to elect to take against the will.

Administration of Estates

38:10 Probate

Probate is the process by which a testator's will is offered to a court after his death to determine that the will is valid. The person offering the will, usually a close relative of the testator, and often the personal representative named in the will, is known as the proponent.

In most instances, having a will admitted to probate is a simple matter. If the attesting witnesses are available, they can testify that the testator signed the will voluntarily and that they believed him to be mentally competent at the time. If the witnesses are not available, the proponent must prove that their signatures on the will are valid. Some states recognize and have statutes providing for what are known as self-proving wills. The advantage of this kind of will is that if all the special statutory requirements are met, the probate court accepts the genuineness of the will without proof. The practical advantage of this procedure is that, at the time of probate, the proponent does not need to locate and produce the attesting witnesses or produce specimens of their signatures for purposes of comparison.

After a will has been admitted to probate, the court officially appoints the personal representative by issuing what are known as letters testamentary. Ordinarily, the person or entity designated by the testator is appointed. If no designation was made, the court usually appoints a close relative or friend of the testator.[2]

Will Contests A will contest arises when one or more persons, referred to as contestants, claim that a will being offered for probate is invalid. A person must, to be eligible as a contestant, have an interest in the estate, and the interest is usually one that will be adversely affected if the will in question is admitted to probate. Typically, the contestant is somebody who was either disinherited or treated less generously in the will than he had expected.

---

[2]Strictly speaking, the term "letters testamentary" refers only to the written authority given to an executor or executrix; the authority given to a personal representative who was not designated by the testator is known as "letters of administration."

The grounds for a will contest might be that the will was revoked, superseded by a later will, or the result of undue influence. Alternatively, a contestant might claim that the entire will is a forgery or that the testator lacked testamentary capacity when he executed it.

Once a will has been contested, the probate court holds a hearing, which is much like a regular trial. The purpose of the hearing is to determine whether the will being offered is valid or, if several wills have been offered, which (if any) is the valid one.

 A testator can attempt to discourage beneficiaries from contesting his will by including in the will what is known as an in terrorem clause. Such a clause, valid in most states, provides that a beneficiary who contests the will forfeits his interest as beneficiary.

38:11   Intestate Succession

When a person dies either without leaving a valid will or leaving a will that fails to dispose of all of his property, the property not passing under a will is distributed according to the state laws governing *intestate succession.* Every state has such laws, although they are not uniform. For example, if a person dies intestate leaving a surviving spouse and children, they will receive the entire estate under the law of most states, but the manner in which the estate is divided among them varies. Division of the estate between the surviving spouse and children, while seemingly fair on first impression, can cause hardship for the spouse.

EXAMPLE
Chris dies intestate, leaving his unskilled wife, Juliene, and two minor children. Under state law, Chris' modest estate is divided in half. One share goes to Juliene, while the other is divided between the children. Because of the children's minority, their shares are held for them in trust until they reach majority. Juliene must support herself and raise the children, but the half of Chris' estate being held for the children is unavailable to her. Juliene's interests—as well as Chris' probable intent had he considered the matter—would have been better served if Chris had left a will naming Juliene as the sole or principal beneficiary.

If a person dies intestate leaving a spouse but no children, the spouse will receive the entire estate. If there are children but no surviving spouse, the children receive the property. Intestacy laws also cover the situation in which one dies leaving neither a spouse nor any children. Relatives who might then receive all or part of a decedent's estate include parents, grandchildren, and siblings. If no surviving heir or ancestor of one who dies intestate can be found, the decedent's estate escheats (passes to) the state.

Appointment of Personal Representative   An intestate estate is administered by a personal representative appointed by the probate court. The appointee is apt to be the same person the court would appoint if the decedent had left a will.

38:12   Role of Personal Representative

The role of a personal representative is somewhat similar to that of a trustee in that a person acting in either capacity manages and is accountable for someone else's property. The major distinctions are that (1) a decedent's estate will be closed after all required administrative procedures have been carried out, while a trust usually exists for a longer time; and (2) the personal representative is often also a beneficiary, while a trustee usually has no personal interest in the trust property. Despite any interest he has in the estate, the representative owes to others interested in the estate a high level of honesty and good faith in carrying out his duties.

Steps in Administering Estate   The steps taken in administering a decedent's estate depend on state law, as does the required procedure for taking them. Important functions of the personal representative include the following:

- Inventorying estate, which might require appraisals
- Collecting debts owed to decedent
- Locating heirs and others interested in estate
- Notifying creditors, to allow submission of claims against estate
- Preparing and filing required tax returns (see 38:14)
- Settling claims against estate
- Distributing estate property in accordance with will or intestacy laws
- Accounting for all estate property

As the following case illustrates, even an apparently straightforward act such as inventorying an estate can lead to a dispute. Note that the case involves a type of trust, known as a totten trust, that has not been discussed in this chapter.

Re Estate of McFetridge
472 Pa 546, 372 A2d 823
(Pennsylvania Supreme Court, 1977)

[*During his lifetime, F.H. McFetridge, the decedent, opened two savings accounts "in trust for J.K. McFetridge," the appellee. After the decedent died, his personal representative, the appellant, included the two accounts in her inventory of the estate. She claimed that the decedent had orally revoked any trusts covering the accounts. The probate court ruled that because the personal representative was a legatee under the decedent's will, her interest was adverse to the decedent's interest, with the result*

that, under a state rule of evidence, she could not be permitted to testify about the revocation. The representative then appealed.]

Roberts, Justice.

*   *   *

Appellant contends her interest is not adverse to decedent's interest. We do not agree. . . . One who deposits money in a savings account in his own name in trust for another establishes a totten trust. . . . A totten trust allows the depositor to retain complete control of the fund during his life and yet secure to the beneficiary any balance standing in the account at the death of the depositor. . . . Prior to decedent's death, appellee had a mere expectancy in the savings accounts since decedent could revoke the totten trusts at will during his lifetime. . . . In the absence of revocation, however, appellee was entitled to the funds in the savings accounts upon decedent's death. . . .

Appellee established by competent evidence that the savings accounts were totten trusts. Totten trusts do not become part of a decedent's estate but rather pass directly to the named beneficiary. . . .

Appellant sought to establish by her testi-mony that decedent orally revoked the totten trusts. Such trusts may be revoked orally without resort to any formalities. . . . If appellant's testimony were admitted and found credible, the funds from the savings accounts would pass by way of the estate and appellant, as a beneficiary under the will, would benefit for the assets would augment her distributive share under the will. Thus, appellant's interest is adverse to decedent's interest insofar as the totten trusts are concerned. Her status as executrix of his estate does not establish that she represents decedent's interest regarding the totten trusts. . . .

[Judgment affirmed.]

A personal representative who fails to carry out his duties properly and consequently causes loss to the estate can be personally liable to the estate for that loss. Personal representatives usually post a bond, which is paid for by the estate, to cover this potential liability.

After all required actions have been taken, the personal representative petitions the court to be discharged. When the petition is granted, the representative is free of further duties concerning the estate, and the estate is closed.

Distributions to Beneficiaries   A person's being named as a will beneficiary does not necessarily mean that he will receive any part of the estate. One reason is that a number of other claims must be paid out of the estate before anything can be distributed to beneficiaries. Included among these priority claims are the following, commonly payable in the order listed:

- Funeral expenses
- Administration expenses (legal expenses; compensation of personal representative and attorney)
- Family allowance (amount paid under state law to surviving spouse or for benefit of children for purchasing necessities during period of administration)
- Amounts owed to federal government, such as income and estate taxes
- Medical expenses for decedent's last illness
- Amounts owed to state and local governments
- Other valid debts of decedent

The priority claims can consume the entire estate, leaving nothing for *any* beneficiaries.

Another situation that prevents a beneficiary from receiving property in accordance with the terms of a will is what is known as ademption of the gift. Ademption occurs under either of two general circumstances. The first is that the specific property described in the will is not part of the estate. The property might never have existed at all or it might have been consumed, lost, destroyed, or transferred earlier.

The second circumstance that can give rise to an ademption is an earlier gift by the testator to the beneficiary. Assume, for example, that in 1981 Walt signs a will leaving $10,000 to his niece, Pat; in 1982 Walt gives Pat $5,000; and in 1983 Walt dies. Should Pat receive $10,000 from Walt's estate? Or should the 1982 payment be treated as a partial satisfaction of the gift provided for in the will? The answer generally depends on the testator's intent, which is a question of fact that the probate court must decide.

A beneficiary might also lose his share of an estate because of abatement. A legacy can abate (be eliminated) when, after the priority claims have been paid, there is sufficient property left in the estate to cover only some of the devises and legacies. The testator's expressed intent governs as to which gifts abate first. If the testator failed to express any intent about the matter, the general rule is that residuary gifts abate first, followed by general gifts. If some but not all gifts of a given class can be made, the beneficiaries of that class take on a pro rata basis.

EXAMPLE
Horace's will provides for the following gifts: his house and its furnishings to Glenda, his wife; $20,000 to his son, Jack; $10,000 to his daughter, Jill; and the residue of his estate to a charitable organization. After all priority claims have been paid, Horace's estate consists of the house, furnishings, and $6,000. Glenda will receive the house and furnishings; Jack $4,000; Jill $2,000; and the charity will receive nothing.

38:13   Avoiding Probate

The term "avoidance of probate" refers to means by which a property owner can transfer his property by means other than his will. It does not involve entire elimination of the probate procedure. If a testator leaves a will, that will must go through probate, although some states provide for short, simple probate procedures for certain small estates. What a testator can do, however, is arrange his affairs so that most of his estate passes independent of the will.

Purposes   There are several reasons why a person might want to avoid probate. Cost is one factor. The fees payable to such people as the personal representative and the attorney often depend on the size of the estate. Another factor is privacy. Probate is a public proceeding, and a person might wish to avoid public disclosure of the size or nature of his estate, or of the manner in which he chose to distribute it.

Methods   Effective methods of avoiding probate include a testator's use of gifts, trusts, life insurance, and joint tenancy. The estate plan for a given estate often contemplates the use of more than one of these methods.

Since a gift is absolute, property given away during the testator's lifetime cannot pass under the testator's will. The same is true as to any property transferred to a living trust that has not been revoked by the time the testator dies. If a testator names his estate as the beneficiary of his life insurance policy, the insurance proceeds will be distributed according to the will. If, however, the beneficiary is a close relative, such as the testator's spouse or child, the proceeds will pass directly to the beneficiary. The distinctive feature of joint tenancy, which is a type of co-ownership of property, is that when one joint tenant dies, title to his interest in the property passes automatically to the surviving joint tenant or tenants.

38:14   Federal and State Taxation

The period required for the administration of a decedent's estate can be lengthy, especially for a large estate. During this time the estate can earn income, which is taxable. For example, the estate might receive interest on certificates of deposit, dividends on stock, or rental income. The estate is a separate entity for federal and state income tax purposes, and special rules govern its income tax liability. The personal representative is responsible for preparing and filing needed tax returns and paying any tax owed. The representative will usually also have to prepare and file final personal income tax returns on behalf of the decedent.

Federal Estate Tax   Depending on its size, an estate might be subject to a federal estate tax. Any tax due is paid out of the estate, before distributions to beneficiaries are made. The personal representative is responsible for preparing and filing the estate tax return and actually paying the tax.

Federal tax used to be payable on even relatively small estates, but changes in the tax laws have tended to eliminate the estate tax as a significant factor in estate planning for many people. Estate planning for larger estates considers the various deductions available under federal law. The marital deduction is the most significant one for many people. A person's entire estate can pass free of estate tax if the estate is left to the surviving spouse. Bear in mind, however, that the surviving spouse's estate, as increased by any amount left to the survivor by the spouse who died, will be taxed when the survivor dies.

 Regardless of the available credits and deductions, if the bulk of an estate consists of a business, the business might have to be sold to generate enough money to pay the federal estate tax unless adequate estate planning has been done to provide another source of the needed money.

State Estate and Inheritance Taxes   Most states also tax decedents' estates, either directly or indirectly, and these taxes are independent of and in addition to the federal estate tax. Because states usually allow fewer and smaller exemptions and deductions from the tax than are available under federal law, the state tax bill is often higher than the federal bill, even though the tax rate is lower.

The majority of states provide for an inheritance tax. The tax is imposed on and paid by each beneficiary after he has received estate property. The amount of tax due depends on both the size of the gift and the beneficiary's relationship to the decedent. For example, on a gift of a given amount or value, the surviving spouse will pay less tax than a sibling of the decedent, and the sibling will pay less than a beneficiary not related to the decedent. Some states impose an estate tax instead of inheritance taxes. Like the federal estate tax, a state estate tax is paid by the personal representative before he distributes any of the estate property to the beneficiaries.

Key Concepts and Terms

- Estate planning helps a person to acquire an estate and dispose of it as he wishes, while keeping loss through taxes to a minimum.
- A trust is a basic estate planning device. Different goals can be achieved by using different types of trusts.
- A living trust is normally created by the trustor's execution of a trust agreement, while the terms of a testamentary trust are included in the trustor's will.
- A trustor is the person who establishes a trust. A trustee is the person who holds the legal title to trust property and is responsible for its management. The beneficiary is the equitable owner of the property and ordinarily receives the income generated by it.
- A trustor can reserve the right to modify or revoke a trust.
- The duration of a private trust, even if irrevocable, is limited by the rule against perpetuities.
- A will is a person's declaration, usually written, of how he wants his estate to be distributed after his death.
- A will is invalid if (1) the testator lacked testamentry capacity, (2) the will was the result of undue influence, or (3) required formalities were not observed.
- A testator has the right to revoke or modify his will at any time, but he can do so only in the manner permitted by law.
- A beneficiary can disclaim his interest under a will, and a testator's surviving spouse can elect to take against the will.
- A decedent's will is admitted to probate after the probate court finds that the will is valid. A will contest occurs if one or more people interested in the estate challenge the validity of a will being offered for probate.
- If a person dies intestate, his estate is distributed according to a state statutory scheme.
- The personal representative of a decedent's estate has the duty of administering the estate in the manner provided by law and in the decedent's will.
- A person can avoid having his property pass through probate by careful use of trusts, gifts, life insurance, and joint tenancy.
- A decedent's estate is taxed on its income. The federal government also imposes

a tax on the estate itself, while most states tax beneficiaries after they have received distributions from an estate.

- Codicil
- Estate Planning
- Intestate Succession
- Living Trust
- Personal Representative
- Probate

- Testamentary Capacity
- Testamentary Trust
- Trust
- Trustee
- Undue Influence
- Will

Questions and Case Problems

1. What is estate planning? Discuss its different goals and how it seeks to achieve them.

2. Discuss the characteristics that distinguish a trust from other devices by which property can be disposed of.

3. Discuss reasons why it is advisable for a person who has signed a will to review that will periodically.

4. Why might a person want to avoid having her property pass under her will or according to the intestate succession laws, and how can this goal be achieved? If a decedent's property does not pass through probate, is that property also ignored for federal estate tax purposes? Explain.

5. Jones is a widower who has two adult children, Allen and Robert. He decides to write his own will, and in the will he wants to disinherit Allen, leave half of his estate to Robert, and leave the other half of his estate to a charity. Jones begins typing a document reflecting these wishes, but the typewriter jams after he has typed the first paragraph, and he writes out the rest of it by hand. He then signs and dates the document. Later that day Jones has both Allen and Robert sign the document as attesting witnesses, but he neglects to inform either son that the document is his will. Six months later Jones dies, and the document is discovered. Allen, Robert, and the charity each claim one half of Jones' estate. How should the estate be divided, and why? Include in the answer any assumptions you have made about the governing state law.

6. The trust property held by a trustee includes 100 shares of Intex Corporation. The trust agreement requires the trustee to distribute trust income each year to the beneficiaries, and it gives the trustee full discretion in allocating receipts and expenses between principal and income. In 1983 Intex declares a two-for-one stock split, with the result that the trustee receives an additional 100 shares of Intex stock. The trustee allocates the new shares to principal, and one of the beneficiaries petitions the court for relief. He argues that the shares should be allocated to income and distributed to him and the other beneficiaries. Should the court interfere with the trustee's action? Why or why not? Would your answer be different if the trust agreement were silent on the matter of allocation? Why?

7. Wilma created a living trust under which she was to receive all trust income until she died. The trustee, a bank, was also authorized to "invade the principal" (make distributions to Wilma out of the trust principal) at the bank's discretion. On Wilma's death, trust income and, at the trustee's discretion, principal are to be paid to Stanley, Wilma's son. On Stanley's death, the trust is to terminate, and the trust

property is to be distributed in equal shares to those of Wilma's eight nieces and nephews listed on a separate schedule to be given to the trustee. Two years after creating the trust Wilma signed a will in which general legacies were made to one niece and one nephew, the others not being mentioned, and Stanley was named as the residuary legatee. Wilma died recently, and the trustee never received the separate schedule indicating the trust remaindermen. The trustee now petitions the court for instructions as to the proper interpretation of the trust agreement. Specifically, the trustee wants to know to whom it will be transferring the trust property after Stanley's death. (a) Why would the trustee seek resolution of this question now, even though the trust will not terminate until the unknown future date of Stanley's death? (b) How should the court answer the trustee's question? Why?

8. Your great-aunt Emily was 94 when she signed her first and last will two years ago. At the time, Emily lived in a rest home and had a nurse to assist her in most of her activities. You visited Emily regularly and talked with her. Usually she recognized you and could carry on a rational conversation, but at times you had to identify yourself, and conversation on those days was difficult. From time to time Emily got her relatives' names mixed up, and she often seemed to be able to recall early events in her life with greater clarity than later ones. Emily died recently, and you discover that in the will she named you as her personal representative and principal beneficiary. Emily's only other heirs are Enid, her niece, and Joe, her nephew. Both Enid and Joe are to receive small bequests under the will, and neither is happy about it. Nevertheless, you offer the will for probate, and Enid and Joe promptly contest it. (a) What is the likely basis of Enid and Joe's claim? (b) What do Enid and Joe stand to gain by contesting the will? (c) As the proponent, what facts do you want to have brought out at the probate hearing? Why? (d) Do Enid and Joe have anything to lose by contesting the will? Explain.

9. Lisa, a widow, has a son, Ralph, and a daughter, Nancy, but she sees little of them since they do not live nearby. Lisa has no other close relatives. For a number of years Lisa has entrusted the management of her property to Maurice, her attorney and advisor. Maurice suggests that Lisa should have a will. After considering the matter, Lisa decides to leave most of her estate to Nancy, with small bequests to Ralph and Maurice. Maurice, who is to be Lisa's personal representative, attempts to convince Lisa that Nancy is unworthy of her mother's bounty because of her immoral lifestyle and radical political views, but Lisa holds firm. She instructs Maurice to draft a will for her signature. Maurice does so, but he intentionally reverses the status of Ralph and Nancy so that Ralph is named as the principal beneficiary. Lisa signs the typed will without reading it, and all required formalities are observed. Soon afterward Lisa dies. How should Lisa's estate be distributed? Why? How, if at all, would your answer differ if Lisa had read the will before signing it?

10. Garfield signed a formal will in which he named his cousin, Odie, the principal beneficiary, and in which he specifically disinherited his son, Nermal. Later, Garfield had a change of heart and decided to substitute Jon, his friend and protege, as the principal beneficiary. Garfield handwrote and signed a codicil making the change, and he sent the document to his attorney with instructions to have it typed. Two days later, while on his way to the attorney's office to sign the typed codicil, Garfield was run over by a truck and killed. Odie and Nermal are Garfield's only surviving relatives. Who, among Odie, Jon, and Nermal, will receive all or the bulk of Garfield's estate? Why?

PART EIGHT

Insurance

Introductory Comments

Insurance is one of the largest industries in the United States. Well over $100 billion was spent in this country in the past year alone on all forms of insurance to protect businesses and individuals alike from the various risks of loss.

The business of insurance is conducted by large corporations operating in this country on a nationwide basis. Despite the national scope and range of the insurance industry, the regulation of this industry has been left largely to the states. The federal government does regulate special areas of insurance, such as securities issued by insurance companies, but it is prevented by law from intervening in the industry's purely intrastate functions. The states retain the power to charter insurance companies, oversee rates, fix the terms of insurance policies, regulate agents and brokers, and monitor a host of other activities undertaken by the insurance industry.

Although the concept of insurance evolved to protect commercial and individual endeavors and could therefore be written in any form, most insurance is now issued in standard form policies written by the insurance companies themselves. These policies are drafted by experts experienced in providing an apparently wide range of coverage tempered by countless exclusions. It is no accident, therefore, that the complex language of most insurance policies is largely incomprehensible to the typical policyholder. A facetious remark about insurance policies that "the front page giveth but the back page taketh away" is not totally inaccurate or inappropriate.

For most individuals insurance represents, after the purchase of a home, perhaps the next largest investment or expenditure that is made during their lifetime. For most businesses, insurance is a key item that must be carefully planned to protect the owners and their assets from risk of loss or liability. For these reasons, insurance is one of the few subject areas that must be discussed and analyzed as a separate unit within business law as a whole.

Chapters 39 and 40 introduce the law of insurance. Chapter 39 focuses on the concept of insurance, the types of risks for which insurance can be purchased, the nature of the insurance business, and how the industry is regulated. In Chapter 40, the various types of commercial, medical, liability, and homeowners' policies are discussed and analyzed. These two chapters provide a solid foundation on which the prudent and well-informed businessperson can base decisions to purchase business and personal insurance.

39 Introduction to the Law of Insurance

39:1 Nature of Insurance

In essence, insurance is an agreement by which one party (the insurer) for a consideration (the premium) promises to pay money to another (the insured or the beneficiary) if a specified event takes place. The event is usually one that causes either (1) the death or injury of a person or (2) the damage, loss, or destruction of property. The written instrument that sets forth the contract of insurance is the policy. As a rule, insurance companies use a standard form of insurance policy for the various types of insurance they offer. Amendments, additions, or deletions to the standard policy are called endorsements or *riders*. In the case of conflicting provisions, an endorsement or rider prevails over a contrary policy.

An insurance contract can be entered into only by someone capable of contracting under insurance law. In the absence of a statute to the contrary, insurance contracts are like other contracts in regard to the capacity of the parties to the contract. Therefore, any individual adult or association of individual adults can make a contract for insurance on property. Similarly, any business has the power to insure the lives of its key employees or officers whose duties and responsibilities are such that a financial loss to the business would result from their death.

Even if a person who wants insurance is insurable or otherwise eligible for insurance, the insurer retains the power to choose with whom it will do business. Any insurance company can decline to issue or renew a policy for any reason it deems proper. However, many states have enacted antidiscrimination statutes that prevent insurers from refusing to issue or renew policies on the basis of an applicant's race, national origin, occupation, age, residence, or similar characteristics. Some statutes also prohibit the cancellation of insurance policies except for nonpayment of premiums or, in regard to automobile insurance, for the loss of a driver's license or vehicle registration.

 An insured can lose the right to collect insurance benefits from an insurance company if he fails to meet his obligations under the insurance policy. These obligations include providing adequate information about the insured person or thing, paying premiums on time, promptly notifying the insurance company about losses covered by the insurance, and cooperating with the insurance agent when a claim is made.

39:2 Kinds of Insurance

It is not unusual for a business to have several insurance policies at the same time to protect against the common risks associated with the operation of the business. There are so many kinds of insurance available today that protection can be bought against almost any conceivable risk or loss. Because risks and losses are always present in the conduct of business or during the course of an individual's lifetime, insurance has become a major planning and preventive tool. It can maintain the integrity or continuity of a business or the assets of an individual when loss occurs.

The following hypothetical example illustrates some common hazards in operating a business and the kinds of risks for which insurance can be purchased.

EXAMPLE

BB&S, Inc. is a corporation that manufactures electronic games in California. Bill and Jill Brooks and Ken Smith own all the corporation's stock, in equal shares. Most of the electronic components used by BB&S in the manufacture of its games are made out of state or are imported from abroad. The company employs 50 workers in its plant, which was recently expanded and remodeled. During the past year, the company was plagued by a run of bad luck that would have driven ordinary mortals out of business:

1. Components imported from abroad were lost at sea, while another shipment of components from New York was destroyed when the plane in which they were being transported crashed.

2. It was discovered that the title to the property purchased by BB&S for its plant expansion was defective. The company was forced to pay an additional sum to perfect its title.

3. A fire at the BB&S plant caused the company to shut down operations for two weeks. As a result, the company suffered considerable loss of profits.

4. Vandals broke into the BB&S warehouse and stole 25 electronic games and caused $50,000 worth of damage to the building itself.

5. A visitor to the plant slipped on a silicon chip, cracked her head, and broke both arms and a leg. She required immediate hospitalization and emergency surgery.

6. The bookkeeper employed by BB&S embezzled $10,000 to pay gambling debts.

7. The driver of a BB&S delivery truck negligently struck another vehicle, causing injuries to that vehicle's driver. The BB&S truck, while being driven back to the plant, was hit by an uninsured motorist.

8. Ken Smith became very apprehensive about illness after his brother died, although a physical examination showed that Ken was in perfect health. In

turn, Bill and Jill became concerned that they would have no money to purchase Ken's interest in the company should he suddenly die.

9. Three employees of BB&S were injured on the job due to unrelated work-site hazards.

10. All 50 employees went out on strike for two weeks demanding that BB&S improve safety conditions at the plant.

11. A purchaser of a BB&S game suffered severe burns when he tried to extinguish a fire that broke out in the game due to a short circuit.

12. Bill Brooks suffered a concussion after being hit with a baseball bat during a practice session of the company's softball team.

All of the business activities, risks, or losses included in the above example can be covered by insurance. Of course, there are many other kinds of insurance regularly used by both businesses and individuals that are designed to cover peculiar needs or activities. Other less common forms of insurance can also be obtained to meet unusual or uncommon risks. Clearly, insurance coverage is limited only by the ingenuity or creativity of the potential insureds and by the willingness of an insurer to accept the risks.

The most common and widely used kinds of insurance are life, health, automobile, and property insurance. These types are discussed briefly below.

Life Insurance   Life insurance is essentially a contract to pay a specified sum, in a lump sum or in installments, either to the person named as the *beneficiary* or to the estate of the insured when the insured dies. Among the kinds of life insurance available are (1) ordinary life, (2) limited-payment life, and (3) term life. Under an *ordinary,* or *straight, life insurance policy,* the insured must pay premiums throughout his life. A limited payment policy requires that premiums be paid during a limited period, such as 10, 15, or 20 years, or until the death of the insured, whichever occurs first. *Term insurance* continues only for a stated period, usually five years. Under level term policies, the benefits payable on the insured's death remain the same—or level—during the term of the policy. The policy can be renewed for additional periods up to age 65, at a higher premium with each renewal since the risk of death increases with the age of the insured. Under decreasing or reducing term policies, the benefits payable gradually decline during the term of the policy. For example, the face value of a policy purchased by a 20-year-old person would decrease throughout his life to zero at age 65. The annual premiums would remain constant because the increased risk of death as the insured ages is offset by the decline in face value of the insurance.

One type of decreasing term insurance is what is known as *credit life insurance.* This is carried by a debtor on his life in connection with a specific credit transaction, and the creditor is named as the beneficiary. The debtor pays the premium, as part of his cost of obtaining the credit. Since the purpose of credit life insurance is to make sure that the creditor is paid, the amount of insurance starts out as the amount of the debt and is reduced as the debt is paid off in installments.

Many life insurance policies include investment features in addition to providing for the payment of benefits when the insured dies. For example, an ordinary life insurance policy with a savings feature allows an insured to borrow against his policy or surrender it for a cash payment. The policy's cash surrender value and the amount that can be borrowed against the policy depend on the total amount of the premium payments that have been made. Endowment policies are another form of investment through insurance. Under this type of policy an insurer pays the insured a fixed sum as guaranteed income when he attains a specified age. If the insured dies before the termination of the endowment period, payments are made to the beneficiaries.

Accident and Health Insurance   Accident insurance covers accidental injury or death from specified perils and under stated conditions. Health, medical, and hospitalization insurance is designed to pay at least part of an insured's expenses that arise from sickness, disability, and hospitalization.

Property Insurance   *Property insurance* covers a great variety of risks. The most common is fire. Fire insurance is a contract by which the insurer agrees to pay the insured a specified amount for loss of or damage to designated property caused by fire. It may include other kinds of insurance as well. Most states have what is known as the standard fire policy, which is a standard contract of insurance prescribed by statute. Frequently, fire insurance policies also insure against damage from (1) wind, hail, and other forces of nature; (2) smoke; and (3) faulty plumbing or plumbing fixtures.

Another kind of property insurance is burglary, robbery, and malicious mischief insurance. It is designed to protect the insured from loss that is due to those crimes.

Title insurance covers the risk or loss due to a defect in the title to property (see Chapter 34).

 A businessperson can protect his business by carrying business interruption insurance and strike or labor dispute insurance to insure against losses that arise from these events. He can also obtain fidelity insurance to insure against losses due to embezzlement or other dishonest acts by employees.

Liability Insurance   Liability insurance is designed to indemnify the insured against liability, loss, or damage on account of the specific acts, conduct, or conditions specified in the policy. For example, products liability insurance protects the producer or manufacturer of goods against losses that result from damages claims filed by users of the goods. The hazards covered by such a policy are usually described as accidents arising out of the handling or use of goods or products manufactured, sold, or distributed by the insured.

Several distinct classes of risks are frequently covered in the same policy. For example, the typical automobile insurance policy covers not only the car but also liability to third persons in connection with the use of the car. Thus, an automobile insurance policy might include (1) "bodily injury" (personal injury) and property damage liability insurance, which protects against personal injuries or property damage sustained by third persons; (2) collision insurance, which protects against damage to the insured vehicle regardless of fault; (3) "comprehensive insurance," which protects the insured from losses due to theft of or certain damage to the vehicle; and (4) uninsured motorist protection, which protects the insured against bodily injuries caused by an uninsured or hit-and-run driver. Automobile insurance can also include medical payments coverage, which provides for accident-related medical and hospital expenses of the insured or any occupant of his car.

No-fault Insurance   *No-fault insurance*, although only recently instituted for automobiles, is not a recent concept. No-fault insurance has been adopted by every state, as well as by the federal government. It takes the form of workers' compensation, unemployment insurance, and Social Security.[1] In the last ten years, various no-fault automobile insurance systems have been adopted by approximately 25 states. Under these plans, payments for automobile accident losses are made to injured parties without a determination of fault. Although details of no-fault insurance vary considerably from state to state, the fundamental concept is that an injured person can recover at least some compensation directly from his own insurance company (or from the government, under some plans), instead of having to wait for a determination of fault or legal responsibility for an accident and then collect accordingly. Most plans eliminate or curtail the payment of benefits for general damages such as pain and suffering. However, most no-fault plans *do* retain conventional tort liability as the basis for compensation in cases of serious injury.

Types of Insurance Policies   A person can obtain a specific type of policy once he has decided on the kind of insurance he needs. Available policies can be classified as being (1) open, (2) valued, (3) commercial block, (4) running, (5) floater, and (6) master.

An open, or unvalued, insurance policy sets forth only a description of the property covered under the policy. The insurer is obligated to pay the actual value of the property up to but not exceeding the stated policy limits.

EXAMPLE
A farmer buys a cotton crop insurance policy. The policy does not fix a value on the insured crop but only provides that (1) the insurer's liability shall not exceed the amount set out in the application for insurance and (2) the amount of insurance depends on the average price per unit actually received for cotton harvested or on the average daily cotton exchange quotations for a specified six-month period. This insurance policy, which does not carry a specific value, is an open policy.

In contrast, a valued policy is one in which the parties have agreed on the value of the insured property in the event of future loss, or the value is fixed by state statute.

A *commercial block policy* insures against several basic but different types of risk as to commercial property. These risks include fire, theft, burglary, water damage, and liability.

A running policy provides continuous or successive insurance that will vary

---

[1]Workers' compensation is discussed in Chapter 51.

from time to time as to the amount of coverage. This type of policy is used to cover an insured's inventory that fluctuates in quantity (and hence value) from day to day. Often associated with a running policy is a floater policy. The distinctive feature of a floater policy is that the insured property is covered as it is moved from one place to another. Thus, for example, a merchant's running policy would cover inventory while it is in the store. However, the merchant might have to obtain a floater policy to cover specific inventory items that are moved elsewhere, as would occur when customers are allowed to remove items from the store to try them out before buying them.

Often, an insured's business or profession requires several policies of insurance of the same type, covering different risks. In such situations a master policy is used. Master policies contain certain general terms, which are incorporated by reference in certificates of insurance issued later. Using a master policy avoids the specific inclusion of detailed policy provisions and general terms in each subsequently issued certificate.

A common example of the use of a master policy is *group insurance,* which is the coverage of a number of individuals by a single policy. Group policies for life or medical insurance are a common fringe benefit of most businesses. The premiums may be paid in whole or in part by the employer. In group insurance the general practice is to issue individual certificates based on a master policy. The master policy itself insures nothing; only the combined terms of the master policy and the certificate of insurance constitute the insurance contract.

The law applicable to group insurance differs from that governing individual policies. For example, the group insurer has no duty to check individually the insurability of each person in a group policy. An insured is bound by the provisions stated in the master policy and not necessarily in the certificate of insurance. Ordinarily, group life insurance is written as term insurance and the premiums are adjusted annually based on each year's experience. Group policies usually limit the coverage of an employee to the time or duration of employment.

 Employees are often concerned about continuing group coverage after they terminate their employment. Most group policies provide conversion to individual coverage. It is important that both the employer and the departing employee know how and when conversion can be made. An employer should also ascertain the deadline for a departing employee to apply for conversion. An employer who fails to give timely and accurate information on how and when to take advantage of a conversion privilege can be liable for lost benefits.

Reinsurance   To protect against huge potential losses under existing insurance policies, most insurers take out what is in effect insurance on their own insurance. This system is known as *reinsurance.* It is a common practice in the insurance industry. Through reinsurance, insurers contract with other companies (reinsurers) for indemnification for all or part of their potential policy losses which might have to be paid under original insurance contracts. In this manner, insurance companies reduce their potential liabilities and apportion risks of loss.

As with other types of insurance, the liability of the reinsurer depends on the terms of the reinsurance contract. In most states, reinsurance contracts and the business of reinsurance are strictly regulated by law. Normally, a reinsurance policy covers the same time period as the original insurance policy that it reinsures. Because reinsurance is primarily an indemnity system, a reinsurer is not liable unless the insurer actually pays an insured's claim.

Reciprocal Insurance   *Reciprocal insurance* is a system in which individuals, partnerships, or corporations, none of which is an insurance company, agree to indemnify each other against certain kinds of losses. The participants, who are referred to as reciprocal insurers, all contribute money to a fund that is maintained for paying claims. Each reciprocal insurer thus becomes both an insurer and an insured at the same time. The practice of creating reciprocal insurance arrangements is limited mostly to businesses that would otherwise have to pay prohibitively large premiums for needed insurance. By use of reciprocal insurance, the businesses can obtain the insurance coverage they need. If there is money left in the fund after the expiration of the indemnity period agreed on, the businesses also share in the distribution of the fund.

39:3   Insurance Companies

In practically all states, statutes have been enacted which, while varying widely in their terms and provisions, provide elaborate systems for the formation and regulation of insurance companies. An insurance company has only the powers that are conferred by one of these statutes. The corporate powers of a life insurance company organized under the laws of one state, for example, cannot be enlarged by the laws of any other state in which the company may be permitted to do business.

A company organized to transact insurance can carry out its activities in the usual and necessary manner as governed by its charter or articles of incorporation (see Chapter 42). For example, an insurance company that is chartered to insure all kinds of property against fire or other casualty can insure against loss by burglary. However, it cannot engage in a transaction or business that is not expressly permitted by its charter and not reasonably incidental to the purposes for which it is organized.

Types of Insurance Companies   In general, there are three kinds of insurance companies: stock, mutual, and mixed. A stock insurance company is a corporation in which the initial capital investment is made by subscribers to the stock. The business is then conducted by a board of directors elected by its stockholders, and the distribution of earnings or profits as between stockholders and policyholders is determined by the board of directors. A stock insurance company has also been tersely defined as one in which stockholders contribute all the capital, pay all the losses, and take all the profits!

A mutual insurance company is a cooperative enterprise whose members (the policyholders) maintain a dual relationship with the company: They are both insurers and insureds. Not only do they contribute to the payment of losses but they are also entitled to receive payment in case of death or other loss and to share in the company's profits. By a system of premiums or assessments, the members contribute to a fund from which losses and liabilities are paid. After these payments are made, any profits from this fund are divided among the members in proportion to their interest.

Policyholders in mutual companies are not generally regarded as stockholders of such companies. Thus, an important difference between stock companies and mutual insurance companies is that stockholders of stock companies have the legal right to elect directors and officers while members of a mutual company do not have that right.

Mixed companies, as the term implies, possess the characteristics of both of the other two types.

There are other types of insurance organizations, more limited in scope, that must be mentioned. These are rating bureaus and advisory organizations. Their functions are distinct from those of regular insurance companies, and they are generally regulated by state statutory provisions applicable exclusively to them. A rating organization exists for the purpose of establishing rates, rating plans, or rating systems. These rates, plans, or systems are then used by insurance companies in establishing the premiums they will charge. An advisory organization prepares forms, makes underwriting rules, or collects and furnishes loss and other statistical information to insurers or rating organizations. An advisory organization acts only in an advisory capacity; it does not establish rates. An insurer can be a member of a rating or an advisory organization and participate in its management. It can also subscribe to the services of rating or advisory organizations of which it is not a member.

Lloyd's of London   At this point it is appropriate to discuss the well-known *Lloyd's of London*, which differs from other insurance companies in a fundamental way. Lloyd's is the oldest insurance organization in existence. The key word here is "organization," for Lloyd's is not a single company. Instead, insurance is written on all types of risks—except ordinary life insurance—by a syndicate or group of individuals, each of whom is personally liable to the extent of the risk assumed. The total membership of Lloyd's exceeds 18,000 wealthy private individuals from 60 countries organized into 436 syndicates. The syndicates range in size from a few individuals to several hundred. Business is offered to these syndicates by approximately 265 brokerage firms that scout around the world for insurance opportunities. For example, assume that an oil company wants to insure its new multimillion-dollar oil tanker. The risk of loss is so great that no single insurer will assume the whole risk. Through Lloyd's, the tanker can be insured by members of a syndicate, and each member becomes potentially liable only for a portion of the tanker's value if it is lost.

39:4   Insurance Agents and Brokers

The business of buying and selling insurance is conducted primarily by insurance agents, brokers, and other persons who act as representatives of buyers or sellers.

An *insurance agent* is a person authorized to represent an insurer in dealing with third persons in matters relating to insurance. The agent owes a permanent allegiance to and sustains a continuing relationship with the insurance company he represents. There are various kinds of insurance agents; frequently, the term is defined by state statute.

In contrast, an *insurance broker* is one who acts as a middleman between the insured and the insurer. The broker is not employed by a specific company. Instead, he holds himself out for hire to the public and solicits insurance business from the public.

The principles of the law of agency apply to the relationship between insurance companies and their agents.[2] An insurance company, like any other principal, is liable for the acts of its agents done within the scope of their authority.

Duty to Follow Instructions in Good Faith   Both an insurance agent and an insurance broker must act in good faith. They must confine their acts to the actual authority granted to them. For example, the insurance agent must obey his company's instructions and use due care and reasonable diligence in transacting the business entrusted to him. If an agent or broker departs from instructions or breaches the duties entrusted to him, he can be liable for losses sustained. Thus, if an insurance company, which is entitled under the terms of a policy to cancel or reduce a risk, directs its agent to cancel the policy but the agent fails to do so, the agent can be liable to the insurer for any amount that the insurer later has to pay under the policy.

The following case illustrates the general obligations of an insurance broker and the circumstances under which a broker or an insurance company can be held liable to an insured for the broker's acts that are beyond the scope of his authority. The same principles apply to agents.

Lewis
v
Michigan Millers Mut. Ins. Co.
154 Conn 660, 228 A2d 803
(Connecticut Supreme Court, 1967)

[Lewis, the plaintiff, obtained from Michigan Millers Mutual Insurance Company, the defendant, a liability insurance policy covering premises Lewis owned on Dixwell Avenue in New Haven. After the policy had been issued, Lewis' insurance broker, Bretzfelder & Cahn, Inc., misconstrued certain instructions and transferred the policy coverage from

the Dixwell Avenue property to other property Lewis owned, on Read Street. Later, Lewis was sued by a woman who claimed to have been injured on the Dixwell Avenue property. Lewis requested that the insurance company defend her, as it had agreed to do in the policy. The insurance company refused, asserting that at the request of Lewis' broker, it had transferred the policy coverage from the Dixwell Avenue property to the Read Street property. After the insurer refused to defend, the lawsuit against Lewis was eventually settled. In the present action, Lewis sought to recover from the insurer the amount of the settlement, plus the reasonable cost

---

[2]The general rights and liabilities of agents are discussed in Chapter 48.

of her attorney's fee. The trial court entered judg-
ment for Michigan Millers, and Lewis appealed.]

Thim, Associate Justice.

*   *   *

The decisive issue in this case is whether Cahn had the authority to seek and obtain a binding endorsement transferring the plaintiff's liability coverage and thereby relieve the defendant of any responsibility concerning subsequent events at the Dixwell Avenue property.

An insurance agent is a person expressly or impliedly authorized to represent an insurance company in its dealings with third persons. . . . An insurance broker is "one who acts as a middleman between the insured and insurer and who solicits insurance from the public under no employment from any special company and who either places an order for insurance with a company selected by the insured, or, in the absence of such selection, with a company the broker selects." . . . It is clear from the record that Cahn was an insurance broker rather than an agent of the defendant.

When procuring insurance for a person such as the plaintiff, a broker becomes the agent of that person for that purpose. . . . Once that purpose is accomplished, however, and the insurance is procured, the agency relationship between the insured and the broker terminates, and the broker is without any authority to do anything which further affects the insured unless expressly or impliedly authorized by the insured to do so. . . .

From an application of the above principles to this case, it is apparent that, when Cahn sought and obtained the renewal policy for one year covering the Dixwell Avenue property, it acted as the plaintiff's agent. It is equally apparent that once the policy was issued, Cahn ceased to be the plaintiff's agent. At this point, in the absence of a new conferral of authority on Cahn by the plaintiff, Cahn could not affect the existing contract of insur-

ance between the plaintiff and the defendant covering the Dixwell Avenue property. Some six months after the renewal policy had been issued and the agency relationship had ceased, the plaintiff notified Cahn that her mail was to be referred to the Read Street address. The finding is unclear as to whether the plaintiff, by this notification, intended to have Cahn in turn notify the defendant of this change of mailing address. Even if we assume, however, that it was the plaintiff's intention to once again utilize Cahn as her agent, this time for the limited purpose of having Cahn inform the defendant of the change of mailing address, this agency did not empower Cahn to procure a binding transfer of liability coverage from the Dixwell Avenue property to the Read Street property. Cahn was not expressly or impliedly authorized by the plaintiff to request such a transfer. Nor did it have the apparent authority to seek and obtain the transfer on the plaintiff's behalf. Apparent authority is that semblance of authority which a principal, through his own acts or inadvertences, causes or allows third persons to believe his agent possesses. . . . To fix the principal's liability for the agent's act, it must be shown either that the principal, by his own acts, causes the mistaken belief that the agent had the requisite authority or that the principal knowingly permitted the agent to engender that belief. . . . Also, of course, the third party must have acted in good faith on the false appearance created by the principal. . . . In the present case, the plaintiff did not hold Cahn out to the defendant as possessing the authority to obtain the endorsement, nor did she knowingly permit Cahn to act as having such authority. Indeed, the plaintiff did not even learn of Cahn's actions until the endorsement transferring coverage was a fait accompli. At that point she expressly protested the transfer. There is no evidence that the defendant relied on anyone other than Cahn before it issued the endorsement. In the absence of actual knowledge to the contrary, it was bound to know that Cahn's authority to represent the plaintiff had terminated six months earlier when the renewal policy was issued. . . . It was not justified in relying solely on Cahn's request to transfer the plaintiff's coverage. The "[a]pparent power of an agent is to be determined not by his own acts but by those of the principal." . . . Here, the plaintiff neither did anything nor knowingly allowed anything to be done which would justify the defendant's acquiescence to Cahn's request to issue the endorsement transferring coverage.

The facts found do not support the conclusion reached by the trial court that Cahn had the authority to procure the endorsement on behalf of the plaintiff. Thus, the endorsement did not deprive the plaintiff of insurance coverage on the Dixwell Avenue property. . . .

Having failed to defend the action instituted against the plaintiff, the defendant must respond in damages for the breach of its contract to do so. . . .

[Judgment set aside and case remanded with directions to render judgment for plaintiff for $2,500.]

Duty to Procure Insurance   An insurance agent or broker must exercise good faith and reasonable diligence to procure insurance on the best terms obtainable. If an agent or broker is employed to keep up insurance, the failure to do so by either renewing an expired policy or properly maintaining an existing policy can render the agent or broker liable to the client for losses sustained. However, if insufficient information is given and, for that reason, no policy is procured, the agent or broker would not be liable for failing to procure insurance since there was actually no valid contract to procure. If insurance cannot be obtained, the agent or broker must notify the client within a reasonable time. Failure to do so can render the agent or broker liable for damages suffered by the client for lack of insurance.

The losses or damages that an aggrieved client can claim when an agent or broker fails to obtain insurance vary from state to state. In most states the damages are equal to the amount that would have been due under a policy had one been obtained. Where no loss occurs, the measure of damages is the amount paid as the premium.

The following case illustrates that, in some states, an agent or broker can be liable for any loss—even lost profits from the interruption of business—sustained when he fails to obtain insurance as he is supposed to do.

Joseph Forest Products, Inc.
v
Pratt
278 Or 477, 564 P2d 1027
(Oregon Supreme Court, 1977)

[Joseph Forest Products requested Pratt, its insurance agent, to obtain fire insurance on a pole-treating plant. Pratt agreed to do so and Joseph paid the required premium. Pratt failed to obtain the insurance. During the period in which coverage was supposedly in effect, Joseph's plant was damaged by fire. Joseph sued Pratt for damages to its plant, equipment, and inventory, as well as damages for lost profits. The trial court ruled that Pratt was liable only for the amount that would have been due under the insurance policy had it been obtained; it *did not allow Joseph to recover damages for lost profits. Joseph appealed.]*

Howell, Justice.

*   *   *

An insurance agent or broker who agrees to procure insurance for another for a fee but fails to do so may be liable for any damage resulting from his omission. Liability may be based upon a breach of contract or upon negligence, or upon both, depending upon the particular circumstances of the case. Normally, causation requirements will limit any recovery to that which the plaintiff would have received through the insurer if coverage had been provided. However, if the plaintiff is able to prove that additional consequential damages resulted from the agent's failure to obtain coverage, he will then be entitled to recover those consequential damages as well. . . .

As a general rule the liability of the agent with respect to a loss, by reason of his breach of duty, is that which would have fallen on the company had the insurance been properly effected, *together with such other damages as proximately result from the breach,* and less the amount of unpaid premiums or cost of the insurance. . . . [Court's emphasis.]

An insurance broker is the agent of the insured in negotiating for a policy, and owes a duty to his principal to exercise reasonable skill, care, and diligence in effecting insurance. Thus he may be held liable where he has breached a contract to procure insurance for his principal. And while such broker is not obligated to assume the duty of procuring a policy, without consideration for his promise, he must exercise ordinary care in the performance of such duty when assumed, the prom-

ise to take the policy being a sufficient consideration. He is charged with the exercise of reasonable care and skill in making inquiries and obtaining information concerning the responsibility of the insurer with whom [he places] the risk, and is liable for *any loss* occasioned by such want of care. [Court's emphasis.]

If a broker or agent of the insured neglects to procure insurance, or does not follow instructions, or if the policy is void or materially defective, through the agent's fault, he is liable to his principal for any loss he may have sustained thereby. . . .

It is true that, as defendant points out, some courts have stated that agents and brokers will be liable for losses only up to the limits of the policy applied for. This statement is correct as a general rule because, even if he were insured, the plaintiff's losses would have been covered only to the extent of the policy limits. . . . However, the rule has no application to additional, consequential losses sustained, not by reason of the occurrence of the contingency insured against (such as fire, theft, etc.), but by reason of defendant's breach of contract or negligent failure to secure coverage (such as loss of profits due to unnecessary delay in obtaining reimbursement for the original loss). We can discern no reason for creating a special exception to normal liability concepts because the case involves an insurance agent.

Of course, in order to recover for additional, consequential damages, the plaintiff must prove that the additional losses were caused by the defendant and that these damages were reasonably foreseeable at the time of application. . . .

[Reversed and remanded.]

Compensation   An insurance agent's right to compensation from an insurance company for selling and writing insurance depends on the terms of the contract existing between the agent and the company. Insurance brokers and agents have a general lien on all policies they procure for their principal—and on all money they receive on such policies—for payment of amounts owed to them for commissions, disbursements, and advances.

39:5   Regulation of Insurance Business

The power to organize an insurance company and conduct the insurance business is not a right. Rather, it is a privilege granted by each state, subject to certain conditions. The business of insurance is one that is affected with a public interest. As such, it is a proper subject of state regulation and control. Thus, each state can regulate the relations between insurer and insured, as well as the internal affairs of insurance companies operating within the state.

The power to regulate the insurance business is very broad. It extends to all persons seeking to engage in the insurance business. For example, state law can confine the business of insurance to corporations. State law can also prescribe reasonable conditions to the conduct of the insurance business by individuals as well as corporations.

Most states have enacted statutes that create regulatory entities, such as insurance boards, superintendents, or commissioners. These boards and officials regulate and supervise the transaction of insurance business to protect the public interest, make uniform rates, execute the insurance laws, and see that violations of the insurance laws are dealt with properly. In some states, the superintendent or commissioner of insurance is given the power to revoke, withhold, or refuse to renew an insurance company's license.

The states' right to regulate and control insurance companies includes the right to manage their dissolution. Indeed, if a company cannot financially continue its operations, it can be dissolved at the instance of the state. Once dissolution proceedings have commenced, or after expiration or forfeiture of an insurance company's charter, the company cannot legally issue an insurance policy. Many states permit the appointment of a receiver in proceedings for either (1) the liquidation and dissolution or (2) the rehabilitation or reorganization of an insurance company. The difficulties encountered in the forced liquidation or reorganization of insurance companies that have assets and liabilities in two or more states led to the adoption by many states of the Uniform Insurers Liquidation Act or statutes patterned after that act. The purpose of the uniform act is to secure equal treatment for all creditors regardless of the state in which they do business.

Federal Regulation of Insurance   For many years insurance was held not to constitute commerce within the meaning of the United States Constitution. Consequently, the industry was left relatively free from federal intervention even though business was conducted on an interstate basis. In 1944, however, the United States Supreme Court held that fire insurance transactions that cross state lines do constitute interstate commerce and are subject to regulation by Congress under the commerce clause. This decision[3] clearly represented a potential change

---

[3]*United States v South-Eastern Underwriters Asso.*, 322 US 533, 88 L Ed 1440, 64 S CT 1162, reh den 323 US 811, 89 L Ed 646, 65 S Ct 26 (1944).

in the regulation of the insurance industry. To nullify the decision, in effect, Congress enacted the McCarran–Ferguson Act (15 USC §§ 1011–1015). By and large, the act limits the federal government's power to regulate the insurance industry.

 Although the federal government is precluded by the McCarran–Ferguson Act from regulating insurance, Congress can still regulate specific practices of the insurance industry through laws affecting *all* businesses and industries. For example, loans extended by insurance companies or certain insurance sales practices that involve credit must conform to the standards set forth in the federal truth in lending laws, as discussed in Chapter 27.

Key Concepts and Terms

- An insurance policy is a contract by which, in consideration of periodic payments called premiums, an insurer promises to pay the insured or a beneficiary a sum of money if an event specified in the policy occurs.

- Different types of insurance cover different risks. These risks include (1) an insured's death, accidental injury, or illness; (2) the damage or destruction of the insured's property; and (3) the insured's becoming liable to some other person.

- Insurance policies can be classified as being (1) open, (2) valued, (3) commercial block, (4) running, (5) floater, or (6) master.

- The three main types of insurance companies are stock companies, mutual companies, and mixed companies.

- The business of buying and selling insurance is primarily carried on by insurance agents and brokers. Agents are employed by and represent specific insurance companies. Brokers are not employed by specific companies; they hold themselves out for hire to and solicit insurance business from the public at large. Agents and brokers must act in good faith and must follow instructions given by their clients. Insurance companies are bound by all acts and contracts of their agents within the scope of their authority.

- The insurance industry is regulated primarily by state law. Specific matters that are regulated or controlled include premiums, provisions of insurance policies, and the conduct of insurance agents and brokers. Federal regulatory powers are limited by the McCarran–Ferguson Act.

- Beneficiary
- Commercial Block Policy
- Credit Life Insurance
- Group Insurance
- Insurance Agent
- Insurance Broker
- Lloyd's of London
- McCarran–Ferguson Act

- No-fault Insurance
- Ordinary (Straight) Life Insurance
- Property Insurance
- Reciprocal Insurance
- Reinsurance
- Rider
- Term Insurance

Questions and Case Problems

1. Consider the following statements:

    a. "The liability insurance system that the automobile insurance companies have developed in the United States to deal with accidental loss and injuries does not work well. For years there have been complaints that automobile insurance company performance is unsatisfactory. Criticism extends from specific company practices, such as arbitrary and unfair cancellation and nonrenewal actions, to rejection of the basic premise—insurance against negligently caused losses—on which the present system of automobile insurance has been erected. The system is slow, incomplete, and expensive. The companies and organizations involved in furnishing this service to the public in many respects do a poor job."

    b. "The basic difficulty with the present automobile insurance system is that the insured event is too complicated, turning as it does on legal liability. You can be paid for a traffic accident only by traversing tricky terrain. First you must claim against the other driver's insurance company. . . . Second, you must claim that the other driver was at fault and that you were free from fault. . . . Third, you must claim for a totally uncertain amount which includes not only your out-of-pocket loss for medical expenses and missed wages, but also payment for so-called pain and suffering."

    In light of these criticisms should no-fault insurance be adopted by all states? Why? To what extent should tortfeasors—and thus their insurers—be liable for injuries and death caused by their negligence or willful misconduct?

2. Stoll, an insurance broker, contacts Collegiate Manufacturing with suggestions for additional insurance. Stoll advises Collegiate to protect itself against fire loss by a policy to provide coverage for the company's fluctuating inventory. Collegiate agrees and Stoll places the insurance. However, the policy insures the inventory only up to a maximum limit of liability that is less than its market value. Collegiate's president fails to read the policy and is thus unaware of the limitation. A fire subsequently occurs, causing $394,000 in damage, but Collegiate receives only partial payment of $280,000, the maximum due under the policy. Collegiate sues Stoll for $114,000—the excess of the loss over the payment—because of Stoll's alleged negligent failure to provide adequate coverage. Stoll denies any negligence and alleges as a defense Collegiate's contributory negligence in failing to advise itself of the protection under the policy. Stoll also asserts that in any case, the coverage that Collegiate thought had been provided is not available from any company Stoll represents. How should the case be decided?

3. Commercial Insurance, through its agent, Leonard, insures an automobile belonging to Ingalls. After issuing the policy, Commercial investigates Ingalls and learns that the automobile is used by Ingalls' son who is deemed by Commercial to be a poor risk. Commercial writes to Leonard, stating that it is canceling Ingalls' insurance policy; it also notifies Ingalls of the cancellation. However, Leonard tells Ingalls to disregard the cancellation and that the insurance is still in effect. Ingalls tells Leonard that if the insurance is not in effect, he will buy insurance elsewhere, but relying on Leonard's statements, Ingalls does not purchase other insur-

ance. Later, the automobile is damaged. Commercial denies liability on the ground that it had previously canceled the policy. Is Ingalls entitled to recover under the policy? Is Leonard liable to Ingalls?

4. Describe the various kinds of insurance and the risks for which each is used.

5. What is the basic difference between liability insurance and the other types of insurance discussed in this chapter?

6. How does Lloyd's of London differ from other insurance companies?

7. In February 1968, a hot water heater owned by Karam exploded, damaging a leased building in which Karam was operating a Laundromat. Two actions for property damage were instituted against Karam and his liability insurer. The actions were settled for $18,500 with the insurer paying $10,000 and Karam paying $8,500. Karam then sued Darbonne, his insurance agent. When Karam had originally sought insurance, he had asked the agent to obtain property damage liability coverage for $100,000. Darbonne had intended to obtain insurance in this amount, but by mistake she had obtained only $10,000 coverage. The invoice sent to Karam by Darbonne billing for the property damage liability coverage indicated that the agent had obtained $100,000 in property damage liability coverage. Is the agent liable to Karam for her failure to obtain adequate liability insurance coverage? If so, in what amount?

8. DiMicco met with an employee of Buckingham-Wheeler Insurance Agency to discuss the placing of insurance on a 20-foot boat that was approximately eleven years old. After the meeting, the agency's employee advised DiMicco that he would insure the boat for $5,000. The employee did this despite the fact that he knew that the insurer would not issue a policy on a boat having a value of $5,000 or greater or a boat that was older than three years of age without a survey as to its condition. Some weeks after the meeting the boat was damaged in a storm and sank. DiMicco sought to recover for her loss. Can the insurance company deny coverage? Is the insurance agency liable to DiMicco? Is the agency liable to the insurance company? Who must pay for the loss?

9. Farmers Mutual issues an insurance policy to George Bechard in connection with George's ownership of a Chevrolet truck. The policy provides the usual liability coverage. It also provides for the payment of benefits to or for the benefit of any person who, while driving or riding in the truck, is killed or injured in an accident. However, a rider to the policy specifically states that accident insurance benefits will not be paid "for death while driving the truck in the course of a person's employment." Mutual's agent tells George that he "is covered" regardless of the circumstances under which he is driving the truck at any time. George is later killed in an accident that occurs while he is driving the truck in the course of his business. His widow claims the accidental death benefit under the policy, but Mutual denies liability, pointing to the rider. Is Mutual bound by the statement of its agent? Should George's widow recover the death benefit?

10. Myles buys a ferryboat at an auction for $2,850. He then seeks to insure it against loss. He knows that the former owner had insured the boat for $100,000. He also knows that other, similar ferries are quite valuable and that he bought his boat at a bargain price. Under these circumstances, is it proper to insure the vessel for $100,000? Should Myles disclose his purchase price to the insurer? Discuss.

40 The Insurance Contract and Coverage

40:1 Formation and Validity of Insurance Contracts

The relationship between an insurer and an insured is purely contractual. A contract of insurance is a voluntary contract, and competent persons can make whatever contract for insurance they see fit to make, provided the contract does not contravene any law or public policy.

A contract of insurance—or any renewal of it—must be assented to by both parties either in person or through their agents. As with other contracts, as discussed in Part Three of this book, there must be a meeting of the minds of the parties on the essential terms and elements of the contract. These terms include (1) the subject matter to be insured, (2) the risk insured against, (3) the commencement and period of the risk undertaken by the insurer, (4) the amount of insurance, and (5) the premium and time at which it is to be paid.

The first step in creating an insurance contract is applying for insurance. The application is an offer or proposal for a contract; it must be accepted by the insurer before a contract of insurance—the policy—is issued. Insurance companies are not compelled to accept every application presented and can stipulate what terms and for what period of time the risks will be accepted. An acceptance makes the insurance binding and effective. Ordinarily, notice of acceptance of the application is sent to the applicant. Neither the delivery of an insurance policy nor the prepayment of the premium is necessary for a valid contract unless the parties so stipulate. Frequently, however, especially in the case of *life insurance*, prepayment of the initial premium is required. When this is the case, an insurance contract is not completed, nor is the risk assumed by the insurer, until payment is made.

Pending formal acceptance of an application, an insurance company can issue a contract for temporary insurance. Temporary insurance covers someone or something for a reasonable time until either a policy can be written or its issuance approved. Temporary insurance is usually evidenced by a binding slip or an interim receipt referred to as a *binder*. A binder differs from an application for insurance in that a binder is itself a contract, albeit an informal one. In view of its informal nature, a binder need not express all the elements of a contract, such as the rate of premium or even the name of the insurer, and it can be an oral agreement.

Although it is usual to name the insured in an insurance policy, it is not essential; the insured can be described in ways other than by name. So long as an insurance company is not misled as to the applicant's identity, it cannot avoid the risk by claiming that the name or description of the insured is not that stated in the policy. For example, the validity of a renewal policy of fire insurance issued to a corporation is not affected by the fact that the insured corporation has changed its name without the insurer's knowledge.

The risk under an insurance policy usually attaches as of the time agreed on or understood by the parties. "Attachment of the risk" refers to the time after which the insurer will be liable for loss or damage under a policy. In some circumstances, the time at which a contract of insurance becomes effective—and the risk attaches—is regulated by statute.

An insurance policy must generally specify the period during which the insurance is to continue. If an exact time period is specified, that specification governs. If no time is expressly indicated, surrounding circumstances can be considered to determine the duration of coverage.

The following case illustrates that insurance coverage might not exist if the requisites of a valid insurance contract are not met, even though the circumstances otherwise weigh strongly in favor of coverage.

Reynolds

v

Guarantee Reserve Life Ins. Co.
44 Ill App 3d 764, 3 Ill Dec 397, 358 NE2d 940
(Illinois Appellate Court, 1976)

[Mark Reynolds applied for life and disability insurance with Guarantee Reserve on September 26, 1974. He named his parents as beneficiaries in the applications and paid the company's agent the required premium on both policies. The applications provided that the insurance would not take effect until the policies were either delivered, issued by the company, or accepted by the applicant. The applications were approved by Guarantee Reserve on October 18, 1974. On October 22, Mark was killed. The news of his death was received by the insurance company before the policies were typed. Guarantee Reserve then returned to Mark's parents the amount of the prepaid premiums and refused to pay the parents the benefits stated in the policies.

Mark's parents sued to compel the company to issue and deliver the insurance policies. The trial court entered judgment for Guarantee Reserve, and Mark's parents appealed.]

Jones, Justice.

*   *   *

At issue here is whether an insurance company can, after accepting the first premium from the applicant and finding him to be an insurable risk, reject the applications for insurance and refuse to issue and deliver policies because of the applicant's death prior to the issuance of the policies. Attending the issue is the fact that the applications for the policies and receipt for the initial premium payments state that no policy will be in effect until either "delivered," "issued by the company," or "accepted" by the applicant. We find that the terms of the agreement must control; therefore, the company may reject the application. . . .

An application for insurance is a mere offer; it creates no rights and imposes no duty on the insurer. . . . The parties to an application for insurance are competent to make any provision for the effective date of insurance. . . . Such provision may be the issuance of the policy, the date of delivery of the policy or the date of acceptance of the policy by the applicant and is binding and not contrary to public policy. . . . Where the application and receipt in connection with an application for insurance provide [that] no insurance will be effective until a policy is issued or delivered, no contract of insurance is created where the applicant dies prior to the time such conditions are performed. . . .

Applying the principles above to the applications, receipt and facts in the instant case, it is apparent that no contract of insurance was in effect prior to the death of plaintiff's son Mark. The applications constituted mere offers; the conditions precedent to the insurance policies taking effect had not been performed prior to Mark's death. There is some ambiguity created as to effective policy dates since the applications' conditions of "delivery," and "acceptance" in the life and disability applications respectively conflict with the condition of "issuance" in the receipt. However, even resolving this ambiguity in favor of the insured, the condition is not met as no policy for Mark Reynolds was ever issued or delivered . . .

The plaintiffs' final contention is that it is unconscionable for the defendant to take a check from the proposed insured, cash it for its own use and refuse to provide any coverage to the proposed insured in return. There is no merit to this contention. It is not conduct that is harsh or shocking to the conscience for an insurance company to accept prepayment of premiums for proposed policies of insurance which clearly will not provide coverage until issued or delivered where the receipt for that prepayment expressly contains a provision that if the company declines to issue a policy the amount received will be refunded. Only hindsight in an unusual and unfortunate situation makes it appear so. The language of the agreement is controlling. . . .

[Judgment affirmed.]

40:2 Insurable Interest

An *insurable interest* is necessary to the validity of an insurance contract. If no insurable interest exists, the contract is void. A distinction must be made between property insurance and life insurance in determining what amounts to an insurable interest. In regard to property, anyone has an insurable interest who derives a benefit from the property's existence or would suffer loss from its destruction. This is true whether or not the insured has title to, a lien on, or possession of the property. For example, a contractor who agrees to construct or repair a building for a stipulated price has an insurable interest in the building, as do persons furnishing materials for use in the work. The owner of the building has an insurable interest to the extent of its value, even though the loss, in the absence of insurance, would fall on the contractor.

The following case provides an excellent illustration of the concept of insurable interest in property. It shows how the issue might arise in a dispute between an insured and an insurance company and what type of interest can be insured.

Constantine

v

Home Ins. Co.
427 F2d 1338
(United States Court of Appeals, Sixth Circuit, 1970)

[Scott sold generators to the Village of Constantine under a conditional sales contract in which he retained title to the generators. Because the contract required him to insure the equipment, Scott applied to the Home Insurance Company for breakdown insurance. He fully informed the company about the transaction and, since he retained title, did not request that the Village be named in the policy. Scott also informed the company that it was his intention to sell the conditional sales contract at a later date. Later, he sold the contract to a bank. The insurance policy was neither assigned nor reissued to the bank. Subsequently, two generators broke down and Home Insurance refused to pay Scott. The insurance company contended that Scott no longer possessed any insurable interest in the property. Both Scott and the Village of Constantine sued the insurance company. The trial court dismissed their complaint, and they appealed.]

Edwards, Circuit Judge.

*   *   *

[The issue before the Court is] whether a Michigan public policy against "wagering contracts" bars enforcement of this insurance policy by Scott because at the time of the breakdown of the machinery involved, Scott no longer possessed any "insurable interest" in the property. The District Court held that it did. . . .

[W]e do not believe that the voidance of an insurance contract because it is a "wagering contract" follows automatically from a holding that an insured has divested himself of any ownership interest in the property insured by the policy. . . . In [the leading Michigan case on this topic the court concluded that]:

"An insurable interest does not, of necessity, depend upon ownership of the property. It may be a special interest entirely disconnected from any title, lien, or possession. If the holder of an interest in property will suffer direct pecuniary loss, by its destruction, he may indemnify himself therefrom by a contract of insurance. The question is not what is his title to the property, but rather, would he be damaged pecuniarily by its loss. If he would, he has an insurable interest. That interest may be derived by possession, enjoyment, or profits of the property, security or lien resting upon it, or it may be other certain benefits growing out of or dependent upon it." . . .

Thus, it seems clear to us that Michigan invokes its rule, one founded upon public policy, to avoid the possibility that someone would be tempted to gamble upon another's life or property when he had nothing at stake in the destruction of either. But it is not a rule designed to serve the purpose of a technical defense to an otherwise valid contract between parties who know exactly what is involved.

Patently, Scott had a real interest in the continued existence and operation of the instant machinery. As of the time of the breakdown of the two generators in question, he was still liable on his undertaking to procure damage insurance. In the event he had failed to do so, or in the event we hold his attempt to do so to have been void, he will become liable to the Village of Constantine for the damage. While Scott had neither ownership interest in the property insured nor anything to gain from it, he clearly did have something to lose. Under Michigan law we believe this was sufficient to take this insurance out of the "wagering contract" class. . . .

[Judgment reversed.]

Life or Health Insurance   Every person has an insurable interest in his own life. He may insure it in good faith for the benefit of his estate or any person. However, a person cannot have an insurable interest in the life of another unless he has a reasonable expectation of benefit or advantage from the continuance of the other's life. In all cases there must be a reasonable relation between the parties—pecuniary or blood or affinity—that gives rise to an expectation of benefit or advantage from the continuance of the insured's life. Clearly, the essential element in determining whether an insurable interest exists in a life or health insurance policy is good faith. It should not be obtained for the purpose of speculating on the hazard of a life in which the insured has no interest.

Key Employee Insurance   It is generally recognized that a business has an insurable interest in the lives of its key officers or employees and has the power to obtain insurance on their lives. For example, a small, closely held corporation can purchase *key employee insurance* and name the company as beneficiary with the intention that it will use the proceeds to purchase the insured's interest in the firm. The mere existence of the relationship of employer and employee is not sufficient in itself to give the employer an insurable interest. It must further be shown that there is a reasonable expectation that the employer would realize a substantial pecuniary gain through the continued life of the employee, or sustain a substantial pecuniary loss if the employee dies.

Credit Life Insurance   A creditor has an insurable interest in the life of his debtor, at least for the amount of the debt and the cost of carrying the insurance on the debtor's life. This interest is subject to the limitation that the amount of the policy must not be so disproportionate to the amount of the debt (plus the cost of carrying the insurance) as to justify the conclusion that the policy is essentially a wagering or speculative one. For example, a credit life policy for $3,000 is really a *wagering policy* and is void if the insured's debt is only $70.

The following case discusses and analyzes the concept of insurable interest in life insurance. It explores most of the relationships in which an insurable interest can exist. Consider whether the reasoning of the court is persuasive.

Mutual Savings Life Ins. Co.
v
Noah
291 Ala 444, 282 So 2d 271,
60 ALR3d 81
(Alabama Supreme Court, 1973)

[Donald Noah was named as the beneficiary in three policies of insurance issued by the Mutual Savings Life Insurance Company on the life of his brother, William Noah. The policies were in force when William died, but the insurer refused to pay the amounts due except for partial payment under a burial insurance policy. It contended that Donald Noah lacked an insurable interest in the life of his deceased brother. Donald filed a declaratory judgment action against the insurance company seeking to have the court declare that the insurer was obligated to pay the death benefits and the balance of the burial benefits prescribed under the policies, plus accidental death benefits provided in all three. The trial court issued judgment in favor of Donald (the *appellee–complainant) and against Mutual Savings (the appellant–respondent) on all three polices in the total amount of $5,065.35, consisting of $5,000 under the life policies and $65.35 under the burial policy, with interest. Mutual Savings appealed.]*

Heflin, Chief Justice.

*   *   *

The most divisive issue with which this court is faced is presented by appellant–respondent's contention that Donald R. Noah has no insurable interest in the life of the insured, and that each of the three policies was invalid by reason thereof. It may be well to note at the outset that this court holds the burial policy not to be subject to the insurable interest requirement. The public policy grounds for requiring an insurable interest, which are discussed below, are not applicable to a burial policy wherein the benefits are substantially restricted to providing burial services. For this reason, it is the named insured in such a policy who is in reality the recipient of the insurance benefits, not the named beneficiary. . . .But, even if it could be said that the burial policy is subject to the insurable interest requirement, this court holds, for the reasons stated below, that Donald R. Noah did have an insurable interest in William's life.

Under the evidence the two life policies were procured or "taken out" . . . by the beneficiary, and thus the long-established rule that the insurance is invalid unless the beneficiary has an "insurable interest" in the life of the insured applies. This rule is to the effect that a person has an unlimited insurable interest in his own life and may designate any person as his beneficiary so long as the insurance was procured or taken out by the insured and the premiums paid by him, but one taking out a policy of insurance for his own benefit, on the life of another person, must have an insurable interest in the continuance of the life of such insured. . . .

Several reasons have been assigned as the

basis for the insurable interest requirement, both of which are grounded upon public policy considerations: a policy taken out by one for his own benefit on the life of another, in whom he has no insurable interest is, in substance, a wagering contract; and such a policy may hold out a temptation to the beneficiary to hasten by improper means the death of the insured. . . .

Certain blood relationships have been held sufficient, in and of themselves to negate the supposition that the beneficiary would take out such a policy for the purpose of wagering on the insured's death, or that such a policy would entice the beneficiary to take the insured's life, and in such cases the relationship alone is said to create an insurable interest. This is true notwithstanding the fact that the beneficiary may have no reasonable expectation of pecuniary advantage through the continued life of the insured or consequent loss by reason of his death, which would otherwise be required in order to find an insurable interest.

The relationship of husband and wife has been held to be sufficiently close to give either an insurable interest in the life of the other. . . . The parent–child relationship has been accorded the same status as that given to husband and wife. . . .

On the other hand, the following relationships have been held not to create an insurable interest on the basis of such relationship alone. Cousin and cousin; . . . the wife of his wife's brother . . . ; aunt and niece . . . ; aunt-in-law and niece . . . ; niece and uncle. . . .

The specific issue presented in the case under review is whether one has an insurable interest in the life of his brother by virtue of the relationship alone. While realizing that this issue is one of first impression in Alabama, and that other jurisdictions are in conflict on this matter, a review of the holdings of other states has convinced this court that the vast majority and best reasoned holdings support the proposition that the brother–brother relationship will, in and of itself, support an insurable interest. . . .

As to what blood relationships are sufficiently close to support an insurable interest, that of brothers is admittedly a borderline case. . . .

The reason most often assigned as the basis of a holding that such relationship will, in and of itself, support an insurable interest is that the natural love and affection prevailing between the two and the expectation that one will render the other aid in time of need is sufficient to overcome any wagering contract argument, as well as any impulse to hasten the death of the insured. This rationale was well stated in [an Arkansas case] as follows:

> "Brothers are so closely related that they are naturally interested in the preservation of the life of each other. Generally, they will lay down their life for each other. As a rule they care for each other in illness to the extent, if necessary, of furnishing all needed comforts and medicinal aid. It would be contrary to human nature for them to speculate on the death of each other, so it may well be that their contracts for insurance on the life of each other should not be classed as wagering contracts."

This view was adopted by Kentucky in [a case] wherein the court stated that an insurable interest may arise from blood relationship alone without regard to whether the beneficiary has any pecuniary interest in the life of the insured or is dependent upon him. If blood relationship alone constitutes an insurable interest, certainly, the court reasoned, the relationship of one brother to another, is sufficiently close for that purpose. The court concluded as follows:

> "[W]here the relationship . . . is so close as to preclude the probability that mercenary motives would induce the sacrifice of life to gain the insurance, the element of pecuniary consideration is not deemed essential to sustain the validity of the policy." . . .

In addition to the cases cited above a number of other jurisdictions have held the blood relationship alone sufficient. . . .

Perhaps the facts of the instant case tend to contradict the closeness and mutual love and affection which the above holdings attribute to the brother–brother relationship, but this court does not write for this case alone. The holding of this court today will govern all future cases, not just the exceptional one where the natural love and affection common to the brother–brother relationship may be missing.

In view of the foregoing it is the conclusion of this court that the brother–brother relationship will, standing alone, support an insurable interest.

This court has reviewed the holdings of various other jurisdictions which are contra to the decision announced by this court today, and finds that the rationale underlying these cases is that one would take out an insurance policy on the life of his brother for the purpose of gambling on the time of his death, or would, by virtue of such policy, be induced to take the life of his brother for a price, which is not, in the opinion of this court, substantiated by the common experience of mankind. . . .

[Affirmed.]

40:3 Premiums

An insurance *premium* is the consideration paid by an insured to an insurer for undertaking to indemnify the insured against peril. The premium and the time at which it is to be paid are essential terms of the insurance contract. The gross premium ordinarily includes the net premium and the loading. The "net premium" is the amount required by the insurer to provide the insurance coverage itself. The "loading" is an amount added to the net premium to cover administrative and other costs, such as brokers' commissions, medical examinations, and the processing of applications.

Policy premiums are calculated on the basis of the relation between the risk of loss and the value of the object insured. For example, as the value of insured property increases, so does the premium. An insurer will determine what the likelihood is that a loss to insured property will occur and what it will have to pay to the insured on such a loss. Of course, a host of variables, such as the location of the property, its value, the nature of the business, how property is used, and its age, would all go into an insurer's calculations of the premium.

Premiums for life insurance are based on mortality tables, interest rates, and administrative expenses required to carry on the business of insurance. Mortality tables are statistical tables that show the probable life expectancy of a normal person according to sex and age. Knowing life expectancy, the insurance company can then compute the interest it will receive on the investment of the premiums paid during the expected life of the insured. This interest, plus the reserves required by law to be maintained by insurance companies, must equal the total required policy or death payments at the assumed mortality rate. In other words, a portion of the premium is theoretically reserved or set aside by the insurer and another portion is invested. These reserves, when added to the interest on the investments over the expected life of an insured as statistically shown in the mortality tables, must equal the face value of the policy to be paid on the insured's death. Any surplus represents the profits made by the insurer.

A statement of the premium, or a statement of the basis and rates on which the final premium is to be determined and paid, is a necessary part of the policy. A binder need not, however, specify the rate of premium or basis for its computation; an agreement to pay the premium or customary rate is implied.

Self-insurance Purchasers of liability and other types of insurance can often save on their premiums by electing to absorb an initial part of a loss through a "deductible." This is a specified amount of monetary damage that an insured must pay first, before the insurer will cover the loss in excess of that amount. The use of this or other devices by which an individual or business voluntarily chooses to bear either a part of, or the entire, risk is sometimes called *self-insurance*. Obviously, it is not insurance in the traditional meaning of the word, since it really signifies the *absence* of insurance.

 Because there are so many kinds of insurance available, an individual or business should consider whether certain risks or losses could very well be self-insured either because the probability of their occurrence is low or the premiums that would be charged are too high to justify coverage.

Return of Premium As a general rule, an insurer is entitled only to such a reasonable premium as the risk carried warrants. A person is entitled to a return of the premium (1) in the case of overinsurance; (2) when the contract is voidable due to the insurer's fraud or misrepresentation; (3) when the contract is voidable because the insured was ignorant of certain facts through no fault of his own; or (4) when, by any default of the insured other than actual fraud, the insurer did not incur any liability under the policy.

40:4   Risks and Coverage

An insurer is at liberty to select the character of the risk it will assume. All foreseeable losses or risks can be insured against except those for which issuance of insurance would be against public policy or prohibited by statute, or those occasioned by the insured's own fraud or misconduct. Within these limits, the parties can make such contracts as they choose and can qualify or limit the liability assumed. Almost any contingent or unknown event that can injure a person having an insurable interest or create a liability against him can be insured against. Of course, the insurer is not liable except on proof that a loss is within the terms of the policy, for these terms determine the measure of the insurer's liability.

 The essence of insurance is that the greater the hazard, the higher the cost. That is why insurance companies investigate how business property is used before they agree to issue an original policy. It is also why they include provisions that suspend or limit insurance coverage when an insured increases the risk without notifying the insurer. Often an insured will mistakenly believe that the provisions of an insurance policy cover all the risks he wants to be insured. An insured must take the time to understand what is and is not being covered under any policy. If essential risks or losses are excluded, additional coverage should be obtained.

40:5   Notice and Proof of Loss

Insurance policies ordinarily contain provisions requiring the insured to give timely notice to the insurer of a loss or occurrence arising under the terms of a policy. The purpose of a provision for notice is to allow the insurer to review its rights and liabilities as well as to afford it an opportunity for investigation and possible settlement or payment of a claim. The insured's failure to give timely notice will not relieve the insurer of liability under a policy unless the insurer is substantially prejudiced by the provision.

The time for giving notice or making proof of loss does not begin to run until the insured has knowledge, or is charged with notice, of the loss or event on which his rights are based. Thus, where the beneficiary of a life or accident policy is ignorant of the existence of the policy, delay in giving notice or furnishing proof of loss is excused until a reasonable time after his discovery of the policy's existence. An insured can be excused for delay or failure to give notice where it appears that he believed that an accident or injury was not covered by the policy or that he was not liable for the accident in question.

No matter what type of insurance policy an individual or business buys, there are time limits incorporated within the policy. These deadlines are not only easily overlooked, but they are often misunderstood. For example, few people realize that the clock continues to run even while negotiations for settlement are continuing with an insurance company. Most insureds, in the absence of legal advice, may not know whether a deadline is approaching or whether an insurer has waived a deadline, as discussed below. Unless the insurer has specifically waived a deadline, it is better to commence litigation before the time expires rather than to wait for the insurance company to act, only to discover that a deadline for filing a claim or commencing litigation has passed, precluding recovery under the policy.

Policy provisions concerning notice or proof of loss can be expressly waived by the insurer or its authorized agent. A waiver will be implied from (1) conduct amounting to a recognition of liability, such as proceeding with payment of a loss or settlement of a claim; (2) the insurer's failure to object to an attempted notice or proof of loss; or (3) the facts of the case, under some circumstances.

40:6   Rights and Obligations of Parties After Loss

Insurance policies usually provide that the insurer has the right to investigate, negotiate, and settle any claim or suit as it deems proper. A policy might also contain a clause that prohibits the insured from voluntarily assuming any liability or interfering in settlement negotiations without the insurer's consent. The purposes of this provision is to prevent collusion and to give the insurer complete control of the defense or compromise of a suit or claim.

Duty of Insurer to Act in Good Faith   An insurer's obligation of good faith and fair dealing is implied in every insurance contract to protect an insured from unwarranted liability. This obligation requires an insurer to settle a claim against its insured even though the express terms of the policy do not impose such a duty. Therefore, an insurer is required to make an intelligent evaluation of a settlement offer in good faith by considering the interests of the insured equally with its own. This evaluation should be based on a reasonable investigation by persons qualified to make a decision respecting the risk involved.

When there is a great risk of a recovery beyond the policy limits so that the most reasonable manner of disposing a claim is a settlement which can be made within policy limits, good faith requires the insurer to settle the claim. Its unwarranted refusal to do so constitutes a breach of the implied covenant of good faith and fair dealing. An insurance company that acts outrageously to deprive an insured of his policy benefits runs the risk of having to pay far more than the policy requires. Its conduct could amount to a tort, which can result in punitive as well as compensatory damages. A wrongful refusal to settle may also constitute a violation of a state consumer protection statute. In at least one state, for example, an insurance company's refusal to deal in good faith has been held to constitute a violation of the state's ban of unfair or deceptive practices by all businesses.[1]

Duty of Insurer to Defend   Most policies of liability insurance contain a clause that obligates the insurer to defend the insured against all lawsuits covered by the policy, even though they might be groundless, false, or fraudulent. If there is doubt as to an insurer's duty to defend, as might exist if there is an ambiguous exclusionary provision in the policy, the courts will generally decide in the insured's favor.

An insurer's unjustified denial of liability and unwarranted refusal to defend a suit against the insured constitutes a breach of its contract, and the insured is thereby released from the obligation of leaving the management of litigation to the insurer. The insured can defend on his own account and make any reasonable compromise of the action. An insurer that wrongfully refuses to defend can be obligated to pay the amount of a judgment rendered against its insured, or of any reasonable settlement made by the insured in good faith (although ordinarily not more than the face amount of the policy).

Duty of Insured to Cooperate   In most liability insurance policies there are provisions that require the insured to cooperate with the insurer in such matters as attending hearings and trials, securing and giving evidence, obtaining the attendance of witnesses, and assisting in making settlements. An insured is required to disclose information reasonably demanded by the insurer to enable it to determine whether it should settle a claim against the insured or whether there is a genuine defense. If an insured breaches a cooperation provision after the insurer has exercised reasonable diligence in securing the insured's cooperation and the insurer is substantially prejudiced by the breach, the insurer has a defense against liability on the policy.

40:7   Proceeds and Beneficiaries

The beneficiary is the person entitled to the proceeds of insurance when the loss, damage, or liability insured against arises.

Ordinarily, the term "beneficiary" refers to the person designated in a life insurance policy as the one who is to receive the benefits that become payable when the insured dies. Should a beneficiary predecease an insured, the right to receive the proceeds depends mainly on the nature of the interest that the deceased beneficiary had. If the policy does not provide for the beneficiary's death and does not reserve the right to change a beneficiary, the named beneficiary has a vested right, which passes to his estate on his death. This right cannot be divested (taken away) by the insured or other owner of the policy (except by permitting the policy to lapse).

---

[1]*Levy v North American Co. for Life & Health Ins.*, 90 Wash 2d 846, 586 P2d 845 (Washington Supreme Court, 1978).

EXAMPLE

Morton takes out a life insurance policy and names his wife, Betty, as beneficiary. The policy provides that Morton can waive the right to change or revoke the beneficiary, and Morton chooses to waive this right. Morton's irrevocable designation of Betty gives her a vested and absolute interest in the policy proceeds that cannot be divested by Morton without her consent.

If a life insurance policy permits a change of beneficiary by the insured, but no other beneficiary is named after the designated beneficiary predeceases the insured, the proceeds of the policy are payable to the estate or legal representative of the insured. A beneficiary of a life insurance policy who murders or feloniously causes the death of an insured forfeits rights under the policy.

As a general rule an insured under any type of insurance policy is limited to recovery of the amount set forth in the policy. Also, if an insured accepts payment of a lesser amount, he cannot recover an additional sum later by showing, for example, that both parties supposed that another insurer was liable for a portion of the loss. On the other hand, if the payment of a loss is procured by the insured's fraud, the insurer can recover the amount it paid. Likewise, an insurer that has made a payment under an erroneous belief induced by mistake of fact is entitled to restitution from the beneficiary even though the insurer contributed to the mistake.

An insured must demand payment if the insurer fails to pay promptly. If an insurer fails or refuses to pay, an insured is generally limited to recovering the proceeds of the policy, plus interest. Special damages are not ordinarily awarded, although some courts are now moving in the direction of allowing additional damages, including even mental and emotional distress caused by the insurer's failure to pay. After an insurer grants the insurer a release from any further obligation to pay, the release is binding on the insured unless it was induced by false representations or fraud.

40:8   Assignment or Transfer of Policy

An insurance policy can be assigned by the insured to a third person, to the insurer, or to the beneficiary.[2] Assignment can be made to secure a debt owed by the assignor to the assignee, to create a trust, as a gift, or for any other legitimate purpose. Unless the assignment is a gift, it generally must be supported by consideration. An ordinary life insurance policy cannot be assigned without the beneficiary's consent. As a general rule, an assignee acquires no greater rights by virtue of the assignment than the assignor enjoyed.

 Insurance policies often require that the insurer be notified about and consent to an assignment. Ordinarily, in the absence of a contrary provision in the policy, an assignee's rights are lost if the insured violates the policy terms, as by failing to obtain the insurer's consent to the assignment.

---

[2]Assignments are discussed in Chapter 17.

No particular language is necessary to make a valid assignment. Unless required by statute or the policy terms, an assignment need not even be in writing.

40:9   Conditions, Concealment, Representations, and Warranties

Insurers can impose any *conditions* on their obligations, so long as the conditions are clearly expressed and are not contrary to law or public policy. Conditions in insurance law are of two kinds—precedent and subsequent. A condition precedent is a condition that must be performed before an insurance contract becomes effective. It calls for the happening of some event or the performance of some act after the terms of the contract have been agreed on, but before the contract becomes binding on the parties. In a life insurance policy, for example, a typical condition precedent is that the policy shall not take effect until delivery and payment of the first premium during the good health of the applicant.

A condition subsequent is a condition that must be present after the risk insured against has attached. For example, a provision in a jewelry store owner's burglary policy that the insured keep 75 percent of the value of his inventory in a safe when the store is closed is a condition subsequent, the breach of which relieves the insurer of liability.

Concealment   Each party to an insurance contract must communicate to the other, in good faith, all facts within his knowledge that are material to the contract and that the other party has no means of ascertaining. A party's failure to communicate what he knows, and ought to communicate, is *concealment*. Concealment of matters that are material to the risk invalidates the policy. The test of materiality is whether a fact, if truly stated, might reasonably have influenced the insurer in its decision to reject or accept the risk, or to charge a higher premium.

 Keeping secrets about a business is often a wise idea. However, it can be costly when an insurance company is kept in the dark. Generally, it is to the insured's advantage to notify the insurer of developments that may affect the risks or the premiums. For example, a change in the structure or ownership of a business, or an improvement that reduces risk, might entitle an insured to a reduced premium. If the insurer is not notified, the insured would not be eligible for lower premiums. When altered circumstances *increase* risks, warranting higher premiums, failure to notify the insurer of the change could lead to retroactive added premiums at best; at worst, it could lead to rejection of otherwise valid claims.

Representations and Misrepresentations   A *representation* is an oral or written statement given by the insured to the insurer before the contract is made. The statement consists of factual information that is intended or necessary to enable the insurer to determine whether it will accept the risk and at what premium. Representations are either affirmative or promissory. Affirmative representations are allegations of fact as they exist at the time they are made; promissory representations refer to what is to happen during the term of the insurance policy.

A representation can be false and yet not have been made with an intent to deceive. In contrast, a misrepresentation is a statement as a fact of something that (1) is untrue, (2) is known to be untrue, and (3) *is* made with an intent to deceive. A misrepresentation can also be a statement that an insured claims is true without knowing it to be true, and which has a tendency to mislead.

EXAMPLE

Broyles bought a car on May 11, 1977. At the same time, he purchased a life insurance policy from Ford Life Insurance Company. Broyles signed a health statement on the application, declaring that he was in "good health" to the best of his knowledge. A place for listing exceptions to or limits on the general statement of health was left blank. In fact, as early as July 1976, Broyles knew he was suffering from some kind of blood disorder. He died of leukemia on October 8, 1977. Broyles had not known that he had leukemia when he applied for the life insurance. However, because he had known that he had a blood disorder, his statement as to good health was untrue and, as such, a misrepresentation.

 If there is a deliberate concealment or misrepresentation in obtaining an insurance policy, the insurer will normally not have to pay for a loss. Even if the insurance contract is valid to begin with, failure to provide current information about a risk can preclude or diminish recovery for a loss. It is not at all unusual for business insurance policies to require the policyholder to promptly report changes in operations, fluctuations in inventory, relocation of the business, and other conditions that might increase the risk of loss. Therefore, the insured should carefully read the policy to ascertain what risk is insured and what information needs to be communicated on a continuing basis to the insurance company.

Warranties   A *warranty* is a statement, description, or undertaking by an insured that appears in the insurance policy and relates to the risk insured against. For example, a provision of a burglary policy by which the insured agrees to install certain locks on the insured premises is an express warranty. A warranty must appear on the face of a policy or be incorporated in some fashion into the policy.

At this point a distinction must be made between a warranty and a representation. A warranty is part of the completed contract, whereas a representation is made during the formation of a contract and is not necessarily incorporated into the policy itself. In other words, a representation tends to induce the insurer to assume the risk more readily, whereas a warranty is a written stipulation in the policy on which the validity of the contract depends. A warranty can be breached regardless of the insured's intent. Breach of a warranty prevents recovery under the insurance policy, even if the warranty does not relate to a matter that is material to the risk. However, a misrepresentation must relate to a material matter and must have been willfully and knowingly made with an intent to defraud in order for an insurer to be relieved of liability.

The following case illustrates the impact of false statements made by an applicant for automobile insurance. Consider how the result depends in large part on whether the misstatements are deemed warranties or representations. Consider, too, the policy of the law as discussed by the court to the end that warranties are to be more strictly construed than misrepresentations and must be incorporated specifically into the terms of an insurance policy.

Allstate Ins. Co.

v

Boggs

27 Ohio St 2d 216, 56 Ohio Ops 2d 130, 271 NE2d 855

(Ohio Supreme Court, 1971)

[In December 1966, cars driven by William Boggs and Dallas Christopher were involved in an automobile accident. Both drivers were killed, and a passenger in Boggs' car was injured. Inland Mutual Insurance Company had in effect a policy issued to Christopher. In the application for that policy Christopher had stated that no driver under 25 years of age would operate the vehicle and that he had been born in 1940. After the accident, Inland learned that Christopher had been born in 1943. Inland therefore canceled Christopher's policy and refused to cover the accident on the ground that his policy was void. Allstate, which was Boggs' insurer, then brought an action seeking to have Christopher's policy declared valid; otherwise, Allstate would be liable under the uninsured motorist provisions of Boggs' policy. At trial, it was stipulated that Inland would not have issued the policy had it known Christopher's correct age. There were no facts tending to show that Christopher deliberately misrepresented his age. The trial court found that Inland's policy was in full force and effect at the time of the accident, and Inland then appealed.]

C. William O'Neill, Chief Justice.

*   *   *

The primary question raised by this cause is whether a misstatement of age by an insured in an application for an automobile liability insurance policy renders the policy void *ab initio* [from the outset].

Statements by an insured fall into two classes—those which constitute warranties, and those which constitute representation.

The consequences of a misstatement of fact by an insured are entirely different, depending on whether the statement is a warranty or a representation. If the statement is a warranty, a misstatement of fact voids the policy *ab initio*. However, if the statement is a representation, a misstatement by the insured will render the policy voidable, if it is fraudulently made and the fact is material to the risk, but it does not void the policy *ab initio*.

In the law of insurance, a representation is a statement made prior to the issuance of the policy which tends to cause the insurer to assume the risk. A warranty is a statement, description or undertaking by the insured of a material fact either appearing on the face of the policy or in another instrument specifically incorporated in the policy. . . .

The insurer's decision to incorporate the statement in or to omit it from the policy generally controls whether the statement is a warranty or a representation.

However, the mere fact that a statement of an insured is incorporated in a policy does not necessarily make such statement a warranty. Courts do not favor warranties, or forfeitures from the breach thereof, and a statement as to conditions does not constitute a warranty unless the language of the policy, construed strictly against the insurer, requires such an interpretation. The fundamental principle is that inasmuch as policies of insurance are in the language selected by the insurer they are to be construed strictly against the insurer, and liberally in favor of the insured. . . .

In other words, an insurer is bound by the provisions which he chooses to incorporate in his policy. If it is his purpose to provide that a misstatement by the insured shall render the policy void *ab initio,* such facts must appear clearly and unambiguously from the terms of the policy.

It should be noted at this point that in the instant case there is no provision in the policy to the effect that any misstatement or misrepresentation made by the insured shall render the policy void.

Thus, the basic issue is whether the insurer in its contract of insurance provided that age was such a material fact that a misrepresentation thereof would make the contract void *ab initio.* It is stipulated that appellant would not have issued this policy if it had been aware of [the insured's] age; but that is a statement *after* the fact. [Court's emphasis.] Furthermore, such stipulation cannot affect the legal conclusion which must be drawn from the policy of insurance as to whether misstatement of age is sufficient, under the terms of the policy, to render the policy void *ab initio.*

The application in the instant case required, among other things, that the applicant state his age, accidents, prior traffic convictions and any prior refusal or cancellation of insurance.

Although the policy provides generally that, "the named insured agrees that the statements in the declarations and in the application for this policy are his agreements and representations, that this policy is issued in reliance upon the truth of such representations," nowhere is the application, as such, incorporated in and made a part of the policy. The mere fact that a policy of insurance refers to the application does not make such application a part of the policy. . . . In order to have an incorporation by reference in an insurance policy, it must be done in unequivocal language on the face of the policy. . . .

Therefore, we must look to the policy itself to determine whether the misstatements of the insured, alone, are sufficient to render the policy void *ab initio.*

The *only place in the policy* where direct reference is made to any of the subject matter contained in the application is that part of the policy designated Combination Automobile Daily Report. [Court's emphasis.] In items 9 and 10 thereof, reference is made to prior convictions and prior policy cancellations. However, no reference is made in the policy to the age of the insured.

Although it is now stipulated that the appellant would not have issued the policy if it had been aware of the insured's age, the insurer did not deem *age* of sufficient importance to incorporate such matter in its policy, even though it did incorporate prior traffic convictions and prior policy cancellations in the body of the policy. [Court's emphasis.]

The insurer in the instant case has chosen to include in its policy only the statements as to prior convictions and prior cancellations, thus giving those representations at least the semblance of warranties which would render the policy void *ab initio* if the misstatement therein was material to the risk. The insurer failed to incorporate the statement as to age. That representation in the application, if shown to be material to the risk and fraudulently made, would be grounds for cancellation of the policy, but does not render the policy void *ab initio,* and may not be used to avoid liability after the accident has occurred.

In order for an insurer to successfully assert that an insured's misstatement as to his age in an insurance policy application is a strict warranty which makes the policy void *ab initio,* the insurer must include a statement in the policy which it issues to the effect that such a representation as to age in the application is a warranty.

[Judgment affirmed.]

40:10 Waiver and Estoppel

In all types of insurance, a party to the contract can waive or be estopped from asserting policy provisions. Waiver and estoppel, which are defined below, are frequently applied in insurance law in favor of the insured or beneficiary to prevent a rescission by the insurer or a forfeiture of the policy. Both doctrines are also applicable in favor of the insurer, however. That is, the insurer can claim that the insured forfeited his policy because of waiver or estoppel.

The terms "waiver" and "estoppel" designate different legal concepts, although in many insurance cases estoppel is used in a vague sense, making its meaning practically synonymous with waiver. Generally, waiver is a voluntary act that implies an abandonment of a right or privilege. Estoppel has been so loosely used as to make it difficult to define. Essential elements of estoppel are the misleading of a party who is entitled to rely on the acts or statements in question, and a consequent change of position to that party's detriment. Thus, any agreement, declaration, or course of action on the insurer's part that leads an insured honestly to believe that by conforming to it his policy will not be forfeited, followed by due conformity on his part, will estop (prevent) the insurer from declaring a forfeiture, even though the insurer may claim that the policy has been forfeited under the express provisions of the contract. It can be seen, therefore, that a distinction does exist between waiver and estoppel, but this distinction is not as clear as the definitions indicate them to be and, in fact, many courts use these terms interchangeably.

The following case illustrates the use of the estoppel doctrine in insurance law. The court's opinion analyzes the limits of the doctrine in the sense that estoppel cannot be used to create or fashion an insurance contract where none previously existed.

Madgett

v

Monroe County Mutual Tornado Ins. Co.
46 Wis 2d 708, 176 NW2d 314
(Wisconsin Supreme Court, 1970)

[On May 15, 1960, the defendant, Monroe Mutual Tornado Insurance Company, issued a policy insuring farm buildings owned by Schlaver against windstorm damage. Four years later, in March 1964, the plaintiff, Madgett, bought the farm from Schlaver. On April 1, 1964, Madgett took possession of the property. No assignment of the insurance policy was made, and no new policy covering windstorm damage was obtained. On April 13, 1964, the buildings on the farm were damaged by a windstorm.

After the storm, Madgett's farm manager went to see one of Monroe Mutual's directors, who lived nearby. The director advised the manager to get the buildings repaired and prepare a list of property damages. Madgett had the buildings repaired, but Monroe Mutual refused to pay the claim on the ground that there was no contract of insurance between it and Madgett. Madgett sued to recover payment and won in the trial court. Monroe Mutual then appealed.]

Robert W. Hansen, Justice.

*   *   *

The plaintiff seeks to recover as the insured from the defendant as insurer under an insurance policy covering windstorm damages. The weakness in plaintiff's case is that he had no policy of insurance with the defendant company on the date when the damages were sustained. The company had issued a windstorm policy to the previous owner but that policy had not been assigned to plaintiff, and no new policy had been issued. The relationship of insurer and insured derives from a contract of insurance. Here it is conceded that there was no contract of insurance between the plaintiff and the defendant company.

Instead, plaintiff claims that the defendant company is estopped from mentioning the absence of any contract of insurance by reason of the acts of its director. When the director of the company told the manager of the farm to have the storm-damaged buildings repaired, such act of defendant's agent estops it from asserting that plaintiff was not its insured, or so the plaintiff argues. Estoppel is a sturdy doctrine, but it cannot sustain so heavy a load.

Estoppel can block, but it cannot create. It is a barricade that can stop a litigant from proceeding down a roadway that, except for estoppel, would be open to him. It is not a bulldozer that can create a roadway where none in fact exists or ever did. Estoppel may prevent an insurer from enforcing certain policy provisions against its insured. However, even where the relationship of insurer and insured exists, estoppel cannot be used to enlarge the coverage of an insurance policy, for then the effect would be to create ". . . a new contract providing coverage for which no premium has been paid." Cases where there was a contract of insurance, or had been an assignment of an existing policy, cannot be relied upon. Here there was no contract and there was no assignment. As this court stated in a case where a husband sought to use estoppel to collect on an insurance policy issued to his wife:

> "But the difficulty of applying the doctrine of estoppel in this case arises from the fact that the plaintiff never had any contractual relations with the defendant companies, and the doctrine of estoppel will not apply to create a contract that never existed. . . . We are asked to create a contract of insurance in the first instance, and then invoke the doctrine of estoppel as to this court-made contract. This cannot be done."

Plaintiff cannot here recover as an insured under a contract of insurance because there was no contract of insurance between plaintiff and defendant. Estoppel cannot be used to create what does not and never did exist. Plaintiff was not an insured. Defendant was not his insurer.

[Judgment reversed.]

40:11   Cancellation

Cancellation is commonly regarded as the right to rescind, abandon, or abrogate a contract of insurance. An insurance contract is not susceptible to cancellation or rescission only in part, at least without the consent of both the insurer and the insured. The cancellation of an insurance policy does not affect any rights that have already accrued under the policy in favor of the insured or a third person. Thus, for example, an insurer cannot avoid liability for a loss by giving notice of its election to terminate the policy *after* the loss has occurred.

Both the form and the sufficiency of a notice of cancellation are determined by policy provisions. Most insurance policies contain provisions allowing cancellation at the request of the insured. For example, an insured's mere physical surrender of his policy does not necessarily terminate the contract. Fire insurance policies and other contracts of insurance on property, in addition to the common provision for cancellation of the policy on the insured's request, generally provide that the insurer can cancel by giving notice to the insured within a prescribed period, usually five or ten days, and returning the unearned portion of the premium paid by the insured. The reason for this provision is to allow the insured ample opportunity to negotiate for other insurance to replace the canceled policy.

Both the insurer and the insured can cancel or rescind an insurance policy on the basis of fraud or misrepresentation. An insured's right to rescind a policy for fraud must be exercised promptly after the insured learns of the fraud. The insurer must give notice that the policy is canceled and must pay back or offer the insured the premiums paid.

40:12   Incontestability Provisions

Life insurance policies usually contain provisions commonly referred to as *incontestability clauses*. An incontestability clause provides that the policy cannot be contested after a certain passage of time. There are two kinds of clauses, one providing that the policy shall be incontestable after a particular date and the other providing that the policy shall be incontestable after a specified period of time. The latter type, which usually designates the period as one or two years, is in general use. The intent of both types of incontestability clauses is to fix a limited time within which an insurer must discover and assert any grounds it may have for rescinding a policy issued by it. Legislation in all but two states—Missouri and Rhode Island—requires that life insurance contracts have incontestability clauses.

If a policy contains an incontestability clause, the insurer must take legal action within the specified time period either by suing to cancel or rescind the policy, or by setting up misrepresentation or fraud in the procurement of the policy as a defense in an action brought by the insured or the beneficiary.

Key Concepts and Terms

- The relationship between an insurer and an insured is purely contractual. A contract of insurance must describe (1) the subject matter to be insured, (2) the risk insured against, (3) the commencement and period of the risk undertaken by the insurer, (4) the amount of insurance, and (5) the premium and time at which it is to be paid.
- Negotiations for the purchase of insurance are ordinarily initiated when a person fills out an application. The application itself is not a contract; it is only an offer. It must be accepted by the insurer before an insurance contract is created.
- A binder is a receipt that an insurer can issue to the insured. It provides temporary insurance coverage.
- An insurance premium is the price at which the insurer agrees to carry the risk insured against. As such, it is the consideration paid by the insured for the insurance.

- An insurer is at liberty to select the character of the risk it will assume. Subject to this right, all foreseeable losses or risks can be insured against unless (1) insuring them is contrary to public policy or prohibited by statute or (2) they are losses caused by the insured's own fraud or other misconduct.

- The insurer is not liable except on proof that a loss within the terms of a policy has occurred.

- An insurable interest is necessary to the validity of an insurance contract. In regard to property, anyone has an insurable interest who derives a benefit from its existence or would suffer loss from its destruction. In regard to life insurance, every person has an insurable interest in his own life. To have an insurable interest in another's life, a person must have a reasonable expectation of benefit or advantage from the continuance of the other's life.

- Most insurance policies require the insured to give timely notice to the insurer of a loss or occurrence arising under the terms of the policy. The purpose of such a provision is to allow the insurer to (1) review its rights and liabilities and (2) investigate claims and perhaps settle them.

- An obligation of good faith and fair dealing on the insurer's part is implied in every insurance contract. This obligation requires an insurer to settle a claim against its insured in an appropriate case even though the policy does not expressly impose such a duty.

- The beneficiary is the person entitled to the proceeds of insurance when the loss, damage, or liability insured against arises. Ordinarily, "beneficiary" refers to the person designated in a life insurance policy as the one who is to receive the benefits that become payable when the insured dies.

- An insured can recover only the amount set forth in his insurance policy. An insured cannot recover additional sums after payment of a loss has been made.

- In all types of insurance, a party to the contract can waive or be estopped from asserting policy provisions. Waiver and estoppel are frequently applied in insurance law in favor of the insured or the beneficiary to prevent the insurer's cancellation of the policy.

- Binder
- Concealment
- Conditions
- Incontestability Clause
- Key Employee Insurance
- Life Insurance

- Premium
- Representation
- Self-insurance
- Wagering Contract
- Warranty

Questions and Case Problems

1. Jesse buys a used Cadillac for $4,100. A comprehensive insurance policy on the car is issued by an insurer. Three days later, the car is stolen. On processing the theft claim, the insurer discovers that Jesse had purchased a stolen vehicle. It then disclaims liability on the ground that Jesse had no insurable interest in the vehicle. Does Jesse have an insurable interest in the stolen car?

2. Prior to October 1964, Mrs. King and her husband owned real property and the building on it, in which they operated a grocery store. On October 12, 1964, Mr. and Mrs. King conveyed the real property to their daughters. For the next several years the daughters and their husbands cared for the Kings and helped run the grocery store. The proceeds from the store were placed in a special bank account and used to meet the Kings' needs. In February 1967, Aetna Insurance Company issued a policy to Mrs. King insuring her against any loss she might sustain from the destruction of the building and its contents by fire. In December 1967 the store and all of its contents were destroyed by fire. Aetna denied Mrs. King's claim for loss on the ground that at the time of the fire she did not have an insurable interest in the store and its contents. How should this case be decided?

3. Dr. Pappas owned an old log-frame house on which he purchased fire insurance in the amount of $5,000. Later, Dr. Pappas deeded the property to his then 6-year-old son. He later purchased an additional fire insurance policy, but never gave notice to either insurance company that he had deeded the property to his son. The house was subsequently completely destroyed by fire. Did the doctor have an insurable interest in this property? Would the fact that the doctor paid for the rehabilitation and remodeling of the home, prior to its loss, have any bearing on the question of insurable interest? Would the doctor's probable control over the insured property during his son's minority affect his insurable interest? Assume that the second insurance company knew at the time its policy was issued that the doctor did not have title to the house. Should a duty to investigate and ascertain the property's true status be imposed on that company? If the insurance company had known that the doctor did not have title to the insured property at the time the policy was issued, should it be estopped or prevented from asserting the doctor's lack of insurable interest?

4. Describe the essential terms and elements of an insurance contract.

5. Walker contracted with Fisher to trim Walker's trees. On the same day Walker called her insurance agent and stated she would like to have an accident policy on Fisher. The agent agreed to issue the policy. The policy was effective for one day and named Fisher as insured and Walker as beneficiary with her relationship to the insured shown as "employer." The premium of 85 cents was paid by Walker. The policy provided in part for accidental death benefits of $10,000. While trimming trees at Walker's residence, Fisher sustained an accidental bodily injury from which he later died. Did Walker have an insurable interest in Fisher's life? Would the result be different if Walker were named only as a nominal beneficiary and at the suggestion of the agent who did not know Fisher's nonfamily status?

6. Analyze and discuss the duty of the insurer to act in good faith.

7. When James Robinson's 16-year-old son died, the death certificate stated, "there were no marks on body that indicated violence; apparently died from natural causes." About seven months before, Robinson had applied to Reliable Life Insurance Company for a life policy on the boy, naming himself as beneficiary. The application stated that the boy had not been treated by a doctor in the past five years, had not had any illness or injury within the past five years, and had never been hospitalized at all. The facts, discovered by Reliable after the boy's death, were that Robinson's son had suffered from sickle-cell anemia for several years, and less than two years earlier had been hospitalized for two weeks for intestinal hemorrhaging and sickle-cell anemia. The false medical history prompted Reliable to refuse to pay on the policy. The statute applicable to the case provided that false

statements in an application for life insurance would not void coverage unless the insurer showed that the matter or thing represented was material to the risk "or actually contributed to the contingency or event on which said policy became due and payable." Should Reliable have to pay the face amount of the life policy?

8. Distinguish between conditions and representations. Why are they so important in the law of insurance?

9. In his application for life insurance, Bunn indicated that he was married and that he did not contemplate a change in occupation or foreign travel. At the time the application was made, however, Bunn was not married, although he had been living with a woman for 15 years and was the father of her two children. Later, Bunn married the woman and left for work in Vietnam. He died there one year later. The insurer denied liability under the policy on the ground that Bunn made two material misrepresentations in his application for the policy. Were both representations material? Should the policy be declared void?

10. Johnston was arrested and taken into custody by state police during a raid at the Tally Ho Restaurant. Johnston claimed that he had innocently wandered into a gambling and stag party, and the state dropped all charges against him. However, Johnston's name had appeared in several newspaper stories in connection with the illegal party and police raid. He sued Tally Ho for negligence in allowing the party, seeking damages for injury to his reputation and business standing. Tally Ho requested its insurer, PMA, to defend the action under the terms of its liability policy. PMA refused, and Tally Ho joined PMA as a third-party defendant in the action. PMA's insurance policy provided as follows:

> "The company will pay on behalf of the insured all sums which the insured shall become legally obligated to pay as damages because of Coverage A (bodily injury) or Coverage B (property damage) to which this insurance applies, caused by an occurrence, and the company shall have the right and duty to defend any suit against the insured seeking damages on account of such bodily injury or property damage, even if any of the allegations of the suit are groundless, false, or fraudulent."

Is Johnston's claim for damage to his reputation and business standing covered by the "property damage" clause of the policy? Does PMA have a duty to defend Tally Ho? Johnston also alleged in his complaint that he was "set upon and arrested by the police." He did not allege specifically that any bodily injury resulted, and he did not claim damages for bodily injury. Does the mere use of the words "set upon and arrested" mean that Johnston was physically injured, obligating the insurance company to defend Tally Ho?

PART NINE

Business Organizations

Introductory Comments

Business in the United States encompasses all economic activity pursued for profit. All business organizations—whether they are sole proprietorships, partnerships, or corporations—have this purpose. Success depends in part on the form and structure of the business enterprise. Obviously, while success in business is not necessarily guaranteed simply by adopting one form of organization over another, the careful crafting of a business does enhance the likelihood of its being successful.

The chapters in this part discuss the basic types of business organizations and cover how they are formed, how they are managed, and how they operate. These chapters provide the business law student with a basic understanding of the legal doctrines affecting the most important business entities.

General and limited partnerships are discussed in Chapter 41. Also discussed in this chapter are other similar forms of businesses, such as joint ventures, which have many partnership characteristics yet differ from partnerships in fundamental ways. Chapters 42 through 45 present the law of corporations, including corporate finance and securities regulation (Chapter 43), corporate management (Chapter 44), and the rights of shareholders (Chapter 45). Chapter 46 focuses on the franchise, which, although not a type of business organization per se, is a common and vital form of business enterprise. The final chapter in this part, Chapter 47, is based on all the materials discussed in Chapters 41 through 46. It analyzes the most important considerations to be weighed in the formation of a new business, how these factors affect the conduct of business, and their relative merit.

Students may find it helpful to focus on the basic issues with which business organizations must deal. These issues, common to all businesses, include (1) formation; (2) control; (3) management; (4) transferability of ownership; (5) liability; and (6) duration. An appreciation of how these issues are handled with respect to the sole proprietorship, the partnership, the corporation, and the franchise—and how they may differ as to each—will help the student to work successfully in the business environment and to use the knowledge gained in this text in a productive, profitable, and legally responsible manner.

41 Partnerships, Limited Partnerships, and Special Ventures

41:1 Nature and Formation of Partnerships

The partnership is a common form of business organization. Many of the doctrines of partnership law developed in Europe under the law merchant during the Middle Ages and in England under the common law. In the United States, most of these doctrines are now codified in the *Uniform Partnership Act* (UPA), which was originally drafted in 1914. The UPA has been adopted in every state except Georgia and Louisiana. Because of the widespread applicability of the UPA throughout the United States, the discussion of partnership law in this chapter will be based on it.[1]

A partnership is an association of two or more persons to carry on a business for profit as co-owners (UPA § 6). A partnership can be formed for any purpose that is not in violation of law or public policy; it can be formed for a single transaction or for a continuing series of transactions.

There are various types of partnerships, each creating different powers and liabilities for partners. The types that will be discussed in this chapter are general partnerships and limited partnerships.

Among *general partnerships,* a distinction is made in some states between trading or commercial partnerships on the one hand, and ordinary or nontrading partnerships on the other. A trading partnership is one that engages in buying or selling. In contrast, a nontrading partnership is one that is not organized for trade or commerce. Partnerships organized for the practice of a profession, such as law, are examples of nontrading partnerships. Although the UPA seems to have abolished these categories, courts in some states have made distinctions between members of trading and nontrading partnerships in regard to such matters as their power both to borrow money and to sell personal property on behalf of the firm.

Creation of Partnership A partnership is created by a contract between or among the parties (the intended partners). The parties must expressly agree to unite their property and services as co-owners to carry on a business for profit and

---

[1]The complete text of the UPA is reproduced in Appendix D.

to share the profits and losses in stated proportions. The contract must be based on valid consideration.

A partnership agreement regulates the duties of the partners and can include virtually any provision desired by them. Certain partnership agreements must be in writing to be effective. For example, an agreement that provides for mandatory continuance of a partnership for more than one year is within the statute of frauds (see Chapter 15) and must be evidenced by a written document. Other partnership agreements do not need to be in writing. For example, an agreement authorizing the partners to deal in real estate need not be in writing insofar as the rights of the partners as to one another are concerned.

 It is suggested that any partnership agreement be in writing so that the partners' understanding of their mutual rights and duties is preserved and protected. If a partnership agreement is not in writing, it may be very difficult to prove that an oral agreement among the partners existed if, for example, one of the partners dies.

Other Business Relationships Compared   In some ways partnerships resemble other forms of business and other types of relationships. Thus, a partnership has certain elements in common with an agency relationship, a joint venture, a corporation, a nonprofit association, the relationship between joint owners of property, and even a trust. At the same time, a partnership has characteristics that are clearly distinguishable from these other relationships. Some of these similarities and differences will now be discussed briefly.

The primary distinction between a partnership and an agency (see Chapter 48) is that a partnership consists of co-owners. Although an agent can receive a share of the profits of the principal's business as compensation for services, the agent is not an owner.

A *joint venture* resembles a partnership in that its members associate as co-owners in a business enterprise, agreeing to share profits and losses (see 41:12). However, a partnership ordinarily engages in a continuing business for an indefinite or fixed period of time, whereas a joint venture is formed for a single transaction or a limited series of transactions.

Unlike a partnership, a corporation is always treated as an artificial person created by law separate and distinct from its shareholders (see Chapter 42). Shareholders of a corporation are generally not personally liable for corporate debts, and no shareholder or corporate officer can bind the corporation without authorization from the board of directors (see Chapter 45). In contrast, each partner has the power to bind each fellow member of the partnership. Each partner is individually liable both for debts and obligations of the partnership and for acts of his copartners that are within the scope of their authority.

Employment relations are also readily distinguishable from partnerships. Unlike a partner, for example, an employee is not empowered to exercise management or control over the work being performed. An employee usually works for a fixed compensation and does not share in the profits and losses of the employer's business as does a partner. Finally, an employee is not viewed as having a fiduciary relationship with his employers, whereas a relationship of trust always exists between partners.

The following case illustrates circumstances under which a partnership can be found to exist. Note that if other requirements necessary for the formation of a partnership are present, a written agreement is not required. Consider the circumstances under which the question of whether a partnership existed arose in the case and why the court held that a partnership had been created.

Cochran

v

Board of Supervisors
85 Cal App 3d 75, 149 Cal Rptr 304
(California Court of Appeal, 1978)

[A county assessor sought to compel a county board of supervisors to uphold certain property tax assessments made by the assessor. The assessments were based on the assessor's conclusion that certain contiguous parcels of land should be valued as separate tracts. All the owners of the parcels were closely related by blood, marriage, or employment. Three businesses, which also held record title to some of the parcels in question, were jointly owned by several of the record owners. The board of supervisors found that an oral partnership had been formed, that all of the parcels of land had the same legal ownership, and that the property should have been assessed as a whole rather than as individual parcels. The county assessor then petitioned the trial court for an order to compel the board of supervisors to uphold his property tax assessments. The trial court found for the board, and the assessor appealed.]

Newsom, J.

*   *   *

On April 1 and 2, 1976, the Del Norte County Board of Supervisors . . . held hearings on the applications of Harold A., Jane S. and Prudence M. Miller, Joanne M. and Theodore Lilley, Achsah J. Graham, Darrell H.

Schroeder, and Miller Redwood Co. (hereinafter applicants) for a reduction in the . . . assessments made by the assessor on land to which variously they hold record title. The assessment was based upon the assessor's conclusion that the lands owned by applicants should have been valued as separate tracts, and, as such, would have been both valued and taxed more highly. As appears in greater detail below, the Board disagreed, and its views were sustained by the trial court, leading to the present appeal.

A perusal of the record reveals that the individual applicants are closely related: Harold and Jane Miller are husband and wife; Prudence Miller, Achsah Graham and Joanne Lilley are their daughters; Theodore Lilley is Joanne's husband; and Darrell Shroeder, though unrelated by blood or marriage to the other applicants, is a key employee of the family lumber enterprise. Miller Redwood Company and Rellim Redwood Company are wholly owned subsidiaries of Stimson Lumber Company, and the individual applicants together own at least 90 percent of the stock of Stimson.

The subject lands are owned of record by the applicants in a variety of combinations. Tracts are held individually by Harold A. Miller, Jane S. Miller, Joanne M. Lilley, Achsah Jane Graham, and Miller Redwood Co. The remaining tracts are held by groups: Harold A., Jane S., Prudence and Achsah Miller are one; Harold A. Miller, Theodore Lilley and Darrell H. Schroeder another; and Harold A. Miller and Darrell H. Schroeder form the third group.

A web of contractual rights binds the tracts together. Rellim has the right to cut timber on all tracts, and title to the timber thereon once the trees are felled. Its parent company, Stimson, has the right of first refusal to purchase any of the lands on the death of the owner. . . .

Indeed, it is fair to say that the applicants have bound themselves in such a manner that no one of them is free to deal with his land except in the manner set forth in these numerous contracts. . . .

A primary factual finding by the Board is that the applicants' timber operations constituted a partnership. A partnership is "an association of two or more persons to carry on as co-owners a business for profit." . . . This definition has been amplified and rephrased as requiring a community of interest in the business and a sharing of profits and losses. . . .

The rules for determining the existence of a partnership . . . provide that co-ownership of any sort and profit-sharing are factors tending to establish partnership. A written agreement is not necessary. . . . The intent of the parties as revealed in the terms of their agreement is, of course, a crucial factor in determining whether a partnership exists, as are the conduct of the parties and the surrounding circumstances. . . . If, using these criteria, a partnership were to be found, it would not be disproved by a finding of unequal duties, contributions or distribution of profits. . . .

Here, the totality of circumstances tends strongly to support the Board's conclusion of a parol [oral] partnership. The record shows without contradiction that the applicants regarded themselves as partners, conducted their business jointly, and distributed profits in proportion to their ownership interests. Indeed, the record shows that Rellim logged all of the subject lands in accordance with the overall needs of the enterprise, and without regard for boundary lines between separate parcels.

Certainly we are bound to say under these circumstances that substantial evidence supports the Board's conclusion that the applicants operated as a partnership. . . .

[Affirmed.]

Who Can Be Partners   In general, any person or entity capable of making a contract can be a partner. Since UPA § 2 is rather broad in its definition of "person," individuals, other partnerships, corporations, and business associations all have the capacity to become partners. Under the UPA a corporation can become a partner, although it might be limited in doing so by state corporation laws.[2] A minor can become a partner, but his contract of partnership might not be valid, with the result that his potential liability as a partner might not be enforceable.[3]

Silent Partners   Occasionally, a partnership is formed in which one or more of the members do not want to be associated publicly with the partnership. These members are known as *silent partners,* and their connection with partnership business is ordinarily concealed. Silent partners sometimes take an active part in partnership affairs, but often they do not.

---

[2]State corporation laws are discussed in Chapter 42.
[3]Legal capacity of parties is discussed in Chapter 13.

Junior and Senior Partners   The terms "junior partner" and "senior partner," while frequently used in law firms and other professional partnerships, generally have no special legal significance other than that which is given the terms in the partnership agreement. In at least one state, it is provided by statute that partners can, by written agreement, establish various classes of partners, such as senior partners, junior partners, and managing partners, and that they can also establish various classes of nonpartner employees.

41:2   Partnership Property

All property brought into a partnership or acquired by it is partnership property [UPA § 8(1)]. Property acquired with partnership funds is also partnership property. Under UPA §§ 8(3) and 8(4), real property can be acquired in the partnership name. In every state, the personal property of a partnership is owned by the partnership itself and not by the partners individually.

Conveyance of Property   Partnership property can be conveyed only in the partnership name [UPA § 8(3)]. Title to real property that is in the names of all of the partners individually can be conveyed if all the partners sign the conveyance; this passes all of their rights to such property [UPA § 10(5)].

   Any partner can convey title to real property by a conveyance signed on behalf of a partnership if title to the property is in the name of the partnership [UPA § 10(1)]. Of course, such a conveyance must also be within the authority of the partner. A conveyance of partnership property by a partner, even though made without authority, cannot be recovered by a partnership if the property has been conveyed for value and the purchaser lacks knowledge or notice that the partner exceeded his authority.

   If title to property is in the name of one or more of the partners, a partner in whose name the title stands can convey title. Thus, for example, if property owned by the Santa Fe partnership is held in the name of Fremont, legal title can be conveyed by Fremont in his own name. However, under UPA § 10(3), a partnership may recover property that is conveyed this way unless it is otherwise bound by the partner's acts.

   Although the UPA regulates the sale of real property, it does not specifically deal with the sale or conveyance of personal property. These transactions are handled by the partners under their general powers to enter into contracts within the customary scope or purpose of partnership business.

Property Rights of Partners   The property rights of an individual partner include (1) the interest in the partnership; (2) the right in specific partnership property held in tenancy in partnership; and (3) the right to participate in management.

   A partner's interest in the partnership is his share of the profit and surplus (UPA § 26). A partner can dispose of his interest in a partnership by selling it to another partner. A partner can also transfer his interest in the partnership to a third person. However, a third person to whom the interest is assigned cannot become a partner without the consent of the existing partners. Indeed, the conveyance of a partner's interest does not entitle the assignee to (1) interfere in the management or administration of partnership business, (2) require any information or account of partnership transactions, or (3) inspect the partnership books [UPA § 18(g)]. The assignee is entitled only to receive the profits to which the assigning partner would otherwise be entitled.

Tenancy in Partnership   Real property that is owned or acquired by a partnership is held under what is called a *tenancy in partnership* [UPA § 25(1)]. Under UPA § 25(2), the characteristics of a tenancy in partnership are that (1) each partner has an equal right to use the property for partnership purposes in the absence of an agreement to the contrary; (2) a partner does not possess in any specific item of partnership property an interest that can be voluntarily sold, assigned, or mortgaged; (3) a creditor of a partner cannot proceed against any specific item of partnership property; and (4) on the death of a partner, the partnership property vests in the surviving partners for partnership purposes and is not subject to the right of survivorship.[4]

41:3   Powers of Partners

The general powers of partners are largely defined by the rules of law applicable to agents (see Chapter 48). In fact, the law of partnership has been called a branch of agency law. In one sense, every partner is a principal. However, for all purposes within the scope of a partnership's business, every partner is also a general and authorized agent of the partnership as well as an agent of all the other partners.

The powers of partners are governed largely by the provisions of the UPA and by the terms of the partnership agreement. Under UPA § 18(c), all partners possess an equal right in the management and conduct of the partnership business, even though some partners may receive a larger percentage of the profits. The conduct of a partnership is usually decided by a majority of the partners. Majority rule does not apply to an act that, by the partners' agreement, must be consented to by all the partners. Also, UPA § 9(3) provides that certain acts usually require the consent of all the partners. These acts are:

- Assigning partnership property for the benefit of creditors[5]
- Disposing of partnership goodwill
- Doing any act that would make it impossible to carry on the ordinary business of the partnership
- Consenting to the entry of a court judgment against the partnership
- Submitting a partnership claim or liability to arbitration

Scope of Authority   A partner's status as such gives him the authority to act as an agent for the partnership in transactions within the usual course of partnership

---

[4]The right of survivorship is discussed in Chapter 32.
[5]Assignments for the benefit of creditors are discussed in Chapter 31.

business [UPA § 9(1)]. The partner need not obtain express permission from other partners to transact partnership business. For example, a partner can use the partnership's assets to pay its debts, and he can enter into contracts in the name of the partnership and bind the firm by these contracts. A partner also has the authority to sign bills and notes or other debt instruments on behalf of the firm, and to collect, release, compromise, and pay claims or debts due the partnership.

A partner's act does not always bind the other partners or the partnership. If, for example, a partner acts without authority on a matter not within the apparent scope of partnership business, neither the partnership nor the other partners are bound by the act unless the other partners later ratify it. Partners can also restrict their authority as agents of the firm. They can even place secret restrictions on one another's authority, and these restrictions will bind all the partners and any other person who may have knowledge of them or be under a duty to make an inquiry in this regard. Secret restrictions usually do not, however, apply to third persons who deal with the firm and have no knowledge about them.

The following case illustrates a creditor's attempt to hold a partnership liable on the theory that one partner's act was binding on the partnership. Note the court's reasoning in arriving at its decision. Note also that the partnership in the case was in the process of being dissolved; dissolution is discussed in 41:6.

Brewer
v
Elks
260 NC 470, 133 SE2d 159
(North Carolina Supreme Court, 1963)

[Brewer filed a claim for $4,000 for amounts due under two notes against a partnership conducted by Elks and Keel doing business as the Friendly Furniture Company. A receiver handling the dissolution of the partnership allowed Brewer's claim for $2,000 under the first note. From the sale of partnership assets, Brewer was paid a portion of the first note, leaving a balance of $963.15. Brewer then sued to collect the balance of the first note as well as the total amount due under the second. At trial, both Elks and Keel admitted liability for the balance owing under the first note signed in the name of the Friendly Furniture Company. Keel denied liability on the second note. He contended that because Elks had personally signed it in his own name, the partnership was not liable. The court dismissed Brewer's claim, finding that the evidence was not sufficient to

establish partnership liability. From this judgment, Brewer appealed.]

Rodman, Justice.

*   *   *

[The question presented for determination is]: Did [Brewer] offer any evidence on which a jury should be permitted to find that the note was in fact a partnership obligation?

Where a contract apparently made for the purpose of carrying on partnership business is executed in the partnership name by a partner, the partnership is liable for a breach of the contract even though the partner was not authorized to so contract, unless the other parties to the contract had knowledge of the lack of authority; but "an act of a partner which is not apparently for the carrying on of the business of the partnership in the usual way does not bind the partnership unless authorized by the other partners." [UPA § 9(2)].

Here the note was not signed in the partnership name; it did not on its face purport to be for the benefit of the partnership. To establish liability, [Brewer] must show that the partner was acting on behalf of the partnership in procuring the loan and was authorized to so act; or that the partners, with knowledge of the transaction, thereafter ratified the acts of their partner.

Defendant Robert Elks testified that he was, on 17 February 1959, the managing partner of the Friendly Furniture Company, having served in that capacity for fourteen years. He asked plaintiff "to sign some notes at the bank for the company with me. Mr. Brewer said that he would and on February 17, 1959, Mr. Brewer and my wife and I went to the Guaranty Bank and Trust Company to sign the notes. Mr. Brewer signed the notes with me and my wife at my request because the Company needed the money." He testified that the proceeds of the loan were by mistake deposited in his personal account; he immediately wrote a check transferring the funds to the credit of Friendly Furniture Company.

The mere fact that a partnership ultimately benefits from a contract made by a partner in his own name does not create a partnership obligation. . . .

Partnership contracts are not usually made in the names of the individual partners. The usual way for a partnership to indicate its liability for money borrowed is to execute the note in its name. Since the note here sued on was not executed in the name of the partnership, [Brewer] had the burden of showing defendants Keel had authorized the transaction. We find nothing in the testimony of plaintiff or . . . Elks to warrant a finding that [Keel had authorized Elks] to borrow for the partnership. . . .

[Judgment reversed on other grounds.]

41:4 Rights and Duties of Partners

The relationship existing among partners is one of trust. They each have an obligation to exercise the utmost good faith and integrity in their dealings with one another with regard to partnership affairs. This relationship, which is a fiduciary one, requires a partner to share with the partnership (1) all business opportunities clearly related to the subject of partnership operations and (2) any personal profit or advantage that he gains from dealings that involve partnership property and affairs. If a partner has promised to devote full time to the partnership business, the partner's time is considered to be a partnership asset. Hence, a partner cannot render services to any other employer, even one that does not compete with the partnership, without the consent of all other partners. If a partner does so, the salary he receives can be considered partnership income.

The rights and duties of partners among themselves are specified in considerable detail by the UPA. Under the UPA, each partner can:

- Share equally in the profits of the firm [UPA § 18(a)]
- Receive repayment of his contributions, whether by way of capital or advances to the partnership profits [UPA § 18(a)]
- Receive indemnification on payments made on behalf of the firm or for personal liabilities incurred [UPA § 18(b)]

- Receive interest on advances and on capital contributions [UPA §§ 18(c), (d)]
- Share in the management and conduct of the business [UPA § 18(e)]
- Have access to the firm's books and records (UPA § 19)
- Have a formal accounting of partnership affairs (UPA § 22)

These rights can be changed by agreement. For example, all the partners can agree to vest the management of the partnership in one or more of the partners or change the general rules about the distribution of profits or sharing of losses. The principle of majority rule can be changed by agreement to require the unanimous decision of partners on certain matters. The partners can also agree to give themselves the right to expel a partner under certain circumstances.

Partners' rights are complemented by a series of duties. Under the UPA, each partner has a duty to:

- Contribute toward losses sustained by the partnership [UPA § 18(a)]
- Work for the partnership without remuneration other than a share of profits [UPA § 18(b)]
- Submit to a majority vote when differences arise among partners as to the conduct of the firm's business [UPA § 18(b)]
- Share with other partners any information regarding partnership matters (UPA § 20)
- Account to the firm for any profit derived from any partnership transaction or from the use of partnership property (UPA § 21)

Profits and Losses   Each partner is entitled to an equal share in the profits of the partnership [UPA § 18(a)]. Unless there is an agreement to the contrary, partners share equally in the profits, even though they may have contributed unequally to capital or services. The sharing of profits can be controlled by an express agreement among the partners, or by an agreement that may be implied from the partners' conduct. Note, however, that a contractual provision limiting only the *salaries* of partners does not limit the partners' rights to participate in the profits of the firm over and above operating expenses. A partner's breach of a partnership agreement, whether or not committed in bad faith, does not cause him to lose his rights to share in partnership profits. However, a partner who refuses to contribute funds essential to the operation of a partnership business can be excluded from participation in the profits. If a partner abandons the business, he can also forfeit some or all of his share of the profits.

UPA § 18(a) provides that unless there is an agreement to the contrary, each partner must contribute toward the losses sustained by a partnership according to his share in the profits. If partners do make a different agreement among themselves as to how losses shall be apportioned, the agreement will be controlling as among the partners. An agreement can provide any reasonable basis for apportioning losses. For example, a partnership agreement can provide that losses shall be shared on an equal basis, or it can limit the liability of particular partners as to losses.

Distributions and Compensation for Services   Each partner can be reimbursed for all expenses paid or incurred in the ordinary conduct of partnership business, plus interest [UPA §§ 18(b), (c)]. However, no partner is entitled to compensation for services on behalf of a partnership except with the consent of all other partners [UPA § 18(f)]. The reason for this rule is that ordinarily a partner is obligated to devote his services to the partnership, giving it all his time, skill, and ability. Therefore, unless there has been some agreement among the partners covering the matter, no partner has any right to a greater share of the partnership profits simply because he has rendered services. The only exception to this rule is that on dissolution, a surviving partner is entitled to reasonable compensation for services in winding up the partnership affairs.

 Ordinarily, provisions of a partnership agreement will expressly regulate the duty of partners to render services to the partnership. It is therefore important to review the partnership agreement to determine the exact nature of a partner's obligation in that regard. This is also true if a partner engages in outside activities for his own benefit. There is nothing inherently fraudulent or against public policy in permitting a partner to engage in his own business pursuits while he is a member of a partnership. However, he must (1) act in good faith toward the other partners and (2) not violate any agreement among the partners preventing him from engaging in the enterprise in question.

Repayment of Contributions   Each partner is entitled to be repaid for his contributions of capital or advances to the partnership property [UPA § 18(a)]. Capital consists of the money that the partnership agreement requires each partner to contribute for starting the business. An advance is an amount paid in by the partner in excess of the investment specified in a partnership agreement. If one partner has contributed a larger amount to the capital of the firm than another, the repayments will be made in the same proportion in which the capital was furnished.

Books and Records   One of the ordinary duties of partners is to keep accurate books and records showing the firm's accounts. On demand, partners must present full and complete information to any other partner on all matters affecting the partnership business (UPA § 20). Each partner is entitled to access to the partnership books and records at all times. These records must be kept at the principal office of the partnership business (UPA § 19). When a partner dies, his personal representative has the same rights with respect to access and inspection of partnership books as the partner himself would have had.

Right to Accounting   Under the UPA, each partner has the right to a formal *accounting* as to partnership affairs. This right arises if a partner is wrongfully excluded from the partnership business or its property by the other partners [UPA § 22(a)], if the right to an accounting exists under the terms of any agreement among the partners [UPA § 22(b)], or whenever other circumstances make it just and reasonable [UPA § 22(d)]. Every partner must also account to the partnership for any benefit and hold for it any profits derived without the consent of the other partners from any transaction connected with the formation, conduct, or liquidation of the partnership.

A partner who requests an accounting and who does not receive it can sue for an accounting. It is not necessary that a partner cause the dissolution of the partnership (see 41:6) to get an accounting. However, to be entitled to a court-ordered accounting, the partner must show that he is in fact a partner and that the transaction giving rise to the demand is connected with the formation, conduct, or liquidation of the partnership.

Liabilities   Given the many rights and duties imposed on partners, it is clear that the potential for litigation between members of a partnership is considerable. A partner can be liable to another partner if he neglects to give a partnership all his time, skill, and ability, or if he neglects to use his knowledge, skill, and ability to promote the common benefit of the business. A partner can also be liable for failing to perform services agreed to be performed, for wrongfully engaging in an enterprise other than partnership business, and for not paying another partner compensation that is due the latter for services rendered the partnership. Finally, a partner can be liable to one or more other partners for breach of the fiduciary relationship that is inherent in a partnership, and for personal injuries and property damage.

Under general partnership law, a legal action cannot be maintained among partners with regard to partnership transactions unless there has been an accounting or settlement of partnership affairs. Under this rule, a partner cannot ordinarily sue to recover (1) a share of the partnership profits, (2) a share of the proceeds of a sale of partnership property, (3) compensation for services rendered, or (4) damages for breach of certain general provisions of a partnership agreement. However, it is frequently possible to avoid the effects of this rule; many states have enacted statutes that permit actions between partners in cases where they would not be maintainable under the common-law rule.

41:5   Liability to Third Persons

The liability of a partner for the acts of his copartners is founded on principles of agency. The UPA prescribes the nature of the liability. Under UPA § 15(b), partners are jointly liable for all debts and obligations resulting from partnership transactions. In regard to liability for torts, partners are jointly and severally liable for torts committed in the course of partnership business. This means that a third person suing for a tort can either sue all of the partners jointly or sue any one partner individually [UPA §§ 13, 15(a)].

Under the doctrine of mutual agency, any member of a partnership is liable for torts even in the absence of participation, ratification, or knowledge. That is, an injured party can single out a partner and hold him liable, even if he was not personally involved in the commission of the tort. However, if a tort requires a showing of malice or wrongful intent, each partner sought to be held liable must also be shown to have acted with malice or possessed wrongful intent.

A silent partner who participates in the profits of a partnership is subject to the same liability as active partners. The law does not permit a silent partner to share secretly in the profits of a firm without taking his share of the risks and without bearing his share of the losses as to third persons. Thus, for example, a creditor is entitled to recover from all the partners, including silent ones, even though one partner might hold himself out as the sole owner of a business and in spite of any agreement entered into among the partners purporting to limit liability.

Torts of Employees   The UPA does not specifically provide that a partnership is liable for the torts of an employee. Rather, it provides that the law of agency applies [UPA § 4(3)]. This rule makes the partnership liable for the torts of employees—as agents of the partnership—committed within the scope of their employment. The members of the partnership are also liable for these torts, and this liability is joint and several. However, if an employee commits a tortious act *outside* the scope of his employment, neither the partnership nor the partners will be held liable.

Conversion and Misapplication of Funds   If a partner, acting within the scope of his apparent authority, receives money or property from a third person and misapplies it, the partnership is liable for the loss (UPA § 14). UPA § 14 also provides that a partnership will be liable if property received by it in the course of its business is misapplied by any partner while it is in the partnership's custody. This rule represents a codification of the common law, which made all partners liable for a conversion of property committed by one member of the firm while acting within the scope of his authority.

Partners are jointly and severally liable for everything chargeable to the partnership due to misapplication of funds [UPA § 15(a)]. Therefore, if one partner converts a third person's money or property, the person can sue all of the partners jointly or any one partner individually. However, neither the partnership nor innocent partners are liable for a conversion or misapplication of funds that does not occur in the course of the firm's business. Thus, for example, if a partner in a law firm embezzles money, the other partners are not liable since the embezzlement was not done in the course of proper partnership business.

Fraud and Misrepresentation   Fraud and fraudulent representations of one partner in the course of partnership business bind the partnership and render it liable. This is so even though other partners are innocent of any participation in the fraud. The reason for this rule is found in the general principle of the liability of firms and partners for unlawful acts committed by their agents within the general scope of their agency. The rule imposing civil liability on an innocent partner for the fraud of a copartner is especially applicable where the innocent partner receives the benefit of the fraudulent conduct.

Indemnification   Because all partners are jointly liable for partnership debts and obligations [UPA § 15(b)], each partner may be required to pay the entire amount of such a debt or obligation himself. When one partner has so paid off a debt or obligation that is jointly owed by the partners, the UPA requires the partnership to indemnify the one who paid. UPA § 18(b) provides for indemnification whenever a partner has made payments or has incurred personal liabilities in the ordinary and proper conduct of partnership business, or for the preservation of its business or property. If a partnership is itself unable to indemnify a partner, the obligation falls on all the other partners.

Criminal Liability   The rule in some states is that a partnership cannot commit a crime since it is not a legal entity. In many states, however, a partnership can be found to have committed a crime, through the acts of one or more of the partners. The penalty in those states is a fine levied against the partnership's property.

A partner is, of course, individually liable for his criminal act, and if all the partners participate in the act, they are criminally liable as well. However, a partner who does not participate in criminal conduct involving other partners will not be held criminally liable. That is, one partner's criminal conduct does not automatically make other partners liable too.

Partnership by Estoppel   In certain circumstances, parties can be held liable as partners as against third persons, even though a partnership does not exist between the parties. Under the UPA, one who has allowed or caused others to believe that he is a partner can be estopped to deny the relationship [UPA § 16(1)].

EXAMPLE
Anderson, the sole proprietor of a retail fabrics business, approaches Zale for a loan. Anderson tells Zale that Goodson is a partner in Anderson's business. Goodson knows about Anderson's statements but does not advise Zale to the contrary, although he could easily do so. Zale relies on Goodson's credit and status in the community in extending the loan to Anderson. Insofar as this loan is concerned, Goodson is estopped from denying that he is a partner with Anderson. Goodson can be held liable to Zale for the amount of the loan as if he were in fact a partner in Anderson's business.

Liability of Third Person to Partnership for Injuries to Partner   Unlike a corporation, which is generally permitted to recover damages for a negligent injury to one of its employees, a partnership usually has no right to recover damages from another person for injuries inflicted on one of the partners. The reason for this rule is that a partner is not considered an employee of the partnership, so no right of action can arise.

EXAMPLE
Armstrong and Sharp are partners doing business as United Steel Supply Company. While on partnership business, Armstrong is injured by Grune's negligent act. Armstrong can recover damages from Grune for loss of income. However, since Armstrong is not considered an employee of United Steel, United Steel cannot recover damages from Grune for its lost earnings and profits due to Armstrong's injury.

41:6   Dissolution of Partnership

"Dissolution of a partnership" is the change in the relation of the partners that is caused by any partner ceasing to be associated in the carrying on of the business (UPA § 29). *Dissolution* is not in itself a termination of the partnership or of the rights and powers of partners. Many of these rights and powers continue during the winding up process that follows dissolution (see 41:7). Although various terms have been applied to the process leading up to the final settlement of all partnership affairs, the term "dissolution" designates that point in time when the partners cease to carry on the business together. The term is thus distinguishable from "winding up" (or "liquidation" as it is also called), which is the process of settling partnership affairs after dissolution, and "termination," which is that point in time when all the partnership affairs are completely wound up.

Causes of Dissolution   UPA § 31(1) provides that even without any violation of a partnership agreement, dissolution is caused by (1) the termination of the definite term or particular undertaking specified in the partnership agreement, (2) the withdrawal of a partner when no definite term or particular undertaking is specified; (3) the mutual consent of all the partners before or after the termination of a specified term or undertaking; or (4) the expulsion of a partner if it is carried out in accordance with the provisions of the partnership agreement. Dissolution is also caused by any event that makes it unlawful for the partnership to be carried on or for its members to carry on in partnership [UPA § 31(3)]; by the death of any partner [UPA § 31(4)]; and by the bankruptcy of any partner or the partnership itself [UPA § 31(5)]. In addition, dissolution can occur if a partner withdraws at any time in violation of the partnership agreement and the circumstances do not permit dissolution under any other provision of the UPA [UPA § 31(2)].

The various causes of dissolution are discussed separately below. It should be noted, however, that the most common potential causes of the dissolution of a large partnership are the death or withdrawal of a partner. As a practical matter, these causes have been eliminated in many large partnerships. The partnership agreements of law, accounting, and stock brokerage firms frequently provide that there will be no dissolution on the death of any individual partner or on his withdrawal, such as by retirement. The validity of these agreements has been authorized by statute in a number of states.

Expiration of Term; Completion of Purpose [UPA § 31(1)(a)]   A partnership agreement can provide that the partnership is to last for a stated period of time, such as one year or two years. If so, the partnership is dissolved when the stated time expires. Similarly, the agreement can state that the partnership is to last until a certain project is completed; completion of the project dissolves a partnership of this type. Note, however, as discussed below, that any partner can effectively end the partnership relationship before its intended term expires. Conversely, on the expiration of a partnership term, the partners can decide to continue the partnership business. If they do, their rights and duties remain the same as they were on the expiration date (UPA § 23).

Withdrawal [UPA §§ 31(1)(b), 31(2)]   Dissolution of a partnership by withdrawal can be accomplished at any time even if it violates an agreement among the partners [see UPA § 31(2)]. Thus, although a given partnership is to exist for a specific period of time, or for the accomplishment of a particular purpose, it can be dissolved by the withdrawal of any partner even at a moment's notice.

The right to dissolve a partnership at any time is deemed implicit in a partnership at will. A withdrawing partner is not liable to other partners even though dissolution of a partnership results in loss to the other partners. However, the right to dissolve a partnership at will must be exercised in good faith. If a partner acts in bad faith—as by attempting to appropriate for himself some special advantage or opportunity that may more properly belong to the partnership—this would be treated as a wrongful dissolution.

If a partnership is for a fixed term, dissolution by withdrawal constitutes a violation of the partnership agreement. Thus, although the withdrawing partner has the *power* to dissolve the partnership in this way, he does not have the *right* to do so. Accordingly, the withdrawing partner in this situation can be held liable to the other partners for any losses caused by the dissolution.

The following case illustrates how a partner's withdrawal causes the dissolution of a partnership. Consider the duties of partners during dissolution and why the partner in this case was deemed to have breached his fiduciary duty to the other partners even though his withdrawal constituted a proper basis for dissolution.

Lavin

v

Ehrlich
80 Misc 2d 247, 363 NYS2d 50
(New York Supreme Court, 1974)

[Ehrlich was one of three partners in a neighborhood tax preparing business. Ehrlich managed the business and the other two partners were essentially investors. In a letter to the other partners, Ehrlich announced his immediate withdrawal from and dissolution of the partnership. Later that same month, he contracted to buy the storefront property in which the partnership operated its business. He then took title to the building and refused to negotiate a new lease with the partnership, which he considered dissolved. The partners sued Ehrlich, contending that he could not unilaterally dissolve the partnership and that he had further breached his fiduciary duties in buying the property. The displaced partners sought a court order holding that Ehrlich held

the property in a constructive trust for the partnership.]

Bertram Harnett, Justice.

*   *   *

A neighborhood tax preparing business depends on many of the same clients returning each year. To this end, the location of the business is important and forms part of its goodwill. Were a partner in the business to buy in his own name the building housing it and then eject the partnership at the end of the lease, that would be an intolerable breach of fiduciary relationship. . . . But, what if that partner first serves notice to dissolve the partnership before buying the building; can he still be held to the same duties to his partners?

[Plaintiffs Lavin and Dillworth] first assert that Ehrlich could not unilaterally dissolve the partnership in contravention of the express withdrawal provisions of the partnership agreement. A contract provision does permit a withdrawing partner to give the others first option to buy him out on terms to be mutually agreeable, and failing in that gives him the right to sell to a stranger. However, there is no stranger poised to buy, nor is there any indication that one portends. Indeed, the provision on withdrawal is at best an agreement to agree. Accordingly, the agreement is not in point here.

Ehrlich argues that the agreement provides no specific term of life for the partnership, and so it is a partnership at will, to be dissolved at the insistence of any partner. . . . This is true, and Ehrlich's letter . . . effectively triggered the dissolution of the partnership, and should have set the winding up in motion towards final termination.

However, this dissolution did not free Ehrlich of all fiduciary relationship to the partnership. "On dissolution the partnership is not terminated, but continues until the winding up of the partnership affairs is completed." . . . There may be a relaxation of a partner's duties to his co-partners in relationships that look to the future of the newly dissolved partnership. . . . But, in dealings effecting the winding up of the partnership and the proper preservation of partnership assets during this time, "the good faith and full disclosure exacted of partners continues." . . .

Moreover, the Court is satisfied on the record that Ehrlich instituted and carried on negotiations for the building's purchase during the vital partnership tenure, and completed them later, without offering the ultimate deal to his partners. The opportunity to purchase the property and insure continued possession of the goodwill asset embodied in the location should have been offered to the partnership. Ehrlich breached his fiduciary duty in not making that offer and in appropriating this important partnership asset to himself. . . .

At the bottom, Ehrlich is doing something hopefully achievable from a technical standpoint, but sadly lacking in equity. He was the actual conductor of the business. He went out and grabbed the building, and now hopes, with this maneuver and his possession of the list of names and past tax return files (which he has undisputedly) to capitalize on the partnership location and goodwill to the exclusion of his partners. We cannot accept his strategy. . . .

Accordingly, the Court finds Ehrlich holds the property in constructive trust for the partnership and must surrender his right, title, and interest to the partnership if offered two-thirds of the purchase price he paid by the remaining partners Lavin and Dillworth. . . .

[Order issued.]

Mutual Consent [UPA § 31(1)(c)]   A partnership can be altered, modified, or dissolved by mutual agreement. A partnership formed under an agreement that does not contain a provision as to its duration lasts no longer than as mutually agreed by the partners. Moreover, even if the time for the dissolution of a partnership is specified in the partnership agreement, the partners can mutually agree to dissolve their relationship before that time. This may be accomplished either by an express agreement for dissolution or by conduct implying an intention to dissolve the partnership. Partners can also agree on terms of a dissolution differing from those originally provided in the partnership agreement. If they do so, the specific dissolution agreement controls, and all the partners are bound by it.

Expulsion of Partner [UPA § 31(1)(d)]   The expulsion of a partner in accordance with a provision in the partnership agreement authorizing expulsion causes a dissolution of the partnership. If the agreement lists specific grounds for expulsion, one or more of those grounds must be shown to exist before an expulsion is justified. The expelling partners are not liable for any losses that the expelled partner sustains as a result of the expulsion. The other partners can be liable, however, if the expulsion is made in bad faith or without any right to expel as authorized by the partnership agreement. If a partner is expelled pursuant to an express provision of a partnership agreement, the remaining partners have the right to continue the business.

The following case involves a partnership's right to expel a partner without notice and without any opportunity to be heard. Note the court's discussion whether a duty of good faith should be imposed in the expulsion of a partner and why the court held that this duty did not exist in the case.

Holman

v

Coie

11 Wash App 195, 522 P2d 515,

72 ALR3d 1209

(Washington Court of Appeals, 1974)

[Francis and William Holman were partners in a law firm that did considerable work for the Boeing Company. In 1965, with the consent of the partnership, Francis was elected to the Washington State House of Representatives. In 1968 he was elected to the Washington State Senate without seeking the firm's approval, but no objection was made by any member of the firm. In 1969 Francis gave a speech before the State Senate that irritated several of Boeing's top officials. Later, the president of Boeing advised the managing partner of the law firm that Boeing did not want Francis to do further legal work on its behalf. Subsequently, the firm's executive committee met in the absence of Francis and William—both of whom were members of the committee—and resolved to expel the brothers. The firm did not permit the brothers to contest their expulsion, and it did not give them any reasons for the action. Francis and William sued the other partners for damages, and the trial court entered judgment

in favor of the partnership. The Holman brothers appealed.]

Munson, Judge.

*   *   *

The partnership agreement, § 1.2, states in part:

> any member may be expelled from the Firm by a majority vote of the Executive Committee.

The agreement does not require giving of notice, a statement of reasons, a showing of good cause, or a hearing. . . .

We find this partnership agreement to [be] unambiguous, and not to require notice, reasons, or an opportunity to be heard. To inject those issues would be to rewrite the agreement of the parties, a function we neither presume nor assume.

Plaintiffs . . . challenge the expulsion on the basis that . . . it was not bona fide, or in good faith, and contend such a requirement should be implied.

[UPA § 31(d)] states: "Dissolution is caused: ... By the expulsion of any partner from the business bona fide in accordance with such a power conferred by the agreement between the partners; ..." The partnership agreement here at issue merely states that a partner may be expelled by majority vote of the executive committee with no provisions for cause, reasons, notice or hearing. "Bona fide" is defined as: "In or with good faith; honestly, openly, and sincerely; without deceit or fraud." Black's Law Dictionary 223 (4th ed. 1951).

Undoubtedly, the general rule of law is that the partners in their dealings with each other must exercise good faith.

> The relation existing between copartners is one requiring the exercise of the utmost good faith. Each partner is a trustee for all, and no individual or group may take an unconscionable advantage of another.

... In [a 1928 New York case] Justice Cardozo stated [that]:

> Joint adventures, like copartners, owe to one another, ... duty of the finest loyalty. Many forms of conduct permissible in a workaday world for those acting at arm's length, are forbidden to those bound by fiduciary ties. ... Not honesty alone, but the punctilio of an honor the most sensitive, is then the standard of behavior.

Likewise, a partner is not permitted to derive any profit or advantage from the partnership relationship except with the full knowledge and consent of the partners. ... That such is the law cannot be questioned. However, the personal relationships between partners to which the terms "bona fide" and "good faith" relate are those which have a bearing upon the business aspects or property of the partnership and prohibit a partner, to-wit, a fuduciary, from taking any personal advantage touching those subjects. ... Plaintiffs' claims do not relate to the business aspects or property rights of this partnership. There is no evidence the

purpose of the severance was to gain any business or property advantage to the remaining partners. Consequently, in that context, there has been no showing of breach of the duty of good faith toward plaintiffs.

There is authority for plaintiffs' contention that the term "bona fide" or "good faith" requires more, *i.e.,* compliance with basic procedural due process standards. ...

An article in [an English law journal] states in part:

> should the situation be one involving an "expulsion" ... and the dispute ... is determined by the majority of partners, it is submitted that the application of the rules of natural justice are an essential legal prerequisite in the determination of the partnership dispute. This is so because partners in this circumstance are acting as a "tribunal or body of persons invested with authority to adjudicate upon matters involving civil consequences to individuals."

The article concludes that prior to expulsion, a partner is entitled to notice, the reasons, and a hearing, much as has been found by our courts under the phrase "due process of law."

We choose not to follow [the author of this article]. These parties in writing the partnership clauses dealing with expulsion, and the defendants who carried them out, chose to adopt the guillotine approach, rather than a more diplomatic approach, to the expulsion of partners. The actions of defendants were within the contemplation of the agreement. While this course of action may shock the sensibilities of some, to others it may be that once the initial decision is made, the traumatic reaction to that decision is more quickly overcome and the end result more merciful. However that course of action may appear to the reader, the possibility of exactly such action occurring is clear from reading the agreement. None of the partners had any reason to believe the agreement required anything more prior to abruptly and brusquely terminating their services.

We conclude that these parties contractually agreed to the very method of expulsion exercised by the defendants, *i.e.*, a clean, quick, and expeditious severance, with a clear method of accounting. It is not difficult to understand why parties to such a professional relationship would find this method desirable. This case, which has consumed nearly 4 years of litigation, and the attendant publicity, illustrates the virtues of this method of expulsion. The foundation of a professional relationship is personal confidence and trust. Once a schism develops, its magnitude may be exaggerated rightfully or wrongfully to the point of destroying a harmonious accord. When such occurs, an expeditious serverance is desirable. To imply terms not expressed in this partnership agreement frustrates the unambiguous language of the agreement and the result contemplated.

[Judgment affirmed.]

Death of Partner [UPA § 31(4)]   The death of a partner causes dissolution of a partnership regardless of whether the partnership is at will or for a fixed period of time. As in the case of dissolution by other causes, the death of a partner does not *terminate* the partnership until its affairs are wound up by the surviving partners. Note, however, that partners can provide by agreement that the partnership shall *not* be dissolved by the death of a partner. Indeed, partners can even set forth the terms by which the partnership will be continued by the surviving partners after the death of one or more of the copartners. For example, it is common for partners to agree that their surviving partners shall have the right or option to purchase a deceased partner's interest in the firm on specified terms and conditions.

Dissolution by Judicial Decree [UPA § 32(1)]   In certain circumstances, a judicial declaration can dissolve a partnership. A court shall, on application by or for a partner, decree dissolution of a partnership in any one of the following instances: (1) when a partner has been declared insane or shown to be of unsound mind; (2) when a partner becomes incapable of performing his part of a partnership contract; (3) when a partner has been guilty of misconduct that prejudicially affects the carrying on of the business; (4) when a partner willfully or persistently commits a breach of the partnership agreement or otherwise so conducts himself that it is not reasonably practical to carry on the business in partnership with him; (5) when the business of the partnership can be carried on only at a loss; and (6) for other circumstances that may render dissolution just and equitable.

A suit for dissolution of a partnership is equitable in nature.[6] A court can consider all of the facts and circumstances before granting or withholding relief. Usually, a court orders partnership assets sold and the proceeds applied to payment of all partnership debts. The balance remaining is then applied to repay each partner's contributions, and to pay current earnings according to each partner's share of the partnership profits (UPA § 40). If there are no partnership debts, a court can order distribution of the partnership assets "in kind," which means distribution of

---

[6]The distinction between equitable and legal remedies is discussed in Chapter 1.

the assets themselves rather than the proceeds from their sale. If there are losses, or if partnership liabilities exceed assets available for distribution, each partner must contribute according to his share of the profits [UPA § 18(a)]. If a partner has not contributed the full share of capital that he originally agreed to, he must pay his share before other partners are required to make up any losses sustained. If one of the partners is insolvent or refuses to contribute his share of the losses, the remaining partners must make up his share proportionately. They will then have the right to sue the defaulting partner to enforce his contribution [UPA §§ 40(d)–(f)].

 When partners fall out, they should invoke judicial dissolution under UPA § 32 and seek an accounting, rather than trying to divide up the assets of the partnership on their own. If one partner does not want to dissolve the partnership under court supervision, at the very least the partners should consider obtaining an independent audit of the partnership's worth.

Misconduct and Breach of Agreement   The UPA provisions dealing with misconduct are drafted in such broad language that they can cover a wide variety of frictions among partners [see UPA §§ 32(1)(c)–(f)]. Because of the difficulty in defining just what misbehavior or what degree of misconduct would authorize judicial dissolution, courts are often cautious about dissolving a partnership for misconduct. They ordinarily require a showing of gross misconduct or willful neglect of partnership obligations before they will grant a decree of dissolution. For example, dissolution will not be decreed for a partner's lack of courtesy to firm customers or for friction among partners that does not affect the success of the business. Nor will dissolution be ordered for trifling causes or temporary grievances involving no permanent mischief. However, if one partner has been guilty of misconduct that is markedly injurious to the interests of an innocent partner, this misconduct will be regarded as sufficient ground for dissolution.

Dissolution can also be decreed if a partner's conduct is inconsistent with continuation of the partnership, if a partner's misconduct materially interferes with the business, or if a partner willfully breaches the partnership agreement. Moreover, the wrongful exclusion of one partner by one or more of his copartners from participation in the business or the management of the partnership amounts to misconduct and constitutes a ground for judicial dissolution.

Admission of New Partner   The UPA does not appear to make the admission of a new partner a cause for dissolution. For example, the admission of a new partner is not listed either as a cause of dissolution or as a ground for obtaining a judicial decree of dissolution (see UPA §§ 31, 32). Moreover, UPA § 18(g) provides that one cannot become a member of a partnership without the consent of all the other partners, thus apparently recognizing the admission of a partner into a continuing partnership.

Effect of Dissolution   When a partnership dissolves, the general agency of one partner for his copartner ceases. The mutual agency is prolonged to a limited degree only until the affairs of the partnership are wound up. In other words, after dissolution no partner has any power whatsoever to act for or bind the others.

Dissolution does, however, leave each of the partners with an equal duty and an equal power to do whatever is necessary to collect the debts due the partnership and to adjust, settle, and pay its debts. Moreover, dissolution of a partnership terminates the authority of a partner to act for the partnership except in limited circumstances (UPA § 33). However, a partner does not lose his authority insofar as it may be necessary for the winding up of partnership affairs.

The dissolution of a partnership works an absolute revocation of all implied authority in any of the partners to bind the others to new contracts or obligations.

Liability for Obligations of Dissolved Firm   The dissolution of a partnership does not dissolve the existing liabilities of any partner [UPA § 36(1)]. The right of third persons to enforce obligations and contracts binding on a firm at the time of its dissolution usually continues after the termination of a partnership. Regardless of the reasons, a partner who leaves a firm remains liable to the partnership's creditors for all existing debts of the firm to the same extent as if he had remained with the partnership. Creditors can agree not to hold a partner liable on his withdrawal from a firm, but they are not required to do so. Thus, a retiring partner cannot absolve himself from liability for firm debts contracted while he was a member of the firm in the absence of an agreement on the part of a creditor [see UPA § 36(2)]. He cannot, however, be held liable for future debts.

When the business of a dissolved partnership is continued by former partners, creditors of the old firm are creditors of the persons or partnership continuing the business (UPA § 41). This rule applies in a variety of situations, such as when a partner retires and transfers his interest to other partners or to third persons. It also applies if all but one partner retire and the retiring partners assign their rights to the continuing partner. However, if a new firm doing business under an old firm's name is composed of entirely different persons, it is not liable for the old firm's debts.

A person admitted as a partner into an existing partnership is liable for all the obligations of the partnership that arose before his admission, as though he had been a partner when the obligations were incurred (UPA § 17). This liability can, however, be satisfied only out of partnership property. It must be emphasized that UPA § 17 applies only to one who enters an *existing partnership*. Thus, for example, one who enters into a partnership with a person who had done business as a sole proprietor does not become liable for the prior debts of the business at the time it was carried on as a proprietorship, and those debts cannot be satisfied out of partnership property.

Notice of Dissolution   To protect innocent third persons, the law imposes on partners the duty of giving *notice of dissolution* of a partnership. Otherwise, they run the risk of being bound to third persons by the subsequent exercise of the authority that they have given to each other as partners. Therefore, under this rule, members of a dissolved partnership continue to be liable to those with whom they have previously dealt as partners and who have no notice or knowledge of the dissolution of the firm, and who in good faith continue to act in the belief that the firm is still in existence [UPA § 35(1)]. For this reason, and as part of any dissolution, a retiring partner generally publishes notice of withdrawal from a firm to protect against future debts incurred by the partners continuing the business.

Both the character and the sufficiency of a notice of dissolution that will be effective to relieve a partner from liability depend in large part on whether the person receiving the notice has had former dealings with the firm. Those who have had actual dealings with the firm are entitled to direct notice of the dissolution. Those who have known of the existence of the firm but have not dealt with it are entitled merely to constructive or general notice. UPA § 3(2) recognizes that notice can be given verbally, by delivery through the mail, or by other means of communication to the recipient's place of business or residence. To avoid liability for contracts with persons who know of a partnership's existence but have not learned of its dissolution, the fact of dissolution must be advertised in a newspaper of general circulation in the place at which the partnership business was regularly conducted [see UPA § 35(1)(b)(II)].

Continuation in Business   The effect of dissolution is generally to permit a partnership to operate only until it is wound up, as discussed in 41:7. However, when dissolution is caused by breach of a partnership agreement, those partners who have not caused the dissolution can continue the business in the same name, provided that they pay the partner who caused the dissolution the value of his interest [UPA § 38(2)(b)]. Moreover, dissolution does not necessarily cause the liquidation of a firm where there has been an agreement among the partners stating that it does not do so. The remaining partners can also continue to operate a partnership if one partner has been expelled pursuant to the terms of a partnership agreement.

41:7   Winding Up

Winding up means the administration of assets of a partnership for the purpose of terminating the business and discharging its obligations. Included in the winding up or liquidation of partnership affairs are (1) the performance of existing contracts, (2) the collection of debts or claims due the firm, and (3) the payment of partnership debts. The right to carry out the winding up is given either to partners who have not wrongfully dissolved the partnership or to the legal representative of the last surviving partner (UPA § 37). Moreover, any partner or his legal representative can have a partnership wound up by court decree. If a partnership is ended by mutual consent or by the expiration of its term, the right to wind up is vested in all partners, and each is under a duty to liquidate partnership affairs.

Liquidating Partners   The partners who have the right to do the winding up can agree that one or more of them shall act as *liquidating partners*. Those who remain in charge of the business during the winding up period occupy a fiduciary relationship to the other partners until the winding up is complete. If partners cannot agree as to who shall wind up, a court can appoint a receiver.

A liquidating partner is considered to have all the power that is necessary for the final settlement of the partnership's affairs. If other partners expressly give their consent, the liquidating partner has broad power to incur obligations. For example, a liquidating partner can incur obligations that are necessary to complete existing contracts after the partnership is dissolved, and he can borrow money to pay partnership debts. However, there are limits to a liquidating partner's powers. For example, a liquidating partner is the sole agent of a partnership *only* for purposes of winding it up. Thus, he normally lacks the power to incur obligations that will bind the firm or the other partners as individuals. He also lacks the power to enter into new contracts or new business on behalf of the firm.

UPA § 18(f) provides that if a partnership is being wound up because one of the partners has died, a surviving partner is entitled to reasonable compensation for his services in winding up the partnership's affairs. This rule, which is an exception to the usual rule that no partner is entitled to remuneration for acting in the partnership business, is included in the UPA because the death of a partner necessarily leaves the entire burden of winding up on the survivors. In certain circumstances, a court might award compensation to the partners who have performed more than their share of work in winding up and liquidating the partnership.

Application of Assets to Liabilities   In settling accounts among partners after dissolution, the liabilities of the partnership rank in order of payment as follows: (1) those owing to creditors other than partners; (2) those owing to partners for other than capital and profits; (3) those owing to partners in respect to capital; and (4) those owing to partners in respect to profits [UPA § 40(b)]. These statutory rules for the distribution of assets apply only in the absence of an agreement among partners on the same subject matter.

After the payment of liabilities, any surplus can be applied to pay in cash the net amount owing to the partners [UPA § 38(1)]. When a partner leaves a firm voluntarily, or involuntarily without assigning his interest to the other partners, he is entitled to receive an amount equal to the value of his interest at dissolution. The same rule applies when a partner dies, except that the decreased partner's share goes to his estate.

41:8   Limited Partnerships

Limited partnerships are entities created by state statutes. They were developed to facilitate commercial investments by those who wanted a financial interest in a business but did not want all the responsibilities and liabilities of partners. In recent years, most states have adopted the *Uniform Limited Partnership Act* (ULPA), which governs the rights, duties, and obligations of limited partnerships. The ULPA was first promulgated in 1916, and the original act was superseded in 1976 by a revised act. The 1916 text, which is reproduced in Appendix E, will probably not be replaced in all states for a number of years. However, the 1976 revised text, reproduced in Appendix F, forms the basis of the discussion of limited partners in this chapter.

A limited partnership is a partnership formed by two or more persons having as its members one or more "general partners" and one or more "limited partners." A general partner is a partner who assumes the management responsibilities of the partnership and full personal liability for the debts of the partnership. A limited partner is a partner who makes a contribution of cash or other property to the partnership and who obtains an interest in the partnership in return. The limited partner, whose liability for partnership debts is also limited, is not active in management.

A person can be both a general partner and a limited partner in the same partnership at the same time. In this case, the partner has in respect to his contribution as a limited partner all the rights he would have if he were not a general partner (ULPA § 303).

41:9　Formation of Limited Partnership

There are certain requirements for the formation of a limited partnership. These requirements concern the certificate of limited partnership that the partners must execute. The certificate sets forth the name of the partnership, the general character of its business, the location of its principal place of business, the name and address of each partner and his capital contributions, a designation of which partners are general and limited, and the respective rights and priorities, if any, of the partners (ULPA § 201). A copy of the certificate must be filed in the office of the Secretary of State (ULPA § 201; see also §§ 204, 206). The certificate can be amended or canceled by following similar formalities (ULPA § 202). If a certificate contains false statements, anyone who suffers a loss by relying on it can hold liable (1) any person who signed the certificate and who knew of the erroneous statements or (2) any general partner who should have known of the erroneous statements, even if he lacked actual knowledge of them [ULPA § 207(1)].

The purpose of the certificate is to give all potential creditors notice of the limited liability of the limited partners. The ULPA requires at least substantial compliance in good faith with these requirements. If there is no substantial compliance, the purported limited partner can be held liable as a general partner. However, a purported limited partner can escape liability as a general partner if, on ascertaining the mistake, he promptly renounces his interest in the profits of the business or in other compensation he receives (ULPA § 304).

The following case illustrates the effect of an partnership's failure to comply with the ULPA provisions in regard to formation. Note that although certain statutory requirements were not followed, the limited partners still retained their status as such under the law.

Garrett

v

Koepke
569 SW2d 568
(Texas Court of Civil Appeals, 1978)

[Koepke and Wood were named as limited partners in a limited partnership agreement. However, the limited partnership agreement was not filed with the Secretary of State as required by state law. When the partnership failed to pay a debt, Koepke and Wood were sued personally. The plaintiffs contended that the failure of the partnership to follow the statutory requirements as to formation caused it to become a general partnership, making Koepke and Wood liable as general partners. Judgment was *for Koepke and Wood in the trial court, and the plaintiffs appealed.]*

Akin, Justice.

*   *   *

The principal question presented by this appeal is whether limited partners lose their limited liability status, as a matter of law, where the partnership had failed to comply with [ULPA § 201], which requires filing with the Secretary of State a certificate setting forth certain information pertaining to the limited partnership. A corollary question is whether certain limited partners lost their status with respect to limited liability where they exercised control over the partnership assets. We hold that since [ULPA § 201] is a notice statute and since appellants already had the information that would have been provided by compliance with the statute prior to dealing with the limited partnership, the failure to comply with [§ 201] does not cause appellees to lose their status as limited partners. . . .

Appellants argue first that since a certificate of limited partnership was never filed with the Secretary of State, a question is presented as to whether the partnership became a general one, thus making appellees liable as general partners. Secondly, they assert that even if a valid limited partnership was formed, an issue exists as to whether when certain of the limited partners took control of the business, they lost their limited liability. Finally, appellants urge that because the limited partners failed to promptly renounce their respective interests in the partnership assets when they discovered that no limited partnership certificate had been filed, they lost their limited liability, citing [ULPA § 304]. We hold, however, that since appellants were on notice that the entity with which they were dealing was in fact a limited partnership, appellees' failure to comply with [§ 201] is immaterial. We hold further that no limited partner took such a part in the control of the business so as to lose his shield of limited liability. In view of these holdings, we do not address whether the limited partners promptly renounced their interests.

Appellees admit that they had failed to file a certificate of limited partnership as required by [§ 201]. Appellants contend, therefore, that appellees are liable for the debt sued upon as general partners. We cannot agree with this contention. We see no logical reason to strip appellees of their limited liability under their partnership agreement merely because they failed to comply with [§ 201]. The purpose of the filing requirements under the act is to provide notice to third persons dealing with the partnership of the essential features of the partnership arrangements. . . . Since appellants knew that the entity with which they were dealing was a limited partnership, as well as the consequences of dealing with such an entity, they were in no way prejudiced by the failure to comply with the statute. We see no compelling policy reason here for holding that appellees became general partners by requiring technical compliance with these notice provisions. Indeed, such was not the intent of the legislature in enacting the statute; instead, its' intent was to provide notice of limited liability of certain partners to third parties dealing with a partnership. . . . The nature and legal existence of a partnership does not depend upon any filing required by a statute. . . . We hold, therefore, that where a party has knowledge that the entity with which he is dealing is a limited partnership, that status is not changed by failing to file under [§ 201]. . . .

[Judgment affirmed.]

41:10   Rights and Liabilities of Limited Partners

The rights of a limited partner are substantially the same as those of a partner in a general partnership, except that the limited partner has no right to take control of the business. Thus, a limited partner has the right of access to the partnership books, the right to an accounting as to the state of the partnership business, the right to inspect the partnership's tax returns, and the right to receive other information regarding the affairs of the partnership as is just and reasonable (ULPA § 305).

In contrast to the liability of a partner in a general partnership for partnership debts, a limited partner has *no* personal liability for partnership debts (ULPA § 303). The maximum loss that a limited partner can sustain is the amount of his investment in the limited partnership. However, if a limited partner is also a general partner, or if he takes part in the management and control of the business, the limited partner then becomes liable as a general partner [ULPA § 303(a)].

41:11   Termination of Limited Partnership

Under ULPA § 801, a limited partnership can be dissolved (1) at the time or on the happening of the events specified in the certificate of limited partnership, (2) on the written consent of all partners, and (3) in the event of a general partner's withdrawal. In certain cases, dissolution of a limited partnership does not have to occur on the withdrawal of a general partner if there is at least one other general partner and the certificate of limited partnership permits the business to be carried on by the remaining general partner. A limited partnership can also be dissolved by court order on application by or for a partner whenever it is not practicable to carry on the business in conformity with the partnership agreement (ULPA § 802).

Settlement and Distribution of Assets (ULPA § 804)   Various priorities must be observed in settling a limited partnership's accounts after dissolution. On dissolution, assets are to be distributed first to creditors in satisfaction of liabilities of the limited partnership; next, to partners and former partners in satisfaction of liabilities for distributions under ULPA §§ 601 and 604; and last, to partners first for the return of their contributions and secondly in proportion to their interest in the partnership. Of course, the members of a limited partnership can include in the partnership agreement different priorities for distribution on winding up of partnership affairs.

41:12   Joint Ventures

A joint venture is an association of persons with the intent to engage in and carry out a single business venture for profit. The joint venturers combine their efforts, property, money, skills, and knowledge without creating a partnership or corporation; each participant stands in the relation of principal as well as agent to each of the others with an equal right to control the means employed to achieve the common purpose of the venture.

A joint venture is very similar to a partnership. Indeed, the rights, duties, and liabilities of joint venturers are often tested by the same rules as those that govern partnerships. However, there are important differences between these two types of business relationships. Perhaps the most significant difference is the single—or ad hoc—nature of a joint venture. In contrast, a partnership is usually formed to conduct a continuing business. Other differences include the eligibility of a corporation for membership in a joint venture but not ordinarily in a partnership, and the fact that joint venturers, unlike partners, can sue each other for damages without resorting to an accounting.

Convenience and expediency have made joint ventures a popular form of enterprise. Today, joint ventures are an almost necessary means of acquiring the great concentration of economic resources, knowledge, and skills required for such large-scale construction projects as public buildings, highways, bridges, dams, and even nuclear reactors. Joint ventures have also been used for the exploitation and development of natural resources, for joint participation in public offerings of stocks and bonds, for commercial shipping ventures, and for the development and sale of real estate subdivisions. Joint ventures also offer certain benefits when used as vehicles for tax-oriented investments, such as real estate or oil and gas projects, because they are taxed as partnerships rather than as corporations.

41:13 Elements of a Joint Venture

The relationship of joint venturers is created when two or more persons combine their money, property, or time in the conduct of some particular line of trade or for some particular business deal. The first requirement for the creation of a joint venture is the parties' intent to create the enterprise. This intent is usually manifested by contract, although little formality is required. The relationship of joint venturers can, however, be created by oral agreement, or its existence can be inferred from the conduct of the parties and from other facts and circumstances surrounding their association.

The second requirement is that all participants combine their property, money, labor, knowledge, or skills in some common undertaking. The contributions of the parties need not be equal or of the same character, but there must be a contribution by each participant of something benefiting the enterprise. Facts showing the joining of funds, property, or labor in a common purpose to obtain a result for the benefit of all parties, in which each participant has a right to direct the conduct of others, is often considered evidence that a joint venture exists.

A third requirement for creating a joint venture is that each person have equal control over the enterprise. There must also be a community of interest in the subject matter of the joint venture. Moreover, a joint proprietary interest in property used pursuant to a joint venture must be shown in some states. In other states, it is only necessary to have a joint interest in the objects and purposes of the venture. The fourth requirement is an agreement among the venturers to share profits.

In addition to satisfying the above requirements, a joint venture must be limited to a single undertaking. It is this characteristic that is most often used to distinguish a joint venture from a partnership. An enterprise must be of limited scope and duration in order to constitute a joint venture. In certain circumstances, however, associations organized for diversified operations of a continuing nature have been recognized as joint ventures. The following case illustrates the elements necessary for the formation of a joint venture and shows that although parties might change the structure of the business, a joint venture relationship will not necessarily end if the parties intend it to continue.

Tate
v
Ballard
68 NW2d 261
(Minnesota Supreme Court, 1955)

[Tate and Ballard formed an association to purchase and operate a factory. Both advanced money toward the purchase price of the plant and for working capital. Later, a corporation was formed to carry out the venture. Still later, Tate sued for dissolution of the association and for an accounting on the ground that the parties had been engaged in a joint venture. Ballard denied that a joint venture had been created. At trial, the court ruled in favor of Tate and held that Ballard was indebted to Tate for $4,000 by the terms of their joint venture agreement. From this judgment, Ballard appealed.]

Thomas Gallaher, Justice.

*   *   *

A joint venture ordinarily is created where two or more persons agree to combine their money, property, time, or skill in a business operation and share in the profits of the enterprise in some fixed proportion. We have held that four prerequisites are essential to its formation, i.e., (1) contribution of money, property, time, or skill, not necessarily in equal proportions, by each of the parties; (2) joint proprietorship and mutuality of control of the subject matter of the venture; (3) an agreement for sharing of profits, though not necessarily the losses, arising from the venture; and (4) a contract express or implied establishing the joint venture relationship.... [Ballard] concedes that in the instant case there is evidence sufficient to establish the elements of *contribu-*

tion and *sharing of profits* but asserts that there is none which would support the essential findings of *contract* covering the venture or *joint proprietorship and control* of the subject matter thereof. [Court's emphasis.]

With respect to the contract prerequisite, [Ballard] contends that the formation of the corporation and transfer of all assets to it effectively terminated any relationship of joint venture which may have existed prior thereto and converted the status of the parties to that of ordinary corporate stockholders. However, it has been held that formation of a corporation to which the assets of a joint venture are transferred is not inconsistent with the continuance of the joint venture relationship between the parties if it can be established that such was their intent.... As expressed in [another case], "The fact that joint adventurers may determine to carry out the purpose of the agreement through the medium of a corporation does not change the essential nature of the relationship."

It is clear from these principles that the purpose or intent of the parties in the formation of the corporation is important in determining whether the joint venture continued thereafter. Such intent may be gathered from the actions of the parties as well as their expressions. Here there was testimony that the corporation was formed primarily for the purpose of saving taxes and thus increasing profits. No corporate meetings of either stockholders or directors were ever held. No minute books were submitted. The enterprise was thereafter conducted by the parties in the same manner as it was before formation of the corporation.... All of such factors lend reasonable support to the trial court's determination that the joint venture relationship continued after the formation of the corporation and that the latter merely constituted an instrument to facilitate and further the operation of the former. . . .

As to the issue of joint or mutual control, defendant argues that the evidence establishes that [Tate] merely controlled the plant at Clovis, while the corporation exercised the over-all proprietary control of all the assets, and that hence this essential prerequisite to joint venture was absent. It must be recalled, however, that the mutuality of control required is that of the parties to the venture and that in this respect, a comparison of the rights of [Tate] with those of the corporation, as suggested by defendant, would not be the determinative factor. Further, a disparity in the exercise of actual control as between the parties to a joint venture does not negate such a venture where, as here, the parties through the exercise of their rights as corporate stockholders, or otherwise, may, if desired, each exercise an equal measure of control therein. . . .

[Judgment affirmed.]

41:14 Rights and Liabilities of Joint Venturers

The rights and duties of joint venturers depend primarily on the terms of the contract by which the relationship was brought into existence. Joint venturers are also affected by general principles of contract and partnership law. The most basic of these is the principle that the relationship of joint venturers is fiduciary in nature. The law imposes on joint venturers the obligation of loyalty to the joint concern and of the utmost good faith, honesty, and fairness in their dealings with each other with regard to matters pertaining to the enterprise.

Profits and Losses In the absence of an agreement to the contrary, joint venturers are entitled to a share of the profits equal to their shares in the business, as set forth in the joint venture agreement. This is true even though contributions of the participants differ in kind or in amount.

Joint venturers are also bound to share losses resulting from an enterprise, if it is so provided in their contract or required by law. A participant in a joint venture who fails to pay his share of sustained losses can be sued for contribution by his associates. For that matter, a joint venturer can also subject himself to liability for damages by failing to contribute his share toward the payment of expenses or to perform other obligations to further the goals of the business.

Property Rights Unless otherwise agreed, property purchased with the funds of a joint venture or with its profits belongs to all the participants for the purposes of the enterprise. A joint venturer who holds or acquires title to property for the venture is a trustee for the other participants, even if the property was purchased with his own funds. Therefore, a joint venturer who retains or appropriates for personal benefit property belonging to the venture, or who acts in any other way to deprive the associates of the benefit of such property, becomes liable for breach of fiduciary duties. Similarly, a joint venturer who purchases or leases property related to the enterprise without full disclosure to the other associates, or who mismanages assets of the enterprise, will be liable to the others.

Withdrawal   A party to a joint venture cannot unilaterally withdraw from or abandon the enterprise before its purposes have been attained. One who does so can be liable to the other parties to the venture for damages resulting from the withdrawal. If, in addition, the withdrawing party then acts independently with respect to the subject matter of the joint venture, he can be compelled to share the benefits with the other parties.

Liability to Third Persons   Each joint venturer has the power to bind the others and to subject them to liability to third parties in matters that are within the scope of the venture. This is consistent with the general rule that each member of a joint venture acts as both principal and agent within the apparent scope of the venture and for its benefit.[7] As to third persons who deal with a member of a joint venture in good faith and without any knowledge of any limit on his authority, the law presumes that the venturer has been accorded the power to bind his associates. Consequently, associates can be liable to third persons even where they have expressly agreed among themselves that no liability should arise.

Key Concepts and Terms

- A partnership is an association of two or more persons to carry on as co-owners a business for profit. It is a voluntary association by agreement, and it is governed by the Uniform Partnership Act in most states. A contract, either express or implied, is ordinarily essential to the formation of a partnership.

- All property brought into a partnership or acquired by it with partnership funds is partnership property. Title of property so acquired can be conveyed only in the partnership name.

- The property rights of an individual partner include rights in specific partnership property, the interest in the partnership, and the right to participate in management.

- A tenancy in partnership arises when property is acquired by a partnership, regardless of whether title was taken in the names of all the partners or in the name of only one. Each partner has an equal right to use the property for partnership purposes. On the death of a partner, property held in tenancy in partnership vests in the surviving partners for partnership purposes; it is not subject to the right of survivorship.

- All partners possess an equal right in the management and conduct of partnership business. Questions that affect a partnership are usually decided by a majority of the partners.

- Each partner is entitled to an equal share in the profits of the partnership unless the partners have agreed to a different arrangement. Losses are also to be shared by all partners equally or in agreed proportions.

---

[7]The agency relationship is discussed in Chapter 48.

- Every partner is not only a principal but also a general and authorized agent of the partnership. The authority of a partner to act as an agent for a partnership is limited to transactions within the scope of the partnership business or within the apparent scope of a partner's authority.

- Among themselves, partners are fiduciaries. An obligation of the utmost good faith and integrity is imposed on partners in their dealings with one another with regard to partnership property and affairs.

- Partners are jointly liable for all debts and obligations that result from partnership transactions. Partners are jointly and severally liable for torts committed in the course of partnership business.

- Dissolution is a change in the relation of the partners caused by any partner's ceasing to be associated in the conduct of the business. Dissolution is followed by winding up of the business, and later by its termination.

- "Winding up" means the administration of a partnership's assets for the purpose of terminating the business and discharging its obligations. It entails the performance of existing contracts, the collection of debts or claims due the firm, and the payment of partnership debts.

- In settling accounts among partners after dissolution, creditors (other than partners) are ordinarily given priority. After these creditors have been paid, debts owing to partners may be paid. Any surplus is then distributed to the partners as return of capital and profits.

- A limited partnership is a partnership formed by two or more persons having as its members one or more general partners and one or more limited partners. It is governed by the Uniform Limited Partnership Act in most states. The general partner assumes the management responsibilities of the partnership and full personal liability for its debts. Each limited partner makes a contribution of cash or other property to the partnership and obtains an interest in the partnership in return. A limited partner, whose liability for partnership debts is limited, cannot be active in management.

- A joint venture is an association of persons with the intent to engage and carry out a single business venture for profit.

- There are generally four essential elements to the formation of a joint venture: (1) an intent to create a joint venture; (2) an agreement to combine property, money, labor, knowledge, and skills in a common undertaking; (3) a right to joint control; and (4) an agreement for the sharing of profits.

- Accounting
- Dissolution
- General Partnership
- Joint Venture
- Limited Partnership
- Liquidating Partner
- Notice of Dissolution
- Partnership by Estoppel
- Silent Partner
- Tenancy in Partnership
- Uniform Limited Partnership Act (ULPA)
- Uniform Partnership Act (UPA)

Questions and Case Problems

1. Paboogian purchases a dental building with his own money but puts title to it in the name of his partnership. Does the building thereby become partnership property? Would the result be different if Paboogian had purchased the building with partnership funds?

2. How is a general partnership formed? How does the formation of a limited partnership differ from that of a general partnership?

3. Holmes signs a loan agreement with the Tenth City Bank to borrow $1 million for a partnership. Unknown to the bank, the partnership agreement provides that no single partner can borrow funds for the partnership without the written consent of all partners. Can the bank enforce the loan agreement against the partnership? On learning of the loan, partner Mendes notifies the Tenth City Bank that she will not be liable on any subsequent partnership debts. Will this notice relieve Mendes of further liability?

4. Potter and Hercule are partners. During a business trip for the partnership, Potter negligently operates his car and injures Tobin. Can Tobin recover from Hercule for Potter's negligent conduct?

5. Tinker, Tabay, and Vargas form a partnership for a three-year period to manufacture a new perfume. Six months later, Tinker elects to dissolve the partnership. Is Tinker liable to the other partners for any damages resulting from dissolution of the partnership? After dissolution, the remaining partners continue to operate the business in the firm name. Can Tinker sue her former partners for compensation accruing after she withdrew from the partnership? Is Tinker liable for debts acquired by the partnership after her withdrawal?

6. Discuss the various causes of the dissolution of a partnership. What is the difference between a partnership's "dissolution" and the winding up of its affairs?

7. Gratch purchases a warehouse with his own funds but records title in the name of a partnership of which he is a partner. Later, in a dispute with the partnership, Gratch alleges that he never intended that the building be partnership property. If the partnership shows that it urgently needed this type of warehouse, is it likely to prevail? If so, why?

8. Shawn, England, and May begin work on an idea to create a "thunder-lizard doll." The doll represents an imaginary lizard that England used in Oklahoma on a radio program about the weather. Eventually, the doll idea develops into a proposed book about Oklahoma weather. England writes a manuscript, Shawn has it typed and edited, and May does the art work. Before completion of the book, Shawn is ejected from the venture. Shawn then sues England and May for an accounting of the profits. England and May contend that a partnership existed only as to the lizard doll idea and that it ended when that idea was dropped. Is Shawn entitled to an accounting? Why?

9. Does property owned by a partnership differ from property owned by individual partners but used for partnership purposes? If so, how?

10. In what ways does a joint venture resemble a partnership? In what ways is it different?

42 Introduction to Corporations

The corporation is a creature of the State. It is presumed to be incorporated for the benefit of the public.

Hale v Henkel,
201 US 43, 50 L Ed 652, 26 S Ct 370
(United States Supreme Court, 1906)

A business corporation is organized and carried on primarily for the profit of the shareholders.

Dodge v Ford Motor Co.,
204 Mich 459, 197 NW 668
(Michigan Supreme Court, 1919)

42:1 General Comments

A corporation is a form of business enterprise that exists as a separate legal entity from the individuals who own or manage it. The owners, known as shareholders, are recognized by the law as distinct from the corporation and, as such, are not liable for the corporation's debts and obligations. A corporation, unlike a partnership (see Chapter 41), has an indefinite existence because an owner's corporate shares can be transferred when he dies. A corporation is managed by officers and directors who are charged by law with specific duties to the corporation and to its shareholders. In short, a corporation has (1) a separate identity, (2) continuity of existence, (3) limited shareholder liability, (4) free transferability of ownership rights, (5) centralized management, and (6) limited powers through its officers and directors.

Traditionally, the power to incorporate is held by the state under its general corporation laws. These statutes prescribe the corporate structure and the relationships between management and shareholders, between the majority and minority shareholders, and between classes of shareholders. They also set forth limits of management accountability.

Model Business Corporation Act   The Model Business Corporation Act (MBCA) provides state legislators, lawyers, and law review commissions with a working model for the revision and modernization of state corporation laws. The MBCA, which is set out as Appendix C to this book, is the result of the American Bar Association's efforts to draft both a federal corporation law and a state model corporation law. It has been adopted in whole or in part by at least 35 states. Because the MBCA is used so widely as a model for state corporation laws, reference will be made to it throughout this and the other chapters on corporations (Chapters 43–45).

Corporate Charter   A company doing business as a corporation is given rights or privileges by the state. The instrument that conveys them is called a corporate charter. Besides these rights and privileges, the charter embraces the state constitution and other statutes that affect the corporation in the state where it is organized. The charter governs the course and conduct of the corporation's business and delineates the proper scope of its activities. The charter is also referred to as the articles of incorporation or the certificate.

42:2   Classes and Types of Corporations

The corporation is the dominant form of business enterprise in the United States. Although corporations represent less than ten percent of the existing business enterprises in number, they employ three-fourths of the nation's labor force and control or own a similar percentage of our national wealth. Most economic activity in the country can be attributed to the large, publicly held corporations. Their size and power have given them the ability to exert great influence on the conduct of society. Generally, corporations are classified as public, private, or quasi-public. These classes are discussed below.

Public Corporation   A public corporation is a corporation that is created for public purposes connected with the administration of government. An incorporated school district and an incorporated municipality are examples of public corporations. Local taxes largely support local public corporations.

Private Corporation   A private corporation, in contrast to a public one, is a corporation created to earn profits for its owners (profit corporation) or to raise funds for charitable purposes (nonprofit corporation). The three most common types of private corporations are the incorporated sole proprietorship, the close corporation, and the publicly held corporation. The characteristics of each type are discussed below.

Incorporated Sole Proprietorship.   As its name suggests, the incorporated sole proprietorship is a corporation that is owned and operated by one person. This person is the director and chief executive officer of the corporation. He is answerable only to himself as long as his actions are within the limits of the law.

Close Corporation.   A *close corporation* has three distinctive features: (1) it is owned by a small number of shareholders, (2) it does not sell its stock to the general public, and (3) its officers and directors are ordinarily shareholders. Often, a close corporation is owned by a family and is operated as a partnership.[1]

Publicly Held Corporation.   A publicly held corporation is a corporation that sells and trades its shares and issues debt obligations to the general public. The nation's largest corporations are publicly held. Because it is the most prevalent form of corporation, the publicly held corporation is the basis of discussion in the rest of this chapter and in the other chapters on corporations.[2]

---

[1]Partnership is discussed in Chapter 41.

[2]The "publicly held" corporation should not be confused with the "public" corporation; "publicly held" refers to the fact that the corporation *is owned by* the public, not that it is *operated for* the public, as is a public corporation.

Other types of private corporations are formed for specific advantages or benefits enjoyed by their owners. These include the Subchapter S corporation, the holding company, the professional corporation, the foreign corporation, and the multinational corporation.

Subchapter S Corporation.   A *Subchapter S corporation* is a close corporation that has elected to be treated as a sole proprietorship or partnership for income tax purposes under the Internal Revenue Code. The term "Subchapter S" is derived from the particular subdivision of the Internal Revenue Code that permits this type of taxation and sets forth the eligibility requirements for this tax status. The Subchapter S provision exempts the corporation from paying corporate income tax and allows the shareholders to be taxed on corporate earnings and to deduct corporate losses directly. Consequently, the Subchapter S corporation avoids the "double taxation" levied on a normal corporation. This double taxation arises because when a normal corporation distributes money or property to its shareholders, the amount of money or the fair market value of the property is taxed as a dividend to the shareholders, but before the distribution it was also taxed as a part of the corporation's profits.

The eligibility requirements for Subchapter S corporations are quite technical under the Internal Revenue Code. Generally, a corporation is eligible if it has less than 15 shareholders, has only one class of stock outstanding, and is a domestic corporation. Furthermore, each shareholder must consent in writing to the election of Subchapter S status. In most cases a corporation's eligibility is not determined by the type of business it conducts.

Subchapter S status can be revoked only with the consent of all shareholders. Once Subchapter S status has been terminated or revoked, the corporation cannot reelect Subchapter S status for five years.[3]

Holding Company.   A *holding company* is a corporation that owns interests in one or more other corporations. The extent to which it owns these interests varies. A holding company can be organized and operated for the sole purpose of holding a controlling interest, and in this sense, it is a supercorporation that dictates the policies and programs of those corporations in which it owns stock. A holding company can also be an ordinary business enterprise that quite incidentally owns stock in another corporation. Another common type of holding company is a large enterprise at the top of an organizational pyramid that owns all the stock and controls the management of its constituent companies or operating divisions.

Professional Corporation.   Accountants, dentists, doctors, lawyers, and other professionals are allowed to incorporate under the laws of many states and by the federal government under the Internal Revenue Code. The professional corporation is formed to obtain the benefits flowing from corporation status: limited liability and federal income tax advantages. State statutes governing professional corporations, however, usually restrict stock ownership to individuals licensed in that state, and they generally forbid a professional corporation from conducting its activities except through professionals.

---

[3]Corporate taxation and the consideration of this factor in selecting the type of business organization is discussed in Chapter 47.

Foreign Corporation.   A *foreign corporation* is a corporation that is created by or organized under the laws of another state or country. Thus, a corporation organized under the laws of one state and operating in another state is a foreign corporation in the latter state. Of course, a corporation transacting business in another state must have the required certificate of authority to do business in that state. Otherwise, it cannot enforce its claims against that state's residents in the state's courts. The same is true for a corporation organized in a foreign country and doing business in the United States.

 Meeting certain requirements to transact business in another state does not involve the same expense or red tape that incorporation in the home state does, but it is inconvenient and can be easily overlooked. Therefore, if business is to be conducted in another state, it is wise to ascertain whether any of these requirements exist before transacting business in that state and to take the appropriate steps to meet those requirements.

Multinational Corporations   Corporations organized under the laws of a state often do business in foreign countries. Corporations formed in other countries also engage in business in the United States. A corporation might manufacture products in this country and sell them directly abroad; or it might obtain raw materials in one country, produce a finished product in the United States, and then market the goods elsewhere. When corporations engage in business in this manner, they are referred to as multinational corporations.

Most of the larger multinational corporations are actually comprised of several constituent companies called subsidiaries. A single, controlling (parent) corporation directs all the activities of the subsidiaries. Multinational corporations that operate in this fashion have three basic characteristics: (1) central control by the parent corporation, (2) a common production and marketing strategy for the entire enterprise, and (3) integration of operations among the subsidiaries and affiliates with the parent.

Quasi-Public Corporation   A *quasi-public*, or public service, *corporation* is a corporation that owes a duty to the public because it has special privileges conferred by the state. These privileges include having freedom from competition and enjoying certain powers of a public nature, such as the power of eminent domain (see Chapter 37), to enable them to discharge their duties for public benefit. In exchange for having freedom from competition, quasi-public corporations are closely regulated and subject to strict governmental scrutiny. For example, power companies and telephone companies are typical quasi-public corporations, and they are closely regulated in such areas as plant expansion and rate increases.

42:3 Promoters

The modern business corporation does not come into being spontaneously. Someone must conceive and initiate the business and bring together people interested in the enterprise. This person is generally referred to as a *promoter*, one who takes part in the formation of a new corporation.

A promoter is not the same as an incorporator. A promoter can aid in establishing a corporation without actually participating in its formation or signing any incorporation documents. He need not be related to the corporation as an officer, director, or shareholder. A promoter's activities can be divided into (1) discovery, (2) investigation, and (3) assembly. Discovery is finding the business opportunity; investigation is analyzing the proposed business to determine its economic feasibility; assembly is bringing together property, money, and personnel to set the business in motion.

A promoter's work begins long before the corporation is organized. The promoter looks for the capital needed to achieve the purposes set forth in the proposed articles of incorporation. He brings together the potential shareholders, aids in procuring stock subscriptions, and sets in motion the machinery that leads to formation of the corporation itself.

Once the corporation is formed, the promoter does not necessarily lose his character as such. If a person continues to perform the acts that characterize promoters, such as inducing persons to subscribe to capital stock or invest in the corporation's securities, his relationship to the corporation as a promoter continues.

Compensation of Promoters   The states have not adopted a uniform approach to compensating promoters for services rendered before incorporation. In some states, in the absence of a provision in the articles of incorporation or statutory provisions, a corporation is not liable to its promoters for services rendered or expenses incurred before incorporation unless the corporation later expressly agrees to make such payments. Under this view, an implied promise to reimburse a promoter cannot be imputed to the corporation, since the corporation did not exist when the services were rendered or the expenses incurred. In other states, a promise to pay a promoter is implied, particularly when the promoter performs necessary and reasonable services in obtaining a charter, in securing stock subscriptions, or in otherwise perfecting the organization. This rule for reimbursing a promoter for preincorporation expenses is based on the notion that it would otherwise be difficult to organize a corporation. No one would render any services, however essential, if the corporation's obligation to pay could not be imputed to it once it comes into existence. Regardless of which approach is adopted by the states, after a corporation has been organized, it can authorize payment of compensation to promoters (MBCA § 22).

Duties and Liabilities of Promoters   A promoter stands in a fiduciary relationship to the prospective corporation and to the subsequent stock subscribers. The promoter must exercise the utmost good faith in dealing with the corporation and its shareholders. He must fully disclose all material facts and fully advise the corporation and its shareholders of any interest that may in any manner affect them. A promoter will not be allowed to benefit by any secret profit or advantage gained at the expense of the corporation or its shareholders unless all material facts have been disclosed. Compensation to promoters for services must be made on the basis of full disclosure as well. For example, a promoter who secretly profits through the sale of property to a corporation has committed a fraud on the corporation and its shareholders. The promoter may be required to account for the profit or return it to the corporation.

In the absence of a statute to the contrary, if a promoter makes a contract for the benefit of a corporation before the corporation exists, the promoter is personally liable on it. This is also true when a promoter conducts the ordinary affairs of a business in the nature of a corporation before it is legally organized or qualified to do business. Of course, the corporation can later enter into a new contract with the same creditor or the same contracting party, thereby releasing the promoter from liability.

 A promoter frequently enters into contracts on behalf of a corporation before it is legally born. Unless the promoter has obtained a corporation's formal ratification of preincorporation contracts as soon as the incorporation is official, the promoter will remain personally liable under the contracts.

The issue in the following case is a promoter's liability for certain conduct in connection with a corporate property transaction. Consider why the court held the promoter liable.

Park City Corp.
v
Watchie
249 Or 493, 439 P2d 587
(Oregon Supreme Court, 1968)

[Watchie acquired options to purchase 965 acres of property for $729,000. He then interested a group of investors to buy the property and acted as a trustee on their behalf. The investors were interested only in holding the property as an investment for later resale, not for development. Watchie organized a corporation to develop the property. After forming the corporation, Watchie, as the investors' trustee, entered into a contract with the corporation to buy the property owned by the syndicate for $1.4 million. None of the corporation's stock subscribers had been advised that the property had been previously acquired by the investors for one-half the purchase price, nor were they advised of Watchie's relationship as trustee for the group. Although extensive plans were made for developing the property acquired by the corporation, development was never carried out. Ultimately, the corporation sued Watchie for violating his fiduciary relationship as a

promoter by realizing such a large profit on the sale of the property to the corporation. At trial, the court ruled that the corporation failed to prove the allegations of its complaint against Watchie. The corporation appealed.]

Sloan, Justice.

*   *   *

Plaintiff's cause of suit is based upon a doctrine originally formulated in this country in the Massachusetts case of Old Dominion Copper Mining & Smelting Co. v. Bigelow, 1909, 203 Mass. 159, 89 N.E. 193, 40 L.R.A., N.S., 314. We read that case to hold that the promoter of a corporation owes to the corporation, and its subsequent subscribers of stock, a fiduciary duty. This duty is violated if he schemes to and does secretly acquire property or the right to buy property which he knows the corporation will require and sells it to the corporation, while he still retains control of the corporation, at a secret profit which is not disclosed to the later subscribers or to an independent board of directors of the corporation. In that event the corporation may bring an action to recover the secret profits. Oregon has adopted this theory in [a 1908 case]. The doctrine is generally recognized. . . .

The best expression we have found of the precise rule which delineates the particular kind of factual situation in which the corporation is permitted the remedy of the recovery of secret profits is in [the 1908 case], and it is this:

> "If two or more persons associate themselves for the purpose of purchasing property, and one of them represents to the others that particular property can be bought for a designated price, which he procures to be paid by the associates, when in truth the purchase is for a less sum, and he has received the difference between the two sums, no doubt he may be compelled to account for such differences, though the property may be worth all that was paid for it. The same principle applies as against promoters of corporations. Hence, if any of them has a secret contract for the purchase of property, the terms of which are more favorable than those disclosed by him, or an agreement that he shall have stock in the corporation without paying therefor, any advantage which he thereby obtains is a fraud on the other shareholders and upon the corporation, and he will not be permitted to retain it. . . . And he may be compelled to account for such difference without rescission of the contract. . . ."

Plaintiff's complaint alleged facts which would bring the case within the factual situation covered by the rule just quoted. As before mentioned, the allegations of the complaint are limited to charges that Watchie was the promoter of plaintiff corporation; that he personally contracted to buy the Skyline property, that he formed plaintiff corporation and while he was in the complete control of it, sold the property to the corporation for double his own purchase price and that Watchie "did not disclose to either the Board of Directors or the stockholders of plaintiff corporation that

[Watchie] would make a profit of $729,000, by reason of said contract." These are the pertinent allegations of the complaint.

The evidence does not sustain the allegations. In the complete transaction, as described in the evidence, the property was bought by the Seattle syndicate. It was not bought with the scheme or design of selling it to this or any other persons or corporation but it was held for sale at the price specified. Contrary to the allegations, Watchie did not participate in any part of the profit made by the Seattle syndicate in the contract for the sale of the property, except for the commission paid to H. R. Watchie & Associates, Inc. In the contract with plaintiff corporation, Watchie was named as the vendor. But he was acting, admittedly, only as the trustee for the Seattle syndicate. He was not the true vendor or the recipient of any of the profits, as alleged. Nor is there any evidence that at any time, Watchie as an individual or as trustee schemed to overload the profit on unsuspecting subscribers. . . .

However, the evidence did establish that Watchie made a personal profit in the form of the commission he received for the transaction. The commission was actually received by H. R. Watchie & Associates, Inc., but it is Watchie's alter ego. Because of his failure to disclose his dual relationship, he should be required to return this personal profit to plaintiff. . . . This means that he should not be charged with the whole commission received. He should be charged with that part which can be said to result from his non-disclosure.

The subscription agreement informed all subscribers that there would be a commission in the present transaction payable to Watchie or H. R. Watchie & Associates, Inc., by the corporation. This commission was described in the subscription agreement as one-ninth of the cost of the property to Watchie or Watchie & Associates, Inc. It also provided that he was to receive his actual costs. Thus everyone that was involved in the venture was aware that there would be a profit to Watchie.

As a result of his non-disclosure, however,

there is an ambiguity concerning what was the cost to Watchie for determining the amount of his authorized profit on the transaction; the price at which he purchased the property for the Seattle syndicate or the price he arranged between the syndicate and the plaintiff corporation. Since this ambiguity is solely the result of Watchie's non-disclosure of his relationship with the syndicate it would seem that the proper course would be to resolve the ambiguity against Watchie and in favor of the corporation that the cost referred to in the subscription agreement was the original cost.

This necessitates a holding that Watchie would only be entitled to a commission based on the initial cost of $729,000, or a commission of $81,000. Plaintiff is, therefore, entitled to a judgment accordingly. But, in addition, Watchie would be entitled to retain the actual costs that either he or that H. R. Watchie & Associates, Inc. incurred in the transaction between the syndicate and plaintiff. These costs we cannot definitely determine from the record.

The decree is modified to the extent stated and the cause remanded to the trial court to make the necessary finding as to the costs for which Watchie should receive credit and to enter a decree accordingly.

42:4   The Process of Incorporation

The right to act as a corporation is a privilege conferred by state law. A corporation comes into existence only by complying with statutory requirements of the state in which it is incorporated. No corporation can exist without the state's authorization.

 When owners of a business incorporate, they create a legal entity having the capacity to contract and incur debts on its own. To achieve freedom from personal liability for corporate debts, the owners, directors, and officers must comply with the requirements set out in the corporation laws of the state of incorporation. Noncompliance can mean suspension of the corporation and potential personal liability of the shareholders, officers, and directors for corporate debts.

Incorporation ordinarily begins by filing articles of incorporation with a designated state official, such as the Secretary of State (MBCA § 55). In a few states, a copy of the articles must also be filed locally, in the county where the corporation's principal office is to be located or where it owns property. The state official with whom articles are filed determines whether they are in the proper form and are entitled to be filed. When articles conforming to the provisions of the state corporation law are presented, the state official must file them and then issue a certificate of incorporation (MBCA § 55). Most states require payment of an incorporation fee before a corporation is permitted to conduct business.

The statutory requirements as to the form and content of the articles of incorporation must be substantially followed. Most states require articles of incorporation to contain certain minimum provisions as set out in the applicable corporation law, which is the law of the place where the corporation is to be organized (see MBCA § 54). Articles of incorporation are usually required to contain the following information: (1) corporate name, (2) corporate purpose, (3) corporation's specific business, (4) location of principal office, (5) name of designated agent for service of process, (6) number of directors, and (7) capital structure (MBCA § 54).

In some states, even though statutory requirements are met, a corporation might still not be qualified to do business. For example, the election of corporate officers, the subscription and payment of capital stock, and other steps may also be necessary. Accordingly, under state statutes of this type, if nothing more is done than filing articles of incorporation in the proper office, no corporation will come into existence. In other states, the existence of a corporation is deemed to commence at the time the articles of incorporation are filed with the state and a certificate of incorporation issued (MBCA § 56). This is true even though such statutes may also require some form of organizational procedure or meeting before the corporation can actually conduct business (MBCA § 57).

After the articles of incorporation have been filed with the state and a certificate of incorporation issued, the corporate board of directors usually holds a meeting to complete all of the steps necessary to its organizational structure (MBCA § 57). At this time, the corporation elects corporate officers and adopts governing rules, which are called *bylaws*. The corporation also (1) obtains authorization to open bank accounts, (2) complies with qualifications for doing business in other states if necessary, (3) obtains approval to lease or purchase property, (4) ratifies promoter contracts, and (5) obtains approval to issue stock and debt securities.

Bylaws   Every corporation has the power to enact bylaws that govern its internal operation. Bylaws supplement the articles of incorporation and contain details of corporate administration, management, and internal operating procedures. Bylaws must be consistent with all state laws and with the articles of incorporation.

The initial bylaws are adopted by the board of directors. The power to alter, amend, or repeal bylaws or to adopt new bylaws, subject to repeal or change by action of the shareholders, is vested in the board of directors unless that power is reserved to the shareholders in the articles of incorporation (MBCA § 27).

Corporate Name   A name is particularly important to the existence of a corporation. The name designates the corporation in the same manner as the name of an individual designates the person. Thus, each corporation must have a name by which it is to do all legal acts, to sue and to be sued. Under MBCA § 8, a corporate name cannot contain any word or phrase indicating or implying that the corporation is organized for any purposes other than those specified in the articles of incorporation. For example, a marine supply corporation cannot call itself a marine shipbuilding corporation. Moreover, a corporate name cannot be the same as or deceptively similar to the name of any other corporation organized or doing business in the state. A corporation may, however, obtain another corporation's written consent to use a similar or identical name. A corporation resulting from a merger or consolidation can take the same name as that used in the state by any of its predecessors (MBCA § 8).

The right to use a corporate name is as much a part of the corporate charter as any other privilege. A significant part of the value of a corporate name is usually that which derives from the rights accorded by the law of trade names, trade-marks, and service marks (see Chapter 53).

To protect corporate names, MBCA § 9 provides that the exclusive right to use a particular name can be reserved by (1) any person intending to organize a corporation, (2) a domestic corporation intending to change its name, (3) a foreign corporation intending to apply for a certificate of authority to transact business in the state, (4) any foreign corporation authorized to transact business in the state and intending to change its name, and (5) any person intending to organize a foreign corporation that will do business in the state. The reservation is made by filing an application with the state to reserve a specified corporate name. If the name is available for corporate use, the state reserves it for the applicant's exclusive use for 120 days. The name can then be registered with the state by filing an application for registration and paying a registration fee (MBCA § 10).

Seal   Under the common law, a corporation could act only by its seal. This technical rule has given way. Today, in the transaction of business, a seal is no more necessary to validate the acts and contracts of a corporation than it is to validate those of an individual. However, it is sometimes desirable to adopt a seal so that all corporate contracts or other acts can be attested to with the seal. The presence of the seal establishes that the instrument to which it is affixed is the act of the corporation, and it is evidence of the proper execution of a contract and that the seal was affixed by proper authority.

Corporate Domicil and Place of Business   One's "domicil" is the place where one lives. The term refers to a relationship that the law creates between an individual—or a corporation—and a particular locality, state, or country. Sometimes the terms "domicil" and "residence" are used synonymously, but the two are actually different in meaning. For example, a person who resides in Florida for the winter but has a permanent home in New York is domiciled in New York, not Florida. Similarly, a corporation can transact business in Florida, and even maintain an office there to further its business, without being domiciled there.

A corporation's domicil belongs exclusively to the state in which it is created. Since a corporation exists only by reason of the law of the state where it is incorporated, it must dwell in that state and cannot migrate at will from state to state. These general rules do not mean, however, that a corporation's existence will not be recognized in other places. A corporation can qualify to transact business in any other state unless otherwise prohibited by law. Certainly, it can transact business in interstate commerce without undue interference from any state other than that of its incorporation.

For nearly 50 years, the state of Delaware has been unofficially recognized as the most desirable corporate domicil. Its liberal promanagement corporation laws and favorable court decisions in cases involving corporations have attracted business enterprises from all over the world. Forty percent of the companies listed on the New York Stock Exchange are domiciled in Delaware, and over 200 of the 500 largest industrial corporations in America are incorporated in this state.

42:5   Defects in the Formation Process

A corporation created in strict compliance with all the mandatory legal conditions for incorporation is termed a de jure corporation—a lawful corporation. It is a separate legal entity and possesses all the attributes or powers incident to a corporation. Such attributes include (1) limited liability, (2) continuity of life, (3) the power to sue and be sued, (4) the power to hold and convey property, (5) the capacity to contract, and (6) the right to exercise other corporate powers. The right of a de jure corporation to exist and act cannot be successfully attacked directly by the state or by any other party. In other words, the law recognizes the corporation character of a de jure corporation.

Occasionally, however, incorporators fail to or improperly perform one or more of the formal requirements for incorporation. In this situation, the corporation lacks de jure status. It does not possess all the attributes and powers ordinarily enjoyed by a corporation that fully complies with the requirements of the law.

In a few states a defective corporation is regarded as a nullity—as though no corporation had been formed at all. For example, lawsuits based on contractual obligations or torts can be defended on the basis that no corporation exists; conveyances made by the defective corporation can also be invalidated. Moreover, associates, shareholders, incorporators, or any other officers of what was purported to be a corporation may be sued and held personally liable on "corporate" obligations.

The soundness of the nullity theory is questionable. In some instances, incorporators may intentionally fail to comply with incorporation requirements—in the hope of gaining some later advantage—leaving investors, employees, customers, and creditors open to liability. In other instances, the failure to comply with state incorporation statutes could be due simply to an attorney's negligence or be an innocent mistake of people trying to form a corporation without legal help. Because the nullity theory can produce harsh results, many courts have been reluctant to apply it.

De Facto Corporation   In many states, a corporation that has not obtained de jure status but has complied sufficiently to be given corporate status against third parties is recognized as a *de facto corporation.* A de facto corporation is an apparent corporate organization, asserted to be a corporation by those running the business, and actually acting as such, but it lacks the legal sanction of the law and corporate status against the state.

As a general rule, a de facto corporation comes into existence when a de jure corporation has not been created because of some irregularity or defect in its formation or because of some failure to comply with the conditions of a state incorporation law. A de facto corporation will be held to exist if there is (1) a valid law under which the corporation might be incorporated, (2) a bona fide attempt to organize under that law, and (3) an actual exercise of corporate powers.

A number of states have eliminated the de jure or de facto concepts, following MBCA § 56. This section provides that a corporation comes into existence only when the certificate of incorporation has actually been issued. If an individual or group of individuals assumes to act as a corporation before the certificate has been issued, they can be held liable under MBCA § 146 for all debts and liabilities incurred. Under the MBCA and in those states that have adopted similar provisions, if a corporation's articles have been approved and a certificate of incorporation has been issued, a valid corporation will be presumed to have been formed, except in certain actions brought by the state.

Corporation by Estoppel   In certain circumstances, an organization that cannot be either a de jure corporation or a de facto one can still be regarded between the parties to a given transaction as a corporation. That is, an organization that has not complied with state statutes and can in no sense be deemed even a de facto corporation for any purpose can obtain corporate status by virtue of an estoppel. The effect of the estoppel is to prevent one or more persons from denying the existence of the corporation. For example, if a person transacts business with an entity holding itself out as a corporation, the entity can be estopped from denying corporate existence if disputes over the transaction occur later. In some states, a corporation must have at least a de facto existence before it can be estopped to deny its existence. In other states, if an entity represents itself as a corporation, it can be estopped from denying corporate existence regardless of its true status.

The following case illustrates how the MBCA has affected the concept of de facto corporations and corporations by estoppel. Consider the court's reasoning in its decision that the model act eliminated these concepts. Note also the precise point at which, according to the court, a corporation comes into existence.

Robertson
v
Levy
197 A2d 443
(District of Columbia Court of Appeals, 1964)

[Robertson entered into an agreement with Levy for the latter to form a corporation and purchase Robertson's business. Levy submitted articles of incorporation to the state on December 27, 1961, but they were rejected on January 2, 1962. Despite the rejection, Levy began operating the business as a corporation. Robertson sold his assets to the corporation and received an installment note in return. A certificate of incorporation was finally issued on January 17, 1962. In June 1962, the corporation ceased doing business, and Levy stopped making payments on the note. Robertson sued Levy personally for the balance due on the note. Judgment was

for Levy, the trial court ruling that Robertson was estopped from denying the existence of the corporation and thus could not hold Levy personally liable for the note. Robertson appealed.]

Hood, Chief Judge.

*   *   *

The case presents the following issues on appeal: Whether the president of an "association" which filed its articles of incorporation, which were first rejected but later accepted, can be held personally liable on an obligation entered into by the "association" before the certificate of incorporation has been issued, or whether the creditor is "estopped" from denying the existence of the "corporation" because, after the certificate of incorporation was issued, he accepted the first installment payment on the note.

The Business Corporation Act of the District of Columbia ... is patterned after the Model Business Corporation Act. . . .

For a full understanding of the problems raised, some historical grounding is not only illuminative but necessary. In early common law times private corporations were looked upon with distrust and disfavor. This distrust of the corporate form for private enterprise was eventually overcome by the enactment of statutes which set forth certain prerequisites before the status was achieved, and by court decisions which eliminated other stumbling blocks. Problems soon arose, however, where there was substantial compliance with the prerequisites of the statute, but not complete formal compliance. Thus the concepts of de jure corporations, de facto corporations, and of "corporations by estoppel" came into being. . . .

One of the reasons for enacting modern corporation statutes was to eliminate problems inherent in the de jure, de facto and estoppel concepts. Thus [MBCA §§ 56 and 146] were enacted as follows:

"[MBCA § 56]. Effect of issuance of incorporation.

"Upon the issuance of the certificate of incorporation, the corporate existence shall begin, and such certificate of incorporation shall be conclusive evidence that all conditions precedent required to be performed by the incorporators have been complied with and that the corporation has been incorporated under this chapter, except as against the District of Columbia in a proceeding to cancel or revoke the certificate of incorporation."

"[MBCA § 146]. Unauthorized assumption of corporate powers.

"All persons who assume to act as a corporation without authority so to do shall be jointly and severally liable for all debts and liabilities incurred or arising as a result thereof."

The first portion of [MBCA § 56] sets forth a *sine qua non* regarding compliance. No longer must the courts inquire into the equities of a case to determine whether there has been "colorable compliance" with the statute. The corporation comes into existence only when the certificate has been issued. Before the certificate issues, there is no corporation de jure, de facto or by estoppel. . . .

The authorities which have considered the problem are unanimous in their belief that [MBCA §§ 56 and 146] have put to rest de facto corporations and corporations by estoppel. Thus the Comment to . . . the Model Act, after noting that de jure incorporation is complete when the certificate is issued, states that:

"Since it is unlikely that any steps short of securing a certificate of incorporation would be held to constitute apparent compliance, the possibility that a de facto corporation could exist under such a provision is remote."

Similarly, Professor Hornstein in his work on Corporate Law and Practice [observes] that: "Statutes in almost half the jurisdictions have virtually eliminated the distinction between de jure and de facto corporations. . . ." . . .

The portion of [MBCA § 56] which states that the certificate of incorporation will be "conclusive evidence" that all conditions precedent have been performed eliminates the problems of estoppel and de facto corporations once the certificate has been issued. The existence of the corporation is conclusive evidence against all who deal with it. Under [MBCA § 146], if an individual or group of individuals assumes to act as a corporation before the certificate of incorporation has been issued, joint and several liability attaches. We hold, therefore, that the impact of these sections, when considered together, is to eliminate the concepts of estoppel and de facto corporateness under the Business Corporation Act of the District of Columbia. It is immaterial whether the third person believed he was dealing with a corporation or whether he intended to deal with a corporation. The certificate of incorporation provides the cut off point; before it is issued, the individuals, and not the corporation, are liable.

Turning to the facts of this case, Penn Ave. Record Shack, Inc. was not a corporation when the original agreement was entered into, when the lease was assigned, when Levy took over Robertson's business, when operations began under the Penn Ave. Record Shack, Inc. name, or when the bill of sale was executed. Only on January 17 did Penn Ave. Record Shack, Inc. become a corporation. Levy is subject to personal liability because, before this date, he assumed to act as a corporation without any authority so to do. Nor is Robertson estopped from denying the existence of the corporation because after the certificate was issued he accepted one payment on the note. An individual who incurs statutory liability on an obligation under [MBCA § 146] because he has acted without authority, is not relieved of that liability where, at a later time, the corporation does come into existence by complying with [MBCA § 56]. Subsequent partial payment by the corporation does not remove this liability. . . .

[Judgment reversed.]

42:6   Corporate Powers and Functions

State laws give generous powers to corporations to enable them to engage in business activities. For example, MBCA § 4 gives a corporation the following rights and powers:

- Right to sue and be sued
- Right to acquire or sell real or personal property
- Right to hold, acquire, or dispose of shares of stock
- Ability to make contracts and become liable on them
- Power to mortgage corporate property
- Right to lend money and guarantee obligations of others
- Right to become a partner of others
- Power to compensate employees
- Right to pursue a nonprofitable objective
- Right to be treated as a separate entity or person
- Right to perpetual existence
- Right to make donations for the public welfare or for charitable, scientific, or educational purposes
- Right to pay pensions and to establish profit-sharing and other incentive plans for corporate directors, officers, and employees

In addition, MBCA § 3 provides that a corporation can engage in any lawful business purpose except banking or insurance.

A corporation has express powers to perform any act authorized by its articles of incorporation or by the general corporation laws of the state of incorporation. If a corporation does not insert provisions relating to corporate powers in its articles of incorporation, it usually means that the corporation has elected to have comprehensive powers to meet the objectives of incorporation. In most states, moreover, corporations also have implied powers to do whatever is reasonably necessary to promote their purposes and aid their express powers unless these powers are prohibited by common or statutory law [see MBCA § 4(q)].

42:7   Ultra Vires Acts

An act of a corporation that is beyond its express or implied powers is said to be *ultra vires*—beyond corporate powers. Ultra vires acts can arise when a corporation acts outside the powers granted in its articles of incorporation or beyond the powers granted under a state corporation law. The ultra vires doctrine seeks to preserve (1) the public's interest that a corporation will not exceed the powers granted to it, (2) the shareholders' interest that their capital will not be subjected to risks not contemplated by the articles of incorporation, and (3) the obligation of all persons dealing with a corporation to take notice of the limits on its power.

The ultra vires doctrine has been used by corporations as a defense. That is, corporations have sought to avoid obligations on the ground that corporate powers were exceeded in undertaking those obligations. The modern trend is to reject this kind of assertion, whether it is urged for or against a corporation, if it will result in legal wrong or inequity. Therefore, in many states—and in the MBCA—the availability of the ultra vires defense is limited (MBCA § 7).

In the following case, the court discusses why a corporation's making charitable contributions is not ultra vires. Consider the court's discussion of the ultra vires doctrine and its application to the facts of the case.

A.P. Smith Mfg. Co.
v
Barlow
13 NJ 145, 98 A2d 581, 39 ALR2d 1179
(New Jersey Supreme Court, 1953)

[A.P. Smith, a corporation, contributed regularly over the years to local charities. In 1951 the corporation's board of directors adopted a resolution appropriating $1,500 to Princeton University. When this action was questioned by shareholders, the corporation sought to have a court determine the propriety of its contribution. At trial, the court ruled that the contribution was proper and constituted a lawful exercise of corporate powers. The shareholders appealed.]

Jacobs, J.

*   *   *

The [trial court], in a well-reasoned opinion ..., determined that a donation by the plaintiff The A.P. Smith Manufacturing Company to Princeton University was *intra vires* [within its powers]. ...

The company was incorporated in 1896 and is engaged in the manufacture and sale of valves, fire hydrants and special equipment, mainly for water and gas industries.... Over the years the company has contributed regularly to the local community chest and on occasions to Upsala College in East Orange and Newark University, now part of Rutgers, the State University. On July 24, 1951 the board of directors adopted a resolution which set forth that it was in the corporation's best interests to join with others in the 1951 Annual Giving to Princeton University, and appropriated the sum of $1,500 to be transferred by the corporation's treasurer to the university as a contribution towards its maintenance....

The objecting stockholders have ... acknowledged that for over two decades there has been state legislation on our books which expresses a strong public policy in favor of corporate contributions such as that being questioned by them. Nevertheless, they have taken the position that (1) the plaintiff's certificate of incorporation does not expressly authorize the contribution and under common-law principles the company does not possess any implied or incidental power to make it....

In his discussion of the early history of business corporations Professor Williston refers to a 1702 publication where the author stated flatly that "The general intent and end of all civil incorporations is for better government." And he points out that the early corporate charters, particularly their recitals, furnish additional support for the notion that the corporate object was the public one of managing and ordering the trade as well as the private one of profit for the members.... However, with later economic and social developments and the free availability of the corporate device for all trades, the end of private profit became generally accepted as the controlling one in all businesses other than those classed broadly as public utilities.... As a concomitant the common-law rule developed that those who managed the corporation could not disburse any corporate funds for philanthropic or other worthy public cause unless the expenditure would benefit the corporation.... During the

19th Century when corporations were relatively few and small and did not dominate the country's wealth, the common-law rule did not significantly interfere with the public interest. But the 20th Century has presented a different climate.... Control of economic wealth has passed largely from individual entrepreneurs to dominating corporations, and calls upon the corporations for reasonable philanthropic donations have come to be made with increased public support. In many instances such contributions have been sustained by the courts within the common-law doctrine upon liberal findings that the donations tended reasonably to promote the corporate objectives....

... [W]e have no hesitancy in sustaining the validity of the donation by the plaintiff. There is no suggestion that it was made indiscriminately or to a pet charity of the corporate directors in furtherance of personal rather than corporate ends. On the contrary, it was made to a preeminent institution of higher learning, was modest in amount and well within the limitations imposed by the statutory enactments, and was voluntarily made in the reasonable belief that it would aid the public welfare and advance the interests of the plaintiff as a private corporation and as part of the community in which it operates. We find that it was a lawful exercise of the corporation's implied and incidental powers under common-law principles ... As has been indicated, there is now widespread belief throughout the nation that free and vigorous nongovernmental institutions of learning are vital to our democracy and the system of free enterprise and that withdrawal of corporate authority to make such contributions within reasonable limits would seriously threaten their continuance. Corporations have come to recognize this and with their enlightenment have sought in varying measures, as has the plaintiff by its contribution, to insure and strengthen the society which gives them existence and the means of aiding themselves and their fellow citizens. Clearly then, the appellants, as individual stockholders whose private interests rest entirely upon the well-being of the plaintiff corporation, ought not be permitted to close their eyes to present-day realities and thwart the long-visioned corporate action in recognizing and voluntarily discharging its high obligations as a constituent of our modern social structure.

[Judgment affirmed.]

42:8   Corporate Tort and Criminal Liability

A corporation can commit and be held liable for almost every kind of tort (see Chapter 5). The fact that a business is incorporated is not a defense in a tort action. Moreover, the agency rule of respondeat superior (see Chapter 48) is also applicable to corporations. Under this rule, a corporation can be held liable for the torts and other wrongful acts of its officers, directors, agents, or employees, so long as the wrongdoer is acting within the scope of his authority or the course of his employment.

Fraud   Corporations can also be held liable for the fraud and deceit of their officers and agents acting within the scope of their corporate authority or employment. A corporation's liability for fraud extends to false statements in certificates, reports, or documents required to be filed with a governmental entity. This is particularly true if the required documents are the sort on which others are to rely and act.

Criminal Liability   It was long held under the common law that a corporation could not be prosecuted criminally. Today, however, a corporation can be held criminally liable for the acts of an officer or employee acting within the scope of his employment.[4] To hold a corporation liable, it is not necessary to show that the criminal acts of an officer or employee were expressly authorized or approved. Indeed, a corporation cannot even escape liability by claiming that it specifically prohibited its officers and employees from violating the law.

A corporation can be punished by fine or by seizure of its property. Because it might be more difficult to punish corporations than to punish individuals, a state can impose different punishment on a corporation than is imposed on an individual for the same criminal offense. For example, a state can properly impose the penalty of mandatory dissolution on a corporation in addition to the penalties imposed on individuals. However, states cannot impose different degrees of punishment for the same act because doing so would violate the constitutional right of equal protection under the law.

42:9   Consolidation and Merger

Various changes can be made in the structure of a corporation. These changes include merger, consolidation, and changes in capital stock. A *merger* is the absorption of one or more corporations into another corporation (MBCA § 71).

4Criminal liability is discussed in Chapter 4. White-collar crime is discussed in Chapter 55.

EXAMPLE

The Crestview Steel Corporation seeks a merger with its competitor, the Bay Iron Corporation. At a meeting of Crestview's board of directors, the vice-president for corporate acquisitions proposes various merger alternatives. These merger proposals are as follows:

1. The first proposal involves a merger by mutual agreement between Crestview and Bay Iron in which Bay Iron shares would be converted into Crestview shares. Bay Iron shareholders would either exchange their existing shares for Crestview shares or would be paid in cash for the value of their Bay Iron shares. Under this alternative, Bay Iron shareholders could continue their investment and could share in Bay Iron's potential growth through their ownership of Crestview shares. Bay Iron would cease to do business as a separate company, however; it would merge with Crestview.

2. The second proposal entails Crestview's formation of a new corporation—the Brannan Steel Corporation. Under this alternative, Crestview would merge Bay Iron by mutual agreement into Brannan Steel by exchanging Brannan stock for the outstanding Bay Iron stock. Dissenting shareholders would be paid the value of their shares. In this manner, Crestview would avoid fusion with Bay Iron but would end up controlling Bay Iron by virtue of its ownership of Brannan Steel. This transaction would be a typical three-party merger. Under this plan, former Bay Iron shareholders would not acquire any Crestview shares.

3. The third merger proposal involves the gradual acquisition of Bay Iron by Crestview. This alternative would be particularly advantageous if Bay Iron shares were depressed or underpriced in the stock market. Under this type of merger, Crestview would purchase a large block of Bay Iron stock at favorable prices. It would then make a cash offer to Bay Iron shareholders to purchase additional shares in order to give it a majority position in Bay Iron. If this tender offer were successful, Crestview would acquire control of Bay Iron, although it would not necessarily purchase all outstanding Bay Iron stock. Some Bay Iron shareholders might not tender their shares to Crestview for purchase. Once in control of Bay Iron, however, Crestview could then propose a merger to Bay Iron's board of directors, which Crestview would control. Under this merger, Bay Iron's minority shares—owned by those who did not tender or sell their stock to Crestview during its tender offer—would be converted into cash.

The merger proposals illustrated in the above example are but three of the many different types of corporate changes in structure and ownership. They are all legitimate business transactions resulting in the merger of one or more corporations.

A *consolidation* is the unification of two or more corporations to form a single new corporation (MBCA § 72). Merger and consolidation are similar in that both reach a similar result. That is, the surviving corporation issues stock for the stock of the absorbed corporations and has the assets of all the combined companies. Every state corporation law contains procedures for merger and consolidation. Either procedure is usually accomplished by action of the boards of directors of the affected corporations. Approval by the required percentage of the shareholders, usually one-half to two-thirds of the shares of the affected companies, is also required (see MBCA §§ 71-77).[5] There is an exception to the prerequisite of shareholder approval of a merger or consolidation: approval is not necessary if one corporation holds an overwhelming majority of the stock of another corporation, usually 90 or 95 percent (see MBCA § 75). For example, merger of a subsidiary corporation can be accomplished by vote of the boards of directors of the corporations involved.

De Facto Mergers   A de facto merger is a transaction that for all practical purposes is a merger but is treated as a sale of assets. In certain situations it is possible for a corporation to cast an intercorporate transaction as a sale of assets rather than a merger, thus preventing a dissenting shareholder from blocking the sale or from receiving the fair value of his shares owned. To remedy this situation, some courts have developed the de facto merger doctrine. Under this doctrine, shareholders who dissent to the sale of assets are given both the opportunity to receive payment of the fair value of their shares and appraisal rights to determine that fair value. In those states that have adopted the MBCA, the problem of de facto mergers has largely ceased to exist. The reason is that MBCA § 79 specifically requires shareholder approval for a sale of assets and gives dissenting shareholders the same right to fair payment for shares owned that they have in a merger or consolidation (see MBCA §§ 80, 81).

Rights and Liabilities of Successor Corporations   Most states provide that the property, powers, and assets that belong to constituent or merged companies at the time of a consolidation or merger pass to the successor corporation (the corporation formed by the consolidation or merger). Even in the absence of a statutory provision, the effect is usually the same.

The extent to which liabilities of the constituent or merged corporations pass to the successor corporation varies from state to state. In some states, the successor's liability is limited to the amount of property or assets it received. In other situations, when a successor corporation merely continues the business of merged or consolidated corporations, the successor can be held liable for *all* of the old corporation's debts, regardless of the amount of property received. In some states this rule is broadly applied, at least with a consolidation. Therefore, when a debtor corporation ceases to exist, the consolidated corporation is answerable to all the old corporation's liabilities. In still other states, liability for the obligations of a corporation that has transferred all its assets to another corporation through consolidation, merger, or otherwise has been imposed by statute. Of course, if a corporation's assets are transferred to a new corporation for the specific purpose of defrauding creditors, the new corporation is held liable for the debts and liabilities of the old corporation, even though these obligations may have come into existence after the transfer.

A consolidated or merged corporation can also be liable for taxes imposed on a

---

predecessor. For example, a consolidated corporation can be held liable for paying a federal tax that one of its constituent corporations was obliged to pay before consolidation.

The following case illustrates a situation in which liability was not imposed on a successor corporation. Consider the reasoning of the dissenting judge and the circumstances under which he would impose liability.

Ortiz

v

South Bend Lathe
46 Cal App 3d 842, 120 Cal Rptr 556
(California Court of Appeal, 1975)

[In 1967 Ortiz was injured at work by a defective punch press. The press had been manufactured in 1955 by the Johnson Machine and Press Company. In 1956 Johnson had been acquired by Bontrager Corporation, and in 1962 the Amsted Corporation bought Bontrager. At the time of the accident, Amsted, through its subsidiary, South Bend Lathe, was manufacturing the Johnson press under that trade name and with facilities that originally belonged to Johnson. Ortiz sued Amsted for damages and was awarded judgment in the trial court. Amsted appealed.]

Compton, J.

*   *   *

The issue which is dispositive of the appeal in this case is whether by tracing the history of Johnson and its assets to their ultimate acquisition by Amsted, the latter became burdened with the liabilities of the former.

In 1956, after the manufacture and sale of the machine in question, Johnson was acquired by Bontrager Corporation (Bontrager) an Indiana corporation. The exact nature of this acquisition is not made clear in the record. Suffice to say that shortly thereafter the physical assets of Johnson were transferred to Bontrager and Johnson became a mere "shell" corporation with no assets. A single outstanding share of stock in Johnson was held by Bontrager and carried on its books as an asset of the latter corporation. The corporate "shell" was preserved in order to continue the Johnson trade name in corporate form. Johnson as an entity, however, transacted no business on its own following the acquisition by Bontrager. Both parties agree that as a result of this acquisition Bontrager did assume the liabilities of Johnson. . . . The primary activity of Bontrager was then the manufacture of the Johnson press line.

In 1962, Amsted, pursuant to a purchase agreement with Bontrager, acquired the principal assets of Bontrager; which assets included a manufacturing facility at Elkhart, Indiana, together with the equipment therein, the trade name and customer lists and the single share of stock in the Johnson "shell." After the acquisition of its assets by Amsted, Bontrager continued in existence for a period of time, holding the cash received in the transaction until it was ultimately liquidated by distributing this cash to its stockholders.

Following the acquisition, as noted earlier, Amsted continued to manufacture the Johnson press line through its subsidiary South Bend Lathe. In August 1965, Johnson was dissolved. Since Johnson's assets had previously been acquired by Bontrager and sold to Amsted, there was at the time of the dissolution no distribution of anything of value to Amsted, the holder of the single share of stock.

The purchase agreement by which Amsted acquired the assets of Bontrager provided that among other things Amsted acquired the right to adopt and use the name Johnson Machine and Press Corporation. The agreement also provided that Amsted would assume certain liabilities of Bontrager but expressly recited that Amsted *would not assume* "any liability, debt or obligation of Bontrager except those expressly . . . assumed under [the] agreement and that Bontrager shall continue to be solely responsible for all its other known or unknown liabilities, debts or obligations arising prior or subsequent to the closing." [Court's emphasis.]

There is no question but what Amsted paid adequate and valid consideration, a sum in excess of $1,000,000, for the assets of Bontrager. Nor is there the slightest hint of any fraud in the transaction. The injury in question, and for which liability is sought to be imposed on Amsted, occurred some five years after this acquisition and two years after the total dissolution of Johnson.

The general rule is where one corporation sells or transfers all of its assets to another corporation, the latter is not liable for the debts and liabilities of the former unless (1) the purchaser expressly or impliedly agrees to such assumption, (2) the transaction amounts to a consolidation or merger of the two corporations, (3) the purchasing corporation is merely a continuation of the selling corporation, or (4) the transaction is entered into fraudulently to escape liability for debts. . . .

By the terms of the purchase agreement between Amsted and Bontrager there was no express or implied assumption of liability. There was, as noted, no fraud in the transaction and the consideration flowing to Bontrager was ample. Bontrager and Amsted dealt at arms' length, there was no mixture of officers or stockholders. The two corporate entities were completely separate and distinct both before and after the sale. Under these facts there was neither a consolidation or merger nor a continuation or reincarnation of Bontrager, the old corporation. . . .

Amsted did not assume the liabilities of Bontrager either by agreement, express or implied, or involuntarily by operation of law. Nor does it make any difference that the assets which were acquired consisted of trade names, customer lists or business good will. . . .

[Ortiz makes] the argument that because Johnson continued in existence as a "shell" corporation after the transfer from Bontrager to Amsted of the single share of stock, Amsted assumed Johnson's liabilities at the time of the dissolution of Johnson.

No consolidation or merger of Johnson with Amsted resulted from the dissolution of the Johnson "shell." Strictly speaking, a consolidation signifies such a union as necessarily results in the creation of a new corporation and the termination of the constituents whereas a merger signifies the "absorption of one corporation by another which retains its name and corporate identity with the added capital, franchises and powers of the merged corporation." . . . The dissolution of the Johnson "shell" did not result in the creation of a new corporation nor did Amsted as a result thereof acquire any added capital, franchise or power that it did not already possess as a result of its purchase of the Bontrager assets. . . .

It is suggested . . . that this corporate change of ownership is an effective way of cutting off anticipated future product liability. However, Ortiz in the present situation is no worse off than if Johnson had gone bankrupt early in the game.

After all is said and done what occurred in this case is simply that Amsted for adequate and valid consideration acquired the assets of another corporation under circumstances which do not warrant, as an exception to the general rule against it, the involuntary imposition on Amsted of the preexisting liability of Bontrager. . . .

[Judgment reversed.]

Fleming, J. [dissenting].

*   *   *

Concededly, the operation of the Johnson machinery business passed through the hands of several different operators in a series of complicated transactions. There was, however, continuity of business operation throughout. Each operator succeeded its predecessor in the business of manufacturing and marketing Johnson machinery, and the latest one, Amsted, acquired the Johnson name, premises, plant, equipment, inventory, customer lists, catalogues, and goodwill from its predecessor and continued to operate the Johnson machinery business to the time of the accident. . . .

Amsted, having undertaken to operate the business, thereby assumed the risks growing out of the continuity of business operation. One of these risks was product liability for defective machinery put in circulation at an earlier time and never corrected. While users of an orphaned product no longer actively manufactured or marketed cannot look to an existing manufacturer for parts, repairs, service, information, and the like, users of a product that continues to be manufactured, marketed, and serviced under its original trade name can

reasonably expect a degree of protection from the entity currently carrying on the business, even though that entity may not be the one that originally manufactured and marketed the particular item involved. This expectation is particularly justifiable when the product consists of heavy machinery of a type that carries a high risk of personal injury. A manufacturer of heavy machinery who undertakes to carry on an existing business must take the good with the bad, and the bad includes defective product liability. . . . Product liability today has become an integral part of a manufacturing business, and the liability attaches to the business like fleas to a dog, where it remains imbedded regardless of changes in ownership of the business. So long as the business retains its distinctive identity and character and continues to be operated as it has in the past, defective product liability adheres to the business and remains there until discharged by bankruptcy or comparable judicial act. . . .

I would affirm the judgment.

42:10   Dissolution and Liquidation

The *dissolution* of a corporation is an event that necessarily leads to termination of the corporation's existence. A corporation's articles of incorporation can limit the lifetime of the corporation to a specified term. If so, the corporation is dissolved— and its existence terminates—when the specified term expires. The dissolution and termination of a corporation can also occur either voluntarily or by what is known as judicial liquidation. Judicial liquidation is involuntary dissolution that is brought about by petition to a court filed by either the corporation's shareholders or its creditors.

 The dissolution of a corporation does not relieve officers and directors from responsibility to the corporation's creditors. All states have enacted statutes that hold directors and officers responsible for winding up company affairs, including the payment of debts and taxes.

Voluntary Dissolution   In many states, the majority of a corporation's shareholders can seek and obtain a dissolution. In states that have adopted the MBCA, a corporation can be voluntarily dissolved by the written consent of all its shareholders (MBCA § 83). A corporation can also be voluntarily dissolved by its incorporators before the business commences or any shares are issued (MBCA § 82), or by the act of the corporation itself when authorized by the board of directors and approved by the shareholders (MBCA § 84).

Involuntary Dissolution or Liquidation Many states have enacted statutes providing in general terms for involuntary dissolution of a corporation by action of a specified number or proportion of its shareholders. This procedure is referred to as the *liquidation* of assets or business of a corporation, rather than a corporation dissolution. However, for all intents and purposes, liquidation is the same as dissolution.

The MBCA provides for the liquidation of a corporation in a legal action by a shareholder when it is established that (1) the directors are deadlocked in the management of corporate affairs, (2) the shareholders are unable to break the deadlock, and (3) irreparable injury is being caused by the deadlock (MBCA § 97). MBCA § 97 also provides for the liquidation of a corporation's assets and business when shareholders are deadlocked in voting power and have failed, for a period that includes at least two consecutive annual meetings, to elect successors to directors whose terms have expired or would have expired on the next election.

Most states also provide by statute for involuntary dissolution or liquidation under the following circumstances: (1) when the directors or those in charge act in an illegal, oppressive, or fraudulent manner; (2) when corporate assets are being misapplied or wasted; (3) when an election or appointment of directors is invalid; or (4) when a corporation has abandoned its business, or the corporation's objectives have fully failed or are entirely abandoned [see MBCA § 97(4)].

In most states, when a corporation is dissolved or liquidated, a trustee or receiver is appointed to oversee the process. Trustees are authorized to enforce a corporation's contractual rights and to meet its obligations that were created prior to dissolution or liquidation. Trustees can also engage in any new transaction incidental to their winding up of corporate affairs. For example, they can compromise and settle claims or convey corporate property for this purpose, and they can distribute the corporation's assets. In this regard, the trustees are merely agents of the corporation and its shareholders.

When a corporation is dissolved, its assets are first used to pay the debts and claims asserted against it by creditors. Secured creditors are entitled to be be satisfied from secured property. The remaining assets can then be distributed among the shareholders. Distributions made to shareholders on liquidation of a corporation are referred to as liquidating dividends.

Key Concepts and Terms

- A corporation is a legal entity created by law. It is separate and distinct from the individuals who own or manage it. The owners of a corporation have limited liability. Debts and liabilities incurred by a corporation belong to the corporation and are not attributed to the shareholders. Management of a corporation is centralized in the officers and directors, who are charged with specific duties to the corporation and its shareholders.

- The common characteristics of corporations include (1) separate identity, (2) continuity of existence, (3) limited shareholder liability, (4) free transferability of ownership rights, (5) centralized management, and (6) limited powers.

- Corporations can be organized for many purposes, public and private. Three common forms in the United States are the incorporated sole proprietorship (the one-person corporation), the close corporation, and the publicly held corporation.

- A promoter is a person who initiates a corporation and brings together persons interested in the enterprise. The promoter must exercise the utmost good faith in dealing with the corporation and its shareholders both before and after incorporation.

- The right to act as a corporation is a special privilege conferred by state law. A corporation comes into existence only by complying with statutory requirements of the state in which it is incorporated.

- Once articles of incorporation have been filed and accepted by the state, a certificate of incorporation is issued and corporate existence commences.

- A corporation that has been regularly created in strict compliance with all the mandatory legal conditions for incorporation is a de jure corporation. A de jure corporation is a separate legal entity and possesses all of the attributes or powers incident to a corporation.

- A corporation has express powers to perform any act authorized by the articles of incorporation. In most states, corporations also have implied powers to do whatever is reasonably necessary to promote their express purposes and aid their express powers.

- An act of a corporation that is beyond its express or implied powers is said to be ultra vires. Ultra vires acts can occur when a corporation acts outside the powers granted in its articles of incorporation, or beyond the powers granted under a state corporation law.

- A corporation can be held liable for the torts of its officers, directors, agents, and employees acting within the scope of their authority or the course of their employment. In many states, a corporation can also be held criminally liable.

- Changes can be made in corporate structure by such acts as merger or consolidation. A merger is the absorption of one or more corporations by another corporation. A consolidation is the unification of two or more corporations to form a single new corporation.

- Property, powers, and assets belonging to a constituent or merged corporation at the time of a consolidation or merger pass to the new or successor corporation. In many states, liabilities of a predecessor corporation pass to the successor as well.

- A corporation can be terminated by (1) voluntary dissolution, or (2) liquidation of the corporation by a court on petition of either the shareholders or the creditors.

- Bylaws
- Close Corporation
- Consolidation
- Corporation by Estoppel
- De Facto Corporation
- Dissolution
- Foreign Corporation

- Holding Company
- Liquidation
- Merger
- Promoter
- Quasi-Public Corporation
- Subchapter S Corporation
- Ultra Vires

Questions and Case Problems

1. The Wilmington Memorial Company sells cemetery markers and monuments, in competition with the Silverbrook Cemetery Company, which sells and erects markers in conjunction with its cemetery operation. Silverbrook's charter provides that it can "sell personal property of every kind and may make all contracts and do all acts necessary" to run its cemetery. Believing that the marker business is beyond Silverbrook's corporate powers, Wilmington sues to enjoin Silverbrook from engaging in this business. How should the court decide the case?

2. Architect Howe enters into a contract with Boss for services to be performed for a corporation not yet formed. When the contract is made, Boss signs it as follows: "Edwin A. Boss, agent for a Minnesota corporation to be formed who will be the obligor." Howe performs services worth $38,000 but is paid only $14,500. The corporation is never formed. Howe sues Boss for the balance. Is Boss personally liable? Why?

3. Preston purchases a tract of land for $240,000. Later she forms a corporation and sells the same land for $350,000. Is the sale proper? Can this question be answered without additional facts? If not, what additional facts must be disclosed?

4. How is a corporation formed, and what are its principal characteristics?

5. How do Subchapter S and close corporations differ from publicly held corporations?

6. Life Science produced a dangerous pesticide called Kepone at its plant in Virginia. Moore and Hundtofte were the managing officers directly responsible for operations. In 1973 and 1974, Life Science failed to file an annual report with the state or to pay certain franchise taxes. Consequently, the corporation was dissolved on June 1, 1975. Despite dissolution, Moore and Hundtofte continued to manufacture Kepone as though Life Science were still a viable corporation. On August 11, 1975, they applied for reinstatement of Life Science's corporate status, and the application was approved two days later. Before reinstatement, however, the federal government fined the corporation and the two directors for violation of certain safety regulations. Moore and Hundtofte opposed the fine, arguing that they were not personally liable. They contended that the reinstatement of Life Science's corporate status in August related back to June, validating as corporate acts all actions taken in its name by the two officers in the interim. Are Moore and Hundtofte personally liable?

7. Why do public corporations such as utility companies have certain privileges that are not available to other corporations?

8. A group of hotel and restaurant owners, supply companies, and several other businesses organized an association to attract conventions to Portland, Oregon. The association financed its activities by contributions from members. Hotel members were asked to deal only with suppliers who paid their assessments. Implementation of the agreement by hotel members to curtail purchases from nonpaying suppliers was a violation of federal law, the Sherman Antitrust Act. The Hilton Hotels Corporation, one of the members of the association, had a corporate policy prohibiting such discrimination against suppliers. Indeed, the Hilton policy was to purchase supplies solely on the basis of price, quality, and service. The manager of the Portland Hilton was clearly aware of this policy and was determined to carry it out to the letter. On two occasions, he called the hotel's purchasing agent into his office and told him plainly that Hilton would not take part in any boycott. Despite his instructions to the contrary, the purchasing agent met with a supplier and threatened loss of Hilton business until the supplier paid the association assessment. Later Hilton Hotels was criminally prosecuted for this violation of the Sherman Act. Was Hilton guilty? Can the hotel be held liable for the criminal acts of its agent, even when the agent acted contrary to his instructions?

9. The United States Coast Guard's observations of an oil refinery led to a prosecution of the oil company for polluting coastal waters. The law under which the corporation was prosecuted authorized the imposition of a fine or imprisonment. After a trial, the oil company was given a suspended fine and placed on probation for six months. As a condition of probation, the company was required to set up a pollution prevention program. Less than delighted with the terms of probation, the oil company went back into court contending that it could only be given a fine. Can the corporation properly be placed on probation, or is it only subject to a fine?

10. Duffy, a promoter for a corporation not yet formed, enters into a contract with Mann on behalf of the corporation. The contract obligates the corporation to employ Mann for two years. Later, the corporation is formed and Mann commences work on the date specified in the contract. One month after beginning work, Mann is fired. He sues both Duffy and the corporation for breach of contract. How should the case be decided?

43 Corporate Finance and Securities Regulation

Corporate Finance

43:1 Introduction to Corporate Finance

There are two basic ways to finance a corporation. The first way, generally referred to as equity financing, is to issue shares of stock. The second way, referred to as debt financing, is to borrow money on the credit of the corporation. The broad term *securities* is used with respect to both types of financial arrangements.

In forming and operating a corporation, promoters, corporate officers, or directors must decide what percentage of the corporation's operating capital should be debt and what percentage should be obtained through the issuance of stock. The possible range of corporate financing may vary from an all-common stock capital structure to one in which common equity is minimal and the corporation's capitalization is represented primarily by debt securities or preferred stock. Obviously, various factors influence the decision as to how much stock should be issued and the extent to which the corporation should borrow funds for its operation. For example, a higher proportion of debt to equity signifies a greater risk to the corporation. If a corporation cannot pay its debt obligations, it may be forced into insolvency or bankruptcy.

Considerations involved in determining the most beneficial debt–equity ratio for a corporation include an assessment of the corporation's growth potential and earning capability, and the projected need for borrowed capital.

43:2 Equity Securities; Stock

The right of a corporation to issue stock is generally controlled by state law. Most state corporation laws require that the articles of incorporation specify whether one or more classes of stock will be issued, how many shares will be authorized, and the amount that must be paid in on stock subscriptions before the corporation can commence business. For example, under the Model Business Corporation Act

(MBCA), the articles of incorporation must set forth the total number of shares that the corporation is authorized to issue, the classes of each share, and a statement of the preferences, limitations, and relative rights in regard to the shares of each class (MBCA § 54).

The amount of stock initially issued by a corporation is determined by the promoters or incorporators. This amount is also governed by practical business considerations and financing agreements. Once the amount of authorized capital stock has been established, it cannot be increased or decreased without amending the articles of incorporation, which requires shareholder consent [see MBCA §§ 58(d), 59]. Frequently, corporations initially authorize more shares than are immediately issued. Consequently, the corporate officers or directors, rather than shareholders, have control over this aspect of corporate financing. In such a case, the officers or directors can authorize the issuance of additional shares without shareholder approval if all of the authorized shares have not been issued.

Once a corporation complies with the statutory requirements governing the issuance of stock, it can issue all, part, or none of the stock authorized as it so chooses. Until shares of stock have actually been issued, they are called authorized or unissued shares (MBCA § 2). Once issued, they are called issued or outstanding shares.

The capital of a corporation is its net worth. It is the total amount of money subscribed and paid in by the shareholders, plus all the gains or profits arising from corporate operations, minus any losses that have been sustained. Capital indicates the assets of a corporation—regardless of their source—that are used in the conduct of corporate business. Working capital is the difference between current assets and current liabilities. It is frequently used as a measure of a company's liquidity and capacity to meet its obligations as they fall due.

Types of Equity Securities   In most states, corporations are generally authorized by statute to issue two or more classes of stock that differ as to their respective rights and interests (see MBCA §§ 15, 16). The most widely used classes of stock are *common* and *preferred*. The purpose in having different types and classes of securities is to allocate the risk of loss among shareholders. In addition, these classes are used to allocate control of the corporation through voting restrictions among shareholders and to establish participation rights in corporate proceeds either through profits or on liquidation.

Other commonly used classes of stock are par value and no-par value stock. The designation of a par value for stock originated from the requirement in early American corporation laws that the value of the outstanding stock must be specified in a total dollar amount. These laws were based on the requirement or assumption that corporations would not commence business until the stock had been fully subscribed or purchased. In contrast, no-par stock has no nominal or par value indicated on the face of the stock certificate. In 1979, amendments to the MBCA eliminated the concepts of par and no-par value.

Common Stock   Common stock, or common shares, confer the ordinary rights of a shareholder to participate in the control of a corporation, in the surplus and profits, and in the distribution of corporate assets on dissolution. Common stock is ordinarily exposed to the greatest risk because it is entitled to receive distributions only after all other claims have been satisfied. On the other hand, common shareholders also have the opportunity to reap the greatest rewards because they are entitled to all amounts available in excess of prior claims. Furthermore, common shareholders control the corporation. They affect the growth of earnings and assets by electing directors who make the fundamental decisions about corporate directions, operations, and investments. In addition, they determine indirectly through the election of directors which portion of corporate earnings or assets will be distributed to security holders as dividends and which shall be retained by the corporation for further investment and operations.

Preferred Stock   Preferred stock represents a type of corporate financing that provides a corporation with a security, coupling the flexibility of common stock with the limited obligation of the bond. The issuance of preferred stock is authorized by MBCA §§ 15 and 16. Preferred stock represents a type of ownership. Unlike common stock, however, preferred stock carries only limited or contingent voting rights. Voting rights may arise, for example, only in case of default in dividend payments or when the attributes of the preferred stock itself are to be changed. Preferred stock does not dilute the voting control residing in the common shareholder. It is thus an excellent financial tool, permitting participation in corporate profits while restricting participation in corporate operations.

EXAMPLE
Stanton has long operated the Crestview Company as a sole proprietorship. He wishes to pass the business on to his children, but be is worried about their ability to run it harmoniously together after he retires. Stanton believes that his daughter, Arcadia, is far more able than is his son, Morley, to run and manage the business. However, he wants Morley to benefit from company profits. Thus, Stanton incorporates Crestview and creates two classes of stock: common and preferred. The preferred shares are given no voting rights. He later transfers the common stock to Arcadia, effectively allowing her to control the corporation through the voting rights conferred on the common shares. Stanton gives Morley the preferred shares, enabling him to participate in the company's profits without the right to interfere in the affairs of the business. Thus, Stanton has ensured the continuity of the business by giving Arcadia voting control via the common stock. At the same time, Stanton has protected Morley by giving him the right to participate in corporate profits via the preferred stock.

The special character of preferred stock lies in its relationship to the common stock. Preferred shareholders normally have preference or first claim when dividends are declared. The favored position of preferred stock also extends to the disposition of assets on corporate liquidation.[1] This priority, however, exists only with reference to the common stock and does not affect the senior position of corporate creditors or bondholders. The preference given to preferred stock on liquidation has meaning and value only if corporate assets remain after creditors have been fully paid.

---

[1]Disposition of assets on liquidation is discussed in Chapter 45.

Fractional Shares Most states, as well as MBCA § 24, authorize corporations to issue fractional shares, or scrip, entitling the holder to combine the fractional shares to acquire whole shares. In some states, the owners of fractional shares are entitled to vote, receive dividends, and participate in the distribution of corporate assets in the event of liquidation.

Acquisition and Redemption of Issued Shares Any corporation can acquire shares originally issued by it (MBCA § 6). In recent years, many large publicly owned corporations have purchased their own stock, often at premium prices. The acquisition of this stock has come largely in response to situations in which investors or other corporations have initially purchased large blocks of a corporation's stock, thereby posing potential takeover problems. To prevent the use of these large blocks in takeover bids, corporations have found it more prudent to acquire them in buy-back transactions. In a few cases, corporations have been sued for reacquiring such blocks from single large shareholders at premium prices. However, state and federal laws do not necessarily forbid the sale of shares back to a company or a corporation's acquisition of its own shares so long as full disclosure is made.

Redemption is the involuntary sale of stock by the owner to the issuing corporation for a fixed price. The fixed or call price at which the stock must be redeemed is generally based on the value of the stock or is set forth in the stock certificate or redemption agreement. The power of a corporation to redeem its stock for retirement or cancellation must be authorized in the articles of incorporation or by appropriate state statute. Once shares are made redeemable, they are generally protected against subsequent impairment or repudiation, although in certain circumstances a corporation may modify redemption rights on shareholder approval (see MBCA §§ 58–60, 65).

It is a common practice for corporations to make preferred stock redeemable. Indeed, some issues of preferred stock or other securities *must* be redeemed. If so, the corporation usually establishes a *sinking fund* for this purpose, although the use of such a fund is not required in all cases (see MBCA §§ 15, 16). To establish a sinking fund, a corporation sets aside funds from its net earnings at various intervals each year specifically to pay for redemptions. The amount of funds set aside is usually a percentage of the total amount of the preferred stock or other redeemable securities that have been issued and are to be redeemed.

43:3 Problems of Capital Formation

In financing a corporation through the issuance of capital stock, two basic questions emerge: (1) what type of consideration can be validly accepted by the corporation in payment for shares issued and (2) who determines whether valid consideration has been paid and what limits are placed on the discretion of those making this decision.

Stock Subscription Agreements In the past, corporations were largely financed through stock subscriptions by which future shareholders agreed to contribute money or other assets for stock issued, or to be issued, by a corporation. These agreements are generally known as *subscription agreements* (see MBCA § 17). Agreements made before the actual formation of a corporation have been termed preincorporation agreements.

The basic problem with preincorporation subscriptions is that a subscriber has no one with whom to contract, since the corporation does not yet exist. Courts in various states have adopted several solutions to resolve this problem. For example, in some states subscribers are deemed to have made a continuing offer in the subscription contract to purchase stock when the corporation actually comes into existence. The subscriber may withdraw an offer at any time until it is accepted. In other states, subscription agreements are deemed to be contracts among the subscribers for the benefit of the corporation. In these states, a subscription agreement cannot be revoked unless the corporation does not come into existence or does not fulfill the terms of the contract. Still other states have enacted laws that make subscriptions irrevocable for a given period of time. For example, under MBCA § 17, a subscription for shares is irrevocable for a period of six months unless otherwise provided by the terms of the subscription agreement or unless all the subscribers consent to the revocation of such a subscription.

Consideration for Shares   Although most states—and the MBCA—specify the types and amount of consideration for which stock can be issued, there are a variety of ways by which purchasers of stock have evaded paying full value. One method, for example, is to issue stock for less than its value as fixed by the board of directors. Stock issued for a lesser value has been called discount stock. In other cases, stock has been simply given away without any consideration whatsoever. This stock is called bonus stock. Stock has also been issued for inadequate consideration. Frequently, for example, property or services given to or rendered a corporation are greatly overvalued. Stock so acquired in this way is called *watered stock*.

Most states now strictly regulate all these practices. For example, MBCA § 18 provides that shares can only be issued for consideration as authorized by the board of directors, either at a fixed price, at a minimum price, or as based on a formula or other method for the determination of the price. Formula pricing methods are frequently used in connection with the issuance of additional shares of a class for which an active trading market already exists, and in competitive bidding transactions such as those used by many public utilities, where the exact price is fixed just before sale. Under MBCA § 19, the consideration for the issuance of shares can be paid in money, in other property, or in labor or services actually performed. However, neither promissory notes nor future services can be used to pay for shares issued by a corporation.

Despite these statutory provisions, problems still arise, particularly over the question of the proper valuation of property received by a corporation in return for shares issued. With discount or bonus stock there is simply a disparity between the value of stock and the money received by the issuing corporation. In such a case, it is relatively easy to establish that a corporation received insufficient consideration. However, with watered stock the primary question is how the valuation of the property was made in return for the issued stock. Obviously, cases can arise in which shares are issued for property or services rendered that seemingly bear little relationship to the value of the shares issued. In most states, as well as under MBCA § 19, the judgment of the board of directors or shareholders as to the value of consideration received for shares is conclusive in the absence of fraud.

 MBCA § 19 and similar provisions give considerable discretion to boards of directors whose judgment will generally be upheld by the courts in these matters. However, if fraud can be proved, all the parties involved in the transaction, including the shareholder who received the stock for the inadequate consideration and board members, can personally be liable in damages for the sums that the corporation should have received when it issued stock.

The following case illustrates the situation in which a promissory note was given in exchange for the issuance of a stock certificate that was to be delivered after payment of the note. Observe that the applicable state statute, patterned after MBCA § 19, provided that a promissory note would *not* constitute payment for the issuance of corporate shares.

Haselbush
v
Alsco of Colorado, Inc.
161 Colo 138,
421 P2d 113
(Colorado Supreme Court, 1966)

[Haselbush sued to cancel a note previously signed by him and given to Alsco, Inc., in return for the issuance of a stock certificate for 10,000 shares of Alsco stock. The certificate was never delivered to Haselbush but was held by the corporation pending payment of the note. The trial court upheld the validity of the note and awarded judgment in favor of the corporation.]

Pringle, Justice.

*   *   *

In seeking to have the note cancelled, Haselbush claims that issuance of the stock certificate and acceptance of the promissory note by Alsco was illegal and void under the Colorado Constitution, Article XV, Sec. 9 and [Colorado statutory law]. The pertinent part of

Article XV, Sec. 9 of the Colorado Constitution reads as follows:

> "No corporation shall issue stocks or bonds, except for labor done, services performed, or money or property actually received, and all fictitious increase of stock or indebtedness shall be void. . . ."

[The pertinent Colorado statute] reads as follows:

> "Neither promissory notes nor future services shall constitute payment or part payment, for shares of a corporation."

In [an earlier case] we held that Article XV, Sec. 9 of the Colorado Constitution is not a defense to an action (in this case a counterclaim) brought on a promissory note given for the stock of a corporation. The statute does not affect that holding and we adhere to the rule in that case.

The statute does not forbid the corporation from taking a note or obligation from a prospective stockholder. On the contrary, it impliedly recognizes the right to do so, but declares that no such note shall be considered as payment, and no certificate shall issue until the note is paid. . . . The issuance of the certificate, if in fact there was such here, does not affect the enforceability of the note.

Both the constitutional provision and the statute are aimed at preventing the watering of corporate stock. Their purpose is to prevent corporations from issuing stock without receiving full value, and so to prevent the diluting of the holdings of innocent stockholders, and the reliance by creditors on false or nonexistent capital resulting from the issuance of watered stock. This purpose would not be served by holding, as Haselbush asks us to hold, that these provisions may be used to defeat an action by the corporation seeking to enforce payment on a promissory note given for the issuance of stock when the transaction has been made in good faith.

The judgment is affirmed.

43:4   Debt Securities; Bonds; Convertible Securities

Most corporations issue debt securities such as *bonds* and *debentures*. All corporate borrowing must be authorized by the board of directors or delegated by the board to the officers of the corporation. Shareholder approval is not ordinarily required to permit a corporation to engage in debt financing.

Debt securities are normally issued with a maturity date on which the principal amount is to be repaid. There is normally a fixed income rate on the principal amount borrowed. Holders of debt securities must be paid interest before any dividends can be paid to shareholders. Moreover, the principal must be paid before anything is paid to shareholders on corporate liquidation. Debt securities are redeemable at the option of the corporation. Occasionally, reduction in the amount of outstanding debt is required by the articles of incorporation. A corporation might even be required to maintain a sinking fund for this purpose.

The holders of debt securities are generally given no voting rights in the election of directors. In a few states, statutes provide that voting rights can be given to holders of debt securities if authorized by the articles of incorporation.

There are basic differences between stock (equity) and debt securities. Stock ordinarily includes voting rights, while debt securities do not. Owners of stock participate via dividends in corporate profits, and the dividends are roughly in proportion to the earnings of the corporation. In contrast, debt receives a fixed rate of interest that must be paid at specified times. On liquidation of a corporation, the holders of debt obligations receive up to the amount of their claims, whereas equity investors receive the residue. Finally, interest on debt is regarded as an expense for accounting purposes and taxation and is therefore deductible by the corporations. Dividends on stock constitute income and are not deductible.

Bonds   A bond is a corporate promise to pay a certain amount of indebtedness. It is secured by the assets of the corporation. A convertible bond carries with it the privilege of conversion into shares of stock at the bondholder's option. An income bond is a bond on which income is payable only if the income is available out of corporate earnings after interest on other corporate indebtedness has been paid. A participating bond—also called a profit-sharing bond—is a bond with a fixed rate of interest plus a right to participate in corporate earnings to the extent provided in the bond. Interest on a participating bond is a fixed charge and must be paid regardless of corporate earnings. In this respect, it differs from the income bond.

Indentures and Trustees   Bonds are generally long-term promissory notes. They contain more elaborate provisions than do simple promissory notes given by one individual to another in a commercial transaction. To enable an issuing corporation to borrow relatively small amounts on identical terms from a large number of persons, the obligation is channeled through a trustee, who administers the payment of interest and principal. The trustee also enforces other obligations on behalf of the bondholders as a group. The borrowing corporation contracts with a trustee through an instrument called an *indenture*. The indenture defines the assorted obligations of the borrower, the rights and remedies of the lenders, and the role of the trustee. The bond itself is simply a promise by the borrower to pay a specified amount on a specified date, plus interest, subject to the conditions spelled out in the indenture.

Trust Indenture Act of 1939   In 1939, Congress enacted the Trust Indenture Act (15 USC §§ 77aaa et seq.) to protect the interest of investors in notes, bonds, and other corporate debt obligations. The act is designed to protect investors by requiring certain trust indentures to conform to specific statutory requirements. Under indentures covered by the act, trustees have a great responsibility for the protection of investors. The act insures that investors will obtain the services of a trustee properly qualified to represent their interests. Under the act, if debt securities worth $1,000,000 or more are offered to the public, they must be issued pursuant to an indenture with a properly qualified trustee. Information must be provided relating to trustees in the indenture under which a debt security is to be issued.

Debentures   A debenture is similar to a bond in that it is a promise to pay a certain amount of indebtedness. Debentures differ from bonds in that no property is pledged as security. In other words, a debenture is an unsecured written corporate promise backed by the general credit of a corporation and not secured by any specific property.

 Not all bonds and debentures rank equally as claims on a corporation. Two frequently encountered variations are the mortgage bond and the subordinated debenture. Holders of the mortgage bond are secured as to the payment of principal and interest by a pledge or mortgage of described assets of the debtor. They have a prior claim to payment of their proceeds against other creditors with respect to the mortgaged property. The subordinated debenture has precisely the opposite effect for its holders. It effectively prevents repayment of the principal in the event of the corporation's liquidation or reorganization until all other creditors to whom it is subordinated are repaid in full.

Convertible securities   *Convertible securities* are equity or debt securities that can be changed into another type of security. For example, preferred shares are frequently made convertible into common shares at the option of the shareholder under specified terms. Bonds are also frequently made convertible into common stock. Convertible securities—whether originally equity or debt—are used primarily as a financing device when new risk capital requires some seniority over the holders of existing securities.

For investors, convertible securities offer some advantages over common stock or debt obligations, such as bonds and debentures. With a fixed income return, convertible securities provide a degree of safety and assured income that protects against a decline in common stock prices or a drop-off in corporate earnings. Convertible securities also provide an opportunity for the shareholder to participate in higher common stock prices if the market value of the security into which a preferred stock or debenture is convertible appreciates.

Securities Regulation

> Since the time to which the memory of man runneth not to the contrary the human animal has been full of cunning and guile. Many of the schemes and artifices have been so sophisticated as almost to defy belief. But the ordinary run of those willing and able to take unfair advantage of others are mere apprentices in the art when compared with the manipulation thought up by those connected in one way or another with transactions in securities.
>
> *Green v Santa Fe Industries, Inc.*, 533 F2d 1283
> (United States Court of Appeals, Second Circuit, 1976)

43:5   State Blue-Sky Laws

Early in this century, there were many fraudulent sales of securities to unwary investors. In every state, the need to protect uninformed investors demanded legislation. As a consequence, state laws were first enacted to stop the sale of stock in fly-by-night companies, visionary oil wells, distant gold mines, and other fraudulent transactions. Because these laws were aimed at speculative schemes which had "no more basis than so many feet of blue sky," they were commonly referred to as blue-sky laws.

Generally, blue-sky laws are based on the premise that most of the public lacks knowledge and sophistication about securities investment. Many people are potentially easy prey for promoters of worthless securities or securities of doubtful value. The primary value of state blue-sky laws is therefore to protect the public from deceit and fraud in intrastate securities transactions. The laws regulate all investment schemes designed to lead investors into enterprises, the earnings and profits of which must come through the management, control, and operation of others. Blue-sky laws are obviously paternalistic in nature in that the states endeavor to shield their citizens from unscrupulous stock promoters and to protect innocent purchasers who may be induced to invest money in speculative enterprises over which they have little or no control.

Blue-sky laws differ widely from state to state. However, while statutory variations do exist, most states now incorporate one or more of three basic types of regulatory techniques: (1) antifraud provisions relating to securities transactions, (2) registration of securities, and (3) registration of brokers or dealers dealing with securities.

While the blue-sky laws are primarily aimed at the prevention of fraud in securities transactions, the controls imposed in some states are not limited to disclosure and antifraud provisions. In a few states, the selling price of securities is regulated. Likewise, maximum brokerage fees can be fixed by statute. In other states, blue-sky laws incorporate concepts embodied in the federal laws (see 43:6) by regulating, for example, takeover bids or market manipulations.

Uniform Securities Act   Over half of the states and the District of Columbia have enacted all or part of the Uniform Securities Act. The Uniform Securities Act is divided into four parts. Each of the first three parts is devoted to the implementation of one of the three basic methods historically employed by the various states in the blue-sky laws to control the sale of and trading in securities. Recognizing that the various states have employed only one or two of the three basic methods of control, the Uniform Securities Act is thus constructed so that each of the first three parts may be enacted individually or in conjunction with one or both of the other two. The fourth part contains general provisions relating to the administration and enforcement of the act.

43:6   Federal Regulation of Securities

The federal regulation of equity and debt securities—and of the stock market—originated largely after the stock market crash in 1929. The crash and subsequent depression prompted congressional investigations, which uncovered many undesirable, deceptive, and highly questionable practices in the marketing and sale of securities. As a consequence of these investigations, various federal laws were enacted, beginning with the Securities Act of 1933 (15 USC §§ 77a et seq.), and followed by the Securities Exchange Act of 1934 (15 USC §§ 78a et seq.), the Investment Company Act of 1940 (15 USC §§ 80a-1 et seq.), the Investment Advisors Act of 1940 (15 USC §§ 80b-1 et seq.), and, more recently, the Securities Investor Protection Act of 1970 (15 USC §§ 78aaa et seq.).

The *Securities Act of 1933* and the *Securities Exchange Act of 1934* are the two principal federal statutes relating to the sale and distribution of securities. The former relates primarily to the initial issuance of securities; the latter regulates the trading of securities after their initial issuance. These two acts are discussed in detail in 43:7 and 43:8.

Investment Company Act of 1940   The Investment Company Act requires registration of all investment companies that use the mail or other interstate facilities of communication. Investment companies must reveal through registration their intent with regard to specific subjects such as diversification, borrowing or lending money, issuing securities, and investing in real estate or commodities. In this manner, the act regulates the selling practices of investment companies, promotes honest and unbiased management, and ensures the availability of financial information to security holders.

Investment Advisors Act of 1940   The Investment Advisors Act requires all persons engaged in giving advice or issuing reports of any securities for compensation to register with the Securities and Exchange Commission (SEC). The act applies to all persons whose primary business enterprise is advising on investments. Fraudulent or deceptive practices by registered advisors are prohibited. The act also prohibits profit-sharing arrangements among advisors and the assignment to third parties of advisory contracts without client consent.

Securities Investor Protection Act of 1970   In 1970, a new federal securities act was adopted to protect securities investors against losses due to the financial failure of brokers or dealers. The act created the Securities Investment Protection Corporation (SIPC), which is composed of all brokers or dealers who are registered under the other federal securities laws. The SIPC is authorized to accumulate and manage an insurance fund to indemnify customers of brokers or dealers for losses suffered on the liquidation of a member broker or dealer. The basic means through which the act implements its purpose is the forced liquidation of any member who fails or is in danger of failing to meet his obligations to customers.

43:7   Securities Act of 1933

The Securities Act of 1933 (1933 act) has two basic objectives. The first is to provide investors with full disclosure of all material investment information in connection with an original interstate issuance of securities from the issuer to the public. The second objective of the act is to prevent fraud and misrepresentation in the interstate sale of securities generally.

The provisions of the Securities Act of 1933 apply only to transactions in interstate commerce. However, the SEC and the federal courts have broadly interpreted the meaning of interstate commerce. Today, interstate commerce is involved whenever one uses the means of conducting interstate commerce, such as the telephone or mail, in any part of a securities transaction.

Issuers, Underwriters, and Dealers   With certain exceptions, the term "issuer" means any person who issues or proposes to issue any security. "Person" in this sense can refer to a natural person, but it also refers to a corporation, whether already formed or in the process of being formed.

The process of distributing securities from an original issuer to the investor or ultimate retail purchaser is called *underwriting*. Firms that contract with an issuer to market securities are known as underwriters. Firms that buy from underwriters and resell to the public are dealers.

Registration   The basic means by which the Securities Act of 1933 attempts to accomplish its purpose of protecting the investing public is advance disclosure. The act requires that before a security can be issued, the issuer must file with the SEC a registration statement containing information with respect to the security, the issuer, and the underwriters. This information must also be made available to the public, generally in the form of a *prospectus*. A prospectus is a digest of the most important information contained in the registration statement. The prospectus must be given to all investors before the sale or delivery of an issuer's security.

 The SEC does not have the authority to rule on what securities may or may not be distributed to the public. It has only the responsibility to see that the required disclosures are met before distribution. However, the SEC *is* empowered to prevent securities from being distributed if the disclosure requirements are not met. It does so by preventing or suspending the effectiveness of an issuer's registration statements. In addition, material misstatements or omissions pertaining to registration statements may subject an issuer to criminal or civil penalties.

Exemptions   Certain types of securities are exempt from registration. An exemption allows a sale or resale of securities without compliance with the registration or prospectus requirements of the act. For example, securities issued or guaranteed by the government or by banks are exempted. Certain types of small offerings of less than a specific value are also exempt from registration. In addition, transactions by persons other than issuers, underwriters, or dealers are exempted. Finally, transactions by an issuer that do not involve a public offering (that is, private offerings of securities) are also exempt from registration. Whether or not an offering is private or public is a question of fact in each case. To resolve this issue the courts consider several factors about an offering, including the investors' need for protection, the availability of material information to aid investors, the number of offerees, the size of the offering, the manner in which the securities are offered, and the marketability of the securities.

 Even though a security is exempt from the registration and prospectus requirements of the 1933 act, there is no exemption from the antifraud provisions contained in Section 12 (15 USC § 77q). Any person who offers or sells a security—whether exempt from registration or not—in interstate commerce and either makes an untrue statement of material fact or omits to state a material fact is liable to the purchaser of the security for all damages sustained.

What Is a Security?   As used in the federal securities laws, the word "security," or "securities," means more than merely stocks and bonds. The term has been applied to everything from annuities to cemetery lots, oil rights, orange groves, and even silver foxes. The 1933 Act defines "security" as any note; stock; treasury stock; bond; debenture; evidence of indebtedness; certificate of interest or participation in any profit-sharing agreement; transferable share; investment contract; voting-trust certificate; certificate of deposit for a security; fractional interest in oil, gas, or other mineral rights; or, in general, any interest commonly known as a security. Although a security ordinarily is a written document, oral agreements come within the scope of the act as well.

"Investment contract" is a term that has been broadly interpreted by the SEC and the Supreme Court, thus bringing many transactions within the scope of federal securities regulation. An investment contract is deemed to be any contract, transaction, or scheme by which a person invests money in a common enterprise and expects profits to accrue solely from the efforts of the promoter or third parties. For example, a scheme in which an investor pays cash to be a distributor of cosmetics, but receives as well the right to recruit other investors as distributors and to receive a portion of the investment of such recruits, is an investment contract subject to the registration provisions of the 1933 act.

Fraudulent Practices The principal antifraud provision in the 1933 act is contained in § 12. This section applies only to the sale of, or an offer to sell, securities, and not to their purchase. It makes it unlawful for any person, with respect to such a sale or offer in interstate commerce or through the use of the mail, to employ any device or scheme to defraud. Section 12 also prohibits any person from (1) obtaining money or property by means of any untrue statements of material facts or any omission to state material facts and (2) engaging in any transaction, practice, or course of business that operates or would operate as a fraud or deceit on a purchaser.

The following case illustrates the scope and coverage of the 1933 act. Note that the stockbroker and brokerage firm were strictly liable for losses sustained by customers in the purchase of unregistered securities.

Lewis
v
Walston & Co.
487 F2d 617
(United States Court of Appeals, Fifth Circuit, 1973)

[Mrs. DeCasenave, a registered representative (stockbroker) of Walston, a brokerage firm, touted stock of Allied Automation to Lewis and McDonald by telephone and whenever they came into Walston's office on business. DeCasenave voiced optimistic opinions about the appreciation potential of Allied's stock and even went so far as to introduce Lewis and McDonald to an officer of the corporation. She arranged a meeting between Lewis and McDonald and officers of the corporation, and they either purchased or agreed to purchase Allied stock

at that time. Walston knew about DeCasenave's efforts in touting Allied stock, but its office manager never asked the broker to halt her efforts in this regard. Allied stock was never registered with the SEC. After sustaining losses, Lewis and McDonald sued Walston and DeCasenave for damages under § 12 of the 1933 act. After a trial, the jury rendered a verdict against both the broker and the brokerage firm. The trial court, however, set aside the verdict against the brokerage firm and granted judgment in its favor notwithstanding the verdict. Both the plaintiffs and DeCasenave then appealed.]

Wisdon, Circuit Judge.

*   *   *

Liability for the sale of unregistered securities is absolute under § 12(1) of the

Securities Act of 1933. A purchaser may recover regardless of whether he can show any degree of fault, negligent or intentional, on the seller's part. Liability is established if the plaintiff proves three elements: (1) that no registration statement covering the securities involved was in effect; (2) that, in the language of the statutes, the defendants were "person[s] who [sold] or offer[ed] to sell" the securities; (3) that the mails, or facilities for interstate transportation or communications were used in making the sale. In this case, since the parties stipulated that the first and third elements were present, the only question for the jury to decide was whether Mrs. DeCasenave "sold" the Allied Automation stock, within the meaning of § 12(1).

Mrs. DeCasenave of course was not a "seller" in the most common sense of that word, that is, she was not the party who parted with the securities sold and received the consideration given in exchange. That, however, is not conclusive under § 12(1), for the courts have recognized that other parties who participate in the negotiations of or arrangements for the sale of unregistered securities "sell" those securities within the meaning of § 12(1). . . . Brokers have long been held liable as sellers under § 12(2), as have other parties responsible for bringing about sales of securities they themselves do not own. . . . In *Hill York*, [an earlier case decided by this court, we] announced the test applied in this Circuit to determine whether a participant in the arrangements for a sale "sells" securities within the meaning of § 12(1). The test is whether the party is the "proximate cause" of the sale.

. . . Mrs. DeCasenave does not dispute the facts that she touted the Allied Automation stock heavily to the plaintiffs, arranged the January 3 meeting, and notified the plaintiffs that there was additional stock available before each of the plaintiffs' later purchases. The jury could permissibly infer from these facts that Mrs. DeCasenave's actions were a "substantial

factor" in bringing about the plaintiffs' purchases, and thus the "proximate cause" of those purchases. Moreover, both plaintiffs testified that throughout their dealings in Allied Automation they had "relied on [their] broker"; and, although they are interested witnesses, the judgment of their credibility was for the jury. Viewing the evidence "in the light and with all reasonable inferences most favorable" to the plaintiffs, it is impossible to say that "the facts and inferences point so strongly and overwhelmingly" in Mrs. DeCasenave's favor that reasonable men could not have found for the plaintiffs. . . . The district court therefore properly denied Mrs. DeCasenave's motion for judgment notwithstanding the verdict. . . .

The plaintiffs attack the award of judgment n.o.v. [notwithstanding the verdict] in Walston's favor by arguing that the evidence was sufficient to support a verdict against Walston on any one of three theories. They contend that the evidence supports (1) the conclusion tht Walston itself proximately caused the sale of stock to the plaintiffs, and thus was a seller" of the securities within the meaning of the *Hill York* case; (2) the conclusion that in taking the actions the jury found proximately caused the sale, Mrs. DeCasenave was clothed with apparent authority from Walston; and (3) that in taking those actions, Mrs. DeCasenave was acting within the line and scope of her employment. We do not address the first two of these contentions, because we find that the evidence supported a verdict against Walston on the third theory, and that the award of judgment n. o. v. in Walston's favor must therefore be reversed. . . .

. . . [W]e think it clear that there was an evidentiary basis for finding that Mrs. DeCasenave was acting within the scope of her employment in taking the actions the jury found constituted the proximate cause of the plaintiffs' purchases. Those actions included touting a stock, making recommendations, keeping customers informed of developments in a company whose securities the customers were considering buying, and arranging the mechanics of a purchase-and-sale transaction. These are "acts commonly done" by brokers. . . . at the very least, they would be "simila[r] in quality" to acts brokers are routinely authorized to perform. Mrs. DeCasenave used the Walston offices regularly in arranging the transaction; and she used her position as the representative who serviced McDonald's and Lewis's accounts to recruit them as purchasers of this new company's stock. Thus, to this extent, the "instrumentality by which the harm [was] done [was] furnished by the master to the servant". . . .

Walston argues that Mrs. DeCasenave was acting beyond the scope of her employment. For example, Walston did not deal in unregistered securities. Moreover, Mrs. DeCasenave and the brokerage house did not perform their usual roles as brokers; that is, the transaction did not involve the broker's placing an order through the house's New York office, which was then executed by the central office. In this regard, they note that Walston never stood to receive, and never did receive, any commission or other financial benefit from the direct and essentially private exchange Mrs. DeCasenave arranged. In addition, Walston points to Gaff's [Walston's office manager's] testimony that he advised Mrs. DeCasenave against dealing in the stock, and to Lewis's testimony that Gaff advised him to the same effect.

None of these superficially supportive bases for Walston's argument precludes the conclusion that Mrs. DeCasenave's actions were within the scope of her employment. That Walston did not deal in unregistered securities addresses only the question whether Mrs. DeCasenave's conduct was authorized; as our discussion above and the quotation from the Restatement indicate, however, conduct may be within the scope of employment even if it is unauthorized, if it is sufficiently similar to authorized conduct. That the transactions did

not involve the execution of an order through the brokerage house also does not necessarily mean that Mrs. DeCasenave's acts were without the scope of her employment. Brokers may and do take many actions in the course of their dealings with customers that do not relate directly to transactions executed through the brokerage house; these actions are not for that reason necessarily beyond the scope of the brokers' employment. That Walston did not receive any financial benefit from the transaction is not of controlling importance. If a particular act is authorized, or sufficiently similar to an authorized act, finding that act to be within the scope of employment does not require that the act have conferred any particular benefit, financial or otherwise, on the employer.

Finally, Gaff's testimony that he advised Mrs. DeCasenave against continuing to hawk Allied Automation does not preclude a finding that Mrs. DeCasenave acted within the scope of her employment. In the first place, the precise wording of Gaff's admonition makes it clear that his words were intended not as an instruction given in his official capacity, but rather as personal counsel to Mrs. DeCasenave. He told her that she should "stick to her own business and run stocks instead of trying to talk about pies in the sky all the time", and that "[f]or every deal that you try to put together on an underwriting or a new issue of something like that, you might work for years before you get one deal". It was to Jackie DeCasenave's personal interest, not the interests of Walston & Co., that Gaff appealed. Second, Gaff, in spite of his position as manager of the office, did nothing beyond issuing this scarcely forbidding warning to Mrs. DeCasenave. Gaff's advice to Lewis also fails to defeat the possibility that Mrs. DeCasenave was acting within the scope of her employment. That too was only investment advice: Gaff told Lewis there were too many listed stocks for him to be investing where there was a "margin of risk". Such advice conveyed no meaning that Mrs.

DeCasenave was acting outside the scope of her authority in promoting Allied Automation.

Thus we find that there was evidence to support the jury's conclusion that Mrs. De-Casenave was acting within the scope of her employment. . . .

The judgment in favor of the plaintiffs against Mrs. DeCasenave is affirmed. The judgment in favor of Walston & Company is reversed and the case is remanded to the district court to enter a judgment for the plaintiffs against Walston & Company in favor of the plaintiffs.

43:8   Securities Exchange Act of 1934

In contrast to the Securities Act of 1933, which was enacted to control the initial issuance of securities, the Securities Exchange Act of 1934 (1934 act) was enacted to regulate securities after their initial issuance. The 1934 act regulates both securities exchanges, such as the New York Stock Exchange, and the securities market. It is intended to make available to persons who buy and sell securities information relating to the issuers of the securities. The act seeks to prevent (1) fraud in securities trading and the manipulation in stock markets and (2) abuses and fraudulent schemes by corporate owners, directors, or officers. It outlaws the use of insider information (discussed later in 43:8) for the financial gain of privileged insiders or persons to whom such inside information is given ("tippees") to the detriment of uninformed security holders. The 1934 act also promotes the self-regulation of business practices by the various stock exchanges and their members to achieve fair and honest markets available for those engaged in the purchase or sale of securities.

Securities and Exchange Commission   Among the most important aspects of the 1934 act was the creation of the *Securities and Exchange Commission* (SEC). This federal agency consists of five commissioners appointed by the President with the advice and consent of the Senate. The SEC administers all the various federal securities laws. The SEC also has certain authority and responsibility over corporate reorganizations under the federal bankruptcy laws.[2]

Registration   The 1934 act requires all stock exchanges, brokers, and dealers to register with the SEC unless exempted by the commission. The SEC has authority to expel or suspend member brokers or dealers from exchanges.

The 1934 act also precludes securities from being listed on a stock exchange unless the issuer registers both with the exchange and with the SEC. An issuer must provide information that is substantially the same as that required for initial issues under the Securities Act of 1933. Registration requirements have been extended as well to securities traded in the over-the-counter market if an issuer has gross assets exceeding $1,000,000 and a minimum of 500 shareholders. Registrants are required to provide the SEC current information by filing regular reports.

---

[2]Bankruptcy is discussed in Chapter 31.

Annual 10-K Report   Every issuer of a security registered under the Securities Exchange Act of 1934 must file periodic reports with the SEC. These reports are intended to keep the information and documents required to be included in or filed with the registration statement reasonably current. Moreover, every issuer of securities must file an annual "10-K" form, which includes a description of the business of the company and its properties, a summary of operations for the last five fiscal years, and a list of parent corporations and subsidiaries. The 10-K reports must contain information concerning legal proceedings and the increase or decrease in outstanding securities and indebtedness, as well as other financial information. The reports must also contain the approximate number of security holders and information concerning compensation paid to executive officers and directors.

Annual Shareholder Report   To prompt greater disclosure of financial information to shareholders, the 1934 act requires every corporation that has registered securities with the SEC to issue an annual shareholder report containing financial information for the last two fiscal years. Annual reports must reflect the financial position of the corporation and the results of operations. They generally contain the same information, but in a briefer form, as that contained in the 10-K forms filed with the SEC. In addition, annual reports must contain a five-year summary of operations and an analysis of corporate operations by management. A brief description of the corporation's business and its various divisions or segments must also be included. Corporations must list corporate directors and executive officers, their principal occupations or businesses, and the name and business of any organization by which these people are employed. The annual reports must also include the annual range of trading prices for the corporate shares for each quarter during the past two fiscal years, the amount of dividends paid, and a statement offering to provide shareholders with a copy of the 10-K form filed with the SEC. Every corporation must send the SEC a copy of its annual report.

Short-Swing Transactions   Because of their positions, corporate officers and employees can use inside information unknown to the general public profitably to personal advantage. Naturally, a person possessing inside information about how a corporation is doing—and hence what the corporation's stock is or will be worth— is at a great advantage over members of the general population who do not possess this information.

Section 16 of the 1934 act (15 USC § 78p) was enacted in response to potential *insider* abuse. It is designed to prevent insiders—defined as any officer, director, or owner of more than ten percent of a corporation's stock—from using inside information to make profits on the sale or purchase of the corporation's securities. Section 16 applies to all corporations that have equity securities registered under § 12 of the act. All insiders must report their beneficial interest of registered securities— stock owned by them or by members of their families—to the SEC. All purchases or sales of stock in the corporation must also be reported. Any profit made by an insider from either a purchase and sale or a sale and purchase of the corporation's stock within less than a six-month period belongs to the corporation.

As a general rule, there are no defenses to an action based on § 16. If an insider purchased or sold a registered security within the specified time period, any profits so made must be turned over to the corporation. It makes no difference that an insider did not have actual access to inside information. Nor does it matter that a person did not use inside information. In short, any person coming within the terms of § 16 is liable for any profit made within the six-month period.

The following case illustrates how § 16 was interpreted with respect to a two-step plan used to sell securities. Consider whether the reasoning of the majority is persuasive, and contrast it with the reasoning of the dissenting justices.

Reliance Electric Co.

v

Emerson Electric Co.
404 US 418, 30 L Ed 2d 575, 92 S Ct 596, reh den 405 US 969, 31 L Ed 2d 244, 92 S Ct 1162
(United States Supreme Court, 1972)

[In June 1967, in an unsuccessful takeover attempt, Emerson Electric acquired 13.2 percent of Dodge Manufacturing Company's stock. Later, Emerson decided to sell its shares when Dodge merged with Reliance Electric Company. Since Emerson owned over 10 percent of the stock and the sale was to take place within six months of purchase, it settled on a two-step plan to minimize the effect of the § 16 restriction on insider transactions. Emerson first sold 37,000 shares of Dodge to bring its holdings down to 9.96 percent. Two weeks later it sold the remainder. Reliance then demanded that Emerson's profits on both sales be turned over to it. Emerson sued in federal court for a declaration that it was not so liable. Emerson contended that at the time of the second sale it had not been a 10 percent shareholder in Dodge, so that § 16 did not apply. The trial court ruled in Emerson's favor, and Reliance appealed.]

Justice Stewart delivered the opinion of the Court.

*   *   *

Section 16(b) of the Securities Exchange Act of 1934 ... provides, among other things, that a corporation may recover for itself the profits realized by an owner of more than 10% of its shares from a purchase and sale of its stock within any six-month period, provided that the owner held more than 10% "both at the time of the purchase and sale." In this case, the respondent, the owner of 13.2% of a corporation's shares, disposed of its entire holdings in two sales, both of them within six months of purchase. The first sale reduced the respondent's holdings to 9.96%, and the second disposed of the remainder. The question presented is whether the profits derived from the second sale are recoverable by the Corporation under § 16(b). We hold that they are not. ...

The history and purpose of § 16(b) have been exhaustively reviewed by federal courts on several occasions since its enactment in 1934. ... Those courts have recognized that the only method Congress deemed effective to curb the evils of insider trading was a flat rule taking the profits out of a class of transactions in which the possibility of abuse was believed to be intolerably great. As one court observed:

"In order to achieve its goals, Congress chose a relatively arbitrary rule capable of easy administration. The objective standard of Section 16(b) imposes strict liability upon substantially all transactions occurring within the statutory time period, regardless of the intent of the insider or the existence of actual speculation. This approach maximized the ability of the rule to eradicate speculative abuses by reducing difficulties in proof. Such arbitrary and sweeping coverage was deemed necessary to insure the optimum prophylactic effect." . . .

Thus Congress did not reach every transaction in which an investor actually relies on inside information. A person avoids liability if he does not meet the statutory definition of an "insider," or if he sells more than six months after purchase. Liability cannot be imposed simply because the investor structured his transaction with the intent of avoiding liability under § 16(b). The question is, rather, whether the method used to "avoid" liability is one permitted by the statute.

Among the "objective standards" contained in § 16(b) is the requirement that a 10% owner be such "both at the time of the purchase and sale . . . of the security involved." Read literally, this language clearly contemplates that a statutory insider might sell enough shares to bring his holdings below 10%, and later—but still within six months—sell additional shares free from liability under the statute. Indeed, commentators on the securities laws have recommended this exact procedure for a 10% owner who, like Emerson, wishes to dispose of his holdings within six months of their purchase.

Under the approach urged by Reliance, and adopted by the District Court, the apparent immunity of profits derived from Emerson's second sale is lost where the two sales, though independent in every other respect, are "interrelated parts of a single plan." . . . But a "plan" to sell that is conceived within six months of purchase clearly would not fall within § 16(b) if the sale were made after the six months had expired, and we see no basis in the statute for a different result where the 10% requirement is

involved rather than the six-month limitation. . . .

The judgment is affirmed.

Justice Douglas, with whom Justice Brennan and Justice White concur, dissenting.

*   *   *

Section 16(b) is a "prophylactic" rule . . . whose wholesome purpose is to control the insiders whose access to confidential information gives them unfair advantage in the trading of their corporation's securities.

The congressional investigations which led to the enactment of the Securities Exchange Act unearthed convincing evidence that disregard by corporate insiders of their fiduciary positions was widespread and pervasive. Indeed, "the flagrant betrayal of their fiduciary duties by directors and officers of corporations who used their positions of trust and the confidential information which came to them in such positions, to aid them in their market activities," was reported by the Senate subcommittee charged with the investigation to be "[a]mong the most vicious practices unearthed at the hearings." . . . The subcommittee did not limit its attack to directors and officers. "Closely allied to this type of abuse was the unscrupulous employment of inside information by large stockholders who, while not directors and officers, exercised sufficient control over the destinies of their companies to enable them to acquire and profit by information not available to others." . . .

Despite its flagrantly inequitable character, the most respected pillars of the business and financial communities considered windfall profits from "sure-thing" speculation in their own company's stock to be one of the usual emoluments of their position. . . .

Section 16(b) was drafted to combat these "predatory operations," . . . by removing all possibility of profit from those short-swing insider trades occurring within the statutory period of six months. The statute is written broadly, and the liability it imposes is strict.

Profits are forfeit without proof of an insider's intent to gain from inside information, and without proof that the insider was even privy to such information.

Today, however, in the guise of an "objective" approach, the Court undermines the statute. By the simple expedient of dividing what would ordinarily be a single transaction into two parts—both of which could be performed on the same day, so far as it appears from the Court's opinion—a more-than-10% owner may reap windfall profits on 10% of his corporation's outstanding stock. This result, " 'plainly at variance with the policy of the legislation as a whole,' " . . . is said to be required because Emerson, owning only 9.96%, was not a "bene-ficial owner" of more than 10% within the meaning of § 16(b) "at the time of" the disposition of this block of Dodge stock.

If § 16(b) is to have the "optimum prophylactic effect" which its architects intended, insiders must not be permitted so easily to circumvent its broad mandate. We should hold that there was only one sale—a plan of distribution conceived "at the time" Emerson owned 13.2% of the Dodge stock, and implemented within six months of a matching purchase. Moreover, in the spirit of the Act we should presume that *any* such "split-sale" by a more-than-10% owner was part of a single plan of disposition for purposes of § 16(b) liability. . . .

Antifraud Provisions The principal antifraud provision of the Securities Exchange Act is § 10(b). This section applies to both the sale and purchase of securities, but it is not self-implementing. Rather, it depends on implementing regulations by the SEC, which the SEC issued as *Rule 10b-5*. Section 10(b) makes it unlawful for any person to use, in connection with the purchase or sale of any security through interstate commerce, or the use of a national securities exchange, any manipulative or deceptive device or contrivance in contravention of any SEC rules or regulations. In turn, SEC Rule 10b-5 is the principal fraud control rule instituted under § 10(b). It is a broad rule outlining fraudulent practices in general, and specifying three general areas of proscribed activities: (1) using any device, scheme, or artifice to defraud; (2) making any untrue statement or omitting any statement of material fact; or (3) engaging in any act, practice, or course of business that does or would operate as a fraud or deceit. Section 10(b) and Rule 10b-5 do not apply exclusively to fraudulent acts or activities directed toward inducing the purchase or sale of securities. Each makes unlawful any such act or activity performed 'in connection with the purchase or sale" of a security. In addition, the United States Supreme Court has held that these provisions are to be read flexibly, not technically or restrictively. Section 10(b) does not expressly authorize a civil remedy for damages, but courts have interpreted the act to permit private actions by those defrauded in securities transactions.

To recover under Rule 10b-5 there must be some fraudulent action or deception in connection with the purchase or sale of securities. A misrepresented or undisclosed fact must be a material one. Furthermore, for liability to exist, it must be shown that one person actually intended to deceive, manipulate, or defraud another.

In addition to its general prohibition of fraudulent activities by Rule 10b-5, the SEC has promulgated a number of other rules under § 10(b) which identify specific activities falling within the scope of the prohibitions of this section. Although these rules do not make any acts unlawful, they define certain activities as constituting "manipulative or deceptive devices or contrivances."

The following case illustrates an application of § 10(b) of the 1934 act and Rule 10b-5. Note the various elements of the case against the defendants, and analyze the soundness of the dissenting opinion. In light of the purpose and policy underlying the 1934 act, which view is correct?

Zweig
v
Hearst Corp.
594 F2d 1261
(United States Court of Appeals, Ninth Circuit, 1979)

[Campbell wrote a weekly newspaper column that frequently discussed the financial condition of small corporations. He often bought the shares of companies that he expected to discuss favorably in his columns, and then sold the shares at a profit soon after publication. In 1969, Campbell interviewed officers of American Systems, Inc. (ASI) and wrote a column that appeared on June 5, 1969. The article contained several erroneous statements that cast the company in a more favorable light than it deserved. Before the publication of his column, Campbell purchased directly from ASI 5,000 shares of its stock. After his column appeared, the price of ASI stock rose swiftly.

The sudden price movement of ASI stock affected Zweig and Bruno. They owned stock in RGC, which had entered into a reorganization plan by which it was to merge into ASI. ASI had agreed to pay the RGC shareholders enough ASI stock to equal a market value of $1,800,000. The number of shares were to be determined by the average closing bid for ASI stock for the five market days preceding June 10, 1969. The artificial price rise in ASI stock after the appearance of Campbell's column on June 5 led to a substantial dilution in the interest in ASI that Zweig and Bruno ultimately received under the merger agreement. As a result, Zweig and Bruno sued Campbell and other defendants for damages alleging that Campbell had violated § 10(b) of the Securities Exchange Act of 1934 and Rule 10b-5.

After a trial, the court dismissed the action against Campbell. Zweig and Bruno then appealed.]

Goodwin, Circuit Judge.

*   *   *

Zweig and Bruno argue that Campbell should be liable under Rule 10b-5 for his omission of these material facts from his column about ASI: (1) that he had invested in ASI stock at a discount price two days before his column was to be published, and intended to sell it on the short-swing rise in price; (2) that he made a practice of "scalping" the stocks of companies about which he wrote by buying their stock shortly before his columns about them were published and then selling the stock at a profit after the columns caused a jump in the market price; and (3) that his favorable columns were often reprinted as advertisements for the subject companies in a financial journal in which Campbell had an interest.

Zweig and Bruno contend that Rule 10b-5 required Campbell to inform his readers of these facts so that the readers could judge for themselves whether Campbell's personal motives for promoting ASI affected his objectivity.

Rule 10b-5 provides:

"It shall be unlawful for any person, directly or indirectly, by the use of any means or instrumentality of interstate commerce, or of the mails or of any facility of any national securities exchange,

(a) To employ any device, scheme, or artifice to defraud,

(b) To make any untrue statement of a material fact or to omit to state a material fact necessary in order to make the statements made, in the light of the circumstances under which they were made, not misleading, or

(c) To engage in any act, practice, or course of business which operates or would operate as a fraud or deceit upon any person,

in connection with the purchase or sale of any security." . . .

The appropriate test for the materiality of an omitted fact is whether there is a substantial likelihood that a reasonable investor would consider the fact important in making his or her investment decision. . . . The facts revealing Campbell's lack of objectivity were material under this test. Reasonable investors who read the column would have considered the motivations of a financial columnist such as Campbell important in deciding whether to invest in the companies touted. . . .

Had Campbell's story objectively reported an undisputed fact or news event, such as the discovery of a valuable mineral deposit or the declaration of a dividend, his ownership of ASI stock might not have been significant in reasonable investors' minds. But given the column's style and tone, with its glowing praise of ASI and conclusion that the firm was a worthy investment despite its risks, the effect of Campbell's stock ownership on his objectivity would be important to his readers. We conclude, therefore, that the omitted facts alleged as violations were material. Unless some doctrine limits Campbell's duty to disclose the facts, he must be held liable for intentionally withholding them. Rule 10b-5 makes no distinction between material misrepresentations and nondisclosure of material facts necessary to keep other statements from being misleading. . . .

Most disclosure cases cited by the parties have involved a corporate insider, or a receiver of a tip, who traded in the corporation's stock without disclosing material facts that, if publicly known, would have affected the stock's market value. . . . In most of these cases, the information withheld was directly relevant to inherent value of the firm's assets and operations, or its potential earnings and growth prospects.

In this case, the information withheld from the public was of a slightly different type. Viewing the evidence in the light most favorable to the plaintiffs, Campbell failed to reveal to investor-readers that he expected to gain personally if they followed his advice. He did not tell them that he had purchased the stock at a bargain price knowing that he would write his column and then sell on the rise, as he had done with other stocks before. He did not reveal that his column would also appear as a paid advertisement for ASI in his journal. This withheld information did not relate directly to the company's value and expected performance, but it was necessary to avoid misleading Campbell's audience on the reliance they could place on the column. We hold that in failing to disclose these facts, Campbell violated Section 10(b) and Rule 10b-5 just as corporate insiders do when they withhold material facts about a corporation's prospects while trading its stock. . . .

. . . Columnists . . . ordinarily have no duty to disclose facts about their personal financial affairs or about the corporations on which they report. But there are instances in which Section 10(b) and Rule 10b-5 require disclosure. Here . . . the defendant assumed those duties when, with knowledge of the stock's market and an intent to gain personally, he encouraged purchases of the securities in the market. Campbell should have told his readers of his stock ownership, of his intent to sell shares that he had bought at a discount for a quick profit, and of the practice of having his columns reprinted verbatim as advertisements in the financial journal in which he had an interest.

In order for Campbell to be liable to non-readers Zweig and Bruno, however, a further duty must be shown. To recover damages, these plaintiffs must prove that Campbell owed them a duty. They must show that they were in a relationship with Campbell similar to his readers' relationship with him. We believe that RGC, and its shareholders Zweig and Bruno, were in a position similar to that of Campbell's readers. RGC and the readers had strikingly similar stakes in the processes of the market.

At the time the Campbell column was published, RGC had already contractually committed itself to sell its assets to ASI. ASI agreed to pay at a future date stock worth $1,800,000 for the RGC assets. The number of ASI shares was to be fixed by the market value of ASI stock on given dates. In making this deal, RGC relied on the existence of an honest market. A market presumes the ability of investors to assess all the relevant data on a stock, including the credibility of those who recommend it, in creating a demand for that stock.

In effect, RGC in good faith placed its fate in the hands of market investors, including Campbell's readers. RGC relied on the forces of a fully informed market. Instead, it was forced to sell in a manipulated market. If Campbell was unaware of RGC's reliance on the market, he could have discovered it with minimal effort by asking ASI or RGC about the terms of the merger, or by checking the reorganization agreement that had been signed several months before. RGC was a foreseeable plaintiff.

Furthermore, the more readers the Campbell column influenced, the greater the distortion of the market. As the price of ASI stock rose, the added losses caused by the deception did not fall upon the readers, but shifted to RGC. Each reader who bought into ASI at the inflated price reduced the number of shares that ASI would have to issue to RGC in the merger. The more shares the readers bought in reliance on Campbell, the less real value the ASI shareholders as a whole had to give up in the merger, and the more RGC had to absorb

the adverse effects of the deception. In this unusual situation, the duty Cambell owed his readers must also extend to RGC. . . .

We are aware that in traditional common-law terms it is difficult to make out a duty owed by Campbell to a corporation that did not, and could not, have read his writings before deciding to purchase ASI stock. But if there had been no RGC merger planned, Campbell would be liable to his readers for losses caused by the $1.10 per share temporary inflation that we must assume was caused by his column. In the unusual fact setting here, someone else, a purchaser of ASI stock that relied on the free and unmanipulated market that the federal securities laws were designed to foster, absorbed part of that loss. That forced purchaser should not be required, in effect, to pay Campbell's damages for him. We believe it fully consistent with the spirit and letter of the securities laws to impose upon Campbell a duty to RGC. As we have illustrated, to extend the obligation of disclosure to the readers but to bar RGC from recovery under the rubrics of reliance or duty would lead to a wholly incongruous result: the more effective Campbell was in elevating the price of the stock for his own benefit, the greater the losses an innocent third party (RGC) would have to absorb.

While Rule 10b-5 should not be extended to require every financial columnist or reporter to disclose his or her portfolio to all of his or her readers, it does cover the activities of one who uses a column as part of a scheme to manipulate the market and deceive the investing public. . . .

The court below asserted that it saw no harm or impropriety in a columnist's "making a nickel" at the same time he tells his readers of what may truly appear to him to be an enterprise with a bright future. The trial court was apprehensive that compelling disclosure of financial interest in such a situation would provide a disincentive to columnists to report on the merits of worthy companies. This observation is true, but it proves too much. If brokers were permitted to make secret profits by self-dealing in the market, they too would be stimulated to find better stocks, in which they could invest personally while passing along the advice to their customers. Moreover, the judgment of corporate directors and officers and controlling shareholders might similarly be spurred if they could expect short-swing profits in the markets for the stocks of the companies they manage. But the federal securities laws, in guarding the public from abuses, strictly circumscribe the opportunities of persons holding certain positions to profit from their positions. We hold that these laws also require a financial columnist, in recommending a security that he or she owns, to provide the public with all material information he or she has on that security, including his or her ownership, and any intent he or she may have (a) to score a quick profit on the recommendation, or (b) to allow or encourage the recommendation to be published as an advertisement in his or her own periodical.

Reversed and remanded.

Ely, Circuit Judge (Dissenting).

*   *   *

While I agree that Campbell's alleged conduct was reprehensible, the District Court rightly concluded that he was not liable to the appellants in this case. The majority effectively removes the substantive content in the requirement of "in connection with" when it holds that Campbell may be liable in damages under Rule 10b-5 to individuals who decided to acquire stock and executed a merger agreement months before the wrongful conduct occurred. . . . Sincerely believing that my Brothers stretch section 10(b) and Rule 10b-5 beyond their breaking point, I would affirm.

Corporate Tender Offers and Takeovers   A cash takeover bid is a public offer made by one corporation to the shareholders of another corporation to purchase a certain number, generally a controlling interest, of the second corporation's voting shares at a specific price. Cash tender offers generally provide hefty premiums to tendering shareholders, and the offer is usually open for a limited time. In 1968 Congress enacted the *Williams Act* [15 USC § 78n(d–f)], which specifically regulates tender offers and corporate takeovers. Under the act, an acquiring corporation making a cash takeover bid for the shares of another corporation must file certain reports with the SEC describing the acquirer's business plans and sources of financing. A minimum tender period is established, requiring that all offers remain open for at least ten days, thus precluding the speedy exchanges of control that occurred before the enactment of the act. The Williams Act also contains a broad proscription of fraud. Its basic purpose is to protect target shareholders by providing them with more information about an acquirer and by giving them more time to decide whether to tender shares for which a bid has been made. It is reasoned that disclosure provisions coupled with greater time for deliberation allow target shareholders to make better decisions. Largely as a consequence of the act, the sudden takeovers characteristic of earlier days are now almost extinct.

Key Concepts and Terms

- A corporation can be capitalized (financed) by issuing stock or borrowing on the credit of the corporation. "Securities" is the term used in connection with corporate financial arrangements, whether based on equity or based on debt.

- Common stock is the basic equity security. Ordinarily its owner is entitled to participate in the control of the corporation, in surplus and profits, and in the distribution of corporate assets on dissolution.

- Preferred stock is another type of equity security. It represents a type of corporate financing that couples the flexibility of common stock with the limited obligation of the bond. Preferred shareholders normally have preference over common stock when dividends are declared and in the disposition of assets on corporate liquidation.

- Most corporations can and do issue debt securities, such as bonds or debentures. A bond is a secured obligation of a corporation. When unsecured, the debt is called a debenture. The holders of debt securities are generally given no voting rights in the election of directors. Debt securities receive a fixed rate of interest that must be paid at specified times. On liquidation of a corporation, the holders of debt securities receive up to the amount of their claims.

- Convertible securities can be either equity or debt securities that can be changed into another type of security. Preferred shares and bonds are frequently made convertible into common stock at the option of the shareholder. Convertible securities—whether equity or debt—are used primarily as a financing device when providers of new risk capital require some seniority over the holders of existing securities.

- A corporation can acquire, redeem, retire, or cancel securities originally issued by it. Redemption is the involuntary sale of securities by the owner to the issuing corporation for a fixed price.

- Almost every state has enacted a blue-sky law or adopted portions of the Uniform Securities Act, which regulates intrastate securities transactions. Most state laws contain (1) antifraud provisions, (2) requirements for the registration of securities, or (3) provisions requiring the registration of brokers or dealers.

- Federal regulation of securities is carried out primarily through the Securities Act of 1933 and the Securities Exchange Act of 1934. The Securities Act relates primarily to the initial issuance of securities, while the Exchange Act regulates the trading of securities after their initial issuance.

- The Securities and Exchange Commission is the federal agency that administers all of the various federal securities laws.

- Bond
- Common Stock
- Convertible Securities
- Debenture

- Indenture
- Insider
- Preferred Stock
- Prospectus

- Rule 10b-5
- Securities Act of 1933
- Securities and Exchange Commission (SEC)
- Securities Exchange Act of 1934
- Security

- Short-Swing Transaction
- Sinking Fund
- Subscription Agreement
- Underwriting
- Watered Stock
- Williams Act

Questions and Case Problems

1. Dodge formed a corporation to buy orange groves in Florida and subdivide them into one-acre plots to sell to investors. Promotion materials painted a rosy picture about the investment potential. These materials showed the anticipated return from 100 trees and a 60-year income projection. In addition to a deed, each purchaser received a grove-care agreement providing for the maintenance of the plot. Are these orange groves securities? Why?

2. What are the two basic methods used to finance a corporation? How do these methods differ?

3. Brown buys 1,000 shares of Ace Corporation common stock, and Green buys 1,000 shares of Ace preferred stock. Compare and contrast the rights of Brown and Green with respect to (a) the receipt of periodic dividends from Ace's earnings, (b) the election of Ace directors, and (c) the receipt of distributions if Ace is dissolved.

4. Portage Plastics, a corporation with a high ratio of debt to equity, borrowed $12,500 from each of two persons who were not shareholders. The loans provided for payment of five percent of the net profits before taxes to the lenders instead of interest. Are the loans actually equity securities despite being termed loans?

5. Pinson reads an article in a newspaper that Minco, a company in which she owns stock, has discontinued its uranium explorations. Because of this article, Pinson sells her stock. At the same time, Durant, a director of Minco, believes a geologist's theory that uranium is indeed present on company property. He makes plans to have the company undertake additional tests. Without disclosing his plans, Durant buys Minco stock. Minco later makes a major uranium strike, causing the value of its stock to skyrocket. Pinson sues Durant for damages. Did Durant have a duty to Pinson or to others to disclose his inside information? To whom did he owe a duty of disclosure? Should Pinson be permitted to recover damages, although she now owns no Minco stock?

6. Mr. Whiting, a director of Dow Chemical Company, bought 21,000 Dow shares. The money for this purchase was given to him by Mrs. Whiting, who sold 29,000 Dow shares in a separate transaction some weeks earlier. Mrs. Whiting maintained her own checking and brokerage accounts, and did not mingle her funds or assets with those of her husband. Although she controlled all transactions involving her property and did not discuss individual trades with Mr. Whiting, the two did discuss mutual financial goals. Must Mr. Whiting give up any profit made on his sale and purchase of Dow shares? Why?

7. Nu-Vo, a Florida corporation, issued 100,000 outstanding shares of common stock traded over the counter. Nu-Vo seeks additional capital through a public offering of 100,000 new shares of common stock. The new stock must be, but as yet has not been, registered under the Securities Act of 1933. Does Rich, Nu-Vo's president,

violate any of the securities laws by offering a friend 10,000 shares when the two happen to meet on a fishing expedition?

8. Douglas, a leading aircraft manufacturer, informed a brokerage company of substantially reduced company earnings. This information was relayed the next day to other employees of the brokerage firm and then to selected companies with which the brokerage firm had dealings. These companies then sold virtually all of their Douglas holdings. When the company publicly announced disappointing earnings a few days later, the price of its stock fell dramatically. What laws, if any, were broken? Would the brokerage firm be liable to persons purchasing Douglas stock after the firm knew of the unfavorable earnings but before they were made public? What remedies exist against those who profited from the inside information? Should Douglas be held liable for failing to disclose its earnings expectations as soon as they were known?

9. Compare and contrast the antifraud provisions of the Securities Act of 1933 with those of the Securities Exchange Act of 1934.

10. Texas Gulf Sulfur (TGS) was engaged in exploration and mining of minerals. In November 1963, it drilled a test hole on property in Canada which revealed significant deposits of copper, zinc, and silver. TGS then began to acquire rights to the surrounding property. The president of TGS instructed employees who knew of the discovery to keep it quiet. By April 1964, rumors of the find had reached New York newspapers. The president therefore had two TGS executives issue a news release on April 12 to discount the rumors and to indicate that insufficient information was available to evaluate a possible ore discovery. The release also stated that additional drilling would be required. On April 16, the company gave out two additional reports which indicated that a discovery had indeed been made. The stock of TGS went from $17.50 per share to over $58 in a few months. The SEC brought an action under Rule 10b-5 against TGS employees who purchased stock before full disclosure of the ore discovery had been made to the public. The SEC also sued TGS for the misleading press release, as well as employees who received options to purchase TGS stock prior to public disclosure of the information. The SEC also joined persons to whom the insiders had given information about the discovery. Did the officers, directors, and employees of TGS violate Rule 10b-5? Can those receiving inside information and purchasing securities based on this information also be held liable? Did TGS violate any of the securities laws by issuing a misleading press release that could have had a material effect on the price of its securities? Can the SEC request a judgment ordering restitution of illegal profits by an individual trading in TGS stock on the basis of undisclosed information?

44 Corporate Management

44:1 Introduction

Every corporation is governed by a board of directors. The board represents the corporation in all business matters; it has the authority to transact all ordinary business within the scope of its articles of incorporation. The directors are responsible for all corporate decisions, and they exercise this decision-making power in meetings usually held at times fixed by the articles of incorporation or the corporate bylaws.[1]

The board's powers are conferred by state corporation laws. Under the MBCA, the directors are authorized to:

- Approve a change in the corporation's registered office or registered agent (MBCA § 13)
- Establish the time of payment of stock subscriptions (MBCA § 17)
- Establish the selling price of corporate stock (MBCA § 18)
- Establish the value of noncash contributions received for shares of stock (MBCA § 19)
- Adopt or change bylaws (MBCA § 27)
- Fill vacancies on the board (MBCA § 38)
- Declare dividends (MBCA § 45)
- Remove officers (MBCA § 51)
- Propose amendments to the articles of incorporation (MBCA §§ 58, 59)
- Approve any plan of merger or consolidation (MBCA §§ 71, 72)
- Recommend the sale of substantially all corporate assets (MBCA § 79)
- Recommend corporate dissolution to shareholders (MBCA § 84)

In addition to exercising these statutory powers, the board makes decisions about the expansion of business, the development of new products, and the nature and extent of corporate borrowing.

---

[1]The election of directors is discussed in Chapter 45.

The board of directors uses its powers to run the corporation at large. Directors may oversee the conduct of corporate officers and the course of corporate business. Internal management, however, is almost always left to the corporate officers, with the board acting as a reviewing body of the actions taken by the president or the chief executive officer. For this reason, it can be said that the boards of most large, publicly owned corporations have no real, independent power in the day-to-day corporate activities. This view of the board's functions is supported by MBCA § 35, which provides that the business and affairs of a corporation shall be managed *under the direction* of the board.

Executive and Audit Committees   The board of directors usually meets officially only a few times each year. Therefore, any business requiring the board's attention is conducted by what is called the executive committee. Normally, an executive committee consists of the chief executive officer of the corporation, one or two inside directors, and one or two outside directors (see 44:2). Under MBCA § 42, an executive committee can exercise all the authority of the board of directors, but it cannot sell major corporate assets, issue stock, or declare dividends.

Another useful committee often appointed by the board of directors is the audit committee. This committee generally reviews the corporation's financial statements with independent auditors. An audit committee may also inquire into the financial practices of the corporation, its accounting practices, and financial reporting. At times it may even evaluate the corporation's financial statements in terms of their content and readability.

44:2   Directors

Most publicly held corporations have two types of directors: inside directors, who are officers of the corporation and full-time employees, and *outside directors*, who are not corporate employees. Inside directors have specific knowledge of corporate operations, while outside directors, who are usually unaffiliated with the corporation, do not. In certain circumstances, an outside director might have a business or professional relationship with a company, as, for example, an investment banker or a lawyer. In closely held corporations, outside directors are often friends or relatives of the principal shareholders. The New York Stock Exchange requires newly listed companies to have at least two outside directors because they help to serve as independent checks on management.

Corporate directors are obligated to be well informed of corporate affairs. The fact that a director is inactive does not excuse him from this obligation. A director must take the initiative to stay informed and to question suspect actions. Otherwise, he may be subject to personal liability.

44:3   Powers and Duties of Officers and Directors

The business of a corporation is conducted through its officers and directors. They are the corporation's agents.[2] Officers and directors are required to act in the

---

[2]The agency relationship is discussed in Chapter 48.

utmost good faith, giving to the business the benefit of their care and judgment, and to exercise their powers solely in the interests of the corporation and its shareholders. Officers and directors must also act only within the scope of their authority, as is expressly conferred by the corporation.

 The question of the exact extent of an officer's authority often arises. This authority can be express, as conferred by the corporation; implied; or apparent, based on what the officer appears to be authorized to do in the regular conduct of business. Since the authority of an officer or employee might affect business dealings with a corporation, it is wise to raise the question of his authority before an agreement is made; otherwise, the agreement could later turn out to be illusory.

President   The president of a corporation is vested with authority in various ways. In some states, the president derives his authority by statute or from the corporation or board of directors. In these states the president has no inherent powers to act for the corporation. The fact that a president owns a majority of the corporate stock or otherwise controls the corporation does not vest the president with any additional authority.

Other states take the broader view that the president is the general manager of corporate affairs and has authority to act for the corporation. This authority allows him to perform all acts within the scope of corporate business and within the scope of his usual duties. He also has implied authority to do any act appropriate in the ordinary course of business. This implied authority does not extend to acts beyond the general scope of the ordinary business of the corporation or for his own benefit. That is, a president who is entrusted with the management of the entire business has not necessarily been delegated all corporate rights and powers, but only the business he is authorized to transact in the name of the corporation.

The following case illustrates the extent of a corporate president's authority to act for or contract on behalf of the corporation. Consider the limits imposed on the officer's authority.

Templeton

v

Nocona Hills Owners Asso.
555 SW2d 534
(Texas Court of Civil Appeals, 1977)

[Templeton entered into a one-year employment contract as manager of the Nocona Hills Country Club. The agreement was signed both by her and by the president of the club, but it was never ratified by Nocona's board of directors. Shortly after a change in ownership, Templeton was discharged by the general manager for disloyalty. She brought suit against the country club to recover the amount she would have received had the written contract been honored. A judgment was entered in favor of the country club, and Templeton appealed.]

Cornelius, Justice.

*   *   *

The authority of an officer to contract for a corporation may be actual or apparent. In

Texas, by statute, the board of directors of a corporation, not its president, is charged generally with the duty of managing the corporation's affairs.... Consequently, actual authority of the president to contract on behalf of the corporation must be found either in specific statutes, in the organic law of the corporation, or in a delegation of authority from the board of directors formally expressed, or must be implied from the nature of his position or from custom or habit of doing business.... As to express authority, there was no proof in this case of any of the provisions of the corporate charter or by-laws, and there was no attempt to prove that the board of directors or the shareholders had invested the president with any authority to make contracts on its behalf.... In fact, the only evidence concerning contracts on behalf of the corporation was [President] Jameson's testimony that only the board could authorize them, and that the board refused to approve the one in question here. As to implied authority, the settled rule in Texas is that a corporation president, merely by virtue of his office, has no inherent power to bind the corporation except as to routine matters arising in the ordinary course of business.... The execution of an employment con-

tract binding the corporation to employ a person in a managerial position for a period of one year could not be considered a matter in the ordinary and usual course of appellee's business.... Especially is this true since the power to hire and discharge employees for [the corporation] was vested in a general manager rather than in the president. Indeed, Jameson had not even taken office as president ... when the contract was executed. Under the record in this case, we are impelled to the conclusion that appellant failed in her burden to establish that Mr. Jameson was invested with actual authority to make the contract sued upon.

There was likewise a failure to produce any evidence that Jameson had apparent authority to make the contract.... The record here contains no evidence of any act on the part of the corporation's board of directors or other authorized person which would lead any reasonable person to believe that Mr. Jameson was invested with the power to execute, without approval of the board of directors, a year's employment contract....

[Judgment affirmed.]

44:4 Compensation of Corporate Officers

A corporation may compensate its officers for services rendered by them on behalf of the corporation. This compensation can take various forms, including salaries, bonuses, stock options, and payments to pension or retirement plans. The manner and total amount of compensation ordinarily is determined by the board of directors, with some limitations. The board must act according to the procedures set forth in the articles of incorporation, the bylaws, the board's resolutions, or applicable state statutes. Furthermore, the board must award salaries that are reasonable and for services actually rendered. In determining whether compensation is reasonable, the total compensation package, including bonuses and other fringe benefits, must be analyzed. For example, spending corporate funds on costly fringe benefits might result in excessive total compensation, even though an officer's base salary is reasonable. The officer's work performance and the nature of the work in light of his qualifications, abilities, and responsibilities must also be examined. In this respect, an officer's contribution in helping a corporation withstand adverse financial circumstances may be considered. Other factors that should be looked at in determining a reasonable salary include the salary paid to other officers of the corporation, the salary paid to officers of corporations engaged in similar businesses, and the general financial condition of the corporation.

44:5   Fiduciary Duty of Officers and Directors

Officers and directors occupy a fiduciary relationship to the corporation and its shareholders. This means that they are bound in good conscience to act in the interests of the corporation and to guard those interests. The transactions of an officer or director for the corporation must be fair and honest. This is an unbending rule of the MBCA (MBCA § 35) and is followed in most states. If an officer or director makes a personal profit while acting in his fiduciary capacity, he may be compelled to account for and return those profits to the corporation.

If an officer or director becomes involved in a transaction against the interests of a corporation or its shareholders, the transaction is void unless (1) the facts of the transaction are disclosed; (2) the transaction is approved by a majority of the disinterested directors or the shareholders; or (3) the transaction, in the final analysis, is fair and reasonable to the corporation (MBCA § 41).

44:6   Duty of Care

Officers and directors, by state law, have a duty to use reasonable care and diligence in performing their designated functions. This means that they must exercise the same degree of care and prudence that people prompted by self-interest generally exercise in their own affairs. In exercising reasonable care, a director can rely on information, reports, opinions, and statements prepared or presented by corporate officers or employees whom the director reasonably believes to be competent in the matters presented. A director can also rely on the specialized knowledge of lawyers, accountants, investment brokers, and board committees.

The following case presents an example of the *duty of care* that is imposed on corporate directors. Consider why the directors in the case were deemed to have met that duty.

Graham
v
Allis-Chalmers Mfg. Co.
188 A2d 125
(Delaware Supreme Court, 1963)

[Two shareholders brought an action on behalf of Allis-Chalmers against its directors and four non-director employees for damages the corporation suffered as a result of antitrust violations committed by the four employees. There was no evidence that any of the directors had actual knowledge of the employees' antitrust activities. The shareholders contended that the directors were liable as a matter of law because they failed to take the action designed to make them aware of and prevent the employees'

antitrust activities. The trial court dismissed the complaint, and the shareholders appealed.]

Wolcott, Justice.

*   *   *

Allis-Chalmers is a manufacturer of a variety of electrical equipment. It employs in excess of 31,000 people, has a total of 24 plants, 145 sales offices, 5000 dealers and distributors, and its sales volume is in excess of $500,000,-000 annually. The operations of the company are conducted by two groups, each of which is under the direction of a senior vice president. . . .

The Board of Directors of fourteen members, four of whom are officers, meets once a month, October excepted, and considers a previously prepared agenda for the meeting. Supplied to the Directors at the meetings are financial and operating data relating to all phases of the company's activities. The Board meetings are customarily of several hours's duration in which all the Directors participate actively. Apparently, the Board considers and decides matters concerning the general business policy of the company. By reason of the extent and complexity of the company's operations, it is not practicable for the Board to consider in detail specific problems of the various divisions.

The indictments to which Allis-Chalmers and the four non-director defendants pled guilty charge that the company and individual non-director defendants, commencing in 1956, conspired with other manufacturers and their employees to fix prices and to rig bids to private electric utilities and governmental agencies in violation of the anti-trust laws of the United States. None of the director defendants in this cause were named as defendants in the indictments. Indeed, the Federal Government acknowledged that it had uncovered no probative evidence which could lead to the conviction of the defendant directors. . . .

Plaintiffs have wholly failed to establish ei-

ther actual notice or imputed notice to the Board of Directors of facts which should have put them on guard, and have caused them to take steps to prevent the future possibility of illegal price fixing and bid rigging. Plaintiffs say that as a minimum in this respect the Board should have taken the steps it took in 1960 when knowledge of the facts first actually came to their attention as a result of the Grand Jury investigation. Whatever duty, however, there was upon the Board to take such steps, the fact of the 1937 decrees has no bearing upon the question, for under the circumstances they were notice of nothing.

Plaintiffs are thus forced to rely solely upon the legal proposition advanced by them that directors of a corporation, as a matter of law, are liable for losses suffered by their corporations by reason of their gross inattention to the common law duty of actively supervising and managing the corporate affairs. Plaintiffs rely mainly upon Briggs v. Spaulding, 141 U.S. 132, 11 S.Ct. 924, 35 L.Ed. 662.

From the Briggs case and others cited by plaintiffs, . . . it appears that directors of a corporation in managing the corporate affairs are bound to use that amount of care which ordinarily careful and prudent men would use in similar circumstances. Their duties are those of control, and whether or not by neglect they have made themselves liable for failure to exercise proper control depends on the circumstances and facts of the particular case.

The precise charge made against these director defendants is that, even though they had no knowledge of any suspicion of wrongdoing on the part of the company's employees, they still should have put into effect a system of watchfulness which would have brought such misconduct to their attention in ample time to have brought it to an end. However, the Briggs case expressly rejects such an idea. On the contrary, it appears that directors are entitled to rely on the honesty and integrity of their subordinates until something occurs to put them on suspicion that something is wrong. If such occurs and goes unheeded, then liability of the directors might well follow, but absent cause for suspicion there is no duty upon the directors to install and operate a corporate system of espionage to ferret out wrongdoing which they have no reason to suspect exists.

The duties of the Allis-Chalmers Directors were fixed by the nature of the enterprise which employed in excess of 30,000 persons, and extended over a large geographical area. By force of necessity, the company's Directors could not know personally all the company's employees. The very magnitude of the enterprise required them to confine their control to the broad policy decisions. That they did this is clear from the record. At the meetings of the Board in which all Directors participated, these questions were considered and decided on the basis of summaries, reports and corporate records. These they were entitled to rely on. . . .

In the last analysis, the question of whether a corporate director has become liable for losses to the corporation through neglect of duty is determined by the circumstances. If he has recklessly reposed confidence in an obviously untrustworthy employee, has refused

or neglected cavalierly to perform his duty as a director, or has ignored either willfully or through inattention obvious danger signs of employee wrongdoing, the law will cast the burden of liability upon him. This is not the case at bar, however, for as soon as it became evident that there were grounds for suspicion, the Board acted promptly to end it and prevent its recurrence.

Plaintiffs say these steps should have been taken long before, even in the absence of suspicion, but we think not, for we know of no rule of law which requires a corporate director to assume, with no justification whatsoever, that all corporate employees are incipient law violators who, but for a tight checkrein, will give free vent to their unlawful propensities.

We therefore affirm the Vice Chancellor's ruling that the individual director defendants are not liable as a matter of law merely because, unknown to them, some employees of Allis-Chalmers violated the anti-trust laws thus subjecting the corporation to loss. . . .

[Judgment affirmed.]

44:7   Duty of Loyalty; Corporate Opportunities

Officers and directors owe a *duty of loyalty* to the corporation—the duty to refrain from participating in personal ventures that exploit their corporate position in any way. Corporate officials are obligated to expend their best efforts to promote the interests of the corporation and its shareholders and place those interests above their own personal gain. Thus, they must refrain from competing with the corporation, engaging in conflicts of interest, usurping corporate opportunities, or oppressing minority shareholders.

Corporate Opportunities   The duty of loyalty requires corporate officers to refrain from appropriating for personal benefit a business opportunity that properly belongs to the corporation. This is known as the *corporate opportunity doctrine*. Under the doctrine, corporate officials cannot divert to themselves opportunities in which the corporation has a right, property interest, or expectancy, or which should properly belong to the corporation. For example, an officer of a corporation is not permitted to use corporate property or assets to develop a business that would be in direct competition with the corporation. Furthermore, an officer or director cannot acquire property in which the corporation is itself interested or which is important to the corporation's business. Thus, for example, if a corporation has leased certain property, a director cannot buy that property.

If an officer or director takes advantage of a corporate opportunity, he must turn over to the corporation all property or profits he acquires through the opportunity. In an appropriate case, damages can also be awarded to the corporation.

EXAMPLE

Acme Packers handled and prepared canned meat products. Acme sold all its output to other manufacturers who in turn sold the canned goods under different labels. Two Acme directors incorporated another company called Acme Fine Meats and began to market under this label products purchased directly from Acme Packers. Although Acme Packers was not engaged in the retail marketing of canned products, it could easily have done so because canned products are within its line of business. Thus, the directors of Acme Fine Meats unfairly acquired a business opportunity rightfully belonging to Acme Packers. All profits of Acme Fine Meats rightfully belong to Acme Packers and must be turned over to it.

The corporate opportunity doctrine appears to be easy to apply, but in most cases it is not. Proper application of the rule generally is a two-step process. First, a court must determine whether the business opportunity in question is actually a corporate opportunity. If it is so determined, the court must then ascertain whether taking advantage of the business opportunity also was a breach of the officer's fiduciary duty to the corporation.

The following case illustrates the application of (1) the corporate opportunity doctrine, (2) the various tests used by courts in determining potential liability for breach of the duty of loyalty, and (3) the two-step procedure used by courts in determining whether liability should be imposed. Note that the court first determines that the appropriated opportunity was in fact a business opportunity rightfully belonging to the corporation before it considers whether the corporate officials violated their fiduciary duties in appropriating that opportunity.

Miller

v

Miller

301 Minn 207, 222 NW2d 71, 77 ALR3d 941

(Minnesota Supreme Court, 1974)

[Miller Waste Mills, Inc. was incorporated by Rudolph and Benjamin Miller to manufacture waste and wiping cloth. Rudolph and Benjamin later formed a partnership, Unit Manufacturing, to

produce cloths in smaller packages, which Miller Waste had not been able to do profitably. Rudolph and Benjamin also developed another business to manufacture a lubricator for diesel locomotives. Then they formed two more corporations to manufacture plastic products. All these other corporations generated business for Miller Waste. One of the companies formed by Rudolph and Benjamin purchased waste from Miller Waste, processed and packaged it, and then sold it back to Miller Waste at a profit. A Miller Waste shareholder sued Rudolph and Benjamin on behalf of the corporation *to recover profits made by them in the other businesses. Following a trial, the shareholder's complaint was dismissed. The trial court found that Rudolph and Benjamin did not appropriate to themselves business opportunities properly belonging to Miller Waste. From this judgment the shareholder appealed.]*

Rogosheke, Justice.

*   *   *

At the outset we acknowledge the well-recognized, common-law principle that one entrusted with the active management of a corporation, such as an officer or director, occupies a fiduciary relationship to the corporation and may not exploit his position as an "insider" by appropriating to himself a business opportunity properly belonging to the corporation. . . .

. . . We have searched the case law and commentary in vain for an all-inclusive or "critical" test or standard by which a wrongful appropriation can be determined and are persuaded that the doctrine is not capable of precise definition. Rather, it appears that courts have opened or closed the business opportunity door to corporate managers upon the facts and circumstances of each case and by application of one or more of three variant but often overlapping tests or standards: (1) The "interest or expectancy" test, which precludes acquisition by corporate officers of the property of a business opportunity in which the corporation has a "beachhead" in the sense of [an] interest or expectancy growing out of a preexisting right or relationship; (2) the "line of business" test, which characterizes an opportunity as corporate whenever a managing officer becomes involved in an activity intimately or closely associated with the existing or prospective activities of the corporation; and (3) the "fairness" test, which determines the existence of a corporate opportunity by applying ethical standards of what is fair and equitable under the circumstances.

. . . [W]e believe a more helpful approach is to combine the "line of business" test with the "fairness" test and to adopt criteria involving a two-step process for determining the ultimate question of when liability for a wrongful appropriation of a corporate opportunity should be imposed. The threshold question to be answered is whether a business opportunity presented is also a "corporate" opportunity, i.e., whether the business opportunity is of sufficient importance and is so closely related to the existing or prospective activity of the corporation as to warrant judicial sanctions against its personal acquisition by a managing officer or director of the corporation. . . .

. . . If [an] opportunity is found to be a corporate one, liability should not be imposed upon the acquiring officer if the evidence establishes that his acquisition did not violate his fiduciary duties of loyalty, good faith, and fair dealing toward the corporation. Thus the second step in the two-step process leading to the determination of the ultimate question of liability involves close scrutiny of the equitable considerations existing prior to, at the time of, and following the officer's acquisition. Resolution will necessarily depend upon a consideration of all the facts and circumstances of each case considered in the light of those factors which control the decision that the opportunity was in fact a corporate opportunity. Significant factors which should be considered are the nature of the officer's relationship to the management and control of the corporation; whether the opportunity was presented to him in his official or individual capacity; his prior disclosure of the opportunity to the board of directors or shareholders and their response; whether or not he used or exploited corporate facilities, assets, or personnel in acquiring the opportunity; whether his acquisition harmed or benefited the corporation; and all other facts and circumstances bearing on the officer's good faith and whether he exercised the diligence, devotion, care, and fairness toward the corporation which ordinarily prudent men would exercise under similar circumstances in like positions. . . .

Applying our interpretation of the doctrine of corporate opportunity to this case, we have no difficulty in affirming the trial court's determination that [the] defendants ... did not wrongfully appropriate to defendant corporations or to themselves any corporate opportunity properly belonging to Miller Waste. ... [U]nder the facts as found, the [defendants] discharged their fiduciary duties of good faith, loyalty, and fair dealing. ... [T]he unrefuted testimony at trial establishes that [the defendants], devoting their best efforts, worked exceedingly long hours at the waste mill; developed new lines of business for it, such as the sale of cotton "cuttings" and the division of plastic trading; loaned Miller Waste money when it needed financial assistance; and transacted all intercorporate activities at a profit to Miller Waste. No corporate assets were used in establishing any of defendant corporations, their activities were fully disclosed, and most important, Miller Waste was supplied with a captive market which has sustained the corporation and made it the "number one waste mill in the United States."

We must conclude therefore, based upon the record, that defendant brothers, by embracing business opportunities and as a result advancing their own self-interest, were not unfair, did not act in bad faith, and did not violate their duty of loyalty to Miller Waste. Accordingly, plaintiff's complaint was properly dismissed.

Affirmed.

44:8 Liabilities of Officers and Directors

State corporation laws generally do not contain long lists of prohibited transactions. They impose few specific liabilities on officers and directors, and of these, most are generally applicable only to directors. For example, MBCA § 48 imposes liability on directors for a distribution to shareholders contrary to statute or charter restrictions. To avoid liability in this situation, a director who attends a board meeting at which an illegal action is taken must record a dissenting vote in the minutes of the corporation (see MBCA § 35); if he approves the act, he must file a written dissent with the corporate secretary immediately after the meeting adjourns to avoid liability.

To avoid liability in other situations, a director must observe the standard of care set forth in MBCA § 35. This standard is that a director must act in good faith in a manner reasonably believed to be in the best interests of the corporation and with such care as an ordinarily prudent person in a like position would use under similar circumstances. In performing his duties, a director can rely on information opinions, reports, and statements of others. A director can also delegate certain functions to the officers and other employees of the corporation.

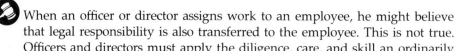 When an officer or director assigns work to an employee, he might believe that legal responsibility is also transferred to the employee. This is not true. Officers and directors must apply the diligence, care, and skill an ordinarily prudent person would apply in the interests of the corporation and its shareholders. Thus, the fact that a particular corporate employee is primarily re-

sponsible for a particular corporate task does not relieve corporate officers or directors from personal liability for the employee's negligence.

In the absence of self-dealing, officers or directors are not usually liable for honest errors or mistakes in judgment. In this regard, courts, in refusing to impose higher standards of care on corporate officers or directors, have typically applied the sentiment that no man of sense would take the office if the law imposed on him a guaranty of the general success of the company as a penalty for any negligence.

If an officer or director violates any of the common-law or statutory duties owed to the corporation or the shareholders, he may be held personally liable. For example, an officer or director can be held liable for engaging in a conflict of interest, seizing corporate opportunities, engaging in transactions unfair to minority shareholders, or otherwise acting to further an interest at the expense of the corporation or its shareholders.

44:9   Business Judgment Rule

One of the basic principles of the corporate system is that the corporation is managed by and acts through its board of directors. The board is primarily responsible for setting corporate policies in such matters as the declaration of dividends, the adequacy of executive compensation, the hiring and firing of employees, marketing, pricing, and mergers or acquisitions. The board is assumed to use unbiased business judgment and to be better equipped than courts would be in making these decisions. Consequently, when a court is confronted with a challenged business decision, it will ordinarily defer to the discretion of the directors. This is known as the *business judgment rule.* The rule arises out of judicial concern that highly qualified individuals will be reticent to serve as corporate directors if the law requires them to use a higher degree of care in the conduct of their office than that which is required of the reasonable, prudent person. The discretion of directors that is permitted by the rule was summarized many years ago by a court as follows: "Questions of policy management, expediency of contracts or action, adequacy of consideration, [and] lawful appropriation of corporate funds to advance corporate interests, are left solely to the [the directors'] honest and unselfish decision, for their powers therein are without limitation and free from restraint, and the exercise of them for the common and general interests of the corporation may not be questioned although the results show that what they did was unwise or inexpedient."[3] Courts have also invoked the business judgment rule to conserve judicial resources by not permitting every business decision to be reviewed or subject to challenge in court.

 The business judgment rule does not allow directors to abdicate all responsibility. As noted by one court that considered the relationship between the

---

3*Pollitz v Wabash R. Co.,* 207 NY 113, 100 NE 721, 724 (New York Court of Appeals, 1912).

directors' duty of due care and the business judgment rule: "When courts say that they will not interfere in matters of business judgment, it is presupposed that judgment . . . has in fact been exercised. A director cannot close his eyes to what is going on about him . . . and have it said that he is exercising business judgment. Courts have properly decided to give directors a wide latitude in the management of the affairs of the corporation provided always a judgment, and that means an honest, unbiased judgment, is reasonably exercised by them."[4]

44:10   Liability Under Federal Securities Laws

Since the 1930s, the federal government has been increasingly active in overseeing corporate financing and the issuing of corporate securities. When corporations issue stock or debt instruments, officers and directors must abide by the terms of the federal laws relating to securities, specifically the Securities Act of 1933 and the Securities Exchange Act of 1934.[5]

Under the Securities Act of 1933 (15 USC §§ 77a et seq.) every corporation seeking to issue securities, unless exempt, must register with the Securities and Exchange Commission (SEC) and disclose pertinent details to the public about the proposed transaction. Section 11 of the 1933 act requires directors and officers to have significant legal, financial, and operational knowledge of a corporation whenever securities are registered with the SEC. If a registration statement contains material misstatements or omissions, officers or directors may be liable in damages to disappointed purchasers under § 11. Section 11 also contains the principal *defense* to a liability action against an officer or director. This defense is that the officer or director exercised *due diligence* in meeting federal registration requirements.

Violation of § 11 is not the only way an officer or director might incur liability under the 1933 act. An officer or director could also be liable under § 12, which requires that a registration statement be filed with the SEC. Any officer or director who has taken an active role in offering or selling an unregistered security is subject to liability. Furthermore, directors may be held liable under § 17, which deals with fraud committed in the offer or sale of securities. Anyone who purchases an unregistered security is entitled to rescind the purchase or obtain damages against the seller.

An officer or director can also incur civil and criminal liability under the Securities Exchange Act of 1934. This liability can be incurred in connection with any of the following:

- Failure to file applications, reports, or documents
- Alteration, misrepresentation, or omission of information in statements as to stock ownership and transactions in such stock
- Manipulation of securities prices

---

[4]*Casey v Woodruff*, 49 NYS2d 625, 643 (New York Supreme Court, 1944).
[5]Corporate finance and the impact of federal securities laws on corporations, generally, is discussed in Chapter 43.

- Use of manipulative and deceptive devices in the offer and sale of securities
- Improper solicitation of proxies
- Unlawful representations
- Concealment of material information

In addition to the Securities Act of 1933 and the Securities Exchange Act of 1934, there are other federal laws that impose responsibilities and liabilities on officers and directors. These laws specifically relate to an officer's or director's position as a controlling person in the corporation, as a conspirator, or as an aider or abettor of offenses committed by others.

 As a result of the federal securities laws, it is extremely important for officers and directors to take all reasonable steps to assure that corporate publicity and reports, for example, are accurate and complete. Complete and timely public disclosure of material developments affecting the corporation should be made when that information has been appropriately verified. All reports and documents filed with the SEC, the states, or other governmental entities should be accurate and free from omissions or misrepresentations.

The following case illustrates the scope of officers' and directors' liability under § 11 of the Securities Act of 1933 and the application of the due diligence defense.

Escott
v
BarChris Constr. Corp.
283 F Supp 643, 2 ALR Fed 86
(United States District Court, SD NY, 1968)

[BarChris Construction Corporation built bowling alleys for resale. Needing funds to finance its operations, BarChris sold debt securities to the public. The company later defaulted on the securities and ultimately went bankrupt. The holders of the securities brought suit under § 11 of the Securities Act of 1933 against each officer and director of BarChris, alleging that the registration statement filed with the SEC contained material false statements and material omissions. Damages were sought from the corporate officers and from nine directors who signed the registration statement. After a trial, all the defendants moved to dismiss the complaint. In his opinion, the district court judge discussed the merits

of the action against each officer and director separately. The court's discussion of the liability of several of these officers and directors is set forth below.]

McLean, District Judge.

*   *   *

RUSSO

Russo was, to all intents and purposes, the chief executive officer of BarChris. He was a member of the executive committee. He was familiar with all aspects of the business. . . . He acted on BarChris's behalf in making the financing statements. . . . He was thoroughly aware of BarChris's stringent financial condition. . . .

In short, Russo knew all the relevant facts. He could not have believed that there were no untrue statements or material omissions in the prospectus. Russo has no due diligence defenses.

VITOLO AND PUGLIESE

They were the founders of the business who stuck with it to the end. Vitolo was president and Pugliese was vice president. Despite their titles, their field of responsibility in the administration of BarChris's affairs during the period in question seems to have been less all-embracing than Russo's. Pugliese in particular appears to have limited his activities to supervising the actual construction work.

Vitolo and Pugliese are each men of limited education. It is not hard to believe that for them the prospectus was difficult reading, if indeed they read it at all.

But whether it was or not is irrelevant. The liability of a director who signs a registration statement does not depend upon whether or not he read it or, if he did, whether or not he understood what he was reading.

And in any case, Vitolo and Pugliese were not as naive as they claim to be. They were members of BarChris's executive committee. At meetings of that committee BarChris's affairs were discussed at length. They must have known what was going on. Certainly they knew of the inadequacy of cash.... They knew of their own large advances to the company which remained unpaid. They knew that they had agreed not to deposit their checks until the financing proceeds were received. They knew and intended that part of the proceeds were to be used to pay their own loans.

All in all, the position of Vitolo and Pugliese is not significantly different, for present purposes, from Russo's. They could not have believed that the registration statement was wholly true and that no material facts had been omitted. And in any case, there is nothing to show that they made any investigation of anything which they may not have known about or understood. They have not proved their due diligence defenses.

KIRCHER

Kircher was treasurer of BarChris and its chief financial officer. He is a certified public accountant and an intelligent man. He was thoroughly familiar with BarChris's financial affairs....

Moreover, as a member of the executive committee, Kircher was kept informed as to those branches of the business of which he did not have direct charge. He knew about the operation of alleys, present and prospective.... In brief, Kircher knew all the relevant facts.

Kircher worked on the preparation of the registration statement.... He supplied information ... about the company's business. He read the prospectus and understood it. He knew what it said and what it did not say.

Kircher's contention is that he had never before dealt with a registration statement, that he did not know what it should contain, and that he relied wholly on [others] to guide him. He claims that it was their fault, not his, if there was anything wrong with it. He says that all the facts were recorded in BarChris's books where these "experts" could have seen them if they had looked. He says that he truthfully answered all their questions. In effect, he says that if they did not know enough to ask the right questions and to give him the proper instructions, that is not his responsibility.

There is an issue of credibility here.... Knowing the facts, Kircher had reason to believe that the expertised portion of the prospectus, i.e., the 1960 figures, was in part incorrect. He could not shut his eyes to the facts and rely on [the auditors] for that portion.

As to the rest of the prospectus, knowing the facts, he did not have a reasonable ground to believe it to be true. On the contrary, he must have known that in part it was untrue. Under these circumstances, he was not entitled to sit back and place the blame on the lawyers for not advising him about it.

Kircher has not proved his due diligence defenses.

TRILLING

Trilling's position is somewhat different from Kircher's. He was BarChris's controller. He signed the registration statement in that capacity, although he was not a director.

Trilling entered BarChris's employ in October 1960. He was Kircher's subordinate. When Kircher asked him for information, he furnished it. On at least one occasion he got it wrong.

Trilling was not a member of the executive committee. He was a comparatively minor figure in BarChris. The description of BarChris's "management" on page 9 of the prospectus does not mention him. He was not considered to be an executive officer.

Trilling may well have been unaware of several of the inaccuracies in the prospectus. But he must have known of some of them. As a financial officer, he was familiar with Bar-Chris's finances and with its books of account. . . . He should have known, although perhaps through carelessness he did not know at the time, that BarChris's contingent liability . . . was greater than the prospectus stated. In the light of these facts, I cannot find that Trilling believed the entire prospectus to be true.

But even if he did, he still did not establish his due diligence defenses. He did not prove that as to the [expertised] parts of the prospectus . . . he had no reasonable ground to believe that it was untrue. He also failed to prove, as to the [non-expertised] parts of the prospectus . . . that he made a reasonable investigation which afforded him a reasonable ground to believe that it was true. As far as appears, he made no investigation. He did what was asked of him and assumed that others would properly take care of supplying accurate data as to the other aspects of the company's business. This would have been well enough but for the fact that he signed the registration statement. As a signer, he could not avoid responsibility by leaving it up to others to make it accurate. Trilling did not sustain the burden of proving his due diligence defenses. . . .

AUSLANDER

Auslander was an "outside" director, i.e., one who was not an officer of BarChris. He was chairman of the board of Valley Stream National Bank in Valley Stream, Long Island. In February 1961 Vitolo asked him to become a director of BarChris. Vitolo gave him an enthusiastic account of BarChris's progress and prospects. As an inducement, Vitolo said that when BarChris received the proceeds of a forthcoming issue of securities, it would deposit $1,000,000 in Auslander's bank.

In February and early March 1961, before accepting Vitolo's invitation, Auslander made some investigation of BarChris. He obtained . . . reports which contained sales and earnings figures for periods earlier than December 31, 1960. He caused inquiry to be made of certain of BarChris's banks and was advised that they regarded BarChris favorably. . . .

On March 3, 1961, Auslander indicated his willingness to accept a place on the board. Shortly thereafter, on March 14, Kircher sent him a copy of BarChris's annual report for 1960. Auslander observed that BarChris's auditors were Peat, Marwick. They were also the auditors for the Valley Stream National Bank. He thought well of them.

Auslander was elected a director on April 17, 1961. The registration statement in its original form had already been filed, of course without his signature. On May 10, 1961, he signed a signature page for the first amendment to the registration statement which was filed [with the SEC] on May 11, 1961. This was a separate sheet without any document attached. Auslander did not know that it was a signature page for a registration statement. He vaguely understood that it was something "for the SEC."

Auslander attended a meeting of BarChris's directors on May 15, 1961. At that meeting he, along with the other directors, signed the signature sheet for the second amendment which constituted the registration statement in its final form. Again, this was only a separate sheet without any document attached. Auslander never saw a copy of the registration statement in its final form.

At the May 15 directors' meeting, however, Auslander did realize that what he was signing was a signature sheet to a registration statement. This was the first time that he had appreciated that fact. A copy of the registration statement in its earlier form as amended on May 11, 1961 was passed around at the meeting. Auslander glanced at it briefly. He did not read it thoroughly.

At the May 15 meeting, Russo and Vitolo stated that everything was in order and that the prospectus was correct. Auslander believed this statement. . . .

. . . Auslander made no investigation of the accuracy of the prospectus. He relied on the assurance of Vitolo and Russo, and upon the information he had received in answer to his inquiries back in February and early March. These inquiries were general ones, in the nature of a credit check. The information which he received in answer to them was also general, without specific reference to the statements in the prospectus, which was not prepared until some time thereafter.

It is true that Auslander became a director on the eve of the financing. He had little opportunity to familiarize himself with the company's affairs. The question is whether, under such circumstances, Auslander did enough to establish his due diligence defense with respect to the . . . prospectus.

Although there is a dearth of authority, . . . an English case . . . is of some value. In [that case] it was held that a director who knew nothing about the prospectus and did not even read it, but who relied on the statement of the company's managing director that it was "all right," was liable for its untrue statements. . . .

Section 11 [of the Securities Act of 1933] imposes liability in the first instance upon a director, no matter how new he is. He is presumed to know his responsibility when he becomes a director. He can escape liability only by using that reasonable care to investi-

gate the facts which a prudent man would employ in the management of his own property. In my opinion, a prudent man would not act in an important matter without any knowledge of the relevant facts, in sole reliance upon representations of persons who are comparative strangers and upon general information which does not purport to cover the particular case. To say that such minimal conduct measures up to the statutory standard would, to all intents and purposes, absolve new directors from responsibility merely because they are new. This is not a sensible construction of Section 11, when one bears in mind its fundamental purpose of requiring full and truthful disclosure for the protection of investors.

I find and conclude that Auslander has not established his due diligence defense with respect to the misstatements and omissions in those portions of the prospectus. . . .

GRANT

Grant became a director of BarChris in October 1960. His law firm was counsel to BarChris in matters pertaining to the registration of securities. Grant drafted the registration statement for the stock issue in 1959 and for the warrants in January 1961. He also drafted the registration statement for the debentures. In the preliminary division of work . . . , Grant took initial responsibility for preparing the registration statement. . . .

Grant is sued as a director and as a signer of the registration statement. This is not an action against him for malpractice in his capacity as a lawyer. Nevertheless, in considering Grant's due diligence defenses, the unique position which he occupied cannot be disregarded. As the director most directly concerned with writing the registration statement and assuring its accuracy, more was required of him in the way of reasonable investigation than could fairly be expected of a director who had no connection with this work.

There is no valid basis for plaintiffs' accusation that Grant knew that the prospectus was

false in some respects and incomplete and misleading in others. Having seen him testify at
length, I am satisfied as to his integrity. I find
that Grant honestly believed that the registration statement was true and that no material
facts had been omitted from it.

In this belief he was mistaken, and the fact
is that for all his work, he never discovered
any of the errors or omissions which have
been recounted at length in this opinion. . . .

Grant contends that a finding that he did
not make a reasonable investigation would be
equivalent to a holding that a lawyer for an
issuing company, in order to show due diligence, must make an independent audit of the
figures supplied to him by his client. I do not
consider this to be a realistic statement of the
issue. There were errors and omissions here
which could have been detected without an
audit. The question is whether, despite his
failure to detect them, Grant made a reasonable effort to that end.

Much of this registration statement is a scis-
sors and paste-pot job. Grant lifted large portions from the earlier prospectuses, modifying
them in some instances to the extent that he
considered necessary. But BarChris's affairs
had changed for the worse by May 1961. Statements that were accurate in January were no
longer accurate in May. Grant never discovered this. He accepted the assurance of
Kircher and Russo that any change which

might have occurred had been for the better,
rather than the contrary.

It is claimed that a lawyer is entitled to rely
on the statements of his client and that to require him to verify their accuracy would set an
unreasonably high standard. This is too broad
a generalization. It is all a matter of degree. To
require an audit would obviously be unreasonable. On the other hand, to require a check of
matters easily verifiable is not unreasonable.
Even honest clients can make mistakes. The
statute imposes liability for untrue statements
regardless of whether they are intentionally
untrue. The way to prevent mistakes is to test
oral information by examining the original
written record.

There were things which Grant could readily have checked which he did not check. . . .

. . . After making all due allowances for the
fact that BarChris's officers misled him, there
are too many instances in which Grant failed
to make an inquiry which he could easily have
made which, if pursued, would have put him
on his guard. In my opinion, this finding on
the evidence in this case does not establish an
unreasonably high standard in other cases for
company counsel who are also directors. Each
case must rest on its own facts. I conclude that
Grant has not established his due diligence defenses except as to the audited 1960 figures. . . .

[Motion to dismiss denied.]

44:11   Indemnification and Insurance

Indemnification in the corporate context is a corporation's payment of an obligation
or liability imposed on an officer or director. As such, it is the most common
method of protecting corporate officers and directors against the cost of defending
lawsuits and the imposition of personal liability. A corporation can pay the obligation directly, or it can make good the loss sustained by the corporate official.

Nearly every state has adopted a statute permitting indemnification. The MBCA
provides for the indemnification of any corporate official, including any officer,
director, employee, or agent who may be made party to litigation by reason of his
position with the corporation (MBCA § 5). Such a lawsuit might be brought by (1)

a corporation; (2) a shareholder challenging the official's performance of duties; (3) a governmental agency; or (4) a private party for breach of contract, tortious conduct, or other violation of law.

It must be noted that under the MBCA indemnification in derivative actions differs from that in third-party actions. A derivative action is one that is initiated by a shareholder on behalf of the corporation. In a derivative action indemnification is restricted to expenses, including attorney's fees. A third-party suit is an action brought for personal recovery in the plaintiff's own name. In a third-party action indemnification is allowed not only for expenses but also for judgments, fines, and amounts paid in settlement. The obvious policy reason for broader coverage of third-party claims is that in a third-party action the individual was presumably working in good faith for the corporate interests and therefore should be protected, whereas in a derivative action the officer or director allegedly violated a duty to the corporation.

The extent of indemnification depends on the corporate official's conduct. The common standard of conduct is that a corporate official must have acted in good faith and in a manner reasonably believed to be in, or not opposed to, the best interests of the corporation. For example, if a director meets the duty of loyalty to the corporation and the duty of care, indemnification is proper.

The amount of the payment also varies: a corporate official who is found to be liable for negligence or misconduct in the performance of his duty to the corporation may be indemnified for expenses only with court approval, but indemnification for expenses is automatic if he is found not to be liable.

In a criminal action, the corporate official may be entitled to indemnification if he had no reasonable cause to believe that his conduct was illegal.

Insurance In recent years, another method of protecting directors and officers from liability has emerged. Many corporations now purchase liability insurance for their officers, directors, and other corporate officials.[6] This insurance generally covers corporate officials against any loss arising from a claim against them in their official capacity. Loss is usually defined as any amount a director or officer is required or permitted to pay in regard to a legal liability for a wrongful act, including damages, judgment, settlements, and expenses incurred in defending suits.

Most liability insurance policies of this type contain exclusions or exceptions from coverage. There is usually no coverage for any claim against an officer or director based on a personal gain or profit to which the officer or director was not legally entitled. Therefore, most insurance will not protect an officer or director from breach of the duty of loyalty or from a conflict of interest. Also, the insurance usually will not protect an officer or director against expenses incurred in actions arising under the federal securities laws.

Key Concepts and Terms

- The board of directors is the governing body of a corporation. The board represents the corporation and has the authority to transact all ordinary business.

---

[6]Insurable risk is discussed in Chapter 40.

- Most publicly owned corporations have both inside and outside directors. The New York Stock Exchange requires newly listed companies to have at least two outside directors.

- The board of directors is primarily responsible for setting corporate policies. Where matters of business judgment are involved, directors meet their responsibility of reasonable care and diligence if they act honestly, in good faith, and with unbiased judgment.

- The officers and directors of a corporation are its agents, through whom the corporation functions and carries on its business.

- Officers and directors are fiduciaries both to the corporation and to the shareholders. They have a duty to avoid using inside information for personal advantage, to preserve corporate opportunities, and generally to be loyal to the corporation and its shareholders. In the absence of self-dealing, officers or directors are not usually liable for honest errors or mistakes of judgment.

- Officers and directors can be held liable under § 11 of the Securities Act of 1933, which requires them to have a significant legal, financial, and operational knowledge of a corporation whenever securities are registered with the SEC before they are issued and sold to the public.

- Officers and directors can be held liable under the Securities Exchange Act of 1934 for misstatements, misrepresentations, half-truths, or the omission of material information in the offer or sale of any securities registered with the SEC. An officer or director can also incur civil and criminal liability under the 1934 act in connection with (1) applications, reports, or documents filed or required to be filed with the SEC; (2) statements as to stock ownership and transactions in such stock; (3) manipulation of securities prices; (4) use of manipulative and deceptive devices in the offer and sale of securities; and (5) concealing material information.

- Indemnification and insurance protect officers and directors against the cost of defending lawsuits and the imposition of personal liability.

• Business Judgment Rule	• Duty of Loyalty
• Corporate Opportunity Doctrine	• Indemnification
• Due Diligence	• Outside Director
• Duty of Care	

Questions and Case Problems

1. Arthur J. Goldberg, former Justice of the United States Supreme Court, observed that "contrary to legal theory, the board of directors of most of our large companies do not in fact control and manage their companies, nor are they equipped to do so." (*New York Times*, 29 Oct. 1972, Sec. 3, p. 1.) Are these views substantiated by the discussion in this chapter of corporate management and the duties of officers and directors? Should directors exert greater control over corporate management?

2. What are the principal powers conferred on the board of directors by the MBCA?

3. Richardson, the president and sole shareholder of a corporation, obtained a loan from Wiebke to meet her business payroll. Richardson gave Wiebke a promissory note, which she signed as an individual. The note did not mention the corporation although Wiebke believed that the loan was to be used in the corporation's business. On obtaining the loan, Richardson put it in her corporation's bank account. A ledger account entitled "Wiebke loan" was set up on the corporate books. Interest paid on the note was carried on the corporation's books as a corporate expense. Later, Richardson defaulted on the note, and Richardson went into personal bankruptcy. Wiebke then sued the corporation and sought to hold it liable. Who would win the lawsuit?

4. What are the basic duties owed by officers and directors to the corporation and its shareholders?

5. Woodtek purchased all the shares of Musulin Forest Products from Matt Musulin and his son. Woodtek's vice-president and general manager executed a promissory note in favor of Musulin. When the time came to pay the note, Woodtek contended that the vice-president had no authority to sign such a note for the corporation. It argued that the board of directors had not authorized the note in the first place and that Musulin should have inquired. Is Woodtek liable?

6. A group of Florida investors organize a corporation to operate a country club and golf course. At a shareholders' meeting, they discuss the possibility of acquiring land adjacent to the golf course, but the matter is not pursued by the corporation. Later, two of the corporation's largest shareholders—its president and vice-president—purchase the adjoining land and sell it for a substantial profit. A minority shareholder sues, charging that the officers have breached their fiduciary duty by taking a corporate opportunity for themselves. The shareholder claims that the officers must give to the corporation all the profits from the sale of the adjoining property. How should the case be decided?

7. Pablo is president and director of Hawaiian International Finances (HIF) and a director of Pablo Realty. On a trip to California in connection with her realty business, Pablo spots attractive real estate investment opportunities and brings them to the attention of the finance company. HIF's board of directors sends Pablo and three other directors back to California to investigate. Eventually, Pablo contracts on behalf of HIF to buy two parcels of land. The sellers are represented by brokers who subsequently split their commissions with Pablo, paying her a total of $22,000. When HIF finds out about these payments some months later, it sues to recover the sums. Must Pablo pay over to HIF the amount of her commissions received? Would the result be affected by the fact that Pablo received no compensation for serving as president and director of HIF?

8. Shelton, the branch manager of Alenco Company, promises Lanier a one-year contract and an annual compensation of $22,000 if Lanier will leave his present job and go to work for Alenco. Lanier accepts and when he starts work with Alenco he is presented with a new offer that differs significantly both in salary and commissions from the one originally offered by Shelton. Lanier therefore sues Alenco for the salary due under the rest of his one-year contract. Alenco argues that Shelton does not have either express or apparent authority to hire anyone for a fixed term. It claims such contracts are against company policy. Alenco asserts that it is up to Lanier to ascertain the limits of Shelton's authority. Is Alenco liable to Lanier for the terms of the contract originally promised by Shelton?

9. Williams requests the U-Vend Corporation to install a hot-drink machine and a soda dispenser in the Radio Shack outlet that she manages. Williams signs a three-year lease for the machines. The lease designates Radio Shack Corporation as the lessee. Williams pays the first month's rent with a personal check, which she signs. Subsequent payments are made by bank money orders signed "Radio Shack Corporation" by various employees of the outlet. Eight months later, U-Vend receives a letter from the treasurer of Radio Shack, requesting that it remove the machine from its outlet since neither Williams nor anyone else had authority to order anything from it. Because Radio Shack continues to refuse to pay for the installed machines, U-Vend sues for damages for the remaining months of the three-year lease. What is the result?

10. Equitable Life held a note of Inland Printing Company that was secured by personal property and real estate. The note came due but was not paid. When Equitable looked for the property, it found that Inland had been sold to another company. Equitable then sued directors and officers of Inland on the ground that they had negligently wasted Inland's assets, resulting in damage to its creditors. Equitable did not assert any fraud or deceit on the part of the officers and directors. How should the case be decided?

45 Rights and Liabilities of Shareholders

45:1 Introduction

A corporation is for most purposes separate and distinct from its individual members or shareholders. Title to corporate property is held by the corporation as a separate entity and not by the shareholders. Shareholders have no power to represent a corporation or act for it in the transaction of its ordinary business, even when all or a majority of the corporation's stock is owned by a single individual.

As a general rule, corporations operate under the principle of majority rule. The holders of a majority of the shares with voting power control the corporation by electing the board of directors. The board of directors, in turn, also acts by majority vote in carrying out its duties and obligations.[1]

45:2 Shareholder Functions

The shareholders' principal function is to elect the board of directors (MBCA § 39). By electing directors, shareholders indirectly control the actions of a corporation and determine its policies and goals. In addition to electing or removing directors, shareholders ordinarily exercise several other functions. They have the power to (1) adopt, amend, or repeal bylaws; (2) amend the articles of incorporation (MBCA § 59); (3) approve loans to officers, as well as stock-option plans offered to directors, officers, or employees (MBCA § 20); (4) approve extraordinary corporate matters or fundamental changes in the corporate structure, such as mergers or consolidations (MBCA § 73); and (5) approve the dissolution of the corporation (MBCA § 84).

Annual Meetings The holding of an annual corporate meeting to elect directors is usually regulated by statute, the articles of incorporation, corporate bylaws, or common-law rules. Annual shareholder meetings are generally called to elect members to the board of directors, review the financial status of the corporation, and vote on various proposals submitted to the shareholders themselves. By stat-

---

[1]The rights, duties, and obligations of directors are discussed in Chapter 44.

ute, written notice must be given each shareholder, stating the place, day, and hour of the meeting (MBCA § 29). The notice must be delivered to the shareholder not less than 10 nor more than 50 days before the date of the meeting. If a special meeting is called, shareholders must be informed of the purpose for which it is called. Moreover, if extraordinary changes, such as a merger, dissolution, or sale of corporate assets not in the regular course of business are contemplated, the shareholders must be given specific notice of the proposal before the meeting (MBCA §§ 73, 79, 84). Any action taken at a meeting for which requisite notice has not been given is a nullity unless the notice requirements have been waived (MBCA § 144).

Quorum   A *quorum* is ordinarily required for a valid shareholder meeting. Most states have enacted statutes specifying the percentage of shares constituting a quorum. For example, MBCA § 32 provides that a majority of the shares entitled to vote, represented in person or by *proxy* (discussed below), constitute a quorum at a meeting of shareholders. If a quorum exists, a vote of the majority of the shares present is sufficient to conduct business, unless the vote of a greater number is required to decide a particular matter.

Shareholder Proposals   To fully participate at an annual meeting, shareholders are given the right to propose corporate amendments, offer resolutions, speak for or against resolutions, and ask questions of the corporate officers present at the meeting. Proposals and questions have run the gamut from individual questions about corporate dividend policies to the offering of resolutions on voting procedures, location of corporate meetings, or other matters of interest to shareholders. In recent years, the actions of large publicly owned corporations have been seriously questioned, particularly through shareholder proposals or resolutions objecting to corporate policy that involves bribery practices, environmental protection, affirmative action, American foreign policy, or investment in South Africa. While the motives of the individuals or groups making these politically or socially oriented proposals might be questioned, and while most of these proposals have garnered only a small percentage of shareholder votes, that is not to say that shareholders should be precluded from offering such proposals in the first place. Indeed, the right of shareholders to speak and to make such proposals are fundamental attributes of corporate ownership—so much so, that the federal securities laws applicable to the solicitation of proxies, for example, require the inclusion of shareholder statements up to 200 words whenever their proposals are deemed to be proper subjects for shareholder deliberation.

45:3   Voting Rights

Unless a class of stock has been created without voting rights, each shareholder is normally entitled to one vote for each outstanding share owned. In many states, special statutory rules govern the voting of jointly held shares, shares held by fiduciaries, shares owned by minors, and shares held by other corporations.

Because of their size, most large corporations find it impractical to determine on the date of the meeting who the shareholders are, the number of their shares, and those entitled to vote. Accordingly, the stock transfer books of corporations are frequently closed on a record date fixed for the determination of shareholder lists before the actual date of the meeting (see MBCA § 30). Only the shareholders listed on this record date are eligible to vote at the next shareholder meeting.

Voting Agreements and Voting Trusts   A group of shareholders may agree to vote their shares in the same way. Such arrangements are called voting or pooling agreements. A more formal arrangement is termed a voting trust. In a voting trust shares are actually transferred to a trustee, who must vote under a legally enforceable trust agreement. Most states regulate voting arrangements and voting trusts.

Cumulative Voting   One of the most important contemporary issues concerning shareholder voting rights is *cumulative voting*. The purpose of cumulative voting is to give minority shareholders representation on the board of directors in proportion to the number of shares owned. Under cumulative voting, a shareholder can give one or more candidates seeking election to the board of directors as many votes as the number of directors to be elected multiplied by the number of votes to which each shareholder is entitled. Thus, for example, if a corporation is to elect five directors to its board, a shareholder owning 20 percent of the voting shares can elect at least one director under cumulative voting. He does so by casting up to all his votes for that one director, rather than splitting his vote among all five of the directorships to be filled. For minority shareholders, cumulative voting is most successful when a greater number of directors are to be elected. In such cases, fewer votes are needed by minority shareholders to elect at least one director. If minority shareholders were not afforded cumulative voting rights, they would have no representation on the board because minority shares would always be outvoted by the majority under straight voting principles.

The constitutional or statutory law of nearly half the states requires some form of cumulative voting. In other states, corporations are authorized to permit this type of voting in their articles of incorporation.

Large, publicly owned corporations recognize the power of minority shareholders under cumulative voting. To avoid that power, most of these corporations are incorporated in states that do not mandate cumulative voting. Some corporations have also attempted to limit the effect of cumulative voting by establishing classes of directors with staggered terms, thereby reducing the number of directors to be elected each year. The fewer the number of directors to be elected, the larger the minority interest must be to enable a shareholder to elect one director. Although the creation of classes of directors has been successfully challenged, particularly in states that require cumulative voting, the MBCA does authorize it (MBCA § 37). However, this authorization is effective only if cumulative voting is not otherwise required, as under the optional provisions of MBCA § 33.

Proxies   If a shareholder grants authority to another to cast his vote at a shareholder meeting, both the authorized person and the instrument empowering him to cast a vote on behalf of another are called proxies. The word "proxy" is a contraction of "procuracy," the act of representing another person as an agent. The person granting the proxy is called the principal.

The shares of publicly owned corporations are usually held by a great number of shareholders who, for one reason or another, do not attend annual meetings. By giving their voting power to proxies, shareholders can exercise their voting rights at these meetings. Corporations also use proxies to obtain a quorum so that a lawful meeting can be held (see MBCA § 32).

A proxy is either general or limited. If a person is given a general proxy, he can vote on all corporate proposals, except on extraordinary matters such as fundamental changes in the articles of incorporation. If a special or limited proxy is given, however, the proxy can only vote in a certain manner or on certain specified matters as required by the principal. Since the proxy relationship is one of agency, it can be revoked by the principal at any time unless it has been made irrevocable. Under MBCA § 33, a proxy is valid only for eleven months unless otherwise provided.

Since publicly owned corporations are characteristically controlled or managed by holders of only a small percentage of the equity of such corporations, the use of proxies at shareholder meetings is essential to conduct corporate activity. If proxies were permitted to be solicited and obtained without explanation as to the matters to be voted on or the manner in which shares would be voted, shareholders effectively would have no voice in the operation of their corporation. Consequently, the solicitation of proxies by corporations or by shareholders, as well as their form and content, are stringently regulated both by the states and by the federal government. The SEC has established disclosure requirements that must be met prior to proxy solicitation. The proxy rules adopted by the SEC are closely patterned after the registration and disclosure procedures of the Securities Act of 1933.[2] The SEC rules require that shareholders be given the opportunity to specify the manner in which their shares are to be voted. Furthermore, proxy solicitations must not mislead shareholders. They must be accurate and complete to enable shareholders to make informed decisions in their capacity as voters. The regulations seek to ensure that shareholder meetings will be meetings of informed parties competent to deliberate on corporate matters and decide them by shareholder vote. In fact, it has been said that the SEC so designed its rules as to make proxies the closest practicable substitute for attendance at a shareholder meeting.

A proxy contest typically results from a conflict between current management and insurgent shareholders who are seeking corporate control. Often, a group of shareholders acquires a substantial position in a corporation and wants to control it through the election of a majority of the directors. This can only be done either by acquiring a majority of the voting shares or by soliciting a sufficient number of proxies from other shareholders to control the election. Proxies, therefore, are invaluable to each factions' efforts to elect its own slate of directors.

45:4   Preemptive Rights

One of the common ways by which a corporation raises more funds for its operation is by issuing additional stock. If a corporation does so, it can give its shareholders preferential treatment by permitting them to purchase the new stock

---

[2]Federal securities regulation is discussed in Chapter 43.

ahead of other shareholders in proportion to the number of shares each share-holder owns. This privilege is called a *preemptive right.* It enables shareholders to maintain the existing ratio of their proprietary interest and voting power in a cor-poration despite the issuance of more stock.

Most states do not require corporations to grant preemptive rights to share-holders. For example, under MBCA § 26 shareholders have no such rights unless authorized in the articles of incorporation.

When a corporation issues new stock, each shareholder usually receives a *war-rant,* or right to purchase the new stock. The warrant sets forth the requirements necessary to purchase one share, the price per share, and the warrant's expiration date. Because new shares are frequently offered below the current market price, such rights ordinarily have a market value of their own and may be actively traded on the stock market. In most cases, preemptive rights and warrants must be sold or exercised within a relatively short time before their expiration.

45:5 Inspection Rights

A fundamental right in corporation law is the right of shareholders to inspect the corporation's books and records. Although in some states only inspection of corpo-rate share registers is permitted, the right of inspection is enforced in all 50 states by statute. The MBCA has a typical inspection provision. It requires each corpora-tion to maintain particular records, grants to certain shareholders the right to in-spect them on written demand, sets forth the penalty for violation of the inspection right, and authorizes courts to compel the production of records for inspection when a demand has been improperly denied (MBCA § 52).

The right of shareholder inspection is not absolute. It must be exercised with restraint and only for a proper purpose. A proper purpose is generally considered to be one that is lawful, made in good faith, reasonable, relevant to the share-holder's interest and status as a shareholder, and not inimical to the corporation. The three purposes that have been consistently held to be proper are (1) investiga-tion of suspected corporate mismanagement; (2) determination of the value of cor-porate stock; and (3) communication with other shareholders. For example, in a proxy contest between management and dissident shareholders, inspection of the shareholder register is absolutely necessary if the dissidents are to communicate with other shareholders and solicit their proxies. Without access to the shareholder register, dissident shareholders would have little or no chance to successfully ob-tain proxies.

To exercise the right of inspection a shareholder must present a written demand to the corporation. The demand must comply with the requirements as to content and demonstrate that the demanding shareholder has the required proper pur-pose. Often, a demand for inspection is refused even though a proper purpose is evident. At this point, the shareholder must seek judicial enforcement of his in-spection rights. The standard practice among large publicly held corporations is for management to deny shareholder demands for inspection unless ordered to do so by a court. Indeed, the right to inspect share registers containing the names and addresses of other shareholders has become the subject of more litigation than any other individual shareholder right.

The right of inspection raises a number of potential problems. For example, it is not always clear who is a shareholder or what entities are corporations within the meaning of the rule. Problems also arise as to the specific books and records that are subject to inspection. Moreover, the right to inspect may not always include the right to copy, and the right of a shareholder to inspect may not extend to agents or other persons employed by the shareholder to assist in making an inspection. Finally, the right to inspect the records of a given corporation may not include the right to inspect the records of a subsidiary corporation even though it is wholly owned by the parent.

45:6   Dividend Rights

A *dividend* is an amount set apart by the board of directors from a corporation's net earnings and surplus funds for distribution to shareholders. The declaration and payment of dividends constitutes a normal and routine part of corporate business, and corporate directors ordinarily have the power to declare cash dividends and to determine their amount (see MBCA § 45). Dividends are usually paid in cash, but they can also be paid in property, including the corporation's own shares.

There are two general prerequisites to the declaration of a dividend: (1) surplus earnings or corporate profits and (2) a resolution by the directors to declare a dividend. Consistent with the first of these requirements, a dividend cannot be declared and paid if the corporation is insolvent or if paying the dividend would make the corporation insolvent. Moreover, a corporation cannot make any dividend payment that would be contrary to a restriction in the articles of incorporation (MBCA § 45).

Bear in mind that just because a corporation has profits does not necessarily mean that the directors will distribute those profits to the shareholders. The directors have wide latitude in determining the circumstances under which dividends will be declared. While they can pay out profits as dividends, they can also plow them back into the business to ensure the corporation's health and growth.

At the time a dividend is declared, each shareholder of record is entitled to his share of the dividend. However, in modern corporate practice, corporations usually declare dividends payable to those who were shareholders of record on a specified date. Normally, the date of payment follows the date of declaration by one or two months. For example, a dividend notice that is dated October 28, 1983, and states: "The directors of the Crestview Corporation have declared a regular quarterly dividend of 40 cents per share, payable on the 5th day of December, 1983, to the shareholders of record on the 20th day of November, 1983," will entitle only the shareholders listed on the record date, and not necessarily those owning Crestview stock either on the date of declaration or on the actual date of payment, to the dividend. Shares of stock sold or transferred on the various stock exchanges after the record date are termed *ex-dividend*, which means that they are sold without dividend rights.

Dividends can be paid in cash, as in the Crestview example above. However, they can also be paid in other forms, such as stock dividends, stock splits, and property dividends. These will now be discussed.

Stock Dividends   A *stock dividend* is a dividend that is payable in the stock of the dividend-paying corporation. The corporation usually issues new stock for this purpose. Since the size of each shareholder's dividend—the amount of new stock the shareholder receives—is based on the number of shares already owned, the distribution does not affect any shareholder's proportionate interest in the corporation. To a large extent, stock dividends are psychological dividends since no assets of the corporation are actually distributed to shareholders. In fact, stock dividends do not increase the holding of shareholders in the distributing corporation. When a stock dividend is declared, the corporation simply transfers to its capital fund an amount of surplus earnings or profits that is equal to the value of the new stock; the corporation reduces its earned surplus by the same amount. This so-called "capitalization of surplus" does not alter the combined total of stated capital, paid-in surplus, and earned surplus on the corporate books. Although the transferred earnings to the capital fund may increase the aggregate value of all the capital stock, the increased equity is reflected merely by an increased number of shares. The book value of each share is diminished, but the ownership interest of each shareholder in the corporation remains unchanged.

Stock Split   In a *stock split*, a shareholder receives two, three, or four times as many shares as previously owned. (In a reverse stock split, the actual number of shares owned by any shareholder is reduced in reverse proportion.) Unlike a stock dividend, a stock split adds *nothing* to the capital fund of a corporation. The split merely increases (or decreases, in the case of a reverse stock split) the total number of shares outstanding, reduces the unit value of each share, and may stimulate the trading of shares in the stock market by making the shares cheaper to buy. Unlike a stock dividend, a stock split must be authorized by an amendment of the articles of incorporation.

Property Dividends   A property dividend is one paid in property belonging to the corporation. For example, a corporation in the liquor distribution business might pay a dividend in liquor. More often, the property paid as a dividend is shares of stock. The shares can be either of a subsidiary of the corporation or of an unaffiliated corporation. When a parent corporation distributes shares of a subsidiary to divest itself of ownership, the transaction is commonly referred to as a spin-off.

Preferred Dividends   Various classes of stock are often created to give shareholders different rights in the corporation. As discussed in Chapter 43, one of these classes is preferred stock. It is often used to give owners a dividend preference over the common shareholders. This preference is entirely a matter of contract and is generally set forth in the articles of incorporation or bylaws and on each stock certificate. Preferred dividends are generally payable only out of net earnings and at the discretion of corporate directors.

Cumulative Dividends   When a dividend is passed or omitted in any year because of deficiency in earnings, the shareholders lose any right to share in the profits for that year. However, this right is not lost if the corporation has provided for the cumulation of dividends on the stock. The right of preferred shareholders to cumulative dividends may differ from that of common shareholders if there is a provision authorizing such right in the corporation's articles of incorporation, the bylaws, or the stock certificates, or a guaranty of dividends issued by the corporation.

EXAMPLE

The earnings of the Crestview Corporation were down last year. Consequently, the board of directors voted to pass (omit) dividends on both the common and preferred stock. This year, the corporation's earnings are sufficient to pay dividends. Crestview's articles of incorporation provide for the payment of passed dividends on the preferred stock, but not on the common stock. Thus, in addition to a dividend for the current year, the preferred stockholders will also receive the omitted dividend that should have been paid last year. Both dividends will be paid out of current earnings. Because the common stock has not been given a similar right of cumulative or passed dividends, the common stockholders will receive a dividend only for the current year. The omitted common stock dividend from last year will not be made up out of current earnings.

45:7   Majority and Minority Shareholders

The power of majority shareholders to control a corporation imposes on them a duty to exercise good faith, care, and diligence in the control of corporate affairs and to protect the interests of minority shareholders. Majority shareholders cannot use their control to benefit themselves alone or to destroy the minority's interest. For example, majority shareholders may not, as against a minority shareholder, dissipate or waste corporate funds or profits. The majority must also act fairly and with due regard to the interests of the minority shareholders in the purchase or sale of property, in contracts with the corporation, and in all other dealings involving minority interests. In turn, minority shareholders must generally submit to the decisions made by the majority so long as the majority acts in good faith and within the limit imposed by law.

The reasons and public policy behind these general rules are apparent. There is an ever-present danger that majority shareholders will use their power, position, or inside information to further their own interests to the detriment of the corporation or minority shareholders. For example, majority shareholders could appoint themselves to key executive positions while denying employment to minority shareholders; they could pay themselves high salaries but refuse to declare dividends (which would also benefit minority shareholders).

To protect minority shareholders, some states have enacted statutes requiring the vote of two-thirds or three-fourths of the shares with voting power before fundamental corporate changes can occur. In other states, if a charter amendment or other fundamental change materially affects the rights of a particular class of stock, an affirmative vote of the shares of that affected class must approve the action, regardless of whether the shares of that class have any general voting power.

Extraordinary Corporate Transactions   Shareholders have certain rights when a corporation participates in a merger, consolidation, or sale of assets. Under the common law, all these transactions (which are described in Chapter 42) require the unanimous consent of the shareholders. Therefore, dissenting shareholders could veto any proposed transaction of this type. In response to this inordinate power of minority shareholders, most states enacted statutes permitting a merger, consolidation, or sale of corporate assets on the affirmative vote of a majority of the voting shares of the corporations involved. For example, the MBCA authorizes a merger or consolidation (§§ 71–73), or a sale of substantially all corporate assets other than in the regular course of business (§ 79) after majority shareholder approval. The procedure set forth in most state statutes and in the MBCA also requires approval by the board of directors and notice to all shareholders.

Short-Form Merger   The MBCA also permits what has been termed a short-form merger. In a merger of this type the owners of at least 90 percent of the shares can approve a merger in a summary manner without notice to or consent of minority shareholders (see MBCA § 75).

Dissenters' Rights   To protect the rights of minority shareholders who object to a merger (other than a short-form merger), consolidation, or sale of assets, most states, as well as the MBCA (§§ 80, 81), give shareholders who dissent from such transactions the right to demand that the corporation pay them the fair value of their shares. For a shareholder to exercise this right, a written objection to the corporate transaction must be filed with the corporation before the shareholders vote on the proposed transaction. If the transaction is approved, the dissenting shareholders must be so advised and offered fair value for their shares. If a dispute arises as to what constitutes fair value, shareholders can seek a more impartial appraisal via judicial relief.

In the following case, the fundamental issue is the relationship of the majority and minority shareholders, and their rights and obligations with regard to a merger. The case illustrates how, although being careful to follow the statutory procedures, the majority shareholders still breached their fiduciary obligations to the minority shareholders, rendering the merger invalid.

Singer

v

Magnavox Co.
380 A2d 969
(Delaware Supreme Court, 1977)

[In 1974, North American Phillips Corporation incorporated North American Phillips Development Corporation (Development) for the purpose of mak-
ing a tender offer for shares of the Magnavox Corporation. Development offered to buy all Magnavox shares for $8 per share. The directors of Magnavox voted to oppose the offer on the grounds of price inadequacy and so notified their shareholders. Later, the respective managements of Magnavox, North American, and Development compromised on their difference over the tender offer. They agreed to terms that included an increase in the offer price to

$9 per share. Two-year employment contracts were signed with 16 Magnavox officers. As part of the agreement, Magnavox withdrew its opposition to the tender offer. Development then acquired approximately 84.1 percent of Magnavox's outstanding common stock. With Development firmly in control of Magnavox, the managements of these two companies then set about to acquire all equity interests in Magnavox through a merger. Development created T.M.C. Development Corporation for this purpose. The directors of Magnavox unanimously agreed to a merger with T.M.C. and scheduled a special shareholders' meeting to vote on the plan. The shareholders were told that approval of the merger was assured since Development's holding alone was large enough to provide the requisite statutory majority. The merger was approved at the shareholders' meeting. The Singers, who were minority shareholders, then filed an action in court alleging that the merger was fraudulent in that it did not serve any business purpose other than the forced removal of public minority shareholders from an equity position in Magnavox at a grossly inadequate price to enable North American, through Development, to obtain sole ownership of Magnavox. The trial court dismissed the complaint, ruling that the merger was not fraudulent merely because it was accomplished without any business purpose other than to eliminate the Magnavox minority shareholders. The court further held that the Singers' remedy for dissatisfaction with the merger was to seek an appraisal of their shares. The Singers then appealed.]

Duffy, Justice (for the majority).

*   *   *

To state the obvious, . . . two (or more) Delaware corporations "may merge into a single corporation." Generally speaking, whether such a transaction is good or bad, enlightened or ill-advised, selfish or generous—these considerations are beside the point. Section 251 [of the Delaware Corporation Law] authorizes a merger and any judicial consideration of that

kind of togetherness must begin from that premise.

Section 251 also specifies in detail the procedures to be followed in accomplishing a merger. Briefly, these include approvals by the directors of each corporation and by "majority [vote] of the outstanding stock of" each corporation, followed by the execution and filing of formal documents. The consideration given to the shareholders of a constituent corporation in exchange for their stock may take the form of "cash, property, rights or securities of any other corporation." . . . A shareholder who objects to the merger or is dissatisfied with the value of the consideration given for his shares may seek an appraisal. . . .

In this appeal it is uncontroverted that defendants complied with the stated requirements of § 251. Thus there is both statutory authorization for the Magnavox merger and compliance with the procedural requirements. But, contrary to defendants' contention, it does not necessarily follow that the merger is legally unassailable. We say this because, (a) plaintiffs invoke the fiduciary duty rule which allegedly binds defendants; and (b) Delaware case law clearly teaches that even complete compliance with the mandate of a statute does not, in every case, make the action valid in law. . . .

. . . As we have noted, § 251, by its terms, makes permissible that which the North American side of this dispute caused to be done: the merger of T.M.C. into Magnavox. We must ascertain, however, what restraint, if any, the duty to minority stockholders placed on the exercise of that right. . . .

Any inquiry into the business purpose of a merger immediately leads to such questions as: "Whose purpose?" or "Whose business?" Is it that of the corporations whose shares are (or were) held by the minority? If so, it may well be that the business purpose of that company . . . is advanced by the merger, but that could be an academic result if the complainants (as here) are no longer shareholders because they have been cashed-out. On the other hand, if the corporation in which the complainants held shares "vanishes" in the merger, inquiry as to purpose may be unrealistic if not academic. And if the business purpose of the parent (or dominant) corporation should be examined (as defendants argue), minority shareholders of the subsidiary (or controlled corporation) may have undue difficulty in raising and maintaining the issue.

The point of this discussion is not that an exploration of the business purpose for a merger is without merit. . . . It seems to us, rather, that the approach to the purpose issue should be made by first examining the competing claims between the majority and minority stockholders of Magnavox. . . .

It is a settled rule of law in Delaware that Development, as the majority stockholder of Magnavox, owed to the minority stockholders of that corporation a fiduciary obligation in dealing with the latter's property. . . . The fiduciary obligation is the cornerstone of plaintiffs' rights in this controversy and the corollary, of course, is that it is likewise the measure of the duty owed by defendants.

Delaware courts have long announced and enforced high standards which govern the internal affairs of corporations chartered here, particularly when fiduciary relations are under scrutiny. It is settled Delaware law, for example, that corporate officers and directors . . . and controlling shareholders . . . owe their corporation and its minority shareholders a fiduciary obligation of honesty, loyalty, good faith, and fairness. . . .

Defendants concede that they owe plaintiffs a fiduciary duty but contend that, in the context of the present transaction, they have met that obligation by offering fair value for the Magnavox shares. And, say defendants, plaintiffs' exclusive remedy for dissatisfaction with the merger is to seek an appraisal. . . . We disagree. In our view, defendants cannot meet their fiduciary obligations to plaintiffs simply by relegating them to a statutory appraisal proceeding.

At the core of defendants' contention is the premise that a shareholder's right is exclusively in the *value* of his investment, not its *form*. [Court's emphasis.]·And, they argue, that right is protected by [an] appraisal which, by definition, results in fair value for the shares. This argument assumes that the right to take is coextensive with the power to take and that a dissenting stockholder has no legally protected right in his shares, his certificate or his company beyond a right to be paid fair value when the majority is ready to do this. . . .

Plaintiffs allege that defendants violated their respective fiduciary duties by participating in the tender offer and other acts which led to the merger and which were designed to enable Development and North American to, among other things:

> "[C]onsummate a merger which did not serve any valid corporate purpose or compelling business need of Magnavox and whose sole purpose was to enable Development and North American to obtain sole ownership of the business and assets of Magnavox at a price determined by defendants which was grossly inadequate and unfair and which was designed to give Development and North American a disproportionate amount of the gain said defendants anticipated would be recognized from consummation of the merger."

Defendants contend, and the [trial court] agreed, that the "business purpose" rule does not have a place in Delaware's merger law. . . .

Plaintiffs contend that the Magnavox merger was fraudulent because it was made without any ascertainable corporate business purpose and was designed solely to freeze out the minority stockholders. . . .

We hold the law to be that a Delaware Court will not be indifferent to the purpose of a merger when a freeze-out of minority stockholders on a cash-out basis is alleged to be its sole purpose. In such a situation, if it is alleged that the purpose is improper because of the fiduciary obligation owed to the minority, the Court is duty-bound to closely examine that allegation even when all of the relevant statutory formalities have been satisfied. . . .

We hold . . . that a § 251 merger, made for the sole purpose of freezing out minority stockholders, is an abuse of the corporate process; and the complaint, which so alleges in this suit, states a cause of action for violation of a fiduciary duty for which the Court may grant such relief as it deems appropriate under the circumstances. . . .

[Judgment reversed.]

Shareholder Deadlock   The operation and management of a corporation requires a high degree of mutual trust, respect, and cooperation. This is particularly true of corporations in which the principal shareholders also serve as corporate officers and directors. If dissension occurs among shareholders, conflicts invariably arise among officers and directors. If corporate control is evenly divided, dissension can lead to deadlock among directors, thereby obstructing even routine corporate business matters.

To remedy the situation, MBCA § 97 provides for the liquidation of a corporation when shareholders are deadlocked in voting power. Liquidation is authorized when shareholders have failed for a period including at least two consecutive annual meeting dates to elect successors to directors whose terms have expired or would have expired on the election of their successors. Many states have enacted similar legislation providing for dissolution in case of shareholder deadlock. Most statutes require that some irreparable harm or injury to the corporation be established before judicial dissolution is authorized. The statutes vary as to the person authorized to bring an action for dissolution, the type of deadlock that must exist, and the nature of the irreparable injury that the corporation must have suffered.

45:8   Shareholder Remedies

There are various remedies that a shareholder can use against or on behalf of the corporation in which he owns shares. First, of course, the shareholder can sue the corporation in his own right if he has sustained an individual loss that is separate and distinct from any loss suffered by other shareholders. However, the shareholder can also (1) file what is called a *derivative action* on behalf of the corporation or (2) file a representative or class action on behalf of himself and other shareholders if the number of persons interested in the action is too large for all to be joined as parties. Derivative and class actions are discussed below.

Derivative Action   A shareholder's derivative action is a legal action that a shareholder files, but that the corporation itself would normally be expected to file. Thus, since the action is brought on the corporation's behalf, the corporation is the real plaintiff, even though it is named as a defendant. The reason the shareholder files the action is that, for some reason, corporate management has refused to do so. For example, this refusal might occur when the wrong that the corporation has allegedly suffered—and on which the derivative action is based—involves management's own wrongdoing. Before a shareholder can successfully assert a derivative action, a demand must be made on the appropriate corporate official to bring the suit. If the demand is refused, the way is clear for the shareholder to proceed. A demand is not required if it is obvious that the demand would be futile, as for example, when the claim is being made against the corporate directors themselves (see MBCA § 49).

EXAMPLE
The directors of the Industrial Loan Corporation were suspected of fraud and mismanagement of corporate affairs. Relatives of the directors had obtained huge loans at low interest rates with little or no collateral given as security. Grimm, who held 100 shares of Industrial at the time these acts were committed, demanded that the directors cease their fraudulent loan transactions and mismanagment. He also demanded that the directors repay to the corporation the excessive compensation that they had awarded themselves during their terms of office. When the board refused to accede to Grimm's demands, he was entitled to file a derivative action on Industrial's behalf to void the fraudulent loans and recover the excessive compensation paid to the directors.

In some states, statutes require shareholders in derivative actions who own less than a specified percentage or dollar amount of shares in the corporation to post security for the reasonable expenses incurred by the corporation. If this security for expenses is not posted, a derivative action could be dismissed despite the validity of the underlying claims. Moreover, a shareholder who initiates a derivative action without reasonable cause may be held liable to the defendants for the reasonable expenses, including attorney's fees incurred in their defense (MBCA § 49). However, it should be noted that most states that have adopted the MBCA have excluded such provisions or have excluded attorney's fees from reasonable expenses. The following case focuses on one of the prerequisites necessary for a shareholder to file a derivative action.

Jepson

v

Peterson

69 SD 388, 10 NW2d 749 (South Dakota Supreme Court, 1943)

[Jepson filed an action alleging that Peterson and two other officers and directors of the Black Hills Amusement Corporation misappropriated assets of the corporation. Jepson's complaint was later dismissed by the trial court because he did not allege in the complaint or establish that he owned shares of the corporation at the time the wrongful acts occurred. Jepson then appealed from the dismissal.]

Roberts, Presiding Judge.

*   *   *

The question presented on appeal is whether a stockholder may maintain a derivative action of this nature charging mismanagement or malfeasance on the part of the officers of the corporation prior to the acquisition of stock. The question has not been decided in this jurisdiction, and there appears to be a direct conflict of authority as to the right of a subsequent stockholder to complain of prior acts. The rule obtaining in the federal courts and in many of the state courts is that to entitle a minority stockholder to attack a wrongful transaction it must appear that he was a stockholder at the time of the commission of the act complained of or that his shares of stock have devolved on him since by operation of law. The [Federal rule requires] the plaintiff in such an action to plead that he "was a shareholder at the time of the transaction of which he complains or that his shares thereafter devolved on him by operation of law." . . .

In [a Nebraska case] the court said: "Sound reason and good authority sustain the rule that a purchaser of stock cannot complain of the prior acts and management of the corporation. . . ." A contrary view is expressed in other jurisdictions to the effect that the cause of action for the wrongdoing of officers and directors is a part of the assets in which a stockholder has a transferable interest, that a transfer of his shares includes the ownership of incidents thereto, and that it is immaterial whether the stockholder who seeks to vindicate the right was such at the time of the wrongful transaction. . . .

An action of this nature by a stockholder on behalf of himself and other stockholders similarly situated has its foundation in equity. If a corporation refuses to prosecute an action in its favor, equity to prevent a failure of justice disregards the corporate entity and permits suit to be brought and maintained by a stockholder to protect rights beneficially belonging to him. The right exists because of special injury to him. We think that the decisions holding that a subsequent stockholder cannot maintain, for want of equity, a derivative suit complaining of the prior acts and management of the corporation, are sound. Plaintiff has not alleged as to when or how he acquired his shares of stock in defendant corporation or that he was a stockholder at the time of the alleged wrongful acts. We conclude as ruled by the court below that the complaint fails to state a cause of action.

The order appealed from is affirmed.

Class Action   As discussed in Chapter 2, a class action is an action that a person brings for his own benefit *and* on behalf of others who have a similar interest in the outcome of the case. Class actions are especially useful in the corporate context, where it is practically impossible to join all shareholders of a widely held public corporation. By lumping claims together, a shareholder who would otherwise be without resources to engage in extended litigation is permitted to stand as a representative for many other shareholders who are similarly situated.

45:9   Shareholder Liability

One of the main reasons for establishing a corporation is to limit personal liability. Shareholders want to protect their personal assets by limiting their potential liability for business obligations to their investment in the corporation's capital stock. Because a corporation is a separate legal entity, distinct from its shareholders, shareholders generally are not liable for any of the corporation's obligations. In the absence of charter, constitutional, or statutory provisions to the contrary, this rule applies to liability for torts as well as to contractual obligations. Except as discussed below, the rule applies to a shareholder who owns a controlling interest, a majority, or even all of the stock of a corporation. It also applies to a shareholder that is itself a corporation.

Liability of Controlling Shareholders   There are some circumstances under which the corporate entity is disregarded and shareholders are held liable for corporate obligations. Courts have coined the phrase "piercing the corporate veil" to refer to this situation.

Perhaps the most common circumstance in which the corporate identity is disregarded is that in which a corporation is merely an alter ego or business conduit of an individual or another corporation. Under what is known as the *alter ego doctrine*, liability may be imposed on a controlling shareholder if there is such unity of interest and ownership that the separation of the individual and the company has ceased to exist. The doctrine applies to the situation in which the corporate structure is a sham and the individual—not the corporation—is doing business behind the corporate shield.

 The alter ego doctrine has been used to impose liability on an individual for torts such as fraud, as well as for debts and other contractual obligations. To avoid having the alter ego doctrine invoked and the corporate veil pierced, shareholders should keep their personal business carefully separated from that of the corporation. Personal funds or other assets should not be mingled with those of the corporation; all dealings with the corporation should be properly documented and kept at arm's length. A common trap is the controlling shareholders' neglect of corporate formalities. The shareholder who runs a corporation as his own personal business is especially vulnerable. He frequently fails to hold required meetings and to keep adequate books and records. A creditor who finds a corporation unable to meet its obligation may discover and use this disregard of formalities to invoke the alter ego doctrine and obtain a judgment against the shareholder personally.

The following case illustrates the application of the alter ego doctrine and the circumstances under which a controlling shareholder might be held personally liable for corporate debts or obligations. Note the facts of this case and the reasons why the court declined to invoke the doctrine.

Holmes

v

Clow

533 SW2d 99

(Texas Court of Civil Appeals, 1976)

[*Holmes sued Mobile Modulars, Inc., and Del Clow, its president, to recover $2,062 for certain blueprints and design work for a housing project. Holmes based his action against Clow individually* on the premise that Clow organized and controlled the corporation for his sole benefit and that the corporation was Clow's alter ego, created to defraud Holmes and other creditors. At trial, judgment was rendered in favor of Holmes against the corporation but not against Clow individually. Holmes then appealed from that part of the judgment denying recovery against Clow as the alter ego of Mobile Modulars.]

Moore, Justice.

*   *   *

Generally speaking, the legal fiction of corporate entity may be disregarded where the fiction is used as a means of perpetrating a fraud or is relied upon to justify a wrong. . . . This rule, however, is an exception to the general rule which forbids disregarding corporate existence or entity and is not to be applied unless it is made to appear that there is such unity that the separateness of the corporation has ceased and the facts are such that adherence to the fiction would, under the particular circumstances, sanction a fraud or promote injustice. . . .

In order to warrant piercing the corporate veil, the courts generally require the presence of one or more of the following factual situations: (1) evidence that the corporate entity amounts to a fraud, promotes injustice or it is relied on to justify a wrong, (2) that it was inadequately capitalized, (3) that an individual controls and manages the entity in such a manner that it becomes his alter ego, and (4) that the corporate formalities were not adhered to by the corporation. Each case must rest on its special facts. . . .

First, we consider the question of the alleged fraud. There is nothing in the evidence indicating bad faith on the part of [Clow] in forming the corporation. Insofar as the record shows, the corporation was formed for the purpose of constructing a large number of houses under a specific F.H.A. commitment. [Clow] testified that prior to incorporation cost figures were prepared on the housing project and it was determined that the undertaking would be profitable. There is no evidence that [Clow] made any false representations to appellant or withheld facts concerning the corporation's financial condition. . . .

Next appellant contends that the corporation was underfinanced to the extent it constituted a fraud on persons dealing with it. The evidence shows that while the corporation had an authorized capital of $500,000.00, the sum of only $1,000.00 was paid in. The trial court found that the paid in capital was adequate at the time of incorporation in view of the fact that it had a commitment from a bank for an interim loan which the incorporators believed sufficient to cover its debts. There is no evidence that [Clow] or any other person misrepresented to appellant the extent of the capital of the company, nor is there any evidence that [Clow] personally received any benefit from the blueprints supplied by appellant. The trial court found that appellant failed to establish that [Clow] used the corporation as a sham to perpetrate a fraud, to avoid personal liability, or to avoid the effect of the statute. Subsequent events, namely the failure of the corporation, cannot afford the basis of finding fraud at the inception of the corporation. . . . It is incumbent upon the one seeking to pierce the corporate veil to show by evidence that the financial setup of the corporation is just a sham and accomplishes an injustice. . . . Under the circumstances, and keeping in mind that the burden of proof on the issue was on appellant, we do not feel that the evidence is such as to require us to hold that, as a matter of law, the corporate entity should be disregarded on the grounds that the financial setup was a mere sham.

Next, appellant contends [Clow] failed to adhere to the requirements concerning the operation of the corporation and that in so doing [Clow] assumed such control over the corporation as to make it, in effect, his alter ego. In this connection appellant argues that there is no evidence showing that corporate minutes were kept and there is no evidence showing that the board of directors ever approved the various corporate transactions. He further contends that the evidence conclusively shows [Clow] exercised control over the directors. As stated above, the only testimony before the trial court concerning the corporate operations was given by [Clow] and his wife. They both testified that while the corporate records could not be located, apparently due to the lapse of time, the directors met and approved all corporate transactions. They further denied that [Clow] exercised control over the directors and testified each director was afforded a right to vote his convictions. There is no direct evidence in the record to the contrary.

Generally speaking the courts will not disregard the corporate entity and treat it as the alter ego of an individual unless it is shown that there is such unity of interest and ownership that the individuality of the corporation and the owner or owners of its stock has ceased and that the observance of the fiction would sanction fraud or promote injustice. Bad faith in one form or another must be shown before the court will disregard the fiction of separate corporate existence. . . . Under the circumstances we do not think this court is required to hold as a matter of law that the corporate entity ceased to exist and became [Clow's] alter ego. . . .

[Judgment affirmed.]

Watered Stock As discussed in Chapter 43, stock acquired in exchange for property or services at an overvaluation or at a discount is called watered stock. Use of watered stock is generally held to constitute a fraud on the corporation's creditors. A subscriber or purchaser to whom watered stock is issued is liable to creditors to the extent of the difference between the value of the shares and the amount actually paid for them. The rule in some states is that if overvalued property has been given to a corporation in exchange for its stock, a fraudulent intent to overvalue the property must be shown to establish a shareholder's liability (see MBCA § 19). Other states, however, have adopted the "true value" rule, under which motive, intent, or good faith are disregarded. In such states, a shareholder is held liable for watered stock regardless of motive or intent.

Illegal Dividends Another exception to the rule of limited shareholder liability may come into play if dividends are illegally declared and paid by a corporation. In this situation, shareholders can be held liable to creditors to the extent of the illegal dividend. In some states, shareholders can be held liable on this basis only if (1) corporate debts existed at the time the dividends were declared, (2) the corporation was insolvent, and (3) the shareholders knew of the illegality of the dividend. Primary liability for illegal dividends is placed on the directors who declared them (MBCA § 48). However, any director against whom a claim is asserted for wrongful payment of a dividend is entitled to contribution from any shareholder who knowingly received the dividend.

45:10 Transfer of Stock

Corporate stock is transferable, just as any other personal property is transferable. The power to transfer or dispose of stock is a right that is incident to ownership and can be limited only by statute or by a valid charter or contract provision. The transfer of stock is generally regulated by Article 8 of the Uniform Commercial Code.

Regulations can be made respecting the mode and formal requirements of the transfer of stock. Restrictions on the power to transfer shares are sometimes imposed by provisions in a corporate charter or by general laws applicable to all corporations. However, such restrictions are strictly interpreted by the courts, and those contained in a corporate charter must be reasonable and not contrary to public policy.

A corporation's power to enact bylaws restricting the sale or transfer of stock generally is regulated by statute. In the absence of statutory authority, a corporation does not have the power, either through its bylaws or through other regulations, to prohibit the transfer or sale of its stock without consent or approval of the corporation, its directors, officers, or other shareholders. To be effective, any restriction on the transfer of stock must appear on the stock certificate itself. Any corporate law that unreasonably restrains a shareholder's ability to transfer corporate stock is against public policy and therefore invalid.

The generally authorized method of transferring is delivery of the stock certificate indorsed to a specific person by the owner named on the certificate. A stock certificate can also be indorsed in blank, which means that the name of the transferee is omitted. This type of certificate is called a *street certificate*. A person can hold a stock certificate in "street name," that is, without being named as the owner or transferee.

Stock can also be transferred by delivery of the certificate accompanied by a separate document containing a written assignment of the certificate or a power of attorney to sell, assign, or transfer the shares.

The purchaser of stock who has obtained its indorsement or who has complied with the reasonable requirements as to transfer is entitled to have the stock transferred in his name on the books of the corporation. This right is enforceable against the corporation and its transfer agents. A corporation may, of course, refuse to make a transfer on its books to protect itself from loss or fraud. It may require that the certificate be surrendered so that it can authenticate it or guarantee the signature of the transferor. If a corporation wrongfully refuses to transfer stock, the transferee can either maintain an action for damages or sue to compel the transfer.

Key Concepts and Terms

- Corporations operate under the principle of majority rule.
- Shareholders exercise control over a corporation through the election of the board of directors, which takes place at the annual shareholder meeting. A quorum is required for a valid shareholder meeting.
- Each shareholder is normally entitled to one vote for each share owned. Only shareholders listed in the books of a corporation on the record date are eligible to vote at a shareholder meeting.
- Cumulative voting is a device permitting shareholders to exercise power in a corporation directly proportional to the percentage of shares owned.
- A proxy is one's authorization to another to act for him in a certain manner or on specified matters. By means of the proxy, shareholders can exercise voting rights when they do not personally attend shareholder meetings.

- A shareholder is ordinarily given preemptive rights to purchase new stock issued by a corporation in proportion to the number of shares he owns.

- A fundamental right in corporation law is the right of shareholders to inspect the books and records of the corporation in which they own stock. The right of inspection can be exercised only for a proper purpose.

- A corporation may declare and pay dividends in cash, its own stock, or other property. Directors are given considerable discretion in declaring dividends.

- The owners of preferred stock often receive dividend preference over the common shareholders. Dividends on preferred stock are generally payable only out of net earnings.

- Shareholders have a variety of remedies to use against or on behalf of a corporation. An individual can sue in his own right, bring a class action, or file a derivative action to redress a wrong done to the corporation.

- A shareholder whose identity is indistinguishable from that of the corporation is personally liable for corporate obligations. This is the alter ego doctrine; the corporation is the alter ego of the shareholder. A shareholder could also be held liable to the corporation for holding watered stock. Directors and controlling shareholders may be held liable for the payment of illegal dividends.

- Corporate stock is inherently transferable. A shareholder's power to transfer or dispose of stock is a right that is incident to ownership and can be limited only by statute, contract, or the articles of incorporation.

- Alter Ego Doctrine
- Cumulative Voting
- Derivative Action
- Dividend
- Ex-Dividend
- Preemptive Right
- Preferred Dividend

- Proxy
- Quorum
- Stock Dividend
- Stock Split
- Street Certificate
- Warrant

Questions and Case Problems

1. The Securities and Exchange Commission has written as follows: "The traditional concept that boards of directors serve as a check on management and that the board is answerable to the shareholders by virtue of their elective power has been questioned in light of the fact that board elections are frequently a ratification of management nominees and that shareholders who wish to participate more fully in the affairs of their corporation are often frustrated and discouraged by the difficulty such participation entails under the present regulatory system." A contrary view has been stated as follows: "[T]here is no reason for [shareholders] to have any voice, direct or representational, in the catalogue of corporate decisions . . . on prices, wages, and investment. They are no more affected than nonshareholding neighbors by these decisions. . . . They deserve the voiceless position in which the modern development [has] left them." [A. Chayes, *The Modern Corporation and the Rule of Law in the Corporation in Modern Society* 25, 40–41 (E. Mason ed. 1959)].

Can these two conflicting views be reconciled? Is it wise to give shareholders greater powers over the course and conduct of corporate affairs? Do not most shareholders in fact follow the so-called "Wall Street rule" that if the shareholder disagrees with management, he sells the stock? In what ways can shareholders influence management besides participation in the election of directors?

2. Ametco is a large multinational corporation with mining operations in South America. An organization that opposes American foreign investment purchases ten shares of Ametco's stock and then seeks to make certain proposals at Ametco's next annual meeting. These include a proposal that Ametco sell its investment in one Latin American country and a proposal that Ametco end the discharge of pollutants into the Pacific Ocean from its smelter in another South American country. Ametco denies that its smelter is polluting the Pacific. What can this dissident organization do to bring its proposals before other shareholders? What are Ametco's obligations to help the organization notify other shareholders of its proposals? Can Ametco prevent the organization from circulating to other shareholders proposals that Ametco believes to be false and injurious to its operations at home and abroad?

3. How do cumulative voting and the use of proxies affect shareholders' voting rights?

4. Mrs. Rettina owns a 20 percent interest in a lumber company. The other 80 percent interest is held by the company's managers, who also own 100 percent of a related business. Extensive intercorporate transactions occur between these two companies. Mrs. Rettina has received no dividend for several years despite handsome salaries and bonuses paid to management. What rights does Mrs. Rettina have and what may she do under the circumstances?

5. Erdman and three others each owned a 25 percent interest in a corporation. After working approximately 18 years, Erdman left the company but held on to his stock. Subsequently, the other three realized $40,000 from the sale of some investments the corporation had made while Erdman was still active. Then, despite declining profits, the three used the $40,000 to grant themselves retroactive salary increases and bonuses. Erdman sued, charging wrongful depletion of corporate assets and demanded a portion of the proceeds in the form of a dividend. How should the case be decided?

6. The board of directors of the Mayflower Hotel Corporation approved a proposed merger of the corporation into the Hilton Corporation. All nine Mayflower directors are nominees of Hilton, having been elected after Hilton acquired 56 percent of Mayflower's outstanding stock. A minority shareholder objects to the merger and seeks to block it in court. She contends that no quorum was present at Mayflower's meeting when the proposed merger was approved. Under the corporate bylaws, a quorum consists of five directors. At the meeting, six of the nine directors were present, but four of them were directly interested in the proposed merger. Mayflower's bylaws permit the counting of interested directors toward a quorum, but the minority shareholder argues that this provision is invalid. Should interested directors be counted toward a quorum? Should the merger be invalidated? Does § 41 of the MBCA affect the outcome? If the merger is upheld, what other rights does the minority shareholder enjoy?

7. Magline consistently showed a profit but never declared a dividend. At the end of the 1978–79 fiscal year, Magline's current assets totaled $3,000,000. The following year that figure increased to $4,000,000. Magline's quick assets (cash and items

quickly convertible to cash) exceeded current liabilities by more than $1,000,000. After repeated defeats at board meetings, two directors (who together owned 41 percent of Magline shares) sued to compel the payment of dividends. Magline's controlling shareholders argued that the company needed a large amount of working capital for diversification of its plant and product line. They also contended that Magline needed reserve funds in case it would have to renegotiate its government contracts. Should Magline be ordered to declare a dividend under the circumstances?

8. The Campbells are the principal shareholders of Royal Development, a home-construction firm. The corporation issued to them 4,500 shares valued at $45,000 for which they paid $33,000 in cash and 25 lots. After commencing building on these 25 lots, Royal Development folded due to lack of funds. Mesa Lumber, which had sold Royal Development $5,000 worth of lumber and building supplies, participated in the liquidation of Royal's assets but recovered very little. Mesa then sued Royal Development and the Campbells individually. Mesa claimed that the Campbells had grossly undercapitalized the corporation, had not paid the full subscription price for their stock, and had so intermingled their personal affairs with those of the company that the corporation had no existence separate and apart from them. To sustain its allegations, what must Mesa prove? Should the Campbells be held individually liable for the debts of their corporation?

9. The directors of Gaines Corporation send out a proxy solicitation on a proposed sale of Gaines to Life Investors, urging approval of the sale. The proxy statement mentions pending lawsuits that charged certain officers of Gaines with paying excessive commissions and fees in connection with acquisition and management of property. After the sale is approved, some minority shareholders sue for rescission. They claim that the proxy statement was defective because (1) it did not mention the fact that the pending lawsuits sought $2,000,000 in damages and that all of the directors and officers of Gaines were charged with fraud, self-dealing, and mismanagement and (2) management did not disclose in its proxy solicitation that the directors and officers of Gaines had a real personal interest in approving the sale because the sale would result in the abandonment of the lawsuits against them. Were all material facts disclosed to the shareholders? Can the sale of Gaines to Life Investors be rescinded? Is a derivative action proper in this case?

10. How are minority shareholders protected from the majority under the common law and the MBCA?

46 Franchises

46:1 Introduction

Franchises are a major component of the American economy. In 1980, sales through franchises exceeded $300 billion and accounted for approximately one-third of all retail sales made.

The system of franchising is relatively simple. Under a franchising agreement, the developer of a product or service (*franchisor*) grants another person (*franchisee*) an exclusive right (franchise) to market the product or service under the franchisor's trademark or trade name through a marketing plan in a specified area for a specified period of time. The franchise is not simply a license to sell a product or service—it entails a close, cooperative relationship between the franchisor and the franchisee. In addition, the franchisor's trade name or trademark identifies the franchisee as part of a larger business enterprise rather than as an independent retailer selling a unique product or service.

There are three basic types of retail franchises: (1) those in which the franchisor is a manufacturer whose basic operation is to distribute trademarked products, such as automobiles, trucks, or gasoline; (2) those in which the franchisor is a wholesaler whose basic purpose is to reduce the expenses involved in the flow of inventory in, for example, drugstores, hardware stores, and the automotive aftermarket; and (3) those in which the franchisor is merely a trademark holder and service sponsor to the retailer who conducts an enterprise, such as a fast-food or motel chain, under a common trade name using similar operating procedures. Retail franchises in which the franchisor is a manufacturer or wholesaler are commonly referred to as *distribution franchises*, while the franchises in which the franchisor is a service sponsor are ordinarily referred to as *business format franchises*.

46:2 Franchisor–Franchisee Relationship

The franchise relationship is considered to be unique under the law. The relationship between franchisor and franchisee combines features of both the agency and the independent contractor relationships,[1] and therefore does not fit precisely into any of the traditional business relationship classifications.

Usually the franchisor offers certain minimum services and legal rights to the franchisee. These services and rights are tied to a system of distribution or marketing that is used by all the franchisees. The distribution or marketing system regulates such matters as purchasing, merchandising, advertising, record-keeping, maintenance, supply, and business format. The franchisor may also train the franchisee's employees, supervise the franchisee, require the use of standardized operating manuals, control quality, and provide other expert services.

Clearly, the franchisor's control over the franchisee is at the heart of the franchisor–franchisee relationship. This control is buttressed by a contractual requirement that the franchisee conform to the standard operating procedures as dictated by the franchisor under threat of losing the franchise. In a distribution franchise, the control exercised by the franchisor might be limited to those matters directly bearing on the product itself, such as storage, handling, display, or servicing. In a business format franchise, however, the franchisor's control usually extends to *every* aspect of the franchisee's business.

46:3 The Franchise Contract

Two documents are generally used in connection with the creation of a franchisor–franchisee relationship and the grant of a franchise. The first document is a deposit receipt, which is also known as a letter of intent, territorial binder, or letter of commitment. It is a temporary agreement in which the franchisor acknowledges receipt of a money deposit from the franchisee, ordinarily called a *franchise fee*, and agrees to perform certain acts leading to the signing of a *franchise contract*. Later, the parties sign the franchise contract, which is a far more detailed document. The contract spells out all the rights and liabilities of the parties.

 Under most franchise arrangements, a franchise fee is required at the time a deposit receipt or franchise contract is actually signed. The franchise fee may be payable in a lump sum or in installments, depending on the agreement between the parties. The businessperson is cautioned about the possibility that the franchise fee may also be "hidden" in payments that the franchisor requires for merchandise or services, in excess of the bona fide wholesale prices of the goods furnished to the franchisee. The fee could also be disguised as contributions to an advertising fund administered by the franchisor.

Clauses in franchise contracts usually stipulate that the franchisor will (1) provide managerial assistance to the franchisee, (2) assist in site selection, (3) conduct traning programs, and (4) provide operating manuals. In return, the franchisee agrees to run the business in a manner stipulated by the franchisor. Most contracts also specify that the franchisor will provide particular equipment, goods, or types of facilities.

---

[1]These relationships are discussed in Chapters 48 (agency) and 49 (independent contractor).

Advertising   The advertising done for a franchise operation is generally originated by the franchisor. Some contracts provide that the franchisor bears the expense of this service. Under other contracts, the franchisee is obligated to pay for his own advertising, generally on the basis of a percentage of sales. A franchise contract may also provide that a certain percentage of the franchisee's gross sales be spent for advertising by the franchisor.

46:4   Duration and Termination of Franchise

Traditionally, franchisees have been at the mercy of franchisors with regard to termination of the franchise contract. Most franchise contracts provide that the franchisor has the right to terminate at will. Thus, there is a need to protect franchisees' rights in their contracts, and state and federal laws exist to serve this purpose. Under these laws, most franchise contracts cannot be canceled arbitrarily if they are performed in a reasonable and satisfactory manner.

By way of illustrating the protective laws referred to above, the termination of automobile dealerships is specifically governed by the federal *Automobile Dealers Day in Court Act* (15 USC §§ 1221–1225) and similar state legislation. These laws, which prevent car manufacturers from terminating dealerships in bad faith, are designed to curtail car manufacturers' coercion and intimidation of retail dealers through threats of terminating the financing of new automobiles. A second purpose of the laws is to prevent a manufacturer from pressuring a dealer, under threat of terminating the dealership, to accept cars, parts, accessories, and supplies that the dealer neither needs nor wants.

A franchisor can, of course, terminate the franchise contract if the franchisee fails to discharge the duties required of him under the contract. For example, if the franchisee of an employment agency franchise agrees in the contract that the business will be conducted in a downtown office but in fact operates only as a telephone service from his home, the franchisor has good cause to terminate the contract.

Most franchise contracts contain notice provisions requiring the franchisor to give the franchisee reasonable notice of termination. The failure to comply with the notice requirement renders the termination invalid, and the franchisor may be liable in damages to the franchisee. The following case illustrates the limits that the courts tend to place on a franchisor's right to terminate a franchise contract, as well as the scope of the contract itself.

Shell Oil Co.
v
Marinello

63 NJ 402, 307 A2d 598, 67 ALR3d 1291
(New Jersey Supreme Court, 1973)

[In 1959, Shell Oil Company leased a service station to Marinello and entered into a written dealership agreement with him. The lease was for a one-year term and was regularly renewed in writing for the next 12 years. In 1972, Shell notified Marinello that it was terminating the lease and dealership agree-

ment. Marinello sued to enjoin the termination. Shell maintained in court that it could terminate the lease under the rules of landlord and tenant law. Marinello argued that the dealership agreement and lease constituted a franchise and could not be terminated without good cause. The trial court agreed with Marinello, ruling that Shell could not terminate the lease without good cause. From this judgment, Shell appealed.]

Sullivan, J.

*   *   *

We are in full agreement with the basic determination of the trial court that Shell had no legal right to terminate its relationship with Marinello except for good cause, i.e., the failure of Marinello to substantially comply with his obligations under the lease and dealer agreement. . . .

Shell argues that its lease of the service station premises to Marinello is independent of its dealer agreement with him, and that its legal rights as a landlord under the lease are absolute and cannot be restricted. This is pure sophistry. The two contractual documents are but part of an integrated business relationship. They were entered into simultaneously, [and] have the same commencement and expiration dates. . . .

The relationship between Shell and Marinello is basically that of franchise. The lease is an integral part of that same relationship. Our Legislature, in enacting the Franchise Practices Act, has declared that distribution and sales through franchise arrangements in New Jersey vitally affect the general economy of the State, the public interest and the public welfare. . . . The Act prohibits a franchisor from terminating, cancelling or failing to re-

new a franchise without good cause, which is defined as the failure by the franchisee to substantially comply with the requirements imposed on him by the franchise. . . .

The Act does not directly control the franchise relationship herein since Marinello's last renewal antedates the effective date of the statue. . . . However, the Act reflects the legislative concern over long-standing abuses in the franchise relationship, particularly provisions giving the franchisor the right to terminate, cancel or fail to renew the franchise. To that extent the provisions of the Act merely put into statutory form the extant public policy of this state. . . .

We hold (1) that the lease and dealer agreement herein are integral parts of a single business relationship, basically that of a franchise, (2) that the provision giving Shell the absolute right to terminate on 10 days' notice is void as against the public policy of this State, (3) that said public policy requires that there be read into the existing lease and dealer agreement, and all future lease and dealer agreements which may be negotiated in good faith between the parties, the restriction that Shell not have the unilateral right to terminate, cancel or fail to renew the franchise, including the lease, in absence of a showing that Marinello has failed to substantially perform his obligations under the lease and dealer agreement, i.e., for good cause, and (4) that good cause for termination has not been shown in this case.

Based on the foregoing, Marinello's franchise, including his lease, would have legal existence for an indefinite period, subject to his substantially performing his obligations thereunder. . . .

[Trial court's judgment modified and, as modified, affirmed.]

46:5   Governmental Regulation of Franchising

Various approaches have been adopted by the states and the federal government to regulate franchises. Under certain circumstances, franchises have been deemed to be securities that are subject to the registration requirements under federal and state securities acts.[2] Franchising has also been subject to regulation through federal and state antitrust laws governing price-fixing, price controls, tie-in buying, and market or territorial domination.[3] The federal mail fraud statute (18 USC § 1341) has also been applied to franchises.

The most important federal legislation applicable to franchises is the *Federal Trade Commission Act*, which prohibits unfair or deceptive acts or practices in commerce [15 USC §§ 45(a)(1) and 45(a)(6)]. Under the authority of this act, the Federal Trade Commission (FTC) has adopted rules and regulations governing the sale of franchises and business opportunities (see 16 CFR Part 436). These rules were adopted in response to widespread abuses in connection with the sale of franchises and business opportunity ventures throughout the country. They reduce the opportunity for deceptive practices by prohibiting certain acts and by requiring the disclosure of information relevant to a proposed sale of franchises. The rules set forth the circumstances under which a franchisor or franchise broker can make claims about the actual or projected sales, income, or profits of existing or potential outlets. They also impose other requirements on franchisors or franchise brokers for establishing franchises.

State Regulation of Franchising   Many states have enacted legislation relating specifically to franchising. This legislation generally authorizes legal action by a franchisee to recover damages for the franchisor's violation of the law. However, the provisions of these state laws vary. In some states these provisions are similar to the federal franchise laws. Laws of this type declare certain acts to be unfair and deceptive practices, or unfair methods of competition, and they require full disclosure of all pertinent information by franchisors before franchises can be sold. Other state laws incorporate principles of the federal securities and antitrust acts, requiring franchisors to register with the state agency before selling franchises, and perhaps requiring that a copy of the franchise prospectus or advertising material used to promote the sale of franchises be filed with a state regulatory agency. Still other state laws require only the franchisors deal with franchisees in good faith.

As is evident, the various franchise laws adopted by the states are not consistent or uniform in approach. Indeed, even the basic definition of terms varies widely from state to state, depending on the particular regulatory approach used. For example, one group of states defines "franchise" on the basis of how much control is exercised by the franchisor and how closely the franchise is associated with the franchisor's marketing plan or system; in the absence of these features, a business venture is not deemed to be a franchise subject to state regulation. A second group of states defines "franchise" in terms of the common interest that the parties to a franchise contract have in the success of the business; typical statutory language in these states refers to "the community of interest among the parties" to a particular business arrangement. A third approach focuses on the mutual financial benefits in a business relationship and requires a continuing financial interest between parties in addition to the licensing of a basic marketing plan. A few states have at-

---

[2]Securities regulation is discussed in Chapter 43.
[3]Antitrust legislation is discussed in Chapter 54.

tempted to define "franchise" in other terms. For example, in some states a franchise is defined as a continuing commercial relationship, while in others a franchisee's business must be substantially reliant on the franchisor for its supply of basic goods in order to constitute a franchise. Obviously, the applicability of a state's franchise legislation to a particular business arrangement or venture depends on the definition of terms, the purpose of the legislation, and the abuses sought to be remedied.

The following case illustrates how a court determines whether a particular business venture is a franchise. Bear in mind that the result might very well have been different had some other regulatory approach or definition of terms been in force.

People
v
Kline
110 Cal App 3d 587, 168 Cal Rptr 185
(California Court of Appeal, 1980)

[Donald Kline was charged with and convicted of the unlawful offer and sale of a franchise in violation of the California Franchise Investment Law, the first franchise disclosure law enacted in the United States. The California law defines franchise on the basis of the control exercised over the franchisee and the existence of a marketing plan or system prescribed by the franchisor. On appeal, Kline contended that his offer and sale of business opportunities did not constitute a franchise within the meaning of the law because no marketing plan or system existed at the time the business opportunities were sold.]

Koford, J.

*   *   *

Appellant Donald Gene Kline was charged by information with . . . one count of unlawful offer and sale of a franchise. . . .

In mid-1977 [Kline] formulated plans to establish a fast food chain which would sell hot dogs from portable kiosks under the name

"Aunt Hilda's Pennsylvania Dutch Steamed Franks." He incorporated a company for this purpose, designated as National Food Service Marketing, Inc. . . .

In June 1977, [Kline] had begun regularly to patronize a restaurant in Tiburon, where he met James Shaul and Caroline Mushet with whom he discussed his plans for the Aunt Hilda's Pennsylvania Dutch Steamed Franks enterprise. He told Mushet that he intended to build many kiosks for the enterprise, and showed her blueprints for the kiosks.

In November 1977, Shaul told Mushet that [Kline] "was offering a very good price for his franchises," and suggested that they become involved in the enterprise as partners, with Shaul as manager and Mushet as investor. On November 21, 1977, Shaul, Mushet, and [Kline] met at Shaul's apartment to discuss the enterprise. [Kline] told Mushet that he was offering a franchise for $25,000 on a very short term basis, which he would soon sell for $40,000 and later would sell for $80,000. Shaul told Mushet that "it was a turn key operation." Mushet understood this to mean that "it was everything complete, ready to go, absolutely supplied and sustained and everything else." She was also told that the menu for the business "would be handled by an expert." She was given a "pro forma" outlining projected sales, operating expenses, payroll expenses, and profits for "Aunt Hilda's Pennsylvania

Dutch Steamed Franks," and [Kline] handed Mushet a newspaper article about franchises and said that he was proposing a similar operation. She testified that, "as I understood it, he was going to have many many franchises. He was going to have a lot of Aunt Hilda's barns all over the place."

Mushet was not given specific details as to a marketing plan or system; both [Kline] and Shaul, however, told her that "everything would be supplied and managed and promoted by National Food Service Marketing." She understood that the day-to-day operation of the business was to be conducted by National Food Service Marketing, Inc., that there would be an ongoing relationship between [Kline's] corporation and her proposed partnership with Shaul, and that [Kline] was in complete control of the operation.

That very evening Mushet decided to enter into the proposed investment. Mushet and Shaul signed a handwritten "partnership agreement" drafted by [Kline] in which Mushet agreed to invest $50,000 in the partnership for the purchase of at least two "Aunt Hilda's Kiosks' Business Opportunities." They also signed as partners a "purchase agreement," also handwritten and drafted by [Kline], to purchase two "Aunt Hilda's Kiosks' Business Opportunities" for $25,000 each from National Food Service Marketing, Inc.

Mushet gave [Kline] $50,000 in two installments ([Kline] later demanded more money from her, and on two occasions she loaned him funds totaling $15,000). . . .

[Kline] contends that the court erred, . . . because [he] did not sell or offer to sell a "franchise." . . . " 'Franchise' means a contract or agreement, either expressed or implied, whether oral or written, between two or more persons by which:

"(a) A franchisee is granted the right to engage in the business of offering, selling or distributing goods or services under a market-ing plan or system prescribed in substantial part by a franchisor; and

"(b) The operation of the franchisee's business pursuant to such plan or system is substantially associated with the franchisor's trademark, service mark, trade name, logotype, advertising or other commercial symbol designating the franchisor or its affiliate; and

"(c) The franchisee is required to pay, directly or indirectly, a franchise fee."

[Kline] argues that the two "business opportunities" sold to the partnership formed by Shaul and Mushet did not as a matter of law constitute a franchise . . . because there was no "marketing plan or system" and even if so, it was not "prescribed in substantial part by a franchisor." . . .

The contract or agreement which constitutes a "franchise" . . . may be expressed or implied, oral or written. In the case at bench there was a written contract binding the franchisor, National Food Service Marketing, Inc., [Kline's] corporation, to "total and continuing support" of the franchisee. [Kline] had agreed orally to assist in advertising and to supply food and supplies and menu planning, etc., through his corporation. The use of identifiable and distinctive kiosks at least implied a prescribed marketing plan or system, and there was an expressed agreement to sell "Aunt Hilda's Pennsylvania Dutch Steamed Franks," surely an indication of a common marketing plan or system. [Kline] also promised that there would be an operational plan which he had "pretty well worked out." He represented to a number of people that he was organizing a national food franchise similar to other well known and successful national franchises. The whole scheme was [Kline's] conception of an integrated operation prescribed and directed by him through National Food Service Marketing, Inc., his corporation. By phrasing his handwritten agreement in terms of sale of a "business opportunity" [he] cannot avoid the requirement of registering this franchise sale.

There was therefore ample evidence from which the trial court could find all of the statutory elements of a franchise; as that court said: "The whole aroma, the whole atmosphere around this sale clearly related to the sale of other than just the kiosk. It was a sale, actually, of a franchise."

[Kline's] argument that there must exist a fully prescribed and detailed marketing plan or system in order to meet the definition of a registerable franchise sale or offer is too narrow a statutory construction. The Legislature expressed concern for the protection of prospective franchisees in enacting the Franchise Investment Law. . . . In fact the specified intent of the law was to prevent such a sale as made by [Kline], where the seller's failure to provide full information "would lead to fraud or a likelihood that the franchisor's promises would not be fulfilled." Therefore it is not appropriate to construe the definition of [franchise] to fully developed franchise schemes. A sale for a fee of a business substantially associated with the seller's trademark, service mark, trade name, logotype, advertising or other commercial symbol, which the seller represents *will constitute* a franchise and will include a marketing plan or system *to be* prescribed in substantial part by the seller is the unlawful sale of an unregistered franchise. [Court's emphasis.] . . .

[Judgment affirmed.]

46:6   Franchisor's Liability for Acts of Franchisee

The franchisor is not liable to third persons for acts of the franchisee under most circumstances. This is so because franchising does not necessarily create an agency relationship in which the acts of the franchisee are imputed to the franchisor. However, if a sufficient degree of control and direction is exercised by a franchisor, an agency relationship may be created. In such cases, the franchisor can be liable to third persons for acts or omissions of the franchisee. In determining whether an agency relationship exists between a franchisor and franchisee under a franchise agreement, the right to control the business is an important factor. If the franchisor has the right to exercise complete control over the operation of the franchise, an agency relationshp may exist, with the franchisor as the principal and the franchisee the agent.

In products liability cases the franchisor may be liable to a third person injured by a product supplied by the franchisor, despite the absence of control over the franchisee's business.[4] For example, if a person is injured by a defective automobile part he purchased from a franchisee, the franchisor or manufacturer can be held liable to the injured person regardless of the precise relationship of the franchisor and franchisee under the franchise agreement.

The liability of a franchisor for acts of the franchisee is exemplified in the case below. Note the circumstances under which the franchisor was held liable and the extent of the franchisor's control over the franchisee.

---

[4]Products liability is discussed in Chapter 7.

Kuchta
v.
Allied Builders Corp.
21 Cal App 3d 541, 98 Cal Rptr 588
(California Court of Appeal, 1971)

[Kuchta contacted the Allied Builders Corporation concerning the construction of an outdoor patio and living area. Allied referred Kuchta to its franchisee, Ralph Weiner. A contract was signed with Weiner, naming him as the contractor. The contract required in part that all construction conform to local and state building codes. Weiner submitted building plans to the appropriate local agency, but they were disapproved. Without Kuchta's knowledge or consent, Weiner submitted other plans that complied with the regulations, and these were approved. However, Weiner built the patio and living area according to the original, noncomplying plans. When the local housing agency discovered what had occurred, Kuchta was required to demolish the patio and restore the area to its original condition. Kuchta then sued both Allied and Weiner for damages. Allied defended, arguing that as the franchisor it was not liable for acts of its franchisee. The trial court entered judgment against both Allied and Wiener, holding them equally responsible in damages to Kuchta. From this judgment, Allied appealed.]

Kerrigan, Acting Presiding Justice.

*　　　*　　　*

The law is clear that a franchisee may be deemed to be the agent of the franchisor. . . . In the field of franchise agreement, the question of whether the franchisee is an independent contractor or an agent is ordinarily one of fact, depending on whether the franchisor exercises complete or substantial control over the franchisee. . . .

In the case under review, there was evidence that Allied Builders exercised strong control over Weiner. The franchise agreement itself gave Allied Builders the right to control the location of the franchisee's place of business, to prescribe minimum display equipment, to regulate the quality of the goods used or sold, to control the standards of construction, to approve the design and utility of all construction, and to assign persons to see that the franchisee performed according to the franchisor's standards. Additionally, Allied enjoyed the right of inspection over the franchisee's plans and specifications, the franchisee's work in progress, and finished jobs, as well as the right to train Weiner's salesmen. Moreover, Allied Builders was entitled to share in the profits of the franchisee and to audit Weiner's books. These elements of control were sufficient to support an implied finding of agency. . . . Both the main office and the branch office answered their phone in the same manner, to wit, "Allied Builders." Both the franchisor and the franchisee did business under the same name at that time, to wit, Allied Builders System. The contract listed "Allied Builders System" as the contractor. Both offices employed common advertising in newspapers and in the yellow pages of the telephone book. Calls to the main office brought swift and certain reaction from the franchisee. Weiner represented to plaintiffs that the firm had been in business for over 50 years, which covered the entire span of Allied's experience in the building business. The plaintiffs' check for payment on the contract price was endorsed and deposited to the account of "Allied Builders System." Consequently, there was ample evidence that Allied Builders either intentionally, or by want of ordinary care, led third persons, including plaintiffs, to believe that the franchisee and Allied Builders were part of the same business operation.

While Allied Builders argues that no agency relationship existed by virtue of the franchise agreement, in that the agreement itself stated that no such agency relationship was created, the declarations of the parties in the agreement respecting the nature of the relationship are not controlling. . . .

Weiner was an agent or ostensible agent of Allied. It is clear that he acted in an important management position. Therefore, the only question remaining is whether a franchisor may be liable in punitive damages for a franchisee's fraud to the same extent as it would for the fraud of an employee, officer or manager.

The franchise agreement provided a plethora of controls and supervisory privileges on behalf of the franchisor. Allied enjoyed a right to cancel the franchise relationship at any time by reason of Weiner's insolvency, failure to maintain sufficient gross sales, or failure to comply with any contractual obligation, including Weiner's duty to comply with all building codes and to obtain necessary building permits. The most significant control an employer has over the acts of an official is the right to terminate his employment for misconduct. Allied had even this control over Weiner. Allied also required the franchisee to make a certain amount of gross sales yearly and the franchise royalty was based entirely upon gross receipts. Thus, Allied received a financial benefit from fraudulently induced contracts. In light of the foregoing indicia of control, it is difficult to distinguish between this agency relationship and that of any managerial official. Weiner may be equated in all respects with an employee, officer or manager. . . .

[Judgment affirmed.]

Key Concepts and Terms

- Under a franchising agreement, the developer of a product or service (franchisor) grants another person (franchisee) an exclusive right (franchise) to market the product or service under the franchisor's trademark or trade name through a marketing plan in a given area for a specified period of time.

- The relationship between franchisor and franchisee combines features of the agency relationship and the independent contractor relationship. At the heart of the franchisor–franchisee relationship is the control the franchisor exercises over the franchisee, including control of site, methods of business operation, merchandising, record-keeping, and quality of the product or service.

- The franchise contract creates the franchisor–franchisee relationship, grants the franchise, and sets forth the parties' rights and duties.

- Termination of a franchise is governed by provisions in the contract and, in some states, by statute.

- Franchises have been regulated by the states and by the federal government through securities legislation, antitrust laws, and mail fraud statutes, as well as through specific franchise disclosure laws.

- Franchisors are ordinarily not liable to third persons for acts or omissions of the franchisee. However, if the franchisor exercises a sufficient degree of control and direction over the franchisee, an agency relationship may be created, rendering the franchisor liable for the franchisee's acts.

- Automobile Dealers Day in Court Act
- Business Format Franchise
- Distribution Franchise
- Federal Trade Commission Act
- Franchisee
- Franchise Contract
- Franchise Fee
- Franchisor

Questions and Case Problems

1. Analyze and discuss the various types of franchise regulatory approaches adopted by the states.

2. National Cleaners sells cleaning solvent to local dry cleaners and prescribes and enforces quality service standards. In return, a local subscribing dry cleaner is granted the right to display a regionally or nationally advertised symbol of quality. A fee is charged for the right to use this symbol. Is this arrangement a franchise? Do the definitions of franchise, as discussed in this chapter, affect the answer?

3. What distinguishes the franchise from other business relationships?

4. Seams is a large department store chain that advertises heavily in newspapers, magazines, and mail-order catalogs. The No-Leak Roofing Company rents space in one of Seams' stores under a typical department store lease and concession arrangement. No-Leak is a roof repair company that actively participates on a cooperative basis in Seams' local advertising program. Under the contract, No-Leak pays Seams a fixed minimum rent plus a percentage of gross sales. No-Leak must maintain certain types and levels of insurance and have all the necessary business permits. Although No-Leak does business under its own name, its invoices state that it is a Seams' authorized roofing contractor. Is this arrangement a franchise? Does the answer depend on the particular definition or approach to franchises in force in the state where No-Leak is doing business?

5. Why is the franchisor ordinarily not liable for wrongful acts of the franchisee? What is the determining factor of a franchisor's liability?

6. Why are franchise terminations particularly the subject of state laws?

7. Murphy sustains personal injuries while she is a guest at a Holiday Inn motel. The motel is operated by Betsy-Lynn Motor Corporation as a franchise. Holiday Inn does not own the premises on which the accident occurred. Can Murphy hold Holiday Inn liable for her personal injuries? Under what circumstances would Holiday Inn be liable?

8. Guild Industries granted area franchises for the distribution of furniture under its "Baby Butler" trade name. All the franchises granted were unsuccessful and were closed after the franchisees sustained substantial losses. Each of the product distribution schemes devised by Guild to be used by its franchisees was inherently fraudulent. Representations made by Guild to prospective franchisees were false. The franchisees also encountered unanticipated costs which precluded realization of the promised profits. In view of these facts, what state and federal remedies exist to protect the public and prospective franchisees from Guild's business scheme? What remedies would be available to franchisees who have gone out of business, despite the representations and assurances of Guild Industries?

9. Gail Coty is injured while operating a meat-slicing machine on the premises of her employer, the Yankee Doodle Dandy Restaurant, a fast-food franchisee. She sues the franchisor for negligence, seeking damages for her personal injuries. The fran-

chise contract imposes on the franchisee numerous restrictions relating to the operation of the restaurant. These restrictions are primarily geared toward protecting the Yankee Doodle trademark and the goodwill associated with it. The franchisor does not retain any day-to-day supervisory control, cannot hire or fire anyone, cannot stop work in the restaurant, and cannot give any orders to the franchisee's employees. Assuming that Gail could prove negligence, is the franchisor liable for the torts of its franchisee?

10. Mr. Steak, Inc., issued franchises for restaurants throughout the country. From 1962, all its franchise agreements prohibited the sale of alcoholic beverages on restaurant premises. A reprinting of the franchise forms in 1968 inadvertently omitted this clause, and various franchises were granted without it. As a result, 27 of the over 200 Mr. Steaks throughout the country served alcohol. The omission was later discovered and reinserted in the franchise forms. Following a slump in sales, Mr. Steak experimented in authorizing the sale of alcoholic beverages in certain of its restaurants; it even issued four written waivers of the prohibition clause. Another ten franchise operators started to sell liquor on their own without any waiver from Mr. Steak. However, when the owners of a Mr. Steak franchise in Colorado told the franchisor of their intent to sell alcohol, Mr. Steak refused to give its permission and sued to enjoin the breach of its franchise. How should the case be decided?

47 Considerations in Choosing Form of Business Organization

47:1 Introduction

One of the most important, and indeed fundamental, issues in launching a business venture is the form and structure the venture will take. In deciding which particular form of business to adopt, one should consider all of the advantages and disadvantages of each type of business entity. The purpose of this chapter is to aid the businessperson in making this selection by reviewing the basic types of business organizations and discussing some of the matters that should be considered before choosing a particular type.

The selection of the best form of business organization depends to a large degree on the nature of the business itself, the general financial conditions and tax situations of the participants, the number of investors involved, the extent to which capital is required, and a host of other factors. In many cases, family relationships must also be considered.

The principal organizational structures for the conduct of business are the sole proprietorship, the partnership (see Chapter 41), and the corporation (see Chapters 42–45). That is not to say, however, that the choice of organization must be from among these basic forms of business enterprise. Other forms, such as the joint venture, business trust, real estate syndicate, or real estate investment trust, are commonly used for particular business purposes. A *joint venture,* for example, is often used to finance special-purpose investments and projects that may require large sums of capital, particularly in real estate development. Moreover, the basic forms of business enterprise are not in themselves uniform in nature or totally separate and distinct, either from a tax or a business point of view. This is particularly true of corporations, which can be one-person ventures, family corporations, or multinational giants with thousands of investors, employees, and managerial personnel. It is also true of the franchise (see Chapter 46), which is not really a distinct form of business organization at all since it can be operated by a partnership, a sole proprietorship, or a corporation. Despite the blending of one form with another, each type of business organization is subject to specific laws based on the nature, attributes, and requirements of its particular structure.

The determination of the best form of business—or at least the one most suited to a particular type of activity—is extremely important and carries serious legal and tax consequences for all participants. In some ventures, participants automatically prefer certain forms of business over others. For example, the limited partnership is by far the most commonly used business entity in real estate because it offers investors both the limited legal liability of a corporation and the tax benefits of a partnership. On the other hand, many persons about to launch a business often think only in terms of operating as a corporation. From an economic standpoint, the great appeal of the corporation stems from the fact that the law treats it as an entity separate and distinct from its shareholders. However, it has often been remarked, "When in doubt, do not incorporate," because in many cases the partnership or sole proprietorship offers far more advantages than does a corporation.

As the following case shows, it is of vital importance for people in business to be aware of the many types of entities capable of doing business and to make certain that the entity chosen conforms to the legal criteria governing that business. Note that although the business here was characterized in one form by its participants, the court considered it to be an entirely different type of entity.

Rizzo
v
Rizzo
3 Ill 2d 291, 120 NE2d 546
Illinois Supreme Court, 1954)

[Rocco Rizzo, Sr., operated a business under the name of Rocco Rizzo & Co. Michael, the oldest son, went to work for his father in 1910; Joseph in 1913; Rocco, Jr., in 1916; and John in 1920. Each son performed definite duties for the business. Michael, the most experienced, was the general manager. None of them received wages, and all the profits were equally divided. In 1915, Rocco, Sr., retired from active participation. In 1929, the father deeded the business property to Michael, who paid no consideration for either the business or the building. After the death of Rocco, Jr., his estate claimed one-quarter of the business, contending that it was a partnership. The other brothers argued that the business was a sole proprietorship owned by Michael. At trial, the court found that the brothers had operated the business as a partnership from 1920 to 1931, when Rocco, Jr., died. Thus, his estate was entitled to a one-fourth interest in the partnership as of the date of his death. The court also ruled that the

plaintiff was entitled to an accounting from the other brothers. From this judgment, the brothers appealed.]

Bristow, Justice.

*   *   *

In the instant case the decree of the court in plaintiff's favor is predicated upon the existence of a partnership relation between plaintiff's deceased husband and his brothers. The requisites of a partnership are that the parties must have joined together to carry on a trade or venture for their common benefit, each contributing property or services, and having a community of interest in the profits. . . .

Defendants contend that the evidence establishes that Michael Rizzo was the sole proprietor of the business on the date of the death of plaintiff's decedent. In support thereof, defendants point out that the business was turned over to Michael in 1915 when his father retired, that the profits were merely the measure of compensation for the brothers, that Michael was regarded as the boss by persons dealing with the firm, and that a formal partnership contract had to be drawn up at the request of the bank in order to negotiate a loan in 1937, indicating that there was no partnership prior thereto.

The fact that Michael, as the oldest son, had more authority in the management than the other brothers does not of itself preclude the existence of a partnership, particularly in view of the custom in such closely-knit immigrant families. In fact, Michael stated that the business was turned over to him because he was the oldest son. Furthermore, it is an accepted partnership practice that one partner may be charged with greater managerial responsibilities.

The fact that the brothers admitted that they all worked in the business, sharing equally in the profits and going without pay if there were none, tends to comply with the essential requirement for a partnership. That interpretation is enhanced by . . . the statement of an employee of 30 years that all the brothers were regarded as the owners.

Furthermore, the fact that the firm name, originally Rocco Rizzo & Co. had been changed to Rocco Rizzo Son & Co. when Michael entered the business, and was again changed to Rocco Rizzo Sons & Co., and was so listed in the telephone book and on the truck during the lifetime of Rocco, Jr., is further evidence of the existence of a partnership between the brothers as of 1931. Changes in the firm name to Jacob Shlem & Sons were deemed significant in establishing the existence of a partnership in [another case, in which] the sons also went to work in the family business.

Under the circumstances in the case at bar, therefore, there is ample evidence that the brothers, Michael, Joseph, John, and Rocco, Jr., were carrying on the business for their common benefit, each contributing his services and having an equal interest in the profits; hence, the finding of the master as approved by the chancellor, that the brothers were partners as of the date of the death of Rocco, Jr., could in no way be deemed to be manifestly against the weight of the evidence. . . .

In the light of our analysis of this cause, the findings of the chancellor are amply supported by the evidence, and the decree entered pursuant thereto is in accordance with the law and should properly be affirmed.

Decree affirmed.

The rest of this chapter focuses on a number of different factors that affect a businessperson's choice of the best type of business organization for a given enterprise. These factors are (1) creation of the organization and continuing requirements following its creation, (2) management, (3) compensation of the participants, (4) capital requirements, (5) duration of the business, (6) transferability of the business or rights in it, (7) personal liability of the participants, and (8) taxation. Bear in mind, however, that it is usually impossible for those about to launch a business venture to avail themselves of all the advantages of every form of business. Instead, the most important factors should be identified, and the advantages and disadvantages of each carefully analyzed. The form of business organization that most meets the needs of the participants should be ultimately chosen. When this is accomplished, the business will be far more likely to succeed than if the various factors discussed in this chapter are ignored and the form of business enterprise is chosen out of whim or for unimportant reasons.

47:2   Creation; Continuing Requirements

A sole proprietorship is the simplest business enterprise to form. It can be commenced at any time, usually by obtaining a business license and paying sales and other taxes. A written agreement is not necessary. Indeed, the states impose very few formal requirements that must be complied with before one can engage in business as a sole proprietor.

Forming a general partnership is also relatively simple. A written agreement is not ordinarily required, except in certain cases. A partnership that will necessarily last longer than one year, for example, must be created by a written agreement because of the statute of frauds (see Chapter 15).

In a limited partnership, the partners must prepare and sign a certificate setting forth prescribed information, including a designation of which partners are general and which are limited (see Chapter 41). The certificate must be filed with a state official, generally the Secretary of State. The certificate may be amended or canceled by following similar formalities.

Once a sole proprietorship or partnership is formed, the states usually do not require it to disclose on a regular basis data or information concerning its operation. Partnerships are required to file an information tax return each year, but they are not otherwise subject to reporting requirements. The information return must disclose each partner's distributive share of the partnership income, gains, losses, deductions, and credits. As discussed further in 47:9, each partner must also disclose his share of these items on his own individual tax return.

Corporations   The requirements for organizing a corporation are more formal. Incorporation is a statutory process requiring strict compliance with the requirements. Every state requires a corporation to file its articles of incorporation before it can lawfully engage in business (see Chapter 42). Usually it must pay a filing fee. It must also pay a license fee to the state in which it desires to do business, even if it is not incorporated in that state, and an annual franchise fee for the privilege of doing business. In addition, a corporation must strictly comply with state and federal securities laws when issuing stock.

 The cost of forming a corporation, including legal fees, as compared against the cost of creating a sole proprietorship or partnership, may be quite high. The amount of the fees and taxes that a corporation must pay, the cost of filing reports and returns with the state or federal government, and the annual upkeep required of the corporation should not be casually overlooked when deciding which form of business venture is most appropriate.

Other formalities that a corporation must observe and that distinguish it from a sole proprietorship or partnership include annual shareholder and formal director meetings, notification to shareholders of various corporate actions, and the taking of detailed minutes of meetings conducted by the board of directors or the shareholders.

47:3 Management

The number of persons involved in a business, and the method by which it will be managed, are obviously important determinants of the appropriate type or structure of business organization. In a general partnership, the partners are all co-managers. Each partner has both the express and implied authority to bind the partnership in dealings with third parties. Each partner also has a technical and legal veto over the other partners as to partnership affairs. If there are many general partners, each capable of acting for the partnership as a whole, the business could lose its sense of purpose, going off in many directions. For this reason, the partnership agreement typically establishes a form of *centralized management* structure.

In a limited partnership, the limited partners cannot participate actively in management. Accordingly, a limited partnership interest represents a passive investment, which may not meet the objectives of participants who want some control over their investment.

The corporate form is much more suitable than a partnership to a business involving large numbers of people. The centralized management, through the election of directors by shareholders and, in turn, the appointment of corporate officers by directors, is often a major reason for incorporating. The ultimate power in a corporation usually resides in the shareholders who own the majority of the voting stock or are in a position to control the corporation; the minority interests may have little or no role in the active management of a corporation. This limitation on the role of minority shareholders is particularly significant when active owners want assurance that inactive owners will not interfere in the business. Therefore, to the extent that an enterprise requires a sophisticated management structure, the corporate form is probably the most preferable type of business organization.

Fiduciary Duties of Management   The legal obligations of partners or corporate managers to act in good faith must be considered when choosing a business form. In a partnership, for example, each partner is bound by the highest duty of loyalty to the other partners. A lesser standard of care is generally applied to corporate officers and directors. They are usually not liable for acts of ordinary negligence; they are presumed to have acted within the broad range of normal business judgment.[1] Clearly, this deference given to corporate management decisions by the courts can be a distinct advantage.

It should be noted, however, that the high standard of care applicable to partners is being more frequently applied to corporate managers in a growing number of states. In addition, the strict compliance required of corporate management to the federal securities laws (see Chapter 44) also tends to reduce the differences in the duty of care between the partnership and the corporation.

---

[1]The business judgment rule is discussed in Chapter 44 (see 44:9).

47:4   Compensation of Participants

Any assessment of the desirability of one business form over another must contain a comparative analysis of the compensation options available with the various types of business organizations. Compensation usually consists of any of the four following elements: (1) basic cash compensation or salary; (2) benefits under pension, retirement, or profit-sharing plans; (3) other fringe benefits, such as group insurance programs, club memberships, and business use of company automobiles; and (4) incentive compensation, which can be most meaningful in terms of both financial rewards and employee motivation.

The corporate form of business offers the most possibilities in terms of compensation. A corporate employee's compensation package can be structured to include all four of the elements listed above. Stock compensation and stock options, unavailable in other forms of business enterprise, are traditionally used as incentive compensation for executives. Furthermore, if a shareholder is also an employee of the corporation, he may be entitled to participate in an accident and health insurance plan and to receive group life insurance or other benefits. The shareholder-employee does not have to pay income tax on benefits paid by the corporation.

The compensation alternatives available to organizational forms other than the corporation are more limited. For example, a sole proprietor is not eligible to participate in a qualified pension plan under the *Internal Revenue Code*, because he cannot be both an employer and employee at the same time within the meaning of the law. Note, however, that the Internal Revenue Code does allow an individual to set aside and deduct up to a prescribed amount of income each year for retirement savings. In a partnership, health or life insurance and other benefits received by a partner might be considered compensation and treated as taxable income.

47:5   Capital Requirements

The choice of organization often depends on how much capital will be required to run the business and whether it will be necessary to retain capital. With a sole proprietorship and general partnership, these considerations might not play a vital role; a person or partnership can engage in business without operating capital and without the need to accumulate profits.

The corporate form offers the greatest ease and flexibility in obtaining capital. The various ways a corporation can raise capital, including issuing equity and debt securities, readily permit the transfer and readjustment of interests of those who own the business. Indeed, this may be the prime advantage to the corporate form. Therefore, to the extent that an enterprise seeks to take advantage of financing alternatives, the corporation can offer a significant advantage.

When capital is acquired through debt financing, the corporate form has an additional advantage in that the corporation, rather than the shareholders, will be held liable for corporate debt obligations. In some situations, however, this aspect of the corporate form is not significant because debt financing might not be available without incurring *personal liability*. For example, creditors of closely held corporations frequently require personal guaranties of the principal shareholders. As to a profitable partnership, on the other hand, a third party might very well extend credit to the partnership with recourse limited to the partnership assets; that is, without the partners being personally liable.

47:6 Duration of the Business

The intended *duration of a business* is another factor to consider in selecting a business structure. Most sole proprietorships terminate on the owner's death. Of course, the business can be taken over by a family member or an associate, or the assets can be sold to permit its continued existence.

Partnerships must be dissolved in order for the business to be terminated. The Uniform Partnership Act lists a number of acts or events that cause dissolution (see Chapter 41). Obviously, the existence of these many causes of dissolution and eventual termination should prompt potential partners to study their relationship in-depth from both the business and personal standpoints. For example, an otherwise successful partnership business might have to be terminated because of personality differences among the partners or simply because one partner dies. Therefore, uncertainty as to a partnership's duration might prompt those about to engage in a business to select another form of enterprise.

Generally, a corporation has perpetual life unless it is dissolved by the shareholders or by court order. If a corporate president or a shareholder dies, for example, a corporation's business is not automatically terminated.

47:7 Transferability of Ownership

A basic concern in the formation of any business is how easily the business (or rights in it) can be transferred or sold. A sole proprietorship is perhaps the easiest type of business to sell. Since a sole proprietor generally answers to no other person, the business can be sold at any time. In contrast, under § 18 of the Uniform Partnership Act, a partner in a general partnership cannot transfer his interest without the other partners' consent. (Such a limitation on the transferability of a partnership interest is often advantageous, particularly if all the participants actively contribute to the success of the business.) For a limited partnership, the partnership's required certificate can provide for the transferability of a limited as well as a general partner's interest.

As for a corporation, corporate shares are generally transferable at any time by the shareholders. Free transferability is often an advantage in forming a business as a corporation, particularly if capital will be raised by issuing equity securities. Note, however, that restrictions similar to those of partnerships can be imposed to limit the transfer or sale of a shareholder's interest. For example, shareholders of a closely held corporation often enter into a restrictive agreement that prevents one shareholder from selling his interest without first offering it to the corporation or the other shareholders. The increasing recognition of special treatment for closely held corporations in state corporation laws has led many courts to be extremely tolerant of share transfer restrictions when challenged.

Although the mechanics differ, *transferability of ownership* varies only slightly between the partnership and corporate forms. In both forms, the interests can be either freely transferable or restricted from transfer. Only in a limited number of situations will transfer limits be better adapted to the corporate form. Accordingly, as with some other factors that would appear to favor the corporation, the significance of this factor in selecting the form of enterprise should not be overestimated.

47:8 Liability of Participants

A businessperson's potential liability varies greatly from one business structure to another. The limited liability of corporate shareholders is often considered the primary advantage of the corporation. Because a corporation is an entity separate and distinct from its shareholders, shareholders are not normally liable for the corporation's obligations. They are only liable to the limited extent of their initial investment, which means that the maximum loss that they can sustain is the value of the stock they own.

There are, however, various judicially created doctrines that have been applied by the courts to extinguish limited shareholder liability. For example, it can be extinguished if a corporation is operated as an alter ego of the principal shareholder (see Chapter 45). Moreover, if a corporation has been inadequately capitalized, the corporate entity might be disregarded and the individual shareholders held personally liable. Although the courts will not casually disregard the corporate entity and impose liability on shareholders, the possibility of their doing so must be considered when choosing the most appropriate business entity.

In close corporations, limited liability of the shareholders may be illusory. Close corporations often receive bank or other loans on the condition that an individual shareholder cosign the promissory note, which makes him personally liable on the debt. Accordingly, at least until a corporate enterprise becomes well established and sufficiently stable in the eyes of creditors, the only protection against liability that the shareholders might have is their insulation from tort liability. The existence of this protection, without more, is not necessarily a valid reason for incorporating. A business venture, whether incorporated or not, can adequately protect itself against tort liability by obtaining various readily available types of insurance coverage (see Chapter 39).

Unlike a corporate shareholder, both a sole proprietor and a partner in a general partnership are individually liable for all obligations incurred by the sole proprietorship or partnership. In a partnership, each partner can also be liable for wrongful acts committed by one or more of the other partners.

Limited partnerships are often formed to protect investors against the potential liability that would exist with a general partnership. The liability of limited partners is akin to the liability of corporate shareholders in that a limited partner is not individually liable for the partnership's obligations. Instead, a limited partner's liability is limited to his stated contribution to the enterprise, provided the partnership agreement is publicly filed and various other rules are observed, including the absolute requirement that the limited partner take no part in the management of the business. A general partner of a limited partnership, in contrast, has unlimited personal liability for partnership obligations.

Of course, either a general or a limited partnership can purchase various types of insurance against the possible imposition of personal liability. However, the nature of a business may make it very difficult for a partnership to obtain *liability insurance*. For example, a fledgling partnership that manufactures an inherently risky product might have considerable difficulty in obtaining product liability coverage, or the cost of the insurance might be inordinately high.

47:9   Taxation

A business can be intentionally structured to create maximum tax savings. There is nothing unethical, immoral, or illegal about planning to minimize state or federal taxes. As the United States Supreme Court has observed, "The legal right of a taxpayer to decrease the amount of what otherwise would be his taxes, or altogether avoid them, by means which the law permits, cannot be doubted."[2]

All individuals in business, including sole proprietors, are subject to a graduated federal tax on their incomes. Each self-employed person must also pay self-employment tax on part or all of his income to help finance Social Security benefits. While Social Security taxes are withheld from the wages of employees, self-employed persons must pay the tax as part of the income tax.

Taxation of Partnerships and Corporations   Like sole proprietors, partners are taxed individually. The partnership files an information tax return which shows the partnership's income and deductions and their allocation among the partners. In turn, each partner reports his allocated share of income and deductions on his individual income tax return.

EXAMPLE
Yellin is a partner with three others in Olé Perfume Enterprise. Each of the four partners shares equally in the profits and losses. In its third year of operation, the partnership has a gross income of $400,000 with deductions of $200,000. Yellin must report on his own income tax return for that year gross income in the amount of $100,000 as his share of the partnership's gross income, but he can take deductions in the amount of $50,000. He must report the income of $100,000 regardless of how much is actually distributed to him.

In calculating his income tax, each partner must include on his own return his share of partnership income and deductions for the taxable year in which they are accrued by the partnership. It does not matter when partnership income is actually distributed to each partner; that is, even if part of the income is distributed during the next year, it must be reported the year it was earned by the partnership. Indeed, a partner is taxed on his proportionate share of partnership income even if *none* of the income is actually distributed.

2*Gregory v Helvering*, 293 US 465, 79 L Ed 596, 55 S Ct 266 (1935).

The principal tax distinction between the corporation and the partnership is that a corporation is a taxable entity, separate and apart from its shareholders. As a result, income generated by a corporation can be taxed twice; once at the corporate level and again at the shareholder level.

EXAMPLE

The Brannan Corporation has earnings of $10 million on which it is taxed by the federal government. From these earnings Brannan distributes $2 million to its shareholders as dividends. The dividends received by the shareholders are also taxed as ordinary income when reported by the shareholders on their annual returns. Thus, $2 million of Brannan's earnings is taxed twice, once at the corporate level and once again when the distributed earnings are received as dividends by the shareholders.

In some states, shareholders are also burdened with an intangible personal property tax on their shares.

Ordinarily a corporation has a *separate legal identity* for tax purposes even if it is wholly owned by a single shareholder or by related shareholders. Therefore, no matter how decisive a sole shareholder's actions will be in determining those of the corporation, once the corporation is active as an entity and is more than the alter ego of the shareholder the two are separate taxpayers.

 One must bear in mind that a business will ordinarily be subject to tax on the basis of its *actual* form and identifiable characteristics, rather than on the basis of its apparent structure. Thus, if a corporation is a sham, serving only as the alter ego of its principal shareholder, the corporate entity might be disregarded for tax purposes. Corporate earnings will then be attributed to the shareholders, who will be taxed in the same manner as are other individuals. Similarly, a partnership that evidences a number of features characteristic of a corporation might end up being taxed as a corporation rather than as a partnership.

Accumulation of Income   A significant drawback to the partnership form is the requirement that accumulated or undistributed earnings be allocated to the individual partners for tax purposes in the year they are earned. In contrast, the law allows a corporation to accumulate up to a prescribed amount of its earnings and profits without adverse tax consequences to the shareholders in most situations. Indeed, the ability to accumulate earnings is one of the primary benefits flowing from corporate status.

Taxation of Joint Ventures   As discussed in Chapter 41, a joint venture is a combination of two or more persons seeking a joint profit in some specific venture without designating themselves as a partnership or a corporation. A joint venture is usually formed for the purpose of engaging in a single project that could require several months or several years for its completion, but in most other respects it resembles a partnership and embodies the idea of the mutual agency of its members. Ordinarily, joint ventures are taxable as partnerships. For example, if two corporations form a business and divide the profits and losses equally, the endeavor is a joint venture, the business is taxed as a partnership, and each corporation must report on its tax return its one-half share of the profits and losses earned from the joint venture.

Subchapter S Corporation   The final business entity that should be considered from the tax standpoint is the *Subchapter S corporation,* which is discussed generally in Chapter 42. To avoid the double taxation that would otherwise be imposed, as discussed above, certain corporations can elect to be taxed under Subchapter S of the Internal Revenue Code instead of under the regular rules governing the taxation of corporations. In effect, a Subchapter S corporation's income is taxed to the shareholders as though it had been distributed to them as a dividend at the end of the corporation's taxable year. Moreover, if the corporation suffers a loss, the loss is treated as the shareholders' loss. For all other tax purposes, the corporation is treated like any other corporation despite the Subchapter S election. Thus, by incorporating and electing to be taxed under Subchapter S, the owners of a small business can enjoy the benefits both of the corporation and the partnership. A Subchapter S corporation can be used to divide business income among children or other relatives for tax purposes without taking the money out of the corporation and without incurring the double tax liability. This often is a simpler, more feasible approach than the family partnership.

Some restrictions on Subchapter S corporations can make the election impractical or unattractive. For example, a Subchapter S corporation is limited to 15 shareholders all of whom must be individuals, except for estates and certain trusts. A Subchapter S corporation can have only one class of stock, and a certain percentage of the business must consist of active rather than passive investments. Additionally, Subchapter S status can be adopted only by unanimous shareholder consent and terminated only by unanimous agreement. If an election is terminated, a corporation is ineligible to regain Subchapter S status for five years.

Key Concepts and Terms

- Selecting the most suitable form of business organization depends to a large degree on (1) the nature of the business, (2) the general financial condition and tax status of the participants, (3) the number of investors involved, (4) and the extent to which capital is required.

- The principal forms available for a business enterprise are the sole proprietorship, the partnership, and the corporation.

- To the extent that an enterprise requires a sophisticated management structure, the corporation is the most preferable form of business organization.

- A business organization must meet certain requirements imposed by the states before it can engage in business. A sole proprietorship or partnership must only apply for a business license and arrange for the payment of sales or other taxes. A limited partnership must file a certificate with the state. A corporation must meet formal requirements regarding incorporation and qualification and may also be required to comply with the requirements of the federal securities laws before stock or other securities may be issued.

- The amount of capital necessary to begin a business varies with its size. Accordingly, most sole proprietorships and partnerships engage in business without having to raise significant amounts of capital. A corporation, however, must generate capital and usually does so by selling shares or issuing debt securities. If flexibility in financing and capital formation are required, the corporation may be the preferable form of business organization.

- The longevity of a business depends on its form. A sole proprietorship usually terminates on the owner's death. Various acts or events may cause the dissolution and eventual termination of a partnership. A corporation can exist indefinitely, even if a shareholder dies or sells his shares.

- The ease of sale or transfer of ownership might be another determining factor. A sole proprietorship is the easiest type of business to sell. A partner cannot sell or transfer a partnership interest without the consent of the other partners. Corporate shares are ordinarily freely transferable at any time by the shareholders, although many smaller, close corporations do restrict the transfer or sale of shareholders' interests.

- The businessperson's personal liability is an important consideration in choosing the most suitable business form. A sole proprietor or general partner is individually liable for all business obligations and torts. A limited partner's liability extends only to the amount of the partner's contribution to the enterprise. Because a corporation is a separate entity under the law, shareholders are not normally liable for any corporate obligations or torts.

- Tax implications are yet another factor in deciding how to organize a business. Both a partnership and a sole proprietorship are treated similarly for income tax purposes. In contrast, income generated by a corporation and distributed as dividends is taxed twice—once at the corporate level and again at the shareholder level.

- Accumulation of Income
- Centralized Management
- Duration of Business
- Internal Revenue Code
- Joint Venture
- Liability Insurance

- Personal Liability
- Separate Legal Identity
- Subchapter S Corporation
- Taxation
- Transferability of Ownership

Questions and Case Problems

1. Dubois is the sole proprietor of a small explosives firm. The net profits of the business in 1980 were $200,000 and constituted the sole source of Dubois' income. Dubois expects that the profits of his business will increase at the rate of about five percent per year over the next ten years. The business has a small sales force and several manufacturing employees. There are two key employees whom Dubois is anxious to keep in the business. Dubois believes that he needs an annual income of about $65,000 per year to cover his living expenses and his federal and state

income taxes. He has no other outside income. Should he incorporate? If so, what are the advantages and disadvantages?

2. Discuss the reasons why organizational and managerial structure are important factors to consider when forming a business.

3. Compare and contrast the question of liability in a corporation, a partnership, and a sole proprietorship.

4. Rolf and Amundsen are interested in starting a business to sell books by mail and public auction. They plan to have an inventory composed exclusively of books and to conduct the business out of their homes. They do not plan to hire any employees. Rolf and Amundsen each contribute approximately $50,000 for the acquisition of rare books and to borrow additional money on a short-term basis from banks. What type of business association should they form and why?

5. Willie and Hope Farmer run a successful lumber business. They want to expand production but do not have the necessary capital to do so. They are reluctant to take on additional debt because of their financial position and the prevailing high interest rates. Winston, who knows of the Farmers' expansion plans, contacts them to discuss possible investment in their business. She does not want to become involved in its management but would like some control over its affairs if she puts up money. What form of organization is most appropriate in this situation? Why?

6. On graduation from college, Bradley Condrake returns home to start a fish and poultry company. He has chosen this particular business venture because his father ran a similar enterprise for a long time. Bradley hopes to benefit from his father's connections with suppliers and outlets and to learn his marketing skills. However, Bradley's father, already retired, does not wish to participate actively in the business. He does plan to invest money and to participate minimally. During the initial stages of the business, Bradley does not plan to employ more than one or two part-time persons as the need arises. He has leased a building for the business with an option to purchase. He will purchase the equipment he will need, particularly refrigeration equipment, from other companies. What type of business organization should Bradley form? Why?

7. Drewes is attempting to form a business renting tools, machinery, and other items to the public. The initial capital needs are so great that Drewes must obtain financing from outside investors or banks. Drewes prefers to manage the business herself but will consider letting one or more of the investors help her run the business. A major problem with a rental business is the potential liability for injuries to persons who rent equipment, and Drewes is concerned about this. She also realizes that she may gain tax benefits from the depreciation of the rental equipment and perhaps from the losses she might sustain during the first year or two of operations. In light of these circumstances, how should the business be formed? Why?

8. Smith works for an accounting partnership owned by Kelley and Galloway. He receives $1,000 per month in salary, travel expenses, and a bonus paid out of the firm's profits. Although Smith is held out to third persons as a partner, and contracts with third parties indicate that Smith is a partner, there is no partnership agreement and he has not contributed to any of the partnership assets. Smith becomes dissatisfied with the firm and leaves. He contends he is entitled as a partner to ten percent of the profits. What type of business arrangement had been created? Is Smith entitled to share in the profits?

9. Discuss the tax differences of the corporation, the Subchapter S corporation, and the partnership.

10. The Allen family owns and operates a pet shop. All three family members participate in the business and own the property on which they operate their store. The net profits are distributed equally to each family member who participates in the business. One of them reads an article about the wisdom of incorporating, but they decide that the business should continue as a family operation. Moreover, even though they would obtain limited liability on incorporation, they realize that no bank would extend the corporation credit without the individual guaranty of the shareholders. They do not foresee a substantial change either in the profits or losses of the business, and they do not have plans for a substantial expansion of the business. They are also somewhat interested in establishing a pension plan or disability insurance program but realize that if they incorporate this may be difficult with only three shareholders. Should the Allens continue their business as a partnership or should they incorporate? Why?

PART TEN

Employment Relationships

Introductory Comments

Broadly defined, "employment" is a person's use of something for a particular purpose. In this part of the book, the term refers to the use of people who are compensated for their services. The discussion focuses on three different types of employment relationships: agency, independent contractor, and employer–employee.

In the agency relationship, one person (the agent) acts for and on behalf of another (the principal). A typical example is the relationship between a homeowner who wishes to sell his house and the person with whom he contracts to find a buyer for the house. A key concept of agency is representation; the agent represents the principal. The agency relationship is discussed in Chapter 48.

An independent contractor is a person who is hired to do a particular job. As discussed in Chapter 49, the employer's interest is in the completed job. Indeed, the distinguishing fea-

ture of an independent contractor relationship is the employer's lack of control over the means by which the contractor accomplishes the job. The relationship exists when, for example, a business contracts with an accounting firm for an audit of its books and preparation of its income tax returns. The accountant is so important an independent contractor from a businessperson's viewpoint that the relationship between an accountant and his client is discussed separately, in Chapter 50.

The traditional employment relationship is that of employer and employee. The distinction between status as an agent and status as an employee is sometimes blurred, but essentially it is that an employee is hired to work for and under the direct control of the employer, rather than to represent him. The basic rights and duties of employers and employees are discussed in Chapter 51.

Chapter 52 discusses two significant aspects

of the employer–employee relationship that are regulated extensively by federal legislation. The first of these is labor relations, which involves the right of employees to organize and bargain collectively with their employer. The second is job discrimination, which, if left unchecked, operates to restrict people's employment rights and opportunities for reasons unrelated to their ability to do the work in question.

The different employment relationships discussed in Part Ten are complex and involve many rights and corresponding duties and liabilities. Clearly, the more complete knowledge a businessperson has about the statutory and court-made law that governs the relationships, the better equipped that person will be to make reasoned decisions in the employment area and, in this way, to minimize future litigation.

48 Agency Relationship

48:1 Introduction

"Let every eye negotiate for itself and trust no agent." So stated William Shakespeare in one of his works. While such advice may have been good counsel in the bard's time, in our modern economy it is virtually impossible to transact business in the absence of agents or the *agency* relationship. Because the use of agents is pervasive in commercial life, it is essential that the businessperson know (1) how to create an agency relationship, (2) how to conduct business using agents, and (3) how to terminate an agency. This chapter is designed to meet these goals.

An agency arises when one person, the principal, enlists the services of another person, the agent, to manage a business or perform a transaction in the principal's name or on his behalf subject to the principal's control. Agency is a *fiduciary relationship,* meaning one of trust or confidence. Any person having the capacity to act may do so through an agent. Once an agency has been established, the acts of the agent become those of the principal.

There are three different kinds of agents: general, special, and universal. A general agent is authorized to perform all activities connected with the projects or tasks for which he is hired. A special agent is authorized to perform only specific activities under particular instructions. A universal agent is authorized to transact all of the principal's business and to do all acts that the principal can delegate; thus, a universal agent is an unlimited general agent.

48:2 Creation of Relationship

The agency relationship is ordinarily created by agreement between the principal and the agent. An agency is created and authority is actually conferred very much as any other contract is made (see Chapters 10 through 15). As between the principal and agent, there must be a meeting of minds in establishing the agency, as well as the consent of both the principal and the agent. The principal must intend that the agent act for him, and the agent must intend to accept the principal's authority and act on it.

While the creation of an agency relationship arises from mutual consent, it is not essential that a formal or written contract be signed by the parties. Thus, although an agency is often express, it can also be implied, based on the conduct of the parties or how they represent their relationship to other persons with whom business is conducted. Bear in mind, too, that the language used in an agreement between persons does not necessarily determine the legal nature of their relationship. Rather, the intention of the parties is controlling. If business performed by one person on behalf of another is essentially in the nature of an agency, an agency relationship is created regardless of what the parties call that relationship. Conversely, the mere use of the words "agent" or "principal" will not necessarily give rise to an agency if the persons do not intend to act as principal and agent.

Agency by Estoppel and Necessity   Two kinds of agencies that are not created by contract are agency by estoppel and agency by necessity. An *agency by estoppel* is created when one person permits another to act for him and, by so doing, causes third persons to reasonably believe that an agency has been created. This relationship between the parties is called an agency by estoppel because the courts will not permit one person who has held out another as his agent to deny the existence of an agency later, during litigation.

Agency by necessity comes into existence when an emergency arises that makes it necessary or proper for one person to act for another without having express authority to do so. The emergency must be a real one; it is not sufficient that the agent only believes that an emergency exists. An agent's authority under this doctrine terminates as soon as the agent has performed the emergency services and has communicated with the principal that certain acts have been performed on his behalf.

48:3   Authority of Agent

The essence of the agency relationship is the authority of the agent to act for and bind the principal. The source of the agent's authority is always the principal. An agent can have (1) actual authority or (2) apparent or ostensible authority. *Actual authority* is express or implied authority granted to the agent by the principal. Express authority, as the name implies, means authority expressly conferred by the principal on the agent. Implied authority is not actually given by the principal to the agent. Instead, it is the authority the agent uses to do whatever acts are incidental, necessary, usual, or proper to the exercise of the express authority actually delegated to him. An agent is usually deemed to have the implied authority to perform business on the principal's behalf in accordance with the general custom, usage, and procedures in that business.

EXAMPLE
Paul, the owner of a used-car lot, contracts with Eric to manage the lot for him and to sell cars for a commission. In operating the lot, Eric begins a marketing campaign that includes newspaper advertising. Eric has the implied authority to contract for advertising because it is a customary part of conducting a used-car business.

Apparent Authority   *Apparent* or *ostensible authority* is authority that, although not actually granted to the agent by the principal, the principal knowingly permits the agent to exercise, or that the principal holds the agent out to third persons as possessing. Thus, if a principal conducts business so as to cause third persons to reasonably believe that the agent possesses authority to act in the principal's name with regard to particular matters, the principal will be bound by the agent's acts within the scope of that apparent authority as to a third person who in good faith reasonably believes that the agent has such authority. For the doctrine of apparent or ostensible authority to be invoked, the following must be established: (1) the principal in some way manifested consent to the exercise of such authority, or at least has knowingly permitted the agent to carry out particular activities; (2) the third person acted reasonably and in good faith in believing that the agent was acting with the principal's authority; and (3) the third person relied on this authority and would suffer injury or loss if the transaction was not binding on the principal.

The following case illustrates the way in which these elements establish the authority of an agent. As the case shows, determination of apparent or ostensible authority is made by examining the actions of the principal, not the actions of the agent. An agent's assumption or representation that he has the authority does not create apparent authority.

R. H. Kyle Furniture Co.
v
Russell Dry Goods Co.
340 SW2d 220, 85 ALR2d 428
(Kentucky Court of Appeals, 1960)

[Kyle Furniture Company sued Russell Dry Goods to recover $1,767.15 for goods alleged to have been sold and delivered to Russell on the order of its manager, Clyde Thomas. Russell contended that it had never bought the goods and that they had not been delivered to its store. It further argued that its manager had lacked the authority to buy the goods and that it was therefore not liable for their cost. The trial court ruled in Russell's favor, holding that it did not have to pay. Kyle Furniture appealed.]

Stanley, Commissioner.

*   *   *

The questions are whether Thomas bought the merchandise for himself and other persons or for the [dry goods] store, of which he was the manager, and whether the plaintiff [Kyle Furniture] could rely upon the apparent or ostensible authority of Thomas to buy the merchandise for the [store].

The plaintiff is a wholesale dealer in furniture, located in Charleston, West Virginia. The defendant conducted a general dry goods store in Russell Springs, Kentucky. It was formerly a partnership in which Thomas was a partner with J. L. Turner and Cal Turner of Scottville, Kentucky; but several years before this transaction the Russell Dry Goods Company became a corporation. Thomas continued in charge as general manager. J. L. Turner and Son is also a corporation. It operates a chain of forty stores in Kentucky and Tennessee, one of which was the Russell Dry Goods Company.

H. T. Burdette, one of plaintiff's traveling salesmen, testified that Thomas first purchased certain items of furniture on October 12, 1955. They were shipped to the charged to the company. There were several other like transactions before February 29, 1956, when Thomas and he discussed the proposition of setting up a special furniture department on the second floor of the Russell building. He submitted a stock order amounting to $2,471.40, subject to being confirmed by Cal Turner. Turner declined to approve it, as "he was not ready to go in the furniture business." There were several isolated orders given by Thomas which were duly shipped and charged to the dry goods company before an order was given on April 28, 1956, for an assortment of rugs, carpeting, dishes, lawnmowers, electric fans and furniture. The order aggregated $1,767.15. It was sent in as having been sold to the dry goods company and its account was charged. When the truck arrived at Russell Springs with the shipment, the store was on fire or had already burned down. At Thomas' request, the goods were taken to his garage and unloaded there. This is the account sued on.

Plaintiff's official having charge of its accounts filed copies of the several invoices showing the goods were bought by the dry goods company, shipped to and charged to it, and the account had been duly credited with payments. The first information the plaintiff had of any limitation upon Thomas' authority was a letter from Cal Turner, president of J. L. Turner and Company, declining to pay the account sued on. . . .

Thomas testified that all of the purchases had been made for himself personally or clerks in the store or friends at wholesale prices. He admits having made a little profit on some of the shipments, but whether for himself or the store is not revealed. . . . Thomas insisted that Burdette knew these were personal transactions. He stated that he would personally pay Burdette for the shipments when he came around on his visits. . . . Burdette denied this and many other affirmative statements. Thomas did not remember anything at all about the particular shipment involved here being received. Other than the evidence of the truckman, the record is silent as to what became of the merchandise.

Cal Turner testified that Thomas and all other managers of his various subsidiary stores had been positively denied authority to make any purchases of stock.

The defendant undertook to show that furniture was not handled in the store. This apparently was to prove that the plaintiff should have known Thomas was not buying the merchandise as stock for the store. But a long-time clerk testified that it had carried in stock household articles, wallpaper, rugs, mattresses, bed springs and, at one time, window fans and some chairs made in a local factory. This tended to show that the defendant did not confine its operations strictly to "dry goods."

The court sustained an objection to an inquiry of the plaintiff's credit manager concerning the custom in the business world to rely upon the authority of the manager of a store to buy merchandise. The witness avowed that store managers normally have full authority to purchase merchandise, and this is generally relied upon. We think this evidence was competent. The evidence had a tendency to prove a presumption of agency. . . .

Authority to contract on behalf of the principal may arise from a usage or custom of business. . . .

It is within well-settled law that the plaintiff, as principal, is bound by the notice or knowledge of its salesman, Burdette, although it was not actually communicated to his company. . . . And further, though it was competent for the principal to limit the authority of an agent, the restriction on the authority of Thomas to buy merchandise for the store is not binding on the plaintiff, for there was no evidence that it had notice or knowledge thereof; and the directive was ineffective to limit the agent's apparent authority in this transaction or relieve the company of an obligation to pay for the merchandise. . . . Therefore, the defendant is bound on this contract of purchase, if it was made by Thomas within the implied or ostensible scope of his authority as manager of the store, unless plaintiff's salesman knew or had reason to know that he was exceeding his authority in ordering the goods on the credit of the company. This is so well recognized that citation of law is scarcely required. . . .

There are many cases of foreign jurisdictions holding that a general manager of a store is presumed to have authority to buy merchandise. . . . In a prefatory note [to the annotation at 55ALR2d 6] it is said:

> "A technical distinction exists between implied authority and apparent authority, implied authority being that which is an incident of the position occupied by the agent and which is more or less indispensable to the performance of the duties of the position, while apparent authority is that which the principal by a course of conduct has held the agent out as possessing, or which he through negligence has allowed the agent to assume, and which third persons dealing with the agent in good faith are justified in relying upon." . . .

As stated in some of the cases summarized, it would be impossible for persons to deal safely with corporations if in each case they were required at their peril to determine the exact scope of the authority of such agents as managers and superintendents; hence, they are justified in relying upon the apparent or implied authority of such agents. We think that is sound law. The term "apparent or implied authority" would not likely apply to the purchase of goods wholly outside the character or line of merchandise carried, e.g., the manager of a men's clothing store buying a large quantity of drugs. In the instant case, the stock of the defendant's country store was not limited to "dry goods," which is generally defined as textile fabrics. . . . It was undenied that the Russell store had previously stocked articles similar in character to those contained in this order. The purchase could well be regarded as having been made in the ordinary and usual course of the business, even though the purchases may have been specially made for individual customers. . . .

We are of the opinion the court should hold as a matter of law that Thomas, as manager of the defendant's store, had ostensible authority to purchase the goods, subject, however, to the jury believing that Burdette, the plaintiff's agent, knew, or should have known by the exercise of ordinary and reasonable prudence, that he did not have such authority. . . .

[Judgment reversed.]

Power of Agent to Bind Principal   The scope of an agent's power to bind the principal depends largely on the powers that the principal has conferred on the agent. Common sense plays a large role in determining the extent of an agent's powers and his authority in any given case. For example, an agent's power to make a contract extends only to contracts that are usual and customary in the business or trade involved. An agent's normal contractual powers clearly would *not* include the authority to modify an agreement after its execution, to waive its conditions, or otherwise to diminish the obligations of the other contracting party.

Authority to borrow money on the principal's credit may be the most important—and also most dangerous—authority that a principal can confer on an agent. This authority does not exist even for a general agent unless it has been expressly given or is necessarily implied by the character of the business.

 An agent who has the slightest doubt as to the propriety of an authorized activity should bring all facts of the prospective transaction to the principal's immediate attention and request written clarification of the action authorized by the principal. In this way, the agent could prevent the principal from later accusing him of exceeding the scope of his authority or acting adversely to the principal's interests.

Subagents   Sometimes a principal expressly authorizes an agent to delegate authority to another person. This person, called a *subagent*, then represents the principal as if he were directly appointed by the principal. An agent's authority to create a subagency can be implied if the nature of the business is such that the principal can reasonably contemplate that the agent's authority will be exercised through subagents. Whether subagents can be appointed is determined on a case-by-case basis. The customs or usage of a particular trade or business are important considerations. If a particular business is ordinarily conducted through subagents, it may be presumed that the principal has impliedly authorized their appointment and use. If a principal has placed personal trust or confidence in the agent, however, the agent's authority cannot be delegated to another without the principal's consent.

48:4   Ratification of Agent's Acts

The principal is not bound by acts exceeding the scope of an agent's authority. A principal can, however, ratify acts that were done in excess of the agent's authority, or even acts that were done by a person who purported to be an agent but actually was not. If the principal does ratify, the rights and duties of all parties concerned are just the same as if the agent—or would-be agent—had had proper authority when the act was done.

To constitute a valid *ratification*, the principal's approval must be given with full knowledge of all facts pertinent to the transaction. A principal's mere acceptance of the benefits derived from the agent's unauthorized acts will not amount to a ratification if the principal has not been supplied with all material facts. The principal must either adopt or reject the entire transaction. He cannot avail himself of those acts that are beneficial and repudiate those that are detrimental.

Ratification as Express or Implied   Ratification of an unauthorized act can be express (either orally or in writing) or implied from the acts or conduct of the principal subsequent to the act. Although particular formalities are not usually required for ratification, it should be noted that to bind the principal, the form of ratification must be of equal dignity to what the original authorization would have been. That is, if the original authorization to create an agency had to be in writing, such as authorization to sell land, then the ratification also must be in writing. However, it need not be a formal document, nor need it necessarily be addressed or delivered to the other party to the contract.

Ratification may arise from the principal's silence as well as from the principal's affirmative act or statements.

EXAMPLE
Without authorization, Alice makes a contract to sell a truckload of George's trac-

tors to Acme Company for a good price. George learns about the contract and, without saying anything, delivers the tractors to Acme. By his conduct, George has ratified the unauthorized contract that his agent made.

Implied ratification is also created by a principal's failure to repudiate an unauthorized act of his agent within a reasonable time. The principal cannot simply wait, retain the benefits of an unauthorized act or contract if it should turn out to be profitable, and yet retain a right to repudiate the act. In other words, the principal must decide whether to ratify or repudiate, and then act promptly on that decision; to promote stability in commercial transactions, it is highly important that persons who transact business with one another act with the knowledge that they will be bound by their actions.

48:5   Rights, Duties, and Liabilities of Principal and Agent

The range of an agent's duties toward the principal are determined by the scope of the authority conferred by the principal. The agent is under a duty to act only as authorized, and an agent who exceeds his authority becomes liable to the principal for damages that result from the unauthorized acts. The agent has a duty to obey all reasonable instructions of the principal. Where the instructions are clear and precise, they must be followed exactly.

An agent, as a fiduciary, has the obligation to disclose to the principal all facts relevant to the agency. For example, if the principal has instructed the agent to sell property on certain specified terms or at a particular price, and the agent later learns that other or more advantageous terms or a better price could be obtained, the agent is obligated to communicate this to the principal. An agent also has a duty not to act against the principal by serving or acquiring any private interest in his capacity as an agent. For example, an agent cannot engage in competition with the principal or gain any unfair advantage or secret profit in an agency transaction. Furthermore, an agent cannot furnish to others or use for himself, in opposition to the principal, any information he receives confidentially from the principal or acquires in the course of the agency. The following case illustrates the situation in which an agent breached his fiduciary duties to the principal.

Baskin
v
Dam
4 Conn Cir 702, 239 A2d 549
(Connecticut Court of Appeals, 1967)

[Baskin sued Erik Dam, Earle Everett, Jr., and the J. D. Real Estate Company for damages. He claimed that he had engaged the defendants as agents to

search for and negotiate the purchase of a building lot in the town of Manchester but that when they found a suitable lot they dealt with it as their own property, breaching their fiduciary relationship to him. The trial court ruled in favor of Baskin, holding that the defendants had breached the terms of their agency relationship with him. The defendants then appealed.]

Dearington, Judge.

*   *   *

The [trial court's] finding . . . indicates that the plaintiff went to the office of the J. D. Real Estate Company on May 9, 1966, and talked with the head of the company and the defendant Everett, one of the company's salesmen, in respect to purchasing a lot in the Middle Heights section of Manchester. The plaintiff instructed Everett to find a lot for him in this area although nothing definite was agreed on as to either the price of such a lot or the commission for finding one. A few days later the defendant Dam, a co-salesman with Everett of the J. D. Real Estate Company, contacted the plaintiff and told him he was working on his account. The defendants gave the plaintiff several leads in the area, and Dam told potential sellers in the area that a Mr. Baskin was looking for a lot to buy. The defendants, while looking for such a lot for the plaintiff, found a lot owned by Paul Hublard. They reported to the plaintiff that they owned a lot in the area (the Hublard lot), and the plaintiff agreed to purchase the lot. The defendants did not then own the Hublard lot but purchased it for $5000 on May 26, 1966, and then rescinded their agreement with the plaintiff and sold the lot to Paul Kiernan for $6700. No disclosure was made to the plaintiff of the circumstances surrounding the purchase of this lot. Kiernan had previously inquired about a lot, but no obligations existed between him and the defendants. During this time the defendants were acting as agents for the plaintiff. . . .

As briefed by the parties, the basic issue relates to an alleged agency. The plaintiff claims an agency was created and that the defendants violated their fiduciary duty in that they acted adversely to his interest in the transaction involving the lot. The defendants maintain that they were acting in a routine manner and had a sale been effected in respect to the plaintiff they would at most have become an agent of the seller. . . .

There appears to be no serious question that the defendants were attempting to locate a lot for the plaintiff in the area designated by him. Their conversations and activities negative any other conclusion. The trial court in its memorandum placed great weight upon the testimony of Lincoln Murphy and Olga Cowles, owners of property in the Middle Heights area, in arriving at its conclusion that agency had been established. Murphy testified that "Mr. Dam approached me and the gist of the conversation was that he did have a client and he was acting to purchase land in the area for . . . one Mr. Baskin. . . ." Mrs. Cowles testified that during the interview "I did ask Mr. Dam—Well, I was a little confused as to what would happen if we had a buyer, and he was the seller of the lot, and of course, we had gone to him asking him to sell the lot for us, who would pay a commission of such a deal, and he said Mr. Baskin would." Such evidence went a long way in destroying the defendants' claim that they were acting in a routine manner and had a sale been effected they would have been agents of the seller. . . .

An agent employed to purchase for another, cannot purchase for himself, whether he be actually or constructively an agent. He is, in such case, a trustee for his employer. . . . The principal must have full knowledge that his agent is purchasing the subject matter and he must consent to it. . . . Nor can a dual agency exist, with the alleged agent attempting to represent adversary parties, unless there be a disclosure and consent by both parties. . . . Nor can an agent who is employed to purchase property purchase it himself and attempt to resell it to his principal at a profit to himself. . . . The very relationship implies that the principal has reposed some trust or confidence in the agent and that the agent or employee is obligated to exercise the utmost good faith, loyalty and honesty toward his principal or employer. . . . This rule is not confined to a particular class of persons but is a rule of universal application to all persons coming within its principle. . . .

[Judgment affirmed.]

Agent's Duty to Hold Money or Property   Money or property held by an agent is held in trust and must be applied for the purposes of the agency. The agent is under a duty to use reasonable care to protect the principal's property by keeping it in a safe place and protecting it from being lost, destroyed, or stolen. Money or property that the agent receives for the principal must be paid promptly to the principal.

Payment made to an agent who has authority to collect payment is equivalent to payment to the principal. This payment is complete when the money is delivered into the agent's hands and discharges any indebtedness the third person owes the principal. The debt is considered paid even though the agent may subsequently misappropriate the money or fail to turn it over to the principal.

Agent's Duty to Exercise Reasonable Care and Skill   An agent must exercise reasonable care and skill in the discharge of his agency. "Reasonable skill" is that skill possessed by persons usually engaged in the same occupation or business. Accordingly, an agent who represents himself as having particular skills and talents in a field assumes an obligation to exercise the care and skill that persons of similar expertise in the same field would have. Errors of judgment *not* due to the agent's lack of reasonable skill will not render the agent liable to the principal.

Principal's Rights   The principal is entitled to all rights and benefits that result from an agent's authorized acts on behalf of the principal. If the principal is named as the contracting party, a third person is bound by a contract made by an agent in the name of the principal and is liable to the principal to the same extent as he would be if the principal had contracted with him directly.

Principal's Duty to Agent   The primary duties of the principal to the agent are those that arise from the agency contract. The principal has a duty to compensate, reimburse, and indemnify the agent for services rendered or money expended in the transaction of agency business. The amount of the agent's compensation for services should be firmly fixed in the agency agreement. If it is not, the law will imply a promise on the principal's part to pay the agent a reasonable amount for those services.

In the absence of contractual provisions to the contrary, a principal is obligated to pay a sales agent commissions on any bona fide sale to a solvent purchaser. This is usually true even if the principal subsequently refuses to fill the order or the customer refuses to receive the goods or pay for them. The exception to this rule is that if the principal has reserved the right to reject orders, the agent is not entitled to the commission on orders rejected.

Remedies   A principal whose agent violates or threatens to violate the duties of the agency relationship has several available legal remedies. These remedies include a lawsuit against the agent (1) for breach of the agency contract or for failure to perform it properly; (2) for money received by the agent for the principal but not turned over by the agent; (3) for a tort, such as fraud or other dishonesty; or (4) for an accounting. In addition to these judicial remedies, the principal can also discharge the agent, rescind or cancel the agency contract, or simply refuse to pay the agreed compensation.

An agent also has remedies against the principal. The agent can, for example, sue to recover compensation that is owed to him for services rendered. An agent who is wrongfully discharged can sue the principal for damages.

48:6   Rights, Duties, and Liabilities as to Third Persons

In relation to third persons, the principal is bound by and liable for all acts performed by his agent within the actual or apparent scope of the agent's authority. This rule of liability is based not on agency principles but on those relating to the law of employer and employee. The principal can also be held liable for the torts an agent commits in the course and scope of his employment, even though the principal did not authorize, ratify, participate in, or even know of the misconduct. Liability for an agent's torts is grounded on the employer–employee principle of *respondeat superior*.[1]

Knowledge and Notice   A principal is chargeable with and bound by knowledge or notice that his agent receives from a third person while the agent is acting within the scope of his authority. Notice chargeable in this way is called *constructive notice*. A principal who has constructive notice of a fact is treated just as if he had actually received the notice. Stated another way, the principal, not the third person, has to bear the responsibility for the agent's failure to communicate. The theory is that between two innocent persons—the principal and the third person—the one setting the situation in motion should suffer the legal consequences of a wrongdoer. The imputation of the agent's knowledge to the principal has been applied in a variety of business situations. For example, an agent's knowledge of the contents of a contract can be imputed to the principal.

 Depending on the scope and purpose of an agency, it may be essential that the principal be fully and currently informed about all or at least some circumstances, as they arise, relating to the subject matter of the agency. If so, when the agency is created, the agent should be instructed as to (1) what information relating to his actions is to be communicated to the principal and (2) how the communications are to be made. The instruction should be in writing. It can be part of the contract creating the agency if a written contract is used.

Liability of Agent   An agent who negotiates and signs a contract with a third person on behalf of a principal is ordinarily not himself a party to the contract and does not intend to be personally liable under it. The agent will not be personally liable if (1) signing the contract is within the scope of the agent's authority and (2) the agent's status as an agent is known to the third person. The agent's status is usually disclosed by his signing the contract in a representative capacity, such as "National Hardware Service, by John Jacobs, Agent." If, however, nothing in the contract indicates an agency relationship between the agent and his principal, the agent might be held liable as one of the contracting parties. Furthermore, if an

---

[1]The doctrine of respondeat superior is further discussed in Chapter 51.

agent purports to act in his agency capacity in making a contract with a third person, but is actually acting without or in excess of his authority, the agent is personally liable for any damages suffered by the third person due to the agent's act.

Agent's Tort Liability   Regardless of the agency relationship, an agent is liable for any torts he commits. The agent's tort liability is based not on a contractual relationship between the principal and agent, but simply on the legal rule that every person must act in a manner that will not be harmful to another. The fact that the principal may *also* be liable for the agent's torts does not excuse the agent from liability; they can be liable jointly.

48:7   Undisclosed Agency

If the other party to a transaction conducted by an agent knows that the agent is acting for a principal and knows the principal's identity, the principal is said to be disclosed. If a third person knows or has reason to know that the agent is, or may be, acting for a principal but is unaware of the principal's identity, the principal is said to be partially disclosed. If the third person has no notice whatsoever of the fact that the agent is acting for another person, the principal—as well as the agency relationship—is said to be *undisclosed*.

Concealment of the identity of a principal is a common and sometimes necessary practice in business. For example, concealment of the identity of the true purchaser of realty may be a wise—and perfectly legal—business technique to prevent business competitors from bidding on the same property. Furthermore, concealment of a principal's true identity might enable the principal to take actions without having to concern himself with the personal feelings of some third person.

Liability of Principal and Agent   In an undisclosed agency situation in which the principal fails to perform as agreed, the other party has the option of holding either the agent or the principal (assuming his discovery of the principal's existence and identity) liable, and he has a reasonable time in which to decide whom to sue. After he decides, he must abide by the decision even though there is ultimately no satisfaction of the liability.

 To avoid the possibility of his own liability on a contract, an agent must, when the contract is made, disclose not only the agency relationship but also the principal's identity. The effect of an agent's failure to do so is illustrated in the following case.

Mawer-Gulden-Annis, Inc.

v

Brazilian & Colombian Coffee Co.
49 Ill App 2d 400, 199 NE2d 222
(Illinois Court of Appeals, 1964)

[Mawer sued Brazilian and Colombian Coffee and its president, Weinshenk, seeking damages for the value of olives that Mawer had ostensibly sold and delivered to Brazilian. In entering into the transaction with Mawer, Weinshenk did not disclose that he and his company were acting for an undisclosed

principal on whose behalf the goods were purchased. At trial, Brazilian contended that it did not purchase the olives in its own right. Brazilian argued that it was acting as a food broker and that Mawer should have known the identity of its principal from the bills of lading. The trial court found Brazilian and Weinshenk liable, and they appealed.]

Kluczynski, Justice.

*   *   *

Defendants denied they purchased the goods in their own right or for an undisclosed principal but stated that their function was as food brokers representing plaintiff in the sale wherein they would obtain a customer for plaintiff. They further state that the goods were actually delivered by plaintiff to the customer defendants obtained for the plaintiff. . . .

In the instant case the trial court, upon hearing and weighing the evidence, and passing upon the credibility of the witnesses, found that Brazilian did not disclose the name of its principal at the time of contracting. We cannot hold that these findings were against the manifest weight of the evidence especially when in its letter of June 20, 1961, . . . eight days after the confirmation and delivery, Brazilian, through Weinshenk, its president, writes, "The writer tried to contact you several times by phone and vice versa to give you the name of the buyer, but as your B/L #OZ 3990 (the bill of lading) indicates, you delivered these goods to our customers, Pantry Queen Food Products Company, and therefore you should have invoiced them for this merchandise directly."

In [an early Illinois case] the court said:

"It is a settled rule in verbal contracts, if the agent does not disclose his agency and name his principal, he binds himself and becomes subject to all liabilities, express and implied, created by the contract and transaction, in the same manner as if he were the principal in

interest. . . . And the fact that the agent is known to be a commission merchant, auctioneer, or other professional agent, makes no difference. . . ."

The duty is upon the agent, who wishes to avoid liability, to disclose the name or identity of his principal clearly and in such a manner as to bring such adequately to the actual notice of the other party, and it is not sufficient that the third person has knowledge of facts and circumstances which would, if reasonably followed by inquiry, disclose the identity of the principal. . . . The reason for the rule is [the] necessity for disclosing who the principals are to give the contracting party the opportunity to make inquiry as to the fact, and then to determine whether he is satisfied that such persons are the principals of the agent, and if they are, then whether such party is willing to extend credit to such principals. . . .

The defendant's argument that the plaintiff is chargeable with knowledge of the principal from the fact that the carrier allegedly called and spoke to the shipping clerk regarding the olives and that the bill of lading made out by the shipping clerk showed Pantry Queen as the consignee, when taken together with the fact that defendant is generally known as a broker, is untenable.

Even if we assume plaintiff, from the above circumstances, had learned the identity of the principal, such information was not so timely as to relieve defendant of liability. To avoid personal liability, disclosure of the principal must be made at the time of contracting, otherwise either the agent or the subsequently disclosed principal may be held. . . . Defendant, not having informed plaintiff of the customer for whom it was purchasing, therefore, contracted as a principal, and cannot now complain if it is held liable as such. . . .

Affirmed.

48:8   Duration and Termination of Agency

Duration of an agency relationship is determined by the agency agreement. If no time is specified, the agency relationship will expire at the end of a reasonable time or on completion of the purpose of the agency.

Principal's Power to Revoke   The principal's power to revoke an agent's authority is not absolute. That is, actions of an agent could continue to bind a principal as to third persons after the principal has revoked the agent's authority if the third person does not know of the revocation and relies on the continued existence of the agency.

 Disputes and litigation can be prevented if a principal who has revoked his agent's authority notifies any persons who have dealt with the agent that the agency relationship no longer exists.

Termination by Operation of Law   In some situations an agency is said to be terminated "by operation of law," meaning simply that the circumstances are such that in the interest of fairness the law automatically terminates the agency. These circumstances include (1) the death of the principal or agent; (2) either party's inability to continue to perform, such as due to illness; (3) loss or destruction of the subject matter of the agreement; and (4) a change in business conditions, value of the subject matter, or identity of the principal.

48:9   Power of Attorney

A *power of attorney* is a written instrument by which a person, acting as a principal, appoints another as his agent, conferring on that person the authority to perform certain acts on his behalf. The writing is sometimes also called a letter of attorney. The word "attorney" is used simply to designate a particular type of principal–agent relationship. An agent acting under a power of attorney is referred to as an attorney in fact and may or may not be an attorney at law.

Some states require a power of attorney to convey real property or any interest in it to be prepared with the same formalities as a deed or mortgage (see Chapters 34 and 35). Some states also require these powers of attorney to be recorded with a designated public official.

Types of Powers   The purpose of a power of attorney is to serve as tangible evidence of the agent's authority to third persons with whom the agent may deal. A power of attorney can be *general*, which means that the agent is authorized to act in any manner consistent with the general business or purposes of the principal. It can also be *special*, which means that the agent can act only to perform specified tasks. A power of attorney can also be partly general and partly special.

EXAMPLE
Prince wants to sell some of his property, tracts 1, 2, and 3. He can grant a sales

agent a general power (sell any or all of the tracts to whoever will pay the best price) or a special power (sell tract 1 to Jones for no less than $10,000). However, Prince can also grant a partly general and partly special power (sell tracts 1 and 3 to whoever will pay the best price, but sell tract 2 only to Balboa for no less than $15,000).

Interpretation of Power of Attorney   The key rule in interpreting a power of attorney is that the parties' intention as it existed when the power was granted is controlling. Furthermore, powers of attorney are strictly construed. This means, for example, that a given instrument will be held to grant *only* those powers that are specified in it. For these reasons, any power of attorney should set forth as many of the important aspects of the agency being created as possible, including the following:

- Status of the principal, such as whether an individual or a business entity
- Type of power of attorney being granted
- Nature of the property and property rights that are to be subject to the power
- Nature of the ownership of the property that is to be subject to the power
- Scope and extent of powers granted
- Effective date of the power, and its duration

Some powers of attorney set forth the manner in which the power being granted is to be executed. If this is done, the attorney in fact must act precisely as directed.

Key Concepts and Terms

- Agency is a fiduciary relationship. It arises when one person (the principal) confides to another (the agent) the management of a business or performance of a transaction to be carried out by the agent in the principal's name and subject to the principal's control. Any person or organization having the capacity to act can act through an agent.
- The agency relationship ordinarily is created by agreement of the principal and agent. The agreement is often express, but it can also be implied if the relationship can be reasonably inferred from the surrounding circumstances.
- Agency can be created when a person permits another to act for him and, by so doing, causes third persons to reasonably believe that an agency has been created. This is called agency by estoppel.
- Agency by necessity is an agency that is created in certain emergency situations in which it is proper for one person to act for another without having the express authority to do so.
- Under the doctrine of apparent or ostensible authority, if the principal conducts business so as to cause third persons to reasonably believe that the agent possesses authority to act in the principal's name, the principal will be bound by the agent's acts. Determination of ostensible authority is made by examining actions of the principal, not the agent.

- A principal sometimes expressly authorizes an agent to delegate the agent's authority to another person, a subagent. The subagent then represents the principal as if he had been directly appointed by the principal.

- Ratification is a principal's adoption of his agent's prior act, which did not bind the principal but was done or professed to be done on his account. It can be express (orally or in writing) or implied from the acts or conduct of the principal subsequent to the act.

- An agent must obey all reasonable instructions of the principal and is required to exercise the utmost good faith, loyalty, and honesty toward the principal. He must also exercise reasonable care and skill. The principal has the duty to compensate, reimburse, and indemnify an agent for services rendered or money spent in the transaction of agency business.

- The principal is liable for torts performed by the agent within the actual or apparent scope of the agent's authority. The agent is also liable for his torts.

- The extent to which an agent conceals the identity of the principal determines whether the agency is disclosed, partially disclosed, or undisclosed.

- Duration of an agency is determined by agreement between the principal and agent. If no time is specified, the agency expires at the end of a reasonable time or on completion of the purpose of the agency. An agency can also be terminated by operation of law.

- A power of attorney is a written instrument by which a person, acting as principal, appoints another as his agent, conferring on the agent the authority to perform certain acts on the principal's behalf.

- Agency
- Agency by Necessity
- Apparent (Ostensible) Authority
- Constructive Notice
- Fiduciary Relationship
- General Power
- Implied Authority

- Power of Attorney
- Ratification
- Respondeat Superior
- Special Power
- Subagent
- Undisclosed Agency

Questions and Case Problems

1. Why is the agency relationship termed a fiduciary relationship between the principal and the agent?

2. Rosen visits Deporter Tours. She brings with her a brochure published under the name of World Trek, advertising an African safari. Deporter agrees to arrange for Rosen to join the safari, which is to begin in Cairo. Rosen pays $1,200 for the tour, and Deporter forwards that sum, minus a ten percent commission, to World Trek. Because Rosen plans to tour Europe on a casual and unscheduled basis for several months before joining the safari, she and Deporter exchange contact addresses. Rosen goes about her travels, and she receives no further word about the safari. On the starting date for the safari, she turns up in Cairo but finds no sign of the safari nor anyone who has even heard of World Trek. Rosen subsequently learns from Deporter that the meeting place for the safari was changed to Nairobi, and that World Trek had been unable to contact her to let her know. This happened

because Deporter had failed to communicate Rosen's contact address to World Trek. Rosen sues Deporter for recovery of the $1,200 tour price, claiming that the agency breached its agreement to arrange the tour and thus prevented her from going on the safari. How should the case be decided?

3. Grimes meets Artug at a party where he offers to help Artug find a publisher for Artug's new book "solely as a friend." Grimes forgets about his promise and does nothing to find a publisher for the manuscript. Has an agency relationship been created? Is Grimes liable to Artug for breach of contract?

4. Delta Corp. is in the business of servicing mobile-home purchase contracts. For a fee, it handles the collection of monthly payments from mobile-home buyers. Delta acquires these accounts by making agreements with dealers in mobile homes, or with the banks that financed them. Donald is a Delta representative in Arizona, and he has authority to solicit accounts from banks and dealers. The president of Western Coach Corporation, a retail seller of mobile homes, tells Donald that she knows of a Texas company that has a portfolio of $2 million in mobile-home contracts that it wants to sell. Donald sees an opportunity to place these contracts in banks with which Delta does business. Thus, he agrees to pay Western Coach Corporation five percent of the gross charges in transferring this portfolio, as a "finder's fee," and he and Western Coach sign a contract to this effect. Subsequently, Delta Corporation refuses to pay the five percent to Western Coach, denying that Donald had any authority to bind it to any such agreement. Did Donald have this authority? Why?

5. What circumstances tend to show that a principal has ratified the actions of his agent? What effect does ratification have?

6. How does an agency created by a power of attorney differ from an ordinary agency relationship? Does it always differ?

7. Ralph's business manager receives a check payable to Ralph. The manager indorses Ralph's name on the check, cashes it, and keeps the money. Ralph sues the bank for the amount of the check. How should the case be decided?

8. Williams is a sales representative for Ace Co, a publisher of books for the medical profession. Her job is to visit doctors, hospitals, and other potential customers, and to solicit orders for books from Ace's line. She is paid a 25 percent commission on all sales. On leaving Dr. Boyd's office after making an unsuccessful sales presentation, Williams notices a valuable painting on the wall of Boyd's waiting room. Angered by her failure to make a sale, Williams defaces the painting. Boyd discovers who ruined his painting and sues Ace for its value. Is Ace liable for Williams' act?

9. Janet frequently buys heavy machinery from various suppliers for the Kendall Construction Co., of which she is the general purchasing agent. Two months after she leaves that job, Janet buys two tractors from a former supplier without stating that the tractors are not being bought for Kendall. After defaulting on the purchase, Janet is sued by the supplier, who also sues Kendall. Discuss the liability of all the parties.

10. Crestview Co. authorizes Haven to buy a new generator for the company plant. Haven enters into an agreement with Genco and signs the agreement, "Crestview Company, by its agent Haven." Can Genco enforce the agreement against Crestview? Against Haven?

49 Independent Contractor Relationship

49:1 Introduction

This chapter examines one of the most common employment relationships, that between an employer and an independent contractor. Like the chapter on agency (Chapter 48), this chapter emphasizes the importance of anticipating problems and preventing disputes that could lead to legal liability. It treats the general principles governing the creation of the relationship, the liability of the employer for injuries caused by his own negligence or by that of his independent contractor, and the liability of the contractor for injuries to others during the course of the job and after its completion.

An *independent contractor* is a person who contracts to render services using his own means and methods to perform the work. He is accountable to the employer only for the final product of the work. In other words, the contractor is not under the *control* of the employer. If, on the other hand, the employer has the power to control not only the nature of the final product of the work but also the order, method, or plan of the work itself, the hired person is an ordinary employee.

A particular worker's status as an independent contractor is of considerable significance to the employer. One reason is that the employer of an independent contractor is usually not liable for the contractor's torts. This sets the employer apart from the principal in an agency relationship, who is liable for the agent's torts (see Chapter 48) and from an ordinary employer, who is liable for his employee's torts (see Chapter 51). Independent contractor status is also important because independent contractors are not usually covered under workers' compensation and other labor legislation. This means that, for example, the employer will not be held accountable for injuries suffered by the contractor on the job.[1]

 An employer cannot always take advantage of the benefits that are available with an independent contractor relationship. For example, if an employer's

---

[1]Workers' compensation is discussed in Chapter 51. Other labor legislation, such as the federal Fair Labor Standards Act, which sets minimum wages, is discussed in Chapters 51 and 52.

words or conduct lead a third person to believe that a worker is an employee, the employer cannot later escape liability for the worker's tort by claiming that the worker was actually an independent contractor. The same is true if the employer has admitted his own liability for the worker's tort and the injured person has sued the employer in reliance on this admission.

49:2   Existence of the Relationship

There is no rigid rule to determine whether a hired worker is an employee or an independent contractor. Each case is decided on its own facts. Over the years the courts have looked to the "realities of the relationship" between the employer and the worker to determine the worker's status. The basic determinative factor is the extent of the employer's control over the worker and the work.

Whether an employer has the right to control the work can sometimes be determined from the contract of employment. If the contract is silent about whether the employer has any right to control the contractor's work methods, the existence or nonexistence of control will be determined from all the circumstances. Some factors that indicate an *absence* of employer control—and therefore an independent contractor relationship—are (1) the existence of a contract for the performance of a certain type or piece of work at a fixed price; (2) the independent nature of the worker's business; (3) the worker's employment of assistants, with the right to supervise their activities; (4) the worker's obligation to furnish necessary tools, supplies, and materials; (5) the worker's right to control the progress of the work; (6) the time for which the worker is employed; (7) payment by job rather than by amount of time worked; and (8) the contracted work not being a part of the employer's regular business.

Factors that indicate the *presence* of employer control over the worker—and therefore an employer–employee relationship—include (1) the employer's right to discharge the worker or terminate the contract; (2) periodic payment rather than payment for either the completed job or completed phases of it; (3) the employer's furnishing or selecting the worker's assistants or equipment; and (4) the employer's possession and control of the premises on which the work is being performed.

In the following decision, the court discusses the factors it considered in determining whether a worker was an independent contractor. Note the court's emphasis on the extent of the employer's control over the worker.

Massey
v
Tube Art Display, Inc.
15 Wash App 782, 551 P2d 1387
(Washington Court of Appeals, 1976)

[Redford was hired by Tube Art Display Company to remove a sign. In so doing, he struck a gas pipeline, causing an explosion that injured people and property. The injured persons sued Tube Art on the theory that as an employer, Tube Art was liable for the negligence of its employee, Redford. Tube Art argued that it was not liable since Redford was only its independent contractor. The trial judge ruled that Redford was an employee and that Tube Art was liable. Tube Art appealed.]

Swanson, Judge.

*   *   *

Traditionally, servants . . . have been looked upon as persons employed to perform services in the affairs of others under an express or implied agreement, and who, with respect to physical conduct in the performance of those services, [are] subject to the other's control or right of control. . . .

An independent contractor, on the other hand, is generally defined as one who contracts to perform services for another, but who is not controlled by the other nor subject to the other's right to control with respect to his physical conduct in performing the services. . . .

In determining whether one acting for another is a servant or independent contractor, several factors must be taken into consideration. These are . . . as follows:

(a) the extent of control which, by the agreement, the master may exercise over the details of the work;

(b) whether or not the one employed is engaged in a distinct occupation or business;

(c) the kind of occupation, with reference to whether, in the locality, the work is usually done under the direction of the employer or by a specialist without supervision;

(d) the skill required in the particular occupation;

(e) whether the employer or the workman supplies the instrumentalities, tools, and the place of work for the person doing the work;

(f) the length of time for which the person is employed;

(g) the method of payment, whether by the time or by the job;

(h) whether or not the work is a part of the regular business of the employer;

(i) whether or not the parties believe they are creating the relation of master and servant; and

(j) whether the principal is or is not in business.

All of these factors are of varying importance in determining the type of relationship involved and, with the exception of the element of control, not all the elements need be present. . . . It is the right to control another's physical conduct that is the essential and oftentimes decisive factor in establishing . . . whether the person controlled is a servant . . . .

In discussing the actual extent to which the element of control must be exercised, we pointed out in [an earlier case] that the plaintiff need not show that the [employer] controlled or had the right to control every aspect of the [employee's] operation in order to incur vicarious liability. Rather,

> [i]t should be sufficient that plaintiff present substantial evidence of . . . control or right of control over those activities from whence the actionable negligence flowed. If the rule were otherwise, then a person wishing to accomplish a certain result through another could declare the other to be an independent contractor generally, and yet retain control over a particularly hazardous part of the undertaking without incurring liability for acts arising out of that part. Such a result would effectively thwart the purpose of the rules of vicarious liability. . . .

In making his ruling that Tube Art was responsible as a matter of law for Redford's actions the trial judge stated,

> I think that under the undisputed evidence in this case they not only had the right to control, but they did control. They controlled the location of the spot to dig. They controlled the dimensions. They controlled the excavation and they got the building permits. They did all of the discretionary work that was necessary before he started to operate. They knew that the method of excavation was going to be by use of a backhoe rather than a pick and shovel which might have made a lit-

tle difference on the exposure in this situation. They in effect created the whole atmosphere in which he worked. And the fact that even though he did not work for them all of the time and they paid him on a piece-work basis for the individual job didn't impress me particularly when they used him the number of times they did. Most of the time they used him for this type of work.. . .

Our review of the evidence supports the trial court's evaluation of both the right and exercise of control even though Redford had been essentially self-employed for about 5 years at the time of trial, was free to work for other contractors, selected the time of day to perform the work assigned, paid his own income and business taxes and did not participate in any of Tube Art's employee programs. The testimony

advanced at trial, which we find determinative, established that during the previous 3 years Redford had worked exclusively for sign companies and 90 percent of his time for Tube Art. He had no employees, was not registered as a contractor or subcontractor, was not bonded, did not himself obtain permits or licenses for his jobs, and dug the holes at locations and in dimensions in exact accordance with the instructions of his employer. In fact, Redford was left no discretion with regard to the placement of the excavations that he dug. Rather, it was his skill in digging holes pursuant to the exact dimensions prescribed that caused him to be preferred over other backhoe operators.. . .

[Judgment affirmed.]

 An employer always has the right to see that the contractor's work is performed according to contract specifications. Thus, the employer's retention of the right to supervise or inspect work for this purpose as it progresses does not change the worker's status from independent contractor to employee.

49:3 Liability of Employer, Generally

The traditional rule is that an employer of an independent contractor is not liable for the contractor's torts committed in the performance of the work the contractor was hired to perform. The theory is that since the employer does not possess the power to control the details of the contractor's work, the employer should not have to answer for injuries resulting from the way the work is carried out. However, so many exceptions to the traditional rule have been created in recent years that the rule now serves primarily as a preamble to the list of its exceptions.

Exceptions to Employer's Nonliability   Exceptions to an employer's nonliability for the contractor's acts are based on the public policy that a person should not be relieved of the consequences of acts simply by delegating performance to another person. These exceptions arise when the employer is in some way at fault in bringing about or contributing to the contractor-caused injuries. Thus, for example, the employer can be liable for injuries sustained where (1) he interferes with the performance of the work and fails to exercise due care over whatever control he has assumed, (2) he has ratified the acts resulting in injury, (3) the work involved unlawful or tortious conduct, (4) he was negligent in selecting the independent contractor (this important exception is discussed further in 49:4), (5) he furnished the contractor with incompetent employees or defective tools, or (6) an employee of the contractor was injured as a result of defects existing on the employer's premises before the work began.

Another important exception to the employer's nonliability for the independent contractor's torts arises where the contractor fails to exercise due care in performing work that is *inherently dangerous*. The employer is liable on the theory that where danger is inherent in the nature of the work, it is only fair that the employer be responsible for injury resulting from it. "Inherently dangerous" work is work necessarily attended with danger no matter how skillfully or carefully it is performed. For example, the construction of a skyscraper in a populous city, the operation of certain types of machinery, and the use of pesticides could be considered inherently dangerous.

 An employer hiring a contractor should make certain that the contract specifically provides that the contractor must assume liability for harm to a third person arising from the contractor's negligence and that the contractor must carry insurance to cover this obligation.

Employer's Nondelegable Duties   Some duties that an employer requests a contractor to assume are *nondelegable*. That is, an employer must retain responsibility for certain acts. For example, if a person is required to perform street repair work in conformance with an ordinance, he cannot relieve himself of that duty by contracting with another to do the work, nor can he escape responsibility on the theory that restoration of the street is under the independent contractor's control.

49:4   Lack of Care in Selecting Independent Contractor

An employer who failed to exercise reasonable care in selecting a competent independent contractor is liable for that contractor's negligence. A competent contractor is one who has the knowledge, skill, equipment, personal characteristics, and experience reasonably necessary to perform the required job without creating an unreasonable risk of harm to third persons.

Criteria of Care in Selection of Contractor   In determining whether an employer has been negligent in checking the qualifications of an independent contractor, the courts have noted that the employer should pay particular attention to the contractor's age, experience, training for the work to be performed, and reputation. Courts have also looked to whether the contractor was licensed to do the work contracted for and was properly equipped to perform the work. The following case illustrates a situation in which an employer failed to take reasonable measures to investigate the competency of the independent contractor and was therefore liable for the contractor's negligence.

Hudgens

v

Cook Industries, Inc.
521 P2d 813, 78 ALR3d 902
(Oklahoma Supreme Court, 1974)

[Edwards, a trucker, was under contract with Cook Industries to haul wheat. While driving his truck, Edwards hit a car and injured Davis, a passenger in the car. Davis sued Cook Industries on the theory that it negligently hired an incompetent driver who used defective equipment. The trial court entered judgment for Cook, and Davis appealed.]

Hodges, Justice.

*   *   *

[The evidence revealed] that: Edwards was a reckless driver with a lengthy history of prior arrests and accidents; he consistently and repeatedly hauled loads in excess of the legal weight limits (some violations occurring during his employment by Cook); he was a person with a lengthy history of drinking intoxicating beverages while operating motor vehicles; he had no permit to haul grain in the State of Oklahoma at the time of the accident; he did not comply with safety regulations promulgated by the Federal Highway Administration; his equipment was grossly defective and unsafe for operation upon the public highways. . . .

Other evidence disclosed that the truck was 13,000 pounds overweight at the time of the accident. . . .

It was Edwards' testimony that Cook did not require him to fill out an application to haul nor did they make any inquiry concerning his ability or equipment.

The testimony of the truck manager for Cook was that Cook did not provide written or oral instructions to him relating to trucker selection. This was left to his discretion. It was

his policy, and therefore that of the company, to make no inquiries as to ability, experience, driving record, traffic violations, criminal offenses, equipment, necessary permits, validity of drivers license, liability or cargo insurance. He just "assumed" everything was in order. It was his assumption that Edwards had the necessary permits and insurance, but no check was ever made to determine if he actually did. Edwards made at least fifty trips for Cook under these assumptions.

The truck manager for Union Equity, who like Cook, was a grain exporter engaged in the purchase of wheat for overseas sale stated that it was the policy of his company to hire no truckers unless they were able to produce a certificate of insurance showing that they possessed both cargo and liability insurance. This requirement was to protect the public and to insure against any loss of cargo. The records maintained by him revealed that Edwards had applied on two occasions to haul wheat for Union Equity, but that he had been rejected on both occasions. . . .

Generally, an employer is not liable for the torts of an independent contractor, but there are many exceptions to the rule. . . .

One of the conditions under which the employer is relieved of liability for the negligent acts of an independent contractor which he has employed is when the employer has borne the duty which requires him to exercise due care in selecting a competent contractor for the necessary work. . . .

"Competent contractor" is defined as one who possesses the knowledge, skill, experience, personal characteristics, and available equipment which a reasonable man would realize that an independent contractor must have in order to do the work which he contracts to do without creating unreasonable risk of injury to others. . . .

Where there is foreseeable risk of harm to others unless precautions are taken, it is the duty of one who is regularly engaged in a

commercial enterprise which involves selection of motor carriers as an integral part of the
business, to exercise reasonable care to select a
competent carrier. . . . If there is competent evidence tending to show that such employer
*knew, or in the exercise of reasonable care should
have known,* that the independent contractor
was not such a driver, and reasonable men
might draw conflicting conclusions on the
matter, then whether or not the employer was
negligent in the discharge of his duty to select
a competent contractor becomes a question to
be determined by the trier of the fact. [Court's
emphasis.] . . .

[Judgment reversed.]

 To minimize legal liability for a contractor's negligence, an employer should,
prior to hiring the contractor, make a careful inquiry about his qualifications.
The extent of the necessary investigation is determined from the nature of
the work to be performed. For example, if the contractor is to be hired for a
job requiring special skills and involving potential danger to the public, such
as driving a gasoline tank truck, a more thorough inquiry into the contractor's qualifications will be necessary than if the job is a routine or unskilled
one.

Employer's Subsequent Knowledge of Contractor's Incompetence   An employer can be liable for the contractor's negligence if, although the employer was
originally unaware that the contractor was careless or incompetent, he acquired
such knowledge after the contractor commenced the work. An employer who permits the contractor to continue working after learning of his incompetence could
be negligent for failure to terminate the relationship, even though there was no
negligence in hiring the contractor.

49:5   Liability of Independent Contractor

An independent contractor who agrees to perform a job makes the implied promise to perform that job in a skillful, safe, and professional manner. Therefore, he is
liable for negligent acts that he or his employees commit. This rule applies regardless of whether the person who hired him is also liable for the contractor's negligence. Furthermore, a contractor has the duty to make sure that the rights of other
persons, be they persons on the premises, employees of the hiring party, or simply
other contractors on the job, are not injured by his work.

Liability after Completion of Work   The general rule is that the liability of an
independent contractor ceases once his work has been completed and turned over
to and accepted by the employer. Under this rule, even though the contractor may
have failed to perform the contract properly or with due care, the employer assumes responsibility for defects once the job is done. There are, however, exceptions to the general rule. For example, an independent contractor may remain
liable after turning over defective work if (1) the defect was so concealed that the
employer could not reasonably detect it; (2) the contractor fraudulently concealed

the defect; or (3) the finished work constituted a nuisance, was inherently dangerous, or was so negligently defective that it was imminently dangerous to third persons.

Key Concepts and Terms

- An independent contractor is a worker who contracts to do certain work according to his own methods, without being subject to the employer's control.
- Factors that indicate independent contractor status are (1) the existence of a contract for performance of a specified job at a fixed price; (2) the independent nature of the contractor's business; (3) the contractor's employment of assistants and retention of the right to supervise their activities; (4) the contractor's duty to furnish his own tools and supplies; and (5) the fact that the work is not part of the employer's regular business.
- An employer always has the right to see that the contract is performed according to specifications. His retention of the right to check over the independent contractor's work as it progresses does not change the contractor's status to that of an employee.
- An independent contractor is liable for negligent acts that he or his employees commit.
- The general rule, subject to several exceptions, is that once a contractor's work has been completed and accepted by the employer, the employer is then liable for later injuries resulting from the work.

- Control
- Independent Contractor
- Inherently Dangerous
- Nondelegable Duties

Questions and Case Problems

1. From an employer's point of view, what is the significance of a worker's being an independent contractor rather than an employee?
2. Hoosier Engineering, an independent contractor, contracts with CG&E, a power and gas company, for the replacement of some of CG&E's power poles, wires, and related equipment. The contract calls for transferring the power from the old circuitry to the new as soon as the work is completed. Tedesco is a Hoosier lineman, one of a crew of four. After completing his work on the last of the new poles being installed, he is about to descend when a short circuit occurs in front of him. The flash temporarily blinds him, and he loses his balance. Because he has failed to secure his safety belt, Tedesco falls and is seriously injured. The new circuitry should not have been "live" at the time of the accident, but another Hoosier employee had turned on the power prematurely. Tedesco sues CG&E for his injuries. How should the court decide the case?
3. Cole Department Store hires the Baker Security Service in an effort to reduce shoplifting. Baker assigns two uniformed and armed security guards to the store. While on duty, one of the guards bends over to tie his shoe. He has forgotten to fasten his pistol in his holster, and the pistol falls to the floor and discharges,

injuring Doris, a customer. Doris sues Cole Department Store for damages. Should she win the case? Why?

4. Roger owns a skyscraper in a large city. He hires a window-washing firm to maintain and clean the windows in his building. During the course of routine window cleaning, one of the workers drops a bucket, which injures a bystander in the street below. Is Roger liable for the injury? Discuss. Would Roger be liable if one of the workers fell while cleaning windows? Discuss.

5. Mark hires an independent contractor to sandblast the outside of a building and supplies him with sandblasting equipment to perform the work. While performing the job, the contractor is injured when the air hose on the sandblaster, which is in bad repair, ruptures. Is Mark liable for the contractor's injury? Discuss. Would it make any difference if the contractor had known before beginning the work that the equipment was defective? Would it make any difference if the hose was new and there was no indication that it was defective?

6. Under what circumstances is an employer not permitted to assert the independent contractor status of a worker even though, at the time in question, the worker was in fact an independent contractor?

7. Brown needs a high retaining wall to be built on her land. The wall must be specially designed because of the steep slope of the land and the unstable condition of the soil. Brown accepts bids for the project from several general contractors, but she rejects all of them as being too high. She then contracts with her friend Peters to do the work for far less than what any of the contractors had quoted. Peters' only relevant experience is that he has built several low divider walls on level ground. Although he has no professional qualifications to do Brown's job, he states that he can do it satisfactorily. The wall designed and built by Peters gives way, damaging adjoining property. The neighbor sues Brown for damages. How should the case be decided? Why?

8. Eddy owns a dump truck. He contracts with Northpoint Gravel Co. for delivering gravel to various of Northpoint's customers. Each day Northpoint gives Eddy the necessary details about gravel orders to be filled that day. Eddy pays all his operating expenses, and he makes all decisions as to the size of each load he hauls, the number of loads hauled each day, and the routes he takes in making deliveries. While making a delivery to one of Northpoint's customers, Eddy negligently runs over and injures Adams, one of the customer's employees. Adams sues Northpoint, claiming that Eddy is its employee. Is Adams correct? Discuss.

9. An amendment to the local fire code requires that an approved smoke detection and sprinkler system be installed in all apartment buildings containing five or more units. Warren owns a large apartment building. She hires Dooley, an independent contractor, to do all the work necessary to upgrade the building in compliance with the new fire code requirement. Without Warren's knowledge, Dooley installs a cheap, nonapproved smoke detection and sprinker system. Before the work is even completed there is a fire, and one of the tenants is injured. It is established that the injury would not have occurred had the work already done by Dooley been in compliance with the fire code requirement. The tenant sues Warren, and Warren denies liability on the ground that Dooley is responsible. How should the court decide the case?

10. Carey owns and operates an apple orchard. He hires an independent contractor to spray the orchard with a pesticide. Carey's neighbor uses land adjoining the orchard for growing vegetables organically, that is, without the use of any chemi-

cals. Organically-grown vegetables are worth twice as much as those grown by conventional methods. While the contractor is spraying Carey's orchard, the wind starts blowing, and it carries some of the pesticide onto the vegetables growing on the adjacent land. Is Carey liable to his neighbor for the damage done to the organic crop? Is the contractor liable to the neighbor?

50 Accountant Relationship

50:1 Introduction

The accountant plays a major role in modern business because it is he who monitors a business' financial system. Clearly, the accountant is regarded as being an expert in money matters. When he is hired, he gains access to a business' confidential financial information and can be called on to perform complicated or technical tasks. The accountant is responsible for, among other things, conducting audits—which entails the examination of business or financial records—preparing tax returns, and consulting with businesses and individuals about money management.

Usually an accountant is hired on a contract basis. The contract creates a relationship between the accountant and the employer, imposing on each person certain duties, rights, and liabilities, which are discussed in this chapter.

Unauthorized Practice of Law Accountants are often asked to give advice on all phases of setting up and running a business. Because the accountant must interpret government rules and regulations in giving advice, he runs the risk of being guilty of practicing law without a license to do so. To a degree, an accountant cannot properly represent his clients without giving some legal advice in connection with the practice of his ordinary work in keeping books and records and in preparing tax returns. At the same time, the accountant is generally barred from giving strictly legal advice or answering legal questions having no connection with his ordinary work. The following case illustrates the often fine line that exists between accounting and the practice of law.

Bancroft

v

Indemnity Ins. Co.
203 F Supp 49
(United States District Court, Louisiana, 1962)

[Bancroft hired an accountant in regard to a tax problem. The accountant gave Bancroft erroneous information, subjecting him to an additional tax assessment. Before paying the additional assessment, however, Bancroft sought further advice from the accountant and the Internal Revenue Service. The accountant erroneously advised Bancroft that the

tax was legal and properly assessed and that he would be unsuccessful if he attempted to obtain a refund. Due to this advice, Bancroft did not apply for a refund, although he was entitled to one. On learning of the accountant's errors, Bancroft sued the accountant and the accountant's liability insurer. In defending its own interest in the case, the insurer argued that (1) the accountant had improperly given legal advice and had therefore committed a crime; (2) the insurance policy did not cover criminal conduct of the insured; and (3) as a result, it was not liable to Bancroft for the loss he suffered due to the accountant's negligence.]

Ben C. Dawkins, Jr., Chief Judge.

*   *   *

Defendant contends that the advice given plaintiffs by the [accountant] was not within the proper area of accounting; that his opinion actually was a legal view which lawfully could be rendered only by a licensed attorney-at-law; that, therefore, the [accountant] committed a crime . . . and that [he cannot] be held liable for his negligently rendering legal advice because plaintiffs knew that he was not licensed to practice law. Defendant urges, [therefore], that its professional liability policy does not extend coverage to the risk of liability for [the] performance of a criminal act.

Without judging the merits of the account-ing profession's [actual] rendition of quasi-legal services, we must take judicial notice of the fact that, in . . . Louisiana, as elsewhere, C.P.A.'s regularly render opinions and advise their clients on matters of federal and state income tax liability as a routine matter in performance of their professional services. As a matter of fact, attorneys-at-law frequently refer clients to C.P.A.'s for such advice, which is in a specialized field; and attorneys also seek such advice directly from C.P.A.'s. In writing the policy here sued upon, defendant is bound to have known of this almost universal practice.

This is further borne out by the testimony of the [accountant], who stated that he has rendered opinions and given advice as to tax consequences of various transactions during the whole of his professional career; and by . . . testimony that the problem was one both of accounting and taxation and it therefore was within the proper province of a C.P.A. to render an opinion on the probable tax results of the proposed stock transfer. We hold, therefore, that had the action been brought against the [accountant], the mixed legal and accounting nature of the opinion would not have been a valid defense on the grounds urged by defendant, i.e., that plaintiff knew the [accountant] could not practice law.

[Judgment for plaintiff.]

50:2 Audits; Tax Return Preparation

Audits represent, by far, the bulk of accounting work and comprise nearly 80 percent of most accounting firms' income. An audit consists of the examination of a business' financial records and the preparation of a report on its financial condition. The audit can be of several types, ranging from a complete audit, in which the total financial condition of a business is scrutinized, to a *test audit*, in which a company's financial position is merely sampled on a selective basis.

Most audits consist of four stages: (1) gathering information and data on which the audit will be based; (2) establishing the appropriate auditing procedures; (3) revising the audit program, if necessary, to comply with the work in progress; and

(4) preparing the audit report based on the accumulated and analyzed data, detailing or summarizing the business' financial condition.

Tax Return Preparation   Many taxpayers have their income tax returns prepared by third persons for a fee, and these third persons are frequently accountants. Indeed, *tax return* preparation has become so large a business that it is now regulated to some extent by federal legislation, as discussed below. In addition, tax preparers may be subject to various state laws, the application of which is far from uniform.

The federal *Tax Reform Act of 1976* contains many rules that apply to income tax preparers. For example, any income tax preparer must furnish a completed copy of each return (the form on which the tax due is computed) to the taxpayer not later than the time the return is given to the taxpayer for his signature. Furthermore, any income tax return preparer must retain for three years after the close of the return period a completed copy of each return he prepared, or retain a list of the names and taxpayer identification numbers of the taxpayers for whom returns were prepared. The preparer must make this copy or list available for inspection by the Internal Revenue Service. Penalties are prescribed for, among other things, failure to furnish a copy of a return to the taxpayer, failure to sign the return, failure to furnish an identifying number, failure to retain a copy or required list, and failure to file a correct information return.

 Various types of tax fraud are made crimes by the *Internal Revenue Code*. For example, any person, including an accountant, who willfully makes and signs a tax return containing a statement under oath that the tax return is correct when he does not believe it to be true, or who willfully assists another person in preparing a false return, is guilty of a felony that is punishable by fine and imprisonment.

50:3 Duty to Client

Accountants are subject to the same rules in their practice as any other professional engaged in rendering skilled professional services for compensation. The accountant must exercise the skill, care, knowledge, and judgment usually possessed by accountants in the community. He must conduct adequate investigations to discover embezzlement when performing an audit and other accounting services. He must also follow standard accounting procedures and perform all the services for which he was hired.

An accountant is not an insurer against damage to a client and does not guarantee correct judgment. However, if he fails to exercise reasonable care according to normal professional standards, he may be held liable to the client for damages. For example, if an accountant uncovers suspicious circumstances, he must inform the client or fully investigate the matter. If he fails to do so, he can be held liable to the client for the resulting loss.

The following case illustrates an accountant's negligent failure to pursue an inquiry into a company's finances where he knew or ought to have known of improper financial transactions. Consider the accountant's duty in such circumstances and the extent of his liability.

1136 Tenants' Corp.
v
Max Rothenberg & Co.
36 App Div 2d 804, 319 NYS2d 1007
(New York Supreme Court, Appellate Division, 1971)

[The plaintiff, a corporation, owned a cooperative apartment house. It hired the defendant accounting firm to go over its books and render a monthly statement showing its financial condition as reflected by its books. Plaintiff's books were based on statements prepared by Riker & Co., a firm of managing agents. Riker & Co. kept its own books, collected the plaintiff's maintenance charges and deposited them in its own account, and paid the plaintiff's bills. Riker, the head of Riker & Co., appropriated certain of the collections to his own use and failed to pay plaintiff's bills. After learning of this embezzlement and suffering money losses caused by it, plaintiff sued the accounting firm for negligent performance of accounting services. The trial court ruled for plaintiff, holding that the accounting firm was liable. The accounting firm appealed.]

Per curiam.

*   *   *

The record amply supports the Trial Court's findings that defendant was engaged to audit and not merely "write-up" plaintiff's books and records and that the procedures performed by defendant were "incomplete, inadequate and improperly employed." One of defendant's senior partners admitted at the trial that defendant performed services for plaintiff which went beyond the scope of a "write-up" and that it actually performed some auditing procedures for plaintiff. Defendant's worksheets indicate that defendant did examine plaintiff's bank statement, invoices and bills and, in fact, one of the worksheets is entitled "Missing Invoices 1/1/63–12/31/63" (plaintiff's exhibit 16-B-6). That sheet alone indicates invoices missing from the records of Riker & Co. which totalled more than $44,000.

Utilization of the simplest audit procedures would have revealed Riker's defalcations [embezzlements]. Moreover, *even if* defendant were hired to perform only "write-up" services, it is clear, beyond dispute, that it did become aware that material invoices purportedly paid by Riker were missing, and, accordingly, had a duty to at least inform plaintiff of this. [Court's emphasis.] But even this it failed to do. Defendant was not free to consider these and other suspicious circumstances as being of no significance and prepare its financial reports as if same did not exist. . . .

[Judgment affirmed.]

50:4   Duty to Third Persons

Until recently, the recognized rule was that an accountant is not liable for his negligence to a third person with whom he had not directly contracted. Under this view of limited liability, an accountant owes no duty to a "stranger"; his duty is only to his client. This is based on the notion that to expose an accountant to liability to third persons would constitute too great a burden on the accounting profession. In the words of one famous judge, "If liability for negligence exists, a thoughtless slip or blunder . . . may expose accountants to a liability in an indeterminate amount for an indeterminate time to an indeterminate class."[1]

In recent years, this policy of limited liability has been rejected in a number of states. In these states, an accountant can be held liable to a third person for his negligence despite the absence of a direct contractual relationship with the third person. Thus, if an accountant knows that his work will be relied on by a particular person or group of persons and that it will be used for a particular purpose, a duty of reasonable care can arise. Breach of this duty of care subjects the accountant to liability to all persons who may have foreseeably relied on his work.

The following case illustrates the accountant's duty of care to third persons. The case is one of the first to extend an accountant's liability. Note how the court discusses public policy in support of its position. Consider the extent of liability and the class of persons in whose favor it can exist.

Shatterproof Glass Corp.
v
James
466 SW2d 873, 46 ALR3d 968
(Texas Court of Civil Appeals, 1971)

[The defendant accountants furnished certified audit reports to four corporations concerning their financial condition. The accountants knew that the reports would be used by Shatterproof Glass and others in connection with loans to be made to the corporations. The reports represented that the corporations were solvent when in fact they were not. Relying on the erroneous reports, Shatterproof loaned money to the four corporations, and later it lost the money because of the corporations' insolvency. Shatterproof sued the accountants, alleging negligence in preparing the reports. The trial court ruled for the accountants on the ground that their liability did not extend to third persons with whom they had not contracted. Shatterproof appealed.]

Langdon, J.

*   *   *

As is evident from recent decisions involving investors and other persons who extend credit to corporations, the courts have replaced "privity" and "primary benefit" with the concepts of "good faith" and "common honesty." . . .

In Escott v BarChris Construction Corporation, 283 F Supp 643 (USDC SDNY, 1968), an accounting firm was held liable to third parties for an incorrect audit. The court said of the accountant:

"... He did not spend an adequate amount of time on a task of this magnitude. Most important of all, he was too easily satisfied with glib answers to his inquiries.

"... [T]here were enough danger signals in the materials which he did examine to require some further investigation on his part. Generally accepted accounting standards required such further investigation under these circumstances. It is not always sufficient merely to ask questions."

---

[1]Justice Benjamin Cardozo in *Ultramares Corp. v Touche*, 255 NY 170, 174 NE 441, 74 ALR 1139 (New York Court of Appeals, 1931).

The facts in Rusch Factors, Inc. v Levin [284 F Supp 85 (1968)] . . . are very nearly the same as in the case at bar. In Rusch a Rhode Island corporation sought financing from the plaintiff and requested certified financial statements. The statements prepared by the defendant accountant represented the corporation to be solvent by a substantial amount whereas in fact the corporation was insolvent. In reliance upon such statements the plaintiff loaned the corporation $337,000 plus. Subsequently, the corporation went into receivership and the plaintiff recovered only a portion of what it had loaned. The plaintiff then instituted suit against the accountant seeking recovery on the grounds that it had been injured as the result of its reliance upon the fraudulent or negligent misrepresentations contained in the financial statements which were certified to by the accountants. . . .

In Rusch the court held that an accountant should be liable in negligence for careless financial misrepresentations relied upon by actually foreseen and limited classes of persons. In that case ". . . the defendant knew that his certification was to be used for, and had as its very aim and purpose, the reliance of potential financiers of the Rhode Island corporation." The [accountants in this case] had the same knowledge. . . .

We find and hold that . . . an accountant may be held liable to third parties who rely upon financial statements, audits, etc., prepared by the accountant in cases where the latter fails to exercise ordinary care in the preparation of such statements, audits, etc., and the third party because of such reliance suffers financial loss or damages. . . .

[Judgment reversed.]

 Since "prevention is better than the best remedy," it is always advisable for an investor to have his own accountant explore any situation in which he intends to make a sizable investment. While the other party to the intended transaction may not always permit the investor to have his own accountant examine the other's books, the reception that the suggestion receives may in itself be a clue as to whether the investment should be made.

Unaudited Financial Statements   Although many states now hold accountants liable to third persons for negligence in the preparation of complete financial statements, as discussed above, they remain divided on the question of accountant liability in regard to working papers or *unaudited financial statements*. This question may arise when materials, supplied by a client to an accountant, are later shown to be false. In most circumstances, the accountant is not negligent—and hence is not liable to third persons—simply because he fails to discover that the materials with which he is supplied are incorrect. However, if he knows or has a reasonable basis for knowing that there are serious discrepancies or falsehoods in the materials supplied, he should make the appropriate inquiries and insist on some independent verification.

50:5   Obligations under Federal Securities Laws

Federal regulation of the securities market emerged from the aftermath of the 1929 stock market crash. Among the laws enacted are the *Securities Act of 1933* and the

Securities Exchange Act of 1934. These acts were designed to (1) provide investors with full disclosure of material information concerning public offerings of securities in commerce; (2) protect investors against fraud; and (3) through the imposition of specified liabilities, promote ethical standards of honesty and fair dealing.[2]

 The importance of the federal securities acts to accountants must be stressed. Under them, an accountant who knowingly prepares or assists in the preparation of false materials in connection with an offering of corporate securities can be liable to anyone who relies on those materials. Therefore, an accountant can be liable for failing to properly prepare or adequately supervise the preparation of a wide variety of materials that are routinely issued by corporations. This liability is illustrated in the following case.

Berkowitz

v

Baron

428 F Supp 1190

(United States District Court, S.D. New York, 1977)

[The plaintiffs bought a corporation's stock after relying on information about the corporation issued in connection with the stock offering. The information was false, and the plaintiffs suffered financial losses. They sued the officers of the corporation and its accountant for making material misrepresentations in a financial statement as part of a fraudulent scheme to induce the public to buy the stock, all in violation of § 10(b) of the Securities Exchange Act of 1934.]

Cannella, District Judge.

*   *   *

The complaint alleges [a] cause of action against . . . the accounting firm responsible for preparation of the [financial statement]. . . .

Rule 10b-5 [issued by the Securities and Exchange Commission] provides in pertinent part that

It shall be unlawful for any person, directly or indirectly, by the use of any means or instrumentality of interstate commerce, or of the mails, or of any facility of any national securities exchange. . . .

> (2) to make any untrue statement of a material fact or to omit to state a material fact necessary in order to make the statements made, in the light of the circumstances under which they were made, not misleading.

The Court finds that the companies' financial statement . . . given to the plaintiffs . . . did not fully and fairly portray the financial condition of the companies and thus violated the Rule.

The most troublesome aspect of the financial statement is the treatment accorded certain items reported therein. One such item is shipping costs and expenses totalling $145,281.76. This sum was included as a component of manufacturing overhead. Expert testimony established that this method of presentation was not in accord with generally accepted accounting principles of the time. The appropriate procedure would have been to treat such shipping costs as an operating expense . . . and take it as a deduction against gross profit, instead of

---

[2]The federal securities acts are discussed in detail in Chapter 43.

including it in cost of goods sold, above the gross profit line.

The effect of this treatment was to cast a false picture of the companies' net income and inventory value. Because manufacturing overhead is a component of cost of goods sold, which in turn is one element of inventory value, improper incorporation of shipping costs and expenses in manufacturing overhead resulted in an overstatement of inventory computed to be approximately $44,560 by plaintiff's expert witness. The enlarged inventory entry had a direct effect on the net loss/net income figure reported in the financial statement. Had the shipping costs and expenses been treated according to generally accepted accounting principles, the companies would have shown a net loss of approximately $24,960 (less the tax effect) for the fiscal year ... instead of a net income of $19,603, as was reported.

Another item, factoring charges, was likewise treated in a manner not in accordance with generally accepted accounting principles. These charges, in the amount of $28,686.41, were shown as a deduction in arriving at net sales and appear above the gross profit line on the balance sheet. Proper accounting procedures required that factoring charges be deducted below the gross profit line. ... This handling of factoring charges, as well as the improper treatment of shipping costs and expenses, resulted in a lowered gross profit figure.

Without going into detail, it can be seen that these charges created a financial picture for the companies that was inaccurate. The slightly inflated inventory figure gave rise to an overoptimistic estimate by plaintiffs of the revenues anticipated from liquidation of the inventory.

Reporting the items above the gross profit line altered the gross profit percentage. The appearance of a small net income instead of a small net loss falsely supported the view that with good management a profit could be made.

Given these conditions, a finding that the financial statement is "materially misleading" is fully supported. Stated generally, the traditional test of materiality in 10b-5 suits is whether the fact is such that a reasonable investor *would* have considered it important in making the decision or *might have* acted otherwise had it not been misleadingly represented. ... [Court's emphasis.]

Similarly, the Court finds that plaintiffs have established reliance on the misrepresentations; they have proved that the misrepresentations were in fact substantial factors in the securities transaction involved. ... Plaintiffs' testimony, though it established little else, established that they relied exclusively on the representations contained in the financial statement and the fact that the factory was in operation when the transaction took place. Moreover, the fact that plaintiffs demanded and received assurance that the net worth of the companies had not changed by more than $30,000 between April 30, the effective date of the financial statement, and the August 26 signing of the contract indicates that the financial picture of the companies as reflected in the financial statement was a substantial factor in plaintiffs' decision to purchase. In sum, plaintiffs were induced to purchase a business that was worth less than they had been led to believe. ...

[Judgment for plaintiffs.]

Section 10(b) of the Securities Exchange Act and SEC Rule 10b-5 are designed to protect the investing public by promoting disclosure and the free flow of information. However, neither the act nor the regulation attempts to create violations for mere misstatements or omissions of a trivial nature. The critical statement or omission in a given case must be "material." Materiality is measured by an objective test that asks whether a reasonable person would attach importance to the misrepresentation or omission in determining his choice of action in the questioned transaction.

Key Concepts and Terms

- An accountant's employment is based on a contract that sets forth the accountant's and employer's rights and duties.
- An accountant is permitted to apply legal knowledge in connection with his accounting work, but he cannot give legal advice or practice law (unless he is also a licensed attorney).
- An accountant is not an insurer of his advice. He is liable to his client only for failing to exercise the reasonable skill, care, knowledge, and judgment possessed by other accountants in the community.
- An accountant is liable for negligent acts and omissions in rendering tax services and in providing erroneous or untimely tax advice.
- An accountant can be liable for his negligence with respect to a third person, despite the absence of any contract between them. This liability can exist if, when preparing a report for a client, the accountant should reasonably have known that the report would be used by a particular third person for a particular purpose.
- Under the federal securities laws, an accountant can be liable for failing to properly prepare, to have prepared, or to supervise the preparation of a corporate client's materials issued in connection with an offering of securities.

- Audit
- Internal Revenue Code
- Securities Act of 1933
- Securities Exchange Act of 1934
- Tax Reform Act of 1976

- Tax Return
- Test Audit
- Unaudited Financial Statement
- Unauthorized Practice of Law

Questions and Case Problems

1. What functions are performed by accountants?
2. Discuss the accountant's principal ethical and legal duties when performing professional services.
3. Under what circumstances is an accountant who fails to discover fraud when performing an audit liable to (a) his client and (b) a third person?
4. Zelkin, an accountant, is hired by Caruso to negotiate with the Internal Revenue Service (IRS) concerning Caruso's tax liability. In preparing for these negotiations, Zelkin performs legal research at several law libraries and reviews pertinent legal documents. This legal research is primarily, although not exclusively, directed at

determining the accounting methods used by other companies having tax problems similar to Caruso's. Is Zelkin guilty of the unauthorized practice of law?

5. Between 1950 and 1970, Velma received annual payments from Bryant Corp., for which her now-deceased husband had worked during his lifetime. The payments were made as part of Bryant's policy of giving continuing financial help to spouses of deceased officers who had rendered faithful service. In 1971, Bryant's accountant determined that the payments constituted taxable income to Velma. Therefore, the accountant withheld and paid to the IRS certain amounts from Velma's payments. In 1983, Velma reads a tax court decision to the effect that a corporation's payments to the spouses of deceased employees do not constitute taxable income. Velma files an income tax refund claim, but the claim is denied due to being filed too late. Velma then sues Bryant's accountant for damages. Is the accountant liable to Velma for the amount withheld from her payments? Is the date of the tax court opinion of any significance?

6. Wills prepares a financial report for Asher, who wants to buy all the assets of the Mondane Company. In preparing his report, Wills fails to follow standard accounting procedures, and his report is grossly misleading. Ultimately, the sale of the Mondane assets to Asher falls through for reasons not involving the financial report. However, Mondane's assets are bought by Wiggons, who somehow acquired Wills' misleading report and read and relied on it. After suffering severe financial losses, Wiggons sues Wills for damages. She alleges that Wills was negligent in the performance of his duties. Is Wills liable to Wiggons?

7. Sharon, a certified public accountant (CPA), is preparing Kenware Corporation's annual corporate tax returns. In so doing, she advises Kenware's president that she believes a particular IRS ruling is unconstitutional and will prepare the tax return ignoring the ruling. She further advises Kenware that, in the event of litigation, Kenware would probably win the case. After the forms are filed, the tax return is contested by the IRS, and Kenware is assessed a substantial penalty. Discuss the liability, if any, of Sharon to Kenware. Would it make any difference if Sharon happened to be an attorney as well as a CPA?

8. Richard, an accountant, prepares an audit for his client, Soho Industries. He prepares the audit negligently, erroneously indicating that Soho has far greater assets than it actually does have. The audit report happens to come into the hands of Ledlow Financial Group. Relying on the report, Ledlow loans money to Soho and then loses the money because of Soho's insufficient capitalization. If Richard's report had not been negligently prepared, Ledlow would not have relied on it, loaned money to Soho, nor suffered the loss. Discuss Richard's liability, if any, to (a) Soho and (b) Ledlow.

9. Lifeline Insurance Company sells life insurance. A Lifeline officer makes a number of false bookkeeping entries to conceal his systematic misappropriation of company funds. An accountant employed by Lifeline discovers the false entries but fails to mention them to the appropriate financial officers of the company. If Zale extends credit to Lifeline, mistakenly believing the company to be solvent when it is not, is the accountant liable to Zale for failing to disclose the false bookkeeping entries? Would it make any difference if the accountant was not hired to perform a complete financial audit and render a formal report?

10. Makey is hired by Sindell to prepare and file Sindell's tax return. Makey is late in filing the return, which results in the assessment of a penalty against Sindell. Sindell settles the matter with the tax officials, paying 50 percent of the assessed penalty. Is Makey liable to Sindell for the amount of the penalty actually paid?

51 Basic Rights and Duties in the Traditional Employer– Employee Relationship

51:1   Introduction

This chapter examines the traditional employment relationship, which exists between employer and employee. At one time, the terms "master" and "servant" were commonly used to indicate the relationship that exists when one person employs another. Today, the words "employer" and "employee" are used, although legal literature and judicial decisions still use the traditional terms at times.

In theory, each person has the right to contract for his labor or services and to abandon employment if conditions of service are not satisfactory. Historically, however, for reasons of poverty, family, employment scarcity, or competition, an employee has had little choice but to accept employment on the terms and conditions offered by the employer. Laws made in recent years regulating employment and labor relations have attempted to alleviate some of the previous inequities of the system.

51:2   The Employment Contract

An employment contract is a contract in which the employer hires the employee to do something for the employer's or a third person's benefit. The relationship of employer and employee is contractual in nature, and its creation is determined by principles governing the formation of other contracts (see Chapters 10 through 15). Employment contracts are often oral and informal. However, whether informal or not, every employment contract includes an implied provision of good faith and fair dealings between employer and employee and an implied provision that neither will do anything that will injure the rights of the other to receive the benefits of the agreement.

Employee Manuals   The employee manual is enjoying increasing popularity as an orientation device for new employees. A good manual can anticipate a wide range of questions and help to clarify them. It can, however, also create problems for an employer who relies on it by, for example, trying to explain a complex benefit plan briefly and simply in the manual, with the result that the explanation is misleading. Since employee manuals are usually written by a company's personnel department rather than by an attorney, the employer should make clear that the manual neither constitutes an employment contract nor is to be "read into" any employment contract as a provision. Also, the employer can include a statement in the manual along the following lines: "All examples used in this manual are merely illustrative. Your own case may be different. For a precise statement of your own benefits and coverage, check with the Personnel Department."

51:3   Employee's Duties to Employer

An employee has certain duties to the employer that exist even if there is no contractual provision imposing them. These duties include reasonable skill, loyalty, and good faith.

Skill   An employee must use care and reasonable skill in managing or controlling any aspects of the employer's business for which he is hired. An employee who fails to exercise reasonable skill can be liable for damage caused to the employer by that failure.

Loyalty to Employer's Interests   An employee has the duty of furthering his employer's interests. The employee is not permitted either to engage in a business detrimental to that of the employer or to perform for his own benefit any activity that would have the effect of destroying the business. Nor can the employee use information he obtains by virtue of his employment to further his own interests. For example, courts have held it a violation of an employee's duties (1) to engage or even participate in a business that competes with that of the employer (even outside working hours) or (2) to seek to obtain for himself the employer's customer accounts. The following case involves whether an employer was justified in discharging an employee for attempting to make secret deals with another person to buy the employer's business.

Wildman

v

Ritter

469 SW2d 446

(Texas Court of Civil Appeals, 1971)

[C & SRM, a computer consulting firm, employed Wildman as vice-president in charge of its technical team. During the employment, Wildman and other corporate officers attempted to interest outsiders in buying C & SRM. However, the company learned of this attempt and fired Wildman. Wildman sued to collect back pay. Judgment was for C & SRM, and Wildman appealed.]

Moore, Justice.

*   *   *

Computer & Systems Resource Management, Inc. (hereinafter referred to as C & S R M), was a corporation formed in May, 1969, to provide professional educational consulting and systems management services to industry. The principal investor, as well as the company's first president, was D. G. Ritter. The Board of Directors of the corporation consisted of D. G. Ritter, Richard A. Favro and appellant, James R. Wildman. Ritter served as president from the inception of the corporation until the first week of August, 1969, when Favro was made president. Appellant, James R. Wildman, served as vice president of the corporation from its inception until the time he was discharged on October 20, 1969. . . . The evidence shows that immediately after appellant was employed he was given instructions as to the scope of his authority. According to Ritter and Favro, Wildman was instructed that it was his duty to handle the "technical team" of the corporation, but was not to make any executive decisions. If any executive decisions arose, he was to consult Mr. Ritter, and in the event he was not available, he was to consult Mr. Favro. Wildman testified that he understood that Favro was his superior and acted for Ritter even though Favro was not president in the early stages of the company. He also admitted that Favro had changed the scope of his duties from time to time.

In early August, 1969, Mr. Favro called a meeting of the technical team composed of appellant, Mr. Biggs, Mr. Jannach and Mr. Barstow. During the course of the meeting Mr. Favro advised them that the income of the corporation had not come up to expectations and that it would be necessary for the company to curtail expenses. As a result of this statement, appellant, Biggs, Jannach and Barstow apparently became apprehensive as to the financial stability of C & S R M. Shortly thereafter, without the knowledge of either Ritter or Favro, they got together and discussed the matter and commenced formulating certain plans whereby C & S R M could be sold or merged with another corporation. It appears that Mr. Biggs knew an investor in Amarillo, Texas, by the name of Royal Jackson whom he thought might be interested in acquiring or

forming some type of enterprise of this nature. As a result, he, Wildman and Barstow prepared a letter to Jackson setting forth three alternate business plans by which a new corporation could be formed or by which C & S R M could be merged with another corporation. The first proposal in the letter was that the "technical team" consisting of Wildman, Biggs, Jannach and Barstow, would leave the employment of C & S R M and would cooperate with Jackson in buying control of another corporation by the name of Iconic Teleprocessors, Inc. Secondly, they proposed the possibility of purchasing control of C & S R M from Ritter. Thirdly, they proposed to form a totally new corporation using the technical team of C & S R M and taking over some of the business of C & S R M. After the letter had been prepared, Biggs took it to Amarillo and discussed the propsoals with Jackson. The proposal was never accepted. Appellant does not dispute the fact that he participated in this entire transaction.

Upon learning of this, Favro, as president of C & S R M, immediately discharged appellant. Appellant then instituted this suit for the remainder of his salary alleged to be due under the contract.

At the close of appellant's evidence, appellees moved for an instructed verdict on the ground that no contract existed, as a matter of law, in that the letter of employment constituted nothing more than a contract to make a contract and therefore was not binding. After overruling the motion, the trial court submitted the cause to the jury. . . . [T]he jury found . . . that Wildman exceeded the course and scope of his authority as executive vice president in submitting the reorganization proposal to Royal Jackson, that such conduct constituted good cause for appellant's discharge, . . . that the participation by Wildman in the formulation of the proposal to Royal Jackson constituted disloyalty, and . . . that such disloyalty constituted good cause for appellant's discharge.

. . . [A]ppellant urges that there is no evidence to sustain the jury's findings that he, Wildman, exceeded his authority or was guilty of disloyalty, or that such conduct constituted good cause for his discharge. We do not agree. There is an implied obligation on the part of the employee to do no act which has a tendency to injure the employer's business, interest or reputation. Any breach of this obligation will justify the employer in discharging the employee from his services. . . .

. . . [W]e are satisfied that the evidence set forth herein is sufficient to constitute at least some evidence . . . in support of the finding that appellant exceeded his authority and was disloyal to his employer. It is without dispute that he participated in a plan to organize a competing business using the technical staff of C & S R M and to take its business. Had he been successful, the business of C & S R M would have been seriously disrupted if not destroyed. In these circumstances we think there was sufficient evidence to support the finding that C & S R M had good cause to discharge appellant.

[Judgment affirmed.]

 An employee's fiduciary duties not to engage in any conflict of interest as to his employer are not limited to officers, directors or other management personnel. Even rank-and-file employees have a duty not to do anything that interferes with an employer's interests. Bear in mind, though, that unless it is specifically prohibited, an employee *can* take on outside work after his regular office hours as long as the work (1) is not inconsistent or an interference with the employer's business and (2) does not reduce the value of the employee's full-time services to the employer.

Employee's Duties as to Property Acquired in Connection with Employment Generally, everything an employee acquires in connection with his employment, except his compensation, belongs to the employer. This is true regardless of whether the acquisition is lawful or unlawful, or whether it is made during or after expiration of the term of employment. This basic rule is simply another expression of the agency rule (see Chapter 48) that an agent cannot use property that is the subject of the agency, or powers conferred on him, for his own benefit. Furthermore, if an employee creates something as part of his duties under the employment, the thing created is the employer's property, unless by agreement the employee retains some right in the product. For example, a chemist who discovers a formula—which may have great economic value—while conducting research for his employer during work hours is not entitled to ownership of the formula. The formula is the property of the employer.

Employer's Profits or Earnings An employee may be required to account for any secret profit, gift, gratuity, or benefit he receives in his capacity as an employee. The employee has the duty to exercise good faith toward the employer and cannot, without the employer's consent, retain profits or earnings received in performing the employer's business or participating in an undertaking that constitutes a breach of duty to the employer or conflicts with the employee's duties to his employer.

51:4   Employer's Duties to Employee

Duties an employer owes to his employee depend on the nature of the employment, provisions of the employment contract, and applicable statutes. An employer generally does not have the duty to provide specific work for the employee. Rather, he can use the employee's services when and how he chooses, so long as he compensates the employee according to the contract.

Employee's Welfare   An implied provision of employment contracts is that the employer will not add to the employment any new conditions involving dangers or inconveniences not within the employee's contemplation at the time he was hired. An employer's general duties are to ensure that the place at which the employee works is reasonably safe and to furnish suitable and safe tools and equipment. This becomes more imperative as the risk increases; the employer's standard of care for the employees' safety must be commensurate with the dangers of the business. Public policy as to care and protection of workers has undergone great change in recent times, and as discussed in 51:10, legislation has been enacted to protect employees' safety and health.

51:5   Employee Privacy

Privacy is an elusive right and one that, in the employer–employee setting, must constantly be balanced against the employer's right to conduct business profitably and successfully. Unlike his counterpart of 50 years ago, today's worker does not sell "his soul" to the employer; he sells only his labor. Nevertheless, federal Labor Department hearings have revealed that using cameras on assembly lines, denying access to records, monitoring employee's conversations (even in washrooms), and using lie detectors are common practices. Conflict between management's desire to control and monitor many aspects of employee life and, on the other hand, the employee's desire for greater self-expression and personal growth free of corporate influence is producing a decided shift toward individual rights.

Lie Detector Tests   The *polygraph*, or lie detector, is an electrical instrument that can measure and record on a graph certain physiological data concerning the person being tested. These data include blood pressure, pulse rate, respiration rate, and galvanic skin response (a measurement of relative skin conductivity). When a polygraph expert questions a person to whom the instrument is attached, the data are recorded. The expert can then examine the resulting chart (polygram) and determine with a high degree of accuracy which questions the individual has answered truthfully. Lie detector tests have long been the subject of controversy. Their use by employers has raised the serious question of invasion of employees' privacy and privilege against self-incrimination.

The giving of preemployment polygraph tests is the most controversial use of the polygraph in private industry. Proponents argue that it gives the employer both protection from employee theft and a cheap way of verifying employee truthfulness. Critics point to the lack of scientific support for the claims that the polygraph can screen dishonest employees from honest ones.

Many union contracts include bans on lie detector tests. Also, legislation in some states prohibits employers from *requiring* prospective employees to undergo lie detector tests, although they can request that applicants do so. In other states, legislation prohibits employers from even requesting a prospective employee to take any test purporting to determine honesty. The following case illustrates how courts construe polygraph legislation strictly, to fulfill the public policy of promoting employee privacy.

State

v

Berkey Photo Inc.
150 NJ Super 56, 374 A2d 1226
(New Jersey Superior Court, Appellate Division, 1977)

[Berkey Photo, the employer and defendant here, was convicted in the trial court of violating a state statute making it an offense for an employer to "influence, request or require an employee to take or submit to a lie detector test as a condition of employment or continued employment." The employer then appealed.]

Per curiam.

*   *   *

Defendant asked certain employees to take a lie detector test as an aid in investigating a theft from its plant in Clifton, New Jersey. On this appeal defendant contends that the statute was not violated primarily because the initial suggestion of using lie detector tests came from the police and, contrary to the trial judge's conclusion, the employees took the tests voluntarily and not as a condition of continued employment within the meaning of the statute.

The underlying facts are not in dispute. On October 22, 1974, defendant reported the theft of a case of cameras to the Clifton Police Department. Two detectives went to the plant and met with defendant's director of security, Jim Ahern. It was established that during the preceding weekend the cameras had been stolen from a small area of the plant which had been accessible to only six employees and an alarm repairman employed by an independent contractor.

The detectives interviewed four of the employees and asked each if [he] would be willing to submit to a polygraph test. The four agreed to do so. Thereafter the detectives recommended to Ahern that polygraph tests be used in the investigation. The detectives also recommended that defendant arrange for the tests privately because the Clifton Police Department did not have a polygraph team and there would be a delay of a month or more if the State Police were asked to perform the test.

Ahern conferred with the personnel director, Thomas Glynn, and they decided to ask the employees to take the test. Ahern and Glynn, and in some cases Ahern alone, asked the six employees as well as the alarm repairman to take the test. All agreed to do so and signed "waiver" forms stating that they were taking the test voluntarily. For the purpose of this appeal we accept the finding that all were informed in advance that under the laws of New Jersey no employer may require a person to take a polygraph test as a condition of employment or continued employment.

The six employees and the alarm repairman submitted to the tests. The questions were limited to establishing knowledge or involvement in the particular theft, except that preliminary questions were asked to relieve tension and nervousness. All persons tested were "cleared of involvement," except one employee. The test established his involvement and he confessed his guilt while the test was being administered.

[The statute] precludes an employer from influencing, requesting or requiring an employee to take or submit to a lie detector test as a condition of employment or continued employment. There is no question that defendant here did request the employees to take or submit to the test. It makes no difference that the police initiated or recommended the procedure. The sole issue before us is whether, in the circumstances of this case, the request to take the test "was a condition of employment or continued employment" within the meaning of the statute. On this issue the opinion of our Supreme Court in [an earlier case] is persuasive and, in our opinion, dispositive.

In [that case] defendant, the operator of a chain of drug stores, used polygraph tests as a screening device in its hiring procedures. Each of the employees involved in the charges brought against defendant was told that he or she did not have to take the test and signed a consent or waiver form. Two of the employees were unaffected by the test results, but one was fired immediately after the test revealed that she had been previously involved in a larceny. In upholding defendant's conviction for three separate violations relating to these employees, the Supreme Court stated: . . . "Nor is there any assurance of true voluntariness for the economic compulsions are generally such that the employee had no realistic choice." The Court went on to say:

We readily reject . . . the defendant's contention that its request was not a condition of employment or continued employment within the statutory contemplation. Surely the employee would understand that it was despite any formal assertion by the employer to the contrary and his understanding would be wholly realistic in view of the employment relationship. . . . In the light of the "breadth of the objectives of the legislation and the common sense of the situation" . . . there can be little doubt that the conduct of the defendant here was violative of the statute. . . .

That a crime was being investigated and the police were involved does not justify the employer's intrusion of a lie detector test into an employment relationship. Nor do these factors lessen the compulsion inherent in the situation. In fact, it may heighten that unspoken compulsion. Here, for example, one employee testified that he "volunteered" to take the test, after being told he did not have to do so and that his refusal would not affect his continued employment, because he was a security guard, he was in the building when the theft occurred and he wanted "to clear" himself of suspicion. Another employee, the plant manager, testified that he had a "duty" to take the test "voluntarily." Surely the employees understood what was expected of them when told that others were taking the test. How else can one explain that the guilty employee, the one who confessed, submitted to the test knowing the risk he was taking? . . .

[Conviction affirmed.]

Employee Surveillance An employer's surveillance of employees raises questions that can only be resolved on balancing the employer's and employee's interests in each case. An employee's personal mail when delivered to him at his place of business is a case in point. Routine mailroom procedures in many companies call for opening all letters, regardless of who the addressee is. If mail marked "personal" is opened by the employer and read without the employee's authority, some courts have found an unjustified intrusion into the private life of the employee. The employer has then been liable for damages.

 Employers who screen all incoming mail should expressly (and in writing) warn employees that their mail is subject to being opened. Such a warning can (1) discourage employees from having personal mail sent to the business and (2) remove any "expectation of privacy" that is essential to an invasion of privacy lawsuit.

Employee surveillance problems can also arise when an employer monitors an employee's telephone conversations. Federal law allows a person to record a conversation so long as the purpose is not to commit a crime or other injurious act. State legislation, however, may be more restrictive. In the absence of particular state or local restrictions, an employer can install a telephone-monitoring device on telephones in departments that deal with the general public. The justification for this practice is that it enables the employer to protect employees from abusive language by irate customers, and allows supervisors to better train and instruct employees on how to communicate with the public. When telephone monitoring is adopted by an employer, the employer should be completely open about it. This means that employees should be advised of the monitoring in advance, to preclude an invasion of privacy suit.

51:6 Injuries to Employees; Workers' Compensation

In the absence of statute, an employer is liable to an employee for injuries received in the course of employment if the injury results from the employer's negligence. The employer's duty is to use reasonable care to provide the employee with a safe working place and with safe tools and equipment. As in other negligence actions, what constitutes reasonable care depends on the surrounding circumstances. A problem from the employee's viewpoint is that the employer can assert defenses ordinarily applicable in negligence cases (see Chapter 6). Thus, the employee's contributory negligence might bar recovery. Also, the doctrine of assumption of risk applies, on the theory that by entering employment, the employee assumes ordinary risks. Moreover, under what is known as the fellow servant doctrine, an employer is not liable to an employee for injuries sustained solely as the result of the negligence of other employees.

In recognition of the problems that employees have when they try to recover from their employers for their injuries, most states have enacted *workers' compensation* legislation. This legislation, which is liberally interpreted by the courts, eliminates the need to prove negligence. Instead, the employee is granted the right to receive compensation for most employment-related injuries without regard to fault. A disadvantage of workers' compensation from the employee's viewpoint is that the amount of compensation that will be paid is limited.

Workers' compensation laws are administered primarily by administrative boards or commissions, rather than by the courts.[1] The amount of compensation to be awarded in any given case is determined in accordance with a prescribed schedule, in an informal administrative proceeding. At that proceeding, the employer might resist the employee's claim by showing that (1) there was no injury or (2) the injury that did occur was either not as severe as claimed or was not job-related. The amount of compensation finally awarded is usually paid by the employer's workers' compensation insurance carrier. At times, however, the employer itself pays all or part of the award.

 In some states, an employee injured on the job must be compensated *solely* under workers' compensation legislation; he does not have the right to sue the employer for damages. In other states, however, the employee can elect whether to take the statutory workers' compensation coverage or waive that coverage and sue the employer for negligence.

Disability Resulting from Mental Stress   Mental or nervous disorders or disabilities resulting from employment-connected *physical* injuries and an accompanying trauma or shock to the nervous system are generally compensable, even though they cannot always be established by objective diagnostic procedures. They are compensable on the theory that the physical injury (however slight) is an identifiable and specific physical or disease-related "cause" for the mental or nervous disorder. The judicial viewpoint has been expressed in this regard that a psychoneurosis resulting from shock due to an accident constitutes a "violence to the physical structure of the body" within compensation statutes and is therefore compensable.[2]

Courts have had difficulty dealing with the situation in which the worker's disability was caused neither by a single injury to the worker nor by a single mental shock, but rather by emotional pressures produced by the job. The following decision, which could have far-reaching consequences, illustrates one court's approach to this problem.

Firemen's Fund Ins. Co.

v

Industrial Com.
119 Ariz 51, 579 P2d 555
(Arizona Supreme Court, 1978)

[The Arizona Industrial Commission awarded medical, hospital, and surgical expenses, as well as other compensation, to a worker on the ground that her disabling injury resulted from the gradual buildup of occupational stress and tension, which con-

stituted an "injury" within the meaning of the workers' compensation legislation. The court of appeals reversed the Commission's holding, after which an appeal was taken to the Arizona Supreme Court.]

Struckmeyer, Vice Chief Justice.

*   *   *

Janice W. Craig, respondent employee, was employed by Drenberg and Associates, an in-

---

[1]Administrative law is discussed in Chapter 3.
[2]*Todd v Goostree*, 493 SW2d 411 (Missouri Court of Appeals, 1973).

surance agency. She had approximately 15 years' experience when she started to work at the Drenberg Agency in August of 1974. She was initially assigned underwriting duties in the personal and commercial line of insurance. About the time respondent started to work, Drenberg began a year of explosive growth. Under normal conditions, an agency with 400,000 accounts could expect to acquire approximately 40,000 new accounts in the period of a year. Drenberg grew from 400,000 to 1,200,000 in just over one year. To keep pace with this growth, the agency's employees worked many extra hours, five and one-half day weeks. Yet, in spite of their best efforts, the agency remained thirty days behind in its accounts.

Respondent was a conscientious employee and a perfectionist. In addition to her duties in the area of the personal and commercial line of insurance, she took over a part of what is described as the commercial desk handling correspondence and renewals and changes. Her working conditions created an atmosphere in which respondent was under constant pressure.

On or about April 1, 1975, Drenberg purchased an agency from Earl Woodland, thereby acquiring 500 new accounts and an additional employee. Respondent was given supervisory responsibility for the new employee and the responsibility for merging the books of the two agencies. The additional responsibility and the mounting pressure began to affect respondent. She began to feel frustrated and ineffective. She experienced difficulty relating to her coworkers and on occasions had heated exchanges with customers. On September 25, 1975, respondent engaged in a particularly emotional telephone conversation with one of the agency's customers, after which she eventually left the office in tears. That night she took a slight overdose of sleeping pills. The following day she sought help at the Tri-City Mental Hospital and was subsequently admitted to Camelback Hospital, where her condition was diagnosed as neurotic depression, or a mental breakdown.

Respondent filed a claim with the Industrial Commission wherein she related facts which established that she was suffering from a disabling mental condition brought on by the gradual buildup of the stress and strain of her employment. . . .

Petitioner [Drenberg's insurance carrier] urges that there must be an unexpected injury-causing event accompanied by physical impact or exertion before there is an accident [within] the meaning of [the Arizona statute, which] provides in part:

"Every employee covered by insurance in the state compensation fund who is injured by accident . . . shall receive such medical, nurse and hospital services and medicines, . . . as provided in this chapter."

Physical impact or exertion is not a necessary element in determining whether an injury has, in fact, occurred. . . .

[According to one authority]:

"There are, in addition, several decisions confirming the conpensability of a disabling nervous condition brought on gradually by strain and worry. A clean-cut illustration is the Michigan holding in *Carter v. General Motors Corporation* [106 NW 2d 105 (1960)]. Here we have the modern industrial tragedy, not at the executive level, but at the level of the assembly line, with a set of facts recalling Charlie Chaplin's losing battle with his inhuman antagonist in *Modern Times*. The claimant, who had considerable emotional trouble in his background to start with, simply could not keep up with the assembly line, as a result of which he found himself constantly berated by his foreman. This in turn filled him with dread of losing his job, and the final result was a disabling psychosis. The Supreme Court of Michigan upheld an award." . . .

We do not have a claimant who was unable to keep up with other workers. Rather, there is here a claimant upon whom more and more work and responsibility was constantly being placed by her employer so that eventually the work and responsibility became more than she could tolerate. At this point, the unanticipated occurred and claimant suffered a mental breakdown. We think under these circum- stances, as the Industrial Commission found, that claimant sustained personal injury arising out of and in the course of her employment within the meaning of the [Workers'] Compen- sation Act.

Award affirmed.

"Dual Purpose" Doctrine   Most workers' compensation statutes require a show- ing that an employee's injury arose out of and in the course and scope of employ- ment before the employer can be required to pay compensation. The relationship of the employee's injury to his employment is important if the injury occurs while the employee is traveling, particularly if the travel is based on motives that are both personal and employer-oriented. Under what is called the *dual purpose doc- trine,* if the employee's work created the necessity for travel, he is in the course and scope of employment even though he is serving some purpose of his own at the same time. In this way, courts have expressed the public policy that it is reasonable to place the risk of injury on the employer if it is established that the business mission was a concurrent cause of the employee's trip.

51:7   Employer's Liability for Employee's Torts

Under what is called the doctrine of *respondeat superior,* an employer is usually held liable for his employee's negligent acts or intentional torts committed during the course of employment. This liability is based on several theories. One is that because the employer can carry insurance as a cost of doing business, he must also assume the risk of his employees committing torts. Another theory is that the employee's acts can be regarded as the employer's acts (because the employee is engaged in the employer's work), so that the employer cannot, simply by delegat- ing work, avoid his duty of due care to others.

An employer's liability under the respondeat superior doctrine is *vicarious.* That is, the liability is secondary and arises simply because the employment relation- ship exists. Depending on the circumstances, however, an employer can also be primarily liable in connection with an employee's tort. For example, the employer might have been negligent in training an employee or in entrusting the employee with a dangerous tool or machine. An employer can also be negligent in hiring or retaining an incompetent or unfit employee.

EXAMPLE
A hospital's hiring policy requires that it obtain from each applicant for employ- ment at least four references and that it check at least two of them before hiring. Despite this policy, the hospital accepts Wilson's application, which lists only two references, and it hires Wilson as an orderly without checking either reference. On the job, Wilson assaults and robs a patient. Proper checking would have revealed

that Wilson has a criminal record and that he was expelled from medical school due to a serious drug problem. The hospital is liable for the patient's loss and injury because it was negligent in hiring Wilson.

An employer who has been held liable for an employee's tort can, of course, sue the employee in an attempt to recover his losses. As a practical matter, however, the lawsuit will usually be in vain. The employer will probably win a money judgment, but the chances of collecting that judgment are poor.

Course and Scope of Employment A frequently disputed issue in respondeat superior cases is whether the employee was acting in the *course and scope of his employment* at the time of the incident in question. Relevant factors include (1) the employee's intent; (2) the nature, time, and place of his conduct; (3) his actual and implied authority; (4) the work he was hired to do; (5) incidental acts that the employer should reasonably have expected to be done; (6) the amount of freedom allowed the employee in performing his duties; and (7) the foreseeability of the employee's act. Note that an employer is not relieved of liability under the respondeat superior doctrine merely because the employee was combining his own business with that of the employer. This is similar to the rule under the dual purpose doctrine, discussed in 51:6. The following case illustrates how the courts usually hold the respondeat superior doctrine to apply so long as the employee's conduct was authorized, even if the specific activity was not required.

United States
v
Romitti
363 F2d 662
(United States Court of Appeals, Ninth Circuit, 1966)

[Moore, a federal employee, was involved in a traffic accident while allegedly traveling on employment-related business. The plaintiff, injured in the accident, sued the federal government for its employee's negligence under the respondeat superior doctrine. The plaintiff was awarded judgment, and the government appealed.]

Browning, Circuit Judge.

*   *   *

To summarize, the trier of fact had before it evidence that Mr. Moore was traveling on direct orders of his employer and for the sole purpose of serving his employer's business; that he was transporting property of the employer and fellow employees (including his supervisor), both necessary to the performance of that business; that he was traveling on the most direct route between two of his employer's work locations; that he was using an expressly authorized means of transportation; that he was driving during regular working hours; and that he was being paid his regular salary plus per diem, plus costs of transportation. This was enough to support a finding that Moore's negligence occurred "in the transaction of the business of the agency," and therefore to justify the conclusion that a private employer would be liable. . . .

. . . As Chief Justice Traynor said in [a California case], "The principal justification for the application of the doctrine of respondeat superior in any case is the fact that the employer may spread the risk through insurance and carry the cost thereof as part of his costs of doing business." This purpose requires that the employer assume those risks which are attributable to the employer's business, rather than to purely personal pursuits of the employee. Since the trip involved in the present case was undertaken to serve the purposes of the United States, the United States should bear the risks incidental to it. This basic fact is not affected by the circumstance that Mr. Moore's normal duties were those of an electronics engineer rather than a chauffeur, and that he was authorized but not required to provide his own automobile for use in his employer's service. The ... courts have imposed respondeat superior liability where the employee was not hired as a driver and the choice of means of conveyance was his. ...

On the other hand, in some situations deviation from usual duties and use of other than required means may add support to an inference that the employee was not engaged in his employer's enterprise, but was on a "frolic of his own." ...

Similarly, the failure of the employer to exercise control over the employee's driving is a factor of varying importance. Existence of the power to control the physical details of the service may be crucial when the question is whether the actor is an agent or an independent contractor, but may be relatively insignificant in determining whether an admitted agent is acting within the scope of his employment.

In this connection it is important to notice a distinction between a principal's liability for his own negligence and his liability for the negligence of his agent. If a principal negligently employs a person who is incapable of performing the task for which he is hired, or negligently fails to exercise proper control over the agent's performance, the principal is liable for injuries due to the principal's own negligence—without regard to the doctrine of respondeat superior. ... But the liability imposed upon the principal by the doctrine of respondeat superior is vicarious and does not rest upon the principal's fault. The fault for which the principal is required to respond is not that of the principal but that of the agent, committed in the course of the principal's business. Thus, when respondeat superior liability is asserted, "we are not ... looking for the master's fault but rather for risks that may fairly be regarded as typical of or broadly incidental to the enterprise he has undertaken." ...

We assume that in exercising the election which the United States gave these employees to use a private vehicle in performing the employer's errand, the employees were motivated at least in part by considerations of personal comfort and convenience. Nevertheless, the choice also served the interests of the United States, and this is enough. ...

[Affirmed.]

51:8 Termination of Employment Relationship, Generally

An employment contract can terminate by (1) expiration of the contractual term of employment, (2) the death or legal incapacity of either the employer or the employee, (3) the employer's discharge of the employee, or (4) the employee's resignation or retirement.

When an employment contract fixes no duration, the term of employment extends for the period that the parties have fixed for paying salary or wages. Hence, an employee paid a monthly salary is said to be hired on a month-to-month basis, while an employee paid weekly is hired on a week-to-week basis; an employee doing piecework is hired for no specified term. Some courts have held that a hiring at a yearly rate is presumed to be for one year, and that this presumption is not changed merely because salary is paid on a monthly basis. A person performing work at an agreed price and for a stated period of time can continue in the same employment after expiration of the term, without a new agreement. In this situation it is presumed that the terms of the original contract are continued.

If an employment contract is for a fixed period, the employer can legally discharge an employee prior to its expiration only for "good cause." What constitutes a good cause is usually specified in the contract. Most business employers expressly reserve the right to discharge employees for such problems as habitual lateness to work, drinking on the job, or simply failure to perform their job satisfactorily.

Contract Requiring Employer's Satisfaction   Generally, where whim, taste, sensibility, or judgment is involved, a contract provision that the employee will perform to the employer's satisfaction makes the employer the sole judge of what this satisfaction is. The theory is that the relation of employer and employee is confidential and personal, and that such a satisfaction stipulation is equivalent to an agreement that the employee's performance depends on his service being agreeable to the employer. This is not to say, however, that the employer can act in bad faith. If the employee can show that the employer's actual reason for discharging the employee was other than dissatisfaction with the employee's services, then the employer has breached the contract, and the employee may be able to recover damages for wrongful discharge.[3]

Employee's Willful Breach of Duty   An employer can terminate the employment contract at any time for an employee's willful breach of duty in the course of employment. An example is disobedience of a reasonable order. A single act of disobedience can justify the employee's discharge, even if no injury results to the employer. If the employer's order is unreasonable or illegal, however, its disobedience does not justify the employee's discharge.

Employee's Remedies   An employee who is discharged without good cause prior to expiration of a fixed term of service can sue for breach of the employment contract (see Chapter 18). The employee also has the option of treating the contract as rescinded and suing the employer under the theory of *quantum meruit*. That is, the employee would seek the reasonable value of the services he has already performed, as if the original contract had never been made.

Employee's Breach of Contract   An employee who breaches an employment contract by unjustifiably refusing to perform the required services is liable to his employer for damages. Employment contracts are not usually subject to specific enforcement, meaning that a court will not compel the employee to perform. However, statutes in some jurisdictions provide that a valid contract to perform a

---

[3]Discrimination against employees is discussed in Chapter 52.

service of unique, extraordinary, or intellectual character, the loss of which cannot be reasonably or adequately compensated in damages, can be enforced against the employee for a term of up to a particular number of years, frequently seven. At times, a contract for the exclusive services of an artist or performer can be enforced indirectly by means of a *negative injunction*, which is an injunction restraining the employee from rendering services to others. The rationale for this approach is that in contracts involving unique personal services of such persons as star performers and athletes, the employer has contracted for the exclusive right to display the celebrity for a given period; part of the right for which the employer had bargained and compensated the celebrity is that no other entrepreneur will have the right to display the celebrity during the contract period.

51:9   Termination of At-Will Contracts

The general rule is that an *at-will employment*—employment having no specified term—can be terminated at the will of either party on notice to the other. Historically, an at-will employment could be terminated by the employer with or without cause. The employer's motive in the termination was immaterial, and the employee was said to suffer no legal wrong even though the employer may have been capricious in discharging him. Today, however, the employer's right to discharge an employee under an at-will contract is often limited by statutes or public policy considerations. For example, an employer is not permitted to discharge an employee for a reason that amounts to discrimination (see Chapter 52).

Retaliatory Discharge   An important judicially created restriction on an employer's otherwise arbitrary right to discharge an at-will employee is the recognition of a civil cause of action for wrongful discharge when an employee is discharged in retaliation for actions that are protected by public policy. This public policy exception to the at-will doctrine has been applied to afford civil relief to an employee discharged under such circumstances as (1) refusing to commit perjury in testimony before a state legislative committee, (2) filing a workers' compensation claim against the employer, (3) designating an attorney to negotiate terms and conditions of employment, (4) participating in legal union activities, and (5) filing a complaint under the Fair Labor Standards Act (discussed in 51:11). The rationale is that a retaliatory discharge is done in bad faith and is not in the best interest of the economic system or the public good.

51:10   Occupational Safety and Health

Each year, many American workers are killed, suffer disabling injuries, or contract occupational diseases such as silicosis, asbestosis, pesticide and chemical poisoning, and lung and liver cancer. Technological advances and new processes in American industry have introduced hazards to the workplace. For example, carcinogenic chemicals, lasers, ultrasonic energy, beryllium metal, epoxy resin, and pesticides all have presented threats to the health of workers. Historically, employers were slow to protect employees from the dangers of industrialization, and the courts' conservatism resulted in a hesitation to extend the employer's common-law liability to fit changed conditions of industrial life. Due in large part to public pressure, states and the federal government began enacting legislation to help alleviate this problem.

OSHA Congress took a major step toward the protection of employees when it enacted the *Occupational Safety and Health Act of 1970* (OSHA) (29 USC §§ 651 et seq.). The purpose of OSHA is to assure every worker safe and healthful working conditions and to preserve the nation's human resources. The legislation is administered by the Occupational Safety and Health Administration, under the Department of Labor. The Secretary of Labor issues mandatory occupational safety and health standards, derived from established federal standards, national consensus standards, and new standards developed under procedures explained in the act's standards-making provision.

OSHA is complex and far-reaching legislation. The core of the statute is the so-called "general duty clause," setting forth duties of employers and employees with respect to occupational health and safety and mandating that employers furnish employees a place of employment free from "recognized hazards" likely to cause death or serious physical harm. A hazard from which an employer must protect the employee is deemed a recognized hazard if it (1) is a condition of common knowledge or general recognition in the particular industry and detectable by means of the senses or (2) is of such wide recognition as a hazard in the industry that even if it is not so detectable, there are generally known and accepted tests for its existence that should make its presence known to the employer. The act provides that each employee and employer must comply with occupational safety and health standards as well as all rules, regulations, and orders issued under the act applicable to his own actions and conduct.

Inspections OSHA provides for inspections and investigations of workplaces by the Secretary of Labor and for the issuance of citations to employers who violate the act's provisions or regulations issued under it. A citation fixes a reasonable time for abatement of the violation; an employer who fails to abate a violation can face severe civil and criminal penalties. Any employer has the right to contest a citation, which is done in an administrative proceeding. Ultimately, the employer can file an appeal to the United States Court of Appeals from an adverse administrative decision.

Periodic Reports Inadequacies in employers' reporting of occupational injuries or illnesses were recognized by Congress in enacting OSHA. As a result, the act sets forth a mandatory system of record-keeping and reporting. Among other things, employers are required to maintain a log of occupational injuries and illnesses, and to compile an annual summary of these injuries and illnesses based on information contained in the log. The shift from voluntary to mandatory compliance in the reporting of injuries and illnesses means that virtually all employers are now required to maintain records of work-related injuries and illnesses and to report their injury experience to the Bureau of Labor Statistics on request.

51:11 Fair Labor Standards Act

In 1938, Congress enacted the *Fair Labor Standards Act* (FLSA) (29 USC § 201 et seq.), which is also known as the Wage and Hour Law. The FLSA regulates hours and wages of employees engaged in commerce or involved in production of goods for commerce, and it prohibits oppressive child labor. It is administered by the Wage and Hour Division of the Department of Labor, which is empowered to establish and use local agencies to assist in carrying out the law. The act places a floor under wages and a ceiling over hours of employment. It also spreads employment among a greater number of workers by putting financial pressure on employers (by requiring extra pay for overtime work) and reinforces employee bargaining power concerning hourly wages (by prohibiting wage rates below certain levels).

The minimum wage provisions of the FLSA are read into and become part of every employment contract that is subject to the terms of the act. The effect of these provisions is to make an employee a creditor of his employer regardless of any actual attempted agreement as to compensation. Thus, the employer and employee are at liberty to contract with reference to hours and compensation in any manner they wish, *as long as the compensation to be paid is not less than the minimum fixed by the act.*

 An employer should have its personnel director and legal counsel meet periodically for a review of how the minimum wage, overtime, equal pay, or hiring practices of the business are affected by recent legislation, amendments, or regulations. A good start is to contact the nearest Wage and Hour Division office for a copy of its latest amendments. Employees, either as individuals or as union members, are advised to do the same.

Key Concepts and Terms

- The relationship of employer and employee is contractual, and its creation is determined by principles governing formation of contracts generally. There is an implied provision of good faith and fair dealing in every employment contract.

- An employee has certain rights in the employment setting as to privacy. For example, there are statutory and judicial limits on the employer's right to administer lie detector tests and to conduct surveillance on employees.

- An employer is liable to an employee for injuries received in the course of employment that results from the employer's negligence. The employer may assert defenses ordinarily applicable in negligence cases.

- Under workers' compensation legislation, enacted in most jurisdictions, the theory of negligence is discarded, common-law defenses are eliminated, and the worker is given a right to compensation for all injuries arising from his employment.

- Under the doctrine of respondeat superior, even though an employer is personally innocent of wrongdoing, he may be vicariously liable for his employees' torts committed within the scope of employment.

- When an employment contract fixes no duration, the term of employment extends for the period that the parties have agreed on for payment of salary or wages. If the contract is for a fixed period, the employer can legally discharge an employee prior to its expiration only for "good cause."

- The general rule is that an at-will employment relationship—employment having no specified term—can be terminated at the will of either party on notice to the other. Historically, at-will employment could be terminated solely at the employer's discretion, but today the employer may be limited in this right by statute or public policy considerations.

- The Occupational Safety and Health Act of 1970 (OSHA) was enacted to give workers safer and healthier working conditions and to help preserve the nation's human resources.

- The Fair Labor Standards Act was enacted by Congress to set minimum wage levels for industries engaged in interstate commerce.

- At-Will Employment
- Course and Scope of Employment
- Dual Purpose Doctrine
- Fair Labor Standards Act
- Negative Injunction
- Occupational Safety and Health Act of 1970

- Polygraph Test
- Quantum Meruit
- Respondeat Superior
- Vicarious Liability
- Workers' Compensation

Questions and Case Problems

1. What is the difference between an employee and (a) an independent contractor and (b) an agent?

2. How is the employer–employee relationship created? How is it terminated?

3. Discuss the extent to which the state and federal statutes discussed in this chapter regulate private employment relationships.

4. What recourse does an employer have against an employee who, although having signed a contract requiring her to do a particular job, refuses to do that job?

5. Gary operates a motor scooter supplied to him by the Rainbow Ice Cream Company for selling ice cream. He operates within an area designated by Rainbow, works whenever he pleases, pays his own expenses (including gas and oil), and sells the ice cream at prices fixed by Rainbow, later accounting to Rainbow for a percentage of the profits. While selling ice cream, Gary is injured when his scooter is struck by a hit-and-run driver. Gary sues Rainbow for his injuries. Should he recover?

6. The Thrush Paper Corporation sponsors an annual company picnic for its employees and their guests. During the course of a picnic, an employee playing in the traditional company baseball game hits a fly ball that leaves the park, strikes Larry, who is walking on the sidewalk adjacent to the park, and seriously injures him.

Larry sues Thrush for his injuries. Will Larry win the case? Would it make any difference if Larry, too, were an employee of Thrush who was leaving the picnic at the time of the accident?

7. Corey is employed by the Maser Electronics Company as its chief physicist. His employment contract specifies that his employment is "conditional on service and conduct being satisfactory to Maser Electronics, who shall be the sole judge in this regard." Later, Maser discharges Corey simply because it cannot afford to pay his high salary any longer. Corey sues Maser for breach of contract. How should the case be decided? Would it make any difference if Maser had discharged Corey so that it could hire a more qualified physicist?

8. Ralph is a salesman for the Reilly Shoe Company and is on the road, showing the new line of Reilly shoes to potential customers. On his way to see a customer, he stops at a local drive-in for lunch. While eating a hamburger, he has a "cafe coronary." That is, a portion of the hamburger becomes lodged in his throat, and he dies from suffocation. Is Ralph's death covered under workers' compensation legislation? Would it make a difference if the incident had occurred after Ralph had seen the customer and was on his way home?

9. Fred is employed by the Delcorte Hardware Company, which has, in the past few months, been subject to losses of items the company believes are being taken by a ring of employees in its main store. For this reason, and unknown to the employees in the main store, Delcorte installs closed-circuit television cameras which maintain continual surveillance on the employees from one-way windows in the ceiling. On discovering this surveillance procedure, Fred sues Delcorte for invasion of privacy, and he is immediately fired for "disloyalty" to the store. Fred sues again, this time for breach of contract. How should the case be decided? Why?

10. An employee of Careless Company has a demonstrated allergy to smoke from cigarettes. She sues to require the company to prohibit cigarette smoking in the vicinity of her work station. She alleges that Careless is subjecting her to work in "unsafe conditions" within the meaning of state occupational health and safety legislation. Should Careless be required to comply with the employee's demand?

52 Labor Relations and Job Discrimination

52:1 Introduction to Labor Relations

The Industrial Revolution brought sweeping changes to the workplace. Growth of industrial empires hiring hundreds, thousands, then tens of thousands of employees spread across the land. This burgeoning created not only a means of livelihood for the common worker, but problems as well. Early labor unions and craft guilds were no match for employers whose interests were nearly always protected by the courts at employee expense. At common law, for example, employees' collective activities, such as a strike for higher wages or safer working conditions, were frequently held to be a criminal conspiracy and enjoined under penalty of heavy fine or imprisonment. It was not until 1914, when Congress enacted the Clayton Antitrust Act (15 USC §§ 12–18), that some remedy was made available. The act narrows the availability of injunctions against labor organizations in cases involving employers and employees. It does so by allowing an injunction only if it is necessary to prevent irreparable harm to property and no adequate legal remedy exists. However, far more by way of legislative action was required before employees were able to organize effectively to bargain for employment rights.

Modern American labor law is grounded on several federal statutes, which are discussed later in this chapter. Together, these statutes establish the right of workers to form unions and bargain with an employer. They prohibit unfair labor practices, recognize industrial arbitration, set forth labor's and management's rights and duties in the labor field, and establish individual employee rights as to employers and unions.

52:2 Right to Strike and Organize

A strike is a cessation of work by employees—or a refusal to work at their usual speed—to obtain more favorable terms from their employer. Historically, while strikes were not illegal as such, courts would frequently halt strikes by temporary injunction on employers' showings that the particular strike was "unjustified" or causing the employer "irreparable harm." Enactment of the Norris–LaGuardia Act of 1932 (29 USC §§ 101 et seq.) was a significant step toward the development of a national labor policy. It accorded full freedom to employees to organize and negotiate the terms and conditions of their employment through representatives of their choosing, and it limited the issuance of restraining orders and injunctions against unions by federal courts. The act expressly makes unenforceable a so-called yellow-dog contract, which is any agreement between employees and a company in which an employee promises either not to become or remain a member of any labor organization or to withdraw from the employment relationship if he joins any labor organization.

The Norris–LaGuardia Act did not place affirmative obligations on employers to negotiate with labor unions, but it assisted union organization and collective bargaining by modifying prior judicial decisions concerning the unions' role. In summary, the act (1) provides employees freedom of organization, association, and designation of representatives; (2) prevents federal courts from issuing injunctions in almost any case "involving or growing out of a labor dispute"; and (3) refuses injunctive relief to any person failing to make "every reasonable effort" to settle labor disputes by negotiation or mediation. In addition, the *National Labor Relations Act* (see 52:3), which expressly guarantees employees the right "to engage in other concerted activities for the purpose of collective bargaining or other mutual aid or protection," safeguards the right to strike for employees in commerce by preventing the states from regulating peaceful strikes in industries affecting commerce.

Picketing   "Picketing" means walking or patrolling in the vicinity of a place of business involved in a labor dispute and, by word of mouth, banner, or placard, undertaking to inform the public about the dispute. Picketing may be intended to persuade workers to stay away from or quit their jobs, or to advise members of the public of the labor dispute and influence them to withhold patronage from the business being picketed. At common law, picketing was lawful in employer–employee controversies only when both its method and its object was legal.

State regulation of peaceful picketing is today subject to two principal limitations. The first is the free speech guaranty of the First Amendment to the Constitution. Although picketing cannot dogmatically be equated with free speech, it has an element of communication, and this element is not lost simply because a labor dispute is involved. Peaceful picketing can, however, be restrained by the state when it is for an unlawful purpose, such as in support of an illegal strike. Picketing carried on with intimidation, threats, coercion, or force is illegal. Also unlawful is picketing conducted with vandalism or other overt criminal activity.

The second principal limitation on state regulation of peaceful picketing is federal preemption of the field (meaning that when the federal government has taken exclusive control over a given legal area, the states cannot act in that area). The National Labor Relations Act, discussed below, provides that a state cannot enjoin peaceful and legal picketing against an industry engaged in interstate commerce. Because so many businesses have been held to be "engaged in interstate commerce" as that phrase has been interpreted by the courts, the federal statute governs more often than not.

52:3   Expansion of Labor's Rights

During the New Deal, following national economic chaos in the early 1930s, Congress continued its movement toward encouraging unionism and collective bargaining. The National Labor Relations Act of 1935 (NLRA) (29 USC §§ 151 et seq.), also known as the Wagner Act, was the genesis of the present-day, comprehensive federal legislation that regulates labor relations affecting interstate commerce. The NLRA's purposes are as follows:

- Removal of obstructions to the free flow of interstate commerce
- Promotion of industrial peace through fair, prompt, and just labor dispute settlements
- Balancing of labor's and management's competing interests
- Protection of employees' right of collective action in securing satisfactory wages, hours, and employment conditions
- Prevention of employers' unfair labor practices
- Establishment of national labor laws uniformly administered and enforced

Constitutionality of the NLRA was upheld by the United States Supreme Court.[1] The Court rejected contentions that the act was beyond congressional authority under the commerce clause, that it invaded Tenth Amendment rights of the states, and that it denied employers due process of law by restricting freedom of contract.

Sections 3 and 4 of the NLRA create the National Labor Relations Board (NLRB), which is given jurisdiction to administer the act and control over *unfair labor practices* and questions of union representation. The NLRB has power to issue and prosecute complaints under the act. Section 7, the heart of the act, guarantees that employees have the right to organize, form, join, or assist labor organizations; bargain collectively through representatives of their choosing; and engage in concerted activities for the purpose of collective bargaining. Section 8 of the act imposes on employers the duty to bargain collectively with the union designated as the exclusive representative for the employees. Section 8 also lists unfair labor practices on the part of employers. Examples are (1) interfering with, restraining, or coercing employees in the exercise of their right to form a union; (2) unlawfully assisting or sponsoring a labor union; (3) discriminating against employees because of union activity; (4) refusing to bargain collectively with a designated employee representative; and (5) discriminating against employees who file charges with the NLRB.

Notwithstanding its significance, the NLRA was not intended as "complete" labor legislation, and three factors particularly influenced subsequent changes and extensions in the law: (1) the act was concerned with the organizing phase of labor relations; (2) it dealt exclusively with restraining *employer* unfair labor practices,

---

[1]*NLRB v Jones & Laughlin Steel Corp.*, 301 US 1, 81 L Ed 839, 57 S Ct 615 (1937).

not union practices; and (3) it left substantive terms of employment entirely to private negotiation.

52:4   The Swing Back Toward Management

As a result of favorable governmental policy toward unionism and sympathetic enforcement of the NLRA, union membership increased from 3 million to 15 million employees between 1935 and 1947. During this period, nationwide strikes occurred in entire industries, at times crippling national production of coal, textiles, lumber, oil, and both maritime and rail transportation. The public became alarmed in the years following, and the pendulum of public sentiment began swinging towards management. Congress responded to this movement in 1947 when it enacted the *Labor Management Relations Act* (LMRA) (29 USC §§ 141–144, 151–158), also known as the Taft–Hartley Act.

The LMRA was intended to lessen industrial disputes and place employers on an equal position with unions in bargaining and labor relations. It attempted to achieve a "balance of obligations" by recognizing that unions, too, could be guilty of unfair labor practices. Under the act, it is an unfair labor practice for a union to (1) refuse to bargain collectively with an employer; (2) coerce or restrain an employee in the exercise of his right to refrain from joining a union; (3) cause, or attempt to cause, an employer to discriminate against an employee who is not a union member; (4) impose excessive initiation fees to join a union; or (5) engage in featherbedding (forcing an employer to pay for unperformed work).

The LMRA provides that the President can intervene in industrywide disputes that would "imperil the national health or safety" if allowed to continue and, by invoking certain machinery under the law, ask a federal district court for an 80-day injunction against a strike or work stoppage imperiling national health or safety. The act also undertakes to regulate certain provisions in the collective bargaining agreement itself by, for example, outlawing the "closed shop" (in which employees have to be union members as a prerequisite to employment). Furthermore, the act provides for legal remedies both to enforce labor agreements and to recover damages for their breach.

52:5   Collective Bargaining

Section 8(d) of the NLRA imposes on both the union and the employer a mandatory duty "to meet at reasonable times and confer in good faith with respect to wages, hours and other terms and conditions of employment." Since the act does not define "wages, hours and other terms and conditions of employment," the NLRB and the courts determine what subjects are within the statutory requirements. An employer sometimes refuses to bargain collectively with a union as to a mandatory bargaining subject [a subject that the NLRB has ruled falls within the scope of § 8(d)]. In that event, the NLRB can petition a United States Court of Appeals for enforcement of its order against the employer to bargain with the union, as illustrated in the following case.

NLRB
v
Gulf Power Co.
384 F2d 822
(United States Court of Appeals, Fifth Circuit, 1967)

[The NLRB petitioned the United States Court of Appeals for enforcement of its order requiring that an employer (Gulf Power Company) bargain collectively with a union as to safety rules and practices. The NLRB argued that safety rules and practices are "other terms and conditions of employment" within the meaning of NLRA § 8 (d).]

Ainsworth, Circuit Judge.

*   *   *

The issue we must decide is whether safety rules and safe work practices are mandatory subjects of collective bargaining under the provisions of Sections 8(d) of the Act relating to the mutual obligation of the employer and the employer and the Union "to meet at reasonable times and confer in good faith with respect to wages, hours and *other terms and conditions of employment....*" [Court's emphasis.]

For more than twenty years the Union has been the exclusive bargaining agent for Gulf Power's employees in an appropriate unit. Gulf Power Company is a public utility engaged in the generation, transmission and sale of electric power, with principal offices at Pensacola, Florida, and is engaged in commerced within the meaning of the Act. A collective bargaining contract was entered into between the Company and the Union on December 27, 1962, effective until August 15, 1964, and from year to year thereafter unless either party should give notice of termination or revision. Article VI of said contract entitled "Safety" contained several provisions relative

to safe employment practices. The Company also embodied other safety provisions in a 60-page "Safe Work Practices" handbook, prepared by it and issued to all employees, which provided also for discipline or discharge of employees who violated its provisions.... On April 30, 1963, the Company unilaterally revised its safety rules. On June 3, 1963, the Union wrote the Company that it protested the Company's action in having on April 30, 1963 unilaterally placed a revised set of safety rules in operation without having bargained on this subject with the Union. The Company replied that it was required by law to provide reasonably safe and healthful places of employment for its employees, to provide compensation for workmen injured in the course of their employment; that this responsibility rested exclusively with it; and that it could not share its obligations with the Union and could not agree that the Union "take any part in the formulation of policy in respect to safety procedures or other matters for which it bears no responsibility under the law." The Union accordingly filed an unfair labor practice charge against the Company which it withdrew shortly thereafter. On June 15, 1964, the Company and the Union notified each other of intention to revise the contract between them....

A number of bargaining sessions were held at which the Union stated that it was concerned about safety and wanted some type or program of cooperation with the Company on safety. The Company replied that it would be glad to discuss safety with the Union but was of the view that it could not delegate its responsibility for promulgating and regularly revising safety rules. After six bargaining sessions the Company steadfastly declined to bargain with reference to the promulgation and revision of safe work practice rules, maintaining that this was exclusively the legal and moral nondelegable responsibility of the Company. The present complaint of unfair labor practice was accordingly filed. The Board held a hearing after which it concluded that the Company's action in declining to bargain with the Union with respect to safe work practices and/or safety rules violated Section 8(a) (5) and (1) of the Act. We agree and accordingly order enforcement of the order. It is inescapable that in a public utility electric generating and transmission company the workers, through their chosen representative, should have the right to bargain with the Company in reference to safe work practices. This is not to say that there are not areas where the Company's obligations to the public are paramount and which may not properly be the subject of an agreement with the Union after a bargain-

ing session is held. Nonetheless, the parties by their own actions in the past have clearly indicated that they consider safety rules and practices a bargainable issue by including several important provisions in Article VI of the contract already referred to. . . .

We hold, therefore, in agreement with the Board, that the phrase "other terms and conditions of employment" contained in Section 8(d) of the Act is sufficiently broad to include safety rules and practices which are undoubtedly conditions of employment, and that Section 8(d) requires good faith bargaining as a mutual obligation of the employer and the Union in connection with such matters. . . .

Enforced.

The end result of successful *collective bargaining* is a *collective bargaining agreement*, the labor contract that sets forth the rights and duties of the employer and the union. This contract is a generalized code to govern situations that those who drafted it could not wholly anticipate. Thus, it is not an ordinary contract governed by general contract principles. Indeed, central to an understanding of labor relations is the concept that the collective bargaining agreement is not a simple product of a consensual relationship, but rather covers the whole employment relationship and calls into being a new common law—the common law of a particular industry or shop.

Section 301 of the LMRA provides that suits to enforce terms of collective bargaining agreements between an employer and a union representing employees in an industry affecting commerce, or between two labor organizations, can be brought in any federal district court having jurisdiction. While § 301 expressly authorizes only "employers and unions" to sue one another for breach of the collective bargaining agreement, the United States Supreme Court has held that even individual employees can sue their employers to vindicate "uniquely personal rights" under the contract, such as special employment conditions or special rates of pay.[2]

52:6 Arbitration and Mediation

Virtually all collective bargaining agreements contain arbitration provisions. In the context of labor relations, *arbitration* is the process by which a dispute that cannot be settled voluntarily through an agreement's grievance procedure is referred to an

---

[2]*Smith v Evening News Asso.*, 371 US 195, 9 L Ed 2d 246, 83 S Ct 267 (1962).

impartial person—the arbitrator—for resolution. Both parties must agree in advance to accept the arbitrator's decision as final and binding. The decision itself is made on the basis of the evidence presented and arguments made at an arbitration hearing. Processing of an employee's grievance under a collective bargaining agreement usually consists of four steps: (1) presentation of the case to the employee's immediate supervisor; (2) if settlement is not obtained, presentation of the case in writing to the proper division superintendent; (3) if no agreement results, submission for determination by a company executive; and finally (4) if the executive's decision it not satisfactory, referral to the impartial arbitrator. The arbitrator acts according to the prevailing rules of arbitration law and the accepted practice and custom that has developed regarding industrial relations. Prior arbitration awards in similar cases are not binding or conclusive, although they have value as persuasive force. Generally, the "controlling law" is the collective bargaining agreement signed by the parties.

 As part of the consideration for an employer's agreement to arbitrate grievances or disputes arising under a collective bargaining agreement, the union usually will agree to a "no strike" clause. This means that the union will agree not to strike or cause work stoppages or slowdowns because of any dispute or grievance that is subject to arbitration.

Judicial Enforcement of Arbitration Agreement   The courts have made it clear that enforcement of arbitration clauses is crucial to industrial peace and that specific performance is the best means of assuring enforcement. Accordingly, when either an employer or a union refuses to arbitrate as provided in the collective bargaining agreement, and the grievance procedure has been followed, as discussed above, the other party can sue in federal court to compel the nonbargaining party to arbitrate according to the terms of the agreement. Arbitration awards can also be enforced in federal court.

The question sometimes arises whether a particular grievance falls within the arbitration clause of a collective bargaining agreement. In such a case, the courts have ruled that all claims or grievances are to be resolved in favor of arbitration. Hence, if the claim of an employer or employee seeking arbitration *on its face* appears to fall within the scope of the arbitration clause, the court must order the opposing party to arbitrate that claim.

Labor Mediation and Conciliation Services   Unlike arbitration, in which disputed issues are decided by a third person, *mediation and conciliation* is a process by which disputing parties are encouraged to reach an agreement on their own initiative. Typically, mediators do not propose settlements, and they never reach "decisions." Rather, they function as intermediaries between the parties, helping to create the proper "atmosphere for settlement." Toward this end, Congress created an independent agency known as the Federal Mediation and Conciliation Service, which has the duty of assisting parties to settle labor disputes through mediation and conciliation. During the course of any strike or protracted labor dispute, it is not unusual for one or both parties to decide that a point has been reached at which settlement must be had at all costs. At this time a labor mediator, whether federal, state, or local, might be able to serve as the catalyst to revive bogged-down negotiations, hastening the end of the strike or dispute.

52:7   Rights of Individuals

The NLRA, amended in 1947 by the LMRA, was further amended by Congress in 1959, when it enacted the *Labor Management Reporting and Disclosure Act* (LMRDA) (29 USC §§ 401, 402 et al.), also known as the Landrum–Griffin Act. The LMRDA is intended to eliminate certain improper practices of both unions and employers that had resulted in frequent deprivation of employees' rights. The act regulates the internal affairs of unions and establishes what has been termed a "bill of rights" for union members. Under the act, union members have (1) equal rights and privileges to nominate union officers and participate and vote in union membership meetings; (2) the right of free speech at union meetings; (3) procedural safeguards as to union dues, fees, and assessments; and (4) due process safeguards against improper union disciplinary actions. The act also gives union members the right to inspect union policy and financial statements, to be informed as to the provisions of the act, and to sue (when the union itself fails to do so) to recover misappropriated union assets.

Job Discrimination

52:8   Introduction

There may be no more fundamental right than the right to work and be treated fairly and equally by an employer. An interference with the right to fairness and equal treatment constitutes job discrimination, and numerous remedies are available to prevent it. For example, several states and municipalities have enacted fair employment practices laws, and an increasing number of collective bargaining agreements contain antidiscrimination provisions. In addition, there are several federal laws prohibiting discrimination in employment.

   The most far-reaching federal statute in this regard is *Title VII of the Civil Rights Act of 1964* (42 USC §§ 2000e et seq.). Title VII forbids discrimination in employment on the basis of race, color, religion, sex, or national origin. This prohibition is directed against most employers, employment agencies, and unions. For example, it applies to any employer (1) engaged in an industry affecting commerce and (2) having 15 or more employees. Title VII does not, however, apply to other types of job discrimination, and it is intended neither to guarantee a job to every person regardless of his or her qualifications nor to command that any person be hired simply because he or she was formerly the subject of discrimination or a member of a minority group. Rather, Title VII forbids discriminatory job preferences for *any* group—minority or majority—by requiring the removal of artificial, arbitrary, and unnecessary barriers to employment when they operate invidiously to discriminate on the basis of impermissible classifications. Title VII is enforced through law-suits both by private individuals and by the federal *Equal Employment Opportunity Commission* (EEOC), an administrative agency.

52:9   Racial Discrimination

Racial discrimination in employment can take a variety of forms and arise in many types of practices. For example, an employer's seniority system might operate to discriminate against persons of a particular race, as might a termination policy. As the following case illustrates, an employer can also be guilty of racial discrimination in connection with hiring policies.

United States
v
Georgia Power Co.
474 F2d 906
(United States Court of Appeals, Fifth Circuit, 1973)

[Georgia Power Company required that any appli-cant for a job with the company have a high school diploma. This and other aspects of Georgia Power's hiring and recruitment policy were challenged in a lawsuit filed under Title VII by the United States Attorney General and a number of individuals. The plaintiffs alleged that Georgia Power's policies were racially discriminatory. The district court ruled that the diploma requirement was invalid, but it upheld certain other of the company's hiring and recruiting practices. The plaintiffs appealed.]

Tuttle, Circuit Judge.

*   *   *

[DIPLOMA REQUIREMENT]

Since we find that the company made no sub-stantial showing that possession of a high school diploma is a business necessity at Geor-gia Power, we affirm the aspect of the district court's decision which strikes down the di-ploma requirement. As the Supreme Court [has noted]:

History is filled with examples of men and women who rendered highly effective per-formance without the conventional badges of accomplishment in terms of certificates, di-plomas, or degrees. Diplomas and tests are useful servants, but Congress has mandated the commonsense proposition that they are not to become masters of reality. . . .

[The] court explicitly held that the use of a high school requirement which has a dis-proportionate racial impact and has not been proven to be a predictor of ultimate job success controverts the congressional mandate of Title VII. As with Georgia Power's testing pro-gram, . . . the issue here is whether or not the company has made a sufficient showing to manifest a relationship between its educational requirement and its job characteristics.

The requirement undoubtedly screens out blacks at a considerably higher rate than whites, because in the 25–44 age group in the South, 64.7% of white males, 35% of black males, 63% of white females, and 34.7% of black females have completed high school. In the Atlanta area, statistics show that for males over 18 years of age, 70.7% of the whites had finished high school compared with only 46.2% of the blacks.

The justification offered at trial for the re-quirement was very weak. As the district court observed:

At best, the only justification for this re-quirement is the obvious eventual need for above-average ability to read and com-

prehend the increasingly technical maintenance manuals, the training bulletins,
operating instructions, forms and the like demanded by the sophisticated industry . . . . In
such a context, the high school education requirement cannot be said to be reasonably related to job performance. This is not to say
that such requirements are not desirable . . . it
simply means that the "diploma test" cannot
be used to measure the qualities. Many high
school courses needed for a diploma (history,
literature, physical education, etc.) are not
necessary for these abilities. A new reading
and comprehension test . . . might legitimately be used for this job need.

Many employees without high school diplomas have mastered the technical literature and
many of the highest-ranking personnel in the
company did not pass the "diploma test", including 47 of 100 foremen, supervisors, and
chief division operators in the Atlanta and
Macon operating division. Such a large percentage of current employees have succeeded
at Georgia Power without a diploma that it
simply cannot be "irrelevant", as the company
urges, that some employees have successfully
performed without possessing diplomas.

The rest of the data presented by the company is equally inconclusive. The proof that
non-high school graduates have recently obtained fewer promotions than graduates is a
non sequitur in light of the company's requirement of the paper qualification as a prerequisite for promotion out of laborer positions
even for pre-1960 employees and in view of
the fact that many of the older (pre-1960) employees not holding diplomas were already at
the top of their lines of progression by 1960.
Therefore, the court appropriately held that
Georgia Power had not demonstrated a business necessity for requiring the diploma. . . .

HIRING AND RECRUITMENT POLICIES

Failure or refusal to hire any individual on account of race is expressly prohibited by Section
703 of Title VII. . . . The private plaintiffs claim
that this prohibition extends to Georgia
Power's practices of (1) word-of-mouth recruiting and (2) recruiting for skilled personnel
only at all-white institutions. The district court
rejected both these contentions, saying:

> Advertisement of existing vacancies by
> word-of-mouth on the part of company em-
> ployees has been the best means for recruit-
> ment, and often for promotion, from time
> immemorial. It has been done by both blacks
> and whites in this company.

Even if it were harmful, there is no known
way to halt it. The mere fact that a company's
personnel has a majority of one race or another does not make such practice chargeable
to the employer as a discriminatory act. Only
if some preference were given the white referrals could the question rise to the point of decision. Nor is there any significance in the places
of conducting interviews for possible management personnel. In short, the court finds no
evidence substantiating a racially motivated
policy of recruiting on the part of the company.

Only 7.2% of the company's labor force was
shown to be black, although this race constituted a much larger percentage of the available labor force. In non-laborer jobs, this
disparity is even greater. Under word-of-
mouth hiring practices, friends of current employees admittedly received the first word
about job openings. Since most current employees are white, word-of-mouth hiring alone
would tend to isolate blacks from the "web of
information" which flows around opportunities at the company. . . . No business necessity compels the company to continue to
rely so heavily on this hiring technique. In
fact, it contends it has already taken action to
convey news of new openings to blacks by
posting job notices on company bulletin
boards which can be read by all personnel.
Since 92.8% of all personnel likely to see these
notices on a regular basis is white, however,
this step is patently inadequate.

We believe that the district court stopped its reasoning short of the considerations which would have led to full equitable relief. Word-of-mouth hiring and interviewing for recruitment only at particular scholastic institutions are practices that are neutral on their face. However, under the facts of the instant case, each operates as a "built-in-headwind" to blacks and neither is justified by business necessity. While the court was without doubt free to leave these practices available for future use, its failure to order them to be supplemented by affirmative action on the part of Georgia Power Company was clearly an abuse of discretion.

At least two courts have already recognized the need to counteract the discriminatory impact of word-or-mouth hiring. [One court] refused to enjoin "apparently neutral referral-type recruitment practices" only because it found that "[t]he Company . . . has initiated substantial changes in its recruitment procedures." . . . Where no effective alternative techniques were used to remedy the lock-in effect of similar recruitment policies, one district court proscribed the use of word-of-mouth hiring altogether.

The built-in headwinds which the present Georgia Power system harbors must be offset by affirmative steps reasonably calculated to encourage black employment and to break through the currently circumscribed web of information. For example, advertisements of openings in newspapers and periodicals accessible to the black communities of Atlanta and other Georgia cities, and public notice that the company is an equal opportunity employer, are common recruiting techniques which should be considered. We again decline to usurp the prerogative of the district court to formulate the exact relief which an overall decree will require on this one facet. We hold only that the present word-of-mouth practice must either be supplemented or changed.

The company's policy of seeking skilled personnel only at white educational institutions is similarly an invidious brake on black employment opportunities for which no business necessity justification was shown. While the company obviously ought not be enjoined to recruit on all college campuses unless it chooses to do so, it also ought not be allowed to continue to restrict its recruitment programs to all—or preponderantly all—white institutions while maintaining such a racially imbalanced work force. The district court is likewise directed to supplement or change this practice. . . .

Full enjoyment of Title VII rights sometimes requires that the court remedy the present effects of past discrimination. . . . This includes both redressing the continuing effects of discriminatory seniority systems . . . and affirmative action to alter a seniority system which is not discriminatory on its face. If the present seniority system in fact operates to lock in the effects of past discrimination, it is subject to judicial alteration under Title VII. . . .

Most courts, in molding appropriate remedies, have adhered to the "rightful place" theory, according to which blacks are assured the first opportunity to move into the next vacancies in positions which they would have occupied but for wrongful discrimination and which they are qualified to fill. . . . This is the theory which should be applied here.

Should company test invalidity be the trial court's ultimate conclusion, then seniority would thereby be extended to all blacks wrongfully deprived of the opportunity to advance beyond the positions of laborer, porter, janitor, or maid by either the testing or the high school education requirements. This relief reaffirms that "[t]he ethic which permeates the American dream is that a person may advance as far as his talents and his merit will carry him." . . .

[Judgment affirmed in part and reversed in part.]

As the *Georgia Power* case suggests, Title VII is the major weapon against racial discrimination in employment. It provides for relief if the court finds that the alleged discriminator "has intentionally engaged in or is intentionally engaging in an unlawful employment practice" as described in the statute. The United States Supreme Court has held that proof that an employer adopted a discriminatory employment practice, *whether purposely discriminatory or not*, establishes a violation of Title VII.[3] Moreover, although Title VII was intended to have prospective application only, relief has been granted to remedy present and continuing effects of past discrimination.

52:10   Sex Discrimination

Women in American society hold more than two of every five jobs in the civilian labor force, yet the average pay for women who work full time is less than three-fifths of the average for men. Congress took one step to alleviate this situation when it enacted the Equal Pay Act of 1963 [29 USC § 206(d)]. This act prohibits discrimination between employees on the basis of sex in determining wages paid for equal work on jobs requiring equal skill, effort, and responsibility, when the jobs are performed under similar working conditions. Amounts due an employee that have been withheld in violation of the act are regarded to be unpaid minimum wages or unpaid overtime compensation, in violation of the Fair Labor Standards Act (discussed in Chapter 51). Accordingly, action to obtain payment of these wages can be brought by the Wage and Hour Administrator of the Department of Labor or by any affected employee.

Title VII of the Civil Rights Act of 1964 also addresses the problem of sex discrimination. Under Title VII, employment decisions cannot be predicated on mere stereotyped impressions about characteristics of males or females. Myth and purely habitual assumptions about the inability of women to perform certain kinds of work are not acceptable reasons for refusing to employ qualified individuals or for paying them less. Furthermore, an employer may not burden female employees in such manner as to deny them employment opportunities because of their gender. For example, an employer's denial of accumulated seniority to female employees who return to work following disability caused by childbirth violates Title VII if the employer permits employees on leave for other nonoccupational disabilities to retain seniority. The following case illustrates a somewhat different type of sex discrimination.

Johnson

v

University of Pittsburgh

359 F Supp 1002

(United States District Court, W.D. Pennsylvania, 1973)

[*Dr. Sharon Johnson was an untenured assistant professor in the biochemistry department of the University of Pittsburgh medical school. She had been hired in 1967 for a three-year term, and in 1970 she was rehired for another three years. In 1971, members of the biochemistry department met*

---

[3]*Griggs v Duke Power Co.*, 401 US 424, 28 L Ed 2d 158, 91 S Ct 849 (1971).

*and decided not to grant Johnson tenure and, in-
stead, to discharge her, purportedly due to her inadequate teaching. Johnson sued the university,
alleging a violation of Title VII. She also sought an
injunction preventing her discharge until her Title
VII claims were resolved. Johnson's right to an injunction depended in large part on her showing a
reasonable probability of eventual success in the Title VII litigation.]*

Knox, District Judge.

*   *   *

The defendant attempted to show that sex
discrimination did not enter into the decision
of tenured faculty to deny plaintiff tenure and
promotion to an associate professorship, and
also introduced evidence, most of it gathered
after the making of the decision to discharge
her, to indicate that she was a poor teacher.
The evidence offered in this case shows that
out of 401 faculty members in the School of
Medicine, only 5 women have tenure. Six Departments in the School have no women at all,
eleven have no tenured women and only
three have women with tenure. The average
salary for male tenured professors is $37,500
while the average salary for women with tenure is $27,000. Increases in salary are granted
at a higher rate to male professors than female.
There are four times as many women eligible
for tenure on this faculty as there are men.
During the last six years, 70 men were given
tenure as compared to 3 women. The figure
sent by the Medical School to the Affirmative
Action office of the University show that the
Medical School plans little by way of affirmative action at any definite time so as to change
these figures and alter the imbalance in any
way. This Affirmative Action office was established after a prior investigation by the Department of Health, Education and Welfare of
sex discrimination at the University.

When the instant matter was taken before
the University Senate Subcommittee on Academic Freedom and Tenure it was indicated
that there was some substance to Dr. Johnson's

charges that there was some discrimination in
this department and it should be investigated.
The evidence with respect to discrimination is
clinched by the fact that the number of
women in the faculty has been decreasing in
the past two years as compared to men
whereas one would expect in the face of
charges such as these some attempt would be
made to increase the number of women.

The defendant introduced a large amount of
evidence indicating that plaintiff was not a satisfactory teacher. It is not the function of this
court to determine what weight should be
given in a university of the high stature of the
University of Pittsburgh to basic and advanced
research versus teaching abilities. Nevertheless
the handbook and guidelines adopted by this
University do indicate various criteria which
are to be used in determining tenure, only one
of which was given any weight in this particular case. As might be expected various individual students rated the plaintiff low in
teaching ability while others rated her
high. . . . When all the evaluations were
gathered in, however, it appeared that there
was only a miniscule difference between
plaintiff's standing and that of a man who was
given tenure. After the decision of the tenured
faculty, opinions derogatory to plaintiff's
teaching ability were sought and received to
justify the decision. The previous head of the
Department, however, contacted in Europe
stated that he thought she should be given
tenure.

In a case such as this the question is
whether there is a disparate treatment of males
and females based upon sex. . . . A review of
the testimony in this case indicates that there
has been such disparate treatment in this medical school. . . .

In arriving at our conclusion, we have also
carefully considered [another decision] where
the court said:

"Nor was the evidence insufficient to support the finding of a violation of Title VII as
to these particular plaintiffs. The evidence, especially the fact that during the six month pe-

riod following the plaintiffs' application (and when the plaintiffs were told that the company was not then hiring) 43 new male employees were hired despite the fact of plaintiffs' prior experience and good work records with the company, does support an inference of discrimination as the district court found. Plaintiffs made out a prima facie case of unlawful discrimination. . . ."

For these reasons, we find there is a strong likelihood of plaintiff's success on the merits. . . .

[The court concludes that:]

(1) This court has jurisdiction over the parties and this cause pursuant to [Title VII].

(2) Plaintiff has made out a prima facie case of intentional discrimination on the basis of her sex which will result in termination of employment as of June 30, 1973, by proof as follows:

(a) statistical evidence of a pattern and practice of discrimination against women in the School of Medicine, University of Pittsburgh. . . .

(b) evidence that a comparable male professor was granted tenure in 1971 in the School of Medicine, through disparate treatment based on sex. . . .

(c) proof that all of the male professors in plaintiff's department, regardless of rank or tenure, were uniformly given increases in compensation of $1,500 per year while plaintiff, the

only woman in the Biochemistry Department during the years 1967–1972, was given raises averaging $1,000 per year.

(d) the procedures here adopted in the Department of Biochemistry were never used prior to this termination.

(e) evidence that the defendants in their affirmative action program have taken no substantial steps to eliminate discrimination against women in the School of Medicine and the Department of Biochemistry.

(f) decreasing the number of women on the faculty of the School of Medicine in the years 1970–1972 while complaints of sex discrimination were pending.

(3) Plaintiff has established a prima facie case of arbitrary denial of equal protection by the actions of the tenure committee, the Chairman of the Department of Biochemistry and the Dean of the School of Medicine. . . .

(4) The evidence establishes a reasonable probability of plaintiff's success on the merits.

(5) A preliminary injunction should be issued to preserve the status quo pending final determination of this case on the merits. . . .

[Injunction issued.]

To find an unlawful sex bias, it is not necessary that the discriminatory practice focus on a characteristic peculiar to one of the genders or be directed at all members of a sex. It is only necessary that gender be a substantial factor in the determination; that is, for example, if a female plaintiff were a man, she would not have been treated in the same manner.

Sexual Harassment   An employer's policy of—or acquiescence in—compelling female employees to submit to sexual advances of male supervisors is unlawful under Title VII on the ground that it creates an artificial barrier to employment or advancement that is placed before one gender and not the other, despite the fact that both genders are similarly situated. Thus, for example, a Title VII violation occurs when (1) a supervisor makes sexual demands on a subordinate employee and conditions that employee's job status, in any manner, on a favorable response to those demands and (2) the employer does not take prompt remedial action after learning of the demands.

According to guidelines issued by the EEOC, *sexual harassment* exists if (1) submission to some "conduct" is either an explicit or implicit term or condition of employment; (2) submission or rejection serves as the basis for an employment decision; or (3) the "conduct" has the purpose or effect of substantially interfering with the individual's work performance or creating an intimidating, hostile, or offensive work environment.

Sexual harassment complaints can take the form of lawsuits filed in court or complaints filed with state, federal, or local administrative agencies. Judgments against employers and supervisors in sexual harassment cases have resulted in substantial monetary recoveries, as well as back wages, unemployment compensation, reinstatement and, in some cases, even payment of the employee's bills for psychiatric treatment.

 To minimize liability for employee sexual harassment, a business or other employer should (1) post a policy against such harassment, (2) include in the policy a workable mechanism for the prompt reporting of instances of harassment and for maintaining the anonymity of complainants, (3) communicate a warning to supervisors against such conduct, and (4) promptly and fully investigate any complaints of harassment received and deal severely with supervisors found to have violated the policy.

52:11   Age Discrimination

The *Age Discrimination in Employment Act of 1967* (ADEA) (29 USC §§ 621 et seq.) prohibits an employer from refusing to hire, discharging, or otherwise discriminating against an individual with respect to compensation, terms, conditions, or privileges of employment, based on age.

The act, which applies to employers, employment agencies, and labor unions, prohibits discrimination against workers between the ages of 40 and 70, and prohibits placing help wanted ads indicating preferences based on age. Nothing in the act affects the jurisdiction of state agencies performing similar functions with regard to discriminatory employment practices on account of age. Furthermore, a state statute that is broader in scope than the federal statute—such as one protecting persons of all ages—can be applied concurrently with the ADEA. To enforce the act, the Secretary of Labor can bring civil actions, and in those actions damages can be collected for the affected employees. However, before suing, the Secretary must attempt to eliminate the discriminatory practices and effect voluntary compliance with the act by conciliation, conference, and persuasion. The ADEA also specifically provides for lawsuits by individuals.

52:12   Religious Discrimination

Title VII makes it an unlawful employment practice for an employer to discriminate against an individual because of religion. "Religion" is defined as including all aspects of religious observance and practice, as well as belief. An obvious case of discrimination exists if an employer refuses to hire—or later discharges—a person because of religion. However, an employer is also required to make a reasonable attempt to accommodate an employee's religious beliefs. The touchstone of religious discrimination under Title VII is whether a "reasonable accommodation" can be reached between employer and employee without undue employer hardship. Although the precise limits of the employer's duty in this regard have not been established, the United States Supreme Court has held that to accommodate the needs of an employee whose religion required him to observe Saturday as his Sabbath, the employer was not required by Title VII to deny shift or job preferences to other employees, to take steps inconsistent with an otherwise valid collective bargaining agreement, or to bear more than a very small cost to effect an accommodation.[4]

 Title VII does not protect only those who are members of "recognized" religious societies. It also protects persons who express their religious views in an unorthodox fashion, as well as atheists and those who merely wish to be free from religious intimidation at work.

52:13   Discrimination Against the Handicapped

Several states have enacted legislation prohibiting job discrimination based on physical handicap. In some instances, this has been accomplished by amending existing antidiscrimination statutes to extend coverage to handicapped individuals. In other instances it has been done by enacting new statutes making nondiscrimination in employment a recognized right of the handicapped. The scope and application of this legislation depends on the language contained in its definitions with respect, for example, to who is to be considered "handicapped" or what constitutes a "physical handicap" under the statute. Availability of relief in each particular case rests on whether the handicap or disability was so related to job performance as to prevent the employee or applicant from actually fulfilling the requirements specified by the employer.

The Federal government has also acted in this area. Section 503(a) of the Rehabilitation Act of 1973 [29 USC § 793(a)] provides that any contract in excess of $2,500 entered into by any federal department or agency for procurement of personal property and nonpersonal services (including construction) for the United States is required to contain a provision requiring that the party contracting with the government will take affirmative action to employ and advance qualified handicapped individuals. This provision also applies to subcontracts in excess of $2,500 entered into by the prime contractor.

---

[4]*Trans World Airlines, Inc. v Hardison*, 432 US 63, 53 L Ed 2d 113, 97 S Ct 2264 (1977).

52:14   Affirmative Action and Reverse Discrimination

An employer may have an obligation under Title VII to fashion and implement an affirmative action program, even if not ordered to do so by a court. According to the EEOC, *affirmative action* means those actions appropriate to overcome effects of past or present practices, policies, or other barriers to equal employment opportunity. It encompasses activities such as soliciting applicants from minority-group organizations, setting goals for hiring or promotion of minority-group persons, instituting sensitivity training for managers and supervisors, and selecting a minority-group person over other applicants where, at least theoretically, all applicants are equally qualified.

There is no separate concept of *reverse discrimination* under Title VII in the EEOC's view; discrimination against *all* individuals because of race, color, religion, sex, or national origin is illegal. Based on several judicial opinions, however, it may be said that reverse discrimination is a policy or practice that favors or prefers minorities over males or whites. Hence, claims of reverse discrimination often challenge the propriety of affirmative action policies.

In reverse discrimination cases involving outright prejudice against particular individuals, the courts have been as zealous in guarding the rights of these people as they have been in guarding the rights of members of minority groups. On the other hand, in cases in which affirmative relief has been sought by minorities in the form of preferential treatment or the imposition of quotas, some courts have granted the relief on the theory that it is usually temporary; is not directed against particular whites or males; and, though not desirable, is justified because it sometimes appears to be the only way in which the effects of past discriminatory practices directed against minority groups can be corrected.

Key Concepts and Terms

- The National Labor Relations Act of 1935 gives employees the right of collective action in securing satisfactory wages, hours, and working conditions. It also lists employers' unfair labor practices and established the National Labor Relations Board to enforce the act.

- The Labor Management Relations Act (Taft–Hartley Act) attempted to place employers on an equal position with unions in bargaining and labor relations. It lists unfair labor practices on the part of unions and undertakes to regulate the collective bargaining process itself.

- The Labor Management Reporting and Disclosure Act (Landrum–Griffin Act) was intended to eliminate certain improper practices on the part of labor unions and employers that had resulted in frequent deprivation of employees' rights. The act imposes what has become known as a "bill of rights" for union members.

- A collective bargaining agreement covers the whole employment relationship and calls into being a new common law—the common law of a particular industry or shop.

- Collective bargaining agreements contain a provision for arbitration, the process by which a labor dispute that cannot be settled voluntarily through the contract's grievance procedure is referred to an impartial person for resolution.

- Federal (as well as state and local) fair employment practices laws have been enacted to prevent job discrimination. The most far-reaching federal statute in this regard is Title VII of the Civil Rights Act of 1964, which forbids discrimination in employment on the basis of race, color, religion, sex, or national origin, by employers, employment agencies, and unions.

- The Federal Age Discrimination in Employment Act of 1967 prohibits an employer from discrimination against an individual with respect to compensation, terms, conditions, or privileges of employment, based on age.

- Under Title VII, an employer may have an obligation to create an affirmative action program, to overcome effects of past or present practices of policies that discriminate against minority groups. Some courts have held that reverse discrimination is also a form of prohibited conduct under Title VII.

- Affirmative Action
- Age Discrimination in Employment Act of 1967
- Arbitration
- Civil Rights Act of 1964
- Collective Bargaining
- Collective Bargaining Agreement
- Equal Employment Opportunity Commission
- Labor Management Relations Act
- Labor Management Reporting and Disclosure Act
- Mediation and Conciliation
- National Labor Relations Act
- Reverse Discrimination
- Sexual Harassment
- Title VII
- Unfair Labor Practice

Questions and Case Problems

1. What is collective bargaining? Discuss its significance in modern industrial relations.

2. What is an unfair labor practice? State examples of unfair labor practices by (a) an employer and (b) a union.

3. Discuss arbitration and the circumstances in which the need for it arises. How does it differ from mediation and conciliation?

4. What is affirmative action? Is it a desirable policy? Why?

5. Croller Power Company maintains a disability plan for employees. Under the plan, disabled employees are paid 65 percent of their normal wages. The plan excludes certain disabilities, including pregnancy. Barbara, who has been unable to work for eight weeks because of her pregnancy, sues Croller. She alleges that the failure of Croller's plan to cover pregnancy is unlawful sex discrimination under Title VII of the Civil Rights Act of 1964. How should the case be decided?

6. Harry, a white salesman for Rallam Carpet Company, has worked for Rallam for 15 years. At the age of 58 he is discharged, and he is told by Rallam that the "economic hard times being experienced by the company" are the sole reason for

the discharge. Shortly before the discharge, however, Harry's manager had told him privately that "You might want to start looking around for a new position; I have word that upper management is seeking 'younger and newer' people." Three days after Harry's departure, Rallam hires a 27-year-old, highly qualified, black woman to replace Harry. On what grounds might Harry sue Rallam? Would his lawsuit be successful?

7. Local 346 of an oil workers union operated under a three-year collective bargaining agreement with Jekko Oil Company. The contract expired on December 31, and negotiations for a new contract between Jekko and Local 346 had begun 35 days before that date. It is now 28 days into the new year, and no new agreement has been reached. Representatives of both sides have met every day. However, Local 346 has submitted none of Jekko's proposals to its members, has made no counteroffers, and has rejected all Jekko contract offers outright. The union's position is that "We've heard nothing from Jekko worth talking about." Has Local 346 refused to bargain in good faith?

8. Alice Jones, the chief flight instructor at Gaynor Airlines, a small intrastate carrier, applies to Arrow Airlines, a large interstate carrier, for a position as pilot. She meets all requirements for Arrow's position except its height requirement; Jones is five feet two inches tall, and Arrow requires that its pilots be between five feet seven inches and six feet two inches in height. Jones sues Arrow under Title VII, alleging sex discrimination. She argues that, statistically, Arrow's height requirement excludes 93 percent of all female pilots but only 26 percent of all male pilots. Arrow argues that any person who is not at least five feet seven inches tall cannot handle the controls of its planes safely because of visibility factors stemming from cockpit design. Has Arrow violated Title VII?

9. A union, in an attempt to organize the employees of Gallagher Iron Works, hands out union leaflets across the street from Gallagher's plant each day just as the employees are entering and leaving the plant during shift changes. Gallagher places large trash containers in front of its plant. Each container has on it a prominent label stating "PUT YOUR UNION TRASH HERE." Gallagher also has several management personnel on the street noting the names of all employees who accept union leaflets. Is Gallagher acting illegally? If so, how and why?

10. Bellow Motor Lines, an interstate trucking line, recruits its drivers primarily by word-of-mouth referrals. It neither publishes help-wanted ads nor recruits through job placement agencies. Statistically, 89 percent of Bellow's drivers are white male; only 11 percent are black, although blacks comprise about 30 percent of the local population. Williams, a black male who is licensed to drive heavy trucks and is an experienced driver, applies for a job with Bellow. He is told that there are no openings for drivers. Later, Williams learns that Bellow hired Jackson, a white male, as a driver one week after refusing to hire Williams. Jackson is the second cousin of one of Bellow's current drivers, by whom he was advised about a job opening. Williams sues Bellow for violation of Title VII. How should the court decide the case?

PART ELEVEN

Unfair Business Practices and White-Collar Crime

Introductory Comments

Businesses of every kind and size can be victims of—and liable for—activities that constitute unfair competition. The law has long recognized the businessperson's right to be protected from these activities, and there is an increasing amount of litigation in this area.

Unfair competition often involves the commission of an unfair business practice, which can consist of a breach of contract, a tort, a violation of a statute, or a combination of these. Examples include wrongfully taking business away from another, engaging in what the law defines as an "unfair trade practice," wrongfully appropriating another's ideas or creations, misusing trade secrets, violating an agreement not to compete, and making false disparaging statements about another's business or products. These practices, and the rights and liabilities of the parties involved, are discussed in Chapter 53.

An extreme example of unfair competition is an agreement or scheme by which competi-

tion is significantly reduced or eliminated altogether. Such an agreement or scheme can involve destructive price discrimination or lead to the creation of a monopoly. This is where the law of antitrust enters the picture. As is clear from the discussion in Chapter 54, an understanding of antitrust law is essential to a businessperson's survival in the marketplace.

It is usually a business, rather than an individual, that commits an unfair business practice or violates an antitrust law. However, a businessperson himself can also be personally liable for engaging in activities that constitute what is known as white-collar crime. Indeed, the notion that a businessperson is "above the law" has been dispelled as evidence of white-collar crime has increased in recent years. Chapter 55 focuses on this problem, discussing the more common types of white-collar crime and pointing out the magnitude of the problem.

53 Unfair Trade Practices and Wrongful Appropriation of Ideas

53:1 Wrongful Interference

Generally, a contract is made between two persons with the intention by both parties to perform exactly according to the agreement. Sometimes, however, a third person acts in such a manner as to prompt one of the contracting parties to breach the agreement. For example, a third person might persuade an independent contractor to terminate his employment with an employer. In other situations, the third person may substantially interfere with the performance of a contract short of causing its actual breach. In still other instances, a third person may dissuade a prospective contracting party from entering into a contract in the first place.

In each of these situations, wrongful *interference* with contract has occurred. The person so interfering with the actual or prospective contractual relationship can be held liable to the injured party. Liability is imposed because the contracting parties have inviolable property rights to fulfill the contract or to have it fulfilled, to reap profits resulting from its performance, and to compel performance by the other party.

Although the existence of a valid contract must usually be shown before an injured party can recover for wrongful interference with contract, it is not necessary in all cases. If a contractual relation would have been created but for the third party's interference, liability may be imposed. Absolute certainty of an impending agreement with another is not required. Rather, reasonable assurance that a contract would have been formed but for the interference, in view of all the circumstances, is sufficient to establish liability.

The law is uncertain as to whether a contract must be legally enforceable before a third person can be held liable for interference. In some states, liability will be imposed even if the underlying contract is unenforceable against the other contracting party because of formal defects, oppressive provisions, or the like. In other states, liability will not be imposed if the contract itself is unenforceable. In view of the public policy to the effect that the basis of liability is the interference with an existing relationship—rather than interference with a contract—the first view appears to be the better approach. Indeed, a majority of states agree and have enacted statutes that impose liability despite the unenforceability of the underlying contract. The following case analyzes the elements of wrongful interference with contract.

Childress
v
Abeles
240 NC 667, 84 SE2d 176
(North Carolina Supreme Court, 1954)

[Childress (the plaintiff) entered into a contract with the Trogdon Furniture Company to manufacture cabinets for Abeles (the defendant). Under the contract, Childress was to be paid a commission for each cabinet Trogdon manufactured for Abeles. Subsequently, a dispute arose between Childress and Abeles. Abeles notified Trogdon that it was to cease paying commissions to Childress and that if it refused to cease, Abeles would not buy any more cabinets. As a result, Trogdon stopped paying commissions to Childress under the Childress–Trogdon contract. Childress then sued Abeles for willful inducement of breach of contract. Judgment was for Childress, and Abeles appealed.]

Parket, Justice.

*   *   *

"The right to make contracts is both a liberty and a property right." ... In consequence, the overwhelming weight of authority in this nation is that an action in tort lies against an outsider who knowingly, intentionally and unjustifiably induces one party to a contract to breach it to the damage of the other party. ...

To subject the outsider to liability for compensatory damages on account of this tort, the plaintiff must allege and prove these essential elements of the wrong: *First,* that a valid contract existed between the plaintiff and a third person, conferring upon the plaintiff some contractual right against the third person. ...

Second, that the outsider had knowledge of the plaintiff's contract with the third person. ... *Third,* that the outsider intentionally induces the third person not to perform his contract with the plaintiff. ... *Fourth,* that in so doing the outsider acted without justification. ... *Fifth,* that the outsider's act caused the plaintiff actual damages. ...

The outsider has knowledge of the contract within the meaning of the second element of the tort if he knows the facts which give rise to the plaintiff's contractual right against the third person. "If he knows those facts, he is subject to liability even though he is mistaken as to their legal significance and believes that there is no contract or that the contract means something other than what it is judicially held to mean." ...

The complaint in substance alleges the existence of a valid contract between the plaintiff and the Trogdon Furniture Co., conferring on plaintiff contractual rights against the Trogdon Furniture Co.; that the defendants had knowledge of this contract; that plaintiff had fully performed and was entitled to the full commissions, and the defendants intentionally and without justification induced the Trogdon Furniture Company not to perform its contract with the plaintiff to the plaintiff's actual damage. The allegations of the complaint ... contain all the essential allegations necessary to recover damages for wrongfully inducing a breach of contract. ...

The evidence in the Record shows that the defendants had full knowledge of the facts which gave rise to the plaintiff's contractual right against the Trogdon Furniture Company, and full knowledge that the Trogdon Furniture Company was paying the plaintiff commissions on the goods manufactured and sold by it to them. Acting with this knowledge they knew that their acts in wrongfully inducing the Trogdon Furniture Company to breach its contract with plaintiff would be highly injurious to him. . . .

[Judgment affirmed.]

Interference with Economic Advantage   By analogy to interference with contract, liability can also be imposed for intentional interference with economic advantage in the absence of contract. Under this theory, a party who has reasonable expectations of acquiring an economic advantage in a business transaction is protected from unjustified interference.

Permissible or Justifiable Interference   In certain situations, a third person is privileged to protect and further his own interests (or those of others) by interfering with another's contract or economic advantage. This privilege is called justification. Whether one is justified in interfering in any particular situation is not determined by precise standards. It is determined by balancing conflicting considerations. The importance of the objective advanced by the interference is weighed against the importance of the interest affected. The interfering party's conduct must be scrutinized, as must the relationship between the contracting parties and all other relevant matters. The line separating permissible behavior and unjustified interference reflects the ethical standards of the community. The question of justification often boils down to whether the third party transgressed generally accepted standards of common morality or whether he merely played by the "rules of the game."

Competition is the most common basis of justifiable interference. This is so because a person has no right to be protected against reasonable competition. Thus, unless wrongful means are employed, or unless a restraint of trade is created, one who intentionally causes another not to enter into (or not to continue) a contractual relation with a competitor is usually not liable for interference. Competition justifies the conduct.

A person is also justified in interfering with a contract or economic advantage of another if he acts to protect a legitimate interest of his own and uses lawful and proper methods in doing so under the circumstances. Thus, a person who, having a financial interest in the business of a third person, intentionally causes that person not to enter into a prospective contractual relationship with another does not interfere improperly so long as he does not employ wrongful means. He is justified in acting in his own interest.

EXAMPLE
Caldwell loans money to Baker for a motion picture. Baker is on the verge of signing Claudine to play the lead role in the film. Caldwell objects to the casting of Claudine, and as a result Baker gives the part to Arcadia. Caldwell's interference with the prospective contract between Claudine and Baker is not improper, and Caldwell is not liable to Claudine. His financial interest in the film justifies his interest and participation in the choice of actresses.

Finally, a person who bears responsibility for another may be permitted to interfere in that person's contractual relations or business activities. So long as the person responsible acts to protect the other's welfare and does not employ wrongful measures, he is justified in interfering in the other person's business activities. This rule applies to situations in which, by ordinary standards of decent conduct, one person is charged with responsibility for protecting another's welfare. This situation may exist, for example, in the relationship of parent and child, minister and member of his congregation, teacher and pupil, attorney and client, and employer and employee.

53:2   Unfair Trade Practices; Trade Secrets

The economy of the United States is based on a compromise between the theory of laissez faire (a policy opposing governmental interference in business) and a policy advocating complete governmental control over business. During the past 80 years, American legislators and courts have adopted a so-called "regulated competition" under which private individuals have the maximum degree of discretion and control over their business activities so long as traditional notions of fairness and ethics are observed. In essence, the law acts as a reference to promote fairness in the marketplace.

The law of *unfair trade practices* originally focused on businesses that palmed off their own goods as being those of a rival business. Subsequently, the law was extended to proscribe parasitism under the theory that a business may not appropriate its competitor's skill, expenditures, or labor. Today, the law regulating unfair trade practices applies to a host of different business practices, including trade secrets, trade libel, unfair packaging and labeling, and false advertising. These are discussed below and in 53:3 through 53:5.

Trade Secrets   The concept of *trade secret* is nebulous; the term has several definitions. Essentially, a trade secret can be any formula, pattern, device, or compilation of information used in business to obtain an advantage over competitors who do not know about it or who do not use it. A trade secret may also be a plan or process, tool, mechanism, or compound, known only to its owner and his key employees. A trade secret differs from other secret business information. Unlike business secrets in general, a trade secret is more than mere information about the conduct of a business, such as contract bids, salaries of key employees, or knowledge of new products. A trade secret is something actually used in a business to its advantage.

Misuse of a trade secret is an unfair business practice. Therefore, an employee who learns of a trade secret cannot use it after leaving his employment. The employee can take and use the general skill or knowledge acquired during the course of his employment, but he is not permitted to disclose the former employer's trade secrets. If he does so, the owner can obtain injunctive relief or even damages in appropriate cases.

Customer information and customer lists may constitute a trade secret. The following case discusses the factors used in determining whether a former employee can use such information acquired during his prior employment.

Town & Country House & Homes Service, Inc.

v

Evans
150 Conn 314, 189 A2d 390
(Connecticut Supreme Court, 1963)

[The plaintiff, the owner of a housecleaning business, sued to enjoin a former employee from soliciting the plaintiff's customers, and for damages for having solicited his customers. The trial judge rendered judgment for the defendant, and the plaintiff appealed.]

Shea, Associate Justice.

*   *   *

The plaintiff conducts a housecleaning business and provides men and machinery for that purpose. The defendant was employed by the plaintiff from May, 1957, to March, 1960. . . . He worked for the plaintiff at the homes of various customers . . . in this state and . . . in New York. During the latter part of his employment, he told a number of the plaintiff's customers that he was planning to enter the housecleaning business for himself, and he solicited business from them. Thereafter, the defendant terminated his employment and started his own housecleaning business. At the time of the trial he had fifteen regular customers, some of whom were former customers of the plaintiff.

The [trial] court found that the defendant solicited customers for his own business before his employment with the plaintiff was terminated. Such action was in direct competition with his employer and was contrary to the employer's interest. It was a betrayal of the employer's trust and confidence in the defendant. . . .

Trade secrets are the property of the employer and cannot be used by the employee for his own benefit. The lack of any express agreement on the part of the employee not to disclose a trade secret is not significant. The law will import into every contract of employment a prohibition against the use of a trade secret by the employee for his own benefit, to the detriment of his employer, if the secret was acquired by the employee in the course of his employment. . . . A list of customers, if their trade and patronage have been secured by years of business effort and advertising and the expenditure of time and money, constitutes an important part of a business and is in the nature of a trade secret. It is the property of the employer and may not be used by the employee as his own property or to his employer's prejudice. . . .

[Judgment reversed.]

 The liability of third persons is quite different from liability imposed on employees for misuse of trade secrets. A third person will be held liable for misuse only if a trade secret has been wrongfully acquired. Therefore, if a competitor discovers another's trade secret by improper means, or has learned of it from a former employee, he may be enjoined from using the secret or held liable in damages to the secret's owner. If a competitor discovers a trade secret by fair means, such as through independent discovery, the owner will not be protected.

Covenants Not to Compete   An employer frequently attempts to protect trade secrets by entering into a contract with employees under which the employees agree not to compete with the employer for a particular length of time within a specific geographical area, after leaving the employer's business. Such an agreement is known as a *covenant not to compete*. Although this kind of agreement was regarded as contrary to public policy and therefore void at common law, today a covenant not to compete is generally valid and enforceable if it is supported by consideration and is reasonable and consistent with the public interest.

A covenant not to compete can take any number of forms, including that of an agreement by the employee to forfeit benefits under a noncontributory retirement plan or profit-sharing trust in the event of postemployment competition. In most states, the restriction must be agreed on when employment first begins. There is no fixed formula for determining whether a particular covenant not to compete is reasonable; the question must be decided on a case-by-case basis. There are, however, certain elements the courts frequently consider in ascertaining reasonableness, including, for example, the consideration supporting the covenant, threatened danger to the employer in the absence of a restriction on competition, economic hardship imposed on the employee as a result of a limit on his ability to compete, and the effect of an anticompetitive covenant on the public interest. Usually, a covenant that is unlimited as to both time and area will be held invalid as being unreasonable.

Whether the employee will suffer an unreasonable economic hardship due to the restriction imposed on his ability to compete has been held to depend on such factors as the general business conditions then prevailing, the employee's ability to continue supporting himself and his family, and the need for the employee to change his occupation or residence.

EXAMPLE

Members of a medical partnership hire an obstetrician for their clinic for a three-year period. Under the contract, the obstetrician covenants that on separation from the clinic for any reason he will refrain from practicing medicine within a 25-mile radius of the city in which the clinic is located. Subsequently, he leaves the clinic and immediately establishes a new practice within the proscribed area. He has violated the anticompetition clause in the contract, and a court can issue an injunction against him because the anticompetitive covenant is reasonable.

 A businessperson should take steps to secure an understanding with and a legally binding commitment from all employees as to the confidential nature of information acquired by the employee during his employment. In this regard, the businessperson may set forth in the employment contract a provision under which the employee promises not to use or disclose any of the employer's trade secrets either during or subsequent to the employment relationship.

Abandonment of Trade Secret   Once a trade secret has been abandoned it is no longer protectable, no longer a trade secret. Abandonment entails a general public disclosure, such as public sale of the article or its description in literature available to the public. Disclosure that destroys trade secret protection can also occur through the voluntary publication of the secret in, for example, technical or trade journals, or advertising material. The filing of a patent application (see 53:8) does not constitute an abandonment of the trade secret. Nor is there an abandonment if the patent application is rejected. Actual issuance of a patent, however, is considered an abandonment.

53:3   Trade Libel

Trade libel, or disparagement as it is also called, arises when a person communicates false or disparaging statements about another's property, goods, or services, resulting in the actual loss of business. A trade libel need not be defamatory.[1] For example, a false statement made to a potential customer, such as "Smythe is out of business, so buy your goods from me" is a trade libel. It is not defamatory, because it does not say anything bad about Smythe.

A lawsuit based on trade libel is difficult to maintain successfully because of the well-recognized business privilege to promote one's own product at the expense of competitors. On the theory that one who offers goods or services in the marketplace opens himself to competitor criticism, the courts have allowed as "fair comment" a very broad scope of critical statements as to products or services without finding that trade libel has been committed. This privilege of fair comment, however, does not extend to the making of specific false claims about another's property, products, or business. For example, one business may claim that its product is "finer," of "higher quality," or performs "better" than another. At the same time, it may not state that another's goods are "seconds" or "prison-made" when in fact they are not.

The following case discusses the public policy considerations underpinning trade libel. Note the discussion of permissible product comparison and when comparisons are deemed unethical and unfair.

Testing Systems, Inc.

v

Magnaflux Corp.
251 F Supp 286, 149 USPQ 129
(United States District Court, ED Pennsylvania, 1966)

[Testing Systems sued its business competitor, Magnaflux Corporation, alleging that Magnaflux had committed trade libel by falsely stating that the federal government had tested Testing Systems' product and found it to be only 40 percent as effec-

tive as its own. Magnaflex defended itself on the grounds that it was permissible to compare products in such a manner and that no trade libel had occurred. The defendant moved for dismissal of the complaint.]

John W. Lord, Jr., District Judge.

*   *   *

This is an action for trade libel or disparagement of property. . . .

---

[1]Defamation is discussed in Chapter 5.

It would serve no useful purpose to dwell at length on the issue of unfavorable comparison. Suffice it to say ... that a statement which takes the form of an unfavorable comparison of products, or which "puffs" or exaggerates the quality of one's own product is not ordinarily actionable....

The fine line that separates healthy competitive effort from underhanded business tactics is frequently difficult to determine. Apart from the tradesman's right of free speech, which must be vigorously safeguarded, the public has a genuine interest in learning the relative merits of particular products, however that may come about. To advance these interests the law of the market place gives the competitor a wide berth in the conduct of his business. As [was said in a 1932 case],

> "[H]e may send out circulars, or give information verbally, to customers of other men, knowing they are bound by contract for a definite term, although acting upon the expectation and with the purpose of getting the trade of such persons for himself.
>
> "[H]e may use any mode of persuasion with such a customer ... which appeals to his self-interest, reason, or even his prejudices.
>
> "[H]e may descant upon the extent of his rival's facilities compared with his own, his rival's means, his insolvency, if it be a fact, and the benefits which will result to the customer in the future from coming to the solicitor rather than remaining where he is. ... 'the law of competition' ... takes little note of the ordinary rules of good neighborhood or abstract morality." ...

Nonetheless, there is an outer perimeter to permissible conduct. The tradesman must be assured that his competitors will not be suffered to engage in conduct which falls below the minimum standard of fair dealing. "[I]t is no answer that they can defend themselves by also resorting to disparagement. A self-respecting business man will not voluntarily adopt, and should not be driven to adopt, a selling method which he regards as undignified, un-

fair, and repulsive. A competitor should not, by pursuing an unethical practice force his rival to choose between its adoption and the loss of his trade." ...

The defendant's comments in the case presently before this Court do not entitle him to the protection accorded to "unfavorable comparison." There is a readily observable difference between saying that one's product is, in general, better than another's (though even this is subject to serious objection) ... and asserting, as here, that such other's is only 40% as effective as one's own. The former, arguably, merely expresses an opinion, the truth or falsity of which is difficult or impossible of ascertainment. The latter, however, is an assertion of fact, not subject to the same frailties of proof, implying that the party making the statement is fortified with the substantive facts necessary to make it. This distinction has never been seriously questioned.... The defendant in this case admittedly circulated to plaintiff's present and prospective customers false statements to the effect that the government had tested both products and found the defendant's to be 60% more effective than plaintiff's. This is not the sort of "comparison" that courts will protect.

Apart from this, there is at least one additional factor which withdraws the defendant's comments from the category of unfavorable comparison. Not content with making the admittedly false statements and allowing them to be evaluated independently of any extraneous influence, the defendant here gave added authenticity to its assertions by invoking the reputation of a third party, the United States Government. It is unnecessary to speculate on the additional force the defendant's remarks must have had when coupled with the purported approval of so highly credible a source. This, of course, is to say nothing of the statements to the effect that the plaintiff had been "thrown out," which by no stretch of the imagination could be termed mere comparison.

For all of the above reasons, it is the judg-

ment of this Court that the defendant's remarks are actionable. . . .

[Motion to dismiss granted on another

ground, relating to damages, unless plaintiff
amended complaint within 30 days to cure the
defect.]

53:4   Packaging and Labeling

Package design is vitally important to successful product marketing. It is often the
sole difference between similar goods. Packaging is also a significant determinant
of buying behavior. The term "trade dress" describes the appearance of a product.
Trade dress consists of the peculiar visual appearance produced by a particular
arrangement or combination of colors, symbols, words, and designs on a label,
package, or product. The arrangement or combination is intended to make the
source of one product distinguishable from another and to promote its sale. Trade
dress is distinct from copyright, trademark, or trade name protection.

The underlying basis of unfair competition law as applied to *trade dress simulation* is the protection of consumers from confusion as to the source of goods. The
law is also based on the goal of preventing one business from trading on the established goodwill of another by simulating the packaging or labeling of an existing
product.

Many states have enacted legislation to protect business from trade dress simulation or from unfair packaging and labeling practices. The most important is the
Uniform Deceptive Trade Practices Act. The act codifies the modern view of trade
dress unfair competition by granting relief to businesses where there is a likelihood of confusion or misunderstanding as to the source of goods or services.

Confusion is especially likely to occur when a particular trade dress has acquired
what is known as a *secondary meaning.* "Secondary meaning" in this context refers
to consumer identification of the trade dress sought to be protected with the producer of the goods. A trade dress acquires a secondary meaning when its total
image has become associated in the public mind with the source or origin of the
goods (rather than with the goods themselves) and a particular manufacturer. In
one case, for example, Clairol, Inc., a cosmetics manufacturer, was successful in
convincing a court that the distinctive trade dress used for its hydrogen peroxide
hair product had acquired a secondary meaning.[2]

53:5   False Advertising

False statements about a particular product constitute an unfair trade practice. The
essence of *false advertising* is fraudulent misrepresentation, which results in injury
to competitors or customers. Whether false advertising has occurred requires, in
each case, a balancing of several interests: the interest of a business to advertise its

---

[2]*Clairol, Inc. v Andrea Dumon, Inc.,* 14 Ill App 3d 641, 303 NE2d 177, 86 ALR3d 493 (Illinois Appellate
  Court, 1973).

goods and services as aggressively and effectively as possible, even to the point of issuing highly misleading overstatements (puffing); the interest of business competitors not to be unjustifiably maligned as to their products; and the interest of the consumer to be told the truth about the products and services offered.

A consumer damaged by false advertising can bring a common-law action against the false advertiser for fraud. The attorney general in some states is authorized to bring an action on behalf of all consumers who have been defrauded. In addition, many states have laws based on the Uniform Deceptive Trade Practices Act, which prohibits deceptive commercial conduct and, among other things, misleading advertising. The act permits "a person likely to be damaged by a deceptive trade practice of another" to sue for injunctive relief to prevent the practice. States that have not adopted the act have strong legislation against false advertising.

Lanham Act   Because of the difficulties in establishing liability for common-law false advertising in state courts, and because the problems of false advertising are nationwide, Congress enacted § 43(a) of the *Lanham Act* [15 USC § 1125(a)] governing the sale of goods or services in interstate commerce. Section 43(a) prohibits competitors from transacting business in a manner that unnecessarily and unfairly harms another's business. It provides legal remedies to competitors who are injured by false advertising in interstate commerce.

EXAMPLE
A pharmaceutical company places advertising in magazines and on television. The ads compare pain relievers and claim that one of the company's drugs is superior to competitive drugs as an analgesic and inflammation reducer. On evidence that such claims are false, the advertising is enjoinable as a misrepresentation under § 43(a).

Liability under § 43(a) of the Lanham Act is not restricted solely to descriptions and representations that are literally false. Relief can also be granted if advertising simply creates a false impression by omission of relevant information. For example, a distributor of foreign-made goods who omits placing the true country of origin of the imported goods on the packaging and uses the phrase "United States" on the package to create the impression of domestic origin creates a false impression; his advertising violates § 43(a).

Section 43(a) has been applied in many different circumstances. By way of illustration, the following acts have been held to constitute false advertising under § 43(a): selling goods by falsely representing that they are endorsed by a particular person or organization, falsely representing that a product was designed or authorized by a particular person, advertising an inferior product by using a picture of a competing product, selling goods from a catalog confusingly similar in format to another's catalog, advertising a product with a false representation of a consumer product testing organization's rating, and palming off an inferior product in response to orders for another product.

Federal Trade Commission   The *Federal Trade Commission Act* (FTCA) declares both "unfair methods of competition" and "unfair or deceptive acts or practices" in commerce to be unlawful [15 USC § 45(a)]. The *Federal Trade Commission* (FTC) has exclusive authority to enforce the FTCA. In determining whether a business practice is unfair, the FTC considers the following factors: (1) whether the practice offends public policy, as established by statutes, the common law, or otherwise; (2) whether it is immoral, unethical, oppressive, or unscrupulous; and (3) whether it causes substantial injury to consumers, competitors, or other businessmen. The FTC is specifically authorized to prevent false advertising of food, drugs, and cosmetics (15 USC § 52).

Several general principles applicable to determining whether particular business practices constitute false advertising under the FTCA have been recognized. Among these is that for an advertisement to be found deceptive, it need not be shown that the advertiser lacked good faith or intended to deceive. Nor need it be shown, if advertisements have a capacity to deceive, that actual deception resulted. Rather, advertisements are judged on the basis of the meaning they convey to an average or unsophisticated person, not an expert.

When the FTC, after a hearing, rules that a particular act, practice, or method of competition is prohibited by the FTCA, the FTC is required to make a written report of its findings. It may issue to the offending business a cease and desist order, which prohibits the method of competition in question. The party against whom a cease and desist order is issued may then appeal and seek judicial relief from the order.

If the FTC finds that a company has engaged in false and deceptive advertising with regard to a particular product, the FTC can also order the company to conduct corrective advertising. This could involve a specific proportion of the company's advertising print space or broadcast time or a specified proportion of the company's total advertising expenditures.

 Many states have so-called "little FTC" laws, which provide that the state attorney general, or a local prosecutor, can sue on behalf of defrauded buyers for injunctive relief or damages. Most state statutes of this sort also permit a consumer to sue a merchant who is engaged in unfair practices. Other states have enacted legislation under which private individuals or companies can sue other companies that have committed deceptive trade practices or false advertising.

Deceptive Television Commercials   Television commercials represent a recurrent problem for the advertiser. The true colors of coffee, orange juice, and iced tea, for example, are lost in transmission on a television screen, and artificial substances must be substituted to obtain a "natural" look. The hot television lights require the use, for example, of mashed potatoes for ice cream, and shaving cream must be used to get the kind of head that is normal on a glass of beer. The use of such mock-ups or props in television commercials is not necessarily an unfair trade practice. However, it is an unfair trade practice to show a product experiment in a television commercial as objective proof of a product claim while conveying to viewers the false impression that they are seeing the experiment for themselves, when in fact they are seeing mock-ups.

53:6 Trademarks

A *trademark* is a word, name, symbol, or device used by a manufacturer to identify his goods and distinguish them from those manufactured or sold by others. Symbols used to identify services, as opposed to goods, are usually called service marks. Since the legal requirements for trademarks and service marks are essentially the same, both are referred to as trademarks. The term "trade name" is used to distinguish partnerships, corporations, and other businesses. Specifically, a trade name is a term or symbol that identifies a business and its goodwill; trademarks and service marks identify and distinguish goods and services.

A trademark or service mark can be any identifying symbol. It may be a well-known word (such as "Jockey" with respect to underwear), a familiar design (such as that on the Kleenex tissue box), a distinctive container (such as the Coca Cola bottle), or a distinctive building design (such as McDonald's golden arches).

A word or symbol qualifies as a trademark if (1) there is a tangible symbol—a word, name, device, symbol, or any combination of these; (2) there is actual adoption and use of the symbol as a mark by a manufacturer or seller of goods or services, and (3) the function of the word or symbol is to identify and distinguish the seller's goods from goods made or sold by others. The symbol must be distinctive enough to identify and distinguish the goods that bear the symbol from other similar goods.

Trademark law serves a dual function: it protects the merchant in the use of his trademarks and it protects the people who rely on the trademarks in purchasing goods or services. The trademark has thus been likened to the "business autograph" of the owner; it is a representation that articles on which it is placed are made or prepared by a particular firm.

Lanham Act   While trademark protection is available under state law, the major source of trademark law is the Federal Trademark Act of 1946 (15 USC §§ 1051–1127), commonly known as the Lanham Act. Any person or business can register a trademark with the United States Patent and Trademark Office if the trademark has been used in interstate commerce. Once a trademark has been registered, the owner has the exclusive right to use it. Anyone who reproduces or copies the trademark in connection with the sale or advertising of goods or services when such use is likely to cause confusion or mistake, or to deceive, is liable in damages to the owner of the trademark.

There is no exact definition of the degree of resemblance that is necessary to constitute trademark *infringement*. However, a rule has been formulated that no merchant can adopt a trademark that so resembles another that ordinary purchasers, buying with ordinary care, are likely to be misled. The likelihood of purchaser confusion is determined by examining many factors. These factors include the type of trademark at issue, similarity of design, similarity of product, identity of retail outlets and purchasers, identity of advertising media utilized, the defendant's intent, and whether actual confusion resulted. These different factors are illustrated in the following decision.

Dallas Cowboys Cheerleaders, Inc.

v

Pussycat Cinema, Ltd.
604 F2d 200
(United States Court of Appeals, Second Circuit, 1979)

[*The Dallas Cowboys Cheerleaders, Inc., sued the owner and distributor of a motion picture for exhibiting a movie in which, without the plaintiff's permission, the actresses wore uniforms essentially identical to uniforms in which the plaintiff had a trademark. The suit alleged trademark infringement under the Lanham Act. At an early stage of the proceeding, the trial court gave the plaintiff temporary relief by issuing a preliminary injunction. The injunction prevented the defendants from exhibiting or distributing the movie until a final decision was reached in the lawsuit. From the court's order, the defendants appealed.*]

Van Graafeiland, Circuit Judge.

*   *   *

At all the football games and public events where plaintiff's cheerleaders appear and on all commercial items depicting the cheerleaders, the women are clad in . . . distinctive uniform. The familiar outfit consists of white vinyl boots, white shorts, a white belt decorated with blue stars, a blue bolero blouse, and a white vest decorated with three blue stars on each side of the front and a white fringe around the bottom. In this action plaintiff asserts that it has a trademark in its uniform and that defendants have infringed . . . that trademark in advertising and exhibiting [the movie entitled] "Debbie Does Dallas."

Pussycat Cinema, Ltd., is a New York corporation which owns a movie theatre in New York City. . . . In November 1978 the Pussycat Cinema began to show "Debbie Does Dallas,"

a gross and revolting sex film. . . . In the movie's final scene Debbie dons a uniform strikingly similar to that worn by the Dallas Cowboys Cheerleaders and for approximately twelve minutes of film footage engages in various sex acts while clad or partially clad in the uniform. Defendants advertised the movie with marquee posters depicting Debbie in the allegedly infringing uniform and containing such captions as "Starring Ex Dallas Cowgirl Cheerleader Bambi Woods" and "You'll do more than cheer for this X Dallas Cheerleader." Similar advertisements appeared in the newspapers. . . .

. . . In the instant case the combination of the white boots, white shorts, blue blouse, and white star-studded vest and belt is an arbitrary design which makes the otherwise functional uniform trademarkable. . . .

Having found that plaintiff has a trademark in its uniform, we must determine whether the depiction of the uniform in "Debbie Does Dallas" violates that trademark. The district court found that the uniform worn in the movie and shown on the marquee closely resembled plaintiff's uniform and that the public was likely to identify it as plaintiff's uniform. Our own comparison of the two uniforms convinces us that the district court was correct, and defendants do not seriously contend that the uniform shown in the movie is not almost identical with plaintiff's. Defendant's contention is that, despite the striking similarity of the two uniforms, the public is unlikely to be confused within the meaning of section 43(a) of the Lanham Act.

Defendants assert that the Lanham Act requires confusion as to the origin of the film, and they contend that no reasonable person would believe that the film originated with plaintiff. Appellants read the confusion requirement too narrowly. In order to be confused, a consumer need not believe that the owner of the mark actually produced the item and placed it on the market. . . . The public's belief that the mark's owner sponsored or otherwise approved the use of the trademark satisfies the confusion requirement. In the instant case, the uniform depicted in "Debbie Does Dallas" unquestionably brings to mind the Dallas Cowboys Cheerleaders. Indeed, it is hard to believe that anyone who had seen defendants' sexually depraved film could ever thereafter disassociate it from plaintiff's cheerleaders. . . .

Plaintiff expects to establish on trial that the public may associate it with defendants' movie and be confused into believing that plaintiff sponsored the movie, provided some of the actors, licensed defendants to use the uniform, or was in some other way connected with the production. The trademark laws are designed not only to prevent consumer confusion but also to protect "the synonymous right of a trademark owner to control his product's reputation." . . .

[Judgment affirmed.]

53:7   Copyright

A person has a common-law property right in the tangible expression of his creative works and can obtain redress against anyone who deprives him of that right or wrongfully copies his work. The common-law *copyright* protects such tangible forms of expression as writings, letters, prints, pictures, paintings, photographs, pictorial illustrations, statues, and other artistic productions, as well as musical, dramatic, and literary compositions, either written or printed. In short, common-law copyright protects virtually all original tangible expressions of a person's intellectual creativity.

The manner of presenting or interpreting a work is a recognized artistic expression and can also be protected by common-law copyright. For example, a news commentator has a common-law copyright in his voice and manner of presentation; an orchestra has an exclusive common-law right in its particular musical rendition of a musical composition, even though the composition is itself not copyrightable; and a broadcast of an athletic event is protected by common-law copyright. Copyright protection does not, however, extend to the *ideas* expressed in subject matter but only to the *form or mode of expression*. For example, the bare scheme or skeleton of a plot is an idea and therefore is not protected by common-law copyright.

Although ideas as such are not protected by copyright, they may be protected by the general principles of unfair competition where there has been a breach of some contractual or fiduciary relationship; for example, ideas can be protected by contract.

Federal Copyright Law   Under the Constitution of the United States, Congress is empowered to grant to authors a limited monopoly (exclusive use) for their writings (Article 1, § 8). This power covers not only literary work, but all works of artistic achievement. A work need not be fine art nor highly creative. It need only be an original creation.

The federal Copyright Act (17 USC §§ 101 et seq.), which was substantially revised in 1978, now provides statutory copyright protection in original works of authorship "fixed in any tangible medium of expression, now known or later developed, from which they can be perceived, reproduced, or otherwise communicated, either directly or with the aid of a machine or device." Such copyrightable works of authorship include literary, musical, or dramatic works, including any accompanying music; pantomimes and choreographic works; motion pictures and other audiovisual works; and sound recordings. The act specifies, however, that in no case does copyright protection for an original work of authorship extend to any idea, procedure, process, system, method of operation, concept, principle, or discovery, regardless of the form in which it is described, explained, illustrated, or embodied in such work [17 USC § 102(b)].

Another section of the act (17 USC § 106) gives the owner of a copyright the exclusive right to do (and to authorize others to do) the following: reproduce the copyrighted work; prepare derivative works based on the copyrighted work; distribute copies of the copyrighted work to the public by sale or other transfer of ownership, or by rental, lease, or lending; perform the copyrighted work publicly (in the case of literary, musical, dramatic, and choreographic works; pantomimes; and motion pictures and other audiovisual works); and display the copyrighted work publicly (in the case of literary, musical, dramatic, and choreographic, or sculptural works, including the individual images of a motion picture or other audiovisual work).

A copyright owner can transfer to another person his rights in a copyright. The transfer of *exclusive* rights to a federal copyright, however, is not valid unless the transfer is in writing and signed by the owner of the rights conveyed or the owner's authorized agent. The transfer of a statutory copyright on a nonexclusive basis does not require a writing.

It is illegal for anyone to infringe on any of the rights provided to the owner of a copyright by the Copyright Act. Infringement will be found if (1) the defendant's "work" is essentially identical to the plaintiff's and (2) the defendant is shown to have had access to the plaintiff's work. The owner of a statutory copyright has a wide choice of remedies in a copyright infringement suit. The act provides for injunction against further infringement; damages against the infringer and recovery of profits made by him; seizure of all infringing copies during the pendency of the lawsuit; and destruction of infringing copies, plates, molds, and other devices necessary to make the infringing copies (17 USC §§ 501–504).

Securing a Statutory Copyright   Under the Copyright Act, copyright is secured *automatically* for "original works of authorship" when the work is created. A work is "created" when it is fixed in a copy or phonorecord for the first time. In general, "copies" are material objects from which a work can be read or visually perceived either directly or with the aid of a machine or a device, such as books, manuscripts, sheet music, film, videotape, or microfilm. "Phonorecords" are material objects embodying fixations of sounds (excluding, by statutory definition, motion picture sound tracks), such as audiotapes and phonograph discs. Thus, for example, a song (the work) can be fixed in sheet music (copies) or in phonograph discs (phonorecords), or both. Prior to 1978, statutory copyright was secured under the

Copyright Act by publication with notice of copyright, assuming compliance with other relevant statutory conditions. Under the copyright law that became effective on January 1, 1978, no publication, registration, or other action in the United States Copyright Office is required to secure copyright.

When a work is published under the authority of the copyright owner, a notice of copyright should be placed on all publicly distributed copies, even works published outside the United States. Failure to comply with the notice requirement can result in loss of certain rights otherwise available to the copyright owner. The notice for visually perceptible copies should contain the following three elements: (1) the symbol © (the letter c in a circle) or the word "copyright", (2) the year of first publication of the work, and (3) the name of the copyright owner.

 In general, copyright registration is a legal formality intended to make a public record of the basic facts of the particular copyright. Even though registration is not generally a requirement for protection, the copyright law provides several inducements to encourage copyright owners to register their copyright. Among these advantages are that the registration establishes a public record of the copyright claim, and registration is ordinarily necessary before an infringement suit can be filed in court. To register a work, the copyright owner sends to the United States Copyright Office, in the same envelope or package, a properly completed application form, a specified fee, and a deposit of the work being registered.

Fair Use Doctrine   In spite of a copyright owner's exclusive rights in copyrighted works, the Copyright Act provides that the "fair use" of a copyrighted work, including such use by reproduction in copies or phonorecords, for purposes such as criticism, comment, news reporting, teaching (including multiple copies for classroom use), scholarship, or research, is not an infringement of copyright. In determining whether the use made of a work in any particular case is a fair use, the factors to be considered include (1) the purpose and character of the use, including whether it is of a commercial nature or is for nonprofit educational purposes; (2) the nature of the copyrighted work; (3) the amount and substantiality of the portion used in relation to the copyrighted work as a whole; and (4) the effect of the use on the potential market for, or value of, the copyrighted work (17 USC § 107).

The *fair use doctrine*, as embodied in § 107, provides a means of balancing the exclusive rights of the copyright holder with the public's interest in the dissemination of information affecting areas of universal concern, such as art, science, history, or industry. Fair use cannot be determined by resort to arbitrary rules but requires examination of the facts in each case.

EXAMPLE

Jeannie is preparing a research paper for publication and, to support her thesis, quotes a paragraph from a copyrighted technical journal, properly crediting the source. Such limited quotation constitutes fair use of the copyrighted material within the meaning and spirit of § 107. Mark, another student, directly quotes more than 2,000 words of a copyrighted technical journal in his research paper. Mark properly cites the journal as the author, but he has probably infringed the copyright; such extensive use of another's work is not fair. If it is necessary for Mark to copy so extensively from copyrighted materials, he should obtain the express written permission of the author and publisher of the copyrighted work.

53:8 Patents

Just as copyright laws protect authors, *patent* laws protect inventors. The Constitution of the United States gives Congress the power to promote the progress of science by securing for limited times to inventors the exclusive right to their discoveries (Article 1, § 8). Congress enacted the first patent law in 1790. The law has undergone many revisions, which have culminated in the Patent Act of 1952 (35 USC §§ 1 et seq.). The act states that subject to the requirements of the statute, any person who invents or discovers any new and useful process, machine, manufacture, or composition of matter (or any new and useful improvements for one of them) can obtain a patent (35 USC § 101). The act established the federal Patent and Trademark Office for administering laws relating to patents.

The purposes of the federal patent system are (1) to foster and reward inventions; (2) to promote disclosure of inventions, to stimulate further innovation, and to permit the public to use the invention once the patent expires; and (3) to assure that ideas in the public domain remain there for the free use of the public.

A patent is personal property and can be sold, bequeathed by a will, or passed to the heirs of a deceased patent owner. The Patent Act provides for the transfer or sale of a patent, or of an application for a patent, by an instrument in writing. This instrument, called an "assignment," can transfer either the entire interest in the patent or only a partial interest. When the patent is assigned, the assignee becomes the owner of the patent and has the same rights as the original patentee.

 Applying for a patent requires knowledge of complex patent law and experience in dealing with the Patent and Trademark Office. Any business or individual inventor should employ a patent attorney to perform this service. The Patent and Trademark Office maintains a register of attorneys and other persons who have the appropriate legal and scientific qualifications to assist persons in obtaining patents.

Patents, Trademarks, and Copyrights Compared and Distinguished The basic distinction between patentable and copyrightable subject matter is that a patent protects the *substance* or the *idea* embodied in a work, while a copyright protects the *mode of expression* of the work. Although patent and copyright protection are derived from the same section of the Constitution, there are different standards for obtaining and enforcing them. For example, a patent must comply with the statutory standards of novelty and lack of obviousness, while the only requirement for obtaining a copyright is that it be original. Trademark law is not concerned either with the content of words or the development of new technology, but rather simply with the protection of identifying symbols.

Although trademark, copyright, and patent are three separate and distinct areas of law, occasionally a single product is protectable by all three at the same time.

For example, various features of a household lamp with a sculptured base are capable of protection by all three categories of law. The lamp base, if it qualifies as a "work of art" could be copyrightable. The electrical circuit or bulb might be protected by a patent. The label on the lamp could function as a trademark to identify and distinguish the manufacturer or seller.

Conditions for Obtaining Patent   For an invention to be patentable it must be "new" as defined in the Patent Act. Under the act, if an invention has been described in a printed publication anywhere in the world, or if it has been in public use or on sale in this country before the date that the applicant *made his invention*, a patent cannot be obtained. In addition, if the invention has been described in a printed publication anywhere or has been in public use or on sale in this country more than one year before the date on which a *patent application is filed*, a valid patent cannot be obtained. In this connection, it is immaterial when the invention was made, or whether the printed publication or public use was by the inventor himself or by someone else.

The Patent Act also provides that a patent cannot be obtained if the differences between the subject matter sought to be patented and the prior art (the "state of the art") are such that the subject matter as a whole would have been obvious at the time the invention was made to a person having ordinary skill in the art to which the subject matter pertains (35 USC § 103). In other words, the subject matter sought to be patented must be sufficiently different from what has been used or described before so that it may be said to amount to an invention. Small advances that would be obvious to a person having ordinary skill in the particular field are not inventions capable of being patented. For example, the substitution of one unimportant material for another, or mere changes in size, are ordinarily not patentable.

Under the Patent Act, it is generally only the inventor who can apply for a patent. If a person who is not the inventor applies for a patent, any patent obtained would be void. Joint inventors can apply for a patent jointly. It should be noted that a person who only makes a financial contribution is not a joint inventor and cannot be joined in the application as an inventor.

Infringement   A patent grants to the patentee the right to exclude others from making, using, or selling the invention throughout the United States for a term of 17 years. Accordingly, infringement of a patent is the unauthorized making, using, or selling of the patented invention during its term. If a patent is infringed, the patentee can sue for relief in federal court. He can seek an injunction to prevent continuation of the infringement and also ask for damages. In an infringement suit, the defendant may question the validity of the patent.

A patentee who makes or sells patented articles is required to mark them with the word "patent" and the number of the patent. The penalty for failure to mark is that the patentee cannot recover damages from an infringer unless the infringer was notified of the infringement and continued to infringe after the notice. Some persons mark articles sold with the terms "patent applied for" or "patent pending." While these phrases have no legal significance, they do give information that an application for a patent has been filed. However, protection afforded by a patent does not start until the actual grant of the patent.

Key Concepts and Terms

- To encourage stability in business expectations, liability is imposed on a person who willfully interferes with another's contractual relations or prospective economic advantage.

- Misuse of a trade secret is actionable; it is based on an abuse of confidence. An employee who leaves a job can take and use skills and knowledge acquired during the employment. However, he cannot disclose his employer's trade secrets, such as processes, methods of doing business, trade routes, and secret customer lists.

- A covenant not to compete is generally valid and enforceable if it is reasonable as to time and place. State statutory provisions frequently regulate such covenants. Some statutes prohibit them.

- A person who communicates false disparaging statements as to the quality of another person's property, goods, or services, resulting in loss of business, is liable for trade libel, also known as trade disparagement. A business is privileged to make general claims about its own product, but the privilege boes not extend to making specific false claims about another's property or business.

- The simulation by one business of the packaging or devices employed by another to identify its product or services is an actionable business tort.

- The manufacturer or supplier of goods or services who makes false statements about a product or service in advertisements commits an actionable unfair trade practice at common law. The federal Lanham Act creates liability for advertising misrepresentations as to goods or services in interstate commerce.

- The Federal Trade Commission Act makes unlawful "unfair methods of competition in commerce" and "unfair or deceptive acts or practices in commerce." The act is administered by the Federal Trade Commission (FTC). The FTC is empowered to prevent deceptive sales approaches, product misrepresentations, and price misrepresentations.

- A copyright protects the mode of expression of a work. A patent protects the substance or idea embodied in the work. While a patent must comply with statutory standards of novelty and lack of obviousness to receive protection, the only requirement for obtaining a copyright is that the work be original. Trademark law is concerned with the protection of symbols that identify particular products or services.

- Under the fair use doctrine, a reasonable portion of a copyrighted work can be reproduced without the author's permission when necessary for a legitimate purpose that is not competitive with the copyright owner's market for his work.

- Copyright
- Covenant Not to Compete
- Fair Use Doctrine
- False Advertising
- Federal Trade Commission (FTC)
- Federal Trade Commission Act
- Infringement
- Interference
- Lanham Act

- Patent
- Secondary Meaning
- Trade Dress Simulation
- Trade Libel
- Trademark
- Trade Secret
- Unfair Trade Practice
- Uniform Deceptive Trade Practices Act

Questions and Case Problems

1. Darrow Company is a manufacturer of gumdrops sold under the trademark "Zest" in a red, white, and blue package bearing a picture of Uncle Sam and the slogan, "America's most American candy." Darrow's competitor, Fowler Company, begins to sell gumdrops under the trademark "Sest." Fowler adopts for its gumdrops red, white, and blue packaging bearing a picture of the American eagle and the slogan, "The best for red-blooded Americans." Can Darrow Company prevent Fowler Company from marketing its gumdrops in the manner it has employed? Why?

2. National Motors is negotiating with Sparko Batteries for the purchase of one million auto batteries. Sparko purchases its battery cases exclusively from Case. National Motors tells Sparko if it wants to do business with National, it will have to purchase all battery cases from another supplier. Can Case recover against National Motors for interference with its contractual relationship with Sparko?

3. What is the difference among a copyright, a trademark, and a patent?

4. Ethel Russell created what she considered to be original ideas for socks. In one design, there was a separate compartment for the big toe; another had a separate section for each toe. Because socks were gaining prominence in young women's casual fashion, the "mitten socks" and "glove socks" had wide appeal. Russell registered her two drawings on copyright forms entitled "registration of a claim to copyright in a work of art or model or design for a work of art." Trimfit, Inc., while acknowledging that the toe socks were Russell's idea, began to manufacture these socks under its own label. Russell sued for copyright infringement, claiming that she had the sole right to manufacture toe socks. How should the case be decided?

5. What is a covenant not to compete? How is it used in business?

6. William Trecker, a salesman at the Columbia Ribbon and Carbon Manufacturing Company, signed an agreement not to disclose to anyone the name, address, or requirements of any customer or prospective customer of Columbia, or to divulge any other information acquired during his employment. The agreement also provided that for two years after leaving Columbia, Trecker would not sell any similar goods within any territory he had covered during the two years prior to leaving. Trecker's territory had been nationwide, and Trecker eventually quit to work for A-One Corporation, a Columbia competitor. Columbia sued to enjoin Trecker from competing with it in the United States for two years and to bar him permanently from soliciting Columbia customers. What relief, if any, should the court give Columbia?

7. What is the fair use doctrine?

8. The Crazy Cola Bottling Company employs Joe as a chemist. Joe subsequently leaves Crazy Cola and sets up his own business, manufacturing another soft drink. Crazy Cola asserts that Joe is using trade secrets he uncovered while employed by Crazy Cola and seeks to enjoin him from continuing the activity. Is Crazy Cola entitled to an injunction?

9. Pioneer Aviation and Aerospace Industries are competing to obtain a government contract. Pioneer's sales manager tells the government procurement officer, "Be careful about acceping any bids from Aerospace. They're in real hot water with their creditors. They could be in bankruptcy any day now." Has an unfair business practice been committed? If so, which type?

10. What is an FTC cease and desist order? How is it used?

54 Antitrust

54:1 Introduction

The area of law known as *antitrust* was born in 1890 when Congress enacted the *Sherman Antitrust Act* (15 USC §§ 1 et seq.). *Trust* in this context means a combination of producers or sellers of a product, the purpose of which is to control prices and suppress competition. The Sherman Act was intended to preserve competition in the marketplace and to prevent further concentration of the vast wealth that had been accumulated by a few corporations and individuals.

This chapter is not intended to explain the complexities and inner workings of antitrust law—a subject to which some attorneys devote their entire practice. Instead, the chapter's purpose is to introduce the major federal antitrust legislation: (1) the Sherman Act, as already mentioned (see 54:2 and 54:3); (2) the Clayton Act (see 54:4 through 54:6); and (3) the Robinson–Patman Act (see 54:7). The chapter discusses the more frequent types of antitrust violations and, in 54:8, the enforcement procedures and remedies that are available when an antitrust violation has occurred.

Antitrust law is both complex and controversial. It seeks to balance conflicting interests. On the one hand, there is the consideration of protecting the public against the power exercisable by vast corporations. On the other, there is the question of the extent to which the capitalistic system of free enterprise is to be permitted to operate. It should also be noted that antitrust legislation is intentionally broad, general, and vague. Phrases such as "restraint of trade," "monopolization," "unfair methods of competition," and "conduct that tends substantially to lessen competition" abound. Necessarily, this language only has definite meaning when courts interpret the statutes and apply them to the facts of particular cases.

 As a result of expanding judicial construction of antitrust laws, a continuously increasing number of antitrust cases has been filed by public and private litigants. There has been a tendency to expand the role of antitrust law from one of maintaining commercial competition and a free market to one of monitoring business activities and producing social reform. It is essential, therefore, that businesspersons be aware of possible antitrust consequences of their activities. Any businessperson who has a potential antitrust problem should seek the advice of an attorney specially trained in the field. It is the antitrust lawyer's role to recommend methods and procedures of business operation that do not violate the antitrust laws.

54:2   Restraint of Trade

Section 1 of the Sherman Act (15 USC § 1) provides that "every contract, combination in the form of trust or otherwise, or conspiracy, in restraint of trade or commerce among the several states, or with foreign nations" is illegal. For there to be a violation of § 1 there must be some combination or common action by two or more persons or businesses.

In interpreting the statute, the courts have equated "restraint of trade" with "restraint of competition." The interstate commerce requirement ("commerce among the several states") was originally interpreted as meaning that the mere manufacture or production of goods was not interstate commerce even if the goods were destined for shipment from one state to another. Today, however, the commerce requirement is satisfied simply by showing that the business or activity in question, even when purely intrastate, has a "substantial economic effect" on other states.

The Rule of Reason and the Per Se Doctrine   In a sense, every business contract restrains trade since it sets terms on which at least one commercial transaction will take place, and thereby removes that transaction from the field of competition. This was obviously not what Congress intended to prohibit. Accordingly, the United States Supreme Court held that the Sherman Act was intended to forbid only "unreasonable" restraints of trade and that it did not impair freedom to enter into ordinary business contracts.[1] Certain types of business conduct, however, have been held to be "unreasonable per se." This means that the conduct is unreasonable in and of itself; proof that the conduct occurred is sufficient to establish a violation of the Sherman Act. Examples of conduct that is unreasonable per se are (1) price-fixing and (2) dividing market territories among competitors.

Price-Fixing   *Price-fixing* means any combination or agreement between or among competitors, formed for the purpose—and having the effect—of raising, depressing, fixing, pegging, or stabilizing the price of goods in interstate commerce. For example, if several corporations form a trade association that fixes prices of the corporations' products and limits sales to a select list of jobbers, the corporations are guilty of illegal price-fixing. There is no defense or recognized justification for price-fixing. For example, it is no defense that the price fixed was actually reasonable, that the purpose of the price-fixing was to end "ruinous competition" in the marketplace, or that the price was fixed to eliminate unstable prices that plagued both producers and consumers.

The courts have been expansive in determining what constitutes price-fixing. Even agreements among competitors fixing minimum prices constitute illegal

---

[1]*Standard Oil Co. v United States*, 221 US 1, 55 L Ed 619, 31 S Ct 502 (1911).

price-fixing. By way of illustration, it has been held that a state bar association's establishment of minimum-fee schedules for legal services constitutes price-fixing.[2] An agreement among competitors on how much they will sell or produce is also an illegal price-fixing scheme (even if no specific fixed price is agreed on), as is an agreement among buyers (1) as to the price they will offer or (2) to limit purchases so as to depress the market price.

The following case involves an antitrust prosecution (see 54:8) against an organization of car dealers that had engaged in a scheme to stabilize and increase prices. Note the court's expressed view that once an illegal agreement to fix prices is made, it will be presumed that a conspiracy to restrain trade exists, regardless whether the price-fixing agreement is actually carried out.

Plymouth Dealers' Asso.
v
United States
279 F2d 128
(United States Court of Appeals, Ninth Circuit, 1960)

[An association of Plymouth dealers published a price list for Plymouth cars, and it circulated the list to its members. The prices were higher than those recommended by the manufacturer, and it was intended that none of the members would sell Plymouths for less than the listed prices. The association was indicted for and found guilty of violation § 1 of the Sherman Act, and it appealed.]

Barnes, Circuit Judge.

*   *   *

The indictment charged that the appellant and certain co-conspirators engaged in "a combination and conspiracy to stabilize the retail prices of Plymouth motor cars and accessories in the San Francisco Bay Area, in unreasonable restraint" of interstate commerce . . .

Appellant urges that agreeing on a fixed uniform list price, and sending it out to a dealers' association's members cannot violate Sec-

tion 1 of the Sherman Act, unless there is proof of something more—that it was adhered to; that it was utilized to fix prices; or that it did actually fix prices.

Inasmuch as automobiles are sold at their cost plus a retained gross profit, and the manufacturer's cost does not vary in the restricted market area involved, the gross profit is the only variable. If sold at the factory's suggested retail price, a 24% gross profit would result; if sold at the association's suggested retail price, a 33⅓% gross profit would result. Thus the list price, argues appellant, was merely a device to permit the giving of larger allowances on trade-ins, a "packing" that did not affect the price, and hence was no restraint of trade.

The difficulty with appellant's position is that the Supreme Court has ruled that certain acts constitute *per se* violation of the antitrust laws, and no explanation of why the act was done, nor what its effect might be in a particular case, is of any consequence or materiality. . . .

[O]nce the agreement to fix a price is made, it is conclusively presumed that a conspiracy to restrain trade exists, and it is "immaterial whether the agreements were ever actually carried out, whether the purpose of the conspiracy was accomplished in whole or in part,

---

[2]*Goldfarb v Virginia State Bar,* 421 US 773, 44 L Ed2d 572, 95 S Ct 2004 (United States Supreme Court, 1975).

or whether an effort was made to carry the object of the conspiracy into effect." . . .

When the term "fix prices" is used, that term is used in its larger sense. A combination or conspiracy formed for the purpose and with the effect of raising, depressing, fixing, pegging or stabilizing the price of a commodity in interstate commerce is unreasonable *per se* under the Sherman Act. . . . The test is not what the actual effect is on prices, but whether such agreements interfere with "the freedom of traders and thereby restrain their ability to sell in accordance with their own judgment." . . . The competition between the Plymouth dealers and the fact that the dealers used the fixed uniform list price in most instances only as a starting point, is of no consequence. It *was* an agreed starting point; it had been agreed upon between competitors; it was in some instances in the record respected and followed; it had to do with, and had its effect upon, price. [Court's emphasis.]

The fact that there existed competition of other kinds between the various Plymouth dealers, or that they cut prices in bidding against each other, is irrelevant. . . .

Nor does the fact that a plan entered into by competitors to control prices, and having an effect thereon, did not ultimately succeed in accomplishing what the parties anticipated, absolve them from their violation of the law.

In a deteriorating market (at least with respect to automobile dealers, as was the case in the market defined as "Plymouth cars sold in the San Francisco Bay Area in 1955–56–57 and –58"), no matter what steps are taken to influence prices, sometimes the power of larger economic factors prevail, and the average retained gross profit of the dealer goes down. The question is not what the profit was, but how it got where it was, and what it would have been had there been no agreement to influence or stabilize prices. The very fact that

this is extremely difficult of proof is probably one of the reasons why, in its wisdom, the Congress has seen fit to establish the law, and the Supreme Court to establish certain *per se* consequences of the proscribed action. . . .

Further, common sense tells us that there is no need for competitors to meet, agree upon content, print and circularize "list prices" that are never to be looked at. There was testimony the fixed list price was created and intended to be used to eliminate public distrust, occasioned by the previous wide variance in quoted retail prices which were determined as a matter of individual dealer judgment, varying to meet competitor's prices.

The "fixed, uniform list price" was not precisely followed in many, in fact in most, instances. It was not intended to be so used. It was fixed "high" so a greater trade-in could be allowed; so that the ultimate percentage of gross profit over the factory price could be higher. It was used by some dealers in seventy-five per cent of their deals. This list price was shown to customers, at times, as "the regular price" of the automobile. By the agreed uniform list price, Plymouth list price became $2,340 in San Francisco, rather than $2,130. . . .

Here the Association members all had to pay the factory price for their Plymouths. To agree to put the starting price for their bargaining at $2,340 instead of $2,130 (the manufacturer's suggested retail price), they were following a minimum price, not within their control, as modified by a hypothetical gross price, controlled by the dealers. This established as a matter of actual practice one boundary of "the range within which . . . sales would be made." . . . This was "a factor which prevents the determination of [market] prices by free competition alone." . . .

[Conviction affirmed.]

Division of Market Territories among Competitors Any agreement among businesses performing similar services or dealing in similar products, whereby the available market is divided up and each is given a share, is illegal per se. As in the case of price-fixing, no justifications or defenses are recognized. The rationale for this rule is that an agreement among competitors to divide the market for a particular product gives each an effective monopoly in its share of the market since even though competitive products may be available, each firm has the power to fix prices as to a particular product.

54:3 Monopolies

Section 2 of the Sherman Act (15 USC § 2) makes it a criminal offense to monopolize, attempt to monopolize, or combine or conspire to monopolize any part of interstate or foreign commerce. To "monopolize" is to acquire or exercise the power to exclude competitors from a market or to control prices within a relevant market. By using that term, rather than *monopoly*, the statute contemplates action rather than merely status.

EXAMPLE
Newspaper B distributes thousands of free copies of its newspaper in a geographical area in which newspaper A is operating. B's free distribution occurs during a four-month period, and much of it is done on Wednesday, the heavy grocery-ad day. Advertising constitutes 80 percent of A's revenue, and a significant portion of that revenue comes from grocery advertising. B has engaged in an illegal attempt to monopolize since, if B succeeds in driving A out of business, a dangerous probability exists that B will achieve a monopolistic position in the daily newspaper market and be able to exploit that position to the disadvantage of the people and businesses in the area.

Relevant Market At some inexact point—the subject of much antitrust litigation—"market power" becomes "monopoly power," the power to control prices and to exclude competitors. To determine whether a company has monopoly power it is necessary to define the *relevant market,* based on what constitutes (1) the revelant geographic market (for example, California, the West, or the nation) and (2) the relevant product market (for example, the market for cellophane wrapping material, or the market for *all* flexible wrapping material). Naturally, an antitrust defendant (a business charged with a violation of the antitrust laws) will argue that it has a large market, which will make its share of the market small, while the party alleging the violation will argue that the defendant's market is small, making its market share relatively large.

The geographic market is generally defined by the area in which the defendant and competing sellers sell the product. If the product is sold nationwide, then the market will be considered national. There may be regional submarkets where a number of local sellers compete with nationwide sellers; the market for beer is an example. In this case, the submarket might be found to be the relevant market.

Transportation cost is the principal factor limiting the size of a geographic market.

The product market is largely determined by consumer preferences and the extent to which physically dissimilar products can fulfill the same consumer need. In *United States v E. I. DuPont De Nemours & Co.*, the so-called *Cellophane Case*,[3] the United States Supreme Court announced the rule that goods reasonably interchangeable by consumers for the same purposes make up that part of the trade or commerce, monopolization of which may be illegal. In the *Cellophane Case*, the relevant market was held to be *all* flexible wrapping material, not merely cellophane wrapping material. The Court stressed the functional interchangeability of those products. Under this rule, photocopiers, for example, are deemed to be interchangeable for antitrust purposes, even among brands using different mechanical processes.

Market Share Courts frequently take the share of the market that an alleged monopolist has *presently* captured as the principal indicator of "monopoly power." Depending on the circumstances, 90 percent, or even 75 percent, is sufficient to constitute "monopoly power." It has been argued that *market share* is an imperfect measure of market power, since it fails to take into account the availability of close substitutes for the product in question and the ease with which new entrants, not presently selling in the market, can enter the market.

54:4   Tying Agreements

A *tying agreement* is an agreement by which a person or corporation agrees to sell a product (the tying product) only on condition that the buyer also purchases a different product (the tied product). For example, a cement company might agree to sell its premixed cement (the tying product) to a building contractor only on condition that the contractor also purchase cement mixers (the tied product) from the cement company.

The tying doctrine originated under § 3 of the *Clayton Act* (15 USC § 14). Section 3 makes it illegal to sell or lease goods in interstate commerce on condition that the purchaser or lessee not use or deal in the goods of a competitor of the seller or lessor, if the effect may be substantially to lessen competition or tend to create a monopoly in any line of commerce. There are three basic requirements for an illegal tie: (1) there must be separate tying and tied products, (2) the seller must have sufficient economic power to restrain competition appreciably in the tied product, and (3) the tying arrangement must affect more than an "insubstantial" amount of commerce. Even though the seller offers the two products as a single unit at a single price, there is no tie if the buyer is free to take either product by itself.

The tying product and the tied product can be related in a variety of ways. For example, they can be products that must both be used in fixed proportions, such as nuts and bolts; the tied product might be designed to be used with the tying product, as data processing cards are used with a computer; or the tied and tying products might be usable either together or separately, as are seed and fertilizer.

---

[3]351 US 377, 100 L Ed 1264, 76 S Ct 994 (1956).

Franchise Tying Agreements   The illegality of certain types of tying agreements has particular significance to the franchising industry. As discussed in Chapter 46, so-called "business format franchises" are characterized by the franchisee's being granted the right to use, within a designated area, a franchisor's service mark; trade name; distinctive building, structure, or style of decor; and techniques of doing business. This type of franchising is essentially based on linking the distinctive image to a standardized operation with, it is hoped, high quality control. Because the commercial success of the franchising usually depends on a nationwide uniform image, the courts tend to allow the franchisor to require the business format franchisee to use particular products to maintain high quality. However, whenever a franchisor insists that services, equipment, or supplies be obtained from the franchisor or a designated source as a condition of receiving and retaining the franchise, a potential tying problem exists. This situation is illustrated in the following case. Note particularly the court's discussion of the antitrust policy for preventing tying agreements, as well as the detailed examination of the defendant's business methods.

Siegel

v

Chicken Delight, Inc.
448 F2d 43, 14 ALR Fed 458
(United States Court of Appeals, Ninth Circuit, 1971)

[Siegel and other franchisees of defendant, Chicken Delight, sued for injuries allegedly resulting from illegal restraints imposed by Chicken Delight's standard form franchise agreements. The restraints consisted of Chicken Delight's contractual requirements that franchisees buy certain essential cooking equipment, dry-mix food items, and trademark-bearing packaging exclusively from Chicken Delight as a condition of obtaining a Chicken Delight trademark license. The trial court ruled that these requirements constituted a tying agreement that was unlawful under § 1 of the Sherman Act. Chicken Delight then appealed.]

Merrill, Circuit Judge.

*   *   *

In order to establish that there exists an unlawful tying arrangement plaintiffs must demonstrate *First,* that the scheme in question involves two distinct items and provides that one (the tying product) may not be obtained unless the other (the tied product) is also purchased.... *Second,* that the tying product possesses sufficient economic power appreciably to restrain competition in the tied product market.... *Third,* that a "not insubstantial" amount of commerce is affected by the arrangement....

Chicken Delight concedes that the third requirement has been satisfied. It disputes the existence of the first two. Further it asserts that, even if plaintiffs should prevail with respect to the first two requirements, there is a *fourth* issue: whether there exists a special justification for the particular tying arrangement in question.... [Court's emphasis.]

The District Court ruled that the license to use the Chicken Delight name, trade-mark, and method of operation was "a tying item in the traditional sense," ... the tied items being the cookers and fryers, packaging products, and mixes.

The court's decision to regard the trademark or franchise license as a distinct tying item is not without precedent.... Nevertheless, Chicken Delight argues that the District Court's conclusion conflicts with the purposes behind the strict rules governing the use of tying arrangements.

The hallmark of a tie-in is that it denies competitors free access to the tied product market, not because the party imposing the arrangement has a superior product in that market, but because of the power or leverage exerted by the tying product. . . . Rules governing tying arrangements are designed to strike, not at the mere coupling of physically separable objects, but rather at the use of a dominant desired product to compel the purchase of a second, distinct commodity. . . . In effect, the forced purchase of the second, tied product is a price exacted for the purchase of the dominant, tying product. By shutting competitors out of the tied product market, tying arrangements serve hardly any purpose other than the suppression of competition. . . .

Chicken Delight urges us to hold that its trade-mark and franchise licenses are not items separate and distinct from the packaging, mixes, and equipment, which it says are essential components of the franchise system. To treat the combined sale of all these items as a tie-in for antitrust purposes, Chicken Delight maintains, would be like applying the antitrust rules to the sale of a car with its tires or a left shoe with the right. Therefore, concludes Chicken Delight, the lawfulness of the arrangement should not be measured by the rules governing tie-ins. We disagree.

In determining whether an aggregation of separable items should be regarded as one or more items for tie-in purposes in the normal cases of sales of products the courts must look to the function of the aggregation. Consideration is given to such questions as whether the amalgamation of products resulted in cost savings apart from those reductions in sales expenses and the like normally attendant upon any tie-in, and whether the items are normally sold or used as a unit with fixed proportions.

Where one of the products sold as part of an aggregation is a trade-mark or franchise li-

cense, new questions are injected. In determining whether the license and the remaining ("tied") items in the aggregation are to be regarded as distinct items which can be traded in distinct markets consideration must be given to the function of trade-marks.

The historical conception of a trade-mark as a strict emblem of source of the product to which it attaches has largely been abandoned. The burgeoning business of franchising has made trade-mark licensing a widespread commercial practice and has resulted in the development of a new rationale for trade-marks as representations of product quality. This is particularly true in the case of a franchise system set up not to distribute the trade-marked goods of the franchisor, but, as here, to conduct a certain business under a common trade-mark or trade name. Under such a type of franchise, the trade-mark simply reflects the goodwill and quality standards of the enterprise which it identifies. As long as the system of operation of the franchisees lives up to those quality standards and remains as represented by the mark so that the public is not misled, neither the protection afforded the trade-mark by law nor the value of the trade-mark to the licensee depends upon the source of the components.

This being so, it is apparent that the goodwill of the Chicken Delight trade-mark does not attach to the multitude of separate articles used in the operation of the licensed system or in the production of its end product. It is not what is used, but how it is used and what results that have given the system and its end product their entitlement to trade-mark protection. It is to the system and the end product that the public looks with the confidence that established goodwill has created.

Thus, sale of a franchise license, with the attendant rights to operate a business in the prescribed manner and to benefit from the goodwill of the trade name, in no way requires the forced sale by the franchisor of some or all of the component articles. Just as the quality of a copyrighted creation cannot by a tie-in be appropriated by a creation to which the copyright does not relate . . . , so here attempts by tie-in to extend the trade-mark protection to common articles (which the public does not and has no reason to connect with the trade-mark) simply because they are said to be essential to production of that which is the subject of the trade-mark, cannot escape antitrust scrutiny.

Chicken Delight's assertions that only a few essential items were involved in the arrangement does not give us cause to reach a different conclusion. The relevant question is not whether the items are essential to the franchise, but whether it is essential to the franchise that the items be purchased from Chicken Delight. This raises not the issue of whether there is a tie-in but rather the issue of whether the tie-in is justifiable, a subject to be discussed below.

We conclude that the District Court was not in error in ruling as matter of law that the arrangement involved distinct tying and tied products. . . .

Chicken Delight contends that the arrangement was a reasonable device for measuring and collecting revenue. There is no authority for justifying a tying arrangement on this ground. Unquestionably, there exist feasible alternative methods of compensation for the franchise licenses, including royalties based on sales volume or fees computed per unit of time, which would neither involve tie-ins nor have undesirable anticompetitive consequences.

Second, Chicken Delight advances as justification the fact that when it first entered the fast food field in 1952 it was a new business and was entitled to . . . protection. . . . As to the period here involved—1963 to 1970—it contends that transition to a different arrangement would be difficult if not economically impossible.

We find no merit in this contention. Whatever claim Chicken Delight might have had to a new business defense in 1952—a question we need not decide—the defense cannot apply to the 1963–70 period. To accept Chicken Delight's argument would convert the new business justification into a perpetual license to operate in restraint of trade. . . .

The third justification Chicken Delight offers is the "marketing identity" purpose, the franchisor's preservation of the distinctiveness, uniformity and quality of its product.

In the case of a trade-mark this purpose cannot be lightly dismissed. Not only protection of the franchisor's goodwill is involved. The licensor owes an affirmative duty to the public to assure that in the hands of his licensee the trade-mark continues to represent that which it purports to represent. For a licensor, through relaxation of quality control, to permit inferior products to be presented to the public under his licensed mark might well constitute a misuse of the mark. . . .

However, to recognize that such a duty exists is not to say that every means of meeting it is justified. Restraint of trade can be justified only in the absence of less restrictive alternatives. . . .

The District Court found factual issues to exist as to whether effective quality control could be achieved by specifications in the case of the cooking machinery and the dip and spice mixes. These questions were given to the jury under instructions; and the jury . . . found against Chicken Delight. . . .

. . . One cannot immunize a tie-in from the antitrust laws by simply stamping a trade-mark symbol on the tied product—at least where the tied product is not itself the product represented by the mark. . . .

[Judgment affirmed.]

Defenses   A defendant might seek to justify a tie on two theories. Under the first—the new industry theory—some courts have permitted a tie instituted in the launching of a new business with a highly uncertain future on the theory that the tie is justified as necessary to ensure proper functioning of special equipment. As the business becomes established, however, tying might no longer be justified. The second defense theory is that of quality control for protection of a business' goodwill. This defense rarely succeeds. Indeed, the only situation in which the protection of goodwill justifies the use of tying is one in which specifications for a substitute would be so detailed that they could not practically be supplied.

54:5   Mergers and Acquisitions

A merger is one company's acquisition of the stock or assets of another company in such a manner that the latter company will be controlled by the former (see Chapter 42). Because mergers can result in concentration of power in a few companies in an industry, they are regulated by antitrust laws. Section 7 of the Clayton Act, as it was later amended (15 USC § 18), provides that a corporation cannot acquire the stock or assets of another corporation engaged in interstate commerce if, in any line of commerce in any section of the country, the effect of the acquisition may be substantially to lessen competition or tend to create a monopoly. The issues in merger cases usually relate to definitions of the product market (the "line of commerce") and the geographic market (the "section of the country"), and to determination of the market shares of the corporations involved, the status of the corporations as actual or potential competitors in the market or markets involved, and the probable effect of the merger.

A merger that violates § 7 of the Clayton Act might also violate the Sherman Act. However, the showing of anticompetitive impact required for a successful prosecution is much less rigorous under § 7 than under the Sherman Act provisions. Consequently, most merger cases are brought under § 7 of the Clayton Act rather than under the Sherman Act provisions.

 The United States Department of Justice issues a set of so-called "merger guidelines," which, although not having the force of law, are used by many courts in analyzing the legality of mergers.

54:6   Interlocking Directorates

Section 8 of the Clayton Act (15 USC § 19) prohibits a person from being on the boards of directors of any two or more corporations if two conditions exist. The first condition is that any of the corporations has capital, surplus, and undivided profits aggregating more than one million dollars and is engaged in commerce (the act excludes banks, banking associations, and common carriers subject to the Interstate Commerce Act). The second condition is that the corporations are or were competitors, so that the elimination of competition by agreement between them would constitute a violation of any provision of any antitrust law. Section 8 has been construed to forbid corporations from having the same director if an agreement between the corporations to fix prices or divide territories would violate § 1 of the Sherman Act. By prohibiting *interlocking directorates*, § 8 seeks to prevent violation of the antitrust laws by removing the opportunity or temptation to enter into illegal arrangements.

54:7   Price Discrimination

The *Robinson–Patman Act* (15 USC § 13) makes it unlawful to discriminate, directly or indirectly, in price among different purchasers of goods of like grade and quality under certain conditions. Those conditions are that (1) any of the transactions is in commerce and (2) the effect of the discrimination may be substantially to (a) lessen competition; (b) tend to create a monopoly; or (c) injure, destroy or prevent competition with any person who grants or knowingly receives the benefit of such a discrimination, or the customers of either. Many types of conduct that amount to *price discrimination* have been held illegal under the act.

EXAMPLE
Foran Corporation is a large national company with a milk-processing plant in Louisville. Foran sells milk in surrounding areas at lower prices than in Louisville, where it has a large share of the market. The surrounding areas are served by local companies, and Foran is trying to obtain a share of that market. Foran's policy is price discrimination, in violation of the Robinson–Patman Act.

   Both the seller who offers and the preferred buyer who knowingly receives discriminatory prices are guilty of violating the act.

Like Grade or Quality   Generally, physical differences in two products that affect their acceptability to buyers will preclude the products from being of "like grade or quality." However, differences in the brand name or label under which the product is sold are not alone sufficient to justify price discrimination.

Defenses   The Robinson–Patman Act expressly provides that nothing in it shall prevent price differentials that make only "due allowance for differences in the cost of manufacture, sale, or delivery" resulting from the differing methods or quantities in which goods are sold or delivered. This defense is rarely relied on in practice, however. For one thing, it is expensive to compile the necessary evidence. For another, according to the Federal Trade Commission's interpretation of the defense, quantity discounts must be based on *actual* cost savings due to the quantity sold, not merely on a generalized policy that larger deliveries are automatically more economical. A seller can also rebut a presumption of price discrimination by showing that his lower price was made in good faith to meet a competitor's equally low price, but this defense is hard to prove.

54:8   Remedies and Enforcement

The variety of lawsuits through which antitrust legislation is enforced is nearly as broad as the scope of the laws themselves, and each type of lawsuit has its own characteristics. The government can commence either a civil damages action or a criminal prosecution against a suspected violator. Damages can also be sought by private persons.

Civil Actions   The Antitrust Division of the United States Department of Justice has primary responsibility for enforcing the Sherman and Clayton Acts. The Antitrust Division investigates alleged antitrust law violations on the basis of complaints received, frequently from businesses that believe themselves injured by a particular practice.

The Department of Justice has authority to commence a civil action to recover damages to the United States Government resulting from violations of antitrust laws. One such violation would be a price-fixing conspiracy that raised prices on goods sold to the government. In cases other than those in which damages are sought, the object of a civil antitrust proceeding by the Department of Justice is a decree to enforce the Sherman Act or Clayton Act by stopping or remedying violations. Antitrust decrees can enjoin whole categories of conduct and permit the Antitrust Division to investigate subsequent business activities of the defendant.

Consent Decrees   Often, the government and an antitrust defendant agree to settle a government antitrust case by a *consent decree*. This type of decree is based on a stipulation by both parties as to what remedy or relief the court should order, without the defendant acknowledging any guilt. The ultimate responsbility in fashioning an antitrust decree lies with the court, however. The court must determine what is or is not in the "public interest," and it is not relieved of this responsibility simply because all parties to the proceeding (including the government) agree on or request a particular form of relief.

Private Antitrust Actions   Section 4 of the Clayton Act (15 USC § 15) allows a private person who has been or will be injured in his business or property by reason of anything forbidden in the antitrust laws—either the Sherman Act or the Clayton Act—to sue in a federal district court. A plaintiff who proves the violation of an antitrust law and resulting injury can recover *treble damages* (three times the amount of the proven damages) plus the costs of the action, including a reasonable attorney's fee. A plaintiff who shows only threatened injury is entitled to injunctive relief, such as the issuance of an injunction prohibiting the illegal conduct.

In recent years, private antitrust lawsuits have been increasingly brought as *class actions*, meaning that all persons similarly injured by the antitrust defendant's conduct have been joined as plaintiffs in the same action. Sometimes, therefore, even very small actual damages attributed to each of many transactions (such as sales of a common but cheap consumer product), when multiplied by a large number of plaintiffs in the class and further multiplied by three under the treble damages provision of the Clayton Act, will become an extremely large sum.

Criminal Prosecutions   The Department of Justice can commence a criminal prosecution if (1) a case involves a "per se violation" of the Sherman Act (see 54:2) and (2) there is evidence of a knowing and willful violation of the law, such as if there has been a planned program of concealment. Most criminal antitrust prosecutions involve price-fixing. Antitrust criminal cases are investigated by grand-jury proceedings, which are conducted, as in other areas of criminal law, through grand-jury subpoenas commanding either the testimony of witnesses, the production of documents, or both.

Administrative Enforcement   The authority to enforce the Clayton Act with respect to business firms that are subject to regulation by particular federal regulatory agencies is vested in those agencies. For example, the Interstate Commerce Commission can enforce the Clayton Act with respect to railroads and motor carriers, while the Civil Aeronautics Board can enforce the act with respect to airlines.

Key Concepts and Terms

- The Sherman Antitrust Act is the foundation of antitrust law. Section 1 prohibits contracts, combinations, or conspiracies in restraint of trade. Only "unreasonable" restraints of trade are prohibited, but certain practices, such as price-fixing, are unreasonable per se.

- Section 2 of the Sherman Act makes illegal monopolizing, attempts to monopolize, or combining or conspiring to monopolize any part of interstate commerce. Monopoly power is the power to control prices or exclude competition in the relevant market.

- Section 4 of the Clayton Act allows private persons injured in their business or property by any violation of the Sherman or Clayton Act to sue in federal court. A winning plaintiff can recover three times the damages sustained. Section 7 prohibits certain corporate mergers, § 3 prohibits tying agreements, and § 8 prohibits certain interlocking directorates of competing corporations.

- The Robinson–Patman Act prohibits illegal price discrimination if the effect may be substantially to lessen competition or tend to create a monopoly. Both the seller who offers and the preferred buyer who knowingly receives discriminatory prices are guilty of violating this act.

- Antitrust legislation is enforced through a wide variety of lawsuits, including civil or criminal proceedings by the Antitrust Division of the United States Department of Justice, private antitrust actions by individuals or classes of individuals, and suits by federal administrative agencies.

- Antitrust
- Class Action
- Clayton Act
- Consent Decree
- Interlocking Directorates
- Market Share
- Monopoly
- Per Se Doctrine
- Price Discrimination

- Price-Fixing
- Relevant Market
- Restraint of Trade
- Robinson–Patman Act
- Sherman Antitrust Act
- Treble Damages
- Trust
- Tying Agreement

Questions and Case Problems

1. Discuss the purpose of Congress' antitrust legislation.

2. Frank, a noted banker, is a director of Peerless Paper Company. If Frank also serves as a director of a large timber and pulp company, is his position actionable under the antitrust laws? Discuss.

3. Ten competitors in the aluminum industry form a jointly managed company to conduct very expensive exploration for undersea ore deposits. Does this violate Sherman Act § 1? Discuss. Would the result be different if the new company were also to allocate all raw materials to the ten joint venturers in fixed proportions? Discuss.

4. Frizzy Company manufactures hair dryers, which it sells through independent retail outlets. Can Frizzy place its dryers with retailers on consignment, setting the retail price and paying the dealer a percentage commission on each sale? Discuss. Suppose Frizzy publishes suggested retail prices for its dryers and follows a policy of terminating dealers who refuse to adhere to the price list; does this conduct violate Sherman Act § 1? Discuss.

5. Daily Dairy sells vanilla ice cream under the "Daily" brand for 85 cents per quart and the same ice cream under the "Gourmet" brand for 99 cents per quart. Is there a possible Robinson–Patman violation? Discuss. Would the result be different if Daily's "Gourmet" brand contained pure vanilla extract (costing an extra two cents per quart), whereas the "Daily" brand used artificial flavoring?

6. Expando Corporation patents a new razor blade that costs much less and lasts much longer than any other blade on the market. If Expando subsequently acquires a monopoly of the razor blade market through sales of the new blade, is there a Sherman Act § 2 violation? Discuss.

7. X Company sells flywheels used in the manufacture of electric motors. Y Motors, a customer, tells X that it can get a better price on flywheels from Z. Can X lower its price to Y without violating the Robinson–Patman Act? Would it make a difference if Z's flywheel were inferior in quality to X's product? Discuss.

8. What is a tying agreement? Discuss the legality of such an agreement.

9. Discuss the means by which antitrust legislation is enforced.

10. A home builder in the Chicago area complains that a lumberyard consistently falls down on its delivery promises but delivers lumber to competing building contractors on schedule. The builder takes her complaint to federal district court in a private suit under the price discrimination provisions of the Robinson–Patman Act. How should the court decide the case? Why?

55 White-Collar Crime

55:1 Introduction

White-collar crime has received considerable attention in recent years. Government agencies and officials, corporations and their officers, individual businesspersons, and average citizens have all become increasingly aware of the existence and cost of white-collar crime. White-collar crime affects all levels and types of business activity. The businessperson who knowingly sells a defective product that results in injury to the consumer, the businessperson who pays a bribe to obtain a contract, and the businessperson who issues securities in violation of the securities laws all may find themselves facing criminal as well as civil sanctions. Numerous other examples could be given. The point to be made is that white-collar crime does not relate solely to one or another of the specific subjects discussed in this book; it relates to all of them.

It might be thought appropriate to discuss white-collar crime as a subcategory of crime generally. This has not been done because white-collar crime is different from street crime in many respects. Moreover, while street crime certainly has an effect on bussinesses and businesspersons, it is not uniquely connected to business in the same way that white-collar crime is.

For the above reasons, it seems preferable to treat white-collar crime as a specific subject. The discussion is presented here, rather than earlier in this book, to make it easier to understand the serious nature of the problem. In addition, consideration of white-collar crime serves as a useful tool for stressing the importance of the various precautions that have been urged throughout this book. The various preventive measures discussed have generally been framed in terms of avoidance of civil liability. It bears emphasizing, however, that adherence to the suggested practices might well save a businessperson the cost, not to mention the damage to business and personal reputation, that a criminal prosecution can entail.

Definitions A major problem in discussing white-collar crime is defining the subject. Professor Sutherland, who coined the phrase "white-collar crime," defined it as "crime committed by a person of respectability and high social status in the course of his occupation."[1] Over the years the concept of white-collar crime has broadened, with emphasis placed more on the nature of the criminal activity than on the social status of the offender. According to the definition now most commonly quoted, white-collar crime is "an illegal act or series of illegal acts committed by non-physical means and by concealment or guile, to obtain money or property, to avoid the payment or loss of money or property, or to obtain business or personal advantage."[2]

Numerous other attempts have been made to define white-collar crime. Most definitions tend to focus on the behavior involved, and certain common characteristics can be identified. The principal attributes of white-collar crime are that (1) it is nonviolent; (2) it is covert in nature, generally involving deceit and concealment; and (3) it is directed toward the acquisition of money, property, or economic or political power. In discussing white-collar crime, emphasis will therefore be placed on crimes involving these characteristics.

It is impossible to discuss all white-collar crimes or all facets of white-collar criminality in one chapter. This chapter will survey some of the more important aspects of the subject. Attention will be given to the magnitude of the problem; to the liability of both business organizations and individuals; and to various specific types of white-collar crimes, both traditional and nontraditional. In addition, two recent federal statutes that have been used to fight white-collar crime will be discussed in some detail. Finally, attention will be given to an emerging problem— computer crime.

55:2   Magnitude of White-Collar Crime

The United States, as a capitalistic nation, has generally encouraged business. Many business practices which today are labeled white-collar crimes were generally accepted only a few years ago. As a result, few people in the past attempted to assess the scope of white-collar crime, since most people did not consider it a serious problem.

Even today, white-collar crime remains largely invisible and therefore difficult to detect. A white-collar crime can be committed by the stroke of a pen or the manipulation of a computer, and the victim or victims may never know that they have been victimized. Indeed, some law-enforcement officials believe that white-collar crime represents the largest category of unreported crime.

Despite the fact that white-collar crime is largely unreported, it has been stated that it is the most serious crime problem in the United States today. Estimates of the total annual cost to the public of white-collar crime range from $40 billion to $200 billion. It has also been estimated that white-collar crime adds 15 percent to the overall price of goods and services and that 20 percent of all business failures, and 30 percent of small-business failures, are due to white-collar crime. Although white-collar crime generally is considered less serious than street crime, most experts believe that the cost of white-collar crime actually exceeds that of street crime. Moreover, white-collar crime can be just as lethal as street crime. For exam-

---

[1]E. Sutherland, *White-Collar Crime* 9 (1949).
[2]H. Edelhertz, *The Nature, Impact, and Prosecution of White-Collar Crime* 3 (1970).

ple, knowingly manufacturing defective products and dumping toxic wastes could result in death, disease, or injury to literally millions of people.

There is great diversity among both white-collar criminals and their victims. Every business organization, every businessperson, and every government worker is a potential white-collar criminal as well as a potential victim of white-collar crime. The businessperson who drives a company car on personal business, the employee who pads an expense account, and the employee who takes office supplies home can all be called white-collar criminals.

55:3   Liability for and Punishment of White-Collar Crime

When an individual commits a crime, he is subject to punishment. When a corporation or other business entity commits a crime, it is not so easy to assign responsibility. Questions arise as to whether the corporation, its responsible officers or employees, or both are liable to criminal prosecution and punishment.

It is clear that corporate officers and employees can be held criminally liable for violations committed on behalf of their corporation, provided the responsible individuals can be identified. However, it is often difficult to pinpoint responsibility on one or more individuals. Situations arise where a crime clearly has been committed, but no person can be identified as the guilty party.

One solution in such a situation is to hold the corporation criminally responsible. At common law, corporations and associations could not be convicted of crimes. Today, however, a corporation can be held criminally responsible, provided the statute in question applies to corporations. If the legislature intended to limit criminal liability to natural persons, a corporation or other artificial entity cannot be found guilty. The question in each case revolves around the legislative intent. The trend today is toward criminal laws generally applicable to corporations and associations.

A prosecutor faced with a corporate violation of a criminal law need not choose between prosecuting the corporation and prosecuting its officers. The corporation and the responsible officers and employees can be prosecuted together and often are. Moreover, it is not necessary to choose between criminal and civil sanctions. In an appropriate case, a corporation and its officers may be subjected both to civil and to criminal liability based on the same acts.

Once a corporation, its officers, or an individual businessperson has been convicted of a white-collar crime, the question of appropriate punishment arises. In the case of corporations, the punishment normally consists of a fine, since a corporation obviously cannot be imprisoned. Under some circumstances, however, a corporate officer might be required to serve a prison sentence on behalf of a corporation. When an individual has been convicted of a white-collar crime, a fine, imprisonment, or both might be imposed as punishment.

The subject of sentencing for white-collar crimes has provoked considerable controversy. In the case of a corporation, questions have been raised as to whether fines really have any deterrent effect. A small fine may well be treated simply as a cost of doing business. In the case of individuals, sentences tend to be lenient. On the one hand, lenient sentences have been justified on the ground that the average white-collar criminal is a highly educated, successful, well-respected person with no prior record, and therefore deserves a light sentence. On the other hand, it has been argued that lenient sentencing of white-collar criminals creates a double standard and causes cynicism among the general public. For example, it has been argued that it is unfair to sentence a bank robber who steals $1,000 to prison for several years, while granting probation to a bank president who embezzles a much larger sum, such as $50,000.

The debate over sentencing is likely to go on for some time. It is unlikely that white-collar criminals will ever be sentenced as severely as street criminals. However, it is quite likely that the sentences for white-collar crimes will become more severe. In addition, it is also probable that the fines imposed on corporations convicted of white-collar crimes will become more substantial.

55:4   Traditional White-Collar Crimes

Traditional white-collar crimes have most often been committed by individuals against their employers rather than by corporations. Any distinction between traditional and nontraditional white-collar crimes is necessarily somewhat artificial, however. As used here, the term "traditional" describes acts that have long been considered wrongful and have in fact resulted in criminal prosecution with some degree of regularity. Acts that only recently have been made criminal or in the past have not resulted in prosecution with any regularity are considered nontraditional (see 55:5). The decision as to which category a given crime falls into has been made by discretion. For example, *mail fraud* has long been a crime, but only in recent years have the mail fraud statutes been used aggressively to combat consumer fraud.

It is impossible to discuss all the various types of traditional white-collar crimes. Discussion here will be limited to three important types of crime: (1) embezzlement, (2) larceny, and (3) tax evasion and avoidance.

Embezzlement   Embezzlement is the fraudulent appropriation of property, often money, by a person to whom it has been voluntarily entrusted. A central element of the crime of embezzlement is the breach of trust. The stereotypical embezzler is a meek bookkeeper, but anyone who is entrusted with the handling of money is a potential embezzler. Embezzlers can do enormous damage to a business. In numerous cases embezzlement has been discovered only after literally thousands of dollars have been siphoned off over a period of 20 or 30 years.

 An employer can take certain steps to minimize the possibility of embezzlement by employees. The most important step is to adopt internal control procedures that will lead to quick detection of any shortages of funds. This can be accomplished by a division of authority among two or more employees. In other words, do not permit one person to do all bookkeeping work without supervision or auditing. An employee who knows that any embezzlement will be rapidly discovered is much less likely to take the risk involved. If the employee does take the risk, detection is much more likely. Finally, without intruding on an employee's privacy, an employer should be alert to any extravagance by individual employees.

Larceny   Larceny is closely related to embezzlement and, like embezzlement, is a form of theft. The basic distinction between embezzlement and larceny is that in embezzlement the original possession is lawful but the property is wrongfully appropriated, while in larceny the original possession is unlawful. From the businessperson's point of view, this distinction may be more theoretical than real. The embezzler is typically someone who has been entrusted with the handling of funds. The larcenist is typically someone who pilfers supplies or inventory items. In both cases, the offender has rightfully had contact with the property taken.

Many businesses treat inventory shortages as a fact of life and a cost of business. Such an approach may have an element of realism. However, an overly fatalistic attitude toward the problem of employee theft may increase the cost to the business far beyond what it would otherwise be and may in fact result in a business' failure. It has been estimated that 60 percent of the crime-related losses sustained by private businesses are due to employee white-collar crime. An employer should therefore adopt all reasonable measures to deter employee pilferage and other forms of employee theft. An important (but often overlooked) fact is that lower-level employees often take their cues from higher management. If the executives of a business adopt high ethical standards and act honestly, they set an example that the employees are more inclined to follow. Other measures can also be adopted to minimize the loss from employee theft. For example, the adoption of warehousing and shipping procedures designed to detect inventory shortages will help minimize losses in that area.

Tax Evasion and Avoidance   Every businessperson is undoubtedly aware that income tax evasion is a crime. However the federal laws governing the evasion or avoidance of taxes may well be the most commonly enforced white-collar crime statutes. Both individuals and corporations can be guilty of income tax evasion. It is the principal tax crime and the one that has resulted in the most prosecutions and convictions. Other tax crimes include (1) willful failure by an employer to withhold and pay over taxes from employees' wages, (2) willful failure to pay any estimated tax or to file any required return or supply any required information, and (3) commission of various kinds of fraud relating to taxes. In addition to criminal penalties, which may consist of both fines and imprisonment, violation of the income tax laws may result in imposition of civil penalties.

55:5   Emerging Emphasis on Other Types of White-Collar Crime

Criminal law is a reflection of society's moral views. Therefore, as these views change, so does the law. Criminal laws affecting white-collar crime have been undergoing this kind of change. There is a distinct trend toward demanding greater corporate and individual responsibility for business decisions and practices, and toward punishing improper business acts as crimes. This section and 55:6 through 55:9 deal with selected aspects of that trend. Emerging criminality in the following areas will be discussed: (1) consumer fraud, (2) marketing or use of defective or harmful products, (3) pollution, and (4) public corruption. Before discussing these individual categories, however, two points should be made. First, these are developing areas, and there are differences of opinion as to what acts do or should constitute crimes. Second, the categories are not mutually exclusive. As examples, a corporation's use and marketing of harmful chemicals can also result in pollution of the environment; a particular consumer fraud might be facilitated by bribing public officials entrusted with its prevention.

55:6   Consumer Fraud

Attempts to impose criminal sanctions for consumer fraud have focused on massive frauds involving numerous consumers. Examples of this type of fraud are not difficult to find; the sale of swampland or barren desert land as prime residential property, the hawking of miracle medical cures, and the sale of products that are never delivered all cause severe financial, and sometimes psychological, hardship to the victims. Traditional civil remedies are often ineffective, either because each individual consumer has lost little, or because the person perpetrating the fraud is effectively judgment-proof (has limited or no funds to pay any damage awards). As a result, there have been increasing demands to hold the perpetrators of such frauds criminally liable. Some states have criminal laws that can be invoked against such consumer frauds. Because many do not, the criminal statute most often applied is the federal mail fraud statute (18 USC § 1341). This statute makes it a crime, punishable by a fine of $1,000, imprisonment up to five years, or both, to use the mail for any scheme to defraud. A companion statute imposes similar penalties on the use of wire, radio, or television communication to defraud (18 USC § 1343). Since most large consumer frauds involve the use of either the mail or another means of communication, these statutes are effective weapons, and the federal government in recent years has made substantial use of them.

The case that follows illustrates the potential reach of the mail fraud statute. As the case shows, a scheme can defraud not only consumers, but also presumably sophisticated businesses.

United States

v

Schall

371 F Supp 912

(United States District Court, W. D. Pennsylvania, 1974)

[Schall, Nikolich, and Torbich were convicted of 26 counts of mail fraud. The convictions arose out of

the defendants' fraudulent execution and financing of home-improvement contracts. After their convictions the defendants filed motions requesting the trial court to acquit them or to grant them new trials, claiming that there was no evidence that the mail was used as part of their scheme to defraud.]

Snyder, District Judge.

The substance of the scheme charged against the Defendants was that through certain home repair companies, homeowners were induced to enter into agreements for the repair and improvement of their residences. Upon the execution of contracts usually calling for installment financed payments, the Defendants would furnish coupon books to the homeowners showing the indebtedness payable to home repair companies or financing companies controlled by the Defendants. At the same time, it was charged, the Defendants would draft home improvement contracts on Associated Town "N" Country Builders (Associated) paper which would contain false information concerning the identity of the debtor and the type and cost of the improvements. The Defendants would then fraudulently affix thereto the signature of the homeowner who had contracted for the original improvement and Associated paper would be presented to Homemakers Loan and Consumer Discount Company (Homemakers), a subsidiary of General Electric Credit Corporation (G. E. Credit), for the purpose of inducing G. E. Credit to purchase these obligations and remit the proceeds to the Defendants. The mastermind of this scheme was alleged to be Gerald Schall. Michael Nikolich, an employee of G. E. Credit, was charged with manipulating the purchase of contracts, knowing them to be false, and then transmitting the proceeds to Gerald Schall. Theodore Torbich was alleged to be involved by going to the homeowners and doing unnecessary work on their furnaces, by intercepting coupon books evidencing the financing of the contracts through G. E. Credit (with whom the homeowners had no contact whatsoever), and by delivering a large portion of the proceeds of these loans to Schall from Homemakers by way of Associated. . . .

It was clear that Homemakers regularly processed their accounts and contracts (including the contracts of Associated) through a computer center in Canton, Ohio. The mailing counts of the Indictment were in pairs; that is, for each alleged fraudulent contract the odd numbered count represented the mailing of a contract from the office in Monroeville, where it was discounted, to G. E. Credit in Canton, Ohio, the processing center; and the second or even numbered counts represented the subsequent mailing from Canton, Ohio of a payment book directly to the homeowner in the Pittsburgh area. . . .

The scope of the crime of Mail Fraud is an extremely broad one and the government ordinarily need prove only (1) the intention of devising a scheme to defraud, and (2) the use of the mails in its furtherance. . . . The scheme is one to defraud if it is reasonably calculated to deceive persons of ordinary prudence and comprehension. . . .

In this case there was a detailed analysis of the findings on which the Court was satisfied beyond a resonable doubt that a scheme to defraud had been intentionally devised. . . .

The Court analyzed at great length the elements of the use of the mails and made specific findings with respect thereto on each count of the Indictment. . . . The law is clear that it is the use of the mails in connection with the scheme when the use of the mails follows in the ordinary course of business. While it is true that the Government's proof did not show that the Defendants mailed anything, there was certainly mailing caused to be done in carrying out the scheme. . . .

The scheme in the instant case involved the execution and *fraudulent financing* of the home improvement contracts through installment loans from Homemakers Loan and Consumer Discount Company, the subsidiary of General Electric Credit Corporation. [Court's emphasis.] The Defendants knew, under all the reasonable inferences to be derived from the testimony present, and particularly from their own efforts in covering up by way of collecting the installment payment books, that the mails would be used by Homemakers in transmitting the installment payment books to the homeowners and that this was a necessary part of the scheme in which they would defraud Homemakers. These Defendants used the mails to secure money for phoney home improvement loans, and intercepted the installment payment coupon books that were sent through the mail by the finance company to the supposed homeowner-borrower. . . .

In brief summary, the Defendants' scheme included the collection of monies for construction work supposedly performed in accordance with home improvement contracts with the various homeowner victims. . . . [T]he defendants were able to avoid performance of their contracts either by not doing the work as required, or by doing some very minor inexpensive cover-up work to make the victims think that the more extensive home improvement repairs contracted for, were being done. . . .

The Defendants, however, did not stop here. Instead, they then forged the homeowners' signatures, ages, and other important credit information on the home improvement installment contracts of Associated Town "N" Country Builders. While Associated was a legitimate broker for Homemakers, obviously these contracts were not. It was then, through Michael Nikolich, that this false information was able to be covered up as he, in effect, knowing that the information on the installment loan applications was false, certified that the contracts were verified in all material respects. . . . After payment was made by draft to the Defendants' companies, Nikolich then would process the contracts through to Can-

ton, Ohio, where the coupon payment books were prepared and sent to the homeowner victims. The effect of this mailing was to carry out a portion of the scheme which had to involve the contract with Canton, Ohio or else Homemakers' books would have been immediately thrown out of balance with the accounts as maintained in Canton. This, again, shows the importance of the mailings in the entire scheme.

But this was not even the end of the scheme, for when the books were sent out and intercepted by the Defendants, either on the pretext that an error had been made in the amount or in the person to whom the book was sent, the next step was then to make payments on the installment loans, and make new contracts with other victims as soon as possible so that their income would always exceed the expenses of covering up their fraudulent activities. Thus, . . . the mailings here were used to assure the other victims of the scheme, Homemakers Loan and Consumer Discount Company and the General Electric Credit Corporation, that the services which had been contracted for had been performed and that the financing agreements were genuine. For this reason the Mail Fraud Statute is applicable because there was a "deliberate, planned use of the mails after the victims' money had been obtained.". . .

[Motions denied.]

State and local governments have also become more involved in consumer fraud in recent years. Using a variety of statutes, they are aggressively prosecuting large consumer frauds. As a result, a particular consumer fraud can be subject to state or local prosecution as well as federal prosecution.

55:7   Marketing or Use of Defective or Harmful Products

Numerous consumer products contain defects that pose dangers to life and health. Employees in manufacturing plants are exposed to chemicals and other products that are potentially hazardous. And it has been shown that customary methods of disposing of certain industrial by-products create health dangers to persons in close proximity to the disposed products.

Examples of these problems abound. Defectively designed automobiles and tires have resulted in numerous injuries and deaths. Poorly designed birth-control devices have caused the death and injury of many women. Use of asbestos and polyvinyl chloride in manufacturing processes has contributed to employees' sterility, cancer, total disability, and even death. Dumping of toxic wastes into waterways has resulted in injuries to nearby residents, and dumping of pesticides has resulted in the pollution of groundwater tables.

The consequences of the above activities are truly tragic. Most people, however, recognize the inevitability that businesses will inadvertently market or use products that prove to be defective or harmful. The real tragedy may lie in the fact that in some instances of the kind described above the businesses involved in fact knew of the dangerous nature of their product. As a matter of economics, they decided that it was preferable to permit customers, employees, or others exposed to the products to suffer the resulting harm than it was to spend the money necessary to eliminate the defect or danger.

The harmful consequences of decisions of this sort have led to calls for the imposition of criminal sanctions, and attempts have been made on the federal and state levels to hold corporations and their management criminally responsible. On the federal level, various statutes have been introduced in Congress, but not adopted. These statutes propose to place criminal liability on corporations and corporate officials who knowingly suppress the fact that their product has harmful defects or may be hazardous to the health of their employees. On the state level, attempts to impose criminal liability have generally taken the form of prosecutions under existing criminal statutes. For example, in one case a corporate automaker was charged with reckless homicide because it marketed a car it allegedly knew to be unsafe. The corporation was acquitted of the criminal charges. It is likely that other corporations will also be charged with criminal homicide in the future, and at least one other case charging corporate homicide has been begun.

Homicide statutes vary in their definition of homicide, but all have typically involved the concept of one natural person killing another. The question therefore arises as to whether a corporation, being an artificial person, can even be charged with homicide. The following case is an example of how one court dealt with that issue.

People
v
Ebasco Services, Inc.
77 Misc 2d 784, 354 NYS2d 807
(New York Supreme Court, 1974)

[Ebasco Services was retained to perform various services in connection with a construction project.

The project entailed construction of a temporary structure called a cofferdam. The cofferdam permitted portions of the East River to be pumped out so that construction work could be performed on the river bottom. On August 17, 1973, a portion of the cofferdam collapsed, killing two workers in the dewatered area. Ebasco, another corporate defendant, and three individual defendants were indicted on *charges of criminally negligent homicide, based on the alleged improper construction of the cofferdam. The defendants filed a motion to dismiss the indictment on various grounds, including the ground that a corporation could not be indicted for criminally negligent homicide.]*

Louis Wallach, Justice.

*   *   *

The motions before the court present. . . the novel issue of whether or not a corporation may be convicted of homicide under the revised [New York] Penal Law. . . .

The killing of a human being by a corporation is an act that can be proscribed by the Legislature. As the [New York] Court of Appeals stated [in a 1909 case]:

> "Within the principles thus and elsewhere declared, we have no doubt that a definition of certain forms of manslaughter might have been formulated which would be applicable to a corporation, and make it criminally liable for various acts of misfeasance and nonfeasance when resulting in death, and amongst which very probably might be included conduct in its substance similar to that here charged against the respondent."

The court stated, however, that it was unable to discover in the statute before it any evidence of an intent by the Legislature to hold a corporation criminally liable for a homicide.

Hence, the issue which this court must decide is: "Does section 125.10 of the Penal Law by its terms encompass corporate defendants?" That section reads as follows:

> "A person is guilty of criminally negligent homicide when, with criminal negligence, he causes the death of another person."

A "person" is defined in the homicide article of the Penal Law (125.05[1]) as follows:

> "'Person,' *when referring to the victim of a homicide,* means a human being who has been born and is alive." [Court's emphasis.]

Defendants assert that, inasmuch as this definition of "person" speaks in terms of a human being, a corporate defendant cannot by its act commit a homicide. This contention flies in the face of the statute which equates "person" with human being only in regard to the victim of the homicide. This statute does not require that the person committing the act of homicide be a human being and the reference to human being is of limited application. As the revisers make clear, the definition contained in section 125.05(1) of the Penal Law was inserted merely to insure that the death of a "person" would not include the abortional killing of an unborn child. . . .

Since no definition of "person" as applied to the actual committing of the homicide has been included by the Legislature in the homicide article, the court must look to the broader definition of "person" contained in the overall definitional article of the Penal Law. Section 10.00(7) defines "person" as follows:

> "'Person' means a human being, and where appropriate, a public or private corporation. . . .

It is apparent from a reading of section 10.00(7) of the Penal Law that whenever the term "person" is used in the Penal Law it includes corporations, except in those instances in which inclusion of a corporation is obviously inappropriate. It would be manifestly inappropriate to apply the definition of "person" to corporation in regard to persons who might be seized and arrested. . .or persons who engage in proscribed sex offenses. . . .

There is, however, no manifest impropriety in applying the broader definition of "person" to a corporation in regard to the commission of a homicide, particularly in view of the statement by the Court of Appeals in [the 1909 case] that the Legislature is empowered to impose criminal liability upon a corporation for a homicide. Accordingly, the court concludes that although a corporation cannot be the victim of a homicide, it may commit that offense and be held to answer therefor. . . .

[Indictment dismissed for other reasons.]

 Corporate criminal liability for defective or harmful products is shifting. Therefore, informed business decisions should be made on the basis of what the law might become, not what it is currently. A businessperson who tries to stay barely within the bounds of the law may find that the law has passed him by. The damage to a business from a criminal prosecution cannot be overestimated. It should also be remembered that, even if a criminal prosecution is unsuccessful, civil proceedings seeking damages might be brought against the business. The prudent businessperson must therefore anticipate developments, rather than merely respond to them.

55:8   Pollution

Federal and state statutes have long declared that certain types of pollution are punishable as crimes. Traditionally, however, these statutes have been laxly enforced. Only over the last few years have demands been made for both stricter laws and greater enforcement of the existing laws. Various statutes and amendments to existing statutes have been enacted in response to these demands. For example, under the *Federal Water Pollution Control Act* (FWPCA) (33 USC §§ 1251–1376), as amended in 1972 and 1977, any person or corporation who willfully or negligently discharges pollutants into water in violation of the act can be criminally prosecuted [33 USC § 1319(c)]. It is noteworthy that the FWPCA provides criminal liability not only for willful pollution, but also for negligent pollution of water. Other federal statutes provide that (1) willful violations of laws governing air pollution; (2) disposal of hazardous wastes; (3) manufacture, distribution, and disposal of toxic substances; and (4) production, distribution, and disposal of pesticides are subject to criminal prosecution. Various state statutes also make certain types of pollution criminal. While some state statutes penalize only knowing or willful pollution, others penalize all prohibited pollution, regardless of the offender's knowledge of the pollution.

55:9   Public Corruption

Since Watergate, increased attention has been paid to corruption of and graft by public officials. As the Watergate incident illustrated, such corruption could involve only certain public officials and their political subordinates. In more typical cases, however, public corruption involves someone in addition to the official or officials involved. Not infrequently, that someone is a corporation or individual businessperson.

Bribery is probably the most commonly encountered crime of public corruption. Bribery consists of the voluntary giving to or receiving by a public official of anything of value, with the intent to influence the public official in his official actions. Both federal and state statutes prohibit bribery of public officials, and these statutes are now being vigorously enforced, as recent convictions of high public officials attest.

Another crime, closely related to bribery, is the exertion of improper influence on public officials. The following case involves this crime and illustrates a court's interpretation of a typical state statute.

State
v
Jacobs
119 Ariz 30, 579 P2d
(Arizona Court of Appeals, 1978)

[Jacobs was convicted of violating an Arizona statute that prohibited a person from seeking to obtain money or any other thing of value on a claim that he can or will improperly influence a public officer's action. Jacobs appealed.]

Schroeder, Judge.

*   *   *

In February, 1976, the appellant, Harvey Udell Jacobs, attempted to secure a large construction contract from a prominent home builder. In the course of those attempts, appellant represented to the builder that, in return for the contract, he would control the vote of a key city councilman on a zoning matter important to the interests of the home builder. Appellant was convicted of violating [§ 13- 281.01 of the Arizona Revised Statutes] making it a criminal offense to seek to "obtain money or any other thing of value" upon a claim or representation that the person seeking the benefit "can or will improperly influence the action of a public officer...." Appellant was sentenced to 20 weekends in the Maricopa County Jail and placed on probation for a period of three years....

The evidence at trial showed that appellant first met with the home builder, John F. Long, on February 2, 1976, to discuss the possibility of appellant obtaining a contract for the installation of floor covering in a new subdivision Long was planning to build. During this conversation, appellant asked Long what it would be worth to him to "get Rosie's vote" on a controversial zoning application sought by one of Long's competitors. Appellant was referring to Phoenix City Councilman Rosendo Gutierrez. Appellant indicated that Gutierrez would vote the way he instructed and stated that Gutierrez owed him a debt which he would cancel in return for the vote on the zoning application. Long told appellant he would have to submit a bid to receive the contract and that he could return to Long's office to pick up the bid specifications.

Long then contacted the Phoenix Police Department and, at its suggestion, recorded his next conversation with appellant. Again, appellant indicated that he could control Gutierrez' vote on the zoning application. Appellant also offered to arrange a meeting with Gutierrez if there would be "no bugging." In short, the evidence showed that appellant represented that he could force Gutierrez to vote in favor of Long's interests if Long in turn awarded appellant the contract....

[Appellant attacks] § 13-281.01 as being overbroad, and asserts that it includes lawful as well as unlawful conduct. In this regard, appellant initially contends that the statute proscribes mere incidental boasting, bragging, or puffing. We disagree. The statute does not proscribe all statements concerning influence of a public official, but only claims or representations of improper influence made with the intent to procure something of value in return. The evidence introduced in this case was more than adequate to enable the jury to find the requisite intent. The statute does not proscribe innocent bravado, nor does it proscribe statements made in connection with legitimate lobbying activity.

Appellant further contends that application of the statute to his activities impinged upon his first amendment rights to free speech. It is true that appellant's conviction was based upon his conversations with Long. However, we reject appellant's notion that an attempt to obtain monetary gain by threatening or prom-

ising unlawful conduct is protected speech. Although appellant points out that he did not, in fact, have any means to control Gutierrez' vote, we are not persuaded that false representations are entitled to greater protection than true ones. Appellant also stresses that his efforts were unsuccessful in that Long did not accept his offer and that he never made any attempt to contact Gutierrez. We believe appellant's contentions are aimed at a fundamental misapplication of the first amendment. Under appellant's reasoning, extortion threats would constitute protected speech. The first amendment is our cherished guardian of freedom in expressing ideas, opinions and information. It is not a shield for criminal activity which has been thwarted at an early stage. . . .

Affirmed.

Illegal political contributions represent another form of criminal public corruption. Both federal and state statutes limit the type and amount of contributions that can be made by various persons and entities, and violation of the statutes can be criminally punishable.

Two crimes that are peripherally related to public corruption deserve mention because of their frequent commission in the prosecution of political corruption. These are *obstruction of justice* and *perjury*. Both crimes are typically committed in an attempt to prevent detection or prosecution of other crimes. Obstruction of justice, which is prohibited by both federal and state laws, consists of interference with the orderly administration of law. Obstruction of justice can involve not only actual obstruction of proceedings before a court, but improper influence of jurors or witnesses and improper obstruction of criminal investigations. Obstruction of justice is often accompanied by perjury. Perjury is the willful giving of a false statement under oath. Originally, perjury could be committed only in judicial proceedings, but many statutes now classify *any* willfully false statement given under oath as perjury. In many cases, public officials and businesspersons have been convicted of obstruction of justice or perjury, even though they were never convicted of, and possibly never even prosecuted for, the crime that originally focused attention on them.

55:10   Racketeer Influenced and Corrupt Organizations Act (RICO)

Here and in 55:11 attention will be focused on two specific statutory schemes enacted by Congress to combat crime. The *Racketeer Influenced and Corrupt*

Organizations Act (RICO) (18 USC §§ 1961–1968), which will be discussed here was originally enacted to control organized crime, but has become the federal government's major weapon in the fight against white-collar crime. The *Foreign Corrupt Practices Act* (FCPA) (15 USC §§ 78a, 78m et seq.), which is discussed in 55:11, was enacted by Congress to fight a specific type of white-collar crime, that of bribery of foreign officials by American businesses.

RICO was passed by Congress primarily to combat organized crime's control of legitimate business organizations. It focuses on certain types of racketeering activities. These are criminal acts such as gambling, arson, bribery, extortion, mail fraud, and obstruction of justice. When a person engages in two or more racketeering activities, the person is engaging in a pattern of racketeering activity. A person engaged in racketeering activity commits a crime under RICO if he engages in any of four specified activities: (1) use of income derived from a pattern of racketeering activity to acquire an enterprise or an interest in an enterprise; (2) acquisition of an interest in or control of an enterprise through a pattern of racketeering activity; (3) conduct of an enterprise's affairs through a pattern of racketeering activity; and (4) conspiracy to commit any of the first three acts.

To come within the coverage of RICO, the prohibited activities must concern an enterprise that engages in or affects interstate or foreign commerce. As a practical matter, this includes all significant business enterprises, since they all have some effect on interstate commerce. The term "enterprise" includes not only individuals, partnerships, corporations, and unions, but also any other legal entity or any group of individuals associated in fact. For example, a government agency can be considered an enterprise.

RICO provides for both criminal and civil liability. The criminal punishment can include a fine of up to $25,000; imprisonment for up to 20 years; or both. In addition, an offender can be required to forfeit any interest he has acquired in the legitimate enterprise, as well as any interest in the enterprise that gave him the source of influence over the legitimate enterprise.

An examination of RICO shows that its coverage is very broad. RICO not only prohibits the acquisition of a business enterprise through illegal methods or with money obtained by illegal methods, but it also prohibits the use of legal business enterprises to commit illegal activities. RICO has been vigorously enforced, and its potential applications are numerous. RICO has been widely used not only in organized crime prosecutions, but also in white-collar crime prosecutions, especially political corruption cases.

EXAMPLE

Wilson has a lucrative income from an illegal gambling operation. To channel his illegal gambling receipts, Wilson purchases a legitimate business, Acme Construction Corporation. Wilson proceeds to bribe local government contract officers to obtain favorable consideration of Acme's bids for government construction jobs. To keep construction costs low, Wilson arranges with a local union leader to unionize his employees. In exchange for payments to the labor leader, the union agrees to a contract for wages below the prevailing wage levels. To save on other construction costs, Wilson pays government inspectors to overlook violations of the building laws. Wilson, the government contract officer, the labor union leader, and the government inspectors are all potential targets of RICO prosecutions. Money derived from a pattern of racketeering activity (gambling) has been used to acquire a legitimate enterprise. The affairs of that legitimate enterprise have been conducted through a pattern of racketeering activity. Finally, the various potential defendants might be found guilty of conspiracy to commit the above offenses.

The court in the following case was called on to interpret the scope of RICO's coverage. The court's decision is typical of the broad construction that most courts have given to RICO.

United States

v

Vignola
464 F Supp 1091
(United States District Court, E. D. Pennsylvania, 1979)

[*Vignola, as President Judge of the Philadelphia Traffic Court, appointed and removed writ-servers to serve arrest warrants issued by the court. Writ-servers received a fee for each warrant they served. Vignola solicited and accepted bribes from certain writ-servers in exchange for directing warrants to them for service. These acts of bribery violated the Pennsylvania bribery statute. Vignola was charged with and convicted by a jury of violating RICO. Vignola then filed a motion requesting the trial court to acquit him, claiming that his actions were not covered by RICO.*]

Joseph S. Lord, III, Chief Judge.

*   *   *

The RICO statute. . .prohibits

". . . any person employed by or associated with any enterprise engaged in, or the activities of which affect, interstate or foreign commerce, [from] conduct[ing] or participat[ing], directly or indirectly, in the conduct of such enterprise's affairs through a pattern of racketeering activity. . ."

18 U.S.C. § 1962(c). The statute defines a "pattern of racketeering activity" as consisting of at least two acts of "racketeering activity," 18 U.S.C. § 1961(5), and sets forth a list of offenses which constitute such activity. Among these offenses is

"any act or threat involving. . . bribery, . . .which is chargeable under State law and punishable by imprisonment for more than one year. . ."

18 U.S.C. § 1961(1). . . .
The defendant's initial claim is that the Philadelphia Traffic Court is not an "enterprise" within the meaning of the RICO statute. We reject this contention as contrary to the plain language of RICO, which defines an enterprise as including

"*any* individual, partnership, corporation, association, or *other legal entity*, and any union or group of individuals associated in fact although not a legal entity,"

18 U.S.C. § 1961(4) [Court's emphasis]. As a creature of statute. . . the Philadelphia Traffic Court is a "legal entity" and is therefore an "enterprise" for the purposes of RICO.

The defendant argues, however, that Congress did not intend RICO to apply to the judiciary, and, in enacting RICO, was not concerned with corruption of that branch of government. We disagree. RICO was enacted as Title IX of the Organized Crime Control Act of 1970; the over-all purpose of that Act is to combat so-called "organized crime," which Congress viewed as a spreading cancer in American society. The major thrust of the 1970 Act is to rid the American economy and the channels of interstate commerce from the influences of "organized crime." Congress has chosen to accomplish this objective not by proscribing the elusive status of "organized crime," but by prohibiting certain behavior, such as syndicated gambling and racketeering, which it has concluded is commonly engaged in by members of "organized crime." This does not mean, however, that Congress intended the 1970 Act to apply *exclusively* to members of "organized crime," and, of course, the Government need not prove that a RICO defendant is a member of "organized crime"...

RICO, or Title IX of the 1970 Act, is aimed at removing racketeering influences from enterprises engaged in, or the activities of which affect, interstate commerce. Through RICO, Congress hoped to reduce the burden placed upon interstate commerce by racketeers, and, to that end, Congress has given "enterprise" the broad definition previously quoted. This definition makes no exception for public entities such as the judiciary, nor do we find any basis in the legislative history for implying one. Indeed, in adopting the 1970 Act, Congress expressed a particular concern for the subversion and corruption of "our democratic processes" and the undermining of the "general welfare of the Nation and its citizens" by "organized crime."

Congress has specifically directed that RICO be "liberally construed to effectuate its remedial purposes...."..., and the courts have recognized and given effect to that mandate. They have been in near-unanimity in rejecting challenges to the characterization of a particular entity as an "enterprise," and have held, for example, that the Pennsylvania Bureau of Cigarette and Beverage Taxes, the Pennsylvania State Senate, a municipal police department, and the Philadelphia Redevelopment Author-

ity are all enterprises within the meaning of RICO...

...The judiciary is as vulnerable to the evils of corruption as any other entity, public or private. We see no reason to read into RICO an exception for that branch of government, nor do we believe Congress intended to create one. We therefore hold that the Philadelphia Traffic Court is an "enterprise" within the meaning of RICO.

The defendant's next contention is that RICO requires the Government to prove not only a connection between the enterprise named in the indictment and interstate commerce, but also between the defendant's pattern of racketeering activity and commerce, and that the Government has failed to prove the latter nexus in his case. We disagree with the defendant's interpretation of RICO, and for the following reasons hold that the Government need not prove that a defendant's racketeering activity in any way affected interstate commerce.

First, the express language of the statute itself requires that the Government prove only that the name *enterprise* be one engaged in, or the activities of which affect, interstate (or foreign) commerce. [Court's emphasis.] 18 U.S.C. § 1962.[18] This specific requirement, coupled with RICO's silence as to the need for any link between a defendant's racketeering activity and interstate commerce, can only mean that Congress intended RICO to apply to racketeering activity with no proven connection to interstate commerce except in connection with

---

[18]The Government met its burden in this regard through uncontroverted testimony that the Philadelphia Traffic Court maintains an "out-of-state" department to collect fines assessed against owners of cars registered out-of-state which have been ticketed in Philadelphia, that drivers whose out-of-state cars have been towed by the Philadelphia Police must go to the Traffic Court and pay all outstanding fines before they can get their cars back, that a large automobile leasing company located in Baltimore, Maryland, has paid fines to the Traffic Court, and that the Traffic Court had a contract with a New Jersey computer firm to provide print-outs of scofflaws.

an enterprise which itself affects interstate commerce. . . .

Second, the legislative history of the 1970 Organized Crime Control Act indicates a congressional intent to reach *all* patterns of racketeering activity engaged in by persons employed by or associated with enterprises whose activities affect interstate commerce. This does not mean that RICO was meant to, nor does it, punish purely state law violations. There is a legitimate federal interest in preventing the corruption and subversion of interstate enterprises, and it is this corruption which RICO seeks to eradicate. The defendant in this case has not been subjected to trial in federal court because he has violated state bribery laws, but because he has corrupted and weakened an enterprise whose activities affect interstate commerce. . . .

. . .We therefore hold that RICO requires no proof that the defendant's racketeering activity in any way affected interstate commerce. . . .

[Motions denied.]

55:11   Foreign Corrupt Practices Act (FCPA)

Following closely on the heels of Watergate came revelations that American businesses were routinely bribing foreign officials to obtain favorable treatment. The apparent extent of such bribery led to calls for new legislation. The response was the Foreign Corrupt Practices Act (FCPA).

The purpose of the FCPA is to deter corporate bribery of foreign officials and governments. To this end, the act contains two major provisions: (1) it prohibits American businesses and their employees from making payments or giving gifts to foreign officials for the purpose of influencing the decisions of such officials or their government and (2) it requires corporations that are required to report to the Securities and Exchange Commission (SEC) to keep records and make reports that reveal any such payments. In short, the act prohibits American businesses from obtaining foreign business by bribing foreign officials and requires disclosure of any such bribery. A business firm that violates the act can be fined up to $1,000,000; an officer, director or stockholder of a business firm who violates the act can be fined up to $10,000; imprisoned for five years; or both.

The FCPA, if vigorously enforced, would provide a powerful deterrent to corporate bribery of foreign officials and governments. To date, however, the FCPA has not been strongly enforced and there have even been calls for its amendment. An examination of the reasons for the FCPA's relative lack of effectiveness provides a good case study in the difficulty of dealing with international white-collar crime.

International white-collar crime is difficult to control under even the best circumstances. Transnational corporations by their nature tend to be large and to have branches and subsidiaries in various countries. If one country outlaws a certain type of activity, a transnational corporation can often evade the law by conducting that activity in another country that does not prohibit it. The fact that different activities can be carried out in different countries also makes it difficult to detect violations of one country's laws. Therefore, the FCPA is inherently difficult to enforce.

It has also been argued that the FCPA puts American corporations at a competitive disadvantage. Different countries have different philosophies concerning the conduct of business. What Americans call a bribe may be viewed in another country as a perfectly acceptable way of obtaining business. If an American corporation does not make the appropriate payment to obtain a contract in such a country, other countries' corporations may. Thus, the argument goes, the FCPA does not prevent bribery of foreign officials; it merely removes American firms from the marketplace.

Whether the FCPA will ultimately prove to be effective or whether it will be amended significantly remains to be seen. If business bribery of foreign officials and foreign governments is to be effectively eliminated, international action may be required. At the present time, the possibility of obtaining any significant degree of cooperation appears remote.

55:12   Computer Crime

It is certain that business will make greater use of more sophisticated computers in both the near and distant future. It is equally certain that white-collar criminals will also make greater use of computers. The possibilities of computer-assisted crime are awesome, and it is fitting to close this chapter with a discussion of the newly emerging field of computer crime.

The computer is a prime target for white-collar criminals because access to much of a business' assets and important information can be gained by use of it. Businesses of all sizes routinely use computers in performing important functions. For example, paychecks are printed by computer, bills are sent by computer, customer lists are maintained in a computer, books are printed by computer, and trade secrets are kept in computers. This increased use of computers has not been accompanied by adequate security systems. Typically, even in a large corporation, there are few people who are familiar with the functioning of computers. Data-processing personnel are given access to a company's computer systems—and thus to the company's assets and trade secrets—with little or nothing in the way of a security check. Companies often have no systematic method of overseeing the use of their computers for the purpose of detecting any improper uses. The result is that it is relatively easy to use a computer to commit criminal acts. The chances of a computer criminal being detected are minimal, and the financial rewards of a successfully completed computer crime are often considerable.

Criminal acts can be directed at computer *hardware* or *software*. Hardware consists of the physical components of the computer. "Software" refers to the programs, procedures, and related documentation involved in the operation of a computer.

Criminal acts involving computer hardware pose no great problems; they are easily detectable and can be punished under traditional criminal laws. Software crimes, however, present great problems. They are extremely difficult to detect, and the existing criminal laws aften are inadequate to deal with the types of misuse that occur. Computer software is vulnerable to misuse in several ways: (1) improper programming (giving erroneous instructions to the computer as to the functions it is to perform), (2) input of improper or erroneous data (feeding the computer incorrect information), (3) alteration or theft of computer output, and (4) obliteration of or other damage to the information stored in the computer. This listing is not exhaustive, but it gives some idea of the potential damage that can be caused by misusing a computer.

Criminal misuse of a computer can take only a few seconds. By punching a key or two, a person can direct a computer to pay large sums of money to persons not authorized to receive them, record outstanding bills as paid, or divulge a company's most important trade secrets to a competitor. Computer crimes also tend to be much more costly from the victims' viewpoint than crimes committed without computer assistance. For example, a single computer theft can involve millions of dollars; in one case, a bank employee was convicted of using the bank's computer to transfer over $10 million to a Swiss bank account. It has been estimated that computer bank thefts average $193,000 per theft; that computer crimes against state and local governments average $329,000 per crime; and that computer crimes against corporations average $621,000 per crime.

Computer criminals are usually highly intelligent, capable persons and frequently are good and trusted employees. Computer crime is intellectually challenging to many people—it involves no violence, detection is difficult, and punishment is lenient.

 Any business that makes substantial use of a computer should adopt some type of security system to lessen the possibility of misuse. The first step to be taken is to consult with a qualified computer consultant as to the weaknesses in the system and the various methods of eliminating or minimizing those weaknesses. If the computer handles financial transactions, an auditing system should be adopted that can detect computer frauds or misappropriations. For example, an auditor should not accept computer-produced records as automatically correct. Computer software packages are available for purposes of auditing computer records. With the aid of such packages, the accuracy of computer-produced records can be checked. The adoption of security procedures and special auditing techniques cannot ensure that a computer will not be misused, but it can lessen the chance of such an occurrence.

Criminal Sanctions   Most criminal laws were enacted long before the advent of computers. Computer misuse often differs substantially from other types of crimes, and it is sometimes difficult to apply the older criminal laws to this new type of misconduct. For example, most states have various types of laws dealing with destruction to or damage of physical property. A person might, however, obliterate the program stored on a computer tape without physically damaging the tape itself. Laws prohibiting physical damage to property obviously were not enacted with such misconduct in mind. The larceny statutes provide another example of the inadequacy of traditional criminal law. Most larceny and other theft statutes were passed to prohibit theft of tangible objects. Computer misuse often involves theft of time or information from the computer. In such cases, the question arises as to whether theft of such intangible objects is prohibited by larceny or other theft statutes. Some courts have held that general theft statutes do apply to theft of intangibles, but a contrary conclusion may be just as logical.

The lack of laws designed to deal specifically with computer crime has forced prosecutors and courts to rely on other types of statutes, such as theft, wire fraud, embezzlement, and forgery statutes. Computer misusers are sometimes convicted under such statutes, sometimes not. In response to the lack of appropriate criminal sanctions against computer misuse, various proposals have been put forward on both federal and state levels.

On the federal level, a *Federal Computer Systems Protection Act* has been proposed, but not yet enacted. This statute would effectively prohibit any unauthorized use of a computer for fraudulent or other illegal purposes. The act would apply to such offenses as embezzlement or theft of money committed by computer, theft of trade secrets committed by computer, and alteration or destruction of computer systems. Violation of the proposed act would be punishable by imprisonment, a substantial fine, or both.

Similar types of statutes on the state level have been proposed, and some states have enacted laws dealing specifically with computer crimes. For example, Florida enacted a Computer Crimes Act (Florida Statutes §§ 815.01–815.07) in 1978, and California passed an act relating to computer crimes (California Penal Code § 502) in 1979. These acts outlaw and punish various types of unauthorized and fraudulent use of computers, as well as damage to or destruction of computer systems and programs.

Key Concepts and Terms

- White-collar crime is crime that is (1) nonviolent; (2) covert, usually involving deceit and concealment; and (3) directed toward acquisition of money, property, or economic or political power. White-collar crime can be committed by and against businesses. Individuals and corporations alike can be found liable for white-collar criminal acts. Punishment of these acts tends to be lenient.

- White-collar crimes that traditionally have resulted in prosecution with some degree of regularity include embezzlement, larceny, and tax evasion and avoidance. In recent years there has been an increased emphasis on other types of white-collar crime, such as consumer fraud, pollution, and public corruption.

- Perpetrators of consumer frauds now are frequently prosecuted criminally, either under the federal mail or wire fraud statutes or under state or local laws.

- Public demands for legislation imposing sanctions on white-collar criminals have resulted in enactment of (1) statutes prohibiting individuals and corporations from knowingly or negligently making or using defective or harmful products; (2) the Federal Water Pollution Control Act (FWPCA), imposing criminal liability both for willful and for negligent acts of pollution; and (3) laws prohibiting bribery, exertion of improper influence, illegal political contributions, obstruction of justice, and perjury.

- The Racketeer Influenced and Corrupt Organizations Act (RICO) prohibits (1) use of income derived from racketeering activities to acquire an enterprise, (2) acquisition of an enterprise through racketeering activities, (3) conduct of an enterprise through racketering activities, and (4) a conspiracy to commit any of the first three acts. RICO was passed to combat organized crime, but the act has been used extensively against white-collar crime, including political corruption.

- The Foreign Corrupt Practices Act (FCPA) prohibits American businesses from bribing foreign officials to obtain business and also requires American businesses to disclose these bribes. The FCPA has not been vigorously enforced to date, partly because of problems perceived in fighting international white-collar crime.

- Computer crime is a growing problem. Existing criminal laws are inadequate to combat computer crime, and proposals have been made for new laws directed specifically against computer crimes. A Federal Computer Systems Protection Act has been proposed, but not yet enacted. Some states have enacted laws dealing specifically with computer crimes.

- Bribery
- Computer Hardware
- Computer Software
- Federal Computer Systems Protection Act
- Federal Water Pollution Control Act (FWPCA)

- Foreign Corrupt Practices Act (FCPA)
- Mail Fraud
- Obstruction of Justice
- Perjury
- Racketeer Influenced and Corrupt Organizations Act (RICO)

Questions and Case Problems

1. It has been said that there will be increased emphasis on "crime in the suites" during the 1980s. What does that statement mean? What are the ramifications of such increased emphasis for businesspersons?

2. Sullivan placed an advertisement for an elixir capable of "curing all your aches and pains" in a small-town newspaper. The newspaper had a total circulation of 5,000 copies, of which 300 copies were delivered to subscribers by mail. In response to the advertisement 50 people purchased the elixir at the price of $25 per bottle. The elixir in fact had no effect on aches and pains, and Sullivan was promptly charged with mail fraud. Should he be convicted? Does it make any difference whether the people who purchased the elixir received their newspapers by mail?

3. Kemp, President of State Bank, wants to attract deposits of county funds to her bank. To this end she pays for a lunch at which she and the County Treasurer discuss business. A month later Kemp pays the County Treasurer's bill for a hotel convention. At Christmas Kemp gives the County Treasurer a gift of a book costing $20. Kemp and the County Treasurer are then charged with three counts of violating a statute that makes it unlawful for any person to offer, promise, or give, and for any public official to receive, any "gift, commission, discount, bonus, or gratuity." Each of the incidents described is the basis of one count. Should Kemp and the County Treasurer be convicted on any of the counts? Does it matter whether county funds were ever deposited in State Bank? Does it matter whether Kemp and the County Treasurer are personal friends?

4. Cohen is convicted of stealing an automobile worth $2,000. Helms is convicted of tax evasion in the amount of $2,000, based on his fraudulent deduction of the cost of operating his personal automobile as a business expense. What is an appropriate sentence for each? Discuss.

5. Peters is president of a toy-manufacturing company. Walsh, a company employee, discovers that a particular toy may have a defect that could injure a child. Walsh tells Peters that one of the company's toys may be dangerous. Peters responds, "I don't want to hear about it." A child is killed by the toy. The local prosecutor charges Peters, Walsh, and the toy company with negligent homicide. Should they be convicted? Discuss the policy reasons underlying your answer.

6. Lodge was mayor of a city and owner of Exotic Imports, a local business. As mayor, Lodge accepted numerous bribes from contractors dealing with the city. Lodge deposited all the bribes directly into Exotic Imports' bank account. Shortly after her term as mayor ended, Lodge sold Exotic Imports and used the proceeds to purchase International Exports, another local business. Shortly thereafter, Lodge was indicted for violation of the Racketeer Influenced and Corrupt Organizations Act (RICO). The indictment alleged that Lodge had used income derived from a pattern of racketeering activity (the bribes) to acquire an enterprise (International Exports). In addition to the other penalties, the prosecutor sought an order forfeiting Lodge's interest in International Exports. Lodge defended on the ground that the income from the bribes had been invested in Exotic Imports, not in International Exports. Should Lodge be convicted? Should she be required to forfeit her interest in International Exports?

7. Should the Foreign Corrupt Practices Act be amended? Explain the reasons for your answer.

8. Optimum Systems, Inc. (OSI) operated a computer at Rockville, Maryland. Seidlitz, an employee of OSI, resigned his job and went to work at his own computer firm in Alexandria, Virginia. Seidlitz began obtaining information from the OSI computer surreptitiously. He did this by means of a remote terminal, which he tied into the OSI computer with a telephone. When Seidlitz's activities were discovered, he was indicted for wire fraud, based on the claim that he had transmitted telephone calls in interstate commerce as part of a scheme to defraud OSI of property. The property involved was the information obtained from the computer. Seidlitz defended on the ground that the information did not constitute property within the meaning of the wire fraud statute. Should Seidlitz's contention be upheld?

9. You want your house repainted. Ford tells you that she will paint it for $1,500, provided that you pay her in cash so that she does not have to report it on her income tax return; otherwise, the price is $2,000. What should you do? Why?

10. Should the average businessperson be concerned about computer crime? Discuss.

Appendix A

THE CONSTITUTION OF THE UNITED STATES

We the People of the United States, in Order to form a more perfect Union, establish Justice, insure domestic Tranquility, provide for the common defense, promote the general Welfare, and secure the Blessings of Liberty to ourselves and our Posterity, do ordain and establish this Constitution for the United States of America.

Article I

Section 1 All legislative Powers herein granted shall be vested in a Congress of the United States, which shall consist of a Senate and House of Representatives.

Section 2 [cl. 1] The House of Representatives shall be composed of Members chosen every second Year by the People of the several States, and the Electors in each State shall have the Qualifications requisite for Electors of the most numerous Branch of the State Legislature.

[cl. 2] No Person shall be a Representative who shall not have attained to the Age of twenty five Years, and been seven Years a Citizen of the United States, and who shall not, when elected, be an Inhabitant of that State in which he shall be chosen.

[cl. 3] Representatives and direct Taxes shall be apportioned among the several States which may be included within this Union, according to their respective Numbers, which shall be determined by adding to the whole Number of free Persons, including those bound to Service for a Term of Years, and excluding Indians not taxed, three fifths of all other Persons. The actual Enumeration shall be made within three Years after the first Meeting of the Congress of the United States, and within every subsequent Term of ten Years, in such Manner as they shall by Law direct. The Number of Representatives shall not exceed one for every thirty Thousand, but each State shall have at Least one Representative; and until such enumeration shall be made, the State of New Hampshire shall be entitled to chuse three, Massachusetts eight, Rhode-Island and Providence Plantations one, Connecticut five, New-York six, New Jersey four, Pennsylvania eight, Delaware one, Maryland six, Virginia ten, North Carolina five, South Carolina five, and Georgia three.

[cl. 4] When vacancies happen in the Representation from any State, the Executive Authority thereof shall issue Writs of Election to fill such Vacancies.

[cl. 5] The House of Representatives shall chuse their speaker and other Officers; and shall have the sole Power of Impeachment.

Section 3 [cl. 1] The Senate of the United States shall be composed of two Senators from each State, chosen by the Legislature thereof, for six Years; and each Senator shall have one Vote.

[cl. 2] Immediately after they shall be assembled in Consequence of the first Election, they shall be divided as equally as may be into three Classes. The Seats of the Senators of the first Class shall be vacated at the Expiration of the second Year, of the second Class at the Expiration of the fourth Year, and of the third Class at the Expiration of the sixth Year, so that one third may be chosen every second Year; and if Vacancies happen by Resignation, or otherwise, during the Recess of the Legislature of any State, the Executive thereof may make temporary Appointments until the next Meeting of the Legislature, which shall then fill such Vacancies.

[cl. 3] No Person shall be a Senator who shall not have attained to the Age of thirty years, and been nine Years a Citizen of the United States, and who shall not, when elected, be an Inhabitant of that State for which he shall be chosen.

[cl. 4] The Vice President of the United States shall be President of the Senate, but shall have no Vote, unless they be equally divided.

[cl. 5] The Senate shall chuse their other Officers, and also a President pro tempore, in the Absence of the Vice President, or when he shall exercise the Office of President of the United States.

[cl. 6] The Senate shall have the sole Power to try all Impeachments. When sitting for that Purpose, they shall be on Oath or Affirmation. When the President of the United States is tried, the Chief Justice shall preside: And no Person shall be convicted without the Concurrence of two thirds of the Members present.

[cl. 7] Judgment in Cases of Impeachment shall not extend further than to removal from Office, and disqualification to hold and enjoy any Office of honor, Trust or Profit under the United States: but the Party convicted shall nevertheless be liable and subject to Indictment, Trial, Judgment and Punishment, according to Law.

Section 4 [cl. 1] The Times, Places and Manner of holding Elections for Senators and Representatives, shall be prescribed in each State by the Legislature thereof; but the Congress may at any time by Law make or alter such Regulations, except as to the Places of chusing Senators.

[cl. 2] The Congress shall assemble at least once in every Year, and such Meeting shall be on the first Monday in December, unless they shall by Law appoint a different Day.

Section 5 [cl. 1] Each House shall be the Judge of the Elections, Returns and Qualifications of its own Members, and a Majority of each shall constitute a Quorum to do Business; but a smaller Number may adjourn from day to day, and may be autorized to compel the Attendance of absent Members, in such Manner, and under such Penalties as each House may provide.

[cl. 2] Each House may determine the Rules of its Proceedings, punish its Members for disorderly Behaviour, and, with the Concurrence of two thirds, expel a Member.

[cl. 3] Each House shall keep a Journal of its Proceedings, and from time to time publish the same, excepting such Parts as may in their Judgment require Secrecy; and the Yeas and Nays of the Members of either House on any question shall, at the Desire of one fifth of those Present, be entered on the Journal.

[cl. 4] Neither House, during the Session of Congress, shall, without the Consent of the other, adjourn for more than three days, nor to any other Place than that in which the two Houses shall be sitting.

Section 6 [cl. 1] The Senators and Representatives shall receive a Compensation for their Services, to be ascertained by Law, and paid out of the Treasury of the United States. They shall in all Cases, excep Treason, Felony and Breach of the Peace, be privileged from Arrest during their Attendance at the Session of their respective Houses, and in going to and returning from the same; and for any Speech or Debate in either House, they shall not be questioned in any other Place.

[cl. 2] No Senator or Representative shall, during the Time for which he was elected, be appointed to any civil Office under the Authority of the United States, which shall have been created, or the Emoluments whereof shall have been encreased during such time; and no Person holding any Office under the United States, shall be a Member of either House during his Continuance in Office.

Section 7 [cl. 1] All Bills for raising Revenue shall originate in the House of Representatives; but the Senate may propose or concur with Amendments as on other Bills.

[cl. 2] Every Bill which shall have passed the House of Representatives and the Senate, shall, before it become a Law, be presented to the President of the United States; If he approve he shall sign it, but if not he shall return it, with his Objections to that House in which it shall have originated, who shall enter the Objections at large on their Journal, and proceed to reconsider it. If after such Reconsideration two thirds of that House shall agree to pass the Bill, it shall be sent, together with the Objections, to the other House, by which it shall likewise be reconsidered, and if approved by two thirds of that House, it shall become a Law. But in all such Cases the Votes of both Houses shall be determined by yeas and Nays, and the Names of the Persons voting for and against the Bill shall be entered on the Journal of each House respectively. If any Bill shall not be returned by the President within ten Days (Sundays excepted) after it shall have been presented to him, the Same shall be a Law, in like Manner as if he had signed it, unless the Congress by their Adjournment prevent its Return, in which Case it shall not be a Law.

[cl. 3] Every Order, Resolution, or Vote to which the Concurrence of the Senate and House of Representatives may be necessary (except on a question of Adjournment) shall be presented to the President of the United States; and before the Same shall take Effect, shall be approved by him, or being disapproved by him, shall be repassed by two thirds of the Senate and House of Representatives, according to the Rules and Limitations prescribed in the Case of a Bill.

Section 8 The Congress shall have Power
[cl. 1] To lay and collect Taxes, Duties, Imposts and Excises, to pay the Debts and provide for the common Defence and general Welfare of the United States; but all Duties, Imposts and Excises shall be uniform throughout the United States;

[cl. 2] To borrow Money on the Credit of the United States;

[cl. 3] To regulate Commerce with foreign Nations, and among the several States and with the Indian Tribes;

[cl. 4] To establish an uniform Rule of Naturalization, and uniform Laws on the subject of Bankruptcies throughout the United States;

[cl. 5] To coin Money, regulate the Value thereof, and of foreign Coin, and fix the Standard of Weights and Measures;

[cl. 6] To provide for the Punishment of counterfeiting the Securities and current Coin of the United States;

[cl. 7] To establish Post Offices and post Roads;

[cl. 8] To promote the Progress of Science and useful Arts, by securing for limited Times to Authors and Inventors the exclusive Right to their respective Writings and Discoveries;

[cl. 9] To constitute Tribunals inferior to the supreme Court;

[cl. 10] To define and punish Piracies and Felonies committed on the high Seas, and Offences against the Law of Nations;

[cl. 11] To declare War, grant Letters of Marque and Reprisal, and make Rules concerning Captures on Land and Water;

[cl. 12] To raise and support Armies, but no Appropriation of Money to that Use shall be for a longer Term than two Years;

[cl. 13] To provide and maintain a Navy;

[cl. 14] To make Rules for the Government and Regulation of the land and naval Forces;

[cl. 15] To provide for calling forth the Militia to execute the Laws of the Union, suppress Insurrections and repel Invasions;

[cl. 16] To provide for organizing arming, and disciplining, the Militia, and for governing such Part of them as may be employed in the Service of the United States, reserving to the States respectively, the Appointment of the Officers, and the Authority of training the Militia according to the discipline prescribed by Congress;

[cl. 17] To exercise exclusive Legislation in all Cases whatsoever, over such District (not exceeding ten Miles square) as may, by Cession of particular States, and the Acceptance of Congress become the Seat of the Government of the United States, and to exercise like Authority over all Places purchased by the Consent of the Legislature of the State in which the Same shall be for the Erection of Forts, Magazines, Arsenals, dock-Yards, and other needful Buildings;—And

[cl. 18] To make all Laws which shall be necessary and proper for carrying into Execution the foregoing Powers, and all other Powers vested by this Constitution in the Government of the United States, or in any Department or Officer thereof.

Section 9 [cl. 1] The Migration or Importation of such Persons as any of the States now existing shall think proper to admit, shall not be prohibited by the Congress prior to the Year one thousand eight hundred and eight, but a Tax or duty may be imposed on such Importation, not exceeding ten dollars for each Person.

[cl. 2] The Privilege of the Writ of Habeas Corpus shall not be suspended, unless when in Cases of Rebellion or Invasion the public Safety may require it.

[cl. 3] No Bill of Attainder or ex post facto Laws shall be passed.

[cl. 4] No Capitation, or other direct, Tax shall be laid, unless in Proportion to the Census or Enumeration herein before directed to be taken.

[cl. 5] No Tax or Duty shall be laid on Articles exported from any State.

[cl. 6] No Preference shall be given by any Regulation of Commerce or Revenue to the Ports of one State over those of another: nor shall Vessels bound to, or from, one State, be obliged to enter, clear, or pay Duties in another.

[cl. 7] No Money shall be drawn from the Treasury, but in Consequence of Appropriations made by Law; and a regular Statement and Account of the Receipts and Expenditures of all public Money shall be published from time to time.

[cl. 8] No Title of Nobility shall be granted by the United States; And no Person holding any Office of Profit or Trust under them, shall, without the Consent of the Congress, accept of any present, Emolument, Office, or Title, of any kind whatever, from any King, Prince, or foreign State.

Section 10 [cl. 1] No State shall enter into any Treaty, Alliance, or Confederation; grant Letters of Marque and Reprisal; coin Money; emit Bills of Credit; make any Thing but gold and silver Coin a Tender in Payment of Debts; pass any Bill of Attainder, ex post facto Law, or Law impairing the Obligation of Contracts, or grant any Title of Nobility.

[cl. 2] No State shall, without the Consent of the Congress, lay any Imposts or Duties on Imports or Exports, except what may be absolutely necessary for executing its inspection Laws: and the net Produce of all Duties and Imposts, laid by any State on Imports or Exports, shall be for the Use of the Treasury of the United States; and all such Laws shall be subject to the Revision and Control of the Congress.

[cl. 3] No State shall, without the Consent of Congress, lay any Duty of Tonnage, keep Troops, or Ships of War in time of Peace, enter into any Agreement or Compact with another State, or with a foreign Power, or engage in War, unless actually invaded, or in such imminent Danger as will not admit of delay.

Article II

Section 1 [cl. 1] the executive Power shall be vested in a President of the Untied States of America. He shall hold his Office during the Term of four Years, and, together with the Vice President, chosen for the same Term, be elected, as follows:

[cl. 2] Each State shall appoint, in such Manner as the Legislature thereof may direct, a Number of Electors, equal to the whole Number of Senators and Representatives to which the State may be entitled in the Congress: but no Senator or Representative, or Person holding an Office of Trust or Profit under the United States, shall be appointed an Elector.

[cl. 3] The Electors shall meet in their respective States, and vote by Ballot for two Persons, of whom one at least shall not be an Inhabitant of the same State with themselves. And they shall make a List of all the Persons voted for, and of the Number of Votes for each; which List they shall sign and certify, and transmit sealed to the Seat of the Government of the United States, directed to the President of the Senate. The President of the Senate shall in the Presence of the Senate and House of Representatives, open all the Certificates, and the Votes shall then be counted. The Person having the greatest Number of Votes shall be the President, if such Number be a Majority of the whole Number of Electors appointed; and if there be more than one who have such Majority, and have an equal Number of Votes, then the House of Representatives shall immediately chuse by Ballot one of them for President; and if no Person have a Majority, then from the five highest on the List the said House shall in like manner chuse the President. But in chusing the President, the Votes shall be taken by States, the Representation from each State having one vote; A quorum for this Purpose shall consist of a Member or Members from two thirds of the States, and a Majority of all the States shall be necessary to a Choice. In every Case, after the Choice of the President, the Person having the greatest Number of Votes of the Electors shall be the Vice President. But if there should remain two or more who have equal Votes, the Senate shall chuse from them by Ballot the Vice President.

[cl. 4] The Congress may determine the Time of chusing the Electors, and the Day on which they shall give their Votes; which Day shall be the same throughout the United States.

[cl. 5] No Person except a natural born Citizen, or a Citizen of the United States, at the time of the Adoption of this Constitution, shall be eligible to the Office of President; neither shall any Person be eligible to that Office who shall not have attained to the Age of thirty-five Years, and been fourteen Years a Resident within the United States.

[cl. 6] In Case of the Removal of the President from Office, or of his Death, Resignation, or Inability to discharge the Powers and Duties of the said Office, the Same shall devolve on the Vice President, and the Congress may by Law provide for the Case of Removal, Death, Resignation or Inability, both of the President and Vice President, declaring what Officer shall then act as President, and such Officer shall act accordingly, until the Disability be removed, or a President shall be elected.

[cl. 7] The President shall, at stated Times, receive for his Services, a Compensation, which shall neither be encreased nor diminished during the Period for which he shall have been elected, and he shall not receive within that Period any other Emolument from the United States or any of them.

[cl. 8] Before he enter on the Execution of his Office, he shall take the following Oath or Affirmation:—"I do solemnly swear (or affirm) that I will faithfully execute the Office of President of the United States, and will to the best of my Ability, preserve, protect and defend the Constitution of the United States."

Section 2 [cl. 1] The President shall be Commander in Chief of the Army and Navy of the United States, and of the Militia of the several States, when called into the actual Service of the United States; he may require the Opinion, in writing, of the principal Officer in each of the executive Departments, upon any Subject relating to the Duties of their respective Offices, and he shall have Power to grant Reprieves and Pardons for Offences against the United States, except in Cases of Impeachment.

[cl. 2] He shall have Power, by and with the Advice and Consent of the Senate, to make Treaties, provided two thirds of the Senators present concur; and he shall nominate, and by and with the Advice and Consent of the Senate, shall appoint Ambassadors, other public Ministers and Consuls, Judges of the supreme Court, and all other Officers of the United States, whose Appointments are not herein otherwise provided for, and which shall be established by Law: but the Congress may by Law vest the Appointment of such inferior Officers, as they think proper, in the President alone, in the Courts of Law, or in the Heads of Departments.

[cl. 3] The President shall have Power to fill up all Vacancies that may happen during the Recess of the Senate, by granting Commissions which shall expire at the End of their next Session.

Section 3 He shall from time to time give to the Congress Information of the State of the Union, and recommend to their Consideration such Measures as he shall judge necessary and expedient; he may, on extraordinary Occasions, convene both Houses, or either of them, and in Case of Disagreement between them, with Respect to the Time of Adjournment, he may adjourn them to such Time as he shall think proper; he shall receive Ambassadors and other public Ministers; he shall take Care that the Laws be faithfully executed, and shall Commission all the Officers of the United States.

Section 4 The President, Vice President and all civil Officers of the United States, shall be removed from Office on Impeachment for, and Conviction of, Treason, Bribery, or other high Crimes and Misdemeanors.

Article III

Section 1 The judicial Power of the United States, shall be vested in one supreme Court, and in such inferior Courts as the Congress may from time to time ordain and establish. The Judges, both of the supreme and inferior Courts, shall hold their Offices during good Behaviour and shall, at stated Times,

receive for their Services, a Compensation, which shall not be diminished during their Continuance in Office.

Section 2 [cl. 1] The judicial Power shall extend to all Cases, in Law and Equity, arising under this Constitution, the Laws of the United States, and Treaties made, or which shall be made, under their Authority;—to all Cases affecting Ambassadors, other public Ministers and Consuls;—to all Cases of admiralty and maritime Jurisdiction;—to Controversies to which the United States shall be a Party;—to Controversies between two or more States;—between a State and Citizens of another State; between Citizens of different States;—between Citizens of the same State claiming Lands under Grants of different States, and between a State, or the Citizens thereof, and foreign States, Citizens or Subjects.

[cl. 2] In all Cases affecting Ambassadors, other public Ministers and Consuls, and those in which a State shall be Party, the supreme Court shall have original Jurisdiction. In all the other Cases before mentioned, the supreme Court shall have appellate Jurisdiction, both as to Law and Fact, with such Exceptions, and under such Regulations as the Congress shall make.

[cl. 3] The Trial of all Crimes, except in Cases of Impeachment, shall be by Jury; and such Trial shall be held in the State where the said Crimes shall have been committed; but when not committed within any State, the Trial shall be at such Place or Places as the Congress may by Law have directed.

Section 3 [cl. 1] Treason against the United States, shall consist only in levying War against them, or in adhering to their Enemies, giving them Aid and Comfort. No Person shall be convicted of Treason unless on the Testimony of two Witnesses to the same overt Act, or on Confession in open Court.

[cl. 2] The Congress shall have Power to declare the Punishment of Treason, but no Attainder of Treason shall work Corruption of Blood, or Forfeiture except during the Life of the Person attainted.

Article IV

Section 1 Full Faith and Credit shall be given in each State to the public Acts, Records, and judicial Proceedings of every other State. And the Congress may by general Laws prescribe the Manner in which such Acts, Records and Proceedings shall be proved, and the Effect thereof.

Section 2 [cl. 1] The Citizens of each State shall be entitled to all Privileges and Immunities of Citizens in the several States.

[cl. 2] A Person charged in any State with Treason, Felony, or other Crime, who shall flee from Justice, and be found in another State, shall on Demand of the executive Authority of the State from which he fled, be delivered up, to be removed to the State having Jurisdiction of the Crime.

[cl. 3] No Person held to Service or Labour in One State, under the Laws thereof, escaping into another, shall, in Consequence of any Law or Regulation therein, be discharged from such Service or Labour, but shall be delivered up on Claim of the Party to whom such Service or Labour may be due.

Section 3 [cl. 1] New States may be admitted by the Congress into this Union; but no new State shall be formed or erected within the Jurisdiction of any other State; nor any State be formed by the Junction of two or more States, or Parts of States, without the Consent of the Legislatures of the States concerned as well as of the Congress.

[cl. 2] The Congress shall have Power to dispose of and make all needful Rules and Regulations respecting the Territory or other Property belonging to the United States; and nothing in this Constitution shall be so construed as to Prejudice any Claims of the United States, or of any particular State.

Section 4 The United States shall guarantee to every State in this Union a Republican Form of Government, and shall protect each of them against Invasion; and on Application of the Legislature, or of the Executive (when the Legislature cannot be convened) against domestic Violence.

Article V

The Congress, whenever two thirds of both Houses shall deem it necessary, shall propose Amendments to this Constitution or, on the Application of the Legislatures of two thirds of the several States, shall call a Convention for proposing Amendments, which, in either Case, shall be valid to all Intents and Purposes, as Part of this Constitution, when ratified by the Legislatures of three fourths of the several States, or by Conventions in three fourths thereof, as the one or the other Mode of Ratification may be proposed by the Congress; Provided that no Amendment which may be made prior to the Year One thousand eight hundred and eight shall in any Manner affect the first and fourth Clauses in the Ninth Section of the first Article; and that no State,

without its Consent, shall be deprived of its equal Suffrage in the Senate.

Article VI

[cl. 1] All Debts contracted and Engagements entered into, before the Adoption of this Constitution shall be as valid against the United States under this Constitution, as under the Confederation.

[cl. 2] This Constitution, and the Laws of the United States which shall be made in Pursuance thereof; and all Treaties made, or which shall be made, under the Authority of the United States, shall be the supreme Law of the Land; and the Judges in every State shall be bound thereby, any Thing in the Constitution or Laws of any State to the Contrary notwithstanding.

[cl. 3] The Senators and Representatives before mentioned, and the Members of the several State Legislatures, and all executive and judicial Officers, both of the United States and of the several States, shall be bound by Oath or Affirmation, to support this Constitution; but no religious Test shall ever be required as a Qualification to any Office or public Trust under the United States.

Article VII

The Ratification of the Conventions of nine States, shall be sufficient for the Establishment of this Constitution between the States so ratifying the Same.

AMENDMENTS

(The first 10 Amendments were adopted December 15, 1791)

Amendment 1

Congress shall make no law respecting an establishment of religion, or prohibiting the free exercise thereof; or abridging the freedom of speech, or of the press; or the right of the people peaceably to assemble, and to petition the Government for a redress of grievances.

Amendment 2

A well regulated Militia, being necessary to the security of a free State, the right of the people to keep and bear Arms, shall not be infringed.

Amendment 3

No Soldier shall, in time of peace be quartered in any house, withouth the consent of the Owner, nor in time of war, but in a manner to be prescribed by law.

Amendment 4

The right of the people to be secure in their persons, houses, papers, and effects, against unreasonable searches and seizures, shall not be violated, and no Warrants shall issue, but upon probable cause, supported by Oath or affirmation, and particularly describing the place to be searched, and the persons or things to be seized.

Amendment 5

No person shall be held to answer for a capital, or otherwise infamous crime, unless on a presentment or indictment of a Grand Jury, except in cases arising in the land or naval forces, or in the Militia, when in actual service in time of War or public danger; nor shall any person be subject for the same offence to be twice put in jeopardy of life or limb; nor shall be compelled in any criminalcase to be a witness against himself, nor be deprived of life, liberty, or property, without due process of law; nor shall private property be taken for public use, without just compensation.

Amendment 6

In all criminal prosecutions, the accused shall enjoy the right to a speedy and public trial, by an impartial jury of the State and district wherein the crime shall have been committed, which district shall have been previously ascertained by law, and to be informed of the nature and cause of the accusation; to be confronted with the witnesses against him; to have compulsory process for obtaining witnesses in his favor, and to have the Assistance of Counsel for his defence.

Amendment 7

In Suits at common law, where the value in controversy shall exceed twenty dollars, the right of trial by jury shall be preserved, and no fact tried by a jury, shall be otherwise re-examined in any Court of the United States, than according to the rules of the common law.

Amendment 8

Excessive bail shall not be required, nor excessive fines imposed, nor cruel and unusual punishments inflicted.

Amendment 9

The enumeration in the Constitution, of certain rights, shall not be construed to deny or disparage others retained by the people.

Amendment 10

The powers not delegated to the United States by the Constitution, nor prohibited by it to the States, are reserved to the States respectively, or to the people.

Amendment 11
(Adopted January 8, 1798)

The Judicial power of the United States shall not be construed to extend to any suit in law or equity, commenced or prosecuted against one of the United States by Citizens of another State, or by Citizens or Subjects of any Foreign State.

Amendment 12
(Adopted September 25, 1804)

The Electors shall meet in their respective states and vote by ballot for President and Vice-President, one of whom, at least, shall not be an inhabitant of the same state with themselves; they shall name in their ballots the person voted for as President, and in distinct ballots the person voted for as Vice-President, and they shall make distinct lists of all persons voted for as President, and of all persons voted for as Vice-President, and of the number of votes for each, which lists they shall sign and certify, and transmit sealed to the seat of the government of the United States, directed to the President of the Senate;—The President of the Senate shall, in the presence of the Senate and House of Representatives, open all the certificates and the votes shall then be counted;— The person having the greatest number of votes for President, shall be the President, if such number be a majority of the whole number of Electors appointed; and if no person have such majority, then from the persons having the highest numbers not exceeding three on the list of those voted for as President, the House of Representatives shall choose immediately, by ballot, the President. But in choosing the President, the votes shall be taken by states, the representation from each state having one vote; a quorum for this purpose shall consist of a member or members from two-thirds of the states, and a majority of all the states shall be necessary to a choice. And if the House of Representatives shall not choose a President whenever the right of choice shall devolve upon them, before the fourth day of March next following, then the Vice-President shall act as President, as in the case of the death or other constitutional disability of the President.—The person having the greatest number of votes as Vice-President, shall be the Vice-President, if such number be a majority of the whole number of Electors appointed, and if no person have a majority, then from the two highest numbers on the list, the Senate shall choose the Vice-President; a quorum for the purpose shall consist of two-thirds of the whole number of Senators, and a majority of the whole number shall be necessary to a choice. But no person constitutionally ineligible to the office of President shall be eligible to that of Vice-President of the United States.

Amendment 13
(Adopted December 18, 1865)

Section 1 Neither slavery nor involuntary servitude, except as a punishment for crime whereof the party shall have been duly convicted, shall exist within the United States, or any place subject to their jurisdiction.

Section 2 Congress shall have power to enforce this article by appropriate legislation.

Amendment 14
(Adopted July 28, 1868)

Section 1 All persons born or naturalized in the United States, and subject to the jurisdiction thereof, are citizens of the United States and of the State wherein they reside. No State shall make or enforce any law which shall abridge the privileges or immunities of citizens of the United States; nor shall any State deprive any person of life, liberty, or property, without due process of law; nor deny to any person within its jurisdiction the equal protection of the laws.

Section 2 Representatives shall be apportioned among the several States according to their respective numbers, counting the whole number of persons in each State, excluding Indians not taxed. But when the right to vote at any election for the choice of electors for President and Vice President of the United States, Representatives in Congress, the Executive and Judicial officers of a State, or the members of the Legislature thereof, is denied to any of the male inhabitants of such State, being twenty-one years of age, and citizens of the United States, or in any way abridged, except for participation in rebellion, or other crime, the basis of representation therein shall be reduced in the proportion which the number of such male citizens shall bear to the whole number of male citizens twenty-one years of age in such State.

Section 3 No person shall be a Senator or Representative in Congress, or elector of President and Vice President, or hold any office, civil or military, under the United States, or under any State, who, having previously taken an oath, as a member of Congress, or as an officer of the United States, or as a member of any State legislature, or as an executive or judicial officer of any State, to support the Constitution of the United States, shall have engaged in insurrection or rebellion against the same, or given aid or comfort to the enemies thereof. But Congress may by a vote of two-thirds of each House, remove such disability.

Section 4 The validity of the public debt of the United States, authorized by law, including debts incurred for payment of pensions and bounties for services in suppressing insurrection or rebellion, shall not be questioned. But neither the United States nor any State shall assume or pay any debt or obligation incurred in aid of insurrection or rebellion against the United States, or any claim for the loss or emancipation of any slave; but all such debts, obligations and claims shall be held illegal and void.

Section 5 The Congress shall have power to enforce, by appropriate legislation, the provisions of this article.

Amendment 15
(Adopted March 30, 1870)

Section 1 The right of citizens of the United States to vote shall not be denied or abridged by the United States or by any State on account of race, color, or previous condition of servitude.

Section 2 The Congress shall have power to enforce this article by appropriate legislation.

Amendment 16
(Adopted February 25, 1913)
The Congress shall have power to lay and collect taxes on incomes, from whatever source derived, without apportionment among the several States, and without regard to any census or enumeration.

Amendment 17
(Adopted May 31, 1913)
The Senate of the United States shall be composed of two Senators from each State, elected by the people thereof, for six years; and each Senator shall have one vote. The electors in each State shall have the

qualifications requisite for electors of the most numerous branch of the State legislatures.

When vacancies happen in the representation of any State in the Senate, the executive authority of such State shall issue writs of election to fill such vacancies: Provided, That the legislature of any State may empower the executive thereof to make temporary appointments until the people fill the vacancies by election as the legislature may direct.

This amendment shall not be so construed as to affect the election or term of any Senator chosen before it becomes valid as part of the Constitution.

Amendment 18
(Adopted January 29, 1919)

Section 1 After one year from the ratification of this article the manufacture, sale, or transportation of intoxicating liquors within, the importation thereof into, or the exportation thereof from the United States and all territory subject to the jurisdiction thereof for beverage purposes is hereby prohibited.

Section 2 The Congress and the several States shall have concurrent power to enforce this article by appropriate legislation.

Section 3 This article shall be inoperative unless it shall have been ratified, as an amendment to the Constitution by the legislatures of the several States, as provided in the Constitution, within seven years from the date of the submission hereof to the States by the Congress.

Amendment 19
(Adopted August 26, 1920)

The right of citizens of the United States to vote shall not be denied or abridged by the United States or by any State on account of sex.

Congress shall have power to enforce this article by appropriate legislation.

Amendment 20
(Adopted February 6, 1933)

Section 1 The terms of the President and Vice President shall end at noon on the 20th day of January, and the terms of Senators and Representatives at noon on the 3d of January, of the years in which such terms would have ended if this article had not been ratified; and the terms of their successors shall then begin.

Section 2 The Congress shall assemble at least once in every year, and such meeting shall begin at noon on the 3d day of January, unless they shall by law appoint a different day.

Section 3 If, at the time fixed for the beginning of the term of the President, the President elect shall have died, the Vice President elect shall become President. If a President shall not have been chosen before the time fixed for the beginning of his term, or if the President elect shall have failed to qualify, then the Vice President elect shall act as President until a President shall have qualified; and the Congress may by law provide for the case wherein neither a President elect nor a Vice-President elect shall have qualified, declaring who shall then act as President, or the manner in which one who is to act shall be selected, and such person shall act accordingly until a President or Vice President shall have qualified.

Section 4 The Congress may by law provide for the case of the death of any of the persons from whom the House of Representatives may choose a President whenever the right of choice shall have developed upon them, and for the case of the death of any of the persons from whom the Senate may choose a Vice President whenever the right of choice shall have devolved upon them.

Section 5 Sections 1 and 2 shall take effect on the 15th day of October following the ratification of this article.

Section 6 This article shall be inoperative unless it shall have been ratified as an amendment to the Constitution by the legislatures of three-fourths of the several States within seven years from the date of its submission.

Amendment 21
(Adopted December 5, 1933)

Section 1 The eighteenth article of amendment to the Constitution of the United States is hereby repealed.

Section 2 The transportation or importation into any State, Territory, or possession of the United States for delivery or use therein of intoxicating liquors, in violation of the laws thereof, is hereby prohibited.

Section 3 This article shall be inoperative unless it shall have been ratified as an amendment to the Constitution by conventions in the several States, as provided in the Constitution, within seven years from the date of submission hereof to the United States by the Congress.

Amendment 22
(Adopted February 26, 1951)

Section 1 No person shall be elected to the office of President more than twice, and no person who has held the office of President, or acted as President, for more than two years of a term to which some other person was elected President shall be elected to the office of the President more than once. But this article shall not apply to any person holding the office of President when this article was proposed by Congress, and shall not prevent any person who may be holding the office of President, or acting as President, during the term within which this article becomes operative from holding the office of President or acting as President during the remainder of such term.

Section 2 This article shall be inoperative unless it shall have been ratified as an amendment to the Constitution by the legislatures of three fourths of the several states within seven years from the date of its submission to the states by the Congress.

Amendment 23
(Adopted April 3, 1961)

Section 1 The District constituting the seat of Government of the United States shall appoint in such manner as the Congress may direct:

A number of electors of President and Vice President equal to the whole number of Senators and Representatives in Congress to which the District would be entitled if it were a State, but in no event more than the least populous State; they shall be in addition to those appointed by the States, but they shall be considered, for the purposes of the election of President and Vice President, to be electors appointed by a State; and they shall meet in the District and perform such duties as provided by the twelfth article of amendment.

Section 2 The Congress shall have power to enforce this article by appropriate legislation.

Amendment 24
(Adopted January 23, 1964)

Section 1 The right of citizens of the United States to vote in any primary or other election for President or Vice President, for electors for President or Vice President, or for Senator or Representative in Congress, shall not be denied or abridged by the United States or any state by reason of failure to pay any poll tax or other tax.

Section 2 The Congress shall have the power to enforce this article by appropriate legislation.

Amendment 25
(Adopted February 10, 1967)

Section 1 In case of the removal of the President from office or of his death or resignation, the Vice President shall become President.

Section 2 Whenever there is a vacancy in the office of the Vice President, the President shall nominate a Vice President who shall take office upon confirmation by a majority vote of both Houses of Congress.

Section 3 Whenever the President transmits to the President pro tempore of the Senate and the Speaker of the House of Representatives his written declaration that he is unable to discharge the powers and duties of his office, and until he transmits to them a written declaration to the contrary, such powers and duties shall be discharged by the Vice President as Acting President.

Section 4 Whenever the Vice President and a majority of either the principal officers of the executive departments or of such other body as Congress may by law provide, transmit to the President pro tempore of the Senate and the Speaker of the House of Representatives their written declaration that the President is unable to discharge the powers and duties of his office, the Vice President shall immediately assume the powers and duties of the office as Acting President.

Thereafter, when the President transmits to the President pro tempore of the Senate and the Speaker of the House of Representatives his written declaration that no inability exists, he shall resume the powers and duties of his office unless the Vice President and a majority of either the principal officers of the executive department or of such other body as Congress may by law provide, transmit within four days to the President pro tempore of the Senate and the Speaker of the House of Representatives their written declaration that the President is unable to discharge the powers and duties of his office. Thereupon Congress shall decide the issue, assembling within forty-eight hours for that purpose if not in session. If the Congress, within twenty-one days after receipt of the latter written declaration, or, if Congress is not in session, within twenty-one days after Congress is required to assemble, determines by two-thirds vote of both Houses that the President is unable to discharge the powers and duties of his office, the Vice President shall continue to discharge the same as Acting President; otherwise, the President shall resume the powers and duties of his office.

Amendment 26
(Adopted July 5, 1971)

Section 1   The right of citizens of the United States, who are eighteen years of age or older, to vote shall not be denied or abridged by the United States or by any State on account of age.

Section 2   The Congress shall have power to enforce this article by appropriate legislation.

Appendix B

ARTICLE 1. GENERAL PROVISIONS

Part 1. Short Title, Construction, Application and Subject Matter of the act

§ 1-101. Short Title. This Act shall be known and may be cited as Uniform Commercial Code.

§ 1-102. Purposes; Rules of Construction; Variation by Agreement.

(1) This Act shall be liberally construed and applied to promote its underlying purposes and policies.

(2) Underlying purposes and policies of this Act are

- (a) to simplify, clarify and modernize the law governing commercial transactions;
- (b) to permit the continued expansion of commercial practices through custom, usage and agreement of the parties;
- (c) to make uniform the law among the various jurisdictions.

(3) The effect of provisions of this Act may be varied by agreement, except as otherwise provided in this Act and except that the obligations of good faith, diligence, reasonableness and care prescribed by this Act may not be disclaimed by agreement but the parties may by agreement determine the standards by which the performance of such obligations is to be measured if such standards are not manifestly unreasonable.

(4) The presence in certain provisions of this Act of the words "unless otherwise agreed" or words of similar import does not imply that the effect of other provisions may not be varied by agreement under subsection (3).

(5) In this Act unless the context otherwise requires

- (a) words in the singular number include the plural, and in the plural include the singular;
- (b) words of the masculine gender include the feminine and the neuter, and when the sense so indicates words of the neuter gender may refer to any gender.

§1-103. Supplementary General Principles of Law Applicable. Unless displaced by the particular provisions of this Act, the principles of law and equity, including the law merchant and the law relative to capacity to contract, principal and agent, estoppel, fraud, misrepresentation, duress, coercion, mistake, bankruptcy, or other validating or invalidating cause shall supplement its provisions.

§ 1-104. Construction Against Implicit Repeal. This Act being a general act intended as a unified coverage of its subject matter, no part of it shall be deemed to be impliedly repealed by subsequent legislation if such construction can reasonably be avoided.

§ 1-105. Territorial Application of the Act; Parties' Power to Choose Applicable Law.

(1) Except as provided hereafter in this section, when a transaction bears a reasonable relation to this state and also to another state or nation the parties may agree that the law either of this state or of such other state or nation shall govern their rights and duties. Failing such agreement this Act applies to transactions bearing an appropriate relation to this state.

(2) Where one of the following provisions of this Act specifies the applicable law, that provision governs and a contrary agreement is effective only to the extent permitted by the law (including the conflict of laws rules) so specified:

Rights of creditors against sold goods. Section 2—402.

Applicability of the Article on Bank Deposits and Collections. Section 4—102.

Bulk transfers subject to the Article on Bulk Transfers. Section 6—102.

Applicability of the Article on Investment Securities. Section 8—106.

Perfection provisions of the Article on Secured Transactions. Section 9—103.

§ 1-106. Remedies to Be Liberally Administered.

(1) The remedies provided by this Act shall be liberally administered to the end that the aggrieved party may be put in as good a position as if the other party had fully performed but neither consequential or special nor penal damages may be had except as specifically provided in this Act or by other rule of law.

(2) Any right or obligation declared by this Act is enforceable by action unless the provision declaring its specifies a different and limited effect.

§ 1-107. Waiver or Renunciation of Claim or Right After Breach.
Any claim or right arising out of an alleged breach can be discharged in whole or in part without consideration by a written waiver or renunciation signed and delivered by the aggrieved party.

§ 1-108. Severability.
If any provision or clause of this Act or application thereof to any person or circumstances is held invalid, such invalidity shall not affect other provisions or applications of the Act which can be given effect without the invalid provision or application, and to this end the provisions of this Act are declared to be severable.

§ 1-109. Section Captions.
Section captions are parts of this Act.

Part 2. General Definitions and Principles of Interpretation

§ 1-201. General Definitions.
Subject to additional definitions contained in the subsequent Articles of this Act which are applicable to specific Articles or Parts thereof, and unless the context otherwise requires, in this Act:

(1) "Action" in the sense of a judicial proceeding includes recoupment, counterclaim, set-off, suit in equity and any other proceedings in which rights are determined.

(2) "Aggrieved party" means a party entitled to resort to a remedy.

(3) "Agreement" means the bargain of the parties in fact as found in their language or by implication from other circumstances including course of dealing or usage of trade or course of performance as provided in this Act (Sections 1—205 and 2—208). Whether an agreement has legal consequences is determined by the provisions of this Act, if applicable; otherwise by the law of contracts (Section 1—103). (Compare "Contract".)

(4) "Bank" means any person engaged in the business of banking.

(5) "Bearer" means the person in possession of an instrument, document of title, or certificated security payable to bearer or indorsed in blank.

(6) "Bill of lading" means a document evidencing the receipt of goods for shipment issued by a person engaged in the business of transporting or forwarding goods, and includes an airbill. "Airbill" means a document serving for air transportation as a bill of lading does for marine or rail transportation, and includes an air consignment note or air waybill.

(7) "Branch" includes a separately incorporated foreign branch of a bank.

(8) "Burden of establishing" a fact means the burden of persuading the triers of fact that the existence of the fact is more probable than its non-existence.

(9) "Buyer in ordinary course of business" means a person who in good faith and without knowledge that the sale to him is in violation of the ownership rights or security interest of a third party in the goods buys in ordinary course from a person in the business of selling goods of that kind but does not include a pawnbroker. All persons who sell minerals or the like (including oil and gas) at wellhead or minehead shall be deemed to be persons in the business of selling goods of that kind. "Buying" may be for cash or by exchange of other property or on secured or unsecured credit and includes receiving goods or documents of title under a pre-existing contract for sale but does not include a transfer in bulk or as security for or in total or partial satisfaction of a money debt.

(10) "Conspicuous": A term or clause is conspicuous when it is so written that a reasonable person against whom it is to operate ought to have noticed it. A printed heading in capitals (as: NON-NEGOTIABLE

BILL OF LADING) is conspicuous. Language in the body of a form is "conspicuous" if it is in larger or other contrasting type or color. But in a telegram any stated term is "conspicuous". Whether a term or clause is "conspicuous" or not is for decision by the court.

(11) "Contract" means the total legal obligation which results from the parties' agreement as affected by this Act and any other applicable rules of law. (Compare "Agreement".)

(12) "Creditor" includes a general creditor, a secured creditor, a lien creditor and any representative of creditors, including an assignee for the benefit of creditors, a trustee in bankruptcy, a receiver in equity and an executor or administrator of an insolvent debtor's or assignor's estate.

(13) "Defendant" includes a person in the position of defendant in a cross-action or counterclaim.

(14) "Delivery" with respect to instruments, documents of title, chattel paper, or certificated securities means voluntary transfer of possession.

(15) "Document of title" includes bill of lading, dock warrant, dock receipt, warehouse receipt or order for the delivery of goods, and also any other document which in the regular course of business or financing is treated as adequately evidencing that the person in possession of it is entitled to receive, hold and dispose of the document and the goods it covers. To be a document of title a document must purport to be issued by or addressed to a bailee and purport to cover goods in the bailee's possession which are either identified or are fungible portions of an identified mass.

(16) "Fault" means wrongful act, omission or breach.

(17) "Fungible" with respect to goods or securities means goods or securities of which any unit is, by nature or usage of trade, the equivalent of any other like unit. Goods which are not fungible shall be deemed fungible for the purposes of this Act to the extent that under a particular agreement or document unlike units are treated as equivalents.

(18) "Genuine" means free of forgery or counterfeiting.

(19) "Good faith" means honesty in fact in the conduct or transaction concerned.

(20) "Holder" means a person who is in possession of a document of title or an instrument or a certificated investment security drawn, issued, or indorsed to him or his order or to bearer or in blank.

(21) To "honor" is to pay or to accept and pay, or where a credit so engages to purchase or discount a draft complying with the terms of the credit.

(22) "Insolvency proceedings" includes any assignment for the benefit of creditors or other proceedings intended to liquidate or rehabilitate the estate of the person involved.

(23) A person is "insolvent" who either has ceased to pay his debts in the ordinary course of business or cannot pay his debts as they become due or is insolvent within the meaning of the federal bankruptcy law.

(24) "Money" means a medium of exchange authorized or adopted by a domestic or foreign government as a part of its currency.

(25) A person has "notice" of a fact when

(a)   he has actual knowledge of it; or

(b)   he has received a notice or notification of it; or

(c)   from all the facts and circumstances known to him at the time in question he has reason to know that it exists.

A person "knows" or has "knowledge" of a fact when he has actual knowledge of it. "Discover" or "learn" or a word or phrase of similar import refers to knowledge rather than to reason to know. The time and circumstances under which a notice or notification may cease to be effective are not determined by this Act.

(26) A person "notifies" or "gives" a notice or notification to another by taking such steps as may be reasonably required to inform the other in ordinary course whether or not such other actually comes to know of it. A person "receives" a notice or notification when

(a)   it comes to his attention; or

(b)   it is duly delivered at the place of business through which the contract was made or at any other place held out by him as the place for receipt of such communications.

(27) Notice, knowledge or a notice or notification received by an organization is effective for a particular transaction from the time when it is brought to the attention of the individual conducting that transaction, and in any event from the time when it would have been brought to his attention if the organization had exercised due diligence. An organization exercises due diligence if it maintains reasonable routines for communicating significant information to the person conducting the transaction and there is reasonable compliance with the routines. Due diligence does not require an individual acting for the

organization to communicate information unless such communication is part of his regular duties or unless he has reason to know of the transaction and that the transaction would be materially affected by the information.

(28) "Organization" includes a corporation, government or governmental subdivision or agency, business trust, estate, trust, partnership or association, two or more persons having a joint or common interest, or any other legal or commercial entity.

(29) "Party", as distinct from "third party", means a person who has engaged in a transaction or made an agreement within this Act.

(30) "Person" includes an individual or an organization (See Section 1—102).

(31) "Presumption" or "presumed" means that the trier of fact must find the existence of the fact presumed unless and until evidence is introduced which would support a finding of its non-existence.

(32) "Purchase" includes taking by sale, discount, negotiation, mortgage, pledge, lien, issue or re-issue, gift or any other voluntary transaction creating an interest in property.

(33) "Purchaser" means a person who takes by purchase.

(34) "Remedy" means any remedial right to which an aggrieved party is entitled with or without resort to a tribunal.

(35) "Representative" includes an agent, an officer of a corporation or association, and a trustee, executor or administrator of an estate, or any other person empowered to act for another.

(36) "Rights" includes remedies.

(37) "Security interest" means an interest in personal property or fixtures which secures payment or performance of an obligation. The retention or reservation of title by a seller of goods notwithstanding shipment or delivery to the buyer (Section 2—401) is limited in effect to a reservation of a "security interest". The term also includes any interest of a buyer of accounts or chattel paper which is subject to Article 9. The special property interest of a buyer of goods on identification of such goods to a contract for sale under Section 2—401 is not a "security interest", but a buyer may also acquire a "security interest" by complying with Article 9. Unless a lease or consignment is intended as security, reservation of title thereunder is not a "security interest" but a consignment is in any event subject to the provisions on consignment sales (Section 2—326). Whether a lease is intended as security is to be determined by the facts of each case; however, (a) the inclusion of an option to purchase does not of itself make the lease one intended for security, and (b) an agreement that upon compliance with the terms of the lease the lessee shall become or has the option to become the owner of the property for no additional consideration or for a nominal consideration does make the lease one intended for security.

(38) "Send" in connection with any writing or notice means to deposit in the mail or deliver for transmission by any other usual means of communication with postage or cost of transmission provided for and properly addressed and in the case of an instrument to an address specified thereon or otherwise agreed, or if there be none to any address reasonable under the circumstances. The receipt of any writing or notice within the time at which it would have arrived if properly sent has the effect of a proper sending.

(39) "Signed" includes any symbol executed or adopted by a party with present intention to authenticate a writing.

(40) "Surety" includes guarantor.

(41) "Telegram" includes a message transmitted by radio, teletype, cable, any mechanical method of transmission, or the like.

(42) "Term" means that portion of an agreement which relates to a particular matter.

(43) "Unauthorized" signature or indorsement means one made without actual, implied or apparent authority and includes a forgery.

(44) "Value". Except as otherwise provided with respect to negotiable instruments and bank collections (Sections 3—303, 4—208 and 4—209) a person gives "value" for rights if he acquires them

(a)   in return for a binding commitment to extend credit or for the extension of immediately available credit whether or not drawn upon and whether or not a chargeback is provided for in the event of difficulties in collection; or

(b)   as security for or in total or partial satisfaction of a pre-existing claim; or

(c)   by accepting delivery pursuant to a pre-existing contract for purchase; or

(d)   generally, in return for any consideration sufficient to support a simple contract.

(45) "Warehouse receipt" means a receipt issued by a person engaged in the business of storing goods for hire.

(46) "Written" or "writing" includes printing,

typewriting or any other intentional reduction to tangible form. Amended in 1962, 1972 and 1977.

§ 1-202. Prima Facie Evidence by Third Party Documents. A document in due form purporting to be a bill of lading, policy or certificate of insurance, official weigher's or inspector's certificate, consular invoice, or any other document authorized or required by the contract to be issued by a third party shall be prima facie evidence of its own authenticity and genuineness and of the facts stated in the document by the third party.

§ 1-203. Obligation of Good Faith. Every contract or duty within this Act imposes an obligation of good faith in its performance or enforcement.

§ 1-204. Time; Reasonable Time; "Seasonably."

(1) Whenever this Act requires any action to be taken within a reasonable time, any time which is not manifestly unreasonable may be fixed by agreement.

(2) What is a reasonable time for taking any action depends on the nature, purpose and circumstances of such action.

(3) An action is taken "seasonably" when it is taken at or within the time agreed or if no time is agreed at or within a reasonable time.

§ 1-205. Course of Dealing and Usage of Trade.

(1) A course of dealing is a sequence of previous conduct between the parties to a particular transaction which is fairly to be regarded as establishing a common basis of understanding for interpreting their expressions and other conduct.

(2) A usage of trade is any practice or method of dealing having such regularity of observance in a place, vocation or trade as to justify an expectation that it will be observed with respect to the transaction in question. The existence and scope of such a usage are to be proved as facts. If it is established that such a usage is embodied in a written trade code or similar writing the interpretation of the writing is for the court.

(3) A course of dealing between parties and any usage of trade in the vocation or trade in which they are engaged or of which they are or should be aware give particular meaning to and supplement or qualify terms of an agreement.

(4) The express terms of an agreement and an applicable course of dealing or usage of trade shall be construed wherever reasonable as consistent with each other; but when such construction is unreasonable express terms control both course of dealing and usage of trade and course of dealing controls usage of trade.

(5) An applicable usage of trade in the place where any part of performance is to occur shall be used in interpreting the agreement as to that part of the performance.

(6) Evidence of a relevant usage of trade offered by one party is not admissible unless and until he has given the other party such notice as the court finds sufficient to prevent unfair surprise to the latter.

§ 1-206. Statute of Frauds for Kinds of Personal Property Not Otherwise Covered.

(1) Except in the cases described in subsection (2) of this section a contract for the sale of personal property is not enforceable by way of action or defense beyond five thousand dollars in amount or value of remedy unless there is some writing which indicates that a contract for sale has been made between the parties at a defined or stated price, reasonably identifies the subject matter, and is signed by the party against whom enforcement is sought or by his authorized agent.

(2) Subsection (1) of this section does not apply to contracts for the sale of goods (Section 2—201) nor of securities (Section 8—319) nor to security agreements (Section 9—203).

§ 1-207. Performance or Acceptance Under Reservation of Rights. A party who with explicit reservation of rights performs or promises performance or assents to performance in a manner demanded or offered by the other party does not thereby prejudice the rights reserved. Such words as "without prejudice", "under protest" or the like are sufficient.

§ 1-208. Option to Accelerate at Will. A term providing that one party or his successor in interest may accelerate payment or performance or require collateral or additional collateral "at will" or "when he deems himself insecure" or in words of similar import shall be construed to mean that he shall have power to do so only if he in good faith believes that the prospect of payment or performance is impaired. The burden of establishing lack of good faith is on the party against whom the power has been exercised.

§ 1-209. Subordinated Obligations. An obligation may be issued as subordinated to payment of another obligation of the person obligated, or a creditor may subordinate his right to payment of an obligation by agreement with either the person obligated or another creditor of the person obligated. Such a subordination does not create a security interest as against either the common debtor or a subordinated creditor. This section shall be construed as declaring the law as it existed prior to the enactment of this section and not as modifying it. Added 1966.

Note: *This new section is proposed as an optional provision to make it clear that a subordination agreement does not create a security interest unless so intended.*

ARTICLE 2. SALES

Part 1. Short Title, General Construction and Subject Matter

§ 2-101. Short Title. This Article shall be known and may be cited as Uniform Commercial Code—Sales.

§ 2-102. Scope; Certain Security and Other Transactions Excluded From This Article. Unless the context otherwise requires, this Article applies to transactions in goods; it does not apply to any transaction which although in the form of an unconditional contract to sell or present sale is intended to operate only as a security transaction nor does this Article impair or repeal any statute regulating sales to consumers, farmers or other specified classes of buyers.

§ 2-103. Definitions and Index of Definitions.

(1) In this Article unless the context otherwise requires

    (a) "Buyer" means a person who buys or contracts to buy goods.

    (b) "Good faith" in the case of a merchant means honesty in fact and the observance of reasonable commercial standards of fair dealing in the trade.

    (c) "Receipt" of goods means taking physical possession of them.

    (d) "Seller" means a person who sells or contracts to sell goods.

(2) Other definitions applying to this Article or to specified Parts thereof, and the sections in which they appear are:

"Acceptance". Section 2—606.
"Banker's credit". Section 2—325.
"Between merchants". Section 2—104.
"Cancellation". Section 2—106(4).
"Commercial unit". Section 2—105.
"Confirmed credit". Section 2—325.

"Conforming to contract". Section 2—106.
"Contract for sale". Section 2—106.
"Cover". Section 2—712.
"Entrusting". Section 2—403.
"Financing agency". Section 2—104.
"Future goods". Section 2—105.
"Goods". Section 2—105.
"Identification". Section 2—501.
"Installment contract". Section 2—612.
"Letter of Credit". Section 2—325.
"Lot". Section 2—105.
"Merchant". Section 2—104.
"Overseas". Section 2—323.
"Person in position of seller". Section 2—707.
"Present sale". Section 2—106.
"Sale". Section 2—106.
"Sale on approval". Section 2—326.
"Sale or return". Section 2—326.
"Termination". Section 2—106.

(3) The following definitions in other Articles apply to this Article:

"Check". Section 3—104.
"Consignee". Section 7—102.
"Consignor". Section 7—102.
"Consumer goods". Section 9—109.
"Dishonor". Section 3—507.
"Draft". Section 3—104.

(4) In addition Article 1 contains general definitions and principles of construction and interpretation applicable throughout this Article.

§2-104. Definitions: "Merchant"; "Between Merchants"; "Financing Agency."

(1) "Merchant" means a person who deals in goods of the kind or otherwise by his occupation holds himself out as having knowledge or skill peculiar to the practices or goods involved in the transaction or to whom such knowledge or skill may be attributed by his employment of an agent or broker or other intermediary who by his occupation holds himself out as having such knowledge or skill.

(2) "Financing agency" means a bank, finance company or other person who in the ordinary course of business makes advances against goods or documents of title or who by arrangement with either the seller or the buyer intervenes in ordinary course to make or collect payment due or claimed under the contract for sale, as by purchasing or paying the seller's draft or making advances against it or by merely taking it for collection whether or not documents of title accompany the draft. "Financing

agency" includes also a bank or other person who similarly intervenes between persons who are in the position of seller and buyer in respect to the goods (Section 2—707).

(3) "Between merchants" means in any transaction with respect to which both parties are chargeable with the knowledge or skill of merchants.

§ 2-105. Definitions: Transferability; "Goods"; "Future" Goods; "Lot"; "Commercial Unit."

(1) "Goods" means all things (including specially manufactured goods) which are movable at the time of identification to the contract for sale other than the money in which the price is to be paid, investment securities (Article 8) and things in action. "Goods" also includes the unborn young of animals and growing crops and other identified things attached to realty as described in the section on goods to be severed from realty (Section 2—107).

(2) Goods must be both existing and identified before any interest in them can pass. Goods which are not both existing and identified are "future" goods. A purported present sale of future goods or of any interest therein operates as a contract to sell.

(3) There may be a sale of a part interest in existing identified goods.

(4) An undivided share in an identified bulk of fungible goods is sufficiently identified to be sold although the quantity of the bulk is not determined. Any agreed proportion of such a bulk or any quantity thereof agreed upon by number, weight or other measure may to the extent of the seller's interest in the bulk be sold to the buyer who then becomes an owner in common.

(5) "Lot" means a parcel or a single article which is the subject matter of a separate sale or delivery, whether or not it is sufficient to perform the contract.

(6) "Commercial unit" means such a unit of goods as by commercial usage is a single whole for purposes of sale and division of which materially impairs its character or value on the market or in use. A commercial unit may be a single article (as a machine) or a set of articles (as a suite of furniture or an assortment of sizes) or a quantity (as a bale, gross, or carload) or any other unit treated in use or in the relevant market as a single whole.

§ 2-106. Definitions: "Contract"; "Agreement"; "Contract for Sale"; "Sale"; "Present Sale"; "Conforming" to Contract; "Termination"; "Cancellation."

(1) In this Article unless the context otherwise requires "contract" and "agreement" are limited to those relating to the present or future sale of goods. "Contract for sale" includes both a present sale of goods and a contract to sell goods at a future time. A "sale" consists in the passing of title from the seller to the buyer for a price (Section 2—401). A "present sale" means a sale which is accomplished by the making of the contract.

(2) Goods or conduct including any part of a performance are "conforming" or conform to the contract when they are in accordance with the obligations under the contract.

(3) "Termination" occurs when either party pursuant to a power created by agreement or law puts an end to the contract otherwise than for its breach. On "termination" all obligations which are still executory on both sides are discharged but any right based on prior breach or performance survives.

(4) "Cancellation" occurs when either party puts an end to the contract for breach by the other and its effect is the same as that of "termination" except that the cancelling party also retains any remedy for breach of the whole contract or any unperformed balance.

§ 2-107. Goods to Be Severed From Realty: Recording.

(1) A contract for the sale of minerals or the like (including oil and gas) or a structure or its materials to be removed from realty is a contract for the sale of goods within this Article if they are to be severed by the seller but until severance a purported present sale thereof which is not effective as a transfer of an interest in land is effective only as a contract to sell.

(2) A contract for the sale apart from the land of growing crops or other things attached to realty and capable of severance without material harm thereto but not described in subsection (1) or of timber to be cut is a contract for the sale of goods within this Article whether the subject matter is to be severed by the buyer or by the seller even though it forms part of the realty at the time of contracting, and the parties can by identification effect a present sale before severance.

(3) The provisions of this section are subject to any third party rights provided by the law relating to realty records, and the contract for sale may be executed and recorded as a document transferring an interest in land and shall then constitute notice to third parties of the buyer's rights under the contract for sale.

Part 2. Form, Formation and Readjustment of Contract

§ 2-201. Formal Requirements; Statute of Frauds.

(1) Except as otherwise provided in this section a contract for the sale of goods for the price of $500 or more is not enforceable by way of action or defense unless there is some writing sufficient to indicate that a contract for sale has been made between the parties and signed by the party against whom enforcement is sought or by his authorized agent or broker. A writing is not insufficient because it omits or incorrectly states a term agreed upon but the contract is not enforceable under this paragraph beyond the quantity of goods shown in such writing.

(2) Between merchants if within a reasonable time a writing in confirmation of the contract and sufficient against the sender is received and the party receiving it has reason to know its contents, it satisfies the requirements of subsection (1) against such party unless written notice of objection to its contents is given within 10 days after it is received.

(3) A contract which does not satisfy the requirements of subsection (1) but which is valid in other respects is enforceable

(a) if the goods are to be specially manufactured for the buyer and are not suitable for sale to others in the ordinary course of the seller's business and the seller, before notice of repudiation is received and under circumstances which reasonably indicate that the goods are for the buyer, has made either a substantial beginning of their manufacture or commitments for their procurement; or

(b) if the party against whom enforcement is sought admits in his pleading, testimony or otherwise in court that a contract for sale was made, but the contract is not enforceable under this provision beyond the quantity of goods admitted; or

(c) with respect to goods for which payment has been made and accepted or which have been received and accepted (Sec. 2—606).

§ 2-202. Final Written Expression: Parol or Extrinsic Evidence.
Terms with respect to which the confirmatory memoranda of the parties agree or which are otherwise set forth in a writing intended by the parties as a final expression of their agreement with respect to such terms as are included therein may not be contradicted by evidence of any prior agreement or of a contemporaneous oral agreement but may be explained or supplemented

(a) by course of dealing or usage of trade (Section 1—205) or by course of performance (Section 2—208); and

(b) by evidence of consistent additional terms unless the court finds the writing to have been intended also as a complete and exclusive statement of the terms of the agreement.

§ 2-203. Seals Inoperative.
The affixing of a seal to a writing evidencing a contract for sale or an offer to buy or sell goods does not constitute the writing a sealed instrument and the law with respect to sealed instruments does not apply to such a contract or offer.

§ 2-204. Formation in General.

(1) A contract for sale of goods may be made in any manner sufficient to show agreement, including conduct by both parties which recognizes the existence of such a contract.

(2) An agreement sufficient to constitute a contract for sale may be found even though the moment of its making is undetermined.

(3) Even though one or more terms are left open a contract for sale does not fail for indefiniteness if the parties have intended to make a contract and there is a reasonably certain basis for giving an appropriate remedy.

§ 2-205. Firm Offers.
An offer by a merchant to buy or sell goods in a signed writing which by its terms gives assurance that it will be held open is not revocable, for lack of consideration, during the time stated or if no time is stated for a reasonable time, but in no event may such period of irrevocability exceed three months; but any such term of assurance on a form supplied by the offeree must be separately signed by the offeror.

§ 2-206. Offer and Acceptance in Formation of Contract.

(1) Unless otherwise unambiguously indicated by the language or circumstances

(a) an offer to make a contract shall be construed as inviting acceptance in any manner and by any medium reasonable in the circumstances;

(b) an order or other offer to buy goods for prompt or current shipment shall be construed as inviting acceptance either by a prompt promise to ship or by the prompt or current shipment of conforming or non-conforming goods, but such a shipment of non-conforming goods does not constitute an acceptance if the seller seasonably notifies the buyer that the shipment is offered only as an accommodation to the buyer.

(2) Where the beginning of a requested performance is a reasonable mode of acceptance an offeror who is not notified of acceptance within a reasonable time may treat the offer as having lapsed before acceptance.

§ 2-207. Additional Terms in Acceptance or Confirmation.

(1) A definite and seasonable expression of acceptance or a written confirmation which is sent within a reasonable time operates as an acceptance even though it states terms additional to or different from those offered or agreed upon, unless acceptance is expressly made conditional on assent to the additional or different terms.

(2) The additional terms are to be construed as proposals for addition to the contract. Between merchants such terms become part of the contract unless:

    (a)   the offer expressly limits acceptance to the terms of the offer;

    (b)   they materially alter it; or

    (c)   notification of objection to them has already been given or is given within a reasonable time after notice of them is received.

(3) Conduct by both parties which recognizes the existence of a contract is sufficient to establish a contract for sale although the writings of the parties do not otherwise establish a contract. In such case the terms of the particular contract consist of those terms on which the writings of the parties agree, together with any supplementary terms incorporated under any other provisions of this Act.

§ 2-208. Course of Performance or Practical Construction.

(1) Where the contract for sale involves repeated occasions for performance by either party with knowledge of the nature of the performance and opportunity for objection to it by the other, any course of performance accepted or acquiesced in without objection shall be relevant to determine the meaning of the agreement.

(2) The express terms of the agreement and any

such course of performance, as well as any course of dealing and usage of trade, shall be construed whenever reasonable as consistent with each other; but when such construction is unreasonable, express terms shall control course of performance and course of performance shall control both course of dealing and usage of trade (Section 1—205).

(3) Subject to the provisions of the next section on modification and waiver, such course of performance shall be relevant to show a waiver or modification of any term inconsistent with such course of performance.

§ 2-209. Modification, Rescission and Waiver.

(1) An agreement modifying a contract within this Article needs no consideration to be binding.

(2) A signed agreement which excludes modification or rescission except by a signed writing cannot be otherwise modified or rescinded, but except as between merchants such a requirement on a form supplied by the merchant must be separately signed by the other party.

(3) The requirements of the statute of frauds section of this Article (Section 2—201) must be satisfied if the contract as modified is within its provisions.

(4) Although an attempt at modification or rescission does not satisfy the requirements of subsection (2) or (3) it can operate as a waiver.

(5) A party who has made a waiver affecting an executory portion of the contract may retract the waiver by reasonable notification received by the other party that strict performance will be required of any term waived, unless the retraction would be unjust in view of a material change of position in reliance on the waiver.

§ 2-210. Delegation of Performance; Assignment of Rights.

(1) A party may perform his duty through a delegate unless otherwise agreed or unless the other party has a substantial interest in having his original promisor perform or control the acts required by the contract. No delegation of performance relieves the party delegating of any duty to perform or any liability for breach.

(2) Unless otherwise agreed all rights of either seller or buyer can be assigned except where the assignment would materially change the duty of the other party, or increase materially the burden or risk imposed on him by his contract, or impair materially his chance of obtaining return performance. A right to damages for breach of the whole contract or a right

arising out of the assignor's due performance of his entire obligation can be assigned despite agreement otherwise.

(3) Unless the circumstances indicate the contrary a prohibition of assignment of "the contract" is to be construed as barring only the delegation to the assignee of the assignor's performance.

(4) An assignment of "the contract" or of "all my rights under the contract" or an assignment in similar general terms is an assignment of rights and unless the language or the circumstances (as in an assignment for security) indicate the contrary, it is a delegation of performance of the duties of the assignor and its acceptance by the assignee constitutes a promise by him to perform those duties. This promise is enforceable by either the assignor or the other party to the original contract.

(5) The other party may treat any assignment which delegates performance as creating reasonable grounds for insecurity and may without prejudice to his rights against the assignor demand assurances from the assignee (Section 2—609).

Part 3. General Obligation and Construction of Contract

§ 2-301. General Obligations of Parties. The obligation of the seller is to transfer and deliver and that of the buyer is to accept and pay in accordance with the contract.

§ 2-302. Unconscionable Contract or Clause.

(1) If the court as a matter of law finds the contract or any clause of the contract to have been unconscionable at the time it was made the court may refuse to enforce the contract, or it may enforce the remainder of the contract without the unconscionable clause, or it may so limit the application of any unconscionable clause as to avoid any unconscionable result.

(2) When it is claimed or appears to the court that the contract or any clause thereof may be unconscionable the parties shall be afforded a reasonable opportunity to present evidence as to its commercial setting, purpose and effect to aid the court in making the determination.

§ 2-303. Allocation or Division of Risks. Where this Article allocates a risk or a burden as between the parties "unless otherwise agreed", the agreement may not only shift the allocation but may also divide the risk or burden.

§ 2-304. Price Payable in Money, Goods, Realty, or Otherwise.

(1) The price can be made payable in money or otherwise. If it is payable in whole or in part in goods each party is a seller of the goods which he is to transfer.

(2) Even though all or part of the price is payable in an interest in realty the transfer of the goods and the seller's obligations with reference to them are subject to this Article, but not the transfer of the interest in realty or the transferor's obligations in connection therewith.

§ 2-305. Open Price Term.

(1) The parties if they so intend can conclude a contract for sale even though the price is not settled. In such a case the price is a reasonable price at the time for delivery if

    (a)   nothing is said as to price; or

    (b)   the price is left to be agreed by the parties and they fail to agree; or

    (c)   the price is to be fixed in terms of some agreed market or other standard as set or recorded by a third person or agency and it is not so set or recorded.

(2) A price to be fixed by the seller or by the buyer means a price for him to fix in good faith.

(3) When a price left to be fixed otherwise than by agreement of the parties fails to be fixed through fault of one party the other may at his option treat the contract as cancelled or himself fix a reasonable price.

(4) Where, however, the parties intend not to be bound unless the price be fixed or agreed and it is not fixed or agreed there is no contract. In such a case the buyer must return any goods already received or if unable so to do must pay their reasonable value at the time of delivery and the seller must return any portion of the price paid on account.

§ 2-306. Output, Requirements and Exclusive Dealings.

(1) A term which measures the quantity by the output of the seller or the requirements of the buyer means such actual output or requirements as may occur in good faith, except that no quantity unreasonably disproportionate to any stated estimate or in the absence of a stated estimate to any normal or otherwise comparable prior output or requirements may be tendered or demanded.

(2) A lawful agreement by either the seller or the buyer for exclusive dealing in the kind of goods concerned imposes unless otherwise agreed an obliga-

tion by the seller to use best efforts to supply the goods and by the buyer to use best efforts to promote their sale.

§ 2-307. Delivery in Single Lot or Several Lots.

Unless otherwise agreed all goods called for by a contract for sale must be tendered in a single delivery and payment is due only on such tender but where the circumstances give either party the right to make or demand delivery in lots the price if it can be apportioned may be demanded for each lot.

§ 2-308. Absence of Specified Place for Delivery.

Unless otherwise agreed

(a) the place for delivery of goods is the seller's place of business or if he has none his residence; but

(b) in a contract for sale of identified goods which to the knowledge of the parties at the time of contracting are in some other place, that place is the place for their delivery; and

(c) documents of title may be delivered through customary banking channels.

§ 2-309. Absence of Specific Time Provisions; Notice of Termination.

(1) The time for shipment or delivery or any other action under a contract if not provided in this Article or agreed upon shall be a reasonable time.

(2) Where the contract provides for successive performances but is indefinite in duration it is valid for a reasonable time but unless otherwise agreed may be terminated at any time by either party.

(3) Termination of a contract by one party except on the happening of an agreed event requires that reasonable notification be received by the other party and an agreement dispensing with notification is invalid if its operation would be unconscionable.

§ 2-310. Open Time for Payment or Running of Credit; Authority to Ship Under Reservation.

Unless otherwise agreed

(a) payment is due at the time and place at which the buyer is to receive the goods even though the place of shipment is the place of delivery; and

(b) if the seller is authorized to send the goods he may ship them under reservation, and may tender the documents of title, but the buyer may inspect the goods after their arrival before payment is due unless such inspection is inconsistent

with the terms of the contract (Section 2—513); and

(c) if delivery is authorized and made by way of documents of title otherwise than by subsection (b) then payment is due at the time and place at which the buyer is to receive the documents regardless of where the goods are to be received; and

(d) where the seller is required or authorized to ship the goods on credit the credit period runs from the time of shipment but post-dating the invoice or delaying its dispatch will correspondingly delay the starting of the credit period.

§ 2-311. Options and Cooperation Respecting Performance.

(1) An agreement for sale which is otherwise sufficiently definite (subsection (3) of Section 2—204) to be a contract is not made invalid by the fact that it leaves particulars of performance to be specified by one of the parties. Any such specification must be made in good faith and within the limits set by commercial reasonableness.

(2) Unless otherwise agreed specifications relating to assortment of the goods are at the buyer's option and except as otherwise provided in subsections (1) (c) and (3) of Section 2—319 specifications or arrangements relating to shipment are at the seller's option.

(3) Where such specification would materially affect the other party's performance but is not seasonably made or where one party's cooperation is necessary to the agreed performance of the other but is not seasonably forthcoming, the other party in addition to all other remedies

(a) is excused for any resulting delay in his own performance; and

(b) may also either proceed to perform in any reasonable manner or after the time for a material part of his own performance treat the failure to specify or to cooperate as a breach by failure to deliver or accept the goods.

§ 2-312. Warranty of Title and Against Infringement; Buyer's Obligation Against Infringement.

(1) Subject to subsection (2) there is in a contract for sale a warranty by the seller that

(a) the title conveyed shall be good, and its transfer rightful; and

(b) the goods shall be delivered free from any security interest or other lien or encumbrance of which the buyer at the time of contracting has no knowledge.

(2) A warranty under subsection (1) will be excluded or modified only by specific language or by circumstances which give the buyer reason to know that the person selling does not claim title in himself or that he is purporting to sell only such right or title as he or a third person may have.

(3) Unless otherwise agreed a seller who is a merchant regularly dealing in goods of the kind warrants that the goods shall be delivered free of the rightful claim of any third person by way of infringement or the like but a buyer who furnishes specifications to the seller must hold the seller harmless against any such claim which arises out of compliance with the specifications.

§ 2-313. Express Warranties by Affirmation, Promise, Description, Sample.

(1) Express warranties by the seller are created as follows:

(a) Any affirmation of fact or promise made by the seller to the buyer which relates to the goods and becomes part of the basis of the bargain creates an express warranty that the goods shall conform to the affirmation or promise.

(b) Any description of the goods which is made part of the basis of the bargain creates an express warranty that the goods shall conform to the description.

(c) Any sample or model which is made part of the basis of the bargain creates an express warranty that the whole of the goods shall conform to the sample or model.

(2) It is not necessary to the creation of an express warranty that the seller use formal words such as "warrant" or "guarantee" or that he have a specific intention to make a warranty, but an affirmation merely of the value of the goods or a statement purporting to be merely the seller's opinion or commendation of the goods does not create a warranty.

§ 2-314. Implied Warranty: Merchantability; Usage of Trade.

(1) Unless excluded or modified (Section 2—316), a warranty that the goods shall be merchantable is implied in a contract for their sale if the seller is a merchant with respect to goods of that kind. Under this section the serving for value of food or drink to be consumed either on the premises or elsewhere is a sale.

(2) Goods to be merchantable must be at least such as

(a) pass without objection in the trade under the contract description; and

(b) in the case of fungible goods, are of fair average quality within the description; and

(c) are fit for the ordinary purposes for which such goods are used; and

(d) run, within the variations permitted by the agreement, of even kind, quality and quantity within each unit and among all units involved; and

(e) are adequately contained, packaged, and labeled as the agreement may require; and

(f) conform to the promises or affirmations of fact made on the container or label if any.

(3) Unless excluded or modified (Section 2—316) other implied warranties may arise from course of dealing or usage of trade.

§ 2-315. Implied Warranty: Fitness for Particular Purpose.

Where the seller at the time of contracting has reason to know any particular purpose for which the goods are required and that the buyer is relying on the seller's skill or judgment to select or furnish suitable goods, there is unless excluded or modified under the next section an implied warranty that the goods shall be fit for such purpose.

§ 2-316. Exclusion or Modification of Warranties.

(1) Words or conduct relevant to the creation of an express warranty and words or conduct tending to negate or limit warranty shall be construed wherever reasonable as consistent with each other; but subject to the provisions of this Article on parol or extrinsic evidence (Section 2—202) negation or limitation is inoperative to the extent that such construction is unreasonable.

(2) Subject to subsection (3), to exclude or modify the implied warranty of merchantability or any part of it the language must mention merchantability and in case of a writing must be conspicuous, and to exclude or modify any implied warranty of fitness the exclusion must be by a writing and conspicuous. Language to exclude all implied warranties of fitness is sufficient if it states, for example, that "There are no

warranties which extend beyond the description on the face hereof."

(3) Notwithstanding subsection (2)

    (a)   unless the circumstances indicate otherwise, all implied warranties are excluded by expressions like "as is", "with all faults" or other language which in common understanding calls the buyer's attention to the exclusion of warranties and makes plain that there is no implied warranty; and

    (b)   when the buyer before entering into the contract has examined the goods or the sample or model as fully as he desired or has refused to examine the goods there is no implied warranty with regard to defects which an examination ought in the circumstances to have revealed to him; and

    (c)   an implied warranty can also be excluded or modified by course of dealing or course of performance or usage of trade.

(4) Remedies for breach of warranty can be limited in accordance with the provisions of this Article on liquidation or limitation of damages and on contractual modification of remedy (Sections 2—718 and 2-719).

§ 2-317. Cumulation and Conflict of Warranties Express or Implied.

Warranties whether express or implied shall be construed as consistent with each other and as cumulative, but if such construction is unreasonable the intention of the parties shall determine which warranty is dominant. In ascertaining that intention the following rules apply:

    (a)   Exact or technical specifications displace an inconsistent sample or model or general language of description.

    (b)   A sample from an existing bulk displaces inconsistent general language of description.

    (c)   Express warranties displace inconsistent implied warranties other than an implied warranty of fitness for a particular purpose.

§ 2-318. Third Party Beneficiaries of Warranties Express or Implied.

Note: *If this Act is introduced in the Congress of the United States this section should be omitted. (States to select one alternative.)*

Alternative A A seller's warranty whether express or implied extends to any natural person who is in the family or household of his buyer or who is a guest in his home if it is reasonable to expect that such person may use, consume or be affected by the goods and who is injured in person by breach of the warranty. A seller may not exclude or limit the operation of this section.

Alternative B A seller's warranty whether express or implied extends to any natural person who may reasonably be expected to use, consume or be affected by the goods and who is injured in person by breach of the warranty. A seller may not exclude or limit the operation of this section.

Alternative C A seller's warranty whether express or implied extends to any person who may reasonably be expected to use, consume or be affected by the goods and who is injured by breach of the warranty. A seller may not exclude or limit the operation of this section with respect to injury to the person of an individual to whom the warranty extends. As amended 1966.

§ 2-319. F.O.B. and F.A.S. Terms.

(1) Unless otherwise agreed the term F.O.B. (which means "free on board") at a named place, even though used only in connection with the stated price, is a delivery term under which

    (a)   when the term is F.O.B. the place of shipment, the seller must at that place ship the goods in the manner provided in this Article (Section 2—504) and bear the expense and risk of putting them into the possession of the carrier; or

    (b)   when the term is F.O.B. the place of destination, the seller must at his own expense and risk transport the goods to that place and there tender delivery of them in the manner provided in this Article (Section 2—503);

    (c)   when under either (a) or (b) the term is also F.O.B. vessel, car or other vehicle, the seller must in addition at his own expense and risk load the goods on board. If the term is F.O.B. vessel the buyer must name the vessel and in an appropriate case the seller must comply with the provisions of this Article on the form of bill of lading (Section 2—323).

(2) Unless otherwise agreed the term F.A.S. vessel

(which means "free alongside") at a named port, even though used only in connection with the stated price, is a delivery term under which the seller must

(a) at his own expense and risk deliver the goods alongside the vessel in the manner usual in that port or on a dock designated and provided by the buyer; and

(b) obtain and tender a receipt for the goods in exchange for which the carrier is under a duty to issue a bill of lading.

(3) Unless otherwise agreed in any case falling within subsection (1) (a) or (c) or subsection (2) the buyer must seasonably give any needed instructions for making delivery, including when the term is F.A.S. or F.O.B. the loading berth of the vessel and in an appropriate case its name and sailing date. The seller may treat the failure of needed instructions as a failure of cooperation under this Article (Section 2—311). He may also at his option move the goods in any reasonable manner preparatory to delivery or shipment.

(4) Under the term F.O.B. vessel or F.A.S. unless otherwise agreed the buyer must make payment against tender of the required documents and the seller may not tender nor the buyer demand delivery of the goods in substitution for the documents.

§ 2-320. C.I.F. and C. & F. Terms.

(1) The term C.I.F. means that the price includes in a lump sum the cost of the goods and the insurance and freight to the named destination. The term C. & F. or C.F. means that the price so includes cost and freight to the named destination.

(2) Unless otherwise agreed and even though used only in connection with the stated price and destination, the term C.I.F. destination or its equivalent requires the seller at his own expense and risk to

(a) put the goods into the possession of a carrier at the port for shipment and obtain a negotiable bill or bills of lading covering the entire transportation to the named destination; and

(b) load the goods and obtain a receipt from the carrier (which may be contained in the bill of lading) showing that the freight has been paid or provided for; and

(c) obtain a policy or certificate of insurance, including any war risk insurance, of a kind and on terms then current at the port of shipment in the usual amount, in the currency of the contract, shown to cover the same goods covered by the bill of lading and providing for payment of loss to the order of the buyer or for the account of whom it may concern; but the seller may add to the price the amount of the premium for any such war risk insurance; and

(d) prepare an invoice of the goods and procure any other documents required to effect shipment or to comply with the contract; and

(e) forward and tender with commercial promptness all the documents in due form and with any indorsement necessary to perfect the buyer's rights.

(3) Unless otherwise agreed the term C. & F. or its equivalent has the same effect and imposes upon the seller the same obligations and risks as a C.I.F. term except the obligation as to insurance.

(4) Under the term C.I.F. or C. & F. unless otherwise agreed the buyer must make payment against tender of the required documents and the seller may not tender nor the buyer demand delivery of the goods in substitution for the documents.

§ 2-321. C.I.F. or C. & F.: "Net Landed Weights"; "Payment on Arrival"; Warranty of Condition on Arrival. Under a contract containing a term C.I.F. or C. & F.

(1) Where the price is based on or is to be adjusted according to "net landed weights", "delivered weights", "out turn" quantity or quality or the like, unless otherwise agreed the seller must reasonably estimate the price. The payment due on tender of the documents called for by the contract is the amount so estimated, but after final adjustment of the price a settlement must be made with commercial promptness.

(2) An agreement described in subsection (1) or any warranty of quality or condition of the goods on arrival places upon the seller the risk of ordinary deterioration, shrinkage and the like in transportation but has no effect on the place or time of identification to the contract for sale or delivery or on the passing of the risk of loss.

(3) Unless otherwise agreed where the contract provides for payment on or after arrival of the goods the seller must before payment allow such preliminary inspection as is feasible; but if the goods are lost

delivery of the documents and payment are due when the goods should have arrived.

§ 2-322. Delivery "Ex-Ship."

(1) Unless otherwise agreed a term for delivery of goods "ex-ship" (which means from the carrying vessel) or in equivalent language is not restricted to a particular ship and requires delivery from a ship which has reached a place at the named port of destination where goods of the kind are usually discharged.

(2) Under such a term unless otherwise agreed

  (a) the seller must discharge all liens arising out of the carriage and furnish the buyer with a direction which puts the carrier under a duty to deliver the goods; and

  (b) the risk of loss does not pass to the buyer until the goods leave the ship's tackle or are otherwise properly unloaded.

§ 2-323. Form of Bill of Lading Required in Overseas Shipment; "Overseas."

(1) Where the contract contemplates overseas shipment and contains a term C.I.F. or C. & F. or F.O.B. vessel, the seller unless otherwise agreed must obtain a negotiable bill of lading stating that the goods have been loaded on board or, in the case of a term C.I.F. or C. & F., received for shipment.

(2) Where in a case within subsection (1) a bill of lading has been issued in a set of parts, unless otherwise agreed if the documents are not to be sent from abroad the buyer may demand tender of the full set; otherwise only one part of the bill of lading need be tendered. Even if the agreement expressly requires a full set

  (a) due tender of a single part is acceptable within the provisions of this Article on cure of improper delivery (subsection (1) of Section 2—508); and

  (b) even though the full set is demanded, if the documents are sent from abroad the person tendering an incomplete set may nevertheless require payment upon furnishing an indemnity which the buyer in good faith deems adequate.

(3) A shipment by water or by air or a contract contemplating such shipment is "overseas" insofar as by usage of trade or agreement it is subject to the commercial, financing or shipping practices characteristic of international deep water commerce.

§ 2-324. "No Arrival, No Sale" Term. Under a

term "no arrival, no sale" or terms of like meaning, unless otherwise agreed,

  (a) the seller must properly ship conforming goods and if they arrive by any means he must tender them on arrival but he assumes no obligation that the goods will arrive unless he has caused the non-arrival; and

  (b) where without fault of the seller the goods are in part lost or have so deteriorated as no longer to conform to the contract or arrive after the contract time, the buyer may proceed as if there had been casualty to identified goods (Section 2—613).

§ 2-325. "Letter of Credit" Term; "Confirmed Credit."

(1) Failure of the buyer seasonably to furnish an agreed letter of credit is a breach of the contract for sale.

(2) The delivery to seller of a proper letter of credit suspends the buyer's obligation to pay. If the letter of credit is dishonored, the seller may on seasonable notification to the buyer require payment directly from him.

(3) Unless otherwise agreed the term "letter of credit" or "banker's credit" in a contract for sale means an irrevocable credit issued by a financing agency of good repute and, where the shipment is overseas, of good international repute. The term "confirmed credit" means that the credit must also carry the direct obligation of such an agency which does business in the seller's financial market.

§ 2-326. Sale on Approval and Sale or Return; Consignment Sales and Rights of Creditors.

(1) Unless otherwise agreed, if delivered goods may be returned by the buyer even though they conform to the contract, the transaction is

  (a) a "sale on approval" if the goods are delivered primarily for use, and

  (b) a "sale or return" if the goods are delivered primarily for resale.

(2) Except as provided in subsection (3), goods held on approval are not subject to the claims of the buyer's creditors until acceptance; goods held on sale or return are subject to such claims while in the buyer's possession.

(3) Where goods are delivered to a person for sale and such person maintains a place of business at which he deals in goods of the kind involved, under

a name other than the name of the person making delivery, then with respect to claims of creditors of the person conducting the business the goods are deemed to be on sale or return. The provisions of this subsection are applicable even though an agreement purports to reserve title to the person making delivery until payment or resale or uses such words as "on consignment" or "on memorandum". However, this subsection is not applicable if the person making delivery

    (a)   complies with an applicable law providing for a consignor's interest or the like to be evidenced by a sign, or

    (b)   establishes that the person conducting the business is generally known by his creditors to be substantially engaged in selling the goods of others, or

    (c)   complies with the filing provisions of the Article on Secured Transactions (Article 9).

(4) Any "or return" term of a contract for sale is to be treated as a separate contract for sale within the statute of frauds section of this Article (Section 2—201) and as contradicting the sale aspect of the contract within the provisions of this Article on parol or extrinsic evidence (Section 2—202).

§ 2-327. Special Incidents of Sale on Approval and Sale or Return.

(1) Under a sale on approval unless otherwise agreed

    (a)   although the goods are identified to the contract the risk of loss and the title do not pass to the buyer until acceptance; and

    (b)   use of the goods consistent with the purpose of trial is not acceptance but failure seasonably to notify the seller of election to return the goods is acceptance, and if the goods conform to the contract acceptance of any part is acceptance of the whole; and

    (c)   after due notification of election to return, the return is at the seller's risk and expense but a merchant buyer must follow any reasonable instructions.

(2) Under a sale or return unless otherwise agreed

    (a)   the option to return extends to the whole or any commercial unit of the goods while in substantially their original condition, but must be exercised seasonably; and

    (b)   the return is at the buyer's risk and expense.

§ 2-328. Sale by Auction.

(1) In a sale by auction if goods are put up in lots each lot is the subject of a separate sale.

(2) A sale by auction is complete when the auctioneer so announces by the fall of the hammer or in other customary manner. Where a bid is made while the hammer is falling in acceptance of a prior bid the auctioneer may in his discretion reopen the bidding or declare the goods sold under the bid on which the hammer was falling.

(3) Such a sale is with reserve unless the goods are in explicit terms put up without reserve. In an auction with reserve the auctioneer may withdraw the goods at any time until he announces completion of the sale. In an auction without reserve, after the auctioneer calls for bids on an article or lot, that article or lot cannot be withdrawn unless no bid is made within a reasonable time. In either case a bidder may retract his bid until the auctioneer's announcement of completion of the sale, but a bidder's retraction does not revive any previous bid.

(4) If the auctioneer knowingly receives a bid on the seller's behalf or the seller makes or procures such a bid, and notice has not been given that liberty for such bidding is reserved, the buyer may at his option avoid the sale or take the goods at the price of the last good faith bid prior to the completion of the sale. This subsection shall not apply to any bid at a forced sale.

Part 4. Title, Creditors and Good Faith Purchasers

§ 2-401. Passing of Title; Reservation for Security; Limited Application of This Section.

Each provision of this Article with regard to the rights, obligations and remedies of the seller, the buyer, purchasers or other third parties applies irrespective of title to the goods except where the provision refers to such title. Insofar as situations are not covered by the other provisions of this Article and matters concerning title become material the following rules apply:

(1) Title to goods cannot pass under a contract for sale prior to their identification to the contract (Section 2—501), and unless otherwise explicitly agreed the buyer acquires by their identification a special property as limited by this Act. Any retention or reservation by the seller of the title (property) in goods

shipped or delivered to the buyer is limited in effect to a reservation of a security interest. Subject to these provisions and to the provisions of the Article on Secured Transactions (Article 9), title to goods passes from the seller to the buyer in any manner and on any conditions explicitly agreed on by the parties.

(2) Unless otherwise explicitly agreed title passes to the buyer at the time and place at which the seller completes his performance with reference to the physical delivery of the goods, despite any reservation of a security interest and even though a document of title is to be delivered at a different time or place; and in particular and despite any reservation of a security interest in the bill of lading

(a)   if the contract requires or authorizes the seller to send the goods to the buyer but does not require him to deliver them at destination, title passes to the buyer at the time and place of shipment; and

(b)   if the contract requires delivery at destination, title passes on tender there.

(3) Unless otherwise explicitly agreed where delivery is to be made without moving the goods,

(a)   if the seller is to deliver a document of title, title passes at the time when and the place where he delivers such documents; or

(b)   if the goods are at the time of contracting already identified and no documents are to be delivered, title passes at the time and place of contracting.

(4) A rejection or other refusal by the buyer to receive or retain the goods, whether or not justified, or a justified revocation of acceptance revests title to the goods in the seller. Such revesting occurs by operation of law and is not a "sale".

§ 2-402. Rights of Seller's Creditors Against Sold Goods.

(1) Except as provided in subsections (2) and (3), rights of unsecured creditors of the seller with respect to goods which have been identified to a contract for sale are subject to the buyer's rights to recover the goods under this Article (Sections 2—502 and 2—716).

(2) A creditor of the seller may treat a sale or an identification of goods to a contract for sale as void if as against him a retention of possession by the seller is fraudulent under any rule of law of the state where the goods are situated, except that retention of possession in good faith and current course of trade by a merchant-seller for a commercially reasonable time after a sale or identification is not fraudulent.

(3) Nothing in this Article shall be deemed to impair the rights of creditors of the seller

(a)   under the provisions of the Article on Secured Transactions (Article 9); or

(b)   where identification to the contract or delivery is made not in current course of trade but in satisfaction of or as security for a pre-existing claim for money, security or the like and is made under circumstances which under any rule of law of the state where the goods are situated would apart from this Article constitute the transaction a fraudulent transfer or voidable preference.

§ 2-403. Power to Transfer; Good Faith Purchase of Goods; "Entrusting".

(1) A purchaser of goods acquires all title which his transferor had or had power to transfer except that a purchaser of a limited interest acquires rights only to the extent of the interest purchased. A person with voidable title has power to transfer a good title to a good faith purchaser for value. When goods have been delivered under a transaction of purchase the purchaser has such power even though

(a)   the transferor was deceived as to the identity of the purchaser, or

(b)   the delivery was in exchange for a check which is later dishonored, or

(c)   it was agreed that the transaction was to be a "cash sale", or

(d)   the delivery was procured through fraud punishable as larcenous under the criminal law.

(2) Any entrusting of possession of goods to a merchant who deals in goods of that kind gives him power to transfer all rights of the entruster to a buyer in ordinary course of business.

(3) "Entrusting" includes any delivery and any acquiescence in retention of possession regardless of any condition expressed between the parties to the delivery or acquiescence and regardless of whether the procurement of the entrusting or the possessor's disposition of the goods have been such as to be larcenous under the criminal law.

(4) The rights of other purchasers of goods and of lien creditors are governed by the Articles on Secured Transactions (Article 9), Bulk Transfers (Article 6) and Documents of Title (Article 7).

Part 5. Performance

§ 2-501. Insurable Interest in Goods; Manner of Identification of Goods.

(1) The buyer obtains a special property and an insurable interest in goods by identification of existing goods as goods to which the contract refers even though the goods so identified are non-conforming and he has an option to return or reject them. Such identification can be made at any time and in any manner explicitly agreed to by the parties. In the absence of explicit agreement identification occurs

(a)   when the contract is made if it is for the sale of goods already existing and identified;

(b)   if the contract is for the sale of future goods other than those described in paragraph (c), when goods are shipped, marked or otherwise designated by the seller as goods to which the contract refers;

(c)   when the crops are planted or otherwise become growing crops or the young are conceived if the contract is for the sale of unborn young to be born within twelve months after contracting or for the sale of crops to be harvested within twelve months or the next normal harvest season after contracting whichever is longer.

(2) The seller retains an insurable interest in goods so long as title to or any security interest in the goods remains in him and where the identification is by the seller alone he may until default or insolvency or notification to the buyer that the identification is final substitute other goods for those identified.

(3) Nothing in this section impairs any insurable interest recognized under any other statute or rule of law.

§ 2-502. Buyer's Right to Goods on Seller's Insolvency.

(1) Subject to subsection (2) and even though the goods have not been shipped a buyer who has paid a part or all of the price of goods in which he has a special property under the provisions of the immediately preceding section may on making and keeping good a tender of any unpaid portion of their price recover them from the seller if the seller becomes insolvent within ten days after receipt of the first installment on their price.

(2) If the identification creating his special property has been made by the buyer he acquires the right to recover the goods only if they conform to the contract for sale.

§ 2-503. Manner of Seller's Tender of Delivery.

(1) Tender of delivery requires that the seller put and hold conforming goods at the buyer's disposition and give the buyer any notification reasonably necessary to enable him to take delivery. The manner, time and place for tender are determined by the agreement and this Article, and in particular

(a)   tender must be at a reasonable hour, and if it is of goods they must be kept available for the period reasonably necessary to enable the buyer to take possession; but

(b)   unless otherwise agreed the buyer must furnish facilities reasonably suited to the receipt of the goods.

(2) Where the case is within the next section respecting shipment tender requires that the seller comply with its provisions.

(3) Where the seller is required to deliver at a particular destination tender requires that he comply with subsection (2) and also in any appropriate case tender documents as described in subsections (4) and (5) of this section.

(4) Where goods are in the possession of a bailee and are to be delivered without being moved

(a)   tender requires that the seller either tender a negotiable document of title covering such goods or procure acknowledgment by the bailee of the buyer's right to possession of the goods; but

(b)   tender to the buyer of a non-negotiable document of title or of a written direction to the bailee to deliver is sufficient tender unless the buyer seasonably objects, and receipt by the bailee of notification of the buyer's rights fixes those rights as against the bailee and all third persons; but risk of loss of the goods and of any failure by the bailee to honor the non-negotiable document of title or to obey the direction remains on the seller until the buyer has had a reasonable time to present the document or direction, and a refusal by the bailee to honor the document or to obey the direction defeats the tender.

(5) Where the contract requires the seller to deliver documents

(a)   he must tender all such documents in correct form, except as provided in this Article with respect to bills of lading in a set (subsection (2) of Section 2—323); and

(b)   tender through customary banking channels is sufficient and dishonor of a draft accompanying the documents constitutes non-acceptance or rejection.

§ 2-504. Shipment by Seller.

Where the seller is required or authorized to send the goods to the buyer and the contract does not require him to deliver them at a particular destination, then unless otherwise agreed he must

(a)   put the goods in the possession of such a carrier and make sure a contract for their transportation as may be reasonable having regard to the nature of the goods and other circumstances of the case; and

(b)   obtain and promptly deliver or tender in due form any document necessary to enable the buyer to obtain possession of the goods or otherwise required by the agreement or by usage of trade; and

(c)   promptly notify the buyer of the shipment.

Failure to notify the buyer under paragraph (c) or to make a proper contract under paragraph (a) is a ground for rejection only if material delay or loss ensues.

§ 2-505. Seller's Shipment Under Reservation.

(1) Where the seller has identified goods to the contract by or before shipment:

(a)   his procurement of a negotiable bill of lading to his own order or otherwise reserves in him a security interest in the goods. His procurement of the bill to the order of a financing agency or of the buyer indicates in addition only the seller's expectation of transferring that interest to the person named.

(b)   a non-negotiable bill of lading to himself or his nominee reserves possession of the goods as security but except in a case of conditional delivery (subsection (2) of Section 2—507) a non-negotiable bill of lading naming the buyer as consignee reserves no security interest even though the seller retains possession of the bill of lading.

(2) When shipment by the seller with reservation of a security interest is in violation of the contract for sale it constitutes an improper contract for transportation within the preceding section but impairs neither the rights given to the buyer by shipment and identification of the goods to the contract nor the seller's powers as a holder of a negotiable document.

§ 2-506. Rights of Financing Agency.

(1) A financing agency by paying or purchasing for value a draft which relates to a shipment of goods acquires to the extent of the payment or purchase and in addition to its own rights under the draft and any document of title securing it any rights of the shipper in the goods including the right to stop delivery and the shipper's right to have the draft honored by the buyer.

(2) The right to reimbursement of a financing agency which has in good faith honored or purchased the draft under commitment to or authority from the buyer is not impaired by subsequent discovery of defects with reference to any relevant document which was apparently regular on its face.

§ 2-507. Effect of Seller's Tender; Delivery on Condition.

(1) Tender of delivery is a condition to the buyer's duty to accept the goods and, unless otherwise agreed, to his duty to pay for them. Tender entitles the seller to acceptance of the goods and to payment according to the contract.

(2) Where payment is due and demanded on the delivery to the buyer of goods or documents of title, his right as against the seller to retain or dispose of them is conditional upon his making the payment due.

§ 2-508. Cure by Seller of Improper Tender or Delivery; Replacement.

(1) Where any tender or delivery by the seller is rejected because non-conforming and the time for performance has not yet expired, the seller may seasonably notify the buyer of his intention to cure and may then within the contract time make a conforming delivery.

(2) Where the buyer rejects a non-conforming tender which the seller had reasonable grounds to believe would be acceptable with or without money allowance the seller may if he seasonably notifies the buyer have a further reasonable time to substitute a conforming tender.

§ 2-509. Risk of Loss in the Absence of Breach.

(1) Where the contract requires or authorizes the seller to ship the goods by carrier

(a)   if it does not require him to deliver them at a particular destination, the risk of loss passes to the buyer when the goods are duly delivered to the carrier even though the shipment is under reservation (Section 2—505); but

(b)   if it does require him to deliver them at a particular destination and the goods are there duly tendered while in the possession of the carrier, the risk of loss passes to the buyer when the goods are there duly so tendered as to enable the buyer to take delivery.

(2) Where the goods are held by a bailee to be delivered without being moved, the risk of loss passes to the buyer

(a)   on his receipt of a negotiable document of title covering the goods; or

(b)   on acknowledgment by the bailee of the buyer's right to possession of the goods; or

(c)   after his receipt of a non-negotiable document of title or other written direction to deliver, as provided in subsection (4) (b) of Section 2—503.

(3) In any case not within subsection (1) or (2), the risk of loss passes to the buyer on his receipt of the goods if the seller is a merchant; otherwise the risk passes to the buyer on tender of delivery.

(4) The provisions of this section are subject to contrary agreement of the parties and to the provisions of this Article on sale on approval (Section 2—327) and on effect of breach on risk of loss (Section 2—510).

§ 2-510. Effect of Breach on Risk of Loss.

(1) Where a tender or delivery of goods so fails to conform to the contract as to give a right of rejection the risk of their loss remains on the seller until cure or acceptance.

(2) Where the buyer rightfully revokes acceptance he may to the extent of any deificiency in his effective insurance coverage treat the risk of loss as having rested on the seller from the beginning.

(3) Where the buyer as to conforming goods already identified to the contract for sale repudiates or is otherwise in breach before risk of their loss has passed to him, the seller may to the extent of any deficiency in his effective insurance coverage treat the risk of loss as resting on the buyer for a commercially reasonable time.

§ 2-511. Tender of Payment by Buyer; Payment by Check.

(1) Unless otherwise agreed tender of payment is a condition to the seller's duty to tender and complete any delivery.

(2) Tender of payment is sufficient when made by any means or in any manner current in the ordinary course of business unless the seller demands payment in legal tender and gives any extension of time reasonably necessary to procure it.

(3) Subject to the provisions of this Act on the effect of an instrument on an obligation (Section 3—802), payment by check is conditional and is defeated as between the parties by dishonor of the check on due presentment.

§ 2-512. Payment by Buyer Before Inspection.

(1) Where the contract requires payment before inspection non-conformity of the goods does not excuse the buyer from so making payment unless

(a)   the non-conformity appears without inspection; or

(b)   despite tender of the required documents the circumstances would justify injunction against honor under the provisions of this Act (Section 5—114).

(2) Payment pursuant to subsection (1) does not constitute an acceptance of goods or impair the buyer's right to inspect or any of his remedies.

§ 2-513. Buyer's Right to Inspection of Goods.

(1) Unless otherwise agreed and subject to subsection (3), where goods are tendered or delivered or identified to the contract for sale, the buyer has a right before shipment or acceptance to inspect them at any reasonable place and time and in any reasonable manner. When the seller is required or authorized to send the goods to the buyer, the inspection may be after their arrival.

(2) Expenses of inspection must be borne by the buyer but may be recovered from the seller if the goods do not conform and are rejected.

(3) Unless otherwise agreed and subject to the provisions of this Article on C.I.F. contracts (subsection (3) of Section 2—321), the buyer is not entitled to inspect the goods before payment of the price when the contract provides

(a)   for delivery "C.O.D." or on other like terms; or

(b)   for payment against documents of title, except where such payment is due only after the goods are to become available for inspection.

(4) A place or method of inspection fixed by the parties is presumed to be exclusive but unless otherwise expressly agreed it does not postpone identification or shift the place for delivery or for passing the risk of loss. If compliance becomes impossible, inspection shall be as provided in this section unless the place or method fixed was clearly intended as an indispensable condition failure of which avoids the contract.

§ 2-514. When Documents Deliverable on Acceptance; When on Payment. Unless otherwise agreed documents against which a draft is drawn are to be delivered to the drawee on acceptance of the draft if it is payable more than three days after presentment; otherwise, only on payment.

§ 2-515. Preserving Evidence of Goods in Dispute. In furtherance of the adjustment of any claim or dispute

   (a)   either party on reasonable notification to the other and for the purpose of ascertaining the facts and preserving evidence has the right to inspect, test and sample the goods including such of them as may be in the possession or control of the other; and

   (b)   the parties may agree to a third party inspection or survey to determine the conformity or condition of the goods and may agree that the findings shall be binding upon them in any subsequent litigation or adjustment.

Part 6. Breach, Repudiation and Excuse

§ 2-601. Buyer's Rights on Improper Delivery. Subject to the provisions of this Article on breach in installment contracts (Section 2—612) and unless otherwise agreed under the sections on contractual limitations of remedy (Sections 2—718 and 2—719), if the goods or the tender of delivery fail in any respect to conform to the contract, the buyer may

   (a)   reject the whole; or

   (b)   accept the whole; or

   (c)   accept any commercial unit or units and reject the rest.

§ 2-602. Manner and Effect of Rightful Rejection.

(1) Rejection of goods must be within a reasonable time after their delivery or tender. It is ineffective unless the buyer seasonably notifies the seller.

(2) Subject to the provisions of the two following sections on rejected goods (Sections 2—603 and 2—604),

   (a)   after rejection any exercise of ownership by the buyer with respect to any commercial unit is wrongful as against the seller; and

   (b)   if the buyer has before rejection taken physical possession of goods in which he does not have a security interest under the provisions of this Article (subsection (3) of Section 2—711), he is under a duty after rejection to hold them with reasonable care at the seller's disposition for a time sufficient to permit the seller to remove them; but

   (c)   the buyer has no further obligations with regard to goods rightfully rejected.

(3) The seller's rights with respect to goods wrongfully rejected are governed by the provisions of this Article on Seller's remedies in general (Section 2—703).

§ 2-603. Merchant Buyer's Duties as to Rightfully Rejected Goods.

(1) Subject to any security interest in the buyer (subsection (3) of Section 2—711), when the seller has no agent or place of business at the market of rejection a merchant buyer is under a duty after rejection of goods in his possession or control to follow any reasonable instructions received from the seller with respect to the goods and in the absence of such instructions to make reasonable efforts to sell them for the seller's account if they are perishable or threaten to decline in value speedily. Instructions are not reasonable if on demand indemnity for expenses is not forthcoming.

(2) When the buyer sells goods under subsection (1), he is entitled to reimbursement from the seller or out of the proceeds for reasonable expenses of caring for and selling them, and if the expenses include no selling commission then to such commission as is usual in the trade or if there is none to a reasonable sum not exceeding ten per cent on the gross proceeds.

(3) In complying with this section the buyer is held only to good faith and good faith conduct hereunder is neither acceptance nor conversion nor the basis of an action for damages.

§ 2-604. Buyer's Options as to Salvage of Rightfully Rejected Goods. Subject to the provisions of the immediately preceding section on perishables if the seller gives no instructions within a reasonable time after notification of rejection the buyer may store the rejected goods for the seller's account or reship them to him or resell them for the seller's account with reimbursement as provided in the preceding section. Such action is not acceptance or conversion.

§ 2-605. Waiver of Buyer's Objections by Failure to Particularize.

(1) The buyer's failure to state in connection with rejection a particular defect which is ascertainable by reasonable inspection precludes him from relying on the unstated defect to justify rejection or to establish breach

    (a)   where the seller could have cured it if stated seasonably; or

    (b)   between merchants when the seller has after rejection made a request in writing for a full and final written statement of all defects on which the buyer proposes to rely.

(2) Payment against documents made without reservation of rights precludes recovery of the payment for defects apparent on the face of the documents.

§ 2-606. What Constitutes Acceptance of Goods.

(1) Acceptance of goods occurs when the buyer

    (a)   after a reasonable opportunity to inspect the goods signifies to the seller that the goods are conforming or that he will take or retain them in spite of their non-conformity; or

    (b)   fails to make an effective rejection (subsection (1) of Section 2—602), but such acceptance does not occur until the buyer has had a reasonable opportunity to inspect them; or

    (c)   does not act inconsistent with the seller's ownership; but if such act is wrongful as against the seller it is an acceptance only if ratified by him.

(2) Acceptance of a part of any commercial unit is acceptance of that entire unit.

§ 2-607. Effect of Acceptance; Notice of Breach; Burden of Establishing Breach After Acceptance; Notice of Claim or Litigation to Person Answerable Over.

(1) The buyer must pay at the contract rate for any goods accepted.

(2) Acceptance of goods by the buyer precludes rejection of the goods accepted and if made with knowledge of a non-conformity cannot be revoked because of it unless the acceptance was on the reasonable assumption that the non-conformity would be seasonably cured but acceptance does not of itself impair any other remedy provided by this Article for non-conformity.

(3) Where a tender has been accepted

    (a)   the buyer must within a reasonable time after he discovers or should have discovered any breach notify the seller of breach or be barred from any remedy; and

    (b)   if the claim is one for infringement or the like (subsection (3) of Section 2—312) and the buyer is sued as a result of such a breach he must so notify the seller within a reasonable time after he receives notice of the litigation or be barred from any remedy over for liability established by the litigation.

(4) The burden is on the buyer to establish any breach with respect to the goods accepted.

(5) Where the buyer is sued for breach of a warranty or other obligation for which his seller is answerable over

    (a)   he may give his seller written notice of the litigation. If the notice states that the seller may come in and defend and that if the seller does not do so he will be bound in any action against him by his buyer by any determination of fact common to the two litigations, then unless the seller after seasonable receipt of the notice does come in and defend he is so bound.

    (b)   if the claim is one for infringement or the like (subsection (3) of Section 2—312) the original seller may demand in writing that his buyer turn over to him control of the litigation including settlement or else be barred from any remedy over and if he also agrees to bear all expense and to satisfy any adverse judgment, then unless the buyer after seasonable receipt of the demand does turn over control the buyer is so barred.

(6) The provisions of subsections (3), (4) and (5) apply to any obligation of a buyer to hold the seller harmless against infringement or the like (subsection (3) of Section 2—312).

§ 2-608. Revocation of Acceptance in Whole or in Part.

(1) The buyer may revoke his acceptance of a lot or commercial unit whose non-conformity substantially impairs its value to him if he has accepted it

(a) on the reasonable assumption that its non-conformity would be cured and it has not been seasonably cured; or

(b) without discovery of such non-conformity if his acceptance was reasonably induced either by the difficulty of discovery before acceptance or by the seller's assurances.

(2) Revocation of acceptance must occur within a reasonable time after the buyer discovers or should have discovered the ground for it and before any substantial change in condition of the goods which is not caused by their own defects. It is not effective until the buyer notifies the seller of it.

(3) A buyer who so revokes has the same rights and duties with regard to the goods involved as if he had rejected them.

§ 2-609. Right to Adequate Assurance of Performance.

(1) A contract for sale imposes an obligation on each party that the other's expectation of receiving due performance will not be impaired. When reasonable grounds for insecurity arise with respect to the performance of either party the other may in writing demand adequate assurance of due performance and until he receives such assurance may if commercially reasonable suspend any performance for which he has not already received the agreed return.

(2) Between merchants the reasonableness of grounds for insecurity and the adequacy of any assurance offered shall be determined according to commercial standards.

(3) Acceptance of any improper delivery or payment does not prejudice the aggrieved party's right to demand adequate assurance of future performance.

(4) After receipt of a justified demand failure to provide within a reasonable time not exceeding thirty days such assurance of due performance as is adequate under the circumstances of the particular case is a repudiation of the contract.

§ 2-610. Anticipatory Repudiation.

When either party repudiates the contract with respect to a performance not yet due the loss of which will substantially impair the value of the contract to the other, the aggrieved party may

(a) for a commercially reasonable time await performance by the repudiating party; or

(b) resort to any remedy for breach (Section 2—703 or Section 2—711), even though he has notified the repudiating party that he would await the latter's performance and has urged retraction; and

(c) in either case suspend his own performance or proceed in accordance with the provisions of this Article on the seller's right to identify goods to the contract notwithstanding breach or to salvage unfinished goods (Section 2—704).

§ 2-611. Retraction of Anticipatory Repudiation.

(1) Until the repudiating party's next performance is due he can retract his repudiation unless the aggrieved party has since the repudiation cancelled or materially changed his position or otherwise indicated that he considers the repudiation final.

(2) Retraction may be by any method which clearly indicates to the aggrieved party that the repudiating party intends to perform, but must include any assurance justifiably demanded under the provisions of this Article (Section 2—609).

(3) Retraction reinstates the repudiating party's rights under the contract with due excuse and allowance to the aggrieved party for any delay occasioned by the repudiation.

§ 2-612. "Installment Contract"; Breach.

(1) An "installment contract" is one which requires or authorizes the delivery of goods in separate lots to be separately accepted, even though the contract contains a clause "each delivery is a separate contract" or its equivalent.

(2) The buyer may reject any installment which is non-conforming if the non-conformity substantially impairs the value of that installment and cannot be cured or if the non-conformity is a defect in the required documents; but if the non-conformity does not fall within subsection (3) and the seller gives adequate assurance of its cure the buyer must accept that installment.

(3) Whenever non-conformity or default with respect to one or more installments substantially impairs the value of the whole contract there is a breach of the whole. But the aggrieved party reinstates the contract if he accepts a non-conforming installment without seasonably notifying of cancellation or if he brings an action with respect only to past installments or demands performance as to future installments.

§ 2-613. Casualty to Identified Goods. Where the contract requires for its performance goods identified when the contract is made, and the goods suffer casualty without fault of either party before the rise of loss passes to the buyer, or in a proper case under a "no arrival, no sale" term (Section 2-324) then

(a)   if the loss is total the contract is avoided; and

(b)   if the loss is partial or the goods have so deteriorated as no longer to conform to the contract the buyer may nevertheless demand inspection and at his option either treat the contract as avoided or accept the goods with due allowance from the contract price for the deterioration or the deficiency in quantity but without further right against the seller.

§ 2-614. Substituted Performance.

(1) Where without fault of either party the agreed berthing, loading, or unloading facilities fail or an agreed type of carrier becomes unavailable or the agreed manner of delivery otherwise becomes commercially impracticable but a commercially reasonable substitute is available, such substitute performance must be tendered and accepted.

(2) If the agreed means or manner of payment fails because of domestic or foreign governmental regulation, the seller may withhold or stop delivery unless the buyer provides a means or manner of payment which is commercially a substantial equivalent. If delivery has already been taken, payment by the means or in the manner provided by the regulation discharges the buyer's obligation unless the regulation is discriminatory, oppressive or predatory.

§ 2-615. Excuse by Failure of Presupposed Conditions. Except so far as a seller may have assumed a greater obligation and subject to the preceding section on substituted performance:

(a)   Delay in delivery or non-delivery in whole or in part by a seller who complies with paragraphs (b) and (c) is not a breach of his duty under a contract for sale if performance as agreed has been made impracticable by the occurrence of a contingency the non-occurrence of which was a basic assumption on which the contract was made or by compliance in good faith with any applicable foreign or domestic governmental regulation or order whether or not it later proves to be invalid.

(b)   Where the causes mentioned in paragraph (a) affect only a part of the seller's capacity to perform, he must allocate production and deliveries among his customers but may at his option include regular customers not then under contract as well as his own requirements for further manufacture. He may so allocate in any manner which is fair and reasonable.

(c)   The seller must notify the buyer seasonably that there will be delay or non-delivery and, when allocation is required under paragraph (b), of the estimated quota thus made available for the buyer.

§ 2-616. Procedure on Notice Claiming Excuse.

(1) Where the buyer receives notification of a material or indefinite delay or an allocation justified under the preceding section he may by written notification to the seller as to any delivery concerned, and where the prospective deficiency substantially impairs the value of the whole contract under the provisions of this Article relating to breach of installment contracts (Section 2-612), then also as to the whole,

(a)   terminate and thereby discharge any unexecuted portion of the contract; or

(b)   modify the contract by agreeing to take his available quota in substitution.

(2) If after receipt of such notification from the seller the buyer fails so to modify the contract within a reasonable time not exceeding thirty days the contract lapses with respect to any deliveries affected.

(3) The provisions of this section may not be negated by agreement except in so far as the sller has assumed a greater obligation under the preceding section.

Part 7. Remedies

§ 2-701. Remedies for Breach of Collateral Contracts Not Impaired. Remedies for breach of any obligation or promise collateral or ancillary to a contract for sale are not impaired by the provisions of this Article.

§ 2-702. Seller's Remedies on Discovery of Buyer's Insolvency.

(1) Where the seller discovers the buyer to be insolvent he may refuse delivery except for cash including payment for all goods theretofore delivered under the contract, and stop delivery under this Article (Section 2-705).

(2) Where the seller discovers that the buyer has

received goods on credit while insolvent he may reclaim the goods upon demand made within ten days after the receipt, but if misrepresentation of solvency has been made to the particular seller in writing within three months before delivery the ten day limitation does not apply. Except as provided in this subsection the seller may not base a right to reclaim goods on the buyer's fraudulent or innocent misrepresentation of solvency or of intent to pay.

(3) The seller's right to reclaim under subsection (2) is subject to the rights of a buyer in ordinary course or other good faith purchaser under this Article (Section 2-403). Successful reclamation of goods excludes all other remedies with respect to them.

§ 2-703. Seller's Remedies in General.
Where the buyer wrongfully rejects or revokes acceptance of goods or fails to make a payment due on or before delivery or repudiates with respect to a part or the whole, then with respect to any goods directly affected and, if the breach is of the whole contract (Section 2-612), then also with respect to the whole undelivered balance, the aggrieved seller may

(a) withhold delivery of such goods;
(b) stop delivery by any bailee as hereafter provided (Section 2-705);
(c) proceed under the next section respecting goods still unidentified to the contract;
(d) resell and recover damages as hereafter provided (Section 2-706);
(e) recover damages for non-acceptance (Section 2-708) or in a proper case the price (Section 2-709);
(f) cancel.

§ 2-704. Seller's Right to Identify Goods to the Contract Notwithstanding Breach or to Salvage Unfinished Goods.

(1) An aggrieved seller under the preceding section may

(a) identify to the contract conforming goods not already identified if at the time he learned of the breach they are in his possession or control;
(b) treat as the subject of resale goods which have demonstrably been intended for the particular contract even though those goods are unfinished.

(2) Where the goods are unfinished an aggrieved seller may in the exercise of reasonable commercial judgment for the purposes of avoiding loss and of effective realization either complete the manufacture and wholly identify the goods to the contract or cease manufacture and resell for scrap or salvage value or proceed in any other reasonable manner.

§ 2-705. Seller's Stoppage of Delivery in Transit or Otherwise.

(1) The seller may stop delivery of goods in the possession of a carrier or other bailee when he discovers the buyer to be insolvent (Section 2-702) and may stop delivery of carload, truckload, planeload or larger shipments of express or freight when the buyer repudiates or fails to make a payment due before delivery or if for any other reason the seller has a right to withhold or reclaim the goods.

(2) As against such buyer the seller may stop delivery until

(a) receipt of the goods by the buyer; or
(b) acknowledgment to the buyer by any bailee of the goods except a carrier that the bailee holds the goods for the buyer; or
(c) such acknowledgment to the buyer by a carrier by reshipment or as warehouseman; or
(d) negotiation to the buyer of any negotiable document of title covering the goods.

(3)
(a) To stop delivery the seller must so notify as to enable the bailee by reasonable diligence to prevent delivery of the goods.
(b) After such notification the bailee must hold and deliver the goods according to the directions of the seller but the seller is liable to the bailee for any ensuing charges or damages.
(c) If a negotiable document of title has been issued for goods the bailee is not obliged to obey a notification to stop until surrender of the document.
(d) A carrier who has issued a non-negotiable bill of lading is not obliged to obey a notification to stop received from a person other than the consignor.

§ 2-706. Seller's Resale Including Contract for Resale.

(1) Under the conditions stated in Section 2-703 on seller's remedies, the seller may resell the goods concerned or the undelivered balance thereof. Where the resale is made in good faith and in a commercially reasonable manner the seller may recover the

difference between the resale price and the contract price together with any incidental damages allowed under the provisions of this Article (Section 2-710), but less expenses saved in consequence of the buyer's breach.

(2) Except as otherwise provided in subsection (3) or unless otherwise agreed resale may be at public or private sale including sale by way of one or more contracts to sell or of identification to an existing contract of the seller. Sale may be as a unit or in parcels and at any time and place and on any terms but every aspect of the sale including the method, manner, time, place and terms must be commercially reasonable. The resale must be reasonably identified as referring to the broken contract, but it is not necessary that the goods be in existence or that any or all of them have been identified to the contract before the breach.

(3) Where the resale is at private sale the seller must give the buyer reasonable notification of his intention to resell.

(4) Where the resale is at public sale

    (a)   only identified goods can be sold except where there is a recognized market for a public sale of futures in goods of the kind; and

    (b)   it must be made at a usual place or market for public sale if one is reasonably available and except in the case of goods which are perishable or threaten to decline in value speedily the seller must give the buyer reasonable notice of the time and place of the resale; and

    (c)   if the goods are not to be within the view of those attending the sale the notification of sale must state the place where the goods are located and provide for their reasonable inspection by prospective bidders; and

    (d)   the seller may buy.

(5) A purchaser who buys in good faith at a resale takes the goods free of any rights of the original buyer even though the seller fails to comply with one or more of the requirements of this section.

(6) The seller is not accountable to the buyer for any profit made on any resale. A person in the position of a seller (Section 2-707) or a buyer who has rightfully rejected or justifiably revoked acceptance must account for any excess over the amount of his security interest, as hereinafter defined (subsection (3) of Section 2-711).

§ 2-707. "Person in the Position of a Seller."

(1) A "person in the position of a seller" includes as against a principal an agent who has paid or become responsible for the price of goods on behalf of his principal or anyone who otherwise holds a security interest or other right in goods similar to that of a seller.

(2) A person in the position of a seller may as provided in this Article withhold or stop delivery (Section 2-705) and resell (Section 2-706) and recover incidental damages (Section 2-710).

§ 2-708. Seller's Damages for Non-acceptance or Repudiation.

(1) Subject to subsection (2) and to the provisions of this Article with respect to proof of market price (Section 2-723), the measure of damages for non-acceptance or repudiation by the buyer is the difference between the market price at the time and place for tender and the unpaid contract price together with any incidental damages provided in this Article (Section 2-710), but less expenses saved in consequence of the buyer's breach.

(2) If the measure of damages provided in subsection (1) is inadequate to put the seller in as good a position as performance would have done then the measure of damages is the profit (including reasonable overhead) which the seller would have made from full performance by the buyer, together with any incidental damages provided in this Article (Section 2-710), due allowance for costs reasonably incurred and due credit for payments or proceeds of resale.

§ 2-709. Action for the Price.

(1) When the buyer fails to pay the price as it becomes due the seller may recover, together with any incidental damages under the next section, the price

    (a)   of goods accepted or of conforming goods lost or damaged within a commercially reasonable time after risk of their loss has passed to the buyer; and

    (b)   of goods identified to the contract if the seller is unable after reasonable effort to resell them at a reasonable price or the circumstances reasonably indicate that such effort will be unavailing.

(2) Where the seller sues for the price he must hold for the buyer any goods which have been identified to the contract and are still in his control except that if resale becomes possible he may resell them at any time prior to the collection of the judgment. The

net proceeds of any such resale must be credited to the buyer and payment of the judgment entitles him to any goods not resold.

(3) After the buyer has wrongfully rejected or revoked acceptance of the goods or has failed to make a payment due or has repudiated (Section 2-610), a seller who is held not entitled to the price under this section shall nevertheless be awarded damages for non-acceptance under the preceding section.

§ 2-710. Seller's Incidental Damages.

Incidental damages to an aggrieved seller include any commercially reasonable charges, expenses or commissions incurred in stopping delivery, in the transportation, care and custody of goods after the buyer's breach, in connection with return or resale of the goods or otherwise resulting from the breach.

§ 2-711. Buyer's Remedies in General; Buyer's Security Interest in Rejected Goods.

(1) Where the seller fails to make delivery or repudiates or the buyer rightfully rejects or justifiably revokes acceptance then with respect to any goods involved, and with respect to the whole if the breach goes to the whole contract (Section 2-612), the buyer may cancel and whether or not he has done so may in addition to recovering so much of the price as has been paid

    (a) "cover" and have damages under the next section as to all the goods affected whether or not they have been identified to the contract; or

    (b) recover damages for non-delivery as provided in this Article (Section 2-713).

(2) Where the seller fails to deliver or repudiates the buyer may also

    (a) if the goods have been identified recover them as provided in this Article (Section 2-502); or

    (b) in a proper case obtain specific performance or replevy the goods as provided in this Article (Section 2-716).

(3) On rightful rejection or justifiable revocation of acceptance a buyer has a security interest in goods in his possession or control for any payments made on their price and any expenses reasonably incurred in their inspection, receipt, transportation, care and custody and may hold such goods and resell them in like manner as an aggrieved seller (Section 2-706).

§ 2-712. "Cover"; Buyer's Procurement of Substitute Goods.

(1) After a breach within the preceding section the buyer may "cover" by making in good faith and without unreasonable delay any reasonable purchase of or contract to purchase goods in substitution for those due from the seller.

(2) The buyer may recover from the seller as damages the difference between the cost of cover and the contract price together with any incidental or consequential damages as hereinafter defined (Section 2-715), but less expenses saved in consequence of the seller's breach.

(3) Failure of the buyer to effect cover within this section does not bar him from any other remedy.

§ 2-713. Buyer's Damages for Non-Delivery or Repudiation.

(1) Subject to the provisions of this Article with respect to proof of market price (Section 2-723), the measure of damages for non-delivery or repudiation by the seller is the difference between the market price at the time when the buyer learned of the breach and the contract price together with any incidental and consequential damages provided in this Article (Section 2-715), but less expenses saved in consequence of the seller's breach.

(2) Market price is to be determined as of the place for tender or, in cases of rejection after arrival or revocation of acceptance, as of the place of arrival.

§ 2-714. Buyer's Damages for Breach in Regard to Accepted Goods.

(1) Where the buyer has accepted goods and given notification (subsection (3) of Section 2-607) he may recover as damages for any non-conformity of tender the loss resulting in the ordinary course of events from the seller's breach as determined in any manner which is reasonable.

(2) The measure of damages for breach of warranty is the difference at the time and place of acceptance between the value of the goods accepted and the value they would have had if they had been warranted, unless special circumstances show proximate damages of a different amount.

(3) In a proper case any incidental and consequential damages under the next section may also be recovered.

§ 2-715. Buyer's Incidental and Consequential Damages.

(1) Incidental damages resulting from the seller's breach include expenses reasonably incurred in inspection, receipt, transportation and care and custody of goods rightfully rejected, any commercially reasonable charges, expenses or commissions

in connection with effecting cover and any other reasonable expense incident to the delay or other breach.

(2) Consequential damages resulting from the seller's breach include

    (a) any loss resulting from general or particular requirements and needs of which the seller at the time of contracting had reason to know and which could not reasonably be prevented by cover or otherwise; and

    (b) injury to person or property proximately resulting from any breach of warranty.

§ 2-716. Buyer's Right to Specific Performance or Replevin.

(1) Specific performance may be decreed where the goods are unique or in other proper circumstances.

(2) The decree for specific performance may include such terms and conditions as to payment of the price, damages, or other relief as the court may deem just.

(3) The buyer has a right of replevin for goods identified to the contract if after reasonable effort he is unable to effect cover for such goods or the circumstances reasonably indicate that such effort will be unavailing or if the goods have been shipped under reservation and satisfaction of the security interest in them has been made or tendered.

§ 2-717. Deduction of Damages From the Price.

The buyer on notifying the seller of his intention to do so may deduct all or part of the damages resulting from any breach of the contract from any part of the price still due under the same contract.

§ 2-718. Liquidation or Limitation of Damages; Deposits.

(1) Damages for breach by either party may be liquidated in the agreement but only at an amount which is reasonable in the light of the anticipated or actual harm caused by the breach, the difficulties of proof of loss, and the inconvenience or nonfeasibility of otherwise obtaining an adequate remedy. A term fixing unreasonably large liquidated damages is void as a penalty.

(2) Where the seller justifiably withholds delivery of goods because of the buyer's breach, the buyer is entitled to restitution of any amount by which the sum of his payments exceeds

    (a) the amount to which the seller is entitled by virtue of terms liquidating the seller's damages in accordance with subsection (1), or

    (b) in the absence of such terms, twenty per cent of the value of the total performance for which the buyer is obligated under the contract or $500, whichever is smaller.

(3) The buyer's right to restitution under subsection (2) is subject to offset to the extent that the seller establishes

    (a) a right to recover damages under the provisions of this Article other than subsection (1), and

    (b) the amount or value of any benefits received by the buyer directly or indirectly by reason of the contract.

(4) Where a seller has received payment in goods their reasonable value or the proceeds of their resale shall be treated as payments for the purposes of subsection (2); but if the seller has notice of the buyer's breach before reselling goods received in part performance, his resale is subject to the conditions laid down in this Article on resale by an aggrieved seller (Section 2-706).

§ 2-719. Contractual Modification or Limitation of Remedy.

(1) Subject to the provisions of subsections (2) and (3) of this section and of the preceding section on liquidation and limitation of damages,

    (a) the agreement may provide for remedies in addition to or in substitution for those provided in this Article and may limit or alter the measure of damages recoverable under this Article, as by limiting the buyer's remedies to return of the goods and repayment of the price or to repair and replacement of non-conforming goods or parts; and

    (b) resort to a remedy as provided is optional unless the remedy is expressly agreed to be exclusive, in which case it is the sole remedy.

(2) Where circumstances cause an exclusive or limited remedy to fail of its essential purpose, remedy may be had as provided in this Act.

(3) Consequential damages may be limited or excluded unless the limitation or exclusion is unconscionable. Limitation of consequential damages for injury to the person in the case of consumer goods is

prima facie unconscionable but limitation of damages where the loss is commercial is not.

§ 2-720. Effect of "Cancellation" or "Rescission" on Claims for Antecedent Breach. Unless the contrary intention clearly appears, expressions of "cancellation" or "rescission" of the contract or the like shall not be construed as a renunciation or discharge of any claim in damages for an antecedent breach.

§ 2-721. Remedies for Fraud. Remedies for material misrepresentation or fraud include all remedies available under this Article for non-fraudulent breach. Neither rescission or a claim for rescission of the contract for sale nor rejection or return of the goods shall bar or be deemed inconsistent with a claim for damages or other remedy.

§ 2-722. Who Can Sue Third Parties for Injury to Goods. Where a third party so deals with goods which have been identified to a contract for sale as to cause actionable injury to a party to that contract.

    (a)   a right of action against the third party is in either party to the contract for sale who has title to or a security interest or a special property or an insurable interest in the goods; and if the goods have been destroyed or converted a right of action is also in the party who either bore the risk of loss under the contract for sale or has since the injury assumed that risk as against the other;

    (b)   if at the time of the injury the party plaintiff did not bear the risk of loss as against the other party to the contract for sale and there is no arrangement between them for disposition of the recovery, his suit or settlement is, subject to his own interest, as a fiduciary for the other party to the contract;

    (c)   either party may with the consent of the other sue for the benefit of whom it may concern.

§ 2-723. Proof of Market Price: Time and Place.

(1) If an action based on anticipatory repudiation comes to trial before the time for performance with respect to some or all of the goods, any damages based on market price (Section 2-708 or Section 2-713) shall be determined according to the price of such goods prevailing at the time when the aggrieved party learned of the repudiation.

(2) If evidence of a price prevailing at the times or places described in this Article is not readily available the price prevailing within any reasonable time before or after the time described or at any other place which in commercial judgment or under usage of trade would serve as a reasonable substitute for the one described may be used, making any proper allowance for the cost of transporting the goods to or from such other place.

(3) Evidence of a relevant price prevailing at a time or place other than the one described in this Article offered by one party is not admissible unless and until he has given the other party such notice as the court finds sufficient to prevent unfair surprise.

§ 2-724. Admissibility of Market Quotations. Whenever the prevailing price or value of any goods regularly bought and sold in any established commodity market is in issue, reports in official publications or trade journals or in newspapers or periodicals of general circulation published as the reports of such market shall be admissible in evidence. The circumstances of the preparation of such a report may be shown to affect its weight but not its admissibility.

§ 2-725. Statute of Limitations in Contracts for Sale.

(1) An action for breach of any contract for sale must be commenced within four years after the cause of action has accrued. By the original agreement the parties may reduce the period of limitation to not less than one year but may not extend it.

(2) A cause of action accrues when the breach occurs, regardless of the aggrieved party's lack of knowledge of the breach. A breach of warranty occurs when tender of delivery is made, except that where a warranty explicitly extends to future performance of the goods and discovery of the breach must await the time of such performance the cause of action accrues when the breach is or should have been discovered.

(3) Where an action commenced within the time limited by subsection (1) is so terminated as to leave available a remedy by another action for the same breach such other action may be commenced after the expiration of the time limited and within six months after the termination of the first action unless the termination resulted from voluntary discontinuance or from dismissal for failure or neglect to prosecute.

(4) This section does not alter the law on tolling of

the statute of limitations nor does it apply to causes of action which have accrued before this Act becomes effective.

ARTICLE 3. COMMERCIAL PAPER

Part 1. Short Title, Form and Interpretation

§ 3-101. Short Title. This Article shall be known and may be cited as Uniform Commercial Code— Commercial Paper.

§ 3-102. Definitions and Index of Definitions.

(1) In this Article unless the context otherwise requires

    (a) "Issue" means the first delivery of an instrument to a holder or a remitter.

    (b) An "order" is a direction to pay and must be more than an authorization or request. It must identify the person to pay with reasonable certainty. It may be addressed to one or more such persons jointly or in the alternative but not in succession.

    (c) A "promise" is an undertaking to pay and must be more than an acknowledgment of an obligation.

    (d) "Secondary party" means a drawer or endorser.

    (e) "Instrument" means a negotiable instrument.

(2) Other definitions applying to this Article and the sections in which they appear are:

"Acceptance." Section 3-410.

"Accommodation party." Section 3-415.

"Alteration." Section 3-407.

"Certificate of deposit." Section 3-104.

"Certification." Section 3-411.

"Check." Section 3-104.

"Definite time." Section 3-109.

"Dishonor." Section 3-507.

"Draft." Section 3-104.

"Holder in due course." Section 3-302.

"Negotiation." Section 3-202.

"Note." Section 3-104.

"Notice of dishonor." Section 3-508.

"On demand." Section 3-108.

"Presentment." Section 3-504.

"Protest." Section 3-509.

"Restrictive Indorsement." Section 3-205.

"Signature." Section 3-401.

(3) The following definitions in other Articles apply to this Article:

"Account." Section 4-104.

"Banking Day." Section 4-104.

"Clearning house." Section 4-104.

"Collecting bank." Section 4-105.

"Customer." Section 4-104.

"Depositary Bank." Section 4-105.

"Documentary Draft." Section 4-104.

"Intermediary Bank." Section 4-105.

"Item." Section 4-104.

"Midnight deadline." Section 4-104.

"Payor bank." Section 4-105.

(4) In addition Article 1 contains general definitions and principles of construction and interpretation applicable throughout this Article.

§ 3-103. Limitations on Scope of Article.

(1) This Article does not apply to money, documents of title or investment securities.

(2) The provisions of this Article are subject to the provisions of the Article on Bank Deposits and Collections (Article 4) and Secured Transactions (Article 9).

§ 3-104. Form of Negotiable Instruments; "Draft"; "Check"; "Certificate of Deposit"; "Note."

(1) Any writing to be a negotiable instrument within this Article must

    (a) be signed by the maker or drawer; and

    (b) contain an unconditional promise or order to pay a sum certain in money and no other promise, order, obligation or power given by the maker or drawer except as authorized by this Article; and

    (c) be payable on demand or at a definite time; and

    (d) be payable to order or to bearer.

(2) A writing which complies with the requirements of this section is

    (a) a "draft" ("bill of exchange") if it is an order;

    (b) a "check" if it is a draft drawn on a bank and payable on demand;

    (c) a "certificate of deposit" if it is an acknowledgment by a bank of receipt of money with an engagement to repay it;

    (d) a "note" if it is a promise other than a certificate of deposit.

(3) As used in other Articles of this Act, and as the context may require, the terms "draft," "check," "certificate of deposit" and "note" may refer to instruments which are not negotiable within this Article as well as to instruments which are so negotiable.

§ 3-105. When Promise or Order Unconditional.

(1) A promise or order otherwise unconditional is not made conditional by the fact that the instrument

(a)   is subject to implied or constructive conditions; or

(b)   states its consideration, whether performed or promised, or the transaction which gave rise to the instrument, or that the promise or order is made or the instrument matures in accordance with or "as per" such transaction; or

(c)   refers to or states that it arises out of a separate agreement or refers to a separate agreement for rights as to prepayment or acceleration; or

(d)   states that it is drawn under a letter of credit; or

(e)   states that it is secured, whether by mortgage, reservation of title or otherwise; or

(f)   indicates a particular account to be debited or any other fund or source from which reimbursement is expected; or

(g)   is limited to payment out of a particular fund or the proceeds of a particular source, if the instrument is issued by a government or governmental agency or unit; or

(h)   is limited to payment out of the entire assets of a partnership, unincorporated association, trust or estate by or on behalf of which the instrument is issued.

(2) A promise or order is not unconditional if the instrument

(a)   states that it is subject to or governed by any other agreement; or

(b)   states that it is to be paid only out of a particular fund or source except as provided in this section.

§ 3-106. Sum Certain.

(1) The sum payable is a sum certain even though it is to be paid

(a)   with stated interest or by stated installments; or

(b)   with stated different rates of interest before and after default or a specified date; or

(c)   with a stated discount or addition if paid before or after the date fixed for payment; or

(d)   with exchange or less exchange, whether at a fixed rate or at the current rate; or

(e)   with costs of collection or an attorney's fee or both upon default.

(2) Nothing in this section shall validate any term which is otherwise illegal.

§ 3-107. Money.

(1) An instrument is payable in money if the medium of exchange in which it is payable is money at the time the instrument is made. An instrument payable in "currency" or "current funds" is payable in money.

(2) A promise or order to pay a sum stated in a foreign currency is for a sum certain in money and, unless a different medium of payment is specified in the instrument, may be satisfied by payment of that number of dollars which the stated foreign currency will purchase at the buying sight rate for that currency on the day on which the instrument is payable or, if payable on demand, on the day of demand. If such an instrument specifies a foreign currency as the medium of payment the instrument is payable in that currency.

§ 3-108. Payable on Demand.

Instruments payable on demand include those payable at sight or on presentation and those in which no time for payment is stated.

§ 3-109. Definite Time.

(1) An instrument is payable at a definite time if by its terms it is payable

(a)   on or before a stated date or at a fixed period after a stated date; or

(b)   at a fixed period after sight; or

(c)   at a definite time subject to any acceleration; or

(d)   at a definite time subject to extension at the option of the holder, or to extension to a further definite time at the option of the maker or acceptor or automatically upon or after a specified act or event.

(2) An instrument which by its terms is otherwise payable only upon an act or event uncertain as to time of occurrence is not payable at a definite time even though the act or event has occurred.

§ 3-110. Payable to Order.

(1) An instrument is payable to order when by its terms it is payable to the order or assigns of any person therein specified with reasonable certainty, or to him or his order, or when it is conspicuously designated on its face as "exchange" or the like and names a payee. It may be payable to the order of

(a)   the maker or drawer; or

(b)   the drawee; or

(c)   a payee who is not maker, drawer or drawee; or

(d)   two or more payees together or in the alternative; or

(e)   an estate, trust or fund, in which case it is payable to the order of the representative of such estate, trust or fund or his successors; or

(f)   an office, or an officer by his title as such in which case it is payable to the principal but the incumbent of the office or his successors may act as if he or they were the holder; or

(g)   a partnership or unincorporated association, in which case it is payable to the partnership or association and may be indorsed or transferred by any person thereto authorized.

(2) An instrument not payable to order is not made so payable by such words as "payable upon return of this instrument properly indorsed."

(3) An instrument made payable both to order and to bearer is payable to order unless the bearer words are handwritten or typewritten.

§ 3-111. **Payable to Bearer.** An instrument is payable to bearer when by its terms it is payable to

(a)   bearer or the order of bearer; or

(b)   a specified person or bearer; or

(c)   "cash" or the order of "cash," or any other indication which does not purport to designate a specific payee.

§ 3-112. **Terms and Omissions Not Affecting Negotiability.**

(1) The negotiability of an instrument is not affected by

(a)   the omission of a statement of any consideration or of the place where the instrument is drawn or payable; or

(b)   a statement that collateral has been given to secure obligations either on the instrument or otherwise of an obligor on the instrument or that in case of default on those obligations the holder may realize on or dispose of the collateral; or

(c)   a promise or power to maintain or protect collateral or to give additional collateral; or

(d)   a term authorizing a confession of judgment on the instrument if it is not paid when due; or

(e)   a term purporting to waive the benefit of any law intended for the advantage or protection of any obligor; or

(f)   a term in a draft providing that the payee by indorsing or cashing it acknowledges full satisfaction of an obligation of the drawer; or

(g)   A statement in a draft drawn in a set of parts (Section 3-801) to the effect that the order is effective only if no other part has been honored.

(2) Nothing in this section shall validate any term which is otherwise illegal.

§ 3-113. **Seal.** An instrument otherwise negotiable is within this Article even though it is under a seal.

§ 3-114. **Date, Antedating, Postdating.**

(1) The negotiability of an instrument is not affected by the fact that it is undated, antedated or postdated.

(2) Where an instrument is antedated or postdated the time when it is payable is determined by the stated date if the instrument is payable on demand or at a fixed period after date.

(3) Where the instrument or any signature thereon is dated, the date is presumed to be correct.

§ 3-115. **Incomplete Instruments.**

(1) When a paper whose contents at the time of signing show that it is intended to become an instrument is signed while still incomplete in any necessary respect it cannot be enforced until completed, but when it is completed in accordance with authority given it is effective as completed.

(2) If the completion is unauthorized the rules as to material alteration apply (Section 3-407), even though the paper was not delivered by the maker or drawer; but the burden of establishing that any completion is unauthorized is on the party so asserting.

§ 3-116. **Instruments Payable to Two or More Persons.** An instrument payable to the order of two or more persons

(a)   if in the alternative is payable to any one of them and may be negotiated, discharged or enforced by any of them who has possession of it;

(b)   if not in the alternative is payable to all of them and may be negotiated, discharged or enforced only by all of them.

§ 3-117. Instruments Payable With Words of Description.
An instrument made payable to a named person with the addition of words describing him

(a)   as agent or officer of a specified person is payable to his principal but the agent or officer may act as if he were the holder;

(b)   as any other fiduciary for a specified person or purpose is payable to the payee and may be negotiated, discharged or enforced by him;

(c)   in any other manner is payable to the payee unconditionally and the additional words are without effect on subsequent parties.

§ 3-118. Ambiguous Terms and Rules of Construction.
The following rules apply to every instrument:

(a)   Where there is doubt whether the instrument is a draft or a note the holder may treat it as either. A draft drawn on the drawer is effective as a note.

(b)   Handwritten terms control typewritten and printed terms, and typewritten control printed.

(c)   Words control figures except that if the words are ambiguous figures control.

(d)   Unless otherwise specified a provision for interest means interest at the judgment rate at the place of payment from the date of the instrument, or if it is undated from the date of issue.

(e)   Unless the instrument otherwise specifies two or more persons who sign as maker, acceptor or drawer or indorser and as a part of the same transaction are jointly and severally liable even though the instrument contains such words as "I promise to pay."

(f)   Unless otherwise specified consent to extension authorizes a single extension for not longer than the original period. A consent to extension, expressed in the instrument, is binding on secondary parties and accommodation makers. A holder may not exercise his option to extend an instrument over the objection of a maker or acceptor or other party who in accordance with Section 3-604 tenders full payment when the instrument is due.

§ 3-119. Other Writings Affecting Instrument.
(1) As between the obligor and his immediate obligee or any transferee the terms of an instrument may be modified or affected by any other written agreement executed as a part of the same transaction, except that a holder in due course is not affected by any limitation of his rights arising out of the separate written agreement if he had no notice of the limitation when he took the instrument.

(2) A separate agreement does not affect the negotiability of an instrument.

§ 3-120. Instruments "Payable Through" Bank.
An instrument which states that it is "payable through" a bank or the like designates that bank as a collecting bank to make presentment but does not of itself authorize the bank to pay the instrument.

§ 3-121. Instruments payable at Bank.

Note: *If this Act is introduced in the Congress of the United States this section should be omitted.*
(States to select either alternative)

Alternative A   A note or acceptance which states that it is payable at a bank is the equivalent of a draft drawn on the bank payable when it falls due out of any funds of the maker or acceptor in current account or otherwise available for such payment.

Alternative B   A note or acceptance which states that it is payable at a bank is not of itself an order or authorization to the bank to pay it.

§ 3-122. Accrual of Cause of Action.
(1) A cause of action against a maker or an acceptor accrues

(a)   in the case of a time instrument on the day after maturity;

(b)   in the case of a demand instrument upon its date or, if no date is stated, on the date of issue.

(2) A cause of action against the obligor of a demand or time certificate of deposit accrues upon demand, but demand on a time certificate may not be made until on or after the date of maturity.

(3) A cause of action against a drawer of a draft or an indorser of any instrument accrues upon demand following dishonor of the instrument. Notice of dishonor is a demand.

(4) Unless an instrument provides otherwise, interest runs at the rate provided by law for a judgment

(a)   in the case of a maker, acceptor or other primary obligor of a demand instrument, from the date of demand;

(b)   in all other cases from the date of accrual of the cause of action.

Part 2. Transfer and Negotiation

§ 3-201. Transfer: Right to Indorsement.

(1) Transfer of an instrument vests in the transferee such rights as the transferor has therein, except that a transferee who has himself been a party to any fraud or illegality affecting the instrument or who as a prior holder had notice of a defense or claim against it cannot improve his position by taking from a later holder in due course.

(2) A transfer of a security interest in an instrument vests the foregoing rights in the transferee to the extent of the interest transferred.

(3) Unless otherwise agreed any transfer for value of an instrument not then payable to bearer gives the transferee the specifically enforceable right to have the unqualified indorsement of the transferor. Negotiation takes effect only when the indorsement is made and until that time there is no presumption that the transferee is the owner.

§ 3-202. Negotiation.

(1) Negotiation is the transfer of an instrument in such form that the transferee becomes a holder. If the instrument is payable to order it is negotiated by delivery with any necessary indorsement; if payable to bearer it is negotiated by delivery.

(2) An indorsement must be written by or on behalf of the holder and on the instrument or on a paper so firmly affixed thereto as to become a part thereof.

(3) An indorsement is effective for negotiation only when it conveys the entire instrument or any unpaid residue. If it purports to be of less it operates only as a partial assignment.

(4) Words of assignment, condition, waiver, guaranty, limitation or disclaimer of liability and the like accompanying an indorsement do not affect its character as an indorsement.

§ 3-203. Wrong or Misspelled Name.
Where an instrument is made payable to a person under a misspelled name or one other than his own he may indorse in that name or his own or both; but signature in both names may be required by a person paying or giving value for the instrument.

§ 3-204. Special Indorsement; Blank Indorsement.

(1) A special indorsement specifies the person to whom or to whose order it makes the instrument payable. Any instrument specially indorsed becomes payable to the order of the special indorsee and may be further negotiated only by his indorsement.

(2) An indorsement in blank specifies no particular indorsee and may consist of a mere signature. An instrument payable to order and indorsed in blank becomes payable to bearer and may be negotiated by delivery alone until specially indorsed.

(3) The holder may convert a blank indorsement into a special indorsement by writing over the signature of the indorser in blank any contract consistent with the character of the indorsement.

§ 3-205. Restrictive Indorsement.
An indorsement is restrictive which either

(a)   is conditional; or

(b)   purports to prohibit further transfer of the instrument; or

(c)   includes the words "for collection," "for deposit," "pay any bank," or like terms signifying a purpose of deposit or collection; or

(d)   otherwise states that it is for the benefit or use of the indorser or of another person.

§ 3-206. Effect of Restrictive Indorsement.

(1) No restrictive indorsement prevents further transfer or negotiation of the instrument.

(2) An intermediary bank, or a payor bank which is not the depositary bank, is neither given notice nor otherwise affected by a restrictive indorsement of any person except the bank's immediate transferor or the person presenting for payment.

(3) Except for an intermediary bank, any transferee under an indorsement which is conditional or includes the words "for collection," "for deposit," "pay any bank," or like terms (sub-paragraphs (a) and (c) of Section 3-205) must pay or apply any value given by him for or on the security of the instrument consistently with the indorsement and to the extent that he does so he becomes a holder for value. In addition such transferee is a holder in due course if

he otherwise complies with the requirements of Section 3-302 on what constitutes a holder in due course.

(4) The first taker under an indorsement for the benefit of the indorser or another person (subparagraph (d) of Section 3-205) must pay or apply any value given by him for or on the security of the instrument consistently with the indorsement and to the extent that he does so he becomes a holder for value. In addition such taker is a holder in due course if he otherwise complies with the requirements of Section 3-302 on what constitutes a holder in due course. A later holder for value is neither given notice nor otherwise affected by such restrictive indorsement unless he has knowledge that a fiduciary or other person has negotiated the instrument in any transaction for his own benefit or otherwise in breach of duty (subsection (2) of Section 3-304).

§ 3-207. Negotiation Effective Although It May Be Rescinded.

(1) Negotiation is effective to transfer the instrument although the negotiation is

    (a)   made by an infant, a corporation exceeding its powers, or any other person without capacity; or

    (b)   obtained by fraud, duress or mistake of any kind; or

    (c)   part of an illegal transaction; or

    (d)   made in breach of duty.

(2) Except as against a subsequent holder in due course such negotiation is in an appropriate case subject to rescission, the declaration of a constructive trust or any other remedy permitted by law.

§ 3-208. Reacquisition.

Where an instrument is returned to or reacquired by a prior party he may cancel any indorsement which is not necessary to his title and reissue or further negotiate the instrument, but any intervening party is discharged as against the reacquiring party and subsequent holders not in due course and if his indorsement has been cancelled is discharged as against subsequent holders in due course as well.

Part 3. Rights of a Holder

§ 3-301. Rights of a Holder.

The holder of an instrument whether or not he is the owner may transfer or negotiate it and, except as otherwise provided in Section 3-603 on payment or satisfaction, discharge it or enforce payment in his own name.

§ 3-302. Holder in Due Course.

(1) A holder in due course is a holder who takes the instrument

    (a)   for value; and

    (b)   in good faith; and

    (c)   without notice that it is overdue or has been dishonored or of any defense against or claim to it on the part of any person.

(2) A payee may be a holder in due course.

(3) A holder does not become a holder in due course of an instrument:

    (a)   by purchase of it at judicial sale or by taking it under legal process; or

    (b)   by acquiring it in taking over an estate; or

    (c)   by purchasing it as part of a bulk transaction not in regular course of business of the transferor.

(4) A purchaser of a limited interest can be a holder in due course only to the extent of the interest purchased.

§ 3-303. Taking for Value.

A holder takes the instrument for value

    (a)   To the extent that the agreed consideration has been performed or that he acquires a security interest in or a lien on the instrument otherwise than by legal process; or

    (b)   when he takes the instrument in payment of or as security for an antecedent claim against any person whether or not the claim is due; or

    (c)   when he gives a negotiable instrument for it or makes an irrevocable commitment to a third person.

§ 3-304. Notice to Purchaser.

(1) The purchaser has notice of a claim or defense if

    (a)   the instrument is so incomplete, bears such visible evidence of forgery or alteration, or is otherwise so irregular as to call into question its validity, terms or ownership or to create an ambiguity as to the party to pay; or

    (b)   the purchaser has notice that the obligation of any party is voidable in whole or in part, or that all parties have been discharged.

(2) The purchaser has notice of a claim against the

instrument when he has knowledge that a fiduciary has negotiated the instrument in payment of or as security for his own debt or in any transaction for his own benefit or otherwise in breach of duty.

(3) The purchaser has notice that an instrument is overdue if he has reason to know

    (a)   that any part of the principal amount is overdue or that there is an uncured default in payment of another instrument of the same series; or

    (b)   that acceleration of the instrument has been made; or

    (c)   that he is taking a demand instrument after demand has been made or more than a reasonable length of time after its issue. A reasonable time for a check drawn and payable within the states and territories of the United States and the District of Columbia is presumed to be thirty days.

(4) Knowledge of the following facts does not of itself give the purchaser notice of a defense or claim

    (a)   that the instrument is antedated or post-dated;

    (b)   that it was issued or negotiated in return for an executory promise or accompanied by a separate agreement, unless the purchaser has notice that a defense or claim has arisen from the terms thereof;

    (c)   that any party has signed for accommodation;

    (d)   that an incomplete instrument has been completed, unless the purchaser has notice of any improper completion;

    (e)   that any person negotiating the instrument is or was a fiduciary;

    (f)   that there has been default in payment of interest on the instrument or in payment of any other instrument, except one of the same series.

(5) The filing or recording of a document does not of itself constitute notice within the provisions of this Article to a person who would otherwise be a holder in due course.

(6) To be effective notice must be received at such time and in such manner as to give a reasonable opportunity to act on it.

§ 3-305. Rights of a Holder in Due Course.
To the extent that a holder is a holder in due course he takes the instrument free from

    (1) all claims to it on the part of any person; and

    (2) all defenses of any party to the instrument with whom the holder has not dealt except

    (a)   infancy, to the extent that it is a defense to a simple contract; and

    (b)   such other incapacity, or duress, or illegality of the transaction, as renders the obligation of the party a nullity; and

    (c)   such misrepresentation as has induced the party to sign the instrument with neither knowledge nor reasonable opportunity to obtain knowledge of its character or its essential terms; and

    (d)   discharge in insolvency proceedings; and

    (e)   any other discharge of which the holder has notice when he takes the instrument.

§ 3-306. Rights of One Not Holder in Due Course.
Unless he has the rights of a holder in due course any person takes the instrument subject to

    (a)   all valid claims to it on the part of any person; and

    (b)   all defenses of any party which would be available in an action on a simple contract; and

    (c)   the defenses of want or failure of consideration, non-performance of any condition precedent, non-delivery, or delivery for a special purpose (Section 3-408); and

    (d)   the defense that he or a person through whom he holds the instrument acquired it by theft, or that payment or satisfaction to such holder would be inconsistent with the terms of a restrictive indorsement. The claim of any third person to the instrument is not otherwise available as a defense to any party liable thereon unless the third person himself defends the action for such party.

§ 3-307. Burden of Establishing Signatures, Defenses and Due Course.

(1) Unless specifically denied in the pleadings each signature on an instrument is admitted. When the effectiveness of a signature is put in issue

    (a)   the burden of establishing it is on the party claiming under the signature; but

    (b)   the signature is presumed to be genuine or authorized except where the action is to enforce the obligation of a purported signer who has died or become incompetent before proof is required.

(2) When signatures are admitted or established, production of the instrument entitles a holder to recover on it unless the defendant establishes a defense.

(3) After it is shown that a defense exists a person claiming the rights of a holder in due course has the burden of establishing that he or some person under whom he claims is in all respects a holder in due course.

Part 4. Liability of Parties

§ 3-401. Signature.

(1) No person is liable on an instrument unless his signature appears thereon.

(2) A signature is made by use of any name, including any trade or assumed name, upon an instrument, or by any word or mark used in lieu of a written signature.

§ 3-402. Signature in Ambiguous Capacity.
Unless the instrument clearly indicates that a signature is made in some other capacity it is an indorsement.

§ 3-403. Signature by Authorized Representative.

(1) A signature may be made by an agent or other representative, and his authority to make it may be established as in other cases of representation. No particular form of appointment is necessary to establish such authority.

(2) An authorized representative who signs his own name to an instrument

    (a)   is personally obligated if the instrument neither names the person represented nor shows that the representative signed in a representative capacity;

    (b)   except as otherwise established between the immediate parties, is personally obligated if the instrument names the person represented but does not show that the representative signed in a representative capacity, or if the instrument does not name the person represented but does show that the representative signed in a representative capacity.

(3) Except as otherwise established the name of an organization preceded or followed by the name and office of an authorized individual is a signature made in a representative capacity.

§ 3-404. Unauthorized Signatures.

(1) Any unauthorized signature is wholly inoperative as that of the person whose name is signed unless he ratifies it or is precluded from denying it; but it operates as the signature of the unauthorized signer in favor of any person who in good faith pays the instrument or takes it for value.

(2) Any unauthorized signature may be ratified for all purposes of this Article. Such ratification does not of itself affect any rights of the person ratifying against the actual signer.

§ 3-405. Impostors; Signature in Name of Payee.

(1) An indorsement by any person in the name of a named payee is effective if

    (a)   an impostor by use of the mails or otherwise has induced the maker or drawer to issue the instrument to him or his confederate in the name of the payee; or

    (b)   a person signing as or on behalf of a maker or drawer intends the payee to have no interest in the instrument; or

    (c)   an agent or employee of the maker or drawer has supplied him with the name of the payee intending the latter to have no such interest.

(2) Nothing in this section shall affect the criminal or civil liability of the person so indorsing.

§ 3-406. Negligence Contributing to Alteration or Unauthorized Signature.
Any person who by his negligence substantially contributes to a material alteration of the instrument or to the making of an unauthorized signature is precluded from asserting the alteration or lack of authority against a holder in due course or against a drawee or other payor who pays the instrument in good faith and in accordance with the reasonable commercial standards of the drawee's or payor's business.

§ 3-407. Alteration.

(1) Any alteration of an instrument is material which changes the contract of any party thereto in any respect, including any such change in

    (a)   the number or relations of the parties; or

    (b)   an incomplete instrument, by completing it otherwise than as authorized; or

    (c)   the writing as signed, by adding to it or by removing any part of it.

(2) As against any person other than a subsequent holder in due course.

    (a)   alteration by the holder which is both fraudulent and material discharges any party whose contract is thereby changed unless that party assents or is precluded from asserting the defense;

(b) no other alteration discharges any party and the instrument may be enforced according to its original tenor, or as to incomplete instruments according to the authority given.

(3) A subsequent holder in due course may in all cases enforce the instrument according to its original tenor, and when an incomplete instrument has been completed, he may enforce it as completed.

§ 3-408. Consideration.

Want or failure of consideration is a defense as against any person not having the rights of a holder in due course (Section 3-305), except that no consideration is necessary for an instrument or obligation thereon given in payment of or as security for an antecedent obligation of any kind. Nothing in this section shall be taken to displace any statute outside this Act under which a promise is enforceable notwithstanding lack or failure of consideration. Partial failure of consideration is a defense pro tanto whether or not the failure is in an ascertained or liquidated amount.

§ 3-409. Draft Not an Assignment.

(1) A check or other draft does not of itself operate as an assignment of any funds in the hands of the drawee available for its payment, and the drawee is not liable on the instrument until he accepts it.

(2) Nothing in this section shall affect any liability in contract, tort or otherwise arising from any letter of credit or other obligation or representation which is not an acceptance.

§ 3-410. Definition and Operation of Acceptance.

(1) Acceptance is the drawee's signed engagement to honor the draft as presented. It must be written on the draft, and may consist of his signature alone. It becomes operative when completed by delivery or notification.

(2) A draft may be accepted although it has not been signed by the drawer or is otherwise incomplete or is overdue or has been dishonored.

(3) Where the draft is payable at a fixed period after sight and the acceptor fails to date his acceptance the holder may complete it by supplying a date in good faith.

§ 3-411. Certification of a Check.

(1) Certification of a check is acceptance. Where a holder procures certification the drawer and all prior indorsers are discharged.

(2) Unless otherwise agreed a bank has no obligation to certify a check.

(3) A bank may certify a check before returning it for lack of proper indorsement. If it does so the drawer is discharged.

§ 3-412. Acceptance Varying Draft.

(1) Where the drawee's proffered acceptance in any manner varies the draft as presented the holder may refuse the acceptance and treat the draft as dishonored in which case the drawee is entitled to have his acceptance cancelled.

(2) The terms of the draft are not varied by an acceptance to pay at any particular bank or place in the United States, unless the acceptance states that the draft is to be paid only at such bank or place.

(3) Where the holder assents to an acceptance varying the terms of the draft each drawer and indorser who does not affirmatively assent is discharged.

§ 3-413. Contract of Maker, Drawer and Acceptor.

(1) The maker or acceptor engages that he will pay the instrument according to its tenor at the time of his engagement or as completed pursuant to Section 3-115 or incomplete instruments.

(2) The drawer engages that upon dishonor of the draft and any necessary notice of dishonor or protest he will pay the amount of the draft to the holder or to any indorser who takes it up. The drawer may disclaim this liability by drawing without recourse.

(3) By making, drawing or accepting the party admits as against all subsequent parties including the drawee the existence of the payee and his then capacity to indorse.

§ 3-414. Contract of Indorser; Order of Liability.

(1) Unless the indorsement otherwise specifies (as by such words as "without recourse") every indorser engages that upon dishonor and any necessary notice of dishonor and protest he will pay the instrument according to its tenor at the time of his indorsement to the holder or to any subsequent indorser who takes it up, even though the indorser who takes it up was not obligated to do so.

(2) Unless they otherwise agree indorsers are liable to one another in the order in which they indorse, which is presumed to be the order in which their signatures appear on the instrument.

§ 3-415. Contract of Accommodation Party.

(1) An accommodation party is one who signs the instrument in any capacity for the purpose of lending his name to another party to it.

(2) When the instrument has been taken for value before it is due the accommodation party is liable in the capacity in which he has signed even though the taker knows of the accommodation.

(3) As against a holder in due course and without notice of the accommodation oral proof of the accommodation is not admissible to give the accommodation party the benefit of discharges dependent on his character as such. In other cases the accommodation character may be shown by oral proof.

(4) An indorsement which shows that it is not in the chain of title is notice of its accommodation character.

(5) An accommodation party is not liable to the party accommodated, and if he pays the instrument has a right of recourse on the instrument against such party.

§ 3-416. Contract of Guarantor.

(1) "Payment guaranteed" or equivalent words added to a signature mean that the signer engages that if the instrument is not paid when due he will pay it according to its tenor without resort by the holder to any other party.

(2) "Collection guaranteed" or equivalent words added to a signature mean that the signer engages that if the instrument is not paid when due he will pay it according to its tenor, but only after the holder has reduced his claim against the maker or acceptor to judgment and execution has been returned unsatisfied, or after the maker or acceptor has become insolvent or it is otherwise apparent that it is useless to proceed against him.

(3) Words of guaranty which do not otherwise specify guarantee payment.

(4) No words of guaranty added to the signature of a sole maker or acceptor affect his liability on the instrument. Such words added to the signature of one of two or more makers or acceptors create a presumption that the signature is for the accommodation of the others.

(5) When words of guaranty are used presentment, notice of dishonor and protest are not necessary to charge the user.

(6) Any guaranty written on the instrument is enforcible notwithstanding any statute of frauds.

§ 3-417. Warranties on Presentment and Transfer.

(1) Any person who obtains payment or acceptance and any prior transferor warrants to a person who in good faith pays or accepts that

(a)   he has a good title to the instrument or is authorized to obtain payment or acceptance on behalf of one who has a good title; and

(b)   he has no knowledge that the signature of the maker or drawer is unauthorized, except that this warranty is not given by a holder in due course acting in good faith

   (i)   to a maker with respect to the maker's own signature; or

   (ii) to a drawer with respect to the drawer's own signature, whether or not the drawer is also the drawee; or

   (iii) to an acceptor of a draft if the holder in due course took the draft after the acceptance or obtained the acceptance without knowledge and the drawer's signature was unauthorized; and

(c)   the instrument has not been materially altered, except that this warranty is not given by a holder in due course acting in good faith

   (i)   to the maker of a note; or

   (ii) to the drawer of a draft whether or not the drawer is also the drawee; or

   (iii) to the acceptor of a draft with respect to an alteration made prior to the acceptance if the holder in due course took the draft after the acceptance, even though the acceptance provided "payable as originally drawn" or equivalent terms; or

   (iv) to the acceptor of a draft with respect to an alteration made after the acceptance.

(2) Any person who transfers an instrument and receives consideration warrants to his transferee and if the transfer is by indorsement to any subsequent holder who takes the instrument in good faith that

(a)   he has a good title to the instrument or is authorized to obtain payment or acceptance on behalf of one who has a good title and the transfer is otherwise rightful; and

(b)   all signatures are genuine or authorized; and

(c)   the instrument has not been materially altered; and

(d)   no defense of any party is good against him; and

(e)   he has no knowledge of any insolvency proceeding instituted with respect to the maker or acceptor or the drawer of an unaccepted instrument.

(3) By transferring "without recourse" the transferor limits the obligation stated in subsection (2) (d) to a warranty that he has no knowledge of such a defense.

(4) A selling agent or broker who does not disclose the fact that he is acting only as such gives the warranties provided in this section, but if he makes such disclosure warrants only his good faith and authority.

§ 3-418. **Finality of Payment or Acceptance.**   Except for recovery of bank payments as provided in the Article on Bank Deposits and Collections (Article 4) and except for liability for breach of warranty on presentment under the preceding section, payment or acceptance of any instrument is final in favor of a holder in due course, or a person who has in good faith changed his position in reliance on the payment.

§ 3-419. **Conversion of Instrument; Innocent Representative.**

(1) An instrument is converted when
(a)   a drawee to whom it is delivered for acceptance refuses to return it on demand; or
(b)   any person to whom it is delivered for payment refuses on demand either to pay or to return it; or
(c)   it is paid on a forged indorsement.

(2) In an action against a drawee under subsection (1) the measure of the drawee's liability is the face amount of the instrument. In any other action under subsection (1) the measure of liability is presumed to be the face amount of the instrument.

(3) Subject to the provisions of this Act concerning restrictive indorsements a representative, including a depositary or collecting bank, who has in good faith and in accordance with the reasonable commercial standards applicable to the business of such representative dealt with an instrument or its proceeds on behalf of one who was not the true owner is not liable in conversion or otherwise to the true owner beyond the amount of any proceeds remaining in his hands.

(4) An intermediary bank or payor bank which is not a depositary bank is not liable in conversion solely by reason of the fact that proceeds of an item

indorsed restrictively (Sections 3-205 and 3-206) are not paid or applied consistently with the restrictive indorsement of an indorser other than its immediate transferor.

Part 5. Presentment, Notice of Dishonor and Protest

§ 3-501. **When Presentment, Notice of Dishonor, and Protest Necessary or Permissible.**

(1) Unless excused (Section 3-511) presentment is necessary to charge secondary parties as follows:
(a)   presentment for acceptance is necessary to charge the drawer and indorsers of a draft where the draft so provides, or is payable elsewhere than at the residence or place of business of the drawee, or its date of payment depends upon such presentment. The holder may at his option present for acceptance any other draft payable at a stated date;
(b)   presentment for payment is necessary to charge any indorser;
(c)   in the case of any drawer, the acceptor of a draft payable at a bank or the maker of a note payable at a bank, presentment for payment is necessary, but failure to make presentment discharges such drawer, acceptor or maker only as stated in Section 3-502(1) (b).

(2) Unless excused (Section 3-511)
(a)   notice of any dishonor is necessary to charge any indorser;
(b)   in the case of any drawer, the acceptor of a draft payable at a bank or the maker of a note payable at a bank, notice of any dishonor is necessary, but failure to give such notice discharges such drawer, acceptor or maker only as stated in Section 3-502(1) (b).

(3) Unless excused (Section 3-511) protest of any dishonor is necessary to charge the drawer and indorsers of any draft which on its face appears to be drawn or payable outside of the states, territories, dependencies and possessions of the United States, the District of Columbia and the Commonwealth of Puerto Rico. The holder may at his option make protest of any dishonor of any other instrument and in the case of a foreign draft may on insolvency of the acceptor before maturity make protest for better security.

(4) Notwithstanding any provision of this section,

neither presentment nor notice of dishonor nor protest is necessary to charge an indorser who has indorsed an instrument after maturity.

§ 3-502. Unexcused Delay; Discharge.

(1) Where without excuse any necessary presentment or notice of dishonor is delayed beyond the time when it is due

(a) any indorser is discharged; and

(b) any drawer or the acceptor of a draft payable at a bank or the maker of a note payable at a bank who because the drawee or payor bank becomes insolvent during the delay is deprived of funds maintained with the drawee or payor bank to cover the instrument may discharge his liability by written assignment to the holder of his rights against the drawee or payor bank in respect of such funds, but such drawer, acceptor or maker is not otherwise discharged.

(2) Where without excuse a necessary protest is delayed beyond the time when it is due any drawer or indorser is discharged.

§ 3-503. Time of Presentment.

(1) Unless a different time is expressed in the instrument the time for any presentment is determined as follows:

(a) where an instrument is payable at or a fixed period after a stated date any presentment for acceptance must be made on or before the date it is payable;

(b) where an instrument is payable after sight it must either be presented for acceptance or negotiated within a reasonable time after date or issue whichever is later;

(c) where an instrument shows the date on which it is payable presentment for payment is due on that date;

(d) where an instrument is accelerated presentment for payment is due within a reasonable time after the acceleration;

(e) with respect to the liability of any secondary party presentment for acceptance or payment of any other instrument is due within a reasonable time after such party becomes liable thereon.

(2) A reasonable time for presentment is determined by the nature of the instrument, any usage of banking or trade and the facts of the particular case.

In the case of an uncertified check which is drawn and payable within the United States and which is not a draft drawn by a bank the following are presumed to be reasonable periods within which to present for payment or to initiate bank collection:

(a) with respect to the liability of the drawer, thirty days after date or issue whichever is later; and

(b) with respect to the liability of an indorser, seven days after his indorsement.

(3) Where any presentment is due on a day which is not a full business day for either the person making presentment or the party to pay or accept, presentment is due on the next following day which is a full business day for both parties.

(4) Presentment to be sufficient must be made at a reasonable hour, and if at a bank during its banking day.

§ 3-504. How Presentment Made.

(1) Presentment is a demand for acceptance or payment made upon the maker, acceptor, drawee or other payor by or on behalf of the holder.

(2) Presentment may be made

(a) by mail, in which event the time of presentment is determined by the time of receipt of the mail; or

(b) through a clearing house; or

(c) at the place of acceptance or payment specified in the instrument or if there be none at the place of business or residence of the party to accept or pay. If neither the party to accept or pay nor anyone authorized to act for him is present or accessible at such place presentment is excused.

(3) It may be made

(a) to any one of two or more makers, acceptors, drawees or other payors; or

(b) to any person who has authority to make or refuse the acceptance or payment.

(4) A draft accepted or a note made payable at a bank in the United States must be pressnted at such bank.

(5) In the cases described in Section 4-210 presentment may be made in the manner and with the result stated in that section.

§ 3-505. Rights of Party to Whom Presentment Is Made.

(1) The party to whom presentment is made may without dishonor require

(a) exhibition of the instrument; and

(b) reasonable identification of the person making presentment and evidence of his authority to make it if made for another; and

(c) that the instrument be produced for acceptance or payment at a place specified in it, or if there be none at any place reasonable in the circumstances; and

(d) a signed receipt on the instrument for any partial or full payment and its surrender upon full payment.

(2) Failure to comply with any such requirement invalidates the presentment but the person presenting has a reasonable time in which to comply and the time for acceptance or payment runs from the time of compliance.

§ 3-506. Time Allowed for Acceptance or Payment.

(1) Acceptance may be deferred without dishonor until the close of the next business day following presentment. The holder may also in a good faith effort to obtain acceptance and without either dishonor of the instrument or discharge of secondary parties allow postponement of acceptance for an additional business day.

(2) Except as a longer time is allowed in the case of documentary drafts drawn under a letter of credit, and unless an earlier time is agreed to by the party to pay, payment of an instrument may be deferred without dishonor pending reasonable examination to determine whether it is properly payable, but payment must be made in any event before the close of business on the day of presentment.

§ 3-507. Dishonor; Holder's Right of Recourse; Term Allowing Re-Presentment.

(1) An instrument is dishonored when

(a) a necessary or optional presentment is duly made and due acceptance or payment is refused or cannot be obtained within the prescribed time or in case of bank collections the instrument is seasonably returned by the midnight deadline (Section 4-301); or

(b) presentment is excused and the instrument is not duly accepted or paid.

(2) Subject to any necessary notice of dishonor and protest, the holder has upon dishonor an immediate right of recourse against the drawers and indorsers.

(3) Return of an instrument for lack of proper indorsement is not dishonor.

(4) A term in a draft or an indorsement thereof allowing a stated time for re-presentment in the event of any dishonor of the draft by nonacceptance of a time draft or by nonpayment if a sight draft gives the holder as against any secondary party bound by the term an option to waive the dishonor without affecting the liability of the secondary party and he may present again up to the end of the stated time.

§ 3-508. Notice of Dishonor.

(1) Notice of dishonor may be given to any person who may be liable on the instrument by or on behalf of the holder or any party who has himself received notice, or any other party who can be compelled to pay the instrument. In addition an agent or bank in whose hands the instrument is dishonored may give notice to his principal or customer or to another agent or bank from which the instrument was received.

(2) Any necessary notice must be given by a bank before its midnight deadline and by any other person before midnight of the third business day after dishonor or receipt of notice of dishonor.

(3) Notice may be given in any reasonable manner. It may be oral or written and in any terms which identify the instrument and state that it has been dishonored. A misdescription which does not mislead the party notified does not vitiate the notice. Sending the instrument bearing a stamp, ticket or writing stating that acceptance or payment has been refused or sending a notice of debit with respect to the instrument is sufficient.

(4) Written notice is given when sent although it is not received.

(5) Notice to one partner is notice to each although the firm has been dissolved.

(6) When any party is in insolvency proceedings instituted after the issue of the instrument notice may be given either to the party or to the representative of his estate.

(7) When any party is dead or incompetent notice may be sent to his last known address or given to his personal representative.

(8) Notice operates for the benefit of all parties who have rights on the instrument against the party notified.

§ 3-509. Protest; Noting for Protest.

(1) A protest is a certificate of dishonor made under the hand and seal of a United States consul or

vice consul or a notary public or other person authorized to certify dishonor by the law of the place where dishonor occurs. It may be made upon information satisfactory to such person.

(2) The protest must identify the instrument and certify either that due presentment has been made or the reason why it is excused and that the instrument has been dishonored by nonacceptance or nonpayment.

(3) The protest may also certify that notice of dishonor has been given to all parties or to specified parties.

(4) Subject to subsection (5) any necessary protest is due by the time that notice of dishonor is due.

(5) If, before protest is due, an instrument has been noted for protest by the officer to make protest, the protest may be made at any time thereafter as of the date of the noting.

§ 3-510. Evidence of Dishonor and Notice of Dishonor.
The following are admissible as evidence and create a presumption of dishonor and of any notice of dishonor therein shown:

(a)   a document regular in form as provided in the preceding section which purports to be a protest;

(b)   the purported stamp or writing of the drawee, payor bank or presenting bank on the instrument or accompanying it stating that acceptance or payment has been refused for reasons consistent with dishonor;

(c)   any book or record of the drawee, payor bank, or any collecting bank kept in the usual course of business which shows dishonor, even though there is no evidence of who made the entry.

§ 3-511. Waived or Excused Presentment, Protest or Notice of Dishonor or Delay Therein.

(1) Delay in presentment, protest or notice of dishonor is excused when the party is without notice that it is due or when the delay is caused by circumstances beyond his control and he exercises reasonable diligence after the cause of the delay ceases to operate.

(2) Presentment or notice or protest as the case may be is entirely excused when

(a)   the party to be charged has waived it expressly or by implication either before or after it is due; or

(b)   such party has himself dishonored the instrument or has countermanded payment or otherwise has no reason to expect or right to require that the instrument be accepted or paid; or

(c)   by reasonable diligence the presentment or protest cannot be made or the notice given.

(3) Presentment is also entirely excused when

(a)   the maker, acceptor or drawee of any instrument except a documentary draft is dead or in insolvency proceedings instituted after the issue of the instrument; or

(b)   acceptance or payment is refused but not for want of proper presentment.

(4) Where a draft has been dishonored by nonacceptance a later presentment for payment and any notice of dishonor and protest for nonpayment are excused unless in the meantime the instrument has been accepted.

(5) A waiver of protest is also a waiver of presentment and of notice of dishonor even though protest is not required.

(6) Where a waiver of presentment or notice or protest is embodied in the instrument itself it is binding upon all parties; but where it is written above the signature of an indorser it binds him only.

Part 6. Discharge

§ 3-601. Discharge of Parties.

(1) The extent of the discharge of any party from liability on an instrument is governed by the sections on

(a)   payment or satisfaction (Section 3-603); or

(b)   tender of payment (Section 3-604); or

(c)   cancellation or renunciation (Section 3-605); or

(d)   impairment of right of recourse or of collateral (Section 3-606); or

(e)   reacquisition of the instrument by a prior party (section 3-208); or

(f)   fraudulent and material alteration (Section 3-407); or

(g)   certification of a check (Section 3-411); or

(h)   acceptance varying a draft (Section 3-412); or

(i)   unexcused delay in presentment or notice of dishonor or protest (Section 3-502).

(2) Any party is also discharged from his liability on an instrument to another party by any other act or

agreement with such party which would discharge his simple contract for the payment of money.

(3) The liability of all parties is discharged when any party who has himself no right of action or recourse on the instrument

    (a)   reacquires the instrument in his own right; or

    (b)   is discharged under any provision of this Article, except as otherwise provided with respect to discharge for impairment of recourse or of collateral (Section 3-606).

§ 3-602. Effect of Discharge Against Holder in Due Course.

No discharge of any party provided by this Article is effective against a subsequent holder in due course unless he has notice thereof when he takes the instrument.

§ 3-603. Payment or Satisfaction.

(1) The liability of any party is discharged to the extent of his payment or satisfaction to the holder even though it is made with knowledge of a claim of another person to the instrument unless prior to such payment or satisfaction the person making the claim either supplies indemnity deemed adequate by the party seeking the discharge or enjoins payment or satisfaction by order of a court of competent jurisdiction in an action in which the adverse claimant and the holder are parties. This subsection does not, however, result in the discharge of the liability

    (a)   of a party who in bad faith pays or satisfies a holder who acquired the instrument by theft or who (unless having the rights of a holder in due course) holds through one who so acquired it; or

    (b)   of a party (other than an intermediary bank or a payor bank which is not a depositary bank) who pays or satisfies the holder of an instrument which has been restrictively indorsed in a manner not consistent with the terms of such restrictive indorsement.

(2) Payment or satisfaction may be made with the consent of the holder by any person including a stranger to the instrument. Surrender of the instrument to such a person gives him the rights of a transferee (Section 3-201).

§ 3-604. Tender of Payment.

(1) Any party making tender of full payment to a holder when or after it is due is discharged to the extent of all subsequent liability for interest, costs and attorney's fees.

(2) The holder's refusal of such tender wholly discharges any party who has a right of recourse against the party making the tender.

(3) Where the maker or acceptor of an instrument payable otherwise than on demand is able and ready to pay at every place of payment specified in the instrument when it is due, it is equivalent to tender.

§ 3-605. Cancellation and Renunciation.

(1) The holder of an instrument may even without consideration discharge any party

    (a)   in any manner apparent on the face of the instrument or the indorsement, as by intentionally cancelling the instrument or the party's signature by destruction or mutilation, or by striking out the party's signature; or

    (b)   by renouncing his rights by a writing signed and delivered or by surrender of the instrument to the party to be discharged.

(2) Neither cancellation nor renunciation without surrender of the instrument affects the title thereto.

§ 3-606. Impairment of Recourse or of Collateral.

(1) The holder discharges any party to the instrument to the extent that without such party's consent the holder

    (a)   without express reservation of rights releases or agrees not to sue any person against whom the party has to the knowledge of the holder a right of recourse or agrees to suspend the right to enforce against such person the instrument or collateral or otherwise discharges such person, except that failure or delay in effecting any required presentment, protest or notice of dishonor with respect to any such person does not discharge any party as to whom presentment, protest or notice of dishonor is effective or unnecessary; or

    (b)   unjustifiably impairs any collateral for the instrument given by or on behalf of the party or any person against whom he has a right of recourse.

(2) By express reservation of rights against a party with a right of recourse the holder preserves

    (a)   all his rights against such party as of the

time when the instrument was originally due; and

(b) the right of the party to pay the instrument as of that time; and

(c) all rights of such party to recourse against others.

Part 7. Advice of International Sight Draft

§ 3-701. Letter of Advice of International Sight Draft.

(1) A "letter of advice" is a drawer's communication to the drawee that a described draft has been drawn.

(2) Unless otherwise agreed when a bank receives from another bank a letter of advice of an international sight draft that drawee bank may immediately debit the drawer's account and stop the running of interest pro tanto. Such a debit and any resulting credit to any account covering outstanding drafts leaves in the drawer full power to stop payment or otherwise dispose of the amount and creates no trust or interest in favor of the holder.

(3) Unless otherwise agreed and except where a draft is drawn under a credit issued by the drawee, the drawee of an international sight draft owes the drawer no duty to pay an unadvised draft but if it does so and the draft is genuine, may appropriately debit the drawer's account.

Part 8. Miscellaneous

§ 3-801. Drafts in a Set.

(1) Where a draft is drawn in a set of parts, each of which is numbered and expressed to be an order only if no other part has been honored, the whole of the parts constitutes one draft but a taker of any part may become a holder in due course of the draft.

(2) Any person who negotiates, indorses or accepts a single part of a draft drawn in a set thereby becomes liable to any holder in due course of that part as if it were the whole set, but as between different holders in due course to whom different parts have been negotiated the holder whose title first accrues has all rights to the draft and its proceeds.

(3) As against the drawee the first presented part of a draft drawn in a set is the part entitled to payment, or if a time draft to acceptance and payment. Acceptance of any subsequently presented part renders the drawee liable thereon under subsection (2). With respect both to a holder and to the drawer payment of a subsequently presented part of a draft payable at sight has the same effect as payment of a check

notwithstanding an effective stop order (Section 4-407).

(4) Except as otherwise provided in this section, where any part of a draft in a set is discharged by payment or otherwise the whole draft is discharged.

§ 3-802. Effect of Instrument on Obligation for Which It Is Given.

(1) Unless otherwise agreed where an instrument is taken for an underlying obligation

(a) the obligation is pro tanto discharged if a bank is drawer, maker or acceptor of the instrument and there is no recourse on the instrument against the underlying obligor; and

(b) in any other case the obligation is suspended pro tanto until the instrument is due or if it is payable on demand until its presentment. If the instrument is dishonored action may be maintained on either the instrument or the obligation; discharge of the underlying obligor on the instrument also discharges him on the obligation.

(2) The taking in good faith of a check which is not postdated does not of itself so extend the time on the original obligation as to discharge a surety.

§ 3-803. Notice to Third Party.

Where a defendant is sued for breach of an obligation for which a third person is answerable over under this Article he may give the third person written notice of the litigation, and the person notified may then give similar notice to any other person who is answerable over to him under this Article. If the notice states that the person notified may come in and defend and that if the person notified does not do so he will in any action against him by the person giving the notice be bound by any determination of fact common to the two litigations, then unless after seasonable receipt of the notice the person notified does come in and defend he is so bound.

§ 3-804. Lost, Destroyed or Stolen Instruments.

The owner of an instrument which is lost, whether by destruction, theft or otherwise, may maintain an action in his own name and recover from any party liable thereon upon due proof of his ownership, the facts which prevent his production of the instrument and its terms. The court may require security indemnifying the defendant against loss by reason of further claims on the instrument.

§ 3-805. Instruments Not Payable to Order or to Bearer. This Article applies to any instrument whose terms do not preclude transfer and which is otherwise negotiable within this Article but which is not payable to order or to bearer, except that there can be no holder in due course of such an instrument.

ARTICLE 4. BANK DEPOSITS AND COLLECTIONS

Part 1. General Provisions and Definitions

§ 4-101. Short Title. This Article shall be known and may be cited as Uniform Commercial Code—Bank Deposits and Collections.

§ 4-102. Applicability.

(1) To the extent that items within this Article are also within the scope of Articles 3 and 8, they are subject to the provisions of those Articles. In the event of conflict the provisions of this Article govern those of Article 3 but the provisions of Article 8 govern those of this Article.

(2) The liability of a bank for action or non-action with respect to any item handled by it for purposes of presentment, payment or collection is governed by the law of the place where the bank is located. In the case of action or non-action by or at a branch or separate office of a bank, its liability is governed by the law of the place where the branch or separate office is located.

§ 4-103. Variation by Agreement; Measure of Damages; Certain Action Constituting Ordinary Care.

(1) The effect of the provisions of this Article may be varied by agreement except that no agreement can disclaim a bank's responsibility for its own lack of good faith or failure to exercise ordinary care or can limit the measure of damages for such lack or failure; but the parties may by agreement determine the standards by which such responsibility is to be measured if such standards are not manifestly unreasonable.

(2) Federal Reserve regulations and operating letters, clearing house rules, and the like, have the effect of agreements under subsection (1), whether or not specifically assented to by all parties interested in items handled.

(3) Action or non-action approved by this Article or pursuant to Federal Reserve regulations or operating letters constitutes the exercise of ordinary care and, in the absence of special instructions, action or non-action consistent with clearing house rules and the like or with a general banking usage not disapproved by this Article, prima facie constitutes the exercise of ordinary care.

(4) The specification or approval of certain procedures by this Article does not constitute disapproval of other procedures which may be reasonable under the circumstances.

(5) The measure of damages for failure to exercise ordinary care in handling an item is the amount of the item reduced by an amount which could not have been realized by the use of ordinary care, and where there is bad faith it includes other damages, if any, suffered by the party as a proximate consequence.

§ 4-104. Definitions and Index of Definitions.

(1) In this Article unless the context otherwise requires

  (a) "Account" means any account with a bank and includes a checking, time, interest or savings account;

  (b) "Afternoon" means the period of a day between noon and midnight;

  (c) "Banking day" means that part of any day on which a bank is open to the public for carrying on substantially all of its banking functions;

  (d) "Clearing house" means any association of banks or other payors regularly clearing items;

  (e) "Customer" means any person having an account with a bank or for whom a bank has agreed to collect items and includes a bank carrying an account with another bank;

  (f) "Documentary draft" means any negotiable or non-negotiable draft with accompanying documents, securities or other papers to be delivered against honor of the draft;

  (g) "Item" means any instrument for the payment of money even though it is not negotiable but does not include money;

  (h) "Midnight deadline" with respect to a bank is midnight on its next banking day following the banking day on which it receives the relevant item or notice or from which the time for taking action commences to run, whichever is later;

  (i) "Properly payable" includes the availability of funds for payment at the time of decision to pay or dishonor;

(j)   "Settle" means to pay in cash, by clearing house settlement, in a charge or credit or by remittance, or otherwise as instructed. A settlement may be either provisional or final;

(k)   "Suspends payments" with respect to a bank means that it has been closed by order of the supervisory authorities, that a public officer has been appointed to take it over or that it ceases or refuses to make payments in the ordinary course of business.

(2) Other definitions applying to this Article and the sections in which they appear are:

"Collecting bank" Section 4-105.

"Depositary bank" Section 4-105.

"Intermediary bank" Section 4-105.

"Payor bank" Section 4-105.

"Presenting bank" Section 4-105.

"Remitting bank" Section 4-105.

(3) The following definitions in other Articles apply to this Article:

"Acceptance" Section 3-410.

"Certificate of deposit" Section 3-104.

"Certification" Section 3-411.

"Check" Section 3-104.

"Draft" Section 3-104.

"Holder in due course" Section 3-302.

"Notice of dishonor" Section 3-508.

"Presentment" Section 3-504.

"Protest" Section 3-509.

"Secondary party" Section 3-102.

(4) In addition Article 1 contains general definitions and principles of construction and interpretation applicable throughout this Article.

§ 4-105. "Depositary Bank"; "Intermediary Bank"; "Collecting Bank"; "Payor Bank"; "Presenting Bank"; "Remitting Bank."

In this Article unless the context otherwise requires:

(a)   "Depositary bank" means the first bank to which an item is transferred for collection even though it is also the payor bank;

(b)   "Payor bank" means a bank by which an item is payable as drawn or accepted;

(c)   "Intermediary bank" means any bank towhich an item is transferred in course of collection except the depositary or payor bank;

(d)   "Collecting bank" means any bank han-

dling the item for collection except the payor bank;

(e)   "Presenting bank" means any bank presenting an item except a payor bank;

(f)   "Remitting bank" means any payor or intermediary bank remitting for an item.

§ 4-106. Separate Office of a Bank.

A branch or separate office of a bank [maintaining its own deposit ledgers] is a separate bank for the purpose of computing the time within which and determining the place at or to which action may be taken or notices or orders shall be given under this Article and under Article 3.

Note: *The brackets are to make it optional with the several states whether to require a branch to maintain its own deposit ledgers in order to be considered to be a separate bank for certain purposes under Article 4. In some states "maintaining its own deposit ledgers" is a satisfactory test. In others branch banking practices are such that this test would not be suitable.*

§ 4-107. Time of Receipt of Items.

(1) For the purpose of allowing time to process items, prove balances and make the necessary entries on its books to determine its position for the day, a bank may fix an afternoon hour of 2 P.M. or later as a cut-off hour for the handling of money and items and the making of entries on its books.

(2) Any item or deposit of money received on any day after a cut-off hour so fixed or after the close of the banking day may be treated as being received at the opening of the next banking day.

§ 4-108. Delays.

(1) Unless otherwise instructed, a collecting bank in a good faith effort to secure payment may, in the case of specific items and with or without the approval of any person involved, waive, modify or extend time limits imposed or permitted by this Act for a period not in excess of an additional banking day without discharge of secondary parties and without liability to its transferor or any prior party.

(2) Delay by a collecting bank or payor bank beyond time limits prescribed or permitted by this Act or by instructions is excused if caused by interruption of communication facilities, suspension of payments by another bank, war, emergency conditions or other circumstances beyond the control of the bank provided it exercises such diligence as the circumstances require.

§ 4-109. **Process of Posting.** The "process of posting" means the usual procedure followed by a payor bank in determining to pay an item and in recording the payment including one or more of the following or other steps as determined by the bank:

(a) verification of any signature;

(b) ascertaining that sufficient funds are available;

(c) affixing a "paid" or other stamp;

(d) entering a charge or entry to a customer's account;

(e) correcting or reversing an entry or erroneous action with respect to the item.

Part 2. Collection of Items: Depositary and Collecting Banks

§ 4-201. **Presumption and Duration of Agency Status of Collecting Banks and Provisional Status of Credits; Applicability of Article; Item Indorsed "Pay Any Bank."**

(1) Unless a contrary intent clearly appears and prior to the time that a settlement given by a collecting bank for an item is or becomes final (subsection (3) of Section 4-211 and Sections 4-212 and 4-213) the bank is an agent or sub-agent of the owner of the item and any settlement given for the item is provisional. This provision applies regardless of the form of indorsement or lack of indorsement and even though credit given for the item is subject to immediate withdrawal as of right or is in fact withdrawn; but the continuance of ownership of an item by its owner and any rights of the owner to proceeds of the item are subject to rights of a collecting bank such as those resulting from outstanding advances on the item and valid rights of setoff. When an item is handled by banks for purposes of presentment, payment and collection, the relevant provisions of this Article apply even though action of parties clearly establishes that a particular bank has purchased the item and is the owner of it.

(2) After an item has been indorsed with the words "pay any bank" or the like, only a bank may acquire the rights of a holder

(a) until the item has been returned to the customer initiating collection; or

(b) until the item has been specially indorsed by a bank to a person who is not a bank.

§ 4-202. **Responsibility for Collection; When Action Seasonable.**

(1) A collecting bank must use ordinary care in

(a) presenting an item or sending it for presentment; and

(b) sending notice of dishonor or non-payment or returning an item other than a documentary draft to the bank's transferor [or directly to the depositary bank under subsection (2) of Section 4-212] (*see note to Section 4-212*) after learning that the item has not been paid or accepted, as the case may be; and

(c) settling for an item when the bank receives final settlement; and

(d) making or providing for any necessary protest; and

(e) notifying its transferor of any loss or delay in transit within a reasonable time after discovery thereof.

(2) A collecting bank taking proper action before its midnight deadline following receipt of an item, notice or payment acts seasonably; taking proper action within a reasonably longer time may be seasonable but the bank has the burden of so establishing.

(3) Subject to subsection (1) (a), a bank is not liable for the insolvency, neglect, misconduct, mistake or default of another bank or person or for loss or destruction of an item in transit or in the possession of others.

§ 4-203. **Effect of Instructions.** Subject to the provisions of Article 3 concerning conversion of instruments (Section 3-419) and the provisions of both Article 3 and this Article concerning restrictive indorsements only a collecting bank's transferor can give instructions which affect the bank or constitute notice to it and a collecting bank is not liable to prior parties for any action taken pursuant to such instructions or in accordance with any agreement with its transferor.

§ 4-204. **Methods of Sending and Presenting; Sending Direct to Payor Bank.**

(1) A collecting bank must send items by reasonably prompt method taking into consideration any relevant instructions, the nature of the item, the number of such items on hand, and the cost of collection involved and the method generally used by it or others to present such items.

(2) A collecting bank may send

(a) any item direct to the payor bank;

(b) any item to any non-bank payor if authorized by its transferor; and

(c)   any item other than documentary drafts to any non-bank payor, if authorized by Federal Reserve regulation or operating letter, clearing house rule or the like.

(3) Presentment may be made by a presenting bank at a place where the payor bank has requested that presentment be made.

§ 4-205. Supplying Missing Indorsement; No Notice from Prior Indorsement.

(1) A depositary bank which has taken an item for collection may supply any indorsement of the customer which is necessary to title unless the item contains the words "payee's indorsement required" or the like. In the absence of such a requirement a statement placed on the item by the depositary bank to the effect that the item was deposited by a customer or credited to his account is effective as the customer's indorsement.

(2) An intermediary bank, or payor bank which is not a depositary bank, is neither given notice nor otherwise affected by a restrictive indorsement of any person except the bank's immediate transferor.

§ 4-206. Transfer Between Banks.

Any agreed method which identifies the transferor bank is sufficient for the item's further transfer to another bank.

§ 4-207. Warranties of Customer and Collecting Bank on Transfer or Presentment of Items; Time for Claims.

(1) Each customer or collecting bank who obtains payment or acceptance of an item and each prior customer and collecting bank warrants to the payor bank or other payor who in good faith pays or accepts the item that

(a)   he has a good title to the item or is authorized to obtain payment or acceptance on behalf of one who has a good title; and

(b)   he has no knowledge that the signature of the maker or drawer is unauthorized, except that this warranty is not given by any customer or collecting bank that is a holder in due course and acts in good faith

(i)   to a maker with respect to the maker's own signature; or

(ii)   to a drawer with respect to the drawer's own signature, whether or not the drawer is also the drawee; or

(iii)   to an acceptor of an item if the holder in due course took the item after the acceptance or obtained the acceptance without knowledge that the drawer's signature was unauthorized; and

(c)   the item has not been materially altered, except that this warranty is not given by any customer or collecting bank that is a holder in due course and acts in good faith

(i)   to the maker of a note; or

(ii)   to the drawer of a draft whether or not the drawer is also the drawee; or

(iii)   to the acceptor of an item with respect to an alteration made prior to the acceptance if the holder in due course took the item after the acceptance, even though the acceptance provided "payable as originally drawn" or equivalent terms; or

(iv)   to the acceptor of an item with respect to an alteration made after the acceptance.

(2) Each customer and collecting bank who transfers an item and receives a settlement or other consideration for it warrants to his transferee and to any subsequent collecting bank who takes the item in good faith that

(a)   he has a good title to the item or is authorized to obtain payment or acceptance on behalf of one who has a good title and the transfer is otherwise rightful; and

(b)   all signatures are genuine or authorized; and

(c)   the item has not been materially altered; and

(d)   no defense of any party is good against him; and

(e)   he has no knowledge of any insolvency proceeding instituted with respect to the maker or acceptor or the drawer of an unaccepted item.

In addition each customer and collecting bank so transferring an item and receiving a settlement or other consideration engages that upon dishonor and any necessary notice of dishonor and protest he will take up the item.

(3) The warranties and the engagement to honor set forth in the two preceding subsections arise notwithstanding the absence of indorsement or words of guaranty or warranty in the transfer or present-

ment and a collecting bank remains liable for their breach despite remittance to its transferor. Damages for breach of such warranties or engagement to honor shall not exceed the consideration received by the customer or collecting bank responsible plus finance charges and expenses related to the item, if any.

(4) Unless a claim for breach of warranty under this section is made within a reasonable time after the person claiming learns of the breach, the person liable is discharged to the extent of any loss caused by the delay in making claim.

§ 4-208. Security Interest of Collecting Bank in Items, Accompanying Documents and Proceeds.

(1) A bank has a security interest in an item and any accompanying documents or the proceeds of either

    (a)   in case of an item deposited in an account to the extent to which credit given for the item has been withdrawn or applied;

    (b)   in case of an item for which it has given credit available for withdrawal as of right, to the extent of the credit given whether or not the credit is drawn upon and whether or not there is a right of charge-back; or

    (c)   if it makes an advance on or against the item.

(2) When credit which has been given for several items received at one time or pursuant to a single agreement is withdrawn or applied in part the security interest remains upon all the items, any accompanying documents or the proceeds of either. For the purpose of this section, credits first given are first withdrawn.

(3) Receipt by a collecting bank of a final settlement for an item is a realization on its security interest in the item, accompanying documents and proceeds. To the extent and so long as the bank does not receive final settlement for the item or give up possession of the item or accompanying documents for purposes other than collection, the security interest continues and is subject to the provisions of Article 9 except that

    (a)   no security agreement is necessary to make the security interest enforceable (subsection (1)(a) of Section 9-203); and

    (b)   no filing is required to perfect the security interest; and

    (c)   the security interest has priority over conflicting perfected security interests in the item, accompanying documents or proceeds.

§ 4-209. When Bank Gives Value for Purposes of Holder in Due Course.

For purposes of determining its status as a holder in due course, the bank has given value to the extent that it has a security interest in an item provided that the bank otherwise complies with the requirements of Section 3-302 on what constitutes a holder in due course.

§ 4-210. Presentment by Notice of Item Not Payable by, Through or at a Bank; Liability of Secondary Parties.

(1) Unless otherwise instructed, a collecting bank may present an item not payable by, through or at a bank by sending to the party to accept or pay a written notice that the bank holds the item for acceptance or payment. The notice must be sent in time to be received on or before the day when presentment is due and the bank must meet any requirement of the party to accept or pay under Section 3-505 by the close of the bank's next banking day after it knows of the requirement.

(2) Where presentment is made by notice and neither honor nor request for compliance with a requirement under Section 3-505 is received by the close of business on the day after maturity or in the case of demand items by the close of business on the third banking day after notice was sent, the presenting bank may treat the item as dishonored and charge any secondary party by sending him notice of the facts.

§ 4-211. Media of Remittance; Provisional and Final Settlement in Remittance Cases.

(1) A collecting bank may take in settlement of an item

    (a)   a check of the remitting bank or of another bank on any bank except the remitting bank; or

    (b)   a cashier's check or similar primary obligation of a remitting bank which is a member of or clears through a member of the same clearing house or group as the collecting bank; or

    (c)   appropriate authority to charge an account of the remitting bank or of another bank with the collecting bank; or

    (d)   if the item is drawn upon or payable by a person other than a bank, a cashier's check, certified check or other bank check or obligation.

(2) If before its midnight deadline the collecting bank properly dishonors a remittance check or authorization to charge on itself or presents or forwards for collection a remittance instrument of or on another bank which is of a kind approved by subsection (1) or has not been authorized by it, the collecting bank is not liable to prior parties in the event of the dishonor of such check, instrument or authorization.

(3) A settlement for an item by means of a remittance instrument or authorization to charge is or becomes a final settlement as to both the person making and the person receiving the settlement

    (a) if the remittance instrument or authorization to charge is of a kind approved by subsection (1) or has not been authorized by the person receiving the settlement and in either case the person receiving the settlement acts seasonally before its midnight deadline in presenting, forwarding for collection or paying the instrument or authorization—at the time the remittance instrument or authorization is finally paid by the payor by which it is payable;

    (b) if the person receiving the settlement has authorized remittance by a non-bank check or obligation or by a cashier's check or similar primary obligation of or a check upon the payor or other remitting bank which is not of a kind approved by subsection (1) (b),—at the time of the receipt of such remittance check or obligation; or

    (c) if in a case not covered by sub-paragraphs (a) or (b) the person receiving the settlement fails to seasonably present, forward for collection, pay or return a remittance instrument or authorization to it to charge before its midnight deadlind,—at such midnight deadline.

§ 4-212. Right of Charge-Back or Refund.

(1) If a collecting bank has made provisional settlement with its customer for an item and itself fails by reason of dishonor, suspension of payments by a bank or otherwise to receive a settlement for the item which is or becomes final, the bank may revoke the settlement given by it, charge back the amount of any credit given for the item to its customer's account or

obtain refund from its customer whether or not it is able to return the items if by its midnight deadline or within a longer reasonable time after it learns the facts it returns the item or sends notification of the facts. These rights to revoke, charge-back and obtain refund terminate if and when a settlement for the item received by the bank is or becomes final (subsection (3) of Section 4-211 and subsections (2) and (3) of Section 4-213).

[(2) Within the time and manner prescribed by this section and Section 4-301, an intermediary or payor bank, as the case may be, may return an unpaid item directly to the depositary bank and may send for collection a draft on the depositary bank and obtain reimbursement. In such case, if the depositary bank has received provisional settlement for the item, it must reimburse the bank drawing the draft and any provisional credits for the item between banks shall become and remain final.]

Note: *Direct returns is recognized as an innovation that is not yet established bank practice, and therefore, Paragraph 2 has been bracketed. Some lawyers have doubts whether it should be included in legislation or left to development by agreement.*

(3) A depositary bank which is also the payor may charge-back the amount of an item to its customer's account or obtain refund in accordance with the section governing return of an item received by a payor bank for credit on its books. (Section 4-301).

(4) The right to charge-back is not affected by

    (a) prior use of the credit given for the item; or

    (b) failure by any bank to exercise ordinary care with respect to the item but any bank so failing remains liable.

(5) A failure to charge-back or claim refund does not affect other rights of the bank against the customer or any other party.

(6) If credit is given in dollars as the equivalent of the value of an item payable in a foreign currency the dollar amount of any charge-back or refund shall be calculated on the basis of the buying sight rate for the foreign currency prevailing on the day when the person entitled to the charge-back or refund learns that it will not receive payment in ordinary course.

§ 4-213. Final Payment of Item by Payor Bank; When Provisional Debits and Credits Become Final; When Certain Credits Become Available for Withdrawal.

(1) An item is finally paid by a payor bank when

the bank has done any of the following, whichever happens first:

(a)   paid the item in cash; or

(b)   settled for the item without reserving a right to revoke the settlement and without having such right under statute, clearing house rule or agreement; or

(c)   completed the process of posting the item to the indicated account of the drawer, maker or other person to be charged therewith; or

(d)   made a provisional settlement for the item and failed to revoke the settlement in the time and manner permitted by statute, clearing house rule or agreement.

Upon a final payment under subparagraphs (b), (c) or (d) the payor bank shall be accountable for the amount of the item.

(2) If provisional settlement for an item between the presenting and payor banks is made through a clearing house or by debits or credits in an account between them, then to the extent that provisional debits or credits for the item are entered in accounts between the presenting and payor banks or between the presenting and successive prior collecting banks seriatim, they become final upon final payment of the item by the payor bank.

(3) If a collecting bank receives a settlement for an item which is or becomes final (subsection (3) of Section 4-211, subsection (2) of Section 4-213) the bank is accountable to its customer for the amount of the item and any provisional credit given for the item in an account with its customer becomes final.

(4) Subject to any right of the bank to apply the credit to an obligation of the customer, credit given by a bank for an item in an account with its customer becomes available for withdrawal as of right

(a)   in any case where the bank has received a provisional settlement for the item,— when such settlement becomes final and the bank has had a reasonable time to learn that the settlement is final;

(b)   in any case where the bank is both a depositary bank and a payor bank and the item is finally paid,—at the opening of the bank's second banking day following receipt of the item.

(5) A deposit of money in a bank is final when made but, subject to any right of the bank to apply the deposit to an obligation of the customer, the deposit becomes available for withdrawal as of right at the opening of the bank's next banking day following receipt of the deposit.

§ 4-214. Insolvency and Preference.

(1) Any item in or coming into the possession of a payor or collecting bank which suspends payment and which item is not finally paid shall be returned by the receiver, trustee or agent in charge of the closed bank to the presenting bank or the closed bank's customer.

(2) If a payor bank finally pays an item and suspends payments without making a settlement for the item with its customer or the presenting bank which settlement is or becomes final, the owner of the item has a preferred claim against the payor bank.

(3) If a payor bank gives or a collecting bank gives or receives a provisional settlement for an item and thereafter suspends payments, the suspension does not prevent or interfere with the settlement becoming final if such finality occurs automatically upon the lapse of certain time or the happening of certain events (subsection (3) of Section 4-211, subsections (1) (d), (2) and (3) of Section 4-213).

(4) If a collecting bank receives from subsequent parties settlement for an item which settlement is or becomes final and suspends payments without making a settlement for the item with its customer which is or becomes final, the owner of the item has a preferred claim against such collecting bank.

Part 3. Collection of Items: Payor Banks

§ 4-301. Deferred Posting; Recovery of Payment by Return of Items; Time of Dishonor.

(1) Where an authorized settlement for a demand item (other than a documentary draft) received by a payor bank otherwise than for immediate payment over the counter has been made before midnight of the banking day of receipt the payor bank may revoke the settlement and recover any payment if before it has made final payment (subsection (1) of Section 4-213) and before its midnight deadline it

(a)   returns the item; or

(b)   sends written notice of dishonor or nonpayment if the item is held for protest or is otherwise unavailable for return.

(2) If a demand item is received by a payor bank for credit on its books it may return such item or send notice of dishonor and may revoke any credit given or recover the amount thereof withdrawn by its customer, if it acts within the time limit and in the manner specified in the preceding subsection.

(3) Unless previous notice of dishonor has been sent an item is dishonored at the time when for purposes of dishonor it is returned or notice sent in accordance with this section.

(4) An item is returned:

    (a)   as to an item received through a clearing house, when it is delivered to the presenting or last collecting bank or to the clearing house or is sent or delivered in accordance with its rules; or

    (b)   in all other cases, when it is sent or delivered to the bank's customer or transferor or pursuant to his instructions.

§ 4-302. Payor Bank's Responsibility for Late Return of Item.

In the absence of a valid defense such as breach of a presentment warranty (subsection (1) of Section 4-207), settlement effected or the like, if an item is presented on and received by a payor bank the bank is accountable for the amount of

    (a)   a demand item other than a documentary draft whether properly payable or not if the bank, in any case where it is not also the depositary bank, retains the item beyond midnight of the banking day of receipt without settling for it or, regardless of whether it is also the depositary bank, does not pay or return the item or send notice of dishonor until after its midnight deadline; or

    (b)   any other properly payable item unless within the time allowed for acceptance or payment of that item the bank either accepts or pays the item or returns it and accompanying documents.

§ 4-303. When Items Subject to Notice, Stop-Order, Legal Process or Setoff; Order in Which Items May Be Charged or Certified.

(1) Any knowledge, notice or stop-order received by, legal process served upon or setoff exercised by a payor bank, whether or not effective under other rules of law to terminate, suspend or modify the bank's right or duty to pay an item or to charge its customer's account for the item, comes too late to so terminate, suspend or modify such right or duty if the knowledge, notice, stop-order or legal process is received or served and a reasonable time for the bank to act thereon expires or the setoff is exercised after the bank has done any of the following:

    (a)   accepted or certified the item;

    (b)   paid the item in cash;

    (c)   settled for the item without reserving a right to revoke the settlement and without having such right under statute, clearing house rule or agreement;

    (d)   completed the process of posting the item to the indicated account of the drawer, maker or other person to be charged therewith or otherwise has evidenced by examination of such indicated account and by action its decision to pay the item; or

    (e)   become accountable for the amount of the item under subsection (1) (d) of Section 4-213 and Section 4-302 dealing with the payor bank's responsibility for late return of items.

(2) Subject to the provisions of subsection (1) items may be accepted, paid, certified or charged to the indicated account of its customer in any order convenient to the bank.

Part 4. Relationship Between Payor Bank and its Customers

§ 4-401. When Bank May Charge Customer's Account.

(1) As against its customer, a bank may charge against his account any item which is otherwise properly payable from that account even though the charge creates an overdraft.

(2) A bank which in good faith makes payment to a holder may charge the indicated account of its customer according to

    (a)   the original tenor of his altered item; or

    (b)   the tenor of his completed item, even though the bank knows the item has been completed unless the bank has notice that the completion was improper.

§ 4-402. Bank's Liability to Customer for Wrongful Dishonor.

A payor bank is liable to its customer for damages proximately caused by the wrongful dishonor of an item. When the dishonor occurs through mistake liability is limited to actual damages proved. If so proximately caused and proved damages may include damages for an arrest or prosecution of the customer or other consequential damages. Whether any consequential damages are proximately caused by the wrongful dishonor is a question of fact to be determined in each case.

§ 4-403. Customer's Right to Stop Payment; Burden of Proof of Loss.

(1) A customer may by order to his bank stop payment of any item payable for his account but the order must be received at such time and in such manner as to afford the bank a reasonable opportunity to act on it prior to any action by the bank with respect to the item described in Section 4-303.

(2) An oral order is binding upon the bank only for fourteen calendar days unless confirmed in writing within that period. A written order is effective for only six months unless renewed in writing.

(3) The burden of establishing the fact and amount of loss resulting from the payment of an item contrary to a binding stop payment order is on the customer.

§ 4-404. Bank Not Obligated to Pay Check More Than Six Months Old.
A bank is under no obligation to a customer having a checking account to pay a check, other than a certified check, which is presented more than six months after its date, but it may charge its customer's account for a payment made thereafter in good faith.

§ 4-405. Death or Incompetence of Customer.

(1) A payor or collecting bank's authority to accept, pay or collect an item or to account for proceeds of its collection if otherwise effective is not rendered ineffective by incompetence of a customer of either bank existing at the time the item is issued or its collection is undertaken if the bank does not know of an adjudication of incompetence. Neither death nor incompetence of a customer revokes such authority to accept, pay, collect or account until the bank knows of the fact of death or of an adjudication of incompetence and has reasonable opportunity to act on it.

(2) Even with knowledge a bank may for 10 days after the date of death pay or certify checks drawn on or prior to that date unless ordered to stop payment by a person claiming an interest in the account.

§ 4-406. Customer's Duty to Discover and Report Unauthorized Signature or Alteration.

(1) When a bank sends to its customer a statement of account accompanied by items paid in good faith in support of the debit entries or holds the statement and items pursuant to a request for instructions of its customer or otherwise in a reasonable manner makes the statement and items available to the customer, the customer must exercise reasonable care and promptness to examine the statement and items to discover his unauthorized signature or any alteration on an item and must notify the bank promptly after discovery thereof.

(2) If the bank establishes that the customer failed with respect to an item to comply with the duties imposed on the customer by subsection (1) the customer is precluded from asserting against the bank.

   (a) his unauthorized signature or any alteration on the item if the bank also establishes that it suffered a loss by reason of such failure; and

   (b) an unauthorized signature or alteration by the same wrongdoer on any other item paid in good faith by the bank after the first item and statement was available to the customer for a reasonable period not exceeding fourteen calendar days and before the bank receives notification from the customer of any such unauthorized signature or alteration.

(3) The preclusion under subsection (2) does not apply if the customer establishes lack of ordinary care on the part of the bank in paying the item(s).

(4) Without regard to care or lack of care of either the customer or the bank a customer who does not within one year from the time the statement and items are made available to the customer (subsection (1)) discover and report his unauthorized signature or any alteration on the face or back of the item or does not within 3 years from that time discover and report any unauthorized indorsement is precluded from asserting against the bank such unauthorized signature or indorsement or such alteration.

(5) If under this section a payor bank has a valid defense against a claim of a customer upon or resulting from payment of an item and waives or fails upon request to assert the defense the bank may not assert against any collecting bank or other prior party presenting or transferring the item a claim based upon the unauthorized signature or alteration giving rise to the customer's claim.

§ 4-407. Payor Bank's Right to Subrogation on Improper Payment.
If a payor bank has paid an item over the stop payment order of the drawer or maker or otherwise under circumstances giving a basis for objection by the drawer or maker, to prevent unjust enrichment and only to the extent necessary

to prevent loss to the bank by reason of its payment of the item, the payor bank shall be subrogated to the rights

(a) of any holder in due course on the item against the drawer or maker; and

(b) of the payee or any other holder of the item against the drawer or maker either on the item or under the transaction out of which the item arose; and

(c) of the drawer or maker against the payee or any other holder of the item with respect to the transaction out of which the item arose.

Part 5. Collection of Documentary Drafts

§ 4-501. Handling of Documentary Drafts; Duty to Send for Presentment and to Notify Customer of Dishonor. A bank which takes a documentary draft for collection must present or send the draft and accompanying documents for presentment and upon learning that the draft has not been paid or accepted in due course must seasonably notify its customer of such fact even though it may have discounted or bought the draft or extended credit available for withdrawal as of right.

§ 4-502. Presentment of "On Arrival" Drafts. When a draft or the relevant instructions require presentment "on arrival," "When goods arrive" or the like, the collecting bank need not present until in its judgment a reasonable time for arrival of the goods has expired. Refusal to pay or accept because the goods have not arrived is not dishonor; the bank must notify its transferor of such refusal but need not present the draft again until it is instructed to do so or learns of the arrival of the goods.

§ 4-503. Responsibility of Presenting Bank for Documents and Goods; Report of Reasons for Dishonor; Referee in Case of Need. Unless otherwise instructed and except as provided in Article 5 a bank presenting a documentary draft

(a) must deliver the documents to the drawee on acceptance of the draft if it is payable more than three days after presentment; otherwise, only on payment; and

(b) upon dishonor, either in the case of presentment for acceptance or presentment for payment, may seek and follow in-

structions from any referee in case of need designated in the draft or if the presenting bank does not choose to utilize his services it must use diligence and good faith to ascertain the reason for dishonor, must notify its transferor of the dishonor and of the results of its effort to ascertain the reasons therefor and must request instructions.

But the presenting bank is under no obligation with respect to goods represented by the documents except to follow any reasonable instructions seasonably received; it has a right to reimbursement for any expense incurred in following instructions and to prepayment of or indemnity for such expenses.

§ 4-504. Privilege of Presenting Bank to Deal With Goods; Security Interest for Expenses.

(1) A presenting bank which, following the dishonor of a documentary draft, has seasonably requested instructions but does not receive them within a reasonable time may store, sell, or otherwise deal with the goods in any reasonable manner.

(2) For its reasonable expenses incurred by action under subsection (1) the presenting bank has a lien upon the goods or their proceeds, which may be foreclosed in the same manner as an unpaid seller's lien.

ARTICLE 5. LETTERS OF CREDIT

§ 5-101. Short Title. This Article shall be known and may be cited as Uniform Commercial Code—Letters of Credit.

§ 5-102. Scope.

(1) This Article applies

(a) to a credit issued by a bank if the credit requires a documentary draft or a documentary demand for payment; and

(b) to a credit issued by a person other than a bank if the credit requires that the draft or demand for payment be accompanied by a document of title; and

(c) to a credit issued by a bank or other person if the credit is not within subparagraphs (a) or (b) but conspicuously states that it is a letter of credit or is conspicuously so entitled.

(2) Unless the engagement meets the requirements of subsection (1), this Article does not apply to engagements to make advances or to honor drafts or

demands for payment, to authorities to pay or purchase, to guarantees or to general agreements.

(3) This Article deals with some but not all of the rules and concepts of letters of credit as such rules or concepts have developed prior to this act or may hereafter develop. The fact that this Article states a rule does not by itself require, imply or negate application of the same or a converse rule to a situation not provided for or to a person not specified by this Article.

§ 5-103. Definitions.

(1) In this Article unless the context otherwise requires

(a) "Credit" or "letter of credit" means an engagement by a bank or other person made at the request of a customer and of a kind within the scope of this Article (Section 5-102) that the issuer will honor drafts or other demands for payment upon compliance with the conditions specified in the credit. A credit may be either revocable or irrevocable. The engagement may be either an agreement to honor or a statement that the bank or other person is authorized to honor.

(b) A "documentary draft" or a "documentary demand for payment" is one honor of which is conditioned upon the presentation of a document or documents. "Document" means any paper including document of title, security, invoice, certificate, notice of default and the like.

(c) An "issuer" is a bank or other person issuing a credit.

(d) A "beneficiary" of a credit is a person who is entitled under its terms to draw or demand payment.

(e) An "advising bank" is a bank which gives notification of the issuance of a credit by another bank.

(f) A "confirming bank" is a bank which engages either that it will itself honor a credit already issued by another bank or that such credit will be honored by the issuer or a third bank.

(g) A "customer" is a buyer or other person who causes an issuer to issue a credit. The term also includes a bank which procures issuance or confirmation on behalf of that bank's customer.

(2) Other definitions applying to this Article and the sections in which they appeal are:

"Notation of Credit." Section 5-108.

"Presenter." Section 5-112(3).

(3) Definitions in other Articles applying to this Article and the sections in which they appear are:

"Accept" or "Acceptance." Section 3-410.

"Contract for sale." Section 2-106.

"Draft." Section 3-104.

"Holder in due course." Section 3-302.

"Midnight deadline." Section 4-104.

"Security." Section 8-102.

(4) In addition, Article 1 contains general definitions and principles of construction and interpretation applicable throughout this Article.

§ 5-104. Formal Requirements; Signing.

(1) Except as otherwise required in subsection (1) (c) of Section 5-102 on scope, no particular form of phrasing is required for a credit. A credit must be in writing and signed by the issuer and a confirmation must be in writing and signed by the confirming bank. A modification of the terms of a credit or confirmation must be signed by the issuer or confirming bank.

(2) A telegram may be a sufficient signed writing if it identifies its sender by an authorized authentication. The authentication may be in code and the authorized naming of the issuer in an advice of credit is a sufficient signing.

§ 5-105. Consideration. No consideration is necessary to establish a credit or to enlarge or otherwise modify its terms.

§ 5-106. Time and Effect of Establishment of Credit.

(1) Unless otherwise agreed a credit is established

(a) as regards the customer as soon as a letter of credit is sent to him or the letter of credit or an authorized written advice of its issuance is sent to the beneficiary; and

(b) as regards the beneficiary when he receives a letter of credit or an authorized written advice of its issuance.

(2) Unless otherwise agreed once an irrevocable credit is established as regards the customer it can be modified or revoked only with the consent of the customer and once it is established as regards the beneficiary it can be modified or revoked only with his consent.

(3) Unless otherwise agreed after a revocable

credit is established it may be modified or revoked by the issuer without notice to or consent from the customer or beneficiary.

(4) Notwithstanding any modification or revocation of a revocable credit any person authorized to honor or negotiate under the terms of the original credit is entitled to reimbursement for or honor of any draft or demand for payment duly honored or negotiated before receipt of notice of the modification or revocation and the issuer in turn is entitled to reimbursement from its customer.

§ 5-107. Advice of Credit; Confirmation; Error in Statement of Terms.

(1) Unless otherwise specified an advising bank by advising a credit issued by another bank does not assume any obligation to honor drafts drawn or demands for payment made under the credit but it does assume obligation for the accuracy of its own statement.

(2) A confirming bank by confirming a credit becomes directly obligated on the credit to the extent of its confirmation as though it were its issuer and acquires the rights of an issuer.

(3) Even though an advising bank incorrectly advises the terms of a credit it has been authorized to advise the credit is established as against the issuer to the extent of its original terms.

(4) Unless otherwise specified the customer bears as against the issuer all risks of transmission and reasonable translation or interpretation of any message relating to a credit.

§ 5-108. "Notation Credit"; Exhaustion of Credit.

(1) A credit which specifies that any person purchasing or paying drafts drawn or demands for payment made under it must note the amount of the draft or demand on the letter or advice of credit is a "notation credit."

(2) Under a notation credit
  (a) a person paying the beneficiary or purchasing a draft or demand for payment from him acquires a right to honor only if the appropriate notation is made and by transferring or forwarding for honor the documents under the credit such a person warrants to the issuer that the notation has been made; and
  (b) unless the credit or a signed statement that an appropriate notation has been made accompanies the draft or demand for payment the issuer may delay honor

until evidence of notation has been procured which is satisfactory to it but its obligation and that of its customer continue for a reasonable time not exceeding thirty days to obtain such evidence.

(3) If the credit is not a notation credit
  (a) the issuer may honor complying drafts or demands for payment presented to it in the order in which they are presented and is discharged pro tanto by honor of any such draft or demand;
  (b) as between competing good faith purchasers of complying drafts or demands the person first purchasing has priority over a subsequent purchaser even though the later purchased draft or demand has been first honored.

§ 5-109. Issuer's Obligation to Its Customer.

(1) An issuer's obligation to its customer includes good faith and observance of any general banking usage but unless otherwise agreed does not include liability or responsibility
  (a) for performance of the underlying contract for sale or other transaction between the customer and the beneficiary; or
  (b) for any act or omission of any person other than itself or its own branch or for loss or destruction of a draft, demand or document in transit or in the possession of others; or
  (c) based on knowledge or lack of knowledge of any usage of any particular trade.

(2) An issuer must examine documents with care so as to ascertain that on their face they appear to comply with the terms of the credit but unless otherwise agreed assumes no liability or responsibility for the genuineness, falsification or effect of any document which appears on such examination to be regular on its face.

(3) A non-bank issuer is not bound by any banking usage of which it has no knowledge.

§ 5-110. Availability of Credit in Portions; Presenter's Reservation of Lien or Claim.

(1) Unless otherwise specified a credit may be used in portions in the discretion of the beneficiary.

(2) Unless otherwise specified a person by presenting a documentary draft or demand for payment under a credit relinquishes upon its honor all claims to the documents and a person by transferring such draft or demand or causing such presentment au-

thorizes such relinquishment. An explicit reservation of claim makes the draft or demand non-complying.

§ 5-111. Warranties on Transfer and Presentment.

(1) Unless otherwise agreed the beneficiary by transferring or presenting a documentary draft or demand for payment warrants to all interested parties that the necessary conditions of the credit have been complied with. This is in addition to any warranties arising under Articles 3, 4, 7 and 8.

(2) Unless otherwise agreed a negotiating, advising, confirming, collecting or issuing bank presenting or transferring a draft or demand for payment under a credit warrants only the matters warranted by a collecting bank under Article 4 and any such bank transferring a document warrants only the matters warranted by an intermediary under Articles 7 and 8.

§ 5-112. Time Allowed for Honor or Rejection; Withholding Honor or Rejection by Consent; "Presenter."

(1) A bank to which a documentary draft or demand for payment is presented under a credit may without dishonor of the draft, demand or credit

    (a) defer honor until the close of the third banking day following receipt of the documents; and

    (b) further defer honor if the presenter has expressly or impliedly consented thereto.

Failure to honor within the time here specified constitutes dishonor of the draft or demand and of the credit [except as otherwise provided in subsection (4) of Section 5-114 on conditional payment].

Note: *The bracketed language in the last sentence of subsection (1) should be included only if the optional provisions of Section 5-114(4) and (5) are included.*

(2) Upon dishonor the bank may unless otherwise instructed fulfill its duty to return the draft or demand and the documents by holding them at the disposal of the presenter and sending him an advice to that effect.

(3) "Presenter" means any person presenting a draft or demand for payment for honor under a credit even though that person is a confirming bank or other correspondent which is acting under an issuer's authorization.

§ 5-113. Indemnities.

(1) A bank seeking to obtain (whether for itself or another) honor, negotiation or reimbursement under a credit may give an indemnity to induce such honor, negotiation or reimbursement.

(2) An indemnity agreement inducing honor, negotiation or reinbursement

    (a) unless otherwise explicitly agreed applies to defects in the documents but not in the goods; and

    (b) unless a longer time is explicitly agreed expires at the end of ten business days following receipt of the documents by the ultimate customer unless notice of objection is sent before such expiration date. The ultimate customer may send notice of objection to the person from whom he received the documents and any bank receiving such notice is under a duty to send notice to its transferor before its midnight deadline.

§ 5-114. Issuer's Duty and Privilege to Honor; Right to Reimbursement.

(1) An issuer must honor a draft or demand for payment which complies with the terms of the relevant credit regardless of whether the goods or documents conform to the underlying contract for sale or other contract between the customer and the beneficiary. The issuer is not excused from honor of such a draft or demand by reason of an additional general term that all documents must be satisfactory to the issuer, but an issuer may require that specified documents must be satisfactory to it.

(2) Unless otherwise agreed when documents appear on their face to comply with the terms of a credit but a required document does not in fact conform to the warranties made on negotiation or transfer of a document of title (Section 7-507) or of a certificated security (Section 8-306) or is forged or fraudulent or there is fraud in the transaction:

    (a) the issuer must honor the draft or demand for payment if honor is demanded by a negotiating bank or other holder of the draft or demand which has taken the draft or demand under the credit and under circumstances which would make it a holder in due course (Section 3-302) and in an appropriate case would make it a person to whom a document of title has been duly negotiated (Section 7-502) or a bona fide purchaser of a certificated security (Section 8-302); and

    (b) in all other cases as against its customer,

an issuer acting in good faith may honor the draft or demand for payment despite notification from the customer of fraud, forgery or other defect not apparent on the face of the documents but a court of appropriate jurisdiction may enjoin such honor.

(3) Unless otherwise agreed an issuer which has duly honored a draft or demand for payment is entitled to immediate reimbursement of any payment made under the credit and to be put in effectively available funds not later than the day before maturity of any acceptance made under the credit.

[(4) When a credit provides for payment by the issuer on receipt of notice that the required documents are in the possession of a correspondent or other agent of the issuer

    (a)   any payment made on receipt of such notice is conditional; and

    (b)   the issuer may reject documents which do not comply with the credit if it does so within three banking days following its receipt of the documents; and

    (c)   in the event of such rejection, the issuer is entitled by charge back or otherwise to return of the payment made.]

[(5) In the case covered by subsection (4) failure to reject documents within the time specified in subparagraph (b) constitutes acceptance of the documents and makes the payment final in favor of the beneficiary.]

Amended in 1977.

Note: *Subsections (4) and (5) are bracketed as optional. If they are included the bracketed language in the last sentence of Section 5-112(1) should also be included.*

§ 5-115. Remedy for Improper Dishonor or Anticipatory Repudiation.

(1) When an issuer wrongfully dishonors a draft or demand for payment presented under a credit the person entitled to honor has with respect to any documents the rights of a person in the position of a seller (Section 2-707) and may recover from the issuer the face amount of the draft or demand together with incidental damages under Section 2-710 on seller's incidental damages and interest but less any amount realized by resale or other use or disposition of the subject matter of the transaction. In the event no resale or other utilization is made the documents, goods or other subject matter involved in the transac-

tion must be turned over to the issuer on payment of judgment.

(2) When an issuer wrongfully cancels or otherwise repudiates a credit before presentment of a draft or demand for payment drawn under it the beneficiary has the rights of a seller after anticipatory repudiation by the buyer under Section 2-610 if he learns of the repudiation in time reasonably to avoid procurement of the required documents. Otherwise the beneficiary has an immediate right of action for wrongful dishonor.

§ 5-116. Transfer and Assignment.

(1) The right to draw under a credit can be transferred or assigned only when the credit is expressly designated as transferable or assignable.

(2) Even though the credit specifically states that it is non-transferable or nonassignable the beneficiary may before performance of the conditions of the credit assign his right to proceeds. Such an assignment is an assignment of an account under Article 9 on Secured Transactions and is governed by that Article except that

    (a)   the assignment is ineffective until the letter of credit or advice of credit is delivered to the assignee which delivery constitutes perfection of the security interest under Article 9; and

    (b)   the issuer may honor drafts or demands for payment drawn under the credit until it receives a notification of the assignment signed by the beneficiary which reasonably identifies the credit involved in the assignment and contains a request to pay the assignee; and

    (c)   after what reasonably appears to be such a notification has been received the issuer may without dishonor refuse to accept or pay even to a person otherwise entitled to honor until the letter of credit or advice of credit is exhibited to the issuer.

(3) Except where the beneficiary has effectively assigned his right to draw or his right to proceeds, nothing in this section limits his right to transfer or negotiate drafts or demands drawn under the credit.

§ 5-117. Insolvency of Bank Holding Funds for Documentary Credit.

(1) Where an issuer or an advising or confirming bank or a bank which has for a customer procured issuance of a credit by another bank becomes insolvent before final payment under the credit and the

credit is one to which this Article is made applicable by paragraphs (a) or (b) of Section 5-102(1) on scope, the receipt or allocation of funds or collateral to secure or meet obligations under the credit shall have the following results:

(a) to the extent of any funds or collateral turned over after or before the insolvency as indemnity against or specifically for the purpose of payment of drafts or demands for payment drawn under the designated credit, the drafts or demands are entitled to payment in preference over deposits or other general creditors of the issuer or bank; and

(b) on expiration of the credit or surrender of the beneficiary's rights under it unused any person who has given such funds or collateral is similarly entitled to return thereof; and

(c) a charge to a general or current account with a bank if specifically consented to for the purpose of indemnity against or payment of drafts or demands for payment drawn under the designated credit falls under the same rules as if the funds had been drawn out in cash and then turned over with specific instructions.

(2) After honor or reimbursement under this section the customer or other person for whose account the insolvent bank has acted is entitled to receive the documents involved.

ARTICLE 6. BULK TRANSFERS

§ 6-101. **Short Title.** This Article shall be known and may be cited as Uniform Commercial Code—Bulk Transfers.

§ 6-102. **"Bulk Transfers"; Transfers of Equipment; Enterprises Subject to This Article; Bulk Transfers Subject to This Article.**

(1) A "bulk transfer" is any transfer in bulk and not in the ordinary course of the transferor's business of a major part of the materials, supplies, merchandise or other inventory (Section 9-109) of an enterprise subject to this Article.

(2) A transfer of a substantial part of the equipment (Section 9-109) of such an enterprise is a bulk transfer if it is made in connection with a bulk transfer of inventory, but not otherwise.

(3) The enterprises subject to this Article are all

those whose principal business is the sale of merchandise from stock, including those who manufacture what they sell.

(4) Except as limited by the following section all bulk transfers of goods located within this state are subject to this Article.

§ 6-103. **Transfers Excepted From This Article.**
The following transfers are not subject to this Article:

(1) Those made to give security for the performance of an obligation;

(2) General assignments for the benefit of all the creditors of the transferor, and subsequent transfers by the assignee thereunder;

(3) Transfers in settlement or realization of a lien or other security interests;

(4) Sales by executors, administrators, receivers, trustees in bankruptcy, or any public officer under judicial process;

(5) Sales made in the course of judicial or administrative proceedings for the dissolution or reorganization of a corporation and of which notice is sent to the creditors of the corporation pursuant to order of the court or administrative agency;

(6) Transfers to a person maintaining a known place of business in this State who becomes bound to pay the debts of the transferor in full and gives public notice of that fact, and who is solvent after becoming so bound;

(7) A transfer to a new business enterprise organized to take over and continue the business, if public notice of the transaction is given and the new enterprise assumes the debts of the transferor and he receives nothing from the transaction except an interest in the new enterprise junior to the claims of creditors;

(8) Transfers of property which is exempt from execution.

Public notice under subsection (6) or subsection (7) may be given by publishing once a week for two consecutive weeks in a newspaper of general circulation where the transferor had its principal place of business in this state an advertisement including the names and addresses of the transferor and transferee and the effective date of the transfer.

§ 6-104. **Schedule of Property, List of Creditors.**

(1) Except as provided with respect to auction sales (Section 6-108), a bulk transfer subject to this Article is ineffective against any creditor of the transferor unless:

(a) The transferee requires the transferor to

furnish a list of his existing creditors prepared as stated in this section; and

(b) The parties prepare a schedule of the property transferred sufficient to identify it; and

(c) The transferee preserves the list and schedule for six months next following the transfer and permits inspection of either or both and copying therefrom at all reasonable hours by any creditor of the transferor, or files the list and schedule in (a public office to be here identified).

(2) The list of creditors must be signed and sworn to or affirmed by the transferor or his agent. It must contain the names and business addresses of all creditors of the transferor, with the amounts when known, and also the names of all persons who are known to the transferor to assert claims against him even though such claims are disputed. If the transferor is the obligor of an outstanding issue of bonds, debentures or the like as to which there is an indenture trustee, the list of creditors need include only the name and address of the indenture trustee and the aggregate outstanding principal amount of the issue.

(3) Responsibility for the completeness and accuracy of the list of creditors rests on the transferor, and the transfer is not rendered ineffective by errors or omissions therein unless the transferee is shown to have had knowledge.

§ 6-105. Notice to Creditors. In addition to the requirements of the preceding section, any bulk transfer subject to this Article except one made by auction sale (Section 6-108) is ineffective against any creditor of the transferor unless at least ten days before he takes possession of the goods or pays for them, whichever happens first, the transferee gives notice of the transfer in the manner and to the persons hereafter provided (Section 6-107).

[§ 6-106. Applications of the Proceeds. In addition to the requirements of the two preceding sections:

(1) Upon every bulk transfer subject to this Article for which new consideration becomes payable except those made by sale at auction it is the duty of the transferee to assure that such consideration is applied so far as necessary to pay those debts of the transferor which are either shown on the list furnished by the transferor (Section 6-104) or filed in writing in the place stated in the notice (Section 6-107) within thirty days after the mailing of such notice. This duty of the transferee runs to all the holders of such debts, and may be enforced by any of them for the benefit of all.

(2) If any of said debts are in dispute the necessary sum may be withheld from distribution until the dispute is settled or adjudicated.

(3) If the consideration payable is not enough to pay all of the said debts in full distribution shall be made pro rata.]

Note: *This section is bracketed to indicate division of opinion as to whether or not it is a wise provision, and to suggest that this is a point on which State enactments may differ without serious damage to the principle of uniformity.*

In any State where this section is omitted, the following parts of sections, also bracketed in the text, should also be omitted, namely:

Section 6-107(2) (e).
6-108(3) (c).
6-109(2).

In any State where this section is enacted, these other provisions should be also.

Optional Subsection (4)

[(4) The transferee may within ten days after he takes possession of the goods pay the consideration into the (specify court) in the county where the transferor had its principal place of business in this state and thereafter may discharge his duty under this section by giving notice by registered or certified mail to all the persons to whom the duty runs that the consideration has been paid into that court and that they should file their claims there. On motion of any interested party, the court may order the distribution of the consideration to the persons entitled to it.]

Note: *Optional subsection (4) is recommended for those states which do not have a general statute providing for payment of money into court.*

§ 6-107. The Notice.

(1) The notice to creditors (Section 6-105) shall state:

(a) that a bulk transfer is about to be made; and

(b) the names and business addresses of the transferor and transferee, and all other business names and addresses used by the transferor within three years last past so far as known to the transferee; and

(c) whether or not all the debts of the transferor are to be paid in full as they fall due as a result of the transaction, and if so, the address to which creditors should send their bills.

(2) If the debts of the transferor are not to be paid in full as they fall due or if the transferee is in doubt on that point then the notice shall state further:

(a) the location and general description of the property to be transferred and the estimated total of the transferor's debts;

(b) the address where the schedule of property and list of creditors (Section 6-104) may be inspected;

(c) whether the transfer is to pay existing debts and if so the amount of such debts and to whom owing;

(d) whether the transfer is for new consideration and if so the amount of such consideration and the time and place of payment; [and]

[(e) if for new consideration the time and place where creditors of the transferor are to file their claims.]

(3) The notice in any case shall be delivered personally or sent by registered or certified mail to all the persons shown on the list of creditors furnished by the transferor (Section 6-104) and to all other persons who are known to the transferee to hold or assert claims against the transforer. As amended 1962.

Note: *The words in brackets are optional. See Note under §6-106.*

§ 6-108. Auction Sales; "Auctioneer."

(1) A bulk transfer is subject to this Article even though it is by sale at auction, but only in the manner and with the results stated in this section.

(2) The transferor shall furnish a list of his creditors and assist in the preparation of a schedule of the property to be sold, both prepared as before stated (Section 6-104).

(3) The person or persons other than the transferor who direct, control or are responsible for the auction are collectively called the "auctioneer." The auctioneer shall:

(a) receive and retain the list of creditors and prepare and retain the schedule of property for the period stated in this Article (Section 6-104);

(b) give notice of the auction personally or by registered or certified mail at least ten days before it occurs to all persons shown on the list of creditors and to all other

persons who are known to him to hold or assert claims against the transferor; [and]

[(c) assure that the net proceeds of the auction are applied as provided in this Article (Section 6-106).]

(4) Failure of the auctioneer to perform any of these duties does not affect the validity of the sale or the title of the purchasers, but if the auctioneer knows that the auction constitutes a bulk transfer such failure renders the auctioneer liable to the creditors of the transferor as a class for the sums owing to them from the transferor up to but not exceeding the net proceeds of the auction. If the auctioneer consists of several persons their liability is joint and several.

Note: *The words in brackets are optional. See Note under § 6-106.*

§ 6-109. What Creditors Protected; [Credit for Payment to Particular Creditors].

(1) The creditors of the transferor mentioned in this Article are those holding claims based on transactions or events occurring before the bulk transfer, but creditors who become such after notice to creditors is given (Sections 6-105 and 6-107) are not entitled to notice.

[(2) Against the aggregate obligation imposed by the provisions of this Article concerning the application of the proceeds (Section 6-106 and subsection (3) (c) of 6-108) the transferee or auctioneer is entitled to credit for sums paid to particular creditors of the transferor, not exceeding the sums believed in good faith at the time of the payment to be properly payable to such creditors.]

Note: *The words in brackets are optional. See Note under § 6-106.*

§ 6-110. Subsequent Transfers.
When the title of a transferee to property is subject to a defect by reason of his non-compliance with the requirements of this Article, then:

(1) a purchaser of any of such property from such transferee who pays no value or who takes with notice of such non-compliance takes subject to such defect, but

(2) a purchaser for value in good faith and without such notice takes free of such defect.

§ 6-111. Limitation of Actions and Levies.
No action under this Article shall be brought nor levy made more than six months after the date on which the transferee took possession of the goods unless the transfer has been concealed. If the transfer has been

concealed, actions may be brought or levies made within six months after its discovery.

Note to Article 6: *Section 6-106 is bracketed to indicate division of opinion as to whether or not it is a wise provision, and to suggest that this is a point on which State enactments may differ without serious damage to the principle of uniformity.*

In any State where Section 6-106 is not enacted, the following parts of sections, also bracketed in the text, should also be omitted, namely:

Sec. 6-107(2) (e).
        6-108(3) (c).
        6-109(2).

In any State where Section 6-106 is enacted, these other provisions should be also.

ARTICLE 7. WAREHOUSE RECEIPTS, BILLS OF LADING AND OTHER DOCUMENTS OF TITLE

Part 1. General

§ 7-101. Short Title. This Article shall be known and may be cited as Uniform Commercial Code— Documents of Title.

§ 7-102. Definitions and Index of Definitions.

(1) In this Article, unless the context otherwise requires:

(a) "Bailee" means the person who by a warehouse receipt, bill of lading or other document of title acknowledges possession of goods and contracts to deliver them.

(b) "Consignee" means the person named in a bill to whom or to whose order the bill promises delivery.

(c) "Consignor" means the person named in a bill as the person from whom the goods have been received for shipment.

(d) "Delivery order" means a written order to deliver goods directed to a warehouseman, carrier or other person who in the ordinary course of business issues warehouse receipts or bills of lading.

(e) "Document" means document of title as defined in the general definitions in Article 1 (Section 1-201).

(f) "Goods" means all things which are treated as movable for the purposes of a contract of storage or transportation.

(g) "Issuer" means a bailee who issues a document except that in relation to an unaccepted delivery order it means the person who orders the possessor of goods to deliver. Issuer includes any person for whom an agent or employee purports to act in issuing a document if the agent or employee has real or apparent authority to issue documents, notwithstanding that the issuer received no goods or that the goods were misdescribed or that in any other respect the agent or employee violated his instructions.

(h) "Warehouseman" is a person engaged in the business of storing goods for hire.

(2) Other definitions applying to this Article or to specified Parts thereof, and the sections in which they appear are:

"Duly negotiate." Section 7-501.

"Person entitled under the document." Section 7-403(4).

(3) Definitions in other Articles applying to this Article and the sections in which they appear are:

"Contract for sale." Section 2-106.

"Overseas." Section 2-323.

"Receipt" of goods. Section 2-103.

(4) In addition Article 1 contains general definitions and principles of construction and interpretation applicable throughout this Article.

§ 7-103. Relation of Article to Treaty, Statute, Tariff, Classification or Regulation. To the extent that any treaty or statute of the United States, regulatory statute of this State or tariff, classification or regulation filed or issued pursuant thereto is applicable, the provisions of this Article are subject thereto.

§ 7-104. Negotiable and Non-Negotiable Warehouse Receipt, Bill of Lading or Other Document of Title.

(1) A warehouse receipt, bill of lading or other document of title is negotiable

(a) if by its terms the goods are to be delivered to bearer or to the order of a named person; or

(b) where recognized in overseas trade, if it runs to a named person or assigns.

(2) Any other document is non-negotiable. A bill of lading in which it is stated that the goods are consigned to a named person is not made negotiable by a provision that the goods are to be delivered only against a written order signed by the same or another named person.

§ 7-105. Construction Against Negative Implication.

The omission from either Part 2 or Part 3 of this Article of a provision corresponding to a provision made in the other Part does not imply that a corresponding rule of law is not applicable.

Part 2. Warehouse Receipts: Special Provisions

§ 7-201. Who May Issue a Warehouse Receipt; Storage Under Government Bond.

(1) A warehouse receipt may be issued by any warehouseman.

(2) Where goods including distilled spirits and agricultural commodities are stored under a statute requiring a bond against withdrawal or a license for the issuance of receipts in the nature of warehouse receipts, a receipt issued for the goods has like effect as a warehouse receipt even though issued by a person who is the owner of the goods and is not a warehouseman.

§ 7-202. Form of Warehouse Receipt; Essential Terms; Optional Terms.

(1) A warehouse receipt need not be in any particular form.

(2) Unless a warehouse receipt embodies within its written or printed terms each of the following, the warehouseman is liable for damages caused by the omission to a person injured thereby:

(a) the location of the warehouse where the goods are stored;

(b) the date of issue of the receipt;

(c) the consecutive number of the receipt;

(d) a statement whether the goods received will be delivered to the bearer, to a specified person, or to a specified person or his order;

(e) the rate of storage and handling charges, except that where goods are stored under a field warehousing arrangement a statement of that fact is sufficient on a non-negotiable receipt;

(f) a description of the goods or of the packages containing them;

(g) the signature of the warehouseman, which may be made by his authorized agent;

(h) if the receipt is issued for goods of which the warehouseman is owner, either solely or jointly or in common with others, the fact of such ownership; and

(i) a statement of the amount of advances made and of liabilities incurred for which the warehouseman claims a lien or security interest (Section 7-209). If the precise amount of such advances made or of such liabilities incurred is, at the time of the issue of the recepit, unknown to the warehouseman or to his agent who issues it, a statement of the fact that advances have been made or liabilities incurred and the purpose thereof is sufficient.

(3) A warehouseman may insert in his receipt any other terms which are not contrary to the provisions of this Act and do not impair his obligation of delivery (Section 7-403) or his duty of care (Section 7-204). Any contrary provisions shall be ineffective.

§ 7-203. Liability for Non-Receipt or Misdescription.

A party to or purchaser for value in good faith of a document of title other than a bill of lading relying in either case upon the description therein of the goods may recover from the issuer damages caused by the non-receipt or misdescription of the goods, except to the extent that the document conspicuously indicates that the issuer does not know whether any part or all of the goods in fact were received or conform to the description, as where the description is in terms of marks or labels or kind, quantity or condition, or the receipt or description is qualified by "contents, condition and quality unknown," "said to contain" or the like, if such indication be true, or the party or purchaser otherwise has notice.

§ 7-204. Duty of Care; Contractual Limitation of Warehouseman's Liability.

(1) A warehouseman is liable for damages for loss of or injury to the goods caused by his failure to exercise such care in regard to them as a reasonably careful man would exercise under like circumstances but unless otherwise agreed he is not liable for damages which could not have been avoided by the exercise of such care.

(2) Damages may be limited by a term in the warehouse receipt or storage agreement limiting the amount of liability in case of loss or damage, and setting forth a specific liability per article or item, or value per unit of weight, beyond which the warehouseman shall not be liable; provided, however, that such liability may on written request of the bailor at the time of signing such storage agreement or within a reasonable time after receipt of the warehouse receipt be increased on part or all of the goods

thereunder, in which event increased rates may be charged based on such increased valuation, but that no such increase shall be permitted contrary to a lawful limitation of liability contained in the warehouseman's tariff, if any. No such limitation is effective with respect to the warehouseman's liability for conversion to his own use.

(3) Reasonable provisions as to the time and manner of presenting claims and instituting actions based on the bailment may be included in the warehouse receipt or tariff.

(4) This section does not impair or repeal . . .

Note: *Insert in subsection (4) a reference to any statute which imposes a higher responsibility upon the warehouseman or invalidates contractual limitations which would be permissible under this Article.*

§ 7-205. Title Under Warehouse Receipt Defeated in Certain Cases.
A buyer in the ordinary course of buisness of fungible goods sold and delivered by a warehouseman who is also in the business of buying and selling such goods takes free of any claim under a warehouse receipt even though it has been duly negotiated.

§ 7-206. Termination of Storage at Warehouseman's Option.
(1) A warehouseman may on notifying the person on whose account the goods are held and any other person known to claim an interest in the goods require payment of any charges and removal of the goods from the warehouse at the termination of the period of storage fixed by the document, or, if no period is fixed, within a stated period not less than thirty days after the notification. If the goods are not removed before the date specified in the notification, the warehouseman may sell them in accordance with the provisions of the section on enforcement of a warehouseman's lien (Section 7-210).

(2) If a warehouseman in good faith believes that the goods are about to deteriorate or decline in value to less than the amount of his lien within the time prescribed in subsection (1) for notification, advertisement and sale, the warehouseman may specify in the notification any reasonable shorter time for removal of the goods and in case the goods are not removed, may sell them at public sale held not less than one week after a single advertisement or posting.

(3) If as a result of a quality or condition of the goods of which the warehouseman had no notice at the time of deposit the goods are a hazard to other property or to the warehouse or to persons, the warehouseman may sell the goods at public or private sale without advertisement on reasonable notification to all persons known to claim an interest in the goods. If the warehouseman after a reasonable effort is unable to sell the goods he may dispose of them in any lawful manner and shall incur no liability by reason of such disposition.

(4) The warehouseman must deliver the goods to any person entitled to them under this Article upon due demand made at any time prior to sale or other disposition under this section.

(5) The warehouseman may satisfy his lien from the proceeds of any sale or disposition under this section but must hold the balance for delivery on the demand of any person to whom he would have been bound to deliver the goods.

§ 7-207. Goods Must Be Kept Separate; Fungible Goods.
(1) Unless the warehouse receipt otherwise provides, a warehouseman must keep separate the goods covered by each receipt so as to permit at all times identification and delivery of those goods except that different lots of fungible goods may be comingled.

(2) Fungible goods so commingled are owned in common by the persons entitled thereto and the warehouseman is severally liable to each owner for that owner's share. Where because of overissue a mass of fungible goods is insufficient to meet all the receipts which the warehouseman has issued against it, the persons entitled include all holders to whom overissued receipts have been duly negotiated.

§ 7-208. Altered Warehouse Receipts.
Where a blank in a negotiable warehouse receipt has been filled in without authority, a purchaser for value and without notice of the want of authority may treat the insertion as authorized. Any other unauthorized alteration leaves any receipt enforceable against the issuer according to its original tenor.

§ 7-209. Lien of Warehouseman.
(1) A warehouseman has a lien against the bailor on the goods covered by a warehouse receipt or on the proceeds thereof in his possession for charges for storage or transportation (including demurrage and terminal charges), insurance, labor, or charges present or future in relation to the goods, and for expenses necessary for preservation of the goods or reasonably incurred in their sale pursuant to law. If

the person on whose account the goods are held is liable for like charges or expenses in relation to other goods whenever deposited and it is stated in the receipt that a lien is claimed for charges and expenses in relation to other goods, the warehouseman also has a lien against him for such charges and expenses whether or not the other goods have been delivered by the warehouseman. But against a person to whom a negotiable warehouse receipt is duly negotiated a warehouseman's lien is limited to charges in an amount or at a rate specified on the receipt or if no charges are so specified then to a reasonable charge for storage of the goods covered by the receipt subsequent to the date of the receipt.

(2) The warehouseman may also reserve a security interest against the bailor for a maximum amount specified on the receipt for charges other than those specified in subsection (1), such as for money advanced and interest. Such a security interest is governed by the Article on Secured Transactions (Article 9).

(3)(a)   A warehouseman's lien for charges and expenses under subsection (1) or a security interest under subsection (2) is also effective against any person who so entrusted the bailor with possession of the goods that a pledge of them by him to a good faith purchaser for value would have been valid but is not effective against a person as to whom the document confers no right in the goods covered by it under Section 7-503.

(b)   A warehouseman's lien on household goods for charges and expenses in relation to the goods under subsection (1) is also effective against all persons if the depositor was the legal possessor of the goods at the time of deposit. "Household goods" means furniture, furnishings and personal effects used by the depositor in a dwelling.

(4) A warehouseman loses his lien on any goods which he voluntarily delivers or which he unjustifiably refuses to deliver.

§ 7-210. Enforcement of Warehouseman's Lien.

(1) Except as provided in subsection (2), a warehouseman's lien may be enforced by public or private sale of the goods in block or in parcels, at any time or place and on any terms which are commercially reasonable, after notifying all persons known to claim an interest in the goods. Such notification must include a statement of the amount due, the nature of the proposed sale and the time and place of any public sale. The fact that a better price could have been obtained by a sale at a different time or in a different method from that selected by the warehouseman is not of itself sufficient to establish that the sale was not made in a commercially reasonable manner. If the warehouseman either sells the goods in the usual manner in any recognized market therefor, or if he sells at the price current in such market at the time of his sale, or if he has otherwise sold in conformity with commercially reasonable practices among dealers in the type of goods sold, he has sold in a commercially reasonable manner. A sale of more goods than apparently necessary to be offered to insure satisfaction of the obligation is not commercially reasonable except in cases covered by the preceding sentence.

(2) A warehouseman's lien on goods other than goods stored by a merchant in the course of his business may be enforced only as follows:

(a)   All persons known to claim an interest in the goods must be notified.

(b)   The notification must be delivered in person or sent by registered or certified letter to the last known address of any person to be notified.

(c)   The notification must include an itemized statement of the claim, a description of the goods subject to the lien, a demand for payment within a specified time not less than ten days after receipt of the notification, and a conspicuous statement that unless the claim is paid within that time the goods will be advertised for sale and sold by auction at a specified time and place.

(d)   The sale must conform to the terms of the notification.

(e)   The sale must be held at the nearest suitable place to that where the goods are held or stored.

(f)   After the expiration of the time given in the notification, an advertisement of the sale must be published once a week for two weeks consecutively in a newspaper of general circulation where the sale is to be held. The advertisement must include a description of the goods, the name of the person on whose account they are being held, and the time and place of the sale. The sale must take place at least fifteen days after the first publication. If there is no newspaper of general circulation where the sale is to be held, the advertisement must be posted at least ten days before the sale in not less than six conspicuous places in the neighborhood of the proposed sale.

(3) Before any sale pursuant to this section any person claiming a right in the goods may pay the amount necessary to satisfy the lien and the reasonable expenses incurred under this section. In that event the goods must not be sold, but must be retained by the warehouseman subject to the terms of the receipt and this Article.

(4) The warehouseman may buy at any public sale pursuant to this section.

(5) A purchaser in good faith of goods sold to enforce a warehouseman's lien takes the goods free of any rights of persons against whom the lien was valid, despite noncompliance by the warehouseman with the requirements of this section.

(6) The warehouseman may satisfy his lien from the proceeds of any sale pursuant to this section but most hold the balance, if any, for delivery on demand to any person to whom he would have been bound to deliver the goods.

(7) The rights provided by this section shall be in addition to all other rights allowed by law to a creditor against his debtor.

(8) Where a lien is on goods stored by a merchant in the course of his business the lien may be enforced in accordance with either subsection (1) or (2).

(9) The warehouseman is liable for damages caused by failure to comply with the requirements for sale under this section and in case of willful violation is liable for conversion.

Part 3. Bills of Lading: Special Provisions

§ 7-301. Liability for Non-Receipt or Misdescription; "Said to Contain"; "Shipper's Load and Count"; Improper Handling.

(1) A consignee of a non-negotiable bill who has given value in good faith or a holder to whom a negotiable bill has been duly negotiated relying in either case upon the description therein of the goods, or upon the date therein shown, may recover from the issuer damages caused by the misdating of the bill or the non-receipt or misdescription of the goods, except to the extent that the document indicates that

the issuer does not know whether any part or all of the goods in fact were received or conform to the description, as where the description is in terms of marks or labels or kind, quantity, or condition or the receipt or description is qualified by "contents or condition of contents of packages unknown," "said to contain," "shipper's weight, load and count" or the like, if such indication be true.

(2) When goods are loaded by an issuer who is a common carrier, the issuer must count the packages of goods if package freight and ascertain the kind and quantity if bulk freight. In such cases "shipper's weight, load and count" or other words indicating that the description was made by the shipper are ineffective except as to freight concealed by packages.

(3) When bulk freight is loaded by a shipper who makes available to the issuer adequate facilities for weighing such freight, an issuer who is a common carrier must ascertain the kind and quantity within a reasonable time after receiving the written request of the shipper to do so. In such cases "shipper's weight" or other words of like purport are ineffective.

(4) The issuer may be inserting in the bill the words "shipper's weight, load and count" or other words of like purport indicate that the goods were loaded by the shipper; and if such statement be true the issuer shall not be liable for damages caused by the improper loading. But their omission does not imply liability for such damages.

(5) The shipper shall be deemed to have guaranteed to the issuer the accuracy at the time of shipment of the description, marks, labels, number, kind, quantity, condition and weight, as furnished by him; and the shipper shall indemnify the issuer against damage caused by inaccuracies in such particulars. The right of the issuer to such indemnity shall in no way limit his responsibility and liability under the contract of carriage to any person other than the shipper.

§ 7-302. Through Bills of Lading and Similar Documents.

(1) The issuer of a through bill of lading or other document embodying an undertaking to be performed in part by persons acting as its agents or by connecting carriers is liable to anyone entitled to recover on the document for any breach by such other persons or by a connecting carrier of its obligation under the document but to the extent that the bill covers an undertaking to be performed overseas or in

territory not contiguous to the continental United States or an undertaking including matters other than transportation this liability may be varied by agreement of the parties.

(2) Where goods covered by a through bill of lading or other document embodying an undertaking to be performed in part by persons other than the issuer are received by any such person, he is subject with respect to his own performance while the goods are in his possession to the obligation of the issuer. His obligation is discharged by delivery of the goods to another such person pursuant to the document, and does not include liability for breach by any other such persons or by the issuer.

(3) The issuer of such through bill of lading or other document shall be entitled to recover from the connecting carrier or such other person in possession of the goods when the breach of the obligation under the document occurred, the amount it may be required to pay to anyone entitled to recover on the document therefor, as may be evidenced by any receipt, judgment, or transcript thereof, and the amount of any expense reasonably incurred by it in defending any action brought by anyone entitled to recover on the document therefor.

§ 7-303. Diversion; Reconsignment; Change of Instructions.

(1) Unless the bill of lading otherwise provides, the carrier may deliver the goods to a person or destination other than that stated in the bill or may otherwise dispose of the goods on instruction from

    (a)   the holder of a negotiable bill; or

    (b)   the consignor on a non-negotiable bill notwithstanding contrary instructions from the consignee; or

    (c)   the consignee on a non-negotiable bill in the absence of contrary instructions from the consignor, if the goods have arrived at the billed destination or if the consignee is in possession of the bill; or

    (d)   the consignee on a non-negotiable bill if he is entitled as against the consignor to dispose of them.

(2) Unless such instructions are noted on a negotiable bill of lading, a person to whom the bill is duly negotiated can hold the bailee according to the original terms.

§ 7-304. Bills of Lading in a Set.

(1) Except where customary in overseas transportation, a bill of lading must not be issued in a set of parts. The issuer is liable for damages caused by violation of this subsection.

(2) Where a bill of lading is lawfully drawn in a set of parts, each of which is numbered and expressed to be valid only if the goods have not been delivered against any other part, the whole of the parts constitute one bill.

(3) Where a bill of lading is lawfully issued in a set of parts and different parts are negotiated to different persons, the title of the holder to whom the first due negotiation is made prevails as to both the document and the goods even though any later holder may have received the goods from the carrier in good faith and discharged the carrier's obligation by surrender of his part.

(4) Any person who negotiates or transfers a single part of a bill of lading drawn in a set is liable to holders of that part as if it were the whole set.

(5) The bailee is obliged to deliver in accordance with Part 4 of this Article against the first presented part of a bill of lading lawfully drawn in a set. Such delivery discharges the bailee's obligation on the whole bill.

§ 7-305. Destination Bills.

(1) Instead of issuing a bill of lading to the consignor at the place of shipment a carrier may at the request of the consignor procure the bill to be issued at destination or at any other place designated in the request.

(2) Upon request of anyone entitled as against the carrier to control the goods while in transit and on surrender of any outstanding bill of lading or other receipt covering such goods, the issuer may procure a substitute bill to be issued at any place designated in the request.

§ 7-306. Altered Bills of Lading.
An unauthorized alteration or filling in of a blank in a bill of lading leaves the bill enforceable according to its original tenor.

§ 7-307. Lien of Carrier.

(1) A carrier has a lien on the goods covered by a bill of lading for charges subsequent to the date of its receipt of the goods for storage or transportation (including demurrage and terminal charges) and for expenses necessary for preservation of the goods incident to their transportation or reasonably incurred in their sale pursuant to law. But against a purchaser for value of a negotiable bill of lading a carrier's lien is limited to charges stated in the bill or

the applicable tariffs, or if no charges are stated then to a reasonable charge.

(2) A lien for charges and expenses under subsection (1) on goods which the carrier was required by law to receive for transportation is effective against the consignor or any person entitled to the goods unless the carrier had notice that the consignor lacked authority to subject the goods to such charges and expenses. Any other lien under subsection (1) is effective against the consignor and any person who permitted the bailor to have control or possession of the goods unless the carrier had notice that the bailor lacked such authority.

(3) A carrier loses his lien on any goods which he voluntarily delivers or which he unjustifiably refuses to deliver.

§ 7-308. Enforcement of Carrier's Lien.

(1) A carrier's lien may be enforced by public or private sale of the goods, in block or in parcels, at any time or place and on any terms which are commercially reasonable, after notifying all persons known to claim an interest in the goods. Such notification must include a statement of the amount due, the nature of the proposed sale and the time and place of any public sale. The fact that a better price could have been obtained by a sale at a different time or in a different method from that selected by the carrier is not of itself sufficient to establish that the sale was not made in a commercially reasonable manner. If the carrier either sells the goods in the usual manner in any recognized market therefor or if he sells at the price current in such market at the time of his sale or if he has otherwise sold in conformity with commercially reasonable practices among dealers in the type of goods sold he has sold in a commercially reasonable manner. A sale of more goods than apparently necessary to be offered to ensure satisfaction of the obligation is not commercially reasonable except in cases covered by the preceding sentence.

(2) Before any sale pursuant to this section any person claiming a right in the goods may pay the amount necessary to satisfy the lien and the reasonable expenses incurred under this section. In that event the goods must not be sold, but must be retained by the carrier subject to the terms of the bill and this Article.

(3) The carrier may buy at any public sale pursuant to this section.

(4) A purchaser in good faith of goods sold to enforce a carrier's lien takes the goods free of any

rights of persons against whom the lien was valid, despite noncompliance by the carrier with the requirements of this section.

(5) The carrier may satisfy his lien from the proceeds of any sale pursuant to this section but must hold the balance, if any, for delivery on demand to any person to whom he would have been bound to deliver the goods.

(6) The rights provided by this section shall be in addition to all other rights allowed by law to a creditor against his debtor.

(7) A carrier's lien may be enforced in accordance with either subsection (1) or the procedure set forth in subsection (2) of Section 7-210.

(8) The carrier is liable for damages caused by failure to comply with the requirements for sale under this section and in case of willful violation is liable for conversion.

§ 7-309. Duty of Care; Contractual Limitation of Carrier's Liability.

(1) A carrier who issues a bill of lading whether negotiable or non-negotiable must exercise the degree of care in relation to the goods which a reasonably careful man would exercise under like circumstances. This subsection does not repeal or change any law or rule of law which imposes liability upon a common carrier for damages not caused by its negligence.

(2) Damages may be limited by a provision that the carrier's liability shall not exceed a value stated in the document if the carrier's rates are dependent upon value and the consignor by the carrier's tariff is afforded an opportunity to declare a higher value or a value as lawfully provided in the tariff, or where no tariff is filed he is otherwise advised of such opportunity; but no such limitation is effective with respect to the carrier's liability for conversion to its own use.

(3) Reasonable provisions as to the time and manner of presenting claims and instituting actions based on the shipment may be included in a bill of lading or tariff.

Part 4. Warehouse Receipts and Bills of Lading: General Obligations

§ 7-401. Irregularities in Issue of Receipt or Bill or Conduct of Issuer. The obligations imposed by this Article on an issuer apply to a document of title regardless of the fact that

(a)   the document may not comply with the

requirements of this Article or of any other law or regulation regarding its issue, form or content; or

(b)   the issuer may have violated laws regulating the conduct of his business; or

(c)   the goods covered by the document were owned by the bailee at the time the document was issued; or

(d)   the person issuing the document does not come within the definition of warehouseman if it purports to be a warehouse receipt.

§ 7-402. Duplicate Receipt or Bill; Overissue.

Neither a duplicate nor any other document of title purporting to cover goods already represented to an outstanding document of the same issuer confers any right in the goods, except as provided in the case of bills in a set, overissue of documents for fungible goods and substitutes for lost, stolen or destroyed documents. But the issuer is liable for damages caused by his overissue or failure to identify a duplicate document as such by conspicuous notation on its face.

§ 7-403. Obligation of Warehouseman or Carrier to Deliver; Excuse.

(1) The bailee must deliver the goods to a person entitled under the document who complies with subsections (2) and (3), unless and to the extent that the bailee establishes any of the following:

(a)   delivery of the goods to a person whose receipt was rightful as against the claimant;

(b)   damage to or delay, loss or destruction of the goods for which the bailee is not liable [, but the burden of establishing negligence in such cases is on the person, entitled under the document];

Note: *The brackets in (1) (b) indicate that State enactments may differ on this point without serious damage to the principle of uniformity.*

(c)   previous sale or other disposition of the goods in lawful enforcement of a lien or on warehouseman's lawful termination of storage;

(d)   the exercise by a seller of his right to stop delivery pursuant to the provisions of the Article on Sales (Section 2-705);

(e)   a diversion, reconsignment or other dis-

position pursuant to the provisions of this Article (Section 7-303) or tariff regulating such right;

(f)   release, satisfaction or any other fact affording a personal defense against the claimant;

(g)   any other lawful excuse.

(2) A person claiming goods covered by a document of title must satisfy the bailee's lien where the bailee so requests or where the bailee is prohibited by law from delivering the goods until the charges are paid.

(3) Unless the person claiming is one against whom the document confers no right under Sec. 7-503(1), he must surrender for cancellation or notation of partial deliveries any outstanding negotiable document covering the goods, and the bailee must cancel the document or conspicuously note the partial delivery thereon or be liable to any person to whom the document is duly negotiated.

(4) "Person entitled under the document" means holder in the case of a negotiable document, or the person to whom delivery is to be made by the terms of or pursuant to written instructions under a nonnegotiable document.

§ 7-404. No Liability for Good Faith Delivery Pursuant to Receipt or Bill.

A bailee who in good faith including observance of reasonable commercial standards has received goods and delivered or otherwise disposed of them according to the terms of the document of title or pursuant to this Article is not liable therefor. This rule applies even though the person from whom he received the goods had no authority to procure the document or to dispose of the goods and even though the person to whom he delivered the goods had no authority to receive them.

Part 5. Warehouse Receipts and Bills of Lading: Negotiation and Transfer

§ 7-501. Form of Negotiation and Requirements of "Due Negotiation."

(1) A negotiable document of title running to the order of a named person is negotiated by his indorsement and delivery. After his indorsement in blank or to bearer any person can negotiate it by delivery alone.

(2)

(a)   A negotiable document of title is also negotiated by delivery alone when by its original terms it runs to bearer.

(b) When a document running to the order of a named person is delivered to him the effect is the same as if the document has been negotiated.

(3) Negotiation of a negotiable document of title after it has been indorsed to a specified person requires indorsement by the special indorsee as well as delivery.

(4) A negotiable document of title is "duly negotiated" when it is negotiated in the manner stated in this section to a holder who purchases it in good faith without notice of any defense against or claim to it on the part of any person and for value, unless it is established that the negotiation is not in the regular course of business or financing or involves receiving the document in settlement or payment of a money obligation.

(5) Indorsement of a non-negotiable document neither makes it negotiable nor adds to the transferee's rights.

(6) The naming in a negotiable bill of a person to be notified of the arrival of the goods does not limit the negotiability of the bill nor constitute notice to a purchaser thereof of any interest of such person in the goods.

§ 7-502. Rights Acquired by Due Negotiation.

(1) Subject to the following section and to the provisions of Section 7-205 on fungible goods, a holder to whom a negotiable document of title has been duly negotiated acquires thereby:

(a) title to the document;

(b) title to the goods;

(c) all rights accruing under the law of agency or estoppel, including rights to goods delivered to the bailee after the document was issued; and

(d) the direct obligation of the issuer to hold or deliver the goods according to the terms of the document free of any defense or claim by him except those arising under the terms of the document or under this Article. In the case of a delivery order the bailee's obligation accrues only upon acceptance and the obligation acquired by the holder in that the issuer and any indorser will procure the acceptance of the bailee.

(2) Subject to the following section, title and rights so acquired are not defeated by any stoppage of the goods represented by the document or by surrender of such goods by the bailee, and are not impaired even though the negotiation or any prior negotiation constituted a breach of duty or even though any person has been deprived of possession of the document by misrepresentation, fraud, accident, mistake, duress, loss, theft or conversion, or even though a previous sale or other transfer of the goods or document has been made to a third person.

§ 7-503. Document of Title to Goods Defeated in Certain Cases.

(1) A document of title confers no right in goods against a person who before issuance of the document had a legal interest or a perfected security interest in them and who neither

(a) delivered or entrusted them or any document of title covering them to the bailor or his nominee with actual or apparent authority to ship, store or sell or with power to obtain delivery under this Article (Section 7-403) or with power of disposition under this Act (Sections 2-403 and 9-307) or other statute or rule of law; nor

(b) acquiesced in the procurement by the bailor or his nominee of any document of title.

(2) Title to goods based upon an unaccepted delivery order is subject to the rights of anyone to whom a negotiable warehouse receipt or bill of lading covering the goods has been duly negotiated. Such a title may be defeated under the next section to the same extent as the rights of the issuer or a transferee from the issuer.

(3) Title to goods based upon a bill of lading issued to a freight forwarder is subject to the rights of anyone to whom a bill issued by the freight forwarder is duly negotiated; but delivery by the carrier in accordance with Part 4 of this Article pursuant to its own bill of lading discharges the carrier's obligation to deliver.

§ 7-504. Rights Acquired in the Absence of Due Negotiation; Effect of Diversion; Seller's Stoppage of Delivery.

(1) A transferee of a document, whether negotiable or non-negotiable, to whom the document has been delivered but not duly negotiated, acquires the

title and rights which his transferor had or had actual authority to convey.

(2) In the case of a non-negotiable document, until but not after the bailee receives notification of the transfer, the rights of the transferee may be defeated

  (a) by those creditors of the transferor who could treat the sale as void under Section 2-402; or

  (b) by a buyer from the transferor in ordinary course of business if the bailee has delivered the goods to the guyer or received notification of his rights; or

  (c) as against the bailee by good faith dealings of the bailee with the transferor.

(3) A diversion or other change of shipping instructions by the consignor in a non-negotiable bill of lading which causes the bailee not to deliver to the consignee defeats the consignee's title to the goods if they have been delivered to a buyer in ordinary course of business and in any event defeats the consignee's rights against the bailee.

(4) Delivery pursuant to a non-negotiable document may be stopped by a seller under Section 2-705, and subject to the requirement of due notification there provided. A bailee honoring the seller's instructions is entitled to be indemnified by the seller against any resulting loss or expense.

§ 7-505. Indorser Not a Guarantor for Other Parties.
The indorsement of a document of title issued by a bailee does not make the indorser liable for any default by the bailee or by previous indorsers.

§ 7-506. Delivery Without Indorsement: Right to Compel Indorsement.
The transferee of a negotiable document of title has a specifically enforceable right to have his transferor supply any necessary indorsement but the transfer becomes a negotiation only as of the time the indorsement is supplied.

§ 7-507. Warranties on Negotiation or Transfer of Receipt or Bill.
Where a person negotiates or transfers a document of title for value otherwise than as a mere intermediary under the next following section, then unless otherwise agreed he warrants to his immediate purchaser only in addition to any warranty made in selling the goods

  (a) that the document is genuine; and

  (b) that he has no knowledge of any fact which would impair its validity or worth; and

  (c) that his negotiation or transfer is rightful

and fully effective with respect to the title to the document and the goods it represents.

§ 7-508. Warranties of Collecting Bank as to Documents.
A collecting bank or other intermediary known to be entrusted with documents on behalf of another or with collection of a draft or other claim against delivery of documents warrants by such delivery of the documents only its own good faith and authority. This rule applies even though the intermediary has purchased or made advances against the claim or draft to be collected.

§ 7-509. Receipt or Bill: When Adequate Compliance With Commercial Contract.
The question whether a document is adequate to fulfill the obligations of a contract for sale or the conditions of a credit is governed by the Articles on Sales (Article 2) and on Letters of Credit (Article 5).

Part 6. Warehouse Receipts and Bills of Lading: Miscellaneous Provisions

§ 7-601. Lost and Missing Documents.

(1) If a document has been lost, stolen or destroyed, a court may order delivery of the goods or issuance of a substitute document and the bailee may without liability to any person comply with such order. If the document was negotiable the claimant must post security approved by the court to indemnify any person who may suffer loss as a result of non-surrender of the document. If the document was not negotiable, such security may be required at the discretion of the court. The court may also in its discretion order payment of the bailee's reasonable costs and counsel fees.

(2) A bailee who without court order delivers goods to a person claiming under a missing negotiable document is liable to any person injured thereby, and if the delivery is not in good faith becomes liable for conversion. Delivery in good faith is not conversion if made in accordance with a filed classification or tariff or, where no classification or tariff is filed, if the claimant posts security with the bailee in an amount at least double the value of the goods at the time of posting to indemnify any person injured by the delivery who files a notice of claim within one year after the delivery.

§ 7-602. Attachment of Goods Covered by a Negotiable Document.
Except where the document

was originally issued upon delivery of the goods by a person who had no power to dispose of them, no lien attaches by virtue of any judicial process to goods in the possession of a bailee for which a negotiable document of title is outstanding unless the document be first surrendered to the bailee or its negotiation enjoined, and the bailee shall not be compelled to deliver the goods pursuant to process until the document is surrendered to him or impounded by the court. One who purchases the document for value without notice of the process or injunction takes free of the lien imposed by judicial process.

§ 7-603. Conflicting Claims; Interpleader. If more than one person claims title or possession of the goods, the bailee is excused from delivery until he has had a reasonable time to ascertain the validity of the adverse claims or to bring an action to compel all claimants to interplead and may compel such interpleader, either in defending an action for non-delivery of the goods, or by original action, whichever is appropriate.

ARTICLE 8. INVESTMENT SECURITIES

Part 1. Short Title and General Matters

§ 8-101. Short Title. This Article shall be known and may be cited as Uniform Commercial Code—Investment Securities.

§ 8-102. Definitions and Index of Definitions.

(1) In this Article, unless the context otherwise requires:

(a)   A "certificated security" is a share, participation, or other interest in property of or an enterprise of the issuer or an obligation of the issuer which is

(i)   represented by an instrument issued in bearer or registered form;

(ii)   of a type commonly dealt in on securities exchanges or markets or commonly recognized in any area in which it is issued or dealt in as a medium for investment; and

(iii)   either one of a class or series or by its terms divisible into a class or series of shares, participations, interests, or obligations.

(b)   An "uncertificated security" is a share, participation, or other interest in prop-

erty or an enterprise of the issuer or an obligation of the issuer which is

(i)   not represented by an instrument and the transfer of which is registered upon books maintained for that purpose by or on behalf of the issuer;

(ii)   of a type commonly dealt in on securities exchanges or markets; and

(iii)   either one of a class or series or by its terms divisible into a class or series of shares, participations, interests, or obligations.

(c)   A "security" is either a certificated or an uncertificated security. If a security is certificated, the terms "security" and "certificated security" may mean either the intangible interest, the instrument representing that interest, or both, as the context requires. A writing that is a certificated security is governed by this Article and not by Article 3, even though it also meets the requirements of that Article. This Article does not apply to money. If a certificated security has been retained by or surrendered to the issuer or its transfer agent for reasons other than registration of transfer, other temporary purpose, payment, exchange, or acquisition by the issuer, that security shall be treated as an uncertificated security for purposes of this Article.

(d)   A certificated security is in "registered form" if

(i)   it specifies a person entitled to the security or the rights it represents; and

(ii)   its transfer may be registered upon books maintained for that purpose by or on behalf of the issuer, or the security so states.

(e)   A certificated security is in "bearer form" if it runs to bearer according to its terms and not by reason of any indorsement.

(2) A "subsequent purchaser" is a person who takes other than by original issue.

(3) A "clearing corporation" is a corporation registered as a "clearing agency" under the federal securities laws or a corporation:

(a)   at least 90 percent of whose capital stock

is held by or for one or more organizations, none of which, other than a national securities exchange or association, holds in excess of 20 percent of the capital stock of the corporation, and each of which is

(i) subject to supervision or regulation pursuant to the provisions of federal or state banking laws or state insurance laws,

(ii) a broker or dealer or investment company registered under the federal securities laws, or

(iii) a national securities exchange or association registered under the federal securities laws; and

(b) any remaining capital stock of which is held by individuals who have purchased it at or prior to the time of their taking office as directors of the corporation and who have purchased only so much of the capital stock as is necessary to permit them to qualify as directors.

(4) A "custodian bank" is a bank or trust company that is supervised and examined by state or federal authority having supervision over banks and is acting as custodian for a clearing corporation.

(5) Other definitions applying to this Article or to specified Parts thereof and the sections in which they appear are:

"Adverse claim." Section 8-302.

"Bona fide purchaser." Section 8-302.

"Broker." Section 8-303.

"Debtor." Section 9-105.

"Financial intermediary." Section 8-313.

"Guarantee of the signature." Section 8-402.

"Initial transaction statement." Section 8-408.

"Instruction." Section 8-308.

"Intermediary bank." Section 4-105.

"Issuer." Section 8-201.

"Overissue." Section 8-104.

"Secured Party." Section 9-105.

"Security Agreement." Section 9-105.

(6) In addition, Article 1 contains general definitions and principles of construction and interpretation applicable throughout this Article.

§ 8-103. Issuer's Lien. A lien upon a security in favor of an issuer thereof is valid against a purchaser only if:

(a) the security is certificated and the right of the issuer to the lien is noted conspicuously thereon; or

(b) the security is uncertificated and a notation of the right of the issuer to the lien is contained in the initial transaction statement sent to the purchaser or, if his interest is transferred to him other than by registration of transfer, pledge, or release, the initial transaction statement sent to the registered owner or the registered pledgee.

§ 8-104. Effect of Overissue; "Overissue."

(1) The provisions of this Article which validate a security or compel its issue or reissue do not apply to the extent that validation, issue, or reissue would result in overissue; but if:

(a) an identical security which does not constitute an overissue is reasonably available for purchase, the person entitled to issue or validation may compel the issuer to purchase the security for him and either to deliver a certificated security or to register the transfer of an uncertificated security to him, against surrender of any certificated security he holds; or

(b) a security is not so available for purchase, the person entitled to issue or validation may recover from the issuer the price he or the last purchaser for value paid for it with interest from the date of his demand.

(2) "Overissue" means the issue of securities in excess of the amount the issuer has corporate power to issue.

§ 8-105. Certificated Securities Negotiable; Statements and Instructions Not Negotiable; Presumptions.

(1) Certificated securities governed by this Article are negotiable instruments.

(2) Statements (Section 8-408), notices, or the like, sent by the issuer of uncertificated securities and instructions (Section 8-308) are neither negotiable instruments nor certificated securities.

(3) In any action on a security:

(a) unless specifically denied in the pleadings, each signature on a certificated security, in a necessary indorsement, on an initial transaction statement, or on an instruction, is admitted;

(b)   if the effectiveness of a signature is put in issue, the burden of establishing it is on the party claiming under the signature, but the signature is presumed to be genuine or authorized;

(c)   if signatures on a certificated security are admitted or established, production of the security entitles a holder to recover on it unless the defendant establishes a defense or a defect going to the validity of the security;

(d)   if signatures on an initial transaction statement are admitted or established, the facts stated in the statement are presumed to be true as of the time of its issuance; and

(e)   after it is shown that a defense or defect exists, the plaintiff has the burden of establishing that he or some person under whom he claims is a person against whom the defense or defect is ineffective (Section 8-202).

§ 8-106. Applicability.   The law (including the conflict of laws rules) of the jurisdiction of organization of the issuer governs the validity of a security, the effectiveness of registration by the issuer, and the rights and duties of the issuer with respect to:

(a)   registration of transfer of a certificated security;

(b)   registration of transfer, pledge, or release of an uncertificated security; and

(c)   sending of statements of uncertificated securities.

§ 8-107. Securities Transferable; Action for Price.

(1) Unless otherwise agreed and subject to any applicable law or regulation respecting short sales, a person obligated to transfer securities may transfer any certificated security of the specified issue in bearer form or registered in the name of the transferee, or indorsed to him or in blank, or he may transfer an equivalent uncertificated security to the transferee or a person designated by the transferee.

(2) If the buyer fails to pay the price as it comes due under a contract of sale, the seller may recover the price of:

(a)   certificated securities accepted by the buyer;

(b)   uncertificated securities that have been transferred to the buyer or a person designated by the buyer; and

(c)   other securities if efforts at their resale would be unduly burdensome or if there is no readily available market for their resale.

§ 8-108. Registration of Pledge and Release of Uncertificated Securities.   A security interest in an uncertificated security may be evidenced by the registration of pledge to the secured party or a person designated by him. There can be no more than one registered pledge of an uncertificated security at any time. The registered owner of an uncertificated security is the person in whose name the security is registered, even if the security is subject to a registered pledge. The rights of a registered pledgee of an uncertificated security under this Article are terminated by the registration of release.

Part 2. Issue—Issuer

§ 8-201. "Issuer."

(1) With respect to obligations on or defenses to a security, "issuer" includes a person who:

(a)   places or authorizes the placing of his name on a certificated security (otherwise than as authenticating trustee, registrar, transfer agent, or the like) to evidence that it represents a share, participation, or other interest in his property or in an enterprise, or to evidence his duty to perform an obligation represented by the certificated security;

(b)   creates shares, participations, or other interests in his property or in an enterprise or undertakes obligations, which shares, participations, interests, or obligations are uncertificated securities;

(c)   directly or indirectly creates fractional interests in his rights or property, which fractional interests are represented by certificated securities; or

(d)   becomes responsible for or in place of any other person described as an issuer in this section.

(2) With respect to obligations on or defenses to a security, a guarantor is an issuer to the extent of his guaranty, whether or not his obligation is noted on a

certificated security or on statements of uncertificated securities sent pursuant to Section 8-408.

(3) With respect to registration of transfer, pledge, or release (Part 4 of this Article), "issuer" means a person on whose behalf transfer books are maintained.

§ 8-202. Issuer's Responsibility and Defenses; Notice of Defect or Defense.

(1) Even against a purchaser for value and without notice, the terms of a security include:

    (a)   if the security is certificated, those stated on the security;

    (b)   if the security is uncertificated, those contained in the initial transaction statement sent to such purchaser or, if his interest is transferred to him other than by registration of transfer, pledge, or release, the initial transaction statement sent to the registered owner or registered pledgee; and

    (c)   those made part of the security by reference, on the certificated security or in the initial transaction statement, to another instrument, indenture, or document or to a constitution, statute, ordinance, rule, regulation, order or the like, to the extent that the terms referred to do not conflict with the terms stated on the certificated security or contained in the statement. A reference under this paragraph does not of itself charge a purchaser for value with notice of a defect going to the validity of the security, even though the certificated security or statement expressly states that a person accepting it admits notice.

(2) A certificated security in the hands of a purchaser for value or an uncertificated security as to which an initial transaction statement has been sent to a purchaser for value, other than a security issued by a government or governmental agency or unit, even though issued with a defect going to its validity, is valid with respect to the purchaser if he is without notice of the particular defect unless the defect involves a violation of constitutional provisions, in which case the security is valid with respect to a subsequent purchaser for value and without notice of the defect. This subsection applies to an issuer that is a government or governmental agency or unit only if either there has been substantial compliance with the legal requirements governing the issue or the issuer has received a substantial consideration for the issue as a whole or for the particular security and a stated purpose of the issue is one for which the issuer has power to borrow money or issue the security.

(3) Except as provided in the case of certain unauthorized signatures (Section 8-205), lack of genuineness of a certificated security or an initial transaction statement is a complete defense, even against a purchaser for value and without notice.

(4) All other defenses of the issuer of a certificated or uncertificated security, including nondelivery and conditional delivery of a certificated security, are ineffective against a purchaser for value who has taken without notice of the particular defense.

(5) Nothing in this section shall be construed to affect the right of a party to a "when, as and if issued" or a "when distributed" contract to cancel the contract in the event of a material change in the character of the security that is the subject of the contract or in the plan or arrangement pursuant to which the security is to be issued or distributed.

§ 8-203. Staleness as Notice of Defects or Defenses.

(1) After an act or event creating a right to immediate performance of the principal obligation represented by a certificated security or that sets a date on or after which the security is to be presented or surrendered for redemption or exchange, a purchaser is charged with notice of any defect in its issue or defense of the issuer if:

    (a)   the act or event is one requiring the payment of money, the delivery of certificated securities, the registration of transfer of uncertificated securities, or any of these on presentation or surrender of the certificated security, the funds or securities are available on the date set for payment or exchange, and he takes the security more than one year after that date; and

    (b)   the act or event is not covered by paragraph (a) and he takes the security more than 2 years after the date set for surrender or presentation or the date on which performance became due.

(2) A call that has been revoked is not within subsection (1).

§ 8-204. Effect of Issuer's Restrictions on

Transfer. A restriction on transfer of a security imposed by the issuer, even if otherwise lawful, is ineffective against any person without actual knowledge of it unless:

(a) the security is certificated and the restriction is noted conspicuously thereon; or

(b) the security is uncertificated and a notation of the restriction is contained in the initial transaction statement sent to the person or, if his interest is transferred to him other than by registration of transfer, pledge, or release, the initial transaction statement sent to the registered owner or the registered pledgee.

§ 8-205. Effect of Unauthorized Signature on Certificated Security or Initial Transaction Statement.

An unauthorized signature placed on a certificated security prior to or in the course of issue or placed on an initial transaction statement is ineffective, but the signature is effective in favor of a purchaser for value of the certificated security or a purchaser for value of an uncertificated security to whom the initial transaction statement has been sent, if the purchaser is without notice of the lack of authority and the signing has been done by:

(a) an authenticating trustee, registrar, transfer agent, or other person entrusted by the issuer with the signing of the security, of similar securities, or of initial transaction statements or the immediate preparation for signing of any of them; or

(b) an employee of the issuer, or of any of the foregoing, entrusted with responsible handling of the security or initial transaction statement.

§ 8-206. Completion or Alteration of Certificated Security or Initial Transaction Statement.

(1) If a certificated security contains the signatures necessary to its issue or transfer but is incomplete in any other respect:

(a) any person may complete it by filling in the blanks as authorized; and

(b) even though the blanks are incorrectly filled in, the security as completed is enforceable by a purchaser who took it for value and without notice of the incorrectness.

(2) A complete certificated security that has been improperly altered, even though fraudulently, remains enforceable, but only according to its original terms.

(3) If an initial transaction statement contains the signatures necessary to its validity, but is incomplete in any other respect:

(a) any person may complete it by filling in the blanks as authorized; and

(b) even though the blanks are incorrectly filled in, the statement as completed is effective in favor of the person to whom it is sent if he purchased the security referred to therein for value and without notice of the incorrectness.

(4) A complete initial transaction statement that has been improperly altered, even though fraudulently, is effective in favor of a purchaser to whom it has been sent, but only according to its original terms.

§ 8-207. Rights and Duties of Issuer With Respect to Registered Owners and Registered Pledgees.

(1) Prior to due presentment for registration of transfer of a certificated security in registered form, the issuer or indenture trustee may treat the registered owner as the person exclusively entitled to vote, to receive notifications, and otherwise to exercise all the rights and powers of an owner.

(2) Subject to the provisions of subsections (3), (4), and (6), the issuer or indenture trustee may treat the registered owner of an uncertificated security as the person exclusively entitled to vote, to receive notifications, and otherwise to exercise all the rights and powers of an owner.

(3) The registered owner of an uncertificated security that is subject to a registered pledge is not entitled to registration of transfer prior to the due presentment to the issuer of a release instruction. The exercise of conversion rights with respect to a convertible uncertificated security is a transfer within the meaning of this section.

(4) Upon due presentment of a transfer instruction from the registered pledgee of an uncertificated security, the issuer shall:

(a) register the transfer of the security to the new owner free of pledge, if the instruction specifies a new owner (who may be the registered pledgee) and does not specify a pledgee;

(b) register the transfer of the security to the new owner subject to the interest of the existing pledgee, if the instruction specifies a new owner and the existing pledgee; or

(c) register the release of the security from the existing pledge and register the pledge of the security to the other pledgee, if the instruction specifies the existing owner and another pledgee.

(5) Continuity of perfection of a security interest is not broken by registration of transfer under subsection (4)(b) or by registration of release and pledge under subsection (4)(c), if the security interest is assigned.

(6) If an uncertificated security is subject to a registered pledge:

(a) any uncertificated securities issued in exchange for or distributed with respect to the pledged security shall be registered subject to the pledge;

(b) any certificated securities issued in exchange for or distributed with respect to the pledge security shall be delivered to the registered pledgee; and

(c) any money paid in exchange for or in redemption of part or all of the security shall be paid to the registered pledgee.

(7) Nothing in this Article shall be construed to affect the liability of the registered owner of a security for calls, assessments, or the like.

§ 8-208. Effect of Signature of Authenticating Trustee, Registrar, or Transfer Agent.

(1) A person placing his signature upon a certificated security or an initial transaction statement as authenticating trustee, registrar, transfer agent, or the like, warrants to a purchaser for value of the certificated security or a purchaser for value of an uncertificated security to whom the initial transaction statement has been sent, if the purchaser is without notice of the particular defect, that:

(a) the certificated security or initial transaction statement is genuine;

(b) his own participation in the issue or registration of the transfer, pledge, or release of the security is within his capacity and within the scope of the authority received by him from the issuer; and

(c) he has reasonable grounds to believe the security is in the form and within the amount the issuer is authorized to issue.

(2) Unless otherwise agreed, a person by so placing his signature does not assume responsibility for the validity of the security in other respects.

Part 3. Transfer

§ 8-301. Rights Acquired by Purchaser.

(1) Upon transfer of a security to a purchaser (Section 8-313), the purchaser acquires the rights in the security which his transferor had or had actual authority to convey unless the purchaser's rights are limited by Section 8-302(4).

(2) A transferee of a limited interest acquires rights only to the extent of the interest transferred. The creation or release of a security interest in a security is the transfer of a limited interest in that security.

§ 8-302. "Bona Fide Purchaser"; "Adverse Claim"; Title Acquired by Bona Fide Purchaser.

(1) A "bona fide purchaser" is a purchaser for value in good faith and without notice of any adverse claim:

(a) who takes delivery of a certificated security in bearer form or in registered form, issued or indorsed to him or in blank;

(b) to whom the transfer, pledge, or release of an uncertificated security is registered on the books of the issuer; or

(c) to whom a security is transferred under the provisions of paragraph (c), (d)(i), or (g) of Section 8-313(1).

(2) "Adverse claim" includes a claim that a transfer was or would be wrongful or that a particular adverse person is the owner of or has an interest in the security.

(3) A bona fide purchaser in addition to acquiring the rights of a purchaser (Section 8-301) also acquires his interest in the security free of any adverse claim.

(4) Notwithstanding Section 8-301(1), the transferee of a particular certificated security who has been a party to any fraud or illegality affecting the security, or who as a prior holder of that certificated security had notice of an adverse claim, cannot improve his position by taking from a bona fide purchaser.

§ 8-303. "Broker."
"Broker" means a person engaged for all or part of his time in the business of buying and selling securities, who in the transaction concerned acts for, buys a security from, or sells a security to, a customer. Nothing in this Article deter-

mines the capacity in which a person acts for purposes of any other statute or rule to which the person is subject.

§ 8-304. Notice to Purchaser of Adverse Claims.

(1) A purchaser (including a broker for the seller or buyer, but excluding an intermediary bank) of a certificated security is charged with notice of adverse claims if:

    (a) the security, whether in bearer or registered form, has been indorsed "for collection" or "for surrender" or for some other purpose not involving transfer; or

    (b) the security is in bearer form and has on it an unambiguous statement that it is the property of a person other than the transferor. The mere writing of a name on a security is not such a statement.

(2) A purchaser (including a broker for the seller or buyer, but excluding an intermediary bank) to whom the transfer, pledge, or release of an uncertificated security is registered is charged with notice of adverse claims as to which the issuer has a duty under Section 8-403(4) at the time of registration and which are noted in the initial transaction statement sent to the purchaser or, if his interest is transferred to him other than by registration of transfer, pledge, or release, the initial transaction statement sent to the registered owner or the registered pledgee.

(3) The fact that the purchaser (including a broker for the seller or buyer) of a certificated or uncertificated security has notice that the security is held for a third person or is registered in the name of or indorsed by a fiduciary does not create a duty of inquiry into the rightfulness of the transfer or constitute constructive notice of adverse claims. However, if the purchaser (excluding an intermediary bank) has knowledge that the proceeds are being used or that the transaction is for the individual benefit of the fiduciary or otherwise in breach of duty, the purchaser is charged with notice of adverse claims.

§ 8-305. Staleness as Notice of Adverse Claims.

An act or event that creates a right to immediate performance of the principal obligation represented by a certificated security or sets a date on or after which a certificated security is to be presented or surrendered for redemption or exchange does not itself constitute any notice of adverse claims except in the case of a transfer:

    (a) after one year from any date set for presentment or surrender for redemption or exchange; or

    (b) after 6 months from any date set for payment of money against presentation or surrender of the security if funds are available for payment on that date.

§ 8-306. Warranties on Presentment and Transfer of Certificated Securities; Warranties of Originators of Instructions.

(1) A person who presents a certificated security for registration of transfer or for payment or exchange warrants to the issuer that he is entitled to the registration, payment, or exchange. But, a purchaser for value and without notice of adverse claims who receives a new, reissued, or re-registered certificated security on registration of transfer or receives an initial transaction statement confirming the registration of transfer of an equivalent uncertificated security to him warrants only that he has no knowledge of any unauthorized signature (Section 8-311) in a necessary indorsement.

(2) A person by transferring a certificated security to a purchaser for value warrants only that:

    (a) his transfer is effective and rightful;

    (b) the security is genuine and has not been materially altered; and

    (c) he knows of no fact which might impair the validity of the security.

(3) If a certificated security is delivered by an intermediary known to be entrusted with delivery of the security on behalf of another or with collection of a draft or other claim against delivery, the intermediary by delivery warrants only his own good faith and authority, even though he has purchased or made advances against the claim to be collected against the delivery.

(4) A pledgee or other holder for security who redelivers a certificated security received, or after payment and on order of the debtor delivers that security to a third person, makes only the warranties of an intermediary under subsection (3).

(5) A person who originates an instruction warrants to the issuer that:

    (a) he is an appropriate person to originate the instruction; and

    (b) at the time the instruction is presented to the issuer he will be entitled to the registration of transfer, pledge, or release.

(6) A person who originates an instruction warrants to any person specially guaranteeing his signature (subsection 8-312 (3)) that:

    (a)   he is an appropriate person to originate the instruction; and

    (b)   at the time the instruction is presented to the issuer

        (i)   he will be entitled to the registration of transfer, pledge, or release; and

        (ii)   the transfer, pledge, or release requested in the instruction will be registered by the issuer free from all liens, security interests, restrictions, and claims other than those specified in the instruction.

(7) A person who originates an instruction warrants to a purchaser for value and to any person guaranteeing the instruction (Section 8-312(6)) that:

    (a)   he is an appropriate person to originate the instruction;

    (b)   the uncertificated security referred to therein is valid; and

    (c)   at the time the instruction is presented to the issuer

        (i)   the transferor will be entitled to the registration of transfer, pledge, or release;

        (ii)   the transfer, pledge, or release requested in the instruction will be registered by the issuer free from all liens, security interests, restrictions, and claims other than those specified in the instruction; and

        (iii)   the requested transfer, pledge, or release will be rightful.

(8) If a secured party is the registered pledgee or the registered owner of an uncertificated security, a person who originates an instruction of release or transfer to the debtor or, after payment and on order of the debtor, a transfer instruction to a third person, warrants to the debtor or the third person only that he is an appropriate person to originate the instruction and, at the time the instruction is presented to the issuer, the transferor will be entitled to the registration of release or transfer. If a transfer instruction to a third person who is a purchaser for value is originated on order of the debtor, the debtor makes to the purchaser the warranties of paragraphs (b), (c)(ii) and (c)(iii) of subsection (7).

(9) A person who transfers an uncertificated security to a purchaser for value and does not originate an instruction in connection with the transfer warrants only that:

    (a)   his transfer is effective and rightful; and

    (b)   the uncertificated security is valid.

(10) A broker gives to his customer and to the issuer and a purchaser the applicable warranties provided in this section and has the rights and privileges of a purchaser under this section. The warranties of and in favor of the broker, acting as an agent are in addition to applicable warranties given by and in favor of his customer.

§ 8-307. Effect of Delivery Without Indorsement; Right to Compel Indorsement. If a certificated security in registered form has been delivered to a purchaser without a necessary indorsement he may become a bona fide purchaser only as of the time the indorsement is supplied; but against the transferor, the transfer is complete upon delivery and the purchaser has a specifically enforceable right to have any necessary indorsement supplied.

§ 8-308. Indorsements; Instructions.

(1) An indorsement of a certificated security in registered form is made when an appropriate person signs on it or on a separate document an assignment or transfer of the security or a power to assign or transfer it or his signature is written without more upon the back of the security.

(2) An endorsement may be in blank or special. An indorsement in blank includes an indorsement to bearer. A special indorsement specifies to whom the security is to be transferred, or who has power to transfer it. A holder may convert a blank indorsement into a special indorsement.

(3) An indorsement purporting to be only of part of a certificated security representing units intended by the issuer to be separately transferable is effective to the extent of the indorsement.

(4) An "instruction" is an order to the issuer of an uncertificated security requesting that the transfer, pledge, or release from pledge of the uncertificated security specified therein be registered.

(5) An instruction originated by an appropriate person is:

    (a)   a writing signed by an appropriate person; or

    (b)   a communication to the issuer in any form agreed upon in a writing signed by the issuer and an appropriate person.

If an instruction has been originated by an appropriate person but is incomplete in any other respect, any person may complete it as authorized and the issuer may rely on it as completed even though it has been completed incorrectly.

(6) "An appropriate person" in subsection (1) means the person specified by the certificated security or by special indorsement to be entitled to the security.

(7) "An appropriate person" in subsection (5) means:

    (a)   for an instruction to transfer or pledge an uncertificated security which is then not subject to a registered pledge, the registered owner; or

    (b)   for an instruction to transfer or release an uncertificated security which is then subject to a registered pledge, the registered pledgee.

(8) In addition to the persons designated in subsections (6) and (7), "an appropriate person" in subsections (1) and (5) includes:

    (a)   if the person designated is described as a fiduciary but is no longer serving in the described capacity, either that person or his successor;

    (b)   if the persons designated are described as more than one person as fiduciaries and one or more are no longer serving in the described capacity, the remaining fiduciary or fiduciaries, whether or not a successor has been appointed or qualified;

    (c)   if the person designated is an individual and is without capacity to act by virtue of death, incompetence, infancy, or otherwise, his executor, administrator, guardian, or like fiduciary;

    (d)   if the persons designated are described as more than one person as tenants by the entirety or with right of survivorship and by reason of death all cannot sign, the survivor or survivors;

    (e)   a person having power to sign under applicable law or controlling instrument; and

    (f)   to the extent that the person designated or any of the foregoing persons may act through an agent, his authorized agent.

(9) Unless otherwise agreed, the indorser of a certificated security by his indorsement or the originator of an instruction by his origination assumes no obligation that the security will be honored by the issuer but only the obligations provided in Section 8-306.

(10) Whether the person signing is appropriate is determined as of the date of signing and an indorsement made by or an instruction originated by him does not become unauthorized for the purposes of this Article by virtue of any subsequent change of circumstances.

(11) Failure of a fiduciary to comply with a controlling instrument or with the law of the state having jurisdiction of the fiduciary relationship, including any law requiring the fiduciary to obtain court approval of the transfer, pledge, or release, does not render his indorsement or an instruction originated by him unauthorized for the purposes of this Article.

§ 8-309. Effect of Indorsement Without Delivery. An indorsement of a certificated security, whether special or in blank, does not constitute a transfer until delivery of the certificated security on which it appears or, if the indorsement is on a separate document, until delivery of both the document and the certificated security.

§ 8-310. Indorsement of Certificated Security in Bearer Form. An indorsement of a certificated security in bearer form may give notice of adverse claims (Section 8-304) but does not otherwise affect any right to registration the holder possesses.

§ 8-311. Effect of Unauthorized Indorsement or Instruction. Unless the owner or pledgee has ratified an unauthorized indorsement or instruction or is otherwise precluded from asserting its ineffectiveness:

    (a)   he may assert its ineffectiveness against the issuer or any purchaser, other than a purchaser for value and without notice of adverse claims, who has in good faith received a new, reissued, or re-registered certificated security on registration of transfer or received an initial transaction statement confirming the registration of transfer, pledge, or release of an equivalent uncertificated security to him; and

    (b)   an issuer who registers the transfer of a certificated security upon the unauthorized indorsement or who registers the transfer, pledge, or release of an uncertificated security upon the unauthorized instruction is subject to liability for improper registration (Section 8-404).

§ 8-312. Effect of Guaranteeing Signature, Indorsement or Instruction.

(1) Any person guaranteeing a signature of an indorser of a certificated security warrants that at the time of signing:

    (a)   the signature was genuine;

    (b)   the signer was an appropriate person to indorse (Section 8-308); and

    (c)   the signer had legal capacity to sign.

(2) Any person guaranteeing a signature of the originator of an instruction warrants that at the time of signing:

    (a)   the signature was genuine;

    (b)   the signer was an appropriate person to originate the instruction (Section 8-308) if the person specified in the instruction as the registered owner or registered pledgee of the uncertificated security was, in fact, the registered owner or registered pledgee of the security, as to which fact the signature guarantor makes no warranty;

    (c)   the signer had legal capacity to sign; and

    (d)   the taxpayer identification number, if any, appearing on the instruction as that of the registered owner or registered pledgee was the taxpayer identification number of the signer or of the owner or pledgee for whom the signer was acting.

(3) Any person specially guaranteeing the signature of the originator of an instruction makes not only the warranties of a signature guarantor (subsection (2) but also warrants that at the time the instruction is presented to the issuer:

    (a)   the person specified in the instruction as the registered owner or registered pledgee of the uncertificated security will be the registered owner or registered pledgee; and

    (b)   the transfer, pledge, or release of the uncertificated security requested in the instruction will be registered by the issuer free from all liens, security interests, restrictions, and claims other than those specified in the instruction.

(4) The guarantor under subsections (1) and (2) or the special guarantor under subsection (3) does not otherwise warrant the rightfulness of the particular transfer, pledge, or release.

(5) Any person guaranteeing an indorsement of a certificated security makes not only the warranties of a signature guarantor under subsection (1) but also warrants the rightfulness of the particular transfer in all respects.

(6) Any person guaranteeing an instruction requesting the transfer, pledge, or release of an uncertificated security makes not only the warranties of a special signature guarantor under subsection (3) but also warrants the rightfulness of the particular transfer, pledge, or release in all respects.

(7) No issuer may require a special guarantee of signature (subsection (3)), a guarantee of indorsement (subsection (5)), or a guarantee of instruction (subsection (6)) as a condition to registration of transfer, pledge, or release.

(8) The foregoing warranties are made to any person taking or dealing with the security in reliance on the guarantee, and the guarantor is liable to the person for any loss resulting from breach of the warranties.

§ 8-313. When Transfer to Purchaser Occurs; Financial Intermediary as Bona Fide Purchaser; "Financial Intermediary."

(1) Transfer of a security or a limited interest (including a security interest) therein to a purchaser occurs only:

    (a)   at the time he or a person designated by him acquires possession of a certificated security;

    (b)   at the time the transfer, pledge, or release of an uncertificated security is registered to him or a person designated by him;

    (c)   at the time his financial intermediary acquires possession of a certificated security specially indorsed to or issued in the name of the purchaser;

    (d)   at the time a financial intermediary, not a clearing corporation, sends him confirmation of the purchase and also by book entry or otherwise identifies as belonging to the purchaser.

        (i)   a specific certificated security in the financial intermediary's possession;

        (ii)   a quantity of securities that constitute or are part of a fungible bulk of certificated securities in the financial intermediary's possession or of uncertificated securities registered in the name of the financial intermediary; or

(iii) a quantity of securities that constitute or are part of a fungible bulk of securities shown on the account of the financial intermediary on the books of another financial intermediary;

(e) with respect to an identified certificated security to be delivered while still in the possession of a third person, not a financial intermediary, at the time that person acknowledges that he holds for the purchaser;

(f) with respect to a specific uncertificated security the pledge or transfer of which has been registered to a third person, not a financial intermediary, at the time that person acknowledges that he holds for the purchaser;

(g) at the time appropriate entries to the account of the purchaser or a person designated by him on the books of a clearing corporation are made under Section 8-320;

(h) with respect to the transfer of a security interest where the debtor has signed a security agreement containing a description of the security, at the time a written notification, which, in the case of the creation of the security interest, is signed by the debtor (which may be a copy of the security agreement) or which, in the case of the release or assignment of the security interest created pursuant to this paragraph, is signed by the secured party, is received by

(i) a financial intermediary on whose books the interest of the transferor in the security appears;

(ii) a third person, not a financial intermediary, in possession of the security, if it is certificated;

(iii) a third person, not a financial intermediary, who is the registered owner of the security, if it is uncertificated and not subject to a registered pledge; or

(iv) a third person, not a financial intermediary, who is the registered pledgee of the security, if it is uncer-

tificated and subject to a registered pledge;

(i) with respect to the transfer of a security interest where the transferor has signed a security agreement containing a description of the security, at the time new value is given by the secured party; or

(j) with respect to the transfer of a security interest where the secured party is a financial intermediary and the security has already been transferred to the financial intermediary under paragraphs (a), (b), (c), (d), or (g), at the time the transferor has signed a security agreement containing a description of the security and value is given by the secured party.

(2) The purchaser is the owner of a security held for him by a financial intermediary, but cannot be a bona fide purchaser of a security so held except in the circumstances specified in paragraphs (c), (d)(i), and (g) of subsection (1). If a security so held is part of a fungible bulk, as in the circumstances specified in paragraphs (d)(ii) and (d)(iii) of subsection (1), the purchaser is the owner of a proportionate property interest in the fungible bulk.

(3) Notice of an adverse claim received by the financial intermediary or by the purchaser after the financial intermediary takes delivery of a certificated security as a holder for value or after the transfer, pledge, or release of an uncertificated security has been registered free of the claim to a financial intermediary who has given value is not effective either as to the financial intermediary or as to the purchaser. However, as between the financial intermediary and the purchaser the purchaser may demand transfer of an equivalent security as to which no notice of adverse claim has been received.

(4) A "financial intermediary" is a bank, broker, clearing corporation, or other person (or the nominee of any of them) which in the ordinary course of its business maintains security accounts for its customers and is acting in that capacity. A financial intermediary may have a security interest in securities held in account for its customer.

§ 8-314. Duty to Transfer, When Completed.

(1) Unless otherwise agreed, if a sale of a security is made on an exchange or otherwise through brokers:

(a) the selling customer fulfills his duty to transfer at the time he:

(i) places a certificated security in the

possession of the selling broker or a person designated by the broker;

(ii) causes an uncertificated security to be registered in the name of the selling broker or a person designated by the broker;

(iii) if requested, causes an acknowledgment to be made to the selling broker that a certificated or uncertificated security is held for the broker; or

(iv) places in the possession of the selling broker or of a person designated by the broker a transfer instruction for an uncertificated security, providing the issuer does not refuse to register the requested transfer if the instruction is presented to the issuer for registration within 30 days thereafter; and

(b) the selling broker, including a correspondent broker acting for a selling customer, fulfills his duty to transfer at the time he:

(i) places a certificated security in the possession of the buying broker or a person designated by the buying broker;

(ii) causes an uncertificated security to be registered in the name of the buying broker or a person designated by the buying broker;

(iii) places in the possession of the buying broker or of a person designated by the buying broker a transfer instruction for an uncertificated security, providing the issuer does not refuse to register the requested transfer if the instruction is presented to the issuer for registration within 30 days thereafter; or

(iv) effects clearance of the sale in accordance with the rules of the exchange on which the transaction took place.

(2) Except as provided in this section or unless otherwise agreed, a transferor's duty to transfer a security under a contract of purchase is not fulfilled until he:

(a) places a certificated security in form to be negotiated by the purchaser in the possession of the purchaser or of a person designated by the purchaser;

(b) causes an uncertificated security to be registered in the name of the purchaser or a person designated by the purchaser; or

(c) if the purchaser requests, causes an acknowledgment to be made to the purchaser that a certificated or uncertificated security is held for the purchaser.

(3) Unless made on an exchange, a sale to a broker purchasing for his own account is within subsection (2) and not within subsection (1).

§ 8-315. Action Against Transferee Based Upon Wrongful Transfer.

(1) Any person against whom the transfer of a security is wrongful for any reason, including his incapacity, as against anyone except a bona fide purchaser, may:

(a) reclaim possession of the certificated security wrongfully transferred;

(b) obtain possession of any new certificated security representing all or part of the same rights;

(c) compel the origination of an instruction to transfer to him or a person designated by him an uncertificated security constituting all or part of the same rights; or

(d) have damages.

(2) If the transfer is wrongful because of an unauthorized indorsement of a certificated security, the owner may also reclaim or obtain possession of the security or a new certificated security, even from a bona fide purchaser, if the ineffectiveness of the purported indorsement can be asserted against him under the provisions of this Article on unauthorized indorsements (Section 8-311).

(3) The right to obtain or reclaim possession of a certificated security or to compel the origination of a transfer instruction may be specifically enforced and the transfer of a certificated or uncertificated security enjoined and a certificated security impounded pending the litigation.

§ 8-316. Purchaser's Right to Requisites for Registration of Transfer, Pledge, or Release on Books.
Unless otherwise agreed, the transferor of a certificated security or the transferor, pledgor, or pledgee of an uncertificated security on due demand must supply his purchaser with any proof of his authority to transfer, pledge, or release or with any other requisite necessary to obtain registration of the transfer, pledge, or release of the security; but if the transfer, pledge, or release is not for value, a transferor, pledgor, or pledgee need not do so unless the

purchaser furnishes the necessary expenses. Failure within a reasonable time to comply with a demand made gives the purchaser the right to reject or rescind the transfer, pledge, or release.

§ 8-317. Creditors' Rights.

(1) Subject to the exceptions in subsections (3) and (4), no attachment or levy upon a certificated security or any share or other interest represented thereby which is outstanding is valid until the security is actually seized by the officer making the attachment or levy, but a certificated security which has been surrendered to the issuer may be reached by a creditor by legal process at the issuer's chief executive office in the United States.

(2) An uncertificated security registered in the name of the debtor may not be reached by a creditor except by legal process at the issuer's chief executive office in the United States.

(3) The interest of a debtor in a certificated security that is in the possession of a secured party not a financial intermediary or in an uncertificated security registered in the name of a secured party not a financial intermediary (or in the name of a nominee of the secured party) may be reached by a creditor by legal process upon the secured party.

(4) The interest of a debtor in a certificated security that is in the possession of or registered in the name of a financial intermediary or in an uncertificated security registered in the name of a financial intermediary may be reached by a creditor by legal process upon the financial intermediary on whose books the interest of the debtor appears.

(5) Unless otherwise provided by law, a creditor's lien upon the interest of a debtor in a security obtained pursuant to subsection (3) or (4) is not a restraint on the transfer of the security, free of the lien, to a third party for new value; but in the event of a transfer, the lien applies to the proceeds of the transfer in the hands of the secured party or financial intermediary, subject to any claims having priority.

(6) A creditor whose debtor is the owner of a security is entitled to aid from courts of appropriate jurisdiction, by injunction or otherwise, in reaching the security or in satisfying the claim by means allowed at law or in equity in regard to property that cannot readily be reached by ordinary legal process.

§ 8-318. No Conversion by Good Faith Conduct.

An agent or bailee who in good faith (including observance of reasonable commercial standards if he is in the business of buying, selling, or otherwise dealing with securities) has received certificated securities and sold, pledged, or delivered them or has sold or caused the transfer or pledge of uncertificated securities over which he had control according to the instructions of his principal, is not liable for conversion or for participation in breach of fiduciary duty although the principal had no right so to deal with the securities.

§ 8-319. Statute of Frauds.

A contract for the sale of securities is not enforceable by way of action or defense unless:

(a) there is some writing signed by the party against whom enforcement is sought or by his authorized agent or broker, sufficient to indicate that a contract has been made for sale of a stated quantity of described securities at a defined or stated price;

(b) delivery of a certificated security or transfer instruction has been accepted, or transfer of an uncertificated security has been registered and the transferee has failed to send written objection to the issuer within 10 days after receipt of the initial transaction statement confirming the registration, or payment has been made, but the contract is enforceable under this provision only to the extent of the delivery, registration, or payment;

(c) within a reasonable time a writing in confirmation of the sale or purchase and sufficient against the sender under paragraph (a) has been received by the party against whom enforcement is sought and he has failed to send written objection to its contents within 10 days after its receipt; or

(d) the party against whom enforcement is sought admits in his pleading, testimony, or otherwise in court that a contract was made for the sale of a stated quantity of described securities at a defined or stated price.

§ 8-320. Transfer or Pledge Within Central Depository System.

(1) In addition to other methods, a transfer, pledge, or release of a security or any interest therein may be effected by the making of appropriate entries on the books of a clearing corporation reducing the

account of the transferor, pledgor, or pledgee and increasing the account of the transferee, pledgee, or pledgor by the amount of the obligation or the number of shares or rights transferred, pledge, or released, if the security is shown on the account of a transferor, pledgor, or pledgee on the books of the clearing corporation; is subject to the control of the clearing corporation; and

(a) if certificated,

(i)   is in the custody of the clearing corporation, another clearing corporation, a custodian bank, or a nominee of any of them; and

(ii) is in bearer form or indorsed in blank by an appropriate person or registered in the name of the clearing corporation, a custodian bank, or a nominee of any of them; or

(b) if uncertificated, is registed in the name of the clearing corporation, another clearing corporation, a custodian bank, or a nominee of any of them.

(2) Under this section entries may be made with respect to like securities or interests therein as a part of a fungible bulk and may refer merely to a quantity of a particular security without reference to the name of the registered owner, certificate or bond number, or the like, and, in appropriate cases, may be on a net basis taking into account other transfers, pledges, or releases of the same security.

(3) A transfer under this section is effective (Section 8–313) and the purchaser acquires the rights of the transferor (Section 8–301). A pledge or release under this section is the transfer of a limited interest. If a pledge or the creation of a security interest is intended, the security interest is perfected at the time when both value is given by the pledgee and the appropriate entries are made (Section 8–321). A transferee or pledgee under this section may be a bona fide purchaser (Section 8–302).

(4) A transfer or pledge under this section is not a registration of transfer under Part 4.

(5) That entries made on the books of the clearing corporation as provided in subsection (1) are not appropriate does not affect the validity or effect of the entries or the liabilities or obligations of the clearing corporation to any person adversely affected thereby.

§ 8–321. Enforceability, Attachment, Perfection and Termination of Security Interests.

(1) A security interest in a security is enforceable

and can attach only if it is transferred to the secured party or a person designated by him pursuant to a provision of Section 8–313(1).

(2) A security interest so transferred pursuant to agreement by a transferor who has rights in the security to a transferee who has given value is a perfected security interest, but a security interest that has been transferred solely under paragraph (i) of Section 8–313(1) becomes unperfected after 21 days unless, within that time, the requirements for transfer under any other provision of Section 8–313(1) are satisfied.

(3) A security interest in a security is subject to the provisions of Article 9, but:

(a) no filing is required to perfect the security interest; and

(b) no written security agreement signed by the debtor is necessary to make the security interest enforceable, except as provided in paragraph (h), (i), or (j) of Section 8–313(1). The secured party has the rights and duties provided under Section 9–207, to the extent they are applicable, whether or not the security is certificated, and, if certificated, whether or not it is in his possession.

(4) Unless otherwise agreed, a security interest in a security is terminated by transfer to the debtor or a person designated by him pursuant to a provision of Section 8–313(1). If a security is thus transferred, the security interest, if not terminated, becomes unperfected unless the security is certificated and is delivered to the debtor for the purpose of ultimate sale or exchange or presentation, collection, renewal, or registration of transfer. In that case, the security interest becomes unperfected after 21 days unless, within that time, the security (or securities for which it has been exchanged) is transferred to the secured party or a person designated by him pursuant to a provision of Section 8–313(1).

Part 4. Registration

§ 8–401. Duty of Issuer to Register Transfer, Pledge, or Release.

(1) If a certificated security in registered form is presented to the issuer with a request to register transfer or an instruction is presented to the issuer with a request to register transfer, pledge, or release, the issuer shall register the transfer, pledge, or release as requested if:

(a) the security is indorsed or the instruction

was originated by the appropriate person or persons (Section 8–308);

(b) reasonable assurance is given that those indorsements or instructions are genuine and effective (Section 8–402);

(c) the issuer has no duty as to adverse claims or has discharged the duty (Section 8–403);

(d) any applicable law relating to the collection of taxes has been complied with; and

(e) the transfer, pledge, or release is in fact rightful or is to a bona fide purchaser.

(2) If an issuer is under a duty to register a transfer, pledge, or release of a security, the issuer is also liable to the person presenting a certificated security or an instruction for registration or his principal for loss resulting from any unreasonable delay in registration or from failure or refusal to register the transfer, pledge, or release.

§ 8–402. Assurance that Indorsements and Instructions Are Effective.

(1) The issuer may require the following assurance that each necessary indorsement of a certificated security or each instruction (Section 8–308) is genuine and effective:

(a) in all cases, a guarantee of the signature (Section 8–312(1) or (2)) of the person indorsing a certificated security or originating an instruction including, in the case of an instruction, a warranty of the taxpayer identification number or, in the absence thereof, other reasonable assurance of identity;

(b) if the indorsement is made or the instruction is originated by an agent, appropriate assurance of authority to sign;

(c) if the indorsement is made or the instruction is originated by a fiduciary, appropriate evidence of appointment or incumbency;

(d) if there is more than one fiduciary, reasonable assurance that all who are required to sign have done so; and

(e) if the indorsement is made or the instruction is originated by a person not covered by any of the foregoing, assurance appropriate to the case corresponding as nearly as may be to the foregoing.

(2) A "guarantee of the signature" in subsection (1) means a guarantee signed by or on behalf of a person reasonably believed by the issuer to be responsible. The issuer may adopt standards with respect to responsibility if they are not manifestly unreasonable.

(3) "Appropriate evidence of appointment or incumbency" in subsection (1) means:

(a) in the case of a fiduciary appointed or qualified by a court, a certificate issued by or under the direction or supervision of that court or an officer thereof and dated within 60 days before the date of presentation for transfer, pledge, or release; or

(b) in any other case, a copy of a document showing the appointment or a certificate issued by or on behalf of a person reasonably believed by the issuer to be responsible or, in the absence of that document or certificate, other evidence reasonably deemed by the issuer to be appropriate. The issuer may adopt standards with respect to the evidence if they are not manifestly unreasonable. The issuer is not charged with notice of the contents of any document obtained pursuant to this paragraph (b) except to the extent that the contents relate directly to the appointment or incumbency.

(4) The issuer may elect to require reasonable assurance beyond that specified in this section, but if it does so and, for a purpose other than that specified in subsection (3)(b), both requires and obtains a copy of a will, trust, indenture, articles of co-partnership, bylaws, or other controlling instrument, it is charged with notice of all matters contained therein affecting the transfer, pledge, or release.

§ 8–403. Issuer's Duty as to Adverse Claims.

(1) An issuer to whom a certificated security is presented for registration shall inquire into adverse claims if:

(a) a written notification of an adverse claim is received at a time and in a manner affording the issuer a reasonable opportunity to act on it prior to the issuance of a new, reissued, or re-registered certificated security and the notification identifies the claimant, the registered owner, and the issue of which the security is a part, and provides an address for communications directed to the claimant; or

(b) the issuer is charged with notice of an adverse claim from a controlling instrument it has elected to require under Section 8–402(4).

(2) The issuer may discharge any duty of inquiry by any reasonable means, including notifying an adverse claimant by registered or certified mail at the address furnished by him or, if there be no such address, at his residence or regular place of business that the certificated security has been presented for registration of transfer by a named person, and that the transfer will be registered unless within 30 days from the date of mailing the notification, either:

    (a)   an appropriate restraining order, injunction, or other process issues from a court of competent jurisdiction; or

    (b)   there is filed with the issuer an indemnity bond, sufficient in the issuer's judgment to protect the issuer and any transfer agent, registrar, or other agent of the issuer involved from any loss it or they may suffer by complying with the adverse claim.

(3) Unless an issuer is charged with notice of an adverse claim from a controlling instrument which it has elected to require under Section 8–402(4) or receives notification of an adverse claim under subsection (1), if a certificated security presented for registration is indorsed by the appropriate person or persons the issuer is under no duty to inquire into adverse claims. In particular:

    (a)   an issuer registering a certificated security in the name of a person who is a fiduciary or who is described as a fiduciary is not bound to inquire into the existence, extent, or correct description of the fiduciary relationship; and thereafter the issuer may assume without inquiry that the newly registered owner continues to be the fiduciary until the issuer receives written notice that the fiduciary is no longer acting as such with respect to the particular security;

    (b)   an issuer registering transfer on an indorsement by a fiduciary is not bound to inquire whether the transfer is made in compliance with a controlling instrument or with the law of the state having jurisdiction of the fiduciary relationship, including any law requiring the fiduciary to obtain court approval of the transfer; and

    (c)   the issuer is not charged with notice of the contents of any court record or file or other recorded or unrecorded document even though the document is in its possession and even though the transfer is made on the indorsement of a fiduciary to the fiduciary himself or to his nominee.

(4) An issuer is under no duty as to adverse claims with respect to an uncertificated security except:

    (a)   claims embodied in a restraining order, injunction, or other legal process served upon the issuer if the process was served at a time and in a manner affording the issuer a reasonable opportunity to act on it in accordance with the requirements of subsection (5);

    (b)   claims of which the issuer has received a written notification from the registered owner or the registered pledgee if the notification was received at a time and in a manner affording the issuer a reasonable opportunity to act on it in accordance with the requirements of subsection (5);

    (c)   claims (including restrictions on transfer not imposed by the issuer) to which the registration of transfer to the present registered owner was subject and were so noted in the initial transaction statement sent to him; and

    (d)   claims as to which an issuer is charged with notice from a controlling instrument it has elected to require under Section 8–402(4).

(5) If the issuer of an uncertificated security is under a duty as to an adverse claim, he discharges that duty by:

    (a)   including a notation of the claim in any statements sent with respect to the security under Sections 8–408(3), (6), and (7); and

    (b)   refusing to register the transfer or pledge of the security unless the nature of the claim does not preclude transfer or pledge subject thereto.

(6) If the transfer or pledge of the security is registered subject to an adverse claim, a notation of the claim must be included in the initial transaction statement and all subsequent statements sent to the transferee and pledgee under Section 8–408.

(7) Notwithstanding subsections (4) and (5), if an

uncertificated security was subject to a registered pledge at the time the issuer first came under a duty as to a particular adverse claim, the issuer has no duty as to that claim if transfer of the security is requested by the registered pledgee or an appropriate person acting for the registered pledgee unless:

(a) the claim was embodied in legal process which expressly provides otherwise;

(b) the claim was asserted in a written notification from the registered pledgee;

(c) the claim was one as to which the issuer was charged with notice from a controlling instrument it required under Section 8–402(4) in connection with the pledgee's request for transfer; or

(d) the transfer requested is to the registered owner. .

§ 8-404. Liability and Non-Liability for Registration.

(1) Except as provided in any law relating to the collection of taxes, the issuer is not liable to the owner, pledgee, or any other person suffering loss as a result of the registration of a transfer, pledge, or release of a security if:

(a) there were on or with a certificated security the necessary indorsements or the issuer had received an instruction originated by an appropriate person (Section 8–308); and

(b) the issuer had no duty as to adverse claims or has discharged the duty (Section 8–403).

(2) If an issuer has registered a transfer of a certificated security to a person not entitled to it, the issuer on demand shall deliver a like security to the true owner unless:

(a) the registration was pursuant to subsection (1);

(b) the owner is precluded from asserting any claim for registering the transfer under Section 8–405(1); or

(c) the delivery would result in overissue, in which case the issuer's liability is governed by Section 8–104.

(3) If an issuer has improperly registered a transfer, pledge, or release of an uncertificated security, the issuer on demand from the injured party shall restore the records as to the injured party to the condition that would have obtained if the improper registration had not been made unless:

(a) the registration was pursuant to subsection (1); or

(b) the registration would result in overissue, in which case the issuer's liability is governed by Section 8–104.

§ 8-405. Lost, Destroyed, and Stolen Certificated Securities.

(1) If a certificated security has been lost, apparently destroyed, or wrongfully taken, and the owner fails to notify the issuer of that fact within a reasonable time after he has notice of it and the issuer registers a transfer of the security before receiving notification, the owner is precluded from asserting against the the issuer any claim for registering the transfer under Section 8–404 or any claim to a new security under this section.

(2) If the owner of a certificated security claims that the security has been lost, destroyed, or wrongfully taken, the issuer shall issue a new certificated security or, at the option of the issuer, an equivalent uncertificated security in place of the original security if the owner:

(a) so requests before the issuer has notice that the security has been acquired by a bona fide purchaser;

(b) files with the issuer a sufficient indemnity bond; and

(c) satisfies any other reasonable requirements imposed by the issuer.

(3) If, after the issue of a new certificated or uncertificated security, a bona fide purchaser of the original certificated security presents it for registration of transfer, the issuer shall register the transfer unless registration would result in overissue, in which event the issuer's liability is governed by Section 8–104. In addition to any rights on the indemnity bond, the issuer may recover the new certificated security from the person to whom it was issued or any person taking under him except a bona fide purchaser or may cancel the uncertificated secutiry unless a bona fide purchaser or any person taking under a bona fide purchaser is then the registered owner or registered pledgee thereof.

§ 8-406. Duty of Authenticating Trustee, Transfer Agent, or Registrar.

(1) If a person acts as authenticating trustee, transfer agent, registrar, or other agent for an issuer in the registration of transfers of its certificated securities or in the registration of transfers, pledges, and releases

of its uncertificated securities, in the issue of new securities, or in the cancellation of surrendered securities:

  (a) he is under a duty to the issuer to exercise good faith and due diligence in performing his functions; and

  (b) with regard to the particular functions he performs, he has the same obligation to the holder or owner of a certificated security or to the owner or pledgee of an uncertificated security and has the same rights and privileges as the issuer has in regard to those functions.

(2) Notice to an authenticating trustee, transfer agent, registrar or other agent is notice to the issuer with respect to the functions performed by the agent.

§ 8-407. Exchangeability of Securities.

(1) No issuer is subject to the requirements of this section unless it regularly maintains a system for issuing the class of securities involved under which both certificated and uncertificated securities are regularly issued to the category of owners, which includes the person in whose name the new security is to be registered.

(2) Upon surrender of a certificated security with all necessary indorsements and presentation of a written request by the person surrendering the security, the issuer, if he has no duty as to adverse claims or has discharged the duty (Section 8-403), shall issue to the person or a person designated by him an equivalent uncertificated security subject to all liens, restrictions, and claims that were noted on the certificated security.

(3) Upon receipt of a transfer instruction originated by an appropriate person who so requests, the issuer of an uncertificated security shall cancel the uncertificated security and issue an equivalent certificated security on which must be noted conspicuously any liens and restrictions of the issuer and any adverse claims (as to which the issuer has a duty under Section 8-403(4)) to which the uncertificated security was subject. The certificated security shall be registered in the name of and delivered to:

  (a) the registered owner, if the uncertificated security was not subject to a registered pledge; or

  (b) the registered pledgee, if the uncertificated security was subject to a registered pledge.

§ 8-408. Statements of Uncertificated Securities.

(1) Within 2 business days after the transfer of an uncertificated security has been registered, the issuer shall send to the new registered owner and, if the security has been transferred subject to a registered pledge, to the registered pledgee a written statement containing:

  (a) a description of the issue of which the uncertificated security is a part;

  (b) the number of shares or units transferred;

  (c) the name and address and any taxpayer identification number of the new registered owner and, if the security has been transferred subject to a registered pledge, the name and address and any taxpayer identification number of the registered pledgee;

  (d) a notation of any liens and restrictions of the issuer and any adverse claims (as to which the issuer has a duty under Section 8-403(4)) to which the uncertificated security is or may be subject at the time of registration or a statement that there are none of those liens, restrictions, or adverse claims; and

  (e) the date the transfer was registered.

(2) Within 2 business days after the pledge of an uncertificated security has been registered, the issuer shall send to the registered owner and the registered pledgee a written statement containing:

  (a) a description of the issue of which the uncertificated security is a part;

  (b) the number of shares or units pledged;

  (c) the name and address and any taxpayer identification number of the registered owner and the registered pledgee;

  (d) a notation of any liens and restrictions of the issuer and any adverse claims (as to which the issuer has a duty under Section 8-403(4)) to which the uncertificated security is or may be subject at the time of registration or a statement that there are none of those liens, restrictions, or adverse claims; and

  (e) the date the pledge was registered.

(3) Within 2 business days after the release from peldge of an uncertificated security has been registered, the issuer shall send to the registered owner and the pledgee whose interest was released a written statement containing:

(a)   a description of the issue of which the uncertificated security is a part;

(b)   the number of shares or units released from pledge;

(c)   the name and address and any taxpayer identification number of the registered owner and the pledgee whose interest was released;

(d)   a notation of any liens and restrictions of the issuer and any adverse claims (as to which the issuer has a duty under Section 8–403(4)) to which the uncertificated security is or may be subject at the time of registration or a statement that there are none of those liens, restrictions, or adverse claims; and

(e)   the date the release was registered.

(4) An "initial transaction statement" is the statement sent to:

(a)   the new registered owner and, if applicable, to the registered pledgee pursuant to subsection (1);

(b)   the registered pledgee pursuant to subsection (2); or

(c)   the registered owner pursuant to subsection (3).

Each initial transaction statement shall be signed by or on behalf of the issuer and must be identified as "Initial Transaction Statement."

(5) Within 2 business days after the transfer of an uncertificated security has been registered, the issuer shall send to the former registered owner and the former registered pledgee, if any, a written statement containing:

(a)   a description of the issue of which the uncertificated security is a part;

(b)   the number of shares or units transferred;

(c)   the name and address and any taxpayer identification number of the former registered owner and of any former registered pledgee; and

(d)   the date the transfer was registered.

(6) At periodic intervals no less frequent than annually and at any time upon the reasonable written request of the registered owner, the issuer shall send to the registered owner of each uncertificated security a dated written statement containing:

(a)   a description of the issue of which the uncertificated security is a part;

(b)   the name and address and any taxpayer

identification number of the registered owner;

(c)   the number of shares or units of the uncertificated security registered in the name of the registered owner on the date of the statement;

(d)   the name and address and any taxpayer identification number of any registered pledgee and the number of shares or units subject to the pledge; and

(e)   a notation of any liens and restrictions of the issuer and any adverse claims (as to which the issuer has a duty under Section 8–403(4)) to which the uncertificated security is or may be subject or a statement that there are none of those liens, restrictions, or adverse claims.

(7) At periodic intervals no less frequent than annually and at any time upon the reasonable written request of the registered pledgee, the issuer shall send to the registered pledgee of each uncertificated security a dated written statement containing:

(a)   a description of the issue of which the uncertificated security is a part;

(b)   the name and address and any taxpayer identification number of the registered owner;

(c)   the name and address and any taxpayer identification number of the registered pledgee;

(d)   the number of shares or units subject to the pledge; and

(e)   a notation of any liens and restrictions of the issuer and any adverse claims (as to which the issuer has a duty under Section 8–403(4)) to which the uncertificated security is or may be subject or a statement that there are none of those liens, restrictions, or adverse claims.

(8) If the issuer sends the statements described in subsections (6) and (7) at periodic intervals no less frequent than quarterly, the issuer is not obliged to send additional statements upon request unless the owner or pledgee requesting them pays to the issuer the reasonable cost of furnishing them.

(9) Each statement sent pursuant to this section must bear a conspicuous legend reading substantially as follows: "This statement is merely a record of the rights of the addressee as of the time of its issuance. Delivery of this statement, of itself, confers no

rights on the recipient. This statement is neither a negotiable instrument nor a security."

ARTICLE 9. SECURED TRANSACTIONS; SALES OF ACCOUNTS AND CHATTEL PAPER

Part 1. Short Title, Applicability and Definitions

§ 9-101. Short Title.
This Article shall be known and may be cited as Uniform Commercial Code—Secured Transactions.

§ 9-102. Policy and Subject Matter of Article.
(1) Except as otherwise provided in Section 9–104 on excluded transactions, this Article applies

    (a)   to any transaction (regardless of its form) which is intended to create a security interest in personal property or fixtures including goods, documents, instruments, general intangibles, chattel paper or accounts; and also

    (b)   to any sale of accounts or chattel paper.

(2) This Article applies to security interests created by contract including pledge, assignment, chattel mortgage, chattel trust, trust deed, factor's lien, equipment trust, conditional sale, trust receipt, other lien or title retention contract and lease or consignment intended as security. This Article does not apply to statutory liens except as provided in Section 9–310.

(3) The application of this Article to a security interest in a secured obligation is not affected by the fact that the obligation is itself secured by a transaction or interest to which this Article does not apply. Amended in 1972.

Note: The adoption of this Article should be accompanied by the repeal of existing statutes dealing with conditional sales, trust receipts, factor's liens where the factor is given a non-possessory lien, chattel mortgages, crop mortgages, mortgages on railroad equipment, assignment of accounts and generally statutes regulating security interests in personal property.

Where the state has a retail installment selling act or small loan act, that legislation should be carefully examined to determine what changes in those acts are needed to conform them to this Article. This Article primarily sets out rules defining rights of a secured party against persons dealing with the debtor; it does not prescribe regulations and controls which may be necessary to curb abuses arising in the small loan business or in the financing of consumer purchases on credit. Accordingly there is no intention to repeal existing regulatory acts in those fields by enactment or re-enactment of Article 9. See Section 9–203(4) and the Note thereto.

§ 9-103. Perfection of Security Interest in Multiple State Transactions.
(1) Documents, instruments and ordinary goods.

    (a)   This subsection applies to documents and instruments and to goods other than those covered by a certificate of title described in subsection (2), mobile goods described in subsection (3), and minerals described in subsection (5).

    (b)   Except as otherwise provided in this subsection, perfection and the effect of perfection or non-perfection of a security interest in collateral are governed by the law of the jurisdiction where the collateral is when the last event occurs on which is based the assertion that the security interest is perfected or unperfected.

    (c)   If the parties to a transaction creating a purchase money security interest in goods in one jurisdiction understand at the time that the security interest attaches that the goods will be kept in another jurisdiction, then the law of the other jurisdiction governs the perfection and the effect of perfection or non-perfection of the security interest from the time it attaches until thirty days after the debtor receives possession of the goods and thereafter if the goods are taken to the other jurisdiction before the end of the thirty-day period.

    (d)   When collateral is brought into and kept in this state while subject to a security interest perfected under the law of the jurisdiction from which the collateral was removed, the security interest remains perfected, but if action is required by Part 3 of this Article to perfect the security interest,

        (i)   if the action is not taken before the expiration of the period of perfection in the other jurisdiction or the end of four months after the collat-

eral is brought into this state, whichever period first expires, the security
interest becomes unperfected at the
end of that period and is thereafter
deemed to have been unperfected as
against a person who became a purchaser after removal;

(ii)   if the action is taken before the expiration of the period specified in
subparagraph (i), the security interest continues perfected thereafter;

(iii) for the purpose of priority over a
buyer of consumer goods (subsection (2) of Section 9–307), the period
of the effectiveness of a filing in the
jurisdiction from which the collateral is removed is governed by the
rules with respect to perfection in
subparagraphs (i) and (ii).

(2) Certificate of title.

(a)   This subsection applies to goods covered
by a certificate of title issued under a statute of this state or of another jurisdiction
under the law of which indication of a security interest on the certificate is required as a condition of perfection.

(b)   Except as otherwise provided in this subsection, perfection and the effect of perfection or non-perfection of the security
interest are governed by the law (including the conflict of laws rules) of the jurisdiction issuing the certificate until four
months after the goods are removed from
that jurisdiction and thereafter until the
goods are registered in another jurisdiction, but in any event not beyond surrender of the certificate. After the
expiration of that period, the goods are
not covered by the certificate of title
within the meaning of this section.

(c)   Except with respect to the rights of a
buyer described in the next paragraph, a
security interest, perfected in another jurisdiction otherwise than by notation on
a certificate of title, in goods brought into
this state and thereafter covered by a certificate of title issued by this state is subject to the rules stated in paragraph (d) of
subsection (1).

(d)   If goods are brought into this state while
a security interest therein is perfected in
any manner under the law of the jurisdiction from which the goods are removed
and a certificate of title is issued by this
state and the certificate does not show
that the goods are subject to the security
interest or that they may be subject to security interests not shown on the certificate, the security interest is subordinate to
the rights of a buyer of the goods who is
not in the business of selling goods of
that kind to the extent that he gives value
and receives delivery of the goods after
issuance of the certificate and without
knowledge of the security interest.

(3) Accounts, general intangibles and mobile
goods.

(a)   This subsection applies to accounts (other
than an account described in subsection
(5) on minerals) and general intangibles
(other than uncertificated securities) and
to goods which are mobile and which are
of a type normally used in more than one
jurisdiction, such as motor vehicles, trailers, rolling stock, airplanes, shipping containers, road building and construction
machinery and commercial harvesting
machinery and the like, if the goods are
equipment or are inventory leased or
held for lease by the debtor to others, and
are not covered by a certificate of title described in subsection (2).

(b)   The law (including the conflict of laws
rules) of the jurisdiction in which the
debtor is located governs the perfection
and the effect of perfection or non-perfection of the security interest.

(c)   If, however, the debtor is located in a jurisdiction which is not a part of the
United States, and which does not provide for perfection of the security interest
by filing or recording in that jurisdiction,
the law of the jurisdiction in the United
States in which the debtor has its major
executive office in the United States governs the perfection and the effect of perfection or non-perfection of the security
interest through filing. In the alternative,
if the debtor is located in a jurisdiction
which is not a part of the United States or

Canada and the collateral is accounts or general intangibles for money due or to become due, the security interest may be perfected by notification to the account debtor. As used in this paragraph, "United States" includes its territories and possessions and the Commonwealth of Puerto Rico.

(d) A debtor shall be deemed located at his place of business if he has one, at his chief executive office if he has more than one place of business, otherwise at his residence. If, however, the debtor is a foreign air carrier under the Federal Aviation Act of 1958, as amended, it shall be deemed located at the designated office of the agent upon whom service of process may be made on behalf of the foreign air carrier.

(e) A security interest perfected under the law of the jurisdiction of the location of the debtor is perfected until the expiration of four months after a change of the debtor's location to another jurisdiction, or until perfection would have ceased by the law of the first jurisdiction, whichever period first expires. Unless perfected in the new jurisdiction before the end of that period, it becomes unperfected thereafter and is deemed to have been unperfected as against a person who became a purchaser after the change.

(4) Chattel paper.

The rules stated for goods in subsection (1) apply to a possessory security interest in chattel paper. The rules stated for accounts in subsection (3) apply to a non-possessory security interest in chattel paper, but the security interest may not be perfected by notification to the account debtor.

(5) Minerals.

Perfection and the effect of perfection or non-perfection of a security interest which is created by a debtor who has an interest in minerals or the like (including oil and gas) before extraction and which attaches thereto as extracted, or which attaches to an account resulting from the sale thereof at the wellhead or minehead are governed by the law (including the conflict of laws rules) of the jurisdiction wherein the wellhead or minehead is located.

(6) Uncertificated securities.

The law (including the conflict of laws rules) of the jurisdiction of organization of the issuer governs the perfection and the effect of perfection or non-perfection of a security interest in uncertificated securities.

§ 9-104. Transactions Excluded From Article.

This Article does not apply

(a) to a security interest subject to any statute of the United States, to the extent that such statute governs the rights of parties to and third parties affected by transactions in particular types of property; or

(b) to a landlord's lien; or

(c) to a lien given by statute or other rule of law for services or materials except as provided in Section 9-310 on priority of such liens; or

(d) to a transfer of a claim for wages, salary or other compensation of an employee; or

(e) to a transfer by a government or governmental subdivision or agency; or

(f) to a sale of accounts or chattel paper as part of a sale of the business out of which they arose, or an assignment of accounts or chattel paper which is for the purpose of collection only, or a transfer of a right to payment under a contract to an assignee who is also to do the performance under the contract or a transfer of a single account to an assignee in whole or partial satisfaction of a preexisting indebtedness; or

(g) to a transfer of an interest in or claim in or under any policy of insurance, except as provided with respect to proceeds (Section 9-306) and priorities in proceeds (Section 9-312); or

(h) to a right represented by a judgment (other than a judgment taken on a right to payment which was collateral); or

(i) to any right of set-off; or

(j) except to the extent that provision is made for fixtures in Section 9-313, to the creation or transfer of an interest in or lien on real estate, including a lease or rents thereunder; or

(k) to a transfer in whole or in part of any claim arising out of tort; or

(l) to a transfer of an interest in any deposit account (subsection (1) of Section 9-105), except as provided with respect to proceeds (Section 9–306) and priorities in proceeds (Section 9–312).

§ 9–105. Definitions and Index of Definitions.

(1) In this Article unless the context otherwise requires:

(a) "Account debtor" means the person who is obligated on an account, chattel paper or general intangible;

(b) "Chattel paper" means a writing or writings which evidence both a monetary obligation and a security interest in or a lease of specific goods, but a charter or other contract involving the use or hire of a vessel is not chattel paper. When a transaction is evidenced both by such a security agreement or a lease and by an instrument or a series of instruments, the group of writings taken together constitutes chattel paper;

(c) "Collateral" means the property subject to a security interest, and includes accounts and chattel paper which have been sold;

(d) "Debtor" means the person who owes payment or other performance of the obligation secured, whether or not he owns or has rights in the collateral, and includes the seller of accounts or chattel paper. Where the debtor and the owner of the collateral are not the same person, the term "debtor" means the owner of the collateral in any provision of the Article dealing with the collateral, the obligor in any provision dealing with the obligation, and may include both where the context so requires;

(e) "Deposit account" means a demand, time, savings, passbook or like account maintained with a bank, savings and loan association, credit union or like organization, other than an account evidenced by a certificate of deposit;

(f) "Document" means document of title as defined in the general definitions of Article 1 (Section 1–201), and a receipt of the kind described in subsection (2) of Section 7–201;

(g) "Encumbrance" includes real estate mortgages and other liens on real estate and all other rights in real estate that are not ownership interests;

(h) "Goods" includes all things which are movable at the time the security interest attaches or which are fixtures (Section 9–313), but does not include money, documents, instruments, accounts, chattel paper, general intangibles, or minerals or the like (including oil and gas) before extraction. "Goods" also includes standing timber which is to be cut and removed under a conveyance or contract for sale, and unborn young of animals, and growing crops;

(i) "Instrument" means a negotiable instrument (defined in Section 3–104), or a certificated security (defined in Section 8–102) or any other writing which evidences a right to the payment of money and is not itself a security agreement or lease and is of a type which is in ordinary course of business transferred by delivery with any necessary indorsement or assignment;

(j) "Mortgage" means a consensual interest created by a real estate mortgage, a trust deed on real estate, or the like;

(k) An advance is made "pursuant to commitment" if the secured party has bound himself to make it, whether or not a subsequent event of default or other event not within his control has relieved or may relieve him from his obligation;

(l) "Security agreement" means an agreement which creates or provides for a security interest;

(m) "Secured party" means a lender, seller or other person in whose favor there is a security interest, including a person to whom accounts or chattel paper have been sold. When the holders of obligations issued under an indenture of trust, equipment trust agreement or the like are represented by a trustee or other person, the representative is the secured party;

(n) "Transmitting utility" means any person primarily engaged in the railroad, street railway or trolley bus business, the electric or electronics communications transmission business, the transmission of goods by pipeline, or the transmission or the production and transmission of electricity, steam, gas or water, or the provision of sewer service.

(2) Other definitions applying to this Article and the sections in which they appear are:

"Account". Section 9–106.
"Attach". Section 9–203.
"Construction mortgage". Section 9–313(1).
"Consumer goods". Section 9–109(1).
"Equipment". Section 9–109(2).
"Farm products". Section 9–109(3).
"Fixture". Section 9–313(1).
"Fixture filing". Section 9–313(1).
"General intangibles". Section 9–106.
"Inventory". Section 9–109(4).
"Lien creditor". Section 9–301(3).
"Proceeds". Section 9–306(1).
"Purchase money security interest". Section 9–107.
"United States". Section 9–103.

(3) The following definitions in other Articles apply to this Article:

"Check". Section 3–104.
"Contract for sale". Section 2–106.
"Holder in due course". Section 3–302.
"Note". Section 3–104.
"Sale". Section 2–106.

(4) In addition Article 1 contains general definitions and principles of construction and interpretation applicable throughout this Article.

§ 9-106. Definitions: "Account"; "General Intangibles". "Account" means any right to payment for goods sold or leased or for services rendered which is not evidenced by an instrument or chattel paper, whether or not it has been earned by performance. "General intangibles" means any personal property (including things in action) other than goods, accounts, chattel paper, documents, instruments, and money. All rights to payment earned or unearned under a charter or other contract involving the use or hire of a vessel and all rights incident to the charter or contract are accounts.

§ 9-107. Definitions: "Purchase Money Security Interest." A security interest is a "purchase money security interest" to the extent that it is

(a)   taken or retained by the seller of the collateral to secure all or part of its price; or
(b)   taken by a person who by making ad-

vances or incurring an obligation gives value to enable the debtor to acquire rights in or the use of collateral if such value is in fact so used.

§ 9-108. When After-Acquired Collateral Not Security for Antecedent Debt. Where a secured party makes an advance, incurs an obligation, releases a perfected security interest, or otherwise gives new value which is to be secured in whole or in part by after-acquired property his security interest in the after-acquired collateral shall be deemed to be taken for new value and not as security for an antecedent debt if the debtor acquires his rights in such collateral either in the ordinary course of his business or under a contract of purchase made pursuant to the security agreement within a reasonable time after new value is given.

§ 9-109. Classification of Goods; "Consumer Goods"; "Equipment"; "Farm Products"; "Inventory." Goods are

(1) "consumer goods" if they are used or bought for use primarily for personal, family or household purposes;

(2) "equipment" if they are used or bought for use primarily in business (including farming or a profession) or by a debtor who is a non-profit organization or a governmental subdivision or agency or if the goods are not included in the definitions of inventory, farm products or consumer goods;

(3) "farm products" if they are crops or livestock or supplies used or produced in farming operations or if they are products of crops or livestock in their unmanufactured states (such as ginned cotton, woolclip, maple syrup, milk and eggs), and if they are in the possession of a debtor engaged in raising, fattening, grazing or other farming operations. If goods are farm products they are neither equipment nor inventory;

(4) "inventory" if they are held by a person who holds them for sale or lease or to be furnished under contracts of service or if he has so furnished them, or if they are raw materials, work in process or materials used or consumed in a business. Inventory of a person is not to be classified as his equipment.

§ 9-110. Sufficiency of Description. For the purposes of this Article any description of personal property or real estate is sufficient whether or not it is specific if it reasonably identifies what is described.

§ 9-111. Applicability of Bulk Transfer Laws.
The creation of a security interest is not a bulk transfer under Article 6 (see Section 6–103).

§ 9-112. Where Collateral Is Not Owned by Debtor.
Unless otherwise agreed, when a secured party knows that collateral is owned by a person who is not the debtor, the owner of the collateral is entitled to receive from the secured party any surplus under Section 9–502(2) or under Section 9–504(1), and is not liable for the debt or for any deficiency after resale, and he has the same right as the debtor

(a)   to receive statements under Section 9–208;

(b)   to receive notice of and to object to a secured party's proposal to retain the collateral in satisfaction of the indebtedness under Section 9–505;

(c)   to redeem the collateral under Section 9–506;

(d)   to obtain injunctive or other relief under Section 9–507(1); and

(e)   to recover losses caused to him under Section 9–208(2).

§ 9-113. Security Interests Arising Under Article on Sales.
A security interest arising solely under the Article on Sales (Article 2) is subject to the provisions of this Article except that to the extent that and so long as the debtor does not have or does not lawfully obtain possession of the goods

(a)   no security agreement is necessary to make the security interest enforceable; and

(b)   no filing is required to perfect the security interest; and

(c)   the rights of the secured party on default by the debtor are governed by the Article on Sales (Article 2).

§ 9-114. Consignment.
(1) A person who delivers goods under a consignment which is not a security interest and who would be required to file under this Article by paragraph (3)(c) of Section 2–326 has priority over a secured party who is or becomes a creditor of the consignee and who would have a perfected security interest in the goods if they were the property of the consignee, and also has priority with respect to identifiable cash proceeds received on or before delivery of the goods to a buyer, if

(a)   the consignor complies with the filing provision of the Article on Sales with respect to consignments (paragraph (3)(c) of Section 2–326) before the consignee receives possession of the goods; and

(b)   the consignor gives notification in writing to the holder of the security interest if the holder has filed a financing statement covering the same types of goods before the date of the filing made by the consignor; and

(c)   the holder of the security interest receives the notification within five years before the consignee receives possession of the goods; and

(d)   the notification states that the consignor expects to deliver goods on consignment to the consignee, describing the goods by item or type.

(2) In the case of a consignment which is not a security interest and in which the requirements of the preceding subsection have not been met, a person who delivers goods to another is subordinate to a person who would have a perfected security interest in the goods if they were the property of the debtor.

Part 2. Validity of Security Agreement and Rights of Parties Thereto

§ 9-201. General Validity of Security Agreement.
Except as otherwise provided by this Act a security agreement is effective according to its terms between the parties, against purchasers of the collateral and against creditors. Nothing in this Article validates any charge or practice illegal under any statute or regulation thereunder governing usury, small loans, retail installment sales, or the like, or extends the application of any such statute or regulation to any transaction not otherwise subject thereto.

§ 9-202. Title to Collateral Immaterial.
Each provision of this Article with regard to rights, obligations and remedies applies whether title to collateral is in the secured party or in the debtor.

§ 9-203. Attachment and Enforceability of Security Interest; Proceeds; Formal Requisites.
(1) Subject to the provisions of Section 4–208 on the security interest of a collecting bank, Section 8–321 on security interests in securities and Section 9–113 on a security interest arising under the Article on Sales, a security interest is not enforceable against the debtor or third parties with respect to the collateral and does not attach unless:

(a) the collateral is in the possession of the secured party pursuant to agreement, or the debtor has signed a security agreement which contains a description of the collateral and in addition, when the security interest covers crops growing or to be grown or timber to be cut, a description of the land concerned;

(b) value has been given; and

(c) the debtor has rights in the collateral.

(2) A security interest attaches when it becomes enforceable against the debtor with respect to the collateral. Attachment occurs as soon as all of the events specified in subsection (1) have taken place unless explicit agreement postpones the time of attaching.

(3) Unless otherwise agreed a security agreement gives the secured party the rights to proceeds provided by Section 9–306.

(4) A transaction, although subject to this Article, is also subject to ....*, and in the case of conflict between the provisions of this Article and any such statute, the provisions of such statute control. Failure to comply with any applicable statute has only the effect which is specified therein.

Note: *At* * *in subsection (4) insert reference to any local statute regulating small loans, retail installment sales and the like.*

The foregoing subsection (4) is designed to make it clear that certain transactions, although subject to this Article, must also comply with other applicable legislation.

This Article is designed to regulate all the "security" aspects of transactions within its scope. There is, however, much regulatory legislation, particularly in the consumer field, which supplements this Article and should not be repealed by its enactment. Examples are small loan acts, retail installment selling acts and the like. Such acts may provide for licensing and rate regulation and may prescribe particular forms of contract. Such provisions should remain in force despite the enactment of this Article. On the other hand if a retail installment selling act contains provisions on filing, rights on default, etc., such provisions should be repealed as inconsistent with this Article except that inconsistent provisions as to deficiencies, penalties, etc., in the Uniform Consumer Credit Code and other recent related legislation should remain because those statutes were drafted after the substantial enactment of the Article and with the intention of modifying certain provisions of this Article as to consumer credit.

§ 9-204. After-Acquired Property; Future Advances.

(1) Except as provided in subsection (2), a security agreement may provide that any or all obligations covered by the security agreement are to be secured by after-acquired collateral.

(2) No security interest attaches under an after-acquired property clause to consumer goods other than accessions (Section 9–314) when given as additional security unless the debtor acquires rights in them within ten days after the secured party gives value.

(3) Obligations covered by a security agreement may include future advances or other value whether or not the advances or value are given pursuant to commitment (subsection (1) of Section 9–105).

§ 9-205. Use or Disposition of Collateral Without Accounting Permissible.

A security interest is not invalid or fraudulent against creditors by reason of liberty in the debtor to use, commingle or dispose of all or part of the collateral (including returned or repossessed goods) or to collect or compromise accounts or chattel paper, or to accept the return of goods or make repossessions, or to use, commingle or dispose of proceeds, or by reason of the failure of the secured party to require the debtor to account for proceeds or replace collateral. This section does not relax the requirements of possession where perfection of a security interest depends upon possession of the collateral by the secured party or by a bailee.

§ 9-206. Agreement Not to Assert Defenses Against Assignee; Modification of Sales Warranties Where Security Agreement Exists.

(1) Subject to any statute or decision which establishes a different rule for buyers or lessees of consumer goods, an agreement by a buyer or lessee that he will not assert against an assignee any claim or defense which he may have against the seller or lessor is enforceable by an assignee who takes his assignment for value, in good faith and without notice of a claim or defense, except as to defenses of a type which may be asserted against a holder in due course of a negotiable instrument under the Article on Commercial Paper (Article 3). A buyer who as part of one transaction signs both a negotiable instrument and a security agreement makes such an agreement.

(2) When a seller retains a purchase money security interest in goods the Article on Sales (Article 2) governs the sale and any disclaimer, limitation or modification of the seller's warranties.

§ 9-207. Rights and Duties When Collateral is in Secured Party's Possession.

(1) A secured party must use reasonable care in the custody and preservation of collateral in his possession. In the case of an instrument or chattel paper reasonable care includes taking necessary steps to preserve rights against prior parties unless otherwise agreed.

(2) Unless otherwise agreed, when collateral is in the secured party's possession

    (a)   reasonable expenses (including the cost of any insurance and payment of taxes or other charges) incurred in the custody, preservation, use or operation of the collateral are chargeable to the debtor and are secured by the collateral;

    (b)   the risk of accidental loss or damage is on the debtor to the extent of any deficiency in any effective insurance coverage;

    (c)   the secured party may hold as additional security any increase or profits (except money) received from the collateral, but money so received, unless remitted to the debtor, shall be applied in reduction of the secured obligation;

    (d)   the secured party must keep the collateral identifiable but fungible collateral may be commingled;

    (e)   the secured party may repledge the collateral upon terms which do not impair the debtor's right to redeem it.

(3) A secured party is liable for any loss caused by his failure to meet any obligation imposed by the preceding subsections but does not lose his security interest.

(4) A secured party may use or operate the collateral for the purpose of preserving the collateral or its value or pursuant to the order of a court of appropriate jurisdiction or, except in the case of consumer goods, in the manner and to the extent provided in the security agreement.

§ 9-208. Request for Statement of Account or List of Collateral.

(1) A debtor may sign a statement indicating what he believes to be the aggregate amount of unpaid indebtedness as of a specified date and may send it to the secured party with a request that the statement be approved or corrected and returned to the debtor. When the security agreement or any other record kept by the secured party identifies the collateral a debtor may similarly request the secured party to approve or correct a list of the collateral.

(2) The secured party must comply with such a request within two weeks after receipt by sending a written correction or approval. If the secured party claims a security interest in all of a particular type of collateral owned by the debtor he may indicate that fact in his reply and need not approve or correct an itemized list of such collateral. If the secured party without reasonable excuse fails to comply he is liable for any loss caused to the debtor thereby; and if the debtor has properly included in his request a good faith statement of the obligation or a list of the collateral or both the secured party may claim a security interest only as shown in the statement against persons misled by his failure to comply. If he no longer has an interest in the obligation or collateral at the time the request is received he must disclose the name and address of any successor in interest known to him and he is liable for any loss caused to the debtor as a result of failure to disclose. A successor in interest is not subject to this section until a request is received by him.

(3) A debtor is entitled to such a statement once every six months without charge. The secured party may require payment of a charge not exceeding $10 for each additional statement furnished.

Part 3. Rights of Third Parties; Perfected and Unperfected Security Interests; Rules of Priority

§ 9-301. Persons Who Take Priority Over Unperfected Security Interests; Rights of "Lien Creditor."

(1) Except as otherwise provided in subsection (2), an unperfected security interest is subordinate to the rights of

    (a)   persons entitled to priority under Section 9-312;

    (b)   a person who becomes a lien creditor before the security interest is perfected;

    (c)   in the case of goods, instruments, documents, and chattel paper, a person who is not a secured party and who is a transferee in bulk or other buyer not in ordinary course of business or is a buyer of farm products in ordinary course of business, to the extent that he gives value and receives delivery of the collateral without knowledge of the security interest and before it is perfected;

(d) in the case of accounts and general intangibles, a person who is not a secured party and who is a transferee to the extent that he gives value without knowledge of the security interest and before it is perfected.

(2) If the secured party files with respect to a purchase money security interest before or within ten days after the debtor receives possession of the collateral, he takes priority over the rights of a transferee in bulk or of a lien creditor which arise between the time the security interest attaches and the time of filing.

(3) A "lien creditor" means a creditor who has acquired a lien on the property involved by attachment, levy or the like and includes an assignee for benefit of creditors from the time of assignment, and a trustee in bankruptcy from the date of the filing of the petition or a receiver in equity from the time of appointment.

(4) A person who becomes a lien creditor while a security interest is perfected takes subject to the security interest only to the extent that it secures advances made before he becomes a lien creditor or within 45 days thereafter or made without knowledge of the lien or pursuant to a commitment entered into without knowledge of the lien.

§ 9-302. When Filing Is Required to Perfect Security Interest; Security Interests to Which Filing Provisions of This Article Do Not Apply.

(1) A financing statement must be filed to perfect all security interests except the following:

(a) a security interest in collateral in possession of the secured party under Section 9–305;

(b) a security interest temporarily perfected in instruments or documents without delivery under Section 9–304 or in proceeds for a 10 day period under Section 9–306;

(c) a security interest created by an assignment of a beneficial interest in a trust or a decedent's estate;

(d) a purchase money security interest in consumer goods; but filing is required for a motor vehicle required to be registered; and fixture filing is required for priority over conflicting interests in fixtures to the extent provided in Section 9–313;

(e) an assignment of accounts which does not alone or in conjunction with other assignments to the same assignee transfer a significant part of the outstanding accounts of the assignor;

(f) a security interest of a collecting bank (Section 4–208) or in securities (Section 8–321) or arising under the Article on Sales (see Section 9–113) or covered in subsection (3) of this section;

(g) an assignment for the benefit of all the creditors of the transferor, and subsequent transfers by the assignee thereunder.

(2) If a secured party assigns a perfected security interest, no filing under this Article is required in order to continue the perfected status of the security interest against creditors of and transferees from the original debtor.

(3) The filing of a financing statement otherwise required by this Article is not necessary or effective to perfect a security interest in property subject to

(a) a statute or treaty of the United States which provides for a national or international registration or a national or international certificate of title or which specifies a place of filing different from that specified in this Article for filing of the security interest; or

(b) the following statutes of this state; [list any certificate of title statute covering automobiles, trailers, mobile homes, boats, farm tractors, or the like and any central filing statute*.]; but during any period in which collateral is inventory held for sale by a person who is in the business of selling goods of that kind, the filing provisions of this Article (Part 4) apply to a security interest in that collateral created by him as debtor; or

(c) a certificate of title statute of another jurisdiction under the law of which indication of a security interest on the certificate is required as a condition of perfection (subsection (2) of Section 9–103).

(4) Compliance with a statute or treaty described in subsection (3) is equivalent to the filing of a financing statement under this Article, and a security interest in property subject to the statute or treaty can be perfected only by compliance therewith except as provided in Section 9–103 on multiple state transactions. Duration and renewal of perfection of a se-

curity interest perfected by compliance with the statute or treaty are governed by the provisions of the statute or treaty; in other respects the security interest is subject to this Article.

Note: *It is recommended that the provisions of certificate of title acts for perfection of security interests by notation on the certificates should be amended to exclude coverage of inventory held for sale.*

§ 9-303. When Security Interest Is Perfected; Continuity of Perfection.

(1) A security interest is perfected when it has attached and when all of the applicable steps required for perfection have been taken. Such steps are specified in Sections 9-302, 9-304, 9-305 and 9-306. If such steps are taken before the security interest attaches, it is perfected at the time when it attaches.

(2) If a security interest is originally perfected in any way permitted under this Article and is subsequently perfected in some other way under this Article, without an intermediate period when it was unperfected, the security interest shall be deemed to be perfected continuously for the purposes of this Article.

§ 9-304. Perfection of Security Interest in Instruments, Documents, and Goods Covered by Documents; Perfection by Permissive Filing; Temporary Perfection Without Filing or Transfer of Possession.

(1) A security interest in chattel paper or negotiable documents may be perfected by filing. A security interest in money or instruments (other than certificated securities or instruments which constitute part of chattel paper) can be perfected only by the secured party's taking possession, except as provided in subsections (4) and (5) of this section and subsections (2) and (3) of Section 9-306 on proceeds.

(2) During the period that goods are in the possession of the issuer of a negotiable document therefor, a security interest in the goods is perfected by perfecting a security interest in the document, and any security interest in the goods otherwise perfected during such period is subject thereto.

(3) A security interest in goods in the possession of a bailee other than one who has issued a negotiable document therefor is perfected by issuance of a document in the name of the secured party or by the bailee's receipt of notification of the secured party's interest or by filing as to the goods.

(4) A security interest in instruments (other than

certificated securities) or negotiable documents is perfected without filing or the taking of possession for a period of 21 days from the time it attaches to the extent that it arises for new value given under a written security agreement.

(5) A security interest remains perfected for a period of 21 days without filing where a secured party having a perfected security interest in an instrument (other than a certificated security), a negotiable document or goods in possession of a bailee other than one who has issued a negotiable document therefor

(a) makes available to the debtor the goods or documents representing the goods for the purpose of ultimate sale or exchange or for the purpose of loading, unloading, storing, shipping, transshipping, manufacturing, processing or otherwise dealing with them in a manner preliminary to their sale or exchange, but priority between conflicting security interests in the goods is subject to subsection (3) of Section 9-312; or

(b) delivers the instrument to the debtor for the purpose of ultimate sale or exchange or of presentation, collection, renewal or registration of transfer.

(6) After the 21 day period in subsections (4) and (5) perfection depends upon compliance with applicable provisions of this Article.

§ 9-305. When Possession by Secured Party Perfects Security Interest Without Filing.
A security interest in letters of credit and advices of credit (subsection (2)(a) of Section 5-116), goods, instruments (other than certificated securities), money, negotiable documents, or chattel paper may be perfected by the secured party's taking possession of the collateral. If such collateral other than goods covered by a negotiable document is held by a bailee, the secured party is deemed to have possession from the time the bailee receives notification of the secured party's interest. A security interest is perfected by possession from the time possession is taken without a relation back and continues only so long as possession is retained, unless otherwise specified in this Article. The security interest may be otherwise perfected as provided in this Article before or after the period of possession by the secured party.

§ 9-306. "Proceeds"; Secured Party's Rights on Disposition of Collateral.

(1) "Proceeds" includes whatever is received

upon the sale, exchange, collection or other disposition of collateral or proceeds. Insurance payable by reason of loss or damage to the collateral is proceeds, except to the extent that it is payable to a person other than a party to the security agreement. Money, checks, deposit accounts, and the like are "cash proceeds". All other proceeds are "non-cash proceeds".

(2) Except where this Article otherwise provides, a security interest continues in collateral notwithstanding sale, exchange or other disposition thereof unless the disposition was authorized by the secured party in the security agreement or otherwise, and also continues in any identifiable proceeds including collections received by the debtor.

(3) The security interest in proceeds is a continuously perfected security interest if the interest in the original collateral was perfected but it ceases to be a perfected security interest and becomes unperfected ten days after receipt of the proceeds by the debtor unless

(a) a filed financing statement covers the original collateral and the proceeds are collateral in which a security interest may be perfected by filing in the office or offices where the financing statement has been filed and, if the proceeds are acquired with cash proceeds, the description of collateral in the financing statement indicates the types of property constituting the proceeds; or

(b) a filed financing statement covers the original collateral and the proceeds are identifiable cash proceeds; or

(c) the security interest in the proceeds is perfected before the expiration of the ten day period.

Except as provided in this section, a security interest in proceeds can be perfected only by the methods or under the circumstances permitted in this Article for original collateral of the same type.

(4) In the event of insolvency proceedings instituted by or against a debtor, a secured party with a perfected security interest in proceeds has a perfected security interest only in the following proceeds:

(a) in identifiable non-cash proceeds and in separate deposit accounts containing only proceeds;

(b) in identifiable cash proceeds in the form of money which is neither commingled with other money nor deposited in a de-

posit account prior to the insolvency proceedings;

(c) in identifiable cash proceeds in the form of checks and the like which are not deposited in a deposit account prior to the insolvency proceedings; and

(d) in all cash and deposit accounts of the debtor in which proceeds have been commingled with other funds, but the perfected security interest under this paragraph (d) is

(i) subject to any right to set-off; and

(ii) limited to an amount not greater than the amount of any cash proceeds received by the debtor within ten days before the institution of the insolvency proceedings less the sum of (I) the payments to the secured party on account of cash proceeds received by the debtor during such period and (II) the cash proceeds received by the debtor during such period to which the secured party is entitled under paragraphs (a) through (c) of this subsection (4).

(5) If a sale of goods results in an account or chattel paper which is transferred by the seller to a secured party, and if the goods are returned to or are repossessed by the seller or the secured party, the following rules determine priorities:

(a) If the goods were collateral at the time of sale, for an indebtedness of the seller which is still unpaid, the original security interest attaches again to the goods and continues as a perfected security interest if it was perfected at the time when the goods were sold. If the security interest was originally perfected by a filing which is still effective, nothing further is required to continue the perfected status; in any other case, the secured party must take possession of the returned or repossessed goods or must file.

(b) An unpaid transferee of the chattel paper has a security interest in the goods against the transferor. Such security interest is prior to a security interest asserted under paragraph (a) to the extent that the transferee of the chattel paper was entitled to priority under Section 9–308.

(c) An unpaid transferee of the account has a

security interest in the goods against the transferor. Such security interest is subordinate to a security interest asserted under paragraph (a).

(d) A security interest of an unpaid transferee asserted under paragraph (b) or (c) must be perfected for protection against creditors of the transferor and purchasers of the returned or repossessed goods.

§ 9-307. Protection of Buyers of Goods.

(1) A buyer in ordinary course of business (subsection (9) of Section 1-201) other than a person buying farm products from a person engaged in farming operations takes free of a security interest created by his seller even though the security interest is perfected and even though the buyer knows of its existence.

(2) In the case of consumer goods, a buyer takes free of a security interest even though perfected if he buys without knowledge of the security interest, for value and for his own personal, family or household purposes unless prior to the purchase the secured party has filed a financing statement covering such goods.

(3) A buyer other than a buyer in ordinary course of business (subsection (1) of this section) takes free of a security interest to the extent that it secures future advances made after the secured party acquires knowledge of the purchase, or more than 45 days after the purchase, whichever first occurs, unless made pursuant to a commitment entered into without knowledge of the purchase and before the expiration of the 45 day period.

§ 9-308. Purchase of Chattel Paper and Instruments.

A purchaser of chattel paper or an instrument who gives new value and takes possession of it in the ordinary course of his business has priority over a security interest in the chattel paper or instrument

(a) which is perfected under Section 9-304 (permissive filing and temporary perfection) or under Section 9-306 (perfection as to proceeds) if he acts without knowledge that the specific paper or instrument is subject to a security interest; or

(b) which is claimed merely as proceeds of inventory subject to a security interest (Section 9-306) even though he knows that the specific paper or instrument is subject to the security interest.

§ 9-309. Protection of Purchasers of Instruments, Documents and Securities.

Nothing in this Article limits the rights of a holder in due course of a negotiable instrument (Section 3-302) or a holder to whom a negotiable document of title has been duly negotiated (Section 7-501) or a bona fide purchaser of a security (Section 8-302) and the holders or purchasers take priority over an earlier security interest even though perfected. Filing under this Article does not constitute notice of the security interest to such holders or purchasers.

§ 9-310. Priority of Certain Liens Arising by Operation of Law.

When a person in the ordinary course of his business furnishes services or materials with respect to goods subject to a security interest, a lien upon goods in the possession of such person given by statute or rule of law for such materials or services takes priority over a perfected security interest unless the lien is statutory and the statute expressly provides otherwise.

§ 9-311. Alienability of Debtor's Rights: Judicial Process.

The debtor's rights in collateral may be voluntarily or involuntarily transferred (by way of sale, creation of a security interest, attachment, levy, garnishment or other judicial process) notwithstanding a provision in the security agreement prohibiting any transfer or making the transfer constitute a default.

§ 9-312. Priorities Among Conflicting Security Interests in the Same Collateral.

(1) The rules of priority stated in other sections of this Part and in the following sections shall govern when applicable: Section 4-208 with respect to the security interests of collecting banks in items being collected, accompanying documents and proceeds; Section 9-103 on security interests related to other jurisdictions; Section 9-114 on consignments.

(2) A perfected security interest in crops for new value given to enable the debtor to produce the crops during the production season and given not more than three months before the crops become growing crops by planting or otherwise takes priority over an earlier perfected security interest to the extent that such earlier interest secures obligations due more than six months before the crops become growing crops by planting or otherwise, even though the person giving new value had knowledge of the earlier security interest.

(3) A perfected purchase money security interest in inventory has priority over a conflicting security interest in the same inventory and also has priority in identifiable cash proceeds received on or before the delivery of the inventory to a buyer if

(a) the purchase money security interest is perfected at the time the debtor receives possession of the inventory; and

(b) the purchase money secured party gives notification in writing to the holder of the conflicting security interest if the holder had filed a financing statement covering the same types of inventory (i) before the date of the filing made by the purchase money secured party, or (ii) before the beginning of the 21 day period where the purchase money security interest is temporarily perfected without filing or possession (subsection (5) of Section 9-304); and

(c) the holder of the conflicting security interest receives the notification within five years before the debtor receives possession of the inventory; and

(d) the notification states that the person giving the notice has or expects to acquire a purchase money security interest in inventory of the debtor, describing such inventory by item or type.

(4) A purchase money security interest in collateral other than inventory has priority over a conflicting security interest in the same collateral or its proceeds if the purchase money security interest is perfected at the time the debtor receives possession of the collateral or within ten days thereafter.

(5) In all cases not governed by other rules stated in this section (including cases of purchase money security interests which do not qualify for the special priorities set forth in subsections (3) and (4) of this section), priority between conflicting security interests in the same collateral shall be determined according to the following rules:

(a) Conflicting security interests rank according to priority in time of filing or perfection. Priority dates from the time a filing is first made covering the collateral or the time the security interest is first perfected, whichever is earlier, provided that there is no period thereafter when there is neither filing nor perfection.

(b) So long as conflicting security interests are unperfected, the first to attach has priority.

(6) For the purposes of subsection (5) a date of filing or perfection as to collateral is also a date of filing or perfection as to proceeds.

(7) If future advances are made while a security interest is perfected by filing, the taking of possession, or under Section 8-321 on securities, the security interest has the same priority for the purposes of subsection (5) with respect to the future advances as it does with respect to the first advance. If a commitment is made before or while the security interest is so perfected, the security interest has the same priority with respect to advances made pursuant thereto. In other cases a perfected security interest has priority from the date the advance is made.

§ 9-313. Priority of Security Interests in Fixtures.

(1) In this section and in the provisions of Part 4 of this Article referring to fixture filing, unless the context otherwise requires

(a) goods are "fixtures" when they become so related to particular real estate that an interest in them arises under real estate law

(b) a "fixture filing" is the filing in the office where a mortgage on the real estate would be filed or recorded of a financing statement covering goods which are or are to become fixtures and conforming to the requirements of subsection (5) of Section 9-402

(c) a mortgage is a "construction mortgage" to the extent that it secures an obligation incurred for the construction of an improvement on land including the acquisition cost of the land, if the recorded writing so indicates.

(2) A security interest under this Article may be created in goods which are fixtures or may continue in goods which become fixtures, but no security interest exists under this Article in ordinary building materials incorporated into an improvement on land.

(3) This Article does not prevent creation of an encumbrance upon fixtures pursuant to real estate law.

(4) A perfected security interest in fixtures has priority over the conflicting interest of an encumbrancer or owner of the real estate where

(a)   the security interest is a purchase money security interest, the interest of the encumbrancer or owner arises before the goods become fixtures, the security interest is perfected by a fixture filing before the goods become fixtures or within ten days thereafter, and the debtor has an interest of record in the real estate or is in possession of the real estate; or

(b)   the security interest is perfected by a fixture filing before the interest of the encumbrancer or owner is of record, the security interest has priority over any conflicting interest of a predecessor in title of the encumbrancer or owner, and the debtor has an interest of record in the real estate or is in possession of the real estate; or

(c)   the fixtures are readily removable factory or office machines or readily removable replacements of domestic appliances which are consumer goods, and before the goods become fixtures the security interest is perfected by any method permitted by this Article; or

(d)   the conflicting interest is a lien on the real estate obtained by legal or equitable proceedings after the security interest was perfected by any method permitted by this Article.

(5) A security interest in fixtures, whether or not perfected, has priority over the conflicting interest of an encumbrancer or owner of the real estate where

(a)   the encumbrancer or owner has consented in writing to the security interest or has disclaimed an interest in the goods as fixtures; or

(b)   the debtor has a right to remove the goods as against the encumbrancer or owner. If the debtor's right terminates, the priority of the security interest continues for a reasonable time.

(6) Notwithstanding paragraph (a) of subsection (4) but otherwise subject to subsections (4) and (5), a security interest in fixtures is subordinate to a construction mortgage recorded before the goods become fixtures if the goods become fixtures before the completion of the construction. To the extent that it is given to refinance a construction mortgage, a mortgage has this priority to the same extent as the construction mortgage.

(7) In cases not within the preceding subsections, a security interest in fixtures is subordinate to the conflicting interest of an encumbrancer or owner of the related real estate who is not the debtor.

(8) When the secured party has priority over all owners and encumbrancers of the real estate, he may, on default, subject to the provisions of Part 5, remove his collateral from the real estate but he must reimburse any encumbrancer or owner of the real estate who is not the debtor and who has not otherwise agreed for the cost of repair of any physical injury, but not for any diminution in value of the real estate caused by the absence of the goods removed or by any necessity of replacing them. A person entitled to reimbursement may refuse permission to remove until the secured party gives adequate security for the performance of this obligation.

§ 9-314. Accessions.

(1) A security interest in goods which attaches before they are installed in or affixed to other goods takes priority as to the goods installed or affixed (called in this section "accessions") over the claims of all persons to the whole except as stated in subsection (3) and subject to Section 9-315(1).

(2) A security interest which attaches to goods after they become part of a whole is valid against all persons subsequently acquiring interests in the whole except as stated in subsection (3) but is invalid against any person with an interest in the whole at the time the security interest attaches to the goods who has not in writing consented to the security interest or disclaimed an interest in the goods as part of the whole.

(3) The security interests described in subsections (1) and (2) do not take priority over

(a)   a subsequent purchaser for value of any interest in the whole; or

(b)   a creditor with a lien on the whole subsequently obtained by judicial proceedings; or

(c)   a creditor with a prior perfected security interest in the whole to the extent that he makes subsequent advances

if the subsequent purchase is made, the lien by judicial proceedings obtained or the subsequent advance under the prior perfected security interest is made or contracted for without knowledge of the security interest and before it is perfected. A purchaser of the whole at a foreclosure sale other than the holder of a perfected security interest purchasing at his own foreclosure sale is a subsequent purchaser within this section.

(4) When under subsections (1) or (2) and (3) a secured party has an interest in accessions which has priority over the claims of all persons who have interests in the whole, he may on default subject to the provisions of Part 5 remove his collateral from the whole but he must reimburse any encumbrancer or owner of the whole who is not the debtor and who has not otherwise agreed for the cost of repair of any physical injury but not for any diminution in value of the whole caused by the absence of the goods removed or by any necessity for replacing them. A person entitled to reimbursement may refuse permission to remove until the secured party gives adequate security for the performance of this obligation.

§ 9-315. Priority When Goods Are Commingled or Processed.

(1) If a security interest in goods was perfected and subsequently the goods or a part thereof have become part of a product or mass, the security interest continues in the product or mass if

(a) the goods are so manufactured, processed, assembled or commingled that their identity is lost in the product or mass; or

(b) a financing statement covering the original goods also covers the product into which the goods have been manufactured, processed or assembled.

In a case to which paragraph (b) applies, no separate security interest in that part of the original goods which has been manufactured, processed or assembled into the product may be claimed under Section 9-314.

(2) When under subsection (1) more than one security interest attaches to the product or mass, they rank equally according to the ratio that the cost of the goods to which each interest originally attached bears to the cost of the total product or mass.

§ 9-316. Priority Subject to Subordination.

Nothing in this Article prevents subordination by agreement by any person entitled to priority.

§ 9-317. Secured Party Not Obligated on Contract of Debtor.

The mere existence of a security interest or authority given to the debtor to dispose of or use collateral does not impose contract or tort liability upon the secured party for the debtor's acts or omissions.

§ 9-318. Defenses Against Assignee; Modification of Contract After Notification of Assignment; Term Prohibiting Assignment Ineffective; Identification and Proof of Assignment.

(1) Unless an account debtor has made an enforceable agreement not to assert defenses or claims arising out of a sale as provided in Section 9-206 the rights of an assignee are subject to

(a) all the terms of the contract between the account debtor and assignor and any defense or claim arising therefrom; and

(b) any other defense or claim of the account debtor against the assignor which accrues before the account debtor receives notification of the assignment.

(2) So far as the right to payment or a part thereof under an assigned contract has not been fully earned by performance, and notwithstanding notification of the assignment, any modification of or substitution for the contract made in good faith and in accordance with reasonable commercial standards is effective against an assignee unless the account debtor has otherwise agreed but the assignee acquires corresponding rights under the modified or substituted contract. The assignment may provide that such modification or substitution is a breach by the assignor.

(3) The account debtor is authorized to pay the assignor until the account debtor receives notification that the amount due or to become due has been assigned and that payment is to be made to the assignee. A notification which does not reasonably identify the rights assigned is ineffective. If requested by the account debtor, the assignee must seasonably furnish reasonable proof that the assignment has been made and unless he does so the account debtor may pay the assignor.

(4) A term in any contract between an account debtor and an assignor is ineffective if it prohibits assignment of an account or prohibits creation of a security interest in a general intangible for money due or to become due or requires the account debtor's consent to such assignment or security interest.

Part 4. Filing

§ 9-401. Place of Filing; Erroneous Filing; Removal of Collateral.

First Alternative Subsection (1)

(1) The proper place to file in order to perfect a security interest is as follows:

(a) when the collateral is timber to be cut or is minerals or the like (including oil and gas) or accounts subject to subsection (5) of Section 9–103, or when the financing statement is filed as a fixture filing (Section 9–313) and the collateral is goods which are or are to become fixtures, then in the office where a mortgage on the real estate would be filed or recorded;

(b) in all other cases, in the office of the [Secretary of State].

Second Alternative Subsection (1)

(1) The proper place to file in order to perfect a security interest is as follows:

(a) when the collateral is equipment used in farming operations, or farm products, or accounts or general intangibles arising from or relating to the sale of farm products by a farmer, or consumer goods, then in the office of the .... in the county of the debtor's residence or if the debtor is not a resident of this state then in the office of the .... in the county where the goods are kept, and in addition when the collateral is crops growing or to be grown in the office of the .... in the county where the land is located;

(b) when the collateral is timber to be cut or is minerals or the like (including oil and gas) or accounts subject to subsection (5) of Section 9–103, or when the financing statement is filed as a fixture filing (Section 9–313) and the collateral is goods which are or are to become fixtures, then in the office where a mortgage on the real estate would be filed or recorded;

(c) in all other cases, in the office of the [Secretary of State].

Third Alternative Subsection (1)

(1) The proper place to file in order to perfect a security interest is as follows:

(a) when the collateral is equipment used in farming operations, or farm products, or accounts or general intangibles arising from or relating to the sale of farm products by a farmer, or consumer goods, then in the office of the ...... in the county of the debtor's residence or if the debtor is not a resident of this state then in the of-

fice of the .... in the county where the goods are kept, and in addition when the collateral is crops growing or to be grown in the office of the ...... in the county where the land is located;

(b) when the collateral is timber to be cut or is minerals or the like (including oil and gas) or accounts subject to subsection (5) of Section 9–103, or when the financing statement is filed as a fixture filing (Section 9–313) and the collateral is goods which are or are to become fixtures, then in the office where a mortgage on the real estate would be filed or recorded;

(c) in all other cases, in the office of the [Secretary of State] and in addition, if the debtor has a place of business in only one county of this state, also in the office of ...... of such county, or, if the debtor has no place of business in this state, but resides in the state, also in the office of ...... of the county in which he resides.

Note: *One of the three alternatives should be selected as subsection (1).*

(2) A filing which is made in good faith in an improper place or not in all of the places required by this section is nevertheless effective with regard to any collateral as to which the filing complied with the requirements of this Article and is also effective with regard to collateral covered by the financing statement against any person who has knowledge of the contents of such financing statment.

(3) A filing which is made in the proper place in this state continues effective even though the debtor's residence or place of business or the location of the collateral or its use, whichever controlled the original filing, is thereafter changed.

Alternative Subsection (3)

[(3) A filing which is made in the proper county continues effective for four months after a change to another county of the debtor's residence or place of business or the location of the collateral, whichever controlled the original filing. It becomes ineffective thereafter unless a copy of the financing statement signed by the secured party is filed in the new county within said period. The security interest may also be perfected in the new county after the expiration of the four-month period; in such case perfection dates from the time of perfection in the new county. A change in the use of the collateral does not impair the effectiveness of the original filing.]

(4) The rules stated in Section 9–103 determine whether filing is necessary in this state.

(5) Notwithstanding the preceding subsections, and subject to subsection (3) of Section 9–302, the proper place to file in order to perfect a security interest in collateral, including fixtures, of a transmitting utility is the office of the [Secretary of State]. This filing constitutes a fixture filing (Section 9–313) as to the collateral described therein which is or is to become fixtures.

(6) For the purposes of this section, the residence of an organization is its place of business if it has one or its chief executive office if it has more than one place of business.

Note: Subsection (6) should be used only if the state chooses the Second or Third Alternative Subsection (1).

§ 9-402. Formal Requisites of Financing Statement; Amendments; Mortgage as Financing Statement.

(1) A financing statement is sufficient if it gives the names of the debtor and the secured party, is signed by the debtor, gives an address of the secured party from which information concerning the security interest may be obtained, gives a mailing address of the debtor and contains a statement indicating the types, or describing the items, of collateral. A financing statement may be filed before a security agreement is made or a security interest otherwise attaches. When the financing statement covers crops growing or to be grown, the statement must also contain a description of the real estate concerned. When the financing statement covers timber to be cut or covers minerals or the like (including oil and gas) or accounts subject to subsection (5) of Section 9–103, or when the financing statement is filed as a fixture filing (Section 9–313) and the collateral is goods which are or are to become fixtures, the statement must also comply with subsection (5). A copy of the security agreement is sufficient as a financing statement if it contains the above information and is signed by the debtor. A carbon, photographic or other reproduction of a security agreement or a financing statement is sufficient as a financing statement if the security agreement so provides or if the original has been filed in this state.

(2) A financing statement which otherwise complies with subsection (1) is sufficient when it is signed by the secured party instead of the debtor if it is filed to perfect a security interest in

    (a)   collateral already subject to a security interest in another jurisdiction when it is

brought into this state, or when the debtor's location is changed to this state. Such a financing statement must state that the collateral was brought into this state or that the debtor's location was changed to this state under such circumstances; or

    (b)   proceeds under Section 9–306 if the security interest in the original collateral was perfected. Such a financing statement must describe the original collateral; or

    (c)   collateral as to which the filing has lapsed; or

    (d)   collateral acquired after a change of name, identity or corporate structure of the debtor (subsection (7)).

(3) A form substantially as follows is sufficient to comply with subsection (1):

Name of debtor (or assignor) ....

Address ....

Name of secured party (or assignee) ....

Address ....

1.   This financing statement covers the following types (or items) of property:

    (Describe) ....

2.   (If collateral is crops) The above described crops are growing or are to be grown on:

    (Describe Real Estate) ....

3.   (If applicable) The above goods are to become fixtures on [where appropriate substitute either "The above timber is standing on _____ " or The above minerals or the like (including oil and gas) or accounts will be financed at the wellhead of the well or mine located on

_____."

    (Describe Real Estate) ....

and this financing statement is to be filed [for record] in the real estate records. (If the debtor does not have an interest of record) The name of a record owner is

....

4.   (If products of collateral are claimed) Products of the collateral are also covered.

(use whichever is applicable) { ....
Signature of Debtor (or Assignor)
....
Signature of Secured Party (or Assignee)

(4) A financing statement may be amended by filing a writing signed by both the debtor and the secured party. An amendment does not extend the

period of effectiveness of a financing statement. If any amendment adds collateral, it is effective as to the added collateral only from the filing date of the amendment. In this Article, unless the context otherwise requires, the term "financing statement" means the original financing statement and any amendments.

(5) A financing statement covering timber to be cut or covering minerals or the like (including oil and gas) or accounts subject to subsection (5) of Section 9–103, or a financing statement filed as a fixture filing (Section 9–313) where the debtor is not a transmitting utility, must show that it covers this type of collateral, must recite that it is to be filed [for record] in the real estate records, and the financing statement must contain a description of the real estate [sufficient if it were contained in a mortgage of the real estate to give constructive notice of the mortgage under the law of this state]. If the debtor does not have an interest of record in the real estate, the financing statement must show the name of a record owner.

(6) A mortgage is effective as a financing statement filed as a fixture filing from the date of its recording if

(a)   the goods are described in the mortgage by item or type; and

(b)   the goods are or are to become fixtures related to the real estate described in the mortgage; and

(c)   the mortgage complies with the requirements for a financing statement in this section other than a recital that it is to be filed in the real estate records; and

(d)   the mortgage is duly recorded.

No fee with reference to the financing statement is required other than the regular recording and satisfaction fees with respect to the mortgage.

(7) A financing statement sufficiently shows the name of the debtor if it gives the individual, partnership or corporate name of the debtor,whether or not it adds other trade names or names of partners. Where the debtor so changes his name or in the case of an organization its name, identity or corporate structure that a filed financing statement becomes seriously misleading, the filing is not effective to perfect a security interest in collateral acquired by the debtor more than four months after the change, unless a new appropriate financing statement is filed before the expiration of that time. A filed financing statement remains effective with respect to collateral transferred by the debtor even though the secured party knows of or consents to the transfer.

(8) A financing statement substantially complying with the requirements of this section is effective even though it contains minor errors which are not seriously misleading.

Note: *Language in brackets is optional.*

Note: *Where the state has any special recording system for real estate other than the usual grantor-grantee index (as, for instance, a tract system or a title registration or Torrens system) local adaptations of subsection (5) and Section 9–403(7) may be necessary. See Mass. Gen. Laws Chapter 106, Section 9–409.*

§ 9–403. What Constitutes Filing; Duration of Filing; Effect of Lapsed Filing; Duties of Filing Officer.

(1) Presentation for filing of a financing statement and tender of the filing fee or acceptance of the statement by the filing officer constitutes filing under this Article.

(2) Except as provided in subsection (6) a filed financing statement is effective for a period of five years from the date of filing. The effectiveness of a filed financing statement lapses on the expiration of the five year period unless a continuation statement is filed prior to the lapse. If a security interest perfected by filing exists at the time insolvency proceedings are commenced by or against the debtor, the security interest remains perfected until termination of the insolvency proceedings and thereafter for a period of sixty days or until expiration of the five year period, whichever occurs later. Upon lapse the security interest becomes unperfected, unless it is perfected without filing. If the security interest becomes unperfected upon lapse, it is deemed to have been unperfected as against a person who became a purchaser or lien creditor before lapse.

(3) A continuation statement may be filed by the secured party within six months prior to the expiration of the five year period specified in subsection (2). Any such continuation statement must be signed by the secured party, identify the original statement by file number and state that the original statement is still effective. A continuation statement signed by a person other than the secured party of record must be accompanied by a separate written statement of assignment signed by the secured party of record and complying with subsection (2) of Section 9–405, including payment of the required fee. Upon timely filing of the continuation statement, the effectiveness of the original statement is continued for five years after the last date to which the filing was effective

whereupon it lapses in the same manner as provided in subsection (2) unless another continuation statement is filed prior to such lapse. Succeeding continuation statements may be filed in the same manner to continue the effectiveness of the original statement. Unless a statute on disposition of public records provides otherwise, the filing officer may remove a lapsed statement from the files and destroy it immediately if he has retained a microfilm or other photographic record, or in other cases after one year after the lapse. The filing officer shall so arrange matters by physical annexation of financing statements to continuation statements or other related filings, or by other means, that if he physically destroys the financing statements of a period more than five years past, those which have been continued by a continuation statement or which are still effective under subsection (6) shall be retained.

(4) Except as provided in subsection (7) a filing officer shall mark each statement with a file number and with the date and hour of filing and shall hold the statement or a microfilm or other photographic copy thereof for public inspection. In addition the filing officer shall index the statement according to the name of the debtor and shall note in the index the file number and the address of the debtor given in the statement.

(5) The uniform fee for filing and indexing and for stamping a copy furnished by the secured party to show the date and place of filing for an original financing statement or for a continuation statement shall be $.......... if the statement is in the standard form prescribed by the [Secretary of State] and otherwise shall be $.........., plus in each case, if the financing statement is subject to subsection (5) of Section 9–402, $....... The uniform fee for each name more than one required to be indexed shall be $.......... The secured party may at his option show a trade name for any person and an extra uniform indexing fee of $.......... shall be paid with respect thereto.

(6) If the debtor is a transmitting utility (subsection (5) of Section 9–401) and a filed financing statement so states, it is effective until a termination statement is filed. A real estate mortgage which is effective as a fixture filing under subsection (6) of Section 9–402 remains effective as a fixture filing until the mortgage is released or satisfied of record or its effectiveness otherwise terminates as to the real estate.

(7) When a financing statement covers timber to be cut or covers minerals or the like (including oil and gas) or accounts subject to subsection (5) of Sec-

tion 9–103, or is filed as a fixture filing, [it shall be filed for record and] the filing officer shall index it under the names of the debtor and any owner of record shown on the financing statement in the same fashion as if they were the mortgagors in a mortgage of the real estate described, and, to the extent that the law of this state provides for indexing of mortgages under the name of the mortgagee, under the name of the secured party as if he were the mortgagee thereunder, or where indexing is by description in the same fashion as if the financing statement were a mortgage of the real estate described.

Note: *In states in which writings will not appear in the real estate records and indices unless actually recorded the bracketed language in subsection (7) should be used.*

§ 9–404. Termination Statement.

(1) If a financing statement covering consumer goods is filed on or after ...., then within one month or within ten days following written demand by the debtor after there is no outstanding secured obligation and no commitment to make advances, incur obligations or otherwise give value, the secured party must file with each filing officer with whom the financing statement was filed, a termination statement to the effect that he no longer claims a security interest under the financing statement, which shall be identified by file number. In other cases whenever there is no outstanding secured obligation and no commitment to make advances, incur obligations or otherwise give value, the secured party must on written demand by the debtor send the debtor, for each filing officer with whom the financing statement was filed, a termination statement to the effect that he no longer claims a security interest under the financing statement, which shall be identified by file number. A termination statement signed by a person other than the secured party of record must be accompanied by a separate written statement of assignment signed by the secured party of record complying with subsection (2) of Section 9–405, including payment of the required fee. If the affected secured party fails to file such a termination statement as required by this subsection, or to send such a termination statement within ten days after proper demand therefor, he shall be liable to the debtor for one hundred dollars, and in addition for any loss caused to the debtor by such failure.

(2) On presentation to the filing officer of such a termination statement he must note it in the index. If he has received the termination statement in duplicate, he shall return one copy of the termination

statement to the secured party stamped to show the time of receipt thereof. If the filing officer has a microfilm or other photographic record of the financing statement, and of any related continuation statement, statement of assignment and statement of release, he may remove the originals from the files at any time after receipt of the termination statement, or if he has no such record, he may remove them from the files at any time after one year after receipt of the termination statement.

(3) If the termination statement is in the standard form prescribed by the [Secretary of State], the uniform fee for filing and indexing the termination statement shall be $......, and otherwise shall be $......, plus in each case an additional fee of $...... for each name more than one against which the termination statement is required to be indexed.

Note: *The date to be inserted should be the effective date of the revised Article 9.*

§ 9-405. Assignment of Security Interest; Duties of Filing Officer; Fees.

(1) A financing statement may disclose an assignment of a security interest in the collateral described in the financing statement by indication in the financing statement of the name and address of the assignee or by an assignment itself or a copy thereof on the face or back of the statement. On presentation to the filing officer of such a financing statement the filing officer shall mark the same as provided in Section 9-403(4). The uniform fee for filing, indexing and furnishing filing data for a financing statement so indicating an assignment shall be $...... if the statement is in the standard form prescribed by the [Secretary of State] and other wise shall be $......, plus in each case an additional fee of $...... for each name more than one against which the financing statement is required to be indexed.

(2) A secured party may assign of record all or part of his rights under a financing statement by the filing in the place where the original financing statement was filed of a separate written statement of assignment signed by the secured party of record and setting forth the name of the secured party of record and the debtor, the file number and the date of filing of the financing statement and the name and address of the assignee and containing a description of the collateral assigned. A copy of the assignment is sufficient as a separate statement if it complies with the preceding sentence. On presentation to the filing officer of such a separate statement, the filing officer

shall mark such separate statement with the date and hour of the filing. He shall note the assignment on the index of the financing statement, or in the case of a fixture filing, or a filing covering timber to be cut, or covering minerals or the like (including oil and gas) or accounts subject to subsection (5) of Section 9-103, he shall index the assignment under the name of the assignor as grantor and, to the extent that the law of this state provides for indexing the assignment of a mortgage under the name of the assignee, he shall index the assignment of the financing statement under the name of the assignee. The uniform fee for filing, indexing and furnishing filing data about such a separate statment of assignment shall be $...... if the statement is in the standard form prescribed by the [Secretary of State] and otherwise shall be $......, plus in each case an additional fee of $...... for each name more than one against which the statement of assignment is required to be indexed. Notwithstanding the provisions of this subsection, an assignment of record of a security interest in a fixture contained in a mortgage effective as a fixture filing (subsection (6) of Section 9-402) may be made only by an assignment of the mortgage in the manner provided by the law of this state other than this Act.

(3) After the disclosure or filing of an assignment under this section, the assignee is the secured party of record.

§ 9-406. Release of Collateral; Duties of Filing Officer; Fees.
A secured party of record may by his signed statement release all or a part of any collateral described in a filed financing statement. The statement of release is sufficient if it contains a description of the collateral being released, the name and address of the debtor, the name and address of the secured party, and the file number of the financing statement. A statement of release signed by a person other than the secured party of record must be accompanied by a separate written statement of assignment signed by the secured party of record and complying with subsection (2) of Section 9-405, including payment of the required fee. Upon presentation of such a statement of release to the filing officer he shall mark the statement with the hour and date of filing and shall note the same upon the margin of the index of the filing of the financing statement. The uniform fee for filing and noting such a statement of release shall be $...... if the statement is in the standard form prescribed by the [Secretary of State] and otherwise shall be $......, plus in each case an additional fee of $......

for each name more than one against which the statement of release is required to be indexed.

[§ 9-407. Information From Filing Officer.]

[(1) If the person filing any financing statement, termination statement, statement of assignment, or statement of release, furnishes the filing officer a copy thereof, the filing officer shall upon request note upon the copy the file number and date and hour of the filing of the original and deliver or send the copy to such person.]

[(2) Upon request of any person, the filing officer shall issue his certificate showing whether there is on file on the date and hour stated therein, any presently effective financing statement naming a particular debtor and any statement of assignment thereof and if there is, giving the date and hour of filing of each such statement and the names and addresses of each secured party therein. The uniform fee for such a certificate shall be $...... if the request for the certificate is in the standard form prescribed by the [Secretary of State] and otherwise shall be $...... Upon request the filing officer shall furnish a copy of any filed financing statement or statement of assignment for a uniform fee of $...... per page.]

Note: This section is proposed as an optional provision to require filing officers to furnish certificates. Local law and practices should be consulted with regard to the advisability of adoption.

§ 9-408. Financing Statements Covering Consigned or Leased Goods.

A consignor or lessor of goods may file a financing statement using the terms "consignor," "consignee," "lessor," "lessee" or the like instead of the terms specified in Section 9-402. The provisions of this Part shall apply as appropriate to such a financing statement but its filing shall not of itself be a factor in determining whether or not the consignment of lease is intended as security (Section 1-201(37)). However, if it is determined for other reasons that the consignment or lease is so intended, a security interest of the consignor or lessor which attaches to the consigned or leased goods is perfected by such filing.

Part 5. Default

§ 9-501. Default; Procedure When Security Agreement Covers Both Real and Personal Property.

(1) When a debtor is in default under a security agreement, a secured party has the rights and remedies provided in this Part and except as limited by subsection (3) those provided in the security agreement. He may reduce his claim to judgment, foreclose or otherwise enforce the security interest by any available judicial procedure. If the collateral is documents the secured party may proceed either as to the documents or as to the goods covered thereby. A secured party in possession has the rights, remedies and duties provided in Section 9-207. The rights and remedies referred to in this subsection are cumulative.

(2) After default, the debtor has the rights and remedies provided in this Part, those provided in the security agreement and those provided in Section 9-207.

(3) To the extent that they give rights to the debtor and impose duties on the secured party, the rules stated in the subsections referred to below may not be waived or varied except as provided with respect to compulsory disposition of collateral (subsection (3) of Section 9-504 and Section 9-505) and with respect to redemption of collateral (Section 9-506) but the parties may by agreement determine the standards by which the fulfillment of these rights and duties is to be measured if such standards are not manifestly unreasonable:

  (a) subsection (2) of Section 9-502 and subsection (2) of Section 9-504 insofar as they require accounting for surplus proceeds of collateral;

  (b) subsection (3) of Section 9-504 and subsection (1) of Section 9-505 which deal with disposition of collateral;

  (c) subsection (2) of Section 9-505 which deals with acceptance of collateral as discharge of obligation;

  (d) Section 9-506 which deals with redemtion of collateral; and

  (e) subsection (1) of Section 9-507 which deals with the secured party's liability for failure to comply with this Part.

(4) If the security agreement covers both real and personal property, the secured party may proceed under this Part as to the personal property or he may proceed as to both the real and the personal property in accordance with his rights and remedies in respect of the real property in which case the provisions of this Part do not apply.

(5) When a secured party has reduced his claim to judgment the lien of any levy which may be made upon his collateral by virtue of any execution based

upon the judgment shall relate back to the date of the perfection of the security interest in such collateral. A judicial sale, pursuant to such execution, is a foreclosure of the security interest by judicial procedure within the meaning of this section, and the secured party may purchase at the sale and thereafter hold the collateral free of any other requirements of this Article.

§ 9-502. Collection Rights of Secured Party.

(1) When so agreed and in any event on default the secured party is entitled to notify an account debtor or the obligor on an instrument to make payment to him whether or not the assignor was theretofore making collections on the collateral, and also to take control of any proceeds to which he is entitled under Section 9-306.

(2) A secured party who by agreement is entitled to charge back uncollected collateral or otherwise to full or limited recourse against the debtor and who undertakes to collect from the account debtors or obligors must proceed in a commercially reasonable manner and may deduct his reasonable expenses of realization from the collections. If the security agreement secures an indebtedness, the secured party must account to the debtor for any surplus, and unless otherwise agreed, the debtor is liable for any deficiency. But, if the underlying transaction was a sale of accounts or chattel paper, the debtor is entitled to any surplus or is liable for any deficiency only if the security agreement so provides.

§ 9-503. Secured Party's Right to Take Possession After Default.

Unless otherwise agreed a secured party has on default the right to take possession of the collateral. In taking possession a secured party may proceed without judicial process if this can be done without breach of the peace or may proceed by action. If the security agreement so provides the secured party may require the debtor to assemble the collateral and make it available to the secured party at a place to be designated by the secured party which is reasonably convenient to both parties. Without removal a secured party may render equipment unusable, and may dispose of collateral on the debtor's premises under Section 9-504.

§ 9-504. Secured Party's Right to Dispose of Collateral After Default; Effect of Disposition.

(1) A secured party after default may sell, lease or otherwise dispose of any or all of the collateral in its then condition or following any commercially rea-

sonable preparation or processing. Any sale of goods is subject to the Article on Sales (Article 2). The proceeds of disposition shall be applied in the order following to

(a) the reasonable expenses of retaking, holding, preparing for sale or lease, selling, leasing and the like and, to the extent provided for in the agreement and not prohibited by law, the reasonable attorneys' fees and legal expenses incurred by the secured party;

(b) the satisfaction of indebtedness secured by the security interest under which the disposition is made;

(c) the satisfaction of indebtedness secured by any subordinate security interest in the collateral if written notification of demand therefor is received before distribution of the proceeds is completed. If requested by the secured party, the holder of a subordinate security interest must seasonably furnish reasonable proof of his interest, and unless he does so, the secured party need not comply with his demand.

(2) If the security interest secures an indebtedness, the secured party must account to the debtor for any surplus, and, unless otherwise agreed, the debtor is liable for any deficiency. But if the underlying transaction was a sale of accounts or chattel paper, the debtor is entitled to any surplus or is liable for any deficiency only if the security agreement so provides.

(3) Disposition of the collateral may be by public or private proceedings and may be made by way of one or more contracts. Sale or other disposition may be as a unit or in parcels and at any time and place and on any terms but every aspect of the disposition including the method, manner, time, place and terms must be commercially reasonable. Unless collateral is perishable or threatens to decline speedily in value or is of a type customarily sold on a recognized market, reasonable notification of the time and place of any public sale or reasonable notification of the time after which any private sale or other intended disposition is to be made shall be sent by the secured party to the debtor, if he has not signed after default a statement renouncing or modifying his right to notification of sale. In the case of consumer goods no other notification need be sent. In other cases notification shall be sent to any other secured party from whom the secured party has received (before send-

ing his notification to the debtor or before the debtor's renunciation of his rights) written notice of a claim of an interest in the collateral. The secured party may buy at any public sale and if the collateral is of a type customarily sold in a recognized market or is of a type which is the subject of widely distributed standard price quotations he may buy at private sale.

(4) When collateral is disposed of by a secured party after default, the disposition transfers to a purchaser for value all of the debtor's rights therein, discharges the security interest under which it is made and any security interest or lien subordinate thereto. The purchaser takes free of all such rights and interests even though the secured party fails to comply with the requirements of this Part or of any judicial proceedings

(a) in the case of a public sale, if the purchaser has no knowledge of any defects in the sale and if he does not buy in collusion with the secured party, other bidders or the person conducting the sale; or

(b) in any other case, if the purchaser acts in good faith.

(5) A person who is liable to a secured party under a guaranty, indorsement, repurchase agreement or the like and who receives a transfer of collateral from the secured party or is subrogated to his rights has thereafter the rights and duties of the secured party. Such a transfer of collateral is not a sale or disposition of the collateral under this Article.

§ 9-505. Compulsory Disposition of Collateral; Acceptance of the Collateral as Discharge of Obligation.

(1) If the debtor has paid sixty per cent of the cash price in the case of a purchase money security interest in consumer goods or sixty per cent of the loan in the case of another security interest in consumer goods, and has not signed after default a statement renouncing or modifying his rights under this Part a secured party who has taken possession of collateral must dispose of it under Section 9-504 and if he fails to do so within ninety days after he takes possession the debtor at his option may recover in conversion or under Section 9-507(1) on secured party's liability.

(2) In any other case involving consumer goods or any other collateral a secured party in possession may, after default, propose to retain the collateral in satisfaction of the obligation. Written notice of such proposal shall be sent to the debtor if he has not signed after default a statement renouncing or modifying his rights under this subsection. In the case of consumer goods no other notice need be given. In other cases notice shall be sent to any other secured party from whom the secured party has received (before sending his notice to the debtor or before the debtor's renunciation of his rights) written notice of a claim of an interest in the collateral. If the secured party receives objection in writing from a person entitled to receive notification within twenty-one days after the notice was sent, the secured party must dispose of the collateral under Section 9-504. In the absence of such written objection the secured party may retain the collateral in satisfaction of the debtor's obligation.

§ 9-506. Debtor's Right to Redeem Collateral.

At any time before the secured party has disposed of collateral or entered into a contract for its disposition under Section 9-504 or before the obligation has been discharged under Section 9-505(2) the debtor or any other secured party may unless otherwise agreed in writing after default redeem the collateral by tendering fulfillment of all obligations secured by the collateral as well as the expenses reasonably incurred by the secured party in retaking, holding and preparing the collateral for disposition, in arranging for the sale, and to the extent provided in the agreement and not prohibited by law, his reasonable attorneys' fees and legal expenses.

§ 9-507. Secured Party's Liability for Failure to Comply With This Part.

(1) If it is established that the secured party is not proceeding in accordance with the provisions of this Part disposition may be ordered or restrained on appropriate terms and conditions. If the disposition has occurred the debtor or any person entitled to notification or whose security interest has been made known to the secured party prior to the disposition has a right to recover from the secured party any loss caused by a failure to comply with the provisions of this Part. If the collateral is consumer goods, the debtor has a right to recover in any event an amount not less than the credit service charge plus ten per cent of the principal amount of the debt or the time price differential plus 10 per cent of the cash price.

(2) The fact that a better price could have been obtained by a sale at a different time or in a different method from that selected by the secured party is not of itself sufficient to establish that the sale was not

made in a commercially reasonable manner. If the secured party either sells the collateral in the usual manner in any recognized market therefor or if he sells at the price current in such market at the time of his sale or if he has otherwise sold in conformity with reasonable commercial practices among dealers in the type of property sold he has sold in a commercially reasonable manner. The principles stated in the two preceding sentences with respect to sales also apply as may be appropriate to other types of disposition. A disposition which has been approved in any judicial proceeding or by any bona fide creditors' committee or representative of creditors shall conclusively be deemed to be commercially reasonable, but this sentence does not indicate that any such approval must be obtained in any case nor does it indicate that any disposition not so approved is not commercially reasonable.

ARTICLE 10. EFFECTIVE DATE AND REPEALER

§ 10-101. Effective Date. This Act shall become effective at midnight on December 31st following its enactment. It applies to transactions entered into and events occurring after that date.

§ 10-102. Specific Repealer; Provision for Transition.

(1) The following acts and all other acts and parts of acts inconsistent herewith are hereby repealed:

(Here should follow the acts to be specifically repealed including the following:

    Uniform Negotiable Instruments Act
    Uniform Warehouse Receipts Act
    Uniform Sales Act
    Uniform Bills of Lading Act
    Uniform Stock Transfer Act
    Uniform Conditional Sales Act
    Uniform Trust Receipts Act
    Also any acts regulating:
      Bank collections
      Bulk sales
      Chattel mortgages
      Conditional sales
      Factor's lien acts
      Farm storage of grain and similar acts
      Assignment of accounts receivable)

(2) Transactions validly entered into before the effective date specified in Section 10-101 and the rights, duties and interests flowing from them remain valid thereafter and may be terminated, completed, consummated or enforced as required or permitted by any statute or other law amended or repealed by this Act as though such repeal or amendment had not occurred.

Note

Subsection (1) should be separately prepared for each state. The foregoing is a list of statutes to be checked.

§ 10-103. General Repealer. Except as provided in the following section, all acts and parts of acts inconsistent with this Act are hereby repealed.

§ 10-104. Laws Not Repealed.

[(1)] The Article on Documents of Title (Article 7) does not repeal or modify any laws prescribing the form or contents of documents of title or the services or facilities to be afforded by bailees, or otherwise regulating bailees' businesses in respects not specifically dealt with herein; but the fact that such laws are violated does not affect the status of a document of title which otherwise complies with the definition of a document of title (Section 1-201).

[(2) This Act does not repeal . . . .
. . . . ,
cited as the Uniform Act for the Simplification of Fiduciary Security Transfers, and if in any respect there is any inconsistency between that Act and the Article of this Act on investment securities (Article 8) the provisions of the former Act shall control.]

Appendix C

MODEL BUSINESS CORPORATION ACT

§ 1. Short Title. This Act shall be known and may be cited as the "_____[insert name of state] Business Corporation Act."

§ 2. Definitions. As used in this Act, unless the context otherwise requires, the term:

(a) "Corporation" or "domestic corporation" means a corporation for profit subject to the provisions of this Act, except a foreign corporation.

(b) "Foreign corporation" means a corporation for profit organized under laws other than the laws of this State for a purpose or purposes for which a corporation may be organized under this Act.

(c) "Articles of incorporation" means the original or restated articles of incorporation or articles of consolidation and all amendments thereto including articles of merger.

(d) "Shares" means the units into which the proprietary interests in a corporation are divided.

(e) "Subscriber" means one who subscribes for shares in a corporation, whether before or after incorporation.

(f) "Shareholder" means one who is a holder of record of shares in a corporation. If the articles of incorporation or the by-laws so provide, the board of directors may adopt by resolution a procedure whereby a shareholder of the corporation may certify in writing to the corporation that all or a portion of the shares registered in the name of such shareholder are held for the account of a specified person or persons. The resolution shall set forth (1) the classification of shareholder who may certify, (2) the purpose or purposes for which the certification may be made, (3) the form of certification and information to be contained therein, (4) if the certification is with respect to a record date or closing of the stock transfer books within which the certification must be received by the corporation and (5) such other provisions with respect to the procedure as are deemed necessary or desirable. Upon receipt by the corporation of a certification complying with the procedure, the persons specified in the certification shall be deemed, for the purpose or purposes set forth in the certification, to be the holders of record of the number of shares specified in place of the shareholder making the certification.

(g) "Authorized shares" means the shares of all classes which the corporation is authorized to issue.

(h) "Employee" includes officers but not directors. A director may accept duties which make him also an employee.

(i) "Distribution" means a direct or indirect transfer of money or other property (except its own shares) or incurrence of indebtedness, by a corporation to or for the benefit of any of its shareholders in respect of any of its shares, whether by dividend or by purchase, redemption or other acquisition of its shares, or otherwise.

§ 3. Purposes. Corporations may be organized under this Act for any lawful purpose or purposes, except for the purpose of banking or insurance.

§ 4. General Powers. Each corporation shall have power:

(a) To have perpetual succession by its corporate name unless a limited period of duration is stated in its articles of incorporation.

(b) To sue and be sued, complain and defend, in its corporate name.

(c) To have a corporate seal which may be altered at pleasure, and to use the same by causing it, or a facsimile thereof, to be impressed or affixed or in any other manner reproduced.

(d) To purchase, take, receive, lease, or otherwise acquire, own, hold, improve, use and otherwise deal in and with, real or personal property, or any interest therein, wherever situated.

(e) To sell, convey, mortgage, pledge, lease, exchange, transfer and otherwise dispose of all or any part of its property and assets.

(f) To lend money and use its credit to assist its employees.

(g) To purchase, take, receive, subscribe for, or otherwise acquire, own, hold, vote, use, employ, sell, mortgage, lend, pledge, or otherwise dispose of, and otherwise use and deal in and with, shares or other interests in, or obligations of, other domestic or foreign corporations, associations, partnerships or individuals, or direct or indirect obligations of the United States or of any other government, state, territory, governmental district or municipality or of any instrumentality thereof.

(h) To make contracts and guarantees and incur liabilities, borrow money at such rates of interest as the corporation may determine, issue its notes, bonds, and other obligations, and secure any of its obligations by mortgage or pledge of all or any of its property, franchises and income.

(i) To lend money for its corporate purposes, invest and reinvest its funds, and take and hold real and personal property as security for the payment of funds so loaned or invested.

(j) To conduct its business, carry on its operations and have offices and exercise the powers granted by this Act, within or without this State.

(k) To elect or appoint officers and agents of the corporation, and define their duties and fix their compensation.

(l) To make and alter by-laws, not inconsistent with its articles of incorporation or with the laws of this State, for the administration and regulation of the affairs of the corporation.

(m) To make donations for the public welfare or for charitable, scientific or educational purposes.

(n) To transact any lawful business which the board of directors shall find will be in aid of governmental policy.

(o) To pay pensions and establish pension plans, pension trusts, profit sharing plans, stock bonus plans, stock option plans and other incentive plans for any or all of its directors, officers and employees.

(p) To be a promoter, partner, member, associate, or manager of any partnership, joint venture, trust or other enterprise.

(q) To have and exercise all powers necessary or convenient to effect its purposes.

§ 5. Indemnification of Directors and Officers.

(a) As used in this section:

(1) *Director* means any person who is or was a director of the corporation and any person who, while a director of the corporation, is or was serving at the request of the corporation as a director, officer, partner, trustee, employee or agent of another foreign or domestic corporation, partnership, joint venture, trust, other enterprise or employee benefit plan.

(2) *Corporation* includes any domestic or foreign predecessor entity of the corporation in a merger, consolidation or other transaction in which the predecessor's existence ceased upon consummation of such transaction.

(3) *Expenses* include attorneys' fees.

(4) *Official capacity* means

(A) when used with respect to a director, the office of director in the corporation, and

(B) when used with respect to a person other than a director, as contemplated in subsection (i), the elective or appointive office in the corporation held by the officer or the employment or agency relationship undertaken by the employee or agent in behalf of the corporation,

but in each case does not include service for any other foreign or domestic corporation or any partnership, joint venture, trust, other enterprise, or employee benefit plan.

(5) *Party* includes a person who was, is, or is threatened to be made, a named defendant or respondent in a proceeding.

(6) *Proceeding* means any threatened, pending or completed action, suit or proceeding, whether civil, criminal, administrative or investigative.

(b) A corporation shall have power to indemnify any person made a party to any proceeding by reason of the fact that he is or was a director if

(1) he conducted himself in good faith; and

(2) he reasonably believed

(A) in the case of conduct in his official capacity with the corporation, that his conduct was in its best interests, and

(B) in all other cases, that his conduct was at least not opposed to its best interests; and

(3) in the case of any criminal proceeding, he had no reasonable cause to believe his conduct was unlawful.

Indemnification may be made against judgments, penalties, fines, settlements and reasonable expenses, actually incurred by the person in connection with the proceeding; except that if the proceeding was by or in the right of the corporation, indemnification may be made only against such reasonable expenses and shall not be made in respect of any proceeding in which the person shall have been adjudged to be liable to the corporation. The termination of any proceeding by judgment, order, settlement, conviction, or upon a plea of nolo contendere or its equivalent, shall not, of itself, be determinative that the person did not meet the requisite standard of conduct set forth in this subsecion (b).

(c) A director shall not be indemnified under subsection (b) in respect of any proceeding charging improper personal benefit to him, whether or not involving action in his official capacity, in which he shall have been adjudged to be liable on the basis that personal benefit was improperly received by him.

(d) Unless limited by the articles of incorporation,

(1) a director who has been wholly successful, on the merits or otherwise, in the defense of any proceeding referred to in subsection (b) shall be indemnified against reasonable expenses incurred by him in connection with the proceeding; and

(2) a court of appropriate jurisdiction, upon application of a director and such notice as the court shall require, shall have authority to order indemnification in the following circumstances:

(A) if it determines a director is entitled to reimbursement under clause (1), the court shall order indemnification, in which case the director shall also be entitled to recover the expenses securing such reimbursement; or

(B) if it determines that the director is fairly and reasonably entitled to indemnification in view of all the relevant circumstances, whether or not he has met the standard of conduct set forth in subsection (b) or has been adjudged liable in the circumstances described in subsection (c), the court may order such indemnification with respect to any proceeding by or in the right of the corporation or in which liability shall have been adjudged in the circumstances described in subsection (c) shall be limited to expenses.

A court of appropriate jurisdiction may be the same court in which the proceeding involving the director's liability took place.

(e) No indemnification under subsection (b) shall be made by the corporation unless authorized in the specific case after a determination has been made that indemnification of the director is permissible in the circumstances because he has met the standard of conduct set forth in subsection (b). Such determination shall be made:

(1) by the board of directors by a majority vote of a quorum consisting of directors not at the time parties to the proceeding; or

(2) If such a quorum cannot be obtained, then by a majority vote of a committee of the board, duly designated to act in the matter by a majority vote of the full board (in which designation directors who are parties may participate), consisting solely of two or more directors not at the time parties to the proceeding; or

(3) by special legal counsel, selected by the board of directors or a committee thereof by vote as set forth in clauses (1) or (2) of this subsection (e), or, if the requisite quorum of the full board cannot be obtained therefor and such committee cannot be established, by a majority vote of the full board (in which selection directors who are parties may participate); or

(4) by the shareholders.

Authorization of indemnification and determination as to reasonableness of expenses shall be made in the same manner as the determination that indemnification is permissible, except that if the determination that indemnification is permissible is made by special legal counsel, authorization of indemnification and determination as to reasonableness of expenses shall be made in a manner specified in clause (3) in the preceding sentence for the selection of such counsel. Shares held by directors who are parties to the proceeding shall not be voted on the subject matter under this subsection (e).

(f) Reasonable expenses incurred by a director who is a party to a proceeding may be paid or reimbursed by the corporation in advance of the final disposition of such proceeding upon receipt by the corporation of

(1) a written affirmation by the director of his good faith belief that he has met the standard of conduct necessary for indemnification by the corporation as authorized in this section, and

(2) a written undertaking by or on behalf of the director to repay such amount if it shall ultimately be determined that he has not met such standard of conduct, and after a determination that the facts then known to those making the determination would not preclude indemnification under this section. The undertaking required by clause (2) shall be an unlimited

general obligation of the director but need not be secured and may be accepted without reference to financial ability to make repayment. Determinations and authorizations of payments under this subsection (f) shall be made in the manner specified in subsection (e).

(g) No provision for the corporation to indemnify or to advance expenses to a director who is made a party to a proceeding, whether contained in the articles of incorporation, the by-laws, a resolution of shareholders or directors, an agreement or otherwise (except as contemplated by subsection (j)), shall be valid unless consistent with this section or, to the extent that indemnity hereunder is limited by the articles of incorporation, consistent therewith. Nothing contained in this section shall limit the corporation's power to pay or reimburse expenses incurred by a director in connection with his appearance as a witness in a proceeding at a time when he has not been made a named defendant or respondent in the proceeding.

(h) For purposes of this section, the corporation shall be deemed to have requested a director to serve an employee benefit plan whenever the performance by him of his duties to the corporation also imposes duties on, or otherwise involves services by, him to the plan or participants or beneficiaries of the plan; excise taxes assessed on a director with respect to an employee benefit plan pursuant to applicable law shall be deemed "fines"; and action taken or omitted by him with respect to an employee benefit plan in the performance of his duties for a purpose reasonably believed by him to be in the interest of the participants and beneficiaries of the plan shall be deemed to be for a purpose which is not opposed to the best interest of the corporation.

(i) Unless limited by the articles of incorporation.

(1) an officer of the corporation shall be indemnified as and to the same extent provided in subsection (d) for a director and shall be entitled to the same extent as a director to seek indemnification pursuant to the provisions of subsection (d);

(2) a corporation shall have the power to indemnify and to advance expenses to an officer, employee or agent of the corporation to the same extent that it may indemnify and advance expenses to directors pursuant to this section; and

(3) a corporation, in addition, shall have the power to indemnify and to advance expenses to an officer, employee or agent who is not a director to such further extent, consistent with law, as may be provided by its articles of incorporation, by-laws, general or specific action of its board of directors, or contract.

(j) A corporation shall have power to purchase and maintain insurance on behalf of any person who is or was a director, officer, employee or agent of the corporation, or who, while a director, officer, employee or agent of the corporation, is or was serving at the request of the corporation as a director, officer, partner, trustee, employee or agent of another foreign or domestic corporation, partnership, joint venture, trust, other enterprise or employee benefit plan, against any liability asserted against him and incurred by him in any such capacity or arising out of his status as such, whether or not the corporation would have the power to indemnify him against such liability under the provisions of this section.

(k) Any indemnification of, or advance of expenses to, a director in accordance with this section, if arising out of a proceeding by or in the right of the corporation, shall be reported in writing to the shareholders with or before the notice of the next shareholders' meeting.

§ 6. Power of Corporation to Acquire its Own Shares.

A corporation shall have the power to acquire its own shares. All of its own shares acquired by a corporation shall, upon acquisition, constitute authorized but unissued shares, unless the articles of incorporation provide that they shall not be reissued, in which case the authorized shares shall be reduced by the number of shares acquired.

If the number of authorized shares is reduced by an acquisition, the corporation shall, not later than the time it files its next annual report under this Act with the Secretary of State, file a statement of cancellation showing the reduction in the authorized shares. The statement of cancellation shall be executed in duplicate by the corporation by its president or a vice president and by its secretary or an assistant secretary, and verified by one of the officers signing such statement, and shall set forth:

(a) The name of the corporation.

(b) The number of acquired shares cancelled, itemized by the classes and series.

(c) The aggregate number of authorized shares, itemized by classes and series, after giving effect to such cancellation.

Duplicate originals of such statements shall be delivered to the Secretary of State. If the Secretary of State finds that such statement conforms to law, he shall, when all fees and franchise taxes have been paid as in this Act prescribed:

(1) Endorse on each of such duplicate originals the word "filed," and the month, day and year of the filing thereof.

(2) File one of such duplicate originals in his office.

(3) Return the other duplicate original to the corporation or its representative.

§ 7. Defense of Ultra Vires.

No act of corporation and no conveyance or transfer of real or personal property to or by a corporation shall be invalid by reason of the fact that the corporation was without capacity or power to do such act or to make or receive such conveyance or transfer, but such lack of capacity or power may be asserted:

(a) In a proceeding by a shareholder against the corporation to enjoin the doing of any act or the transfer of real or personal property by or to the corporation. If the unauthorized act or transfer sought to be enjoined is being, or is to be, performed or made pursuant to a contract to which the corporation is a party, the court may, if all of the parties to the contract are parties to the proceeding and if it deems the same to be equitable, set aside and enjoin the performance of such contract, and in so doing may allow to the corporation or to the other parties to the contract, as the case may be, compensation for the loss or damage sustained by either of them which may result from the action of the court in setting aside and enjoining the performance of such contract, but anticipated profits to be derived from the performance of the contract shall not be awarded by the court as a loss or damage sustained.

(b) In a proceeding by the corporation, whether acting directly or through a receiver, trustee, or other legal representative, or through shareholders in a representative unit, against the incumbent or former officers or directors of the corporation.

(c) In a proceeding by the Attorney General, as provided in this Act, to dissolve the corporation, or in a proceeding by the Attorney General to enjoin the corporation from the transaction of unauthorized business.

§ 8. Corporate Name.

The corporate name:

(a) Shall contain the word "corporation," "company," "incorporated" or "limited," or shall contain an abbreviation of one of such words.

(b) Shall not contain any word or phrase which indicates or implies that it is organized for any purpose other than one or more of the purposes contained in its articles of incorporation.

(c) Shall not be the same as, or deceptively similar to, the name of any domestic corporation existing under the laws of this State or any foreign corporation authorized to transact business in this State, or a name the exclusive right to which is, at the time, reserved in the manner provided in this Act, or the name of a corporation which has in effect a registration of its corporate name as provided in this Act, except that this provision shall not apply if the applicant files with the Secretary of State either of the following: (1) the written consent of such other corporation or holder of a reserved or registered name to use the same or deceptively similar name and one or more words are added to make such name distinguishable from such other name, or (2) a certified copy of a final decree of a court of competent jurisdiction establishing the prior right of the applicant to the use of such name in this State.

A corporation with which another corporation, domestic or foreign, is merged, or which is formed by the reorganization or consolidation of one or more domestic or foreign corporations or upon a sale, lease or other disposition to or exchange with, a domestic corporation of all or substantially all the assets of another corporation, domestic or foreign, including its name, may have the same name as that used in this State by any of such corporations if such other corporation was organized under the laws of, or is authorized to transact business in, this State.

§ 9. Reserved Name.

The exclusive right to the use of a corporate name may be reserved by:

(a) Any person intending to organize a corporation under this Act.

(b) Any domestic corporation intending to change its name.

(c) Any foreign corporation intending to make application for a certificate of authority to transact business in this State.

(d) Any foreign corporation authorized to transact business in this state and intending to change its name.

(e) Any person intending to organize a foreign corporation and intending to have such corporation make application for a certificate of authority to transact business in this State.

The reservation shall be made by filing with the Secretary of State an application to reserve a specified corporate name, executed by the applicant. If the Secretary of State finds that the name is available for corporate use, he shall reserve the same for the exclusive use of the applicant for a period of one hundred and twenty days.

The right to the exclusive use of a specified corporate name so reserved may be transferred to any other person or corporation by filing in the office of the Secretary of State a notice of such transfer, executed by the applicant for whom the name was reserved, and specifying the name and address of the transferee.

§ 10. Registered Name.
Any corporation organized and existing under the laws of any state or territory of the United States may register its corporate name under this Act, provided its corporate name is not the same as, or deceptively similar to, the name of any domestic corporation existing under the laws of this State, or the name of any foreign corporation authorized to transact business in this State, or any corporate name reserved or registered under this Act.

Such registration shall be made by:

(a) Filing with the Secretary of State (1) an application for registration executed by the corporation by an officer thereof, setting forth the name of the corporation, the state or territory under the laws of which it is incorporated, the date of its incorporation, a statement that it is carrying on or doing business, and a brief statement of the business in which it is engaged, and (2) a certificate setting forth that such corporation is in good standing under the laws of the state or territory wherein it is organized, executed by the Secretary of State of such state or territory or by such other official as may have custody of the records pertaining to corporations, and

(b) Paying to the Secretary of State a registration fee in the amount of _____ for each month, or fraction thereof, between the date of filing such application and December 31st of the calendar year in which such application is filed.

Such registration shall be effective until the close of the calendar year in which the application for registration is filed.

§ 11. Renewal of Registered Name.
A corporation which has in effect a registration of its corporate name, may renew such registration from year to year by annually filing an application for renewal setting forth the facts required to be set forth in an original application for registration and a certificate of good standing as required for the original registration and by paying a fee of _____. A renewal application may be filed between the first day of October and the thirty-first day of December in each year, and shall extend the registration for the following calendar year.

§ 12. Registered Office and Registered Agent.
Each corporation shall have and continuously maintain in this state:

(a) A registered office which may be, but need not be, the same as its place of business.

(b) A registered agent, which agent may be either an individual resident in this State whose business office is identical with such registered office, or a domestic corporation, or a foreign corporation authorized to transact business in this State, having a business office identical with such registered office.

§ 13. Change of Registered Office or Registered Agent.
A corporation may change its registered office or change its registered agent, or both, upon filing in the office of the Secretary of State a statement setting forth:

(a) The name of the corporation.

(b) The address of its then registered office.

(c) If the address of its registered office is to be changed, the address to which the registered office is to be changed.

(d) The name of its then registered agent.

(e) If its registered agent is to be changed, the name of its successor registered agent.

(f) That the address of its registered office and the address of the business office of its registered agent, as changed, will be identical.

(g) That such change was authorized by resolution duly adopted by its board of directors.

Such statement shall be executed by the corporation by its president, or a vice president, and verified by him, and delivered to the Secretary of State. If the Secretary of State finds that such statement conforms to the provisions of this Act, he shall file such statement in his office, and upon such filing the change of address of the registered office, or the appointment of a new registered agent, or both, as the case may be, shall become effective.

Any registered agent of a corporation may resign

as such agent upon filing a written notice thereof, executed in duplicate, with the Secretary of State, who shall forthwith mail a copy thereof to the corporation at its registered office. The appointment of such agent shall terminate upon the expiration of thirty days after receipt of such notice by the Secretary of State.

If a registered agent changes his or its business address to another place within the same _____ [supply designation of jurisdiction, such as county, etc., in accordance with local practice], he or it may change such address and the address of the registered office of any corporation of which he or it is registered agent by filing a statement as required above except that it need be signed only by the registered agent and need not be responsive to (e) or (g) and must recite that a copy of the statement has been mailed to the corporation.

§ 14. Service of Process on Corporation.

The registered agent so appointed by a corporation shall be an agent of such corporation upon whom any process, notice or demand required or permitted by law to be served upon the corporation may be served.

Whenever a corporation shall fail to appoint or maintain a registered agent in this State, or whenever its registered agent cannot with reasonable diligence be found at the registered office, then the Secretary of State shall be an agent of such corporation upon whom any such process, notice or demand may be served. Service on the Secretary of State of any such process, notice, or demand shall be made by delivering to and leaving with him, or with any clerk having charge of the corporation department of his office, duplicate copies of such process, notice or demand. In the event any such process, notice or demand is served on the Secretary of State, he shall immediately cause one of the copies thereof to be forwarded by registered mail, addressed to the corporation at its registered office. Any service so had on the Secretary of State shall be returnable in not less than thirty days.

The Secretary of State shall keep a record of all processes, notices and demands served upon him under this section, and shall record therein the time of such service and his action with reference thereto.

Nothing herein contained shall limit or affect the right to serve any process, notice or demand required or permitted by law to be served upon a corporation in any other manner now or hereafter permitted by law.

§ 15. Authorized shares.

Each corporation shall have power to create and issue the number of shares stated in its articles of incorporation. Such shares may be divided into one or more classes with such designations, preferences, limitations, and relative rights as shall be stated in the articles of incorporation. The articles of incorporation may limit or deny the voting rights of or provide special voting rights for the shares of any class to the extent not inconsistent with the provisions of this Act.

Without limiting the authority herein contained, a corporation, when so provided in its articles of incorporation, may issue shares of preferred or special classes:

(a) Subject to the right of the corporation to redeem any of such shares at the price fixed by the articles of incorporation for the redemption thereof.

(b) Entitling the holders thereof to cumulative, noncumulative or partially cumulative dividends.

(c) Having preference over any other class or classes of shares as to the payment of dividends.

(d) Having preference in the assets of the corporation over any other class or classes of shares upon the voluntary or involuntary liquidation of the corporation.

(e) Convertible into shares of any other class or into shares of any series of the same or any other class, except a class having prior or superior rights and preferences as to dividends or distribution of assets upon liquidation.

§ 16. Issuance of Shares of Preferred or Special Classes in Series.

If the articles of incorporation so provide, the shares of any preferred or special class may be divided into and issued in series. If the shares of any such class are to be issued in series, then each series shall be so designated as to distinguish the shares thereof from the shares of all other series and classes. Any or all of the series of any such class and the variations in the relative rights and preferences as between different series may be fixed and determined by the articles or incorporation, but all shares of the same class shall be identical except as to the following relative rights and preferences, as to which there may be variations between different series:

    (A) The rate of dividend.

    (B) Whether shares may be redeemed and, if so, the redemption price and the terms and conditions of redemption.

    (C) The amount payable upon shares in event of voluntary and involuntary liquidation.

    (D) Sinking fund provisions, if any, for the redemption or purchase of shares.

    (E) The terms and conditions, if any, on which shares may be converted.

    (F) Voting rights, if any.

If the articles of incorporation shall expressly vest authority in the board of directors, then, to the extent that the articles of incorporation shall not have established series and fixed and determined the variations in the relative rights and preferences as between series, the board of directors shall have authority to divide any or all of such classes into series and, within the limitations set forth in this section and in the articles of incorporation, fix and determine the relative rights and preferences of the shares of any series so established.

In order for the board of directors to estbalish a series, where authority so to do is contained in the articles of incorporation, the board of directors shall adopt a resolution setting forth the designation of the series and fixing and determining the relative rights and preferences thereof, or so much thereof as shall not be fixed and determined by the articles of incorporation.

Prior to the issue of any shares of a series established by resolution adopted by the board of directors, the corporation shall file in the office of the Secretary of State a statement setting forth:

    (a)   The name of the corporation.

    (b)   A copy of the resolution establishing and designating the series, and fixing and determining the relative rights and preferences thereof.

    (c)   The date of adoption of such resolution.

    (d)   That such resolution was duly adopted by the board of directors.

Such statement shall be executed in duplicate by the corporation by its president or a vice president and by its secretary or an assistant secretary, and verified by one of the officers signing such statement, and shall be delivered to the Secretary of State. If the Secretary of State finds that such statement conforms to law, he shall, when all franchise taxes and fees have been paid as in this Act prescribed:

    (1) Endorse on each of such duplicate originals the word "Filed," and the month, day, and year of the filing thereof.

    (2) File one of such duplicate originals in his office.

    (3) Return the other duplicate original to the corporation or its representative.

Upon the filing of such statement by the Secretary of State, the resolution establishing and designating the series and fixing and determining the relative rights and preferences thereof shall become effective and shall constitute an amendment of the articles of incorporation.

§ 17. Subscriptions for Shares. A subscription for shares of a corporation to be organized shall be irrevocable for a period of six months, unless otherwise provided by the terms of the subscription agreement or unless all of the subscribers consent to the revocation of such subscription.

Unless otherwise provided in the subscription agreement, subscriptions for shares, whether made before or after the organization of a corporation, shall be paid in full at such time, or in such installments and at such times, as shall be determined by the board of directors. Any call made by the board of directors for payment on subscriptions shall be uniform as to all shares of the same class or as to all shares of the same series, as the case may be. In case of default in the payment of any installment or call when such payment is due, the corporation may proceed to collect the amount due in the same manner as any debt due the corporation. The by-laws may prescribe other penalties for failure to pay installments or calls that may become due, but no penalty working a forfeiture of a subscription, or of the amounts paid theron, shall be declared as against any subscriber unless the amount due thereon shall remain unpaid for a period of twenty days after written demand has been made therefor. If mailed, such written demand shall be deemed to be made when deposited in the United States mail in a sealed envelope addressed to the subscriber at his last post-office address known to the corporation, with postage thereon prepaid. In the event of the sale of any shares by reason of any forfeiture, the excess of proceeds realized over the amount due and unpaid on such shares shall be paid to the delinquent subscriber or to his legal representative.

§ 18. Issuance of Shares. Subject to any restrictions in the articles of incorporation:

(a)   Shares may be issued for such consideration as shall be authorized by the board of directors establishing a price (in money or other consideration) or a minimum price or general formula or method by which the price will be determined; and

(b)   Upon authorization by the board of directors, the corporation may issue its own shares in exchange for or in conversion of its outstanding shares, or distribute its own shares, pro rata to its shareholders or the shareholders of one or more classes or series, to effectuate stock dividends or splits, and any such transaction shall not require consideration; provided, that no such issuance of shares of any class or series shall be made to the holders of shares of any other class or series unless it is either expressly provided for in the articles of incorporation, or is authorized by an affirmative vote or the written consent of the holders of at least a majority of the outstanding shares of the class or series in which the distribution is to be made.

§ 19. Payment for Shares.

The consideration for the issuance of shares may be paid, in whole or in part, in money, in other property, tangible or intangible, or in labor or services actually performed for the corporation. When payment of the consideration for which shares are to be issued shall have been received by the corporation, such shares shall be nonassessable.

Neither promissory notes nor future services shall constitute payment or part payment for the issuance of shares of a corporation.

In the absence of fraud in the transaction, the judgment of the board of directors or the shareholders, as the case may be, as to the value of the consideration received for shares shall be conclusive.

§ 20. Stock Rights and Options.

Subject to any provisions in respect thereof set forth in its articles of incorporation, a corporation may create and issue, whether or not in connection with the issuance and sale of any of its shares or other securities, rights or options entitling the holders thereof to purchase from the corporation shares of any class or classes. Such rights or options shall be evidenced in such manner as the board of directors shall approve and, subject to the provisions of the articles of incorporation, shall set forth the terms upon which, the time or times within which and the price or prices at which such shares may be purchased from the corporation upon the exercise of any such right or option. If such rights or options are to issued to directors, officers or employees as such of the corporation or of any subsidiary thereof, and not to the shareholders generally, their issuance shall be approved by the affirmative vote of the holders of a majority of the shares entitled to vote thereon or shall be authorized by and consistent with a plan approved or ratified by such a vote of shareholders. In the absence of fraud in the transaction, the judgment of the board of directors as to the adequacy of the consideration received for such rights or options shall be conclusive.

§ 21. Determination of Amount of Stated Capital. [This section was repealed in 1979.]

§ 22. Expenses of Organization, Reorganization and Financing.

The reasonable charges and expenses of organization or reorganization of a corporation, and the reasonable expenses of and compensation for the sale or underwriting of its shares, may be paid or allowed by such corporation out of the consideration received by it in payment for its shares without thereby rendering such shares non-assessable.

§ 23. Shares Represented by Certificates and Uncertificated Shares.

The shares of a corporation shall be represented by certificates or shall be uncertificated shares. Certificates shall be signed by the chairman or vice-chairman of the board of directors or a vice president and by the treasurer or an assistant treasurer or the secretary or an assistant secretary of the corporation, and may be sealed with the seal of the corporation or a facsimile therof. Any of or all the signatures upon a certificate may be a facsimile. In case any officer, transfer agent or registrar who has signed or whose facsimile signature has been placed upon such certificate shall have ceased to be such officer, transfer agent or registrar before such certificate is issued, it may be issued by the corporation with the same effect as if he were such officer, transfer agent or registrar at the date of its issue.

Every certificate representing shares issued by a corporation which is authorized to issue shares of more than one class shall set forth upon the face or back of the certificate, or shall state that the corporation will furnish to any shareholder upon request and without charge, a full statement of the designations, preferences, limitations, and relative rights of the shares of each class authorized to be issued, and if the corporation is authorized to issue any preferred or special class in series, the variations in the relative rights and preferences between the shares of each such series so far as the same have been fixed and determined and the authority of the board of directors to fix and determine the relative rights and preferences of subsequent series.

Each certificate representing shares shall state upon the face thereof:

(a) That the corporation is organized under the laws of this State.

(b) The name of the person to whom issued.

(c) The number and class of shares, and the designation of the series, if any, which such certificate represents.

No certificate shall be issued for any share until the consideration established for its issuance shall have been paid.

Unless otherwise provided by the articles of incorporation or by-laws, the board of directors of a corporation may provide by resolution that some or all of any or all classes and series of its shares shall be uncertificated shares, provided that such resolution shall not apply to shares represented by a certificate until such certificate is surrendered to the corporation. Within a reasonable time after the issuance or transfer of uncertificated shares, the corporation shall send to the registered owner thereof a written notice containing the information required to be set forth or stated on certificates pursuant to the second and third paragraphs of this section. Except as otherwise expressly provided by law, the rights and obligations of the holders of uncertificated shares and the rights and obligations of the holders of certificates representing shares of the same class and series shall be identical.

§ 24. Fractional Shares. A corporation may (1) issue fractions of a share, either represented by a certificate or uncertificated, (2) arrange for the disposition of fractional interests by those entitled thereto, (3) pay in money the fair value of fractions of a share as of a time when those entitled to receive such fractions are determined, or (4) issue scrip in registered or bearer form which shall entitle the holder to receive a certificate for a full share or an uncertificated full share upon the surrender of such scrip aggregating a full share. A certificate for a fractional share or an uncertificated fractional share shall, but scrip shall not unless otherwise provided

therein, entitle the holder to exercise voting rights, to receive dividends thereon, and to participate in any of the assets of the corporation in the event of liquidation. The board of directors may cause scrip to be issued subject to the condition that it shall become void if not exchanged for certificates representing full shares or uncertificated full shares before a specified date, or subject to the condition that the shares for which scrip is exchangeable may be sold by the corporation and the proceeds thereof distributed to the holders of scrip, or subject to any other conditions which the board of directors may deem advisable.

§ 25. Liability of Subscribers and Shareholders. A holder of or subscriber to shares of a corporation shall be under no obligation to the corporation or its creditors with respect to such shares other than the obligation to pay to the corporation the full consideration for which such shares were issued or to be issued.

Any person becoming an assignee or transferee of shares or of a subscription for shares in good faith and without knowledge or notice that the full consideration therefor has not been paid shall not be personally liable to the corporation or its creditors for any unpaid portion of such consideration.

An executor, administrator, conservator, guardian, trustee, assignee for the benefit of creditors, or receiver shall not be personally liable to the corporation as a holder of or subscriber to shares of a corporation but the estate and funds in his hands shall be so liable.

No pledgee or other holder of shares as collateral security shall be personally liable as a shareholder.

§ 26. Shareholders' Preemptive Rights. The shareholders of a corporation shall have no preemptive right to acquire unissued shares of the corporation, or securities of the corporation convertible into or carrying a right to subscribe to or acquire shares, except to the extent, if any, that such right is provided in the articles of incorporation.

§ 26A. Shareholders' Preemptive Rights [Alternative]. Except to the extent limited or denied by this section or by the articles of incorporation, shareholders shall have a preemptive right to acquire unissued shares or securities convertible into such shares or carrying a right to subscribe to or acquire shares.

Unless otherwise provided in the articles of incorporation,

(a) No preemptive right shall exist

(1) to acquire any shares issued to directors, officers or employees pursuant to approval by the affirmative vote of the holders of a majority of the shares entitled to vote thereon or when authorized by and consistent with a plan theretofore approved by such a vote of shareholders; or

(2) to acquire any shares sold otherwise than for money.

(b) Holders of shares of any class that is preferred or limited as to dividends or assets shall not be entitled to any preemptive right.

(c) Holders of shares of common stock shall not be entitled to any preemptive right to shares of any class that is preferred or limited as to dividends or assets or to any obligations, unless convertible into shares of common stock or carrying a right to subscribe to or acquire shares of common stock.

(d) Holders of common stock without voting power shall have no preemptive right to shares of common stock with voting power.

(e) The preemptive right shall be only an opportunity to acquire shares or other securities under such terms and conditions as the board of directors may fix for the purpose of providing a fair and reasonable opportunity for the exercise of such right.

§ 27. By-Laws. The initial by-laws of a corporation shall be adopted by its board of directors. The power to alter, amend or repeal the by-laws or adopt new by-laws, subject to repeal or change by action of the shareholders, shall be vested in the board of directors unless reserved to the shareholders by the articles of incorporation. The by-laws may contain any provisions for the regulation and management of the affairs of the corporation not inconsistent with law or the articles of incorporation.

§ 27A. By-Laws and Other Powers in Emergency [Optional]. The board of directors of any corporation may adopt emergency by-laws, subject to repeal or change by action of the shareholders, which shall, notwithstanding any different provision elsewhere in this Act or in the articles of incorporation or by-laws, be operative during any emergency in the conduct of the business of the corporation resulting from an attack on the United States or any nuclear or atomic disaster. The emergency by-laws may make any provision that may be practical and necessary for the circumstances of the emergency, including provisions that:

(a) A meeting of the board of directors may be called by any officer or director in such manner and under such conditions as shall be prescribed in the emergency by-laws;

(b) The director or directors in attendance at the meeting, or any greater number fixed by the emergency by-laws, shall constitute a quorum; and

(c) The officers or other persons designated on a list approved by the board of directors before the emergency, all in such order of priority and subject to such conditions, and for such period of time (not longer than reasonably necessary after the termination of the emergency) as may be provided in the emergency by-laws or in the resolution approving the list shall, to the extent required to provide a quorum at any meeting of the board of directors, be deemed directors for such meeting.

The board of directors, either before or during any such emergency, may provide, and from time to time modify, lines of succession in the event that during such an emergency any or all officers or agents of the corporation shall for any reason be rendered incapable of discharging their duties.

The board of directors, either before or during any such emergency, may, effective in the emergency, change the head office or designate several alternative head offices or regional offices, or authorize the officers so to do.

To the extent not inconsistent with any emergency by-laws so adopted, the by-laws of the corporation shall remain in effect during any such emergency and upon its termination the emergency by-laws shall cease to be operative.

Unless otherwise provided in emergency by-laws, notice of any meeting of the board of directors during any such emergency may be given only to such of the directors as it may be feasible to reach at the time and by such means as may be feasible at the time, including publication or radio.

To the extent required to constitute a quorum at any meeting of the board of directors during any such emergency, the officers of the corporation who are present shall, unless otherwise provided in emergency by-laws, be deemed, in order of rank and within the same rank in order of seniority, directors for such meeting.

No officer, director or employee acting in accordance with any emergency by-laws shall be liable except for willful misconduct. No officer, director or employee shall be liable for any action taken by him in good faith in such an emergency in furtherance of the ordinary business affairs of the corporation even though not authorized by the by-laws then in effect.

§ 28. Meetings of Shareholders.
Meetings of shareholders may be held at such place within or without this State as may be stated in or fixed in accordance with the by-laws. If no other place is stated or so fixed, meetings shall be held at the registered office of the corporation.

An annual meeting of the shareholders shall be held at such time as may be stated in or fixed in accordance with the by-laws. If the annual meeting is not held within any thirteen-month period the Court of _____ may, on the application of any shareholder, summarily order a meeting to be held.

Special meetings of the shareholders may be called by the board of directors, the holders of not less than one-tenth of all the shares entitled to vote at the meeting, or such other persons as may be authorized in the articles of incorporation or the by-laws.

§ 29. Notice of Shareholders' Meetings.
Written notice stating the place, day and hour of the meeting and, in case of a special meeting, the purpose or purposes for which the meeting is called, shall be delivered not less than ten nor more than fifty days before the date of the meeting, either personally or by mail, by or at the direction of the president, the secretary, or the officer or persons calling the meeting, to each shareholder of record entitled to vote at such meeting. If mailed, such notice shall be deemed to be delivered when deposited in the United States mail addressed to the shareholder at his address as it appears on the stock transfer books of the corporation, with postage thereon prepaid.

§ 30. Closing of Transfer Books and Fixing Record Date.
For the purpose of determining shareholders entitled to notice of or to vote at any meeting of shareholders or any adjournment thereof, or entitled to receive payment of any dividend, or in order to make a determination of shareholders for any other proper purpose, the board of directors of a corporation may provide that the stock transfer books shall be closed for a stated period but not to exceed, in any case, fifty days. If the stock transfer books shall be closed for the purpose of determining

shareholders entitled to notice of or to vote at a meeting of shareholders, such books shall be closed for at least ten days immediately preceding such meeting. In lieu of closing the stock transfer books, the by-laws, or in the absence of an applicable by-law the board of directors, may fix in advance a date as the record date for any such determination of shareholders, such date in any case to be not more than fifty days and, in case of a meeting of shareholders, not less than ten days prior to the date on which the particular action, requiring such determination of share holders, is to be taken. If the stock transfer books are not closed and no record date is fixed for the determination of shareholders entitled to notice of or to vote at a meeting of shareholders, or shareholders entitled to receive payment of a dividend, the date on which notice of the meeting is mailed or the date on which the resolution of the board of directors declaring such dividend is adopted, as the case may be, shall be the record date for such determination of shareholders. When a determination of shareholders entitled to vote at any meeting of shareholders has been made as provided in this section, such determination shall apply to any adjournment thereof.

§ 31. Voting Record.
The officer or agent having charge of the stock transfer books for shares of a corporation shall make a complete record of the shareholders entitled to vote at such meeting or any adjournment thereof, arranged in alphabetical order, with the address of and the number of shares held by each. Such record shall be produced and kept open at the time and place of the meeting and shall be subject to the inspection of any shareholder during the whole time of the meeting for the purposes thereof. Failure to comply with the requirements of this section shall not affect the validity of any action taken at such meeting.

An officer or agent having charge of the stock transfer books who shall fail to prepare the record of shareholders, or produce and keep it open for inspection at the meeting, as provided in this section, shall be liable to any shareholder suffering damage on account of such failure, to the extent of such damage.

§ 32. Quorum of Shareholders.
Unless otherwise provided in the articles of incorporation, a majority of the shares entitled to vote, represented in person or by proxy, shall constitute a quorum at a meeting of shareholders, but in no event shall a quorum consist of less than one-third of the shares entitled to vote at

the meeting. If a quorum is present, the affirmative vote of the majority of the shares represented at the meeting and entitled to vote on the subject matter shall be the act of the shareholders, unless the vote of a greater number or voting by classes is required by this Act or the articles of incorporation or by-laws.

§ 33. Voting of Shares. Each outstanding share, regardless of class, shall be entitled to one vote on each matter submitted to a vote at a meeting of shareholders, except as may be otherwise provided in the articles of incorporation. If the articles of incorporation provide for more or less than one vote for any share, on any matter, every reference in this Act to a majority or other proportion of shares shall refer to such a majority or other proportion of votes entitled to be cast.

Shares held by another corporation if a majority or the shares entitled to vote for the election of directors of such other corporation is held by the corporation, shall not be voted at any meeting or counted in determining the total number of outstanding shares at any given time.

A shareholder may vote either in person or by proxy executed in writing by the shareholder or by his duly authorized attorney-in-fact. No proxy shall be valid after eleven months from the date of its execution, unless otherwise provided in the proxy.

[Either of the following prefatory phrases may be inserted here: "The articles of incorporation may provide that" or "Unless the articles of incorporation otherwise provide"]. . .at each election for directors every shareholder entitled to vote at such election shall have the right to vote, in person or by proxy, the number of shares owned by him for as many persons as there are directors to be elected and for whose election he has a right to vote, or to cumulate his votes by giving one candidate as many votes as the number of such directors multiplied by the number of his shares shall equal, or by distributing such votes on the same principle among any number of such candidates.

Shares standing in the name of another corporation, domestic or foreign, may be voted by such officer, agent or proxy as the by-laws of such other corporation may prescribe, or, in the absence of such provision, as the board of directors of such other corporation may determine.

Shares held by an administrator, executor, guardian or conservator may be voted by him, either in person or by proxy, without a transfer of such shares into his name. Shares standing in the name of a trustee may be voted by him, either in person or by proxy, but no trustee shall be entitled to vote shares held by him without a transfer of such shares into his name.

Shares standing in the name of a receiver may be voted by such receiver, and shares held by or under the control of a receiver may be voted by such receiver without the transfer thereof into his name if authority so to do be contained in an appropriate order of the court by which such receiver was appointed.

A shareholder whose shares are pledged shall be entitled to vote such shares until the shares have been transferred into the name of the pledgee, and thereafter the pledge shall be entitled to vote the shares so transferred.

On and after the date on which written notice of redemption of redeemable shares has been mailed to the holders thereof and a sum sufficient to redeem such shares has been deposited with a bank or trust company with irrevocable instruction and authority to pay the redemption price to the holders thereof upon surrender of certificates therefor, such shares shall not be entitled to vote on any matter and shall not be deemed to be outstanding shares.

§ 34. Voting Trusts and Agreements Among Shareholders. Any number of shareholders of a corporation may create a voting trust for the purpose of conferring upon a trustee or trustees the right to vote or otherwise represent their shares, for a period of not to exceed ten years, by entering into a written voting trust agreement specifying the terms and conditions of the voting trust, by depositing a counterpart of the agreement with the corporation at its registered office, and by transferring their shares to such trustee or trustees for the purposes of the agreement. Such trustee or trustees shall keep a record of the holders of voting trust certificates evidencing a beneficial interest in the voting trust, giving the names and addresses of all such holders and the number and class of the shares in respect of which the voting trust certificates held by each are issued, and shall deposit a copy of such record with the corporation at its registered office. The counterpart of the voting trust agreement and the copy of such record so deposited with the corporation shall be subject to the same right of examination by a shareholder of the corporation, in person or by agent or attorney, as are the books and records of the corporation, and such counterpart and such copy of such record shall be subject to examination by any holder of record of voting trust certificates, either in person or by agent or attorney, at any reasonable time for any proper purpose.

Agreements among shareholders regarding the voting of their shares shall be valid and enforceable in accordance with their terms. Such agreements shall not be subject to the provisions of this section regarding voting trusts.

§ 35. **Board of Directors.** All corporate powers shall be exercised by or under authority of, and the business and affairs of a corporation shall be managed under the direction of, a board of directors except as may be otherwise provided in this Act or the articles of incorporation, the powers and duties conferred or imposed upon the board of directors by this Act shall be exercised or performed to such extent and by such person or persons as shall be provided in the articles of incorporation. Directors need not be residents of this State or shareholders of the corporation unless the articles of incorporation or by-laws so require. The articles of incorporation or by-laws may prescribe other qualifications for directors. The board of directors shall have authority to fix the compensation of directors unless otherwise provided in the articles of incorparation.

A director shall perform his duties as a director, including his duties as a member of any committee of the board upon which he may serve, in good faith, in a manner he reasonably believes to be in the best interests of the corporation, and with such care as an ordinarily prudent person in a like position would use under similar circumstances. In performing his duties, a director shall be entitled to rely on information, opinions, reports or statements, including financial statements and other financial data, in each case prepared or presented by:

(a) one or more officers or employees of the corporation whom the director reasonably believes to be reliable and competent in the matters presented,

(b) counsel, public accountants or other persons as to matters which the director reasonably believes to be within such person's professional or expert competence, or

(c) a committee of the board upon which he does not serve, duly designated in accordance with a provision of the articles of

incorporation or the by-laws, as to matters within its designated authority, which committee the director reasonably believes to merit confidence,

but he shall not be considered to be acting in good faith if he has knowledge concerning the matter in question that would cause such reliance to be unwarranted. A person who so performs his duties shall have no liability by reason of being or having been a director of the corporation.

A director of a corporation who is present at a meeting of its board of directors at which action on any corporate matter is taken shall be presumed to have assented to the action taken unless his dissent shall be entered in the minutes of the meeting or unless he shall file his written dissent to such action with the secretary of the meeting before the adjournment thereof or shall forward such dissent by registered mail to the secretary of the corporation immediately after the adjournment of the meeting. Such right to dissent shall not apply to a director who voted in favor of such action.

§ 36. **Number and Election of Directors.** The board of directors of a corporation shall consist of one or more members. The number of directors shall be fixed by, or in the manner provided in, the articles of incorporation or the by-laws, except as to the number constituting the initial board of directors, which number shall be fixed by the articles of incorporation. The number of directors may be increased or decreased from time to time by amendment to, or in the manner provided in, the articles of incorporation or the by-laws, but no decrease shall have the effect of shortening the term of any incumbent director. In the absence of a by-law providing for the number of directors, the number shall be the same as that provided for in the articles of incorporation. The names and addresses of the members of the first board of directors shall be stated in the articles of incorporation. Such persons shall hold office until the first annual meeting of shareholders, and until their successors shall have been elected and qualified. At the first annual meeting of shareholders and at each annual meeting thereafter the shareholders shall elect directors to hold office until the next succeeding annual meeting, except in case of the classification of directors as permitted by this Act. Each director shall hold office for the term for which he is elected and until his successor shall have been elected and qualified.

§ 37. Classification of Directors. When the board of directors shall consist of nine or more members, in lieu of electing the whole number of directors annually, the articles of incorporation may provide that the directors be divided into either two or three classes, each class to be as nearly equal in number as possible, the term of office of directors of the first class to expire at the first annual meeting of shareholders after their election, that of the second class to expire at the second annual meeting after their election, and that of the third class, if any, to expire at the third annual meeting after their election. At each annual meeting after such classification the number of directors equal to the number of the class whose term expires at the time of such meeting shall be elected to hold office until the second succeeding annual meeting, if there be two classes, or until the third succeeding annual meeting, if there be three classes. No classification of directors shall be effective prior to the first annual meeting of shareholders.

§ 38. Vacancies. Any vacancy occurring in the board of directors may be filled by the affirmative vote of a majority of the remaining directors though less than a quorum of the board of directors. A director elected to fill a vacancy shall be elected for the unexpired term of his predecessor in office. Any directorship to be filled by reason of an increase in the number of directors may be filled by the board of directors for a term of office continuing only until the next election of directors by the shareholders.

§ 39. Removal of Directors. At a meeting of shareholders called expressly for that purpose, directors may be removed in the manner provided in this section. Any director or the entire board of directors may be removed, with or without cause, by a vote of the holders of a majority of the shares then entitled to vote at an election of directors.

In the case of a corporation having cumulative voting, if less than the entire board is to be removed, no one of the directors may be removed if the votes cast against his removal would be sufficient to elect him if then cumulatively voted at an election of the entire board of directors, or, if there be classes of directors, at an election of the class of directors of which he is a part.

Whenever the holders of the shares of any class are entitled to elect one or more directors by the provisions of the articles of incorporation, the provisions of this section shall apply, in respect to the removal of a director or directors so elected, to the vote of the holders of the outstanding shares of that class and not to the vote of the outstanding shares as a whole.

§ 40. Quorum of Directors. A majority of the number of directors fixed by or in the manner provided in the by-laws or in the absence of a by-law fixing or providing for the number of directors, then of the number stated in the articles of incorporation, shall constitute a quorum for the transaction of business unless a greater number is required by the articles of incorporation or the by-laws. The act of the majority of the directors present at a meeting at which a quorum is present shall be the act of the board of directors, unless the act of a greater number is required by the articles of incorporation or the by-laws.

§ 41. Director Conflicts of Interest. No contract or other transaction between a corporation and one or more of its directors or any other corporation, firm, association or entity in which one or more of its directors are directors or officers or are financially interested, shall be either void or voidable because of such relationship or interest or because such director or directors are present at the meeting of the board of directors or a committee thereof which authorized, approves or ratifies such contract or transaction or because his or their votes are counted for such purpose, if:

(a) the fact of such relationship or interest is disclosed or known to the board of directors or committee which authorizes, approves or ratifies the contract or transaction by a vote or consent sufficient for the purpose without counting the votes or consents of such interested directors; or

(b) the fact of such relationship or interest is disclosed or known to the shareholders entitled to vote and they authorize, approve or ratify such contract or transaction by vote or written consent; or

(c) the contract or transaction is fair and reasonable to the corporation.

Common or interested directors may be counted in determining the presence of a quorum at a meeting of the board of directors or a committee thereof which authorizes, approves or ratifies such a contract or transaction.

§ 42. Executive and Other Committees. If the articles of incorporation or the by-laws so provide, the board of directors, by resolution adopted by a majority of the full board of directors, may designate from among its members an executive committee and one or more other committees each of which, to the extent provided in such resolution or in the articles of incorporation or the by-laws of the corporation, shall have and may exercise all the authority of the board of directors, except that no such committee shall have authority to (i) authorize distributions, (ii) approve or recommend to shareholders actions or proposals required by this Act to be approved by shareholders, (iii) designate candidates for the office of director, for purposes of proxy solicitation or otherwise, or fill vacancies on the board of directors or any committee thereof, (iv) amend the by-laws, (v) approve a plan of merger not requiring shareholder approval, (vi) authorize or approve the reacquisition of shares unless pursuant to a general formula or method specified by the board of directors, or (vii) authorize or approve the issuance or sale of, or any contract to issue or sell, shares or designate the terms of a series of a class of shares, provided that the board of directors, having acted regarding general authorization for the issuance or sale of shares, or any contract therefor, and, in the case of a series, the designation thereof, may, purboard by resolution or by adoption of a stock option or other plan, authorize a committee to fix the terms of any contract for the sale of the shares and to fix the terms upon which such shares may be issued or sold, including, without limitation, the price, the dividend rate, provisions for redemption, sinking fund, conversion, voting or preferential rights, and provisions for other features of a class of shares, or a series of a class of shares, with full power in such committee to adopt any final resolution setting forth all terms thereof and to authorize the statement of the terms of a series for filing with the Secretary of State under this Act.

Neither the designation of any such committee, the delegation thereto of authority, nor action by such committee pursuant to such authority shall alone constitute compliance by any member of the board of directors, not a member of the committee in question, with his responsibility to act in good faith, in a manner he reasonably believes to be in the best interests of the corporation, and with such care as an ordinarily prudent person in a like position would use under similar circumstances.

§ 43. Place and Notice of Directors' Meetings; Committee Meetings. Meetings of the board of directors, regular or special, may be held either within or without this State.

Regular meetings of the board of directors or any committee designated thereby may be held with or without notice as prescribed in the by-laws. Special meetings of the board of directors or any committee designated thereby shall be held upon such notice as is prescribed in the by-laws. Attendance of a director at a meeting shall constitute a waiver of notice of such meeting, except where a director attends a meeting for the express purpose of objecting to the transaction of any business because the meeting is not lawfully called or convened. Neither the business to be transacted at, nor the purpose of, any regular or special meeting of the board of directors or any committee designated thereby need be specified in the notice or waiver of notice of such meeting unless required by the by-laws.

Except as may be otherwise restricted by the articles of incorporation or by-laws, members of the board of directors or any committee designated thereby may participate in a meeting of such board or committee by means of a conference telephone or similar communications equipment by means of which all persons participating in the meeting can hear each other at the same time and participation by such means shall constitute presence in person at a meeting.

§ 44. Action by Directors Without a Meeting.
Unless otherwise provided by the articles of incorporation or by-laws, any action required by this Act to be taken at a meeting of the directors of a corporation, or any action which may be taken at a meeting of the directors or of a committee, may be taken without a meeting if a consent in writing, setting forth the action so taken, shall be signed by all of the directors, or all of the members of the committee, as the case may be. Such consent shall have the same effect as a unanimous vote.

§ 45. Distributions to Shareholders. Subject to any restrictions in the articles of incorporation, the board of directors may authorize and the corporation may make distributions, except that no distribution may be made if, after giving effect thereto, either:

(a)   the corporation would be unable to pay its debts as they become due in the usual course of its business; or

(b)   the corporation's total assets would be less than the sum of its total liabilities and (unless the articles of incorporation otherwise permit) the maximum amount that then would be payable, in any liquidation, in respect of all outstanding shares having preferential rights in liquidation.

Determinations under subparagraph (b) may be based upon (i) financial statements prepared on the basis of accounting practices and principles that are reasonable in the circumstances, or (ii) a fair valuation or other method that is reasonable in the circumstances.

In the case of a purchase, redemption or other acquisition of a corporation's shares, the effect of a distribution shall be measured as of the date money or other property is transferred or debt is incurred by the corporation, or as of the date the shareholder ceases to be a shareholder of the corporation with respect to such shares, whichever is earlier. In all other cases, the effect of a distribution shall be measured as of the date of its authorization if payment occurs 120 days or less following the date of authorization, or as of the date of payment if payment occurs more than 120 days following the date of authorization.

Indebtedness of a corporation incurred or issued to a shareholder in a distribution in accordance with this Section shall be on a parity with the indebtness of the corporation to its general unsecured creditors except to the extent subordinated by agreement.

§ 46. Distribution From Capital Surplus. [This section was repealed in 1979.]

§ 47. Loans to Employees and Directors. A corporation shall not lend money to or use its credit to assist its directors without authorization in the particular case by its shareholders, but may lend money to and use its credit to assist any employee of the corporation or of a subsidiary, including any such employee who is a director of the corporation, if the board of directors decides that such loan or assistance may benefit the corporation.

§ 48. Liabilities of Directors in Certain Cases. In addition to any other liabilities, a director who votes for or assents to any distribution contrary to the provisions of this Act or contrary to any restrictions contained in the articles of incorporation, shall, unless he complies with the standard provided in this Act for the performance of the duties of directors, be liable to the corporation, jointly and severally with all other directors so voting or assenting, for the amount of such dividend which is paid or the value

of such distribution in excess of the amount of such distribution which could have been made without a violation of the provisions of this Act or the restrictions in the articles of incorporation.

Any director against whom a claim shall be asserted under or pursuant to this section for the making of a distribution and who shall be held liable thereon, shall be entitled to contribution from the shareholders who accepted or received any such distribution, knowing such distribution to have been made in violation of this Act, in proportion to the amounts received by them.

Any director against whom a claim shall be asserted under or pursuant to this section shall be entitled to contribution from any other director who voted for or assented to the action upon which the claim is asserted and who did not comply with the standard provided in this Act for the performance of the duties of directors.

§ 49. Provisions Relating to Actions by Shareholders. No action shall be brought in this State by a shareholder in the right of a domestic or foreign corporation unless the plaintiff was a holder of record of shares or of voting trust certificates therefor at the time of the transaction of which he complains, or his shares or voting trust certificates thereafter devolved upon him by operation of law from a person who was a holder of record at such time.

In any action hereafter instituted in the right of any domestic or foreign corporation by the holder or holders of record of shares of such corporation or of voting trust certificates therefor, the court having jurisdiction, upon final judgment and a finding that the action was brought without reasonable cause, may require the plaintiff or plaintiffs to pay to the parties named as defendant the reasonable expenses, including fees of attorneys, incurred by them in the defense of such action.

In any action now pending or hereafter instituted or maintained in the right of any domestic or foreign corporation by the holder or holders of record of less than five per cent of the outstanding shares of any class of such corporation or of voting trust certificates therefor, unless the shares or voting trust certificates so held have a market value in excess of twenty-five thousand dollars, the corporation in whose right such action is brought shall be entitled at any time before final judgment to require the plaintiff or plaintiffs to give security for the reasonable expenses, including fees of attorneys, that may be incurred by it in connection with such action or may be incurred by other parties named as defendant for which it may become legally liable. Market value shall be determined as of the date that the plaintiff institutes the action or, in the case of an intervenor, as of the date that he becomes a party to the action. The amount of such security may from time to time be increased or decreased in the discretion of the court, upon showing that the security provided has or may become inadequate or is excessive. The corporation shall have recourse to such security in such amount as the court having jurisdiction shall determine upon the termination of such action, whether or not the court finds the action was brought without reasonable cause.

§ 50. Officers.   The officers of a corporation shall consist of a president, one or more vice presidents as may be prescribed by the by-laws, a secretary, and a treasurer, each of whom shall be elected by the board of directors at such time and in such manner as may be prescribed by the by-laws. Such other officers and assistant officers and agents as may be deemed necessary may be elected or appointed by the board of directors or chosen in such other manner as may be prescribed by the by-laws. Any two or more officers may be held by the same person, except the offices of president and secretary.

All officers and agents of the corporation, as between themselves and the corporation, shall have such authority and perform such duties in the management of the corporation as may be provided in the by-laws, or as may be determined by resolution of the board of directors not inconsistent with the by-laws.

§ 51. Removal of Officers.   Any officer or agent may be removed by the board of directors whenever in its judgment the best interests of the corporation will be served thereby, but such removal shall be without prejudice to the contract rights, if any, of the person so removed. Election or appointment of an officer or agent shall not of itself create contract rights.

§ 52. Books and Records: Financial Reports to Shareholders; Examination of Records.   Each corporation shall keep correct and complete books and records of account and shall keep minutes of the proceedings of its shareholders and board of directors and shall keep at its registered office or principal place of business, or at the office of its transfer agent or registrar, a record of its shareholders, giving the names and addresses of all shareholders and the number and class of the shares held by each. Any books, records and minutes may be in written form or in any other form capable of being converted into written form within a reasonable time.

Any person who shall have been a holder of record of shares or of voting trust certificates therefor at least six months immediately preceding his demand or shall be the holder of record of, or the holder of record of voting trust certificates for, at least five per cent of all the outstanding shares of the corporation, upon written demand stating the purpose thereof, shall have the right to examine, in person, or by agent or attorney, at any reasonable time or times, for any proper purpose its relevant books and records of accounts, minutes, and record of shareholders and to make extracts therefrom.

Any officer or agent who, or a corporation which, shall refuse to allow any such shareholder or holder of voting trust certificates, or his agent or attorney, so to examine and make extracts from its books and records of account, minutes, and record of shareholders, for any purpose, shall be liable to such shareholder or holder of voting trust certificates in a penalty of ten per cent of the value of the shares owned by such shareholder, or in respect of which such voting trust certificates are issued, in addition to any other damages or remedy afforded him by law. It shall be a defense to any action for penalties under this section that the person suing therefor has within two years sold or offered for sale any list of shareholders or of holders of voting trust certificates for shares of such corporation or any other corporation or has aided or abetted any person in procuring any list of shareholders or of holders of voting trust certificates for any such purpose, or has improperly used any information secured through any prior examination of the books and records of account, or minutes, or record of shareholders or of holders of voting trust certificates for shares of such corporation or any other corporation, or was not acting in good faith or for a proper purpose in making his demand.

Nothing herein contained shall impair the power of any court of competent jurisdiction, upon proof by a shareholder or holder of voting trust certificates of proper purpose, irrespective of the period of time during which such shareholder or holder of voting trust certificates shall have been a shareholder of record or a holder of record of voting trust certificates, and irrespective of the number of shares held by him or represented by voting trust certificates held by him, to compel the production for examination by such shareholder or holder of voting trust certificates of the books and records of account, minutes and record of shareholders of a corporation.

Each corporation shall furnish to its shareholders annual financial statements, including at least a balance sheet as of the end of each fiscal year and a statement of income for such fiscal year, which shall be prepared on the basis of generally accepted accounting principles, if the corporation prepares financial statements for such fiscal year on that basis for any purpose, and may be consolidated statements of the corporation and one or more of its subsidiaries. The financial statements shall be mailed by the corporation to each of its shareholders within 120 days after the close of each fiscal year and, after such mailing and upon written request, shall be mailed by the corporation to any shareholder (or holder of a voting trust certificate for its shares) to whom a copy of the most recent annual financial statements has not previously been mailed. In the case of statements audited by a public accountant, each copy shall be accompanied by a report setting forth his opinion thereon; in other cases, each copy shall be accompanied by a statement of the president or the person in charge of the corporation's financial accounting records (1) stating his reasonable belief as to whether or not the financial statements were prepared in accordance with generally accepted accounting principles and, if not, describing the basis of presentation, and (2) describing any respects in which the financial statements were not prepared on a basis consistent with those prepared for the previous year.

§ 53. **Incorporators.** One or more persons, or a domestic or foreign corporation, may act as incorporator or incorporators of a corporation by signing and delivering in duplicate to the Secretary of State articles of incorporation for such corporation.

§ 54. **Articles of Incorporation.** The articles of incorporation shall set forth:

(a) The name of the corporation.
(b) The period of duration, which may be perpetual.
(c) The purpose or purposes for which the corporation is organized which may be stated to be, or to include, the transaction of any or all lawful business for which

corporations may be incorporated under this Act.

(d) The aggregate number of shares which the corporation shall have authority to issue and, if such shares are to be divided into classes, the mumber of shares of each class.
(e) If the shares are to be divided into classes, the designation of each class and a statement of the preferences, limitations and relative rights in respect of the shares of each class.
(f) If the corporation is to issue the shares of any preferred or special class in series, then the designation of each series and a statement of the variations in the relative rights and preferences as between series insofar as the same are to be fixed in the articles of incorporation, and a statement of any authority to be vested in the board of directors to establish series and fix and determine the variations in the relative rights and preferences as between series.
(g) If any preemptive right is to be granted to shareholders, the provisions therefor.
(h) The address of its initial registered office, and the name of its initial registered agent at such address.
(i) The number of directors constituting the initial board of directors and the names and addresses of the persons who are to serve as directors until the first annual meeting of shareholders or until their successors be elected and qualify.
(j) The name and address of each incorporator.

In addition to provisions required therein, the articles of incorporation may also contain provisions not inconsistent with law regarding:

(1) the direction of the management of the business and the regulation of the affairs of the corporation;
(2) the definition, limitation and regulation of the powers of the corporation, the directors, and the shareholders, or any class of the shareholders, including restrictions on the transfer of shares;
(3) the par value of any authorized shares or class of shares;
(4) any provision which under this Act is required or permitted to be set forth in the by-laws.

It shall not be necessary to set forth in the articles

of incorporation any of the corporate powers enumerated in this Act.

§ 55. Filing of Articles of Incorporation.
Duplicate originals of the articles of incorporation shall be delivered to the Secretary of State. If the Secretary of State finds that the articles of incorporation conform to law, he shall, when all fees have been paid as in this Act prescribed:

    (a)   Endorse on each of such duplicate originals the word "Filed," and the month, day and year of the filing thereof.

    (b)   File one of such duplicate originals in his office.

    (c)   Issue a certificate of incorporation to which he shall fix the other duplicate original.

The certificate of incorporation, together with the duplicate original of the articles of incorporation affixed thereto by the Secretary of State, shall be returned to the incorporators or their representative.

§ 56. Effect of Issuance of Certificate of Incorporation.
Upon the issuance of the certificate of incorporation, the corporate existence shall begin, and such certificate of incorporation shall be conclusive evidence that all conditions precedent required to be performed by the incorporators have been complied with and that the corporation has been incorporated under this Act, except as against this State in a proceeding to cancel or revoke the certificate of incorporation or for involuntary dissolution of the corporation.

§ 57. Organization Meeting of Directors.
After the issuance of the certificate of incorporation an organization meeting of the board of directors named in the articles of incorporation shall be held, either within or without this State, at the call of a majority of the directors named in the articles of incorporation, for the purpose of adopting by-laws, electing officers and transacting such other business as may come before the meeting. The directors calling the meeting shall give at least three days' notice thereof by mail to each director so named, stating the time and place of the meeting.

§ 58. Right to Amend Articles of Incorporation.
A corporation may amend its articles of incorporation, from time to time, in any and as many respects as may be desired, so long as its articles of incorporation as amended contain only such provisions as might be lawfully contained in original articles of incorporation at the time of making such amendment, and, if a change in shares or the rights of shareholders, or an exchange, reclassification or cancellation of shares or rights of shareholders is to be made, such provisions as may be necessary to effect such change, exchange, reclassification or cancellation.

In particular, and without limitation upon such general power of amendment, a corporation may amend its articles of incorporation, from time to time, so as:

    (a)   To change its corporate name.

    (b)   To change its period of duration.

    (c)   To change, enlarge or diminish its corporate purposes.

    (d)   To increase or decrease the aggregate number of shares, or shares of any class, which the corporation has authority to issue.

    (e)   To provide, change or eliminate any provision with respect to the par value of any shares or class of shares.

    (f)   To exchange, classify, reclassify or cancel all or any part of its shares, whether issued or unissued.

    (g)   To change the designation of all or any part of its shares, whether issued or unissued, and to change the preferences, limitations, and the relative rights in respect of all or any part of its shares, whether issued or unissued.

    (h)   To change the shares of any class, whether issued or unissued into a different number of shares of the same class or into the same or a different number of shares of other classes.

    (i)   To create new classes of shares having rights and preferences either prior and superior or subordinate and inferior to the shares of any class then authorized, whether issued or unissued.

    (j)   To cancel or otherwise affect the right of the holders of the shares of any class to receive dividends which have accrued but have not been declared.

    (k)   To divide any preferred or special class of shares, whether issued or unissued, into series and fix and determine the designations of such series and the variations in the relative rights and preferences as between the shares of such series.

(l)   To authorize the board of directors to establish, out of authorized but unissued shares, series of any preferred or special class of shares and fix and determine the relative rights and preferences of the shares of any series so established.

(m)   To authorize the board of directors to fix and determine the relative rights and preferences of the authorized but unissued shares of series theretofore established in respect of which either the relative rights and preferences have not been fixed and determined or the relative rights and preferences theretofore fixed and determined are to be changed.

(n)   To revoke, diminish, or enlarge the authority of the board of directors to establish series out of authorized but unissued shares of any preferred or special class and fix and determine the relative rights and preferences of the shares of any series so established.

(o)   To limit, deny or grant to shareholders of any class the preemptive right to acquire additional shares of the corporation, whether then or thereafter authorized.

§ 59. Procedure to Amend Articles of Incorporation.

Amendments to the articles of incorporation shall be made the following manner:

(a)   The board of directors shall adopt a resolution setting forth the proposed amendment and, if shares have been issued, directing that it be submitted to a vote at a meeting of shareholders, which may be either the annual or a special meeting. If no shares have been issued, the amendment shall be adopted by resolution of the board of directors and the provisions for adoption by shareholders shall not apply. If the corporation has only one of shares outstanding, an amendment solely to change the number of authorized shares to effectuate a split of, or stock dividend in, the corporation's own shares, or solely to do so and to change the number of authorized shares in proportion thereto, may be adopted by the board of directors; and the provisions for adoption

by shareholders shall not apply, unless otherwise provided by the articles of incorporation. The resolution may incorporate the proposed amendment in restated articles of incorporatoin which contain a statement that except for the designated amendment the restated articles of incorporation correctly set forth without change the corresponding provisions of the articles of incorporation as theretofore amended, and that the restated articles of incorporation together with the designated amendment supersede the original articles of incorporation and all amendments thereto.

(b)   Written notice setting forth the proposed amendment or a summary of the changes to be affected thereby shall be given to each shareholder of record entitled to vote thereon within the time and in the manner provided in the Act for the giving of notice of meetings of shareholders. If the meeting be an annual meeting, the proposed amendment of each summary may be included in the notice of such annual meeting.

§ 60. Class Voting on Amendments.

The holders of the outstanding shares of a class shall be entitled to vote as a class upon a proposed amendment, whether or not entitled to vote thereon by the provisions of the articles of incorporation, if the amendment would:

(a)   Increase or decrease the aggregate number of authorized shares of such class.

(b)   Effect an exchange, reclassification or cancellation of all or part of the shares of such class.

(c)   Effect an exchange, or create a right of exchange, of all or any part of the shares of another class into the shares of such class.

(d)   Change the designations, preferences, limitations or relative rights of the shares of such class.

(e)   Change the shares of such class into the same or a different number of shares of the same class or another class or classes.

(f)   Create a new class of shares having rights and preferences prior and superior to the shares of such class, or increase the rights and preferences or the number of authorized shares, of any class having rights and preferences prior or superior to the shares of such class.

(g) In the case of a preferred or special class of shares, divide the shares of such class into series and fix and determine the designation of such series and the variations in the relative rights and preferences between the shares of such series, or authorize the board of directors to do so.

(h) Limit or deny any existing preemptive rights of the shares of such class.

(i) Cancel or otherwise affect dividends on the shares of such class which have accrued but have not been declared.

§ 61. Articles of Amendment. The articles of amendment shall be executed in duplicate by the corporation by its president or a vice president and by its secretary or an assistant secretary, and verified by one of the officers signing such articles, and shall set forth:

(a) The name of the corporation.

(b) The amendments so adopted.

(c) The date of the adoption of the amendment by the shareholders, or by the board of directors where no shares have been issued.

(d) The number of shares outstanding, and the number of shares entitled to vote thereon, and if the shares of any class are entitled to vote thereon as a class, the designation and number of outstanding shares entitled to vote thereon of each such class.

(e) The number of shares voted for and against such amendment, respectively, and, if the shares of any class are entitled to vote thereon as a class, the number of shares of each such class voted for and against such amendment, respectively, or if no shares have been issued, a statement to that effect.

(f) If such amendment provides for an exchange, reclassification or cancellation of issued shares, and if the manner in which the same shall be effected is not set forth in the amendment, then a statement of the manner in which the same shall be effected.

§ 62. Filing of Articles of Amendment. Dupli-

cate originals of the articles of amendment shall be delivered to the Secretary of State. If the Secretary of State finds that the articles of amendment conform to law, he shall, when all fees and franchise taxes have been paid as in this Act prescribed:

(a) Endorse on each of such duplicate originals the word "Filed," and the month, day and year of the filing thereof.

(b) File one of such duplicate originals in his office.

(c) Issue a certificate of amendment to which he shall affix the other duplicate original.

The certificate of amendment, together with the duplicate original of the articles of amendment affixed thereto by the Secretary of State, shall be returned to the corporation or its representative.

§ 63. Effect of Certificate of Amendment. The amendment shall become effective upon the issuance of the certificate of amendment by the Secretary of State, or on such later date, not more than thirty days subsequent to the filing thereof with the Secretary of State, as shall be provided for in the articles of amendment.

No amendment shall affect any existing cause of action in favor of or against such corporation, or any pending suit to which such corporation shall be a party, or the existing rights of persons other than shareholders; and, in the event the corporate name shall be changed by amendment, no suit brought by or against such corporation under its former name shall abate for that reason.

§ 64. Restated Articles of Incorporation. A domestic corporation may at any time restate its articles of incorporation as theretofore amended, by a resolution adopted by the board of directors.

Upon the adoption of such resolution, restated articles of incorporation shall be executed in duplicate by the corporation by its president or a vice president and by its secretary or assistant secretary and verified by one of the officers signing such articles and shall set forth all of the operative provisions of the articles of incorporation as theretofore amended together with a statement that the restated articles of incorporation correctly set forth without change the corresponding provisions of the articles of incorporation as theretofore amended and that the restated articles of incorporation supersede the original articles of incorporation and all amendments thereto.

Duplicate originals of the restated articles of incorporation shall be delivered to the Secretary of State. If the Secretary of State finds that such restated articles of incorporation conform to law, he shall, when all fees and franchise taxes have been paid as in this Act prescribed:

(1) Endorse on each of such duplicate originals the word "Filed," and the month, day and year of the filing thereof.

(2) File one of such duplicate originals in his office.

(3) Issue a restated certificate of incorporation, to which he shall affix the other duplicate original.

The restated certificate of incorporation, together with the duplicate original of the restated articles of incorporation affixed thereto by the Secretary of State, shall be returned to the corporation or its representative.

Upon the issuance of the restated certificate of incorporation by the Secretary of State, the restated articles of incorporation shall be become effective and shall supersede the original articles of incorporation and all amendments thereto.

§ 65. Amendment of Articles of Incorporation in Reorganization Proceedings.

When a plan of reorganization of a corporation has been confirmed by decree or order of a court of competent jurisdiction in proceedings for the reorganization of such corporation, pursuant to the provisions of any applicable statute of the United States relating to reorganizations of corporations, the articles of incorporation of the corporation may be amended, in the manner provided in this section, in as many respects as may be necessary to carry out the plan and put it into effect, so long as the articles of incorporation as amended contain only such provisions as might be lawfully contained in original articles of incorporation at the time of making such amendment.

In particular and without limitation upon such general power of amendment, the articles of incorporation may be amended for such purpose so as to:

(A) Change the corporate name, period of duration or corporate purposes of the corporation;

(B) Repeal, alter or amend the by-laws of the corporation;

(C) Change the aggregate number of shares or shares of any class, which the corporation has authority to issue;

(D) Change the preferences, limitations and relative rights in respect of all or any part of the shares of the corporation, and classify, reclassify

or cancel all or any part thereof, whether issued or unissued;

(E) Authorize the issuance of bonds, debentures or other obligations of the corporation, whether or not convertible into shares of any class or bearing warrants or other evidences of optional rights to purchase or subscribe for shares of any class, and fix the terms and conditions thereof; and

(F) Constitute or reconstitute and classify or reclassify the board of directors of the corporation, and appoint directors and officers in place of or in addition to all or any of the directors or officers then in office.

Amendments to the articles of incorporation pursuant to this section shall be made in the following manner:

(a) Articles of amendment approved by decree or order of such court shall be executed and verified in duplicate by such person or persons as the court shall designate or appoint for the purpose, and shall set forth the name of the corporation, the amendments of the articles of incorporation approved by the court, the date of the decree or order approving the articles of amendment, the title of the proceedings in which the decree or order was entered, and a statement that such decree or order was entered by a court having jurisdiction of the proceedings for the reorganization of the corporation pursuant to the provisions of an applicable statute of the United States.

(b) Duplicate originals of the articles of amendment shall be delivered to the Secretary of State. If the Secretary of State finds that the articles of amendment conform to law, he shall, when all fees and franchise taxes have been paid as in this Act prescribed:

(1) Endorse on each of such duplicate originals the word "Filed," and the month, day and year of the filing thereof.

(2) File one of such duplicate originals in his office.

(3) Issue a certificate of amendment to which he shall affix the other duplicate original.

The certificate of amendment, together with the duplicate original of the articles of amendment affixed thereto by the Secretary of State, shall be returned to the corporation or its representative.

The amendment shall become effective upon the issuance of the certificate of amendment by the Secretary of State, or on such later date, not more than thirty days subsequent to the filing thereof with the

Secretary of State, as shall be provided for in the articles of amendment without any action thereon by the directors or shareholders of the corporation and with the same effect as if the amendments had been adopted by unanimous action of the directors and shareholders of the corporation.

§ 66. Restriction on Redemption or Purchase of Redeemable Shares. [This section was repealed in 1979.]

§ 67. Cancellation of Redeemdable Shares by Redemption or Purchase. [This section was repealed in 1979.]

§ 68. Cancellation of Other Reacquired Shares. [This section was repealed in 1979.]

§ 69. Reduction of Stated Capital in Certain Cases. [This section was repealed in 1979.]

§ 70. Special Provisions Relating to Surplus and Reserves. [This section was repealed in 1979.]

§ 71. Procedure for Merger. Any two or more domestic corporations may merge into one of such corporations pursuant to a plan of merger approved in the manner provided in this Act.

The board of directors of each corporation shall, by resolution adopted by each such board, approve a plan of merger setting forth:

(a) The names of the corporations proposing to merge, and the name of the corporation into which they propose to merge, which is hereafter designated as the surviving corporation.

(b) The terms and conditions of the proposed merger.

(c) The manner and basis of converting the shares of each corporation into shares, obligations or other securities of the surviving corporation or of any other corporation or, in whole or in part, into cash or other property.

(d) A statement of any changes in the articles of incorporation of the surviving corporation to be effected by such merger.

(e) Such other provisions with respect to the proposed merger as are deemed necessary or desirable.

§ 72. Procedure for Consolidation. Any two or more domestic corporations may consolidate into a new corporation pursuant to a plan of consolidation approved in the manner provided in this Act.

The board of directors of each corporation shall, by a resolution adopted by each such board, approve a plan of consolidation setting forth:

(a)   The names of the corporations proposing to consolidate, and the name of the new corporation into which they propose to consolidate, which is hereinafter designated as the new corporation.

(b)   The terms and conditions of the proposed consolidation.

(c)   The manner and basis of converting the shares of each corporation into shares, obligations or other securities of the new corporation or of any other corporation or, in whole or in part, into cash or other property.

(d)   With respect to the new corporation, all of the statements required to be set forth in articles of incorporation for corporations organized under this Act.

(e)   Such other provisions with respect to the proposed consolidation as are deemed necessary or desirable.

§ 72A. Procedure for Share Exchange. All the issued or all the outstanding shares of one or more classes of any domestic corporation may be acquired through the exchange of all such shares of such class or classes by another domestic or foreign corporation pursuant to a plan of exchange approved in the manner provided in this Act.

The board of directors of each corporation shall, by resolution adopted by each such board, approve a plan of exchange setting forth:

(a)   The name of the corporation the shares of which are proposed to be acquired by exchange and the name of the corporation to acquire the shares of such corporation in the exchange, which is hereinafter designated as the acquiring corporation.

(b)   The terms and conditions of the proposed exchange.

(c)   The manner and basis of exchanging the shares to be acquired for shares, obligations or other securities of the acquiring corporation or any other corporation, or, in whole or in part, for cash or other property.

(d)   Such other provisions with respect to the proposed exchange as are deemed necessary or desirable.

The procedure authorized by this section shall not be deemed to limit the power of a corporation to acquire all or part of the shares of any class or classes of a corporation through a voluntary exchange or otherwise by agreement with the shareholders.

§ 73. Approval by Shareholders.

(a) The board of directors of each corporation in the case of a merger or consolidation, and the board of directors of the corporation the shares of which are to be acquired in the case of an exchange, upon approving such plan of merger, consolidation or exchange, shall, by resolution, direct that the plan be submitted to a vote at a meeting of its shareholders,which may be either an annual or a special meeting. Written notice shall be given to each shareholder of record, whether or not entitled to vote at such meeting, not less than twenty days before such meeting, in the manner provided in this Act for the giving of notice of meetings of shareholders, and, whether the meeting be an annual or a special meeting, shall state that the purpose or one of the purposes is to consider the proposed plan of merger, consolidation or exchange. A copy or a summary of the plan of merger, consolidation or exchange, as the case may be, shall be included in or enclosed with such notice.

(b) At each such meeting, a vote of the shareholders shall be taken on the proposed plan. The plan shall be approved upon receiving the affirmative vote of the holders of a majority of the shares entitled to vote thereon of each such corporation, unless any class of shares of any such corporation is entitled to vote thereon as a class, in which event, as to such corporation, the plan shall be approved upon receiving the affirmative vote of the holders of a majority of the shares of each class of shares entitled to vote thereon as a class and of the total shares entitled to vote thereon. Any class of shares of any such corporation shall be entitled to vote as a class if any such plan contains any provision which, if contained in a proposed amendment to articles of incorporation, would entitle such class of shares to vote as a class and, in the case of an exchange, if the class is included in the exchange.

(c) After such approval by a vote of the shareholders of each such corporation, and at any time prior to the filing of the articles of merger, consolidation or exchange, the merger, consolidation or exchange may be abandoned pursuant to provisions therefor, if any, set forth in the plan.

(d) (1) Notwithstanding the provisions of subsections (a) and (b), submission of a plan of merger to a vote at a meeting of shareholders of a surviving corporation shall not be required if:

(i) the articles of incorporation of the surviving corporation do not differ except in name from those of the corporation before the merger,

(ii) each holder of shares of the surviving corporation which were outstanding immediately before the effective date of the merger is to hold the same number of shares with identical rights immediately after,

(iii) the number of voting shares outstanding immediately after the merger, plus the number of voting shares issuable on conversion of other securities issued by virtue of the terms of the merger and on exercise of rights and warrants so issued, will not exceed by more than 20 per cent the number of voting shares outstanding immediately before the merger, and

(iv) the number of participating shares outstanding immediately after the merger, plus the number of participating shares issuable on conversion of other securities issued by virtue of the terms of the merger and on exercise of rights and warrants so issued, will not exceed by more than 20 per cent the number of participating shares outstanding immediately before the merger.

(2) As used in this subsection:

(i) "voting shares" means shares which entitle their holders to vote unconditionally in elections of directors;

(ii) "participating shares" means shares

which entitle their holders to participate without limitation in distribution of earnings or surplus.

§ 74. Articles of Merger, Consolidation or Exchange.

(a) Upon receiving the approvals required by Sections 71, 72 and 73, articles of merger or articles of consolidation shall be executed in duplicate by each corporation by its president or a vice president and by its secretary or an assistant secretary, and verified by one of the officers of each corporation signing such articles, and shall set forth:

(1) The plan of merger or the plan of consolidation;

(2) As to each corporation, either (i) the number of shares outstanding, and, if the shares of any class are entitled to vote as a class, the designation and number of outstanding shares of each such class, or (ii) a statement that the vote of shareholders is not required by virtue of subsection 73(d);

(3) As to each corporation the approval of whose shareholders is required, the number of shares voted for and against such plan, respectively, and, if the shares of any class are entitled to vote as a class, the number of shares of each such class voted for and against such plan, respectively.

(b) Duplicate originals of the articles of merger, consolidation or exchange shall be delivered to the Secretary of State. If the Secretary of State finds that such articles conform to law, he shall, when all fees and franchise taxes have been paid as in this Act prescribed:

(1) Endorse on each of such duplicate originals the word "Filed," and the month, day and year of the filing thereof.

(2) File one of such duplicate originals in his office.

(3) Issue a certificate of merger, consolidation or exchange to which he shall affix the other duplicate original.

(c) The certificate of merger, consolidation or exchange together with the duplicate original of the articles affixed thereto by the Secretary of State, shall be returned to the surviving, new or acquiring corporation, as the case may be, or its representative.

§ 75. Merger of Subsidiary Corporation.

Any corporation owning at least ninety per cent of the outstanding shares of each class of another corporation may merge such other corporation into itself

without approval by a vote of the shareholders of either corporation. Its board of directors shall, by resolution, approve a plan of merger setting forth:

(A) The name of the subsidiary corporation and the name of the corporation owning at least ninety per cent of its shares, which is hereinafter designated as the surviving corporation.

(B) The manner and basis of converting the shares of the subsidiary corporation into shares, obligations or other securities of the surviving corporation or of any other corporation or, in whole or in part, into cash or other property.

A copy of such plan of merger shall be mailed to each shareholder of record of the subsidiary corporation.

Articles of merger shall be executed in duplicate by the surviving corporation by its president or a vice president and by its secretary or an assistant secretary, and verified by one of its officers signing such articles, and shall set forth:

(a)   The plan of merger;

(b)   The number of outstanding shares of each class of the subsidiary corporation and the number of such shares of each class owned by the surving corporation; and

(c)   The date of the mailing to shareholders of the subsidiary corporation of a copy of the plan of merger.

On and after the thirtieth day after the mailing of a copy of the plan of merger to shareholders of the subsidiary corporation or upon the waiver thereof by the holders of all outstanding shares duplicate originals of the articles of merger shall be delivered to the Secretary of State. If the Secretary of State finds that such articles conform to law, he shall, when all fees and franchise taxes have been paid as in this Act prescribed:

(1) Endorse on each of such duplicate originals the word "Filed," and the month, day and year of the filing thereof,

(2) File one of such duplicate originals in his office, and

(3) Issue a certificate of merger to which he shall affix the other duplicate original.

The certificate of merger, together with the duplicate original of the articles of merger affixed thereto by the Secretary of State, shall be returned to the surviving corporation or its representative.

§ 76. Effect of Merger, Consolidation or Exchange.

A merger, consolidation or exchange shall

become effective upon the issuance of a certificate of merger, consolidation or exchange by the Secretary of State, or on such later date, not more than thirty days subsequent to the filing thereof with the Secretary of State, as shall be provided for in the plan.

When a merger or consolidation has become effective:

(a) The several corporations parties to the plan of merger or consolidation shall be a single corporation, which, in the case of a merger, shall be that corporation designated in the plan of merger as the surviving corporation, and, in the case of a consolidation, shall be the new corporation provided for in the plan of consolidation.

(b) The separate existence of all corporations parties to the plan of merger or consolidation, except the surviving or new corporation, shall cease.

(c) Such surviving or new corporation shall have all the rights, privileges, immunities and powers and shall be subject to all the duties and liabilities of a corporation organized under this Act.

(d) Such surviving or new corporation shall thereupon and thereafter possess all the rights, privileges, immunities, and franchises, of a public as well as of a private nature, of each of the merging or consolidating corporations; and all property, real, personal and mixed, and all debts due on whatever account, including subscriptions to shares, and all other choses in action, and all and every other interest of or belonging to or due to each of the corporations so merged or consolidated, shall be taken and deemed to be transferred to and vested in such single corporation without further act or deed; and the title to any real estate, or any interest therein, vested in any of such corporations shall not revert or be in any way impaired by reason of such merger or consolidation.

(e) Such surviving or new corporation shall thenceforth be responsible and liable for all the liabilities and obligations of each of the corporations so merged or consolidated; and any claim existing or action or proceeding pending by or against any of such corporations may be prosecuted as if such merger or consolidation had not taken place, or such surviving or new corporation may be substituted in its place. Neither the rights of creditors nor any liens upon the property of any such corporation shall be impaired by such merger or consolidation.

(f) In the case of a merger, the articles of incorporation of the surviving corporation shall be deemed to be amended to the extent, if any, that changes in its articles of incorporation are stated in the plan of merger; and, in the case of a consolidation, the statements set forth in the articles of consolidation and which are required or permitted to be set forth in the articles of incorporation of corporations organized under this Act shall be deemed to be the original articles of incorporation of the new corporation.

When a merger, consolidation or exchange has become effective, the shares of the corporation or corporations party to the plan that are, under the terms of the plan, to be converted or exchanged, shall cease to exist, in the case of a merger or consolidation, or be deemed to be exchanged in the case of an exchange, and the holders of such shares shall thereafter be entitled only to the shares, obligations, other securities, cash or other property into which they shall have been converted or for which they shall have been exchanged, in accordance with the plan, subject to any rights under Section 80 of this Act.

§ 77. Merger, Consolidation or Exchange of Shares Between Domestic and Foreign Corporations. One or more foreign corporations and one or more domestic corporations may be merged or consolidated, or participate in an exchange, in the following manner, if such merger, consolidation or exchange is permitted by the laws of the state under which each such foreign corporation is organized:

(a) Each domestic corporation shall comply with the provisions of this Act with respect to the merger, consolidation or exchange, as the case may be, of domestic corporations and each foreign corporation shall comply with the applicable provisions of the laws of the state under which it is organized.

(b) If the surviving or new corporation in a merger or consolidation is to be governed by the laws of any state other than this State, it shall comply with the provisions of this Act with respect to foreign corporations if it is to transact business in this State, and in every case it shall file with the Secretary of State of this State:

(1) An agreement that it may be served with process in this State in any proceeding for the enforcement of any obligation of any domestic corporation which is a party to such merger or consolidation and in any proceeding for the enforcement of the rights of a dissenting shareholder of any such domestic corporation against the surviving or new corporation;

(2) An irrevocable appointment of the Secretary of State of this State as its agent to accept service of process in any such proceeding; and

(3) An agreement that it will promptly pay to the dissenting shareholders of any such domestic corporation, the amount, if any, to which they shall be entitled under provisions of this Act with respect to the rights of dissenting shareholders.

§ 78. Sale of Assets in Regular Course of Business and Mortgage or Pledge of Assets. The sale, lease, exchange, or other disposition of all, or substantially all, the property and assets of a corporation in the usual and regular course of its business and the mortgage or pledge of any or all property and assets of a corporation whether or not in the usual and regular course of business may be made upon such terms and conditions and for such consideration, which may consist in whole or in part of cash or other property, including shares, obligations or other securities of any other corporation, domestic or foreign, as shall be authorized by its board of directors; and in any such case no authorization or consent of the shareholders shall be required.

§ 79. Sale of Assets Other Than in Regular Course of Business. A sale, lease, exchange, or other disposition of all, or substantially all, the property and assets, with or without the good will, of a corporation, if not in the usual and regular course of its business, may be made upon such terms and conditions and for such consideration, which may consist in whole or in part of cash or other property, including shares, obligations or other securities of any other corporation, domestic or foreign, as may be authorized in the following manner:

(a) The board of directors shall adopt a resolution recommending such sale, lease, exchange, or other disposition and directing the submission thereof to a vote at a meeting of shareholders, which may be either an annual or a special meeting.

(b) Written notice shall be given to each shareholder of record, whether or not entitled to vote at such meeting, not less than twenty days before such meeting, in the manner provided in this Act for the giving of notice of meetings of shareholders, and, whether the meeting be an annual or a special meeting, shall state that the purpose, or one of the purposes is to consider the proposed sale, lease, exchange, or other disposition.

(c) At such meeting the shareholders may authorize such sale, lease, exchange, or other disposition and may fix, or may authorize the board of directors to fix, any or all of the terms and conditions thereof and the consideration to be received by the corporation therefor. Such authorization shall require the affirmative vote of the holders of a majority of the shares of the corporation entitled to vote thereon, unless any class of shares is entitled to vote thereon as a class, in which event such authorization shall require the affirmative vote of the holders of a majority of the shares of each class of shares entitled to vote as a class thereon and of the total shares entitled to vote thereon.

(d) After such authorization by a vote of shareholders, the board of directors nevertheless, in its discretion, may abandon such sale, lease, exchange, or other disposition of assets, subject to the rights of third parties under any contracts relating thereto, without further action or approval by shareholders.

§ 80. Right of Shareholders to Dissent and Obtain Payment For Shares.

(a) Any shareholder of a corporation shall have the right to dissent from, and to obtain payment for his shares in the event of, any of the following corporate actions:

(1) Any plan of merger or consolidation to which the corporation is a party, except as provided in subsection (c);

(2) Any sale or exchange of all or substantially all of the property and assets of the corporation not made in the usual or regular course of its business, including a sale in dissolution, but not including a sale pursuant to an order of a court having jurisdiction in the premises or a sale for cash on terms requiring that all or substantially all of the net proceeds of sale be distributed to the shareholders in accordance with their respective interests within one year after the date of sale;

(3) Any plan of exchange to which the corporation is a party as the corporation the shares of which are to be acquired;

(4) Any amendment of the articles of incorporation which materially and adversely affects the rights appurtenant to the shares of the dissenting shareholders in that it:

    (i) alters or abolishes a preferential right of such shares;

    (ii) creates, alters or abolishes a right in respect of the redemption of such shares, including a provision respecting a sinking fund for the redemption or repurchase of such shares;

    (iii) alters or abolishes a preemptive right of the holder of such shares to acquire shares or other securities;

    (iv) excludes or limits the right of the holder of such shares to vote on any matter, or to cumulate his votes, except as such right may be limited by dilution through the issuance of shares or other securities with similar voting rights; or

(5) Any other corporate action taken pursuant to a shareholder vote with respect to which the articles of incorporation, the bylaws, or a resolution of the board of directors directs that dissenting shareholders shall have a right to obtain payment for their shares.

(b)(1) A record holder of shares may assert dissenters' rights as to less than all of the shares registered in his name only if he dissents with respect to all the shares beneficially owned by any one person, and discloses the name and address of the person or persons on whose behalf he dissents. In that event, his rights shall be determined as if the shares as to which he has dissented and his other shares were registered in the names of different shareholders.

(2) A beneficial owner of shares who is not the record holder may assert dissenters' rights with respect to shares held on his behalf, and shall be treated as a dissenting shareholder under the terms of this section and Section 31 if he submits to the corporation at the time of or before the assertion of these rights a written consent of the record holder.

(c) The right to obtain payment under this section shall not apply to the shareholders of the surviving corporation in a merger if a vote of the shareholders of such corporation is not necessary to authorize such merger.

(d) A shareholder of a corporation who has a right under this section to obtain payment for his shares shall have no right at law or in equity to attack the validity of the corporate action that gives rise to his right to obtain payment, nor to have the action set aside or rescinded, except when the corporate action is unlawful or fraudulent with regard to the complaining shareholder or to the corporation.

§ 81. Procedures for Protection of Dissenters' Rights.

(a) As used in this section:

(1) "Dissenter" means a shareholder or beneficial owner who is entitled to and does assert dissenters' rights under Section 80, and who has performed every act required up to the time involved for the assertion of such rights.

(2) "Corporation" means the issuer of the shares held by the dissenter before the corporate action, or the successor by merger or consolidation of that issuer.

(3) "Fair value" of shares means their value immediately before the effectuation of the corporate action to which the dissenter objects, excluding any appreciation or depreciation in anticipation of such corporate action unless such exclusion would be inequitable.

(4) "Interest" means interest from the effective date of the corporate action until the date of payment, at the average rate currently paid by the corporation on its principal bank loans, or, if none, at such rate as is fair and equitable under all the circumstances.

(b) If a proposed corporate action which would give rise to dissenters' rights under Section 80(a) is submitted to a vote at a meeting of shareholders, the notice of meeting shall notify all shareholders that they have or may have a right to dissent and obtain payment for their shares by complying with the terms of this section, and shall be accompanied by a copy of Sections 80 and 81 of this Act.

(c) If the proposed corporate action is submitted to a vote at a meeting of shareholders, any shareholder who wishes to dissent and obtain payment for his shares must file with the corporation, prior to the vote, a written notice of intention to demand that he be paid fair compensation for his shares if the proposed action is effectuated, and shall refrain from voting his shares in approval of such action. A shareholder who fails in either respect shall acquire no right to payment for his shares under this section or Section 80.

(d) If the proposed corporate action is approved by the required vote at a meeting of shareholders, the corporation shall mail a further notice to all shareholders who gave due notice of intention to demand payment and who refrained from voting in favor of the proposed action. If the proposed corporate action is to be taken without a vote of shareholders, the corporation shall send to all shareholders who are entitled to dissent and demand payment for their shares a notice of the adoption of the plan of corporate action. The notice shall (1) state where and when a demand for payment must be sent and certificates of certificated shares must be deposited in order to obtain payment, (2) inform holders of uncertificated shares to what extent transfer of shares will be restricted from the time that demand for payment is received, (3) supply a form for demanding payment which includes a request for certification of the date on which the shareholder, or the person on whose behalf the shareholder dissents, acquired beneficial ownership of the shares, and (4) be accompanied by a copy of Sections 80 and 81 of this Act. The time set for the demand and deposit shall be not less than 30 days from the mailing of the notice.

(e) A shareholder who fails to demand payment, or fails (in the case of certificated shares) to deposit certificates, as required by a notice pursuant to subsection (d) shall have no right under this section or Section 80 to receive payment for his shares. If the shares are not represented by certificates, the corporation may restrict their transfer from the time of receipt of demand for payment until effectuation of the proposed corporate action, or the release of restrictions under the terms of subsection (f). The dissenter shall retain all other rights of a shareholder until these rights are modified by effectuation of the proposed corporate action.

(f) (1) Within 60 days after the date set for demanding payment and depositing certificates, if the corporation has not effectuated the proposed corporate action and remitted payment for shares pursuant to paragraph (3), it shall return any certificates that have been deposited, and release uncertificated shares from any transfer restrictions imposed by reason of the demand for payment.

(2) When uncertificated shares have been released from transfer restrictions, and deposited certificates have been returned, the corporation may at any later time send a new notice conforming to the requirements of subsection (d), with like effect.

(3) Immediately upon effectuation of the proposed corporate action, or upon receipt of demand for payment if the corporate action has already been effectuated, the corporation shall remit to dissenters who have made demand and (if their shares are certificated) have deposited their certificates the amount which the corporation estimates to be the fair value of the shares, with interest if any has accrued. The remittance shall be accompanied by:

(i) the corporation's closing balance sheet and statement of income for a fiscal year ending not more than 16 months before the date of remittance, together with the latest available interim financial statements;

(ii) a statement of the corporation's estimate of fair value of the shares; and

(iii) a notice of the dissenter's right to demand supplemental payment, accompanied by a copy of Sections 80 and 81 of this Act.

(g) (1) If the corporation fails to remit as required by subsection (f), or if the dissenter believes that the amount remitted is less than the fair value of his shares, or that the interest is not correctly determined, he may send the corporation his own estimate of the value of the shares or of the interest, and demand payment of the deficiency.

(2) If the dissenter does not file such an estimate within 30 days after the corporation's mailing of its remittance, he shall be entitled to no more than the amount remitted.

(h) (1) Within 60 days after receiving a demand for payment pursuant to subsection (g), if any such demands for payment remain unsettled, the corporation shall file in an appropriate court a petition requesting that the fair value of the shares and interest thereon be determined by the court.

(2) An appropriate court shall be a court of competent jurisdiction in the county of this state where the registered office of the corporation is located. If, in the case of a merger or consolidation or exchange of shares, the corporation is a foreign corporation without a registered office in this state, the petition shall be filed in the county where the registered office of the domestic corporation was last located.

(3) All dissenters, wherever residing, whose demands have not been settled shall be made parties to the proceeding as in an action against their shares. A copy of the petition shall be served on each such dissenter; if a dissenter is a nonresident, the copy may be served on him by registered or certified mail or by publication as provided by law.

(4) The jurisdiction of the court shall be plenary and exclusive. The court may appoint one or more

persons as appraisers to receive evidence and recommend a decision on the question of fair value. The appraisers shall have such power and authority as shall be specified in the order of their appointment or in any amendment thereof. The dissenters shall be entitled to discovery in the same manner as parties in other civil suits.

(5) All dissenters who are made parties shall be entitled to judgment for the amount by which the fair value of their shares is found to exceed the amount previously remitted, with interest.

(6) If the corporation fails to file a petition as provided in paragraph (1) of this subsection, each dissenter who made a demand and who has not already settled his claim against the corporation shall be paid by the corporation the amount demanded by him, with interest, and may sue therefor in an appropriate court.

(i) (1) The costs and expenses of any proceeding under subsection (h), including the reasonable compensation and expenses of appraisers appointed by the court, shall be determined by the court and assessed against the corporation, except that any part of the costs and expenses may be apportioned and assessed as the court may deem equitable against all or some of the dissenters who are parties and whose action in demanding supplemental payment the court finds to be arbitrary, vexatious, or not in good faith.

(2) Fees and expenses of counsel and of experts for the respective parties may be assessed as the court may deem equitable against the corporation and in favor of any or all dissenters if the corporation failed to comply substantially with the requirements of this section, and may be assessed against either the corporation or a dissenter, in favor of any other party, if the court finds that the party against whom the fees and expenses are assessed acted arbitrarily, vexatiously, or not in good faith in respect to the rights provided by this section and Section 80.

(3) If the court finds that the services of counsel for any dissenter were of substantial benefit to other dissenters similarly situated, and should not be assessed against the corporation, it may award to these counsel reasonable fees to be paid out of the amounts awarded to the dissenters who were benefited.

(j) (1) Notwithstanding the foregoing provisions of this section, the corporation may elect to withhold the remittance required by subsection (f) from any dissenter with respect to shares of which the dissenter (or the person on whose behalf the dissenter acts)

was not the beneficial owner on the date of the first announcement to news media or to shareholders of the terms of the proposed corporate action. With respect to such shares, the corporation shall, upon effectuating the corporate action, state to each dissenter its estimate of the fair value of the shares, state the rate of interest to be used (explaining the basis thereof), and offer to pay the resulting amounts on receiving the dissenter's agreement to accept them in full satisfaction.

(2) If the dissenter believes that the amount offered is less than the fair value of the shares and interest determined according to this section, he may within 30 days after the date of mailing of the corporation's offer, mail the corporation his own estimate of fair value and interest, and demand their payment. If the dissenter fails to do so, he shall be entitled to no more than the corporation's offer.

(3) If the dissenter makes a demand as provided in paragraph (2), the provisions of subsections (h) and (i) shall apply to further proceedings on the dissenter's demand.

§ 82. Voluntary Dissolution by Incorporators.

A corporation which has not commenced business and which has not issued any shares, may be voluntarily dissolved by its incorporators at any time in the following manner:

(a) Articles of dissolution shall be executed in duplicate by a majority of the incorporators, and verified by them, and shall set forth:

(1) The name of the corporation.

(2) The date of issuance of its certificate of incorporation.

(3) That none of its shares has been issued.

(4) That the corporation has not commenced business.

(5) That the amount, if any, actually paid in on subscriptions for its shares, less any part thereof disbursed for necessary expenses, has been returned to those entitled thereto.

(6) That no debts of the corporation remain unpaid.

(7) That a majority of the incorporators elect that the corporation be dissolved.

(b) Duplicate originals of the articles of dissolution shall be delivered to the Secretary of State. If the Secretary of State finds that the articles of dissolution conform to law, he shall, when all fees and franchise taxes have been paid as in this Act prescribed:

(1) Endorse on each of such duplicate originals the

word "Filed," and the month, day and year of the filing thereof.

(2) File one of such duplicate originals in his office.

(3) Issue a certificate of dissolution to which he shall affix the other duplicate original.

The certificate of dissolution, together with the duplicate original of the articles of dissolution affixed thereto by the Secretary of State, shall be returned to the incorporators or their representative. Upon the issuance of such certificate of dissolution by the Secretary of State, the existence of the corporation shall cease.

§ 83. Voluntary Dissolution By Consent of Shareholders. A corporation may be voluntarily dissolved by the written consent of all of its shareholders.

Upon the execution of such written consent, a statement of intent to dissolve shall be executed in duplicate by the corporation by its president or a vice president and by its secretary or an assistant secretary, and verified by one of the officers signing such statement, which statement shall set forth:

(a) The name of the corporation.

(b) The names and respective addresses of its officers.

(c) The names and respective addresses of its directors.

(d) A copy of the written consent signed by all shareholders of the corporation.

(e) A statement that such written consent has been signed by all shareholders of the corporation or signed in their names by their attorneys thereunto duly authorized.

§ 84. Voluntary Dissolution By Act of Corporation. A corporation may be dissolved by the act of the corporation, when authorized in the following manner:

(a) The board of directors shall adopt a resolution recommending that the corporation be dissolved, and directing that the question of such dissolution be submitted to a vote at a meeting of shareholders, which may be either an annual or a special meeting.

(b) Written notice shall be given to each shareholder of record entitled to vote at such meeting within the time and in the manner provided in this Act for the giv-

ing of notice of meetings of shareholders, and, whether the meeting be an annual or special meeting shall state that the purpose, or one of the purposes, of such meeting is to consider the advisability of dissolving the corporation.

(c) At such meeting a vote of shareholders entitled to vote thereat shall be taken on a resolution to dissolve the corporation. Such resolution shall be adopted upon receiving the affirmative vote of the holders of a majority of the shares of the corporation entitled to vote thereon, unless any class of shares is entitled to vote thereon as a class, in which event the resolution shall be adopted upon receiving the affirmative vote of the holders of a majority of the shares of each class of shares entitled to vote thereon as a class and of the total shares entitled to vote thereon.

(d) Upon the adoption of such resolution, a statement of intent to dissolve shall be executed in duplicate by the corporation by its president or a vice president and by its secretary or an assistant secretary, and verified by one of the officers signing such statement, which statement shall set forth:

(1) The name of the corporation.

(2) The names and respective addresses of its officers.

(3) The names and respective addresses of its directors.

(4) A copy of the resolution adopted by the shareholders authorizing the dissolution of the corporation.

(5) The number of shares outstanding, and, if the shares of any class are entitled to vote as a class, the designation and number of outstanding shares of each such class.

(6) The number of shares voted for and against the resolution, respectively, and, if the shares of any class are entitled to vote as a class, the number of shares of each such class voted for and against the resolution, respectively.

§ 85. Filing of Statement of Intent to Dissolve. Duplicate originals of the statement of intent to dissolve, whether by consent of shareholders or by act of the corporation, shall be delivered to the Secretary of State. If the Secretary of State finds that such statement conforms to law, he shall, when all fees and franchise taxes have been paid as in this Act prescribed:

- (a) Endorse on each of such duplicate originals the word "Filed," and the month, day and year of the filing thereof.
- (b) File one of such duplicate originals in his office.
- (c) Return the other duplicate original to the corporation or its representative.

§ 86. Effect of Statement of Intent to Dissolve.
Upon the filing by the Secretary of State of a statement of intent to dissolve, whether by consent of shareholders or by act of the corporation, the corporation shall cease to carry on its business, except insofar as may be necessary for the winding up thereof, but its corporate existence shall continue until a certificate of dissolution has been issued by the Secretary of State or until a decree dissolving the corporation has been entered by a court of competent jurisdiction as in this Act provided.

§ 87. Procedure After Filing of Statement of Intent to Dissolve.
After the filing by the Secretary of State of a statement of intent to dissolve:

- (a) The corporation shall immediately cause notice thereof to be mailed to each known creditor of the corporation.
- (b) The corporation shall proceed to collect its assets, convey and dispose of such of its properties as are not to be distributed in kind to its shareholders, pay, satisfy and discharge its liabilities and obligations and do all other acts required to liquidate its business and affairs, and, after paying or adequately providing for the payment of all its obligations, distribute the remainder of its assets, either in cash or in kind, among its shareholders according to their respective rights and interests.
- (c) The corporation, at any time during the liquidation of its business and affairs, may make application to a court of competent jurisdiction within the state and judicial subdivision in which the registered office or principal place of business of the corporation is situated, to have the liquidation continued under the supervision of the court as provided in this Act.

§ 88. Revocation of Voluntary Dissolution Proceedings By Consent of Shareholders.
By the written consent of all of its shareholders, a corporation may, at any time prior to the issuance of a certificate of dissolution by the Secretary of State, revoke voluntary dissolution proceedings theretofore taken, in the following manner:

Upon the execution of such written consent, a statement of revocation of voluntary dissolution proceedings shall be executed in duplicate by the corporation by its president or a vice president and by its secretary or an assistant secretary, and verified by one of the officers signing such statement, which statement shall set forth:

- (a) The name of the corporation.
- (b) The names and respective addresses of its officers.
- (c) The names and respective addresses of its directors.
- (d) A copy of the written consent signed by all shareholders of the corporation revoking such voluntary dissolution proceedings.
- (e) That such written consent has been signed by all shareholders of the corporation or signed in their names by their attorneys thereunto duly authorized.

§ 89. Revocation of Voluntary Dissolution Proceedings By Act of Corporation.
By the act of the corporation, a corporation may, at any time prior to the issuance of a certificate of dissolution by the Secretary of State, revoke voluntary dissolution proceedings theretofore taken, in the following manner:

- (a) The board of directors shall adopt a resolution recommending that the voluntary dissolution proceedings be revoked, and directing that the question of such revocation be submitted to a vote at a special meeting of shareholders.
- (b) Written notice, stating that the purpose or one of the purposes of such meeting is to consider the advisability of revoking the voluntary dissolution proceedings, shall be given to each shareholder of record entitled to vote at such meeting within the time and in the manner provided in this Act for the giving of notice of special meetings of shareholders.
- (c) At such meeting a vote of the shareholders entitled to vote thereat shall be

taken on a resolution to revoke the voluntary dissolution proceedings, which shall require for its adoption the affirmative vote of the holders of a majority of the shares entitled to vote thereon.

(d)   Upon the adoption of such resolution, a statement of revocation of voluntary dissolution proceedings shall be executed in duplicate by the corporation by its president or a vice president and by its secretary or an assistant secretary, and verified by one of the officers signing such statement, which statement shall set forth:

(1) The name of the corporation.

(2) The names and respective addresses of its officers.

(3) The names and respective addresses of its directors.

(4) A copy of the resolution adopted by the shareholders revoking the voluntary dissolution proceedings.

(5) The number of shares outstanding.

(6) The number of shares voted for and against the resolution, respectively.

§ 90. Filing of Statement of Revocation of Voluntary Dissolution Proceedings. Duplicate originals of the statement of revocation of voluntary dissolution proceedings, whether by consent of shareholders or by act of the corporation, shall be delivered to the Secretary of State. If the Secretary of State finds that such statement conforms to law, he shall, when all fees and franchise taxes have been paid as in this Act prescribed:

(a)   Endorse on each of such duplicate originals the word "Filed," and the month, day and year of the filing thereof.

(b)   File one of such duplicate originals in his office.

(c)   Return the other duplicate original to the corporation or its representative.

§ 91. Effect of Statement of Revocation of Voluntary Dissolution Proceedings. Upon the filing by the Secretary of State of a statement of revocation of voluntary dissolution proceedings, whether by consent of shareholders or by act of the corporation, the revocation of the voluntary dissolution proceedings shall become effective and the corporation may again carry on its business.

§ 92. Articles of Dissolution. If voluntary dis-

solution proceedings have not been revoked, then when all debts, liabilities and obligations of the corporation have been paid and discharged, or adequate provision has been made therefor, and all of the remaining property and assets of the corporation have been distributed to its shareholders, articles of dissolution shall be executed in duplicate by the corporation by its president or a vice president and by its secretary or an assistant secretary, and verified by one of the officers signing such statement, which statement shall set forth:

(a)   The name of the corporation.

(b)   That the Secretary of State has theretofore filed a statement of intent to dissolve the corporation, and the date on which such statement was filed.

(c)   That all debts, obligations and liabilities of the corporation have been paid and discharged or that adequate provision has been made therefor.

(d)   That all the remaining property and assets of the corporation have been distributed among its shareholders in accordance with their respective rights and interests.

(e)   That there are no suits pending against the corporation in any court, or that adequate provision has been made for the satisfaction of any judgment, order or decree which may be entered against it in any pending suit.

§ 93. Filing of Articles of Dissolution. Duplicate originals of such articles of dissolution shall be delivered to the Secretary of State. If the Secretary of State finds that such articles of dissolution conform to law, he shall, when all fees and franchise taxes have been paid as in this Act prescribed:

(a)   Endorse on each of such duplicate originals the word "Filed," and the month, day and year of the filing thereof.

(b)   File one of such duplicate originals in his office.

(c)   Issue a certificate of dissolution to which he shall affix the other duplicate original.

The certificate of dissolution, together with the duplicate original of the articles of dissolution affixed thereto by the Secretary of State, shall be returned to the representative of the dissolved corporation. Upon the issuance of such certificate of dissolution the existence of the corporation shall cease, except for the purpose of suits, other proceedings and appropriate corporate action by shareholders, directors and officers as provided in this Act.

§ 94. **Involuntary Dissolution.** A corporation may be dissolved involuntarily by a decree of the _____ court in an action filed by the Attorney General when it is established that:

(a) The corporation has failed to file its annual report within the time required by this Act, or has failed to pay its franchise tax on or before the first day of August of the year in which such franchise tax becomes due and payable; or

(b) The corporation procured its articles of incorporation through fraud; or

(c) The corporation has continued to exceed or abuse the authority conferred upon it by law; or

(d) The corporation has failed for thirty days to appoint and maintain a registered agent in this State; or

(e) The corporation has failed for thirty days after change of its registered office or registered agent to file in the office of the Secretary of State a statement of such change.

§ 95. **Notification to Attorney General.** The Secretary of State, on or before the last day of December of each year, shall certify to the Attorney General the names of all corporations which have failed to file their annual reports or to pay franchise taxes in accordance with the provisions of this Act, together with the facts pertinent thereto. He shall also certify, from time to time, the names of all corporations which have given other cause for dissolution as provided in this Act, together with the facts pertinent thereto. Whenever the Secretary of State shall certify the name of a corporation to the Attorney General as having given any cause for dissolution, the Secretary of State shall concurrently mail to the corporation at its registered office a notice that such certification has been made. Upon the receipt of such certification, the Attorney General shall file an action in the name of the State against such corporation for its dissolution. Every such certificate from the Secretary of State to the Attorney General pertaining to the failure of a corporation to file an annual report or pay a franchise tax shall be taken and received in all courts as prima facie evidence of the facts therein stated. If, before action is filed, the corporation shall file its annual report or pay its franchise tax, together with all penalties thereon, or shall appoint or maintain a registered agent as provided in this Act, or shall file with the Secretary of State the required statement of change of registered office or registered agent, such fact shall be forthwith certified by the Secretary of State to the Attorney General and he shall not file an action against such corporation for such cause. If, after action is filed, the corporation shall file its annual report or pay its franchise tax, together with all penalties thereon, or shall appoint or maintain a registered agent as provided in this Act, or shall file with the Secretary of State the required statement of change of registered office or registered agent, and shall pay the costs of such action, the action for such cause shall abate.

§ 96. **Venue and Process.** Every action for the involuntary dissolution of a corporation shall be commenced by the Attorney General either in the _____ court of the county in which the registered office of the corporation is situated, or in the _____ court of _____ county. Summons shall issue and be served as in other civil actions. If process is returned not found, the Attorney General shall cause publication to be made as in other civil cases in some newspaper published in the county where the registered office of the corporation is situated, containing a notice of the pendency of such action, the title of the court, the title of the action, and the date on or after which default may be entered. The Attorney General may include in one notice the names of any number of corporations against which actions are then pending in the same court. The Attorney General shall cause a copy of such notice to be mailed to the corporation at its registered office within ten days after the first publication thereof. The certificate of the Attorney General of the mailing of such notice shall be prima facie evidence thereof. Such notice shall be published at least once each week for two successive weeks, and the first publication thereof may begin at any time after the summons has been returned. Unless a corporation shall have been served with summons, no default shall be taken against it earlier than thirty days after the first publication of such notice.

§ 97. **Jurisdiction of Court to Liquidate Assets and Business of Corporation.** The _____ courts shall have full power to liquidate the assets and business of a corporation:

(a) In an action by a shareholder when it is established:

(1) That the directors are deadlocked in the management of the corporate affairs and the shareholders are unable to break the deadlock, and that irreparable injury to the corporation is being suffered or is threatened by reason thereof; or

(2) That the acts of the directors or those in control of the corporation are illegal, oppressive or fraudulent; or

(3) That the shareholders are deadlocked in voting power, and have failed, for a period which includes at least two consecutive annual meeting dates, to elect successors to directors whose terms have expired or would have expired upon the election of their successors; or

(4) That the corporate assets are being misapplied or wasted.

(b) In an action by a creditor:

(1) When the claim of the creditor has been reduced to judgment and an execution thereon returned unsatisfied and it is established that the corporation is insolvent; or

(2) When the corporation has admitted in writing that the claim of the creditor is due and owing and it is established that the corporation is insolvent.

(c) Upon application by a corporation which has filed a statement of intent to dissolve, as provided in this Act, to have its liquidation continued under the supervision of the court.

(d) When an action has been filed by the Attorney General to dissolve a corporation and it is established that liquidation of its business and affairs should precede the entry of a decree of dissolution.

Proceedings under clause (a), (b) or (c) of this section shall be brought in the county in which the registered office or the principal office of the corporation is situated.

It shall not be necessary to make shareholders parties to any such action or proceeding unless relief is sought against them personally.

§ 98. Procedure in Liquidation of Corporation by Court. In proceedings to liquidate the assets and business of a corporation the court shall have power to issue injunctions, to appoint a receiver or receivers pendente lite, with such powers and duties as the court, from time to time, may direct, and to take such other proceedings as may be requisite to preserve the corporate assets wherever situated, and carry on the business of the corporation until a full hearing can be had.

After a hearing had upon such notice as the court may direct to be given to all parties to the proceedings and to any other parties in interest designated by the court, the court may appoint a liquidating receiver or receivers with authority to collect the assets of the corporation, including all amounts owing to the corporation by subscribers on account of any unpaid portion of the consideration for the issuance of shares. Such liquidating receiver or receivers shall sell, convey and dispose of all or any part of the assets of the corporation wherever situated, either at public or private sale. The assets of the corporation or the proceeds resulting from a sale, conveyance or other disposition thereof shall be applied to the expenses of such liquidation and to the payment of the liabilities and obligations of the corporation, and any remaining assets or proceeds shall be distributed among its shareholders according to their respective rights and interests. The order appointing such liquidating receiver or receivers shall state their powers and duties. Such powers and duties may be increased or diminished at any time during the proceedings.

The court shall have power to allow from time to time as expenses of the liquidation compensation to the receiver or receivers and to attorneys in the proceeding, and to direct the payment thereof out of the assets of the corporation or the proceeds of any sale or disposition of such assets.

A receiver of a corporation appointed under the provisions of this section shall have authority to sue and defend in all courts in his own name as receiver of such corporation. The court appointing such receiver shall have exclusive jurisdiction of the corporation and its property, wherever situated.

§ 99. Qualifications of Receivers. A receiver shall in all cases be a natural person or a corporation authorized to act as receiver, which corporation may be a domestic corporation or a foreign corporation authorized to transact business in this State, and shall in all cases give such bond as the court may direct with such sureties as the court may require.

§ 100. Filing of Claims in Liquidation Proceedings. In proceedings to liquidate the assets and business of a corporation the court may require all creditors of the corporation to file with the clerk of the court or with the receiver, in such form as the court may prescribe, proofs under oath of their respective claims. If the court requires the filing of claims it shall fix a date, which shall be not less than four months from the date of the order, as the last day for the filing of claims, and shall prescribe the notice that shall be given to creditors and claimants of the date so fixed. Prior to the date so fixed, the court may extend the time for the filing of claims. Creditors and claimants failing to file proofs of claim on or before the date so fixed may be barred, by order of court, from participating in the distribution of the assets of the corporation.

§ 101. **Discontinuance of Liquidation Proceedings.** The liquidation of the assets and business of a corporation may be discontinued at any time during the liquidation proceedings when it is established that cause for liquidation no longer exists. In such event the court shall dismiss the proceedings and direct the receiver to redeliver to the corporation all its remaining property and assets.

§ 102. **Decree of Involuntary Dissolution.** In proceedings to liquidate the assets and business of a corporation, when the costs and expenses of such proceedings and all debts, obligations and liabilities of the corporation shall have been paid and discharged and all of its remaining property and assets distributed to its shareholders, or in case its property and assets are not sufficient to satisfy and discharge such costs, expenses, debts and obligations, all the property and assets have been applied so far as they will go to their payment, the court shall enter a decree dissolving the corporation, whereupon the existence of the corporation shall cease.

§ 103. **Filing of Decree of Dissolution.** In case the court shall enter a decree dissolving a corporation, it shall be the duty of the clerk of such court to cause a certified copy of the decree to be filed with the Secretary of State. No fee shall be charged by the Secretary of State for the filing thereof.

§ 104. **Deposit With State Treasurer of Amount Due Certain Shareholders.** Upon the voluntary or involuntary dissolution of a corporation, the portion of the assets distributable to a creditor or shareholder who is unknown or cannot be found, or who is under disability and there is no person legally competent to receive such distributive portion, shall be reduced to cash and deposited with the State Treasurer and shall be paid over to such creditor or share-holder or to his legal representative upon proof satisfactory to the State Treasurer of his right thereto.

§ 105. **Survival of Remedy After Dissolution.** The dissolution of a corporation either (1) by the issuance of a certificate of dissolution by the Secretary of State, or (2) by a decree of court when the court has not liquidated the assets and business of the corporation as provided in this Act, or (3) by expiration of its period of duration, shall not take away or impair any remedy available to or against such corporation, its directors, officers, or shareholders, for any right or claim existing, or any liability incurred, prior to such dissolution if action or other proceeding thereon is commenced within two years after the date of such dissolution. Any such action or proceeding by or against the corporation may be prosecuted or defended by the corporation in its corporate name. The shareholders, directors and officers shall have power to take such corporate or other action as shall be appropriate to protect such remedy, right or claim. If such corporation was dissolved by the expiration of its period of duration, such corporation may amend its articles of incorporation at any time during such period of two years so as to extend its period of duration.

§ 106. **Admission of Foreign Corporation.** No foreign corporation shall have the right to transact business in this State until it shall have procured a certificate of authority so to do from the Secretary of State. No foreign corporation shall be entitled to procure a certificate of authority under this Act to transact in this State any business which a corporation organized under this Act is not permitted to transact. A foreign corporation shall not be denied a certificate of authority by reason of the fact that the laws of the state or country under which such corporation is organized governing its organization and internal affairs differ from the laws of this State, and nothing in this Act contained shall be construed to authorize this State to regulate the organization or the internal affairs of such corporation.

Without excluding other activities which may not constitute transacting business in this State, a foreign corporation shall not be considered to be transacting business in this State, for the purposes of this Act, by reason of carrying on in this State any one or more of the following activities:

(a) Maintaining or defending any action or suit or any administrative or arbitration proceeding, or effecting the settlement thereof or the settlement of claims or disputes.

(b)   Holding meetings of its directors or shareholders or carrying on other activities concerning its internal affairs.

(c)   Maintaining bank accounts.

(d)   Maintaining offices or agencies for the transfer, exchange and registration of its securities, or appointing and maintaining trustees or depositaries with relation to its securities.

(e)   Effecting sales through independent contractors.

(f)   Soliciting or procuring orders, whether by mail or through employees or agents or otherwise, where such orders require acceptance without this State before becoming binding contracts.

(g)   Creating as borrower or lender, or acquiring, indebtedness or mortgages or other security interests in real or personal property.

(h)   Securing or collecting debts or enforcing any rights in property securing the same.

(i)   Transacting any business in interstate commerce.

(j)   Conducting an isolated transaction completed within a period of thirty days and not in the course of a number of repeated transactions of like nature.

§ 107. Powers of Foreign Corporation.   A foreign corporation which shall have received a certificate of authority under this Act shall, until a certificate of revocation or of withdrawal shall have been issued as provided in this Act, enjoy the same, but no greater, rights and privileges as a domestic corporation organized for the purposes set forth in the application pursuant to which such certificate of authority is issued; and, except as in this Act otherwise provided, shall be subject to the same duties, restrictions, penalties and liabilities now or hereafter imposed upon a domestic corporation of like character.

§ 108. Corporate Name of Foreign Corporation.
No certificate of authority shall be issued to a foreign corporation unless the corporate name of such corporation:

(a)   Shall contain the word "corporation," "company," "incorporated," or "limited,"

or shall contain an abbreviation of one of such words, or such corporation shall, for use in this State, add at the end of its name one of such words or an abbreviation thereof.

(b)   Shall not contain any word or phrase which indicates or implies that it is organized for any purpose other than one or more of the purposes contained in its articles of incorporation or that it is authorized or empowered to conduct the business of banking or insurance.

(c)   Shall not be the same as, or deceptively similar to, the name of any domestic corporation existing under the laws of this State or any other foreign corporation authorized to transact business in this State, or a name the exclusive right to which is, at the time, reserved in the manner provided in this Act, or the name of a corporation which has in effect a registration of its name as provided in this Act except that this provision shall not apply if the foreign corporation applying for a certificate of authority files with the Secretary of State any one of the following:

(1) a resolution of its board of directors adopting a fictitious name for use in transacting business in this State which fictitious name is not deceptively similar to the name of any domestic corporation or of any foreign corporation authorized to transact business in this State or to any name reserved or registered as provided in this Act, or

(2) the written consent of such other corporation or holder of a reserved or registered name to use the same or deceptively similar name and one or more words are added to make such name distinguishable from such other name, or

(3) a certified copy of a final decree of a court of competent jurisdiction establishing the prior right of such foreign corporation to the use of such name in this State.

§ 109. Change of Name by Foreign Corporation.   Whenever a foreign corporation which is authorized to transact business in this State shall change its name to one under which a certificate of authority would not be granted to it on application therefor, the certificate of authority of such corporation shall be suspended and it shall not thereafter transact any business in this State until it has changed its name to a name which is available to it under the laws of this State or has otherwise complied with the provisions of this Act.

§ 110. Application for Certificate of Authority.

A foreign corporation, in order to procure a certificate of authority to transact business in this State, shall make application therefor to the Secretary of State, which application shall set forth:

(a) The name of the corporation and the state or country under the laws of which it is incorporated.

(b) If the name of the corporation does not contain the word "corporation," "company," "incorporated," or "limited," or does not contain an abbreviation of one of such words, then the name of the corporation with the word or abbreviation which it elects to add thereto for use in this state.

(c) The date of incorporation and the period of duration of the corporation.

(d) The address of the principal office of the corporation in the state or country under the laws of which it is incorporated.

(e) The address of the proposed registered office of the corporation in this State, and the name of its proposed registered agent in this State at such address.

(f) The purpose or purposes of the corporation which it proposes to pursue in the transaction of business in this State.

(g) The names and respective addresses of the directors and officers of the corporation.

(h) A statement of the aggregate number of shares which the corporation has authority to issue, itemized by classes and series, if any, within a class.

(i) A statement of the aggregate number of issued shares itemized by class and by series, if any, within each class.

(j) An estimate, expressed in dollars, of the value of all property to be owned by the corporation for the following year, wherever located, and an estimate of the value of the property of the corporation to be located within this State during such year, and an estimate, expressed in dollars, of the gross amount of business which will be transacted by the corpora-

tion during such year, and an estimate of the gross amount thereof which will be transacted by the corporation at or from places of business in this State during such year.

(k) Such additional information as may be necessary or appropriate in order to enable the Secretary of State to determine whether such corporation is entitled to a certificate of authority to transact business in this State and to determine and assess the fees and franchise taxes payable as in this Act prescribed.

Such application shall be made on forms prescribed and furnished by the Secretary of State and shall be executed in duplicate by the corporation by its president or a vice president and by its secretary or an assistant secretary, and verified by one of the officers signing such application.

§ 111. Filing of Application for Certificate of Authority.

Duplicate originals of the application of the corporation for a certificate of authority shall be delivered to the Secretary of State, together with a copy of its articles of incorporation and all amendments thereto, duly authenticated by the proper officer of the state or country under the laws of which it is incorporated.

If the Secretary of State finds that such application conforms to law, he shall, when all fees and franchise taxes have been paid as in this Act prescribed:

(a) Endorse on each of such documents the word "Filed," and the month, day and year of the filing thereof.

(b) File in his office one of such duplicate originals of the application and the copy of the articles of incorporation and amendments thereto.

(c) Issue a certificate of authority to transact business in this State to which he shall affix the other duplicate original application.

The certificate of authority, together with the duplicate original of the application affixed thereto by the Secretary of State, shall be returned to the corporation or its representative.

§ 112. Effect of Certificate of Authority.

Upon the issuance of a certificate of authority by the Secretary of State, the corporation shall be authorized to transact business in this State for those purposes set forth in its application, subject, however, to the right of this State to suspend or to revoke such authority as provided in this Act.

§ 113. Registered Office and Registered Agent of Foreign Corporation.

Each foreign corporation authorized to transact business in this State shall have and continuously maintain in this State:

(a)   A registered office which may be, but need not be, the same as its place of business in this State.

(b)   A registered agent, which agent may be either an individual resident in this State whose business office is identical with such registered office, or a domestic corporation, or a foreign corporation authorized to transact business in this State, having a business office identical with such registered office.

§ 114. Change of Registered Office or Registered Agent of Foreign Corporation.

A foreign corporation authorized to transact business in this State may change its registered office or change its registered agent, or both, upon filing in the office of the Secretary of State a statement setting forth:

(a)   The name of the corporation.

(b)   The address of its then registered office.

(c)   If the address of its registered office be changed, the address to which the registered office is to be changed.

(d)   The name of its then registered agent.

(e)   If its registered agent be changed, the name of its successor registered agent.

(f)   That the address of its registered office and the address of the business office of its registered agent, as changed, will be identical.

(g)   That such change was authorized by resolution duly adopted by its board of directors.

Such statement shall be executed by the corporation by its president or a vice president, and verified by him, and delivered to the Secretary of State. If the Secretary of State finds that such statement conforms to the provisions of this Act, he shall file such statement in his office, and upon such filing the change of address of the registered office, or the appointment of a new registered agent, or both, as the case may be, shall become effective.

Any registered agent of a foreign corporation may resign as such agent upon filing a written notice

thereof, executed in duplicate, with the Secretary of State, who shall forthwith mail a copy thereof to the corporation at its principal office in the state or country under the laws of which it is incorporated. The appointment of such agent shall terminate upon the expiration of thirty days after receipt of such notice by the Secretary of State.

If a registered agent changes his or its business address to another place within the same _____ [supply designation of jurisdiction, such as county, etc., in accordance with local practice], he or it may change such address and the address of the registered office of any corporation of which he or it is registered agent by filing a statement as required above except that it need by signed only by the registered agent and need not be responsive to (e) or (g) and must recite that a copy of the statement has been mailed to the corporation.

§ 115. Service of Process on Foreign Corporation.

The registered agent so appointed by a foreign corporation authorized to transact business in this State shall be an agent of such corporation upon whom any process, notice or demand required or permitted by law to be served upon the corporation may be served.

Whenever a foreign corporation authorized to transact business in this State shall fail to appoint or maintain a registered agent in this State, or whenever any such registered agent cannot with reasonable diligence be found at the registered office, or whenever the certificate of authority of a foreign corporation shall be suspended or revoked, then the Secretary of State shall be an agent of such corporation upon whom any such process, notice, or demand may be served. Service on the Secretary of State of any such process, notice or demand shall be made by delivering to and leaving with him, or with any clerk having charge of the corporation department of his office, duplicate copies of such process, notice or demand. In the event any such process, notice or demand is served on the Secretary of State, he shall immediately cause one of such copies thereof to be forwarded by registered mail, addressed to the corporation at its principal office in the state or country under the laws of which it is incorporated. Any service so had on the Secretary of State shall be returnable in not less than thirty days.

The Secretary of State shall keep a record of all processes, notices and demands served upon him under this section, and shall record therein the time of such service and his action with reference thereto.

Nothing herein contained shall limit or affect the right to serve any process, notice or demand, required or permitted by law to be served upon a foreign corporation in any other manner now or hereafter permitted by law.

§ 116. Amendment to Articles of Incorporation of Foreign Corporation.

Whenever the articles of incorporation of a foreign corporation authorized to transact business in this State are amended, such foreign corporation shall, within thirty days after such amendment become effective, file in the office of the Secretary of State a copy of such amendment duly authenticated by the proper officer of the state or country under the laws of which it is incorporated; but the filing thereof shall not of itself enlarge or alter the purpose or purposes which such corporation is authorized to pursue in the transaction of business in this State, nor authorize such corporation to transact business in this State under any other name than the name set forth in its certificate of authority.

§ 117. Merger of Foreign Corporation Authorized to Transact Business in This State.

Whenever a foreign corporation authorized to transact business in this State shall be a party to a statutory merger permitted by the laws of the state or country under the laws of which it is incorporated, and such corporation shall be the surviving corporation, it shall, within thirty days after such merger becomes effective, file with the Secretary of State a copy of the articles of merger duly authenticated by the proper officer of the state or country under the laws of which such statutory merger was effected; and it shall not be necessary for such corporation to procure either a new or amended certificate of authority to transact business in this State unless the name of such corporation be changed thereby or unless the corporation desires to pursue in this State other or additional purposes than those which it is then authorized to transact in this State.

§ 118. Amended Certificate of Authority.

A foreign corporation authorized to transact business in this State shall procure an amended certificate of authority in the event it changes its corporate name, or desires to pursue in this State other or additional purposes than those set forth in its prior application for a certificate of authority, by making application therefor to the Secretary of State.

The requirements in respect to the form and contents of such application, the manner of its execution, the filing of duplicate originals thereof with the Secretary of State, the issuance of an amended certificate of authority and the effect thereof, shall be the same as in the case of an original application for a certificate of authority.

§ 119. Withdrawal of Foreign Corporation.

A foreign corporation authorized to transact business in this State may withdraw from this State upon procuring from the Secretary of State a certificate of withdrawal. In order to procure such certificate of withdrawal, such foreign corporation shall deliver to the Secretary of State an application for withdrawal, which shall set forth:

(a) The name of the corporation and the state or country under the laws of which it is incorporated.

(b) That the corporation is not transacting business in this State.

(c) That the corporation surrenders its authority to transact business in this State.

(d) That the corporation revokes the authority of its registered agent in this State to accept service of process and consents that service of process in any action, suit or proceeding based upon any cause of action arising in this State during the time the corporation was authorized to transact business in this State may thereafter be made on such corporation by service thereof on the Secretary of State.

(e) A post-office address to which the Secretary of State may mail a copy of any process against the corporation that may be served on him.

(f) A statement of the aggregate number of shares which the corporation has authority to issue, itemized by class and series, if any, within each class, as of the date of such application.

(g) A statement of the aggregate number of issued shares, itemized by class and series, if any, within each class, as of the date of such application.

(h) Such additional information as may be necessary or appropriate in order to enable the Secretary of State to determine and assess any unpaid fees or franchise taxes payable by such foreign corporation as in this Act prescribed.

The application for withdrawal shall be made on forms prescribed and furnished by the Secretary of State and shall be executed by the corporation by its president or a vice president and by its secretary or an assistant secretary, and verified by one of the officers signing the application, or, if the corporation is in the hands of a receiver or trustee, shall be executed on behalf of the corporation by such receiver or trustee and verified by him.

§ 120. Filing of Application for Withdrawal.

Duplicate originals of such application for withdrawal shall be delivered to the Secretary of State. If the Secretary of State finds that such application conforms to the provisions of this Act, he shall, when all fees and franchise taxes have been paid as in this Act prescribed:

(a) Endorse on each of such duplicate originals the word "Filed," and the month, day and year of the filing thereof.

(b) File one of such duplicate originals in his office.

(c) Issue a certificate of withdrawal to which he shall affix the other duplicate original.

The certificate of withdrawal, together with the duplicate original of the application for withdrawal affixed thereto by the Secretary of State, shall be returned to the corporation or its representative. Upon the issuance of such certificate of withdrawal, the authority of the corporation to transact business in this State shall cease.

§ 121. Revocation of Certificate of Authority.

The certificate of authority of a foreign corporation to transact business in this State may be revoked by the Secretary of State upon the conditions prescribed in this section when:

(a) The corporation has failed to file its annual report within the time required by this Act, or has failed to pay any fees, franchise taxes or penalties prescribed by this Act when they have become due and payable; or

(b) The corporation has failed to appoint and maintain a registered agent in this State as required by this Act; or

(c) The corporation has failed, after change of its registered office or registered agent, to file in the office of the Secretary of State a statement of such change as required by this Act; or

(d) The corporation has failed to file in the office of the Secretary of State any amendment to its articles of incorporation or any articles of merger within the time prescribed by this Act; or

(e) A misrepresentation has been made of any material matter in any application, report, affidavit, or other document submitted by such corporation pursuant to this Act.

No certificate of authority of a foreign corporation shall be revoked by the Secretary of State unless (1) he shall have given the corporation not less than sixty days' notice thereof by mail addressed to its registered office in this State, and (2) the corporation shall fail prior to revocation to file such annual report, or pay such fees, franchise taxes or penalties, or file the required statement of change of registered agent or registered office, or file such articles of amendment or articles of merger, or correct such misrepresentation.

§ 122. Issuance of Certificate of Revocation.

Upon revoking any such certificate of authority, the Secretary of State shall:

(a) Issue a certificate of revocation in duplicate.

(b) File one of such certificates in his office.

(c) Mail to such corporation at its registered office in this State a notice of such revocation accompanied by one of such certificates.

Upon the issuance of such certificate of revocation, the authority of the corporation to transact business in this State shall cease.

§ 123. Application to Corporations Heretofore Authorized to Transact Business in This State.

Foreign corporations which are duly authorized to transact business in this State at the time this Act takes effect, for a purpose or purposes for which a corporation might secure such authority under this Act, shall, subject to the limitations set forth in their respective certificates of authority, be entitled to all the rights and privileges applicable to foreign corporations procuring certificates of authority to transact business in this State under this Act, and from the time this Act takes effect such corporations shall be subject to all the limitations, restrictions, liabilities, and duties prescribed herein for foreign corporations procuring certificates of authority to transact business in this State under this Act.

§ 124. Transacting Business Without Certificate of Authority. No foreign corporation transacting business in this State without a certificate of authority shall be permitted to maintain any action, suit or proceeding in any court of this State, until such corporation shall have obtained a certificate of authority. Nor shall any action, suit or proceeding be maintained in any court of this State by any successor or assignee of such corporation on any right, claim or demand arising out of the transaction of business by such corporation in this State, until a certificate of authority shall have been obtained by such corporation or by a corporation which has acquired all or substantially all of its assets.

The failure of a foreign corporation to obtain a certificate of authority to transact business in this State shall not impair the validity of any contract or act of such corporation, and shall not prevent such corporation from defending any action, suit or proceeding in any court of this State.

A foreign corporation which transacts business in this State without a certificate of authority shall be liable to this State, for the years or parts thereof during which it transacted business in this State without a certificate of authority, in an amount equal to all fees and franchise taxes which would have been imposed by this Act upon such corporation had it duly applied for and received a certificate of authority to transact business in this State as required by this Act and thereafter filed all reports required by this Act, plus all penalties imposed by this Act for failure to pay such fees and franchise taxes. The Attorney General shall bring proceedings to recover all amounts due this State under the provisions of this Section.

§ 125. Annual Report of Domestic and Foreign Corporations. Each domestic corporation, and each foreign corporation authorized to transact business in this State, shall file, within the time prescribed by this Act, an annual report setting forth:

(a) The name of the corporation and the state or country under the laws of which it is incorporated.

(b) The address of the registered office of the corporation in this State, and the name of its registered agent in this State at such address, and, in case of a foreign corporation, the address of its principal office in the state or country under the laws of which it is incorporated.

(c) A brief statement of the character of the business in which the corporation is actually engaged in this State.

(d) The names and respective addresses of the directors and officers of the corporation.

(e) A statement of the aggregate number of shares which the corporation has authority to issue, itemized by class and series, if any, within each class.

(f) A statement of the aggregate number of issued shares, itemized by class and series, if any, within each class.

(g) A statement, expressed in dollars, of the value of all the property owned by the corporation, wherever located, and the value of the property of the corporation located within this State, and a statement, expressed in dollars, of the gross amount of business transacted by the corporation for the twelve months ended on the thirty-first day of December preceding the date herein provided for the filing of such report and the gross amount thereof transacted by the corporation at or from places of business in this State. If, on the thirty-first day of December preceding the time herein provided for the filing of such report, the corporation had not been in existence for a period of twelve months, or in the case of a foreign corporation had not been authorized to transact business in this State for a period of twelve months, the statement with respect to business transacted shall be furnished for the period between the date of incorporation or the date of its authorization to transact business in this State, as the case may be, and such thirty-first day of December. If all the property of the corporation is located in this State and all of its business is transacted at or from places of business in this State, then the information required by this subparagraph need not be set forth in such report.

(h) Such additional information as may be necessary or appropriate in order to enable the Secretary of State to determine and assess the proper amount of franchise taxes payable by such corporation.

Such annual report shall be made on forms prescribed and furnished by the Secretary of State, and the information therein contained shall be given as of the date of the execution of the report, except as to the information required by subparagraphs (g) and (h) which shall be given as of the close of business on the thirty-first day of December next preceding the date herein provided for the filing of such report. It shall be executed by the corporation by its president, a vice president, secretary, an assistant secretary, or treasurer, and verified by the officer executing the report, or, if the corporation is in the hands of a receiver or trustee, it shall be executed on behalf of the corporation and verified by such receiver or trustee.

§ 126. Filing of Annual Report of Domestic and Foreign Corporations. Such annual report of a domestic or foreign corporation shall be delivered to the Secretary of State between the first day of January and the first day of March of each year, except that the first annual report of a domestic or foreign corporation shall be filed between the first day of January and the first day of March of the year next succeeding the calendar year in which its certificate of incorporation or its certificate of authority, as the case may be, was issued by the Secretary of State. Proof to the satisfaction of the Secretary of State that prior to the first day of March such report was deposited in the United States mail in a sealed envelope, properly addressed, with postage prepaid, shall be deemed a compliance with this requirement. If the Secretary of State finds that such report conforms to the requirements of this Act, he shall file the same. If he finds that it does not so conform, he shall promptly return the same to the corporation for any necessary corrections, in which event the penalties hereinafter prescribed for failure to file such report within the time hereinabove provided shall not apply, if such report is corrected to conform to the requirements of this Act and returned to the Secretary of State within thirty days from the date on which it was mailed to the corporation by the Secretary of State.

§ 127. Fees, Franchise Taxes and Charges to be Collected by Secretary of State. [Text omitted.]

§ 128. Fees for Filing Documents and Issuing Certificates. [Text omitted.]

§ 129. Miscellaneous Charges. [Text omitted.]

§ 130. License Fees Payable by Domestic Corporations. [Text omitted.]

§ 131. License Fees Payable by Foreign Corporations. [Text omitted.]

§ 132. Franchise Taxes Payable by Domestic Corporations. [Text omitted.]

§ 133. Franchise Taxes Payable by Foreign Corporations. [Text omitted.]

§ 134. Assessment and Collection of Annual Franchise Taxes. It shall be the duty of the Secretary of State to collect all annual franchise taxes and penalties imposed by, or assessed in accordance with, this Act.

Between the first day of March and the first day of June of each year, the Secretary of State shall assess against each corporation, domestic and foreign, required to file an annual report in such year, the franchise tax payable by it for the period from July 1 of such year to July 1 of the succeeding year in accordance with the provisions of this Act, and, if it has failed to file its annual report within the time prescribed by this Act, the penalty imposed by this Act upon such corporation for its failure so to do; and shall mail a written notice to each corporation against which such tax is assessed, addressed to such corporation at its registered office in this State, notifying the corporation (1) of the amount of franchise tax assessed against it for the ensuing year and the amount of penalty, if any, assessed against it for failure to file its annual report; (2) that objections, if any, to such assessment will be heard by the officer making the assessment on or before the fifteenth day of June of such year, upon receipt of a request from the corporation; and (3) that such tax and penalty shall be payable to the Secretary of State on the first day of July next succeeding the date of the notice. Failure to receive such notice shall not relieve the corporation of its obligation to pay the tax and any penalty assessed, or invalidate the assessment thereof.

The Secretary of State shall have power to hear and determine objections to any assessment of franchise tax at any time after such assessment and, after hearing, to change or modify any such assessment. In the event of any adjustment of franchise tax with respect to which a penalty has been assessed for failure to file an annual report, the penalty shall be adjusted in accordance with the provisions of this Act imposing such penalty.

All annual franchise taxes and all penalties for failure to file annual reports shall be due and payable on the first day of July of each year. If the annual franchise tax assessed against any corporation subject to the provisions of this Act, together with all penalties assessed thereon, shall not be paid to the Secretary of State on or before the thirty-first day of July of the year in which such tax is due and payable, the Secretary of State shall certify such fact to the Attorney General on or before the fifteenth day of November of such year, whereupon the Attorney General may institute an action against such corporation in the name of this State, in any court of competent jurisdiction, for the recovery of the amount of such franchise tax and penalties, together with the cost of suit, and prosecute the same to final judgment.

For the purpose of enforcing collection, all annual franchise taxes assessed in accordance with this Act, and all penalties assessed thereon and all interest and costs that shall accrue in connection with the collection thereof, shall be a prior and first lien on the real and personal property of the corporation from and including the first day of July of the year when such franchise taxes become due and payable until such taxes, penalties, interest, and costs shall have been paid.

§ 135. Penalties Imposed Upon Corporations.

Each corporation, domestic or foreign, that fails or refuses to file its annual report for any year within the time prescribed by this Act shall be subject to a penalty of ten per cent of the amount of the franchise tax assessed against it for the period beginning July 1 of the year in which such report should have been filed. Such penalty shall be assessed by the Secretary of State at the time of the assessment of the franchise tax. If the amount of the franchise tax as originally assessed against such corporation be thereafter adjusted in accordance with the provisions of this Act, the amount of the penalty shall be likewise adjusted to ten per cent of the amount of the adjusted franchise tax. The amount of the franchise tax and the amount of the penalty shall be separately stated in any notice to the corporation with respect thereto.

If the franchise tax assessed in accordance with the provisions of this Act shall not be paid on or before the thirty-first day of July, it shall be deemed to be delinquent, and there shall be added a penalty of one per cent for each month or part of month that the same is delinquent, commencing with the month of August.

Each corporation, domestic or foreign, that fails or refuses to answer truthfully and fully within the time prescribed by this Act interrogatories propounded by the Secretary of State in accordance with the provisions of this Act, shall be deemed to be guilty of a misdemeanor and upon conviction thereof may be fined in any amount not exceeding five hundred dollars.

§ 136. Penalties Imposed Upon Officers and Directors.

Each officer and director of a corporation, domestic or foreign, who fails or refuses within the time prescribed by this Act to answer truthfully and fully interrogatories propounded to him by the Secretary of State in accordance with the provisions of this Act, or who signs any articles, statement, report, application or other document filed with the Secretary of State which is known to such officer or director to be false in any material respect, shall be deemed to be guilty of a misdemeanor, and upon conviction thereof may be fined in any amount not exceeding _____ dollars.

§137. Interrogatories by Secretary of State.

The Secretary of State may propound to any corporation, domestic or foreign, subject to the provisions of this Act, and to any officer or director thereof, such interrogatories as may be reasonably necessary and proper to enable him to ascertain whether such corporation has complied with all the provisions of this Act applicable to such corporation. Such interrogatories shall be answered within thirty days after the mailing thereof, or within such additional time as shall be fixed by the Secretary of State, and the answers thereto shall be full and complete and shall be made in writing and under oath. If such interrogatories be directed to an individual they shall be answered by him, and if directed to a corporation they shall be answered by the president, vice president, secretary or assistant secretary thereof. The Secretary of State need not file any document to which such interrogatories relate until such interrogatories be answered as herein provided, and not then if the answers thereto disclose that such document is not in conformity with the provisions of this Act. The Secretary of State shall certify to the Attorney General, for such action as the Attorney General may deem appropriate, all interrogatories and answers thereto which disclose a violation of any of the provisions of this Act.

§ 138. Information Disclosed by Interrogatories.

Interrogatories propounded by the Secretary of State and the answers thereto shall not be open to public inspection nor shall the Secretary of State disclose any facts or information obtained therefrom except insofar as his official duty may require the same to be made public or in the event such interrogatories or the answers thereto are required for evidence in any criminal proceedings or in any other action by this State.

§ 139. Powers of Secretary of State. The Secretary of State shall have the power and authority reasonably necessary to enable him to administer this Act efficiently and to perform the duties therein imposed upon him.

§ 140. Appeal From Secretary of State. If the Secretary of State shall fail to approve any articles of incorporation, amendment, merger, consolidation or dissolution, or any other document required by this Act to be approved by the Secretary of State before the same shall be filed in his office, he shall, within ten days after the delivery thereof to him, give written notice of his disapproval to the person or corporation, domestic or foreign, delivering the same, specifying the reasons therefor. From such disapproval such person or corporation may appeal to the _____ court of the county in which the registered office of such corporation is, or is proposed to be, situated by filing with the clerk of such court a petition setting forth a copy of the articles or other documents sought to be filed and a copy of the written disapproval thereof by the Secretary of State; whereupon the matter shall be tried de novo by the court, and the court shall either sustain the action of the Secretary of State or direct him to take such action as the court may deem proper.

If the Secretary of State shall revoke the certificate of authority to transact business in this State of any foreign corporation, pursuant to the provisions of this Act, such foreign corporation may likewise appeal to the _____ court of the county where the registered office of such corporation in this State is situated, by filing with the clerk of such court a petition setting forth a copy of its certificate of authority to transact business in this State and a copy of the notice of revocation given by the Secretary of State; whereupon the matter shall be tried de novo by the court, and the court shall either sustain the action of the Secretary of State or direct him to take such action as the court may deem proper.

Appeals from all final orders and judgments entered by the _____ court under this section in review of any ruling or decision of the Secretary of State may be taken as in other civil actions.

§ 141. Certificates and Certified Copies to be Received in Evidence. All certificates issued by the Secretary of State in accordance with the provisions of this Act, and all copies of documents filed in his office in accordance with the provisions of this Act when certified by him, shall be taken and received in all courts, public offices, and official bodies as prima facie evidence of the facts therein stated. A certificate by the Secretary of State under the great seal of this State, as to the existence or non-existence of the facts relating to corporations shall be taken and received in all courts, public offices, and official bodies as prima facie evidence of the existence or non-existence of the facts therein stated.

§ 142. Forms to be Furnished by Secretary of State. All reports required by this Act to be filed in the office of the Secretary of State shall be made on forms which shall be prescribed and furnished by the Secretary of State. Forms for all other documents to be filed in the office of the Secretary of State shall be furnished by the Secretary of State on request therefor, but the use thereof, unless otherwise specifically prescribed in this Act, shall not be mandatory.

§ 143. Greater Voting Requirements. Whenever, with respect to any action to be taken by the shareholders of a corporation, the articles of incorporation, require the vote or concurrence of the holders of a greater proportion of the shares, or of any class or series thereof, than required by this Act with respect to such action, the provisions of the articles of incorporation shall control.

§ 144. Waiver of Notice. Whenever any notice is required to be given to any shareholder or director of a corporation under the provisions of this Act or under the provisions of the articles of incorporation or by-laws of the corporation, a waiver thereof in writing signed by the person or persons entitled to such notice, whether before or after the time stated therein, shall be equivalent to the giving of such notice.

§ 145. Action by Shareholders Without a Meeting. Any action required by this Act to be taken at a meeting of the shareholders of a corporation, or any action which may be taken at a meeting of the shareholders, may be taken without a meeting if a consent in writing, setting forth the action so taken shall be signed by all of the shareholders entitled to vote with respect to the subject matter thereof.

Such consent shall have the same effect as a unanimous vote of shareholders, and may be stated as such in any articles or document filed with the Secretary of State under this Act.

§ 146. Unauthorized Assumption of Corporate Powers. All persons who assume to act as a corporation without authority so to do shall be jointly and severally liable for all debts and liabilities incurred or arising as a result thereof.

§ 147. **Application to Existing Corporations.** The provisions of this Act shall apply to all existing corporations organized under any general act of this State providing for the organization of corporations for a purpose or purposes for which a corporation might be organized under this Act, where the power has been reserved to amend, repeal or modify the act under which such corporation was organized and where such act is repealed by this Act.

§ 148. **Application to Foreign and Interstate Commerce.** The provisions of this Act shall apply to commerce with foreign nations and among the several states only insofar as the same may be permitted under the provisions of the Constitution of the United States.

§ 149. **Reservation of Power.** The _____ [insert name of legislative body] shall at all times have power to prescribe such regulations, provisions and limitations as it may deem advisable, which regulations, provisions and limitations shall be binding upon any and all corporations subject to the provisions of this Act, and the _____ [insert name of legislative body] shall have power to amend, repeal or modify this Act at pleasure.

§ 150. **Effect of Repeal of Prior Acts.** The repeal of a prior act by this Act shall not affect any right accrued or established, or any liability or penalty incurred, under the provisions of such act, prior to the repeal thereof.

§ 151. **Effect of Invalidity of Part of This Act.** If a court of competent jurisdiction shall adjudge to be invalid or unconstitutional any clause, sentence, paragraph, section or part of this Act, such judgment or decree shall not affect, impair, invalidate or nullify the remainder of this Act, but the effect thereof shall be confined to the clause, sentence, paragraph, section or part of this Act so adjudged to be invalid or unconstitutional.

§ 152. **Exclusivity of Certain Provisions. [Optional Provision.]** In circumstances to which section 45 and related sections of this Act are applicable, such provisions supersede the applicability of any other statutes of this state with respect to the legality of distributions.

§ 153. **Repeal of Prior Acts.** _____ [Insert appropriate provisions.]

Appendix D

UNIFORM PARTNERSHIP ACT

Part 1. Preliminary Provisions

§ 1. Name of Act. This act may be cited as Uniform Partnership Act.

§ 2. Definition of Terms. In this act, "Court" includes every court and judge having jurisdiction in the case.

"Business" includes every trade, occupation, or profession.

"Person" includes individuals, partnerships, corporations, and other associations.

"Bankrupt" includes bankrupt under the Federal Bankruptcy Act or insolvent under any state insolvent act.

"Conveyance" includes every assignment, lease, mortgage, or encumbrance.

"Real property" includes land and any interest or estate in land.

§ 3. Interpretation of Knowledge and Notice.

(1) A person has "knowledge" of a fact within the meaning of this act not only when he has actual knowledge thereof, but also when he has knowledge of such other facts as in the circumstances shows bad faith.

(2) A person has "notice" of a fact within the meaning of this act when the person who claims the benefit of the notice:

   (a) States the fact to such person, or

   (b) Delivers through the mail, or by other means of communication, a written statement of the fact to such person or to a proper person at his place of business or residence.

§ 4. Rules of Construction.

(1) The rule that statutes in derogation of the common law are to be strictly construed shall have no application to this act.

(2) The law of estoppel shall apply under this act.

(3) The law of agency shall apply under this act.

(4) This act shall be so interpreted and construed as to effect its general purpose to make uniform the law of those states which enact it.

(5) This act shall not be construed so as to impair the obligations of any contract existing when the act goes into effect, nor to affect any action or proceedings begun or right accrued before this act takes effect.

§ 5. Rules for Cases Not Provided for in This Act. In any case not provided for in this act the rules of law and equity, including the law merchant, shall govern.

Part 2. Nature of Partnership

§ 6. Partnership Defined.

(1) A partnership is an association of two or more persons to carry on as co-owners a business for profit.

(2) But any association formed under any other statute of this state, or any statute adopted by authority, other than the authority of this state, is not a partnership under this act, unless such association would have been a partnership in this state prior to the adoption of this act; but this act shall apply to limited partnerships except in so far as the statutes relating to such partnerships are inconsistent herewith.

§ 7. Rules for Determining the Existence of a Partnership. In determining whether a partnership exists, these rules shall apply:

(1) Except as provided by section 16 persons who are not partners as to each other are not partners as to third persons.

(2) Joint tenancy, tenancy in common, tenancy by the entireties, joint property, common property, or part ownership does not of itself establish a partnership, whether such co-owners do or do not share any profits made by the use of the property.

(3) The sharing of gross returns does not of itself establish a partnership, whether or not the persons sharing them have a joint or common right or interest in any property from which the returns are derived.

(4) The receipt by a person of a share of the profits of a business is prima facie evidence that he is a partner in the business, but no such inference shall be drawn if such profits were received in payment:

    (a)   As a debt by installments or otherwise,

    (b)   As wages of an employee or rent to a landlord,

    (c)   As an annuity to a widow or representative of a deceased partner,

    (d)   As interest on a loan, though the amount of payment vary with the profits of the business,

    (e)   As the consideration for the sale of a good-will of a business or other property by installments or otherwise.

§ 8. Partnership Property.

(1) All property originally brought into the partnership stock or subsequently acquired by purchase or otherwise, on account of the partnership, is partnership property.

(2) Unless the contrary intention appears, property acquired with partnership funds is partnership property.

(3) Any estate in real property may be acquired in the partnership name. Title so acquired can be conveyed only in the partnership name.

(4) A conveyance to a partnership in the partnership name, though without words of inheritance, passes the entire estate of the grantor unless a contrary intent appears.

Part 3. Relations of Partners to Persons Dealing with the Partnership

§ 9. Partner Agent of Partnership as to Partnership Business.

(1) Every partner is an agent of the partnership for the purpose of its business, and the act of every partner, including the execution in the partnership name of any instrument, for apparently carrying on in the usual way the business of the partnership of which he is a member binds the partnership, unless the partner so acting has in fact no authority to act for the partnership in the particular matter, and the person with whom he is dealing has knowledge of the fact that he has no such authority.

(2) An act of a partner which is not apparently for the carrying on of the business of the partnership in the usual way does not bind the partnership unless authorized by the other partners.

(3) Unless authorized by the other partners or unless they have abandoned the business, one or more but less than all the partners have no authority to:

    (a)   Assign the partnership property in trust for creditors or on the assignee's promise to pay the debts of the partnership.

    (b)   Dispose of the good-will of the business,

    (c)   Do any other act which would make it impossible to carry on the ordinary business of a partnership,

    (d)   Confess a judgment,

    (e)   Submit a partnership claim or liability to arbitration or reference.

(4) No act of a partner in contravention of a restriction on authority shall bind the partnership to persons having knowledge of the restriction.

§ 10. Conveyance of Real Property of the Partnership.

(1) Where title to real property is in the partnership name, any partner may convey title to such property by a conveyance executed in the partnership name; but the partnership may recover such property unless the partner's act binds the partnership under the provisions of paragraph (1) of section 9, or unless such property has been conveyed by the grantee or a person claiming through such grantee to a holder for value without knowledge that the partner, in making the conveyance, has exceeded his authority.

(2) Where title to real property is in the name of the partnership, a conveyance executed by a partner, in his own name, passes the equitable interest of the partnership, provided the act is one within the authority of the partner under the provisions of paragraph (1) of section 9.

(3) Where title to real property is in the name of

one or more but not all the partners, and the record does not disclose the right of the partnership, the partners in whose name the title stands may convey title to such property, but the partnership may recover such property if the partners' act does not bind the partnership under the provisions of paragraph (1) of section 9, unless the purchaser or his assignee, is a holder for value, without knowledge.

(4) Where the title to real property is in the name of one or more of all the partners, or in a third person in trust for the partnership, a conveyance executed by a partner in the partnership name, or in his own name, passes the equitable interest of the partnership, provided the act is one within the authority of the partner under the provisions of paragraph (1) of section 9.

(5) Where the title to real property is in the names of all the partners a conveyance executed by all the partners passes all their rights in such property.

§ 11. Partnership Bound by Admission of Partner.

An admission or representation made by any partner concerning partnership affairs within the scope of his authority as conferred by this act is evidence against the partnership.

§ 12. Partnership Charged with Knowledge of or Notice to Partner.

Notice to any partner of any matter relating to partnership affairs, and the knowledge of the partner acting in the particular matter, acquired while a partner or then present to his mind, and the knowledge of any other partner who reasonably could and should have communicated it to the acting partner, operate as notice to or knowledge of the partnership, except in the case of a fraud on the partnership committed by or with the consent of that partner.

§ 13. Partnership Bound by Partner's Wrongful Act.

Where, by any wrongful act or omission of any partner acting in the ordinary course of the business of the partnership or with the authority of his copartners, loss or injury is caused to any person, not being a partner in the partnership, or any penalty is incurred, the partnership is liable therefor to the same extent as the partner so acting or omitting to act.

§ 14. Partnership Bound by Partner's Breach of Trust.

The partnership is bound to make good the loss:

(a)   Where one partner acting within the scope of his apparent authority receives

money or property of a third person and misapplies it; and

(b)   Where the partnership in the course of its business receives money or property of a third person and the money or property so received is misapplied by any partner while it is in the custody of the partnership.

§15. Nature of Partner's Liability.

All partners are liable.

(a)   Jointly and severally for everything chargeable to the partnership under sections 13 and 14.

(b)   Jointly for all other debts and obligations of the partnership; but any partner may enter into a separate obligation to perform a partnership contract.

§ 16. Partner by Estoppel.

(1) When a person, by words spoken or written or by conduct, represents himself, or consents to another representing him to any one, as a partner in an existing partnership or with one or more persons not actual partners, he is liable to any such person to whom such representation has been made, who has, on the faith of such representation, given credit to the actual or apparent partnership, and if he has made such representation or consented to its being made in a public manner he is liable to such person, whether the representation has or has not been made or communicated to such person so giving credit by or with the knowledge of the apparent partner making the representation or consenting to its being made.

(a)   When a partnership liability results, he is liable as though he were an actual member of the partnership.

(b)   When no partnership liability results, he is liable jointly with the other persons, if any, so consenting to the contract or representation as to incur liability, otherwise separately.

(2) When a person has been thus represented to be a partner in an existing partnership, or with one or more persons not actual partners, he is an agent of the persons consenting to such representation to bind them to the same extent and in the same manner as though he were a partner in fact, with respect to persons who rely upon the representation. Where all the members of the existing partnership consent

to the representation, a partnership act or obligation results; but in all other cases it is the joint act or obligation of the person acting and the persons consenting to the representation.

§ 17. Liability of Incoming Partner. A person admitted as a partner into an existing partnership is liable for all the obligations of the partnership arising before his admission as though he had been a partner when such obligations were incurred, except that this liability shall be satisfied only out of partnership property.

Part 4. Relations of Partners to One Another

§ 18. Rules Determining Rights and Duties of Partners. The rights and duties of the partners in relation to the partnership shall be determined, subject to any agreement between them, by the following rules:

(a) Each partner shall be repaid his contributions, whether by way of capital or advances to the partnership property and share equally in the profits and surplus remaining after all liabilities, including those to partners, are satisfied; and must contribute towards the losses, whether of capital or otherwise, sustained by the partnership according to his share in the profits.

(b) The partnership must indemnify every partner in respect of payments made and personal liabilities reasonably incurred by him in the ordinary and proper conduct of its business, or for the preservation of its business or property.

(c) A partner, who in aid of the partnership makes any payment or advance beyond the amount of capital which he agreed to contribute, shall be paid interest from the date of the payment or advance.

(d) A partner shall receive interest on the capital contributed by him only from the date when repayment should be made.

(e) All partners have equal rights in the management and conduct of the partnership business.

(f) No partner is entitled to remuneration for acting in the partnership business, except that a surviving partner is entitled to reasonable compensation for his services in winding up the partnership affairs.

(g) No person can become a member of a partnership without the consent of all the partners.

(h) Any difference arising as to ordinary matters connected with the partnership business may be decided by a majority of the partners; but no act in contravention of any agreement between the partners may be done rightfully without the consent of all the partners.

§ 19. Partnership Books. The partnership books shall be kept, subject to any agreement between the partners, at the principal place of business of the partnership, and every partner shall at all times have access to and may inspect and copy any of them.

§ 20. Duty of Partners to Render Information. Partners shall render on demand true and full information of all things affecting the partnership to any partner or the legal representative of any deceased partner or partner under legal disability.

§ 21. Partner Accountable as a Fiduciary.

(1) Every partner must account to the partnership for any benefit, and hold as trustee for it any profits derived by him without the consent of the other partners from any transaction connected with the formation, conduct, or liquidation of the partnership or from any use by him of its property.

(2) This section applies also to the representatives of a deceased partner engaged in the liquidation of the affairs of the partnership as the personal representatives of the last surviving partner.

§ 22. Right to an Account. Any partner shall have the right to a formal account as to partnership affairs:

(a) If he is wrongfully excluded from the partnership business or possession of its property by his co-partners,

(b) If the right exists under the terms of any agreement,

(c) As provided by section 21,

(d) Whenever other circumstances render it just and reasonable.

§ 23. Continuation of Partnership Beyond Fixed Term.

(1) When a partnership for a fixed term or particular undertaking is continued after the termination of

such term or particular undertaking without any express agreement, the rights and duties of the partners remain the same as they were at such termination, so far as is consistent with a partnership at will.

(2) A continuation of the business by the partners or such of them as habitually acted therein during the term, without any settlement or liquidation of the partnership affairs, is prima facie evidence of a continuation of the partnership.

Part 5. Property Rights of a Partner

§ 24. Extent of Property Rights of a Partner. The property rights of a partner are (1) his rights in specific partnership property, (2) his interest in the partnership, and (3) his right to participate in the management.

§ 25. Nature of a Partner's Right in Specific Partnership Property.

(1) A partner is co-owner with his partners of specific partnership property holding as a tenant in partnership.

(2) The incidents of this tenancy are such that:

(a) A partner, subject to the provisions of this act and to any agreement between the partners, has an equal right with his partners to possess specific partnership property for partnership purposes; but he has no right to possess such property for any other purpose without the consent of his partners.

(b) A partner's right in specific partnership property is not assignable except in connection with the assignment of rights of all the partners in the same property.

(c) A partner's right in specific partnership property is not subject to attachment or execution, except on a claim against the partnership. When partnership property is attached for a partnership debt the partners, or any of them, or the representatives of a deceased partner, cannot claim any right under the homestead or exemption laws.

(d) On the death of a partner his right in specific partnership property vests in the surviving partner or partners, except where the deceased was the last surviving partner, when his right in such property vests in his legal representative. Such surviving partner or partners, or the legal repre-

sentative of the last surviving partner, has no right to possess the partnership property for any but a partnership purpose.

(e) A partner's right in specific partnership property is not subject to dower, curtesy, or allowances to widows, heirs, or next of kin.

§ 26. Nature of Partner's Interest in the Partnership. A partner's interest in the partnership is his share of the profits and surplus, and the same is personal property.

§ 27. Assignment of Partner's Interest.

(1) A conveyance by a partner of his interest in the partnership does not of itself dissolve the partnership, nor, as against the other partners in the absence of agreement, entitle the assignee, during the continuance of the partnership, to interfere in the management or administration of the partnership business or affairs, or to require any information or account of partnership transactions, or to inspect the partnership books; but it merely entitles the assignee to receive in accordance with his contract the profits to which the assigning partner would otherwise be entitled.

(2) In case of a dissolution of the partnership, the assignee is entitled to receive his assignor's interest and may require an account from the date only of the last account agreed to by all the partners.

§ 28. Partner's Interest Subject to Changing Order.

(1) On due application to a competent court by any judgment creditor of a partner, the court which entered the judgment, order, or decree, or any other court, may charge the interest of the debtor partner with payment of the unsatisfied amount of such judgment debt with interest thereon; and may then or later appoint a receiver of his share of the profits, and of any other money due or to fall due to him in respect of the partnership, and make all other orders, directions, accounts and inquiries which the debtor partner might have made, or which the circumstances of the case may require.

(2) The interest charged may be redeemed at any time before foreclosure, on in case of a sale being directed by the court may be purchased without therby causing a dissolution:

(a) With separate property, by any one or more of the partners, or

(b) With partnership property, by any one or

more of the partners with the consent of all the partners whose interests are not so charged or sold.

(3) Nothing in this act shall be held to deprive a partner of his right, if any, under the exemption laws, as regards his interest in the partnership.

Part 6. Dissolution and Winding Up

§ 29. **Dissolution Defined.** The dissolution of a partnership is the change in the relation of the partners caused by any partner ceasing to be associated in the carrying on as distinguished from the winding up of the business.

§ 30. **Partnership not Terminated by Dissolution.** On dissolution the partnership is not terminated, but continues until the winding up of partnership affairs is completed.

§ 31. **Causes of Dissolution.** Dissolution is caused:

(1) Without violation of the agreement between the partners,

   (a) By the termination of the definite term or particular undertaking specified in the agreement,

   (b) By the express will of any partner when no definite term or particular undertaking is specified,

   (c) By the express will of all the partners who have not assigned their interests or suffered them to be charged for their separate debts, either before or after the termination of any specified term or particular undertaking,

   (d) By the expulsion of any partner from the business bona fide in accordance with such a power conferred by the agreement between the partners;

(2) In contravention of the agreement between the partners, where the circumstances do not permit a dissolution under any other provision of this section, by the express will of any partner at any time;

(3) By any event which makes it unlawful for the business of the partnership to be carried on or for the members to carry it on in partnership;

(4) By the death of any partner;

(5) By the bankruptcy of any partner or the partnership;

(6) By decree of court under section 32.

§ 32. **Dissolution by Decree of Court.**

(1) On application by or for a partner the court shall decree a dissolution whenever:

   (a) A partner has been declared a lunatic in any judicial proceeding or is shown to be of unsound mind,

   (b) A partner becomes in any other way incapable of performing his part of the partnership contract,

   (c) A partner has been guilty of such conduct as tends to affect prejudicially the carrying on of the business,

   (d) A partner wilfully or persistently commits a breach of the partnership agreement, or otherwise so conducts himself in matters relating to the partnership business that it is not reasonably practicable to carry on the business in partnership with him,

   (e) The business of the partnership can only be carried on at a loss,

   (f) Other circumstances render a dissolution equitable.

(2) On the application of the purchaser of a partner's interest under sections 27 or 28:

   (a) After the termination of the specified term or particular undertaking,

   (b) At any time if the partnership was a partnership at will when the interest was assigned or when the charging order was issued.

§ 33. **General Effect of Dissolution on Authority of Partner.** Except so far as may be necessary to wind up partnership affairs or to complete transactions begun but not then finished, dissolution terminates all authority of any partner to act for the partnership.

(1) With respect to the partners,

   (a) When the dissolution is not by the act, bankruptcy or death of a partner; or

   (b) When the dissolution is by such act, bankruptcy or death or a partner, in cases where section 34 so requires.

(2) With respect to persons not partners, as declared in section 35.

§ 34. **Right of Partner to Contribution from Copartners after Dissolution.** Where the dissolution is caused by the act, death or bankruptcy of a partner, each partner is liable to his co-partners for his share of any liability created by any partner acting for the partnership as if the partnership had not been dissolved unless

(a)   The dissolution being by act of any partner, the partner acting for the partnership had knowledge of the dissolution, or

(b)   The dissolution being by the death or bankruptcy of a partner, the partner acting for the partnership had knowledge or notice of the death or bankruptcy.

§ 35. Power of Partner to Bind Partnership to Third Persons after Dissolution.

(1) After dissolution a partner can bind the partnership except as provided in Paragraph (3).

(a)   By any act appropriate for winding up partnership affairs or completing transactions unfinished at dissolution;

(b)   By any transaction which would bind the partnership if dissolution had not taken place, provided the other party to the transaction

(I)   Had extended credit to the partnership prior to dissolution and had no knowledge or notice of the dissolution; or

(II)   Though he had not so extended credit, had nevertheless known of the partnership prior to dissolution, and, having no knowledge or notice of dissolution, the fact of dissolution had not been advertised in a newspaper of general circulation in the place (or in each place if more than one) at which the partnership business was regularly carried on.

(2) The liability of a partner under Paragraph (1b) shall be satisfied out of partnership assets alone when such partner had been prior to dissolution

(a)   Unknown as a partner to the person with whom the contract is made; and

(b)   So far unknown and inactive in partnership affairs that the business reputation of the partnership could not be said to have been in any degree due to his connection with it.

(3) The partnership is in no case bound by any act of a partner after dissolution

(a)   Where the partnership is dissolved because it is unlawful to carry on the business, unless the act is appropriate for winding up partnership affairs; or

(b)   Where the partner has become bankrupt; or

(c)   Where the partner has no authority to wind up partnership affairs; except by a transaction with one who

(I)   Had extended credit to the partnership prior to dissolution and had no knowledge or notice of his want of authority; or

(II)   Had not extended credit to the partnership prior to dissolution, and, having no knowledge or notice of his want of authority, the fact of his want or authority has not been advertised in the manner provided for advertising the fact of dissolution in Paragraph 1bII).

(4) Nothing in this section shall affect the liability under Section 16 of any person who after dissolution represents himself or consents to another representing him as a partner in a partnership engaged in carrying on a business.

§ 36. Effect of Dissolution on Partner's Existing Liability.

(1) The dissolution of the partnership does not of itself discharge the existing liability of any partner.

(2) A partner is discharged from any existing liability upon dissolution of the partnership by an agreement to that effect between himself, the partnership creditor and the person or partnership continuing the business; and such agreement may be inferred from the course of dealing between the creditor having knowledge of the dissolution and the person or partnership continuing the business.

(3) Where a person agrees to assume the existing obligations of a dissolved partnership, the partners whose obligations have been assumed shall be discharged from any liability to any creditor of the partnership who, knowing of the agreement, consents to a material alteration in the nature or time of payment of such obligations.

(4) The individual property of a deceased partner shall be liable for all obligations of the partnership incurred while he was a partner but subject to the prior payment of his separate debts.

§ 37. Right to Wind Up.
Unless otherwise agreed the partners who have not wrongfully dissolved the partnership or the legal representative of the last surviving partner, not bankrupt, has the right to wind up the partnership affairs; provided, however, that

any partner, his legal representative or his assignee, upon cause shown, may obtain winding up by the court.

§ 38. Rights of Partners to Application of Partnership Property.

(1) When dissolution is caused in any way, except in contravention of the partnership agreement, each partner, as against his co-partners and all persons claiming through them in respect of their interests in the partnership, unless otherwise agreed, may have the partnership property applied to discharge its liabilities, and the surplus applied to pay in cash the net amount owing to the respective partners. But if dissolution is caused by expulsion of a partner, bona fide under the partnership agreement and if the expelled partner is discharged from all partnership liabilities, either by payment or agreement under section 36(2), he shall receive in cash only the net amount due him from the partnership.

(2) When dissolution is caused in contravention of the partnership agreement the rights of the partners shall be as follows:

(a) Each partner who has not caused dissolution wrongfully shall have,

I. All the rights specified in paragraph (1) of this section, and

II. The right, as against each partner who has caused the dissolution wrongfully, to damages for breach of the agreement.

(b) The partners who have not caused the dissolution wrongfully, if they all desire to continue the business in the same name, either by themselves or jointly with others, may do so, during the agreed term for the partnership and for that purpose may possess the partnership property, provided they secure the payment by bond approved by the court, or pay to any partner who has caused the dissolution wrongfully, the value of his interest in the partnership at the dissolution, less any damages recoverable under clause (2a II) of this section, and in like manner indemnify him against all present or future partnership liabilities.

(c) A partner who has caused the dissolution wrongfully shall have

I. If the business is not continued under the provisions of paragraph (2b) all the rights of a partner under paragraph (1), subject to clasue (2a II), of this section,

II. If the business is continued under paragraph (2b) of this section the right as against his co-partners and all claiming through them in respect of their interests in the partnership, to have the value of his interest in the partnership, less any damages caused to his co-partners by the dissolution, ascertained and paid to him in cash, or the payment secured by bond approved by the court, and to be released from all existing liabilities of the partnership; but in ascertaining the value of the partner's interest the value of the goodwill of the business shall not be considered.

§ 39. Rights Where Partnership is Dissolved for Fraud or Misrepresentation.

Where a partnership contract is rescinded on the ground of the fraud or misrepresentation of one of the parties thereto, the party entitled to rescind is, without prejudice to any other right, entitled,

(a) To a lien on, or a right of retention of, the surplus of the partnership property after satisfying the partnership liabilities to third persons for any sum of money paid by him for the purchase of an interest in the partnership and for any capital or advances contributed by him; and

(b) To stand, after all liabilities to third persons have been satisfied, in the place of the creditors or the partnership for any payments made by him in respect of the partnership liabilities; and

(c) To be indemnified by the person guilty of the fraud or making the representation against all debts and liabilities of the partnership.

§ 40. Rules for Distribution.

In settling accounts between the partners after dissolution, the following rules shall be observed, subject to any agreement to the contrary:

(a) The assets of the partnership are:

I. The partnership property,

II. The contributions of the partners necessary for the payment of all the liabilities specified in clause (b) of this paragraph.

(b)   The liabilities of the partnership shall rank in order of payment, as follows:

I.   Those owing to creditors other than partners,

II.   Those owing to partners other than for capital and profits,

III.   Those owing to partners in respect of capital,

IV.   Those owing to partners in respect of profits.

(c)   The assets shall be applied in order of their declaration in clause (a) of this paragraph to the satisfaction of the liabilities.

(d)   The partners shall contribute, as provided by section 18 (a) the amount necessary to satisfy the liabilities; but if any, but not all, of the partners are insolvent, or, not being subject to process, refuse to contribute, the other partners shall contribute their share of the liabilities, and, in the relative proportions in which they share the profits, the additional amount necessary to pay the liabilities.

(e)   An assignee for the benefit of creditors or any person appointed by the court shall have the right to enforce the contributions specified in clause (d) of this paragraph.

(f)   Any partner or his legal representative shall have the right to enforce the contributions specified in clause (d) of this paragraph, to the extent of the amount which he has paid in excess of his share of the liability.

(g)   The individual property of a deceased partner shall be liable for the contributions specified in clause (d) of this paragraph.

(h)   When partnership property and the individual properties of the partners are in possession of a court for distribution, partnership creditors shall have priority on partnership property and separate creditors on individual property, saving the rights of lien or secured creditors as heretofore.

(i)   Where a partner has become bankrupt or his estate is insolvent the claims against his separate property shall rank in the following order:

I.   Those owing to separate creditors,

II.   Those owing to partnership creditors,

III.   Those owing to partners by way of contribution.

§ 41. Liability of Persons Continuing the Business in Certain Cases.

(1) When any new partner is admitted into an existing partnership, or when any partner retires and assigns (or the representative of the deceased partner assigns) his rights in partnership property to two or more of the partners, or to one or more of the partners and one or more third persons, if the business is continued without liquidation of the partnership affairs, creditors of the first or dissolved partnership are also creditors of the partnership so continuing the business.

(2) When all but one partner retire and assign (or the representative of a deceased partner assigns) their rights in partnership property to the remaining partner, who continues the business without liquidation of partnership affairs, either alone or with others, creditors of the dissolved partnership are also creditors of the person or partnership so continuing the business.

(3) When any partner retires or dies and the business of the dissolved partnership is continued as set forth in paragraphs (1) and (2) of this section, with the consent of the retired partners or the representative of the deceased partner, but without any assignment of his right in partnership property, rights of creditors of the dissolved partnership and of the creditors of the person or partnership continuing the business shall be as if such assignment had been made.

(4) When all the partners or their representatives assign their rights in partnership property to one or more third persons who promise to pay the debts and who continue the business of the dissolved partnership, creditors of the dissolved partnership are also creditors of the person or partnership continuing the business.

(5) When any partner wrongfully causes a dissolution and the remaining partners continue the business under the provisions of section 38(2b), either alone or with others, and without liquidation of the partnership affairs, creditors of the dissolved partnership are also creditors of the person or partnership continuing the business.

(6) When a partner is expelled and the remaining partners continue the business either alone or with others, without liquidation of the partnership affairs,

creditors of the dissolved partnership are also creditors of the person or partnership continuing the business.

(7) The liability of a third person becoming a partner in the partnership continuing the business, under this section, to the creditors of the dissolved partnership shall be satisfied out of partnership property only.

(8) When the business of a partnership after dissolution is continued under any conditions set forth in this section the creditors of the dissolved partnership, as against the separate creditors of the retiring or deceased partner or the representative of the deceased partner, have a prior right to any claim of the retired partner or the representative of the deceased partner against the person or partnership continuing the business, on account of the retired or deceased partner's interest in the dissolved partnership or on account of any consideration promised for such interest or for his right in partnership property.

(9) Nothing in this section shall be held to modify any right of creditors to set aside any assignment on the ground of fraud.

(10) The use by the person or partnership continuing the business of the partnership name, or the name of a deceased partner as part thereof, shall not of itself make the individual property of the deceased partner liable for any debts conttracted by such person or partnership.

§ 42. **Rights of Retiring or Estate of Deceased Partner When the Business is Continued.** When any partner retires or dies, and the business is con-

tinued under any of the conditions set forth in section 41 (1, 2, 3, 5, 6), or section 38(2b) without any settlement of accounts as between him or his estate and the person or partnership continuing the business, unless otherwise agreed, he or his legal representative as against such persons or partnership may have the value of his interest at the date of dissolution ascertained, and shall receive as an ordinary creditor an amount equal to the value of his interest in the dissolved partnership with interest, or, at his option or at the option of his legal representative, in lieu of interest, the profits attributable to the use of his right in the property of the dissolved partnership; provided that the creditors of the dissolved partnership as against the separate creditors, or the representative of the retired or deceased partner, shall have priority on any claim arising under this section, as provided by section 41(8) of this act.

§ 43. **Accural of Actions.** The right to an account of his interest shall accrue to any partner, or his legal representative, as against the winding up partners or the surviving partners or the person or partnership continuing the business, at the date of dissolution, in the absence of any agreement to the contrary.

Part 7. Miscellaneous Provisions

§ 44. **When Act Takes Effect.** This act shall take effect on the _____ day of _____ one thousand nine hundred and _____.

§ 45. **Legislation Repealed.** All acts or parts of acts inconsistent with this act are hereby repealed.

Appendix E

§ 1. **Limited Partnership Defined.** A limited partnership is a partnership formed by two or more persons under the provisions of Section 2, having as members one or more general partners and one or more limited partners. The limited partners as such shall not be bound by the obligations of the partnership.

§ 2. **Formation.**

(1) Two or more persons desiring to form a limited partnership shall

(a) Sign and swear to a certificate, which shall state

I. The name of the partnership,

II. The character of the business,

III. The location of the principal place of business,

IV. The name and place of residence of each member; general and limited partners being respectively designated,

V. The term for which the partnership is to exist,

VI. The amount of cash and a description of and the agreed value of the other property contributed by each limited partner,

VII. The additional contributions, if any, agreed to be made by each limited partner and the times at which or events on the happening of which they shall be made,

VIII. The time, if agreed upon, when the contribution of each limited partner is to be returned,

IX. The share of the profits or the other compensation by way of income which each limited partner shall receive by reason of his contribution,

X. The right, if given, of a limited partner to substitute an assignee as contributor in his place, and the terms and conditions of the substitution,

XI. The right, if given, of the partners to admit additional limited partners,

XII. The right, if given, of one or more of the limited partners to priority over other limited partners, as to contributions or as to compensation by way of income, and the nature of such priority.

XIII. The right, if given, of the remaining general partner or partners to continue the business on the death, retirement or insanity of a general partner, and

XIV. The right, if given, of a limited partner to demand and receive property other than cash in return for his contribution.

(b) File for record the certificate in the office of [here designate the proper office].

(2) A limited partnership is formed if there has been substantial compliance in good faith with the requirements of paragraph (1).

§ 3. **Business Which May Be Carried On.** A limited partnership may carry on any business which a partnership without limited partners may carry on, except [here designate the business to be prohibited]

§ 4. **Character of Limited Partner's Contribution.** The contributions of a limited partner may be cash or other property, but not services.

§ 5. **A Name Not to Contain Surname of Limited Partner; Exceptions.**

(1) The surname of a limited partner shall not appear in the partnership name, unless

(a) It is also the surname of a general partner, or

(b) Prior to the time when the limited partner became such the business had been carried on under a name in which his surname appeared.

(2) A limited partner whose name appears in a

---

*The text of this act was obtained from the National Conference of Commissioners on Uniform State Laws, and is reprinted with the Commission's consent.

partnership name contrary to the provisions of paragraph (1) is liable as a general partner to partnership creditors who extend credit to the partnership without actual knowledge that he is not a general partner.

§ 6. Liability For False Statements in Certificate.

If the certificate contains a false statement, one who suffers loss by reliance on such statement may hold liable any party to the certificate who knew the statement to be false.

(a) At the time he signed the certificate, or

(b) Subsequently, but within a sufficient time before the statement was relied upon to enable him to cancel or amend the certificate, or to file a petition for its cancellation or amendment as provided in Section 25(3).

§ 7. Limited Partner Not Liable to Creditors.

A limited partner shall not become liable as a general partner unless, in addition to the exercise of his rights and powers as a limited partner, he takes part in the control of the business.

§ 8. Admission of Additional Limited Partners.

After the formation of a limited partnership, additional limited partners may be admitted upon filing an amendment to the original certificate in accordance with the requirements of Section 25.

§ 9. Rights, Powers and Liabilities of a General Partner.

(1) A general partner shall have all the rights and powers and be subject to all the restrictions and liabilities of a partner in a partnership without limited partners, except that without the written consent or ratification of the specific act by all the limited partners, a general partner or all of the general partners have no authority to

(a) Do any act in contravention of the certificate,

(b) Do any act which would make it impossible to carry on the ordinary business of the partnership,

(c) Confess a judgment against the partnership,

(d) Possess partnership property, or assign their rights in specific partnership property, for other than a partnership purpose,

(e) Admit a person as a general partner,

(f) Admit a person as a limited partner, unless the right so to do is given in the certificate,

(g) Continue the business with partnership property on the death, retirement or in-

sanity of a general partner, unless the right so to do is given in the certificate.

§ 10. Rights of a Limited Partner.

(1) A limited partner shall have the same rights as a general partner to

(a) Have the partnership books kept at the principal place of business of the partnership, and at all times to inspect and copy any of them.

(b) Have on demand true and full information of all things affecting the partnership, and a formal account of partnership affairs whenever circumstances render it just and reasonable, and

(c) Have dissolution and winding up by decree of court.

(2) A limited partner shall have the right to receive a share of the profits or other compensation by way of income, and to the return of his contribution as provided in Sections 15 and 16.

§ 11. Status of Person Erroneously Believing Himself a Limited Partner.

A person who has contributed to the capital of a business conducted by a person or partnership erroneously believing that he has become a limited partner in a limited partnership, is not, by reason of his exercise of the rights of a limited partner, a general partner with the person or in the partnership carrying on the business, or bound by the obligations of such person or partnership; provided that on ascertaining the mistake he promptly renounces his interest in the profits of the business, or other compensation by way of income.

§ 12. One Person Both General and Limited Partner.

(1) A person may be a general partner and a limited partner in the same partnership at the same time.

(2) A person who is a general, and also at the same time a limited partner, shall have all the rights and powers and be subject to all the restrictions of a general partner; except that, in respect to his contribution, he shall have the rights against the other members which he would have had if he were not also a general partner.

§ 13. Loans and Other Business Transactions With Limited Partner.

(1) A limited partner also may loan money to and transact other business with the partnership, and, unless he is also a general partner, receive on account of resulting claims against the partnership, with general creditors, a pro rata share of the assets. No limited partner shall in respect to any such claim

(a) Receive or hold as collateral security any partnership property, or

(b) Receive from a general partner or the partnership any payment, conveyance, or release from liability, if at the time the assets of the partnership are not sufficient to discharge partnership liabilities to persons not claiming as general or limited partners,

(2) The receiving of collateral security, or a payment, conveyance, or release in violation of the provisions of paragraph (1) is a fraud on the creditors of the partnership.

§ 14. Relation of Limited Partners Inter Se.

Where there are several limited partners the members may agree that one or more of the limited partners shall have a priority over other limited partners as to the return of their contributions, as to their compensation by way of income, or as to any other matter. If such an agreement is made it shall be stated in the certificate, and in the absence of such a statement all the limited partners shall stand upon equal footing.

§ 15. Compensation of Limited Partner.

A limited partner may receive from the partnership the share of the profits or the compensation by way of income stipulated for in the certificate; provided, that after such payment is made, whether from the property of the partnership or that of a general partner, the partnership assets are in excess of all liabilities of the partnership except liabilities to limited partners on account of their contributions and to general partners.

§ 16. Withdrawal or Reduction of Limited Partner's Contribution.

(1) A limited partner shall not receive from a general partner or out of partnership property any part of his contribution until

(a) All liabilities of the partnership, except liabilities to general partners and to limited partners on account of their contributions, have been paid or there remains property of the partnership sufficient to pay them,

(b) The consent of all members is had, unless the return of the contribution may be rightfully demanded under the provisions of paragraph (2), and

(c) The certificate is cancelled or so amended as to set forth the withdrawal or reduction.

(2) Subject to the provisions of paragraph (1) a limited partner may rightfully demand the return of his contribution

(a) On the dissolution of a partnership, or

(b) When the date specified in the certificate for its return has arrived, or

(c) After he has given six months' notice in writing to all other members, if no time is specified in the certificate either for the return of the contribution or for the dissolution of the partnership,

(3) In the absence of any statement in the certificate to the contrary or the consent of all members, a limited partner, irrespective of the nature of his contribution, has only the right to demand and receive cash in return for his contribution.

(4) A limited partner may have the partnership dissolved and its affairs wound up when

(a) He rightfully but unsuccessfully demands the return of his contribution, or

(b) The other liabilities of the partnership have not been paid, or the partnership property is insufficient for their payment as required by paragraph (1a) and the limited partner would otherwise be entitled to the return of his contribution.

§ 17. Liability of Limited Partner to Partnership.

(1) A limited partner is liable to the partnership

(a) For the difference between his contribution as actually made and that stated in the certificate as having been made, and

(b) For any unpaid contribution which he agreed in the certificate to make in the future at the time and on the conditions stated in the certificate.

(2) A limited partner holds as trustee for the partnership

(a) Specific property stated in the certificate as contributed by him, but which was not contributed or which has been wrongfully returned, and

(b) Money or other property wrongfully paid or conveyed to him on account of his contribution.

(3) The liabilities of a limited partner as set forth in this section can be waived or compromised only by the consent of all members; but a waiver or compromise shall not affect the right of a creditor of a

partnership who extended credit or whose claim arose after the filing and before a cancellation or amendment of the certificate, to enforce such liabilities.

(4) When a contributor has rightfully received the return in whole or in part of the capital of his contribution, he is nevertheless liable to the partnership for any sum, not in excess of such return with interest, necessary to discharge its liabilities to all creditors who extended credit or whose claims arose before such return.

§ 18. Nature of Limited Partner's Interest in Partnership.
A limited partner's interest in the partnership is personal property.

§ 19. Assignment of Limited Partner's Interest.

(1) A limited partner's interest is assignable.

(2) A substituted limited partner is a person admitted to all the rights of a limited partner who has died or has assigned his interest in a partnership.

(3) An assignee, who does not become a substituted limited partner, has no right to require any information or account of the partnership transactions or to inspect the partnership books; he is only entitled to receive the share of the profits or other compensation by way of income, or the return of his contribution, to which his assignor would otherwise be entitled.

(4) An assignee shall have the right to become a substituted limited partner if all the members (except the assignor) consent thereto or if the assignor, being thereunto empowered by the certificate, gives the assignee that right.

(5) An assignee becomes a substituted limited partner when the certificate is appropriately amended in accordance with Section 25.

(6) The substituted limited partner has all the rights and powers, and is subject to all the restrictions and liabilities of his assignor, except those liabilities of which he was ignorant at the time he became a limited partner and which could not be ascertained from the certificate.

7. The substitution of the assignee as a limited partner does not release the assignor from liability to the partnership under Sections 6 and 17.

§ 20. Effect of Retirement, Death or Insanity of a General Partner.
The retirement, death or insanity of a general partner dissolves the partnership, unless the business is continued by the remaining general partners

(a) Under a right so to do stated in the certificate, or

(b) With the consent of all members.

§ 21 Death of Limited Partner.

(1) On the death of a limited partner his executor or administrator shall have all the rights of a limited partner for the purpose of settling his estate, and such power as the deceased had to constitute his assignee a substituted limited partner.

(2) The estate of a deceased limited partner shall be liable for all his liabilities as a limited partner.

§ 22. Rights of Creditors of Limited Partner.

(1) On due application to a court of competent jurisdiction by any judgment creditor of a limited partner, the court may charge the interest of the indebted limited partner with payment of the unsatisfied amount of the judgment debt; and may appoint a receiver, and make all other orders, directions, and inquires which the circumstances of the case may require.

(2) The interest may be redeemed with the separate property of any general partner, but may not be redeemed with partnership property.

(3) The remedies conferred by paragraph (1) shall not be deemed exclusive of others which may exist.

(4) Nothing in this act shall be held to deprive a limited partner of his statutory exemption.

§ 23. Distribution of Assets.

(1) In settling accounts after dissolution of liabilities of the partnership shall be entitled to payment in the following order:

(a) Those to creditors, in the order of priority as provided by law, except those to limited partners on account of their contributions, and to general partners,

(b) Those to limited partners in respect to their share of the profits and other compensation by way of income on their contributions,

(c) Those to limited partners in respect to the capital of their contributions,

(d) Those to general partners other than for capital and profits,

(e) Those to general partners in respect to profits,

(f) Those to general partners in respect to capital.

(2) Subject to any statement in the certificate or to subsequent agreement, limited partners share in the

partnership assets in respect to their claims for capital, and in respect to their claims for profits or for compensation by way of income on their contributions respectively, in proportion to the respective amounts of such claims.

§ 24. When Certificate Shall be Cancelled or Amended.

(1) The certificate shall be cancelled when the partnership is dissolved or all limited partners cease to be such.

(2) A certificate shall be amended when

    (a)   There is a change in the name of the partnership or in the amount or character of the contribution of any limited partner,

    (b)   A person is substituted as a limited partner,

    (c)   An additional limited partner is admitted,

    (d)   A person is admitted as a general partner,

    (e)   A general partner retires, dies or becomes insane, and the business is continued under Section 20,

    (f)   There is a change in the character of the business of the partnership,

    (g)   There is a false or erroneous statement in the certificate,

    (h)   There is a change in the time as stated in the certificate for the dissolution of the partnership or for the return of a contribution,

    (i)   A time is fixed for the dissolution of the partnership, or the return of a contribution, no time having been specified in the certificate, or

    (j)   The members desire to make a change in any other statement in the certificate in order that it shall accurately represent the agreement between them.

§ 25. Requirements for Amendment and for Cancellation of Certificate.

(1) The writing to amend a certificate shall

    (a)   Conform to the requirements of Section 2 (1a) as far as necessary to set forth clearly the change in the certificate which it is desired to make, and

    (b)   Be signed and sworn to by all members, and an amendment substituting a limited partner or adding a limited or general partner shall be signed also by the member to be substituted or added, and when

a limited partner is to be substituted, the amendment shall also be signed by the assigning limited partner.

(2) The writing to cancel a certificate shall be signed by all members.

(3) A person desiring the cancellation or amendment of a certificate, if any person designated in paragraphs (1) and (2) as a person who must execute the writing refuses to do so, may petition the [here designate the proper court] to direct a cancellation or amendment thereof.

(4) If the court finds that the petitioner has a right to have the writing executed by a person who refuses to do so, it shall order the [here designate the responsible official in the office designated in Section 2] in the office where the certificate is recorded to record the cancellation or amendment of the certificate; and where the certificate is to be amended, the court shall also cause to be filed for record in said office a certified copy of its decree setting forth the amendment.

(5) A certificate is amended or cancelled when there is filed for record in the office [here designate the office designated in Section 2] where the certificate is recorded.

    (a)   A writing in accordance with the provisions of paragraph (1), or (2) or

    (b)   A certified copy of the order of court in accordance with the provisions of paragraph (4).

(6) After the certificate is duly amended in accordance with this section, the amended certificate shall thereafter be for all purposes the certificate provided for by this act.

§ 26. Parties to Actions.
A contributor, unless he is a general partner, is not a proper party to proceedings by or against a partnership, except where the object is to enforce a limited partner's right against or liability to the partnership.

§ 27. Name of Act.
This act may be cited as The Uniform Limited Partnership Act.

§ 28. Rules of Construction.

(1) The rule that statutes in derogation of the common law are to be strictly construed shall have no application to this act.

(2) This act shall be so interpreted and construed as to effect its general purpose to make uniform the law of those states which enact it.

(3) This act shall not be so construed as to impair

the obligations of any contract existing when the act goes into effect, nor to affect any action or proceedings begun or right accrued before this act takes effect.

§ 29. Rules for Cases Not Provided for in This Act.
In any case not provided for in this act the rules of law and equity, including the law merchant, shall govern.

§ 30. Provisions for Existing Limited Partnerships.

(1) A limited partnership formed under any statute of this state prior to the adoption of this act, may become a limited partnership under this act by complying with the provisions of Section 2; provided the certificate set forth

    (a)   The amount of the original contribution of each limited partner, and the time when the contribution was made, and

    (b)   That the property of the partnership exceeds the amount sufficient to discharge its liabilities to persons not claiming as general or limited partners by an amount greater than the sum of the contributions of its limited partners.

(2) A limited partnership formed under any statute of this state prior to the adoption of this act, until or unless it becomes a limited partnership under this act, shall continue to be governed by the provisions of [here insert proper reference to the existing limited partnership act or acts], except that such partnership shall not be renewed unless so provided in the original agreement.

§ 31. Act (Acts) Repealed.
Except as affecting existing limited partnerships to the extent set forth in Section 30, the act (acts) of [here designate the existing limited partnership act or acts] is (are) hereby repealed.

Appendix F

REVISED UNIFORM LIMITED PARTNERSHIP
ACT (1976)*

Article 1. General Provisions

§ 101. Definitions. As used in this Act, unless the context otherwise requires:

(1) "Certificate of limited partnership" means the certificate referred to in Section 201, and the certificate as amended.

(2) "Contribution" means any cash, property, services rendered, or a promissory note or other binding obligation to contribute cash or property or to perform services, which a partner contributes to a limited partnership in his capacity as a partner.

(3) "Event of withdrawal of a general partner" means an event that causes a person to cease to be a general partner as provided in Section 402.

(4) "Foreign limited partnership" means a partnership formed under the laws of any State other than this State and having as partners one or more general partners and one or more limited partners.

(5) "General partner" means a person who has been admitted to a limited partnership as a general partner in accordance with the partnership agreement and named in the certificate of limited partnership as a general partner.

(6) "Limited partner" means a person who has been admitted to a limited partnership as a limited partner in accordance with the partnership agreement and named in the certificate of limited partnership as a limited partner.

(7) "Limited partnership" and "domestic limited partnership" mean a partnership formed by 2 or more persons under the laws of this State and having one or more general partners and one or more limited partners.

(8) "Partner" means a limited or general partner.

(9) "Partnership agreement" means any valid agreement, written or oral, of the partners as to the affairs of a limited partnership and the conduct of its business.

(10) "Partnership interest" means a partner's share of the profits and losses of a limited partnership and the right to receive distributions of partnership assets.

(11) "Person" means a natural person, partnership, limited partnership (domestic or foreign), trust, estate, association, or corporation.

(12) "State" means a state, territory, or possession of the United States, the District of Columbia, or the Commonwealth of Puerto Rico.

§ 102. Name. The name of each limited partnership as set forth in its certificate of limited partnership:

(1) shall contain without abbreviation the words "limited partnership";

(2) may not contain the name of a limited partner unless (i) it is also the name of a general partner or the corporate name of a corporate general partner, or (ii) the business of the limited partnership had been carried on under that name before the admission of that limited partner;

(3) may not contain any word or phrase indicating or implying that it is organized other than for a purpose stated in its certificate of limited partnership;

(4) may not be the same as, or deceptively similar to, the name of any corporation or limited partnership organized under the laws of this State or li-

---

*The text of this act was obtained from the National Conference of Commissioners on Uniform State Laws, and is reprinted with the Commission's consent.

censed or registered as a foreign corporation or limited partnership in this State; and

(5) may not contain the following words [here insert prohibited words].

§ 103. Reservation of Name.

(a) The exclusive right to the use of a name may be reserved by:

(1) any person intending to organize a limited partnership under this Act and to adopt that name;

(2) any domestic limited partnership or any foreign limited partnership registered in this State which, in either case, intends to adopt that name;

(3) any foreign limited partnership intending to register in this State and adopt that name; and

(4) any person intending to organize a foreign limited partnership and intending to have it register in this State and adopt that name.

(b) The reservation shall be made by filing with the Secretary of State an application, executed by the applicant, to reserve a specified name. If the Secretary of State finds that the name is available for use by a domestic or foreign limited partnership, he shall reserve the name for the exclusive use of the applicant for a period of 120 days. Once having so reserved a name, the same applicant may not again reserve the same name until more than 60 days after the expiration of the last 120-day period for which that applicant reserved that name. The right to the exclusive use of a reserved name may be transferred to any other person by filing in the office of the Secretary of State a notice of the transfer, executed by the applicant for whom the name was reserved and specifying the name and address of the transferee.

§ 104. Specified Office and Agent.
Each limited partnership shall continuously maintain in this State:

(1) an office, which may but need not be a place of its business in this State, at which shall be kept the records required by Section 105 to be maintained; and

(2) an agent for service of process on the limited partnership, which agent must be an individual resident of this State, a domestic corporation, or a foreign corporation authorized to do business in this State.

§ 105. Records to Be Kept.
Each limited partnership shall keep at the office referred to in Section 104(1) the following: (1) a current list of the full name and last known business address of each partner set forth in alphabetical order, (2) a copy of the certificate of limited partnership and all certificates of amend-

ment thereto, together with executed copies of any powers of attorney pursuant to which any certificate has been executed, (3) copies of the limited partnership's federal, state, and local income tax returns and reports, if any, for the 3 most recent years, and (4) copies of any then effective written partnership agreements and of any financial statements of the limited partnership for the 3 most recent years. Those records are subject to inspection and copying at the reasonable request, and at the expense, of any partner during ordinary business hours.

§ 106. Nature of Business.
A limited partnership may carry on any business that a partnership without limited partners may carry on except [here designate prohibited activities].

§ 107. Business Transactions of Partner With the Partnership.
Except as provided in the partnership agreement, a partner may lend money to and transact other business with the limited partnership and, subject to other applicable law, has the same rights and obligations with respect thereto as a person who is not a partner.

Article 2. Formation; Certificate of Limited Partnership.

§ 201. Certificate of Limited Partnership.

(a) In order to form a limited partnership two or more persons must execute a certificate of limited partnership. The certificate shall be filed in the office of the Secretary of State and set forth:

(1) the name of the limited partnership;

(2) the general character of its business;

(3) the address of the office and the name and address of the agent for service of process required to be maintained by Section 104;

(4) the name and the business address of each partner (specifying separately the general partners and limited partners);

(5) the amount of cash and a description and statement of the agreed value of the other property or services contributed by each partner and which each partner has agreed to contribute in the future;

(6) the times at which or events on the happening of which any additional contributions agreed to be made by each partner are to be made;

(7) any power of a limited partner to grant the right to become a limited partner to an assignee of any part of his partnership interest, and the terms and conditions of the power;

(8) if agreed upon, the time at which or the events on the happening of which a partner may terminate his membership in the limited partnership and the amount of, or the method of determining, the distribution to which he may be entitled respecting his partnership interest, and the terms and conditions of the termination and distribution;

(9) any right of a partner to receive distributions of property, including cash from the limited partnership;

(10) any right of a partner to receive, or of a general partner to make, distributions to a partner which include a return of all or any part of the partner's contribution;

(11) any time at which or events upon the happening of which the limited partnership is to be dissolved and its affairs wound up;

(12) any right of the remaining general partners to continue the business on the happening of an event of withdrawal of a general partner; and

(13) any other matters the partners determine to include therein.

(b) A limited partnership is formed at the time of the filing of the certificate of limited partnership in the office of the Secretary of State or at any later time specified in the certificate of limited partnership if, in either case, there has been substantial compliance with the requirements of this section.

§ 202. Amendment to Certificate.

(a) A certificate of limited partnership is amended by filing a certificate of amendment thereto in the office of the Secretary of State. The certificate shall set forth:

(1) the name of the limited partnership;

(2) the date of filing of the certificate; and

(3) the amendment to the certificate.

(b) Within 30 days after the happening of any of the following events an amendment to a certificate of limited partnership reflecting the occurrence of the event or events shall be filed:

(1) a change in the amount or character of the contribution of any partner, or in any partner's obligation to make a contribution;

(2) the admission of a new partner;

(3) the withdrawal of a partner; or

(4) the continuation of the business under Section 801 after an event of withdrawal of a general partner.

(c) A general partner who becomes aware that any

statement in a certificate of limited partnership was false when made or that any arrangements or other facts described have changed, making the certificate inaccurate in any respect, shall promptly amend the certificate, but an amendment to show a change of address of a limited partner need be filed only once every 12 months.

(d) A certificate of limited partnership may be amended at any time for any other proper purpose the general partners may determine.

(e) No person has any liability because an amendment to a certificate of limited partnership has not been filed to reflect the occurrence of any event referred to in subsection (b) of this Section if the amendment is filed within the 30-day period specified in subsection (b).

§ 203. Cancellation of Certificate.

A certificate of limited partnership shall be cancelled upon the dissolution and the commencement of winding up of the partnership or at any other time there are no limited partners. A certificate of cancellation shall be filed in the office of the Secretary of State and set forth:

(1) the name of the limited partnership;

(2) the date of filing of its certificate of limited partnership;

(3) the reason for filing the certificate of cancellation;

(4) the effective date (which shall be a date certain) of cancellation if it is not to be effective upon the filing of the certificate; and

(5) any other information the general partners filing the certificate determine.

§ 204. Execution of Certificates.

(a) Each certificate required by this Article to be filed in the office of the Secretary of State shall be executed in the following manner:

(1) an original certificate of limited partnership must be signed by all partners named therein;

(2) a certificate of amendment must be signed by at least one general partner and by each other partner designated in the certificate as a new partner or whose contribution is described as having been increased; and

(3) a certificate of cancellation must be signed by all general partners;

(b) Any person may sign a certificate by an attorney-in-fact, but a power of attorney to sign a certificate relating to the admission, or increased contribution, of a partner must specifically describe the admission or increase.

(c) The execution of a certificate by a general partner constitutes an affirmation under the penalties of perjury that the facts stated therein are true.

§ 205. Amendment or Cancellation by Judicial Act.

If a person required by Section 204 to execute a certificate of amendment or cancellation fails or refuses to do so, any other partner, and any assignee of a partnership interest, who is adversely affected by the failure or refusal, may petition the [here designate the proper court] to direct the amendment or cancellation. If the court finds that the amendment or cancellation is proper and that any person so designated has failed or refused to execute the certificate, it shall order the Secretary of State to record an appropriate certificate of amendment or cancellation.

§ 206. Filing in Office of Secretary of State.

(a) Two signed copies of the certificate of limited partnership and of any certificates of amendment or cancellation (or of any judicial decree of amendment or cancellation) shall be delivered to the Secretary of State. A person who executes a certificate as an agent or fiduciary need not exhibit evidence of his authority as a prerequisite to filing. Unless the Secretary of State finds that any certificate does not conform to law, upon receipt of all filing fees required by law he shall:

(1) endorse on each duplicate original the word "Filed" and the day, month, and year of the filing thereof;

(2) file one duplicate original in his office; and

(3) return the other duplicate original to the person who filed it or his representative.

(b) Upon the filing of a certificate or amendment (or judicial decree of amendment) in the office of the Secretary of State, the certificate of limited partnership shall be amended as set forth herein, and upon the effective date of a certificate of cancellation (or a judicial decree thereof), the certificate of limited partnership is cancelled.

§ 207. Liability for False Statement in Certificate.

If any certificate or limited partnership or certificate of amendment or cancellation contains a false statement, one who suffers loss by reliance on the statement may recover damages for the loss from:

(1) any person who executes the certificate, or causes another to execute it on his behalf, and knew,

and any general partner who knew or should have known, the statement to be false at the time the certificate was executed; and

(2) any general partner who thereafter knows or should have known that any arrangement or other fact described in the certificate has changed, making the statement inaccurate in any respect within a sufficient time before the statement was relied upon reasonably to have enabled that general partner to cancel or amend the certificate, or to file a petition for its cancellation or amendment under Section 205.

§ 208. Notice.

The fact that a certificate of limited partnership is on file in the office of the Secretary of State is notice that the partnership is a limited partnership and the persons designated therein as limited partners are limited partners, but it is not notice of any other fact.

§ 209. Delivery of Certificates to Limited Partners.

Upon the return by the Secretary of State pursuant to Section 206 of a certificate marked "Filed," the general partners shall promptly deliver or mail a copy of the certificate of limited partnership and each certificate to each limited partner unless the partnership agreement provides otherwise.

Article 3. Limited Partners

§ 301. Admission of Additional Limited Partners.

(a) After the filing of a limited partnership's original certificate of limited partnership, a person may be admitted as an additional limited partner:

(1) in the case of a person acquiring a partnership interest directly from the limited partnership, upon the compliance with the partnership agreement or, if the partnership agreement does not so provide, upon the written consent of all partners; and

(2) in the case of an assignee of a partnership interest of a partner who has the power, as provided in Section 704, to grant the assignee the right to become a limited partner, upon the exercise of that power and compliance with any conditions limiting the grant or exercise of the power.

(b) In each case under subsection (a), the person acquiring the partnership interest becomes a limited partner only upon amendment of the certificate of limited partnership reflecting that fact.

§ 302. Voting.

Subject to Section 303, the partnership agreement may grant to all or a specified group of the limited partners the right to vote (on a per capita or other basis) upon any matter.

§ 303. Liability to Third Parties.

(a) Except as provided in subsection (d), a limited partner is not liable for the obligations of a limited partnership unless he is also a general partner or, in addition to the exercise of his rights and powers as a limited partner, he takes part in the control of the business. However, if the limited partner's participation in the control of the business is not substantially the same as the exercise of the powers of a general partner, he is liable only to persons who transact business with the limited partnership with actual knowledge of his participation in control.

(b) A limited partner does not participate in the control of the business within the meaning of subsection (a) solely by doing one or more of the following:

(1) being a contractor for or an agent or employee of the limited partnership or of a general partner;

(2) consulting with and advising a general partner with respect to the business of the limited partnership;

(3) acting as surety for the limited partnership;

(4) approving or disapproving an amendment to the partnership agreement; or

(5) voting on one or more of the following matters:

(i) the dissolution and winding up of the limited partnership;

(ii) the sale, exchange, lease, mortgage, pledge, or other transfer of all or substantially all of the assets of the limited partnership other than in the ordinary course of its business;

(iii) the incurrence of indebtedness by the limited partnership other than in the ordinary course of its business;

(iv) a change in the nature of the business; or

(v) the removal of a general partner.

(c) The enumeration in subsection (b) does not mean that the possession or exercise of any other powers by a limited partner constitutes participation by him in the business of the limited partnership.

(d) A limited partner who knowingly permits his name to be used in the name of the limited partnership, except under circumstances permitted by Section 102(2)(i), is liable to creditors who extend credit to the limited partnership without actual knowledge that the limited partner is not a general partner.

§ 304. Person Erroneously Believing Himself Limited Partner.

(a) Except as provided in subsection (b), a person who makes a contribution to a business enterprise and erroneously but in good faith believes that he has become a limited partner in the enterprise is not a general partner in the enterprise and is not bound by its obligations by reason of making the contribution, receiving distributions from the enterprise, or exercising any rights of a limited partner, if, on ascertaining the mistake, he:

(1) causes an appropriate certificate of limited partnership or a certificate of amendment to be executed and filed; or

(2) withdraws from future equity participation in the enterprise.

(b) A person who makes a contribution of the kind described in subsection (a) is liable as a general partner to any third party who transacts business with the enterprise (i) before the person withdraws and an appropriate certificate is filed to show withdrawal, or (ii) before an appropriate certificate is filed to show his status as a limited partner and, in the case of an amendment, after expiration of the 30-day period for filing an amendment relating to the person as a limited partner under Section 202, but in either case only if the third party actually believed in good faith that the person was a general partner at the time of the transaction.

§ 305. Information.
Each limited partner has the right to:

(1) inspect and copy any of the partnership records required to be maintained by Section 105; and

(2) obtain from the general partners from time to time upon reasonable demand (i) true and full information regarding the state of the business and financial condition of the limited partnership, (ii) promptly after becoming available, a copy of the limited partnership's federal, state, and local income tax returns for each year, and (iii) other information regarding the affairs of the limited partnership as is just and reasonable.

Article 4. General Partners

§ 401. Admission of Additional General Partners.
After the filing of a limited partnership's original certificate of limited partnership, additional

general partners may be admitted only with the specific written consent of each partner.

§ 402. Events of Withdrawal. Except as approved by the specific written consent of all partners at the time, a person ceases to be a general partner of a limited partnership upon the happening of any of the following events:

(1) the general partner withdraws from the limited partnership as provided in Section 602;

(2) the general partner ceases to be a member of the limited partnership as provided in Section 702;

(3) the general partner is removed as a general partner in accordance with the partnership agreement;

(4) unless otherwise provided in the certificate of limited partnership, the general partner; (i) makes an assignment for the benefit of creditors; (ii) files a voluntary petition in bankruptcy; (iii) is adjudicated a bankrupt or insolvent; (iv) files a petition or answer seeking for himself any reorganization, arrangement, composition, readjustment, liquidation, dissolution, or similar relief under any statute, law, or regulation; (v) files an answer or other pleading admitting or failing to contest the material allegations of a petition filed against him in any proceeding of this nature; or (vi) seeks, consents to, or acquiesces in the appointment of a trustee, receiver, or liquidator of the general partner or of all or any substantial part of his properties;

(5) unless otherwise provided in the certificate of limited partnership, [120] days after the commencement of any proceeding against the general partner seeking reorganization, arrangement, composition, readjustment, liquidation, dissolution, or similar relief under any statute, law, or regulation, the proceeding has not been dismissed, or if within [90] days after the appointment without his consent or acquiescence of a trustee, receiver, or liquidator of the general partner or of all or any substantial part of his properties, the appointment is not vacated or stayed, or within [90] days after the expiration of any such

(6) in the case of a general partner who is a natural person,

    (i) his death; or

    (ii) the entry by a court of competent jurisdiction adjudicating him incompetent to manage his person or his estate;

(7) in the case of a general partner who is acting as a general partner by virtue of being a trustee of a trust, the termination of the trust (but not merely the substitution of a new trustee);

(8) in the case of a general partner that is a separate partnership, the dissolution and commencement of winding up of the separate partnership;

(9) in the case of a general partner that is a corporation, the filing of a certificate of dissolution, or its equivalent, for the corporation or the revocation of its charter; or

(10) in the case of an estate, the distribution by the fiduciary of the estate's entire interest in the partnership.

§ 403. General Powers and Liabilities. Except as provided in this Act or in the partnership agreement, a general partner of a limited partnership has the rights and powers and is subject to the restrictions and liabilities of a partner in a partnership without limited partners.

§ 404. Contributions by a General Partner. A general partner of a limited partnership may make contributions to the partnership and share in the profits and losses of, and in distributions from, the limited partnership as a general partner. A general partner also may make contributions to and share in profits, losses, and distributions as a limited partner. A person who is both a general partner and a limited partner has the rights and powers, and is subject to the restrictions and liabilities, of a general partner and, except as provided in the partnership agreement, also has the powers, and is subject to the restrictions, of a limited partner to the extent of his participation in the partnership as a limited partner.

§ 405. Voting. The partnership agreement may grant to all or certain identified general partners the right to vote (on a per capita or any other basis), separately or with all or any class of the limited partners, on any matter.

Article 5. Finance

§ 501. Form of Contribution. The contribution of a partner may be in cash, property, or services rendered, or a promissory note or other obligation to contribute cash or property or to perform services.

§ 502. Liability for Contributions.

    (a)   Except as provided in the certificate of limited partnership, a partner is obligated to the limited partnership to perform any promise to contribute cash or property or to perform services, even if he is unable to perform because of death, disability or any other reason. If a partner does not make the required contribution of property or services, he is obligated at the option of the limited partnership to contribute cash equal to that portion of the value (as stated in the certificate of limited partnership) of the stated contribution that has not been made.

(b) Unless otherwise provided in the partnership agreement, the obligation of a partner to make a contribution or return money or other property paid or distributed in violation of this Act may be compromised only by consent of all the partners. Notwithstanding the compromise, a creditor of a limited partnership who extends credit, or whose claim arises, after the filing of the certificate of limited partnership or an amendment thereto which, in either case, reflects the obligation, and before the amendment or cancellation thereof to reflect the compromise, may enforce the original obligation.

§ 503. Sharing of Profits and Losses. The profits and losses of a limited partnership shall be allocated among the partners, and among classes of partners, in the manner provided in the partnership agreement. If the partnership agreement does not so provide, profits and losses shall be allocated on the basis of the value (as stated in the certificate of limited partnership) of the contributions made by each partner to the extent they have been received by the partnership and have not been returned.

§ 504. Sharing of Distributions. Distributions of cash or other assets of a limited partnership shall be allocated among the partners, and among classes of partners, in the manner provided in the partnership agreement. If the partnership agreement does not so provide, distributions shall be made on the basis of the value (as stated in the certificate of limited partnership) of the contributions made by each partner to the extent they have been received by the partnership and have not been returned.

Article 6. Distributions and Withdrawal

§ 601. Interim Distributions. Except as provided in this Article, a partner is entitled to receive dis-

tributions from a limited partnership before his withdrawal from the limited partnership and before the dissolution and winding up thereof:

(1) to the extent and at the times or upon the happening of the events specified in the partnership agreement; and

(2) if any distribution constitutes a return of any part of his contribution under Section 609(c), to the extent and at the times or upon the happening of the events specified in the certificate of limited partnership.

§ 602. Withdrawal of General Partner. A general partner may withdraw from a limited partnership at any time by giving written notice to the other partners, but if the withdrawal violates the partnership agreement, the limited partnership may recover from the withdrawing general partner damages for breach of the partnership agreement and offset the damages against the amount otherwise distributable to him.

§ 603. Withdrawal of Limited Partner. A limited partner may withdraw from a limited partnership at the time or upon the happening of events specified in the certificate of limited partnership and in accordance with the partnership agreement. If the certificate does not specify the time or the events upon the happening of which a limited partner may withdraw or a definite time for the dissolution and winding up of the limited partnership, a limited partner may withdraw upon not less than 6 months' prior written notice to each general partner at his address on the books of the limited partnership at its office in this State.

§ 604. Distribution Upon Withdrawal. Except as provided in this Article, upon withdrawal any withdrawing partner is entitled to receive any distribution to which he is entitled under the partnership agreement and, if not otherwise provided in the agreement, he is entitled to receive, within a reasonable time after withdrawal, the fair value of his interest in the limited partnership as of the date of withdrawal based upon his right to share in distributions from the limited partnership.

§ 605. Distribution in Kind. Except as provided in the certificate of limited partnership, a partner, regardless of the nature of his contribution, has no right to demand and receive any distribution from a limited partnership in any form other than cash. Except as provided in the partnership agreement, a partner may not be compelled to accept a distribution of any asset in kind from a limited partnership to the extent that the percentage of the asset distributed to him exceeds a percentage of that asset which is equal to the percentage in which he shares in distributions from the limited partnership.

§ 606. Right to Distribution.   At the time a partner becomes entitled to receive a distribution, he has the status of, and is entitled to all remedies available to, a creditor of the limited partnership with respect to the distribution.

§ 607. Limitations on Distribution.   A partner may not receive a distribution from a limited partnership to the extent that, after giving effect to the distribution, all liabilities of the limited partnership, other than liabilities to partners on account of their partnership interests, exceed the fair value of the partnership assets.

§ 608. Liability Upon Return of Contribution.
  (a)   If a partner has received the return of any part of his contribution without violation of the partnership agreement or this Act, he is liable to the limited partnership for a period of one year thereafter for the amount of the returned contribution, but only to the extent necessary to discharge the limited partnership's liabilities to creditors who extended credit to the limited partnership during the period the contribution was held by the partnership.
  (b)   If a partner has received the return of any part of his contribution in violation of the partnership agreement or this Act, he is liable to the limited partnership for a period of 6 years thereafter for the amount of the contribution wrongfully returned.
  (c)   A partner receives a return of his contribution to the extent that a distribution to him reduces his share of the fair value of the net assets of the limited partnership below the value (as set forth in the certificate of limited partnership) of his contribution which has not been distributed to him.

Article 7. Assignment of Partnership Interests

§ 701. Nature of Partnership Interest.   A partnership interest is personal property.

§ 702. Assignment of Partnership Interest.   Ex-cept as provided in the partnership agreement, a partnership interest is assignable in whole or in part. An assignment of a partnership interest does not dissolve a limited partnership or entitle the assignee to become or to exercise any rights of a partner. An assignment entitles the assignee to receive, to the extent assigned, only the distribution to which the assignor would be entitled. Except as provided in the partnership agreement, a partner ceases to be a partner upon assignment of all his partnership interest.

§ 703. Rights of Creditor.   On application to a court of competent jurisdiction by any judgment creditor of a partner, the court may charge the partnership interest of the partner with payment of the unsatisfied amount of the judgment with interest. To the extent so charged, the judgment creditor has only the rights of an assignee of the partnership interest. This Act does not deprive any partner of the benefit of any exemption laws applicable to his partnership interest.

§ 704. Right of Assignee to Become Limited Partner.
  (a) An assignee of a partnership interest, including an assignee of a general partner, may become a limited partner if and to the extent that (1) the assignor gives the assignee that right in accordance with authority described in the certificate of limited partnership, or (2) all other partners consent.
  (b) An assignee who has become a limited partner has, to the extent assigned, the rights and powers, and is subject to the restrictions and liabilities, of a limited partner under the partnership agreement and this Act. An assignee who becomes a limited partner also is liable for the obligations of his assignor to make and return contributions as provided in Article 6. However, the assignee is not obligated for liabilities unknown to the assignee at the time he became a limited partner and which could not be ascertained from the certificate of limited partnership.
  (c) If an assignee of a partnership interest becomes a limited partner, the assignor is not released from his liability to the limited partnership under Sections 207 and 502.

§ 705. Power of Estate of Deceased or Incompetent Partner.   If a partner who is an individual dies or a court of competent jurisdiction adjudges him to be incompetent to manage his person or his property, the partner's executor, administrator, guardian, conservator, or other legal representative may exercise all of the partner's rights for the purpose of settling his estate or administering his property, including any power the partner had to give an assignee the right to become a limited partner. If a partner is a corporation, trust, or other entity and is dissolved or terminated, the powers of that partner may be exercised by its legal representative or successor.

Article 8. Dissolution

§ 801. Nonjudicial Dissolution. A limited partnership is dissolved and its affairs shall be wound up upon the happening of the first to occur of the following:

(1) at the time or upon the happening of events specified in the certificate of limited partnership;

(2) written consent of all partners;

(3) an event of withdrawal of a general partner unless at the time there is at least one other general partner and the certificate of limited partnership permits the business of the limited partnership to be carried on by the remaining general partner and that partner does so, but the limited partnership is not dissolved and is not required to be wound up by reason of any event of withdrawal if, within 90 days after the withdrawal, all partners agree in writing to continue the business of the limited partnership and to the appointment of one or more additional general partners if necessary or desired; or

(4) entry of a decree of judicial dissolution under Section 802.

§ 802. Judicial Dissolution. On application by or for a partner the [here designate the proper court] court may decree dissolution of a limited partnership whenever it is not reasonably practicable to carry on the business in conformity with the partnership agreement.

§ 803. Winding Up. Except as provided in the partnership agreement, the general partners who have not wrongfully dissolved a limited partnership or, if none, the limited partners, may wind up the limited partnership's affairs: but the [here designate the proper court] court may wind up the limited partnership's affairs upon application of any partner, his legal representative, or assignee.

§ 804. Distribution of Assets. Upon the winding up of a limited partnership, the assets shall be distributed as follows:

(1) to creditors, including partners who are creditors, to the extent otherwise permitted by law, in satisfaction of liabilities of the limited partnership other than liabilities for distributions to partners under Section 601 or 604;

(2) except as provided in the partnership agreement, to partners and former partners in satisfaction of liabilities for distributions under Section 601 or 604; and

(3) except as provided in the partnership agreement, to partners *first* for the return of their contributions and *secondly* respecting their partnership interests, in the proportions in which the partners share in distributions.

Article 9. Foreign Limited Partnerships

§ 901. Law Governing. Subject to the Constitution of this State, (1) the laws of the state under which a foreign limited partnership is organized govern its organization and internal affairs and the liability of its limited partners, and (2) a foreign limited partnership may not be denied registration by reason of any difference between those laws and the laws of this State.

§ 902. Registration. Before transacting business in this State, a foreign limited partnership shall register with the Secretary of State. In order to register, a foreign limited partnership shall submit to the Secretary of State, in duplicate, an application for registration as a foreign limited partnership, signed and sworn to by a general partner and setting forth:

(1) the name of the foreign limited partnership and, if different, the name under which it proposes to register and transact business in this State;

(2) the state and date of its formation;

(3) the general character of the business it proposes to transact in this State;

(4) the name and address of any agent for service of process on the foreign limited partnership whom the foreign limited partnership elects to appoint; the agent must be an individual resident of this State, a domestic corporation, or a foreign corporation having a place of business in, and authorized to do business in this State;

(5) a statement that the Secretary of State is appointed the agent of the foreign limited partnership for service of process if no agent has been appointed under paragraph (4) or, if appointed, the agent's authority has been revoked or if the agent cannot be found or served with the exercise of reasonable diligence;

(6) the address of the office required to be maintained in the State of its organization by the laws of that State or, if not so required, of the principal office of the foreign limited partnership; and

(7) if the certificate or limited partnership filed in the foreign limited partnership's state of organization is not required to include the names and business addresses of the partners, a list of the names and addresses.

§ 903. Issuance of Registration.

(a) If the Secretary of State finds that an application for registration conforms to law and all requisite fees have been paid, he shall:

(1) endorse on the application the word "Filed", and the month, day, and year of the filing thereof;

(2) file in his office a duplicate original of the application; and

(3) issue a certificate of registration to transact business in this State.

(b) The certificate of registration, together with a duplicate original of the application, shall be returned to the person who filed the application or his representative.

§ 904. Name.
A foreign limited partnership may register with the Secretary of State under any name (whether or not it is the name under which it is registered in its state of organization) that includes without abbreviation the words "limited partnership" and that could be registered by a domestic limited partnership.

§ 905. Changes and Amendments.
If any statement in the application for registration of a foreign limited partnership was false when made or any arrangements or other facts described have changed, maing the application inaccurate in any respect, the foreign limited partnership shall promptly file in the office of the Secretary of State a certificate, signed and sworn to by a general partner, correcting such statement.

§ 906. Cancellation or Registration.
A foreign limited partnership may cancel its registration by filing with the Secretary of State a certificate of cancellation signed and sworn to by a general partner. A cancellation does not terminate the authority of the Secretary of State to accept service of process on the foreign limited partnership with respect to [claims for relief] [causes of action] arising out of the transactions of business in this State.

§ 907. Transaction of Business Without Registration.

(a)   A foreign limited partnership transacting business in this State may not maintain any action, suit, or proceeding in any court of this State until it has registered in this State.

(b)   The failure of a foreign limited partnership to register in this State does not impair the validity of any contract or act of the foreign limited partnership or prevent the foreign limited partnership from defending any action, suit, or proceeding in any court of this State.

(c)   A limited partner of a foreign limited partnership is not liable as a general partner of the foreign limited partnership solely by reason of having transacted business in this State without registration.

(d)   A foreign limited partnership, by transacting business in this State without registration, appoints the Secretary of State as its agent for service of process with respect to [claims for relief] [causes of action] arising out of the transaction of business in this State.

§ 908. Action by Appropriate Official.
The [appropriate official] may bring an action to restrain a foreign limited partnership from transacting business in this State in violation of this Article.

Article 10. Derivative Actions

§ 1001. Right of Action.
A limited partner may bring an action in the right of a limited partnership to recover a judgment in its favor if general partners with authority to do so have refused to bring the action or if an effort to cause those general partners to bring the action is not likely to succeed.

§ 1002. Proper Plaintiff.
In a derivative action, the plaintiff must be a partner at the time of bringing the action and (1) at the time of the transaction of which he complains or 2) his status as a partner had devolved upon him by operation of law or pursuant to the terms of the partnership agreement from a person who was a partner at the time of the transaction.

§ 1003. Pleading.
In a derivative action, the complaint shall set forth with particularity the effort of

the plaintiff to secure initation of the action by a general partner or the reasons for not making the effort.

§ 1004. Expenses.   If a derivative action is successful, in whole or in part, or if anything is received by the plaintiff as a result of a judgment, compromise, or settlement of an action or claim, the court may award the plaintiff reasonable expenses, including reasonable attorney's fees, and shall direct him to remit to the limited partnership the remainder of those proceeds received by him.

Article 11. Miscellaneous

§ 1101. Construction and Application.   This Act shall be so applied and construed to effectuate its general purpose to make uniform the law with respect to the subject of this Act among states enacting it.

§ 1102. Short Title.   This Act may be cited as the Uniform Limited Partnership Act.

§ 1103. Severability.   If any provision of this Act or its application to any person or circumstance is held invalid, the invalidity does not affect other provisions or applications of the Act which can be given effect without the invalid provision or application, and to this end the provisions of this Act are serverable.

§ 1104. Effective Date, Extended Effective Date and Repeal.   Except as set forth below, the effective date of this Act is _____ and the following Acts [list prior limited partnership acts] are hereby repealed:

(1) The existing provisions for execution and filing of certificates of limited partnerships and amendments thereunder and cancellations thereof continue in effect until [specify time required to create central filing system], the extended effective date, and Sections 102, 103, 104, 105, 201, 202, 203, 204 and 206 are not effective until the extended effective date.

(2) Section 402, specifying the conditions under which a general partner ceases to be a member of a limited partnership, is not effective until the extended effective date, and the applicable provisions of existing law continue to govern until the extended effective date.

(3) Sections 501, 502 and 608 apply only to contributions and distributions made after the effective date of this Act.

(4) Section 704 applies only to assignments made after the effective date of this Act.

(5) Article 9, dealing with registration of foreign limited partnerships, is not effective until the extended effective date.

§ 1105. Rules for Cases Not Provided for in This Act.   In any case not provided for in this Act the provisions of the Uniform Partnership Act govern.

Glossary

Abstract of Title A summary of the condition of the title to property based on an examination of public records.

Abuse of Process A tort, the basis of which is a person's intentional use of a proper legal procedure for an improper purpose.

Acceleration Clause A clause, usually in a promissory note or installment contract, providing that if the debtor fails to make a payment when it is due or breaches any other covenant in the instrument, the balance of the obligation can be declared immediately due and payable.

Acceptance The offeree's assent to an offer as made by an offeror, as a result of which an agreement is made and the parties become bound as contracting parties.

Accord and Satisfaction A method of discharging a contract. An accord is an agreement by the parties to the contract to give and accept some performance different than that originally promised; a satisfaction is the actual performance of the substituted obligation.

Accounting The act or system of recording, auditing, and balancing a business' financial transactions and verifying and reporting the results; a legal proceeding to settle the accounts of parties to a business transaction under court supervision.

Adhesion Contract A contract drafted unilaterally, then presented on a take-it-or-leave-it basis to a weaker party who has no true opportunity to bargain about its terms.

Administrative Law The branch of law dealing with the operation and actions of administrative agencies.

Adverse Possession A method of acquiring real property based on an adverse or hostile, continued use of another person's property for a statutorily prescribed period of time.

Affirmative Action A policy, often adopted by or imposed on an employer, that is designed to overcome the effects of past or present discrimination against one or more classes of persons.

Agency A fiduciary relationship that arises when one person (the principal) entrusts to another person (the agent) the management of some business to be transacted in the principal's name or on his account and under his control, and by which the agent assumes to do the business and render an account of it.

Agency by Necessity An agency that arises when an emergency makes it necessary or proper for one person to act as another's agent even though he lacks express authority to do so.

Agent A party to the agency relationship; the person who acts on behalf of and represents the other party (the principal).

Alter Ego Doctrine A doctrine under which a corporate entity is disregarded, the corporation and its primary or sole shareholder being treated as one and the same.

Annual Percentage Rate (APR) Essentially, the cost of consumer credit for one year, expressed as a percentage.

Anticipatory Breach Breach of contract committed before the time for performance of the contract has arrived.

Antitrust A term used to describe the area of the law that is concerned with preserving competition in the marketplace by breaking up trusts or otherwise limiting the power of their members.

Apparent Authority An agent's authority that, although not expressly granted by the principal, the principal either allows the agent to have or holds the agent out to third persons as having.

Appraisal   An estimate of the real or market value of real estate or other property.

Appraisal Right   The right of dissident or minority shareholders who object to a corporate merger or other fundamental change to have their shares appraised and to receive the appraised value in cash.

Appurtenance   Anything incidental or belonging to land that is considered part of the real property, such as an improvement or easement.

Arbitration   A method of resolving a dispute by which the dispute is brought before a private person (the arbitrator) chosen by both parties to hear the case. An arbitrator's award is enforceable by a court.

Articles of Incorporation   The publicly filed document of a corporation giving it power to transact business.

Assignment   A transfer of a right or interest.

Assignment for Creditors   A debtor relief device by which a debtor transfers property to a third person who liquidates the property and pays off creditors to the extent possible; also known as an assignment for the benefit of creditors.

Assumption of Mortgage   A buyer's acceptance of responsibility for an outstanding indebtedness secured by real property, in connection with his taking title to that property.

Assumption of Risk   A defense to a negligence action. Its basis is that the plaintiff voluntarily encountered a known danger and, by his conduct, expressly or impliedly consented to accept the risk.

Attachment   A prejudgment remedy by which a person suing on a debt has property of the debtor seized so it may later be used to satisfy a judgment.

Attachment of Security Interest   Under UCC Article 9, the process by which a security interest is created.

Attractive Nuisance Doctrine   The doctrine that a landowner who creates or maintains a condition that attracts children but is dangerous to them owes a duty to protect children coming on the land, even if they are trespassers.

At-Will Contract   A contract, frequently of employment, having no specified term and termina-

ble at the will of either party at any time on notice to the other.

Audit   In the accounting sense, an examination of a business' financial records and preparation of a report on its financial condition; in tax law, the process by which a taxpayer's tax return is examined by the taxing authority and the taxpayer is required to substantiate disputed items.

Bailee's Lien   The lien that a bailee has on bailed property for the reasonable value of his services with respect to the property.

Bailment   The relationship arising when an owner of personal property temporarily transfers possession of the property to another, usually for a particular purpose. A bailment can be for the sole benefit of either party or for the mutual benefit of both parties.

Bankruptcy   A federal statutory scheme by which a financially troubled debtor places his property under a court's control, after which either the property is liquidated and creditors are paid to the extent possible, or a plan for the debtor's financial rehabilitation is prepared and executed.

Beneficiary   A person entitled to receive a benefit under a contract, trust, or will; in insurance law, the person entitled to the insurance proceeds on occurrence of the event insured against.

Bill of Lading   A document of title or receipt issued by a land or marine shipper evidencing the receipt of goods for shipment.

Binder   A temporary contract of insurance intended to operate for a short time and couched in brief and general terms to be supplanted later by an insurance policy in which all of the contractual terms are set forth in detail.

Blank Indorsement   An indorsement that specifies no particular indorsee.

Blue-Sky Laws   State statutes regulating the sale of securities.

Board of Directors   The group of persons elected by shareholders of a corporation who are entrusted with the responsibility for managing the corporation.

Bona Fide Purchaser   One who gives a valuable consideration for property and is unaware of any defect in the seller's title.

Bond   A corporate promise to pay a fixed amount

of indebtedness secured by the assets of the corporation; any undertaking in writing binding one party to pay a fixed sum on the happening of a specified event.

Bonus Stock   Stock issued by a corporation without valid consideration.

Breach of Warranty   The breaking of or failure to live up to the terms of an express or implied warranty.

Bribery   A crime that consists of making a gift to a public official for the purpose of influencing the official in his official actions; also, the official's acceptance of such a gift.

Brief   A concise statement of legal issues and authorities prepared by a lawyer, usually for submission to an appellate court.

Bulk Transfer   Under UCC Article 6, the transfer, in a single transaction that is not in the ordinary course of the transferor's business, of a major part of the goods of a transferor whose principal business is the sale of merchandise from stock.

Business Judgment Rule   A judicial doctrine of noninterference in management of corporate affairs on questions of policy, contracts, dividends, executive compensation, and other internal corporate matters.

Bylaws   A document consisting of the internal regulations of a corporation and that, unlike the articles of incorporation, need not be filed with the state.

Capital   The net worth of a corporation. It consists of the sums subscribed and paid in by shareholders, together with all gains or profits arising from corporate operations, minus any losses that have been sustained.

Capital Stock   The declared money value of the outstanding stock of a corporation. It is the amount of money, property, or other assets authorized by the articles of incorporation and contributed, or agreed to be contributed, by the shareholders, and it forms the financial basis of corporate operations. As commonly used, the term refers to a corporation's issued and outstanding stock.

Carmack Amendment   A portion of the Interstate Commerce Act that codifies the common-law rule that a common carrier, although not an absolute

insurer of goods transported, is liable for damage or loss to such goods unless the carrier can show that damage was caused by an act of God, the public enemy, an act of the shipper, an act by public authorities, or the inherent nature of the goods themselves.

Case Law   A rule of law expressed in a judicial decision, rather than in a constitution, statute, ordinance, or regulation.

Cease and Desist Order   An order issued by an administrative agency requiring that practices specified in the order be stopped.

Chain of Title   The chronological list of recorded instruments affecting title to land, beginning with the earliest evidence of ownership and concluding with the latest.

Chapter 11 Plan   A debtor rehabilitation plan prepared in a proceeding under Chapter 11 of the Bankruptcy Code.

Chapter 13 Plan   A debtor rehabilitation plan prepared in a proceeding under Chapter 13 of the Bankruptcy Code.

Charge-Back   Under UCC Article 4, the process by which a collecting bank reverses a provisional credit given earlier on a deposited check that has been dishonored.

Charter   As commonly used, a corporation's articles of incorporation, although the term also includes the statutes and other laws giving the corporation power to act.

Chattel Mortgage   A mortgage on personal property.

Chattels   Personal property that is visible, tangible, and capable of being moved.

Civil Action   An action brought to enforce a private right, as distinguished from a criminal action.

Civil Liability   Liability to be sued in a civil action, as distinguished from criminal liability.

Civil Rights   Broadly, all rights the law will enforce; in the more restricted sense, rights created by state and federal constitutional and statutory provisions designed to prevent discrimination by reason of a person's age, race, color, sex, religion, or national origin.

Class Action   A lawsuit brought by one or more persons on behalf of a larger group of persons, all having a common interest in the subject of the lawsuit.

Clifford Trust   An irrevocable living trust having a term of more than 10 years. It is primarily a tax-planning tool.

Close Corporation   A corporation owned by a small number of shareholders and the shares of which are not offered for sale to the public.

Closed-End Credit   Consumer credit extended in a single transaction rather than on a continuing basis.

Closing   The completion of a real estate transaction as evidenced by the escrow agent's delivery of a deed to the buyer and his contemporaneous transfer to the seller of the balance of the purchase price remaining after payment of all charges assessed against the seller.

Cloud on Title   A claim, or some semblance of title, that appears to be in legal form but is in fact invalid.

Code of Federal Regulations (CFR)   An official federal publication setting forth the rules and regulations of the federal administrative agencies.

Codicil   A document executed with the same formalities as a will and used to change the terms of a will.

Collateral   Under UCC Article 9, the property in which a security interest exists; in a broader sense, any property used as security for an extension of credit.

Collecting Bank   Under UCC Article 4, any bank in the collection chain other than the payor bank.

Collective Bargaining Agreement   An agreement reached by bargaining as to wages and working conditions, entered into between a union and an employer.

Commerce Clause   The provision of the United States Constitution (Art. I, § 8, cl. 3) that grants to Congress the power to regulate commerce with foreign nations and among the states.

Commercial Block Policy   A comprehensive insurance policy that insures against several basic, but different, types of risk with respect to commercial property.

Commercial Paper   Various types of paper that represent cash value in commercial transactions. Commercial paper includes orders to pay money (drafts and checks) and promises to pay money (notes and certificates of deposit), and it can be negotiable or nonnegotiable.

Common Carrier   A bailee who engages in the business of transporting persons or property from place to place for compensation.

Common Law   Legal principles, rules, and usages based on court decisions rather than on statutes or a constitution; in a broader sense, the general Anglo-American system of legal concepts forming the basis of the law of most states.

Common Stock   The most common type of equity security. The issuance of common stock is a basic corporate financing device. The owner of one or more shares has the right to participate in the control of the corporation, in surplus and profits, and in the distribution of corporate assets on dissolution.

Community Property   A system of property rights, adopted in eight western states, under which the earnings of a spouse belong to the "community," which is the entity of husband and wife.

Comparative Negligence   The apportionment of damages between negligent parties in proportion to their respective fault.

Composition with Creditors   A contractual debtor relief arrangement under which creditors agree to accept in full satisfaction of the debts owed to them less than is actually due.

Concealment   The failure to disclose a fact that a person knows and, under the circumstances, should communicate to another. In insurance law, the intentional withholding of any fact material to the risk that the insured in honesty and good faith ought to communicate to the insurer.

Condemnation   The taking of private property for public use through exercise of the power of eminent domain.

Condition   A provision in a contract that makes a party's duty to perform contingent on the occurrence or nonoccurrence of some event. A condition precedent is one that must occur as a prerequisite to a party's duty to perform. A condition subsequent is one that relieves a party of an obligation to perform, while a condition concurrent requires simultaneous performance by the parties.

Conditional Sale   A sale on credit according to the terms of which the seller retains title to the goods sold until the entire purchase price is paid.

Consent Decree   A court judgment or decree that

is based on a stipulation by the parties to a lawsuit, usually criminal in nature, commenced by a government entity. The stipulation sets forth the remedy or relief that the court should order, but without an acknowledgment of guilt by the defendant.

Consideration The promises or performances that the parties to a contract exchange with each other and on which the contract is based.

Consignment A bailment by which goods are delivered to another with the understanding that the recipient will either sell the goods for the owner or return the goods if they are not sold. The person delivering the goods is the consignor, while the person receiving them is the consignee.

Consolidation The formation of a new corporation by the combination of two or more existing corporations.

Constitution Generally, a system of fundamental laws or principles for governing a nation, state, or society. See also *United States Constitution*.

Constructive Eviction A substantial interference with a tenant's possession by a landlord that either renders premises unfit for the purposes for which they were leased or deprives the tenant of the enjoyment of the premises.

Constructive Notice Circumstances deemed by the law to be the equivalent of actual notice.

Consumer In a broad sense, any individual or business buying or leasing goods or services for consumption or use. In the sense used in consumer credit protection legislation, the term refers to an individual who uses goods or services for personal, family, or household purposes, rather than for business purposes.

Consumer Goods or Services Goods or services bought primarily for personal, family, or household purposes.

Consumer Report Under the federal Fair Credit Reporting Act, a report about a consumer's credit standing and related matters, and which is used in determining the consumer's eligibility for credit, insurance, or employment.

Consumer-Reporting Agency Under the federal Fair Credit Reporting Act, a credit agency that prepares consumer reports.

Contract An agreement, based on consideration, to do or refrain from doing a particular lawful thing.

Contributory Negligence A plaintiff's conduct that contributes to his own harm and falls below the required standard of care.

Conversion The intentional and wrongful acquisition, damage, use, or withholding of the property of another. The interest protected is that of possession or control of property.

Convertible Security Any equity or debt security that can be changed into another type of security.

Conveyance In common usage, a deed transferring title to land; in its broadest sense, any transfer of real or personal property or an interest in it.

Copyright A person's basic right in the tangible expression of his creative works against anyone who deprives him of such works by copying or wrongfully reproducing or using them. See also *Statutory Copyright*.

Corporate Opportunity Doctrine A common law legal doctrine imposing on corporate officers and directors a duty of loyalty to the corporation they serve to refrain from appropriating for personal benefit a business opportunity that properly belongs to the corporation.

Corporation An association of persons, created under a statute as a legal entity, vested with authority to act separately from its members.

Corporation by Estoppel A business organization that, although not having complied with state incorporation laws, holds itself out as a corporation and therefore is prevented from denying its corporate status.

Course and Scope of Employment A term that describes any activity of an employee that is a required or authorized part of the employee's job. The question whether a given activity was within the course and scope of employment usually arises in cases involving an employee's right to workers' compensation benefits or an employer's liability under the respondeat superior doctrine.

Covenant A promise, usually that the person making it will do or refrain from doing something.

Covenant Not to Compete A provision in an employment contract by which the employee agrees, within prescribed limits, not to compete with the employer after leaving the employer's business. Also, a similar provision in a contract for the sale of a business, limiting the seller's activities after the sale.

Covenant of Quiet Enjoyment A covenant or promise that the grantee of land or an interest in it shall have legal and peaceful possession.

Covenant Running with the Land A covenant in a deed, the legal effect of which is binding on subsequent purchasers, although they have not contractually assumed any responsibility or obligation for its performance.

Credit Life Insurance Term insurance carried by a debtor in connection with a credit transaction and of which the creditor is the beneficiary.

Crime An offense against society for which the government can seek redress by instituting a criminal prosecution against the accused.

Criminal Law That branch of law concerned with prosecuting and defending persons accused of having committed crimes.

Cumulative Voting The method of voting for corporate directors whereby each shareholder can cast a number of votes equal to the number of his shares multiplied by the number of directors to be elected, with the option of giving all his votes to a single candidate or of distributing them among two or more candidates.

Customer List A list of names of customers of a particular business or of persons who have demonstrated their preference for a particular product or service. Such a list is usually entitled to protection against use or disclosure as a trade secret.

Damages Money that the law awards as pecuniary compensation for an injury done or other loss sustained as a result of another's wrongful conduct.

Debenture An unsecured corporate promise to pay a fixed amount of money back only by the general credit of the corporation.

Declaratory Judgment A type of equitable legal procedure in which a person can petition a court to resolve a question before he sustains actual injury.

Dedication Donation of land by the owner for public use.

Deductible In insurance law, the initial amount of a loss that must be paid by the insured, the insurer then paying for the balance of the loss, up to the limit specified in the policy.

Deed A written instrument used to pass legal title of real property from one person to another. It is ordinarily recorded to provide public notice of the transaction.

Deed of Trust Essentially, a three-party mortgage. The owner (trustor) conveys property to a trustee to hold for the benefit of the lender (beneficiary) to secure payment of a debt or obligation owed to the beneficiary.

De Facto Corporation A corporation that has not complied with all the mandatory requirements to obtain de jure status. It is an apparent corporation, asserted to be a corporation by its members, and actually acting as such, but lacking legal sanction.

Defamation Injury to a person's reputation by the publication of false statements, usually tending to expose the person to hatred, ridicule, or contempt.

Default The nonperformance of a duty arising under a note, mortgage, deed of trust, security agreement, or contract.

Defendant The party against whom a civil lawsuit or criminal action is brought.

Deficiency Judgment A judgment for the portion of a secured debt that remains outstanding after the collateral has been sold and any available proceeds have been applied to the debt.

De Jure Corporation A corporation that has been regularly created in strict compliance with all the mandatory legal conditions for incorporation.

Depositary Bank Under UCC Article 4, the bank in which a check or other item is deposited.

Deposition An oral, out-of-court, pretrial examination of a party or witness under oath, that is recorded by an official court reporter.

Deposit Receipt A form of contract employed by real estate brokers in initiating the purchase and sale of real estate; so called because it takes the form of a firm offer made by a prospective buyer to the owner for the purchase of his property, accompanied by a money deposit.

Derivative Action An action initiated on behalf of a corporation by one or more shareholders. The derivative action is one that the corporation itself could bring, but for some reason does not do so.

Discharge of Debtor Under the Bankruptcy Code, the freeing of a debtor from liability on certain debts, whether paid or not.

Disclosed Principal In agency law, a principal whose existence and identity are known by a party who is dealing with the agent.

Dishonor Under UCC Article 4, a payor bank's refusal to pay a check or other item.

Disparagement See *Trade Libel.*

Dissolution Any change in the partnership relation that ultimately culminates in its termination; an event that necessarily leads to the termination of a corporation's existence.

Dividend A division of profits among shareholders set apart by the board of directors from a corporation's net earnings or surplus funds to be paid to the shareholders in money, stock, or other property.

Dominant Tenement Land obtaining the benefit of an easement appurtenant.

Down Payment The cash that a buyer must pay initially in making a purchase, the balance of the price being covered by a loan or other credit arrangement.

Draft A negotiable instrument that is a written direction that a designated party pay a stated amount of money. An example of a draft is a check.

Dual Purpose Doctrine A doctrine under which a travelling employee's injury is considered to have occurred in the course and scope of employment even though, at the time of the injury, the employee was serving some purpose of his own. The only requirement is that the employee's work have created the need for the trip.

Due Care Care that a reasonably prudent individual would exercise under the particular circumstances.

Due-on-Sale Clause A clause in a mortgage or deed of trust providing that if the mortgagor or trustor sells or transfers the property, the balance of the secured obligation can be declared immediately due.

Due Process Those principles implicit in the concept of ordered liberty and so rooted in the traditions and conscience of the American people as to be considered fundamental. Every person's right to due process of law is guaranteed by the United States Constitution as to both the federal government (Fifth Amendment) and the states (Fourteenth Amendment).

Easement A limited, nonpossessory right or interest in land of another entitling the holder to some use, privilege, or benefit from the land.

Easement Appurtenant An easement created for the benefit of a parcel of land.

Easement in Gross An easement created for the benefit of an individual apart from ownership of land. An example is a public utility easement.

Electronic Funds Transfer (EFT) A cashless transfer of money made by use of an electronic terminal, a telephone, a computer, or magnetic tape.

Eminent Domain The governmental power to take private property for public use, limited only by the Fifth Amendment to the United States Constitution, which requires that compensation be given for property so taken.

Encumbrance A right to or interest in real property that reduces the interest of the property owner. A common example is a mortgage.

Enironmental Impact Statement A report, prepared in compliance with the National Environmental Policy Act, that analyzes the effect that federal legislation and other major federal actions will have on the environment.

Equal Employment Opportunity Commission (EEOC) A federal administrative agency established by Congress under Title VII of the Civil Rights Act of 1964. Its function is to enforce Title VII, which forbids employment discrimination.

Equitable Mortgage An instrument that, although technically invalid as a mortgage because it fails to meet some legal requirement, is nonetheless treated as a mortgage by the courts.

Equity of Redemption The right of a mortgagor to redeem his property after some covenant of the mortgage has been breached, usually by failing to make a payment when due, and the mortgagee has elected to exercise its rights under an acceleration clause.

Equity Security A security that represents a shareholder's interest in a corporation rather than a creditor's interest.

Escrow The conditional delivery of a written instrument or deed to a third party who delivers it unconditionally to a grantee or transferee on the happening of a specified condition or event. The third party who holds the instrument for delivery is the escrow holder or escrow agent.

Estate   The degree, quantity, nature, and extent of a person's interest in real property; in a broader sense, all the property a person owns at a given time.

Estate at Sufferance   A type of tenancy by which a person goes into possession of property lawfully, but later occupies it without right or title.

Estate at Will   A tenancy for an indefinite period of time at the pleasure of both the lessor and lessee.

Estate by Entireties   A term referring to the estate held by a husband and wife as co-owners with the right of survivorship (surviving spouse takes entire estate).

Estate Planning   An activity intended to identify and increase a person's estate, minimize loss through taxation, and allow disposition of the estate in the manner desired by the person.

Estoppel   A bar precluding a person from denying or asserting anything, even if true, to the contrary of what has been represented. Its essential elements are the misleading of a party entitled to rely on the acts or statements in question, and that party's consequent change of position to his detriment.

Eviction   A landlord's act that deprives a tenant of possession, expels him from the premises, or deprives him of enjoyment of the premises.

Excess Insurance   Insurance that covers only loss or damage in excess of the coverage provided by one or more other insurance policies.

Exclusive Agency   A term that embraces several different relationships between a principal and an agent. For example, in a sales agency, the principal might be permitted to make direct sales yet be deprived of the right to appoint other agents; or the agent might be the only person with any right to sell; or the agent might have the right to commissions on all sales, whether made through the agent or not.

Ex-Dividend   Without dividend. The term is used to describe corporate stock that is sold or transferred soon after a dividend was declared and does not carry with it the right to receive the dividend.

Execute   To sign a deed or other document; to perform a contract.

Executed Contract   A contract completely performed by both parties.

Execution   A statutory method by which payment of a money judgment can be enforced, the judgment debtor's property being seized and sold, and the sale proceeds applied to the judgment debt; in a broader sense, the act of signing a document or having performed a contract.

Executive Agreement   An agreement made by the President of the United States, acting within his exclusive powers as the Chief Executive, with the authorized representative of a foreign government.

Executory Contract   A contract that has not yet been performed.

Exemplary Damages   Damages awarded to a victim as a civil penalty against the wrongdoer rather than to compensate the victim for his loss; also known as punitive damages.

Exempt Property   A debtor's property that is not subject to the claims of his creditors.

Exhaustion of Administrative Remedies   With respect to a person's obtaining judicial review of an administrative order, that person's having first used all available administrative appeal procedures without success.

Express Agency   An agency created as the result of an express oral or written agreement between a principal and an agent.

Express Warranty   In sales law, a warranty that is written or orally stated rather than being implied; in insurance law, an agreement set forth in an insurance policy by which the insured stipulates that certain facts relating to the risk are or will be true or that certain acts relating to the risk have been or will be done.

Factor   A person in the business of selling goods on consignment; also called a commission merchant.

Fair Use Doctrine   The doctrine that permits a person to use a reasonable portion of a copyrighted work, even without the author's permission, when necessary for a legitimate purpose that is not competitive with the copyright owner's market for his work, such as to parody, review, or criticize the copyrighted work.

False Advertising   The making of fraudulent misrepresentations about a product, resulting in injury to competitors or customers.

False Arrest   The unlawful restraint by one person of the physical liberty of another under an asserted legal authority to enforce processes of law.

False Imprisonment   The detention of a person for a given period, the person being aware of the detention, and the detaining person's intent being to obstruct or detain the other person without privilege or the other person's consent.

Federal Register   A daily official federal publication of proposed and approved executive, legislative, and administrative regulations and actions.

Federal Trade Commission (FTC)   A federal administrative agency empowered to prevent the use of methods or practices declared unlawful by the Federal Trade Commission Act. The FTC is also partly responsible for enforcing federal antitrust laws.

Fee Simple   The estate in real property that gives the owner the greatest possible right to and control over the property.

Fellow Servant Doctrine   The common-law rule that absolves an employer from liability to one engaged in his employment for injuries incurred solely as the result of the negligence of others who are in the service of the employer and engaged in the same general employment.

Felony   A criminal offense punishable by state or federal imprisonment for more than one year.

Fiduciary   A person, such as a trustee, who holds a position of trust and confidence in a relationship with one or more other persons.

Finance Charge   Essentially, the total cost of credit; a term that must be used in credit transactions governed by the federal Truth in Lending Act.

Financing Statement   Under UCC Article 9, the document filed to perfect a security interest.

First Mortgage   A first lien on property pledged as security, the holder of which has rights superior to the rights of any other mortgagee.

Fixture   Personal property that has been attached to real property and become a part of it.

Floating Lien   A lien on inventory or other property that is changing or apt to change.

Foreclosure   The legal process by which a mortgagor or other debtor is deprived of his interest in property covered by a mortgage or other security arrangement. It usually occurs because of a default in paying the secured debt.

Foreign Corporation   A corporation created by or organized under the laws of another state or country.

Forfeiture   An action by a state to terminate a corporation's existence because of a violation of law, the failure to observe a provision or condition contained in its articles of incorporation, or the commission of other illegal acts.

Franchise   A system of marketing by which the developer of a product or service (the franchisor) grants to another person (the franchisee) an exclusive right to market the product or service under the franchisor's trademark or trade name through a marketing plan in a given area for a specified period of time.

Fraud   Deceit, deception, or trickery operating prejudicially on the rights of another and inducing him to part with property or surrender some legal right.

Fraudulent Conveyance   A transaction by which an owner transfers property or a property right to another to hinder, delay, or defraud the transferor's creditors.

Freedom of Information Act   Federal legislation allowing access to most public records, and setting forth the procedure for obtaining that access.

Freeze Out   The process by which the influence of minority shareholders is eliminated by other shareholders through their use of inside information, powers of control, or stategic position in the corporation.

Freight Forwarder   A person in the business of arranging for the transportation of one or more consignors' goods.

Fungible Goods   Goods of such nature that one unit is identical to and replaceable by another unit. The classic example is grain.

Future Interest   A property interest that, although presently in existence, will not come into the possession of or be enjoyed by the holder until some time in the future.

Garnishment   A prejudgment remedy by which a person suing on a debt can have withheld from the debtor property that, although owned by or owed to the debtor, is in someone else's possession.

Gift A transfer of real or personal property to another without consideration.

Going Public The process by which a close corporation offers its stock for sale to the public. It requires either compliance with the registration and prospectus provisions of the Securities Act of 1933 or the availability of one of the act's exemptions.

Good Faith Fairness and equity; acting with a sincere belief that the accomplishment intended is neither unlawful nor harmful to another.

Goods Under UCC Article 9, all tangible personal property; in a broader sense, merchandise held for sale.

Good Samaritan Legislation Legislation to the effect that a doctor or nurse who aids a stranger in an emergency will not be held liable for negligence.

Gratuitous Bailment A bailment for which neither the bailee nor the bailor receives compensation.

Gross Negligence The equivalent of a conscious and deliberate disregard of a high probability that someone will be injured; a state of mind between negligence and intention.

Group Insurance Insurance that covers a number of individuals by means of a single or blanket insurance policy.

Guest Statute Legislation making a driver liable to a guest passenger (one not paying a fare) only for injuries resulting from the driver's gross negligence.

Highest and Best Use The use of property that is capable of producing the greatest net investment return to the owner.

Holder Any person in possession of a bill or note payable, issued, or indorsed to him.

Holder in Due Course (HDC) Under the UCC, a person who takes a negotiable instrument, document of title, or investment security (1) for value, (2) in good faith, and (3) without notice that there is any defense against it.

Holding Company A corporation that holds a controlling interest in one or more other corporations.

Holding Over A tenant who remains in possession of leased premises after the termination of a lease without the landlord's consent.

Home-Solicitation Sale A credit sale to a consumer made at other than the creditor's place of business.

Homestead Exemption The statutory exemption of all or part of the value of a person's dwelling from the claims of creditors (other than a creditor holding a security interest in the dwelling).

Implied Agency An agency, the existence of which is proven by inferences from facts and circumstances of the case as, for example, by a prior course of dealing between the parties.

Implied Contract A contract inferred from conduct of the parties rather than expressed in words.

Implied Warranty In sales law, a seller's warranty that is imposed by operation of law rather than being based on express language. Implied warranties cover the quality and condition of goods sold.

Imputed Negligence Negligence that is charged to a person by reason of his relationship with the person who was actually negligent.

Incidental Beneficiary A person to whom the benefits of a contract accrue simply as an incident to performance of the contract.

Incontestability Clause A clause in a life insurance contract fixing a limited time within which the insurer must discover and assert any grounds it may have to justify rescission of the contract.

Incorporators Persons who organize a corporation and who sign its articles of incorporation.

Indemnification In the corporate context, a corporation's payment of an obligation or liability imposed on an officer or director; in a broader sense, any right a person has to be saved by another from the legal consequences of his or someone else's conduct.

Indenture A written agreement between a corporation seeking to borrow money and a trustee who represents a group of lenders. The indenture defines the borrower's obligations, the lenders' rights and remedies, and the trustee's role.

Independent Contractor A person who is hired to perform work or render a service according to his own methods and using his own employees and equipment.

Independent Covenant A portion of a lease, contract, or deed, the performance of which does not depend on performance of any other covenant by the same or other party.

Indorsement A signature written on an instrument that is already negotiable, or on a paper so firmly attached to the instrument as to become a part thereof, to negotiate the instrument.

Infraction A minor offense or violation, such as illegal parking or littering, that is distinguishable from a misdemeanor or felony and is usually punishable by a small fine.

Infringement Wrongful use or copying of a copyrighted work, patent, trademark, or trade name.

Inherently Dangerous A term used to describe an activity that is dangerous no matter how skillfully or carefully it is performed.

Injunction An order by a court that a party do or refrain from doing a certain act.

Insider A person who has special access to information concerning a corporation because of his financial interests or role in management.

Insolvent Unable to pay debts as they become due; in bankruptcy, having a lesser amount of assets than liabilities.

Inspection Right The power conferred on shareholders to inspect books and records of the corporation in which they own stock.

Insurance An agreement by which one party (the insurer), for a consideration (the premium), promises to pay money to another (the insured or beneficiary) on the occurrence of a specified type of loss caused by one or more specified events.

Insurance Agent A person expressly or impliedly authorized to represent an insurer in dealing with third persons in matters relating to insurance.

Insurance Broker One who acts as a middleman between an insured and insurer, solicits insurance from the public, and is not generally employed by a particular company.

Insured The person in whose favor a contract of insurance operates and who is indemnified, or is to receive a certain sum on the happening of a specified contingency or event.

Intent A person's fixed and determined purpose. Tortious or criminal intent means the intent to affect a legally protected interest in a way not permitted by law.

Intentional Infliction of Mental Distress A tort characterized by the plaintiff's severe mental suffering resulting from emotional disturbance without physical impact, caused by the defendant's highly aggravated or outrageous words or acts with intent to cause the plaintiff's mental suffering.

Interference A tort consisting of a person's violating the right of another to be secure in his business and contractual relationships or in his relationship with another as an employer or employee.

Interlocking Directors Directors holding seats on the boards of two or more corporations.

Interrogatories Written questions propounded by one party in litigation to the other party, which must be answered under oath prior to trial.

Intestate Succession The distribution of a decedent's property to the persons prescribed by state law, rather than as provided in a will.

Inventory Goods held for sale or lease, or to be furnished under service contracts.

Inverse Condemnation Property taken for public use or damaged by governmental action without a formal taking or eminent domain proceeding.

Invitee A person who directly or impliedly is invited by a landowner to enter land for some purpose of interest or advantage to the owner.

Joint Tenancy Title held by two or more natural persons in equal shares, with right of survivorship (surviving joint tenant or tenants take share of deceased joint tenant).

Joint Tortfeasors Two or more persons who unite in committing a tort or whose acts concur in producing an injury to a third person.

Joint Venture The relationship created when two or more persons combine in a joint business enterprise for their mutual benefit with the understanding that they are to share in the profits or losses and each is to have voice in the management.

Judgment A court's final determination of the rights of the parties on matters submitted to the court in an action or proceeding.

Judgment Debt The debt arising from a judgment ordering the payment of money. The person against whom the judgment is issued is the judgment debtor.

Judgment Lien A lien on the property (usually only real property) of a judgment debtor.

Junior Mortgage A mortgage held by a mortgagee whose rights in the property covered are inferior to the rights of one or more other mortgagees.

Key Employee Insurance Insurance obtained and paid for by a business on the life of one or more of the business' key or most important officers or employees.

Labor Law That body of law, comprised of constitutional provisions, statutes, ordinances, administrative regulations, and court decisions, that regulates such labor relations matters as hours of labor, wages, and working conditions.

Landlord The lessor under a lease of real property.

Land Sales Contract A contract used in connection with the sale of real property under which the seller retains legal title until the buyer pays all or a prescribed part of the purchase price.

Last Clear Chance A doctrine under which the plaintiff's negligence does not bar recovery for the defendant's negligence if, by having exercised reasonable care after noticing the plaintiff's peril, the defendant could have avoided injuring the plaintiff.

Latent Defect A hidden defect that cannot be discovered by ordinary observation or inspection.

Lawsuit An action or proceeding in a civil court, as contrasted with a ciminal prosecution.

Lease An agreement giving rise to the relationship of lessor and lessee.

Leasehold A lessee's estate or interest in property under a lease.

Lessee A person who receives possession of and has the right to use real or personal property under a lease.

Lessor The owner of real or personal property who transfers possession of it to a lessee under a lease.

Liability Insurance Insurance protecting the insured against loss due to his killing or injuring another person or damaging or destroying another's property.

Libel Defamatory material published in the form of printing, writing, or pictures.

License A privilege to do something; in real property law, a privilege to go on another's land and do something, such as hunting or fishing, that otherwise would constitute a trespass.

Licensee In property law, a person who is invited or permitted by a landowner to enter the property for his own convenience, pleasure, or benefit, or for personal reasons not connected with the landowner's interests; in a more general sense, anyone to whom a license has been issued.

Lien A charge on property for the payment or discharge of a debt or duty.

Lien Theory In the law of real property security arrangements, the view that the mortgagee acquires only a lien on the mortgaged property rather than title to it.

Life Estate An estate measured in duration by the life of a natural person.

Life Insurance A contract to pay a specified sum, in a lump sum or installments, to a named beneficiary or to the estate of the insured, on the insured's death.

Limited Partner A partner in a limited partnership who (1) makes a contribution of cash or other property to the partnership and obtains an interest in the partnership in return, but (2) takes no active part in managing the partnership. A limited partner has limited liability for partnership debts.

Liquidation The process of converting property and other assets to cash; in a narrower sense, the process of settling partnership affairs after dissolution.

Listing Agreement A contract of employment between a seller of real property and a real estate broker for the broker's services in selling or offering to sell the property.

Listing of Securities Placing a corporation's securities with a stock exchange so that the securities can be traded publicly.

Litigant A person engaged in litigation as a party.

"Little FTC Laws" State legislation, patterned after the Federal Trade Commission Act, authorizing the attorney general or a local prosecutor to sue for damages or an injunction on behalf of a defrauded buyer.

Living Trust A trust created by a living trustor rather than by the terms of a decedent's will; also known as an inter vivos trust.

Lloyd's of London The oldest existing insurance organization. It does not offer insurance itself. Instead, insurance for a given risk is offered by a syndicate formed for that purpose, each syndicate being comprised of individual members of Lloyd's.

Long Arm Legislation Legislation that gives a state jurisdiction over a nonresident, even though the nonresident is not personally served with process within the state.

Mail Fraud Use of the mail for any scheme to defraud other persons. It is illegal under federal law.

Malice A state of mind of ill will, hatred, or hostility entertained by one person toward another; the state of mind that prompts the intentional doing of a wrongful act without legal justification or excuse.

Malicious Prosecution A tort, the basis of which is one person's having wrongfully commenced a legal proceeding against another.

Marketable Title A title good as a matter of law, its validity not depending on the determination of any question of fact; title that a person of reasonable intelligence and prudence would be willing to take and pay for according to its fair value; with respect to real property, title that is free of encumbrances and of anything else to which a reasonable buyer would object.

Market Share In antitrust law, the share of a given market that an alleged monopolist holds.

Married Women's Acts Statutes or constitutional provisions adopted in most states to benefit married women by abolishing common-law restrictions on the right to contract, to sue and be sued, and to acquire, hold, and convey property in their own right free from interference by their husbands.

Master Policy An insurance policy, commonly used in group insurance, containing certain general terms that are incorporated by reference into a certificate of insurance issued later.

Mechanic's Lien A lien created by statute in favor of persons who have performed work in or furnished materials for the erection or repair of a building.

Mediation and Conciliation A process by which the parties to a dispute are encouraged by a neutral third person to reach agreement on their own initiative.

Merchantable Of good quality and sellable, but not necessarily the best; reasonably suitable for the ordinary uses of the item.

Merger One corporation's acquisition of the stock or assets of another in such manner that the acquired corporation becomes part of the acquiring one.

Merger Doctrine The doctrine that, after a purchaser accepts a deed, the contract of sale is superseded by the deed, and only the rights and remedies contained in the deed are available to the purchaser.

Metes and Bounds Measurements and boundaries, as used in describing real property.

Minor A person under the age of majority; often referred to as an infant in legal writing.

Misdemeanor A criminal offense less serious than a felony and punishable by a fine or up to one year's imprisonment in jail.

Misrepresentation An all-embracing term characterized as one person's false representation of a material fact on which another person justifiably relies to his detriment; in insurance law, a statement of fact that is false, made with intent to deceive, and material to the risk.

Mitigation of Damages The reduction of damages from what they otherwise would be.

Model Business Corporation Act (MBCA) A uniform law governing the incorporation and operation of corporations. It was drafted by the American Bar Association (ABA) and has been adopted in whole or in part by approximately 35 states. See Appendix C.

Monopoly The power to exclude competitors from a market or to control prices within a relevant market.

Mortgage A contract by which specific property is designated or conveyed as security for the performance of an act or, most often, payment of a debt.

Mortgagee The lending party in a mortgage transaction.

Mortgagor The borrowing party in a mortgage transaction.

Motion An application to a court, frequently made orally, to obtain an order or ruling.

Multinational Corporation A corporation characterized by the melding of foreign affiliates or subsidiaries with domestic operations of the parent corporation.

Multiple Listing Agency Contract A device used by groups of real estate brokers to obtain a wider market for the sale of property. It entails the common listing among them of all property they are offering for sale.

Mutual Insurance Company A cooperative enterprise in which members contribute to the creation of a fund by a system of premiums or assessments from which members' losses and liabilities are paid. Any profits are divided among the members in proportion to their interests.

Mutuality of Obligation A phrase expressing the requirement that a contract impose binding obligations on both parties to be deemed valid and enforceable as to either one.

National Labor Relations Board (NLRB) The federal administrative agency created to administer the National Labor Relations Act, certify unions as proper bargaining representatives of employees, and handle unfair labor practice proceedings.

Necessaries In contract law, such things as are essential to the life or health of a person, such as medical services, food, clothing, and education.

Negative Injunction An injunction that prohibits certain conduct.

Negligence The failure of a person owing a duty to another to do what a reasonably prudent person would have done under the same or similar circumstances.

Negotiable Instrument Commercial paper that meets the requirements of UCC Article 3 for negotiability (transferability). Examples include drafts, checks, certificates of deposit, and notes.

No-Fault Insurance A system of self-insurance under which compensation for losses is made independently of a fault determination. No-fault au-

tomobile insurance typically provides that an insured will receive compensation for losses from his own insurer, and tort liability is abolished, at least to the extent of the benefits received.

Nonconforming Use A use of property that violates a zoning ordinance but is nevertheless permitted to continue because it was in existence when the ordinance was enacted.

Nonfreehold Estate At common law, an estate that conveyed possession and use of real property, but not title to it; the modern equivalent is a leasehold.

Nonnegotiable Instrument Commercial paper not meeting the requirements for negotiability (transferability) specified in UCC Article 3.

Nonprofit Corporation A corporation, ordinarily without shareholders, created for purposes that are often charitable, and that do not involve making a profit.

No-Strike Clause A provision in some labor contracts by which a union agrees not to strike or cause work stoppages or slowdowns because of labor disputes or grievances; frequently given in exchange for the employer's agreement to arbitrate grievances.

Note A written promise to pay another a certain sum of money at a certain time; a kind of commercial paper.

Notice of Dishonor A notice that a bill, note, or draft has been dishonored by nonacceptance or nonpayment.

Notice to Creditors Under UCC Article 6, the advance notice of a bulk transfer required to be given to the transferor's creditors.

Notice to Quit A notice to a tenant to perform a lease covenant or condition (most commonly that to pay rent due) or else leave the premises. It is preliminary to the eviction of the tenant.

Novation A contract that immediately discharges a previous contractual duty and creates a new contractual duty, including as a party one who neither owed the previous duty nor was entitled to its performance.

Nuisance An invasion of another person's interest in the use or enjoyment of property. A private nuisance interferes with the private use or enjoyment of property, while a public nuisance interferes with a right common to the general public.

Obstruction of Justice A crime that consists of an

interference with the orderly administration of justice.

Offer A proposal of terms made with the purpose of securing their acceptance by another, thereby completing a contract.

Offeree One to whom an offer is made.

Offeror One who makes an offer.

Offset A creditor practice by which a debtor's money already in the creditor's possession is applied directly to the debt.

Open-End Credit A continuing consumer credit arrangement, such as a charge account with a retail store. To be distinguished from closed and credit.

Open-End Mortgage A mortgage or deed of trust that permits and secures additional, future advances on the original loan.

Option A continuing offer, usually limited in time and supported by consideration, to do or perform a certain thing on certain terms and conditions, and that the party to whom it is given can accept within the time allowed.

Ordinance A city or county's local law of a general and permanent nature, covering such matters of local rather than statewide concern as safety, parking, and elections.

Ordinary Care Care that a reasonably prudent individual would exercise under the particular circumstances.

Ordinary Life Insurance Life insurance for which premiums at a fixed rate are paid throughout the insured's life; also known as straight life insurance.

Output Contract A contract in which the buyer promises to purchase the seller's entire production in exchange for the seller's promise to sell the entire production to the buyer.

Outside Director A corporate director who is not an officer or employee of the corporation and is otherwise unaffiliated with it.

Overdraft The situation that arises when a payor bank pays a check drawn for more than is in the drawer's account at the time of payment.

Par The standardized value attributed by law to a share of stock.

Parent Corporation A corporation that owns a controlling interest in another corporation.

Parol Evidence Rule The rule excluding evidence of prior or contemporaneous oral agreements that would vary a written contract.

Partition Action A court action by which co-owners of property can sever their joint ownership, either by a division of land into separate parcels or by a sale of the property and a division of the proceeds according to the respective interests of each owner.

Partnership An association of two or more persons to carry on a business for profit as co-owners.

Patent The exclusive right of manufacture, sale, or use secured by the Federal Patent Act to a person who invents or discovers a new, nonobvious, and useful device or process.

Patent and Trademark Office The federal bureau that processes patent applications and where all records, drawings, models, specifications, and other papers pertaining to patents are required by law to be kept and preserved.

Payor Bank Under UCC Article 4, the bank that is ultimately responsible for paying (or refusing to pay) a check or other item.

Perfection Under UCC Article 9, the process by which a secured party maximizes his rights with respect to the collateral.

Performance The doing of the acts required by a contract at the time and place specified and in the manner stipulated.

Periodic Tenancy A tenancy that continues for fixed periods of time, such as from year to year, until terminated by notice at the end of one of the periods.

Perjury The willful giving of a false statement under oath.

Per Se Doctrine In antitrust law, the doctrine that certain business conduct is considered to be an unreasonable restraint of trade, and hence illegal, without proof that it has caused actual loss or injury.

Personal Property All property other than real property and fixtures.

Personal Representative The person who administers the estate of a deceased person.

Picketing Walking or patrolling in the vicinity of a place of business involved in a labor dispute and, by mouth, banner, or placard, undertaking to inform the public about the dispute.

Plaintiff   The party who begins a lawsuit by filing a complaint against the other party (the defendant).

Pleadings   The formal written documents filed in court. An example is the complaint by which a civil lawsuit is ordinarily initiated.

Pledge   A type of secured transaction in which possession of the collateral is temporarily given to the secured party.

Police Power   The power inherent in a state to regulate its affairs and ensure the welfare and best interests of its citizens.

Polygraph   An electrical instrument that, by measuring and recording certain physiological data concerning a person being tested, can indicate when the person is telling the truth and when he is not; commonly known as a lie detector.

Posting Process   Under UCC Article 4, the usual procedure by which a payor bank decides to pay a check and then records the payment.

Power of Attorney   A written instrument that serves as tangible evidence that the agent is acting for and on behalf of the principal; also known as a letter of attorney or warrant of attorney.

Power of Sale   A provision in a mortgage (or deed of trust) that empowers the mortgagee (or trustee), without resort to any judicial procedures, to sell the property in the event of default and to apply the sale proceeds to satisfy the secured debt.

Precedent   A court decision that serves as the basis of and authority for a subsequent decision by the same court or another court in the same jurisdiction.

Preemptive Right   The preferential right of shareholders to purchase newly issued stock in proportion to the number of shares each shareholder already owns.

Preferential Transfer   In bankruptcy law, a transfer that involves the debtor's property and can be avoided by the trustee because it gives the transferee creditor an advantage over other creditors.

Preferred Dividend   A dividend paid on preferred stock and usually payable only out of the corporation's net earnings.

Preferred Stock   An equity security that has priority over the common stock as to the payment of dividends. It also has priority as to the repayment of the sum originally paid in to the corporation (usually termed the liquidation preference).

Prejudgment Remedy   A statutory means by which, before a creditor suing on a debt is awarded a judgment, the creditor can obtain an interest in property owned by the debtor.

Premises Liability   The area of tort law that concerns the duties of a landowner, land occupier, or person exercising direct control over land to persons entering the land or injured by activities occurring on the land.

Premium   The agreed price for assuming and carrying an insurable risk; the consideration paid an insurer for undertaking to indemnify the insured against a specified peril.

Prepayment Penalty   A penalty exacted from the borrower for the right to repay a debt before it actually becomes due.

Prescriptive Easement   An easement acquired by adverse possession.

Pretrial Conference   A conference conducted by a judge prior to trial at which the judge and attorneys isolate the issues for trial and sometimes settle the case.

Price Discrimination   The practice by which a seller offers goods of like quality to different buyers at different prices. Certain price discrimination is illegal under the federal Robinson–Patman Act.

Price Fixing   An unlawful agreement among manufacturers or dealers to maintain specified prices.

Principal   As used in agency, the person for whom another acts and from whom he derives authority to act; as used with respect to a loan transaction, the unpaid balance of the amount borrowed, as opposed to interest or monetary penalties.

Priority   The superiority of one person's rights over the rights of other persons. The term is often used with respect to one creditor's right to be paid before other creditors can be.

Privilege   A legal right to engage in particular conduct.

Privileged Communication   In defamation law, a statement that, although apparently defamatory, does not constitute actionable defamation because of its character or the occasion on which it was made; in a broader sense, any communication that, because of the relationship between the parties, the recipient should not disclose and cannot be required to disclose.

Privity An elusive term, used to indicate a relationship by which one person is sufficiently related to another that certain legal consequences follow. In law, privity means that there is an identity of interest between persons such that the interest of one person is measured by the same legal right as that of the other.

Probate The procedure by which a court finds that a document is the valid will of a decedent.

Process The means of compelling a defendant to appear in a civil or criminal case; a writ, warrant of arrest, or other means of subjecting a person or property to a court's jurisdiction.

Products Liability The liability of a manufacturer, processor, or seller of a product for injury caused by the condition of or a defect in the product.

Products Liability Insurance Insurance designed to protect a producer or manufacturer against loss by reason of injury to persons or property caused by use of its products.

Profit In a broad sense, gains, such as the excess of receipts over expenses. In real property law, a profit (or profit *a prendre*) is a right to take off or from another's land something that is part of the land, such as timber.

Promise A pledge to perform; a declaration giving the person to whom it is made a right to expect or claim the performance of some particular thing; in commercial paper, a person's undertaking to pay an instrument.

Promissory Estoppel The doctrine that an estoppel may arise from the making of a promise, even though without consideration, if it was intended that the promise be relied on and, in fact, it was relied on, and if a refusal to enforce it would result in an injustice.

Promoter A person who initiates the formation of a corporation.

Property Insurance Insurance that protects against the loss of, damage to, or destruction of personal property, fixtures, or improvements to real property.

Pro Rata Clause An insurance policy clause limiting the insurer's liability for a loss covered by the policy to only a fraction of the total loss, the fraction being determined by dividing the face amount of the policy by the total amount of insurance covering the risk in question.

Prospectus A document required to be furnished to a prospective purchaser of securities and giving all relevant financial information needed for making a decision whether to purchase those securities.

Provisional Settlement Under UCC Article 4, a conditional (as opposed to final) payment, charge, or credit of a check or other item.

Proximate Cause As an element of tort liability, that cause which, in a natural and continuous sequence, unbroken by any intervening cause, produced the injury, and without which the injury would not have occurred.

Proxy The authority given by a shareholder to another person to vote his shares of stock at a stockholder meeting; the person so authorized to vote.

Public Corporation A corporation created for public purposes connected with the administration of government.

Publicly Held Corporation A large corporation whose securities are owned by a large number of people and traded over a national or regional stock exchange.

Public Offering The offer or sale of securities to a number of persons in such a way that the exemption offered to private placements by the Securities Act of 1933 is not available.

Public Use Use of property by or for the public at large rather than by or for a private owner.

Punitive Damages See *Exemplary Damages.*

Purchase Money Security Interest An interest taken or retained in collateral to secure payment of the purchase price of that collateral. If the interest is a mortgage, it is called a purchase money mortgage.

Purchaser in Good Faith See *Bona Fide Purchaser.*

Qualified Indorsement An indorsement of a negotiable instrument to which "without recourse" or words of similar meaning are added to the signature of the indorser.

Quantum Meruit Literally, "as much as it is worth." It is the basis on which a party can try to recover for a breach of contract by suing for the reasonable value of the work actually done or services actually rendered.

Quasi-Contract A fiction of the law, adopted to achieve justice and enforce legal duties by means of implying that a contract exists even though there is no true contract.

Quiet Title Suit A suit to cause removal of a cloud on title to real property.

Quitclaim Deed A deed that conveys only whatever present right, title, or interest the grantor has in the property.

Quorum The number of a corporation's directors or shares required to be present or represented at a meeting in order to conduct business.

Ratification Treating as authorized or valid an earlier act, often done by somebody else, that otherwise could have been disavowed.

Reaffirmation of Debt A debtor's agreement to pay all or part of a debt that would otherwise be discharged, or was discharged, in a bankruptcy case.

Real Property Land and things that are permanent, fixed, and immovable, such as vegetation, buildings, and other permanent structures.

Reasonable Care Care required by the circumstances of the case; due care under the circumstances.

Receiver A person appointed by a court to take temporary custody of the property of another.

Reciprocal Insurance A system by which individuals or business entities, none of which is an insurance company, agree to indemnify each other against certain kinds of risks.

Recordation The filing of a conveyance of encumbrance in a county office to give constructive notice of a title or other interest affecting real property.

Redemption A corporation's purchase of its own securities; under UCC Article 9, the debtor's reacquisition of property that has been repossessed.

Refinancing The process of obtaining a new loan in place of an old one, the proceeds from the new loan being used in part to pay off the old loan.

Reformation An equitable remedy by which parties rectify or reform a written instrument when they failed, through accident, mistake, or fraud, to express their real agreement or intention in the instrument.

Regulation Z The administrative regulations issued by the Board of Governors of the Federal Re-serve System to clarify and interpret the federal Truth in Lending Act.

Regulatory Agencies Administrative agencies that have authority to regulate economic activities of individuals and businesses by making rules, deciding disputes, and imposing fines.

Rehabilitation Plan A plan for restoring a debtor's failing business or personal finances to a sound financial position, prepared under Chapter 11 or 13 of the Federal Bankruptcy Code.

Reinsurance Insurance obtained by an insurer to protect itself against large potential losses under policies issued by it. Reinsurance has the effect of apportioning risks of loss among several insurers.

Rejection Words or acts of an offeree indicating that he declines the offer.

Release A document by which, for a consideration, a person gives up to another person any claim or further claim he might have against that person.

Relevant Market A term used in antitrust law to describe both the geographic market and the product market of a business that is alleged to hold a monopoly.

Remainder A property interest that will give the holder the right to possession of the property only after the expiration of a prior estate.

Rent The consideration paid by a lessee to a lessor for the use of property under a lease.

Reorganization A term often loosely used to cover various rearrangements of corporate financial structures. Included within its scope are mergers, consolidations, sales or exchanges of stock, insolvency proceedings, and even amendments to the articles of incorporation.

Replevin A legal action by which the owner of specific property, or one having rights in it, seeks to recover that property from whoever has possession of it.

Repossession The act by which a secured party takes possession of the collateral after the debtor's default.

Representation A statement of fact that is intended to be relied on by the person to whom the statement is made; in insurance law, a statement by an insured to the insurer, made before the completion of an insurance contract, giving information about a fact that is relevant to the insurance and that is intended to enable the insurer to determine whether it will accept the risk and at what premium.

Repudiation of Contract Renunciation of liability under a contract; either a refusal to recognize the existence of a contract or the doing of an act that is inconsistent with its existence.

Requirements Contract A contract in which the seller agrees to supply all of a certain material required for the operation of the buyer's business over a specified time, in exchange for the buyer's promise to purchase all of that material from the seller.

Rescission Termination of a contract by a court, by mutual consent of the parties, or pursuant to a condition contained in the contract.

Res Ipsa Loquitur Literally, the thing speaks for itself. The term refers to a doctrine sometimes used in negligence cases. It permits an inference that the defendant was negligent without specific proof of any negligent conduct.

Res Judicata The doctrine that a final court judgment rendered on the merits of a case is conclusive of all causes of action and all issues litigated in that case as to the parties.

Respondeat Superior The doctrine under which the employer is liable to injured third persons for the acts of his employees committed during the course and scope of their employment.

Restatements of the Law A series of publications, published by the American Law Institute, that sets forth scholarly comments as to rules of law. While the Restatements do not constitute actual law, they are given weight in many judicial decisions.

Restitution Returning to a person something of which he was wrongfully deprived.

Restraint of Trade Business combinations and practices interfering unreasonably with the normal production and supply of commodities by the suppression of competition.

Restrictive Covenant A private restriction set forth in a deed, limiting the property owner's use of the property.

Restrictive Indorsement An indorsement that in some way limits the effect of the indorsement.

Retail Installment Contract A contract for the credit sale of goods or services to a consumer and requiring payment of the purchase price in periodic installments.

Retaliatory Eviction The eviction of a tenant by a landlord because the tenant complained to a governmental agency about the condition of rented property, its habitability, or other defects. It is unlawful in most states.

Retraction A statement of such nature and published in such manner as to manifest an honest intention to repair the harm done to an injured reputation by a defamatory statement.

Reverse Discrimination A policy or practice that, by favoring minorities over majority groups, operates to discriminate against members of the majority.

Reversion The interest in property remaining after the grant of a particular estate or leasehold less than a fee simple.

Revocation The act of canceling a document by, in effect, withdrawing it; in contract law, an offeror's withdrawal of an offer before it has been accepted.

Rider An attachment to an insurance policy, made a part of the entire policy to modify or change it.

Right of Survivorship The right to automatically acquire the interest of a deceased joint owner. It is the distinguishing feature of a joint tenancy.

Right-of-Way A right to cross or pass over a parcel of land. It can be a right to use a road or driveway, to construct power lines through or over land, or to place pipes underground.

Riparian Rights The right of a landowner to water bordering on his land, such as a stream or lake.

Rule 10b-5 A regulation adopted by the SEC implementing the antifraud provisions of § 10(b) of the Securities Act of 1934 and proscribing the use of fraud, materially untrue statements, or other deceitful business practices in connection with the purchase and sale of securities in interstate commerce.

Sale Transfer of property for a consideration.

Secondary Meaning A term used to describe a trade dress, the total image of which has become associated in the public mind with the manufacturer of the goods rather than with the goods themselves. A common example is the distinctively-shaped Coca Cola bottle.

Second Mortgage A junior mortgage covering property that is also encumbered by a first mortgage.

Secured Party One holding a security interest in property.

Secured Transaction Any transaction in which an interest in personal property or fixtures is given to secure payment of a debt or performance of some other obligation.

Securities and Exchange Commission (SEC) The federal regulatory agency that administers the federal securities acts.

Security A broad term signifying corporate financing devices, including stocks and bonds.

Security Deposit A sum of money (or other property) given by a lessee before the commencement of a lease to protect the lessor if the lessee fails to perform any of his obligations under the lease.

Security Interest An interest in property intended to secure or guarantee payment of a debt or performance of some other obligation.

Self-Insurance The absence of conventional insurance covering any or, more often, part of a given risk. For example, the owner of a car is self-insured to the extent of any "deductible" stated in his collision coverage.

Servient Tenement An estate burdened by an easement.

Settlement Under UCC Article 4, a general term that includes within its scope payment, giving a credit, or imposing a charge with respect to a check or other item. Such a settlement can be either provisional or final. With respect to a lawsuit, the term refers to an out-of-court agreement between the parties by which all or some of the disputed issues are resolved.

Sexual Harassment Unwelcome sexual overtures, whether verbal or physical, that the Equal Employment Opportunity Commission has held constitutes a violation of Title VII of the Civil Rights Act of 1964 prohibiting employment discrimination.

Short-Form Merger A merger without notice to or consent of the minority shareholders, permitted by statute if approved by a high percentage of the shares.

Short Sale Sale of a security that the seller does not own. The seller delivers to the buyer a security borrowed from another party, gambling that the price of the security will go down and that it will be possible to "cover," that is, to buy the security at a lower price and restore it to the lender.

Short Swing A term used to describe securities transactions in which a purchase and sale by the same person occurs within a six-month period. Such transactions are subject to regulation under § 16 of the Securities Exchange Act of 1934.

Silent Partner A member of a partnership who is not publicly associated with it and whose connection with partnership business is ordinarily concealed.

Sinking Fund A special fund accumulated by a debtor, usually a corporation, and used as security for the payment of a debt at maturity.

Slander Defamatory material communicated orally or by acts or gestures.

Slander of Title False and malicious statements, oral or written, that disparage a person's title to real or personal property, causing him damage.

Small Claims Court A court, sometimes existing independently and at other times constituting a separate division of a trial court, that is available for litigation of small claims not exceeding a specified amount. Small claims court proceedings are often informal, and the parties cannot be represented by attorneys.

Special Agent An agent authorized to do one or more specific acts under particular instructions.

Special Indorsement An indorsement that specifies the person to whom or to whose order it makes the instrument payable.

Special Power Power or authority granted to an agent under a power of attorney and allowing the agent to perform only specified tasks. In contrast, a general power allows the agent to act in any manner consistent with the principal's business or purposes.

Specific Performance The equitable remedy of compelling performance of a contract according to its precise terms, as distinguished from the legal remedy of awarding damages for breach of contract.

Squeeze Out Elimination of certain shareholders in a corporation or other business enterprise by one or more of the other shareholders or owners.

Standing to Sue The capacity to maintain a lawsuit as a plaintiff. A person has standing to sue when he has an actual interest in the lawsuit.

Stare Decisis The doctrine that judicial decisions should stand as precedents or guidance for similar cases arising in the future.

Statute of Frauds A statute requiring certain classes of contracts to be in writing.

Statute of Limitations A statute limiting the period, after an event, during which a lawsuit relating to that event can be commenced.

Statutory Copyright Copyright protection under the Federal Copyright Act. It gives the copyright owner the exclusive right to reproduce, perform, or display the copyrighted work.

Statutory Law Law based on legislative enactments of a state or the federal government.

Statutory Lien A lien arising under a statute.

Stay of Agency Action A court order placing an administrative order or decision in abeyance until the court has reviewed that order or decision.

Stock Bonus Shares of stock given by an issuing corporation to one of its executives or officers as a reward, often measured in terms of corporate earnings.

Stock Dividend A corporation's issuance of stock to existing shareholders without consideration and usually as a symbolic substitute for a cash dividend.

Stock Split A division of the par or stated value of a corporation's shares. It adds nothing to the capital fund of a corporation, merely increasing (or decreasing in the case of a reverse stock split) the total number of shares outstanding, and reducing (or increasing) the unit value of each share.

Stop-Payment Order An order directed to a payor bank by its customer and instructing the bank not to pay a specified check drawn on the bank.

Street Certificate A stock certificate that is endorsed in blank and does not name the owner or transferee when sold.

Strict Liability Liability without fault, based on the public policy that some activities are so dangerous that one who performs them should be liable for injuries, even in the absence of negligence.

Strike A cessation of work by employees to obtain more favorable employment terms from their employer.

Subagent A person to whom an agent delegates authority to act on behalf of the principal; in effect, an agent's agent.

Subchapter S Corporation An ordinary corporation that has elected to be treated as a sole proprietorship or partnership for income tax purposes under the Internal Revenue Code.

Sublease A landlord–tenant relationship created by a lessee (the sublessor) who leases the property to another (the sublessee) for a period not longer than that of the original lease.

Subordinate Inferior or of lower priority. For example, a debt security is referred to as being subordinate or subordinated if its principal, interest, or both will not be repaid until some other class of indebtedness has been repaid.

Subpoena A court order compelling the attendance of a person in court at a stated time and place, and the violation of which may constitute grounds for arrest or contempt of court.

Subscription Agreement An agreement by a potential future shareholder to contribute money or other assets for stock issued, or to be issued, by a corporation.

Subsidiary A corporation controlled by another corporation.

Substantial Performance Performance of a contract which, while not a full performance, is performance in good faith and in compliance with the contract except perhaps for minor and relatively unimportant deviations.

Supremacy Clause The provision of the United States Constitution (Art. VI, cl. 2) that the Constitution, laws, and treaties of the United States shall be the supreme law of the land, anything in the Constitution or laws of any state to the contrary notwithstanding.

Surplus In corporate accounting terms, what is left over after liabilities and capital have been subtracted from assets. It does not necessarily mean that a corporation has cash to pay a dividend, although no dividend can be paid if there is no surplus.

Survivorship In a broad sense, the fact of outliving one or more other persons; in the context of property law, the right of a surviving joint tenant under which the deceased tenant's interest in the property passes automatically to the survivor.

Tax Return The form showing required information about a taxpayer's tax liability and on which the tax due is computed. It is submitted to the Internal Revenue Service or other taxing authority.

Tenancy As commonly used, a tenant's right to the possession of real property; in a broader sense, any right to possession of real property.

Tenancy at Sufferance The tenancy of one who continues in possession of premises after his original, lawful right to possession has terminated.

Tenancy at Will A tenancy that continues for as long as desired by both parties. Either party can terminate it at any time.

Tenancy by the Entireties A modification of a joint tenancy that can exist between husband and wife. It has the quality of survivorship, but neither spouse can convey his or her interest to break the joint tenancy.

Tenancy for Years A tenancy in which the beginning and end are fixed in advance. The term is misleading because, although the tenancy can be for a number of years, it can also be for a number of days, weeks, or months.

Tenancy in Common Ownership of property by any two or more persons in undivided interests (not necessarily equal) without the right of survivorship.

Tenant The lessee under a lease of real property.

Term Insurance Life insurance for a specified period of time, and the premium for which is paid during the specified term only and increases with each renewal period.

Testamentary Capacity The legal ability to make a valid will, the relevant factors being the testator's age and mental competence.

Testamentary Trust A trust created by a decedent's will rather than by a living person.

Test Audit An audit in which a business' financial condition is merely sampled on a selective basis rather than being fully examined.

Thin Incorporation A term used to describe a corporation whose capitalization is so inadequate in relation to its obligations and risks as to be vulnerable to a challenge by its creditors or the Internal Revenue Service.

Third-Party Beneficiary The beneficiary of a contract made between two other persons.

Time of the Essence A term used to describe a contract provision that requires one party's performance at or within the time specified in the contract as a prerequisite to the other party's performance.

Title Insurance An agreement under which, for a consideration, the insurer agrees to indemnify the insured in a specified amount against loss through a defective title to real estate in which the insured has an interest.

Title VII The popular name for that part of the Civil Rights Act of 1964 that forbids discrimination on the basis of race, color, religion, sex, or national origin.

Title Theory In the law of real property security arrangements, the view that the mortgagee acquires title to the mortgaged property rather than simply a lien on it.

Tort A civil wrong other than a breach of contract.

Tortfeasor A person guilty of a tort.

Trade Dress The format in which goods are presented to the public; an element of package design, consisting of the peculiar visual appearance produced by a particular arrangement or combination of colors, symbols, words, and designs impressed on a label, package, or product, distinct from any technical copyright or trademark.

Trade Dress Simulation An unfair trade practice by which one business intentionally packages its goods in a manner deceptively similar to that used by a competitor.

Trade Fixtures Personal property affixed to land and used for carrying on a trade or business.

Trade Libel A business tort arising when a person communicates false disparaging statements as to the quality of another's property, goods, or services, resulting in the other person's actual loss of business; also known as disparagement.

Trademark A sign, device, or mark by which articles produced by a particular person or organization are distinguished from those produced by others.

Trade Name A name, word, or phrase employed by one engaged in business, as a means of identifying his products, business, or services, and of establishing goodwill.

Trade Secret Information respecting the business

or process of production of a dealer or producer and that would be of special value to competitors.

Trade Usage A uniform course of conduct followed in a particular trade, occupation, or business.

Treble Damages Three times the actual damages.

Trust As usually used, an arrangement by which one party holds property for the benefit of one or more others; in antitrust law, a combination of producers or sellers of a product, the purpose of which is to control prices and suppress competition.

Trustee In trust law, the party having legal title to, but not the beneficial ownership of, the trust property; under a deed of trust, the party holding legal title to the property to secure payment of the debt.

Trustor The person who creates a trust; in a real property security transaction, the borrower under a deed of trust.

Trust Receipt A security device by which a lender retains title to inventory items until they are sold.

Tying Agreement An agreement under which a party agrees to sell a product (the tying product) only on condition that the buyer also purchases a different product (the tied product).

Ultra Vires A term used to describe a corporate act that is beyond the scope of the corporation's powers; also used to describe a similar unauthorized act by an administrative agency.

Unauthorized Practice of Law The giving of legal advice or performance of legal services by a person, such as an accountant, who is not a licensed attorney.

Unconscionable Contract A contract, usually made when one of the parties was in a position of disadvantage, that is oppressive, and especially one unreasonably restricting a party's liberty to earn a living or imposing an extortionate rate of interest.

Underwriter One who purchases securities from an issuer with a view to their resale or distribution. In general, the term refers to those persons who make a regular business of distributing securities.

Undisclosed Agency A situation in which a person dealing with another neither knows nor has reason to know that he is dealing with an agent or that an agency relationship exists.

Undivided Interest The interest of each co-owner in property owned in common.

Undue Influence A type of fraud by which a person's free will is destroyed and the will of another person is substituted in its place.

Unfair Competition Wrongful acts that injure or destroy the business of a competitor.

Unfair Labor Practice Any of a number of specific employer or employee acts that are so labeled in federal labor legislation and the commission of which can lead to sanctions.

Unfair Trade Practice A commercial policy or practice that is illegal because it is used to gain an unfair advantage over business competitors.

Uniform Commercial Code (UCC) A uniform code created through the joint efforts of the National Conference of Commissioners on Uniform State Laws and the American Law Institute. The UCC deals with most aspects of modern business transactions and concerns such matters as sale of goods, commercial paper, bank deposits and collections, documents of title, and secured transactions. The UCC has been adopted by all states except Louisiana, which has adopted only portions of the UCC. See Appendix B.

Uniform Laws A series of proposed types of legislation, created by the National Conference of Commissioners on Uniform State Laws, and proposed for adoption by the state legislatures. Many uniform laws have been widely adopted, most notably the Uniform Commercial Code.

Unilateral Contract A contract in which there is a promise on one side only, the consideration being an act or something other than another promise.

Unilateral Mistake A mistake on the part of only one of the parties to a transaction.

Union An association of workers existing for the purpose of securing, through united action and collective bargaining, more favorable wages, hours of labor, and working conditions for its members.

United States Constitution The fundamental document of the American system of government, constituting the supreme law of the land, as adopted by the people of the United States through their representatives in the Convention of 1787 and since amended. See Appendix A.

United States Supreme Court The highest court in the federal court system, established by the United States Constitution. It occupies a unique position within the dual system of federal and state government in view of its power to review and set aside certain decisions of the highest state courts.

Unlawful Detainer A summary eviction procedure, provided for by statute, by which a landlord is supposed to be able to recover possession of leased property quickly and at low cost.

Unliquidated Debt A debt, the amount of which is disputed.

Unsecured Creditor A creditor who has only the debtor's promise to pay, as distinguished from a secured creditor.

Variance The relief granted to an affected property owner from a general zoning ordinance in cases of undue hardship unique or peculiar to particular real property.

Vendor's Lien The implied lien of a real estate seller who has conveyed legal title, as security for the unpaid purchase money; the common-law lien of a seller of goods for the unpaid portion of the purchase price of the goods, where he has parted with title but not possession.

Vested Right A right, usually relating to property, that presently exists, as distinguished from a contingent right, which may or may not exist in the future.

Vicarious Liability Liability imposed by law on one person because of the act or omission of another, such as his employee.

Voidable Contract A contract that, although defective so that it *can* be avoided by one of the parties, is valid and binding until it *is* avoided.

Void Contract A contract having no legal effect whatsoever.

Voluntary Bankruptcy The term used to describe a bankruptcy proceeding in which the debtor, rather than one or more of his creditors, filed the bankruptcy petition.

Voluntary Conveyance A conveyance for which no valuable consideration was received.

Voting Trust An agreement among a group of shareholders by which shares are transferred to a trustee to vote in a certain specified manner under a legally enforceable voting trust agreement.

Wagering Contract An insurance contract that is void because of the insured's lack of an insurable interest in the subject matter of the insurance.

Waiver The abandonment or relinquishment of a right or privilege.

Warehouser A person who stores bailed goods for compensation; traditionally referred to as a warehouseman.

Warehouse Receipt A receipt issued by a person engaged in the business of storing goods for hire.

Warrant A negotiable document issued by a corporation and giving the owner an option to purchase the corporation's stock at a specified price.

Warranty A guaranty, either express or implied, that information is correct, that standards will apply, or that particular activities will take place. In insurance law, a description or undertaking on the part of the insured, appearing in the insurance policy or in another instrument, relating to the risk insured against.

Warranty Deed A deed containing express warranties of title and quiet possession.

Warranty of Fitness An implied warranty by the seller of goods sold for a particular use that the goods are fit for that purpose, provided the buyer is relying on the skill, judgment, or experience of the seller.

Warranty of Habitability An express or implied warranty, given by a landlord at the commencement of a lease, that there are no defects in the rented facilities vital to the use of the premises for residential purposes.

Waste Damage to property by willful neglect, abuse, or misuse.

Watered Stock Stock issued in exchange for property or services at an over valuation or at a discount. The term originated in reference to the practice in agricultural communities of causing cattle to ingest large quantities of water to increase their weight—and hence value—when sold.

White-Collar Crime An illegal act, or a series of illegal acts, committed by non-physical means to (1) obtain money or property, (2) avoid paying or losing money or property, or (3) obtain a business or personal advantage.

Will The document by which a person indicates the desired disposition of his property after his death.

Winding Up The process of settling partnership affairs after dissolution.

Workers' Compensation State legislation providing for compensation for loss resulting from the injury, disability, or death of workers by industrial accident, casualty, or disease. These laws have the common feature of providing compensation in accordance with a fixed schedule rather than on the basis of tort liability.

Working Capital The difference between a corporation's current assets and its current liabilities. It is frequently used as a measure of a company's liquidity and capacity to meet its obligations as they fall due.

Wraparound Mortgage A second mortgage securing a promissory note, the face amount of which is the sum of the unpaid principal secured by the first mortgage plus the amount advanced by the second mortgage.

Writ A court's direction authorizing a person's arrest or the seizure of property, or compelling a person to take certain actions.

Zoning The division of a municipality into districts (zones) according to specific uses or permissible activities. Most zoning ordinances separate commercial or industrial districts from residential districts and prohibit the establishment of places of business or industry in those districts designated as residential.

Table of Statutes

CODE OF FEDERAL REGULATIONS

UNIFORM COMMERCIAL CODE

Index

Notes

Notes

Notes

Notes

Notes

Notes

Notes

Notes

Notes

Notes

Notes

Notes

8 ৮ 7 1